The Longman Anthology
of British Literature

✦ ✤✦✤ ✦

VOLUME 1A

THE MIDDLE AGES

David Damrosch
COLUMBIA UNIVERSITY

Christopher Baswell
UNIVERSITY OF CALIFORNIA, LOS ANGELES

Clare Carroll
QUEENS COLLEGE, CITY UNIVERSITY OF NEW YORK

Kevin J. H. Dettmar
SOUTHERN ILLINOIS UNIVERSITY

Heather Henderson

Constance Jordan
CLAREMONT GRADUATE UNIVERSITY

Peter J. Manning
STATE UNIVERSITY OF NEW YORK, STONY BROOK

Anne Howland Schotter
WAGNER COLLEGE

William Chapman Sharpe
BARNARD COLLEGE

Stuart Sherman
FORDHAM UNIVERSITY

Jennifer Wicke
UNIVERSITY OF VIRGINIA

Susan J. Wolfson
PRINCETON UNIVERSITY

The Longman Anthology of British Literature
Second Edition

David Damrosch

General Editor

VOLUME 1A

THE MIDDLE AGES
Christopher Baswell *and* Anne Howland Schotter

Longman

New York   San Francisco   Boston
London   Toronto   Sydney   Tokyo   Singapore   Madrid
Mexico City   Munich   Paris   Cape Town   Hong Kong   Montreal

Vice President and Editor-in-Chief: *Joseph Terry*
Development Editor: *Mark Getlein*
Assistant Development Editor: *Lai Moy*
Development Manager: *Janet Lanphier*
Senior Marketing Manager: *Melanie Craig*
Supplements Editor: *Donna Campion*
Media Supplements Editor: *Nancy Garcia*
Senior Production Manager: *Valerie Zaborski*
Project Coordination, Text Design, and Page Makeup: *TechBooks*
Cover Design Manager: *Nancy Danahy*
Cover Designer: *Kay Petronio*
On the Cover: *Anne, Duchess of Bedford, Kneeling Before the Virgin Mary and Saint Anne,* from
the *Bedford Hours,* early 15th century. By permission of The British Library.
Photo Researcher: *Julie Tesser*
Manufacturing Buyer: *Lucy Hebard*
Printer and Binder: *Quebecor-World/Taunton*
Cover Printer: *The Lehigh Press, Inc.*

For permission to use copyrighted material, grateful acknowledgment is made to the copyright
holders on pages xli–xlii, which are hereby made part of this copyright page.

Library of Congress Cataloging-in-Publication Data

The Longman anthology of British literature / David Damrosch, general
     editor. — 2nd ed.
          p.   cm.
     Includes bibliographical references and index.
     Contents: v. 1. The Middle Ages / Christopher Baswell and Anne Howland
Schotter. The early modern period / Constance Jordan and Clare
Carroll. The Restoration and the 18th century / Stuart Sherman —
v. 2. The romantics and their contemporaries / Susan Wolfson and Peter
Manning. The Victorian age / Heather Henderson and William Sharpe.
The twentieth century / Kevin Dettmar and Jennifer Wicke.
     ISBN 0-321-09388-7 (v. 1). — ISBN 0-321-09389-5 (v. 2)
     1. English literature.   2. Great Britain—Literary collections.
I. Damrosch, David.
PR1109.L67   2002
820.8—dc21   2002066148

Please visit our website at http://www.ablongman.com/damrosch.

ISBN Single Volume Edition, Volume I: 0-321-09388-7
ISBN Volume 1A, The Middle Ages: 0-321-10667-9
ISBN Volume 1B, The Early Modern Period: 0-321-10578-8
ISBN Volume 1C, The Restoration and the 18th Century: 0-321-10668-7

34567890—QWT—05 04 03

CONTENTS

LIST OF ILLUSTRATIONS

PREFACE

Literature has a double life. Born in one time and place and read in another, literary works are at once products of their age and independent creations, able to live on long after their original world has disappeared. The goal of this anthology is to present a wealth of poetry, prose, and drama from the full sweep of the literary history of the British Isles, and to do so in ways that will bring out both the works' original cultural contexts and their lasting aesthetic power. These aspects are, in fact, closely related: Form and content, verbal music and social meanings, go hand in hand. This double life makes literature, as Aristotle said, "the most philosophical" of all the arts, intimately connected to ideas and to realities that the writer transforms into moving patterns of words. The challenge is to show these works in the contexts in which, and for which, they were written, while at the same time not trapping them within those contexts. The warm response this anthology received from the hundreds of teachers who adopted it in its first edition reflects the growing consensus that we do not have to accept an "either/or" choice between the literature's aesthetic and cultural dimensions. Our users' responses have now guided us in seeing how we can improve our anthology further, so as to be most pleasurable and stimulating to students, most useful to teachers, and most responsive to ongoing developments in literary studies. This preface can serve as a road map to the new phase in this book's life.

LITERATURE IN ITS TIME—AND IN OURS

When we engage with a rich literary history that extends back over a thousand years, we often encounter writers who assume their readers know all sorts of things that are little known today: historical facts, social issues, literary and cultural references. Beyond specific information, these works will have come out of a very different literary culture than our own. Even the contemporary British Isles present a cultural situation—or a mix of cultures—very different from what North American readers encounter at home, and these differences only increase as we go farther back in time. A major emphasis of this anthology is to bring the works' original cultural moment to life: not because the works simply or naively reflect that moment of origin, but because they do refract it in fascinating ways. British literature is both a major heritage for modern North America and, in many ways, a very distinct culture; reading British literature will regularly give an experience both of connection and of difference. Great writers create imaginative worlds that have their own compelling internal logic, and a prime purpose of this anthology is to help readers to understand the formal means—whether of genre, rhetoric, or style—with which these writers have created works of haunting beauty. At the same time, as Virginia Woolf says in A Room of One's Own, the gossamer threads of the artist's web are joined to reality "with bands of steel." This anthology pursues a range of strategies to bring out both the beauty of these webs of words and their points of contact with reality.

The Longman Anthology brings related authors and works together in several ways:

☞ PERSPECTIVES: **Broad groupings that illuminate underlying issues in a variety of the major works of a period.**

☞ AND ITS TIME: **A focused cluster that illuminates a specific cultural moment or a debate to which an author is responding.**

☞ COMPANION READINGS: **Pairings of works in dialogue with each other.**

These groupings provide a range of means of access to the literary culture of each period. The Perspectives sections do much more than record what major writers thought about an issue: they give a variety of views in a range of voices, to illustrate the wider culture within which the literature was being written. An attack on tobacco by King James the First; theological reflections by the pioneering scientist Isaac Newton; haunting testimony by Victorian child workers concerning their lives; these and many other vivid readings give rhetorical as well as social contexts for the poems, plays, and stories around them. Perspectives sections typically relate to several major authors of the period, as with a section on Government and Self-Government that relates broadly to Sir Thomas More's *Utopia*, to Spenser's *Faerie Queene*, and to Milton's *Paradise Lost*. Most of the writers included in Perspectives sections are important figures of the period who could be neglected if they were listed on their own with just a few pages each; grouping them together has proven to be useful pedagogically as well as intellectually. Perspectives sections may also include work by a major author whose primary listing appears elsewhere in the period; thus, a Perspective section on the abolition of slavery—a hotly debated issue in England from the 1790s through the 1830s—includes poems and essays on slavery by Wordsworth, Coleridge, and Barbauld, so as to give a rounded presentation of the issue in ways that can inform the reading of those authors in their individual sections.

When we present a major work "And Its Time," we give a cluster of related materials to suggest the context within which the work was written. Thus Sir Philip Sidney's great *Apology for Poetry* is accompanied by readings showing the controversy that was raging at the time concerning the nature and value of poetry. Some of the writers in these groupings and in our Perspectives sections have not traditionally been seen as literary figures, but all have produced lively and intriguing works, from medieval clerics writing about saints and sea monsters, to a polemical seventeenth-century tract giving *The Arraignment of Lewd, Idle, Froward, and Unconstant Women*, to rousing speeches by Winston Churchill as the British faced the Nazis during World War II.

Also, we include "Companion Readings" to present specific prior texts to which a work is responding: when Sir Thomas Wyatt creates a beautiful poem, *Whoso list to hunt*, by making a free translation of a Petrarch sonnet, we include Petrarch's original (with a literal translation) as a companion reading. For Conrad's *Heart of Darkness*, companion texts include Conrad's diary of the Congo journey on which he based his novella, and a bizarre lecture by Sir Henry Morton Stanley, the explorer-adventurer whose travel writings Conrad parodies.

CULTURAL EDITIONS

This edition also sees the establishment of an important new series of companion volumes, the Longman Cultural Editions, which carry further the anthology's emphases by presenting major texts along with a generous selection of contextual material. Five initial volumes are devoted to *King Lear*; a pairing of *Othello* and Elizabeth Cary's *Tragedie of Mariam*; *Pride and Prejudice*; *Frankenstein*; and *Hard Times*. More are currently being developed. The *Othello/Mariam* and *Frankenstein* volumes build on material derived from the first edition of the anthology; presenting these works separately—available free, for course use, with the anthology itself—has helped to free up space for our many additions to this edition, from the medieval play *Mankind*, to a substantial increase in seventeenth-century lyric poetry, to the addition of Sheridan's hilarious eighteenth-century play *The School for Scandal*, to *Doctor Jekyll and Mr. Hyde* in the Victorian period and *Mrs. Dalloway* in the twentieth century. Taken together, our new edition and the Longman Cultural Editions offer an unparalleled set of materials for the enjoyment and study of British literary culture from its first beginnings to the present.

ILLUSTRATING VISUAL CULTURE

Another important context for literary production has been a different kind of culture: the visual. We have newly added in this edition a suite of color plates in each volume, and we also have one hundred black-and-white illustrations throughout the anthology, chosen to show artistic and cultural images that figured importantly for literary creation. Sometimes, a poem refers to a specific painting, or more generally emulates qualities of a school of visual art. At other times, more popular materials like advertisements may underlie scenes in Victorian or Modernist writing. In some cases, visual and literary creation have merged, as in Hogarth's series *A Rake's Progress*, included in Volume 1, or Blake's illustrated engravings of his *Songs of Innocence and of Experience*, several of whose plates are reproduced in color in Volume 2.

AIDS TO UNDERSTANDING

We have attempted to contextualize our selections in suggestive rather than exhaustive ways, trying to enhance rather than overwhelm the experience of reading the texts themselves. Thus, when difficult or archaic words need defining in poems, we use glosses in the margins, so as to disrupt the reader's eye as little as possible; footnotes are intended to be concise and informative, rather than massive or interpretive. Important literary and social terms are defined when they are used; for convenience of reference, there is also an extensive glossary of literary and cultural terms at the end of each volume, together with useful summaries of British political and religious organization, and of money, weights, and measures. For further reading, carefully selected, up-to-date bibliographies for each period and for each author can be found at the end of each volume.

LOOKING—AND LISTENING—FURTHER

Beyond the boundaries of the anthology itself, along with this edition we are introducing a pair of CDs, one for each semester, giving a wide range of readings of texts in the anthology and of selections of music from each period. It is only in the past century or two that people usually began to read literature silently; most literature has been written in the expectation that it would be read aloud, or even sung in the case of lyric poetry ("lyric" itself means a work meant to be sung to the accompaniment of a lyre or other instruments). The aural power and beauty of these works is a crucial dimension of their experience. For further explorations, we have also expanded our Web site, available to all users at www.awlonline.com/damrosch; this site gives a wealth of information, annotated links to related sites, and an archive of texts for further reading. For instructors, we have revised and expanded our popular companion volume, *Teaching British Literature*, written directly by the anthology editors, 600 pages in length, available free to everyone who adopts the anthology.

WHAT IS BRITISH LITERATURE?

Turning now to the book itself, let us begin by defining our basic terms: What is "British" literature? What is literature itself? And just what should an anthology of this material look like at the present time? The term "British" can mean many things, some of them contradictory, some of them even offensive to people on whom the name has been imposed. If the term "British" has no ultimate essence, it does have a history. The first British were Celtic people who inhabited the British Isles and the northern coast of France (still called Brittany) before various Germanic tribes of Angles and Saxons moved onto the islands in the fifth and sixth centuries. Gradually the Angles and Saxons amalgamated into the Anglo-Saxon culture that became dominant in the southern and eastern regions of Britain and then spread outward; the old British people were pushed west, toward what became known as Cornwall, Wales, and Ireland, which remained independent kingdoms for centuries, as did Celtic Scotland to the north. By an ironic twist of linguistic fate, the Anglo-Saxons began to appropriate the term British from the Britons they had displaced, and they took as a national hero the early, semi-mythic Welsh King Arthur. By the seventeenth century, English monarchs had extended their sway over Wales, Ireland, and Scotland, and they began to refer to their holdings as "Great Britain." Today, Great Britain includes England, Wales, Scotland, and Northern Ireland, but does not include the Republic of Ireland, which has been independent from England since 1922.

This anthology uses "British" in a broad sense, as a geographical term encompassing the whole of the British Isles. For all its fraught history, it seems a more satisfactory term than to speak simply of "English" literature, for two reasons. First: most speakers of English live in countries that are not the focus of this anthology; second, while the English language and its literature have long been dominant in the British Isles, other cultures in the region have always used other languages and have produced great literature in these languages. Important works by Irish, Welsh, and Scots writers appear regularly in the body of this anthology, some of them written directly in their languages and presented here in translation, and others written in an English inflected by the rhythms, habits of thought, and modes of expression characteristic of these other languages and the people who use them.

We use the term "literature" in a similarly capacious sense, to refer to a range of artistically shaped works written in a charged language, appealing to the imagination at least as much as to discursive reasoning. It is only relatively recently that creative writers have been able to make a living composing poems, plays, and novels, and only in the past hundred years or so has creating "belles lettres" or high literary art been thought of as a sharply separate sphere of activity from other sorts of writing that the same authors would regularly produce. Sometimes, Romantic poets wrote sonnets to explore the deepest mysteries of individual perception and memory; at other times, they wrote sonnets the way a person might now write an Op-Ed piece, and such a sonnet would be published and read along with parliamentary debates and letters to the editor on the most pressing contemporary issues.

WOMEN'S WRITING, AND MEN'S

Literary culture has always involved an interplay between central and marginal regions, groupings, and individuals. A major emphasis in literary study in recent years has been the recovery of writing by women writers, some of them little read until recently, others major figures in their time. The first edition of this anthology included more women, and more writing by the women we included, than any other anthology had ever done or does even today. This edition increases the presence of women writers still more, with new inclusions of such important voices as Christine de Pizan, Stevie Smith, and Eavan Boland, while also highlighting Virginia Woolf with the inclusion of the complete text of her great novel *Mrs. Dalloway*. Attending to these voices gives us a new variety of compelling works, and helps us rethink the entire periods in which they wrote. The first third of the nineteenth century, for example, can be defined more broadly than as a "Romantic Age" dominated by six male poets; looking closely at women's writing as well as at men's, we can deepen our understanding of the period as a whole, including the specific achievements of Blake, William Wordsworth, Coleridge, Keats, Percy Shelley, and Byron, all of whom continue to have a major presence in these pages as most of them did during the nineteenth century.

VARIETIES OF LITERARY EXPERIENCE

Above all, we have striven to give as full a presentation as possible to the varieties of great literature produced over the centuries in the British Isles, by women as well as by men, in outlying regions as well as in the metropolitan center of London, and in prose, drama, and verse alike. We have taken particular care to do justice to prose fiction: we include entire novels or novellas by Charles Dickens, Robert Louis Stevenson, Joseph Conrad, and Virginia Woolf, as well as a wealth of short fiction from the eighteenth century to the present. For the earlier periods, we include More's entire *Utopia*, and we give major space to narrative poetry by Chaucer, Spenser, and Milton, among others. Drama appears throughout the anthology, from the medieval *Second Play of the Shepherds* and *Mankind* to a range of twentieth-century plays: George Bernard Shaw's *Pygmalion*, a radio play by Dylan Thomas, Samuel Beckett's *Krapp's Last Tape*, and Caryl Churchill's gender-bending comedy *Cloud 9*. Finally, lyric poetry appears in profusion throughout the anthology, from early lyrics by anonymous Middle English poets and the trenchantly witty Dafydd ap Gwilym to the powerful contemporary voices of Philip Larkin, Seamus Heaney, Eavan Boland, Thom Gunn, and Derek Walcott—himself a product of colonial British education, heir of Shakespeare and James Joyce—who closes the anthology with poems about Englishness abroad and foreignness in Britain.

As topical as these contemporary writers are, we hope that this anthology will show that the great works of earlier centuries can also speak to us compellingly today, their value only increased by the resistance they offer to our views of ourselves and our world. To read and reread the full sweep of this literature is to be struck anew by the degree to which the most radically new works are rooted in centuries of prior innovation. Even this preface can close in no better way than by quoting the words written eighteen hundred years ago by Apuleius of Madaura—both a consummate artist and a kind of anthologist of extraordinary tales—when he concluded the prologue to his masterpiece *The Golden Ass*: Attend, reader, and pleasure is yours.

David Damrosch

ACKNOWLEDGMENTS

In planning and preparing the second edition of our anthology, the editors have been fortunate to have the support, advice, and assistance of many people. Our editor, Joe Terry, has been unwavering in his enthusiasm for the book and his commitment to it; he and his associates Roth Wilkofsky, Janet Lanphier, and Melanie Craig have supported us in every possible way throughout the process, ably assisted by Michele Cronin, Lai Moy, and Alison Main. Our developmental editor Mark Getlein guided us and our manuscript from start to finish with unfailing acuity and Wildean wit. Our copyeditor, Stephanie Magean, marvelously integrated the work of a dozen editors. Daniel Kline and Peter Meyers have devoted enormous energy and creativity to revising our Web site and developing our new audio CD. Joyce Riemer cleared our many permissions, and Julie Tesser tracked down and cleared our many new illustrations. Finally, Valerie Zaborski oversaw the production with sunny good humor and kept the book successfully on track on a very challenging schedule, working closely with Kevin Bradley, and then Kelly Ricci at TechBooks.

Our plans for the new edition have been shaped by comments and suggestions from many faculty who have used the book over the past four years. We are specifically grateful for the thoughtful advice of our reviewers for this edition, Robert Barrett (University of Pennsylvania), Mary Been (Clovis Community College), Stephen Behrendt (University of Nebraska), James Campbell (University of Central Florida), Linda McFerrin Cook (McLellan Community College), Kevin Gardner (Baylor University), Peter Greenfield (University of Puget Sound), Natalie Grinnell (Wofford College), Wayne Hall (University of Cincinnati), Donna Hamilton (University of Maryland), Carrie Hintz (Queens College), Eric Johnson (Dakota State College), Roxanne Kent-Drury (Northern Kentucky University), Adam Komisaruk (West Virginia University), John Laflin (Dakota State University), Paulino Lim (California State University, Long Beach), Ed Malone (Missouri Western State College), William W. Matter (Richland College), Evan Matthews (Navarro College), Lawrence McCauley (College of New Jersey), Peter E. Medine (University of Arizona), Charlotte Morse (Virginia Commonwealth University), Mary Morse (Rider University), Richard Nordquist (Armstrong Atlantic State University), John Ottenhoff (Alma College), Joyce Cornette Palmer (Texas Women's University), Leslie Palmer (University of North Texas), Rebecca Phillips (West Virginia University), William Rankin (Abilene Christian University), Sherry Rankin (Abilene Christian University), Luke Reinsma (Seattle Pacific University), David Rollison (College of Marin), Kathryn Rummel (California Polytechnic), R. G. Siemens (Malaspina University-College), Brad Sullivan (Florida Gulf Coast University), Brett Wallen (Cleveland Community College), Daniel Watkins (Duquesne University), and Julia Wright (University of Waterloo).

We remain grateful as well for the guidance of the many reviewers who advised us on the creation of the first edition, the base on which this new edition has been built. In addition to several of the people named above, we would like to thank Lucien Agosta (California State University, Sacramento), Anne W. Astell (Purdue University), Derek Attridge (Rutgers University), Linda Austin (Oklahoma State University), Joseph Bartolomeo (University of Massachusetts, Amherst), Todd Bender (University of Wisconsin, Madison), Bruce Boehrer (Florida State University),

Joel J. Brattin (Worcester Polytechnic Institute), J. Douglas Canfield (University of Arizona), Paul A. Cantor (University of Virginia), George Allan Cate (University of Maryland, College Park), Eugene R. Cunnar (New Mexico State University), Earl Dachslager (University of Houston), Elizabeth Davis (University of California, Davis), Andrew Elfenbein (University of Minnesota), Margaret Ferguson (University of California, Davis), Sandra K. Fisher (State University of New York, Albany), Allen J. Frantzen (Loyola University, Chicago), Kate Garder Frost (University of Texas), Leon Gottfried (Purdue University), Mark L. Greenberg (Drexel University), James Hala (Drew University), Wendell Harris (Pennsylvania State University), Richard H. Haswell (Washington State University), Susan Sage Heinzelman (University of Texas, Austin), Standish Henning (University of Wisconsin, Madison), Jack W. Herring (Baylor University), Maurice Hunt (Baylor University), Colleen Juarretche (University of California, Los Angeles), R. B. Kershner (University of Florida), Lisa Klein (Ohio State University), Rita S. Kranidis (Radford University), Elizabeth B. Loizeaux (University of Maryland), John J. Manning (University of Connecticut), Michael B. McDonald (Iowa State University), Celia Millward (Boston University), Thomas C. Moser, Jr. (University of Maryland), Jude V. Nixon (Baylor University), Violet O'Valle (Tarrant County Junior College, Texas), Richard Pearce (Wheaton College), Renée Pigeon (California State University, San Bernardino), Tadeusz Pioro (Southern Methodist University), Deborah Preston (Dekalb College), Elizabeth Robertson (University of Colorado), Deborah Rogers (University of Maine), Brian Rosenberg (Allegheny College), Charles Ross (Purdue University), Harry Rusche (Emory University), Kenneth D. Shields (Southern Methodist University), Clare A. Simmons (Ohio State University), Sally Slocum (University of Akron), Phillip Snyder (Brigham Young University), Isabel Bonnyman Stanley (East Tennessee University), Margaret Sullivan (University of California, Los Angeles), Herbert Sussmann (Northeastern University), Ronald R. Thomas (Trinity College), Theresa Tinkle (University of Michigan), William A. Ulmer (University of Alabama), Jennifer A. Wagner (University of Memphis), Anne D. Wallace (University of Southern Mississippi), Jackie Walsh (McNeese State University, Louisiana), John Watkins (University of Minnesota), Martin Wechselblatt (University of Cincinnati), Arthur Weitzman (Northeastern University), Bonnie Wheeler (Southern Methodist University), Dennis L. Williams (Central Texas College), and Paula Woods (Baylor University).

Other colleagues brought our developing book into the classroom, teaching from portions of the work-in-progress. Our thanks go to Lisa Abney (Northwestern State University), Charles Lynn Batten (University of California, Los Angeles), Brenda Riffe Brown (College of the Mainland, Texas), John Brugaletta (California State University, Fullerton), Dan Butcher (Southeastern Louisiana University), Lynn Byrd (Southern University at New Orleans), David Cowles (Brigham Young University), Sheila Drain (John Carroll University), Lawrence Frank (University of Oklahoma), Leigh Garrison (Virginia Polytechnic Institute), David Griffin (New York University), Rita Harkness (Virginia Commonwealth University), Linda Kissler (Westmoreland County Community College, Pennsylvania), Brenda Lewis (Motlow State Community College, Tennessee), Paul Lizotte (River College), Wayne Luckman (Green River Community College, Washington), Arnold Markely (Pennsylvania State University, Delaware County), James McKusick (University of Maryland, Baltimore), Eva McManus (Ohio Northern University), Manuel Moyrao (Old Dominion University), Kate Palguta (Shawnee State University, Ohio), Paul Puccio (University of Central Florida), Sarah Polito (Cape Cod Community College), Meredith Poole (Virginia Western Community College), Tracy Seeley (University of San Francisco), Clare Simmons (Ohio State University), and Paul Yoder (University of Arkansas, Little Rock).

As if all this help weren't enough, the editors also drew directly on friends and colleagues in many ways, for advice, for information, sometimes for outright contributions to headnotes and footnotes, even (in a pinch) for aid in proofreading. In particular, we wish to thank David Ackiss, Marshall Brown, James Cain, Cathy Corder, Jeffrey Cox, Michael Coyle, Pat Denison, Tom Farrell, Andrew Fleck, Jane Freilich, Laurie Glover, Lisa Gordis, Joy Hayton, Ryan Hibbet, V. Lauryl Hicks, Nelson Hilton, Jean Howard, David Kastan, Stanislas Kemper, Andrew Krull, Ron Levao, Carol Levin, David Lipscomb, Denise MacNeil, Jackie Maslowski, Richard Matlak, Anne Mellor, James McKusick, Melanie Micir, Michael North, David Paroissien, Stephen M. Parrish, Peter Platt, Cary Plotkin, Desma Polydorou, Gina Renee, Alan Richardson, Esther Schor, Catherine Siemann, Glenn Simshaw, David Tresilian, Shasta Turner, Nicholas Watson, Michael Winckleman, Gillen Wood, and Sarah Zimmerman for all their guidance and assistance.

The pages on the Restoration and the eighteenth century are the work of many collaborators, diligent and generous. Michael F. Suarez, S. J. (Campion Hall, Oxford) edited the Swift and Pope sections; Mary Bly (Fordham University) edited Sheridan's *School for Scandal*; Michael Caldwell (University of Chicago) edited the portions of "Reading Papers" on *The Craftsman* and the South Sea Bubble. Steven N. Zwicker (Washington University) co-wrote the period introduction, and the headnotes for the Dryden section. Bruce Redford (Boston University) crafted the footnotes for Dryden, Gay, Johnson, and Boswell. Susan Brown, Christine Coch, Tara Czechowski, Paige Reynolds, and Andrew Tumminia helped with texts, footnotes, and other matters throughout; William Pritchard gathered texts, wrote notes, and prepared the bibliography. To all, abiding thanks.

It has been a pleasure to work with all of these colleagues in the ongoing collaborative process that has produced this book and brought it to this new stage of its life and use. This book exists for its readers, whose reactions and suggestions we warmly welcome, as these will in turn reshape this book for later users in the years to come.

POLITICAL AND RELIGIOUS ORDERS

One political order that cannot be ignored by readers of British literature and history is the monarchy, since it provides the terms by which historical periods are even today divided up. Thus much of the nineteenth century is often spoken of as the "Victorian" age or period, after Queen Victoria (reigned 1837–1901), and the writing of the period is given the name Victorian literature. By the same token, writing of the period 1559–1603 is often called "Elizabethan" after Elizabeth I, and that of 1901–1910 "Edwardian" after Edward VII. This system however is based more on convention than logic, since few would call the history (or literature) of late twentieth-century Britain "Elizabethan" any more than they would call the history and literature of the eighteenth century "Georgian," though four king Georges reigned between 1714 and 1820. Where other, better terms exist these are generally adopted.

As these notes suggest, however, it is still common to think of British history in terms of the dates of the reigning monarch, even though the political influence of the monarchy has been strictly limited since the seventeenth century. Thus, where an outstanding political figure has emerged it is he or she who tends to name the period of a decade or longer; for the British, for example, the 1980s was the decade of "Thatcherism" as for Americans it was the period of "Reaganomics." The monarchy, though, still provides a point of common reference and has up to now shown a remarkable historical persistence, transforming itself as occasion dictates to fit new social circumstances. Thus, while most of the other European monarchies disappeared early in the twentieth century, if they had not already done so, the British institution managed to transform itself from imperial monarchy, a role adopted in the nineteenth century, to become the head of a welfare state and member of the European Union. Few of the titles gathered by Queen Victoria, such as Empress of India, remain to Elizabeth II (reigns 1952–), whose responsibilities now extend only to the British Isles with some vestigial role in Australia, Canada, and New Zealand among other places.

The monarchy's political power, like that of the aristocracy, has been successively diminished over the past several centuries, with the result that today both monarch and aristocracy have only formal authority. This withered state of today's institutions, however, should not blind us to the very real power they wielded in earlier centuries. Though the medieval monarch King John had famously been obliged to recognize the rule of law by signing the Magna Carta ("Great Charter") in 1215, thus ending arbitrary rule, the sixteenth- and seventeenth-century English monarchs still officially ruled by "divine right" and were under no obligation to attend to the wishes of Parliament. Charles I in the 1630s reigned mostly without summoning a parliament, and the concept of a "constitutional monarchy," being one whose powers were formally bound by statute, was introduced only when King William agreed to the Declaration of Right in 1689. This document, together with the contemporaneous Bill of Rights, while recognizing that sovereignty still rests in the monarch, formally transferred executive and legislative powers to Parliament. Bills still have to receive Royal Assent, though this was last denied by Queen Anne in 1707; the monarch still holds "prerogative" powers, though these, which include the appointment of certain officials, the dissolution of Parliament and so on, are, in practice wielded by the prime minister. Further information on the political character of various historical periods can be found in the period introductions.

Political power in Britain is thus held by the prime minister and his or her cabinet, members of which are also members of the governing party in the House of Commons. As long as the government is able to command a majority in the House of Commons, sometimes by a coalition of several parties but more usually by the absolute majority of one, it both makes the laws and carries them out. The situation is therefore very different from the American doctrine of the "Separation of Powers," in which Congress is independent of the President and can even be controlled by the opposing party. The British state of affairs has led to the office of prime minister being compared to that of an "elected dictatorship" with surprising frequency over the past several hundred years.

British government is bicameral, having both an upper and a lower house. Unlike other bicameral systems, however, the upper house, the House of Lords, is not elected, its membership being largely hereditary. Membership can come about in four main ways: (1) by birth, (2) by appointment by the current prime minister often in consultation with the Leader of the Opposition, (3) by virtue of holding a senior position in the judiciary, and (4) by being a bishop of the Established Church (the Church of England). In the House of Commons, the lower house, the particular features of the British electoral system have meant that there are never more than two large parties, one of which is in power. These are, together, "Her Majesty's Government and Opposition." Local conditions in Northern Ireland and Scotland have meant that these areas sometimes send members to Parliament in London who are members neither of the Conservative nor of the Labour parties; in general, however, the only other group in the Commons is the small Liberal Party.

Taking these categories in turn, all members of the hereditary aristocracy (the "peerage") have a seat in the House of Lords. The British aristocracy, unlike those of other European countries, was never formally dispossessed of political power (for example by a revolution), and though their influence is now limited, nevertheless all holders of hereditary title—dukes, marquesses, earls, viscounts and barons, in that order of precedence—sit in the Lords. Some continue to do political work and may be members of the Government or of the Opposition, though today it would be considered unusual for a senior member of government to sit in the House of Lords. The presence of the hereditary element in the Lords tends to give the institution a conservative tone, though the presence of the other members ensures this is by no means always the case. Secondly there are "life peers," who are created by the monarch on the prime minister's recommendation under legislation dating from 1958. They are generally individuals who have distinguished themselves in one field or another; retiring senior politicians from the Commons are generally elevated to the Lords, for example, as are some senior civil servants, diplomats, business and trade union leaders, academics, figures in the arts, retiring archbishops, and members of the military. Some of these take on formal political responsibilities and others do not. Finally, senior members of the judiciary sit in the Lords as Law Lords, while senior members of the Church of England hierarchy also sit in the Lords and frequently intervene in political matters. It has been a matter of some controversy whether senior members of other religious denominations, or religions, should also sit in the House of Lords. Within the constitution (by the Parliament Act of 1911 and other acts) the powers of the House of Lords are limited mostly to the amendment and delay of legislation; from time to time the question of its reform or abolition is raised.

In addition, there are minor orders of nobility that should be mentioned. A baronet is a holder of a hereditary title, but he is not a member of the peerage; the style is Sir (followed by his first and last names), Baronet (usually abbreviated as Bart. or Bt.). A knight is a member of one of the various orders of British knighthood, the oldest of which dates back to the Middle Ages (the Order of the Garter), the majority to the eighteenth or nineteenth centuries (the Order of the Thistle, the Bath, Saint Michael, and Saint George, etc.). The title is nonhereditary and is given for various services; it is marked by various initials coming after the name. K.C.B., for example, stands for "Knight Commander of the Bath," and there are many others.

In the House of Commons itself, the outstanding feature is the dominance of the party system. Party labels, such as "Whigs" and "Tories," were first used from the late seventeenth century, when groups of members began to form opposing factions in a Parliament now freed of much of the power of the king. The "Tories," for example, a name now used to refer to the modern Conservative Party, were originally members of that faction that supported James II (exiled in 1689); the word "Tory" comes from the Irish (Gaelic) for outlaw or thief. The "Whigs," on the other hand, supported the constitutional reforms associated with the 1689 Glorious Revolution; the word "whig" is obscurely related to the idea of regicide. The Whig faction largely dominated the political history of the eighteenth century, though the electorate was too small, and politics too controlled by the patronage of the great aristocratic families, for much of a party system to develop. It was only in the middle decades of the nineteenth century that the familiar party system in parliament and the associated electioneering organization in the country at large came into being. The Whigs were replaced by the Liberal Party around the mid-century, as the Liberals were to be replaced by the Labour Party in the early decades of the twentieth century; the Tories had become firm Conservatives by the time of Lord Derby's administrations in the mid-nineteenth century.

The party system has always been fertile ground for a certain amount of parliamentary theater, and it has fostered the emergence of some powerful personalities. Whereas the eighteenth-century Whig prime minister Sir Robert Walpole owed his authority to a mixture of personal patronage and the power made available through the alliances of powerful families, nineteenth-century figures such as Benjamin Disraeli (Conservative prime minister 1868, 1874–1880) and William Ewart Gladstone (Liberal prime minister 1868–1874; 1880–1885; 1885; 1892–1894), were at the apex of their respective party machines. Disraeli, theatrical, personable and with a keen eye for publicity (he was, among other things, a close personal friend of Queen Victoria), formed a great contrast to the massive moral appeals of his parliamentary opponent Gladstone. One earlier figure, William Pitt (1759–1806), prime minister at twenty-four and leader of the country during the French Revolution and earlier Napoleonic wars, stands comparison with these in the historical record; of twentieth-century political figures, David Lloyd-George, Liberal prime minister during World War I, and Winston Churchill, Conservative, during World War II, deserve special mention.

Though political power in the United Kingdom now rests with Parliament at Westminster in London, this has not always been the only case. Wales, which is now formally a principality within the political construction "England and Wales," was conquered by the English toward the end of the thirteenth century—too early for indigenous representative institutions to have fallen into place. Scotland, on the other hand, which from 1603 was linked with England under a joint monarchy but only became part of the same political entity with the Act of Union in 1707, did develop discrete institutions. Recent votes in both Scotland and Wales are leading toward greater local legislative control over domestic issues in both Scotland and Wales. Many Scottish institutions—for example, the legal and educational systems—are substantially different from those of England, which is not true in the case of Wales. The Church of Scotland in particular has no link with the Church of England, having been separately established in 1690 on a Presbyterian basis; this means that authority in the Scottish church is vested in elected pastors and lay elders and not in an ecclesiastical hierarchy of priests and bishops. But the most vexed of the relationships within the union has undoubtedly been that between England and Ireland.

There has been an English presence in Ireland from the Middle Ages on, and this became dominant in the later sixteenth century when English policy was deliberately to conquer and colonize the rest of the country. The consequence of this policy, however, was that an Irish Protestant "Ascendancy" came to rule over a largely dispossessed Catholic Irish peasantry; in 1689 at the Battle of the Boyne this state of affairs was made permanent, as Irish Catholic support for the exiled and Catholic-sympathizing James II was routed by the invading troops of the new Protestant king, William III. An Irish parliament met in Dublin, but this was restricted to Protestants; the Church of Ireland was the established Protestant church in a country where most of the population was Catholic. Irish political representation was shifted to Westminster by Pitt in 1800 under the formal Act of Union with Ireland; the Church of Ireland was disestablished by Gladstone later in the century. In the twentieth century, continuing agita-

tion in the Catholic south of the country first for Home Rule and subsequently for independence from Britain—agitation that had been a feature of almost the whole nineteenth century
at greater or lesser levels of intensity—led to the establishment first of the Irish Free State
(1922) and later of the Republic (1948). In the Protestant North of the country, a local parliament met from 1922 within the common framework of the United Kingdom, but this was suspended in 1972 and representation returned to Westminster, as renewed violence in the
province threatened local institutions. In Northern Ireland several hundred years of conflict
between Protestants, who form the majority of the population in the province, and Catholics
have led to continuing political problems.

Since the Reformation in the sixteenth century Britain has officially been a Protestant
country with a national church headed by the monarch. This "Established Church," the
Church of England or Anglican Church, has its own body of doctrine in the Thirty-Nine Articles and elsewhere, its own order of services in the Book of Common Prayer, and its own translation of the Bible (the "Authorized Version"), commissioned by James I (reigned 1603–1625)
as Head of the Church. There is an extensive ecclesiastical hierarchy and a worldwide communion that includes the American Episcopalian Church.

The Reformation in England was not an easy business, and it has certain negative consequences even today. Some of these have been touched upon above in the case of Ireland.
Those professing Roman Catholicism were excluded from political office and suffered other
penalties until 1829, and a Catholic hierarchy parallel to that of the Church of England only
came into being in Britain in the later nineteenth century. Though many of the restrictions on
Roman Catholics enacted by Act of Parliament at the end of the seventeenth century were
considerably softened in the course of the eighteenth, nevertheless they were very real.

English Protestantism, however, is far from being all of a piece. As early as the sixteenth
century, many saw the substitution of the King's authority and that of the national ecclesiastical hierarchy for that of the Pope to be no genuine Protestant Reformation, which they
thought demanded local autonomy and individual judgment. In the seventeenth century many
"dissenting" or "Non-Conformist" Protestant sects thus grew up or gathered strength (many
becoming "Puritans"), and these rejected the authority of the national church and its bishops
and so the authority of the king. They had a brief moment of freedom during the Civil War
and the Commonwealth (1649–1660) following the execution of Charles I, when there was a
flowering of sects from Baptists and Quakers, which still exist today, to Ranters, Shakers,
Anabaptists, Muggletonians, etc., which in the main do not (except for some sects in the
United States). The monarchy and the Church were decisively reestablished in 1660, but subsequent legislation, most importantly the Act of Toleration (1689), suspended laws against
dissenters on certain conditions.

Religious dissent or nonconformity remained powerful social movements over the following centuries and received new stimulus from the "New Dissenting" revivalist movements of
the eighteenth century (particularly Methodism, though there was also a growth in the Con-
gregationalist and Baptist churches). By the nineteenth century, the social character and geographical pattern of English dissent had been established: religious nonconformity was a feature of the new working classes brought into being by the Industrial Revolution in the towns of
the Midlands and North of England. Anglicanism, which was associated with the pre-industri-
al traditional order, was rejected also by many among the rising bourgeoisie and lower middle
classes; almost every major English novel of the mid-nineteenth century and beyond is written
against a background of religious nonconformity or dissent, which had complex social and
political meanings. Nonconformity was also a particular feature of Welsh society.

Under legislation enacted by Edward I in 1290, the Jews were expelled from England, and
there were few of them in the country until the end of the seventeenth century, when well-
established Jewish communities began to appear in London (the medieval legislation was
repealed under the Commonwealth in the 1650s). Restrictions on Jews holding public office

continued until the mid-nineteenth century, and at the end of the century large Jewish communities were formed in many English cities by refugees from Central and Eastern European anti-Semitism.

Britain today is a multicultural country and significant proportions of the population, many of whom came to Britain from former British Empire territories, profess Hinduism or Islam, among other religions. The United Kingdom has been a member of the European Union since the early 1970s, and this has further loosened ties between Britain and former empire territories or dominions, many of which are still linked to Britain by virtue of the fact that the British monarch is Head of the "Commonwealth," an organization to which many of them belong. In some cases, the British monarch is also Head of State. Most importantly, however, British membership of the European Union has meant that powers formerly held by the national parliament have been transferred either to the European Parliament in Strasbourg, France, or to the European Commission, the executive agency in Brussels, Belgium, or, in the case of judicial review and appeal, to the European Court of Justice. This process seems set to generate tensions in Britain for some years to come.

David Tresilian

ENGLISH MONARCHS

Before the Norman conquest (1066), these included:

Alfred the Great	871–899
Edmund I	940–946
Ethelred the Unready	948–1016
Edward the Confessor	1042–1066
Harold II	1066

The following monarchs are divided by the dynasty ("House") to which they belong:

Normandy

William I the Conqueror	1066–1087
William II, Rufus	1087–1100
Henry I	1100–1135

Blois

Stephen	1135–1154

Plantagenet

Henry II	1154–1189
Richard I "Coeur de Lion"	1189–1199
John	1199–1216
Henry III	1216–1272
Edward I	1272–1307
Edward II	1307–1327
Edward III	1327–1377
Richard II	1377–1399

Lancaster

Henry IV	1399–1413
Henry V	1413–1422
Henry VI	1422–1471

York

Edward IV	1461–1483
Edward V	1483
Richard III	1483–1485

Tudor

Henry VII	1485–1509
Henry VIII	1509–1547
Edward VI	1547–1553
Mary I	1553–1558
Elizabeth I	1558–1603

Kings of England and of Scotland:

Stuart

James I (James VI of Scotland)	1603–1625
Charles I	1625–1649
Commonwealth (Republic)	
Council of State	1649–1653
Oliver Cromwell, Lord Protector	1653–1658
Richard Cromwell	1658–1660

Stuart

Charles II	1660–1685
James II	1685–1688
(Interregnum 1688–1689)	
William III and Mary II	1685–1701 (Mary dies 1694)
Anne	1702–1714

Hanover

George I	1714–1727
George II	1727–1760
George III	1760–1820
George IV	1820–1830
William IV	1830–1837
Victoria	1837–1901

Saxe-Coburg and Gotha

Edward VII	1901–1910

Windsor

George V	1910–1936
Edward VIII	1936
George VI	1936–1952
Elizabeth II	1952–

MONEY, WEIGHTS, AND MEASURES

The possibility of confusion by the British monetary system has considerably decreased since 1971, when decimalization of the currency took place. There are now 100 pence to a pound (worth about $1.60 in the late 1990s). Prior to this date the currency featured a gallery of other units as well. These coins—shillings, crowns, half-crowns, florins, threepenny-bits, and farthings—were contemporary survivals of the currency's historical development. As such they had a familiar presence in the culture, which was reflected in the slang terms used to refer to them in the spoken language. At least one of these terms, that of a "quid" for a pound, is still in use today.

The old currency divided the pound into 20 shillings, each of which contained 12 pence. There were, therefore, 240 pence in 1 pound. Five shillings made a crown, a half-crown was 2½ shillings, and a florin was 2 shillings; there was also a sixpence, a threepenny-bit, and a farthing (a quarter of a penny). In slang, a shilling was a "bob," a sixpence a "tanner," and a penny a "copper." Sums were written as, for example, £12. 6s. 6d. or £12/6/6 (12 pounds, 6 shillings, and 6 pence; the "d." stands for "denarius," from the Latin). Figures up to £5 were often expressed in shillings alone: the father of the novelist D. H. Lawrence, for instance, who was a coal miner, was paid around 35 shillings a week at the beginning of the twentieth century— i.e., 1 pound and 15 shillings, or £1/15/–. At this time two gold coins were also still in circulation, the sovereign (£1) and the half-sovereign (10s.), which had been the principal coins of the nineteenth century; the largest silver coin was the half-crown (2 / 6). Later all coins were composed either of copper or an alloy of copper and nickel. The guinea was £1/1/– (1 pound and 1 shilling, or 21 shillings); though the actual coin had not been minted since the beginning of the nineteenth century, the term was still used well into the twentieth to price luxury items and to pay professional fees.

The number of dollars that a pound could buy has fluctuated with British economic fortunes. The current figure has been noted above; in 1912 it was about $5.00. To get a sense of how much the pound was worth to those who used it as an everyday index of value, however, we have to look at what it could buy within the system in which it was used. To continue the Lawrence example, a coal miner may have been earning 35 shillings a week in the early years of the twentieth century, but of this he would have to have paid six shillings as rent on the family house; his son, by contrast, could command a figure of £300 as a publisher's advance on his novel *The Rainbow* (pub. 1915), a sum which alone would have placed him somewhere in the middle class. In *A Room of One's Own* (1928) Virginia Woolf recommended the figure of £500 a year as necessary if a woman were to write; at today's values this would be worth around £25,000 ($41,000)—considerably more than the pay of, for example, a junior faculty member at a British university, either then or now.

In earlier periods an idea of the worth of the currency, being the relation between wages and prices, can similarly be established by taking samples from across the country at specific dates. Toward the end of the seventeenth century, for example, Poor Law records tell us that a family of five could be considered to subsist on an annual income of £13/14/-, which included £9/14/– spent on food. At the same time an agricultural laborer earned around £15/12/– annually, while at the upper end of the social scale, the aristocracy dramatically recovered and increased their wealth in the period after the restoration of the monarchy in 1660. By 1672 the early industrialist Lord Wharton was realizing an annual profit of £3,200 on his lead mine and smelting plant in the north of England; landed aristocratic families such as the Russells, sponsors of the 1689 Glorious Revolution and later dukes of Bedford, were already worth £10,000 a year in 1660. Such details allow us to form some idea of the value of the £10 the poet John Milton received for *Paradise Lost* (pub. 1667), as well as to see the great wealth that went into building the eighteenth-century estates that now dot the English countryside.

By extending the same method to the analysis of wage-values during the Industrial Revolution over a century and a half later, the economic background to incidents of public disorder in the period, such as the 1819 "Peterloo Massacre" in London, can be reconstructed, as can the background to the poems of Wordsworth, for example, many of which concern vagrancy and the lives of the rural poor. Thus the essayist William Cobbett calculated in the 1820s that £1/4/– a week was needed to support a family of five, though actual average earnings were less than half this sum. By contrast, Wordsworth's projection of "a volume which consisting of 160 pages might be sold at 5 shillings" (1806)—part of the negotiations for his *Poems in Two Volumes* (1807)—firmly establishes the book as a luxury item. Jane Austen's contemporaneous novel *Mansfield Park* (1814), which gives many details about the economic affairs of the English rural gentry, suggests that at least £1000 a year is a desirable income.

Today's pound sterling, though still cited on the international exchanges with the dollar, the deutsche mark, and the yen, decisively lost to the dollar after World War I as the central currency in the international system. At present it seems highly likely that, with some other European national currencies, it will shortly cease to exist as the currency unit of the European Union is adopted as a single currency in the constituent countries of the Union.

British weights and measures present less difficulty to American readers since the vast inertia permeating industry and commerce following the separation of the United States from Britain prevented the reform of American weights and measures along metric lines, which had taken place where the monetary system was concerned. Thus the British "Imperial" system, with some minor local differences, was in place in both countries until decimalization of the British system began in stages from the early 1970s on. Today all British weights and measures, with the exception of road signs, which still generally give distances in miles, are metric in order to bring Britain into line with European Union standards. Though it is still possible to hear especially older people measuring area in acres and not in hectares, distances in miles and not in kilometers, or feet and yards and not centimeters and meters, weight in pounds and ounces and not in grams and kilograms, and temperature in Fahrenheit and not in centigrade, etc., it is becoming increasingly uncommon. Measures of distance that might be found in older texts— such as the league (three miles, but never in regular use), the furlong (220 yards), and the ell (45 inches)—are now all obsolete; the only measure still heard in current use is the stone (14 pounds), and this is generally used for body weight.

David Tresilian

BIBLIOGRAPHY

The Middle Ages

Dictionaries, Encyclopedias • Miranda Green, ed., *Dictionary of Celtic Mythology*, 1992. • Hans Kurath et al., eds., *The Middle English Dictionary*, 1952–. • Norris J. Lacy, ed., *The New Arthurian Encyclopedia*, 1991. • Paul E. Szarmach, M. Teresa Tavormina, Joel T. Rosenthal, eds., *Medieval England: an encyclopedia*, 1998 • Joseph Strayer, gen. ed., *The Dictionary of the Middle Ages*, 13 vols., 1982–1989. • David Wallace, ed., *The Cambridge History of Medieval English Literature*, 1999.

Journals • *Celtica* • *Exemplaria: A Journal of Theory in Medieval and Renaissance Studies* • *Medium Aevum* • *Speculum*, vol. 1–64 (1926–1989) available on-line through JSTOR ("Journal Storage"): http://www.jstor.org

On-Line Sources • Reference material and on-line texts: • Internet Medieval Sourcebook (IMS) (historical and literary texts, both extracts and complete works, some in out-of-date translations): www.fordham.edu/halsall/sbook.html • The Labyrinth: Resources for Medieval Studies (the best clearing-house for access to more specialized sites): www.georgetown.edu/labyrinth/ • *The Medieval Review* (book review journal): http://www.hti.umich.edu/t/tmr/ • The Online Reference Book for Medieval Studies (ORB): http://orb.rhodes.edu/ • NetSERF: The Internet Connection for Medieval Resources: http://netserf.cua.edu

Images From Medieval Manuscripts and Entire Digitized Manuscripts: • Pages from the Beowulf manuscript in color facsimile: http://www.uky.edu/~kiernan/eBeowulf/main.htm • The Piers Plowman Electronic Archive: www.iath.virginia.edu/piers/tcontents.html • The pages run by the Bibliothèque Nationale (Paris) are especially good, and can be searched by subject: http://www.bnf.fr/enluminures/aaccueil.htm • Medieval Illuminated Manuscripts, a joint project of the National Library of the Netherlands and the Museum Meermanno: http://www.kb.nl/kb/manuscripts/ • The Danish Royal Library at Copenhagen (Det Kongelige Bibliotek) has digitized a number of its manuscripts in their entireties, including several of English origin: http://www.kb.dk/kb/dept/nbo/ha/manuskripter/index2-en.htm • The *Très Riches Heures* of Jean, Duc de Berry, is a wonderful trove of images of courtly life, agriculture, and later medieval piety. Much of it is at: http://metalab.unc.edu/wm/rh • All the calendar pages, with some introduction, are at: http://humanities.uchicago.edu/images/heures/heures.html • The late fourteenth-century *Petites Heures* is at: http://www.bnf.fr/enluminures/texte/atx3_02.htm • A famous 13th-century English manuscript of an Anglo-Norman verse life of King Edward "The Confessor," densely illustrated: http://www.lib.cam.ac.uk/MSS/Ee.3.59 • The 12th-century "Aberdeen Bestiary," in a beautifully designed and educational site: http://www.clues.abdn.ac.uk:8080/besttest/firstpag.html

The British Isles Before the Norman Conquest
• D. A. Binchy, *Celtic and Anglo-Saxon Kingship*, 1970. • Peter Hunter Blair, *Roman Britain and Early England, 55 B.C.–A.D. 871*, 1963. • Peter Hunter Blair, *Introduction to Anglo-Saxon England*, 2nd ed., 1977. • H. M. Chadwick, *The Heroic Age*, 1912. • Nora K. Chadwick, *The Celts*, 1970. • Liam de Paor, *The Peoples of Ireland*, 1986. • Myles Dillon and Nora K. Chadwick, *The Celtic Realms*, 1972. • *English Historical Documents*, vol. I, c. 500–1042, ed. Dorothy Whitelock, 1953. [Primary sources in English translation; introductions provide excellent context.] • Nicholas Howe, *Migration and Mythmaking in Anglo-Saxon England*, 1989. • Hugh A. MacDougall, *Racial Myth in English History: Trojans, Teutons, and Anglo-Saxons*, 1982. • Kim McCone, *Pagan past and Christian present in early Irish literature*, 1990. • Nerys Patterson, *Cattle Lords and Clansmen: The Social Structure of Early Ireland*, 2nd ed., 1996. • Frank M. Stenton, "Anglo-Saxon England," *The Oxford History of England*, vol. 2, 1971. • Dorothy Whitelock, *The Beginnings of English Society*, 1952. • David M. Wilson, *The Anglo-Saxons*, 1960. • Charles D. Wright, *The Irish Tradition in Old English Literature*, 1993.

The Norman Conquest and Its Impact • Jonathan Alexander and Paul Binski, *Age of Chivalry: Art in Plantagenet England 1200–1400*, 1987. • Christopher Brooke, *From Alfred to Henry III, 871–1272*, 1961. • R. Allen Brown, *The Normans*, 1984. • Marjorie Chibnall, *Anglo-Norman England, 1066–1166*, 1984. • Michael Clanchy, *England and Its Rulers, 1066–1307*, 1983. • *English Historical Documents*, vol. II, *1042–1189*, eds. David C. Douglas and George W. Greenaway, 1953; vol. III, *1189–1327*, ed. Harry Rothwell, 1975. • Elizabeth Hallam, *Plantagenet Chronicles*, 1986. Chronicle sources, fine illustrations. • H. W. Koch, *Medieval Warfare*, 1978. • A. L. Poole, *From Domesday Book to Magna Carta*, The Oxford History of England, 1955. • F. M. Powicke, *The Thirteenth Century, 1216–1307*, The Oxford History of England, vol. 4, 1953. • Pauline Stafford, *Unification and Conquest: A Political and Social History of England in the Tenth and Eleventh Centuries*, 1989. • Philip Warner, *The Medieval Castle*, 1971.

Continental and Insular Cultures • Judson B. Allen, *The Friar as Critic: Literary Attitudes in the Later Middle Ages*, 1971. • Erich Auerbach, *Mimesis: The Representation of Reality in Western Literature*, trans. Willard R. Trask, 1957. • William Calin, *The French Tradition and the Literature of Medieval England*, 1994. • Marcia Colish, *The Mirror of Language*, rev. ed., 1983. • Ernst Robert Curtius, *European Literature and the Latin Middle Ages*, trans. Willard R. Trask, 1953. • Peter Dronke, *Medieval Latin and the Rise of the European Love Lyric*, 2nd ed., 2 vols., 1968. • Robert W. Hanning, *The Individual in Twelfth-Century Romance*, 1978. • Johan Huizinga, *The Autumn of the Middle Ages*, trans. Rodney J. Payton and Ulrich Mammitzsch, 1996. • W. P. Ker, *Epic and Romance*, 1957. • C. S. Lewis, *The Discarded Image: An Introduction to Medieval and Renaissance Literature*, 1964. • A. J. Minnis, *Medieval Theory of Authorship: Scholastic Literary Attitudes in the Later Middle Ages*, 2nd ed., 1988. • Nigel Saul, ed., *England in Europe 1066–1453*, 1994. • Rosamund Tuve, *Allegorical Imagery: Some Medieval Books and their Posterity*, 1966.

Politics and Society in the Fourteenth and Fifteenth Centuries • David Aers, ed., *Culture and History, 1350–1600*, 1992. • R. B. Dobson, *The Peasants' Revolt of 1381*, 2nd ed., 1983. • *English Historical Documents*, vol. IV, *1327–1485*, ed. A. R. Myers, 1969. • Chris Given-Wilson, *The English Nobility in the Late Middle Ages*, 1987. • Rodney H. Hilton, *Bond Men Made Free: Medieval Peasant Movements and the English Rising of 1381*, 1973. • Ernest F. Jacob, "The Fifteenth Century," *The Oxford History of England*, vol. 6, 1961. • Maurice Keen, *English Society in the Later Middle Ages*, 1990. • Gordon Leff, *The Dissolution of the Medieval Outlook: An Essay on Intellectual and Spiritual Change in the Fourteenth Century*, 1976. • Gervase Matthew, *The Court of Richard II*, 1968. • May McKisack, *The Fourteenth Century, 1307–1399*, 1959. • Colin Platt, *The English Medieval Town*, 1976. • Paul Strohm, *England's empty throne: usurpation and the language of legitimation, 1399–1422*, 1998. • Juliet Vale, *Edward III and Chivalry: Chivalric Society and Its Context 1270–1350*, 1982. • David Wallace, ed., *Bodies and Disciplines: Intersections of Literature and History in Fifteenth-Century England*, 1996. • Scott L. Waugh, *England in the Reign of Edward III*, 1991. [extensive and helpful bibliography]

Religious Institutions and Cultures • Margaret Aston, *Lollards and Reformers*, 1994. • Renate Blumenfeld-Kosinski and Timea Szell, eds., *Images of Sainthood in Medieval Europe*, 1991. • Janet Burton, *Monastic and Religious Orders in Britain, 1000–1300*, 1994. • M. D. Chenu, *Nature, Man, and Society in the Twelfth Century*, eds. and trans. Jerome Taylor and Lester K. Little, 1968. • Ronald C. Finucane, *Miracles and Pilgrims: Popular Beliefs in Medieval England*, 1977. • Thomas Heffernan, *Sacred Biography: Saints and Their Biographers in the Middle Ages*, 1988. • Anne Hudson, *The Premature Reformation: Wycliffite Texts and Lollard History*, 1988. • W. A. Pantin, *The English Church in the Fourteenth Century*, 1980.

Gender, Sexuality, Courtliness, Marriage • John Boswell, *Christianity, Social Tolerance, and Homosexuality: Gay People in Western Europe from the Beginning of the Christian Era to the Fourteenth Century*, 1980. • Christopher Brooke, *The Medieval Idea of Marriage*, 1989. • Glenn Burger and Steven F. Krueger, eds., *Queering the Middle Ages*, 2001. • Jeffrey J. Cohen and Bonnie Wheeler, eds., *Becoming male in the Middle Ages*, 1997. • Susan Crane, *Insular Romance: Politics, Faith, and Culture in Anglo-Norman and Middle English Literature*, 1986. • Georges Duby, *The Knight, the Lady, and the Priest: The Making of Modern Marriage* in *Medieval France*, trans. Barbara Bray, 1983. • Frances and Joseph Gies, *Marriage and the Family in the Middle Ages*, 1987. • Henry A. Kelly, *Love and Marriage in the Age of Chaucer*, 1975. • Clare A. Lees, ed., *Medieval Masculinities: Regarding Men in the Middle Ages*, 1994. • C. S. Lewis, *The Allegory of Love*, 1938. • V. J. Scattergood and J. W. Sherborne, eds., *English Court Culture in the Later Middle Ages*, 1983.

Women, Work, and Religion • Judith Bennett, *Women in the Medieval English Countryside*, 1986. • Caroline Walker Bynum, *Holy Feast and Holy Fast: The Religious Significance of Food to Medieval Women*, 1987. • Sharon Elkins, *Holy Women of Twelfth Century England*, 1988. • Mary Erler and Maryanne Kowaleski, eds., *Women and Power in the Middle Ages*, 1988. • Christine Fell, *Women in Anglo-Saxon England*, 1986. • Penny Schine Gold, *The Lady and the Virgin: Image, Attitude, and Experience in Twelfth-Century France*, 1985. • Barbara Hanawalt, ed., *Women and Work in Preindustrial Europe*, 1986. • Martha Howell, *Women, Production and Patriarchy in Late Medieval Cities*, 1986. • C. E. Meek and M. K. Simms, eds., *The Fragility of Her Sex? Medieval Irish Women in Their European Context*, 1995. • Barbara Newman, *From Virile Woman to Woman Christ: Studies in Medieval Religion and Literature*, 1995. • Lesley Smith and Jane H. M. Taylor, eds., *Women, the Book, and the Godly*, 1995. • Pauline Stafford, *Queens, Concubines, and Dowagers: The King's Wife in the Early Middle Ages*, 1983. • Ulrike Wiethaus, ed., *Maps of Flesh and Light: The Religious Experience of Medieval Women Mystics*, 1993. • Jocelyn Wogan-Browne, *Saints' lives and women's literary culture c. 1150–1300 : virginity and its authorizations*, 2001.

Modes of Transmission: Orality, Literacy, Manuscripts, Languages • Janet Backhouse, *Books of Hours*, 1985. • Mary Carruthers, *The Book of Memory: A Study of Memory in Medieval Culture*, 1990. • Roger Chartier, ed., *The Culture of Print: Power and the Uses of Print in Early Modern Europe*, 1989. • M. T. Clanchy, *From Memory to Written Record: England, 1066–1307*, 2nd ed., 1993. • Janet Coleman, *Medieval Readers and Writers, 1350–1400*, 1981. • Joyce Coleman, *Public Reading and the Reading Public in Late Medieval England and France*, 1996. • Christopher de Hamel, *A History of Illuminated Manuscripts*, 1986. •

John H. Fisher, *The Emergence of Standard English*, 1996. • John Miles Foley, *The Theory of Oral Composition: History and Methodology*, 1988. • Jeremy Griffiths and Derek Pearsall, eds., *Book Production and Publishing in Britain, 1375–1475*, 1989. • Seth Lerer, *Literacy and Power in Anglo-Saxon England*, 1991. • Jeff Opland, *Anglo-Saxon Oral Poetry: A Study of the Traditions*, 1979. • Nicholas Orme, *From Childhood to Chivalry: The Education of the English Kings and Aristocracy 1066–1530*, 1984.

Old English Literature • Journals. • *Anglo-Saxon England* • *Old English Newsletter*

Bibliography. • Stanley B. Greenfield and Fred C. Robinson, *Bibliography of Publications on Old English Literature*, 1980.

Studies and Guides. • Michael Alexander, *Old English Literature*, 1983. • Jess B. Bessinger and Stanley J. Kahrl, eds., *Essential Articles for the Study of Old English Poetry*, 1968. • Jane Chance, *Woman as Hero in Old English Literature*, 1986. • Helen Damico and Alexandra Hennessey Olsen, eds., *New Readings on Women in Old English Literature*, 1990. • Allen J. Franzten, *The Desire for Origins: New Language, Old English, and Teaching the Tradition*, 1990. • Allen J. Franzten, ed., *Speaking Two Languages: Traditional Disciplines and Contemporary Theory in Medieval Studies*, 1991. • Malcolm Godden and Michael Lapidge, eds., *The Cambridge Companion to Old English Literature*, 1991. • Stanley B. Greenfield, *Hero and Exile: The Art of Old English Poetry*, 1989. • Stanley B. Greenfield and Daniel G. Calder, *A New Critical History of Old English Literature*, 1986. • Britton J. Harwood and Gillian Overing, eds., *Class and Gender in Early English Literature: Intersections*, 1994. • Katherine O'Brien O'Keeffe, ed., *Old English Shorter Poems: Basic Readings*, 1994. • Charles D. Wright, *The Irish Tradition in Old English Literature*, 1993.

Middle English Language and Literature • Middle English Grammar. • John A. Burrow and Thorlac Turville-Petre, *A Book of Middle English*, 1996. • Joseph Wright and Elizabeth Mary Wright, *An Elementary Middle English Grammar*, 1979.

On-Line Sources. • TEAMS (The Consortium for the Teaching of the Middle Ages) publishes a series of Middle English texts, also available on-line: http://www.lib.rochester.edu/camelot/teams/tmsmenu.htm • The "Middle

English Compendium" contains texts, a hyper-bibliography, and the *Middle English Dictionary* on-line: http://ets.umdl.umich.edu/m/mec/

Texts. • Jocelyn Wogan-Browne et al., eds., *The Idea of the Vernacular: An Anthology of Middle English Literary Theory, 1280–1520*, 1999.

Studies. • David Aers, *Community, Gender, and Individual Identity: English Writing 1360–1430*, 1988. • H. S. Bennett, "Chaucer and the Fifteenth Century," *The Oxford History of English Literature*, vol. 2, part 1, 1947. • J. A. W. Bennett and Douglas Gray, "Middle English Literature," *The Oxford History of English Literature*, vol. 1, part 2, 1986. • J. A. Burrow, *Ricardian Poetry: Chaucer, Gower, Langland, and the Gawain*, 1971. • William Calin, *The French Tradition and the Literature of Medieval England*, 1994. • Rita Copeland, ed., *Criticism and Dissent in the Middle Ages*, 1996. • E. K. Chambers, "English Literature at the Close of the Middle Ages," *The Oxford History of English Literature*, vol. 2, part 2, 1961. • Basil Cottle, *The Triumph of English 1350–1400*, 1969. • Carolyn Dinshaw, *Getting Medieval: Sexualities and Communities, Pre- and Postmodern*, 1999. • A. S. G. Edwards, *Middle English Prose: A Critical Guide to Major Authors and Genres*, 1984. • Ruth Evans and Lesley Johnson, eds., *Feminist Readings in Middle English Literature: The Wife of Bath and All Her Sect*, 1994. • Laurie A. Finke and Martin B. Schichtman, eds., *Medieval Texts and Contemporary Readers*, 1987. • Richard Firth Green, *A Crisis of Truth: Literature and Law in Ricardian England*, 1999. • Boris Ford, *Medieval Literature: Chaucer and the Alliterative Tradition*, 1982. • Stephen Justice, *Writing and Rebellion: England in 1381*, 1994. • Karma Lochrie, *Covert Operations: The Medieval Uses of Secrecy*, 1999. • Carol M. Meale, ed., *Women and Literature in Britain, c. 1150–1500*, 1993. • Charles Muscatine, *Poetry and Crisis in the Age of Chaucer*, 1972. • Glending Olson, *Literature as Recreation in the Later Middle Ages*, 1982. • Lee Patterson, ed., *Literary Practice and Social Change in Britain, 1380–1530*, 1990. • Lee Patterson, *Negotiating the Past: The Historical Understanding of Medieval Literature*, 1987. • Larry Scanlon, *Narrative, Authority, and Power: The Medieval Exemplum and the Chaucerian Tradition*, 1994. • A. C. Spearing, *Readings in Medieval Poetry*, 1987. • Paul Strohm, *Hochon's Arrow: The Social Imagination of Fourteenth-Century Texts*, 1992. • Thorlac Turville-Petre, *The Alliterative Revival*, 1977. • Thorlac Turville-Petre, *England*

the Nation: Language, Literature, and National Identity, 1290–1340, 1996.

Celtic Culture and Literature • Bibliography. • Rachel Bromwich, *Medieval Celtic Literature: A Select Bibliography*, 1974.

Studies. • Miranda J. Green, ed., *Celtic Goddesses: Warriors, Virgins, and Mothers*, 1995. • Miranda J. Green, ed., *The Celtic World*, 1995.

Irish Culture and Literature (including Early Irish Verse) • Translations. • James Carney, *Medieval Irish Lyrics with "The Irish Bardic Poet,"* 1985. • Tom Peete Cross and Clark Harris Slover, eds., *Ancient Irish Tales*, 1936; repr. with updated bibliography, 1969. • Patrick K. Ford, trans., *The Celtic poets: songs and tales from early Ireland and Wales*, 1999. • Jeffrey Gantz, *Early Irish Myths and Sagas*, 1981. • Kenneth Hurlstone Jackson, *A Celtic Miscellany: Translations from the Celtic Literatures*, 1951. • Kuno Meyer, trans., *Ancient Irish Poetry*, 1994. • Frank O'Connor, trans., *Kings, Lords, and Commons: An Anthology from the Irish*, 1959. • H. P. A. Oskamp, ed. and trans., [translation used], *The Voyage of Máel Dúin*, 1970.

Studies. • Lisa M. Bitel, *Isle of the saints: monastic settlement and Christian community in early Ireland*, 1990. • Lisa M. Bitel, *Land of women: tales of sex and gender from early Ireland*, 1996. • James Carney, *Studies in Irish Literature and History*, 1979. • Doris Edel, ed., *Cultural Identity and Cultural Integration: Ireland and Europe in the Early Middle Ages*, 1995. • Jeffrey Gantz, *Early Irish Myths and Sagas*, 1981. • Kim McKone, *Pagan Past and Christian Present in Early Irish Literature*, 1990. • Brian Murdoch, *In Pursuit of the Caillech Berre: An Early Irish Poem and the Medievalist at Large*, Zeitschrift fur celtische Philologie 44 (1991): 80–127. • Donncha Ó hAodha, *The Lament of the Old Woman of Beare*, in Donnchadh Ó Corráin et al., eds., *Sages, Saints, and Storytellers: Celtic Studies in Honor of Professsor James Carney*, 1989, pp. 308–31. • Nerys Patterson, *Cattle Lords and Clansmen: The Social Structure of Early Ireland*, 2nd ed., 1996. • Alwyn Rees and Brinley Rees, *Celtic Heritage*, 1961. • J. E. Caerwyn Williams and Patrick K. Ford, *The Irish Literary Tradition*, 1992.

Scottish Culture and Literature • Adam J. Aitken et al., eds., *Bards and Makars: Scottish Language and Literature, Medieval and Renaissance*, 1977.

Welsh Culture and Literature • Translations. • Joseph Clancy, *The Earliest Welsh Poetry*, 1970. • Anthony Conran, *The Penguin Book of Welsh Verse*, 1967. • D. Johnston, ed. and trans., *Medieval Welsh Erotic Poetry*, 1991.

Bibliography. • Rachel Bromwich, *Medieval Celtic Literature: A Select Bibliography*, 1974. Studies. • Stephen S. Evans, *The Heroic Poetry of Dark-Age Britain*, 1997. • Kenneth Jackson, *Language and History in Early Britain*, 1953. • A. O. H. Jarman, *The Cynfeirdd: Early Welsh Poets and Poetry*, 1981. • A. O. H. Jarman and Gwilym Rees Hughes, eds., *A Guide to Welsh Literature*, vol. I, 1976. • A. T. E. Matonis, "Traditions of Panegyric in Welsh Poetry: The Heroic and the Chivalric," *Speculum* 53 (1978): 667–87. • Jenny Rowland, *Early Welsh Saga Poetry*, 1990. • Sir Ifor Williams, *The Beginnings of Welsh Poetry: Studies*, 1980. • J. E. C. Williams, *The Poet of the Welsh Princes*, 1994.

Perspectives: Arthurian Myth in the History of Britain • Translations. • Geoffrey of Monmouth, *History of the Kings of Britain*, trans. Lewis Thorpe, 1966. • Gerald of Wales, *The Journey through Wales and The Description of Wales*, trans. L. Thorpe, 1978. • E. L. G. Stones, ed. and trans., *Anglo-Scottish Relations 1174–1328: Some Selected Documents*, 1965.

Studies. • Christopher Brooke, "Geoffrey of Monmouth as a Historian," in C. Brooke et al., eds., *Church and Government in the Middle Ages*, 1976. • Michael J. Curley, *Geoffrey of Monmouth*, 1994. • John Gillingham, *The Context and Purposes of Geoffrey of Monmouth's History of the Kings of Britain*, Anglo-Norman Studies, vol. 13, 1990. • Robert W. Hanning, *The Vision of History in Early Britain: From Gildas to Geoffrey of Monmouth*, 1966. • Francis Ingledew, "The Book of Troy and the Genealogical Construction of History: The Case of Geoffrey of Monmouth's Historia Regum Britanniae," *Speculum* 69(1994): 665–704. • Roger Sherman Loomis, ed., *Arthurian Literature in the Middle Ages*, 1959. • Monika Otter, *Inventiones: Fiction and Referentiality in Twelfth-Century Historical Writing*, 1996. • Michael Prestwich, *Edward the First*, 1988. • E. L. G. Stones, *Edward I*, 1968. • J. S. P. Tatlock, *The Legendary History of Britain*, 1950.

Arthurian Romance • Bibliography. • Norris J. Lacy, ed., *Medieval Arthurian Literature: A Guide to Recent Research*, 1996.

Encyclopedia. • Norris J. Lacy, ed., *The New Arthurian Encyclopedia*, 1991.

Journals. • *Arthuriana*: http://www2.smu.edu/arthuriana • *Arthurian Literature*

Studies. • John Darrah, *Paganism in Arthurian Romance*, 1994. • Thelma Fenster, ed., *Arthurian Women: A Casebook*, 1996. • Maureen Fries and Jeanie Watson, eds., *Approaches to Teaching the Arthurian Tradition*, 1992. • Edward D. Kennedy, ed., *King Arthur: A Casebook*, 1996. • Stephen Knight, *Arthurian Literature and Society*, 1983. • Roger Sherman Loomis, ed., *Arthurian Literature in the Middle Ages: A Collaborative History*, 1969. • Martin Schichtman and James Carley, eds., *Culture and the King: the Social Implications of the Arthurian Legend*, 1994. • Eugene Vinaver, *The Rise of Romance*, 1984.

Late Medieval Allegory • Ann W. Astell, *Political Allegory in Late-Medieval England*, 1999. • Angus Fletcher, *Allegory, The Theory of a Symbolic Mode*, 1964 • Rosamond Tuve, *Allegorical Imagery: Some Medieval Books and Their Posterity*, 1966. • Carolynn Van Dyke, *The Fiction of Truth: Structures of Meaning in Narrative and Dramatic Allegory*, 1985. • John Whitman, *Allegory: The Dynamics of an Ancient and Medieval Technique*, 1987.

Medieval Drama • Studies. • *Contexts for Early English Drama*, eds. Marianne Briscoe and John Coldewey, 1989. • John D. Cox and David Scott Kastan, eds., *A New History of Early English Drama*, 1997. • Clifford Davidson and John Stroupe, eds., *Drama in the Middle Ages*, 1982 • Jody Enders, *The Medieval Theater of Cruelty: Rhetoric, Memory, Violence*, 1999. • Claire Sponsler, *Drama and Resistance: Bodies, Goods, and Theatricality in Late Medieval England*, 1997. • Rosemary Woolf, *The English Mystery Plays*, 1972.

Middle Scots Poetry • Walter Scheps and J. Anna Looney, eds., *Middle Scots Poets: A Reference Guide to James I of Scotland, Robert Henryson, William Dunbar, and Gavin Douglas*, 1986.

Mystical Writings • Bibliography. • Michael E. Sawyer, *A Bibliographical Index of Five English Mystics: Richard Rolle, Julian of Norwich, the Author of* The Cloud of Unknowing, *Walter Hilton, Margery Kempe*, 1978.

General Studies. • David Aers and Lynn Staley, *The Powers of the Holy: Religion, Politics, and Gender in Late Medieval English Culture*,

1996. • Sarah Beckwith, *Christ's Body: Identity, Culture, and Society in Late Medieval Writings,* 1993. • Frances Beer, *Women and Mystical Experience in the Middle Ages,* 1992. • Marion Glasscoe, *English Medieval Mystics: Games of Faith,* 1993. • Marion Glasscoe, ed., *The Medieval Mystical Tradition in England,* Exeter Symposium, vols. 1–5, 1980–1992. • Wolfgang Riehle, *The Middle English Mystics,* trans. Bernard Standring, 1981. • Paul Szarmach, ed., *An Introduction to the Medieval Mystics of Europe,* 1984. • A. K. Warren, *Anchorites and their Patrons in Medieval England,* 1985.

Vernacular Religion and Repression • Texts. • Anne Hudson and H. L. Spencer, "Old Author, New Work: the Sermons of MS Longleat 4," *Medium Aevum* 53 (1984), pp. 231–32 [source for "Preaching and Teaching in the Vernacular"] • Jocelyn Wogan-Browne et al., eds., *The Idea of the Vernacular: An Anthology of Middle English Literary Theory, 1280–1520,* 1999 [source for "The Holy Prophet David"] • Anne Hudson, ed., *Selections from English Wycliffite Writings,* 1997 [source for several modernized texts]. • William Matthews, *Later Medieval English Prose,* 1963 [source for Mirk, *Festial*] • Michael Sargent, ed., *Nicholas Love's "Mirrour of the Blessed Lyf of Jesus Christ Oure Lord,"* 1992 [source used].

Studies • Rita Copeland, *Pedagogy, Intellectuals, and Dissent in the Later Middle Ages,* 2001 • Anne Hudson, *The Premature Reformation: Wycliffite Texts and Lollard History,* 1988. • Anthony Kenny, *Wyclif,* 1985. • K. B. McFarlane, *Lancastrian Kings and Lollard Knights,* 1972.

King Alfred and Asser's *Life of Alfred* • Translations. • Kevin Crossley-Holland, ed., *The Anglo-Saxon World: An Anthology,* 1983. [translation used] • L. C. Jane, trans., *Asser's Life of King Alfred,* 1926. [translation used] • Simon Keynes and Michael Lapidge, trans., *Alfred the Great: Asser's Life of King Alfred and Other Contemporary Sources,* 1983.

Studies. • Alfred P. Smyth, *King Alfred the Great,* 1995. • David J. Sturdy, *Alfred the Great,* 1995. • Dorothy Whitelock, *The Genuine Asser,* 1968.

The Anglo-Saxon Chronicle • Translation. • Anne Savage, trans., *The Anglo-Saxon Chronicles,* 1982.

Study. • Stephen Morillo, ed., *The Battle of Hastings: Sources and Interpretations,* 1996.

Bede • Translation. • Bertram Colgrave and R. A. B. Mynors, eds. and trans., *Bede's Ecclesiastical History of the English People,* 1969.

Studies. • Peter Hunter Blair, *The World of Bede,* 1970. • George H. Brown, *Bede, the Venerable,* 1987. • Robert T. Farrell, ed., *Bede and Anglo-Saxon England,* 1978. • J. M. Wallace-Hadrill, *Bede's Ecclesiastical History of the English People: A Historical Commentary,* 1993. • Benedicta Ward, *The Venerable Bede,* 1990.

Beowulf • Edition. • Frederick Klaeber, ed., *Beowulf and the Fight at Finnsburg,* rev. W. F. Bolton, 1973. [standard edition]

Translations. • Howell D. Chickering, Jr., trans., *Beowulf: A Dual-Language Edition,* 1977. • Kevin Crossley-Holland, trans., *Beowulf,* 1968. • E. T. Donaldson, trans., *Beowulf,* ed. Joseph E. Tuso, 1975. [Norton Critical Edition] • Seamus Heaney, trans. *Beowulf: A New Verse Translation,* 2000. • Alan Sullivan and Timothy Murphy, trans., *Beowulf,* 2003. [translation used]

Bibliography. • Robert J. Hasenfratz, *Beowulf Scholarship: An Annotated Bibliography, 1979–1990,* 1993.

Studies. • Peter S. Baker, *Beowulf: Basic Readings,* 1995. • Adrien Bonjour, *The Digressions in Beowulf,* 1950. • R. W. Chambers, *Beowulf: An Introduction to the Study of the Poem,* 3rd ed., suppl. C. L. Wrenn, 1959. • George Clark, *Beowulf,* 1990. • John Miles Foley, *Traditional Oral Epic: The Odyssey, Beowulf, and the Serbo-Croatian Return Song,* 1990. • Donald K. Fry, ed. *The Beowulf Poet,* 1968. • R. D. Fulk, ed., *Interpretations of Beowulf: A Critical Anthology,* 1991. • Edward B. Irving, Jr., *Rereading Beowulf,* 1989. • J. D. A. Ogilvy and Donald C. Baker, *Reading Beowulf: An Introduction to the Poem, Its Background, and Its Style,* 1983. • Gillian Overing, *Language, Sign, and Gender in Beowulf,* 1990. • Fred C. Robinson, *Beowulf and the Appositive Style,* 1985. • J. R. R. Tolkien, *Beowulf, the Monsters, and the Critics,* 1937.

Chaucer • Editions. • E. Talbot Donaldson, ed., *Chaucer's Poetry,* 1957. [edition used] • Larry D. Benson, gen. ed., *The Riverside Chaucer,* 3rd ed., 1987. [standard edition] • V. A. Kolve and

Glending Olson, eds., The Canterbury Tales: Nine Tales and the "General Prologe," 1989. [Norton Critical Edition] • Peter G. Beidler, ed., Geoffrey Chaucer: "The Wife of Bath": Complete, Authoritative Text with Biographical and Historical Context, Critical History, and Essays from Five Contemporary Critical Perspectives, 1996.

On-Line Sources. • Chaucer Metapage: http://www.unc.edu/depts/chaucer/ • Harvard Chaucer Page: http://icg.fas.harvard.edu/~chaucer/ • Text with electronic glosses: http://www.librarius.com • The Wife of Bath's Portrait, from the Ellesmere Chaucer, is at http://www.huntington.org/LibraryDiv/ChaucerPict.html

Electronic Editions. • Chaucer: Life and Times, CD-ROM, Primary Sources Media 1995. [with full text from The Riverside Chaucer; notes and glosses in pull-down windows] • Peter Robinson, ed., The Wife of Bath's Prologue, Cambridge University Press 1996. [challenging format, but complete survey of manuscripts]

Biographies. • Martin M. Crow and C. Olson, eds., Chaucer Life-Records, 1966. • Donald R. Howard, Chaucer: His Life, His Works, His World, 1987. • Derek Pearsall, The Life of Geoffrey Chaucer, 1992.

Bibliography. • "An Annotated Chaucer Bibliography," annually in Studies in the Age of Chaucer; most recent, for 1999, compiled and edited by Mark Allen and Bege K. Bowers, SAC 23 (2001): 615–99. • John Leyerle and Anne Quick, Chaucer: A Bibliographical Introduction, 1986.

Journals. • Studies in the Age of Chaucer • Chaucer Review • Chaucer Yearbook: A Journal of Late Medieval Studies

Handbooks and Source Collections. • Larry D. Benson and Theodore Anderson, eds., The Literary Context of Chaucer's Fabliaux, 1971. • Piero Boitani and Jill Mann, eds., Cambridge Chaucer Companion, 1986. • Robert P. Miller, ed., Chaucer: Sources and Backgrounds, 1977. • Beryl Rowland, ed., Companion to Chaucer Studies, 2nd ed., rev. 1979.

General Studies. • Susan Crane, Gender and Romance in Chaucer's Canterbury Tales, 1994. • Alfred David, The Strumpet Muse: Art and Morals in Chaucer's Poetry, 1976. • Carolyn Dinshaw, Chaucer's Sexual Poetics,

1989. • E. Talbot Donaldson, Speaking of Chaucer, 1970. • John M. Fyler, Chaucer and Ovid, 1979. • John Ganim, Chaucerian Theatricality, 1990. • Peggy Knapp, Chaucer and the Social Contest, 1990. • Stephen Knight, Geoffrey Chaucer, 1986. • V. A. Kolve, Chaucer and the Imagery of Narrative, 1984. • Seth Lerer, Chaucer and His Readers: Imagining the Author in Late-Medieval England, 1993. • A. J. Minnis, Chaucer and Pagan Antiquity, 1982. • Charles Muscatine, Chaucer and the French Tradition, 1957. • Paul A. Olson, The Canterbury Tales and the Good Society, 1986. • Lee Patterson, Chaucer and the Subject of History, 1991. • D. W. Robertson Jr., Chaucer's London, 1968. • D. W. Robertson Jr., A Preface to Chaucer, 1962. • Donald M. Rose, ed., New Perspectives in Chaucer Criticism, 1981. • Paul Strohm, Social Chaucer, 1989. • David Wallace, Chaucerian Polity: Absolutist Lineages and Associational Forms in England and Italy, 1997.

Studies, Parliament of Fowls. • Jerome Mitchell and William Provost, eds., Chaucer the Love Poet, 1973. • Robert O. Payne, The Key of Remembrance, 1963. • Winthrop Wetherbee, Platonism and Poetry in the Twelfth Century: The Literary Influence of the School of Chartres, 1972.

Studies, Canterbury Tales. • C. David Benson, Chaucer's Drama of Style: Poetic Variety and Contrast in The Canterbury Tales, 1986. • Muriel Bowden, A Commentary on the General Prologue to The Canterbury Tales, 1948. • Donald R. Howard, The Idea of The Canterbury Tales, 1976. • H. Marshall Leicester Jr., The Disenchanted Self: Representing the Subject in The Canterbury Tales, 1990. • Carl Lindahl, Earnest Games: Folkloric Patterns in The Canterbury Tales, 1987. • Jill Mann, Chaucer and the Medieval Estates Satire, 1973. • Paul A. Olson, The Canterbury Tales and the Good Society, 1986. • Winthrop Wetherbee, Geoffrey Chaucer: The Canterbury Tales, 1989.

Christine de Pizan • Editions. • English translation by Bryan Anslay, London 1521. [source for modernized text] • Renate Blumenfeld-Kosinski and Kevin Brownlee, trans., The Selected Writings of Christine de Pizan, 1997.

Studies. • Marilyn Desmond, ed. Christine de Pizan and the Categories of Difference, 1998. • J. C. Laidlaw, Christine de Pizan, the Earl of Salisbury and Henry IV, French Studies 36 (1982): 129–43. • Maureen Quilligan, The Allegory of Female Authority: Christine de Pizan's

"Cité des Dames," 1991. • Charity Cannon Willard, Christine de Pizan: Her Life and Works, 1984.

The Cloud of Unknowing • Edition. • The Cloud of Unknowing, ed. James Walsh, 1981.

Translation. • The Cloud of Unknowing, trans. Clifton Wolters, 1978.

Study. • A. J. Burrow, "Fantasy and Language in The Cloud of Unknowing," Essays in Criticism, vol. 27, 1977.

Dayfydd ap Gwilym • Translations. • Rolfe Humphries, trans., Nine Thorny Thickets: Selected Poems by Dafydd ap Gwilym in New Arrangements by Jon Roush, 1969. [edition used] • Rachel Bromwich, trans., Dafydd ap Gwilym: A Selection of Poems, 1982. • Richard Morgan Loomis, trans., Dafydd ap Gwilym: The Poems, 1982.

Studies. • Rachel Bromwich, Aspects of the Poetry of Dafydd ap Gwilym: Collected Papers, 1986. • Helen Fulton, Dafydd ap Gwilym and the European Context, 1989.

The Dream of the Rood • Edition. • The Dream of the Rood, ed. Michael Swanton, 1970.

Translation. • Kevin Crossley-Holland, ed., The Anglo-Saxon World: An Anthology, 1983.

Studies. • Martin Irvine, "Anglo-Saxon Literary Theory Exemplified in Old English Poems: Interpreting the Cross in The Dream of the Rood and Elene," Old English Shorter Poems, ed. Katherine O'Brien O'Keeffe, 1994. • Rosemary Woolf, "Doctrinal Influences in The Dream of the Rood," Medium Aevum, vol. 27, 1958.

William Dunbar • Edition. • William Dunbar: Poems, ed. James Kinsley, 1958.

Studies. • Priscilla Bawcutt, Dunbar the Maker, 1992. • Edmund Reiss, William Dunbar, 1978. • Florence Ridley, "Studies in Dunbar and Henryson: The Present Situation," Fifteenth-Century Studies: Recent Essays, ed. Robert F. Yeager, 1984. • Ian Simpson Ross, William Dunbar, 1981.

Robert Henryson • Edition. • Robert Henryson: Poems, ed. Charles Elliott, 1963.

Critical Studies. • Douglas Gray, Robert Henryson, 1979. • Robert L. Kindrick, Robert Henryson, 1974.

Judith • Edition. • Judith, ed. B. J. Timmer, 1966.

Translation. • S. A. J. Bradley, trans., Anglo-Saxon Poetry, 1982.

Studies. • Karma Lochrie, "Gender, Sexual Violence, and the Politics of War in the Old English Judith," Class and Gender in Early English Literature, eds. Britton J. Harwood and Gillian Overing, 1994. • Helen Damico, "The Valkyrie Reflex in Old English Literature," New Readings on Women in Old English Literature, eds. Helen Damico and Alexandra Hennessey Olsen, 1990.

Julian of Norwich • Translation. • Showings, trans. Edmund Colledge and James Walsh, 1978.

Studies. • Denise Nowakowski Baker, Julian of Norwich's Showings: From Vision to Book, 1994. • Nicholas Watson, "'Yf Wommen Be Double Naturelly': Remaking 'Woman' in Julian of Norwich's Revelation of Love," Exemplaria 8 (1996): 1–34.

Margery Kempe • Translation. • The Book of Margery Kempe, trans. B. A. Windeatt, 1985.

On-Line Sources. • Mapping Margery Kempe: www.holycross.edu/department/visarts/projects.kempe

Studies. • Clarissa W. Atkinson, Mystic and Pilgrim: The Book and the World of Margery Kempe, 1983. • Karma Lochrie, Margery Kempe and Translations of the Flesh, 1991. • Sandra McEntire, ed., Margery Kempe: A Book of Essays, 1992. • Lynn Staley, Margery Kempe's Dissenting Fictions, 1994.

William Langland, Piers Plowman • Editions. • Derek Pearsall, ed., Piers Plowman by William Langland: An Edition of the C-Text, 1979. • A. V. C. Schmidt, ed., Piers Plowman: A Parallel-Text Edition of the A, B, C, and Z Versions, 2 vols., 1995. • A. V. C. Schmidt, ed., The Vision of Piers Plowman: a critical edition of the B-Text, 1978.

Translations. • E. T. Donaldson, trans., Piers Ploughman: An Alliterative Verse Translation, 1990. [translation used] • J. F. Goodridge, trans., Langland: Piers the Ploughman, rev. 1966.

Bibliography. • Anthony J. Colaianne, Piers Plowman: An Annotated Bibliography of Editions and Criticism 1550–1977, 1978.

Studies. • David Aers, *Chaucer, Langland, and the Creative Imagination*, 1980. • John A. Alford, *A Companion to* Piers Plowman, 1988. • Anna Baldwin, *The Theme of Government in* Piers Plowman, 1981. • Morton Bloomfield, *"Piers Plowman" as a Fourteenth-Century Apocalypse*, 1962. • J. A. Burrow, *Langland's Fictions*, 1993. • F. R. H. DuBoulay, *The England of* Piers Plowman, 1991. • S. S. Hussey, ed., Piers Plowman: *Critical Approaches*, 1969. • Steven Justice and Kathryn Kerby-Fulton, eds., *Written Work: Langland, Labor, and Authorship*, 1997. • Kathryn Kerby-Fulton, *Reformist Apocalypticism and* Piers Plowman, 1990. • Jeanne Krochalis and Edward Peters, *The World of* Piers Plowman, 1975. • Elizabeth Salter, Piers Plowman: *An Introduction*, 1962. • James Simpson, Piers Plowman: *An Introduction to the B-Text*, 1990.

Piers Plowman in Context • Editions. • R. B. Dobson, *The Peasants' Revolt of 1381*, 1970. • Rossell Hope Robbins, ed., *Historical Poems of the XIVth and XVth Centuries*, 1959. • Eric W. Stockton, trans., *The Major Latin Works of John Gower*, 1962.

Studies. • David Aers, *Community, Gender, and Individual Identity: English Writing 1360–1430*, 1988. • Allen Frantzen, ed., *The Work of Work: Servitude, Slavery, and Work in Medieval England*, 1994. • Jesse Gellrich, *Discourse and Dominion in the Fourteenth Century*, 1995. • Barbara Hanawalt, ed., *Chaucer's England: Literature in Historical Context*, 1992. • Stephen Justice, *Writing and Rebellion: England in 1381*, 1994.

John Lydgate • Text. • John Lydgate, *The pilgrimage of the life of man*, ed. F. J. Furnivall, EETS (Early English Text Society) extra series, no. 77, 83, 92. [source of modernized text]

Studies. • Derek Pearsall, *John Lydgate*, 1970. • Rosamund Tuve, "Guillaume's Pilgrimage," in *Allegorical Imagery: Some Medieval Books and Their Posterity*, 1966, pp. 145–218.

The Mabinogi • Translation. • Patrick Ford, trans., *The Mabinogi and Other Medieval Welsh Tales*, 1977. [translation used] • Gwyn and Thomas Jones, trans., *The Mabinogion*, 1949.

Studies. • W. J. Gruffyd, *Folklore and Myth in* The Mabinogion, 1994. • Sioned Davies, *The Four Branches of* The Mabinogi, 1993. • Proinsias MacCana, *The Mabinogi*, 1992. •

Caitlin Matthews, *Mabon and the Mysteries of Britain: An Exploration of* The Mabinogion, 1987.

Sir Thomas Malory • Editions. • Thomas Malory, *Le Morte d'Arthur*, ed. Janet Cowen, intro. John Lawlor, 2 vols., 1969. • Thomas Malory, *King Arthur and his Knights: Selected Tales*, ed. E. Vinaver, 1975. [edition used] • *The Works of Sir Thomas Malory*, ed. Eugene Vinaver, 1977.

Guides and Studies. • Elizabeth Archibald and A. S. G. Edwards, *A Companion to Malory*, 1996. • Larry D. Benson, *Malory's* Morte Darthur, 1976. • Burt Dillon, *A Malory Handbook*, 1978. • P. J. C. Field, *The Life and Times of Sir Thomas Malory*, 1993. • Beverly Kennedy, *Knighthood in the* Morte d'Arthur, 1985. • Terence McCarthy, *An Introduction to Malory*, rev. ed., 1991. • William Matthews, *The Ill-Framed Knight: A Skeptical Inquiry into the Identity of Sir Thomas Malory*, 1966. • Charles Moorman, *The Book of Kyng Arthur: The Unity of Malory's* Morte Darthur, 1965. • Felicity Riddy, *Sir Thomas Malory*, 1987. • Toshiyuki Takamiya and Derek Brewer, eds., *Aspects of Malory*, 1981. • Muriel Whitaker, *Arthur's Kingdom of Adventure: The World of Malory's* Morte Darthur, 1984.

Mankind • Edition. • David Bevington, ed., *Medieval Drama*, 1975. [edition used]

Studies. • David M. Bevington, *From Mankind to Marlowe*, 1962. • Clifford Davidson, *Visualizing the Moral Life: Medieval Iconography and the Macro Moralities*, 1989. • Michael R. Kelley, *Flamboyant Drama: A Study of the "Castle of Perseverance," "Mankind" and "Wisdom,"* 1979. • Robert Potter, *The English Morality Play: Origin, History, and Influence of a Dramatic Tradition*, 1975. • Victor I. Scherb, *Staging Faith: East Anglian Drama in the Later Middle Ages*, 2001.

Marie de France • Translations. • Glyn S. Burgess and Keith Busby, trans., *The Lais of Marie de France*, 1986. • Robert Hanning and Joan Ferrante, *The Lais of Marie de France*, 1978. [translation used]

Bibliography. • Glyn S. Burgess, *Marie de France: An Analytical Bibliography*, 1977; suppl. no. 1, 1986.

Studies. • Margaret M. Boland, *Architectural Structure in the Lais of Marie de France*, 1995. • Glyn S. Burgess, *The Lais of Marie de France: Text and Context*, 1987. • Paula M. Clifford,

Marie de France, Lais, 1982. • Emanuel J. Mickel, Marie de France, 1974.

Middle English Lyrics • Editions. • Maxwell S. Luria and Richard L. Hoffman, eds., Middle English Lyrics, 1974. [Norton Critical Edition; edition used] • R. T. Davies, Medieval English Lyrics: A Critical Anthology, 1963. [edition used] • Theodore Silverstein, ed., English Lyrics Before 1500, 1971. • Celia Sisam and Kenneth Sisam, eds., The Oxford Book of Medieval English Verse, 1970.

Translations. • Frederick Goldin, trans., The Lyrics of the Troubadours and Trouvères: Original Texts, with Translations and Introductions, 1973. • James J. Wilhelm, Lyrics of the Middle Ages: An Anthology, 1990.

Studies. • Peter Dronke, The Medieval Lyric, 3rd ed., 1996. • Douglas Gray, Themes and Images in the Medieval English Religious Lyric, 1972. • David L. Jeffrey, The Early English Lyric and Franciscan Spirituality, 1975. • John F. Plummer, ed., Vox Feminae: Studies in Medieval Woman's Song, 1981. • Rosemary Woolf, The English Religious Lyric in the Middle Ages, 1968.

Ohthere's Journey • Translation and Study. • Niels Lund, ed., and Christine Fell, trans., Two Voyagers at the Court of King Alfred: The Ventures of Ohthere and Wulfstan, 1984.

Riddles • Edition. • Frederick Tupper Jr., ed., The Riddles of the Exeter Book, repr. 1968.

Translations. • Michael J. Alexander, trans. Old English Riddles from the Exeter Book, 1980. [translation used] • James Hall Pitman, ed. and trans., The Riddles of Aldhelm: Text and Verse Translation, 1925. [translation used] • Craig Williamson, trans., A Feast of Creatures: Anglo-Saxon Riddle Songs, 1982.

Study. • Nancy Porter Stork, Through a Gloss Darkly: Aldhelm's Riddles in the British Library, ms. Royal 12.c.xxiii, 1990.

Richard Rolle • Translation. • The Fire of Love, trans. Clifton Wolters, 1972.

Study. • Nicholas Watson, Richard Rolle and the Invention of Authority, 1992.

Second Play of the Shepherds • Editions. • Peter Happé, English Mystery Plays: A Selection, 1975. [edition used] • David Bevington, ed., Medieval Drama, 1975. • Martin Stevens and A. C. Cawley, eds., The Townley Plays, 2 vols., 1994.

Bibliography. • Sidney E. Berger, ed., Medieval English Drama: An Annotated Bibliography of Recent Criticism, 1990.

Studies and Guides. • Richard Beadle, ed., The Cambridge Companion to Medieval English Theatre, 1994. • Richard K. Emmerson, ed., and V. A. Kolve, intro., Approaches to Teaching Medieval English Drama, 1990. • O. B. Hardison Jr., Christian Rite and Christian Drama in the Middle Ages, 1965. • V. A. Kolve, The Play Called Corpus Christi, 1966. • Martin Stevens, Four Middle English Mystery Cycles: Textual, Contextual, and Critical Interpretations, 1987.

Sir Gawain and the Green Knight • Translations. • Marie Borroff, trans., Sir Gawain and the Green Knight, 1967. [translation used] • W. R. J. Barron, ed. and trans., Sir Gawain and the Green Knight, 1974.

Bibliography. • Malcolm Andrew, The Gawain-Poet: An Annotated Bibliography, 1839–1977, 1979.

Guides and Studies. • Ross Arthur, Medieval Sign Theory and Sir Gawain and the Green Knight, 1987. • Larry D. Benson, Art and Tradition in Sir Gawain and the Green Knight, 1965. • Robert J. Blanch et al., eds., Text and Matter: New Critical Perspectives of the Pearl-Poet, 1991. • Robert J. Blanch and Julian Wasserman, From Pearl to Gawain: Forme to Fynisment, 1995. • Marie Borroff, Sir Gawain and the Green Knight: A Stylistic and Metrical Study, 1973. • Derek Brewer and Jonathan Gibson, eds., A Companion to the Gawain-Poet, 1997. • Elisabeth Brewer, comp., Sir Gawain and the Green Knight: Sources and Analogues, 1992. • John Burrow, A Reading of Sir Gawain and the Green Knight, 1966. • Wendy Clein, Concepts of Chivalry in Sir Gawain and the Green Knight, 1987. • Lynn Staley Johnson, The Voice of the Gawain-Poet, 1984. • Sandra Pierson Prior, The Pearl Poet Revisited, 1994. • Ad Putter, An Introduction to the Gawain-Poet, 1996. • Allen Shoaf, The Poem as Green Girdle: Commercium in Sir Gawain and the Green Knight, 1984. • A. C. Spearing, The Gawain-Poet: a Critical Study, 1970. • Meg Stainsby, Sir Gawain and the

Green Knight: *An Annotated Bibliography*, 1978–1989, 1992.

The Táin • Translations. • Cecile O'Rahilly, ed. and trans., Táin bó Cúalnge *from the* Book of Leinster, 1967. [translation used] • Thomas Kinsella, trans., *The Tain*, 1985. [a powerful translation, assembled and slightly rearranged from several Old Irish versions]

Studies. • Kenneth H. Jackson, *The Oldest Irish Tradition: A Window on the Iron Age*, 1964. • J. P. Mallory, ed., *Aspects of* The Tain, 1992.

Taliesin • Translation. • Ifor and J. Caerwyn Williams, trans., *The Poems of Taliesin*, 1968.

Study. • J. E. Caerwyn Williams, *The Poets of the Welsh Princes*, 1994.

The Voyage of St. Brendan • Translation. • J. F. Webb, trans., *Lives of the Saints*, 1965.

Studies • Geoffrey Ashe, *Land to the West: St. Brendan's Voyage to America*, 1962. • Frederick Buechner, *Brendan*, 1987.

The Wanderer • Editions. • T. P. Dunning and A. J. Bliss, eds., *The Wanderer*, 1969. • Anne L. Klinck, *The Old English Elegies: A Critical Edition and Genre Study*, 1992.

Translation. • Kevin Crossley-Holland, ed., *The Anglo-Saxon World: An Anthology*, 1983.

Study. • Martin Green, ed., *The Old English Elegies: New Essays in Criticism and Research*, 1983.

The Wife's Lament • Edition. • Anne L. Klinck, *The Old English Elegies: A Critical Edition and Genre Study*, 1992.

Translation. • Kevin Crossley-Holland, ed., *The Anglo-Saxon World: An Anthology*, 1983.

Studies. • Helen T. Bennett, "Exile and the Semiosis of Gender in Old English Elegies," *Class and Gender in Early English Literature*, eds. Britton J. Harwood and Gillian Overing, 1994. • Barrie Ruth Strauss, "Women's Words as Weapons in *The Wife's Lament*," *Old English Shorter Poems*, ed. Katharine O'Brien O'Keeffe, 1994.

Wulf and Eadwacer • Edition. • Anne L. Klinck, *The Old English Elegies: A Critical Edition and Genre Study*, 1992.

Translation. • Kevin Crossley-Holland, ed., *The Anglo-Saxon World: An Anthology*, 1983.

Studies. • Helen T. Bennett, "Exile and the Semiosis of Gender in Old English Elegies" *Class and Gender in Early English Literature*, ed. Britton J. Harwood and Gillian Overing, 1994. • Pat Bellanoff, "Women's Songs, Women's Language: *Wulf and Eadwacer* and *The Wife's Lament*," *New Readings on Women in Old English Literature*, eds. Helen Damico and Alexandra Hennessey Olsen, 1990. • Marilyn Desmond, "The Voice of Exile: Feminist Literary History and the Anonymous Anglo-Saxon Elegy," *Critical Inquiry*, vol. 16, 1990.

York Crucifixion • Edition: • *The Crucifixion*. In *York Mystery Plays: A Selection in Modern Spelling*. Ed. Richard Beadle and Pamela M. King, 1984. [edition used]

Studies. • Clifford Davidson, *From Creation To Doom: The York Cycle of Mystery Plays*, 1984. • Ruth Evans, "Body Politics: Engendering Medieval Cycle Drama," in *Feminist Readings in Middle English Literature: The Wife of Bath and All Her Sect*, eds. Ruth Evans and Lesley Johnson, 1994, pp. 112–39.

CREDITS

TEXT CREDITS

"The Anonimalle Chronicle" from THE PEASANTS' REVOLT OF 1381, edited by R. B. Dobson. Reprinted by permission of Macmillan Ltd.

Bede: From BEDE'S ECCLESIASTICAL HISTORY OF THE ENGLISH PEOPLE edited by Bertram Colgrave and R. A. B. Mynors (1969). Reprinted by permission of Oxford University Press.

BEOWULF translated by Alan Sullivan. Reprinted by permission of Alan Sullivan.

Boland, Eavan: "From the Irish of Pangur the Cat" from AN ORIGIN LIKE WATER: COLLECTED POEMS 1967–1987 by Eavan Boland. Copyright © 1996 by Eavan Boland. Used by permission of W. W. Norton & Company.

Chaucer, Geoffrey: from CHAUCER'S POETRY, selected and edited by E. T. Donaldson. Copyright © 1958, 1975 HarperCollins Publishers. Reprinted by permission of Pearson Education, Inc.

The Cloud of Unknowing: From THE CLOUD UNKNOWING translated by Clifton Wolters (Penguin Classics, 1961) copyright © Clifton Wolters, 1961. Reprinted by permission of Penguin Books Ltd.

Dafydd ap Gwilym: "Aubade," "One Saving Place," "The Girls of Llanbadarn," "Tales of a Wayside Inn," "The Hateful Husband," "The Winter," "The Ruin," from NINE THORNY THICKETS: SELECTED POEMS BY DAFYDD AP GWILYM, arrangements by Rolfe Humphries. Copyright © 1969 Rolfe Humphries. Reprinted by permission of Kent State University Press.

"De Heretico Comburendo," 1401 from ENGLISH HISTORICAL DOCUMENTS 1327–1485 edited by A. R. Myers. Reprinted by permission of International Thomson Publishing Services Ltd.

"The Dream of the Rood," "The Wanderer," "Wulf and Eadwacer," and "The Wife's Lament" translated by Kevin Crossley-Holland from THE EXETER BOOK RIDDLES, 1993. Copyright © 1993 Kevin Crossley-Holland. Reproduced by permission of the author c/o Rogers, Coleridge & White Ltd., 20 Powis Mews, London W11 1JN.

Geoffrey of Monmouth: From HISTORY OF KINGS OF BRITAIN by Geoffrey of Monmouth, translated by Lewis Thorpe. (Penguin Classics, 1966) Translation copyright © Lewis Thorpe, 1966.

Gerald of Wales: Excerpts from GERALD OF WALES: THE JOURNEY THROUGH WALES AND THE DESCRIPTION OF WALES translated by Lewis Thorpe. Middlesex, England: Penguin Books Ltd., 1978.

Glossary of Literary and Cultural Terms: Excerpts from THE HARPER HANDBOOK TO LITERATURE, 2/E by Northrop Frye, et al. Copyright © 1997 by Addison-Wesley Educational Publishers Inc. Reprinted by permission of the publisher.

Gower, John: "The Voice of Crying" by John Gower, from THE MAJOR WORKS OF JOHN GOWER, edited by Eric W. Stockton. Copyright © 1962 by the University of Washington Press. Reprinted by permission.

"The Holi Prophete Davie Seith" from THE IDEA OF THE VERNACULAR edited by Jocelyn Wogan-Browne, Nicholas Watson, Andrew Taylor and Ruth Evans, pp. 151–53. Copyright © 1990 The Pennsylvania State University. Reproduced by permission of the publisher.

"Judith" from ANGLO-SAXON POETRY: AN ANTHOLOGY OF OLD ENGLISH POEMS, translated by S. A. J. Bradley. Copyright © 1982 by David Campbell Publishers Ltd. Reprinted by permission of David Campbell Publishers Ltd.

Julian of Norwich: From JULIAN OF NORWICH SHOWINGS. Copyright © 1978 by The Missionary Society of St. Paul the Apostle in the State of New York. Used with permission of Paulist Press www.paulistpress.com.

Kempe, Margery: From THE BOOK OF MARGERY KEMPE translated by B. A. Windeatt (Penguin Classics, 1965). Copyright © B. A. Windeatt, 1965. Reprinted by permission of Penguin Books Ltd.

Langland, William: From PIERS PLOWMAN: AN ALLITERATIVE VERSE TRANSLATION by William Langland, translated by E. Talbot Donaldson. Copyright © 1990 by W. W. Norton & Company. Used by permission of W. W. Norton & Company.

Love, Nicholas: From NICHOLAS LOVE'S MIRROR OF THE BLESSED LIFE OF JESUS CHRIST edited by Michael G. Sargent. Reproduced by permission of Routledge, Inc., part of The Taylor & Francis Group.

Malory, Sir Thomas: From KING ARTHUR AND HIS KNIGHTS: SELECTED TALES FROM SIR THOMAS MALORY, edited by Eugene Vinaver, copyright © 1975, 1968, 1956 by Eugene Vinaver. Used by permission of Oxford University Press. Excerpt from CAXTON'S MALORY: A NEW EDITION OF SIR THOMAS MALORY'S LE MORTE DARTHUR translated & edited by James W. Spisak & William Matthews. Copyright © 1983 The Regents of the University of California. Reprinted by permission of University of California Press.

Mankind: Footnotes to "Mankind" from MEDIEVAL DRAMA, David Bevington, editor. Copyright © 1975 by Houghton Mifflin Company. Used with permission.

Marie de France: From THE LAIS OF MARIE DE FRANCE by Robert Hanning and Joan Ferrante. Reprinted by permission of Baker Book House Company.

Ohthere's Journeys: "Ohthere's Journeys" from TWO VOYAGERS AT THE COURT OF KING ALFRED edited by Niels Lund, trans. by Christine E. Fell, 1984. Reprinted by permission of Sessions of York.

Petrarch: Reprinted by permission of the publisher from PETRARCH'S LYRIC POEMS, translated and edited by Robert M. Durling, Cambridge, Mass.: Harvard University Press, Copyright © 1976 by Robert M. Durling.

Riddles: Five Old English Riddles from THE ANGLO-SAXON WORLD, 1982 translated by Kevin Crossley-Holland. Copyright © 1982 Kevin Crossley-Holland. Reproduced by permission of the author c/o Rogers, Coleridge & White Ltd., 20 Powis Mews, London W11 1JN.

The Riddles of Aldhelm: From THE RIDDLES OF ALDHELM, translated by James Hall Pitman. Reprinted by permission of Yale University Press.

Rolle, Richard: From THE FIRE OF LOVE by Richard Rolle, translated by Clifton Wolters (Penguin Classics, 1972) copyright © Clifton Wolters, 1971. Reprinted by permission of Penguin Books Ltd.

Sir Gawain and the Green Knight: From SIR GAWAIN AND THE GREEN KNIGHT: A NEW VERSE TRANSLATION, translated by Marie Borroff. Copyright © 1967 by W. W. Norton & Company, Inc. Used by permission of W. W. Norton & Company, Inc.

Stones, E. L. G.: ANGLO-SAXON RELATIONS, 1174–1328. London: Thomas Nelson and Sons Ltd., 1965, pp. 97–114.

Táin bó Cuailnge: Excerpt from TÁIN BÓ CUAILNGE FROM THE BOOK OF LEINSTER edited by Cecile O'Rahilly. Reprinted by permission of The Governing Board of the School of Celtic Studies of the Dublin Institute for Advanced Studies.

Taliesin: "The Tale of Taliesin" from THE MABINOGI AND OTHER MEDIEVAL WELSH TALES, translated by Patrick K. Ford. Copyright © 1977 by The Regents of the University of California. Reprinted by permission of the University of California Press. "The War-Band's Return" from THE EARLIEST WELSH POETRY by Joseph P. Clancy. Copyright © 1970 by Joseph P. Clancy. Reprinted by permission of the author. "Urien Yechwydd" translated by Saunders Lewis. Reprinted by permission of Mair Saunders. "The Battle of Aargoed Llwyfain" translated by Anthony Conran. Reprinted by permission of Anthony Conran. "Lament For Owain Son of Urien" translated by Anthony Conran. Reprinted by permission of Anthony Conran.

"To Crinog" and "The Viking Terror" from ANCIENT IRISH POETRY, translated by Kuno Meyer. Reprinted by permission of Constable & Robinson Publishing Ltd.

Whitelock, Dorothy, and David Douglas: Excerpts from THE ANGLO-SAXON CHRONICLE. London: Eyre & Spottiswoode, 1961.

Writing in the Wood: From "Writing in the Wood" from EARLY IRISH VERSE, translated and edited by Ruth P. M. Lehmann. Copyright © 1982 by the University of Texas Press. Reprinted by permission.

York Play of the Crucifixion: pp. 212–21 from YORK MYSTERY PLAYS: A SELECTION IN MODERN SPELLING edited by Richard Beadle and Pamela M. King (Oxford World's Classics, 1999) © Richard Beadle and Pamela M. King 1984. Used by permission of Oxford University Press.

ILLUSTRATION CREDITS

Cover: Reproduced by permission of The British Library. Page 2: © Durham University Library. Page 10: The Bridgeman Art Library International Ltd. Page 12: By permission of The British Library. Page 14: © The Conway Library, Courtauld Institute of Art/The Master & Fellows of Corpus Christi College, Cambridge. Page 18: © Bodleian Library, University of Oxford. Page 19: By permission of The British Library. Page 38: © Conway Librarian/Courtauld Institute of Art. Page 127: © Department of Archaeology, University of Durham. Page 144: © Giraudon/Art Resource, NY. Page 178: © Giraudon/Art Resource, NY. Page 219: By permission of the British Library. Page 281: © The Huntington Library Art Collection & Botanical Gardens, San Marino, California/Superstock, Inc. Page 389: © Museum of London. Page 437: By permission of the British Library. Page 455: Photography by Christopher Guy. Reproduced by permission of the Chapter of Worcester Cathedral. Page 515: Ms. Bodley, 758, Fol. 1r. Bodleian Library, University of Oxford. Page 551: By permission of The British Library. Page 633: By permission of The British Library.

The Longman Anthology
of British Literature

VOLUME 1A

THE MIDDLE AGES

Laurence, Prior of Durham, depicted as a scribe, from a 12th-century manuscript.

The Middle Ages

✦ ☷◈☷ ✦

> At the present time, there are five languages in Britain, just as
> the divine law is written in five books, all devoted to seeking out
> and setting forth one and the same kind of wisdom, namely the
> knowledge of sublime truth and of true sublimity. These are the
> English, British, Irish, Pictish, as well as the Latin languages;
> through the study of the scriptures, Latin is in general use among
> them all.
>
> *Bede, Ecclesiastical History of the English People*

The Venerable Bede's famous and enormously influential *Ecclesiastical History of the English People*, written in the early 700s, reflects a double triumph. First, its very title acknowledges the dominance by Bede's day of the Anglo-Saxons, who, centuries earlier, had established themselves on an island already inhabited by Celtic Britons and by Picts. Second, the Latin of Bede's text and his own life as a monk point to the presence of ancient Mediterranean influences in the British Isles, earlier through Rome's military colonization of ancient Britain and later through the conversion of Bede's people to Roman Christianity.

In this first chapter of his first book, Bede shows a complex awareness of the several populations still active in Britain and often resisting or encroaching on Anglo-Saxon rule, and much of his *History* narrates the successive waves of invaders and missionaries who had brought their languages, governments, cultures, and beliefs to his island. This initial emphasis on peoples and languages should not be taken as early medieval multiculturalism, however: Bede's brief comparison to the single truth embodied in the five books of divine law also shows us his eagerness to draw his fragmented world into a coherent and transcendent system of Latin-based Christianity.

It is useful today, however, to think about medieval Britain, before and long after Bede, as a multilingual and multicultural setting, densely layered with influences and communities that divide, in quite different ways, along lines of geography, language, and ethnicity, as well as religion, gender, and class. These elements produced extraordinary cultures and artistic works, whose richness and diversity challenge the modern imagination. The medieval British Isles were a meeting place, but also a point of resistance, for wave after wave of cultural and political influences. Awareness of these multiple origins, moreover, persisted. In the mid-thirteenth century, Matthew Paris's map of England (Color Plate 4) reflects an alertness to the complex geography of history and settlement on his island. Six hundred years after Bede we encounter a historian like Sir Thomas Gray complaining that recent disorders were "characteristic of a medley of different races. Wherefore some people are of the opinion that the diversity of spirit among the English is the cause of their revolutions" (*Scalacronica*, c. 1363).

This complex mixture sometimes resulted from systematic conquest, as with the Romans and, three centuries after Bede, the famous Norman Conquest of 1066; sometimes it was from slower, less unified movements of ethnic groups, such as the Celts, Anglo-Saxons, the Irish in Scotland, and the Vikings. Other important influences arrived more subtly: various forms of Christianity, classical Latin literature and learning, continental French culture in the thirteenth century, and an imported Italian humanism toward the close of the British Middle Ages.

Our understanding of this long period and our very name for it also reflect a long history of multiple influences and cultural and political orders. The term "medieval" began as a condescending and monolithic label, first applied by Renaissance humanists who were eager to distinguish their revived classical scholarship from what they interpreted as a "barbarous" past. They and later readers often dismissed the Middle Ages as rigidly hierarchical, feudal, and Church-dominated. Others embraced the period for equally tendentious reasons, rosily picturing "feudal" England and Europe as a harmonious society of contented peasants, chivalrous nobles, and holy clerics. It is true that those who exercised political and religious control during the Middle Ages—the Roman church and the Anglo-Norman and then the English monarchy—sought to impose hierarchy on their world and created explicit ideologies to justify doing so. They were not unopposed, however; those who had been pushed aside continued to resist—and to contribute to Britain's multiple and dynamic literatures.

The period that we call "the Middle Ages" is vast and ungainly, spanning eight hundred years by some accounts. Scholars traditionally divide medieval English literature into the Old English period, from about 700 to 1066 (the date of the Norman Conquest), and the Middle English period, from 1066 to about 1500. Given the very different state of the English language during the two periods and given the huge impact of the Norman Conquest, this division is reasonable and is reflected in this collection under the headings "Before the Norman Conquest" and "After the Norman Conquest." There were substantial continuities, nevertheless, before and after the Conquest, especially in the Celtic areas beyond the Normans' immediate control.

THE CELTS

It is with the Celts, in fact, that the recorded history of Britain begins, and their literatures continue to the present day in Ireland and Wales. The Celts first migrated to Britain about 400 B.C., after spreading over most of Europe in the two preceding centuries. In England these "Brittonic" Celts absorbed some elements of Roman culture and social order during Rome's partial occupation of the island from the first to the fifth centuries A.D. After the conversion of the Roman emperor Constantine in the fourth century and the establishment of Christianity as the official imperial religion, many British Celts adopted Christianity. The language of these "British" to whom Bede refers gave rise to Welsh. The Celts maintained contact with their people on the Continent, who were already being squeezed toward what is now Brittany, in the west of France. The culture of the Brittonic Celts was thus not exclusively insular, and their myths and legends came to incorporate these cross-Channel memories, especially in the stories of King Arthur.

Celts also arrived in Ireland; and as one group, the "Goidelic" Celts, achieved linguistic and social dominance there, their language split off from that of the

Britons. Some of these Irish Celts later established themselves in Argyll and the western isles of Scotland, "either by friendly treaty or by the sword," says Bede, and from them the Scottish branch of the Celtic languages developed. Bede mentions this language as the "Irish" that is spoken in Britain. The Irish converted to Christianity early but slowly, without the pressure of a Christianized colonizer. When the great Irish monasteries flourished in the sixth century, their extraordinary Latin scholarship seems to have developed alongside the traditional learning preserved by the rigorous schools of vernacular poetry, as we see in the section "Early Irish Verse" (pages 111–20). If anything, Irish monastic study was stimulated by these surviving institutions of a more poetic and priestly class. The Irish monasteries in turn became the impetus behind Irish and Anglo-Saxon missionaries who carried Christianity to the northern and eastern reaches of Europe. Both as missionaries and as scholars, insular Christians had great impact on continental Europe, especially in the eighth and ninth centuries.

By 597 when Pope Gregory the Great sent Augustine (later "of Canterbury") to expand the Christian presence in England, there was already a flourishing Christian Celtic society, especially in Ireland. Ensuing disagreements over Celtic versus Roman ways of worship were ultimately resolved in favor of the Roman liturgy and calendar, but the cultural impact of Celts on British Christianity remained enormous. The Irish *Book of Kells* (page 10), and the Lindisfarne Gospels (Color Plate 1), produced in England, are enlivened by the swirls, interlace, and stylized animals long evident in the work of pagan Celtic craftsmen on the continent. The monks who illuminated such magnificent gospel books also copied classical Latin texts, notably Virgil's *Aeneid* and works by Cicero and Seneca, thereby helping keep ancient Roman literature alive when much of continental Europe fell into near chaos during the Germanic invasions that led to the fall of Rome.

Included in this anthology are examples from the two great literatures written in Celtic languages, Irish and Welsh. Passages from the Irish *Táin Bó Cuailnge* reveal a heroic spirit and an acceptance of the magical which can be compared with aspects of *Beowulf*. Like much Irish heroic narrative, though, the *Táin* also reveals a far more prominent and assertive role for women, some of whom retain resemblances to the goddess figures of Ireland's pagan era. Welsh literature is represented first by lyrics attributed to the early, shadowy poet Taliesin and second by a much later story about his accomplishments which serves to show some of the continuities of Welsh literary culture. Wales also absorbed Latin and later European influences, as represented by fourteenth-century lyrics from the marvelously sophisticated Dafydd ap Gwilym, who resembles Chaucer in his use of continental poetry.

THE GERMANIC MIGRATIONS

While Celtic culture flourished in Ireland, the British Celts and their faith suffered a series of disastrous reversals after the withdrawal of the Romans and the aggressive incursions of the pagan Angles, Saxons, and Jutes from the continent. The Picts and Scots in the north, never Romanized, had begun to harass the Britons, who responded by inviting allies from among the Germanic tribes on the continent in the mid-fifth century. These protectors soon became predators, demanding land and establishing small kingdoms of their own in roughly the eastern half of modern-day England.

Uneasy and temporary treaties followed. The Britons retained a presence in the northwest, in the kingdoms of Rheged and of the Strathclyde Welsh; others were slowly pressed toward present-day Wales in the southwest.

The Angles, Saxons, and Jutes were not themselves a monolithic force, though. Divided into often warring states, they faced resistance, however diminishing, from the Britons and still had to battle the aggressive Picts and Scots, who were the original reason for their arrival. Their own culture was further changed as they converted to Christianity. The piecemeal Anglo-Saxon colonization of England in the sixth and seventh centuries and the island's conversion and later reconversion to Christianity present a complex picture, then—one that could be retold very differently depending on the perspectives of later historians. As the Angles and Saxons settled in and extended their control, the emerging "English" culture drew on new interpretations of the region's history. The most influential account of all was Bede's *Ecclesiastical History*, completed in 731. Our most reliable and eloquent source for early British history, Bede nonetheless wrote as an Anglo-Saxon. He presented his people's history from a providential perspective, seeing their role in Britain and their conversion to Christianity as a crucial part of a divine plan. King Alfred extended this world view when, in the late ninth century, he wrote of his people's struggle against the invading pagan Vikings.

Bede thus adopts an approach to history that reflects his own devout Christian faith and the disciplined religious practices of his monastic brethren in Northumberland. Nevertheless, Bede lived in a wider culture still deeply imbued with the tribal values of its Germanic and pagan past, a culture that maintained at least a nostalgic regard for the kind of individual heroic glory that rarely looks beyond this world. Even in Bede's day, most kings died young and on the battlefield. And natural disasters such as those in 664 (a plague, and the deaths of a king and an archbishop occurring on the day of an eclipse) could send the Anglo-Saxons back to pagan worship. The two worlds, one with its roots in Mediterranean Christianity and the other in Germanic paganism, overlapped and interpenetrated for generations.

The pagan culture that is the setting for the epic *Beowulf* still strongly resembled that of the Germanic "barbarians" described by the Roman historian Tacitus in the first century. The heroic code of the Germanic warrior bands—what Tacitus called the "*comitatus*"—valued courage in battle above all, followed by loyalty to the tribal leader and the warband. These formed the core of heroic identity. A warrior whose leader fell in battle was obliged to seek vengeance at any cost; it was an indelible shame to survive an unavenged leader. Family links were also profound, however, and a persistent tragic theme in Germanic and Anglo-Saxon heroic narrative pits the claims of vengeance against those of family loyalty.

Early warrior culture in the British Isles, as elsewhere, was fraught with violence, as fragile truces between warring tribes and clans were continually broken. The tone of Old English poetry (as of much of Old Irish heroic narrative) is consequently somber, often suffused with a sense of doom. Even moments of high festivity are darkened by allusions to later disasters. Humor often occurs through a kind of ironic understatement: a poet may state that a warrior strode less swiftly into battle, for example, when the warrior in fact is dead. Similarly Cet, an Irish warrior, claims that if his brother were in the house, he would overcome his opponent, Conall. Conall replies, "But he is in the house," and almost casually flings the brother's head at Cet. A lighter tone is found mostly in shorter forms, such as the playful Anglo-Saxon riddles and in some Old Irish poetry.

The Angles and Saxons had come to England as military opportunists, and they in turn faced attacks and settlement from across the Channel. Their increasingly ordered political world and their thriving monastic establishments, such as Bede's monastery of Jarrow, were plundered by Vikings in swift attacks by boat as early as the end of the eighth century. Irish monastic culture faced similar depradations. This continued for a hundred years, and eventually resulted in widespread Scandinavian settlements north of the Thames, in areas called the Danelaw, and around modern-day Dublin. By the 890s Christian Viking kings reigned at York and in East Anglia, extending a history of independence from the southern kingdoms. The period of raids and looting was largely over by 900, but even King Alfred (d. 899) faced Viking incursions in Wessex and consciously depicted himself as a Christian hero holding the line against pagan invaders. Only his kingdom, in fact, resisted their attacks with complete success. Vikings also intermarried with Anglo-Saxons and expanded their influence by political means. Profiting from English dynastic disorder around the turn of the eleventh century, aristocrats in the Danelaw became brokers of royal power. From 1016 to 1035 the Danish Cnut (Canute) was king of both England and Denmark, briefly uniting the two in a maritime empire. The Scandinavian presence was not exclusively combative, however. They sent peaceful traders to the British Isles—among them Ohthere, whose tale of his voyages is included here. They also left their mark on literature and language, as in the early Middle English romance *Havelock the Dane*, which contains many words borrowed from Old Norse.

PAGAN AND CHRISTIAN: TENSION AND CONVERGENCE

Given that writing in the Roman alphabet was introduced to pre-Conquest England by churchmen, it is not surprising that most texts from the period are written in Latin on Christian subjects. Most writing even in the Old English language was also religious. In Anglo-Saxon England and in the Celtic cultures, vernacular literature tended at first to be orally composed and performed. The body of written vernacular Anglo-Saxon poetry that survives is thus very small indeed, although there are plenty of prose religious works. It is something of a miracle that *Beowulf*, which celebrates the exploits of a pagan hero, was deemed worthy of being copied by scribes who were almost certainly clerics. (In fact, almost all the greatest Anglo-Saxon poetry survives in only a single copy—so tenuous is our link to that past.) Yet the copying of *Beowulf* also hints at the complex interaction of the pagan and Christian traditions in Anglo-Saxon culture.

The conflict between the two traditions was characterized (and perhaps exaggerated) by Christian writers and readers as a struggle between pagan violence and Christian values of forgiveness. The old, deep-seated respect for treasure as a sign of power and achievement seemed to conflict with Christian contempt for worldly goods. In fact, however, pagan Germanic and Christian values were alike in many respects and coexisted with various degrees of mutual influence.

Old English poets explored the tensions as well as the overlap between the two sets of values in two primary poetic modes—the heroic and the elegiac. The heroic mode, of which *Beowulf* is the supreme example, celebrates the values of bravery, loyalty, vengeance, and desire for treasure. The great buckle from Sutton Hoo burial (Color Plate 2) is a surviving artifact of such treasure. The elegiac mode, by contrast, calls the value of these things into question, as at best transient and at worst a worldly distraction from spiritual life. The elegiac speaker, usually an exile, laments the loss of earthly goods—his lord, his comrades, the joys of the mead hall—and, in the case of the short poem known as *The Wanderer*, turns his thoughts to heaven. *Beowulf*, composed most likely by a Christian poet looking back at the deeds of his pagan Scandinavian ancestors, uses elements of both the heroic and the elegiac to focus on the overlap of pagan and Christian virtues. A similar, though less adversarial, interaction of a heroic code and the new religion is also encountered in medieval Irish literature, such as the examples of early Irish verse offered here.

The goals of earthly glory and heavenly salvation that concern Old English poetry are presented primarily as they affect men. Recent scholarship, however, reveals the active roles played in society by Anglo-Saxon women, particularly aristocratic ones. One of these is Aethelflaed, daughter of King Alfred, who co-ruled the kingdom of Mercia with her brother Edward at the turn of the tenth century, taking an active military role in fighting off the Danes. Better known today is Abbess Hilda, who founded and ran the great monastery at Whitby from 657 until her death in 680; five Whitby monks became bishops across England during her rule. Nevertheless, women generally take a marginal role in Old English poetry. In secular works marriages are portrayed as being arranged to strengthen military alliances, in efforts (often doomed) to heal bloody rifts between clans. Women thus function primarily as "peace weavers," a term referring occasionally to their active diplomacy in settling disputes but more often to their passive role in marriage exchanges. This latter role was fraught with danger, for if a truce were broken between the warring groups, the woman would face tragically conflicting loyalties to husband and male kin.

The effect of the Germanic heroic code on women is explored in two tantalizingly short poems that invest the elegiac mode with women's voices: *Wulf and Eadwacer* and *The Wife's Lament*. In both, a woman speaker laments her separation from her lord, whether husband or lover, through some shadowy events of heroic warfare. More indicative of the actual power of aristocratic and religious women in Anglo-Saxon society, perhaps, is the Old English poem *Judith*, a biblical narrative which uses heroic diction reminiscent of that in *Beowulf* to celebrate the heroine's military triumph over the pagan Holofernes.

ORAL POETRY, WRITTEN MANUSCRIPTS

For all their deep linguistic differences and territorial conflicts, the Celts and Anglo-Saxons had affinities in the heroic themes and oral settings of their greatest surviving narratives and in the echoes of a pre-Christian culture that endure there. Indeed, these can be compared to conditions of authorship in oral cultures worldwide, from Homer's Greece to parts of contemporary Africa. In a culture with little or no writing, the singer of tales has an enormously important role as the conservator of the past. In *Beowulf*, for instance, the traditional content and verbal formulas of the poetry of praise are swiftly reworked to celebrate the hero's killing of the monster Grendel:

> Meanwhile a man
> skilled as a singer,   versed in old stories,
> wove a new lay   of truly-linked words.
> So the scop started   his song of Beowulf's
> wisdom and strength,   setting his spell
> with subtle staves.

A poet of this kind (in Anglo-Saxon, a *scop* or "shaper") does not just enhance the great warrior's prestige by praising his hero's ancestors and accomplishments. He also recalls and performs the shared history and beliefs of the entire people, in great feats of memory that make the poet virtually the encyclopedia of his culture. A poet from the oral tradition might also become a singer of the new Christian cosmology, like the illiterate herdsman Caedmon, whom Bede describes as having been called to monastic vows by the Abbess Hilda, in honor of his Christian poems composed in the vernacular oral mode.

In Celtic areas, oral poets had even greater status. The ancient class of learned Irish poets were honored servants of noblemen and kings; they remained as a powerful if reduced presence after the establishment of Christianity. The legal status of such a poet (a *fili*) was similar to that of a bishop, and indeed the *fili* carried out some functions of spells and divination inherited from the pagan priestly class, the druids. The ongoing influence of these poets in Irish politics and culture is reflected in the body of surviving secular literature from medieval Ireland, which is considerably larger than that from Anglo-Saxon England. A comparable situation prevailed in Wales. Even in the quite late Welsh *Tale of Taliesin*, the poet Taliesin appears as a public performer before the king as well as a possessor of arcane wisdom, magic, and prophecy.

In a culture in which a poet has such a wide and weighty role, ranging from entertainer to purveyor of the deepest reaches of religious belief, possession of the word bestows tremendous, even magical power. In a text that describes the wonders of the Irish epic the *Táin*, we hear about the promise of "a year's protection to him to whom it is recited." Even when these tales were copied into manuscripts, their written versions were essentially scripts for later performance, or for memorization. In a twelfth-century Irish manuscript, the copyist wishes "A blessing on everyone who will memorize the *Táin* with fidelity in this form and will not put any other form on it."

This attitude of awe toward the word as used by the oral poet was only enhanced by the arrival of Christianity, a faith that attributes creation itself to an act of divine speech. Throughout the Middle Ages and long after orally composed poetry had retreated from many centers of high culture, the power of the word also inhered in its written form, as encountered in certain prized books. Chief among these were the Bible and other books of religious story, especially by such church fathers as Saints Augustine and Jerome, and books of the liturgy. Since these texts bore the authority of divine revelation, the manuscripts that contained them shared in their charisma.

The power of these manuscripts was both reflected and aided by their visual grandeur. Among the highest expressions of the fervor and discipline of early insular monasticism is its production of beautifully copied and exquisitely decorated books of the Bible. The extreme elaboration of their production and the great labor and expense lavished on them suggest their almost holy status. Figures depicted holding a book in the late eighth-century *Book of Kells* (page 10), or writing in the Lindisfarne Gospels, indicate this importance; a fascination with the new technology is suggested by Old English riddles whose answers are "a hand writing," "a book worm," or "a bookcase."

Saint John, from the
Book of Kells. Late 8th
century.

The cost and effort of making manuscript books and their very scarcity contributed to their aura. Parchment was produced from animal skins, stretched and scraped. The training and discipline involved in copying texts, especially sacred texts, were great. The decoration of the most ambitious manuscripts involved rare colors, gold leaf, and often supreme artistry. Thus these magnificent manuscripts could become almost magical icons: Bede, for example, tells of scrapings from Irish manuscripts which mixed with water cured the bites of poisonous snakes.

Manuscripts slowly became more widely available. By the twelfth century we hear more of manuscripts in private hands and the beginning of production outside ecclesiastical settings. By the fourteenth century merchants and private scholars were buying books from shops that resembled modern booksellers. The glamour and prestige of beautiful manuscripts remained, though, even if the sense of their magic faded to a degree. Great families would donate psalters and gospels to religious foundations, with the donor carefully represented in the decoration presenting the book to the Virgin Mary or the Christ child. Spectacular books of private devotion were at once a medium for spiritual meditation and proof of great wealth (see Color Plate 10). Stories of epic conquest like the *Aeneid* would sometimes feature their aristocratic owners' coat of arms.

THE NORMAN CONQUEST

By the time of these developments in book production, though, a gigantic change had occurred. In a single year, 1066, England witnessed the death of the Anglo-Saxon King Edward and the coronation of his disputed successor King Harold, the invasion and triumph of the foreigner William of Normandy, and his own coronation as King William. These events are recorded, from very different perspectives, in *The Anglo-Saxon Chronicle* and the Bayeux Tapestry (page 144). The Normans conquered, with relative ease, an Anglo-Saxon kingdom disordered by civil strife. The monastic movement had lost much of its earlier fervor and discipline, despite reform in the tenth century. Baronial interests had weakened severely the reign of the late King Edward "the Confessor." On an island that already perceived itself as repeatedly colonized, 1066 nonetheless represented a climactic change, experienced and registered at virtually all levels of social, religious, and cultural experience.

One sign of how great a breach had been opened in England, paradoxically, is the multifaceted effort put forth by conquerors and conquered to maintain—or invent—continuity with the pre-Conquest past. In religious institutions, in dynastic genealogies, in the intersection of history and racial myth, in the forms and records of social institutions, the generations after 1066 sought to absorb a radically changed world yet to ground their world in an increasingly mythicized Anglo-Saxon or Briton antiquity. The Normans and their dynastic successors the Angevins eagerly took up and adapted to their own preoccupations ancient Briton political myths such as that of King Arthur and his court, and the stories of such saintly Anglo-Saxon kings as Oswald and Edward the Confessor.

They promoted narratives of their ancestors, like Wace's *Roman de Rou,* the story of the Normans' founder Rollo, commissioned by Henry II. Geoffrey of Monmouth dedicated his *History of the Kings of England* partly to Henry II's uncle, Robert Duke of Gloucester. In that work Geoffrey links the Celtic myths of King Arthur and his followers to an equally ancient myth that England was founded by descendants of the survivors of Troy; he makes his combined, largely fictive but enormously appealing work available to a Norman audience by writing it in Latin. Geoffrey's story was soon retold in "romance," the French from which vernacular texts took their name. The Angevin court also supported the "romances of antiquity," poems in French that narrate the story of Troy (the *Roman de Troie*), its background (*Roman de Thèbes*), and its aftermath (*Roman d'Eneas*), thus creating a model in the antique past for the Normans and their westward conquest of England. And the *Song of Roland,* the great crusading narrative celebrating the heroic death of Charlemagne's nephew as he protected Christendom from the Spanish Moslems, was probably written in the milieu of Henry II's court.

The Normans brought with them a new system of government, a freshly renovated Latin culture, and most important a new language. Anglo-Saxon sank into relative insignificance at the level of high culture and central government. Norman French became the language of the courts of law, of literature, and of most of the nobility. By the time English rose again to widespread cultural significance, about 250 years later, it was a hybrid that combined Romance and Germanic elements.

Latin offered a lifeline of communication at some social levels of this initially fractured society. The European clerics who arrived under the immigrant archbishops Lanfranc and Anselm brought a new and different learning, and often new and deeply unwelcome religious practices: a celibate priesthood, skepticism about local

The Three Living and the Three Dead, from *The De Lisle Psalter.* The transience of life, especially of worldly glory, was never far from the medieval imagination. In this image from a Psalter made in the early 14th century for Baron Robert de Lisle, three kings in elegant courtly array face three rotting corpses. While most of the Psalter is in French and Latin, this scene has a "caption" in rhymed Middle English at the top. The kings say in turn (in modernized form), "I am afeared. Lo, what I see! I think that here are devils three." The corpses reply, "I was well fair. Such shall thou be. For God's love beware by me."

saints, and newly disciplined monasticism. Yet despite these differences and the tensions that accompanied them, clerics of European or British origin were linked by a common liturgy, a considerable body of shared reading, and most of all a common learned language. Secular as well as religious society were coming to be based more and more on the practical use of the written word: the letter, the charter, the documentary record, and the written book. Whereas Anglo-Saxon England had been governed by the word enacted and performed—a law of oral witness and a culture of oral poets—Norman England increasingly became a land of documents and books.

SOCIAL AND RELIGIOUS ORDER

The famed Domesday Book is a first instance of many of these developments. The Domesday survey was a gigantic undertaking, carried out with a speed that still astonishes between Christmas 1085 and William the Conqueror's death in September 1087. A county-by-county survey of the lands of King William and those held by his tenants-in-chief and subtenants, Domesday also records the obligations of landholders and thus reflects a new feudal system by which, increasingly, land was held in post-Conquest England.

Under the Normans, a nobleman held land from the king as a fief, in exchange for which he owed the king certain military and judicial services, including the provision of armed knights. These knights in turn held land from their lord, to whom they also owed military service and other duties. Some of this land they might keep for their own farming and profit, and the rest they divided among serfs (who were obliged, in theory, to stay on the land to which they were born) and free peasantry. Both groups owed their knight or lord labor and either a portion of their agricultural produce or rents in cash. This system of land tenure was surely more complex and irregular in practice than in the theoretical model called feudalism. For instance, services at all levels were sometimes (and increasingly) commuted to cash payment, and while fiefs were theoretically held only by an individual for a lifetime, increasingly there were expectations that they would be inherited. Royal power gradually grew during the thirteenth and fourteenth centuries, yet the local basis of landholding and social order always acted as a counterbalance, even a block, to royal ambition.

The Domesday Book was only one piece of the multifaceted effort by which the Norman and later kings sought to extend and centralize royal power in their territories. William and his successors established a system of royal justices who traveled throughout the realm and reported ultimately to the king, and an organized royal bureaucracy began to appear. The most powerful and learned of these Anglo-Norman kings was William the Conqueror's great-grandson, Henry II, who ruled from 1154 to 1189. Under Henry, royal justice, bureaucracy, and record-keeping made great advances; the production of documents was centralized and took on more standardized forms, and copies of these documents (called "pipe rolls") began to be produced for later reference and proof.

Along with a stronger royal government, the Normans brought a clergy invigorated both by new learning and by the spirituality of recent monastic reforms. Saint Anselm, the second of the Norman archbishops of Canterbury, was a great prelate and the writer of beautiful and widely influential texts and prayers of private devotion. The Victorines and the Cistercians (inspired in part by Saint Bernard of Clairvaux) also brought a strong mystical streak to English monasticism. All these would bear fruit once again in the fourteenth century in a group of mystics writing in Latin and in English.

On the other hand, the Norman prelates, like their kings, brought an urge toward centralized order in the church and a belief that the church and its public justice (the "canon law") should be independent of secular power. This created frequent conflict with kings and aristocrats, who wanted to extend their judicial power and expected to wield considerable influence in the appointment of church officials.

The most explosive moment in this ongoing controversy occurred in the disagreements between Henry II and Thomas Becket, who was Henry's Chancellor and then Archbishop of Canterbury. Becket's increasingly public refusal to accommodate the king, either in the judicial sphere or the matter of clerical appointments, finally led to his murder by Henry's henchmen in 1170 at the altar of Canterbury Cathedral and his canonization very soon thereafter. A large body of hagiography (narratives of his martyrdom and posthumous miracles) swiftly developed, adding to an already rich tradition of writing about the lives of English saints. As Saint Thomas, Becket became a powerful focus for ecclesiastical ambition, popular devotion and pilgrimage, and religious and secular narrative. In fact, the characters of Chaucer's *Canterbury Tales* tell their stories while making a pilgrimage to his shrine.

At least in theory, feudal tenure involved an obligation of personal loyalty between lord and vassal that was symbolically enacted in the rituals of enfeoffment, in which the lord would bestow a fief on his vassal. This belief was elaborated in a large body of secular literature in the twelfth century and after. Yet feudal loyalty was always fragile and ideologically charged. Vassals regularly resisted the wills of their lord or king when their interests collided, sometimes to the

The Murder of Thomas Becket, from Matthew Paris's *Historia Major,* mid-13th century.

extent of officially withdrawing from the feudal bond. Connected to feudal relations was the notion of a chivalric code among the knightly class (those who
fought on horses, *chevaliers*), which involved not just loyalty to the lord but also
honorable behavior within the class, even among enemies. Chivalric literature is
thus full of stories of captured opponents being treated with the utmost politeness,
as indeed happened when Henry II's son Richard was held hostage for years in
Germany, awaiting ransom.

Similarly, although medieval theories of social order had some basis in fact, they
exercised shifting influence within a much more complex social reality. For instance,
medieval society was often analyzed by the model of the "three estates"—those who
fought (secular aristocrats), those who prayed (the clergy), and those who worked the
land (the free and servile peasantry). This model appears more or less explicitly in
the poetry of William Langland and Chaucer. Such a system, though, did not allow
for the gradual increase in manufacturing (weaving, pottery, metalwork, even the
copying of books) or for the urban merchants who traded in such products. As society
became more complex, a model of the "mystical social body" gained popularity, especially in the fourteenth century. Here a wider range of classes and jobs was compared
to limbs and other body parts. Even this more flexible image was strictly hierarchical,
though. Peasants and laborers were the feet, knights (on the right) and merchants
(on the left) were hands, and townspeople were the heart, but the head was made up
of kings, princes, and prelates of the church.

CONTINENTAL AND INSULAR CULTURES

The arrival of the Normans, and especially the learned clerics who came then and
after, opened England to influences from a great intellectual current that was stirring
on the continent, the "renaissance of the twelfth century," which was to have a significant impact in the centuries that followed. A period of comparative political stability and economic growth made travel easier, and students and teachers were on

the move, seeking new learning in Paris and the Loire valley, in northern Italy, and in Toledo with its Arab and Jewish cultures. Schools were expanding beyond the monasteries and into the precincts of urban cathedrals and other religious foundations. Along with offering traditional biblical and theological study, these schools sparked a revived interest in elegant Latin writing, Neoplatonic philosophy, and science deriving from Aristotle.

Because the Normans and Angevins ruled large territories on the Continent, movement across the Channel was frequent; by the mid-twelfth century learned English culture was urbane and international. English clerics like John of Salisbury studied at Chartres and Paris, and texts by eminent speculative and scientific writers like William of Conches and Bernard Silvestris came to England. As these foreign works entered England, education became more ambitious and widely available, and its products show growing contact with the works of classical Latin writers such as Horace, Virgil, Terence, Cicero, Seneca, and Ovid in his erotic as much as in his mythological poetry.

The renewed attention to these works went along with a revival of interest in the *trivium*, the traditional division of the arts of eloquence: grammar, rhetoric, and dialectic. The most aggressive of these was dialectic, a form of logic developed by the Greeks and then rediscovered by Christian Europe from Arab scholars who had preserved and pursued Greek learning. John of Salisbury, who promoted dialectic in his *Metalogicon*, described it with metaphors of military prowess, as though it were an extension of knightly jousting. "Since dialectic is carried on between two persons," he writes, Aristotle's *Topics* "teaches the matched contestants whom it trains and provides with reasons and topics, to handle their proper weapons and engage in verbal, rather than physical conflict." Rhetoric was elaborately codified in technical manuals of poetry. Though in one sense it was merely ornamental, teaching how to flesh out a description or incident with figures of speech, rhetoric could be as coercive as dialectic, though, since it specified strategies of persuasion in a tradition deriving from ancient oratory. Rhetorical texts also instructed the student in letter-writing, increasingly important as an administrative skill and as a form of elevated composition.

The study of the *trivium* generated many Latin school texts and helped foster a high level of Latinity and a self-consciously sophisticated, classicizing literature in the second half of the twelfth century. Some school texts had great influence on vernacular literature, such as the *Poetria Nova* by Geoffrey of Vinsauf, a rhetorical handbook filled with vivid poetic examples. More intriguing is *Pamphilus*, a short Ovidian poem about a seduction, aided by Venus, which turns into a rape. It is thought to have been an exercise in *disputatio*, the oral form that dialectic assumed in the classroom. The poem was immensely popular in the next few centuries and was translated into many vernacular languages. *Pamphilus* was a conduit at once for Ovidian eroticism and for the language of debate on love. Chaucer mentions it as a model of passionate love and seems to have adapted some of its plot devices in his *Troilus and Criseyde*.

While classical Latin literature was often read with a frank interest in pagan ideas and practices, commentators also offered allegorical interpretations that drew pagan stories into the spiritual and cosmological preoccupations of medieval Christianity. Ovid's *Metamorphoses* were thus interpreted in a French poem, the *Ovide Moralisé*, that was clearly known to Chaucer, and in Latin commentaries such as the

Ovidius moralizatus of Pierre Bersuire. For instance, Ovid describes Jupiter, in the form of a bull, carrying the Tyrian princess Europa into the sea to rape her. Bersuire interprets this as Christ taking on human flesh in order to take up the human soul he loves. Alternatively, he offers an explicitly misogynist allegory, casting Europa as young women who like to see handsome young men—bulls: "They are drawn through the stormy sea of evil temptations and are raped." Neither text is often very subtle in the extraction of Christian or moral analogies from Ovid's stories, yet both were popular and influential, if only because they also tell Ovid's tales before allegorizing them.

Allegory became a complex and fruitful area of the medieval imagination, with profound implications not only for reading, but for artistic production as well. In its simplest sense, an allegorical text takes a metaphor and extends it into narrative, often personifying a quality as a character. For instance, the enormously popular dream vision the *Roman de la Rose* by Guillaume de Lorris and Jean de Meun (which Chaucer translated into English) presents a lady's ambivalence toward courtship as the conflict between such personifications as "Reserve" and "Fair Welcome," both aspects of her own mind. When Christine de Pizan came to challenge the misogynist texts of Western tradition—the *Roman de la Rose* among them—she too chose the allegorical mode. In the *Book of the City of Ladies*, it is three virtues personified as ladies—Reason, Rectitude, and Justice—who refute the slanders of men and who encourage the poet to build a city celebrating female achievements. (The continuing influence of this text is reflected by the English translation printed in 1521.) The English morality play *Mankind* uses allegory to portray external forces, presenting its hero as tempted by the vices of the modern age, "New-Guise" (trendy behavior), "Nowadays," and "Nought." Medieval writers also employed an allegorical method known as typology, derived from biblical interpretation, in which Old Testament events are seen as literally true but also symbolically predictive of, and fulfilled by, events in the New Testament. An example of this occurs in *Piers Plowman*, which, among all its other allegorical devices, presents Abraham both as an Old Testament Patriarch, and, in his willingness to sacrifice his son, a type of Faith.

The Continent, particularly France, provided a variety of vernacular influences. French was the international language of aristocratic culture and an important literary language in England; continental French literature was crucial in the rise of courtly literature in Middle English. Many English Arthurian works, including *Sir Gawain and the Green Knight* and Sir Thomas Malory's *Morte Darthur*, are less indebted to English sources than to French romances, whether written on the Continent or in England by authors such as Marie de France and Thomas of Britain. Chaucer borrowed the conventions and imagery of the love poetry of Guillaume de Machaut and Eustache Deschamps, and even the meter of his earlier poetry derives from their French octosyllabic couplets. To a lesser extent, influences from Italy can be seen in Chaucer's use of Dante's *Divine Comedy*, and his extensive borrowing from Petrarch and Boccaccio. Such continental vernacular literatures infiltrated even the Celtic cultures, as we see in the witty mix of Welsh and European traditions in the poems of Dafydd ap Gwilym.

If such writers and records reflect the higher achievements of education in England of the twelfth century and later, literacy was also diffusing in wider circles and new venues. In a society like England's that continued to produce considerable oral and public literature, indeed, the divide between literacy and illiteracy was always unstable and permeable. A secular aristocrat might have a clerk read to him or her; an urbanite could attend and absorb parts of public rituals that involved poems and orations; even a peasant would be able to pick up Latin tags from sermons or the liturgy. Thus a fourteenth-century writer like William Langland could expect his wide and mixed audience to recognize at least some of the Latin phrases he used along with English; and Chaucer could imagine a character like the Wife of Bath who, at best semiliterate, could still quote bits of the Latin liturgy. Access to texts and the self-awareness fostered by private reading may have helped promote the social ambitions and disruptions within the mercantile and even peasant classes during the later Middle Ages.

WOMEN, COURTLINESS, AND COURTLY LOVE

Access to books also increased the self-awareness of women. Possession of books that encouraged prayer and private devotion, such as psalters and Books of Hours, appears to have facilitated early language training in the home. The many images in manuscripts of women reading—especially the Virgin Mary and her mother, Saint Anne—have interesting implications for our understanding of women's literacy and cultural roles. (See for instance the illumination from the *Bedford Hours*, Color Plate 10.) A number of aristocratic Norman and Angevin women received good educations at convents. Women in the holy life possessed at least some literacy, though this often may have been minimal indeed. Even well-educated women were more likely to read English or French than Latin, with the exception of liturgical books.

The roles of women in the society and cultural imagination of post-Conquest England are complex and contradictory. No Anglo-Norman woman held ecclesiastical prestige like the Anglo-Saxon abbess Hilda or other Anglo-Saxon holy women. Women's power seems to have declined in the long term, both in worldly affairs and in the church, as the Normans consolidated their hold on England and imposed their order on society. Nevertheless, ambitious women could have great influence, especially when they siezed upon moments of disruption. In civil strife over the succession to King Henry I, the Empress Matilda organized an army, issued royal writs, and in the end guaranteed the accession of her son Henry II. If Henry II's wife, Eleanor of Aquitaine, spent the latter decades of her husband's reign under virtual house arrest, it was largely because she had conspired with her sons to raise an army against her own husband.

Despite the limitations of their actual power, women were the focus, often the worshiped focus, of much of the best imaginative literature of the twelfth and thirteenth centuries; and women were central to the social rituals we associate with courtliness and the idea of courtly love. Despite her later imprisonment, Eleanor of Aquitaine was a crucial influence in the diffusion of courtly ideas from the continent, especially the south of France; and among the great writers of the century was Marie de France, who was probably related to Henry II. Scholars continue to debate whether the observances of "courtly love" were in fact widely practiced and whether its worship of women was empowering or restrictive: the

Grotesques and a Courtly Scene, from the *Ormesby Psalter,* c. 1310–1325.

image of the distant, adored lady implies immobility and even silence on her part. Certainly lyrics and narratives that embody courtly values are widespread, even if they often question what they celebrate; and the ideals of courtliness may have had as great an impact through these imaginative channels as through actual enactment.

The ideas and rituals of courtliness reach back to Greek and Roman models of controlled and stylized behavior in the presence of great power. In the Middle Ages, values of discretion and modesty also may have filtered into the secular world from the rigidly disciplined setting of the monasteries. As the society of western Europe took on a certain degree of order in the eleventh and twelfth centuries, courtly attainments began to converge and even compete with simple martial prowess in the achievement of worldly power. The presence of large numbers of armed and ambitious men at the great courts provided at once an opportunity for courtly behavior and the threat of its disruption.

Whatever its historical reality, courtly love as a literary concept had an immense influence. In this it adopted the vocabulary of two distinct traditions: the veneration of the Virgin Mary and the love poetry of Ovid and his heirs. Mariolatry, which has a particularly rich tradition in England, celebrates the perfection of Mary as a woman and mother, who undid the sins of Eve and now intercedes for fallen mankind. Ovid, with his celebration of sensuality and cynical instructions for achieving the lover's desire, provided medieval Europe with a whole catalog of love psychology and erotic persuasion.

The self-conscious command of fine manners, whether the proper way of hunting, dressing, addressing a superior, or wooing a lady, became a key mark of an aristocrat. Great reputations grew around courtly attainment, as in the legends that circulated about Richard I. Centuries later, the hero of *Sir Gawain and the Green Knight* is tested as much through his courtly behavior as through his martial bravery. A literature of etiquette emerged as early as the reign of Henry I in England and continued through the thirteenth century. In the court of Henry II, Daniel of Beccles wrote *Urbanus Magnus,* a verse treatise in Latin on courtesy. In this poem he offers detailed advice in

A Knight, early 14th century. This rubbing from a funerary brass depicts a knight as he presented himself to eternity, sheathed in chain mail and fully armed but with his hands joined in prayer. The dog at his feet is a symbol of fidelity.

many arenas of specific behavior at court: avoiding frivolity, giving brief counsel, and especially comporting oneself among the wealthy:

> Eating at the table of the rich, speak little
> Lest you be called a chatterbox among the diners.
> Be modest, make reverence your companion.

In a mildly misogynist passage, Daniel especially warns against becoming involved with the lord's wife, even if she makes an overture, as occurs in Marie de France's

Lanval. Should this happen, Daniel offers polite evasive strategies, skills we see demonstrated in *Sir Gawain and the Green Knight*.

ROMANCE

Courtliness was expressed both in lyric poetry and in a wide range of vernacular narratives that we now loosely call "romances"—referring both to their genre and to the romance language in which they were first written. The Arthurian tradition, featured in this anthology, is only one of many romance traditions; others include the legends of Tristan and Isolde, Alexander, and Havelock the Dane. In romances that focus on courtly love, the hero's devotion to an unapproachable lady tends to elevate his character. Although many courtly romances conclude in a happy and acceptable marriage of hero and heroine, others begin with such a marriage and move to complications (as does Chaucer's *Franklin's Tale*) or warn of the dangers of transgressive love (as does Marie's *Lanval*). To the extent that they portray women as disruptive agents of erotic desire, some romances take on elements of the misogynist tradition that persisted in clerical thought alongside the adoration of the Virgin. Near the end of *Sir Gawain and the Green Knight*, even the courtly Gawain explodes in a virulent diatribe against women.

Love was not the only subject of romance, however. Stories of love and war typically lead the protagonists into encounters with the uncanny, the marvelous, the taboo. This is not so surprising when we recall the practices of medieval Christianity that brought the believer into daily contact with such miracles as the Eucharist; even chronicles of saints' lives regularly showed the divine will breaking miraculously into everyday life. We may say today that romance looses the hero and heroine onto the landscape of the private or social subconscious; a medieval writer might have stressed that nature itself is imbued with mystery both by God and by other, more shadowy, spiritual forces.

In romances, the line between the mundane and the extraordinary is often highly permeable: an episode may move swiftly from a simple ride to a meeting with a magical lady or malevolent dwarf, as often occurs in Thomas Malory. In *The Franklin's Tale*, Chaucer pokes gentle fun at this tendency by having a magician agree to create the illusion of rocks disappearing from the sea, and then bargain with his client over the price of this service. Romance also seems to be a form of imaginative literature in which medieval society could acknowledge the transgressions of its own ordering principles: adultery, incest, unmotivated martial violence. And it often revisits areas of belief and imagination that official culture long had put aside: *Sir Gawain and the Green Knight*, for instance, features a magical knight who can survive having his head cut off and a powerful aged woman who is called a goddess. Both characters reach back, however indirectly, to pre-Christian figures encountered in early Irish and Welsh stories.

THE RETURN OF ENGLISH

The romances are another of the dense points of contact among the many languages and ethnicities of the medieval British Isles. These powerful and evocative narratives often feature figures of Celtic origin like the British King Arthur and his court who came to French- and English-language culture through the Latin *History* of Geoffrey of Monmouth. Such transmission is typical of the linguistic mix in post-Conquest England. The language of the aristocracy was French, used in government and law as well as in the nascent vernacular literature. A few conservative monasteries continued the famed *Anglo-Saxon Chronicle* in its original language after the Conquest. But increasingly English or an evolving form of Anglo-Saxon was the working language of the peasantry. Mixed-language households must have appeared as provincial Anglo-Saxon gentry began, quite quickly, to intermarry with the Normans and their descendants. The twelfth-century satirist Nigel of Canterbury (or "Wireker"), author of the *Mirror of Fools*, came from just such a mixed family.

Few writings in Middle English survive from the late twelfth century, and very little of value besides the extraordinary *Brut* of Layamon, which retranslates much of Geoffrey of Monmouth's *History* from a French version. A manuscript containing the earliest English lyric in this collection, the thirteenth-century *Cuckoo Song*, can suggest the linguistic complexity of the era: it contains lyrics in English and French, and instructions for performance in Latin.

English began to reenter the world of official discourse in the thirteenth century. Communications between the church and the laity took place increasingly in English, and by the late 1250s, Archbishop Sewal of York tended to reject papal candidates for bishoprics if they did not have good English. In 1258 King Henry III issued a proclamation in Latin, French, and English, though the circumstances were unusual. Teaching glossaries include a growing number of English words, as well as the French traditionally used to explain difficult Latin.

The fourteenth century inaugurated a distinct change in the status of English, however, as it became the language of parliament and a growing number of governmental activities. We hear of Latin being taught in the 1340s through English rather than French. In 1362 a statute tried (but failed) to switch the language of law courts from French to English, and in 1363 Parliament was opened in English. The period also witnesses tremendous activity in translating a wide range of works into English, including Chaucer's version of Boethius' *Consolation of Philosophy* and the Wycliffite translations of the Bible, completed by 1396. Finally, at the close of the century, the Rolls of Parliament record in Latin the overthrow of Richard II, but they feature Henry IV (in what was probably a self-consciously symbolic gesture) claiming the throne in a brief, grave speech in English and promising to uphold "the gude lawes and custumes of the Rewme."

The reemergence of English allowed an extraordinary flowering of vernacular literature, most notably the achievements of Chaucer, Langland, and the anonymous genius who wrote *Sir Gawain and the Green Knight*. It would be more accurate, nevertheless, to speak of the reemergence of "Englishes" in the second half of the fourteenth century. The language scholars now call Middle English divides into four quite distinct major dialects in different regions of the island. These dialects were in many ways mutually unintelligible, so that Chaucer, who was from London in the Southeast Midlands, might have been hard-pressed to understand *Sir Gawain and the Green Knight*, written in the West Midlands near Lancashire. (Certainly Chaucer was aware of dialects and mimics some northern vocabulary in his *Canterbury Tales*.) London was the center of government and commerce in this era and later the place of early book printing, which served to stabilize the language. Thus Chaucer's dialect ultimately dominated and developed into modern English. Therefore English-speaking students today can read Chaucer in the original without much difficulty, whereas Langland's *Piers Plowman* is very challenging and *Sir Gawain* may seem virtually a foreign tongue. As a result, the latter two works are offered in translation in this anthology. (For a practical guide to Chaucer's Middle English, also helpful in reading some of the lyrics and plays in this section, see pages 282–84.)

Not only are *Piers Plowman* and *Sir Gawain* written in dialects different from that of Chaucer's London, they also employ a quite distinct poetic style which descends from the alliterative meter of Old English poetry, based on repetitions of key consonants and on general patterns of stress. By contrast, the rhymed syllabic style used by poets like Chaucer developed under the influence of medieval French poetry and its many lyric forms. Fourteenth-century alliterative poetry was part of a revival that occurred in the North and West of the country, at a time when the form would have seemed old fashioned to many readers in the South. In the next two centuries, in a region even more distant from London, alliterative poetry or its echoes persisted in the Middle Scots poetry of William Dunbar, Robert Henryson, and Gavin Douglas.

POLITICS AND SOCIETY IN THE FOURTEENTH CENTURY

The fourteenth-century authors wrote in a time of enormous ferment, culturally and politically as well as linguistically. During the second half of the fourteenth century, new social and theological movements shook past certainties about the divine right of kings, the division of society among three estates, the authority of the church, and the role of women. An optimistic backward view can see in that time the struggle of the peasantry for greater freedom, the growing power of the Commons in Parliament, and the rise of a mercantile middle class. These changes often appeared far darker at the time, though, with threatening, even apocalyptic implications, as can be seen in *Piers Plowman*.

The forces of nature also cast a shadow across the century. In a time that never produced large agricultural surpluses, poor harvests led to famine in the second and third decades of the century, and an accompanying deflation drove people off the land. In 1348 the Black Death arrived in England, killing at least 35 percent of the population by 1350. Plague struck violently three more times before 1375, emptying whole villages. Overall, as much as half the population may have died.

The kingship was already in trouble. After the consolidation of royal power under Henry II and the Angevins in the twelfth century, the regional barons began to reassert their power. In a climactic confrontation in 1215, they forced King John to sign the Magna Carta, guaranteeing (in theory at least) their traditional rights and privileges as well as due process in law and judgment by peers. In the fourteenth century the monarchy came under considerable new pressures. Edward II (1307–1327) was deposed by one of his barons, Roger de Mortimer, and with the connivance of his own queen, Isabella. His son Edward III had a long and initially brilliant reign, marked by great military triumphs in a war against France, but the conflict dragged on so long that it became known as the Hundred Years' War. Edward III's reign was marked at home by famine, deflation, and then, most horribly, plague. His later years

Color Plate 1 First page of the Gospel of Matthew, from the *Lindisfarne Gospels*, c. 698. This illustrated gospel book was made on the "holy island" of Lindisfarne off the coast of Northumberland, partly in honor of St. Cuthbert, who had died there 11 years earlier and whose cult was fast developing at the time. The manuscript reflects an extraordinary flowering of artistic production during these years, and the meeting of world cultures that occurred in Northumbrian monastic life: Mediterranean Latin language and imagery, Celtic interlace, and Germanic animal motifs. In the 10th century an Anglo-Saxon translation was added in the margins and between the lines. (By permission of The British Library.)

Color Plate 2   Gold buckle, from the Sutton Hoo ship-burial, c. 625–630. Fragments of a remarkably preserved ship-burial, probably for an Anglo-Saxon king, were discovered among other burial mounds at Sutton Hoo, in Suffolk, England, in 1939. The burial mound contained numerous coins and 41 objects in gold, among them this magnificent buckle. Stylized animal heads (including two dragons in the circle at bottom) invite comparison with the powerful animal imagery in *Beowulf.* Other objects in the ship include two silver spoons inscribed "Saul" and "Paul," signs of the mixing of pagan practices and Christian influences in this era. (Copyright The British Museum.)

Color Plate 3   The Ardagh Chalice, c. 9th century. This greatest surviving piece of medieval Celtic metalwork was found near the site of an ancient fort at Ardagh, in County Limerick in the southwest of Ireland. Measuring 9.5 inches across and 7 inches tall, the chalice was probably used for wine on great holidays like Easter, when laypeople took Communion. In the 7th century, the learned Irish monk Adamnan had described the chalice of the Last Supper as a silver cup with two opposite handles. The Ardagh Chalice is very similar. It is made of silver alloy, magnificently decorated with gilt and enamel. Its elaborate interlace decoration uses a wide range of Celtic motifs, including fearsomely toothed animal heads. In a band running around the entire bowl are the names of the 12 apostles, further linking its liturgical role to the Last Supper. (National Museum of Ireland.)

Color Plate 4 Map of England, from Matthew Paris's *Historia Major*, mid-13th century. A monk of St. Albans, Matthew Paris wrote a monumental *History of England*, of which two illustrated copies in his own hand survive. Matthew's richly detailed map of England, including counties and major towns, illustrates the geographical knowledge of his day. It further suggests how alert he was to the ethnic divisions that still crossed his island and to the settlements and invasions, both mythic and actual, that had given rise to them. His inscription near the depiction of Hadrian's Wall, for example, informs us that the wall "once divided the English and the Picts." Recalling the claim that the original Britons were Trojan refugees, he writes about Wales (left center): "The people of this region are descended from the followers of Brutus." The story of Arthur's conception may have led Paris to identify Tintagel ("Tintaiol," lower left). Matthew also links geography and racial character, as in his comment on northern Scotland (top center): "A mountainous, woody region producing an uncivilized people." (By permission of The British Library.)

Color Plate 8 *Richard II with His Regalia*, 1394–1395. Richard himself commissioned this splendid life-size and unusually lifelike portrait soon after the death of his beloved first wife, Anne of Bohemia. It was probably mounted at the back of the King's private pew at Westminster Abbey in London, but it also may suggest his wish to be perpetually near Anne, who was entombed nearby. At the same time, the throne, crown, orb, and scepter are all signs of Richard's sense of kingship and secular authority. (© Dean and Chapter of Westminster.)

Color Plate 9 Opening page of *The Wife of Bath's Tale,* from the Ellesmere manuscript of Chaucer's *Canterbury Tales,* 1405–1410. One of the two earliest surviving manuscripts of the *Tales,* it was owned for centuries by the Egerton family, who became Earls of Ellesmere in the nineteenth century. The Ellesmere Chaucer was probably made in London, by then the center of book production in England. Its elaborate decoration and illustration are all the more striking, given how few Middle English texts received such treatment. The portrait of the Wife of Bath is positioned to highlight the beginning of her tale. Her red clothing, whip, and large hat follow details of her description in the *General Prologue* of the *Tales,* and her own words in the prologue to her tale. The grandeur of the treatment of text and decoration in this manuscript—clearly meant both for display and reading—reflect the speed with which Chaucer became a "canonical" author in the years after his death in 1400, and perhaps the wish of wealthy patrons to associate themselves and their interests with his work. It is partly the same wish that ultimately led the American railroad tycoon Henry E. Huntington to buy the manuscript in 1917 and leave it to his library in San Marino, California. (This item is reproduced by permission of The Huntington Library, San Marino, California. EL26C9F72r.)

Color Plate 10 *Anne, Duchess of Bedford, Kneeling Before the Virgin Mary and Saint Anne,* from the *Bedford Hours,* early 15th century. A book of hours was a prayerbook used by laypeople for private devotion. The *Bedford Hours* was produced in a Paris workshop for the Duke of Bedford, a brother of Henry V, and his wife, Anne of Burgundy. Here, Saint Anne is shown teaching her daughter, the Virgin Mary, to read; another book lies open on a lectern in front of the kneeling Anne of Burgundy. (By permission of The British Library.)

were marked by premature senility and control by a court circle. These years were further darkened by the death of that paragon of chivalry, Edward's son and heir-apparent, Edward "The Black Prince." Edward's successor, the Black Prince's son Richard II, launched a major peace initiative in the Hundred Years' War and became a great patron of the arts, but he was also capable of great tyranny. In 1399 like his great-grandfather, he was deposed. An ancient and largely creaky royal bureaucracy had difficulty running a growing mercantile economy, and when royal justice failed to control crime in the provinces, it was increasingly replaced by local powers.

The aristocracy too experienced pressures from the increased economic power of the urban merchants and from the peasants' efforts to exploit labor shortages and win better control over their land. The aristocrats responded with fierce, though only partly successful, efforts to limit wages and with stricter and more articulate divisions within society, even between the peerage and gentry. It is not clear, however, that fourteenth-century aristocrats perceived themselves as a threatened order. If anything, events may have pressed them toward a greater class cohesion, a more self-conscious pursuit of chivalric culture and values. The reign of Edward III saw the foundation of the royal Order of the Garter, a select group of nobles honored for their chivalric accomplishments as much as their power (the order is almost certainly evoked at the close of *Sir Gawain and the Green Knight*). Edward further exploited the Arthurian myth in public rituals such as tournaments and Round Tables. The ancient basis of the feudal tie, land tenure, began to give way to contract and payment in the growing, hierarchicalized retinues of the period. These were still lifelong relationships between lord and retainer, nevertheless, and contemporary historians of aristocratic sympathies like Jean Froissart idealize an ongoing community of chivalric conduct that could reach even across combating nations.

The second estate, the church, was also troubled—in part, paradoxically, because of the growing and active piety of the laity. Encouraged by the annual confession that had been required since the Fourth Lateran Council of 1215, laymen increasingly took control of their own spiritual lives. But the new emphasis on confession also led to clerical corruption. Mendicant (begging) friars, armed with manuals of penance, spread across the countryside to confess penitents in their own homes and sometimes accepted money for absolving them. Whether or not these abuses were truly widespread, they inspired much anticlerical satire—as is reflected in the works of Chaucer and Langland—and the Church's authority diminished in the process. The traditional priesthood, if better educated, was also more worldly than in the past, increasingly pulled from parish service into governmental bureaucracy; it too faced widespread literary satire. Well aware of clerical venality, the church nevertheless fearfully resisted the criticisms and innovations of "reforming clerics" like John Wycliffe and his supporters among the gentry, the "Lollard knights." The church's control over religious experience was further complicated and perhaps undermined by the rise of popular mysticism, among both the clergy and the laity, which was difficult to contain within the traditional ecclesiastical hierarchy. Mystical writing by people as varied as Richard Rolle, Julian of Norwich, the anonymous author of *The Cloud of Unknowing*, and the emotive Margery Kempe all promulgate the notion of an individual's direct experience of the divine. Many of these developments—and the efforts to stop them—appear in the section "Vernacular Religion and Repression" (page 514). Finally, and on a much broader scale, all of Christian

Europe was rocked by the Great Schism of 1378, when believers faced the disconcerting spectacle of two popes ruling simultaneously.

The third estate, the commoners, was the most problematic and rapidly evolving of the three in the fourteenth century. The traditional division of medieval society into three estates had no place for the rising mercantile bourgeoisie and grouped them with the peasants who worked the land. In fact the new urban wealthy formed a class quite of their own. Patrons and consumers of culture, they also served in the royal bureaucracy under Edward III, as is illustrated by the career of Geoffrey Chaucer who came from just such a background. Yet only the wealthiest married into the landed gentry, and poor health conditions in the cities made long mercantile dynasties uncommon. Cities in anything like a modern sense were few and retained rural features. Houses often had gardens, even orchards, and pigs (and pig dung) filled the narrow, muddy streets. Only magnates built in stone; only they and ecclesiastical institutions had the luxury of space and privacy. Otherwise, cities were crowded and dirty—the suburbs especially disreputable—and venues for communicable disease.

The peasants too had a new sense of class cohesion. Events had already loosened the traditional bond of serfs to the land on which they were born, and the plagues further shifted the relative economic power of landowning and labor. As peasants found they could demand better pay, fiercely repressive laws were passed to stop them. These and other discontents, like the arrival of foreign labor and technologies, led to the Rising of 1381 (also known as the Peasants' Revolt). Led by literate peasants and renegade priests, the rebels attacked aristocrats, foreigners, and some priests. They were swiftly and violently put down, but the event was nevertheless a watershed and haunted the minds of the English.

When one leader of the revolt, the priest John Ball, cited Langland's fictional character Piers Plowman with approval, Langland reacted with dismay and revised his poem to emphasize the proper place of peasants. Even more conservative, Chaucer's friend John Gower wrote a horrified Latin allegory on the revolt, *Vox Clamantis* (*The Voice of One Crying*), where he compared the rebels to beasts. By contrast, Chaucer virtually ignored the revolt, aside from a brief comic reference in *The Nun's Priest's Tale*; it remains unclear, though, whether Chaucer's silence reflects comfortable bourgeois indifference or stems from deep anxiety and discomfort. At the same time, these disruptions introduced a period of cultural ferment, and the mercantile middle class also provided a creative force, appearing (though not without some nervous condescension) in some of Chaucer's most enduring characters like *The Canterbury Tales'* Merchant, the Wife of Bath, and the Miller.

It is both from this new middle class and from the established upper class that wider choices in the lives of women emerged in the later Middle Ages. Their social and political power had been curtailed both by clerical antifeminism and by the increasingly centralized government during the twelfth and thirteenth centuries. Starting in the fourteenth century, however, women began to regain an increased voice and presence. Among the aristocracy, Edward II's wife Isabella was an important player in events that brought about the king's deposition. And at the end of the century, Edward III's mistress Alice Perrers was widely criticized for her avarice and her influence on the aging king (for instance by William Langland who refers to her in the allegorical figure Lady Meed).

Women were also important in the spread of lay literacy among the middle class. In France, Christine de Pizan reexamined whole areas of her culture, especially ancient and biblical narrative, from a feminist perspective; her work was known and translated in England. Important autobiographical works were composed in Middle English by Julian of Norwich and Margery Kempe. Julian was an anchoress, living a cloistered religious life but able to speak to visitors such as Margery herself; Margery was an illiterate but prosperous townswoman, daughter of a mayor, who dictated to scribes her experiences of wifehood and rebellion against it, of travel to holy places, and of spiritual growth. Still, for the representation of women's voices in this period we are largely dependent on the fictional creations of men. Chaucer's famous Wife of Bath, for instance, strikes many modern readers as an articulate voice opposing women's repression and expressing their ambitions, but for all her critique of the antifeminist stereotypes of the church, she is in many ways their supreme embodiment. And in a number of Middle English lyrics, probably by men, the woman's voice may evoke scorn rather than pity as she laments her seduction and abandonment by a smooth-talking man, usually a cleric.

THE SPREAD OF BOOK CULTURE IN THE FIFTEENTH CENTURY

Geoffrey Chaucer died in 1400, a convenient date for those who like their eras to end with round numbers. Certainly literary historians have often closed off the English Middle Ages with Chaucer and left the fifteenth century as a sort of drab and undefined waiting period before the dawn of the Renaissance. Yet parts of fifteenth-century England are sites of vital and burgeoning literary culture. Book ownership spread more and more widely. Already in the late fourteenth century, Chaucer had imagined a fictional Clerk of Oxford with a solid collection of university texts despite his relative poverty. More of the urban bourgeoisie bought books and even had appealing collections assembled for them. When printing came to England in the later fifteenth century, books became even more available, though still not cheap.

Whether in manuscript or print, a swiftly growing proportion of these books was in English. The campaigns of Henry V in the second decade of the fifteenth century and his death in 1422 mark England's last great effort to reclaim the old Norman and Angevin territories on the continent. With the loss of all but a scrap of this land and the decline of French as a language of influence, these decades consolidate a notion of cultural and nationalistic Englishness. The Lancastrian kings, Henry the Fourth, Fifth, and Sixth, seem to have adopted English as the medium for official culture and patronized translators like Lydgate. Later in the period William Caxton made a great body of French and English texts available to aristocratic and middle-class readers, both by translating and by diffusing them in the new medium of print.

Ancient aristocratic narratives continued to evolve, as in Thomas Malory's retelling of the Arthurian story in his *Morte Darthur*, one of the books printed by Caxton. Malory works mostly from French prose versions but trims back much of the exploration of love and the uncanny; the result is a recharged tale of chivalric battle and familial and political intrigue. Other continental and local traditions are revived in another courtly setting by a group of Scots poets including William Dunbar and Robert Henryson.

As more and more commoners had educational and financial access to books, they also participated in a lively public literary culture in towns and cities. The fifteenth century sees the flowering of the great dramatic "mystery cycles," sets of plays on religious themes produced and in part performed by craft guilds of larger towns in the Midlands and North. Included here are two brilliant samples, the play of the *Crucifixion* from York and *The Second Play of the Shepherds* from Wakefield. Probably written by clerics, these plays are nonetheless dense with the preoccupations of contemporary working people and enriched by implicit analogies between the lives of their actors and the biblical events they portray. Lyrics and political poems continue to flourish. Sermons remain a popular and widespread form of religious instruction and literary production. And highly literary public rituals, such as Henry V's triumphal civic entries as he returned from his French campaigns, are part of Lancastrian royal propaganda.

By the time Caxton was editing and printing Malory in 1485 with an eye to sales and profit, over eight hundred years had passed since Caedmon is said to have composed his first Christian hymn under angelic direction. The idea of the poet had moved from a version of magician and priest to something more like a modern author; and the dominant model of literary transmission was shifting from listening to an oral performance to reading a book privately. Chaucer, that most bookish of poets, is a case in point. Many of his early poems refer to the pleasures of reading, not only for instruction but even as a mere pastime, often to avoid insomnia. He opens the dream vision *The Parliament of Fowls* with the poet reading a classical Latin text, Cicero's *Dream of Scipio*. Chaucer, of course, read his books and disseminated his own work in handwritten manuscript; in his humorous lyric *To His Scribe Adam* he expresses his frustration with copyists who might mistranscribe his words.

Despite such private bookishness, however, a more public and oral literary culture never disappeared from medieval Britain. Considerable interdependence between oral and literate modes of communication remained; poetry was both silently read and orally performed. In *The Canterbury Tales*, for instance, when the pilgrim Chaucer apologizes for the bawdiness of *The Miller's Tale*, he suggests that if the listener/reader does not like what he *hears*, he should simply turn the *page* and choose another tale. At the same time, literate clerics practiced what we might call learned orality, through lectures or disputations at Oxford and Cambridge or from the pulpit in a more popular setting. Langland imitates such sophisticated oral practice in the theological debates in *Piers Plowman*, and Chaucer uses the sermon form in *The Wife of Bath's Prologue, The Pardoner's Tale*, and *The Parson's Tale*. The popular orality of minstrel performance, harking back however distantly to the world of the Anglo-Saxon *scop* and the Irish *fili*, was also exploited with great self-consciousness by literate poets. Langland expresses harsh disapproval of those minstrels who were mere entertainers, undercutting the serious work of preachers. *Sir Gawain and the Green Knight* presents itself as an oral performance, based on a tale that the narrator has heard recited. By contrast, Chaucer gently twits minstrels in his marvelous parody of popular romance, *Sir Thopas*. Chaucer remains a learned poet whose greatest achievement, paradoxically, was the presentation of fictional oral performances—the tale-telling of the Canterbury pilgrims.

The speed with which communication technologies are changing in our own era has heightened our awareness of such changes in the past. We are now closing the era of the book and moving into the era of the endlessly malleable electronic text. In many ways the means by which we have come to receive and transmit information— television, radio, CD-ROM, Internet—mix orality and literacy in a fashion wholly new yet also intriguingly reminiscent of the later Middle Ages. In contrast to the seeming fixity of texts in the intervening centuries, contemporary literary culture may be recovering the sense of textual and cultural fluidity that brought such dynamism to literary creation in the Middle Ages.

Before the Norman Conquest

⊷ ⚹ ⊶

Beowulf

Beowulf has come down to us as if by chance, for it is preserved only in a single manuscript now in the British Library, Cotton Vitellius A.xv, which almost perished in a fire in 1731. An anonymous poem in the West Saxon dialect of Old English, it may stretch back as early as the late eighth century, although recent scholars think the version we now have was composed within one hundred years of its transcription in the late tenth century. If the later date is correct, this first "English epic" could have appealed to one of the Viking kings who ruled in northern and eastern England. This would help explain a king's burial at sea, a Viking practice, that occurs early in the poem (page 32), and the setting of most of the poem's action in Scandinavia (see map, page 28). Although it was studied by a few antiquarians during the early modern period, *Beowulf* remained virtually unknown until its first printing in 1815, and it was only in the twentieth century that it achieved a place in the canon, not just as a cultural artifact or a good adventure story but as a philosophical epic of great complexity and power.

Several features of *Beowulf* make its genre problematic: the vivid accounts of battles with monsters link it to the folktale, and the sense of sorrow for the passing of worldly things mark it as elegiac. Nevertheless, it is generally agreed to be the first postclassical European epic. Like the *Iliad* and the *Odyssey*, it is a primary epic, originating in oral tradition and recounting the legendary wars and exploits of its audience's tribal ancestors from the heroic age.

The values of Germanic tribal society are indeed central to *Beowulf*. The tribal lord was held to ideals of extraordinary martial valor. More practically, he rewarded his successful followers with treasure that symbolized their mutual obligations. A member of the lord's *comitatus*—his band of warriors—was expected to follow a rigid code of heroic behavior stressing bravery, loyalty, and willingness to avenge lord and comrades at any cost. He would suffer the shame of exile if he should survive his lord in battle; the speaker of *The Wanderer* (pages 130–33) may be such a man. Such values are explicitly invoked at the end of *Beowulf*, when Wiglaf, the hero's only loyal retainer, upbraids his comrades for having abandoned Beowulf to the dragon: he says that their prince wasted his war gear on them, and predicts the demise of their people, the Geats, once their ancient enemies, the Swedes, hear that Beowulf is dead.

Beowulf offers an extraordinary double perspective, however. First, for all its acceptance of the values of pagan heroic code, it also refers to Christian concepts that in many cases conflict with them. Although all characters in the poem—Danes, Swedes, and Geats, as well as the monsters— are pagan, the monster Grendel is described as descended from Cain and destined for hell. It is the joyous song of creation at Hrothgar's banquet, reminiscent of Genesis 1, that inspires Grendel to renew his attacks. Furthermore, while violence in the service of revenge is presented as the proper way for Beowulf to respond to inhuman assailants such as Grendel's mother, the narrator expresses a regretful view, perhaps influenced by Christianity, of the unending chain of violence engaged in by feuding tribes. And although the Danish king Hrothgar uses wealth as a kind of social sacrament when he lavishly rewards Beowulf for his military aid, he simultaneously invokes God in a "sermon" warning him against excessive pride in his youthful strength. This rich division of emotional loyalty probably arises from a poet and audience of Christians who look back at their pagan ancestors with both pride and grief, stressing the intersection of pagan and Christian values in an effort to reconcile the two. By restricting his biblical references to events in the Old Testament, the poet shows the Germanic revenge ethic as consistent with the Old Law of retribution, and leaves implicit its conflict with the New Testament injunction to forgive one's enemies.

Peoples and places in *Beowulf,* after F. Klaeber.

The style *of Beowulf* is simultaneously a challenge and a reward to the modern reader. Some of its features, such as the variation of an idea in different words—which would have been welcomed by a listening, and often illiterate, audience—can seem repetitious to a literate audience. The poem's somewhat archaic diction can make it seem difficult as well, although the translators of the version included here have adopted a more straightforward and colloquial style than was often used in the past. By rendering the opening word "Hwaet!" as "So!" rather than "Hark!" or "Lo!" they have avoided the stuffiness of earlier versions. They have also tried to reduce the confusion arising from the poem's use of patronymics—phrases identifying a character by his father's name. Though they generally retain the designations of Beowulf as "Ecgtheow's son," they often substitute the name of a minor character for the poem's patronymic, rendering "Ecglaf's son" as "Unferth," for instance.

Two other stylistic features that are indebted to the poem's oral origin are highly admired today. First, like other Old English poems, *Beowulf* uses alliteration as a structural principle, beginning three of the four stressed words in a line with the same letter. The translators have sought the same effect, even when departing considerably from the original language, as when they render the line, "waes se grimma gaest Grendel haten" in the passage below as "a horror from hell, hideous Grendel." The poet also uses compound words, such as *mearcstapa* ("borderland-prowler") and *fifelcynnes* ("of monsterkind"), with unusual inventiveness and force. A specific type of compound used for powerful stylistic effects is the "kenning," a kind of compressed metaphor, such as "swan-road" for "ocean" or "wave-courser" for "ship." The kennings resemble the Old English riddles in their teasing, enigmatic quality.

On a larger narrative level is another stylistic feature, also traceable to the poem's oral roots: the tendency to digress into stories tangential to the action of the main plot. The poet's digressions, however, actually contribute to his artistry of broad contrasts—youth and age, joy and sorrow, good and bad kingship. For instance, Hrothgar, while urging humility and generosity on the victorious Beowulf, tells the story of the proud and parsimonious King Heremod. Similarly, when Beowulf returns home in glory to the kingdom of the Geats, the poet praises his uncle Hygelac's young Queen Hygd by contrasting her with the bad Queen Modthryth, who lost her temper and sent her suitors to death.

These episodes also return to prominent themes like nobility, heroic glory, and the distribution of treasure. Such return to key themes, as well as the poem's formulaic repetition and stylistic variation, all bear comparison to insular art of its time. As seen in the page from the *Book of Kells* illustrated on page 10, the dense repetition of lines and intertwined curves, even zoomorphic shapes (often called interlace), competes for attention with the central image of Saint John. This intricately crafted biblical image, like the royal treasure from Sutton Hoo ship burial (Color Plate 2), help remind us that the extraordinary artistic accomplishments of Anglo-Saxon culture went hand-in-hand with its nostalgia for heroic violence.

The poet uses digression and repetition in an especially subtle way to foreshadow dark events to come. To celebrate Beowulf's victory over Grendel, the scop at Hrothgar's hall sings of events of generations earlier, in which a feud caused the deaths of a Danish princess's brother and son. Although this story has nothing to do with the main plot of the poem, there is an implied parallel a few lines later, when, ominously, Hrothgar's queen Wealtheow hints that her husband's nephew Hrothulf should treat her young sons honorably, remembering the favors Hrothgar has shown him, and soon after, she urges Beowulf also to be kind to them. The original audience would have known that after Hrothgar's death, his queen will suffer a disaster like that of the princess in the song. The poet thus applies his broad principle of comparison and contrast to complex narrative situations as well as to simpler concepts such as good and bad kings. It is the often tragic tenor of these digressions that evokes much of the dark mood that suffuses *Beowulf*, even in its moments of heroic triumph.

The following passage from the original Old English, which has been translated literally, illustrates some of the stylistic features of *Beowulf* discussed above.*

      Swā ðā drihtguman   drēamum lifdon,
100   ēadiglice,   oð ðæt ān ongan
      fyrene fre(m)man   fēond on helle;
      wæs se grimma gǣst   Grendel hāten,
      mǣre mearcstapa,   sē þe mōras hēold,
      fen ond fæsten;   fifelcynnes eard
105   wonsǣli wer   weardode hwile,
      siþðan him Scyppend   forscrifen haefde
      in Cāines cynne—   þone cwealm gewraec
      ēce Drihten,   þaes þe hē Abel slōg;
      ne gefeah hē þǣre fǣðe,   ac hē hine feor forwraec,
110   Metod for þy māne   mancynne fram.

      And so the warriors   lived in joy
100   happily   until one began
      the commit crimes,   a fiend from hell
      the grim demon   was called Grendel,
      notorious borderland-prowler   who dwelt in the moors
      fen and stronghold;   the home of monsterkind
105   this cursed creature   occupied for a long while
      since the Creator   had condemned him
      as the kin of Cain—   he punished the killing,
      the Eternal Lord,   because he slew Abel;
      He did not rejoice in that evil deed,   but He banished him far
110   from mankind,   God, in return for the crime.

*The passage is taken from *Beowulf and the Fight at Finnsburg*, 3rd ed., ed. Frederick Klaeber (Boston: D. C. Heath, 1950). The translation is by Anne Schotter.

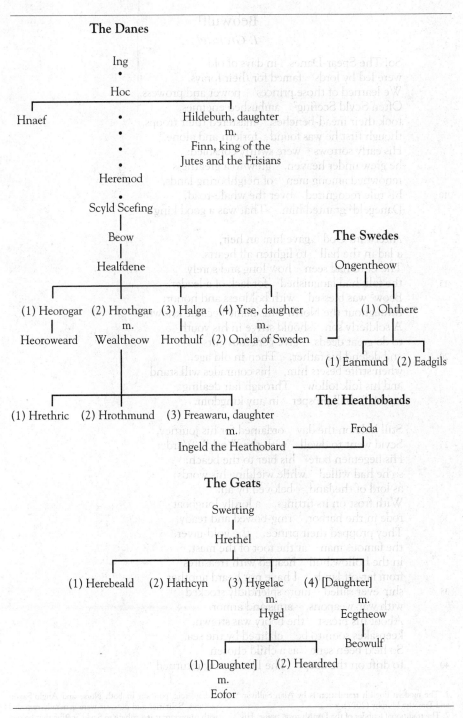

The Danes

Ing
•
Hoc

Hnaef   •   Hildeburh, daughter
               •   m.
               •   Finn, king of the
               •   Jutes and the Frisians

Heremod
•
Scyld Scefing
|
Beow   **The Swedes**
|
Healfdene   Ongentheow

(1) Heorogar (2) Hrothgar (3) Halga (4) Yrse, daughter   (1) Ohthere
                  m.   m.
Heoroweard   Wealtheow   Hrothulf (2) Onela of Sweden

                                                    (1) Eanmund   (2) Eadgils

(1) Hrethric (2) Hrothmund (3) Freawaru, daughter   **The Heathobards**
                             m.
                 Ingeld the Heathobard ———   Froda

The Geats

Swerting
|
Hrethel

(1) Herebeald (2) Hathcyn (3) Hygelac (4) [Daughter]
                                m.   m.
                            Hygd   Ecgtheow
                                             |
                                          Beowulf

(1) [Daughter] (2) Heardred
      m.
    Eofor

Royal genealogies of the Northern European tribes according to the *Beowulf* text.

Beowulf[1]

I. Grendel

So! The Spear-Danes   in days of old
were led by lords   famed for their forays.
We learned of those princes'   power and prowess.
Often Scyld Scefing[2]   ambushed enemies,
5   took their mead-benches,   mastered their troops,
though first he was found   forlorn and alone.[3]
His early sorrows   were swiftly consoled:
he grew under heaven,   grew to a greatness
renowned among men   of neighboring lands,
10   his rule recognized   over the whale-road,
Danegeld[4] granted him.   That was a good king!

Afterward God   gave him an heir,
a lad in the hall   to lighten all hearts.
The Lord had seen   how long and sorely
15   the folk had languished   for lack of a leader.
Beow[5] was blessed   with boldness and honor;
throughout the North   his name became known.
A soldierly son   should strive in his youth
to do great deeds,   give generous gifts
20   and defend his father.   Then in old age,
when strife besets him,   his comrades will stand
and his folk follow.   Through fair dealing
a prince shall prosper   in any kingdom.

Still hale on the day   ordained for his journey,
25   Scyld went to dwell   with the World's Warder.
His liegemen bore   his bier to the beach:
so he had willed   while wielding his words
as lord of the land,   beloved by all.
With frost on its fittings,   a lordly longboat
30   rode in the harbor,   ring-bowed and ready.
They propped their prince,   the gold-giver,
the famous man   at the foot of the mast,
in the hollow hull   heaped with treasures
from far-off lands.   I have not heard another
35   ship ever sailed   more splendidly stocked
with war-weapons,   arms and armor.
About his breast   the booty was strewn,
keepsakes soon to be   claimed by the sea.
So he'd been sent   as a child chosen
40   to drift on the deep.   The Danes now returned

---

1. The modern English translation is by Alan Sullivan and Timothy Murphy (2002).
2. The traditional founder of the Danish royal house. His name means "shield" or "protection" of the "sheaf," suggesting an earlier association in Norse mythology with the god of vegetation. The Danes are known afterward as "Scyldings," descendants of Scyld.
3. Scyld Scefing arrives among the Danes as a foundling,

a dangerous position in both Norse and Anglo-Saxon cultures. Solitaries and outcasts were generally regarded with suspicion; it is a tribute to Scyld Scefing that he surmounted these obstacles to become the leader and organizer of the Danish people.
4. Gold paid as tribute to the Danes.
5. The manuscript reads "Beowulf" here, the copyist's mind having skipped ahead to the story's protagonist.

treasures no less   than those they had taken,
and last they hoisted   high overhead
a golden banner   as they gave the great one
back to the brine   with heavy hearts
45   and mournful minds.   Men cannot say,
though clever in council   or strong under sky,
who might have landed   that shipload of loot.

But the son of Scyld   was hailed in the strongholds
after the father   had fared far away,
50   and he long ruled   the lordly Scyldings.
A son was born   unto Beow also:
proud Healfdene,   who held his high seat,
battle-hardened   and bold in old age.
Four offspring   descended from Healfdene,
55   awake in the world: Heorogar, Hrothgar,
kindly Halga;   I have heard that the fourth
was Onela's queen[6]   and slept with the sovereign
of warlike Swedes.
                          Hrothgar was granted
swiftness for battle   and staunchness in strife,[7]
60   so friends and kinfolk   followed him freely.
His band of young soldiers   swelled to a swarm.
In his mind he mulled   commanding a meadhall
higher than humankind   ever had heard of,
and offering everyone,   young and old,
65   all he could give   that God had granted,
save common land   and commoners' lives.
Then, I am told,   he tackled that task,
raising the rafters   with craftsmen summoned
from many kingdoms   across Middle-Earth.
70   They covered it quickly   as men count the time,
and he whose word   held the land whole
named it Heorot,[8]   highest of houses.
The prince did not fail   to fulfill his pledge:
feasts were given,   favor and fortune.
75   The roof reared up;   the gables were great,
awaiting the flames   which would flare fiercely
when oaths were broken,   anger awakened;
but Heorot's ruin   was not yet at hand.[9]

Each day, one evil   dweller in darkness
80   spitefully suffered   the din from that hall
where Hrothgar's men   made merry with mead.
Harp-strings would sound,   and the song of the scop

6. The daughters of Germanic royal families were married to the heads of opposing tribes in an attempt to cement military alliances. Often, as here, they are not named in the poem.

7. Significantly, Hrothgar is not the first-born of his generation. Leadership of the tribe was customarily conferred by acclamation upon the royal candidate who showed the greatest promise and ability.

8. The name of Hrothgar's hall in Anglo-Saxon literally means "hart" or "stag," a male deer. The epithet "adorned with horns," which is applied to Heorot later, may further suggest its function as a hunting lodge.

9. The peace concluded between the Danes and the Heathobards through intermarriage is already doomed before it has taken place. The events foreshadowed here will occur long after the time of the poem.

would recount the tales   told of time past:
whence mankind had come,   and how the Almighty
85   had fashioned the world   with its fair fields
set in wide waters,   with sun and moon
lifted on high   and lighting the lands
for Earth's first dwellers,   with forests everywhere
branching and blooming,   with life breathing
90   in all kinds of creatures.
                    So the king's thanes
gathered in gladness;   then crime came calling,
a horror from hell,   hideous Grendel,
wrathful rover   of borders and moors,
holder of hollows,   haunter of fens.
95   He had lived long   in the land of the loathsome,
born to the band   whom God had banished
as kindred of Cain,   thereby requiting
the slayer of Abel.[1]   Many such sprang
from the first murderer: monsters and misfits,
100   elves and ill-spirits,   also those giants
whose wars with the Lord   earned them exile.

After nightfall   he nosed around Heorot,
saw how swordsmen   slept in the hall,
unwary and weary   with wine and feasting,
105   numb to the sorrows   suffered by men.
The cursed creature,   cruel and remorseless,
swiftly slipped in.   He seized thirty thanes
asleep after supper,   shouldered away
what trophies he would,   and took to his lair
110   pleased with the plunder,   proud of his murders.

When daylight dawned   on the spoils of slaughter,
the strength of the fiend   was readily seen.
The feast was followed   by fits of weeping,
and cries of outrage   rose in the morning.
115   Hrothgar the strong   sank on his throne,
helpless and hopeless   beholding the carnage,
the trail of the terror,   a trouble too wrathful,
a foe too ferocious,   too steadfast in rage,
ancient and evil.   The evening after
120   he murdered again   with no more remorse,
so fixed was his will   on that wicked feud.
Henceforth the fearful   were easily found
elsewhere, anywhere   far from the fiend,
bedding in barns,   for the brutal hall-thane
125   was truly betokened   by terrible signs,
and those who escaped   stayed safer afar.

So wrath fought alone   against rule and right;
one routed many;   the mead-hall stood empty.
Strongest of Spear-Danes,   Hrothgar suffered

1. See Genesis 4.3–16.

130   this fell affliction   for twelve winters' time.
           As his woes became known   widely and well,
           sad songs were sung   by the sons of men:
           how season on season,   with ceaseless strife,
           Grendel assailed   the Scylding's sovereign.
135   The monster craved   no kinship with any,
           no end to the evil   with wergeld[2] owed;
           nor might a king's   council have reckoned
           on quittance come   from the killer's hand.
           The dark death-shadow   daunted them all,
140   lying in ambush   for old and young,
           secretly slinking   and stalking by night.
           No man knows where   on the misty moor
           the heathen keepers   of hell-runes[3] wander.

           So over and over   the loathsome ogre
145   mortally menaced   mankind with his crimes.
           Raiding by night,   he reigned in the hall,
           and Heorot's high   adornments were his,
           but God would not grant   throne-gifts to gladden
           a scourge who spurned   the Sovereign of Heaven.

150   Stricken in spirit,   Hrothgar would often
           closet his council   to ponder what plan
           might be deemed best   by strong-minded men.
           Sometimes the elders   swore before altars
           of old war-idols,   offering prayers
155   for the soul-slayer   to succor their people.[4]
           Such was their habit,   the hope of heathens:
           with hell in their hearts,   they were lost to the Lord.
           Their inmost minds   knew not the Almighty;
           they never would worship   the world's true protector.
160   Sorry is he   who sears his soul,
           afflicted by flames   he freely embraced.
           No cheer for the chastened!   No change for the better!
           But happy is he   who trusts in heaven
           and lives to his last   in the Lord's keeping.

165   So in his sorrow   the son of Healfdene[5]
           endlessly weighed   how a wise warrior
           might fend off harm.   The hardship this foe
           of his folk inflicted   was fierce and long-lasting,
           most ruinous wrath   and wracking night-evil.

170   A thane[6] of Hygelac   heard in his homeland

2. A cash payment for someone's death. *Wergeld* was regarded as an advance over violent revenge, and Grendel is marked as uncivilized because he refuses to acknowledge this practice.
3. By rendering the Old English *helrunan*, which means "those adept in the mysteries of hell," as "heathen keepers of hell-runes," the translators are taking the liberty of suggesting that "demons" such as Grendel are familiar with runes—the letters of the early Germanic alphabet.
4. In their fear, the Danes resume heathen practices. In Christian belief, the pagan gods were transformed into devils.
5. Hrothgar. He is referred to by his patronymic, his father's name, as is frequent with male characters in the poem.
6. One of the king's principal retainers, chief among these being the earls.

of Grendel's deeds.   Great among Geats,[7]
this man was more mighty   than any then living.
He summoned and stocked   a swift wave-courser,
and swore to sail   over the swan-road
175   as one warrior should   for another in need.
His elders could find   no fault with his offer,
and awed by the omens,   they urged him on.
He gathered the bravest   of Geatish guardsmen.
One of fifteen,   the skilled sailor
180   strode to his ship   at the ocean's edge.

He was keen to embark: his keel was beached
under the cliff   where sea-currents curled
surf against sand;   his soldiers were ready.
Over the longboat's   bow they boarded,
185   bearing below   their burnished weapons
and gilded gear   to hoard in the hull.
Other men shoved   the ship from the shore,
and off went the band,   their wood-braced vessel
bound for the venture   with wind on the waves
190   and foam under bow,   like a fulmar in flight.[8]

On the second day   their upswept prow
slid into sight   of a steep-sided coast,
the goal of their voyage,   gained in good time.
Sea-cliffs and stacks   shone before them,
195   flat-topped capes   at the close of their crossing.
Swiftly the sailors   steered for the shore,
moored their boat   and debarked on the berm.
Clad in corselets   of clattering mail,
they saluted the Lord   for their smooth sailing.

200   From the post he held   high on the headland,
a Scylding had spied   the strangers bearing
bright bucklers   and battle-armor
over their gangplank.   Avid for answers
and minded to know   what men had come hence,
205   Hrothgar's thane   hastened on horseback
down to the beach   where he brusquely brandished
spear-haft in hand   while speaking stern words:

"What warriors are you,   wearers of armor,
bearers of byrnies,   daring to bring
210   your lofty longboat   over the sea-lane?
Long have I looked   out on the ocean
so foreign foes   might never float hither
and harry our homeland   with hostile fleets.
No men have ever   more brazenly borne
215   shields to our shores,   nor have you sought

---

7. A Germanic tribe who lived along the southwestern
coast of what is now Sweden.   8. Gull-like sea bird of the far north Atlantic.

leave from our lords   to land in this place,
nor could you have known   my kin would consent.
I have never beheld   an earl on this earth
more mighty in arms   than one among you.
220   This is no hall-warmer,   handsome in harness,
showy with shield,   but the noblest of knights
unless looks belie him.   Now let me know
who are your fathers   before you fare further
or spy on the Danes.   I say to you, sailors
225   far from your homes: hear me and hasten
to answer me well.   Whence have you wandered?
Why have you come?"
                              Wisest with words,
the eldest offered   an answer for all:
"From Geat-land we come;   we are Geatish men,
230   sharers of Hygelac's   hearth and hall.
My father was famous   among our folk
as a lordly leader   who lived many winters
before, full of years,   he departed our fastness.
His name was Ecgtheow.   All over Earth
235   every wise man   remembers him well.
We have landed in friendship   to look for your lord,
the son of Healfdene,   sovereign of Scyldings.
Give us good guidance: a great errand
has driven us hence   to the holder of Danes.
240   Our purpose is open;   this I promise;
but you could attest   if tales tell the truth.
They speak of some scourge,   none can say what,
secretly stalking   by night among Scyldings,
the shadowy shape   of his malice to men
245   shown by a shameful   shower of corpses.
I offer Hrothgar,   with honest heart,
the means to make   an end to this menace.
Wise and good,   he will win his reward,
the scaling surges   of care will be cooled
250   if ever such awful   evil is vanquished.
So his sorrows   shall swiftly be soothed
or else his anguish   haunt him, unaltered,
as long as his house   holds on the hilltop."

Astride his steed,   the guard spoke again:
255   "A sharp-witted warrior   often must weigh
words against works   when judging their worth.
This I have learned: you honor our lord.
Thus you may come,   though clad in corselets
and weaponed for war.   I shall show you the way.
260   Meanwhile those thanes   who are mine to command
shall stand by the ship   you steered to our shore.
No thief will trouble   your newly-tarred craft
before you return   and take to the tide.
A swan-necked bow   will bear you back

Boar, from a bas-relief carving on Saint Nicholas Church, Ipswich, England. Although this large and vigorous boar dates from the 12th century, it retains stylistic elements of earlier Anglo-Saxon and Viking art. An ancient totem of power, boars were often depicted on early medieval weapons and helmets.

265   to your windward coast. Most welcome of men,
   may you be granted good fortune in battle,
   enduring unharmed the deed you would do."

   So they set out while the ship sat at rest,
   the broad-beamed longboat bound to the beach,
270   lashed by its lines. Lustrous boar-icons
   glinted on cheek-guards. Adorned with gold,
   the flame-hardened helms defended their lives.
   Glad of their mettle while marching together,
   the troop hastened until they beheld
275   the highest of halls raised under heaven,
   most famed among folk in foreign lands.
   Sheathed with gold and grandly gabled,
   the roof of the ruler lit up his realm.
   The foremost warrior waved them forward
280   and bade the band go straight to that building,
   court of the king and his brave kinsmen.
   Reining his steed, he spoke a last word:
   "It is time I returned. May All-Ruling Father
   favor your errand. I'm off to the ocean,
285   to watch and ward away wrathful marauders."

   A stone-paved street steered the men hence.
   They strode on together, garbed in glinting
   jackets of chain-mail whose jingling rings,
   hard and hand-linked, sang on harnesses
290   borne toward the hall by that battle-armed band.

Still sea-weary,   they set their broad-shields
of well-seasoned wood   against Heorot's wall.
Their byrnies clanged   as they bent to a bench
and stood their sturdy   spears in a row,
295   gray from the ash grove,   ground to sharp points.
This was a war party   worthy of weapons.

Then a proud prince   questioned their purpose:
"Where are you bringing   these burnished bosses,
these gray mail-shirts,   grimly-masked helms
300   and serried spears?   I am Hrothgar's
herald and door-ward.   I have never beheld
a band of wanderers   with bearings so brave.
I believe that boldness   has brought you to Hrothgar,
not banishment's shame."
                              The eldest answered,
305   hard and hardy   under his helmet,
a warlike prince   of the Weder[9] people:
"We are Hygelac's   hearth-companions.
My name is Beowulf;   my purpose, to bear
unto Healfdene's son,   your lordly leader,
310   a message meant   for that noblest of men,
if he will allow us   leave to approach."

Wise Wulfgar,   man of the Wendels,
known to many   for boldness in battle,
stoutly spoke out: "I shall ask our sovereign,
315   well-wisher of Danes   and awarder of wealth,
about this boon   you have come to request
and bear you back,   as soon as may be,
whatever answer   the great man offers."

He went straightaway   where Hrothgar waited,
320   old and gray-haired,   with earls gathered round.
Squarely he stood   for his king to assess him.
Such was the Scylding   custom at court,
and so Wulfgar spoke   to his sovereign and friend:
"Far-sailing Geats   have come to our kingdom
325   across the wide water.   These warriors call
their leader *Beowulf*   and bid me bring
their plea to our prince,   if it pleases him
to allow them entrance   and offer them audience.
I implore you to hear them,   princely Hrothgar,
330   for I deem them worthy   of wearing their armor
and treating with earls.   Truly the elder
who led them hither   is a lord of some stature."

Helm of the Scyldings,   Hrothgar held forth:
"I knew him once.   He was only a lad.

9. An alternate name for Geat.

335 His honored father,   old Ecgtheow,
was dowered the daughter   of the Geat, Hrethel.
The son now seeks us   solely from friendship.
Seamen have said,   after sailing hence
with gifts for the Geats,   that his hand-grip would match
340 the might and main   of thirty strong men.
The West-Danes[1] have long   awaited God's grace.
Here is our hope   against Grendel's dread,
if I reckon rightly   the cause of his coming.
I shall give this brave man   boons for boldness.
345 Bring him in quickly.   The band of my kinsmen
is gathered together.   Welcome our guest
to the dwelling of Danes."
                    Then Wulfgar went
through the hall's entry   with word from within:
"I am ordered to answer   that the lord of East-Danes
350 honors your father   and offers you welcome,
sailors who sought us   over the sea-waves,
bravely bent   on embarking hither.
Now you may march   in your mail and masks
to behold Hrothgar.   Here you must leave
355 war-shields and spears   sharpened for strife.
Your weapons can wait   for words to be spoken."

The mighty one rose   with many a man
marshaled about him,   though some were bidden
to stay with the weapons   and stand on watch.
360 Under Heorot's roof   the rest hastened
when Beowulf brought them   boldly before
the hearth of Hrothgar.   Helmed and hardy,
the war-chief shone   as he stood in skillfully
smithed chain-mail   and spoke to his host:

365 "Hail to you, Hrothgar!   I am Hygelac's
kinsman and comrade,   esteemed by the king
for deeds I have done   in the years of youth.
I heard in my homeland   how Grendel grieves you.
Seafarers say   that your splendid hall
370 stands idle and useless   after the sun
sinks each evening   from Heaven's height.
The most honored among us,   earls and elders,
have urged me to seek you,   certain my strength
would serve in your struggle.   They have seen me return
375 bloody from binding   brutish giants,
a family of five   destroyed in our strife;
by night in the sea   I have slain monsters.
Hardship I had,   but our harms were avenged,
our enemies mastered.   Now I shall match

---

1. Hrothgar is, in fact, king of all the Danes: North, South, East, and West. The different terms merely conform to the Anglo-Saxon alliterative pattern established in each line.

380 my grip against Grendel's and get you an end
to this feud with the fiend. Therefore one favor
I ask from you, Hrothgar, sovereign of Spear-Danes,
shelter of shield-bearers, friend to your folk:
that I and my officers, we and no others,
385 be offered the honor of purging your hall.
I have also heard that the rash thing reckons
the thrust of a weapon no threat to his thews,[2]
so I shall grab and grapple with Grendel.
Let my lord Hygelac hear and be glad
390 I foreswore my sword and strong shield
when I fought for life with that fearsome foe.
Whomever death takes, his doom is doubtless
decreed by the Lord. If I let the creature
best me when battle begins in this building,
395 he will freely feast as he often has fed
on men of much mettle. My corpse will require
no covering cloth. He will carry away
a crushed carcass clotted with gore,
the fiend's fodder gleefully eaten,
400 smearing his lonesome lair on the moor.
No need to worry who buries my body
if battle takes me. Send back to my sovereign
this best of shirts which has shielded my breast,
this choice chain-mail, Hrethel's heirloom
405 and Weland's work.[3] Fate goes as it will."

Helm of the Scyldings, Hrothgar answered:
"It is fair that you seek to defend us, my friend,
in return for the favor offered your father
when a killing fanned the fiercest of feuds
410 after he felled the Wylfing, Heatholaf.
Wary of war, the Weder-Geats wanted
Ecgtheow elsewhere, so over the sea-swells
he sought the South-Danes, strong Scyldings.
I had lately become king of my kinsmen,
415 a youth ruling this jewel of a realm,
this store-house of heroes, with Heorogar gone,
my brother and better, born of Healfdene.
I calmed your father's quarrel with wergeld
sent over sea straight to the Wylfings,
420 an ancient heirloom; and Ecgtheow's oath
I took in return.
     "It pains me to tell
what grief Grendel has given me since,
what harm in Heorot, hatred and shame
at his sudden onset. My circle is shrunken;
425 my guardsmen are gone, gathered by fate
into Grendel's grip. How simply the Sovereign
of Heaven could hinder deeds of this hell-fiend!

2. Well-developed sinew or muscle.   3. Legendary blacksmith of the Norse gods.

Beer-swollen boasters,   brave in their ale-cups,
often have sworn   to stay with their swords
430   drawn in the dark,   to strike down the demon.
Then in the morning   the mead-hall was drenched,
blood on the bench-boards,   blood on the floor,
the highest of houses   a horror at dawn.
Fewer were left   to keep faith with their lord
435   since those dear retainers   were taken by death.
But sit now to sup   and afterward speak
of soldierly pride,   if the spirit prompts you."

A bench was then cleared,   there in the beer-hall
so all of the Geats   could sit together,
440   sturdy soldiers,   proud and stout-hearted.
A dutiful Dane   brought them bright ale-cups
and poured sweet mead   while the scop was singing
high-voiced in Heorot.   That host of warriors,
Weders and Scyldings,   shared in the wassails.

445   But envious Unferth,[4]   Ecglaf's son,
spat out his spite   from the seat he took
at his sovereign's feet.   The seafarer's quest
grieved him greatly,   for he would not grant
any man ever,   in all middle-earth,
450   more fame under heaven   than he himself had.

"Are you that Beowulf   Breca bested
when both of you bet   on swimming the straits,
daring the deep   in a dire struggle,
risking your lives   after rash boasting?
455   Though friend or foe,   no man could deflect
your foolhardy foray.   Arms flailing,
you each embraced   the billowing stream,
spanned the sea-lane   with swift-dipping hands
and wended over   the warring ocean.
460   Winter-like waves   were roiling the waters
as the two of you toiled   in the tumult of combers.
For seven nights   you strove to outswim him,
but he was the stronger   and saw at sunrise
the sea had swept him   to Heathoraem[5] shores.
465   Breca went back   to his own homeland,
his burg on the bluff,   stronghold of Brondings,
fair folk and wealthy.   The wager was won;
Beanstan's son   had brought off his boast.
However you fared   in onslaughts elsewhere,
470   I doubt you will live   the length of a night
if you dare to linger   so near Grendel."

---

4. Hrothgar's spokesman or court jester; his rude behavior toward Beowulf is consistent with other figures in epics and romances who taunt the hero before he undertakes his exploits. "Unferth" may mean "strife."
5. Coastal tribe of central Sweden near the Norwegian border.

Then Beowulf spoke,   son of Ecgtheow:
"Listen, Unferth,   my fuddled friend
brimful of beer,   you blabber too much
475   about Breca's venture.   I tell you the truth:
my force in the flood   is more than a match
for any man   who wrestles the waves.
Boys that we were,   brash in our youth
and reckless of risk,   both of us boasted
480   that each one could swim   the open ocean.
So we set forth,   stroking together
sturdily seaward   with swords drawn
hard in our hands   to ward off whale-fish.
No swifter was he   in those heaving seas;
485   each of us kept   close to the other,
floating together   those first five nights.
Then the storm-surges   swept us apart:
winter-cold weather   and warring winds
drove from the north   in deepening darkness.
490   Rough waves rose   and sea-beasts raged,
but my breast was wound   in a woven mail-shirt.
Hard and hand-linked,   hemmed with gold,
it kept those creatures   from causing me harm.
I was drawn to the depths,   held fast by the foe,
495   grim in his grasp;   yet granted a stab,
I stuck in my sword-point,   struck down the horror.
The mighty sea-monster   met death by my hand.

"Often afterward   snatchers of swimmers
snapped at my heels.   With my strong sword
500   I served them fitly.   I would fatten no foes,
feed no man-banes   munching their morsels
when setting to feast   on the floor of the sea.
Instead at sunrise   the sword-stricken
washed up in windrows   to lie lifelessly,
505   lodged by the tide-line,   and nevermore trouble
sailors crossing   the steep-cliffed straits.
As God's beacon   brightened the East,
I spied a cape   across calming seas,
a windward wall.   So I was spared,
510   for fate often favors   an unmarked man
if he keeps his courage.   My sword was the slayer
of nine nixies.[6]   I have not heard of many
who fought a more fearsome   assault in the night
while hurled by the waves   under heaven's vault.
515   Yet I broke the beasts' grip   and got off alive,
weary of warfare.   Swiftly surging
after the storm,   the sea-current swept me
to Finland's coast.
                    "Such close combat
or stark sword-strokes   you have not seen,
520   you or Breca.   No yarn has boasted

6. Fabulous sea creatures.

how either of you two   ever attempted
so bold a deed   done with bright sword,
though I would not bruit   a brother's bane
if the killing of kin   were all I'd accomplished.
525   For that you are certain   to suffer in Hell,
doomed with the damned   despite your swift wit.
I say straight out,   son of Ecglaf,
that ghastly Grendel,   however gruesome,
would never have done   such dreadful deeds,
530   harming your lord   here in his hall,
if your spirit were stern,   your will, warlike,
as you have affirmed.   The foe has found
that he need not reckon   with wrathful swords
or look with alarm   on the likes of you,
535   Scylding victor.   He takes his tribute,
sparing no man,   snatching and supping
whenever he wishes   with wicked delight,
expecting no strife   with spear-bearing Danes.
But soon, very soon,   I shall show him the strength
540   and boldness of Geats   giving him battle.
When morning comes   to light up the land,
you may go again   and gladly get mead
as the bright sun   beams in the South
and starts a new day   for the sons of men."

545   Gray-haired Hrothgar,   giver of hoard-wealth,
was happy to hear   Beowulf bolster
hope for his folk   with forthright avowal.
About the Bright-Danes'   battle-leader
rang warriors' laughter   and winsome words.
550   The queen, Wealtheow,[7]   courtly by custom,
greeted the party   aglitter with gold
and bore the full cup   first to her lord,
the keeper of East-Danes,   dear to his people,
bidding him drink   and be glad of his beer.
555   That soldierly sovereign   quaffed and supped
while his Helming princess   passed through the hall
offering everyone,   young man and old,
the dole he was due.   Adorned with rings,
she bore the burnished   mead-bowl to Beowulf,
560   last of them all,   and honored the Geat
with gracious words,   firm in her wisdom
and grateful to God   for granting her wish.
Here was the prayed-for   prince who would help
to end the ill deeds.   He emptied the cup
565   Wealtheow offered;   then the willing warrior,
Ecgtheow's son,   spoke as one ready
for strife and slaughter:
                    "When I set my ship
to sail on the sea   and hunched in her hull

---

7. "Weal theow" means "foreign slave," and she may be British or Celtic in origin. Even after her marriage to Hrothgar, she continues to maintain her identity as the "lady of the Helmings," an epithet recalling her father Helm.

with my squadron of swords,   I swore to fulfill
570   the will of the Scyldings   or die in the deed,
fall with the slain,   held fast by the foe,
my last day lived out   here in your hall."

The wife was well-pleased   with Beowulf's words,
this oath from the Geat;   and glinting with gold
575   the queen, Wealtheow,   went to her king.
Boasts were bandied   once more in the beer-hall,
the hearty speech   of a hopeful household,
a forceful folk.   But soon the sovereign,
son of Healfdene,   hankered for sleep.
580   He knew how the brute   brooded on bloodshed
all day from dawn   until deepening dusk.
Covered by darkness,   the creature would creep,
a shade among shadows.   The company stood.
One man to another,   Hrothgar hailed
585   brave Beowulf,   wishing him well
and granting him leave   to guard the wine-hall.

"So long as my hand   has hefted a shield,
I never have yielded   the Danes' mansion
to any man else,   whatever his mettle.
590   Now you shall hold   this highest of houses.
Be mindful of fame;   make your might known;
but beware of the wicked.   You will want no boon
if you tackle this task   and live to request it."

Hrothgar and his princes   departed the hall;
595   the warder of Danes   went to his woman,
couched with his queen.   The King of Glory
had granted a guard   against Grendel's wrath,
as all had now learned.   One man had offered
to take on this task   and watch for the terror.
600   The leader of the Geats   would gladly trust
the force of God's favor.   He flung off his mail-shirt,
then handed his helmet   and inlaid sword
to the squire assigned   safe-keeping of iron
and gilded war-gear.   Again the bold
605   Beowulf boasted   while bound for his bed:

"I am no weaker   in works of war,
no less a grappler   than Grendel himself.
Soon I shall sink him   into his death-sleep,
not with my sword   but solely by strength.
610   He is unschooled in skills   to strike against me,
to shatter my shield,   though feared for his fierceness.
So I shall bear   no blade in the night
if he sees fit   to fight without weapons.
May God in His wisdom   grant whom He wills
615   blessing in battle."
                 The brave soldier

settled in bed,   and a bolster pillowed
his proud cheekbone.   About him were stretched
the strong sea-warriors,   each one wondering
whether he ever   would walk once again
620   his beloved land,   or find his own folk
from childhood's time   in an untroubled town.
All had been told   how often before
dreadful death   had swept up the Danes
who lay in this hall.   But the Lord lent them
625   aid in their anguish,   weaving their war-luck,
for one man alone   had the might and main
to fight off the fiend,   crush him in combat,
proving who ruled   the races of men,
then and forever: God, the Almighty.[8]

630   Cunningly creeping,   a spectral stalker
slinked through the gloom.   The bowmen were sleeping
who ought to have held   the high-horned house,
all except one,   for the Lord's will
now became known: no more would the murderer
635   drag under darkness   whomever he wished.
Wrath was wakeful,   watching in hatred;
hot-hearted Beowulf   was bent upon battle.

Then from the moor   under misty hillsides,
Grendel came gliding,   girt with God's anger.
640   The man-scather sought   someone to snatch
from the high hall.   He crept under clouds
until he caught sight   of the king's court
whose gilded gables   he knew at a glance.
He often had haunted   Hrothgar's house;
645   but he never found,   before or after,
hardier hall-thanes   or harder luck.
The joyless giant   drew near the door,
which swiftly swung back   at the touch of his hand
though bound and fastened   with forge-bent bars.
650   The building's mouth   had been broken open,
and Grendel entered   with ill intent.
Swollen with fury,   he stalked over flagstones
and looked round the manse   where many men lay.
An unlovely light   most like a flame
655   flashed from his eyes,   flared through the hall
at young soldiers dozing   shoulder to shoulder,
comradely kindred.   The cruel creature laughed
in his murderous mind,   thinking how many
now living would die   before the day dawned,
660   how glutted with gore   he would guzzle his fill.
It was not his fate   to finish the feast

8. This interpolation of Christian belief into what is essentially a pagan tradition has been taken as evidence of a conscious rewriting of much earlier material. The narrative assures its reader that Christian beliefs were still valid, regardless of what the characters in the story may have believed.

he foresaw that night.

                  Soon the Stalwart,
Hygelac's kinsman,   beheld how the horror,
not one to be idle,   went about evil.

665   For his first feat   he suddenly seized
a sleeping soldier,   slashed at the flesh,
bit through bones   and lapped up the blood
that gushed from veins   as he gorged on gobbets.
Swiftly he swallowed   those lifeless limbs,

670   hands and feet whole;   then he headed forward
with open palm   to plunder the prone.
One man angled   up on his elbow:
the fiend soon found   he was facing a foe
whose hand-grip was harder   than any other

675   he ever had met   in all Middle-Earth.
Cravenly cringing,   coward at heart,
he longed for a swift   escape to his lair,
his bevy of devils.   He never had known
from his earliest days   such awful anguish.

680   The captain, recalling   his speech to the king,
straightaway stood   and hardened his hold.
Fingers fractured.   The fiend spun round;
the soldier stepped closer.   Grendel sought
somehow to slip   that grasp and escape,

685   flee to the fens;   but his fingers were caught
in too fierce a grip.   His foray had failed;
the harm-wreaker rued   his raid on Heorot.
From the hall of the Danes   a hellish din
beset every soldier   outside the stronghold,

690   louder than laughter   of ale-sodden earls.
A wonder it was   the wine-hall withstood
this forceful affray   without falling to earth.
That beautiful building   was firmly bonded
by iron bands   forged with forethought

695   inside and out.   As some have told it,
the struggle swept on   and slammed to the floor
many mead-benches   massive with gold.
No Scylding elders   ever imagined
that any would harm   their elk-horned hall,

700   raze what they wrought,   unless flames arose
to enfold and consume it.   Frightful new sounds
burst from the building,   unnerved the North-Danes,
each one and all   who heard those outcries
outside the walls.   Wailing in anguish,

705   the hellish horror,   hateful to God,
sang his despair,   seized by the grip
of a man more mighty   than any then living.

That shielder of men   meant by no means
to let the death-dealer   leave with his life,

710   a life worthless   to anyone elsewhere.

Then the young soldiers   swung their old swords
again and again   to save their guardian,
their kingly comrade,   however they could.
Engaging with Grendel   and hoping to hew him
715   from every side,   they scarcely suspected
that blades wielded   by worthy warriors
never would cut   to the criminal's quick.
The spell was spun   so strongly about him
that the finest iron   of any on earth,
720   the sharpest sword-edge   left him unscathed.
Still he was soon   to be stripped of his life
and sent on a sore   sojourn to Hell.
The strength of his sinews   would serve him no more;
no more would he menace   mankind with his crimes,
725   his grudge against God,   for the high-hearted kinsman
of King Hygelac   had hold of his hand.
Each found the other   loathsome while living;
but the murderous man-bane   got a great wound
as tendons were torn,   shoulder shorn open,
730   and bone-locks broken.   Beowulf gained
glory in war;   and Grendel went off
bloody and bent   to the boggy hills,
sorrowfully seeking   his dreary dwelling.
Surely he sensed   his life-span was spent,
735   his days upon days;   but the Danes were grateful:
their wish was fulfilled   after fearsome warfare.

Wise and strong-willed,   the one from afar
had cleansed Heorot,   hall of Hrothgar.
Great among Geats,   he was glad of his night-work
740   ending the evil,   his fame-winning feat,
fulfilling his oath   to aid the East-Danes,
easing their anguish,   healing the horror
they suffered so long,   no small distress.
As token of triumph,   the troop-leader hung
745   the shorn-off shoulder   and arm by its hand:
the grip of Grendel   swung from the gable!

Many a warrior   met in the morning
around Hrothgar's hall,   so I have heard.
Folk-leaders fared   from near and far
750   over wide wolds   to look on the wonder,
the track of the terror,   glad he had taken
leave of his life   when they looked on footprints
wending away   to the mere of monsters.
Weary and weak,   defeated in war,
755   he dripped his blood-spoor   down to dark water,
tinting the terrible   tide where he sank,
spilling his lifeblood   to swirl in the surge.
There the doomed one   dropped into death
where he long had lurked   in his joyless lair,
760   and Hell harrowed   his heathen soul.

Many went hence: young men and old
mounted white mares   and rode to the mere,
a joyous journey   on brave battle-steeds.
There Beowulf's   prowess was praised
765   and applauded by all.   Everyone said
that over the Earth   and under bright sky,
from north to south   between sea and sea,
no other man   was more worthy of wearing
corselet or crown,   though no one denied
770   the grace of Hrothgar: that was a good king.

Sometimes they galloped   great-hearted bays;
races were run   where roads were smooth
on open upland.   Meanwhile a man
skilled as a singer,   versed in old stories,
775   wove a new lay   of truly-linked words.
So the scop started   his song of Beowulf's
wisdom and strength,   setting his spell
with subtle staves.   Of Sigemund[9] also
he said what he knew: many marvels,
780   deeds of daring   and distant journeys,
the wars of Waels' son,   his wildness, his sins,
unsung among men   save by Fitela,
Sigemund's nephew,   who knew his secrets
and aided his uncle   in every conflict
785   as comrade-at-need.   A whole clan of ogres
was slain by the Waelsing   wielding his sword.
No small esteem   sprang up for Sigemund
after his death-day.   Dauntless in war,
he struck down a serpent   under gray stone
790   where it held its hoard.   He fared alone
on this fearsome foray,   not with Fitela;
but fate allowed him   to lunge with his blade,
spitting the scaly   worm to the wall.
His pluck repaid,   Sigemund was pleased
795   to take his pick   of the piled-up treasure
and load bright arms   in his longboat's breast
while the molten worm   melted away.

Thus that wayfarer   famed far and wide
among nations of men,   that mighty war-maker,
800   shelter of shield-bearers,   outshone another:
unhappy Heremod,[1]   king of the Danes,
whose strength, spirit,   and courage were spent.
He fell among foes,   was taken by traitors
and swiftly dispatched.   So his sorrows
805   ended at last.   Too long had lords

9. The story of Sigemund is also told in the Old Norse *Volsunga Saga* and with major variations in the Middle High German *Niebelungenlied*. The scop's comparison of Sigemund with Beowulf is ironic in that the order and the outcome of Beowulf's later encounter with a dragon will be reversed.

1. Heremod, an earlier Danish king, was the stock illustration of the unjust and unwise ruler. After bringing bloodshed upon his own house, Heremod took refuge among the Jutes, who eventually put him to death.

and commoners suffered,   scourged by their king,
who ought to have honored   his father's office,
defending his homeland,   his hoard and folk.
Evil had entered him.   Dearer to Danes
810   and all humankind   was Hygelac's kinsman.

Still running heats,   the horses hurtled
on sandy lanes.   The light of morning
had swung to the south,   and many men sped,
keen to behold   the hall of the king,
815   the strange sights inside.   Hrothgar himself,
keeper of treasures   and leader of troops,
came from the queen's   quarters to march
with measured tread   the track to his mead-hall;
the queen and her maidens   also came forth.
820   He stopped on the stairs   and gazed at the gable,
glinting with gold   behind Grendel's hand.

"My thanks for this sight   go straight to Heaven!
Grendel has given me   grief and grievance;
but God often works   wonders on wonders.
825   Not long ago   I had no hope at all
of living to see   relief from my sorrows
while slaughter stained   the highest of houses,
wide-spilling woes   the wisest advisors
despaired of stanching.   None of them knew
830   how to fend off our foes: the ghosts and ghasts
afflicting our folk   here in our fastness.
Now, praise Heaven,   a prince has proven
this deed could be done   that daunted us all.
Indeed the mother   who bore this young man
835   among mankind   may certainly say,
if she still is living,   that the Lord of Old
blessed her child-bearing.   Henceforth, Beowulf,
best of the brave,   I shall hold you in heart
as close as a son.   Keep our new kinship,
840   and I shall award you   whatever you wish
that is mine to command.   Many a time
I have lavished wealth   on lesser warriors,
slighter in strife.   You have earned your esteem.
May the All-Wielder   reward you always,
845   just as He gives you   these goods today."

Beowulf spoke,   son of Ecgtheow:
"We gladly engaged   in this work of war
and freely faced   the unknowable foe,
but I greatly regret   that you were not granted
850   the sight of him broken,   slathered with blood.
I sought to grip him   swiftly and strongly,
wrestle him down   to writhe on his death-bed
as life left him,   unless he broke loose.

It was not my fate   to fasten the man-bane
855 firmly enough.   The fiend was so fierce
he secured his escape   by leaving this limb
to ransom his life,   though little the wretch
has gained for his hurt,   held in the grip
of a dire wound,   awaiting death
860 as a savage man,   besmirched by his sins,
might wait to learn   what the Lord wills."

Unferth was silent.   He spoke no more boasts
about works of war   when warriors gazed
at the hand hanging   from Heorot's roof,
865 the fiend's fingers   jutting in front,
each nail intact,   those terrible talons
like spikes of steel.   Everyone said
that the strongest sword   from smithies of old,
the hardest iron   edge ever forged,
870 would never have harmed   that monstrous mauler,
those bloody claws   crooked for combat.

II. Grendel's Mother

Inside Heorot   many hands hastened
at Hrothgar's command: men and women
washed out the wine-hall,   unfurled on the walls
875 gold-woven hangings   to gladden their guests,
each of whom gazed   wide-eyed in wonder.
Though bound with iron,   the bright building
was badly battered,   its hinges broken.
Only the roof   had escaped unscathed
880 before the fell creature   cringed and fled,
stained by his sin   and despairing of life.
Flee it who will,   a well-earned fate
is not often altered,   for every earth-dweller
and soul-bearing son   must seek out a spot
885 to lay down his body,   lie on his death-bed,
sleep after feasting.
                            So came the season
for Healfdene's son   to stride through his hall:
the king himself   would sup with his kin.
I have never heard   in any nation
890 of such a great host   so graciously gathered,
arrayed on benches   around their ruler,
glad of his fame   and glad for the feast.
Many a mead-cup   those masterful kinsmen
Hrothgar and Hrothulf   raised in the hall.
895 All were then friends   who filled Heorot,
treason and treachery   not yet contrived.[1]

---

1. Possibly an allusion to the later usurpation of the Danish throne by Hrothgar's nephew Hrothulf.

Crowning his conquest,   the King of the Danes
bestowed on the Stalwart   a battle-standard
embroidered with gold,   a helmet, a byrnie,
900   and an unblemished blade   borne out while ranks
of warriors watched.   Then Beowulf drank
a flagon before them: he would feel no shame
facing bold spearmen   with boons such as these.
Not many men   on mead benches
905   have given another   four golden gifts
in friendlier fashion.   The head-guard was flanged
with windings of wire.   Facing forward,
it warded off harm   when the wearer in war
was obliged to bear shield   against enemy blades
910   that were hammer-hardened   and honed by files.
The sovereign ordered   eight swift steeds
brought to the court   on braided bridles.
One bore a saddle   studded with gems
and glinting gold-work: there the great king,
915   son of Healfdene,   would sit during sword-strife,
never faltering,   fierce at the front,
working his will   while the wounded fell.
Then Hrothgar awarded   horses and weapons
both to Beowulf,   bade that he keep them
920   and wield them well.   So from his hoard
he paid the hero   a princely reward
of heirlooms and arms   for braving the battle;
no man could fairly   or truthfully fault them.

That lord also lavished   gifts on the Geats
925   whom Beowulf brought   over broad seas,
and wergeld he gave   for the one Grendel
had wickedly killed,   though the creature would surely
have murdered more   had God in his wisdom,
man in his strength   failed to forestall it.
930   So the Almighty   has always moved men;
yet man must consistently   strive to discern
good from evil,   evil from good
while drunk with days   he dwells in this world.

Music and story   now sounded together
935   as Hrothgar's scop   sang for the hall-fest
a tale often told   when harp was held:[2]
how Finn's followers,   faithless Jutes,
fell to fighting   friends in his fortress;
how Hnaef the Half-Dane,   hero of Scyldings,
940   was fated to fall   in Frisian warfare;

---

2. The following episode is one of the most obscure in *Beowulf*. It seems that Hnaef and Hildeburh are both children of an earlier Danish king named Hoc and that Hildeburh has been sent to marry Finn, the son of Folcwalda and king of the Jutes and Frisians, in order to conclude a marriage alliance and thus settle a prior blood feud between the two tribes. Upon going to visit his sister and her husband, Hnaef is treacherously ambushed and killed by Finn's men; Hildeburh's son by Finn is also killed. In her role as peace-weaver, Hildeburh is torn by conflicting allegiances, foreshadowing the fate of Hrothgar's own daughter Freawaru in her marriage to Ingeld.

how by shield-swagger   harmless Hildeburh,
faithful to Finn   though daughter of Danes,
lost her beloved   brother and son
who were both born   to be struck by spears.
945 Not without cause   did Hoc's daughter
bewail the Lord's will   when morning awoke:
she who had known   nothing but happiness
beheld under heaven   the horror of kin-strife.

War had taken   its toll of attackers;
950 few men remained   for Finn to muster,
too few to force   the fight against Hengest,
a dutiful earl   who had rallied the Danes.
As tokens of truce   Finn offered these terms:
a haven wholly   emptied of foes,
955 hall and high seat,   with an equal share
in gifts given   his own gathered kin.
Each time he treated   his sons to treasures
plated with gold,   a portion would go
to sweeten Hengest's   stay in his hall.
960 The two sides swore   a strict treaty;
and Finn freely   affirmed to Hengest
that all would honor   this oath to the Danes,
as his council decreed,   and further declared
no Frisian would ever,   by word or work,
965 challenge the peace   or mention with malice
the plight of survivors   deprived of their prince
and wintered-in   at the slayer's stronghold.
Should any Frisian   enter in anger,
the sword's edge   would settle the quarrel.

970 That oath offered,   the hoard was opened
for gold to array   the greatest of War-Danes.
Iron-hard guardians   gilded with gold,
bloody byrnies   and boar-tusked helms
were heaped on his bier,   awaiting the balefire.
975 Many a warrior,   weakened by wounds,
had faltered and fallen   with foes he had slain.
Hildeburh ordered   her own dear son
be placed on the pyre,   the prince and his uncle
shoulder to shoulder.   Their bodies were burned
980 while the stricken lady   sang out her sorrow.
Streamers of smoke   burst from the bier
as corpses kindled   with cruelest of flames.
Faces withered,   flesh-wounds yawned
and blood boiled out   as the blaze swallowed
985 with hateful hunger   those whom warfare
had borne away,   the best of both houses.
Their glory was gone.
                         The Frisians were fewer
heading for home;   their high stronghold

990
was empty of allies.   For Hengest also
that winter was woeful,   walled up in Frisia,
brooding on bloodshed   and longing to leave,
though knowing his longboat   never could breast
the wind-darkened swells   of a wide ocean
seething with storms,   or break the ice-bindings

995
that barred his bow   from the bitter waters.
Constrained to wait   for kindlier weather,
he watched until spring,   season of sunlight,
dawned on men's dwellings   as ever it did
and still does today.   Winter withdrew

1000
and Earth blossomed.
                        Though the exile was eager
to end his visit,   he ached for vengeance
before sailing home.   Loathe to foreswear
the way of this world,   he schemed to assail
the sons of slayers.   So Hengest heeded

1005
Hunlaf's son,   who laid on his lap
the sword War-Flame,   feared by all foes,
asking its edge   be offered the Jutes.
His heart was hot;   he could hold back no more;
gladly he answered   Guthlaf and Oslaf,

1010
who wrathfully spoke   of the wrong they suffered,
the shame of Scyldings   sharing their plight.
Then fierce-hearted Finn   fell in his turn,
stricken by swords   in his own stronghold.
The building was bloody   with bodies of foemen:

1015
the king lay slain,   likewise his kin;
and the queen was captured.   Scyldings carried
off in their ship   all of the chattels
found in Finn's fortress,   gemstones and jewels.
The lady was borne   to the land of her birth.

1020
So that story   was sung to its end,
then mirth once more   mounted in Heorot.
Revelry rang   as wine-bearers brought
finely-wrought flagons   filled to the brim.
Wearing her circlet,   Wealtheow walked

1025
where uncle and nephew,   Hrothgar and Hrothulf,
were sitting in peace,   two soldiers together,
each still believing   the other was loyal.
Likewise the officer,   Unferth, was honored
to sit at the feet   of the Scylding sovereign.

1030
Everyone thought him   honest and trustworthy,
blameless and brave,   though his blade had unjustly
stricken a kinsman.
                        So the queen spoke:
"Quaff from your cup,   king of the Scyldings,
giver of gold;   quaff and be glad;

1035
greet the Geats mildly   as well a man might,
mindful of gifts   graciously given
from near and far,   now in your keeping.

They say you would name   that knight as a son
for purging the ring-hall.   Employ as you please
1040 wealth and rewards,   but bequeath to your kin
rule of this realm   when the Ruler of All
holds that you must.   I know that Hrothulf
will honor our trust   and treat these youths well
if you have to leave   this life before him.
1045 I am counting on him   to recall our kindness
when he was a child   and repay our children
for presents we gave   and pleasures we granted."

She turned to the bench   where her sons were seated,
Hrethric and Hrothmund.   Between the two brothers
1050 Beowulf sat;   and the cup-bearer brought him
words of welcome,   willingly gave him
as tokens of favor   two braided arm-bands,
jerkin, corselet,   and jeweled collar
grander than any   other on Earth.[3]
1055 I have heard under heaven   of no higher treasure
hoarded by heroes   since Hama stole off
to his fair fortress   with Freya's necklace,
shining with stones   set by the Fire-Dwarves.
So Hama earned   Eormanric's anger,
1060 and fame for himself.   Foolhardy Hygelac,
grandson of Swerting   and sovereign of Geats,
would wear it one day   on his final foray.
He fell in the fray   defending his treasure,
the spoils he bore   with his battle-standard.
1065 Recklessly raiding   the realm of Frisia,
the prince in his pride   had prompted misfortune
by crossing the sea   while clad in that collar.
He fell under shield,   fell to the Franks,
weaker warriors   stripping the slain
1070 of armor and spoil   after the slaughter.
Hygelac held   the graveyard of Geats.

The hall applauded   the princely prize
bestowed by the queen,   and Wealtheow spoke
for the host to hear: "Keep this collar,
1075 beloved Beowulf;   and bear this byrnie,
wealth of our realm;   may it ward you well.
Swear that your strength   and kindly counsel
will aid these youngsters,   and I shall reward you.
Now your renown   will range near and far;
1080 your fame will wax wide,   as wide as the water
hemming our hills,   homes of the wind.
Be blessed, Beowulf,   with abundant treasures
as long as you live;   and be mild to my sons,
a model admired.   Here men are courtly,

3. The narrative jumps ahead beyond Beowulf's return home to the Geats. His uncle, Hygelac, the king, will not only receive the collar from Beowulf but will die with it in battle among the Frisians. The collar thus connects different events at different times.

1085   honest and true,   each to the other,
all to their ruler;   and after the revels,
well-bolstered with beer,   they do as I bid."

The lady left him   and sat on her seat.
The feast went on;   wine was flowing.
1090   Men could not know   what fate would befall them,
what evil of old   was decreed to come
for the earls that evening.   As always, Hrothgar
headed for home,   where the ruler rested.
A great many others   remained in the hall,
1095   bearing bright benches   and rolling out beds
while one drunkard,   doomed and death-ripened,
sprawled into sleep.   They set at their heads
round war-shields,   well-adorned wood.
Above them on boards,   their battle-helms rested,
1100   ringed mail-shirts   and mighty spear-shafts
waiting for strife.   Such was their wont
at home or afield,   wherever they fared,
in case their king   should call them to arms.
That was a fine folk.
                    They sank into slumber,
1105   but one paid sorely   for sleep that evening,
as often had happened   when grim Grendel
held the gold-hall,   wreaking his wrongs
straight to the end: death after sins.
It would soon be perceived   plainly by all
1110   that one ill-wisher   still was alive,
maddened by grief: Grendel's mother,
a fearsome female   bitterly brooding
alone in her lair   deep in dread waters
and cold currents   since Cain had killed
1115   the only brother   born of his father.
Marked by murder,   he fled from mankind
and went to the wastes.   Doomed evil-doers
issued from him.   Grendel was one,
but the hateful Hell-walker   found a warrior
1120   wakefully watching   for combat in Heorot.
The monster met there   a man who remembered
strength would serve him,   the great gift of God,
faith in the All-Wielder's   favor and aid.
By that he mastered   the ghastly ghoul;
1125   routed, wretched,   the hell-fiend fled,
forlornly drew near   his dreary death-place.
Enraged and ravenous,   Grendel's mother
swiftly set out   on a sorrowful journey
to settle the score   for her son's demise.

1130   She slipped into Heorot,   hall of the Ring-Danes,
where sleeping earls   soon would suffer
an awful reversal.   Her onslaught was less

by as much as a woman's   mettle in war
is less than a man's   wielding his weapon:
1135 the banded blade   hammered to hardness,
a blood-stained sword   whose bitter stroke
slashes a boar-helm   borne into battle.
In the hall, sword-edge   sprang from scabbard;
broadshield was swung   swiftly off bench,
1140 held firmly in hand.   None thought of helmet
or sturdy mail-shirt   when terror assailed him.

Out she hastened,   out and away,
keen to keep living   when caught in the act.
She fastened on one,   then fled to her fen.
1145 He was Hrothgar's   highest counselor,
boon companion   and brave shield-bearer
slain in his bed.   Beowulf slept
elsewhere that evening,   for after the feast
the Geat had been given   a different dwelling.
1150 A din of dismay   mounted in Heorot:
the gory hand   was gone from the gable.
Dread had retaken   the Danes' dwelling.
That bargain was bad   for both barterers,
costing each one   a close comrade.

1155 It was grim for the sovereign,   the grizzled soldier,
to learn his old thane   was no longer living,
to know such a dear one   was suddenly dead.
Swiftly he sent   servants to fetch
battle-blessed Beowulf   early from bed,
1160 together with all   the great-hearted Geats.
He marched in their midst,   went where the wise one
was wondering whether   the All-Wielder
ever would alter   this spell of ill-fortune.
That much-honored man   marched up the floor,
1165 and timbers dinned   with the tread of his troop.
He spoke soberly   after the summons,
asking how soundly   the sovereign had slept.

Hrothgar answered,   head of his house:
"Ask not about ease!   Anguish has wakened
1170 again for the Danes.   Aeschere is dead.
He was Yrmenlaf's   elder brother,
my rune-reader   and keeper of counsel,
my shoulder's shielder,   warder in war
when swordsmen struck   at boar-headed helms.
1175 Whatever an honored   earl ought to be,
such was Aeschere.   A sleepless evil
has slipped into Heorot,   seized and strangled.
No one knows where   she will wander now,
glad of the gory   trophy she takes,
1180 her fine fodder.   So she requites

her kinsman's killer   for yesterday's deed,
when you grabbed Grendel   hard in your hand-grip.
He plagued and plundered   my people too long.
His life forfeit,   he fell in the fray;
1185   but now a second   mighty man-scather
comes to carry   the feud further,
as many a thane   must mournfully think,
seeing his sovereign   stricken with grief
at the slaying of one   who served so well.

1190   "I have heard spokesmen   speak in my hall,
country-folk saying   they sometimes spotted
a pair of prodigies   prowling the moors,
evil outcasts,   walkers of wastelands.
One, they descried,   had the semblance of woman;
1195   the other, ill-shapen,   an aspect of man
trudging his track,   ever an exile,
though superhuman   in stature and strength.
In bygone days   the border-dwellers
called him Grendel.   What creature begot him,
1200   what nameless spirit,   no one could say.
The two of them trekked   untraveled country:
wolf-haunted heights   and windy headlands,
the frightening fen-path   where falling torrents
dive into darkness,   stream beneath stone
1205   amid folded mountains.   That mere⁴ is not far,
as miles are measured.   About it there broods
a forest of fir trees   frosted with mist.
Hedges of wood-roots   hem in the water
where each evening   fire-glow flickers
1210   forth on the flood,   a sinister sight.
That pool is unplumbed   by wits of the wise;
but the heath-striding hart   hunted by hounds,
the strong-antlered stag   seeking a thicket,
running for cover,   would rather be killed
1215   than bed on its bank.   It is no pleasant place
where water-struck waves   are whipped into clouds,
surging and storming,   swept by the winds,
so the heights are hidden   and heaven weeps.
Now you alone   can relieve our anguish:
1220   look, if you will,   at the lay of the land;
and seek, if you dare,   that dreadful dale
where the she-demon dwells.   Finish this feud,
and I shall reward you   with age-old wealth,
twisted-gold treasures,   if you return."

1225   Beowulf spoke,   son of Ecgtheow:
"Grieve not, good man.   It is better to go
and avenge your friend   than mourn overmuch.
We all must abide   an end on this earth,

4. A small lake.

Hidden wrath   took root in his heart,
1520   bloodthirsty thoughts.   He would give no gifts
to honor others.   Loveless, he lived,
a lasting affliction   endured by the Danes
in sorrow and strife.   Consider him well,
his life and lesson.

       "Wise with winters,
1525   I tell you this tale   as I mull and marvel
how the Almighty   metes to mankind
the blessings of reason,   rule and realm.
He arranges it all.   For a time He allows
the mind of a man   to linger in love
1530   with earthly honors.   He offers him homeland
to hold and enjoy,   a fort full of folk,
men to command   and might in the world,
wide kingdoms   won to his will.
In his folly, the fool   imagines no ending.
1535   He dwells in delight   without thought of his lot.
Illness, old age,   anguish or envy:
none of these gnaw   by night at his mind.
Nowhere are swords   brandished in anger;
for him the whole world   wends as he wishes.
1540   He knows nothing worse   till his portion of pride
waxes within him.   His soul is asleep;
his gate, unguarded.   He slumbers too soundly,
sunk in small cares.   The slayer creeps close
and shoots a shaft   from the baneful bow.
1545   The bitter arrow   bites through his armor,
piercing the heart   he neglected to guard
from crooked counsel   and evil impulse.
Too little seems all   he has long possessed.
Suspicious and stingy,   withholding his hoard
1550   of gold-plated gifts,   he forgets or ignores
what fate awaits him,   for the world's Wielder
surely has granted   his share of glory.
But the end-rune   is already written:
the loaned life-home   collapses in ruin;
1555   some other usurps   and openly offers
the hoarded wealth,   heedless of worry.

"Beloved Beowulf,   best of defenders,
guard against anger   and gain for yourself
perpetual profit.   Put aside pride,
1560   worthiest warrior.   Now for awhile
your force flowers,   yet soon it shall fail.
Sickness or age   will strip you of strength,
or the fangs of flame,   or flood-surges,
the sword's bite   or the spear's flight,
1565   or fearful frailty   as bright eyes fade,
dimming to darkness.   Afterward death
will sweep you away,   strongest of war-chiefs.

"I ruled the Ring-Danes   a hundred half-years,
stern under clouds   with sword and spear
1570   that I wielded in war   against many nations
across Middle-Earth,   until none remained
beneath spacious skies   to reckon as rivals.
Recompense happened   here in my homeland,
grief after gladness   when Grendel came,
1575   when the ancient enemy   cunningly entered.
Thereafter I suffered   constant sorrows
and cruelest cares.   But God has given me
long enough life   to look at this head
with my own eyes,   as enmity ends
1580   spattered with gore.   Sit and be glad,
war-worthy one: the feast is forthcoming,
and many gifts   will be granted tomorrow."

Gladly the Geat   sought out his seat
as the Ancient asked.   With all of his men,
1585   the famous one feasted   finely once more.
The helm of Heaven   darkened with dusk,
and the elders arose.   The oldest of Scyldings
was ready to rest   his hoary-haired head
at peace on his pillow.   Peerless with shield,
1590   the leader of Geats   was equally eager
to lie down at last.   A thane was appointed
to serve as his squire.   Such was the courtesy
shown in those days   to weary wayfarers,
soldiers sojourning   over the ocean.

1595   Beneath golden gables   the great-hearted guest
dozed until dawn   in the high-roofed hall,
when the black raven   blithely foretold
joy under Heaven.   Daybreak hastened,
sun after shadow.   The soldiers were ardent,
1600   the earls eager   to hurry homeward;
the stern minded man   would make for his ship,
fare back to his folk.   But first he bade
that Hrunting be sent   to the son of Ecglaf,
a treasure returned   with thanks for the loan
1605   of precious iron.   He ordered the owner
be told he considered   the sword a fine friend,
blameless in battle.   That was a Gallant!
Keen for the crossing,   his weapons secure,
the warrior went   to the worthy Dane;
1610   the thane sought the throne   where a sovereign sat,
that steadfast hero,   Hrothgar the Great.

Beowulf spoke,   son of Ecgtheow:
"Now we must say   as far-sailing seamen,
we wish to make way   homeward to Hygelac.

1615 Here we were well   and warmly received.
If anything further   would earn your favor,
some deed of war   that remains to be done
for the master of men,   I shall always be ready.
Should word ever wend   over wide ocean
1620 that nearby nations   menace your marches,
as those who detest you   sometimes have tried,
I shall summon a thousand   thanes to your aid.
I know Hygelac,   though newly-anointed
the nation's shepherd,   will surely consent
1625 to honor my offer   in word and action.
If you ever need men,   I shall muster at once
a thicket of spears   and support you in strength.
Should Hrethric, your son,   sail overseas,
he shall find friends   in the fort of the Geats.
1630 It is well for the worthy   to fare in far countries."

Hrothgar offered   these answering words:
"Heaven's Sovereign   has set in your heart
this vow you have voiced.   I never have known
someone so young   to speak more wisely.
1635 You are peerless in strength,   princely in spirit,
straightforward in speech.   If a spear fells
Hrethel's son,   if a hostile sword-stroke
kills him in combat   or after, with illness,
slays your leader   while you still live,
1640 the Sea-Geats surely   could name no better
to serve as their king   and keeper of treasure,
should you wish to wield   rule in your realm.
I sensed your spirit   the instant I saw you,
precious Beowulf,   bringer of peace
1645 for both our peoples: War-Danes and Weders,
so often sundered   by strife in the past.
While I wield the rule   of this wide realm,
men will exchange   many more greetings
and riches will ride   in ring-bowed ships
1650 bearing their gifts   where the gannets bathe.
I know your countrymen   keep to old ways,
fast in friendship,   and war as well."

Then the hall's holder,   Healfdene's son,
gave his protector   twelve more treasures,
1655 bidding he bear   these tokens safely
home to his kin,   and quickly return.
The good king kissed   that noblest of knights;
the hoary-haired warrior   hugged him and wept,
too well aware   with the wisdom of age
1660 that he never might see   the young man again
coming to council.   So close had they grown,
so strong in esteem,   he could scarcely endure
the secret sorrow   that surged in his heart;

the flame of affection   burned in his blood.
1665   But Beowulf walked   away with his wealth;
proud of his prizes,   he trod on the turf.
Standing at anchor,   his sea-courser
chafed for its captain.   All the way home
Hrothgar's gifts   were often honored.
1670   That was a king   accorded respect
until age unmanned him,   like many another.

High-hearted,   the band of young braves
strode to the sea,   wrapped in their ring-mesh,
linked and locked shirts.   The land-watcher spied
1675   the fighters faring,   just as before.
He called no taunts   from the top of the cliff
but galloped to greet them   and tell them the Geats
would always be welcome,   armored warriors
borne on their ship.   The broad longboat
1680   lay on the beach,   laden with chain-mail,
chargers and treasures   behind its tall prow.
The mast soared high   over Hrothgar's hoard.

The boat-guard was given   a gold-bound sword;
thereafter that man   had honor enhanced,
1685   bearing an heirloom   to Heorot's mead-bench.
They boarded their vessel,   breasted the deep,
left Denmark behind.   A halyard hoisted
the sea-wind's shroud;   the sail was sheeted,
bound to the mast,   and the beams moaned
1690   as a fair wind wafted   the wave-rider forward.
Foamy-throated,   the longboat bounded,
swept on the swells   of the swift sea-stream
until welcoming capes   were sighted ahead,
the cliffs of Geat-land.   The keel grounded
1695   as wind-lift thrust it   straight onto sand.

The harbor-guard hastened   hence from his post.
He had looked long   on an empty ocean
and waited to meet   the much-missed men.
He moored the broad-beamed   bow to the beach
1700   with woven lines   lest the backwash of waves
bear off the boat.   Then Beowulf ordered
treasures unloaded,   the lordly trappings,
gold that was going   to Hygelac's hall,
close to the cliff-edge,   where the ring-giver kept
1705   his comrades about him.
                            That building was bold
at the hill's crown;   and queenly Hygd,
Haereth's daughter,   dwelt there as well.
Wise and refined,   though her winters were few,
she housed in her bower,   enclosed by the keep,
1710   and granted generous   gifts to the Geats,

most unlike Modthryth,[6]   a maiden so fierce
that none but her father   dared venture near.
The brave man who gazed   at Modthryth by day
might reckon a death-rope   already twisted,
1715   might count himself quickly   captured and killed,
the stroke of a sword   prescribed for his trespass.
Such is no style   for a queen to proclaim:
though peerless, a woman   ought to weave peace,
not snatch away life   for illusory slights.

1720   Modthryth's madness   was tamed by marriage.
Ale-drinkers say   her ill-deeds ended
once she was given   in garlands of gold
to Hemming's kinsman.   She came to his hall
over pale seas,   accepted that prince,
1725   a fine young heir,   at her father's behest.
Thenceforth on the throne,   she was famed for fairness,
making the most   of her lot in life,
sustained by loving   her lordly sovereign.
That king, Offa,   was called by all men
1730   the ablest of any   ruling a realm
between two seas,   so I am told.
Gifted in war,   a wise gift-giver
everywhere honored,   the spear-bold soldier
held his homeland   and also fathered
1735   help for the heroes   of Hemming's kindred:
war-worthy Eomer,   grandson of Garmund.

Brave Beowulf   marched with his band,
strode up the sands   of the broad beach
while the sun in the south   beamed like a beacon.
1740   The earls went eagerly   up to the keep
where the strong sovereign,   Ongentheow's slayer,
the young war-king   doled out gold rings.
Beowulf's coming   was quickly proclaimed.
Hygelac heard   that his shoulder-shielder
1745   had entered the hall,   whole and unharmed
by bouts of battle.   The ruler made room
for the foot-guest crossing   the floor before him.

Saluting his lord   with a loyal speech
earnestly worded,   the winner in war
1750   sat facing the king,   kinsman with kinsman.
A mead-vessel moved   from table to table
as Haereth's daughter,   heedful of heroes,
bore the wine-beaker   from hand to hand.
Keen to elicit   his comrade's account
1755   in the high-roofed hall,   Hygelac graciously
asked how the Sea-Geats   fared on their foray:

---

6. "Modthryth" may mean "arrogant in temper"; it may be a reference to an arrogant woman rather than a proper name.

"Say what befell   from your sudden resolve
to seek out strife   over salt waters,
to struggle in Heorot.   Have you helped Hrothgar
1760   ward off the well-known   cares of his kingdom?
You have cost me disquiet,   angst and anguish.
Doubting the outcome,   dearest of men,
for anyone meeting   that murderous demon,
I sought to dissuade you   from starting the venture.
1765   The South-Danes themselves   should have settled their feud
with ghastly Grendel.   Now I thank God
that I see you again,   safe and sound."

Beowulf spoke,   son of Ecgtheow:
"For a great many men   our meeting's issue
1770   is hardly hidden,   my lord Hygelac.
What a fine fracas   passed in that place
when both of us battled   where Grendel had brought
sore sorrow   on scores of War-Scyldings!
I avenged every one,   so that none of his kin
1775   anywhere need   exult at our night-bout,
however long   the loathsome race lives,
covered with crime.   When Hrothgar came
and heard what had happened   there in the ring-hall,
he sat me at once   with his own two sons.

1780   "The whole of his host   gathered in gladness;
all my life long   I never have known
such joy in a hall   beneath heaven's vault.
The acclaimed queen,   her kindred's peace-pledge,
would sometimes circle   the seated youths,
1785   lavishing rings   on delighted young lords.
Hrothgar's daughter   handed the elders
ale-cups aplenty,   pouring for each
old trooper in turn.   I heard the hall-sitters
calling her Freawaru   after she proffered
1790   the studded flagon.   To Froda's fair son
that maiden is sworn.   This match seems meet
to the lord of Scyldings,   who looks to settle
his Heatho-Bard feud.   Yet the best of brides
seldom has stilled   the spears of slaughter
1795   so swiftly after   a sovereign was stricken.

"Ingeld and all   his earls will be rankled,
watching that woman   walk in their hall
with high-born Danes   doing her bidding.
Her escorts will wear   ancient heirlooms:
1800   Heatho-Bard swords   with braided steel blades,
weapons once wielded   and lost in war
along with the lives   of friends in the fray.
Eyeing the ring-hilts,   an old ash-warrior
will brood in his beer   and bitterly pine

1805 for the stark reminders   of men slain in strife.
He will grimly begin   to goad a young soldier,
testing and tempting   a troubled heart,
his whispered words   waking war-evil:

"'My friend, have you spotted   the battle-sword
1810 that your father bore   on his final foray?
Wearing his war-mask,   Withergyld fell
when foemen seized   the field of slaughter.
His priceless blade   became battle-plunder.
Now some son   of the Scylding who slew him
1815 struts on our floor,   flaunting his trophy,
an heirloom that you   should rightfully own.'

"He will prick and pique   with pointed words
time after time   till the challenge is taken,
the maiden's attendant   is murdered in turn,
1820 blade-bitten   to sleep in his blood,
forfeit his life   for his father's feat.
Another will run,   knowing the road.
So on both sides   oaths will be broken;
and afterward Ingeld's   anger will grow
1825 hotter, unchecked,   as he chills toward his wife.
Hence I would hold   the Heatho-Bards likely
to prove unpeaceable   partners for Danes."

"Now I shall speak   of my strife with Grendel,
further acquainting   the kingdom's keeper
1830 with all that befell   when our fight began.
Heaven's gem   had gone overhead;
in darkness the dire   demon stalked us
while we stood guard   unharmed in Heorot.
Hondscioh was doomed   to die with the onslaught,
1835 first to succumb,   though clad for combat
when grabbed by Grendel,   who gobbled him whole.
That beloved young thane   was eaten alive.
Not one to leave   the hall empty-handed,
the bloody-toothed terror   intended to try
1840 his might upon me.   A curious creel
hung from his hand,   cunningly clasped
and strangely sewn   with devilish skill
from skin of a dragon.   The demon would stuff me,
sinless, inside   like so many others;
1845 but rising in wrath,   I stood upright.
It is too long a tale,   how the people's plaguer
paid for his crimes   with proper requital;
but the feat reflected   finely, my lord,
on the land you lead.   Though the foe fled
1850 to live awhile longer,   he left behind him
as spoor of the strife   a hand in Heorot.
Humbled, he fell   to the floor of the mere.

"The warder of Scyldings   rewarded my warfare
with much treasure   when morning arrived,
1855 and we sat for a feast   with songs and sagas.
He told many tales   he learned in his lifetime.
Sometimes a soldier   struck the glad harp,
the sounding wood;   sometimes strange stories
were spoken like spells,   tragic and true,
1860 rightly related.   The large-hearted lord
sometimes would start   to speak of his youth,
his might in war.   His memories welled;
ancient in winters,   he weighed them all.

"So we delighted   the livelong day
1865 until darkness drew   once more upon men.
Then Grendel's mother,   mourning her son,
swiftly set out   in search of revenge
against warlike Geats.   The grisly woman
wantonly slew   a Scylding warrior:
1870 aged Aeschere,   the king's counselor,
relinquished his life.   Nor in the morning
might death-weary Danes   bear off his body
to burn on a bier,   for the creature clutching him
fled to her fastness   under a waterfall.
1875 This was the sorest   of sorrows that Hrothgar
suffered as king.   Distraught, he beseeched me
to do in your name   a notable deed.
If I dived in the deep,   heedless of danger,
to war underwater,   he would reward me.

1880 "Under I went,   as now is well-known;
and I found the hideous   haunter of fens.
For a time we two   contested our hand-strength;
then I struck off her head   with a huge sword
that her battle-hall held,   and her hot blood
1885 boiled in the lake.   Leaving that place
was no easy feat,   but fate let me live.
Again I was granted   gifts that the guardian,
Healfdene's son,   had sworn to bestow.
The king of that people   kept his promise,
1890 allotting me all   he had earlier offered:
meed for my might,   with more treasures,
my choice from the hoard   of Healfdene's son.
These, my lord,   I deliver to you,
as proof of fealty.   My future depends
1895 wholly on you.   I have in this world
few close kin   but my king, Hygelac."

He bade the boar-banner   now be brought in,
the high helmet,   hard mail-shirt,
and splendid sword,   describing them thus:
1900 "When Hrothgar gave me   this hoarded gear,

the sage sovereign   entreated I tell
the tale of his gift: this treasure was held
by Heorogar, king,   who long was the lord
of Scylding people.   It should have passed
1905   to armor the breast   of bold Heoroweard,
the father's favorite,   faithful and brave;
but he willed it elsewhere,   so use it well."

I have heard how horses   followed that hoard,
four dappled mounts,   matching and fleet.
1910   He gave up his gifts,   gold and horses.
Kinsmen should always   act with honor,
not spin one another   in snares of spite
or secretly scheme   to kill close comrades.
Always the nephew   had aided his uncle;
1915   each held the other's   welfare at heart.
He gave to Queen Hygd   the golden collar,
wondrously wrought,   Wealtheow's token,
and also three steeds,   sleek and bright-saddled.
Thereafter her breast   was graced by the gift.

1920   So Ecgtheow's son   won his repute
as a man of mettle,   acting with honor,
yet mild-hearted   toward hearth-companions,
harming no one   when muddled with mead.
Bold in battle,   he guarded the guerdon
1925   that God had granted,   the greatest strength
of all humankind,   though once he was thought
weak and unworthy,   a sloucher and slacker,
mocked for meekness   by men on the mead-bench,
and given no gifts   by the lord of the Geats.
1930   Every trouble   untwined in time
for the glory-blessed man.
A blade was brought
at the king's request,   Hrethel's heirloom
glinting with gold.   No greater treasure,
no nobler sword   was held in his hoard.
1935   He lay that brand   on Beowulf's lap
and also bestowed   a spacious estate,
hall and high seat.   When land and lordship
were left to them both,   by birthright and law,
he who ranked higher   ruled the wide realm.

III. The Dragon

1940   It happened long after,   with Hygelac dead,
that war-swords slew   Heardred, his son,
when Battle-Scylfings   broke his shield-wall
and hurtled headlong   at Hereric's nephew.
So Beowulf came   to rule the broad realm.
1945   For fifty winters   he fostered it well;

then the old king,   keeper of kinfolk,
heard of a dragon   drawn from the darkness.
He had long lain   in his lofty fastness,
the steep stone-barrow,   guarding his gold;
1950   but a path pierced it,   known to no person
save him who found it   and followed it forward.
That stranger seized   but a single treasure.
He bore it in hand   from the heathen hoard:
a finely-worked flagon   he filched from the lair
1955   where the dragon dozed.   Enraged at the robber,
the sneaking thief   who struck while he slept,
the guardian woke   glowing with wrath,
as his nearest neighbors   were soon to discern.

It was not by choice   that the wretch raided
1960   the wondrous worm-hoard.   The one who offended
was stricken himself,   sorely distressed,
the son of a warrior   sold as a slave.
Escaping his bondage,   he braved the barrens
and guiltily groped   his way below ground.
1965   There the intruder   trembled with terror
hearing the dragon   who drowsed in the dark,
an ancient evil   sleepily breathing.
His fate was to find   as fear unmanned him
his fingers feeling   a filigreed cup.

1970   Many such goblets   had gone to the earth-house,
legacies left   by a lordly people.
In an earlier age   someone unknown
had cleverly covered   those costly treasures.
That thane held the hoard   for the lifetime allowed him,
1975   but gold could not gladden   a man in mourning.
Newly-built   near the breaking waves,
a barrow stood   at the base of a bluff,
its entrance sculpted   by secret arts.
Earthward the warrier   bore the hoard-worthy
1980   portion of plate,   the golden craftwork.
The ringkeeper spoke   these words as he went:

"Hold now, Earth,   what men may not,
the hoard of the heroes,   earth-gotten wealth
when it first was won.   War-death has felled them,
1985   an evil befalling   each of my people.
The long-house is mirthless   when men are lifeless.
I have none to wear sword,   none to bear wine
or polish the precious   vessels and plates.
Gone are the brethren   who braved many battles.
1990   From the hard helmet   the hand-wrought gilding
drops in the dust.   Asleep are the smiths
who knew how to burnish   the war-chief's mask
or mend the mail-shirts   mangled in battle.

Shields and mail-shirts   molder with warriors
1995   and follow no foes   to faraway fields.
No harp rejoices   to herald the heroes,
no hand-fed hawk   swoops through the hall,
no stallion stamps   in the keep's courtyard.
Death has undone   many kindreds of men."

2000   Stricken in spirit,   he spoke of his sorrow
as last of his line,   drearily drifting
through day and dark   until death's flood-tide
stilled his heart.   The old night-scather
was happy to glimpse   the unguarded hoard.
2005   Balefully burning,   he seeks out barrows.
Naked and hateful   in a raiment of flame,
the dragon dreaded   by outland dwellers
must gather and guard   the heathen gold,
no better for wealth   but wise with his winters.

2010   For three hundred winters   the waster of nations
held that mighty   hoard in his earth-hall
till one man wronged him,   arousing his wrath.
The wretched robber   ransomed his life
with the prize he pilfered,   the plated flagon.
2015   Beholding that marvel   men of old made,
his fief-lord forgave   the skulker's offense.
One treasure taken   had tainted the rest.
Waking in wrath,   the worm reared up
and slid over stones.   Stark-hearted,
2020   he spotted the footprints   where someone had stepped,
stealthily creeping   close to his jaws.
The fortunate man   slips swiftly and safely
through the worst dangers   if the World's Warder
grants him that grace.
                                    Eager and angry,
2025   the hoard-guard hunted   the thief who had haunted
his hall while he slept.   He circled the stone-house,
but out in that wasteland   the one man he wanted
was not to be found.   How fearsome he felt,
how fit for battle!   Back in his barrow
2030   he tracked the intruder   who dared to tamper
with glorious gold.   Fierce and fretful,
the dragon waited   for dusk and darkness.
The rage-swollen holder   of headland and hoard
was plotting reprisal: flames for his flagon.
2035   Then day withdrew,   and the dragon, delighted,
would linger no longer   but flare up and fly.
His onset was fearful   for folk on the land,
and a cruel ending   soon came for their king.

The ghastly specter   scattered his sparks
2040   and set their buildings   brightly burning,

flowing with flames   as homesteaders fled.
He meant to leave   not one man alive.
That wreaker of havoc   hated and harried
the Geatish folk   fleeing his flames.
2045   Far and wide   his warfare was watched
until night waned   and the worm went winging
back to the hall   where his hoard lay hidden,
sure of his stronghold,   his walls and his war,
sure of himself,   deceived by his pride.

2050   Then terrible tidings   were taken to Beowulf:
how swiftly his own   stronghold was stricken,
that best of buildings   bursting with flames
and his throne melting.   The hero was heart-sore;
the wise man wondered   what wrong he had wrought
2055   and how he trangressed   against old law,
the Lord Everlasting,   Ruler of All.
His grief was great,   and grim thoughts
boiled in his breast   as never before.
The fiery foe   had flown to his coastlands,
2060   had sacked and seared   his keep by the sea.
For that the war-king   required requital.
He ordered a broad-shield   fashioned of iron,
better for breasting   baleful blazes
than the linden-wood   that warded his warriors.
2065   Little was left   of the time lent him
for life in the world;   and the worm as well,
who had haughtily held   his hoard for so long.
Scorning to follow   the far-flying foe
with his whole host,   the ring-giver reckoned
2070   the wrath of a dragon   unworthy of dread.
Fearless and forceful,   he often had faced
the straits of struggle   blessed with success.
Beowulf braved   many a battle
after ridding Hrothgar's   hall of its horrors
2075   and grappling with Grendel's   gruesome kin.

Not least of his clashes   had come when the king
Hygelac fell   while fighting the Frisians
in hand-to-hand combat.   His friend and fief-lord,
the son of Hrethel,   was slain in the onslaught,
2080   stricken to death   by a blood-drinking blade.
Beowulf battled   back to the beach
where he proved his strength   with skillful swimming,
for he took to the tide   bearing the trophies
of thirty earls   he had felled in the field.
2085   None of the Hetware   needed to boast
how they fared on foot,   flaunting their shields
against that fierce fighter,   for few remained
after the battle   to bear the tale home.

Over wide waters   the lone swimmer went,
2090   the son of Ecgtheow   swept on the sea-waves
back to his homeland,   forlorn with his loss,
and hence to Hygd   who offered her hoard:
rings and a realm,   a throne for the thane.
With Hygelac dead   she doubted her son
2095   could guard the Geats   from foreigners' forays.
Refusing her boon,   Beowulf bade
the leaderless lords   to hail the lad
as their rightful ruler.   He chose not to reign
by thwarting his cousin   but to counsel the king
2100   and guide with good will   until Heardred grew older.

It was Heardred who held   the Weder-Geats' hall
when outcast Scylfings   came seeking its safety:
Eanmund and Eadgils,   nephews of Onela.
That strong sea-king   and spender of treasures
2105   sailed from Sweden   pursuing the rebels
who challenged his right   to rule their realm.
For lending them haven,   Hygelac's son
suffered the sword-stroke   that spilled out his life.
The Swede headed home   when Heardred lay dead,
2110   leaving Beowulf,   lordship of Geats.
That was a good king,   keeping the gift-seat;
yet Heardred's death   dwelled in his thoughts.
A long time later   he offered his aid
to end the exile   of destitute Eadgils.
2115   He summoned an army   for Ohthere's son,
sent weapons and warriors   over wide waters,
a voyage of vengeance   to kill off a king.

Such were the struggles   and tests of strength
the son of Ecgtheow   saw and survived.
2120   His pluck was proven   in perilous onslaughts
till that fateful day   when he fought the dragon.
As leader of twelve   trailing that terror,
the greatest of Geats   glowered with rage
when he looked on the lair   where the worm lurked.
2125   By now he had found   how the feud flared,
this fell affliction   befalling his kingdom,
for the kingly cup   had come to his hand
from the hand of him   who raided the hoard.
That sorry slave   had started the strife,
2130   and against his will   he went with the warriors,
a thirteenth man   bringing the band
to the barrow's brink   which he alone knew.
Hard by the surge   of the seething sea
gaped a cavern   glutted with golden
2135   medallions and chains.   The murderous manbane
hunkered within,   hungry for warfare.

No taker would touch   his treasures cheaply:
the hoard's holder   would drive a hard bargain.

The proud war-king   paused on the sea-point
2140 to lighten the hearts   of his hearth-companions,
though his heart was heavy   and hankered for death.
It was nearing him now.   That taker of treasure
would sunder the soul   from his old bones and flesh.
So Beowulf spoke,   the son of Ecgtheow,
2145 recalling the life   he was loathe to lose:

"From boyhood I bore   battles and bloodshed,
struggles and strife: I still see them all.
I was given at seven   to house with King Hrethel,
my mother's father'   and friend of our folk.
2150 He kept me fairly   with feasts and fine gifts.
I fared no worse   than one of his sons:
Herebeald, Hathcyn,   or princely Hygelac
who was later my lord.   The eldest, Herebeald,
unwittingly went   to a wrongful death
2155 when Hathcyn's horn-bow   hurled an arrow.
Missing the mark,   it murdered the kinsman;
a brother was shot   by the blood-stained shaft.
This blow to the heart   was brutal and baffling.
A prince had fallen.   The felon went free.[1]

2160 "So it is sore   for an old man to suffer
his son swinging   young on the gallows,
gladdening ravens.   He groans in his grief
and loudly laments   the lad he has lost.
No help is at hand   from hard-won wisdom
2165 or the march of years.   Each morning reminds him
his heir is elsewhere,   and he has no heart
to wait for a second   son in his stronghold
when death has finished   the deeds of the first.
He ceaselessly sees   his son's dwelling,
2170 the desolate wine-hall,   the windswept grave-sward
where swift riders   and swordsmen slumber.
No harp-string sounds,   no song in the courtyard.
He goes to his bed   sighing with sorrow,
one soul for another.   His home is hollow;
2175 his field, fallow.
                    "So Hrethel suffered,
hopeless and heart-sore   with Herebeald gone.
He would do no deed   to wound the death-dealer
or harrow his household   with hatred and anger;
but bitter bloodshed   had stolen his bliss,

1. Even in cases of involuntary manslaughter, punishment was required to avenge the dead. In this instance, it seems that a ritual, sacrificial hanging was performed to spare Hathcyn for murdering his brother Herebeald.

2180   and he quit his life   for the light of the Lord.
        Like a luckier man,   he could leave his land
        in the hands of a son,   though he loved him no longer.

        "Then strife and struggle   of Geats and Swedes
        crossed the wide water.   Warfare wounded
2185   both sides in battle   when Hrethel lay buried.
        Ongentheow's sons,   fierce and unfriendly,
        suddenly struck   at Hreosna-Beorh
        and bloodied the bluff   with baneful slaughter.
        Our foes in this feud   soon felt the wrath
2190   of my kinsman the king   claiming our due,
        though the counterblow   cost his own life.
        Hathcyn was killed,   his kingship cut short.
        The slayer himself   was slain in the morning.
        I have heard how Eofor   struck the old Scylfing.
2195   Sword-ashen,   Ongentheow sank
        with his helm split: heedful of harm,
        to kinsman and king,   the hand would not halt
        the death-blow it dealt.
                                "My own sword-arm
        repaid my prince   for the gifts he granted.
2200   He gave me a fiefdom,   the land I have loved.
        He never had need   to seek among Spear-Danes,
        Gifthas or Swedes   and get with his gifts
        a worse warrior.   I wielded my sword
        at the head of our host;   so shall I hold
2205   this blade that I bear   boldly in battle
        as long as life lasts.   It has worn well
        since the day when Daeghrefn   died by my hand,
        the Frankish foe   who fought for the Frisians,
        bearing their banner.   He broke in my grip,
2210   never to barter   the necklace he robbed
        from Hygelac's corpse.   I crushed that killer;
        his bones snapped,   and his life-blood spilled.
        I slew him by strength,   not by the sword.
        Now I shall bear   his brand into battle:
2215   hand and hard sword   will fight for the hoard."

        Now Beowulf spoke   his last battle-boast:
        "In boyhood I braved   bitter clashes;
        still in old age   I would seek out strife
        and gain glory   guarding my folk
2220   if the man-bane comes   from his cave to meet me."

        Then he turned to his troop   for the final time,
        bidding farewell   to bold helmet-bearers,
        fast in friendship: "I would wear no sword,
        no weapon at all   to ward off the worm
2225   if I knew how to fight   this fiendish foe
        as I grappled with Grendel   one bygone night.

But here I shall find   fierce battle-fire
and breath envenomed,   therefore I bear
this mail-coat and shield.   I shall not shy
2230   from standing my ground   when I greet the guardian,
follow what will   at the foot of his wall.
I shall face the fiend   with a firm heart.
Let the Ruler of men   reckon my fate:
words are worthless   against the war-flyer.
2235   Bide by the barrow,   safe in your byrnies,
and watch, my warriors,   which of us two
will better bear   the brunt of our clash.
This war is not yours;   it is meted to me,
matching my strength,   man against monster.
2240   I shall do this deed   undaunted by death
and get you gold   or else get my ending,
borne off in battle,   the bane of your lord."

The hero arose,   helmed and hardy,
a war-king clad   in shield and corselet.
2245   He strode strongly   under the stone-cliff:
no faint-hearted man,   to face it unflinching!
Stalwart soldier   of so many marches,
unshaken when shields   were crushed in the clash,
he saw between stiles   an archway where steam
2250   burst like a boiling   tide from the barrow,
woeful for one   close to the worm-hoard.
He would not linger long   unburned by the lurker
or safely slip   through the searing lair.
Then a battle-cry broke   from Beowulf's breast
2255   as his rightful wrath   was roused for the reckoning.
His challenge sounded   under stark stone
where the hateful hoard-guard   heard in his hollow
the clear-voiced call   of a man coming.

No quarter was claimed;   no quarter given.
2260   First the beast's breath   blew hot from the barrow
as battle-bellows   boomed underground.
The stone-house stormer   swung up his shield
at the ghastly guardian.   Then the dragon's grim heart
kindled for conflict.   Uncoiling, he came
2265   seeking the Stalwart;   but the swordsman had drawn
the keen-edged blade   bequeathed him for combat,
and each foe confronted   the other with fear.
His will unbroken,   the warlord waited
behind his tall shield,   helm and hauberk.
2270   With fitful twistings   the fire-drake hastened
fatefully forward.   His fender held high,
Beowulf felt   the blaze blister through
hotter and sooner   than he had foreseen.
So for the first time   fortune was failing
2275   the mighty man   in the midst of a struggle.
Wielding his sword,   he struck at the worm

and his fabled blade   bit to the bone
through blazoned hide: bit and bounced back,
no match for the foe   in this moment of need.

2280   The peerless prince   was hard-pressed in response,
for his bootless blow   had maddened the monster
and fatal flames   shot further than ever,
lighting the land.   The blade he bared
failed in the fray,   though forged from iron.
2285   No easy end   for the son of Ecgtheow:
against his will   he would leave this world
to dwell elsewhere,   as every man must
when his days are done.   Swiftly the death-dealer
moved to meet him.   From the murderous breast
2290   bellows of breath   belched fresh flames.
Enfolded in fire,   he who formerly
ruled a whole realm   had no one to help him
hold off the heat,   for his hand-picked band
of princelings had fled,   fearing to face
2295   the foe with their lord.   Loving honor
less than their lives,   they hid in the holt.
But one among them   grieved for the Geats
and balked at the thought   of quitting a kinsman.

This one was Wiglaf,   son of Weohstan,
2300   kinsman of Aelfhere,   earl among Scylfings.
Seeing his liege-lord   suffering sorely
with war-mask scorched   by the searing onslaught,
the thankful thane   thought of the boons
his sovereign bestowed: the splendid homestead
2305   and folk-rights his father   formerly held.
No shirker could stop him   from seizing his shield
of yellow linden   and lifting the blade
Weohstan won   when he slew Eanmund,
son of Ohthere.   Spoils of that struggle,
2310   sword and scabbard,   smithwork of giants,
a byrnie of ring-mail   and bright burnished helm
were granted as gifts,   a thane's war-garb,
for Onela never   acknowledged his nephews
but struck against both   of his brother's sons.
2315   When Eadgils avenged   Eanmund's death,
Weohstan fled.   Woeful and friendless,
he saved that gear   for seasons of strife,
foreseeing his son   someday might crave
sword and corselet.   He came to his kinsman,
2320   the prince of the Geats,   and passed on his heirlooms,
hoping Wiglaf   would wear them with honor.
Old then, and wise,   he went from the world.

This war was the first   young Wiglaf would fight
helping the king.   His heart would not quail
2325   nor weapon fail   as the foe would find

going against him;   but he made his grim mood
known to the men: "I remember the time
when taking our mead   in the mighty hall,
all of us offered   oaths to our liege-lord.
2330   We promised to pay   for princely trappings
by staunchly wielding   sword-blades in war
if need should arise.   Now we are needed
by him who chose,   from the whole of his host,
twelve for this trial,   trusting our claims
2335   as warriors worthy   of wearing our blades,
bearing keen spears.   Our king has come here
bent on battling   the man-bane alone,
because among warriors   one keeper of kinfolk
has done, undaunted,   the most deeds of daring.
2340   But this day our lord   needs dauntless defenders
so long as the frightful   fires keep flaring.
God knows I would gladly   give my own body
for flames to enfold   with the gold-giver.
Shameful, to shoulder   our shields homeward!
2345   First we must fell   this fearsome foe
and protect the life   of our people's lord.
It is wrong that one man   be wrathfully racked
for his former feats   and fall in this fight,
guarding the Geats.   We shall share our war-gear:
2350   shield and battle-shirt,   helm and hard sword."

So speaking, he stormed   through the reek of smoke,
with helmet on head,   to help his lord.
"Beloved Beowulf,   bear up your blade.
You pledged in your youth,   powerful prince,
2355   never to let   your luster lessen
while life was left you.   Now summon your strength.
Stand steadfast.   I shall stand with you."

After these words   the worm was enraged.
For a second time   the spiteful specter
2360   flew at his foe,   and he wreathed in flames
the hated human   he hungered to harm.
His dreadful fire-wind   drove in a wave,
charring young Wiglaf's   shield to the boss,
nor might a byrnie   bar that breath
2365   from burning the brave   spear-bearer's breast.
Wiglaf took cover   close to his kinsman,
shielded by iron   when linden was cinder.
Then the war-king,   recalling past conquests,
struck with full strength   straight at the head.
2370   His battle-sword, Naegling,   stuck there and split,
shattered in combat,   so sharp was the shock
to Beowulf's great   gray-banded blade.
He never was granted   the gift of a sword
as hard and strong   as the hand which held it.

2375   I have heard that he broke   blood-hardened brands,
        so the weapon-bearer   was none the better.

        The fearful fire-drake,   scather of strongholds,
        flung himself forward   a final time,
        wild with wounds   yet wily and sly.
2380   In the heat of the fray,   he hurtled headlong
        to fasten his fangs   in the foe's throat.
        Beowulf's life-blood   came bursting forth
        on those terrible tusks.   Just then, I am told,
        the second warrior   sprang from his side,
2385   a man born for battle   proving his mettle,
        keen to strengthen   his kinsman in combat.
        He took no heed   of the hideous head
        scorching his hand   as he hit lower down.
        The sword sank in,   patterned and plated;
2390   the flames of the foe   faltered, faded.
        Though gored and giddy,   Beowulf gathered
        strength once again   and slipped out his sheath-knife,
        the keen killing-blade   he kept in his corselet.
        Then the Geats' guardian   gutted the dragon,
2395   felling that fiend   with the help of his friend,
        two kinsmen together   besting the terror.
        So should a thane   succor his sovereign.

        That deed was the king's   crowning conquest;
        Beowulf's work   in the world was done.
2400   He soon felt his wound   swelling and stinging
        where fell fangs   had fastened upon him,
        and evil venom   enveloped his heart.
        Wisely he sought   a seat by the stone-wall,
        and his gaze dwelled   on the dark doorway
2405   delved in the dolmen,   the straight stiles
        and sturdy archway   sculpted by giants.
        With wonderful kindness   Wiglaf washed
        the clotting blood   from his king and kinsman;
        his hands loosened   the lord's high helm.
2410   Though banefully bitten,   Beowulf spoke,
        for he knew his lifetime   would last no longer.
        The count of his days   had come to a close.
        His joys were done.   Death drew near him.

        "Now I would wish   to will my son
2415   these weapons of war,   had I been awarded
        an heir of my own,   holder of heirlooms.
        I fathered our folk   for fifty winters.
        No warlike lord   of neighboring lands
        dared to assail us   or daunt us with dread.
2420   A watchful warden,   I waited on fate
        while keeping the Geats   clear of quarrels.
        I swore many oaths;   not one was wrongful.

So I rejoice,   though sick with my death-wound,
that God may not blame me   for baseless bloodshed
2425   or killing of kin   when breath quits my body.
Hurry below   and look on the hoard,
beloved Wiglaf.   The worm lies sleeping
under gray stone,   sorely stricken
and stripped of his gold.   Go swiftly and seize it.
2430   Get me giltwork   and glittering gems:
I would set my sight   on that store of wealth.
Loath would I be   to leave for less
the life and lordship   I held for so long."

I have heard how swiftly   the son of Weohstan
2435   hastened to heed   his wounded and weakening
war-lord's behest.   In his woven mail-shirt,
his bright byrnie,   he entered the barrow;
and passing its threshold,   proud and princely,
he glimpsed all the gold   piled on the ground,
2440   the walled-in wealth   won by the worm,
that fierce night-flyer.   Flagons were standing,
embossed wine-beakers   lying unburnished,
their inlays loosened.   There were lofty helmets
and twisted arm-rings   rotting and rusting.
2445   Gold below ground   may betray into grief
any who hold it: heed me who will!

Wiglaf saw also   a gold-woven standard,
a wonder of handiwork,   finger-filigreed,
high above ground.   It gave off a glow
2450   that let him behold   the whole of the hoard.
I am told he took   from that trove of giants
goblets and platters   pressed to his breastplate,
and the golden banner   glinting brightly.
He spotted no sign   of the stricken worm.
2455   The iron-edged brand   old Beowulf bore
had mortally wounded   the warder of wealth
and fiery foe   whose flames in the night
welled so fiercely   before he was felled.

Bent with his burden,   the messenger hastened
2460   back to his master,   burning to know
whether the brave   but wound-weakened
lord of the Weders   was lost to the living.
Setting his spoils   by the storied prince
whose lifeblood blackened   the ground with gore,
2465   Wiglaf wakened   the war-lord with water,
and these words thrust   like spears through his breast
as the ancient one grimly   gazed on the gold:

"I offer my thanks   to the Almighty Master,
the King of Glory,   for granting my kindred
2470   for these precious things   I look upon last.

Losing my life,   I have bought this boon
to lighten my leave-day.   Look to our people,
for you shall be leader;   I lead no longer.
Gather my guard   and raise me a grave-mound
2475   housing my ashes   at Hronesnaesse,
reminding my kin   to recall their king
after his pyre   has flared on the point.
Seafarers passing   shall say when they see it
'Beowulf's Barrow'   as bright longboats
2480   drive over darkness,   daring the flood."

So the stern prince   bestowed on his sword-thane
and keen spear-wielder   the kingly collar,
his gold-plated helm   and hammered hauberk.
He told him to bear them   bravely in battle:
2485   "Farewell, Wiglaf,   last Waegmunding.
I follow our fathers,   foredestined to die,
swept off by fate,   though strong and steadfast."
These heartfelt words   were the warrior's last
before his body   burned in the bale-fire
2490   and his soul sought   the doom of the truthful.

Smitten with sorrow,   the young man saw
the old lord he loved   lying in pain
as life left him.   Slain and slayer
died there together: the dread earth-dragon,
2495   deprived of his life,   no longer would lurk
coiled on the hoard.   Hard-hammered swords
had felled the far-flyer   in front of his lair.
No more would he sport   on the midnight sky,
proud of his wealth,   his power and pomp.
2500   He sprawled on stone   where the war-chief slew him.
Though deeds of daring   were done in that land,
I have heard of no man   whose might would suffice
to face the fire-drake's   fuming breath
or help him escape   if he handled the hoard
2505   once he had woken   its warder from sleep.
Beowulf paid   for that lode with his life;
his loan of days   was lost to the dragon.

Before long the laggards   limped from the woods,
ten cowards together,   the troth-breakers
2510   who had failed to bare   their blades in battle
at the moment their master   needed them most.
In shame they shouldered   their shields and spears.
Armored for war,   they went to Wiglaf
who sorrowfully sat   at their sovereign's shoulder.
2515   Laving his leader,   the foot-soldier failed
to waken the fallen   fighter one whit,
nor could he will   his lord back to life.
The World's Warden   decided what deeds

men might achieve   in those days and these.

2520 A hard answer   was easily offered
by young Wiglaf,   Weohstan's son.
With little love   he looked on the shirkers:
"I tell you in truth,   takers of treasure,
bench-sitting boasters   brave in the hall:
2525 Beowulf gave you   the gear that you wear,
the best helms and hauberks   found near or far
for a prince to proffer   his thankless thanes;
but he wasted his wealth   on a worthless troop
who cast off their king   at the coming of war.
2530 Our lord had no need   to laud his liege-men;
yet God, giver   of glory and vengeance,
granted him strength   to stand with his sword.
I could do little   to lengthen his life
facing that foe,   but I fought nonetheless:
2535 beyond my power   I propped up my prince.
The fire-drake faltered   after I struck him,
and his fuming jaws   flamed less fiercely,
but too few friends   flew to our king
when evil beset him.   Now sword-bestowing
2540 and gold-getting   shall cease for the Geats.
You shall have no joy   in the homeland you love.
Your farms shall be forfeit,   and each man fare
alone and landless   when foreign lords
learn of your flight,   your failure of faith.
2545 Better to die   than dwell in disgrace."

Then Wiglaf bade   that the battle-tidings
be sent to the camp   over the sea-cliff
where warriors waited   with shields unslung,
sadly sitting   from dawn until noon
2550 to learn if their lord   and beloved leader
had seen his last sunrise   or soon would return.
The herald would leave them   little to doubt;
he sped up the headland   and spoke to them all:

"Now the wish-granter,   warlord of Weders,
2555 lies on his death-bed.   The leader of Geats
stays in the slaughter-place,   slain by the worm
sprawled at his side.   Dagger-stricken,
the slayer was felled,   though a sword had failed
to wound the serpent.   Weohstan's son,
2560 Wiglaf is waiting   by Beowulf's body;
a living warrior   watches the lifeless,
sad-heartedly   sitting to guard
the loved and the loathed.   Look now for war
as Franks and Frisians   learn how the king
2565 has fallen in combat.   Few foreigners love us,

for Hygelac angered   the harsh Hugas
when his fleet forayed   to far-off Frisia.
Fierce Hetware   met him with forces
bigger than his.   They broke him in battle;
2570   that mail-clad chieftain   fell with his men.
Hygelac took   no trophies to thanes;
no king of the Meroving   wishes us well.

"I also foresee   strife with the Swedes,
feud without end,   for all know Ongentheow
2575   slew Hrethel's son   when Hathcyn first forayed
near Ravenswood   with hot-headed Geats
and raided the realm   of Scylf-land's ruler.
That fearsome old foe,   father of Ohthere,
quickly struck back.   He cut down our king
2580   to rescue the queen   Hathcyn had captured.
Her captors had shorn   the crone of her gold,
dishonored the aged   mother of Onela.
Ongentheow followed   hard on their heels.
Wounded, weary   and fiercely-harried,
2585   those left unslain   by Swedish swords
limped off leaderless,   hid in the holt.
A huge army   beleaguered them there.
All night long   Ongentheow taunted
the wretched raiders.   At daybreak, he swore,
2590   he would slice them to slivers.   Some would swing
slung on his gallows,   sport for the ravens.
But gladness came   again to grim Geats
hearing Hygelac's   horns in the morning,
the trumpet calls   of the troop that tracked them.
2595   Hathcyn's brother,   bold with his band,
had rallied for battle.
                              "A bloody swath
Scylfings and Geats   left on the landscape,
everywhere gored   with spoor of the stricken.
So the two folks   stirred further feuds.
2600   Wise in warfare,   old Ongentheow
grimly stood off,   seeking the safety
of higher ground.   He had heard of Hygelac's
strength in struggles,   his pride and prowess.
Mistrusting his force   to fend off the foray,
2605   he feared for his family   and fell back to guard
the hoard hidden   behind his earthworks.
Then Hrethel's people   pressed the pursuit:
the standards of Hygelac   stormed the stronghold.
There the Swede   was snared between swords.
2610   Eofor humbled   that hoary-haired leader,
though Wulf struck first,   fierce with his weapon,
and a cut vein colored   the king's white head.
Undaunted, Ongentheow   warded him off;

Wulf was wounded   the worse in return:
2615   Ongentheow's blow   broke open his helm,
hurled him headlong,   helpless and bleeding
though not destined   to die on that day.
Then Eofor faced   the folk-lord alone.
Sternly he stood   when his brother slumped:
2620   Hygelac's soldier   with broadsword in hand
and helmet on head,   hoarded smithwork
shaped by old crafts,   shattered the shield-wall.
The king crumpled,   struck to the quick.

"Now the Geats gathered   after the slaughter.
2625   Some bound the wound   of Eofor's brother
and bundled him off   the field of battle.
Meanwhile one warrior   plundered the other:
Eofor stripped   the hard-hilted sword,
helm and corselet   from Ongentheow's corpse.
2630   He handed that heap   of armor to Hygelac.
Pleased with his prizes,   the king pledged in turn
to reward war-strokes   as lord of the Weders.
He gave great riches   to Wulf and Eofor.
Once they were home,   he honored each one
2635   with a hundred thousand   in land and linked rings.
No man in middle-earth   ever begrudged them
the favor and fortune   bestowed for their feat.
Yet a further honor   was offered Eofor:
the king's only daughter   adorned his house,
2640   awarded in wedlock   to Wonred's son.

"Full of this feud,   this festering hatred,
the Swedes, I am certain,   will swiftly beset us,
as soon as they learn   our lord lies lifeless
who held his hoard,   his hall and his realm
2645   against all foes   when heroes had fallen,
who fostered his folk   with fair kingship.
Now must we hasten,   behold our sovereign,
and bear him for burial.   The brave one shall not
be beggared of booty   to melt on his bier.
2650   Let funeral flames   greedily fasten
on gold beyond measure,   grimly gotten,
lucre our leader   bought with his life.
No earl shall take   tokens to treasure
nor maiden be made   fairer with finery
2655   strung at her throat.   Stripped of their wealth,
they shall wander woefully   all their lives long,
lordless and landless   now that their king
has laid aside laughter,   sport and song.
Their hands shall heft   many a spear-haft,
2660   cold in the morning.   No call of the harp

shall waken warriors   after their battles;
but the black raven   shall boast to the eagle,
crowing how finely   he fed on the fated
when, with the wolf,   he went rending the slain."

2665   Thus the terrible   tidings were told,
and the teller had not   mistaken the truth.
The warriors all rose   and woefully went
to look on the wonder   with welling tears.
They found on the sand   under Earnanaess
2670   their lifeless lord   laid there to rest,
beloved giver   of gifts and gold rings,
the war-king come   at the close of his days
to a marvelous death.   At first the monster
commanded their gaze: grim on the ground
2675   across from the king's   the creature had crumpled,
scaly and scorched,   a fearsome fire-drake
fifty feet long.   He would fly no more,
free in the darkness,   nor drop to his den
at the break of dawn.   Death held the dragon;
2680   he never would coil   in his cavern again.
Beyond the serpent   stood flagons and jars,
plated flatware   and priceless swords
rotting in ruin,   etched out with rust.
These riches had rested   in Earth's embrace
2685   for a thousand winters,   the heritage held
by warders of old,   spell-enwoven
and toilfully tombed   that none might touch them,
unless God Himself,   granter of grace,
true Lord of glory,   allotted release
2690   to one of His choosing   and opened the hoard.

It little profited   him who had wrongfully
hidden the hand-wrought   wealth within walls.
His payment was scant   for slaying the one
with courage to claim it: the kill was quickly
2695   and harshly requited.   So the kingly
may come to strange ends   when their strength is spent
and time meted out.   They may not remain
as men among kin,   mirthful with mead.
Beowulf goaded   the gold's guardian,
2700   raised up the wrath,   not reckoning whether
his death-day had dawned,   not knowing the doom
solemnly sworn   by princes who placed
their hoard in that hollow: the thief who held it
would fall before idols,   forge himself hell-bonds,
2705   waste in torment   for touching the treasure.
He failed to consider   more fully and sooner
who rightfully owned   such awesome riches.

So spoke Wiglaf,   son of Weohstan:
"By the whim of one man,   many warriors
2710   sometimes may suffer,   as here has happened.
No means were at hand   to move my master;
no counsel could sway   the kingdom's keeper
never to trouble   the treasure's taker,
but leave him lying   where long he had hidden,
2715   walled with his wealth   until the world's ending.
He kept to his course,   uncovered the hoard.
Fate was too strongly   forcing him hither.
I have entered that hall,   beheld everything
golden within,   though none too glad
2720   for the opening offered   under its archway.
In haste I heaved   much from the hoard,
and a mighty burden   I bore from the barrow
straight to my sovereign.   He still was alive.
His wits were clear;   his words came quickly.
2725   In anguish, the Ancient   asked that I say
he bade you to build   a barrow for him
befitting the deeds   of a fallen friend.
You shall heap it high   over his ashes,
since he was the world's   worthiest warrior,
2730   famed far and wide   for the wealth of his fortress.

"Now let us hurry   hence to the hoard.
For a second time   I shall see that splendor
under the cliff-wall,   those wonders of craftwork.
Come, I shall take you   close to the trove,
2735   where you may behold   heaps of broad gold.
Then let a bier   be readied to bear
our beloved lord   to his long dwelling
under the watch   of the World's Warden."

Then Weohstan's heir   ordered the earls,
2740   heads of houses   and fief holders,
to fetch firewood   fit for the folk-leader's
funeral pyre.   "Flames shall now flare,
feed on the flesh   and fade into darkness,
an ending for him   who often endured
2745   the iron showers   shot over shield-walls
when string-driven storms   of arrows arose
with feathered fins   to steer them in flight
with barbed arrowheads   eager to bite."

Wisely Wiglaf,   son of Weohstan,
2750   summoned the seven   most steadfast thanes.
They went in together,   eight earls entering
under the evil   arch of the earth-house
with one man bearing   a blazing torch.
No lot was cast   to learn which liege-man

2755   would plunder the loot   lying unguarded,
       as each searcher   could see for himself;
       yet none was unhappy   to hurry that hoard
       out into daylight.   They heaved the dragon
       over the sea-cliff   where surges seized him:
2760   the treasure's keeper   was caught by the tide.
       Then they filled a wain   with filigreed gold
       and untold treasures;   and they carried the king,
       their hoary-haired warlord,   to Hronesnaess.

       There the king's kinsmen   piled him a pyre,
2765   wide and well-made   just as he willed it.
       They hung it with helmets,   shields and hauberks,
       then laid in its midst   their beloved lord,
       renowned among men.   Lamenting their loss,
       his warriors woke   the most woeful fire
2770   to flare on the bluff.   Fierce was the burning,
       woven with weeping,   and wood-smoke rose
       black over the blaze,   blown with a roar.
       The fire-wind faltered   and flames dwindled,
       hot at their heart   the broken bone-house.
2775   Sunken in spirit   at Beowulf's slaying,
       the Geats gathered   grieving together.
       Her hair wound up,   a woebegone woman
       sang and resang   her dirge of dread,
       foretelling a future   fraught with warfare,
2780   kinfolk sundered,   slaughter and slavery
       even as Heaven   swallowed the smoke.

       High on the headland   they heaped his grave-mound
       which seafaring sailors   would spy from afar.
       Ten days they toiled   on the scorched hilltop,
2785   the cleverest men   skillfully crafting
       a long-home built   for the bold in battle.
       They walled with timbers   the trove they had taken,
       sealing in stone   the circlets and gems,
       wealth of the worm-hoard   gotten with grief,
2790   gold from the ground   gone back to Earth
       as worthless to men   as when it was won.
       Then sorrowing swordsmen   circled the barrow,
       twelve of his earls   telling their tales,
       the sons of nobles   sadly saluting
2795   deeds of the dead.   So dutiful thanes
       in liege to their lord   mourn him with lays
       praising his peerless   prowess in battle
       as it is fitting   when life leaves the flesh.
       Heavy-hearted   his hearth-companions
2800   grieved for Beowulf,   great among kings,
       mild in his mien,   most gentle of men,
       kindest to kinfolk   yet keenest for fame.

+∙ ╪◇╪ ∙+

The Táin Bó Cuailnge

The Táin Bó Cuailnge (The Cattle Raid of Cooley), the chief work in the "Ulster Cycle" of Irish heroic narratives, was already a famed and ancient story by the twelfth century, when it was copied into the manuscript now called the Book of Leinster. That manuscript also contains a legend about the recovery of the whole *Táin* by the poets of Ireland, who knew it only in fragments. Followers of the chief poet set out for Brittany, the story reports, where a complete copy had been carried. In the course of their journey, though, they pass the grave of Fergus mac Roich, an earlier poet and a hero in the events of the *Táin*. Alone at the grave, the chief poet's son calls up the spirit of Fergus, who recites to him the tale in its entirety.

This legend offers a window on Irish literary culture and its sense of the past at the time when the *Táin* was written down. The legend comes from a world of written books that could be sought out and copied; yet it also recalls the prestige and priority of an oral tradition in which the ghost of Fergus might chant the work across three days and nights. The rigorous education of Irish poets, and their habits of composition in the vernacular, remained largely oral for centuries after a usable alphabet and books had come into circulation. Further, the story evokes the aura of magic surrounding poets in medieval Ireland and the poets' own sense of themselves as spiritual and even genealogical heirs of an ancient calling which stretched back into the mythic past. Ireland had developed a deeply Christian culture yet celebrated its native secular stories and did so with a vigor that has little of the elegiac nostalgia and biblical echoes seen in *Beowulf*. The highest class of poets, the *filid* (singular *fili*), also inherited practices like divination which had been the work of other learned classes, such as the druids, in the pagan era. Poets were advisors to great men, at once honored for their arcane learning and feared for the satires in which they might reproach and humiliate even the most powerful king.

If the Book of Leinster thus displays a lively but complicated connection to a rich literary past, the *Táin* itself looks backward to a still more ancient world of warring heroes, magical weapons, shape-shifters, and wondrous beasts, in which the line between mortals and gods was blurry and often crossed. The earliest version of the *Táin* stems from an oral tradition perhaps as early as the fourth century, but the society it depicts—with warriors riding in battle chariots, fighting naked, and taking the heads of conquered enemies—mirrors what we know of Celtic peoples on the Continent as early as the second century B.C. The Roman geographer Strabo called the "whole race . . . madly fond of war, high-spirited and quick to battle." Some of their habits persisted in Ireland but were long over by the sixth century A.D. Other social practices—such as clientship, rigid standards of hospitality, and the obligation to safeguard anyone taken under protection—continued late into the medieval period.

Four great stories converge in the *Táin*. It draws, first, on the history of the bulls Finnbennach the White Horned and Donn Cuailnge the Brown Bull of Cooley, who originated as two pig-keepers and passed through a series of animal forms before the moment of the main narrative. Second, the immediate occasion of the cattle raid emerges from a debate between Ailill, king of Connacht, and his wife, Medb. Medb's quest to match the wealth of Ailill leads her into an armed attempt to take Donn Cuailnge from its owner on the borderlands of Ulster. To achieve this end, third, Medb and Ailill gather an army to march against Ulster. Finally, the hero Cú Chulainn single-handedly protects Ulster's borders until the men of Ulster can recover from a seasonal debility with which they have been long cursed.

The debate of Ailill and Medb introduces one of the most powerful women in medieval Irish literature, stemming partly from a pagan goddess of sovereignty. Medb and similar women reflect a persistent aspect of mythic and literary imagination in the Irish heroic narratives, although in medieval Irish law women actually had fewer rights than their Anglo-Saxon counterparts. The story acknowledges Medb's power as a wealthy woman, leader of armies, and queen, but constantly places that power in question. Indeed, several important men are openly hostile to Medb's strong will; even the bull Finnbennach is in Ailill's herds because he refused to be owned by a woman. Yet Medb's role is emphasized in the version of the *Táin* translated here, which transfers to her a number of key actions that other versions attribute to her husband. Medb's power is explicitly sexual. Far from the passive object of desire that we often meet elsewhere in the period, she uses her sexuality as an active force, often frankly used for political gain. Yet Medb is much more than a cunning body; she exploits her wealth and is willing to debate and even to battle with her own ally and husband over issues of military strategy.

The armies that gather against the Ulstermen are replete with heroic fighters and complex allegiances, and the *Táin*'s emotional weight lies in the passionate devotion and divided loyalties of its warriors. There is particular sadness in the plight of a group of Ulstermen, among them Fergus mac Roich, whose own king Conchobor had killed men taken under their protection; they have fled his court and placed themselves in the service of Ailill. Even more personal is the repeated clash between political fidelity and the quasi-familial link of fosterage in the story.

These issues press hard on the *Táin*'s heroic center, Cú Chulainn, the preeminent hero of the Ulster Cycle. The line between the heroic, the superhuman, and the monstrous can be fluid in the *Táin*, as it is in the curious links between Beowulf and Grendel. Cú Chulainn is of divine birth, and has performed a series of wondrous boyhood exploits, before the events of the *Táin*. Even within the *Táin*, he is persistently boyish in appearance and often distracted by activities that approach play. We witness Cú Chulainn coming into his maturity as he fights an exhausting series of border combats single-handedly and unwaveringly, and as he finally must face and defeat his foster-brother Ferdia. Despite this poignant humanity, Cú Chulainn possesses godlike strength and skill with weapons; yet his heroic rage works a physical distortion on him that is almost monstrous, eliciting comparisons with a giant or "a man from the sea-kingdom."

Geography is as important as heroism in the *Táin*. Battles, wonders, and other events repeatedly lead to the naming of a locale, so that the story virtually maps the mythic significance of place in the northern parts of Ireland. It also enfolds much of the genealogy of its legendary heroes. In style and theme, too, the *Táin* counterbalances the wonders of superhuman force by the works of human skill, with elaborate descriptions of clothing, ornament, and decorated weaponry. It narrates the physical beauty of men and women alike with an exquisite attention not found in *Beowulf*. Like much narrative that derives closely from its oral background, the *Táin* is as much the encyclopedia of a people's beliefs and values—or a commemoration of its past beliefs and their impact on current values—as it is a single story of heroic action.

These indications are imprecise but give a rough sense of how key names in the *Táin* sounded in Old Irish. The spelling -*ch* is slightly guttural, as in *loch* or *Bach*.

Ailill	AL-*ill*	Finnbennach	*finn-*VEN-*ach*
Bricriu	BRIK-*roo*	Láeg	*loig*
Cet	*ket*	Medb	*maive*
Conchobor	CON-*cho-wer*	Morrígu	MO-*ree-ga*
Cú Chulainn	*coo-*CHULL-*in*	Nemain	NE-*van*
Dubthach Dáel Ulad	DUV-*thach doil* U-*lad*	Ráth Crúachain	*rawth* CROO-*a-chan*
Emain Macha	EV-*in* MA-*cha*	Samain	SA-*win*
Feidelm	FETH-*elm*	Sid	*sheethe*
Ferdia	*fer-*DEE-*a*	Táin Bó Cuailnge	*toin bow* COO-*ling-e*
Findabair	FIN-*a-wer*		

from **The Táin**[1]

[THE PILLOW TALK]

Once when their royal bed had been prepared for them in Ráth Crúachain[2] in Connacht, Ailill and Medb spoke together as they lay on their pillow. "In truth, woman,"
said Ailill, "she is a well-off woman who is the wife of a nobleman." "She is indeed,"
said the woman; "why do you think so?" "I think so," said Ailill, "because you are better off today than when I married you." "I was well-off before marrying you," said
Medb. "It was wealth that we had not heard of and did not know of," said Ailill, "but
you were a woman of property, and foes from lands next to you were carrying off
spoils and booty from you."

"I was not so," said Medb, "but my father was in the high-kingship of Ireland:[3]
Eochu Feidlech mac Find meic Findomain meic Findeoin meic Findguill meic Rotha
meic Rigéoin meic Blathachta meic Beothechta meic Enna Agnig meic Óengusa
Turbig. He had six daughters: Derbriu, Ethne and Éle, Clothru, Mugain and Medb. I
was the noblest and worthiest of them. I was the most generous of them in bounty
and the bestowal of gifts. I was best of them in battle and fight and combat.[4] I had fifteen hundred royal mercenaries of the sons of strangers exiled from their own land
and as many of the sons of native freemen within the province. And there were ten
men for each mercenary of these, and nine men for every mercenary and eight men
for every mercenary, and seven for every mercenary, and six for every mercenary,
and five for every mercenary, and four for every mercenary, and three for every mercenary, and two for every mercenary, and one mercenary for every mercenary. I had
these as my standing household," said Medb, "and for that reason my father gave me
one of the provinces of Ireland, the province of Crúachu. So I am called Medb
Chrúachna.

"Messengers came from Find mac Rosa Rúaid, the King of Leinster, to court me,
and from Cairbre Nia Fer mac Rosa, the King of Tara, and they came from Conchobor mac Fachtna, the King of Ulster, and they came from Eochu Bec. But I did not
consent, for I demanded a strange bride-gift such as no woman before me had asked
of a man of the men of Ireland: a husband without miserliness, without jealousy,
without fear. If my husband should be miserly, it would not be fitting for us to be
together, for I am generous in largesse and the bestowal of gifts and it would be a
reproach for my husband that I should be better than he in generosity, but it would
be no reproach if we were equal, provided that both of us were generous. Nor would
it be fitting for us to be together if my husband were timorous, for single-handed I
am victorious in battles and contests and combats, and it would be a reproach to my
husband that his wife should be more courageous than he, but it is no reproach if
they are equal, provided that both are courageous. Nor would it be fitting if the man

---

1. Translated by Cecile O'Rahilly, in a translation
accompanying her scholarly edition of *The Táin* for the
Irish Texts Society (1967). As given here, some phrasings
have been modified to improve its readability as a free-
standing text.
2. Ráth Crúachain, the royal fortress of Connacht. Like
many fortress towns in Irish legend, it was founded by a
woman (Cruacha) and retained traces of its ancient role
as a sacred place.
3. Early Ireland was ruled by a shifting company of petty

kings, some of whom entered into clientship, a relationship of dependence and service, with "high kings." The
idea of a high king of all Ireland was pure legend until
long after the era of the *Táin*. The genealogy that follows
(both "mac" and "meic" mean "son of") grounds the
claim to kingship.
4. Medb's wealth and military resources probably derive
from her namesake, the goddess of sovereignty on whose
assent (and sometimes sexual favors) the kingship
depended.

with whom I should be were jealous, for I was never without one lover quickly succeeding another.

Now I have just such a husband: you, Ailill mac Rosa Rúaid of Leinster. You are
not miserly, you are not jealous, you are not inactive. I gave you a contract and a
bride-price as befits a woman: the raiment of twelve men, a chariot worth thrice seven
cumala,[5] the breadth of your face in red gold, the weight of your left arm in white
bronze. Whoever brings shame and annoyance and confusion on you, you have no
claim for compensation or for honor-price for it except what claim I have," said
Medb, "for you are a man dependent on a woman's marriage-portion."

"I was not so," said Ailill, "but I had two brothers, one of them reigning over Tara,
the other over Leinster, Find over Leinster and Cairbre over Tara. I left the rule to them
because of their seniority but they were no better in bounty and the bestowal of gifts than
I. And I heard of no province in Ireland dependent on a woman except this province
alone, so I came and assumed the kingship here in virtue of my mother's rights, for Máta
Muirisc the daughter of Mága was my mother. And what better queen could I have than
you, for you are the daughter of the high-king of Ireland." "Nevertheless," said Medb,
"my property is greater than yours." "I marvel at that," said Ailill, "for there is none who
has greater possessions and riches and wealth than I, and I know that there is not."

They had brought to them what was least valuable among their possessions that
they might know which of them had more goods and riches and wealth. They had
brought to them their wooden cups and their vats and their iron vessels, their cans, their
washing-basins and their tubs. They had brought to them their rings and their bracelets
and their thumb-rings, their treasures of gold and their garments, purple as well as blue
and black and green, yellow and vari-colored and gray, dun and checkered and striped.

Their great flocks of sheep were brought from fields and lawns and open plains.
They were counted and reckoned and it was recognized that they were equal, of the
same size and of the same number. Among Medb's sheep there was a splendid ram
which was the equivalent of a *cumal* in value, but among Ailill's sheep was a ram corresponding to him. From grazing lands and paddocks were brought their horses and
steeds. In Medb's horse-herd there was a splendid horse which might be valued at a
cumal. Ailill had a horse to match him. Then their great herds of swine were brought
from woods and sloping glens and solitary places. They were counted and reckoned
and recognized. Medb had a special boar and Ailill had another. Then their herds of
cows, their cattle and their droves were brought to them from the woods and waste
places of the province. They were counted and reckoned and recognized, and they
were of equal size and equal number.

But among Ailill's cows there was a special bull. He had been a calf of one of
Medb's cows, and his name was Findbennach.[6] But he deemed it unworthy of him to
be counted as a woman's property, so he went and took his place among the king's
cows. It seemed to Medb as if she owned not a penny of possessions since she had not
a bull as great as that among her kine.

Then Mac Roth the herald was summoned to Medb and she asked him to find
out where in any province of Ireland there might be a bull such as he. "I know
indeed," said Mac Roth, "where there is a bull even better and more excellent than

---

5. An amount usually set at the value of three milch cows.
6. A gigantic, blood-red bull with white head and feet.
He and Donn Cúailnge, the Brown Bull of Cooley, are
the final incarnation of two pig-keepers who fought over
their supernatural powers in a series of animal and human
shapes.

he, in the province of Ulster in the cantred of Cúailnge[7] in the house of Dáire mac Fiachna. Donn Cúailnge is his name." "Go you there, Mac Roth, and ask of Dáire for me a year's loan of Donn Cúailnge. At the year's end he will get the fee for the bull's loan, namely, fifty heifers, and Donn Cúailnge himself returned. And take another offer with you, Mac Roth: if the people of that land and country object to giving that precious possession Donn Cúailnge, let Dáire himself come with his bull and he shall have the extent of his own lands in the level plain of Mag Aí and a chariot worth thrice seven *cumala,* and he shall have my own intimate friendship."

Then the messengers proceeded to the house of Dáire mac Fiachna. The number of Mac Roth's embassy was nine messengers. Mac Roth was welcomed in the house of Dáire. That was only right for Mac Roth was the chief herald of all. Dáire asked Mac Roth what was the cause of his journey and why he had come. The herald told why he had come and related the contention between Medb and Ailill. "So I have come to ask for a loan of the Donn Cúailnge to match the Findbennach," he said, "and you shall get the fee for his loan, fifty heifers and the return of Donn Cúailnge himself. And there is something more: come yourself with your bull and you shall get an area equal to your own lands in the level plain of Mag Aí and a chariot worth thrice seven *cumala* and Medb's intimate friendship to boot." Dáire was well pleased with that and in his pleasure he shook himself so that the seams of the flock-bed cushions beneath him burst asunder, and he said: "By the truth of my conscience, even if the Ulstermen object, this precious possession Donn Cúailnge, will now be taken to Ailill and Medb in the land of Connacht." Mac Roth was pleased to hear what Mac Fiachna said.

Then they were attended to and straw and fresh rushes were strewn underfoot for them. The choicest food was served to them and a drinking feast provided until they were merry. And a conversation took place between two of the messengers. "Truly," said one messenger, "our host is generous." "Generous indeed," said the other. "Is there any Ulsterman who is more generous than he?" said the first messenger. "There is indeed," said the second. "More generous is Conchobor[8] whose vassal Dáire is, and it would be no shame if all Ulstermen should rally round Conchobor." "A great act of generosity it is indeed for Dáire to have given Donn Cúailnge to us nine messengers! It would have been the work of the four great provinces of Ireland to carry him off from the land of Ulster." Then a third messenger joined their conversation. "And what are you saying?" he asked. "That messenger says that the man in whose house we are is a generous man." "He is generous indeed," says another. "Is there any Ulsterman who is more generous than he?" asks the first messenger. "There is indeed," says the second. "Conchobor, whose vassal Dáire is, is more generous, and if all Ulstermen adhered to him it would indeed be no shame for them. It was generous of Dáire to give to us nine messengers what only the four great provinces of Ireland could carry off from the land of Ulster." "I should like to see a gush of blood and gore from the mouth that says that, for if the bull were not given willingly, he would be given perforce."

Then Dáire mac Fiachna's butler came into the house with a man carrying liquor and another carrying meat, and he heard what the messengers said. He flew into a passion and laid down the meat and drink for them; he did not invite them to consume it, nor did he tell them not to consume it. He went to the house where Dáire mac Fiachna was and said: "Was it you who gave that excellent treasure, the Donn

---

7. An outlying district on the east coast of Ireland.   8. High king of Ulster and the husband of Medb before her marriage to Ailill.

Cúailnge, to the messengers?" "It was I indeed", said Dáire. "Where he was given may there be no proper rule, for they rightly say that if you do not give him of your own free will, you will give him by force, thanks to the armies of Ailill and Medb and the guidance of Fergus mac Róig."[9] "I swear by the gods whom I worship,"[1] Dáire replied, "unless they take him by force, they shall not take him by fair means." They spent the night talking until morning.

Early next day the messengers arose and went into the house where Dáire was. "Guide us, noble sir, to the spot where Donn Cúailnge is." "Not so indeed," said Dáire, "but if it were my custom to deal treacherously with messengers or travelers or voyagers not one of you should escape alive." "What is this?" said Mac Roth. "There is great cause for it," said Dáire. "You said that if I did not give the bull willingly, then I should give him under compulsion from the army of Ailill and Medb and the sure guidance of Fergus." "Nay," said Mac Roth, "whatever messengers might say as a result of indulging in your meat and drink, it should not be heeded or noticed nor accounted as a reproach to Ailill and Medb." "Yet I shall not give my bull, Mac Roth, on this occasion."

The messengers went on their way home and reached Ráth Crúachan in Connacht. Medb asked tidings of them. Mac Roth told her that they had not brought back his bull from Dáire. "What was the cause of that?" asked Medb. Mac Roth told her the reason. "There is no necessity to 'smooth the knots,' Mac Roth, for it was certain," said Medb, "that he would not be given freely if he were not given by force. So he shall be given by force."

Messengers went from Medb to the Maines[2] to bid them come to Crúachu, the seven Maines with their seven divisions of three thousand, namely, Maine Máithremail, Maine Aithremail, Maine Condagaib Uile, Maine Míngor, Maine Mórgor and Maine Conda Mó Epert. Other messengers went to the sons of Mágu,[3] namely Cet mac Mágach, Anlúan mac Mágach, Mac Corb mac Mágach, Baiscell mac Mágach, Én mac Mágach, Dóche mac Mágach and Scannal mac Mágach. These arrived, in number three thousand armed men. Other messengers went from them to Cormac Cond Longas mac Conchobuir[4] and to Fergus mac Róig, and they too came, in number three thousand.

The first band of all had shorn heads of hair. Green cloaks about them with silver brooches in them. Next to their skin they wore shirts of gold thread with insertions of red gold. They carried swords with white grips and handles of silver. "Is that Cormac yonder?" they all asked. "It is not indeed," said Medb.

The second band had newly shorn heads of hair. They wore gray cloaks and pure white shirts next to their skins. They carried swords with round guards of gold and silver handles. "Is that Cormac yonder?" they all asked. "It is not he indeed," said Medb.

The last band had flowing hair, fair-yellow, golden, streaming manes. They wore purple embroidered cloaks with golden inset brooches over their breasts. They had smooth, long, silken shirts reaching to their insteps. All together they would lift their feet and set them down again. "Is that Cormac yonder?" they all asked. "It is he indeed," said Medb.

---

9. Fergus mac Róig (or mac Roich) warrior, poet, and prophet—had been king of Ulster before Conchobor took the throne from him. Conchobor had further violated Fergus's honor by arranging the murder of men who were under his protection, after which Fergus and Ulstermen loyal to him fled into Connacht. He became an advisor to Ailill and one of Medb's many lovers.

1. A conscious historicizing reference to the polytheism of the era of the Táin.

2. The seven sons of Medb and Ailill. Only six are listed here: their names mean the Motherlike, the Fatherlike, he of All the Qualities, the Sweetly Dutiful, the Strongly Dutiful, and Above Description.

3. Another group of Connacht warriors; Cet ultimately kills Conchobor.

4. Cormac, "Leader of the Exiles," is a son of Conchobor who had fled with Fergus and entered the service of Ailill and Medb.

That night they pitched their camp and stronghold and there was a dense mass of smoke and fire from their camp-fires between the four fords of Aí, Áth Moga, Áth mBercna, Áth Slissen and Áth Coltna. And they stayed for a full fortnight in Ráth Crúachan of Connacht drinking and feasting and merrymaking so that their journey and hosting should be the lighter for them. And then Medb bade her charioteer harness her horses for her that she might go to speak with her druid[5] to seek foreknowledge and prophecy from him.

When Medb came to where her druid was, she asked foreknowledge and prophecy of him. "There are many who part here today from comrades and friends," said Medb, "from land and territory, from father and mother, and if not all return safe and sound, it is on me their grumbles and their curses will fall. Yet none goes forth and none stays here who is any dearer to us than we ourselves. And find out for us whether we shall come back or not." And the druid said: "Whoever comes or comes not back, you yourself will come."

The driver turned the chariot and Medb returned. She saw something that she deemed wonderful, a woman coming towards her by the shaft of the chariot. The girl was weaving a fringe, holding a weaver's beam of white bronze in her right hand with seven strips of red gold on its points. She wore a spotted, green-speckled cloak, with a round, heavy-headed brooch in the cloak above her breast. She had a crimson, rich-blooded countenance, a bright, laughing eye, thin, red lips. She had shining pearly teeth; you would have thought they were showers of fair pearls which were displayed in her head. Like new *partaing* [crimson] were her lips. The sweet sound of her voice and speech was as melodious as the strings of harps plucked by the hands of masters. As white as snow falling at night was the luster of her skin and body shining through her garments. She had long and very white feet with pink, even, round and sharp nails. She had long, fair-yellow, golden hair; three tresses of her hair wound round her head, another tress falling behind which touched the calves of her legs.

Medb gazed at her. "And what are you doing here now, girl?" said Medb. "I am promoting your interest and your prosperity, gathering and mustering the four great provinces of Ireland with you to go into Ulster for Táin Bó Cúailnge." "Why do you do that for me?" said Medb. "I have good reason to do so. I am a bondmaid of your people." "Who of my people are you?" said Medb. "That is not hard to tell. I am Feidelm the prophetess from Síd Chrúachna."[6] "Well then, Feidelm Prophetess, how do you see our army?" "I see red on them. I see crimson."

"Conchobor is suffering in his debility in Emain,"[7] said Medb. "My messengers have gone to him. There is nothing we fear from the Ulstermen. But tell the truth, Feidelm. O Feidelm Prophetess, how do you see our army?" "I see red on them. I see crimson."

"Cuscraid Mend Macha mac Conchobuir is in Inis Cuscraid in his debility.[8] My messengers have gone to him. There is nothing we fear from the Ulstermen. But speak truth, Feidelm. O Feidelm Prophetess, how do you see our army?" "I see red upon them. I see crimson."

---

5. Another archaizing touch. The Druids had been a pagan priestly class, expert in prophecy.
6. The *Síd* was a fairy mound or underground dwelling of the superhuman races who preceded men in Ireland; Feidelm claims to come from one near Medb's capital. Her weaving may be a part of prophetic ritual.
7. Macha, a goddess of war, had come among the Ulstermen in human guise. Conchobor forced her to race with his horses even though she was pregnant. She won but gave birth just over the finish line; she cursed the Ulstermen to suffer in times of danger a period of weakness like that of a woman in labor. Only women, children, and Cú Chulainn were exempt. Emain is Conchobor's capital.
8. Cuscraid is a son of Conchobor, suffering at his island fort.

"Eogan mac Durthacht is at Ráth Airthir in his debility. My messengers have gone to him. There is nothing we fear from the Ulstermen. But speak truth to us, Feidelm. O Feidelm Prophetess, how do you see our army?" "I see red on them. I see crimson."

"Celtchair mac Cuthechair is in his fortress in his debility. My messengers have reached him. There is nothing we fear from the Ulstermen. But speak truth, Feidelm. O Feidelm Prophetess, how do you see our army?" "I see red on them. I see crimson."

"I care not for your reasoning, for when the men of Ireland[9] gather in one place, among them will be strife and battle and broils and affrays, in dispute as to who shall lead the van or bring up the rear or first cross ford or river or first kill swine or cow or stag or game. But speak truth to us, Feidelm. O Feidelm Prophetess, how do you see our army?" "I see red on them. I see crimson."

And Feidelm began to prophesy and foretell Cú Chulainn[1] to the men of Ireland, and she chanted a lay:

"I see a fair man who will perform weapon-feats,
with many a wound in his fair flesh.
The hero's light is on his brow,
his forehead is the meeting-place of many virtues.

"Seven gems of a hero are in his eyes.
His spear-heads are unsheathed.
He wears a red mantle with clasps.

"His face is the fairest. He amazes womenfolk,
a young lad of handsome countenance;
yet in battle he shows a dragon's form.

"His strength is that of Cú Chulainn of Muirthemne;
I know not who is this Cú Chulainn from Muirthemne,
but this I know:
this army will be bloodstained from him.

"Four excellent daggers he has in each hand;
he will manage to ply them on the host.
Each weapon has its own special use.

"When he carries his *ga bulga*[2]
and his sword and spear,
this man wrapped in red
sets his foot on every battle-field.

"His two spears across his chariot's wheel-rim,
high above valor is the distorted one.[3]
So he has appeared to me before,
but he will change his appearance again.

9. The alliance of armies grouped against Ulster, sometimes specifically those allies who are not men of Connacht. In legendary times, Ulster had been the dominant province, and the *Táin* may reflect early conflicts that reduced Ulster's power and size.
1. Cú Chulainn, the "hound of Culann," so named for a boyhood feat in which he killed the savage guard dog of Culann the Smith, then offered to guard Culann's house in the dog's place.
2. The "belly spear" is one of Cú Chulainn's magical weapons, the gift of the woman warrior who trained him in arms. Once it enters the body, it opens into 30 barbs.
3. In his battle frenzy Cú Chulainn undergoes a monstrous distortion or "warp-spasm," one eye swelling over his cheek, a beam of light leaping from his forehead, and blood erupting from his skull.

"He has moved forward to the battle.
If he is not warded off, there will be destruction.
It is he who seeks you in combat:
Cú Chulainn mac Sualtaim.

"He will lay low your entire army,
and he will slaughter you in dense crowds.
Ye shall leave with him all your heads—
the prophetess Feidelm conceals it not.

"Blood will flow from heroes' bodies.
Long will it be remembered:
Men's bodies will be hacked, women will lament,
through the Hound of the Smith that I see."

This has been the prophecy and augury, and the prelude to the tale, the basis of its invention and composition, and the pillow-talk held by Ailill and Medb in Crúachu.

[The Táin Begins]

This is the route of the Táin and the beginning of the army's march together with the names of the roads on which the men of the four great provinces of Ireland traveled into the land of Ulster:[1]

To Mag Cruinn, by way of Tuaim Móna, by Turloch Teóra Crích, by Cúl Sílinne, by Dubfid, by Badbna, by Coltan, across the river Shannon, by Glúine Gabur, by Mag Trega, by northern Tethba, by southern Tethba, by Cúil, by Ochain, by Uata northwards, by Tiarthechta eastwards, by Ord, by Slass, across the river Inneoin, by Carn, across Meath, by Ortrach, by Findglassa Asail, by Drong, by Delt, by Duelt, by Deland, by Selach, by Slabra, by Slechta which was cleared by swords for Medb and Ailill's passage, by Cúil Siblinne, by Dub, by Ochan, by Catha, by Cromma, by Tromma, by Fodromma, by Sláine by Gort Sláine, by Druimm Licci, by Áth nGabla, by Ardachad, by Feoraind, by Findabair, by Aisse, by Airne, by Aurthaile, by Druimm Salaind, by Druimm Caín, by Druimm Caimthechta, by Druimm mac nDega, by Eódond Bec, by Eódond Mór, by Méide in Togmaill, by Méide ind Eoin, by Baile, by Aile, by Dall Scena, by Ball Scena, by Ros Mór, by Scúap, by Timscúap, by Cend Ferna, by Ammag, by Fid Mór in Crannach Cúailnge, by Druimm Caín to Slige Midlúachra.

After the first day's march, the armies spent that night in Cúil Silinne and Ailill mac Rosa's tent was pitched for him. Fergus mac Róich's tent was on his right hand. Cormac Cond Longas mac Conchobuir was beside Fergus. Íth mac Étgaíth was next, then Fiachu mac Fir Aba, then Goibnend mac Lurgnig. Such was the placing of Ailill's tent on his right during that hosting, and thus were the thirty hundred men of Ulster at his right hand so that the confidential talk and discourse and the choicest portions of food and drink might be nearer to them. Medb Chrúachna was on Ailill's left with Findabair[2] beside her. Then came Flidais Fholtchaín, the wife of Ailill Find, who had slept with Fergus on Táin Bó Cúailnge, and it was she who every seventh night on that hosting quenched with milk the thirst of all the men of Ireland, king and queen and prince, poet and learner. Medb was the last of the hosts that day for

---

1. The following catalog of place-names, along with genealogies elsewhere, is typical of the encyclopedic impulse in the *Táin*. Much of the list can be traced on a map, though it diverges from the armies' route in the nar-rative that follows.

2. The daughter of Medb and Ailill, used more than once by Medb as a sexual pawn.

she had been seeking foreknowledge and prophecy and tidings, to learn who was loath and who was eager to go on the expedition. Medb did not permit her chariot to be let down or her horses to be unyoked until she had made a circuit of the encampment.

[THE LAST BATTLE][1]

In the same night Dubthach Dáel Ulad spoke these words among the men of Ireland in Slemain Mide: *Móra maitne. . . .* [2]

Then Dubthach awoke from his sleep and the Nemain[3] brought confusion on the host so that they made a clangor of arms with the points of their spears and their swords, and a hundred warriors of them died on the floor of their encampment through the fearsomeness of the shout they had raised. This was not the most peaceful night ever experienced by the men of Ireland, because of the prophecies and the predictions and because of the specters and visions which appeared to them.

Then said Ailill: "I have succeeded in laying waste Ulster and the land of the Picts from the Monday at the beginning of Samain until the beginning of spring.[4] We have carried off their women-folk, their sons and their youths, their horses and steeds, their flocks and herds and cattle. We have leveled their hills behind them into lowlands, so that they might be of equal height. So I shall not wait here for them any longer, but let them give me battle on Mag Aí if they like. And yet though we say this, let some one go forth to reconnoiter the broad plain of Meath to see whether the Ulstermen come there, and if they do, I shall not retreat, for it is not the good custom of a king ever to retreat." "Who should go there?" everyone said: "Who but Mac Roth, the chief messenger yonder."

Mac Roth went out to reconnoiter the great plain of Meath. Soon he heard a noise and a tumult and a clamor. It seemed to him almost as if the sky had fallen onto the surface of the earth, or as if the fish-abounding, blue-bordered sea had swept across the face of the world, or as if the earth had split in an earthquake, or as if the trees of the forest had all fallen into each other's forked trunks and branches. The wild beasts were fleeing across the plain in such numbers that the surface of the plain of Meath was not visible beneath them.

Mac Roth went to where Ailill was with Medb and Fergus and the nobles of the men of Ireland. He related those tidings to them. "What was that, Fergus?" asked Ailill. "Not difficult to tell," said Fergus. "The noise and clamor and tumult that he heard, the din and the thunder and the uproar, were the Ulstermen attacking the wood, the throng of champions and warriors cutting down the trees with their swords in front of their chariots. It was that which scattered the wild beasts across the plain so that the surface of the plain of Meath is not visible beneath them."

1. In the intervening episodes, the men of Ireland do succeed in seizing the Brown Bull of Cooley. The armies of Medb and Ailill also move around a large part of central and northern Ireland, trying to penetrate the borders of Ulster. Cú Chulainn repeatedly prevents this, despite the continuing weakness of the Ulstermen. He first places impassable taboo signs along their route, then stages night raids on the armies, and finally conducts an exhausting series of single combats, mostly at fords, which climax in a three-day battle with his beloved foster-brother Ferdia. In the face of his onslaught and the gathering army of the now-strong Ulstermen, the men of Ireland have retreated into Meath, moving back toward Connacht. Near collapse, Cú Chulainn is guarded by his father the god Lug and tied down with wooden hoops lest

he return to battle and injure himself mortally.
2. The black-tongued, another Ulster warrior, appears to have a prophetic vision in his sleep and calls out to the men around him. His words are in a form and vocabulary of virtually untranslatable obscurity, called "rosc." A series of such archaic and obscure prophecies punctuates the later parts of the story (see page 106) and is left untranslated here.
3. Panic, one of a group of war goddesses and wife of the war god, Net.
4. Samain is a pre-Christian festival in late fall. The Ulstermen have suffered from their debility for most of the time from then until spring, which may link their weakness and returning strength to seasonal cycles and even vegetation ritual.

Once more Mac Roth scanned the plain. He saw a great gray mist which filled the void between heaven and earth. He seemed to see islands in lakes above the slopes of the mist. He seemed to see yawning caverns in the forefront of the mist itself. It seemed to him that pure-white linen cloths or sifted snow dropping down appeared through a rift in the same mist. He seemed to see a large flock of varied, wonderful birds, or the shimmering of shining stars on a bright, frosty night, or the sparks of a blazing fire. He heard a noise and a tumult, a din and thunder, a clamor and uproar. He went to tell those tidings to Ailill and Medb and Fergus and the nobles of the men of Ireland. He told them these things.

"What was that, Fergus?" asked Ailill. "Not difficult to tell," said Fergus. "The gray mist he saw which filled the void between earth and sky was the breathing of horses and heroes, and the cloud of dust from the ground and from the roads which rises above them driven by the wind so that it becomes a heavy, deep-gray mist in the clouds and in the air.

"The islands in lakes which he saw there, and the tops of hills and mounds rising above the valleys of the mist, were the heads of the heroes and warriors above their chariots and the chariots themselves. The yawning caverns he saw there in the forefront of the same mist were the mouths and nostrils of horses and heroes, exhaling and inhaling the sun and the wind with the swiftness of the host.

"The pure-white linen cloths he saw there or the sifted snow dropping down were the foam and froth that the bits of the reins cast from the mouths of the strong, stout steeds with the fierce rush of the host. The large flock of varied, wonderful birds which he saw there was the dust of the ground and the surface of the earth which the horses flung up from their feet and their hooves and which rose above them with the driving of the wind.

"The noise and the tumult, the din and the thunder, the clamor and the outcry which he heard there was the shock of shields and the smiting of spears and the loud striking of swords, the clashing of helmets, the clangor of breastplates, the friction of the weapons and the vehemence of the feats of arms, the straining of ropes, the rattle of wheels, the trampling of the horses' hoofs and the creaking of chariots, and the loud voices of heroes and warriors coming towards us here.

"The shimmering of shining stars on a bright night that he saw there, or the sparks of a blazing fire, were the fierce, fearsome eyes of the warriors and heroes from the beautiful, shapely, ornamented helmets, eyes full of the fury and anger with which they came, against which neither equal combat nor overwhelming number prevailed at any time and against which none will ever prevail until the day of doom."

"We make little account of it," said Medb. "Goodly warriors and goodly soldiers will be found among us to oppose them." "I do not count on that, Medb," said Fergus, "for I pledge my word that you will not find in Ireland or in Alba a host which could oppose the Ulstermen when once their fits of wrath come upon them."

The four great provinces of Ireland made their encampment at Clártha that night. They left a band to keep watch and guard against the Ulstermen lest they should come upon them unawares.

Conchobor and Celtchair set forth with thirty hundred chariot-fighters armed with spears and halted in Slemain Mide[5] in the rear of the host. But though we say "halted," they did not halt completely, but soon came forward to the encampment of Medb and Ailill in an attempt to be the first to shed blood. * * *[6]

---

5. In Meath, between Ulster and Connacht. The men of Ulster are now pursuing Medb and Ailill.

6. At this point more Ulster warriors assemble to oppose Medb and Ailill.

"Come now, men of Ireland," said Ailill, "let someone go to reconnoiter the broad plain of Meath to find out how the Ulstermen come to the hill in Slemain Mide and to give us an account of their arms and equipment, their heroes and soldiers and their battle-champions and the people of their land. It will be all the more pleasant for us to listen to him now." "Who should go there?" asked they all. "Who but Mac Roth, the chief messenger," said Ailill.

Mac Roth came forward and took up his station in Slemain Mide to await the Ulstermen. The Ulstermen began to muster on that hill and continued doing so from the twilight of early morning until sunset. In all that time the ground was hardly bare of them as they came with every division round its king, every band round its leader, and every king and every leader and every lord with the full number of his own forces and his army, his muster and his gathering. Before the hour of evening sunset all the Ulstermen had reached that hill in Slemain Mide.

Mac Roth went to Ailill and Medb and Fergus and the nobles of the men of Ireland, bringing an account of the first band. Ailill and Medb asked tidings of him on his arrival. "Well now, O Mac Roth," said Ailill, "in what guise and fashion do the men of Ulster come to the hill in Slemain Mide?"

"This is all I know," said Mac Roth. "There came a fierce, powerful, well-favored band onto that hill in Slemain Mide. It seems, if one looks at it, as if it numbered thirty hundred. They all cast off their garments and dug up a mound of turf as a seat for their leader. A warrior, slender, very tall, of great stature and of proud mien, at the head of that band. Finest of the princes of the world was he among his troops, in fearsomeness and horror, in battle and in contention. Fair yellow hair he had, curled, well-arranged, ringletted, cut short. His countenance was comely and clear crimson. An eager gray eye in his head, fierce and awe-inspiring. A forked beard, yellow and curly, on his chin. A purple mantle fringed, five-folded, about him and a golden brooch in the mantle over his breast. A pure-white, hooded shirt with inserts of red gold he wore next to his white skin. He carried a white shield ornamented with animal designs in red gold. In one hand he had a gold-hilted, ornamented sword, in the other a broad, gray spear. That warrior took up position at the top of the hill and everyone came to him and his company took their places around him.

"There came also another band to the same hill in Slemain Mide," said Mac Roth. "It numbered almost thirty hundred. A handsome man in the forefront of that same band. Fair yellow hair he had. A bright and very curly beard on his chin. A green mantle wrapped around him. A pure silver brooch in the mantle over his breast. A dark-red, soldierly tunic with insertion of red gold next to his fair skin and reaching to his knees. A spear like the torch of a royal palace in his hand, with bands of silver and rings of gold. Wonderful are the feats and games performed by that spear in the warrior's hand. The silver bands revolve round the golden rings alternately from butt to socket, and the golden rings revolve round the silver bands from socket to thong. He bore a smiting shield with scalloped rim. On his left side a sword with guards of ivory and ornament of gold thread. That warrior sat on the left hand of the warrior who had first come to the hill, and his company sat around him. But though we say that they sat, yet they did not really do so, but knelt on the ground with the rim of their shields at their chins, in their eagerness to be let at us. And yet it seemed to me that the tall, fierce warrior who led that company stammered greatly.

"Yet another company came to the same hill in Slemain Mide," said Mac Roth, "very like the preceding one in number and appearance and apparel. A handsome, broad-headed warrior in the van of that company. Thick, dark-yellow hair he had.

An eager, dark-blue, restless eye in his head. A bright and very curly beard, forked and tapering, on his chin. A dark-gray, fringed cloak wrapped about him. A leaf-shaped brooch of white bronze in the cloak over his breast. A white-hooded shirt next to his skin. A white shield with animal ornaments of silver he carried. A sword with rounded hilt of bright silver in a warlike scabbard at his waist. A spear like the pillar of a palace on his back. This warrior sat on the turfy mound in front of the warrior who had come first to the hill, and his company took up their positions around him. But sweeter I thought than the sound of lutes in the hands of expert players was the melodious tone of the voice and speech of that warrior as he addressed the warrior who had come first to the hill and gave him counsel."

"Who are those?" asked Ailill of Fergus. "We know them indeed," said Fergus. "The first warrior for whom the sodded mound was cast up on the top of the hill until they all came to him was Conchobor mac Fachtna Fáthaig meic Rosa Rúaid meic Rudraige, the high-king of Ulster and the son of the high-king of Ireland. The great stammering hero who took up his position on the left of Conchobor was Causcraid Mend Macha, the son of Conchobar, with the sons of the Ulster princes around him and the sons of the kings of Ireland who are with him. The spear with silver bands and rings of gold that Mac Roth saw in his hand is called the Torch of Causcraid. With that spear, the silver bands do not revolve around the golden rings except shortly before some victory, and not at any other time, and it is likely that they are now revolving just before victory.

"The handsome, broad-headed warrior who sat on the mound in front of the warrior who had first come to the hill was Sencha mac Ailella meic Máilchló, the eloquent speaker of Ulster, the man who appeases the armies of the men of Ireland. But I pledge my word that he is not giving his lord counsel of cowardice or fear in this day of battle, but counsel to act with valor and bravery, courage and might. And I pledge my word too," said Fergus, "that those who rose up around Conchobor in the early morning today are fine men who can carry out such deeds." "We care little for them," said Medb. "There will be found among us fine heroes and fine warriors to answer them." "I don't count on that," said Fergus, "but I swear that you will not find in Ireland or in Alba an army which can answer the Ulstermen when once their fits of wrath have come upon them."[7] * * *

"Yet another company came to the same hill in Slemain Mide," said Mac Roth, "which numbered no less than thirty hundred. Fierce, bloodstained warrior bands. Fair, clear, blue and crimson men. They had long, fair-yellow hair, beautiful, brilliant countenances, clear kingly eyes. Shining, beautiful garments they wore. Wonderful, golden brooches on their bright-hued arms. Silken, fine-textured shirts. Shining, blue spears they carried. Yellow, smiting shields. Gold-hilted ornamented swords are set on their thighs. Loud-voiced care has come to them. Sad are all the horsemen. Sorrowful are the royal leaders. Orphaned the bright company without their protecting lord who used to defend their borders." "Who are these?" asked Ailill of Fergus. "We know them indeed," said Fergus. "They are fierce lions. They are champions of battle. They are the thirty hundred from Mag Muirtheimne. The reason they are downcast, sorrowful and joyless, is because their territorial king is not among them— Cú Chulainn, the restraining, victorious, red-sworded, triumphant one." "They have good cause," said Medb, "to be downcast, sorrowful and joyless, for there is no evil we have not wrought on them. We have plundered them and we have ravaged them

---

7. In the following section, omitted here, Mac Roth continues with a catalog of 16 more war bands and their leaders, coming to support Conchobor.

from the Monday at the beginning of Samain until the beginning of spring. We have carried off their women and their sons and their youths, their horses and their steeds, their herds and their flocks and their cattle. We have cast down their hills behind them on to their slopes until they were of equal height." "You have no reason to boast over them, Medb," said Fergus, "for you did no harm or wrong to them that the leader of that fine band yonder has not avenged on you, since every mound and every grave, every tombstone and every tomb from here to the eastern part of Ireland is a mound and a grave, a tombstone and a tomb for some fine hero or for some brave warrior slain by the valiant leader of yonder band. Fortunate is he whom they will uphold! Woe to him whom they will oppose! They alone will be as much as half an army against the men of Ireland when they defend their lord in the battle tomorrow morning."

"I heard a great outcry there," said Mac Roth, "to the west of the battle or to the east of the battle." "What outcry was that?" asked Ailill of Fergus. "We know it indeed," said Fergus. "That was Cú Chulainn trying to come to the battle when he was being laid prostrate on his sick-bed in Fert Sciach, with wooden hoops and restraining bands and ropes holding him down, for the Ulstermen do not allow him to come because of his wounds and gashes, for he is unfit for battle and combat after his fight with Ferdia."

It was as Fergus said. That was Cú Chulainn being laid prostrate on his sick-bed in Fert Sciach, held down with hoops and restraining bands and ropes.

Then two female satirists called Fethan and Collach came out of the encampment of the men of Ireland. They pretended to weep and lament over Cú Chulainn, telling him that the Ulstermen had been routed and that Conchobor had been killed and that Fergus had fallen in the fight against them.

It was on that night that the Morrígu daughter of Ernmas[8] came and sowed strife and dissension between the two encampments on either side, and she spoke these words: *Crennait brain*. . . . She whispered to the Érainn[9] that they will not fight the battle which lies ahead.

Then said Cú Chulainn to Láeg mac Riangabra[1]: "Alas for you, my friend Láeg, if anything happens today between the two battle-forces that you don't find out for me." "Whatever I find out, little Cú," said Láeg, "shall be told to you. But see a little flock coming from the west out of the encampment now onto the plain. There is a band of youths after them to check and hold them. See too a band of youths coming from the east out of the encampment to seize them." "That is true indeed," said Cú Chulainn. "It is the omen of a mighty combat and a cause of great strife. The little flock will go across the plain and the youths from the east will encounter those from the west." It was as Cú Chulainn said: The little flock went across the plain and the youths met. "Who gives battle now, my friend Láeg?" asked Cú Chulainn. "The people of Ulster," said Láeg, "that is, the youths."[2] "How do they fight?" asked Cú Chulainn. "Bravely," said Láeg. "The champions who come from the east will make a breach through the battle-line to the west. The champions from the west will make a breach through the battle-line to the east." "Alas that I am not strong enough to go afoot among them! For if I were, my breach too would be clearly seen there today like

8. Morrígu (or Morrigan, later Morgan), Great Queen or Queen of Demons, the major goddess of war, a shapeshifter and sower of discord.
9. The men of Ireland, that is the allies of Medb and Ailill from outside Connacht, who now begin to withdraw their allegiance.
1. Láeg is Cú Chulainn's charioteer and trusted advisor.

2. These are probably the three boy troops who train in mock battles around Conchobor's capital. Cú Chulainn, when still a boy and untutored in the ways of court, had first challenged and then joined them. Because of their age they are untouched by the debility of the Ulstermen and rush into battle before their elders.

that of the rest." "Nay then, little Cú," said Láeg, "it is no disgrace to your valor and no reproach to your honor. You have done bravely before and you will do bravely again." "Well now, friend Láeg," said Cú Chulainn, "rouse the Ulstermen to the battle now; it is time for them to go."

Láeg came and roused the Ulstermen to the battle, and he spoke these words: *Coméirget ríg Macha*. . . .

Then all the Ulstermen rose up at the call of their king and at the behest of their lord and to answer the summons of Láeg mac Riangabra. They all arose stark naked except for their weapons which they bore in their hands. Each man whose tent door faced east would break westwards through his tent westwards, thinking it too long to go around.

"How do the men of Ulster rise for battle now, friend Láeg?" asked Cú Chulainn. "Bravely," answered Láeg. "All are stark naked. Each man whose tent-door faces east rushed westwards through his tent, thinking it too long to go around." "I pledge my word," said Cú Chulainn, "that their early rising around Conchobor is speedy help in answer to a call of alarm."

Then Conchobor said to Sencha mac Ailella: "Good master Sencha, hold back the men of Ulster, and do not let them come to the battle until omens and auguries are strongly in their favor and until the sun rises into the vaults of heaven and fills the glens and slopes, the hills and mounds of Ireland." There they remained until a good omen was strengthened and sunshine filled the glens and slopes and hills and mounds of the province.

"Good master Sencha," said Conchobor, "rouse the men of Ulster for battle; it is time for them to go." Sencha roused the men of Ulster for the fight, and he spoke the words: *Coméirget ríg Macha*. . . .

Láeg had not been there long when he saw all the men of Ireland rising together and taking up their shields and their spears and their swords and their helmets, and driving the troops before them to the battle. All the men of Ireland began to strike and smite, to hew and cut, to slay and slaughter the others for a long while. Then Cú Chulainn asked Láeg, his charioteer, when a bright cloud covered the sun: "How are they fighting the battle now, my friend Láeg?" "Bravely," said Láeg. "If we were to mount, I into my chariot and Conall's charioteer Én into his, and if we were to go in two chariots from one wing of the army to the other along the tips of their weapons, not a hoof nor a wheel nor an axle nor a shaft of those chariots would touch the ground, so densely, so firmly and so strongly are their weapons held in the hands of the soldiers." "Alas that I have not the strength to be among them!" said Cú Chulainn, "for if I had, my attack would be clearly seen there today like that of the rest." "Nay then, little Cú," said Láeg, "it is no disgrace to your valor and no reproach to your honor. You have done bravely before and you will do bravely again."

Then the men of Ireland began again to strike and smite, to hew and cut, to slay and slaughter the others for a long while. The nine chariot-fighters of the warriors of Irúad arrived and three men on foot together with them, and the nine chariot-riders were no swifter than the three on foot.

Then came also the *ferchuitredaig*, the triads of the men of Ireland, and their sole function in the battle was to slay Conchobor if he should be defeated and to rescue Ailill and Medb if it were they who were overcome. * * * [3]

---

3. There follows a catalog of these triads of warriors.

Then said Medb to Fergus: "It would be fitting for you to aid us unstintingly in fighting today, for you were banished from your territory and your land, and we gave you territory and land and property and showed you much kindness." "If I had my sword today," said Fergus, "I would cut them down so that the trunks of men would be piled high on the trunks of men and arms of men piled high on arms of men and the crowns of men's heads piled on the crowns of men's heads and men's heads piled on the edges of shields, and all the Ulstermen's limbs I would scatter to the east and to the west would be as numerous as pebbles between two dry fields along which a king's horses drive: if only I had my sword." Then Ailill said to his own charioteer, Fer Loga: "Bring me quickly the sword that wounds men's flesh, O fellow. I pledge my word that if you take worse care of it today than on the day when I gave it to you on the hillside at Crúachna Aí, even if the men of Ireland and of Alba are protecting you against me today, not all of them will save you."[4] Fer Loga came forward and brought the sword in all the beauty of its fair condition, shining bright as a torch, and the sword was given into Ailill's hand. Ailill gave the sword to Fergus and Fergus welcomed the sword: "Welcome to you, O Caladbolg, the sword of Leite," he said. "The champions of the war-goddess are weary. On whom shall I ply this sword?" asked Fergus. "On the hosts that surround you on all sides," said Medb. "Let none receive mercy or quarter from you today except a true friend."

Then Fergus seized his weapons and went forward to the battle. Ailill seized his weapons. Medb seized her weapons and came to the battle. Three times they were victorious in the battle northwards, until a phalanx of spears and swords forced them to retreat again. Conchobor heard from his place in the battle-line that the battle had three times gone against him in the north. Then he said to his people, the intimate household of the Cráebrúad: "Take my place a while, my men, so I can go and see who is victorious three times to the north of us." Then his household said: "We shall do so, for heaven is above us and earth beneath us and the sea all around us, and unless the firmament with its showers of stars fall upon the surface of the earth, or unless the blue-bordered fish-abounding sea come over the face of the world, or unless the earth quake, we shall never retreat one inch from this spot until you come back to us again."

Conchobor went where he had heard the rout of battle against him three times in the north, and against the shield of Fergus mac Róig he raised his shield, the Óchaín Conchobuir, with its four golden corners and its four coverings of red gold. Then Fergus gave three strong, warlike blows on the Óchaín Conchobuir and Conchobor's shield groaned. Whenever Conchobor's shield groaned, the shields of all the Ulstermen groaned. Strongly and violently as Fergus struck Conchobor's shield, just as stoutly and as bravely did Conchobor hold the shield, so that the corner of the shield did not even touch Conchobor's ear.

"Alas, my men!" said Fergus, "who is it who holds his shield against me today, in this day of conflict where the four great provinces of Ireland meet at Gáirech and Ilgáirech in the battle of the Foray of Cúailnge?" "There is a man here younger and mightier than you, whose father and mother were nobler, one who banished you from your land and territory and estate, one who drove you to dwell with deer and hare and fox, one who did not permit you to hold even the length of your own stride in

---

4. Ailill's charioteer had taken the sword when he spotted Fergus having sex with Medb, and Fergus was reduced to carrying a wooden sword. Ailill here reminds Fergus that he knows of the affair and leaves a hint of threat if Fergus does not use it well.

your land and territory, one who made you dependent on a woman of property, one who once outraged you by slaying the three sons of Usnech despite your safeguard, one who today will ward you off in the presence of the men of Ireland: Conchobor mac Fachtna Fáthaig meic Rossa Rúaid meic Rudraigi, the high king of Ulster and the son of the high king of Ireland."

"That is indeed what has happened," said Fergus. And Fergus grasped the Caladbolg in both hands and swung it back behind him so that its point touched the ground, and his intent was to strike three terrible and warlike blows on the Ulstermen so that their dead might outnumber their living. Cormac Cond Longas, the son of Conchobor, saw him; he rushed towards Fergus and clasped his arms about him. "Ready, yet not ready, my master Fergus. This is hostile and not friendly, my master Fergus. Ungentle but thoughtless, my master Fergus. Do not slay and destroy the Ulsterman with your mighty blows, but take thought for their honor on this day of battle." "Begone from me, lad," said Fergus, "for I shall not live if I do not strike my three mighty, warlike blows upon the Ulstermen today so that their living outnumber their dead."

"Turn your hand level," said Cormac Cond Longas, "and strike off the tops of the hills over the heads of the hosts; that will appease your anger." "Tell Conchobor to come then into his battle-position," Fergus replied. Conchobor came to his place in the battle.

Now that sword, the sword of Fergus, was the sword of Leite from the elfmounds. When one wished to strike with it, it was as big as a rainbow in the air. Then Fergus turned his hand level above the heads of the hosts and cut off the tops of the three hills which are still there in the marshy plain as evidence. Those are the three Máela of Meath.

Now as for Cú Chulainn, when he heard the Óchaín Conchobuir being struck by Fergus mac Róig, he said: "Come now, my friend Láeg, who dares to smite the Óchaín of Conchobor my master while I am alive?" "This huge sword, as big as a rainbow, sheds blood, increase of slaughter," said Láeg. "It is the hero Fergus mac Róig. The chariot sword was hidden in the fairy mounds. The horsemen of my master Conchobor have reached the battlefield."

"Quick, loosen the wooden hoops over my wounds, fellow," said Cú Chulainn. Then Cú Chulainn gave a mighty spring and the wooden hoops flew from him to Mag Túaga in Connacht. The bindings of his wounds went from him to Bacca in Corco M'ruad.[5] The dry wisps of tow which plugged his wounds soared into the uppermost air as high as larks soar on a day of fair weather when there is no wind. His wounds broke out afresh and the trenches and furrows in the earth were filled with his blood and the plugs from his wounds.

The first exploit which Cú Chulainn performed after rising from his sickbed was against the two female satirists, Fethan and Colla, who had been feigning to weep and lament over him. He dashed their two heads together so that he was red with their blood and gray with their brains. None of his weapons had been left beside him apart from his chariot. And he took his chariot on his back and came towards the men of Ireland, and with his chariot he smote them until he reached the spot where Fergus mac Róig stood. "Turn this way, my master Fergus," said Cú Chulainn. Fergus did not answer for he did not hear him. Cú Chulainn said again: "Turn this way, my

---

5. Mag Túaga, the Plain of Hoops, named for the hazel hoops that had held Cú Chulainn. Corco M'ruad, modern Corcomroe in County Clare.

master Fergus, or if you do not, I shall grind you as a mill grinds fine grain, I shall belabor you as flax-heads are belabored in a pool, I shall entwine you as a vine entwines trees, I shall swoop on you as a hawk swoops on little birds." "That is indeed what has happened," said Fergus. "Who dares to speak those proud, warlike words to me here where the four great provinces of Ireland meet at Gáirech and Ilgáirech in the battle of the Foray of Cúailnge?" "Your own fosterson," said Cú Chulainn, "and the fosterson of Conchobor and of the rest of the men of Ulster, Cú Chulainn mac Sualtaim. You promised that you would flee before me when I should be wounded, bloody and pierced with stabs in the battle of the Táin, for I fled before you in your own battle of the Táin."

Fergus heard that, and he turned and took three mighty, heroic strides, and when he turned, all the men of Ireland turned and were routed westwards over the hill. The conflict was centred against the men of Connacht. At midday Cú Chulainn had come to the battle. It was sunset in the evening when the last band of the men of Connacht fled westwards over the hill. By that time there remained in Cú Chulainn's hand only a fistful of the spokes around the wheel and a handful of shafts around the body of the chariot, but he kept on slaying and slaughtering the four great provinces of Ireland during all that time.

Then Medb covered the retreat of the men of Ireland and she sent the Donn Cúailnge around to Crúachu together with fifty of his heifers and eight of Medb's messengers, so that whoever might reach Crúachu or whoever might not, at least the Donn Cúailnge would arrive there as she had promised. Then her issue of blood came upon Medb and she said: "O Fergus, cover the retreat of the men of Ireland that I may pass my water." "By my conscience," said Fergus, "It is ill-timed and it is not right to do so." "Yet I must," said Medb, "for I shall not live unless I do." Fergus came then and covered the retreat of the men of Ireland. Medb passed her water and it made three great trenches in each of which a household can fit. Hence the place is called Fúal Medba.[6]

Cú Chulainn came upon her thus engaged but he did not wound her for he would not strike her from behind. "Grant me a favor today, Cú Chulainn," said Medb. "What favor do you ask?" said Cú Chulainn. "That this army may be under your protection and safeguard till they have gone westwards past Áth Mór."[7] "I grant it," said Cú Chulainn. Cú Chulainn came around the men of Ireland and covered their retreat on one side to protect them. The triads of the men of Ireland came on the other side, and Medb came into her own position and covered their retreat in the rear. In that fashion they took the men of Ireland westwards past Áth Mór.

Then Cú Chulainn's sword was given to him and he smote a blow on the three blunt-topped hills at Áth Luain, as a counterblast to the three Máela Mide, and cut off their three tops.

Fergus began to survey the host as they went westwards from Áth Mór. "This day was indeed a fitting one for those who were led by a woman," said Fergus. . . .[8] said Medb to Fergus. "This host has been plundered and despoiled today. As when a mare goes before her band of foals into unknown territory, with none to lead or counsel them, so this host has perished today."

As for Medb, she gathered and assembled the men of Ireland to Crúachu that they might see the combat of the bulls.

---

6. The Foul Place of Medb.
7. The Ford of Mor, also called Áth Luain (modern Athlone), on the River Shannon at the border of Connacht. Medb is asking Cú Chulainn to spare her army in its retreat.
8. There is a gap in the manuscript text here.

When the Donn Cúailnge saw the beautiful strange land, he bellowed loudly three times. The Findbennach of Aí heard him. Because of the Findbennach no male animal between the four fords of all Mag Aí, (Áth Moga and Áth Coltna, Áth Slissen and Áth mBercha) dared utter a sound louder than the lowing of a cow. The Findbennach tossed his head violently and came forward to Crúachu to meet the Donn Cúailnge.

The men of Ireland asked who should be an eye-witness for the bulls, and they all decided that it should be Bricriu mac Garbada.[9] A year before these events in the Foray of Cúailnge, Bricriu had come from one province to another begging from Fergus, and Fergus had retained him in his service waiting for his chattels and wealth. And a quarrel arose between him and Fergus as they were playing chess, and Bricriu spoke very insultingly to Fergus. Fergus struck him with his fist and with the chessman that he held in his hand and drove the chessman into his head and broke a bone in his skull. While the men of Ireland were on the hosting of the Táin, Bricriu was being cured in Crúachu, and the day they returned from the hosting was the day Bricriu rose from his sickness. The reason they chose Bricriu in this manner was because he was no fairer to his friend than to his enemy. So Bricriu was brought to a gap in front of the bulls.

Each of the bulls caught sight of the other and they pawed the ground and cast the earth over them. They dug up the ground and threw it over their shoulders and their withers, and their eyes blazed in their heads like distended balls of fire. Their cheeks and nostrils swelled like smith's bellows in a forge. And each collided with the other with a crashing noise. Each of them began to gore and to pierce and to slay and slaughter the other. Then the Findbennach Aí took advantage of the confusion of the Donn Cúailnge's journeying and wandering and traveling, and thrust his horn into his side and visited his rage on him. Their violent rush took them to where Bricriu stood and the bulls' hooves trampled him a man's length into the ground after they had killed him.

Hence that is called the Tragical Death of Bricriu.

Cormac Cond Longas, the son of Conchobor, saw this happening and he took a spear which filled his grasp and struck three blows on the Donn Cúailnge from his ear to his tail. "This beast will be no wonderful, lasting possession for us," said Cormac, "since he cannot repel a calf of his own age." Donn Cúailnge heard this for he had human understanding, and he attacked the Findbennach, and for a long while they fought together until night fell on the men of Ireland. And when night fell, all the men of Ireland could do was to listen to their noise and their uproar. That night the bulls traversed the whole of Ireland.

Not long after the men of Ireland arrived early the next day, they saw the Donn Cúailnge coming past Crúachu from the west with the Findbennach Aí a mangled mass on his antlers and horns. The men of Ireland arose and they did not know which of the bulls was there. "Well now, men," said Fergus, "leave him alone if it is the Findbennach Aí, and if it is Donn Cúailnge, leave him his triumph. I swear that what has been done concerning the bulls is but little in comparison with what will be done now."

The Donn Cúailnge arrived. He turned his right side to Crúachu and left there a heap of the liver of the Findbennach. Whence the name Crúachna Áe. He came forward to the brink of Áth Mór and there he left the loin of the Findbennach. Whence

9. Bricriu "of the Poison Tongue," often a troublemaker among the heroes of the Ulster Cycle.

the name Áth Luain. He came eastwards into the land of Meath to Áth Troim and there he left the liver of the Findbennach. He tossed his head fiercely and shook off the Findbennach over Ireland. He threw his thigh as far as Port Lárge. He threw his rib-cage as far as Dublin which is called Áth Clíath. After that he faced towards the north and recognized the land of Cúailnge and came towards it. There there were women and boys and children lamenting the Donn Cúailnge. They saw the forehead of the Donn Cúailnge coming towards them. "A bull's forehead comes to us!" they cried. Hence the name Taul Tairb ever since.

Then the Donn Cúailnge attacked the women and boys and children of the territory of Cúailnge and inflicted great slaughter on them. After that he turned his back to the hill and his heart broke like a nut in his breast.

So far the account and the story and the end of the Táin.

A blessing on every one who shall faithfully memorize the Táin as it is written here and shall not add any other form to it.

But I who have written this story, or rather this fable, give no credence to the various incidents related in it. For some things in it are the deceptions of demons, others poetic figments; some are probable, others improbable; while still others are intended for the delectation of foolish men.

•—•━◆━•—•

Early Irish Verse

Although copied by clerics in a world of written manuscripts, the *Táin* looks backward to an age of oral tales about legendary heroes and heroines, many of them still closely linked to the native gods and goddesses of pre-Christian Ireland. The following samples of Irish verse from the ninth and tenth centuries suggest some of the complex but enormously fruitful interactions of those native Irish traditions and the new Christian culture.

Ireland began to be Christianized from the mid-fifth century, but Christianity came to Ireland more by genuine and gradual conversion than by the point of a sword. The learned monks and hermits, well established by the ninth and tenth centuries, encountered far more disruption from the raids of Vikings, beginning in A.D. 795, than from surviving Irish pre-Christian cultures. Instead, the ancient native dynasties of learned poets, genealogists, and diviners interacted with the new learning of Latin Christianity. Indeed, Saint Columba (c. 521–597) was partly educated by the *fili* Gemmán, the chief poet of Leinster. (*Fili*, plural *filid*, was the highest class of poet in medieval Ireland. See the introduction to the *Táin Bó Cuailnge*, page 92.) One of Columba's few returns to Ireland after founding his monastery on the isle of Iona was to defend the native poets from clerical forces that wanted them suppressed. In fact we know that many monks were also vernacular poets; and conversely, secular *filid* wrote praise poems to clerics, most famously to Saint Columba himself. Their cultural prestige and preservation of ancient learning continued, even as their religious and quasi-magical activity dwindled. All this led to a rich and persistent convergence (not without competition) of native and Christian elements in medieval Irish culture.

The figure addressed in *To Crinog*, for instance, is at once a wise crone—a traditional figure of initiation—and a book of Christian wisdom, perhaps a Latin primer. Irish myths report instruction in craft or battle by a wise woman, with whom the apprentice also enjoys physical intimacy (as a youthful Cú Chulainn had with the woman warrior Scáthach), although in this poem Crinog's teaching is explicitly chaste. Monks also began using the resources of Irish poetry to record religious study—the Word, to which their faith was so attached—and the making of written books. *Pangur the Cat* explores the solitary pleasures of the monk or hermit, and the challenge of textual interpretation, in contrast with the more heroic mold of many saints' lives or contemporary heroic tales: "Fame comes second to the peace / Of study. . . ." *Writing in the Wood* is a poem of labor, but undertaken in a holiday spirit, away from the monastic scriptorium where books were usually copied.

Other voices look to the legendary past with open regret. *A Grave Marked with Ogam* evokes a disastrous battle in which the speaker, now quite alone, fought on the losing side. *Findabair Remembers Fróech* is a yearning lament for a lost lover. It is quite unconnected to monasticism, but a similar history of passions that efface the present also informs the powerful monologue *The Old Woman of Beare*; there the contrast also involves the shift from a lost world of secular heroes to declining mortality in a convent. Her name, and the memories she has of past generations and eras, may link the Old Woman of Beare to a mythic figure of sovereignty, rejuvenated by each man to whom she gives her body and her powers. At the same time, she is a voice of wise lament on the passing of greater times (not unlike many moments in *Beowulf*); she is a rich concubine who has lost her beauty and become a nun; and—in a land where women's powers were usually quite limited—she is a woman who has gone her own way and made choices that now leave her poor, unprotected, and rueful, but not regretful. *The Old Woman of Beare* records the unresolved dialogue between the era of heroic legend and the era of Christ, between joys mortal and immortal: "for Mary's Son / too soon redeems."

The Voyage of Máel Dúin shows us, perhaps most clearly of all, how native secular genres and attitudes persisted, but were revised, under the influence of Christianity. Both in structure and detail, the *Voyage* echoes the *immrana*, native tales of wondrous voyages to otherworldly islands, places both of terror and sybaritic pleasures. Máel Dúin and his companions visit many such islands, but they also pause at the island homes of four Christian hermits, themselves not without magical qualities. Máel Dúin's own genealogy mirrors this meeting of traditions; he is the illegitimate child of a nun and a great warrior. His father has been killed by raiders, he learns, and his voyage is a quest to find them and take obligatory vengeance in the heroic style. The fourth hermit he meets, though, convinces Máel Dúin to forgive his father's murderers and return home in peace. At the levels of genre, genealogy, and narrative, then, the *Voyage* enacts at once a preservation and revision of native traditions under Christian influence.

To Crinog[1]

Crinog, melodious is your song.
Though young no more you are still bashful.
We two grew up together in Niall's[2] northern land,
When we used to sleep together in tranquil slumber.

5   That was my age when you slept with me.
O peerless lady of pleasant wisdom:
A pure-hearted youth, lovely without a flaw,
A gentle boy of seven sweet years.

We lived in the great world of Banva[3]
10   Without sullying soul or body,
My flashing eyes full of love for you,
Like a poor innocent untempted by evil.

---

1. Translated by Kuno Meyer.
2. Legendary Irish king, whose dynasty ruled Ulster and

other areas.
3. An early name for Ireland

Your just counsel is ever ready,
Wherever we are to seek it:
15   To love your penetrating wisdom is better
Than glib discourse with a king.

Since then you have slept with four men after me,
Without folly or falling away:
I know, I hear it on all sides,
20   You are pure, without sin from man.

At last, after weary wanderings,
You have come to me again,
Darkness of age has settled on your face:
Sinless your life draws near its end.

25   You are still dear to me, faultless one,
You shall have welcome from me without stint:
You will not let us be drowned in torment;
We will earnestly practice devotion with you.

The lasting world is full of your fame.
30   Far and wide you have wandered on every track:
If every day we followed your ways,
We should come safe into the presence of dread God.

You leave an example and a bequest
To every one in this world,
35   You have taught us by your life:
Earnest prayer to God is no fallacy.

Then may God grant us peace and happiness!
May the countenance of the King
Shine brightly on us
40   When we leave behind us our withered bodies.

Pangur the Cat[1]

Myself and Pangur, cat and sage
Go each about our business;
I harass my beloved page,
He his mouse.

5   Fame comes second to the peace
Of study, a still day.
Unenvious, Pangur's choice
Is child's play.

Neither bored, both hone
10   At home a separate skill,
Moving, after hours alone,
To the kill.

1. Translated by Eavan Boland.

On my cell wall here,
His sight fixes. Burning.
15   Searching. My old eyes peer
At new learning.

His delight when his claws
Close on his prey
Equals mine, when sudden clues
20   Light my way.

So we find by degrees
Peace in solitude,
Both of us—solitaries—
Have each the trade

25   He loves. Pangur, never idle
Day or night
Hunts mice. I hunt each riddle
From dark to light

Writing in the Wood[1]

Overwatched by woodland wall
    merles make melody full well;
above my book—lined, lettered—
    birds twittered a soothing spell.

5   Cuckoos call clear—fairest phrase—
    cloaked in grays, from leafy leas.
Lord's love, what blessings show' ring!
    Good to write 'neath tow' ring trees.

The Viking Terror[1]

Bitter is the wind to-night,
It tosses the ocean's white hair:
To-night I fear not the fierce warriors of Norway
Coursing on the Irish Sea.

The Old Woman of Beare[1]

The ebbing that has come on me
is not the ebbing of the sea.
What knows the sea of grief or pain?—
Happy tide will flood again.

1. Translated by Ruth P. M. Lehmann. This translation aims to reproduce much of the complex internal rhyme and end-rhyme, assonance, and alliteration of the original; it takes minor liberties with the literal sense.
1. Translated by Kuno Meyer.
1. Translated by James Carney. The speaker's name, "caillech," "veiled one," can mean old woman, hag, widow, and nun. The hag figure has resonance with teachers of crafts and wisdom, as well as early mythic female figures of sovereignty and initiation, rejuvenated when they are embraced by a chosen hero.

5   I am the hag of Bui and Beare—[2]
the richest cloth I used to wear.
Now with meanness and with thrift
I even lack a change of shift.

It is wealth
10   and not men that you love.
In the time that we lived
it was men that we loved.

Those whom we loved, the plains
we ride today bear their names;
15   gaily they feasted with laughter
nor boasted thereafter.

To-day they gather in the tax
but, come to handing out, are lax;
the very little they bestow
20   be sure that everyone will know.

Chariots there were, and we
had horses bred for victory.
Such things came in a great wave;
pray for the dead kings who gave.

25   Bitterly does my body race
seeking its destined place;
now let God's Son come and take
that which he gave of his grace.

These arms, these scrawny things you see,
30   scarce merit now their little joy
when lifted up in blessing
    over sweet student boy.

These arms you see,
    these bony scrawny things,
35   had once more loving craft
    embracing kings.

When Maytime comes
    the girls out there are glad,
and I, old hag, old bones,
40   alone am sad.

No wedding wether killed for me,
an end to all coquetry;
a pitiful veil I wear
on thin and faded hair.

45   Well do I wear
plain veil on faded hair;

---

2. A peninsula in Munster, in the far southwest of Ireland, or a tiny island off its coast. "Bui" may be the small nearby island of Dursey.

many colors I wore
and we feasting before.

Were it not for Feven's plain[3]
    I'd envy nothing old;
I have a shroud of aged skin,
    Feven's crop is gold.

Ronan's city there in Bregon[4]
    and in Feven the royal standing stone,
why are their cheeks not weathered,
    only mine alone?

Winter comes and the sea will rise
    crying out with welcoming wave;
but no welcome for me from nobleman's son
    or from son of a slave.

What they do now, I know, I know:
    to and fro they row and race;
but they who once sailed Alma's ford[5]
    rest in a cold place.

It's more than a day
    since I sailed youth's sea,
beauty's years not devoured
    and sap flowing free.

It's more than a day, God's truth,
    that I'm lacking in youth;
I wrap myself up in the sun—
I know Old Age, I see him come.

There was a summer of youth
    nor was autumn the worst of the year,
but winter is doom
    and its first days are here.

God be thanked, I had joy in my youth.
    I swear that it's true,
if I hadn't leapt the wall
    this old cloak still were not new.

The Lord on the world's broad back
    threw a lovely cloak of green;
first fleecy, then it's bare,
    and again the fleece is seen.

All beauty is doomed.
    God! Can it be right
to kneel in a dark prayer-house
    after feasting by candlelight?

---

3. In inland Munster; connected with power and wealth.
4. Probably an 8th-century king who ruled in the area

of Feven.
5. An unidentified site.

I sat with kings drinking wine and mead
90   for many a day,
and now, a crew of shriveled hags,
      we toast in whey.

Be this my feast, these cups of whey;
      and let me always count as good
95 the vexing things that come of Christ
      who stayed God's ire with flesh and blood.

The mind is not so clear,
      there's mottling of age on my cloak,
gray hairs sprouting through skin,
100   I am like a stricken oak.

For deposit on heaven
      of right eye bereft,
I conclude the purchase
      with loss of the left.

105 Great wave of flood
      and wave of ebb and lack!
What flooding tide brings in
      the ebbing tide takes back.

Great wave of flood
110   and wave of ebbing sea,
the two of them I know
      for both have washed on me.

Great wave of flood
      brings no step to silent cellar floor;
115 a hand fell on all the company
      that feasted there before.

The Son of Mary knew right well
      he'd walk that floor one day;
grasping I was, but never sent
120   man hungry on his way.

Pity Man!—
      If only like the elements he could
come out of ebbing in the very way
      that he comes out of flood.

125 Christ left with me on loan
      flood tide of youth, and now it seems
there's ebb and misery, for Mary's Son
      too soon redeems.

Blessed the island in the great sea
130   with happy ebb and happy flood.
For me, for me alone, no hope:
      the ebbing is for good.

Findabair Remembers Fróech[1]

This, thereafter, is what Findabair used to say,
seeing anything beautiful:
it would be more beautiful for her
to see Fróech crossing the dark water,
5   body for shining whiteness,
hair for loveliness,
face for shapeliness,
eye for blue-grayness,
a well-born youth
10   without fault or blemish,
face broad above, narrow below,
and he straight and perfect,
the red branch with its berries
between throat and white face.
15   This is what Findabair used to say:
She had never seen
anything a half
or a third as beautiful as he.

A Grave Marked with Ogam[1]

Ogam in stone on grave stead,
    where men sometimes tread on course;
king's son of Ireland cut low,
    hit by spear's throw hurled from horse.

5   Cairpre let a quick cast fly
    from high on horseback, stout steed;
ere he wearied his hand struck,
    cut down Oscar, cruel deed.[2]

Oscar hurled a hard throw, crude,
10   like a lion, rude his rage;
killed Con's kin, Cairpre proud,
    ere they bowed on battle stage.

Tall, keen, cruel were the lads
    who found their death in the strife,
15   just before their weapons met;
    more were left in death than life.

I myself was in the fight
    on right, south of Gabair green;

1. Translated by James Carney. Findabair (*FIN-a-wer*) was a daughter of Medb and Ailill (central characters in the *Táin*). She falls in love with the famously handsome warrior Fróech (*Froich*, guttural *-ch*) but her parents resist their marriage. When Fróech is killed by Cú Chulainn, Findabair ultimately dies of heartbreak.
1. Translated by Ruth P. M. Lehmann. This translation again aims to reproduce much of the rhyme, assonance, and alliteration of the original; it takes minor liberties with the literal sense. Ogam is the earliest Irish alphabet, used before the Latin alphabet was applied to Irish. It is a system of long lines marked with short dashes, cross-hatches, and small figures. Most often found in inscriptions or associated with secret messages and divination, it is too awkward an alphabet for writing longer texts.
2. Characters from the "Finn Cycle," a group of tales even more popular than the Ulster Cycle and its central epic the *Táin*. Oscar is Finn's grandson and the cycle's greatest warrior. He and Cairpre, high king of Ireland, kill one another at the Battle of Gabair (*GAV-ar*), which ends the power of Finn's people.

20   twice fifty warriors I killed,
            my skilled hand slew them, clear, clean.

        I'd play for pirates in bale,
            the while the trail I must tread,
        in holy holt boar I'd fell,
            or would snatch the snell bird's egg.

25   That ogam there in the stone,
        around which the slain fall prone,
            if Finn the fighter could come,
            long would he think on ogam.

from The Voyage of Máel Dúin[1]

        They went to an island with a high enclosure of the color of a swan
        In which they found a noble pavilion, a dwelling of brightness.
        Silver brooches, gold-hilted swords, large necklets,
        Beautiful beds, excellent food, golden rows.
5   Strengthening delicate food in the midst of the house, sound savory liquor;
        With fierce greediness upon a high pillar a seemly very quick cat.
        It leapt then over the pillars, a speedy feat;
        Not very big was the guardian of the meat, it was not repulsive.
        One of the three foster brothers of the powerful chief, it was a
            courageous action,
10   Takes with him—it was a proud ounce-weight—a golden necklet.[2]
        The fiery claw of the mysterious cat rent his body,
        The guilty body of the unfortunate man was burnt ash.
        The large necklet was brought back, it created friendship again,
        The ashes of the unfortunate man were cast into the ocean.

* * *

        Then they saw in a small island a psalm-singing old man;
        Excellent was his dignified noble appearance, holy were his words.
        Hair of his noble head—delightful the bright covering—a garment
            with whiteness,
        A brilliant large mantle; bright-covered coloring covering was around him.
5   The excellent chief said to him: "Whence were you sent?"
        "I shall not hide from you what you ask: from Ireland.
        My pilgrimage brought me without any penance
        In the body of a boat over the swift sea; I did not regret it.
        My prowed boat came apart under me on the very violent sea;
10   A bitter, twisting, active, big-waved course put me ashore.
        I cut a sod from the gray-green surface of my fatherland;
        To the place in which I am a breeze brought me: small is the fame.
        The star-strong King established under me out of the miraculous sod
        A delightful island with the color of a seagull over the dark sea.
15   A foot was added to the island every year—

---

1. Verse redaction of chs. 11, 19, and 34, translated by H. P. A. Oskamp. Máel Dúin (*Moil Doon*), the illegitimate son of a nun and a warrior, is brought up by a queen. Learning at the same time of his father's death, he sets out on a sea journey to find and take vengeance on his father's killers. Máel Dúin and his companions came upon a series of islands, each with its marvel or danger. 2. Máel Dúin's foster brothers had swum to his boat as it departed, violating a druid's prohibition; none return from the journey.

It is a victorious achievement—and a tree above the sea's crest.
A clear well came to me—everlasting food—
By the grace of angels, sound beautiful food—a holy gathering.
You will all reach your countries, a fruitful company along the ocean's track,
20   Though it will be a long journey; all except one man."[3]
By the grace of the angels to each single man of them
Came a complete half-loaf and a noble morsel of fish as provision.

* * *

Then they went to an island full of flocks, a famed halting-place,
A victorious achievement; they found there an Irish falcon.
Then they rowed after it, swift to encounter,
Over the crest of the waves to an island in which was their enemy.
5   They made peace there with the swift Máel Dúin, in the presence of
         every swift man;
After true pledging they went to their country, a prosperous journey.
Many remarkable things, many marvels, many mysteries
Was their pleasant story, as swift Máel Dúin told.
A long life and peace while I am in the famous world,
10   May I have cheerful company with virtue from my King of Kings.
When I die may I then reach heaven past the fierce, violent host of demons
In the Kingdom of angels, a famous affair, a very high dwelling.

Judith

The Old English poem *Judith*, concerning the legendary beheader of the Assyrian general Holofernes, has been seen most often as a heroic poem, like *Beowulf*, which it immediately follows in the same unique manuscript. It expresses the same fierce love of battle, and uses the same heroic poetic conventions—archaic diction, formulas, and themes. *Judith* achieves ironic effects, however, by placing these conventions in unexpected contexts, for instance calling Holofernes a "brave man" as he hides behind a net to spy on his retainers. Similarly, it presents his raucous feast as an antifeast—a symbol of misrule rather than of social harmony—and his henchmen as a parody of the traditional band of loyal retainers, as they flee in terror to save their lives.

In addition to *Beowulf*, *Judith* has affinities with Old English poems based on the Old Testament, like *Exodus* and *Daniel*, whose heroes devote their military zeal to the glory of God. Like them, it assumes the timeless perspective of Christian salvation history, so that the apparent anachronisms of Judith's praying to the Trinity or Christ's abhorring Holofernes are entirely appropriate. Based on the Book of Judith in the Latin Bible, which the Anglo-Saxons considered canonical, this poem, like many others in Old English, exists only in fragmentary form. The original audience would have known that Holofernes had entered Judea to besiege the Hebrew city of Bethulia. At the point where the Old English poem begins, the "wickedly promiscuous" general, after his drunken feast, orders the beautiful Hebrew maiden Judith to be brought to his bed. Finding him stretched out in a drunken stupor, she first prays for help and then decapitates him. She thereupon returns to her camp, brandishing the head and exhorting the Hebrews to battle with a stirring speech, which inspires them to victory over the leaderless Assyrians.

---

3. One of the three foster brothers still remains with the voyagers at this point. A later hermit prophesies, "though you will meet your enemies, you will not slay them."

The poem does not simply express the timeless Christian theme of the struggle of God's people against the pagans, but also comments on the immediate social and historical context of its time. It seems to reflect the resistance of the Christian Anglo-Saxons against the pagan Danes during the ninth-century invasions, perhaps exaggerating the Assyrians' drunkenness in order to comment on the notorious Danish drinking habits. Furthermore, Holofernes' plan to rape Judith may evoke the rape of Anglo-Saxon women by Danish soldiers in the presence of their husbands and fathers.

Judith's identity as a woman warrior also puts the poem in the social context of the time. The poem's emphasis on her power, in contrast to the biblical source's emphasis on God's power to operate through the hand of a mere woman, reflects the relatively strong role of aristocratic women in England before the Norman Conquest. (Other Old English poems that reflect this strength include *Juliana*, a typical saint's legend whose heroine is martyred while resisting a Roman general's advances, and *Elene*, whose heroine—Constantine's mother Saint Helen—was believed to have discovered the true cross.) Finally, Judith's heroic action has been seen as an inversion of the rape which Holofernes himself intends to commit upon her, as, seeing him unconscious on his bed, she "took the heathen man by the hair, dragged him ignominiously towards her with her hands, and carefully laid out the debauched and odious man."

Judith[1]

. . . She was suspicious of gifts in this wide world. So she readily met with a helping hand from the glorious Prince when she had most need of the supreme Judge's support and that he, the Prime Mover, should protect her against this supreme danger. The illustrious Father in the skies granted her request in this because she always had firm faith in the Almighty.

I have heard, then, that Holofernes cordially issued invitations to a banquet and had dishes splendidly prepared with all sorts of wonderful things, and to it this lord over men summoned all the most senior functionaries. With great alacrity those shield-wielders complied and came wending to the puissant prince, the nation's chief person. That was on the fourth day after Judith, shrewd of purpose, the woman of elfin beauty first visited him.

So they went and settled down to the feasting, insolent men to the wine-drinking, all those brash armored warriors, his confederates in evil. Deep bowls were borne continually along the benches there and brimming goblets and pitchers as well to the hall-guests. They drank it down as doomed men, those celebrated shield-wielders—though the great man, the awesome lord over evils, did not foresee it. Then Holofernes, the bountiful lord of his men, grew merry with tippling. He laughed and bawled and roared and made a racket so that the children of men could hear from far away how the stern-minded man bellowed and yelled, insolent and flown with mead, and frequently exhorted the guests on the benches to enjoy themselves well. So the whole day long the villain, the stern-minded dispenser of treasure, plied his retainers with wine until they lay unconscious, the whole of his retinue drunk as though they had been struck dead, drained of every faculty.

Thus the men's elder commanded the hall-guests to be ministered to until the dark night closed in on the children of men. Then, being wickedly promiscuous, he commanded the blessed virgin, decked with bracelets and adorned with rings, to be fetched in a hurry to his bed. The attendants promptly did as their master, the ruler

1. Prose translation by S. A. J. Bradley.

of armored warriors, required them. They went upon the instant to the guest-hall where they found the astute Judith, and then the shield-wielding warriors speedily conducted the noble virgin to the lofty pavilion where the great man always rested of a night, Holofernes, abhorrent to the Savior.

There was an elegant all-golden fly-net there, hung about the commandant's bed so that the debauched hero of his soldiers could spy through on every one of the sons of men who came in there, but no one of humankind on him, unless, brave man, he summoned one of his evilly renowned soldiers to go nearer to him for a confidential talk.

Hastily, then, they brought the shrewd lady to bed. Then they went, stout-hearted heroes, to inform their master that the holy woman had been brought to his pavilion. The man of mark, lord over cities, then grew jovial of mood: he meant to defile the noble lady with filth and with pollution. To that heaven's Judge, Shepherd of the celestial multitude, would not consent but rather he, the Lord, Ruler of the hosts, prevented him from the act.

So this species of fiend, licentious, debauched, went with a crowd of his men to seek his bed—where he was to lose his life, swiftly, within the one night: he had then come to his violent end upon earth, such as he had previously deserved, the stern-minded prince over men, while he lived in this world under the roof of the skies.

Then the great man collapsed in the midst of his bed, so drunk with wine that he was oblivious in mind of any of his designs. The soldiers stepped out of his quarters with great alacrity, wine-glutted men who had put the perjurer, the odious persecutor, to bed for the last time.

Then the glorious handmaid of the Savior was sorely preoccupied as to how she might most easily deprive the monster of his life before the sordid fellow, full of corruption, awoke. Then the ringletted girl, the Maker's maiden, grasped a sharp sword, hardy in the storms of battle, and drew it from its sheath with her right hand. Then she called by name upon the Guardian of heaven, the Savior of all the world's inhabitants, and spoke these words:

"God of beginnings, Spirit of comfort, Son of the universal Ruler, I desire to entreat you for your grace upon me in my need, Majesty of the Trinity. My heart is now sorely anguished and my mind troubled and much afflicted with anxieties. Give me, Lord of heaven, victory and true faith so that with this sword I may hew down this dispenser of violent death. Grant me my safe deliverance, stern-minded Prince over men. Never have I had greater need of your grace. Avenge now, mighty Lord, illustrious Dispenser of glory, that which is so bitter to my mind, so burning in my breast."

Then the supreme Judge at once inspired her with courage—as he does every single man dwelling here who looks to him for help with resolve and with true faith. So hope was abundantly renewed in the holy woman's heart. She then took the heathen man firmly by his hair, dragged him ignominiously towards her with her hands and carefully laid out the debauched and odious man so as she could most easily manage the wretch efficiently. Then the ringletted woman struck the malignant-minded enemy with the gleaming sword so that she sliced through half his neck, so that he lay unconscious, drunk and mutilated.

He was not then yet dead, not quite lifeless. In earnest then the courageous woman struck the heathen dog a second time so that his head flew off on to the floor. His foul carcass lay behind, dead; his spirit departed elsewhere beneath the deep ground and was there prostrated and chained in torment ever after, coiled about by snakes, trussed up in tortures and cruelly prisoned in hellfire after his going hence.

Never would he have cause to hope, engulfed in darkness, that he might get out of that snake-infested prison, but there he shall remain forever to eternity henceforth without end in that murky abode, deprived of the joys of hope.

Judith then had won outstanding glory in the struggle according as God the Lord of heaven, who gave her the victory, granted her. Then the clever woman swiftly put the harrier's head, all bloody, into the bag in which her attendant, a pale-cheeked woman, one proved excellent in her ways, had brought food there for them both; and then Judith put it, all gory, into her hands for her discreet servant to carry home. From there the two women then proceeded onwards, emboldened by courage, until they had escaped, brave, triumphant virgins, from among the army, so that they could clearly see the walls of the beautiful city, Bethulia, shining. Then the ring-adorned women hurried forward on their way until, cheered at heart, they had reached the rampart gate.

There were soldiers, vigilant men, sitting and keeping watch in the fortress just as Judith the artful-minded virgin had enjoined the despondent folk when she set out on her mission, courageous lady. Now she had returned, their darling, to her people, and quickly then the shrewd woman summoned one of the men to come out from the spacious city to meet her and speedily to let them in through the gate of the rampart; and to the victorious people she spoke these words:

"I can tell you something worthy of thanksgiving: that you need no longer grieve in spirit. The ordaining Lord, the Glory of kings, is gracious to you. It has been revealed abroad through the world that dazzling and glorious success is impending for you and triumph is granted you over those injuries which you long have suffered."

Then the citizens were merry when they heard how the saintly woman spoke across the high rampart. The army was in ecstasies and the people rushed towards the fortress gate, men and women together, in flocks and droves; in throngs and troops they surged forward and ran towards the handmaid of the Lord, both old and young in their thousands. The heart of each person in that city of mead-halls was exhilarated when they realized that Judith had returned home; and then with humility they hastily let her in.

Then the clever woman ornamented with gold directed her attentive servant-girl to unwrap the harrier's head and to display the bloody object to the citizens as proof of how she had fared in the struggle. The noble lady then spoke to the whole populace:

"Victorious heroes, leaders of the people; here you may openly gaze upon the head of that most odious heathen warrior, the dead Holofernes, who perpetrated upon us the utmost number of violent killings of men and painful miseries, and who intended to add to it even further, but God did not grant him longer life so that he might plague us with afflictions. I took his life, with God's help. Now I want to urge each man among these citizens, each shield-wielding soldier, that you immediately get yourselves ready for battle. Once the God of beginnings, the steadfastly gracious King, has sent the radiant light from the east, go forth bearing shields, bucklers in front of your breasts and mail-coats and shining helmets into the ravagers' midst; cut down the commanders, the doomed leaders, with gleaming swords. Your enemies are sentenced to death and you shall have honor and glory in the fight according as the mighty Lord has signified to you by my hand."

Then an army of brave and keen men was quickly got ready for the battle. Renowned nobles and their companions advanced; they carried victory-banners;

beneath their helms the heroes issued forth straight into battle from out of the holy city upon the very dawning of the day. Shields clattered, loudly resonated. At that, the lean wolf in the wood rejoiced, and that bird greedy for carrion, the black raven. Both knew that the men of that nation meant to procure them their fill among those doomed to die; but in their wake flew the eagle, eager for food, speckled-winged; the dark-feathered, hook-beaked bird sang a battle-chant.

On marched the soldiers, warriors to the warfare, protected by their shields, hollowed linden bucklers, they who a while previously had been suffering the abuse of aliens, the blasphemy of heathens. This was strictly repaid to all the Assyrians in the spear-fight once the Israelites under their battle-ensigns had reached the camp. Firmly entrenched, they vigorously let fly from the curved bow showers of darts, arrows, the serpents of battle. Loudly the fierce fighting-men roared and sent spears into their cruel enemies' midst. The heroes, the in-dwellers of the land, were enraged against the odious race. Stern of mood they advanced; hardened of heart they roughly roused their drink-stupefied enemies of old. With their hands, retainers unsheathed from scabbards bright-ornamented swords, proved of edge, and set about the Assyrian warriors in earnest, intending to smite them. Of that army they spared not one of the men alive, neither the lowly nor the mighty, whom they could overpower.

Thus in the hour of morn those comrades in arms the whole time harried the aliens until those who were their adversaries, the chief sentries of the army, acknowledged that the Hebrew people were showing them very intensive sword-play. They went to inform the most senior officers of this by word of mouth and they roused those warriors and fearfully announced to them in their drunken stupor the dreadful news, the terror of the morning, the frightful sword-encounter.

Then, I have heard, those death-doomed heroes quickly shook off their sleep and thronged in flocks, demoralized men, to the pavilion of the debauched Holofernes. They meant to give their lord warning of battle at once, before the terror and the force of the Hebrews descended upon him; all supposed that the men's leader and that beautiful woman were together in the handsome tent, the noble Judith and the lecher, fearsome and ferocious. Yet there was not one of the nobles who dared awaken the warrior to inquire how it had turned out for the soldier with the holy virgin, the woman of the Lord.

The might of the Hebrews, their army, was drawing closer; vehemently they fought with tough and bloody weapons and violently they indemnified with gleaming swords their former quarrels and old insults: in that day's work the Assyrians' repute was withered, their arrogance abased. The men stood around their lord's tent, extremely agitated and growing gloomier in spirit. Then all together they began to cough and loudly make noises and, having no success, to chew the grist with their teeth, suffering agonies. The time of their glory, good fortune and valorous doings was at an end. The nobles thought to awaken their lord and friend; they succeeded not at all.

Then one of the soldiers belatedly and tardily grew so bold that he ventured pluckily into the pavilion as necessity compelled him. Then he found his lord lying pallid on the bed, deprived of his spirit, dispossessed of life. Straightway then he fell chilled to the ground, and distraught in mind he began to tear his hair and his clothing alike and he uttered these words to the soldiers who were waiting there miserably outside:

"Here is made manifest our own perdition, and here it is imminently signalled that the time is drawn near, along with its tribulations, when we must perish and be destroyed together in the strife. Here, hacked by the sword, decapitated, lies our lord."

Then distraught in mind they threw down their weapons; demoralized they went scurrying away in flight. The nation magnified in strength attacked them in the rear until the greatest part of the army lay on the field of victory levelled by battle, hacked by swords, as a treat for the wolves and a joy to the carrion-greedy birds. Those who survived fled from the linden spears of their foes. In their wake advanced the troop of Hebrews, honoured with the victory and glorified in the judgment: the Lord God, the almighty Lord, had come handsomely to their aid. Swiftly then with their gleaming swords those valiant heroes made an inroad through the thick of their foes; they hacked at targes and sheared through the shield-wall. The Hebrew spear-throwers were wrought up to the fray; the soldiers lusted mightily after a spear-contest on that occasion. There in the dust fell the main part of the muster-roll of the Assyrian nobility, of that odious race. Few survivors reached their native land.

The soldiers of royal renown turned back in retirement amidst carnage and reeking corpses. That was the opportunity for the land's in-dwellers to seize from those most odious foes, their old dead enemies, bloodied booty, resplendent accoutrements, shield and broad sword, burnished helmets, costly treasures. The guardians of their homeland had honorably conquered their enemies on the battlefield and destroyed with swords their old persecutors. In their trail lay dead those who of living peoples had been most inimical to their existence.

Then the whole nation, most famous of races, proud, curled-locked, for the duration of one month were carrying and conveying into the beautiful city, Bethulia, helmets and hip-swords, gray mail-coats, and men's battle-dress ornamented with gold, more glorious treasures than any man among ingenious men can tell. All that the people splendidly gained, brave beneath their banners in the fray, through the shrewd advice of Judith, the courageous woman. As a reward the celebrated spearmen brought back for her from the expedition the sword and the bloodied helmet of Holofernes as well as his huge mail-coat adorned with red gold; and everything the ruthless lord of the warriors owned of riches or personal wealth, of rings and of beautiful treasures, they gave it to that beautiful and resourceful lady.

For all this Judith gave glory to the Lord of hosts who granted her esteem and renown in the realm of earth and likewise too a reward in heaven, the prize of victory in the glory of the sky because she always had true faith in the Almighty. Certainly at the end she did not doubt the reward for which she long had yearned.

For this be glory into eternity to the dear Lord who created the wind and the clouds, the skies and the spacious plains and likewise the cruel seas and the joys of heaven, through his peculiar mercy.

The Dream of the Rood

The Dream of the Rood is a remarkable tenth-century poem, a mystical dream vision whose narrator tells of his dream that the rood—Christ's cross—appeared to him and told the story of its unwilling role in the crucifixion. The poem is an excellent illustration of how the conventions of Old English heroic poems like Beowulf were adapted to the doctrines of Christianity. Christ's Passion is converted into a heroic sacrifice as the cross reports that it watched him—the young hero—strip himself naked, as if preparing for battle, and bravely ascend it. In the same vein, the cross presents itself as a thane (retainer) forced into disloyalty, as it watches—and participates in—the crucifixion, unable to avenge its beloved Lord.

In addition to heroic poetry, *The Dream of the Rood* recalls Old English genres such as the riddle and the elegy. In riddle fashion, the cross asks, "What am I?"—that started as a tree, became an instrument of torture, and am now a beacon of victory, resplendent with jewels. In the manner of elegies like *The Wanderer*, the speaker, stained with sin, presents himself as a lonely exile whose companions have left him and gone to heaven. After his vision, he resolves to seek the fellowship of his heavenly Lord and his former companions, which he pictures as taking place in a celestial mead hall: "the home of joy and happiness, / where the people of God are seated at the feast / in eternal bliss."

One of the most striking poetic effects of *The Dream of the Rood* is its focus on the Incarnation, God's taking on human flesh. The poet often juxtaposes references to Christ's humanity and divinity in the same line, thereby achieving a powerful effect of paradox, as when he tells of the approach of "the young warrior, God Almighty." It is noteworthy that the aspect of Christ's humanity which the poet stresses is the heroism rather than the pathos which was to become so prominent in later medieval poetry and art. This heroism provides a context for a cryptic passage at the end of the poem, where the dreamer refers to Christ's "journey" to bring "those who before suffered burning" victoriously to heaven. In *The Harrowing of Hell* (based on the apocryphal Gospel of Nicodemus), Christ heroically freed the virtuous Old Testament patriarchs from damnation and led them to eternal bliss.

The fame of *The Dream of the Rood* appears to have been widespread in its own time. Our knowledge of it comes from three sources: the huge stone Ruthwell Cross in southern Scotland built in the eighth century (on which a short version is inscribed in runic letters); the silver Brussels Cross, made in England in the tenth century; and the manuscript found written in Vercelli in northern Italy, also written in the tenth century—the only complete version of the poem. These varied locations are a testament to the wide influence of Anglo-Saxon scholars, not only in the British Isles but on the Continent as well.

The Dream of the Rood[1]

Listen! I will describe the best of dreams
which I dreamed in the middle of the night
when, far and wide, all men slept.
It seemed that I saw a wondrous tree
5   soaring into the air, surrounded by light,
the brightest of crosses; that emblem was entirely
cased in gold; beautiful jewels
were strewn around its foot, just as five
studded the cross-beam. All the angels of God,
10   fair creations, guarded it. That was no cross
of a criminal, but holy spirits and men on earth
watched over it there—the whole glorious universe.

Wondrous was the tree of victory, and I was stained
by sin, stricken by guilt. I saw this glorious tree
15   joyfully gleaming, adorned with garments,
decked in gold; the tree of the Ruler
was rightly adorned with rich stones;
yet through that gold I could see the agony
once suffered by wretches, for it had bled
20   down the right hand side. Then I was afflicted,

1. Translated by Kevin Crossley-Holland.

The Ruthwell Cross, north side, top section, 7th–8th century. Preserved in a church in southern Scotland, this 18-foot stone cross is carved with many Christian scenes, including this depiction of Saint John the Baptist, bearded and holding the Lamb of God. The Latin inscription beneath the saint is written in runes—the traditional Germanic alphabet, used for ritualistic purposes. Runic inscriptions elsewhere on the cross reproduce portions of *The Dream of the Rood* in Old English. Still other inscriptions are in Latin and employ the Roman alphabet. Thus, like *The Dream of the Rood* itself, whose Christlike hero resembles a Germanic warrior, the Ruthwell Cross illustrates the fusion of Mediterranean and Germanic traditions in Anglo-Saxon Christian culture.

frightened at this sight; I saw that sign often change
its clothing and hue, at times dewy with moisture,
stained by flowing blood, at times adorned with treasure.
Yet I lay there for a long while
25   and gazed sadly at the Savior's cross
until I heard it utter words;
the finest of trees began to speak:
"I remember the morning a long time ago
that I was felled at the edge of the forest
30   and severed from my roots. Strong enemies seized me,
bade me hold up their felons on high,
made me a spectacle. Men shifted me
on their shoulders and set me on a hill.
Many enemies fastened me there. I saw the Lord of Mankind
35   hasten with such courage to climb upon me.
I dared not bow or break there

against my Lord's wish, when I saw the surface
of the earth tremble. I could have felled
all my foes, yet I stood firm.
40   Then the young warrior, God Almighty,
stripped Himself, firm and unflinching. He climbed
upon the cross, brave before many, to redeem mankind.
I quivered when the hero clasped me,
yet I dared not bow to the ground,
45   fall to the earth. I had to stand firm.
A rood was I raised up; I bore aloft the mighty King,
the Lord of Heaven. I dared not stoop.
They drove dark nails into me; dire wounds are there to see,
the gaping gashes of malice; I dared not injure them.
50   They insulted us both together; I was drenched in the blood
that streamed from the Man's side after He set His spirit free.

"On that hill I endured many grievous trials;
I saw the God of Hosts stretched
on the rack; darkness covered the corpse
55   of the Ruler with clouds, His shining radiance.
Shadows swept across the land, dark shapes
under the clouds. All creation wept,
wailed for the death of the King; Christ was on the cross.
Yet men hurried eagerly to the Prince
60   from afar; I witnessed all that too.
I was oppressed with sorrow, yet humbly bowed to the hands of men,
and willingly. There they lifted Him from His heavy torment,
they took Almighty God away. The warriors left me standing there,
stained with blood; sorely was I wounded by the sharpness of spear-shafts.
65   They laid Him down, limb-weary; they stood at the corpse's head,
they beheld there the Lord of Heaven; and there He rested for a while,
worn-out after battle. And then they began to build a sepulchre;
under his slayers' eyes, they carved it from the gleaming stone,
and laid therein the Lord of Victories. Then, sorrowful at dusk,
70   they sang a dirge before they went, weary,
from their glorious Prince; He rested in the grave alone.
But we still stood there, weeping blood,
long after the song of the warriors
had soared to heaven; the corpse grew cold,
75   the fair human house of the soul. Then our enemies
began to fell us; that was a terrible fate.
They buried us in a deep pit; but friends
and followers of the Lord found me there
and girded me with gold and shimmering silver.

80   "Now, my loved man, you have heard
how I endured bitter anguish
at the hands of evil men. Now the time is come
when men far and wide in this world,
and all this bright creation, bow before me;
85   they pray to this sign. On me the Son of God
suffered for a time; wherefore I now stand on high,

glorious under heaven; and I can heal
all those who stand in awe of me.
Long ago I became the worst of tortures,
90   hated by men, until I opened
to them the true way of life.
Lo! The Lord of Heaven, the Prince of Glory,
honored me over any other tree
just as He, Almighty God, for the sake of mankind
95   honored Mary, His own mother,
before all other women in the world.
Now I command you, my loved man,
to describe your vision to all men;
tell them with words this is the tree of glory
100   on which the Son of God suffered once
for the many sins committed by mankind,
and for Adam's wickedness long ago.
He sipped the drink of death. Yet the Lord rose
with His great strength to deliver man.
105   Then He ascended into heaven. The Lord Himself,
Almighty God, with His host of angels,
will come to the middle-world again
on Domesday to reckon with each man.
Then He who has the power of judgment
110   will judge each man just as he deserves
for the way in which he lived this fleeting life.
No-one then will be unafraid
as to what words the Lord will utter.
Before the assembly, He will ask where that man is
115   who, in God's name, would undergo the pangs of death,
just as He did formerly upon the cross.
Then men will be fearful and give
scant thought to what they say to Christ.
But no-one need be numbed by fear
120   who has carried the best of all signs in his breast;
each soul that has longings to live with the Lord
must search for a kingdom far beyond the frontiers of this world."

Then I prayed to the cross, eager
and light-hearted, although I was alone
125   with my own poor company. My soul
longed for a journey, great yearnings
always tugged at me. Now my hope in this life
is that I can turn to that tree of victory
alone and more often than any other man
130   and honor it fully. These longings master
my heart and mind, and my help comes
from holy cross itself. I have not many friends
of influence on earth; they have journeyed on
from the joys of this world to find the King of Glory,
135   they live in heaven with the High Father,
dwell in splendor. Now I look day by day
for that time when the cross of the Lord,

which once I saw in a dream here on earth,
will fetch me away from this fleeting life
140   and lift me to the home of joy and happiness
where the people of God are seated at the feast
in eternal bliss, and set me down
where I may live in glory unending and share
the joy of the saints. May the Lord be a friend to me,
145   He who suffered once for the sins of men
here on earth on the gallows-tree.
He has redeemed us; He has given life to us,
and a home in heaven.
                    Hope was renewed,
blessed and blissful, for those who before suffered burning.
150   On that journey the Son was victorious,
strong and successful. When He, Almighty Ruler,
returned with a thronging host of spirits
to God's kingdom, to joy among the angels
and all the saints who lived already
155   in heaven in glory, then their King,
Almighty God, entered His own country.

═╪═ PERSPECTIVES ╪═
Ethnic and Religious Encounters

In the centuries of their insurgency and the consolidation of their influence in Britain, the Angles and Saxons negotiated a series of encounters that left them, and England, profoundly transformed. They arrived from the distant coasts of northwest continental Europe as self-conscious foreigners, divided into large tribal groups and often warring among themselves. They were pagans and masters of a great but essentially oral culture. By the end of their dominance, in 1066, they were long-Christianized and increasingly had come to perceive themselves as a single people. Moreover, their conversion involved a new commitment to the practical uses of writing and the talismanic power of the written book, as well as a heightened sense of the conflicting claims and uses of their ancient vernacular and of Latin. They now experienced England as their native place and registered their ancestral geography on the Continent as an area of nostalgic exploration or, equally, the source of hostile invasion.

All this was the work of centuries. It was not an unconscious or "natural" development, however. The passages in this section, in their different ways, offer key moments in the lengthy and complex process by which the Germanic newcomers encountered other peoples, religions, textual cultures, and geographies.

The initial contact between the Germanic invaders and the prior inhabitants of England—Britons, the "Irish" of the northwest, and the Picts—was based on military service which turned into military aggression. Relatively soon, though, and even as their territorial ambitions continued, the Angles and Saxons developed other contacts, especially with the Britons. The British were already Christian, and the Angles and Saxons first came to Christianity through British models if not by British hands. Later, the Anglo-Saxons themselves would face invasion by Vikings, who ultimately settled north of the Humber in the "Danelaw." Much of Asser's *Life of King Alfred* documents Alfred's struggle against Viking raiders.

Though he celebrated Alfred's West Saxon kingship and culture, Asser was himself a Welshman. His presence at Alfred's court is a sign of how Latin learning had declined in the disordered era of Viking incursions; Alfred was obliged to turn to other peoples to restore education in his own realm. The Norwegian trader Ohthere, too, came to Alfred's court even while the King was fending off Viking raiders. Ohthere seems to have sparked lively interest in his own people and their social order, as well as in his visits to what the Anglo-Saxons knew was their ancestral home.

Christianization was also a slow, complex, and incomplete process of acculturation. Bede recounts a number of moments when the differing responses to a single event register the encounters of pagan and Christian, literate and illiterate, and Latin and Germanic traditions. The conversion of King Edwin, for instance, involved not just the King fulfilling a promise made in a vision but also his nobles learning to imagine a new spiritual geography which went far beyond the brief joys of their warrior cohort. In the story of Imma, the magical loosing of a prisoner's chains is seen by some as the effect of an ancient pagan "loosing spell," but by Imma (and Bede's Christian readers) as the effect of masses said for his soul.

Language and literacy equally figure in the conversion of the Angles and Saxons and in the slow emergence of the idea of an "English" people. Imma is freed by the uncanny (and somewhat misdirected) power of the Latin mass. The high level of Bede's own Latin suggests how that language was becoming a cohesive force, at least among clerics. Yet in one of his tenderest stories, Bede tells about the illiterate Caedmon who learned, by divine intervention, to tell biblical stories in vernacular poetry. Bede admits that his Latin version of *Caedmon's Hymn* is inadequte, which suggests that Anglo-Saxon could assume its own place in the operations of the sacred. And Asser celebrates Alfred's childhood love of Saxon poems, laments Alfred's illiteracy, yet tells how the illiterate prince competed for the gift of a book he valued almost as a talisman. Alfred's acquisition of literacy and of Latin is part of his rise to successful kingship, and he caps his own reign with the series of translations that bring crucial texts of Latin Christianity into an Anglo-Saxon that Alfred now seems to see as a unifying national tongue.

Finally, even as some Anglo-Saxons aspire to nationhood, they do so by nostalgic memories of their foreign past, as seen in the information they draw from the Norwegian visitor Ohthere. At the same time, though, they mark themselves off from this geography and see themselves as the sinning victims of invasions that will end their power, just as their own successful invasions had punished and subdued the earlier Britons. This is repeatedly made explicit in *The Anglo-Saxon Chronicle*'s report of the twin battles fought by King Harold against Norwegian aggressors in the North and then against the triumphant Normans in the South. Their sense of nationhood and of being folded into processes of Christian history is clearest as the Chronicler witnesses the close of Anglo-Saxon dominance.

Bede
672–735

Bede was born on lands belonging to the abbey of Wearmouth-Jarrow. He entered that monastery at the age of seven and never traveled more than seventy-five miles away. Bede is the most enduring product of the golden age of Northumbrian monasticism. In the generations just preceding his, a series of learned abbots had brought Roman liturgical practices and monastic habits to Wearmouth-Jarrow, as well as establishing there the best library in England. Out of this settled life and disciplined religious culture Bede created a diverse body of writings that are learned both in scholarly research and in the purity of their Latin. They include biblical commentaries, school texts from spelling to metrics, treatises on the liturgical calendar, hymns, and lives of saints.

Bede's *An Ecclesiastical History of the English People*, completed in 731, marks the apex of his achievement. Given the localism of his life, Bede's grasp of English history is extraordinary, not just in terms of his eager pursuit of information, but equally in his balanced and complex sense of the broad movement of history. Bede registers a persistent concern about his sources and their reliability. He prefers written and especially documentary evidence, but he will use oral reports if they come from several sources and are close enough to the original event.

The *Ecclesiastical History* suggests the contours of a national history, even a providential history, in the arrival of the Angles and Saxons, and in the island's uneven conversion to Christianity. Despite his frequent stories of battles among the Germanic peoples in Britain, Bede speaks of the English people emphatically in the singular. Nevertheless, Bede is delicately aware of the historical layering brought about by colonization and the ongoing resistance of earlier inhabitants. Further, he is always alert to profoundly transformative influences, aside from ethnicity, that color his time: the process of conversion to Christianity, and the variable coexistence of Christian and pagan instincts in individual minds; the interplay of oral and written culture; the status in religious and official life of Latin and the Anglo-Saxon vernaculars.

from An Ecclesiastical History of the English People[1]
[THE CONVERSION OF KING EDWIN][2]

King Edwin hesitated to accept the word of God which Paulinus[3] preached but, as we have said, used to sit alone for hours at a time, earnestly debating within himself what he ought to do and what religion he should follow. One day Paulinus came to

---

1. Edited and translated by Bertram Colgrave and R. A. B. Mynors.
2. From bk. 2, chs. 12–14. Edwin became king of Northumbria in 616, aided by Raedwald, king of the East Angles. Exiled at Raedwald's court, Edwin had a vision wherein he promised a shadowy visitor he would convert if he achieved the crown. The visitor laid his right hand on Edwin's head as a sign to remember that promise when the gesture was repeated.
3. Later archbishop of York, Paulinus had been sent to Northumbria from Kent with Edwin's Christian wife after Edwin had promised tolerance of Christian worship.

him and, placing his right hand on the king's head, asked him if he recognized this sign. The king began to tremble and would have thrown himself at the bishop's feet but Paulinus raised him up and said in a voice that seemed familiar, "First you have escaped with God's help from the hands of the foes you feared; secondly you have acquired by His gift the kingdom you desired; now, in the third place, remember your own promise; do not delay in fulfilling it but receive the faith and keep the commandments of Him who rescued you from your earthly foes and raised you to the honor of an earthly kingdom. If from henceforth you are willing to follow His will which is made known to you through me, He will also rescue you from the everlasting torments of the wicked and make you a partaker with Him of His eternal kingdom in heaven."

When the king had heard his words, he answered that he was both willing and bound to accept the faith which Paulinus taught. He said, however, that he would confer about this with his loyal chief men and his counselors so that, if they agreed with him, they might all be consecrated together in the waters of life. Paulinus agreed and the king did as he had said. A meeting of his council was held and each one was asked in turn what he thought of this doctrine hitherto unknown to them and this new worship of God which was being proclaimed.

Coifi, the chief of the priests, answered at once, "Notice carefully, King, this doctrine which is now being expounded to us. I frankly admit that, for my part, I have found that the religion which we have hitherto held has no virtue nor profit in it. None of your followers has devoted himself more earnestly than I have to the worship of our gods, but nevertheless there are many who receive greater benefits and greater honor from you than I do and are more successful in all their undertakings. If the gods had any power they would have helped me more readily, seeing that I have always served them with greater zeal. So it follows that if, on examination, these new doctrines which have now been explained to us are found to be better and more effectual, let us accept them at once without any delay."

Another of the king's chief men agreed with this advice and with these wise words and then added, "This is how the present life of man on earth, King, appears to me in comparison with that time which is unknown to us. You are sitting feasting with your ealdormen and thegns[4] in winter time; the fire is burning on the hearth in the middle of the hall and all inside is warm, while outside the wintry storms of rain and snow are raging; and a sparrow flies swiftly through the hall. It enters in at one door and quickly flies out through the other. For the few moments it is inside, the storm and wintry tempest cannot touch it, but after the briefest moment of calm, it flits from your sight, out of the wintry storm and into it again. So this life of man appears but for a moment; what follows or indeed what went before, we know not at all. If this new doctrine brings us more certain information, it seems right that we should accept it."[5] Other elders and counselors of the king continued in the same manner, being divinely prompted to do so.

Coifi added that he would like to listen still more carefully to what Paulinus himself had to say about God. The king ordered Paulinus to speak, and when he had said his say, Coifi exclaimed, "For a long time now I have realized that our religion is worthless; for the more diligently I sought the truth in our cult, the less I found it. Now I confess openly that the truth shines out clearly in this teaching which can

4. Ealdorman: the highest Anglo-Saxon rank below king; thegn: a noble warrior still serving within the king's household.

5. This famous simile is put in the mouth of a lay nobleman, not the pagan priest Coifi whose argument for conversion was based on disappointed self-interest.

bestow on us the gift of life, salvation, and eternal happiness. Therefore I advise your Majesty that we should promptly abandon and commit to the flames the temples and the altars which we have held sacred without reaping any benefit." Why need I say more? The king publicly accepted the gospel which Paulinus preached, renounced idolatry, and confessed his faith in Christ. When he asked the high priest of their religion which of them should be the first to profane the altars and the shrines of the idols, together with their precincts, Coifi answered, "I will; for through the wisdom the true God has given me no one can more suitably destroy those things which I once foolishly worshiped, and so set an example to all." And at once, casting aside his vain superstitions, he asked the king to provide him with arms and a stallion; and mounting it he set out to destroy the idols. Now a high priest of their religion was not allowed to carry arms or to ride except on a mare. So, girded with a sword, he took a spear in his hand and mounting the king's stallion he set off to where the idols were. The common people who saw him thought he was mad. But as soon as he approached the shrine, without any hesitation he profaned it by casting the spear which he held into it; and greatly rejoicing in the knowledge of the worship of the true God, he ordered his companions to destroy and set fire to the shrine and all the enclosures. The place where the idols once stood is still shown, not far from York, to the east, over the river Derwent. Today it is called Goodmanham, the place where the high priest, through the inspiration of the true God, profaned and destroyed the altars which he himself had consecrated.[6]

So King Edwin, with all the nobles of his race and a vast number of the common people, received the faith and regeneration by holy baptism in the eleventh year of his reign, that is in the year of our Lord 627 and about 180 years after the coming of the English to Britain. He was baptized at York on Easter Day, 12 April, in the church of Saint Peter the Apostle, which he had hastily built of wood while he was a catechumen and under instruction before he received baptism. He established an episcopal see for Paulinus, his instructor and bishop, in the same city.

[THE STORY OF IMMA][7]

In this battle in which King Aelfwine[8] was killed, a remarkable incident is known to have happened which in my opinion should certainly not be passed over in silence, since the story may lead to the salvation of many. During the battle one of the king's retainers, a young man named Imma was struck down among others; he lay all that day and the following night as though dead, among the bodies of the slain, but at last he recovered consciousness, sat up, and bandaged his wounds as best he could; then, having rested for a short time, he rose and set out to find friends to take care of him. But as he was doing so, he was found and captured by men of the enemy army and taken to their lord, who was a *gesith*[9] of King Aethelred. On being asked who he was, he was afraid to admit that he was a thegn; but he answered instead that he was a poor peasant and married; and he declared that he had come to the army in company with other peasants to bring food to the soldiers. The *gesith* took him and had his wounds attended to. But when Imma began to get better, he ordered him to be bound at night to prevent his escape. However, it proved impossible to bind him, for no sooner had those who chained him gone, than his fetters were loosed.

6. This detail is typical of Bede's liking for textual or archaeological authentication.
7. Bk. 4, ch. 22.
8. A battle in 679, between King Ecgfrith of Northumbria and Aethelred king of the Mercians caused the death of this under-king and brother of Ecgfrith.
9. A nobleman, serving a king but having his own household of retainers and servants.

Now he had a brother whose name was Tunna, a priest and abbot of a monastery in a city which is still called *Tunnacaestir* after him. When Tunna heard that his brother had perished in the fight, he went to see if he could find his body; having found another very like him in all respects, he concluded that it must be his brother's body. So he carried it to the monastery, buried it with honor, and took care to offer many masses for the absolution of his soul. It was on account of these celebrations that, as I have said, no one could bind Imma because his fetters were at once loosed. Meanwhile the *gesith* who kept him captive grew amazed and asked him why he could not be bound and whether he had about him any loosing spells such as are described in stories. But Imma answered that he knew nothing of such arts. "However," said he, "I have a brother in my country who is a priest and I know he believes me to be dead and offers frequent masses on my behalf; so if I had now been in another world, my soul would have been loosed from its punishment by his intercessions." When he had been a prisoner with the *gesith* for some time, those who watched him closely realized by his appearance, his bearing, and his speech that he was not of common stock as he had said, but of noble family. Then the *gesith* called him aside and asked him very earnestly to declare his origin, promising that no harm should come to him, provided that he told him plainly who he was. The prisoner did so, revealing that he had been one of the king's thegns. The *gesith* answered, "I realized by every one of your answers that you were not a peasant, and now you ought to die because all my brothers and kinsmen were killed in the battle: but I will not kill you for I do not intend to break my promise."

As soon as Imma had recovered, the *gesith* sold him to a Frisian in London; but he could neither be bound on his way there nor by the Frisian. So after his enemies had put every kind of bond on him and as his new master realized that he could not be bound, he gave him leave to ransom himself if he could. Now the bonds were most frequently loosed from about nine in the morning, the time when masses were usually said. So having sworn that he would either return or send his master the money for his ransom, he went to King Hlothhere of Kent, who was the son of Queen Aethelthryth's sister already mentioned, because he had once been one of Aethelthryth's thegns; he asked for and received the money from him for his ransom and sent it to his master as he had promised.[1]

He afterwards returned to his own country, where he met his brother and gave him a full account of all his troubles and the comfort that had come to him in those adversities; and from what his brother told him, he realized that his bonds had generally been loosed at the time when masses were being celebrated on his behalf; so he perceived that the other comforts and blessings which he had experienced during his time of danger had been bestowed by heaven, through the intercession of his brother and the offering up of the saving Victim. Many who heard about this from Imma were inspired to greater faith and devotion, to prayer and almsgiving and to the offering up of sacrifices to God in the holy oblation, for the deliverance of their kinsfolk who had departed from the world; for they realized that the saving sacrifice availed for the everlasting redemption of both body and soul.

This story was told me by some of those who heard it from the very man to whom these things happened; therefore since I had so clear an account of the incident, I thought that it should undoubtedly be inserted into this *History*.

1. Imma had been thegn to Aethelthryth, wife of King Ecgfrith, before he entered Aelfwine's service. He now turns to her nephew, implicitly invoking obligations of kinship, for help with his ransom.

[CAEDMON'S HYMN][2]

In the monastery of this abbess[3] there was a certain brother who was specially marked out by the grace of God, so that he used to compose godly and religious songs; thus, whatever he learned from the holy Scriptures by means of interpreters, he quickly turned into extremely delightful and moving poetry, in English, which was his own tongue. By his songs the minds of many were often inspired to despise the world and to long for the heavenly life. It is true that after him other Englishmen attempted to compose religious poems, but none could compare with him. For he did not learn the art of poetry from men nor through a man but he received the gift of song freely by the grace of God. Hence he could never compose any foolish or trivial poem but only those which were concerned with devotion and so were fitting for his devout tongue to utter. He had lived in the secular habit until he was well advanced in years and had never learned any songs.[4] Hence sometimes at a feast, when for the sake of providing entertainment, it had been decided that they should all sing in turn, when he saw the harp approaching him, he would rise up in the middle of the feasting, go out, and return home.

On one such occasion when he did so, he left the place of feasting and went to the cattle byre, as it was his turn to take charge of them that night. In due time he stretched himself out and went to sleep, whereupon he dreamed that someone stood by him, saluted him, and called him by name: "Caedmon," he said, "sing me something." Caedmon answered, "I cannot sing; that is why I left the feast and came here because I could not sing." Once again the speaker said, "Nevertheless you must sing to me." "What must I sing?" said Caedmon. "Sing," he said, "about the beginning of created things." Thereupon Caedmon began to sing verses which he had never heard before in praise of God the Creator, of which this is the general sense: "Now we must praise the Maker of the heavenly kingdom, the power of the Creator and his counsel, the deeds of the Father of glory and how He, since he is the eternal God, was the Author of all marvels and first created the heavens as a roof for the children of men and then, the almighty Guardian of the human race, created the earth." This is the sense but not the order of the words which he sang as he slept. For it is not possible to translate verse, however well composed, literally from one language to another without some loss of beauty and dignity. When he awoke, he remembered all that he had sung while asleep and soon added more verses in the same manner, praising God in fitting style.

In the morning he went to the reeve[5] who was his master, telling him of the gift he had received, and the reeve took him to the abbess. He was then bidden to describe his dream in the presence of a number of the more learned men and also to recite his song so that they might all examine him and decide upon the nature and origin of the gift of which he spoke; and it seemed clear to all of them that the Lord had granted him heavenly grace. They then read to him a passage of sacred history or doctrine, bidding him make a song out of it, if he could, in metrical form. He undertook the task and went away; on returning next morning he repeated the passage he had been given, which he had put into excellent verse. The abbess, who

---

2. Bk. 4, ch. 24.
3. Hild, an aristocratic woman famed for her piety, who had founded and ruled the abbey of Whitby.
4. Monks, who devoted their lives to prayer and the cele-

bration of the liturgy, needed to be literate in Latin. Caedmon was one of the lay brothers, who performed menial tasks and were often uneducated.
5. Person responsible for running the monastery's estates.

recognized the grace of God which the man had received, instructed him to renounce his secular habit and to take monastic vows. She and all her people received him into the community of the brothers and ordered that he should be instructed in the whole course of sacred history. He learned all he could by listening to them and then, memorizing it and ruminating over it, like some clean animal chewing the cud, he turned it into the most melodious verse: and it sounded so sweet as he recited it that his teachers became in turn his audience. He sang about the creation of the world, the origin of the human race, and the whole history of Genesis, of the departure of Israel from Egypt and the entry into the promised land and of many other of the stories taken from the sacred Scriptures: of the incarnation, passion, and resurrection of the Lord, of His ascension into heaven, of the coming of the Holy Spirit and the teaching of the apostles. He also made songs about the terrors of future judgment, the horrors of the pains of hell, and the joys of the heavenly kingdom. In addition he composed many other songs about the divine mercies and judgments, in all of which he sought to turn his hearers away from delight in sin and arouse in them the love and practice of good works. He was a most religious man, humbly submitting himself to the discipline of the Rule; and he opposed all those who wished to act otherwise with a flaming and fervent zeal. It was for this reason that his life had a beautiful ending.

When the hour of his departure drew near he was afflicted, fourteen days before, by bodily weakness, yet so slight that he was able to walk about and talk the whole time. There was close by a building to which they used to take those who were infirm or who seemed to be at the point of death. On the night on which he was to die, as evening fell, he asked his attendant to prepare a place in this building where he could rest. The attendant did as Caedmon said though he wondered why he asked, for he did not seem to be by any means at the point of death. They had settled down in the house and were talking and joking cheerfully with each of those who were already there and it was past midnight, when he asked whether they had the Eucharist in the house. They answered, "What need have you of the Eucharist? You are not likely to die, since you are talking as cheerfully with us as if you were in perfect health." "Nevertheless," he repeated, "bring me the Eucharist." When he had taken it in his hand he asked if they were all charitably disposed towards him and had no complaint nor any quarrel nor grudge against him. They answered that they were all in charity with him and without the slightest feeling of anger; then they asked him in turn whether he was charitably disposed towards them. He answered at once, "My sons, I am in charity with all the servants of God." So, fortifying himself with the heavenly viaticum, he prepared for his entrance into the next life. Thereupon he asked them how near it was to the time when the brothers had to awake to sing their nightly praises to God. They answered, "It will not be long." And he answered, "Good, let us wait until then." And so, signing himself with the sign of the holy cross, he laid his head on the pillow, fell asleep for a little while, and so ended his life quietly. Thus it came about that, as he had served the Lord with a simple and pure mind and with quiet devotion, so he departed into His presence and left the world by a quiet death; and his tongue which had uttered so many good words in praise of the Creator also uttered its last words in His praise, as he signed himself with the sign of the cross and commended his spirit into God's hands; and from what has been said, it would seem that he had foreknowledge of his death.

Bishop Asser
? – c. 909

When Bede died in 735, he left an island that was very unstable in its political geography but apparently ever more stable and accomplished in its religion and learning. By the end of the century, that world was shattered. In 793 Vikings sacked the monastery of Lindisfarne, not far from Wearmouth-Jarrow. Waves of raiders and then settlers followed. Monastic communities fled inland, and some shifted for generations before resettling finally. However sporadic and temporary may have been the worldly impact of these Viking raiders, however quickly they became peaceful settlers, they had a disastrous effect on the kind of disciplined learning witnessed by the life of Bede. By the time of Asser, Latin learning in most of England was fragmented and in decline, though not so bad as it suits Alfred to claim. Asser, a Welsh monk and later bishop of Sherborne, was summoned to Wessex by King Alfred as part of a project to revive learning and extend its audience beyond those who read Latin. Alfred accomplished this, in part, by looking to men like Asser, from areas such as Wales which had preserved some traditions of classical learning.

Asser's worshipful and disorganized but lively *Life of King Alfred* was written in Latin during the king's life, about 893. It depicts the origins of the king's scholarly ambitions, interwoven with the struggles by which Alfred established and extended his rule and resisted renewed Viking incursions. Asser thus offers a double narrative of texts and conquests which make one another possible and worthy. The diffusion of learning and revival of religious discipline become enmeshed in a logic that also includes Alfred's ambitions to rule all the Anglo-Saxons.

from The Life of King Alfred[1]
[ALFRED'S BOYHOOD]

Now he was greatly cherished above all his brothers by the united and ardent love of his father and mother, and indeed of all people; and he was ever brought up entirely at the royal court. As he passed through his infancy and boyhood he surpassed all his brothers in beauty, and was more pleasing in his appearance, in his speech, and in his manners. From his earliest childhood the noble character of his mind gave him a desire for all things useful in this present life, and, above all, a longing for wisdom; but, alas! the culpable negligence of his relations, and of those who had care of him, allowed him to remain ignorant of letters until his twelfth year, or even to a later age. Albeit, day and night did he listen attentively to the Saxon poems, which he often heard others repeating, and his retentive mind enabled him to remember them.

An ardent hunter, he toiled persistently at every form of that art, and not in vain. For in his skill and success at this pursuit he surpassed all, as in all other gifts of God. And this skill we have ourselves seen on many occasions.

Now it chanced on a certain day that his mother showed to him and to his brothers a book of Saxon poetry, which she had in her hand, and said, "I will give this book to that one among you who shall the most quickly learn it." Then, moved at these words, or rather by the inspiration of God, and being carried away by the beauty of the initial letter in that book, anticipating his brothers who surpassed him in years but not in grace, he answered his mother, and said, "Will you of a truth give that book to one of us? To him who shall soonest understand it and repeat it to you?"

1. Translated by L. C. Jane.

And at this she smiled and was pleased, and affirmed it, saying, "I will give it to him."
Then forthwith he took the book from her hand and went to his master, and read it;
and when he had read it he brought it back to his mother and repeated it to her.

After this he learnt the Daily Course, that is, the services for each hour, and
then some psalms and many prayers. These were collected in one book, which, as we
have ourselves seen, he constantly carried about with him everywhere in the fold of
his cloak, for the sake of prayer amid all the passing events of this present life. But,
alas! the art of reading which he most earnestly desired he did not acquire in accordance with his wish, because, as he was wont himself to say, in those days there were
no men really skilled in reading in the whole realm of the West Saxons.

With many complaints, and with heartfelt regrets, he used to declare that among
all the difficulties and trials of this life this was the greatest. For at the time when he
was of an age to learn, and had leisure and ability for it, he had no masters; but when
he was older, and indeed to a certain extent had anxious masters and writers, he
could not read. For he was occupied day and night without ceasing both with illnesses
unknown to all the physicians of that island, and with the cares of the royal office
both at home and abroad, and with the assaults of the heathen by land and sea.[2]
None the less, amid the difficulties of this life, from his infancy to the present day, he
has not in the past faltered in his earnest pursuit of knowledge, nor does he even now
cease to long for it, nor, as I think, will he ever do so until the end of his life.

[ALFRED'S KINGSHIP]

Yet amid the wars and many hindrances of this present life, and amid the assaults of
the pagans, and his daily illness, the king ceased not from the governance of the
kingdom and from the pursuit of every form of hunting. Nor did he omit to instruct
also his goldsmiths and all his artificers, his falconers and his huntsmen and the keepers of his dogs; nor to make according to new designs of his own articles of goldsmiths' work, more venerable and more precious than had been the wont of all his
predecessors. He was constant in the reading of books in the Saxon tongue, and more
especially in committing to memory the Saxon poems, and in commanding others to
do so. And he by himself labored most zealously with all his might.

Moreover he heard the divine offices daily, the Mass, and certain psalms and
prayers. He observed the services of the hours by day and by night, and oftentimes
was he wont, as we have said, without the knowledge of his men, to go in the nighttime to the churches for the sake of prayer. He was zealous in the giving of alms, and
generous towards his own people and to those who came from all nations. He was
especially and wonderfully kindly towards all men, and merry. And to the searching
out of things not known did he apply himself with all his heart.

Moreover many Franks, Frisians and Gauls, pagans, Britons, Scots and Armori-
cans, of their own free will, submitted them to his rule, both nobles and persons of
low degree. All these he ruled, according to his excellent goodness, as he did his
own people, and loved them and honored them, and enriched them with money
and with power.

He was eager and anxious to hear the Holy Scripture read to him by his own
folk, but he would also as readily pray with strangers, if by any chance one had come
from any place. Moreover he loved with wonderful affection his bishops and all the

2. Alfred's patient suffering in illness is one of several patterns by which Asser implies analogies with the lives of saints.

clergy, his ealdormen and nobles, his servants and all his household. And cherishing their sons, who were brought up in the royal household, with no less love than he bore towards his own children, he ceased not day and night, among other things, himself to teach them all virtue and to make them well acquainted with letters.

But it was as though he found no comfort in all these things. For, as if he suffered no other care from within or without, in anxious sorrow, day and night, he would make complaint to the Lord and to all who were joined to him in close affection, lamenting with many sighs for that Almighty God had not made him skilled in divine wisdom and in the liberal arts.

<hr/>

King Alfred
849–899

Alfred, king of the West Saxons, had ambitions to be king of all England, at least south of the Humber. He spent much of his reign in a series of campaigns against Viking raiders. After a decisive victory at the battle of Edington in 878, Alfred negotiated a peace that included the departure of the Danes from Wessex and the baptism of their king Guthrum. In the later years of his reign, starting about 890, he embarked on a quite different, but ultimately more influential, campaign of conquest and Christian conversion, through the series of Anglo-Saxon translations from Latin produced by his own hand and under his patronage. Pope Gregory the Great's *Pastoral Care* (c. 591), a handbook for bishops, was the first. This effort assuredly had charitable and scholarly motivations, but it also takes on interesting national overtones when it assumes that Anglo-Saxon is one language and known by all, and even more when it is linked to earlier translations and the westward movement of ancient power.

Preface to Saint Gregory's *Pastoral Care*[1]

King Alfred bids greet Bishop Waerferth[2] with his words lovingly and with friendship; and I let it be known to thee that it has very often come into my mind what wise men there formerly were throughout England, both of sacred and secular orders; and what happy times there were then throughout England; and how the kings who had power over the nation in those days obeyed God and His ministers; how they preserved peace, morality, and order at home, and at the same time enlarged their territory abroad; and how they prospered both with war and with wisdom; and also how zealous the sacred orders were both in teaching and learning, and in all the services they owed to God; and how foreigners came to this land in search of wisdom and instruction, and how we should now have to get them from abroad if we were to have them. So general was its decay in England that there were very few on this side of the Humber who could understand their rituals in English, or translate a letter from Latin into English; and I believe that there were not many beyond the Humber. There were so few of them that I cannot remember a single one south of the Thames when I came to the throne. Thanks be to Almighty God that we have any teachers among us now. And therefore I command thee to do as I believe thou art willing, to disengage thyself from worldly matters as often as thou canst, that thou mayest apply

1. Translated by Kevin Crossley-Holland.
2. Waerferth, bishop of Worcester, had earlier translated

Gregory's *Dialogues* for Alfred and perhaps inspired the king's more ambitious program.

the wisdom which God has given thee wherever thou canst. Consider what punishments would come upon us on account of this world, if we neither loved it [wisdom]
ourselves nor suffered other men to obtain it: we should love the name only of
Christian, and very few the virtues. When I considered all this, I remembered also
that I saw, before it had been all ravaged and burned, how the churches throughout
the whole of England stood filled with treasures and books; and there was also a
great multitude of God's servants, but they had very little knowledge of the books,
for they could not understand anything of them, because they were not written in
their own language. As if they had said: "Our forefathers, who formerly held these
places, loved wisdom, and through it they obtained wealth and bequeathed it to us.
In this we can still see their tracks, but we cannot follow them, and therefore we
have lost both the wealth and the wisdom, because we would not incline our hearts
after their example." When I remembered all this, I wondered extremely that the
good and wise men who were formerly all over England, and had perfectly learned
all the books, had not wished to translate them into their own language. But again I
soon answered myself and said: "They did not think that men would ever be so careless, and that learning would so decay; through that desire they abstained from it,
since they wished that the wisdom in this land might increase with our knowledge
of languages." Then I remembered how the law was first known in Hebrew, and
again, when the Greeks had learned it, they translated the whole of it into their
own language, and all other books besides. And again the Romans, when they had
learned them, translated the whole of them by learned interpreters into their own
language. And also all other Christian nations translated a part of them into their
own language.[3] Therefore it seems better to me, if you think so, for us also to translate some books which are most needful for all men to know into the language
which we can all understand, and for you to do as we very easily can if we have tranquility enough, that is, that all the youth now in England of free men, who are rich
enough to be able to devote themselves to it, be set to learn as long as they are not
fit for any other occupation, until they are able to read English writing well: and let
those be afterwards taught more in the Latin language who are to continue in learning, and be promoted to a higher rank. When I remembered how the knowledge of
Latin had formerly decayed throughout England, and yet many could read English
writing, I began, among other various and manifold troubles of this kingdom, to
translate into English the book which is called in Latin *Pastoralis*, and in English
Shepherd's Book, sometimes word by word, and sometimes according to the sense, as
I had learned it from Plegmund my archbishop, and Asser my bishop, and Grimbald
my mass-priest, and John my mass-priest. And when I had learned it as I could best
understand it, and as I could most clearly interpret it, I translated it into English;
and I will send a copy to every bishopric in my kingdom; and in each there is a
book-mark worth fifty mancuses.[4] And I command in God's name that no man take
the book-mark from the book, or the book from the monastery. It is uncertain how
long there may be such learned bishops as now, thanks be to God, there are nearly
everywhere; therefore I wish them always to remain in their places unless the bishop
wish to take them with him, or they be lent out anywhere, or any one be making a
copy from them.

3. An early statement of the widespread medieval idea of
the persistent westward movement of learning, *translatio
studii*, in parallel with the westward movement of power,
translatio imperii. If Alfred will now revive learning in
England, he may imply, should he not also consolidate
power?
4. Gold coins.

~+ ≍◊≍ +~

Ohthere's Journeys

Along with religious and speculative works like *Pastoral Care* and Boethius's *Consolation of Philosophy*, Alfred also sponsored the translation of histories, both Bede's *Ecclesiastical History of the English People* and the early fifth-century *Seven Books of History against the Pagans*, of Paulus Orosius. In the latter, Orosius's opening survey of geography is expanded to include lands north of the Alps, and the translator inserts the following account of two northern voyages by the Norwegian trader Ohthere, who later came to Alfred's court.

Ohthere describes two journeys, one made largely for curiosity (but also for walrus tusks) and the other mostly for trade. In the first, he heads north along the west coast of Norway, around the north edge of modern Sweden and Finland, and into the White Sea—a little-known area, inhabited only by hunters and fishermen. In the second he goes to the main trading town of his nation, Sciringes-heal (on the south coast of modern Norway), and then to a large town and trading center, Hedeby (modern Schleswig in northern Germany). Along with keen details of fauna and almost anthropological observation of local tribes, Ohthere notes the great exports of his area: furs, amber, and ivory—some of which he has brought to King Alfred. Throughout the passage, an implicit, curious interlocutor mediates between the interests (and ignorance) of the English audience and the foreign traveler.

Ohthere's Journeys[1]

Ohthere told his lord, King Alfred,[2] that he lived the furthest north of all Norwegians. He said that he lived in the north of Norway on the coast of the Atlantic. He also said that the land extends very far north beyond that point, but it is all uninhabited, except for a few places here and there where the *Finnas*[3] have their camps, hunting in winter, and in summer fishing in the sea.

He told how he once wished to find out how far the land extended due north, or whether anyone lived to the north of the unpopulated area. He went due north along the coast, keeping the uninhabited land to starboard and the open sea to port continuously for three days. He was then as far north as the whale hunters go at their furthest. He then continued due north as far as he could reach in the second three days. There the land turned due east, or the sea penetrated the land he did not know which—but he knew that he waited there for a west-northwest wind, and then sailed east along the coast as far as he could sail in four days. There he had to wait for a due northern wind, because there the land turned due south, or the sea penetrated the land he did not know which. Then from there he sailed due south along the coast as far as he could sail in five days. A great river went up into the land there. They turned up into the river, not daring to sail beyond it without permission, since the land on the far side of the river was fully settled. He had not previously come across any settled district since he left his own home, but had, the whole way, land to starboard that was uninhabited apart from fishers and bird-catchers and hunters, and they were all *Finnas*. To port he always had the open sea. The *Beormas* had extensive settlements in their country but the Norwegians did not dare to venture there. But the land of the *Terfinnas* was totally uninhabited except where hunters made camp, or fishermen or bird-catchers.

1. Translated by Christine E. Fell.
2. As a foreign visitor, Ohthere would need the official protection of the king, who is thus "his lord."
3. The *Finnas* (modern Lapps) are a nomadic people who

give tribute to the Norwegians. They herd deer, hunt, and fish. They are not the peoples we now call Finns, whom Ohthere called *Beormas* and *Cwenas*.

The *Beormas* told him many stories both about their own country and about the lands which surrounded them, but he did not know how much of it was true because he had not seen it for himself. It seemed to him that the *Finnas* and the *Beormas* spoke almost the same language. His main reason for going there, apart from exploring the land, was for the walruses, because they have very fine ivory in their tusks—they brought some of these tusks to the king—and their hide is very good for ship-ropes. This whale [i.e., walrus] is much smaller than other whales; it is no more than seven ells long. The best whale-hunting is in his own country; those are forty-eight ells long, the biggest fifty ells long; of these he said that he, one of six, killed sixty in two days.

He was a very rich man in those possessions which their riches consist of, that is in wild deer. He had still, when he came to see the king, six hundred unsold tame deer. These deer they call "reindeer." Six of these were decoy-reindeer. These are very valuable among the *Finnas* because they use them to catch the wild reindeer. He was among the chief men in that country, but he had not more than twenty cattle, twenty sheep and twenty pigs, and the little that he plowed he plowed with horses. Their wealth, however, is mostly in the tribute which the *Finnas* pay them. That tribute consists of the skins of beasts, the feathers of birds, whale-bone, and ship-ropes made from whale-hide and sealskin. Each pays according to his rank. The highest in rank has to pay fifteen marten skins, five reindeer skins, one bear skin and ten measures of feathers, and a jacket of bearskin or otterskin and two ship-ropes. Each of these must be sixty ells long, one made from whale-hide the other from seal.

He said that the land of the Norwegians is very long and narrow. All of it that can be used for grazing or plowing lies along the coast and even that is in some places very rocky. Wild mountains lie to the east, above and alongside the cultivated land. In these mountains live the *Finnas*. The cultivated land is broadest in the south, and the further north it goes the narrower it becomes. In the south it is perhaps sixty miles broad or a little broader; and in the middle, thirty or broader; and to the north, he said, where it is narrowest, it might be three miles across to the mountains. The mountains beyond are in some places of a width that takes two weeks to cross, in others of a width that can be crossed in six days.

Beyond the mountains Sweden borders the southern part of the land as far as the north, and the country of the *Cwenas* borders the land in the north. Sometimes the *Cwenas* make raids on the Norwegians across the mountains, and sometimes the Norwegians make raids on them. There are very large fresh-water lakes throughout these mountains, and the *Cwenas* carry their boats overland onto the lakes and from there make raids on the Norwegians. They have very small, very light boats.

Ohthere said that the district where he lived is called *Halgoland*.[4] He said no-one lived to the north of him. In the south part of Norway there is a trading-town which is called *Sciringes heal*. He said that a man could scarcely sail there in a month, assuming he made camp at night, and each day had a favorable wind. He would sail by the coast the whole way. To starboard is first of all *Iraland*[5] and then those islands which are between *Iraland* and this land, and then this land until he comes to *Sciringes heal*, and Norway is on the port side the whole way. To the south of *Sciringes heal* a great sea penetrates the land; it is too wide to see across. Jutland is on the far side and after that *Sillende*.[6] This sea flows into the land for many hundred miles.

4. The northernmost province of Norway, much of it within the polar circle.

5. Possibly a corruption of Iceland.

6. Probably southern Jutland, modern North Schleswig.

The Death of Harold, from *The Bayeux Tapestry,* c. 1073–1088. This narrative tapestry was made within living memory of the Conquest, and the scenes depicted on it overlap much of the story as told in the *Anglo-Saxon Chronicle.* The tapestry is an extraordinary production: a roll about 20 inches high and some 230 feet long thought to have been embroidered by English women, whose needlework had international fame. In this climactic scene, at left King Harold is cut down by a mounted Norman knight; at center, Anglo-Saxon foot soldiers parry spears thrown by mounted Normans. In the marginal decoration at top, birds of prey and lions face off, emblems perhaps of the noble combatants; at the bottom, in a very different tone, lie the corpses and arms of fallen soldiers.

From *Sciringes heal* he said that he sailed in five days to the trading-town called Hedeby, which is situated among Wends, Saxons and Angles and belongs to the Danes. When he sailed there from *Sciringes heal* he had Denmark to port and the open sea to starboard for three days. Then two days before he arrived at Hedeby he had Jutland and *Sillende* and many islands to starboard. The Angles lived in these districts before they came to this land. On the port side he had, for two days, those islands which belong to Denmark.

The Anglo-Saxon Chronicle

The Anglo-Saxon Chronicle began to be assembled in the 890s at Winchester, in the heart of King Alfred's Wessex and at the high point of his reign. The decision to use Anglo-Saxon in this originally monastic product reflects the influence of Alfred's translation projects. The original version of the *Chronicle* was distributed to a number of monasteries, which made their own additions sometimes as late as the mid-twelfth century. If the various *Chronicles* began as a gesture of common language and shared history, though, their later entries—like the one below—increasingly record dynastic struggle and civil strife. And the *Chronicles* themselves, in their extensions after the Conquest, emblematize the fate of the Anglo-Saxon vernacular and culture: increasingly isolated, fragmentary, and recorded in a disappearing tongue.

from **The Anglo-Saxon Chronicle**[1]

STAMFORD BRIDGE AND HASTINGS

1066   In this year King Harold came from York to Westminster at the Easter following the Christmas that the king died,[2] and Easter was then on 16 April. Then over all England there was seen a sign in the skies such as had never been seen before. Some said it was the star "comet" which some call the long-haired star; and it first appeared on the eve of the Greater Litany, that is 24 April, and so shone all the week. And soon after this Earl Tosti came from overseas into the Isle of Wight with as large a fleet as he could muster and both money and provisions were given him.[3] And King Harold his brother assembled a naval force and a land force larger than any king had assembled before in this country, because he had been told that William the Bastard[4] meant to come here and conquer this country. This was exactly what happened afterwards. Meanwhile Earl Tosti came into the Humber with sixty ships and Earl Edwin came with a land force and drove him out, and the sailors deserted him. And he went to Scotland with twelve small vessels, and there Harold, king of Norway, met him with three hundred ships, and Tosti submitted to him and became his vassal; and they both went up the Humber until they reached York. And there Earl Edwin and Morcar his brother fought against them; but the Norwegians had the victory. Harold, king of the English, was informed that things had gone thus; and the fight was on the Vigil of Saint Matthew. Then Harold our king came upon the Norwegians by surprise and met them beyond York at Stamford Bridge with a large force of the English people; and that day there was a very fierce fight on both sides. There was killed Harold Fairhair and Earl Tosti, and the Norwegians who survived took to flight; and the English attacked them fiercely as they pursued them until some got to the ships. Some were drowned, and some burned, and some destroyed in various ways so that few survived and the English remained in command of the field. The king gave quarter to Olaf, son of the Norse king, and their bishop and the earl of Orkney and all those who survived on the ships, and they went up to our king and swore oaths that they would always keep peace and friendship with this country; and the king let them go home with twenty-four ships. These two pitched battles were fought within five nights.

Then Count William came from Normandy to Pevensey on Michaelmas Eve, and as soon as they were able to move on they built a castle at Hastings. King Harold was informed of this and he assembled a large army and came against him at the hoary apple-tree. And William came against him by surprise before his army was drawn up in battle array. But the king nevertheless fought hard against him, with the men who were willing to support him, and there were heavy casualties on both sides. There King Harold was killed and Earl Leofwine his brother, and Earl Gyrth his brother, and many good men, and the French remained masters of the field, even as God granted it to them because of the sins of the people. Archbishop Aldred and the citizens of London wanted to have Edgar *Cild*[5] as king, as was his proper due; and Edwin and Morcar promised him that they would fight on his side; but always the more it ought to have been forward the more it got behind, and the worse it grew

1. Translated by Kevin Crossley-Holland.
2. Edward "the Confessor" ruled 1042–1066. Harold claims the throne through his sister Edith, Edward's widow.
3. Tosti was Harold's estranged brother, and now supported the rival claim of Harold Fairhair, king of Norway.

4. William of Normandy, "the Conqueror."
5. Son of Edgar the Exile, grandson and great-grandson of kings; his great-uncle King Edward had titled him "Aetheling," or "throne-worthy." He was still a minor in 1066 and would have had to rule through a regent.

from day to day, exactly as everything came to be at the end. The battle took place on the festival of Calixtus the pope. And Count William went back to Hastings, and waited there to see whether submission would be made to him. But when he understood that no one meant to come to him, he went inland with all his army that was left to him, and that came to him afterwards from overseas, and ravaged all the region that he overran until he reached Berkhamstead. There he was met by Archbishop Aldred and Edgar *Cild*, and Earl Edwin and Earl Morcar, and all the chief men from London. And they submitted out of necessity after most damage had been done— and it was a great piece of folly that they had not done it earlier, since God would not make things better, because of our sins. And they gave hostages and swore oaths to him, and he promised them that he would be a gracious liege lord, and yet in the meantime they ravaged all that they overran. Then on Christmas Day, Archbishop Aldred consecrated him king at Westminster. And he promised Aldred on Christ's book and swore moreover (before Aldred would place the crown on his head) that he would rule all this people as well as the best of the kings before him, if they would be loyal to him. All the same he laid taxes on people very severely, and then went in spring overseas to Normandy, and took with him Archbishop Stigand, and Aethelnoth, abbot of Glastonbury, and Edgar *Cild* and Earl Edwin and Earl Morcar, and Earl Waltheof, and many other good men from England. And Bishop Odo and Earl William stayed behind and built castles far and wide throughout this country, and distressed the wretched folk, and always after that it grew much worse. May the end be good when God wills!

▶══◀ END OF PERSPECTIVES: ETHNIC AND RELIGIOUS ENCOUNTERS ◀══▶

▶═◆═◀

Taliesin

The name of Taliesin resonated through Welsh literary imagination for more than a millennium, from the late sixth century until the end of the Middle Ages. Only a small cluster of about a dozen poems can be securely identified with him, all of them praise poems and elegies for contemporary kings. These must have circulated for generations in oral form. They appear in their earliest surviving manuscript, the late thirteenth-century Book of Taliesin, already embedded within a nimbus of intriguing legends and falsely attributed works that had been attached to the prestige of his name across the centuries. (For one such legend, see *The Tale of Taliesin*, page 565.)

Despite this central role, Taliesin was not a poet of "Wales" in anything like its modern geography. In the later sixth century when he was active, Welsh-speaking kingdoms survived in the north and west of Britain and into modern Scotland. They were embattled, pressured by the expanding Anglo-Saxon kingdoms to the east and south, by Picts in the north, and by Irish Celts in the kingdom of Dalriada to the far northwest. Among these unstable Welsh kingdoms, especially Rheged around the Solway Firth, Taliesin became an important court poet.

The warrior kings in the Welsh north, such as Taliesin's chief patrons Urien king of Rheged and his son Owain, were extolled in a poetic culture that celebrated treasure and heroic violence, yet did so in forms of considerable intricacy and language of dramatic spareness. Taliesin's poems use ambitious meters and stanzas involving internal rhyme, end rhyme, and alliteration. They do not merely glory in armed bloodshed but also explore the boasts and emotions leading up to battle; they often display a haunting visual sense of its grisly aftermath.

Taliesin further celebrates the generosity and gaiety of the triumphant court: in ways reminiscent of the Anglo-Saxon *Wanderer*, one poem here registers the poet's terror at the thought of
losing his patron and protector. In an elegy for Owain ap Urien, Taliesin combines all these
elements, yet brackets them with a suddenly broadened and suggestively discordant perspective, a Christian plea for the needs of Owain's soul.

Urien Yrechwydd[1]

	Urien of Yrechwydd	most generous of Christian men,
	much do you give	to the people of your land;
	as you gather	so also you scatter,
	the poets of Christendom	rejoice while you stand.
5	More is the gaiety	and more is the glory
	that Urien and his heirs	are for riches renowned,
	and he is the chieftain,	the paramount ruler,
	the far-flung refuge,	first of fighters found.
	The Lloegrians[2] know it	when they count their numbers,
10	death have they suffered	and many a shame,
	their homesteads a-burning,	stripped their bedding,
	and many a loss	and many a blame,
	and never a respite	from Urien of Rheged.
	Rheged's defender,	famed lord, your land's anchor,
15	all that is told of you	has my acclaim.
	Intense is your spear-play	when you hear ploy of battle,
	when to battle you come	'tis a killing you can,
	fire in their houses ere day	in the lord of Yrechwydd's way,
	Yrechwydd the beautiful	and its generous clan.
20	The Angles are succorless.	Around the fierce king
	are his fierce offspring.	Of those dead, of those living,
	of those yet to come,	you head the column.
	To gaze upon him	is a widespread fear;
	Gaiety clothes him,	the ribald ruler,
25	gaiety clothes him	and riches abounding,
	gold king of the Northland	and of kings king.

The Battle of Argoed Llwyfain[1]

There was a great battle Saturday morning
From when the sun rose until it grew dark.
The fourfold hosts of Fflamddwyn[2] invaded,
Goddau and Rheged gathered in arms,
5   Summoned from Argoed as far as Arfynydd[3]—
They might not delay by as much as a day.

With a great blustering din, Fflamddwyn shouted,
"Have these the hostages come? Are they ready?"[4]

1. "I-*rech*-ooeed" (gutural "ch"), or Rheged. Like many
Anglo-Saxon poems, this poem uses a break (caesura) in
midline. Translated by Saunders Lewis.
2. The Angles and Saxons.
1. "Ar-goid Lloo-*ee*-vine, the Welsh "ll" rather like "tl"
pronounced quickly as a single sound. Translated by
Anthony Conran.

2. "Flom-*thoo*-een," the Flame-bearer, identity uncertain.
3. "Goddau ("*Go*-thy,") and Arfynydd ("Ar-*vi*-nith")
British territories.
4. Fflamddwyn arrogantly demands hostages, guarantees
of submission, before the battle. The use of direct quotation is unique among Taliesin's poems.

To him then Owain, scourge of the eastlands,
10   "They've not come, no! they're not, nor shall they be ready."
And a whelp of Coel would indeed be afflicted
Did he have to give any man as a hostage!

And Urien, lord of Erechwydd, shouted,
"If they would meet us now for a treaty,
15   High on the hilltop let's raise our ramparts,
Carry our faces over the shield rims,
Raise up our spears, men, over our heads
And set upon Fflamddwyn in the midst of his hosts
And slaughter him, ay, and all that go with him!"

20   There was many a corpse beside Argoed Llwyfain;
From warriors ravens grew red
And with their leader a host attacked.
For a whole year I shall sing to their triumph.

The War-Band's Return[1]

Through a single year
This man has poured out
Wine, bragget, and mead,
Reward for valor.
5   A host of singers,
A swarm about spits,
Their torques round their heads,
Their places splendid.
Each went on campaign,
10   Eager in combat,
His steed beneath him,
Set to raid Manaw
For the sake of wealth,
Profit in plenty,
15   Eight herds alike
Of calves and cattle,
Milch cows and oxen,
And each one worthy.

I could have no joy
20   Should Urien be slain,
So loved before he left,
Brandishing his lance,
And his white hair soaked,
And a bier his fate,
25   And gory his cheek
With the stain of blood,
A strong, steadfast man,
His wife made a widow,
My faithful king,

---

1. Translated by Joseph P. Clancy.

30   My faithful trust,
My bulwark, my chief,
Before savage pain.

Go, lad, to the door:
What is that clamor?
35   Is the earth shaking?
Is the sea in flood?
The chant grows stronger
From marching men!

Were a foe in hill,
40   Urien will stab him;
Were a foe in dale,
Urien has pierced him;
Were foe in mountain,
Urien conquers him;
45   Were foe on hillside,
Urien will wound him;
Were foe on rampart,
Urien will smite him:
Foe on path, foe on peak,
50   Foe at every bend,
Not one sneeze or two
He permits before death.
No famine can come,
Plunder about him.
55   Like death his spear
Piercing a foeman.
And until I die, old,
By death's strict demand,
I shall not be joyful
60   Unless I praise Urien.

Lament for Owain Son of Urien[1]

God, consider the soul's need
  Of Owain son of Urien!
Rheged's prince, secret in loam:
  No shallow work to praise him.

5   A straight° grave, a man much praised,   *narrow*
  His whetted spear the wings of dawn:
That lord of bright Llwyfenydd,
  Where is his peer?

Reaper of enemies; strong of grip;
10   One kind with his fathers;
Owain, to slay Fflamddwyn,
  Thought it no more than sleep.

1. Translated by Saunders Lewis.

Sleepeth the wide host of England
      With light in their eyes,
15   And those that had not fled
      Were braver than were wise.

Owain dealt them doom
      As the wolves devour sheep;
That warrior, bright of harness,
20   Gave stallions for the bard.

Though he hoarded wealth like a miser
      For his soul's sake he gave it.
God, consider the soul's need
      Of Owain son of Urien!

———— ✦ ————

The Wanderer

In the Exeter Book, a manuscript copied about 975 and donated to the Bishop of Exeter, are preserved some of the greatest short poems in Old English, including a number of poems referred to as elegies—laments that contrast past happiness with present sorrow and remark on how fleeting is the former. Along with *The Wanderer*, the elegies include its companion piece *The Seafarer*; *The Ruin*; *The Husband's Message*; *The Wife's Lament*; and *Wulf and Eadwacer*. While the last two are exceptional in dealing with female experience, elegies for the most part focus on male bonds and companionship, particularly the joys of the mead hall. Old English poetry as a whole is almost entirely devoid of interest in romantic love between men and women and focuses instead on the bond between lord and retainer; elegiac poems such as *The Wanderer* have in fact been called "the love poetry of a heroic society."

The Wanderer opens with an appeal to a Christian concept, as the third-person narrator speaks of the wanderer's request for God's mercy. The body of the poem, however—primarily a first-person account in the wanderer's voice—reflects more pagan values in its regret for the loss of earthly joys. Though the poem's structure is somewhat confusing, one can discern two major parts. In the first, the wanderer laments his personal situation: he was once a member of a warrior band, but his lord—his beloved "gold-friend"—has died, leaving him a homeless exile. He dreams that he "clasps and kisses" his lord, but he then wakes to see only the dark waves, the snow, and the sea birds.

The second part of the poem turns from personal narrative to a more general statement of the transitoriness of all earthly things. The speaker (possibly someone other than the wanderer at this point), looking at the ruin of ancient buildings, is moved to express the ancient Roman motif known as *"ubi sunt"* (Latin for "where are"): "Where has the horse gone? Where the man? Where the giver of gold? / Where is the feasting place? And where the pleasures of the hall?" In the concluding five lines, the reader is urged to seek comfort in heaven.

There has been much debate about the degrees of Christianity and paganism in this tenth-century poem. The positions range from the view that the Christian opening and closing are totally extraneous to the poem and have been tacked on by a monkish copyist, to the view that the poem is a Christian allegory about a soul exiled from his heavenly home, longing for his lord Jesus Christ. It is now generally held that the poem is authentically Christian, in a literal rather than an allegorical way, but that the values of pagan society still exert a powerful pull in it.

The Wanderer[1]

Often the wanderer pleads for pity
and mercy from the Lord; but for a long time,
sad in mind, he must dip his oars
into icy waters, the lanes of the sea;
5   he must follow the paths of exile: fate is inflexible.

Mindful of hardships, grievous slaughter,
the ruin of kinsmen, the wanderer said:
"Time and again at the day's dawning
I must mourn all my afflictions alone.
10   There is no one still living to whom I dare open
the doors of my heart. I have no doubt
that it is a noble habit for a man
to bind fast all his heart's feelings,
guard his thoughts, whatever he is thinking.
15   The weary in spirit cannot withstand fate,
a troubled mind finds no relief:
wherefore those eager for glory often
hold some ache imprisoned in their hearts.
Thus I had to bind my feelings in fetters,
20   often sad at heart, cut off from my country,
far from my kinsmen, after, long ago,
dark clods of earth covered my gold-friend;
I left that place in wretchedness,
plowed the icy waves with winter in my heart;
25   in sadness I sought far and wide
for a treasure-giver, for a man
who would welcome me into his mead-hall,
give me good cheer (for I boasted no friends),
entertain me with delights. He who has experienced it
30   knows how cruel a comrade sorrow can be
to any man who has few loyal friends:
for him are the ways of exile, in no wise twisted gold;
for him is a frozen body, in no wise the fruits of the earth.
He remembers hall-retainers and treasure
35   and how, in his youth, his gold-friend
entertained him. Those joys have all vanished.
A man who lacks advice for a long while
from his loved lord understands this,
that when sorrow and sleep together
40   hold the wretched wanderer in their grip,
it seems that he clasps and kisses
his lord, and lays hands and head
upon his lord's knee as he had sometimes done
when he enjoyed the gift-throne in earlier days.
45   Then the friendless man wakes again
and sees the dark waves surging around him,
the sea-birds bathing, spreading their feathers,
frost and snow falling mingled with hail.

1. Translated by Kevin Crossley-Holland.

"Then his wounds lie more heavy in his heart,
50   aching for his lord. His sorrow is renewed;
the memory of kinsmen sweeps through his mind;
joyfully he welcomes them, eagerly scans
his comrade warriors. Then they swim away again.
Their drifting spirits do not bring many old songs
55   to his lips. Sorrow upon sorrow attend
the man who must send time and again
his weary heart over the frozen waves.

"And thus I cannot think why in the world
my mind does not darken when I brood on the fate
60   of brave warriors, how they have suddenly
had to leave the mead-hall, the bold followers.
So this world dwindles day by day,
and passes away; for a man will not be wise
before he has weathered his share of winters
65   in the world. A wise man must be patient,
neither too passionate nor too hasty of speech,
neither too irresolute nor too rash in battle;
not too anxious, too content, nor too grasping,
and never too eager to boast before he knows himself.
70   When he boasts a man must bide his time
until he has no doubt in his brave heart
that he has fully made up his mind.
A wise man must fathom how eerie it will be
when all the riches of the world stand waste,
75   as now in diverse places in this middle-earth
old walls stand, tugged at by winds
and hung with hoar-frost, buildings in decay.
The wine-halls crumble, lords lie dead,
deprived of joy, all the proud followers
80   have fallen by the wall: battle carried off some,
led them on journeys; the bird carried one
over the welling waters; one the gray wolf
devoured; a warrior with downcast face
hid one in an earth-cave.
85   Thus the Maker of Men laid this world waste
until the ancient works of the giants stood idle,
hushed without the hubbub of inhabitants.
Then he who has brooded over these noble ruins,
and who deeply ponders this dark life,
90   wise in his mind, often remembers
the many slaughters of the past and speaks these words:
Where has the horse gone? Where the man? Where the giver of gold?
Where is the feasting-place? And where the pleasures of the hall?
I mourn the gleaming cup, the warrior in his corselet,
95   the glory of the prince. How that time has passed away,
darkened under the shadow of night as if it had never been.
Where the loved warriors were, there now stands a wall
of wondrous height, carved with serpent forms.
The savage ash-spears, avid for slaughter,

100   have claimed all the warriors—a glorious fate!
       Storms crash against these rocky slopes,
       sleet and snow fall and fetter the world,
       winter howls, then darkness draws on,
       the night-shadow casts gloom and brings
105   fierce hailstorms from the north to frighten men.
       Nothing is ever easy in the kingdom of earth,
       the world beneath the heavens is in the hands of fate.
       Here possessions are fleeting, here friends are fleeting,
       here man is fleeting, here kinsman is fleeting,
110   the whole world becomes a wilderness."
       So spoke the wise man in his heart as he sat apart in thought.
       Brave is the man who holds to his beliefs; nor shall he ever
       show the sorrow in his heart before he knows how he
       can hope to heal it. It is best for a man to seek
115   mercy and comfort from the Father in heaven, the safe home that awaits us all.

⊷ ⧓ ⊶

Wulf and Eadwacer *and* The Wife's Lament

Old English literature focuses largely on masculine and military concerns and lacks a concept of romantic love—what the twelfth-century French would later call *"fine amour."* Against this backdrop *Wulf and Eadwacer* and *The Wife's Lament* stand out, first, by their use of woman's voice and second, by their treatment of the sorrows of love.

Though the exact genre of these poems is problematic, some scholars classifying them as riddles and others as religious allegories, most group them with a class of Old English poems known as elegies, with which they are preserved in the same manuscript, the Exeter Book. The elegies lament the loss of earthly goods, comradeship, and the "hall joys," often, as in *The Wanderer* and *The Seafarer*, by a speaker in exile. *The Wife's Lament* and *Wulf and Eadwacer* differ from the other elegies in that the speakers, as women, had no experience of comradeship to lose, as their main function was to be exchanged in marriage to cement relationships between feuding tribes. They are in a sense twice exiled, first from the noble brotherhood by their gender, and second from their beloved by their personal history. Furthermore, unlike the speakers in *The Wanderer* and *The Seafarer*, they do not look forward to the consolation of a heavenly kingdom imagined as a warlord with his group of retainers.

Although the two elegies in woman's voice are unique in the Old English corpus, they have analogues within the larger tradition of continental woman's song, which flourished in medieval Latin and the vernaculars from the eleventh century on. Their composition was so early—990 at the latest—that this tradition could not have influenced them, although the Roman poet Ovid's *Heroides* (verse letters of abandoned heroines to their faithless lovers) could have done so. One critic has raised the question of female authorship, on the grounds that continental nuns in the eighth century were criticized for writing romantic songs. As the critic Marilynn Desmond has suggested, perhaps Virginia Woolf's speculation that "anonymous was a woman" is true of these poems.

Though scholars agree that *Wulf and Eadwacer* is "heartrending" and "haunting," they cannot agree on the dramatic situation—each translation is an act of interpretation. The present translator, Kevin Crossley-Holland, sees the poem as involving the female speaker; her husband (Eadwacer); her lover (Wulf), from whom she is separated; and her child (a "cub"). Although what transpired before is unclear, she wistfully concludes, "men easily savage what was never secure, our song together." The dramatic setting of *The Wife's Lament* is similarly ambiguous; it is not clear whether the woman's anger is directed toward her husband or to a third person who plotted to separate them.

Wulf and Eadwacer

Prey, it's as if my people have been handed prey.
They'll tear him to pieces if he comes with a troop.

O, we are apart.

Wulf is on one island, I on another,
5   a fastness that island, a fen-prison.
Fierce men roam there, on that island;
they'll tear him to pieces if he comes with a troop.

O, we are apart.

How I have grieved for my Wulf's wide wanderings.
10   When rain slapped the earth and I sat apart weeping,
when the bold warrior wrapped his arms about me,
I seethed with desire and yet with such hatred.
Wulf, my Wulf, my yearning for you
and your seldom coming have caused my sickness,
15   my mourning heart, not mere starvation.
Can you hear, Eadwacer? Wulf will spirit
our pitiful whelp to the woods.
Men easily savage what was never secure,
our song together.

The Wife's Lament[1]

I draw these words from my deep sadness,
my sorrowful lot. I can say that,
since I grew up, I have not suffered
such hardships as now, old or new.
5   I am tortured by the anguish of exile.

First my lord forsook his family
for the tossing waves; I fretted at dawn
as to where in the world my lord might be.
In my sorrow I set out then,
10   a friendless wanderer, to search for my man.
But that man's kinsmen laid secret plans
to part us, so that we should live
most wretchedly, far from each other
in this wide world; I was seized with longings.

15   My lord asked me to live with him here;
I had few loved ones, loyal friends
in this country; that is reason for grief.
Then I found my own husband was ill-starred,
sad at heart, pretending, plotting
20   murder behind a smiling face. How often

1. Translated by Kevin Crossley-Holland.

we swore that nothing but death should ever
divide us; that is all changed now;
our friendship is as if it had never been.
Early and late, I must undergo hardship
25 because of the feud of my own dearest loved one.
Men forced me to live in a forest grove,
under an oak tree in the earth-cave.
This cavern is age-old; I am choked with longings.
Gloomy are the valleys, too high the hills,
30 harsh strongholds overgrown with briars:
a joyless abode. The journey of my lord so often
cruelly seizes me. There are lovers on earth,
lovers alive who lie in bed,
when I pass through this earth-cave alone
35 and out under the oak tree at dawn;
there I must sit through the long summer's day
and there I mourn my miseries,
my many hardships; for I am never able
to quiet the cares of my sorrowful mind,
40 all the longings that are my life's lot.

Young men must always be serious in mind
and stout-hearted; they must hide
their heartaches, that host of constant sorrows,
behind a smiling face.
                              Whether he is master
45 of his own fate or is exiled in a far-off land—
sitting under rocky storm-cliffs, chilled
with hoar-frost, weary in mind,
surrounded by the sea in some sad place—
my husband is caught in the clutches of anguish;
over and again he recalls a happier home.
50 Grief goes side by side with those
who suffer longing for a loved one.

Riddles

Riddles were a popular genre in Anglo-Saxon England, appealing to a taste for intellectual puzzles, which we also see in *Beowulf*, with its kennings; *The Dream of the Rood*, with its speaking cross; and *Wulf and Eadwacer*, with its cryptic dramatic situation. In the Exeter Book, one of the four major manuscripts containing Anglo-Saxon poetry (including *The Wanderer*, *The Wife's Lament*, and *Wulf and Eadwacer*) there are nearly a hundred riddles in Old English, dating from the seventh to the tenth centuries. They were in some cases modeled on collections of a hundred Latin riddles by the seventh-century Anglo-Saxon scholar Aldhelm, but they also derive in large part from indigenous folk tradition. In fact, they mark an important point of intersection between literate and oral culture in Anglo-Saxon England: though designed to be recited, they are written and sometimes focus on the technology of writing.

The three Anglo-Latin riddles of Aldhelm included here reveal an attitude of awe toward writing, conceived as an almost magical act, partly because of its novelty in a recently oral culture, but more because of its ownership by a priestly class in control of Christianity, the religion of "the Book." Aldhelm gives a sense of the tremendous effort that went into book-making—scratching treated animal skins with a quill pen or cutting into tablets made of wax, wood, and leather—and the resultant splendid object, adorned with "artful windings," cut into a "fair design." In the *Alphabet*, he makes the personified letters express their pride in the paradox of writing as voiceless speech: "We / in silence quickly bring out hoarded words." The pen in the riddle of that name speaks of its origin as a bird's feather and of its ability, despite its present earthbound state, to help lead the virtuous to heaven.

Of the Old English riddles included here, four also have to do with writing, an activity important in the daily life of priests. Old English Riddle 2 traces the making of a book by speaking as a sheep slain for its skin to make parchment, describing the "bird's feather" leaving tracks on its surface, and concluding in the person of the Bible itself, decorated with "the wondrous work of smiths," sacred and useful at the same time. Old English Riddle 5 similarly traces a tool from its origin in nature to its status as a manufactured thing. The narrator speaks of its life growing by the water (as a plant), the paradox that, though "mouthless," it should "sing / to men sitting at the mead-bench" (as a flute), and the "miracle" by which it can send a private message (as a pen).

In contrast to those Old English riddles concerned with writing, the majority deal with aspects of Anglo-Saxon secular life, with answers such as a shield, a storm, an iceberg, or a ship. The poem of this sort included here, Old English Riddle 1, explores areas of experience usually ignored by Old English epic, elegiac, and religious poetry. Beginning traditionally, "I'm a strange creature," it treats domestic activity—the storage and preparation of food—by a lower-class woman, a churl's daughter. One of several sexual riddles in the Exeter Book, it is a finely sustained *double entendre*, showing that there was indeed humor in Old English poetry.

(Following the manuscripts, Aldhelm's riddles are printed with the titles that state their solutions, while those from the Exeter Book—which offers no solutions—are followed by solutions given by modern editors).

Three Anglo-Latin Riddles by Aldhelm[1]
Alphabet

We seventeen sisters, voiceless all, declare
Six others bastards are, and not of us.
Of iron we are born, and find our death
Again by iron; or at times we come
From pinion of a lofty-flying bird.
Three brothers got us of an unknown mother.
To him who thirsts for instant counsel, we
In silence quickly bring out hoarded words.

Writing Tablets

Of honey-laden bees I first was born,
But in the forest grew my outer coat;
My tough backs came from shoes. An iron point
In artful windings cuts a fair design,
And leaves long, twisted furrows, like a plow.
From heaven unto that field is borne the seed
Or nourishment, which brings forth generous sheaves
A thousandfold. Alas, that such a crop,
A holy harvest, falls before grim war.

1. Translated by James Hall Pitman.

Pen

The shining pelican, whose yawning throat
Gulps down the waters of the sea, long since
Produced me, white as he. Through snowy fields
I keep a straight road, leaving deep-blue tracks
Upon the gleaming way, and darkening
The fair champaign with black and tortuous paths;
Yet one way through the plain suffices not,
For with a thousand bypaths runs the road,
And them who stray not from it, leads to heaven.

Five Old English Riddles[2]

1

I'm a strange creature, for I satisfy women,
a service to the neighbors! No one suffers
at my hands except for my slayer.
I grow very tall, erect in a bed,
5   I'm hairy underneath. From time to time
a good-looking girl, the doughty daughter
of some churl dares to hold me,
grips my russet skin, robs me of my head
and puts me in the pantry. At once that girl
10   with plaited hair who has confined me
remembers our meeting. Her eye moistens.

2

An enemy ended my life, took away
of my bodily strength; then he dipped me
in water and drew me out again,
15   and put me in the sun where I soon shed
all my hair. The knife's sharp edge
bit into me once my blemishes had been scraped away;
fingers folded me and the bird's feather
often moved across my brown surface,
20   sprinkling useful drops; it swallowed the wood-dye
(part of the stream) and again traveled over me
leaving black tracks. Then a man bound me,
he stretched skin over me and adorned me
with gold; thus I am enriched by the wondrous work
25   of smiths, wound about with shining metal.
Now my clasp and my red dye
and these glorious adornments bring fame far and wide
to the Protector of Men, and not to the pains of hell.
If the sons of men would make use of me
30   they would be the safer and more sure of victory,

2. Translated by Kevin Crossley-Holland.

their hearts would be bolder, their minds more at ease,
their thoughts wiser, they would have more friends,
companions and kinsmen (true and honorable,
brave and kind) who would gladly increase
35   their honor and prosperity, and heap
benefits upon them, holding them fast
in love's embraces. Ask what I am called,
of such use to men. My name is famous,
of service to men and sacred in itself.

3

A moth devoured words. When I heard
of that wonder it struck me as a strange event
that a worm should swallow the song of some man,
a thief gorge in the darkness on fine phrases
and their firm foundation. The thievish stranger
was not a whit the wiser for swallowing words.

4

I watched four curious creatures
traveling together; their tracks were swart,
each imprint very black. The birds' support
moved swiftly; it flew in the air,
dived under the wave. The toiling warrior
worked without pause, pointing the paths
to all four over the beaten gold.

5

I sank roots first of all, stood
near the shore, close by the dyke
and dash of waves; few men
saw my home in that wilderness,
5   but each dawn, each dusk,
the tawny waves surged and swirled
around me. Little did I think
that I, mouthless, should ever sing
to men sitting at the mead-bench,
10   varying my pitch. It is rather puzzling,
a miracle to men ignorant of such arts,
how a knife's point and a right hand
(mind and implement moving as one)
could cut and carve me—so that I
15   can send you a message without fear,
and no one else can overhear
or noise abroad the words we share.

Solutions: 1. Penis or onion; 2. Bible; 3. Book worm; 4. Pen and fingers; 5. Reed.

After the Norman Conquest

⇒ PERSPECTIVES ⇐

Arthurian Myth in the History of Britain

Almost since it first appeared, the story of King Arthur has occupied a contested zone between myth and history. Far from diminishing the Arthurian tradition, though, this ambiguity has lent it a tremendous and protean impact on the political and cultural imagination of Europe, from the Middle Ages to the present. Probably no other body of medieval legend remains today as widely known and as often revisited as the Arthurian story.

One measure of Arthur's undiminished importance is the eager debate, eight centuries old and going strong, about his historical status. Whether or not a specific "Arthur" ever existed, legends and attributes gathered around his name from a very early date, mostly in texts of Welsh background. Around 600 a Welsh poem refers briefly to Arthur's armed might, and by about 1000, the story *Culhwch and Olwen*, from the Mabinogion, assumes knowledge of Arthur as a royal warlord. Other early Welsh texts begin to give him more-than-mortal attributes, associating Arthur with such marvels as an underworld quest and a mysterious tomb. In the ninth century, the Latin *History of the Britons* by the Welshman Nennius confidently speaks of Arthur as a great leader and lists his twelve victories ending with that at Mount Badon.

Some of this at least fits with better-documented history and with less-shadowy commanders who might have been models for an Arthurian figure, even if they were not "Arthur." When the Romans withdrew in 410, the romanized Britons soon faced territorial aggression from the Saxons and Picts. In the decades after midcentury, the Britons mounted a successful defense, led in part by Aurelius Ambrosius and culminating, it appears, with the battle of Badon in roughly 500, after which Saxon incursions paused for a time. In those same years of territorial threat, some Britons had emigrated to what is now Brittany, and in the 460s or 470s a warlord named Riothamus led an army, probably from Britain, and fought successfully in Gaul in alliance with local rulers sympathetic to Rome. His name was latinized from a British title meaning "supreme king." Both Riothamus and Aurelius Ambrosius correspond to parts of the later narratives of Arthur: his role as high king, his triumphs against the Saxons, his links to Rome (both friendly and hostile), and his campaigns on the continent.

Whether the origins of Arthur's story lie in fact or in an urge among the Welsh to imagine a great leader who once restored their power against the ever-expanding Anglo-Saxons, he was clearly an established figure in Welsh oral and written literature by the ninth century. Arthur, however, also held a broader appeal for other peoples of England. The British Isles were felt to lie at the outer edge of world geography, but the story of Arthur and his ancestor Brutus served to create a Britain with other kinds of centrality. The legend of Brutus made Britain the end point of an inexorable westward movement of Trojan imperial power, the *translatio imperii*, and Arthur's forebears became linked to Roman imperial dynasties. Finally, the general movement of Arthur's continental campaigns neatly reversed the patterns of Roman and then Norman colonization.

In the later Middle Ages and after, Arthur and his court are most often encountered in works that lay little claim to historical accuracy. Rather, they exploit the very uncertainty of Arthurian narrative to explore the highest (if sometimes self-deceiving) yearnings of private emotion and social order. These Arthurian romances also probe, often in tragic terms, the limits and taboos that both define and subvert such ideals, including the mutual threats posed by private emotion and social order.

Nevertheless, the Arthurian tradition has also been pulled persistently into the realm of the real. It was presented as serious historical writing from the twelfth century through the end of the Middle Ages. Political agents have used Arthur's kingship as a model or precedent for their own aspirations, as seen in the Kennedy administration's portrayal as a version of Camelot. Even elements of the Christian church wrote their doctrines into Arthurian narrative or claimed Arthur as a patron.

The texts in this section present three illuminating moments of Arthur's emergence into history and politics. Geoffrey of Monmouth's *History of the Kings of Britain*, finished around 1138, was the fullest version yet of Arthur's origin and career. Geoffrey was the first to make Arthur such a central figure in British history, and it was largely through Geoffrey's Latin "history" that Arthur became so widespread a feature of cultural imagination in the Middle Ages and beyond. Writing at the close of the twelfth century, Gerald of Wales narrates an occasion, possibly orchestrated by Henry II, in which Arthurian tradition was slightly altered and folded into emergent Norman versions of British antiquity. The section ends with two politically charged versions of national origin, English and Scottish, proposed in 1301 as part of Edward I's efforts to influence royal succession in Scotland.

•━╅═╈━•

Geoffrey of Monmouth
c. 1100–1155

From the perspective of surviving British peoples in Wales and Cornwall, the Norman Conquest of 1066 was only the last among successive waves of invasion by Romans, Picts, Anglo-Saxons, and Vikings. The Celtic Britons had long been pushed into the far southwest by the time the Normans arrived, where they continued to resist colonization. The Welsh maintained a vital language, culture, and ethnic mythology, including a memory of their fellow Celts in Brittany and a divided nostalgia for the long-departed Romans. Thus a whole Celtic linguistic and political world offered an alternative to the languages and legends of the Normans, much of which derived ultimately from Mediterranean antiquity. Arthur, king of the Britons, emerged as a key figure as these peoples and cultures began to articulate the complex new forms of political and private identity precipitated by the Conquest.

No one was more important in this process than Geoffrey of Monmouth. He was prior of the Abbey of Monmouth in Wales and later was named bishop of Saint Asaph, though civil disorder prevented his taking the post. Yet he was also active in the emerging schools of Oxford, he was patronized by Norman nobles and bishops, and he wrote in Latin. Geoffrey's learning reflects this double allegiance. Well schooled in the Latin curriculum that embraced ancient Roman and Christian literature, he was also deeply versed in the oral and written culture of Wales. As a creative negotiater between Welsh and Anglo-Norman legends and languages, his influence was without parallel.

Both of Geoffrey's surviving prose works, the *Prophecies of Merlin* (finished around 1135) and the *History of the Kings of Britain* (about 1138) present themselves as translations of ancient texts from Wales or Brittany. Geoffrey also wrote a *Life of Merlin* in Latin verse. He probably synthesized a number of sources and added material of his own in his "translations." It was a pointed gesture, nevertheless, to posit a Celtic text whose authority rivaled the Latin culture and legends that had underwritten later Anglo-Saxon and then Norman power in England. Geoffrey daringly inverted the general hierarchy of Latin and vernaculars in his time; instead, he offered "British" as the ancient tongue that he wanted to make more broadly accessible for Latin-reading newcomers.

Geoffrey's central heroes are Brutus, the exiled Trojan descendant who colonized and named Britain, and Arthur, who reunified England after Saxon and Pictish attacks, and repulsed Roman efforts to re-establish power there. Geoffrey's own purposes in the *History* were complex but he was responding in part to contemporary events. The 1130s were a decade of civil strife in England, as nobles shifted their allegiances between King Stephen and the other claimant to the throne, the future Henry II. Welsh nobles took advantage of this disorder to rebel and set up their own principalities. Scholars remain divided as to whether Geoffrey was more interested in a return to strong and unified rule in Norman England, or wanted rather to encourage the Welsh princes with the story of a great predecessor who might one day return.

Geoffrey's narrative carefully presents itself as history, in a century of great historical writing. He uses the typical armature of documentary and other written records, archaeological evidence, and claims to well-founded witness. Casting the story of Arthur into this respected form allows Geoffrey to employ but also to counter the dominant master-narrative of Christian history in England, which was Bede's. Rather than a story of Anglo-Saxon arrival and conversion, Geoffrey offers a story of an earlier foundation and a prior conversion; he thus creates imaginative space for a convergence between Norman power and the culture and ambitions of people and languages at its edges. Moreover, the *History* generates an exterior (if now conveniently absent) common enemy in the imperial Romans. Geoffrey pulls in yet more ancient models by frequently echoing Virgil's *Aeneid* and its story of exile and refoundation, and by placing his story within biblical, Trojan, and Roman chronologies. And he points forward to his own time by inserting the earlier *Prophecies of Merlin* in the midst of the *History*.

The continued influence of Geoffrey's *History* on later literature is testimony to the powerful themes he folded into his story. Much that is developed in later romance explorations of the Arthurian world is already here: the tragedy of a people bravely battling its own decline; the danger and overwhelming attraction of illicit sexual desire; the ambivalent position of Mordred as cousin or nephew; the Arthurian realm brought down, ultimately, by the treachery of the king's own kin and by a transgression of the marriage bed that echoes Arthur's own conception.

The following selections from Geoffrey's *History* feature the Trojan background of Britain and the birth and early kingship of Arthur. Other texts in this section and following trace later episodes in his evolving legend: the development of Arthur's court, the celebration and tragedy of romantic desire, and the death of the king.

from History of the Kings of Britain[1]
Dedication

Whenever I have chanced to think about the history of the kings of Britain, on those occasions when I have been turning over a great many such matters in my mind, it has seemed a remarkable thing to me that, apart from such mention of them as Gildas and Bede had each made in a brilliant book on the subject, I have not been able to discover anything at all on the kings who lived here before the Incarnation of Christ, or indeed about Arthur and all the others who followed on after the Incarnation. Yet the deeds of these men were such that they deserve to be praised for all time. What is more, these deeds were handed joyfully down in oral tradition, just as if they had been committed to writing, by many peoples who had only their memory to rely on.

At a time when I was giving a good deal of attention to such matters, Walter, Archdeacon of Oxford, a man skilled in the art of public speaking and well-informed about the history of foreign countries, presented me with a certain very ancient book written in the British language.[2] This book, attractively composed to form a consecutive

1. Translated by Lewis Thorpe (1966).
2. Walter and Geoffrey were both associated with an early Oxford college, and their names appear together on sev-

eral legal documents. In two of these, Geoffrey calls himself a *magister*, a teacher at an advanced level.

and orderly narrative, set out all the deeds of these men, from Brutus, the first King of the Britons, down to Cadwallader, the son of Cadwallo.[3] At Walter's request I have taken the trouble to translate the book into Latin, although, indeed, I have been content with my own expressions and my own homely style and I have gathered no gaudy flowers of speech in other men's gardens. If I had adorned my page with high-flown rhetorical figures, I should have bored my readers, for they would have been forced to spend more time in discovering the meaning of my words than in following the story.

I ask you, Robert, Earl of Gloucester,[4] to do my little book this favor. Let it be so emended by your knowledge and your advice that it must no longer be considered as the product of Geoffrey of Monmouth's small talent. Rather, with the support of your wit and wisdom, let it be accepted as the work of one descended from Henry, the famous King of the English; of one whom learning has nurtured in the liberal arts and whom his innate talent in military affairs has put in charge of our soldiers, with the result that now, in our own lifetime, our island of Britain hails you with heartfelt affection, as if it had been granted a second Henry.

You too, Waleran, Count of Mellent, second pillar of our kingdom, give me your support, so that, with the guidance provided by the two of you, my work may appear all the more attractive when it is offered to its public.[5] For indeed, sprung as you are from the race of the most renowned King Charles, Mother Philosophy has taken you to her bosom, and to you she has taught the subtlety of her sciences. What is more, so that you might become famous in the military affairs of our army, she has led you to the camp of kings, and there, having surpassed your fellow-warriors in bravery, you have learned, under your father's guidance, to be a terror to your enemies and a protection to your own folk. Faithful defender as you are of those dependent on you, accept under your patronage this book which is published for your pleasure. Accept me, too, as your writer, so that, reclining in the shade of a tree which spreads so wide, and sheltered from envious and malicious enemies, I may be able in peaceful harmony to make music on the reed-pipe of a muse who really belongs to you.

[TROY, AENEAS, BRUTUS' EXILE][6]

After the Trojan war, Aeneas fled from the ruined city with his son Ascanius and came by boat to Italy. He was honorably received there by King Latinus, but Turnus, King of the Rutuli, became jealous of him and attacked him. In the battle between them Aeneas was victorious. Turnus was killed and Aeneas seized both the kingdom of Italy and the person of Lavinia, who was the daughter of Latinus.[7]

When Aeneas' last day came, Ascanius was elected King. He founded the town of Alba on the bank of the Tiber and became the father of a son called Silvius. This Silvius was involved in a secret love-affair with a certain niece of Lavinia's; he married her and made her pregnant. When this came to the knowledge of his father Ascanius, the latter ordered his soothsayers to discover the sex of the child which the

---

3. Bede's *Ecclesiastical History of the English People* was the source most used by 12th-century historians, but it has little to say about England before the coming of the Angles and Saxons. Geoffrey offers a (perhaps fictive) source for a more ancient history of the people who preceded the Saxons.
4. An illegitimate son of King Henry I. He had a hand in the education of the future Henry II, his nephew.
5. Waleran de Beaumont, Count of Meulan (1104–1166)

moved in the same circles as the Earl of Gloucester, and was patron of the Norman Abbey of Bec, a great center of learning. Geoffrey's fulsome tone is typical of dedications to great magnates in the period.
6. From bk. 1, ch. 3.
7. This summarizes the political narrative of Virgil's *Aeneid*, a text Geoffrey knew well and echoed frequently throughout his *History*.

girl had conceived. As soon as they had made sure of the truth of the matter, the soothsayers said that she would give birth to a boy, who would cause the death of both his father and his mother; and that after he had wandered in exile through many lands this boy would eventually rise to the highest honor.

The soothsayers were not wrong in their forecast. When the day came for her to have her child, the mother bore a son and died in childbirth. The boy was handed over to the midwife and was given the name Brutus. At last, when fifteen years had passed, the young man killed his father by an unlucky shot with an arrow, when they were out hunting together. Their beaters drove some stags into their path and Brutus, who was under the impression that he was aiming his weapon at these stags, hit his own father below the breast. As the result of this death Brutus was expelled from Italy by his relations, who were angry with him for having committed such a crime. He went in exile to certain parts of Greece; and there he discovered the descendants of Helenus, Priam's son, who were held captive in the power of Pandrasus, King of the Greeks. After the fall of Troy, Pyrrhus, the son of Achilles, had dragged this man Helenus off with him in chains, and a number of other Trojans, too. He had ordered them to be kept in slavery, so that he might take vengeance on them for the death of his father.

When Brutus realized that these people were of the same race as his ancestors, he stayed some time with them. However, he soon gained such fame for his military skill and prowess that he was esteemed by the kings and princes more than any young man in the country.

[The Naming of Britain][8]

[Brutus conquers the Greek king (reversing the Greek conquest of his ancestral Troy), marries the king's daughter Ignoge, and leads the Trojan descendants off to seek a new land. They pass through continental Europe, where they do battle with the Gauls.]

In their pursuit the Trojans continued to slaughter the Gauls, and they did not abandon the bloodshed until they had gained victory.

Although this signal triumph brought him great joy, Brutus was nevertheless filled with anxiety, for the number of his men became smaller every day, while that of the Gauls was constantly increasing. Brutus was in doubt as to whether he could oppose the Gauls any longer; and he finally chose to return to his ships in the full glory of his victory while the greater part of his comrades were still safe, and then to seek out the island which divine prophecy had promised would be his. Nothing else was done. With the approval of his men Brutus returned to his fleet. He loaded his ships with all the riches which he had acquired and then went on board. So, with the winds behind him, he sought the promised island, and came ashore at Totnes.

At this time the island of Britain was called Albion. It was uninhabited except for a few giants. It was, however, most attractive, because of the delightful situation of its various regions, its forests and the great number of its rivers, which teemed with fish; and it filled Brutus and his comrades with a great desire to live there. When they had explored the different districts, they drove the giants whom they had discovered into the caves in the mountains. With the approval of their leader they divided the land among themselves. They began to cultivate the fields and to build houses, so that in a short time you would have thought that the land had always been inhabited.

8. From bk. 1, chs. 15–18 and bk. 2, ch. 1.

Brutus then called the island Britain from his own name, and his companions he called Britons. His intention was that his memory should be perpetuated by the derivation of the name. A little later the language of the people, which had up to then been known as Trojan or Crooked Greek, was called British, for the same reason.[9]

[BRUTUS BUILDS NEW TROY]

Once he had divided up his kingdom, Brutus decided to build a capital. In pursuit of this plan, he visited every part of the land in search of a suitable spot. He came at length to the River Thames, walked up and down its banks and so chose a site suited to his purpose. There then he built his city and called it Troia Nova. It was known by this name for long ages after, but finally by a corruption of the word it came to be called Trinovantum. * * *

When the above-named leader Brutus had built the city about which I have told you, he presented it to the citizens by right of inheritance, and gave them a code of laws by which they might live peacefully together. At that time the priest Eli was ruling in Judea and the Ark of the Covenant was captured by the Philistines. The sons of Hector reigned in Troy, for the descendants of Antenor had been driven out. In Italy reigned Aeneas Silvius, son of Aeneas and uncle of Brutus, the third of the Latin Kings. * * *[1]

In the meantime Brutus had consummated his marriage with his wife Ignoge. By her he had three sons called Locrinus, Kamber and Albanactus, all of whom were to become famous. When their father finally died, in the twenty-third year after his landing, these three sons buried him inside the walls of the town which he had founded. They divided the kingdom of Britain between them in such a way that each succeeded to Brutus in one particular district. Locrinus, who was the first-born, inherited the part of the island which was afterwards called Loegria after him. Kamber received the region which is on the further bank of the River Severn, the part which is now known as Wales but which was for a long time after his death called Kambria from his name. As a result the people of that country still call themselves Kambri today in the Welsh tongue. Albanactus, the youngest, took the region which is nowadays called Scotland in our language. He called it Albany, after his own name.

[MERLIN AND THE FIRST CONQUEST OF IRELAND][2]

[*The descendants of Brutus' three sons include Leir (Shakespeare's King Lear), the brothers Brennius and Belinus who conquer Rome, and Lud who rebuilds New Troy and names it Kaerlud after himself (whence "London"). In the reign of Lud's brother, Julius Caesar invades England; generations of Britons resist, until King Coel makes peace with the Roman legate Constantius. The latter succeeds Coel, marries Coel's daughter, and sires Constantine who becomes emperor of Rome. The Romans tire of defending Britain against invaders and withdraw from the island. Vortigern usurps the throne from the Briton line, then holds it in alliance with the Saxons Hengist and Horsa. The Saxons become aggressors, and Vortigern flees them but is overcome by the brothers Aurelius Ambrosius and Utherpendragon, who restore the Briton royal line and drive the Saxons into the north. Aurelius reigns, restoring churches and the rule of law; he wants to commemorate the Britons who died fighting off the Saxons.*]

9. With this detail, Geoffrey creates a linguistic history in which early Welsh is as ancient as classical Latin, and more purely "Trojan."

1. Medieval historians often made such parallels between biblical and secular chronologies.
2. From bk. 8, chs. 10–13.

Aurelius collected carpenters and stone-masons together from every region and ordered them to use their skill to contrive some novel building which would stand forever in memory of such distinguished men. The whole band racked their brains and then confessed themselves beaten. Then Tremorinus, Archbishop of the City of the Legions,[3] went to the King and said: "If there is anyone anywhere who has the ability to execute your plan, then Merlin, the prophet of Vortigern, is the man to do it.[4] In my opinion, there is no one else in your kingdom who has greater skill, either in the foretelling of the future or in mechanical contrivances. Order Merlin to come and use his ability, so that the monument for which you are asking can be put up."

Aurelius asked many questions about Merlin; then he sent a number of messengers through the various regions of the country to find him and fetch him. They traveled through the provinces and finally located Merlin in the territory of the Gewissei, at the Galabes Springs, where he often went. They explained to him what they wanted of him and then conducted him to the King. The King received Merlin gaily and ordered him to prophesy the future, for he wanted to hear some marvels from him. "Mysteries of that sort cannot be revealed," answered Merlin, "except where there is the most urgent need for them. If I were to utter them as an entertainment, or where there was no need at all, then the spirit which controls me would forsake me in the moment of need."

He gave the same refusal to everyone present. The King had no wish to press him about the future, but he spoke to him about the monument which he was planning. "If you want to grace the burial-place of these men with some lasting monument," replied Merlin, "send for the Giants' Ring which is on Mount Killaraus in Ireland. In that place there is a stone construction which no man of this period could ever erect, unless he combined great skill and artistry. The stones are enormous and there is no one alive strong enough to move them. If they are placed in position round this site, in the way in which they are erected over there, they will stand forever."

At these words of Merlin's Aurelius burst out laughing. "How can such large stones be moved from so far-distant a country?" he asked. "It is hardly as if Britain itself is lacking in stones big enough for the job!" "Try not to laugh in a foolish way, your Majesty," answered Merlin. "What I am suggesting has nothing ludicrous about it. These stones are connected with certain secret religious rites and they have various properties which are medicinally important. Many years ago the Giants transported them from the remotest confines of Africa and set them up in Ireland at a time when they inhabited that country. Their plan was that, whenever they felt ill, baths should be prepared at the foot of the stones; for they used to pour water over them and to run this water into baths in which their sick were cured. What is more, they mixed the water with herbal concoctions and so healed their wounds. There is not a single stone among them which hasn't some medicinal virtue."

When the Britons heard all this, they made up their minds to send for the stones and to make war on the people of Ireland if they tried to hold them back. In the end the King's brother, Utherpendragon, and fifteen thousand men, were chosen to carry out the task. Merlin, too, was co-opted, so that all the problems which had to be met could have the benefit of his knowledge and advice. They made ready their ships and they put to sea. The winds were favorable and they arrived in Ireland.

---

3. Also called Caerusk or Caerleon; Geoffrey mentions it often and may have had some connection with it.
4. Merlin, son of a Briton princess and a demonic spirit, has already appeared; he triumphed over Vortigern's magicians and uttered a series of prophecies. Merlin's roles as a royal advisor, a prophet, and even a shape-shifter can be compared to those of poets in early Celtic cultures.

At that time there reigned in Ireland a young man of remarkable valor called Gillomanius. As soon as he heard that the Britons had landed in the country, he collected a huge army together and hurried to meet them. When he learned the reason of their coming, Gillomanius laughed out loud at those standing round him. "I am not surprised that a race of cowards has been able to devastate the island of the Britons," said he, "for the Britons are dolts and fools. Who ever heard of such folly? Surely the stones of Ireland aren't so much better than those of Britain that our realm has to be invaded for their sake! Arm yourselves, men, and defend your fatherland, for as long as life remains in my body they shall not steal from us the minutest fragment of the Ring."

When he saw that the Irish were spoiling for a fight, Uther hurriedly drew up his own line of battle and charged at them. The Britons were successful almost immediately. The Irish were either mangled or killed outright, and Gillomanius was forced to flee. Having won the day, the Britons made their way to Mount Killaraus. When they came to the stone structure, they were filled with joy and wonder. Merlin came up to them as they stood round in a group. "Try your strength, young men," said he, "and see whether skill can do more than brute strength, or strength more than skill, when it comes to dismantling these stones!"

At his bidding they all set to with every conceivable kind of mechanism and strove their hardest to take the Ring down. They rigged up hawsers and ropes and they propped up scaling-ladders, each preparing what he thought most useful, but none of these things advanced them an inch. When he saw what a mess they were making of it, Merlin burst out laughing. He placed in position all the gear which he considered necessary and dismantled the stones more easily than you could ever believe. Once he had pulled them down, he had them carried to the ships and stored on board, and they all set sail once more for Britain with joy in their hearts.

The winds were fair. They came to the shore and then set off with the stones for the spot where the heroes had been buried. The moment that this was reported to him, Aurelius dispatched messengers to all the different regions of Britain, ordering the clergy and the people to assemble and, as they gathered, to converge on Mount Ambrius, where they were with due ceremony and rejoicing to re-dedicate the burial-place which I have described. At the summons from Aurelius the bishops and abbots duly assembled with men from every rank and file under the King's command. All came together on the appointed day. Aurelius placed the crown on his head and celebrated the feast of Whitsun in right royal fashion, devoting the next three days to one long festival. * * *

Once he had settled these matters, and others of a similar nature, Aurelius ordered Merlin to erect round the burial-place the stones which he had brought from Ireland. Merlin obeyed the King's orders and put the stones up in a circle round the sepulchre, in exactly the same way as they had been arranged on Mount Killaraus in Ireland, thus proving that his artistry was worth more than any brute strength.

[UTHERPENDRAGON SIRES ARTHUR][5]

[Vortigern's son attacks Aurelius Ambrosius and Utherpendragon. They drive him off, though Aurelius is poisoned through Saxon treachery. A miraculous star appears, which Merlin interprets as a sign of Uther's destined kingship, the coming of Arthur, and the rule of Uther's dynasty. At the same time, however, Merlin prophesies the decline of the Britons. As king, Uther fights off more Saxon incursions.]

5. From bk. 8, chs. 19–24.

The next Eastertide Uther told the nobles of his kingdom to assemble in that same town of London, so that he could wear his crown and celebrate so important a feast-day with proper ceremony. They all obeyed, traveling in from their various cities and assembling on the eve of the feast. The King was thus able to celebrate the feast as he had intended and to enjoy himself in the company of his leaders. They, too, were all happy, seeing that he had received them with such affability. A great many nobles had gathered there, men worthy of taking part in such a gay festivity, together with their wives and daughters.

Among the others there was present Gorlois, Duke of Cornwall, with his wife Ygerna, who was the most beautiful woman in Britain. When the King saw her there among the other women, he was immediately filled with desire for her, with the result that he took no notice of anything else, but devoted all his attention to her. To her and to no one else he kept ordering plates of food to be passed and to her, too, he kept sending his own personal attendants with golden goblets of wine. He kept smiling at her and engaging her in sprightly conversation. When Ygerna's husband saw what was happening, he was so annoyed that he withdrew from the court without taking leave. No one present could persuade him to return, for he was afraid of losing the one object that he loved better than anything else. Uther lost his temper and ordered Gorlois to come back to court, so that he, the King, could seek satisfaction for the way in which he had been insulted. Gorlois refused to obey. The King was furious and swore an oath that he would ravage Gorlois' lands, unless the latter gave him immediate satisfaction.

Without more ado, while the bad blood remained between the two of them, the King collected a huge army together and hurried off to the Duchy of Cornwall, where he set fire to towns and castles. Gorlois' army was the smaller of the two and he did not dare to meet the King in battle. He preferred instead to garrison his castles and to bide his time until he could receive help from Ireland. As he was more worried about his wife than he was about himself, he left her in the castle of Tintagel,[6] on the sea-coast, which he thought was the safest place under his control. He himself took refuge in a fortified camp called Dimilioc,[7] so that, if disaster overtook them, they should not both be endangered together. When the King heard of this, he went to the encampment where Gorlois was, besieged it and cut off every line of approach.

Finally, after a week had gone by, the King's passion for Ygerna became more than he could bear. He called to him Ulfin of Ridcaradoch, one of his soldiers and a familiar friend, and told him what was on his mind. "I am desperately in love with Ygerna," said Uther, "and if I cannot have her I am convinced that I shall suffer a physical breakdown. You must tell me how I can satisfy my desire for her, for otherwise I shall die of the passion which is consuming me." "Who can possibly give you useful advice," answered Ulfin, "when no power on earth can enable us to come to her where she is inside the fortress of Tintagel? The castle is built high above the sea, which surrounds it on all sides, and there is no other way in except that offered by a narrow isthmus of rock. Three armed soldiers could hold it against you, even if you stood there with the whole kingdom of Britain at your side. If only the prophet Merlin would give his mind to the problem, then with his help I think you might be able to obtain what you want." The King believed Ulfin and ordered Merlin to be sent for, for he, too, had come to the siege.

6. Tin-*ta*-jel, on the rocky northwestern coast of Cornwall.

7. Di-*mi*-li-oc, perhaps a site roughly five miles from Tintagel.

Merlin was summoned immediately. When he appeared in the King's presence, he was ordered to suggest how the King could have his way with Ygerna. When Merlin saw the torment which the King was suffering because of this woman, he was amazed at the strength of his passion. "If you are to have your wish," he said, "you must make use of methods which are quite new and until now unheard-of in your day. By my drugs I know how to give you the precise appearance of Gorlois, so that you will resemble him in every respect. If you do what I say, I will make you exactly like him, and Ulfin exactly like Gorlois' companion, Jordan of Tintagel. I will change my own appearance, too, and come with you. In this way you will be able to go safely to Ygerna in her castle and be admitted."

The King agreed and listened carefully to what he had to do. In the end he handed the siege over to his subordinates, took Merlin's drugs, and was changed into the likeness of Gorlois. Ulfin was changed into Jordan and Merlin into a man called Britaelis, so that no one could tell what they had previously looked like. They then set off for Tintagel and came to the Castle in the twilight. The moment the guard was told that his leader was approaching, he opened the gates and the men were let in. Who, indeed, could possibly have suspected anything, once it was thought that Gorlois himself had come? The King spent that night with Ygerna and satisfied his desire by making love with her. He had deceived her by the disguise which he had taken. He had deceived her, too, by the lying things that he said to her, things which he planned with great skill. He said that he had come out secretly from his besieged encampment so that he might make sure that all was well with her, whom he loved so dearly, and with his castle, too. She naturally believed all that he said and refused him nothing that he asked. That night she conceived Arthur, the most famous of men, who subsequently won great renown by his outstanding bravery.

Meanwhile, when it was discovered at the siege of Dimilioc that the King was no longer present, his army, acting without his instructions, tried to breach the walls and challenge the beleaguered Duke to battle. The Duke, equally ill-advisedly, sallied forth with his men, imagining apparently that he could resist such a host of armed men with his own tiny band. As the struggle between them swayed this way and that, Gorlois was among the first to be killed. His men were scattered and the besieged camp was captured. The treasure which had been deposited there was shared out in the most inequitable way, for each man seized in his greedy fist whatever good luck and his own brute strength threw in his way.[8]

Not until the outrages which followed this daring act had finally subsided did messengers come to Ygerna to announce the death of the Duke and the end of the siege. When they saw the King sitting beside Ygerna in the likeness of their leader, they blushed red with astonishment to see that the man whom they had left behind dead in the siege had in effect arrived there safely before them. Of course, they did not know of the drugs prepared by Merlin. The King put his arms round the Duchess and laughed aloud to hear these reports. "I am not dead," he said. "Indeed, as you see, I am very much alive! However, the destruction of my camp saddens me very much and so does the slaughter of my comrades. What is more, there is great danger that the King may come this way and capture us in this castle. I will go out to meet him and make peace with him, lest even worse should befall us."

---

8. Geoffrey emphasizes the destructive potential of private greed, private ambition, and brute force, even in the rule of a strong king like Uther. This becomes a dominant theme in Geoffrey and later Arthurian narratives.

The King set out and made his way towards his own army, abandoning his disguise as Gorlois and becoming Utherpendragon once more. When he learned all that had happened, he mourned for the death of Gorlois; but he was happy, all the same, that Ygerna was freed from her marital obligations. He returned to Tintagel Castle, captured it and seized Ygerna at the same time, she being what he really wanted. From that day on they lived together as equals, united by their great love for each other; and they had a son and a daughter. The boy was called Arthur and the girl Anna.

[ANGLO-SAXON INVASION]

As the days passed and lengthened into years, the King fell ill with a malady which affected him for a long time. Meanwhile the prison warders who guarded Octa and Eosa,[9] as I have explained above, led a weary life. In the end they escaped with their prisoners to Germany and in doing so terrified the kingdom: for rumor had it that they had already stirred up Germany, and had fitted out a huge fleet in order to return to the island and destroy it. This, indeed, actually happened. They came back with an immense fleet and more men than could ever be counted. They invaded certain parts of Albany[1] and busied themselves in burning the cities there and the citizens inside them. The British army was put under the command of Loth of Lodonesia, with orders that he should keep the enemy at a distance. This man was one of the leaders, a valiant soldier, mature both in wisdom and age. As a reward for his prowess, the King had given him his daughter Anna and put him in charge of the kingdom while he himself was ill. When Loth moved forward against the enemy he was frequently driven back again by them, so that he had to take refuge inside the cities. On other occasions he routed and dispersed them, forcing them to fly either into the forests or to their ships. Between the two sides the outcome of each battle was always in doubt, it being hard to tell which of them was victorious. Their own arrogance was a handicap to the Britons, for they were unwilling to obey the orders of their leaders. This undermined their strength and they were unable to beat the enemy in the field.

Almost all the island was laid waste. When this was made known to the King, he fell into a greater rage than he could really bear in his weakened state. He told all his leaders to appear before him, so that he could rebuke them for their overweening pride and their feebleness. As soon as he saw them all assembled in his presence, he reproached them bitterly and swore that he himself would lead them against the enemy. He ordered a litter to be built, so that he could be carried in it; for his weakness made any other form of progress impossible. Then he instructed them all to be in a state of preparedness, so that they could advance against the enemy as soon as the opportunity offered. The litter was constructed immediately, the men were made ready to start and the opportunity duly came.

They put the King in his litter and set out for Saint Albans, where the Saxons I have told you about were maltreating all the local population * * *

[*Despite his illness, Uther prevails. Octa and Eosa are killed.*]

Once the Saxons had been defeated, as I have explained above, they did not for that reason abandon their evil behavior. On the contrary, they went off to the north-

---

9. A son and a kinsman of the Saxon Hengist; Uther had imprisoned them in London. Geoffrey closely connects the resurgence of the Saxon invaders with Uther's adul-

tery and the disorder within his own army.
1. That is, Scotland, named for Brutus's son Albanactus.

ern provinces and preyed relentlessly upon the people there. King Uther was keen to pursue them, as he had proposed, but his princes dissuaded him from it, for after his victory his illness had taken an even more serious turn. As a result the enemy became bolder still in their enterprises, striving by every means in their power to take complete control of the realm. Having recourse, as usual, to treachery, they plotted to see how they could destroy the King by cunning. When every other approach failed, they made up their minds to kill him with poison. This they did: for while Uther lay ill in the town of St. Albans, they sent spies disguised as beggars, who were to discover how things stood at court. When the spies had obtained all the information that they wanted, they discovered one additional fact which they chose to use as a means of betraying Uther. Near the royal residence there was a spring of very limpid water which the King used to drink when he could not keep down any other liquids because of his illness. These evil traitors went to the spring and polluted it completely with poison, so that all the water which welled up was infected. When the King drank some of it, he died immediately. Some hundred men died after him, until the villainy was finally discovered. Then they filled the well in with earth. As soon as the death of the King was made known, the bishops of the land came with their clergy and bore his body to the monastery of Ambrius and buried it with royal honors at the side of Aurelius Ambrosius, inside the Giants' Ring.

[ARTHUR OF BRITAIN][2]

After the death of Utherpendragon, the leaders of the Britons assembled from their various provinces in the town of Silchester and there suggested to Dubricius, the Archbishop of the City of the Legions, that as their King he should crown Arthur, the son of Uther. Necessity urged them on, for as soon as the Saxons heard of the death of King Uther, they invited their own countrymen over from Germany, appointed Colgrin as their leader and began to do their utmost to exterminate the Britons. They had already over-run all that section of the island which stretches from the River Humber to the sea named Caithness.[3]

Dubricius lamented the sad state of his country. He called the other bishops to him and bestowed the crown of the kingdom upon Arthur. Arthur was a young man only fifteen years old; but he was of outstanding courage and generosity, and his inborn goodness gave him such grace that he was loved by almost all the people. Once he had been invested with the royal insignia, he observed the normal custom of giving gifts freely to everyone. Such a great crown of soldiers flocked to him that he came to an end of what he had to distribute. However, the man to whom open-handedness and bravery both come naturally may indeed find himself momentarily in need, but poverty will never harass him for long. In Arthur courage was closely linked with generosity, and he made up his mind to harry the Saxons, so that with their wealth he might reward the retainers who served his own household. The justness of his cause encouraged him, for he had a claim by rightful inheritance to the kingship of the whole island. He therefore called together all the young men whom I have just mentioned and marched on York. * * *[4]

[Arthur and his followers attack Colgrin and ultimately subdue the Saxons; then they repel armies of Scots, Picts, and Irish. Arthur restores Briton dynasties throughout England, marries Guinevere, and establishes a stable peace.]

2. From bk. 9, chs. 1–11.
3. That is, Northumberland and Scotland.
4. Geoffrey links the ancient practice of a king's largesse to his warrior band together with the claim of dynastic genealogy. Arthur will again use the latter claim when he decides to invade Gaul and then march toward Rome.

Arthur then began to increase his personal entourage by inviting very distinguished men from far-distant kingdoms to join it. In this way he developed such a code of courtliness in his household that he inspired peoples living far away to imitate him. The result was that even the man of noblest birth, once he was roused to rivalry, thought nothing at all of himself unless he wore his arms and dressed in the same way as Arthur's knights. At last the fame of Arthur's generosity and bravery spread to the very ends of the earth; and the kings of countries far across the sea trembled at the thought that they might be attacked and invaded by him, and so lose control of the lands under their dominion. They were so harassed by these tormenting anxieties that they rebuilt their towns and the towers in their towns, and then went so far as to construct castles on carefully chosen sites, so that, if invasion should bring Arthur against them, they might have a refuge in their time of need.

All this was reported to Arthur. The fact that he was dreaded by all encouraged him to conceive the idea of conquering the whole of Europe.

━━ ⇥◆⇤ ━━

Gerald of Wales
c. 1146–1222

Geoffrey of Monmouth's *History of the Kings of Britain* was soon translated into French, early Middle English, and Welsh, and it reappears in other languages for centuries. Contemporary historians, especially those interested in pre-Saxon history, were enthusiastic about this new story. Others were skeptical. Nevertheless, Geoffrey's narrative was soon accepted widely as fact, adopted, and revised to serve the interests of the Angevin dynasty.

The discovery of Arthur's bones at Glastonbury Abbey in 1191, as reported by the prolific writer Gerald of Wales, is a particularly rich instance of this habit, benefiting both the status of Henry II and the prestige of the abbey. Glastonbury faced a crisis common among Anglo-Saxon monastic foundations after the Norman Conquest. It was, in fact, probably the earliest Christian community in Britain; nonetheless, the oral tradition of its antiquity was weakened as the Normans took power, bringing with them a new insistence on written documentation. Glastonbury had little proof of its claims to ancient privilege, either by way of charters (and those mostly spurious) or the related prestige of holy relics. At the same time, Henry II was interested in ancient narratives that might legitimize his imperial aims.

Gerald's version of events both suggests Henry's almost wondrous wisdom in identifying the very spot of Arthur's burial and implies the existence of early written records at Glastonbury. To have Arthur as a patron, authenticated by King Henry himself, greatly substantiated the abbey's other claims. At the same time, Henry's knowledge mysteriously linked him to Arthur, and the corpse itself neatly altered Arthurian tradition, certifying Arthur's actual death and perhaps damping Welsh hopes for a messianic return.

from The Instruction of Princes[1]

The memory of Arthur, that most renowned King of the Britons, will endure forever. In his own day he was a munificent patron of the famous Abbey at Glastonbury, giving many donations to the monks and always supporting them strongly, and he is highly praised in their records. More than any other place of worship in his kingdom he loved the church of the Blessed Mary, Mother of God, in Glastonbury, and he

---

1. Translated by Lewis Thorpe. Gerald reports the same events again in a later text, the *Speculum Ecclesiae*.

fostered its interests with much greater loving care than that of any of the others. When he went out to fight, he had a full-length portrait of the Blessed Virgin painted on the front of his shield, so that in the heat of battle he could always gaze upon her; and whenever he was about to make contact with the enemy he would kiss her feet with great devoutness.

In our lifetime Arthur's body was discovered at Glastonbury, although the legends had always encouraged us to believe that there was something otherworldly about his ending, that he had resisted death and had been spirited away to some far-distant spot.[2] The body was hidden deep in the earth in a hollowed-out oak-bole and between two stone pyramids which had been set up long ago in the churchyard there. They carried it into the church with every mark of honor and buried it decently there in a marble tomb. It had been provided with most unusual indications which were, indeed, little short of miraculous, for beneath it—and not on top, as would be the custom nowadays—there was a stone slab, with a leaden cross attached to its underside. I have seen this cross myself and I have traced the lettering which was cut into it on the side turned towards the stone, instead of being on the outer side and immediately visible. The inscription read as follows: HERE IN THE ISLE OF AVALON LIES BURIED THE RENOWNED KING ARTHUR, WITH GUINEVERE, HIS SECOND WIFE.

There are many remarkable deductions to be made from this discovery. Arthur obviously had two wives, and the second one was buried with him. Her bones were found with those of her husband, but they were separate from his. Two-thirds of the coffin, the part towards the top end, held the husband's bones, and the other section, at his feet, contained those of his wife. A tress of woman's hair, blond, and still fresh and bright in color, was found in the coffin. One of the monks snatched it up and it immediately disintegrated into dust. There had been some indications in the Abbey records that the body would be discovered on this spot, and another clue was provided by lettering carved on the pyramids, but this had been almost completely erased by the passage of the years. The holy monks and other religious had seen visions and revelations. However, it was Henry II, King of England, who had told the monks that, according to a story which he had heard from some old British soothsayer,[3] they would find Arthur's body buried at least sixteen feet in the ground, not in a stone coffin but in a hollowed-out oak-bole. It had been sunk as deep as that, and carefully concealed, so that it could never be discovered by the Saxons, whom Arthur had attacked relentlessly as long as he lived and whom, indeed, he had almost wiped out, but who occupied the island [of Britain] after his death. That was why the inscription, which was eventually to reveal the truth, had been cut into the inside of the cross and turned inwards towards the stone. For many a long year this inscription was to keep the secret of what the coffin contained, but eventually, when time and circumstance were both opportune, the lettering revealed what it had so long concealed.

What is now known as Glastonbury used in ancient times to be called the Isle of Avalon. It is virtually an island, for it is completely surrounded by marshlands. In Welsh it is called "Ynys Avallon," which means the Island of Apples. "Aval" is the Welsh word for apple, and this fruit used to grow there in great abundance.[4] After the

2. In his other version (the *Speculum Ecclesiae*) Gerald is more nervously dismissive: "In their stupidity the British people maintain that he is still alive. . . . According to them, once he has recovered from his wounds this strong and all-powerful King will return to rule over the Britons in the normal way."

3. In the *Speculum Ecclesiae*, Gerald says that Henry learned this "from the historical accounts of the Britons and from their bards."

4. Citing and explaining words from the various British vernaculars is a widespread habit in Latin historical writing as early as Bede.

Battle of Camlann,[5] a noblewoman called Morgan, who was the ruler and patroness of these parts as well as being a close blood-relation of King Arthur, carried him off to the island now known as Glastonbury, so that his wounds could be cared for. Years ago the district had also been called "Ynys Gutrin" in Welsh, that is the Island of Glass, and from these words the invading Saxons later coined the place-name "Glastingebury." The word "glass" in their language means "vitrum" in Latin, and "bury" means "castrum" [camp] or "civitas" [city].

You must know that the bones of Arthur's body which were discovered there were so big that in them the poet's words seem to be fulfilled:

All men will exclaim at the size of the bones they've exhumed.[6]

The Abbot showed me one of the shin-bones. He held it upright on the ground against the foot of the tallest man he could find, and it stretched a good three inches above the man's knee. The skull was so large and capacious that it seemed a veritable prodigy of nature, for the space between the eyebrows and the eye-sockets was as broad as the palm of a man's hand. Ten or more wounds could clearly be seen, but they had all mended except one. This was larger than the others and it had made an immense gash. Apparently it was this wound which had caused Arthur's death.

1193

<hr>

Edward I
1239–1307

Beginning in 1291, King Edward I of England revived an ancient claim to be feudal overlord of Scotland and thereby sought to control a disputed succession to its throne. By 1293 the Scottish king John Balliol had become Edward's vassal, but rebelled and was forced to abdicate in 1296. The military and diplomatic struggle (later called the "Great Cause") stretched across the decade. By the turn of the fourteenth century, in an extraordinary move, both the English and Scots had turned to the court of Pope Boniface VIII for a legal decision. In pursuing Edward's claim, his agents ransacked chronicles—including Geoffrey of Monmouth's *History*—as well as ancient charters, to compile a dossier of historical and legal precedents. Despite his own bureaucratic reforms requiring documentary proof for most legal claims, Edward was ready to invoke common memory and ancient legends to support his position regarding Scotland. Knowing that such chronicle material would have no status in court, in May of 1301 Edward resorted to the letter below before Pope Boniface ruled in the matter.

The written letter was a highly developed and self-conscious genre during the Middle Ages. Letters were often meant to be public and could carry the force of law. Indeed, the form of many legal documents had developed from royal letters. Letter writing became an area for textbooks and school study, the *ars dictaminis*. Elaborate formulas of salutation and closing, and other rhetorical figures, were taught and used for important correspondence as a way of establishing the sender's learning and prestige. The papal curia employed a particularly challenging system of prose rhythm called the *cursus*, which was imitated in some royal chanceries and is found in the Latin of Edward's letter.

<hr>

5. Arthur's last battle, fought against the rebel army of his kinsman Mordred. Arthur kills Mordred but is himself mortally wounded.
6. Virgil, *Georgics*, 1.497.

Letter sent to the Papal Court of Rome
Concerning the king's rights in the realm of Scotland¹

To the most Holy Father in Christ lord Boniface, by divine providence the supreme pontiff of the Holy Roman and Universal Church, Edward, by grace of the same providence king of England, lord of Ireland, and duke of Aquitaine offers his humblest devotion to the blessed saints.² What follows we send to you not to be treated in the form or manner of a legal plea, but altogether extrajudicially, in order to set the mind of your Holiness at rest. The All-Highest, to whom all hearts are open, will testify how it is graven upon the tablets of our memory with an indelible mark, that our predecessors and progenitors, the kings of England, by right of lordship and dominion, possessed, from the most ancient times, the suzerainty of the realm of Scotland and its kings in temporal matters, and the things annexed thereto, and that they received from the self-same kings, and from such magnates of the realm as they so desired, liege homage and oaths of fealty. We, continuing in the possession of that very right and dominion, have received the same acknowledgments in our time, both from the king of Scotland, and from the magnates of that realm; and indeed such prerogatives of right and dominion did the kings of England enjoy over the realm of Scotland and its kings, that they have even granted to their faithful folk the realm itself, removed its kings for just causes, and constituted others to rule in their place under themselves. Beyond doubt these matters have been familiar from times long past and still are, though perchance it has been suggested otherwise to your Holiness' ears by foes of peace and sons of rebellion, whose elaborate and empty fabrications your wisdom, we trust, will treat with contempt.

Thus, in the days of Eli and of Samuel the prophet, after the destruction of the city of Troy, a certain valiant and illustrious man of the Trojan race called Brutus, landed with many noble Trojans, upon a certain island called, at that time, Albion.³ It was then inhabited by giants, and after he had defeated and slain them, by his might and that of his followers, he called it, after his own name, Britain, and his people Britons, and built a city which he called Trinovant, now known as London. Afterwards he divided his realm among his three sons, that is he gave to his first born, Locrine, that part of Britain now called England, to the second, Albanact, that part then known as Albany, after the name of Albanact, but now as Scotland, and to Camber, his youngest son, the part then known by his son's name as Cambria and now called Wales, the royal dignity being reserved for Locrine, the eldest. Two years after the death of Brutus there landed in Albany a certain king of the Huns, called Humber, and he slew Albanact, the brother of Locrine. Hearing this, Locrine, the king of the Britons, pursued him, and he fled and was drowned in the river which from his name is called Humber, and thus Albany reverted to Locrine. * * * Again, Arthur, king of the Britons, a prince most renowned, subjected to himself a rebellious Scotland, destroyed almost the whole nation, and afterwards installed as king of Scotland one Angusel by name. Afterwards, when King Arthur held a most famous feast at Caerleon, there were present there all the kings subject to him, and among them

---

1. Translated by E. L. G. Stones (1965). Although sent in the name of the King, a Latin letter of such formality would have been written by notaries in his chancery. A French draft also survives, which might have been used by Edward himself.
2. A flowery opening formula was typical of formal letters

between persons of power; it also provided a place for Edward to make ambitious (and in the case of Aquitaine, highly optimistic) territorial claims.
3. Here the letter borrows closely from Geoffrey of Monmouth's foundation narrative; see page 163.

Angusel, king of Scotland, who manifested the service due for the realm of Scotland by bearing the sword of King Arthur before him; and in succession all the kings of Scotland have been subject to all the kings of the Britons. Succeeding kings of England enjoyed both monarchy and dominion in the island, and subsequently Edward, known as the elder, son of Alfred, king of England, had subject and subordinate to him, as lord superior, the kings of the Scots, the Cumbrians, and the Strathclyde Welsh. * * *

Since, indeed, from what has been said already, and from other evidence, it is perfectly clear and well-known that the realm of Scotland belongs to us of full right, by reason of property and of possession, and that we have not done and have not dared to do anything, as indeed we could not do, in writing or in action, by which any prejudice may be implied to our right or possession, we humbly beseech your Holiness to weigh all this with careful meditation, and to condescend to keep it all in mind when making your decision, setting no store, if you please, by the adverse assertions which come to you on this subject from our enemies, but, on the contrary, retaining our welfare and our royal rights, if it so please you, in your fatherly regard. May the Most High preserve you, to rule his Holy Church through many years of prosperity.

Kempsey, 7 May 1301, the twenty-ninth year of our reign.

<hr>

COMPANION READING
A Report to Edward I[1]

Sir, seeing that you have lately sent a statement to the pope concerning your right to Scotland, the Scots are making efforts to nullify that statement by certain objections which are given below. * * * They say that in that letter you ground your right on old chronicles, which contain various falsehoods and lies, and are abrogated and made void by the subsequent contrary actions of your predecessors and of yourself, which vitiate all the remaining part of your letter, and therefore one should give no credence to such a document. And they say further, that with only this unworthy and feeble case to rely upon, you are striving to evade the cognizance of your true judge, and to suppress the truth, and unlawfully, by force of arms, to repel your weaker neighbors, and to prevent the pope from pursuing the examination of this case. * * *

Again, they say that the old chronicles that you use as evidence of your right could not assist you, even if they were authenticated, as is not the case, they say, because it is notorious that these same old chronicles are utterly made naught and of no avail by other subsequent documents of greater significance, by contrary agreements and actions, and by papal privileges. * * * Then, sir, in order that credence be not given to the documents, histories, and deeds described in your statement, they say that allegations like those recounted in your narrative are put out of court by the true

1. The Scots learned about Edward's letter and made their own response to the pope; this report to Edward, written in the French he would actually have used with his counselors, specifies the Scots' rebuttal. The Scots carefully assert the superior force of later charters and other legal instruments, and dismiss Edward's reliance on unauthenticated legends. In case Edward's story should carry weight with Boniface, however, they also provide a counternarrative of their own national foundation by Scota, daughter of the Pharaoh, and how she expelled British influence from her land. The English and Scots diplomats thus tell opposing prehistories that underwrite their current claims. Just as important, though, they are negotiating around an unusually articulate moment in the contest between different forms of textuality—legendary and chronicle tradition versus legal documents—in the creation of contemporary political power.

facts, and they endeavor to demonstrate their assertion by chronicles and narratives of a contrary purport. Brutus divided between his three sons the island once called Britain, and now England, and gave to one son Loegria, to another Wales, and to the third what is now called Scotland, and made them peers, so that none of them was subject to another. Afterwards came a woman named Scota, daughter of Pharaoh of Egypt, who came via Spain and occupied Ireland, and afterwards conquered the land of Albany, which she had called, after her name, *Scotland*,[2] and one place in that land she had called after the names of her son Erk and her husband Gayl, wherefore that district was called *Ergaill* [Argyll], and they drove out the Britons, and from that time the Scots, as a new race and possessing a new name, had nothing to do with the Britons, but pursued them daily as their enemies, and were distinguished from them by different ranks and customs, and by a different language. Afterwards they joined company with the Picts, by whose strength they destroyed the Britons, and the land which is now called England, and for this reason the Britons gave tribute to the Romans, to obtain the help of the Roman emperor, whose name was Severus, against the Scots, and by his help the Britons made a wall between themselves and the Scots, having a length of 130 leagues in length from one sea to the other, and they say that by this it appears that Scotland was not at any time under the lordship of the Britons.[3] But they do not deny that King Arthur by his prowess conquered Denmark, France, Norway and also Scotland, and held them until he and Mordred were slain in battle, and from that time the realm of Scotland returned to its free status. They say that the Britons were then expelled by the Saxons, and then the Saxons by the Danes, and then the Danes by the Saxons, and that in the whole period of the Saxon kings the Scots remained free without being subject to them, and at that time, by the relics of Saint Andrew which came from Greece, they were converted to the faith five hundred years before the English became Christians, and from that time the realm of Scotland, with the king and the realm [*sic*], were under the lordship of the Roman church without any intermediary, and by it were they defended against all their enemies. * * *

⚬

✠ END OF PERSPECTIVES: ARTHURIAN MYTH IN THE HISTORY OF BRITAIN ✠

ARTHURIAN ROMANCE

Marie de France
(fl. 2nd half of the 12th century)

In a famous line from the prologue to her *Lais*, Marie de France suggested that serious readers could approach an obscure old book and "supply its significance from their own wisdom." The original French text, "*de lur sen le surplus mettre,*" implies that such readers add on something

---

2. This neatly replicates Brutus's trajectory from the eastern Mediterranean, across part of continental Europe, and thence to the British Isles.
3. The Scots artfully shift the emphasis found in Geoffrey of Monmouth. Roman colonization and Hadrian's wall become evidence of an ancient ethnic division and Scots independence both from the Britons and from the Britons' later invaders.

that is missing. In part a gesture of respect toward the study of pagan Latin literature in a Christian setting, this statement also seems to permit Marie herself a dramatically new perspective when she encounters the long-established Arthurian story, in *Lanval*. Starting with a scene of war that readers of Geoffrey of Monmouth might recognize, Marie swiftly brings into play elements that had been largely absent in the historicizing stories of Arthur: bodily desire and its dangers, romantic longing, the realm of the uncanny, the power of women, the force of wealth and influence in even the noblest courts.

Marie's specific identity remains obscure, but it is clear that she was a woman of French origin writing in England in the later decades of the twelfth century, widely educated, and in touch with the royal court. She dedicates her book of *Lais* to a "noble King" who was probably Henry II, and she may have been his kinswoman, possibly an illegitimate half-sister. Marie's works draw into that courtly culture the languages and traditions of the English and Celtic past. She rewrote a Latin narrative about the origin of "Saint Patrick's Purgatory" and the adventure of an Irish knight there; and she retold the fables of Aesop using an English translation that she attributed to King Alfred. The *Lais*, she says, came to her through oral transmission, and she connects them with the Bretons. Indeed, the best early copy of the *Lais*, Harley manuscript 978 in the British Library, is itself a multilingual compilation that includes the early Middle English poem *The Cuckoo Song* ("Sumer is icumen in"; see page 550).

Writing a generation after Geoffrey of Monmouth and not long before Gerald of Wales, Marie brings a quite different and rather critical set of preoccupations to her Arthurian story. She opens her tale with a realistic and admirable occasion of male power and strong kingship: Arthur's battle for territory and his reward of faithful vassals. A bleaker side of that courtly world, and perhaps of Marie's own, is also implicit, however. With a terseness and indirection typical of her *lais*, Marie shows women as property in the king's gift, knights forgotten when their wealth runs out, and the perversion of judicial process.

Marvels and erotic desire dominate her tale, though, and women's power, for good or ill, is its primary motivating force. Guinevere, in a hostile portrait of adulterous aggression and vengeful dishonesty, nonetheless manages to manipulate Arthur and his legal codes when Lanval rejects her advances. The queen is countered by Lanval's supernatural mistress, who commands luxurious riches that dwarf Arthur's; she rescues Lanval by being an unimpeachable legal witness in his defense. Indeed, she arrives on her white palfrey as the moment of judgment nears, almost like a knightly champion in a trial by battle. Lanval vanishes into a timeless world of fulfilled desire and limitless wealth that has analogies in much older Celtic tradition—for instance, in *The Voyage of Máel Dúin* (page 119). This closing scene defies the reintegration of male courtly order that is typical even in the erotic romances of Marie's contemporary Chrétien de Troyes.

The realm of eroticism and women's power in *Lanval*, though, is not automatically any more virtuous or stable than the ostentatious wealth and corruptible law of the world of Arthurian men. If Lanval's mysterious lady is beautiful and generous, she also takes his knightliness from him. Lanval is last seen riding behind the lady, and not on a warhorse but on a palfrey. Guinevere swiftly reduces Arthur to a weak and temporizing king. And in her initial explosion after Lanval rejects her, Guinevere accuses him of homosexuality. For all its absurdity, the moment articulates unnerving implications of the profound bonds among men in the Arthurian world, implications that could interrupt genealogical transmission of wealth and power. Marie's Guinevere again voices fears the tradition has left unsaid.

Marie de France may be trying less to propound a critique of the received stories of Arthur than to recall her readers' attention to elements that tradition has left aside, as she suggests in her prologue. Some of this is no more troubling than a delightful fantasy of wealth and pleasure, outside time and without consequences. Other elements imply, with startling economy, forces that (in the hands of later romancers) tear the Arthurian world to pieces.

Marie de France Writing, from an illuminated manuscript of her works. While most images of writing feature men, women were also writers and copyists as well as readers (see Color Plate 10). Here, in a late-13th-century manuscript of her poems, Marie de France is shown at her writing desk, strikingly similar in posture and detail (and in authority) to Laurence of Durham more than a century earlier (see page 2).

from LAIS[1]
Prologue

Whoever has received knowledge
and eloquence in speech from God
should not be silent or secretive
but demonstrate it willingly.

5   When a great good is widely heard of,
then, and only then, does it bloom,
and when that good is praised by many,
it has spread its blossoms.
The custom among the ancients—

10   as Priscian[2] testifies—
was to speak quite obscurely
in the books they wrote,
so that those who were to come after
and study them

15   might gloss the letter
and supply its significance from their own wisdom.[3]
Philosophers knew this,
they understood among themselves
that the more time they spent,

20   the more subtle their minds would become
and the better they would know how to keep themselves
from whatever was to be avoided.
He who would guard himself from vice
should study and understand

25   and begin a weighty work

1. Translated by Robert Hanning and Joan Ferrante.
2. A famed grammarian of the late Roman empire, Priscian remained widely influential in the study of Latin language and literature in the 12th century.
3. Marie refers to the practice of supplying glosses— explanatory notes such as this one—to school texts; she also implies that later readers bring their own perspective to earlier works, a point relevant to her own free adaptation of earlier Arthurian stories.

by which he might keep vice at a distance,
and free himself from great sorrow.
That's why I began to think
about composing some good stories
30 and translating from Latin to Romance;[4]
but that was not to bring me fame:
too many others have done it.
Then I thought of the *lais* I'd heard.[5]
I did not doubt, indeed I knew well,
35 that those who first began them
and sent them forth
composed them in order to preserve
adventures they had heard.
I have heard many told;
40 and I don't want to neglect or forget them.
To put them into word and rhyme
I've often stayed awake.

In your honor, noble King,[6]
who are so brave and courteous,
45 repository of all joys
in whose heart all goodness takes root,
I undertook to assemble these *lais*
to compose and recount them in rhyme.
In my heart I thought and determined,
50 sire, that I would present them to you.
If it pleases you to receive them,
you will give me great joy;
I shall be happy forever.
Do not think me presumptuous
55 if I dare present them to you.
Now hear how they begin.

Lanval

I shall tell you the adventure of another *lai*,
just as it happened:
it was composed about a very noble vassal;
in Breton, they call him Lanval.[1]

5 Arthur, the brave and the courtly king,
was staying at Cardoel,[2]
because the Scots and the Picts
were destroying the land.[3]
They invaded Logres°   *England*
10 and laid it waste.

4. That is, to French.
5. A *lai* was typically a short verse narrative, meant for oral performance with music. A particular group of these, often including Arthurian tales, was especially connected with Brittany.
6. Probably Henry II.

1. Marie seems to imply knowledge of Breton, a Celtic language related to Welsh. In other works, she shows knowledge of English as well, and excellent Latin.
2. Carlisle, in the north of England.
3. Scots and Picts were Arthur's traditional enemies.

At Pentecost, in summer,[4]
the king stayed there.
He gave out many rich gifts:
to counts and barons,

15   members of the Round Table—
such a company had no equal in all the world—
he distributed wives and lands,
to all but one who had served him.
That was Lanval; Arthur forgot him,

20   and none of his men favored him either.
For his valor, for his generosity,
his beauty and his bravery,
most men envied him;
some feigned the appearance of love

25   who, if something unpleasant happened to him,
would not have been at all disturbed.
He was the son of a king of high degree
but he was far from his heritage.
He was of the king's household

30   but he had spent all his wealth,
for the king gave him nothing
nor did Lanval ask.
Now Lanval was in difficulty,
depressed and very worried.

35   My lords, don't be surprised:
a strange man, without friends,
is very sad in another land,
when he doesn't know where to look for help.
The knight of whom I speak,

40   who had served the king so long,
one day mounted his horse
and went off to amuse himself.
He left the city
and came, all alone, to a field;

45   he dismounted by a running stream
but his horse trembled badly.
He removed the saddle and went off,
leaving the horse to roll around in the meadow.
He folded his cloak beneath his head

50   and lay down.
He worried about his difficulty,
he could see nothing that pleased him.
As he lay there
he looked down along the bank

55   and saw two girls approaching;
he had never seen any lovelier.
They were richly dressed,
tightly laced,

4. "Summer" here refers to late spring. The feast of Pentecost commemorates the descent of the Holy Spirit among
Christ's apostles; it is often the occasion of Arthurian stories, especially those that involve marvels.

in tunics of dark purple;
60   their faces were very lovely.
The older one carried basins,
golden, well made, and fine;
I shall tell you the truth about it, without fail.
The other carried a towel.
65   They went straight
to where the knight was lying.
Lanval, who was very well bred,
got up to meet them.
They greeted him first
70   and gave him their message:
"Sir Lanval, my lady,
who is worthy and wise and beautiful,
sent us for you.
Come with us now.
75   We shall guide you there safely.
See, her pavilion is nearby!"
The knight went with them;
giving no thought to his horse
who was feeding before him in the meadow.
80   They led him up to the tent,[5]
which was quite beautiful and well placed.
Queen Semiramis,
however much more wealth,
power, or knowledge she had,
85   or the emperor Octavian[6]
could not have paid for one of the flaps.
There was a golden eagle on top of it,
whose value I could not tell,
nor could I judge the value of the cords or the poles
90   that held up the sides of the tent;
there is no king on earth who could buy it,
no matter what wealth he offered.
The girl was inside the tent:
the lily and the young rose
95   when they appear in the summer
are surpassed by her beauty.
She lay on a beautiful bed—
the bedclothes were worth a castle—
dressed only in her shift.
100   Her body was well shaped and elegant;
for the heat, she had thrown over herself,
a precious cloak of white ermine,
covered with purple alexandrine,°   *embroidery*
but her whole side was uncovered,
105   her face, her neck and her bosom;

---

5. Elaborate tents are often found in contemporary narratives of kings going out to battle.
6. Semiramis, legendary queen of Assyria and builder of Babylon, led armies of conquest; she is also a conventional figure of uncontrolled sexual desire. She is interestingly placed here as a female counterpart to Octavian (Augustus Caesar), the first Roman emperor.

she was whiter than the hawthorn flower.
The knight went forward
and the girl addressed him.
He sat before the bed.
110 "Lanval," she said, "sweet love,
because of you I have come from my land;
I came to seek you from far away.
If you are brave and courtly,
no emperor or count or king
115 will ever have known such joy or good;
for I love you more than anything."
He looked at her and saw that she was beautiful;
Love stung him with a spark
that burned and set fire to his heart.
120 He answered her in a suitable way.
"Lovely one," he said, "if it pleased you,
if such joy might be mine
that you would love me,
there is nothing you might command,
125 within my power, that I would not do,
whether foolish or wise.
I shall obey your command;
for you, I shall abandon everyone.
I want never to leave you.
130 That is what I most desire."
When the girl heard the words
of the man who could love her so,
she granted him her love and her body.
Now Lanval was on the right road!
135 Afterward, she gave him a gift:
he would never again want anything,
he would receive as he desired;
however generously he might give and spend,
she would provide what he needed.
140 Now Lanval is well cared for.
The more lavishly he spends,
the more gold and silver he will have.
"Love," she said, "I admonish you now,
I command and beg you,
145 do not let any man know about this.
I shall tell you why:
you would lose me for good
if this love were known;
you would never see me again
150 or possess my body."
He answered that he would do
exactly as she commanded.
He lay beside her on the bed;
now Lanval is well cared for.
155 He remained with her
that afternoon, until evening

and would have stayed longer, if he could,
and if his love had consented.
"Love," she said, "get up.
160   You cannot stay any longer.
Go away now; I shall remain
but I will tell you one thing:
when you want to talk to me
there is no place you can think of
165   where a man might have his mistress
without reproach or shame,
that I shall not be there with you
to satisfy all your desires.
No man but you will see me
170   or hear my words."
When he heard her, he was very happy,
he kissed her, and then got up.
The girls who had brought him to the tent
dressed him in rich clothes;
175   when he was dressed anew,
there wasn't a more handsome youth in all the world;
he was no fool, no boor.
They gave him water for his hands
and a towel to dry them,
180   and they brought him food.
He took supper with his love;
it was not to be refused.
He was served with great courtesy,
he received it with great joy.
185   There was an entremet°   *side dish*
that vastly pleased the knight
for he kissed his lady often
and held her close.
When they finished dinner,
190   his horse was brought to him.
The horse had been well saddled;
Lanval was very richly served.
The knight took his leave, mounted,
and rode toward the city,
195   often looking behind him.
Lanval was very disturbed;
he wondered about his adventure
and was doubtful in his heart;
he was amazed, not knowing what to believe;
200   he didn't expect ever to see her again.
He came to his lodging
and found his men well dressed.
That night, his accommodations were rich
but no one knew where it came from.
205   There was no knight in the city
who really needed a place to stay
whom he didn't invite to join him

to be well and richly served.
Lanval gave rich gifts,
210 Lanval released prisoners,
Lanval dressed jongleurs,°   *performers*
Lanval offered great honors.
There was no stranger or friend
to whom Lanval didn't give.
215 Lanval's joy and pleasure were intense;
in the daytime or at night,
he could see his love often;
she was completely at his command.

In that same year, it seems to me,
220 after the feast of Saint John,
about thirty knights
were amusing themselves
in an orchard beneath the tower
where the queen was staying.
225 Gawain was with them
and his cousin, the handsome Yvain;[7]
Gawain, the noble, the brave,
who was so loved by all, said:
"By God, my lords, we wronged
230 our companion Lanval,
who is so generous and courtly,
and whose father is a rich king,
when we didn't bring him with us."
They immediately turned back,
235 went to his lodging
and prevailed on Lanval to come along with them.
At a sculpted window
the queen was looking out;
she had three ladies with her.
240 She saw the king's retinue,
recognized Lanval and looked at him.
Then she told one of her ladies
to send for her maidens,
the loveliest and the most refined;
245 together they went to amuse themselves
in the orchard where the others were.
She brought thirty or more with her;
they descended the steps.
The knights came to meet them,
250 because they were delighted to see them.
The knights took them by the hand;
their conversation was in no way vulgar.
Lanval went off to one side,
far from the others; he was impatient

---

7. Gawain and Yvain serve to place Marie's hero in the context of more famous Arthurian episodes. Gawain, nephew of Arthur and distinguished both for bravery and courtesy, increasingly acts as Lanval's sponsor in the rest of the *lai*.

255   to hold his love,
        to kiss and embrace and touch her;
        he thought little of others' joys
        if he could not have his pleasure.
        When the queen saw him alone,
260   she went straight to the knight.
        She sat beside him and spoke,
        revealing her whole heart:
        "Lanval, I have shown you much honor,
        I have cherished you, and loved you.
265   You may have all my love;
        just tell me your desire.
        I promise you my affection.
        You should be very happy with me."
        "My lady," he said, "let me be!
270   I have no desire to love you.
        I've served the king a long time;
        I don't want to betray my faith to him.
        Never, for you or for your love,
        will I do anything to harm my lord."
275   The queen got angry;
        in her wrath, she insulted him:
        "Lanval," she said, "I am sure
        you don't care for such pleasure;
        people have often told me
280   that you have no interest in women.
        You have fine-looking boys
        with whom you enjoy yourself.
        Base coward, lousy cripple,
        my lord made a bad mistake
285   when he let you stay with him.
        For all I know, he'll lose God because of it."
        When Lanval heard her, he was quite disturbed;
        he was not slow to answer.
        He said something out of spite
290   that he would later regret.
        "Lady," he said, "of that activity
        I know nothing,
        but I love and I am loved
        by one who should have the prize
295   over all the women I know.
        And I shall tell you one thing;
        you might as well know all:
        any one of those who serve her,
        the poorest girl of all,
300   is better than you, my lady queen,
        in body, face, and beauty,
        in breeding and in goodness."
        The queen left him
        and went, weeping, to her chamber.
305   She was upset and angry

because he had insulted her.
She went to bed sick;
never, she said, would she get up
unless the king gave her satisfaction
310   for the offense against her.
The king returned from the woods,
he'd had a very good day.
He entered the queen's chambers.
When she saw him, she began to complain.
315   She fell at his feet, asked his mercy,
saying that Lanval had dishonored her;
he had asked for her love,
and because she refused him
he insulted and offended her:
320   he boasted of a love
who was so refined and noble and proud
that her chambermaid,
the poorest one who served her,
was better than the queen.
325   The king got very angry;
he swore an oath:
if Lanval could not defend himself in court
he would have him burned or hanged.
The king left her chamber
330   and called for three of his barons;
he sent them for Lanval
who was feeling great sorrow and distress.
He had come back to his dwelling,
knowing very well
335   that he'd lost his love,
he had betrayed their affair.
He was all alone in a room,
disturbed and troubled;
he called on his love, again and again,
340   but it did him no good.
He complained and sighed,
from time to time he fainted;
then he cried a hundred times for her to have mercy
and speak to her love.
345   He cursed his heart and his mouth;
it's a wonder he didn't kill himself.
No matter how much he cried and shouted,
ranted and raged,
she would not have mercy on him,
350   not even let him see her.
How will he ever contain himself?
The men the king sent
arrived and told him
to appear in court without delay:
355   the king had summoned him
because the queen had accused him.

Lanval went with his great sorrow;
they could have killed him, for all he cared.
He came before the king;
360   he was very sad, thoughtful, silent;
his face revealed great suffering.
In anger the king told him:
"Vassal, you have done me a great wrong!
This was a base undertaking,
365   to shame and disgrace me
and to insult the queen.
You have made a foolish boast:
your love is much too noble
if her maid is more beautiful,
370   more worthy, than the queen."
Lanval denied that he'd dishonored
or shamed his lord,
word for word, as the king spoke:
he had not made advances to the queen;
375   but of what he had said,
he acknowledged the truth,
about the love he had boasted of,
that now made him sad because he'd lost her.
About that he said he would do
380   whatever the court decided.
The king was very angry with him;
he sent for all his men
to determine exactly what he ought to do
so that no one could find fault with his decision.
385   They did as he commanded,
whether they liked it or not.
They assembled,
judged, and decided,
that Lanval should have his day;
390   but he must find pledges for his lord
to guarantee that he would await the judgment,
return, and be present at it.[8]
Then the court would be increased,
for now there were none but the king's household.
395   The barons came back to the king
and announced their decision.
The king demanded pledges.
Lanval was alone and forlorn,
he had no relative, no friend.
400   Gawain went and pledged himself for him,
and all his companions followed.
The king addressed them: "I release him to you
on forfeit of whatever you hold from me,
lands and fiefs, each one for himself."

8. Marie introduces judicial procedures that may have recalled those in Henry's reign: summons and accusation, setting a day for judgment, the rise of royal jurisdiction, the possibility of a champion, and trial by battle.

405 When Lanval was pledged, there was nothing else to do.
     He returned to his lodging.
     The knights accompanied him,
     they reproached and admonished him
     that he give up his great sorrow;
410 they cursed his foolish love.
     Each day they went to see him,
     because they wanted to know
     whether he was drinking and eating;
     they were afraid that he'd kill himself.
415 On the day that they had named,
     the barons assembled.
     The king and the queen were there
     and the pledges brought Lanval back.
     They were all very sad for him:
420 I think there were a hundred
     who would have done all they could
     to set him free without a trial
     where he would be wrongly accused.
     The king demanded a verdict
425 according to the charge and rebuttal.
     Now it all fell to the barons.
     They went to the judgment,
     worried and distressed
     for the noble man from another land
430 who'd gotten into such trouble in their midst.
     Many wanted to condemn him
     in order to satisfy their lord.
     The Duke of Cornwall said:
     "No one can blame us;
435 whether it makes you weep or sing
     justice must be carried out.
     The king spoke against his vassal
     whom I have heard named Lanval;
     he accused him of felony,
440 charged him with a misdeed—
     a love that he had boasted of,
     which made the queen angry.
     No one but the king accused him:
     by the faith I owe you,
445 if one were to speak the truth,
     there should have been no need for defense,
     except that a man owes his lord honor
     in every circumstance.
     He will be bound by his oath,
450 and the king will forgive us our pledges
     if he can produce proof;
     if his love would come forward,
     if what he said,
     what upset the queen, is true,
455 then he will be acquitted,

because he did not say it out of malice.
But if he cannot get his proof,
we must make it clear to him
that he will forfeit his service to the king;
460   he must take his leave."
They sent to the knight,
told and announced to him
that he should have his love come
to defend and stand surety for him.
465   He told them that he could not do it:
he would never receive help from her.
They went back to the judges,
not expecting any help from Lanval.
The king pressed them hard
470   because of the queen who was waiting.
When they were ready to give their verdict
they saw two girls approaching,
riding handsome palfreys.
They were very attractive,
475   dressed in purple taffeta,
over their bare skin.
The men looked at them with pleasure.
Gawain, taking three knights with him,
went to Lanval and told him;
480   he pointed out the two girls.
Gawain was extremely happy, and begged him
to tell if his love were one of them.
Lanval said he didn't know who they were,
where they came from or where they were going.
485   The girls proceeded
still on horseback;
they dismounted before the high table
at which Arthur, the king, sat.
They were of great beauty,
490   and spoke in a courtly manner:
"King, clear your chambers,
have them hung with silk
where my lady may dismount;
she wishes to take shelter with you."
495   He promised it willingly
and called two knights
to guide them up to the chambers.
On that subject no more was said.
The king asked his barons
500   for their judgment and decision;
he said they had angered him very much
with their long delay.
"Sire," they said, "we have decided.
Because of the ladies we have just seen
505   we have made no judgment.
Let us reconvene the trial."

Then they assembled, everyone was worried;
there was much noise and strife.
While they were in that confusion,
510   two girls in noble array,
dressed in Phrygian silks
and riding Spanish mules,
were seen coming down the street.
This gave the vassals great joy;
515   to each other they said that now
Lanval, the brave and bold, was saved.
Gawain went up to him,
bringing his companions along.
"Sire," he said, "take heart.
520   For the love of God, speak to us.
Here come two maidens,
well adorned and very beautiful;
one must certainly be your love."
Lanval answered quickly
525   that he did not recognize them,
he didn't know them or love them.
Meanwhile they'd arrived,
and dismounted before the king.
Most of those who saw them praised them
530   for their bodies, their faces, their coloring;
each was more impressive
than the queen had ever been.
The older one was courtly and wise,
she spoke her message fittingly:
535   "King, have chambers prepared for us
to lodge my lady according to her need;
she is coming here to speak with you."
He ordered them to be taken
to the others who had preceded them.
540   There was no problem with the mules.
When he had seen to the girls,
he summoned all his barons
to render their judgment;
it had already dragged out too much.
545   The queen was getting angry
because she had fasted so long.
They were about to give their judgment
when through the city came riding
a girl on horseback:
550   there was none more beautiful in the world.
She rode a white palfrey,
who carried her handsomely and smoothly:
he was well apportioned in the neck and head,
no finer beast in the world.
555   The palfrey's trappings were rich;
under heaven there was no count or king
who could have afforded them all
without selling or mortgaging lands.

She was dressed in this fashion:
560 in a white linen shift
that revealed both her sides
since the lacing was along the side.
Her body was elegant, her hips slim,
her neck whiter than snow on a branch,
565 her eyes bright, her face white,
a beautiful mouth, a well-set nose,
dark eyebrows and an elegant forehead,
her hair curly and rather blond;
golden wire does not shine
570 like her hair in the light.
Her cloak, which she had wrapped around her,
was dark purple.
On her wrist she held a sparrow hawk,
a greyhound followed her.
575 In the town, no one, small or big,
old man or child,
failed to come look.
As they watched her pass,
there was no joking about her beauty.
580 She proceeded at a slow pace.
The judges who saw her
marveled at the sight;
no one who looked at her
was not warmed with joy.
585 Those who loved the knight
came to him and told him
of the girl who was approaching,
if God pleased, to rescue him.
"Sir companion, here comes one
590 neither tawny nor dark;
this is, of all who exist,
the most beautiful woman in the world."
Lanval heard them and lifted his head;
he recognized her and sighed.
595 The blood rose to his face;
he was quick to speak.
"By my faith," he said, "that is my love.
Now I don't care if I am killed,
if only she forgives me.
600 For I am restored, now that I see her."
The lady entered the palace;
no one so beautiful had ever been there.
She dismounted before the king
so that she was well seen by all.
605 And she let her cloak fall
so they could see her better.
The king, who was well bred,
rose and went to meet her;
all the others honored her
610 and offered to serve her.

When they had looked at her well,
when they had greatly praised her beauty,
she spoke in this way,
she didn't want to wait:
615   "I have loved one of your vassals:
you see him before you—Lanval.
He has been accused in your court—
I don't want him to suffer
for what he said; you should know
620   that the queen was in the wrong.
He never made advances to her.
And for the boast that he made,
if he can be acquitted through me,
let him be set free by your barons."
625   Whatever the barons judged by law
the king promised would prevail.
To the last man they agreed
that Lanval had successfully answered the charge.
He was set free by their decision
630   and the girl departed.
The king could not detain her,
though there were enough people to serve her.
Outside the hall stood
a great stone of dark marble
635   where heavy men mounted
when they left the king's court;
Lanval climbed on it.
When the girl came through the gate
Lanval leapt, in one bound,
640   onto the palfrey, behind her.
With her he went to Avalun,[9]
so the Bretons tell us,
to a very beautiful island;
there the youth was carried off.
645   No man heard of him again,
and I have no more to tell.

Sir Gawain and the Green Knight

As a subject of literary romance, Arthurian tradition never had the centrality in later medieval England it had gained in France. It was only one of a wide range of popular topics like Havelok the Dane, King Horn, and the Troy story. Nevertheless Arthur and his court played an ongoing role in English society, written into histories and emulated by aristocrats and kings. And in the later fourteenth or early fifteenth century, several very distinguished Arthurian poems appeared, such as the alliterative Morte Arthure and the Awntyrs (Adventures) off Arthure.

9. Avalon is the mysterious island to which Arthur is also carried, mortally wounded, after his final battle. Marie's contemporary Gerald of Wales expresses far older associations of Avalon with powerful women (see pages 172–73).

Sir Gawain and the Green Knight is the greatest of the Arthurian romances produced in England. The poem embraces the highest aspirations of the late medieval aristocratic world, both courtly and religious, even while it eloquently admits the human failings that threaten those values. A knight's troth and word, a Christian's election and covenant, the breaking point of a person's or a society's virtues, all come in for celebration and painful scrutiny during Gawain's adventure.

Like *Beowulf*, *Sir Gawain and the Green Knight* comes down to us by the thread of a single copy. Its manuscript contains a group of poems (*Sir Gawain, Pearl, Purity,* and *Patience*) that mark their anonymous author as a poet whose range approaches that of his contemporary Chaucer, and whose formal craft is in some ways more ambitious than Chaucer's.

Gawain is the work of a highly sophisticated provincial court poet (likely in the northwest Midlands), working in a form and narrative tradition that is conservative in comparison with Chaucer's. The poet uses the alliterative long line, a meter with its roots in Anglo-Saxon poetry; the unrhymed alliterative stanzas, of irregular length, each end with five shorter rhymed lines often called a "bob-and-wheel" stanza. (For a further discussion of the alliterative style, see the introduction to William Langland, page 423.) Within these traditional constraints, however, the poem achieves an apex of medieval courtly literature, as a superlatively crafted and stylized version of quest romance.

The romance never aims to detach itself from society or history, though. It opens and closes by referring to Troy, the ancient, fallen empire whose survivors were legendary founders of Britain, a connection well known through Geoffrey of Monmouth. Arthur, their ultimate heir, went on later in his myth to pursue imperial ambitions that, like those of Troy, were foiled by adulterous desire and political infidelity. *Sir Gawain* also echoes its contemporary world in the technical language of architecture, crafts, and arms. This helps draw in the kind of conservative, aristocratic court for which the poem seems to have been written, probably in Cheshire or Lancashire, a somewhat backward region whose nobles remained loyal to Richard II. Along with the pleasure it takes in fine armor and courtly ritual, the poem seems to enfold anxieties about the economic pressures of maintaining chivalric display in a period of costly new technology, inflation, and declining income from land.

By the time this poem was written, toward the close of the fourteenth century, Gawain was a famous Arthurian hero. His reputation was ambiguous, though; he was both Arthur's faithful retainer and nephew, but also a suave seducer. Which side of Gawain would dominate in this particular poem? Would he stand for a civilization of Christian chivalry or one of cynical sophistication?

The test that begins to answer this question occurs during Arthur's ritual celebrations of Christmas and the New Year, and within the civilized practices of Eucharist and secular feast. A gigantic green knight interrupts Arthur's banquet to offer a deadly game of exchanged ax-blows, to be resolved in one year's time. Although the Green Knight, with his ball of holly leaves, seems at first to come from the tradition of the Wild Man—a giant force of nature itself—he is also a sophisticated knight, gorgeously attired. He knows, too, just how to taunt a young king without quite overstepping the bounds of courtly behavior. Gawain takes up the challenge, but a still greater marvel ensues.

As the term of the agreement approaches, Gawain rides off, elaborately armed, to find the Green Knight and fulfill his obligation, even if that means his death. What Gawain encounters first, though, are temptations of character and sexuality even trickier and more crucial than they at first seem.

Sir Gawain and the Green Knight is remarkable not only for the intricacy of its plot but also for the virtuosity of its descriptions, such as the almost elegiac review of the passing seasons ("And so the year moves on in yesterdays many"). The poem rejoices in the masterful exercise of skill as the mark of civilization. Beautifully crafted knots appear everywhere, and we encounter artisanal craft as well in narrative elements like the Green Knight's dress (a dazzling mixture of leafy green and jeweler's gold), Gawain's decorated shield and arms, and the expertise of the master of the hunt who carves up the prey of Gawain's host with ritual precision. Even Gawain's exquisite courtly manners appear as a civilizing artifice.

The ambition of the poem's own craft is equally evident in its extraordinary range of formal devices. Preeminent among these is the symbolic register of number. The poem can be seen as a single unit, circling back to the Trojan scene with which it begins. It has a double structure, too, as it shifts between the courts of Arthur and Gawain's mysterious host. In the manuscript it is divided into four parts ("fits") that respond to the seasonal description at the opening of Part 2. The narrative proper ends by echoing the very start of the poem, at line 2525, itself a multiple of fives that recalls the pentangle on Gawain's shield symbolizing his virtues. The final rhyming stanza, with its formula of grace and salvation, brings the line total to 2530, whose individual digits add up to ten, a number associated with the divine in medieval numerology.

This symbolic structure can seem sometimes overdetermined. A range of elements, however, invites the reader to come at the poem from other perspectives. The poem's very circularity, narrative and formal, allows it to be viewed from beginning or ending. From the front it is a poem of male accomplishment, largely celebrating *men's* courts and *men's* virtues (even men's horses). At the other end, however, it focuses on a court presided over by an old woman (later called a goddess), a court whose irruption into the Arthurian world is explained as the playing out of an old and mysterious rivalry between two queens. Male, even patriarchal from one direction, the poem seems matriarchal, almost pagan, from the other. For all its formal cohesion and celebration of craft, the poem also pulls the reader back and keeps its mysteries intact by leaving many narrative loose ends and unanswered questions.

Unresolvable ambiguities reside most clearly in the pentangle on Gawain's shield and in the "green girdle" whose true owner remains uncertain. For all their differences, both are figures that insist on repetition, end where they begin, and possess a geometry that can be traced forward or backward. Yet the static perfection of the pentangle is subtly set against the protean green girdle, which passes through so many hands, alters its shape (being untied and retied repeatedly), and connects with so many issues in the poem: mortality, women's power, Gawain's fault and the acceptance of that fault by the whole Arthurian court. The girdle becomes an image both of flaw and triumph and of all the loose ends in this early episode of the Arthurian myth.

The girdle also serves to link *Sir Gawain* to political and social issues of the poet's own time, particularly efforts to revalidate a declining system of chivalry. After the last line in the manuscript, a later medieval hand has added "Hony Soyt Qui Mal Pence" ("shamed be he who thinks ill thereof"), the motto of the royal Order of the Garter, founded by Edward III in 1349 to promote a revival of knighthood. The Arthurian myth had already been redeployed to buttress royal power when Edward III refounded a Round Table in 1344. King Arthur's wisdom at the close of Gawain's adventure lies in transforming Gawain's shame, rage, and humiliated sense of sin into an emblem at once of mortal humanity and aristocratic cohesion. This is the place—back with the king and ritually connected with the Order of the Garter—where the closed circle of the poem opens to the social, historical world of empire, court, and kingship.

Sir Gawain and the Green Knight[1]
Part 1

Since the siege and the assault was ceased at Troy,
The walls breached and burnt down to brands and ashes,
The knight that had knotted the nets of deceit

---

1. This translation, remarkably faithful to the original alliterative meter and stanza form, is by Marie Borroff (1967).

Was impeached for his perfidy, proven most true.
5   It was high-born Aeneas[2] and his haughty race
That since prevailed over provinces, and proudly reigned
Over well-nigh all the wealth of the West Isles.[3]
Great Romulus to Rome repairs in haste;
With boast and with bravery builds he that city
10   And names it with his own name, that it now bears.
Ticius to Tuscany,[4] and towers raises,
Langobard[5] in Lombardy lays out homes,
And far over the French Sea, Felix Brutus[6]
On many broad hills and high Britain he sets,
15   most fair.
Where war and wrack and wonder
By shifts have sojourned there,
And bliss by turns with blunder
In that land's lot had share.

20   And since this Britain was built by this baron great,
Bold boys bred there, in broils delighting,
That did in their day many a deed most dire.
More marvels have happened in this merry land
Than in any other I know, since that olden time,
25   But of those that here built, of British kings,
King Arthur was counted most courteous of all,
Wherefore an adventure I aim to unfold,
That a marvel of might some men think it,
And one unmatched among Arthur's wonders.
30   If you will listen to my lay but a little while,
As I heard it in hall, I shall hasten to tell
                          anew.
As it was fashioned featly
In tale of derring-do,
35   And linked in measures meetly
By letters tried and true.

This king lay at Camelot[7] at Christmastide;
Many good knights and gay his guests were there,
Arrayed of the Round Table[8] rightful brothers,
40   With feasting and fellowship and carefree mirth.
There true men contended in tournaments many,
Joined there in jousting these gentle knights,

2. Aeneas led the survivors of Troy to Italy, after a series of ambiguous omens and misadventures. In medieval tradition, he was also said to have plotted to betray his own city. "The knight" in line 3, though, may refer to the Trojan Antenor, also said to have betrayed Troy.
3. Perhaps Europe, or just the British Isles. Many royal houses traced their ancestry to Rome and Troy.
4. Possibly Titus Tatius, ancient king of the Sabines.
5. Ancestor of the Lombards, and a nephew of Brutus.
6. According to Geoffrey of Monmouth and others, a great-grandson of Aeneas, exiled after accidentally killing

his father and later the founder of Britain.
7. Arthur's capital; its location is uncertain, probably in Wales, and perhaps it is to be connected with Caerleon-on-Usk where Arthur had been crowned. Knights were expected to gather at his court, in celebration and homage, on the five liturgical holidays on which Arthur wore his crown: Easter, Ascension, Pentecost, All Saints' Day, and Christmas.
8. Its shape symbolized the unity of Arthur's knights but also avoided disputes over precedence.

Then came to the court for carol-dancing,
For the feast was in force full fifteen days,
45   With all the meat and the mirth that men could devise,
Such gaiety and glee, glorious to hear,
Brave din by day, dancing by night.
High were their hearts in halls and chambers,
These lords and these ladies, for life was sweet.
50   In peerless pleasures passed they their days,
The most noble knights known under Christ,
And the loveliest ladies that lived on earth ever,
And he the comeliest king, that that court holds,
For all this fair folk in their first age[9]
55   were still.
      Happiest of mortal kind,
      King noblest famed of will;
      You would now go far to find
      So hardy a host on hill.

60   While the New Year was new, but yesternight come,
This fair folk at feast two-fold was served,
When the king and his company were come in together,
The chanting in chapel achieved and ended.
Clerics and all the court acclaimed the glad season,
65   Cried Noel anew, good news to men;
Then gallants gather gaily, hand-gifts to make,
Called them out clearly, claimed them by hand,
Bickered long and busily about those gifts.
Ladies laughed aloud, though losers they were,
70   And he that won was not angered, as well you will know.[1]
All this mirth they made until meat was served;
When they had washed them worthily, they went to their seats,
The best seated above, as best it beseemed,
Guenevere the goodly queen gay in the midst
75   On a dais[2] well-decked and duly arrayed
With costly silk curtains, a canopy over,
Of Toulouse and Turkestan tapestries rich,
All broidered and bordered with the best gems
Ever brought into Britain, with bright pennies
80   to pay.
      Fair queen, without a flaw,
      She glanced with eyes of gray.
      A seemlier that once he saw,
      In truth, no man could say.

85   But Arthur would not eat till all were served;
So light was his lordly heart, and a little boyish;

9. Arthur is emphatically a young king here, even "boyish." The phrase may also recall the Golden Age, an era of uncorrupted happiness.
1. The distribution of gifts at New Year displayed the king's wealth and power; it was also the occasion here of some courtly game of exchange, in which the loser perhaps gave up a kiss.
2. A medieval nobleman's hall typically had a raised platform at one end, on which the "high table" stood.

His life he liked lively—the less he cared
To be lying for long, or long to sit,
So busy his young blood, his brain so wild.
90   And also a point of pride pricked him in heart,
For he nobly had willed, he would never eat
On so high a holiday, till he had heard first
Of some fair feat or fray some far-borne tale,
Of some marvel of might, that he might trust,
95   By champions of chivalry achieved in arms,
Or some suppliant came seeking some single knight
To join with him in jousting, in jeopardy each
To lay life for life, and leave it to fortune
To afford him on field fair hap or other.
100 Such is the king's custom, when his court he holds
At each far-famed feast amid his fair host
                    so dear.
          The stout king stands in state
          Till a wonder shall appear;
105   He leads, with heart elate,
          High mirth in the New Year.

So he stands there in state, the stout young king,
Talking before the high table of trifles fair.
There Gawain the good knight by Guenevere sits,
110 With Agravain à la dure main on her other side,
Both knights of renown, and nephews of the king.
Bishop Baldwin above begins the table,
And Yvain,[3] son of Urien, ate with him there.
These few with the fair queen were fittingly served;
115 At the side-tables sat many stalwart knights.
Then the first course comes, with clamor of trumpets
That were bravely bedecked with bannerets bright,
With noise of new drums and the noble pipes.[4]
Wild were the warbles that wakened that day
120 In strains that stirred many strong men's hearts.
There dainties were dealt out, dishes rare,
Choice fare to choose, on chargers so many
That scarce was there space to set before the people
The service of silver, with sundry meats,
125   on cloth.
          Each fair guest freely there
          Partakes, and nothing loth;
          Twelve dishes before each pair;
          Good beer and bright wine both.

130 Of the service itself I need say no more,
For well you will know no tittle was wanting.

---

3. Another nephew of Arthur. The relationship of uncle
and nephew is close in many Arthurian romances, and
noble youths were often sent to be raised by an uncle on
the mother's side.
4. Holiday banquets were formalized, almost theatrical.

Another noise and a new was well-nigh at hand,
That the lord might have leave his life to nourish;
For scarce were the sweet strains still in the hall,

135   And the first course come to that company fair,
There hurtles in at the hall-door an unknown rider,
One the greatest on ground in growth of his frame:
From broad neck to buttocks so bulky and thick,
And his loins and his legs so long and so great,

140   Half a giant on earth I hold him to be,
But believe him no less than the largest of men,
And that the seemliest in his stature to see, as he rides,
For in back and in breast though his body was grim,
His waist in its width was worthily small,

145   And formed with every feature in fair accord
                          was he.
              Great wonder grew in hall
              At his hue most strange to see,
              For man and gear and all

150   Were green as green could be.

And in guise all of green, the gear and the man:
A coat cut close, that clung to his sides,
And a mantle to match, made with a lining
Of furs cut and fitted—the fabric was noble,

155   Embellished all with ermine, and his hood beside,
That was loosed from his locks, and laid on his shoulders.
With trim hose and tight, the same tint of green,
His great calves were girt, and gold spurs under
He bore on silk bands that embellished his heels,

160   And footgear well-fashioned, for riding most fit.
And all his vesture verily was verdant green;
Both the bosses on his belt and other bright gems
That were richly ranged on his raiment noble
About himself and his saddle, set upon silk,

165   That to tell half the trifles would tax my wits,
The butterflies and birds embroidered thereon
In green of the gayest, with many a gold thread.
The pendants of the breast-band, the princely crupper,
And the bars of the bit were brightly enameled;

170   The stout stirrups were green, that steadied his feet,
And the bows of the saddle and the side-panels both,
That gleamed all and glinted with green gems about.
The steed he bestrides of that same green
                          so bright.

175   A green horse great and thick;
              A headstrong steed of might;
              In broidered bridle quick,
              Mount matched man aright.

Gay was this goodly man in guise all of green,

180   And the hair of his head to his horse suited;
Fair flowing tresses enfold his shoulders;

A beard big as a bush on his breast hangs,
That with his heavy hair, that from his head falls,
Was evened all about above both his elbows,
185   That half his arms thereunder were hid in the fashion
Of a king's cap-à-dos,[5] that covers his throat.
The mane of that mighty horse much to it like,
Well curled and becombed, and cunningly knotted
With filaments of fine gold amid the fair green,
190   Here a strand of the hair, here one of gold;
His tail and his foretop twin in their hue,
And bound both with a band of a bright green
That was decked adown the dock with dazzling stones
And tied tight at the top with a triple knot
195   Where many bells well burnished rang bright and clear.
Such a mount in his might, nor man on him riding,
None had seen, I dare swear, with sight in that hall
so grand.
As lightning quick and light
200   He looked to all at hand;
It seemed that no man might
His deadly dints withstand.

Yet had he no helm, nor hauberk[6] neither,
Nor plate, nor appurtenance appending to arms,
205   Nor shaft pointed sharp, nor shield for defense,
But in his one hand he had a holly bob
That is goodliest in green when groves are bare,
And an ax in his other, a huge and immense,
A wicked piece of work in words to expound:
210   The head on its haft was an ell long;
The spike of green steel, resplendent with gold;
The blade burnished bright, with a broad edge,
As well shaped to shear as a sharp razor;
Stout was the stave in the strong man's gripe,
215   That was wound all with iron to the weapon's end,
With engravings in green of goodliest work.
A lace lightly about, that led to a knot,
Was looped in by lengths along the fair haft,
And tassels thereto attached in a row,
220   With buttons of bright green, brave to behold.
This horseman hurtles in, and the hall enters;
Riding to the high dais, recked he no danger;
Not a greeting he gave as the guests he o'erlooked,
Nor wasted his words, but "Where is," he said,
225   "The captain of this crowd? Keenly I wish
To see that sire with sight, and to himself say
my say."
He swaggered all about
To scan the host so gay;
230   He halted, as if in doubt
Who in that hall held sway.

---

5. Probably a hooded cape, fastened under the chin.   6. A tunic of chain mail.

There were stares on all sides as the stranger spoke,
For much did they marvel what it might mean
That a horseman and a horse should have such a hue,
235 Grow green as the grass, and greener, it seemed,
Than green fused on gold more glorious by far.
All the onlookers eyed him, and edged nearer,
And awaited in wonder what he would do,
For many sights had they seen, but such a one never,
240 So that phantom and faerie the folk there deemed it,
Therefore chary of answer was many a champion bold,
And stunned at his strong words stone-still they sat
In a swooning silence in the stately hall.
As all were slipped into sleep, so slackened their speech
245   apace.
              Not all, I think, for dread,
              But some of courteous grace
              Let him who was their head
              Be spokesman in that place.

250 Then Arthur before the high dais that entrance beholds,
And hailed him, as behooved, for he had no fear,
And said "Fellow, in faith you have found fair welcome;
The head of this hostelry Arthur am I;
Leap lightly down, and linger, I pray,
255 And the tale of your intent you shall tell us after."
"Nay, so help me," said the other, "He that on high sits,
To tarry here any time, 'twas not mine errand;
But as the praise of you, prince, is puffed up so high,
And your court and your company are counted the best,
260 Stoutest under steel-gear on steeds to ride,
Worthiest of their works the wide world over,
And peerless to prove in passages of arms,
And courtesy here is carried to its height,
And so at this season I have sought you out.
265 You may be certain by the branch that I bear in hand
That I pass here in peace,[7] and would part friends,
For had I come to this court on combat bent,
I have a hauberk at home, and a helm beside,
A shield and a sharp spear, shining bright,
270 And other weapons to wield, I ween well, to boot,
But as I willed no war, I wore no metal.
But if you be so bold as all men believe,
You will graciously grant the game that I ask
                      by right."
275   Arthur answer gave
              And said, "Sir courteous knight,
              If contest here you crave,
              You shall not fail to fight."

---

7. A holly branch could symbolize peace and was used in games of the Christmas season.

"Nay, to fight, in good faith, is far from my thought;
280   There are about on these benches but beardless children,
Were I here in full arms on a haughty steed,
For measured against mine, their might is puny.
And so I call in this court for a Christmas game,
For 'tis Yule and New Year, and many young bloods about;
285   If any in this house such hardihood claims,
Be so bold in his blood, his brain so wild,
As stoutly to strike one stroke for another,
I shall give him as my gift this gisarme[8] noble,
This ax, that is heavy enough, to handle as he likes,
290   And I shall bide the first blow, as bare as I sit.
If there be one so willful my words to assay,
Let him leap hither lightly, lay hold of this weapon;
I quitclaim it forever, keep it as his own,
And I shall stand him a stroke, steady on this floor,
295   So you grant me the guerdon to give him another,
                          sans blame.
                  In a twelvemonth and a day
                  He shall have of me the same;
                  Now be it seen straightway
300   Who dares take up the game."

If he astonished them at first, stiller were then
All that household in hall, the high and the low;
The stranger on his green steed stirred in the saddle,
And roisterously his red eyes he rolled all about,
305   Bent his bristling brows, that were bright green,
Wagged his beard as he watched who would arise.
When the court kept its counsel he coughed aloud,
And cleared his throat coolly, the clearer to speak:
"What, is this Arthur's house," said that horseman then,
310   "Whose fame is so fair in far realms and wide?
Where is now your arrogance and your awesome deeds,
Your valor and your victories and your vaunting words?
Now are the revel and renown of the Round Table
Overwhelmed with a word of one man's speech,
315   For all cower and quake, and no cut felt!"
With this he laughs so loud that the lord grieved;
The blood for sheer shame shot to his face,
                          and pride.
                  With rage his face flushed red,
320   And so did all beside.
                  Then the king as bold man bred
                  Toward the stranger took a stride.

And said "Sir, now we see you will say but folly,
Which whoso has sought, it suits that he find.
325   No guest here is aghast of your great words.

8. A long-handled ax with a spike at the end.

Give to me your gisarme, in God's own name,
And the boon you have begged shall straight be granted."
He leaps to him lightly, lays hold of his weapon;
The green fellow on foot fiercely alights.
330 Now has Arthur his ax, and the haft grips,
And sternly stirs it about, on striking bent.
The stranger before him stood there erect,
Higher than any in the house by a head and more;
With stern look as he stood, he stroked his beard,
335 And with undaunted countenance drew down his coat,
No more moved nor dismayed for his mighty dints
Than any bold man on bench had brought him a drink
                          of wine.
                  Gawain by Guenevere
340   Toward the king doth now incline:
              "I beseech, before all here,
              That this melee may be mine."

"Would you grant me the grace," said Gawain to the king,
"To be gone from this bench and stand by you there,
345 If I without discourtesy might quit this board,
And if my liege lady misliked it not,
I would come to your counsel before your court noble.
For I find it not fit, as in faith it is known,
When such a boon is begged before all these knights,
350 Though you be tempted thereto, to take it on yourself
While so bold men about upon benches sit,
That no host under heaven is hardier of will,
Nor better brothers-in-arms where battle is joined;
I am the weakest, well I know, and of wit feeblest;
355 And the loss of my life would be least of any;
That I have you for uncle is my only praise;
My body, but for your blood, is barren of worth;
And for that this folly befits not a king,
And 'tis I that have asked it, it ought to be mine,
360 And if my claim be not comely let all this court judge,
                          in sight."
                  The court assays the claim,
                  And in counsel all unite
                  To give Gawain the game
365   And release the king outright.

Then the king called the knight to come to his side,
And he rose up readily, and reached him with speed,
Bows low to his lord, lays hold of the weapon,
And he releases it lightly, and lifts up his hand,
370 And gives him God's blessing, and graciously prays
That his heart and his hand may be hardy both.
"Keep, cousin," said the king, "what you cut with this day,
And if you rule it aright, then readily, I know,
You shall stand the stroke it will strike after."

375 Gawain goes to the guest with gisarme in hand,
And boldly he bides there, abashed not a whit.
Then hails he Sir Gawain, the horseman in green:
"Recount we our contract, ere you come further.
First I ask and adjure you, how you are called
380 That you tell me true, so that trust it I may."
"In good faith," said the good knight, "Gawain am I
Whose buffet befalls you, whate'er betide after,
And at this time twelvemonth take from you another
With what weapon you will, and with no man else
385   alive."
              The other nods assent:
              "Sir Gawain, as I may thrive,
              I am wondrous well content
              That you this dint shall drive."

390 "Sir Gawain," said the Green Knight, "By God, I rejoice
That your fist shall fetch this favor I seek,
And you have readily rehearsed, and in right terms,
Each clause of my covenant with the king your lord,
Save that you shall assure me, sir, upon oath,
395 That you shall seek me yourself, wheresoever you deem
My lodgings may lie, and look for such wages
As you have offered me here before all this host."
"What is the way there?" said Gawain, "Where do you dwell?
I heard never of your house, by Him that made me,
400 Nor I know you not, knight, your name nor your court.
But tell me truly thereof, and teach me your name,
And I shall fare forth to find you, so far as I may,
And this I say in good certain, and swear upon oath."
"That is enough in New Year, you need say no more,"
405 Said the knight in the green to Gawain the noble,
"If I tell you true, when I have taken your knock,
And if you handily have hit, you shall hear straightway
Of my house and my home and my own name;
Then follow in my footsteps by faithful accord.
410 And if I spend no speech, you shall speed the better:
You can feast with your friends, nor further trace
                                          my tracks.
              Now hold your grim tool steady
              And show us how it hacks."
415   "Gladly, sir; all ready,"
              Says Gawain; he strokes the ax.

The Green Knight upon ground girds him with care:
Bows a bit with his head, and bares his flesh:
His long lovely locks he laid over his crown,
420 Let the naked nape for the need be shown.
Gawain grips to his ax and gathers it aloft—
The left foot on the floor before him he set—
Brought it down deftly upon the bare neck,

That the shock of the sharp blow shivered the bones
425 And cut the flesh cleanly and clove it in twain,
That the blade of bright steel bit into the ground.
The head was hewn off and fell to the floor;
Many found it at their feet, as forth it rolled;
The blood gushed from the body, bright on the green,
430 Yet fell not the fellow, nor faltered a whit,
But stoutly he starts forth upon stiff shanks,
And as all stood staring he stretched forth his hand,
Laid hold of his head and heaved it aloft,
Then goes to the green steed, grasps the bridle,
435 Steps into the stirrup, bestrides his mount,
And his head by the hair in his hand holds,
And as steady he sits in the stately saddle
As he had met with no mishap, nor missing were
                    his head.
440   His bulk about he haled,
              That fearsome body that bled;
              There were many in the court that quailed
              Before all his say was said.

For the head in his hand he holds right up;
445 Toward the first on the dais directs he the face,
And it lifted up its lids, and looked with wide eyes,
And said as much with its mouth as now you may hear:
"Sir Gawain, forget not to go as agreed,
And cease not to seek till me, sir, you find,
450 As you promised in the presence of these proud knights.
To the Green Chapel come, I charge you, to take
Such a dint as you have dealt—you have well deserved
That your neck should have a knock on New Year's morn.
The Knight of the Green Chapel I am well-known to many,
455 Wherefore you cannot fail to find me at last;
Therefore come, or be counted a recreant knight."
With a roisterous rush he flings round the reins,
Hurtles out at the hall-door, his head in his hand,
That the flint-fire flew from the flashing hooves.
460 Which way he went, not one of them knew
Nor whence he was come in the wide world
                    so fair.
              The king and Gawain gay
              Make game of the Green Knight there,
465   Yet all who saw it say
              'Twas a wonder past compare.

Though high-born Arthur at heart had wonder,
He let no sign be seen, but said aloud
To the comely queen, with courteous speech,
470 "Dear dame, on this day dismay you no whit;
Such crafts are becoming at Christmastide,
Laughing at interludes,[9] light songs and mirth,

---

9. Brief performances between the courses of the banquet.

Amid dancing of damsels with doughty knights.
Nevertheless of my meat now let me partake,
475   For I have met with a marvel, I may not deny."
He glanced at Sir Gawain, and gaily he said,
"Now, sir, hang up your ax,[1] that has hewn enough,"
And over the high dais it was hung on the wall
That men in amazement might on it look,
480   And tell in true terms the tale of the wonder.
Then they turned toward the table, these two together,
The good king and Gawain, and made great feast,
With all dainties double, dishes rare,
With all manner of meat and minstrelsy both,
485   Such happiness wholly had they that day
               in hold.
         Now take care, Sir Gawain,
         That your courage wax not cold
         When you must turn again
490   To your enterprise foretold.

Part 2

This adventure had Arthur of handsels[2] first
When young was the year, for he yearned to hear tales;
Though they wanted for words when they went to sup,
Now are fierce deeds to follow, their fists stuffed full.
495   Gawain was glad to begin those games in hall,
But if the end be harsher, hold it no wonder,
For though men are merry in mind after much drink,
A year passes apace, and proves ever new:
First things and final conform but seldom.
500   And so this Yule to the young year yielded place,
And each season ensued at its set time;[3]
After Christmas there came the cold cheer of Lent,
When with fish and plainer fare our flesh we reprove;
But then the world's weather with winter contends:
505   The keen cold lessens, the low clouds lift;
Fresh falls the rain in fostering showers
On the face of the fields; flowers appear.
The ground and the groves wear gowns of green;
Birds build their nests, and blithely sing
510   That solace of all sorrow with summer comes
               ere long.
         And blossoms day by day
         Bloom rich and rife in throng;
         Then every grove so gay
515   Of the greenwood rings with song.

And then the season of summer with the soft winds,
When Zephyr sighs low over seeds and shoots;

---

1. A literal suggestion, but also an invitation to put the matter aside.
2. New Year's gifts.

3. This famous passage on the cycle of seasons draws both on Germanic conventions of the battle of Winter and Summer, and on Romance springtime lyrics, the *reverdies*.

Glad is the green plant growing abroad,
When the dew at dawn drops from the leaves,
520 To get a gracious glance from the golden sun.
But harvest with harsher winds follows hard after,
Warns him to ripen well ere winter comes;
Drives forth the dust in the droughty season,
From the face of the fields to fly high in air.
525 Wroth winds in the welkin wrestle with the sun,
The leaves launch from the linden and light on the ground,
And the grass turns to gray, that once grew green.
Then all ripens and rots that rose up at first,
And so the year moves on in yesterdays many,
530 And winter once more, by the world's law,
                                   draws nigh.
                    At Michaelmas the moon[4]
                    Hangs wintry pale in sky;
                    Sir Gawain girds him soon
535   For travails yet to try.

Till All-Hallows' Day[5] with Arthur he dwells,
And he held a high feast to honor that knight
With great revels and rich, of the Round Table.
Then ladies lovely and lords debonair
540 With sorrow for Sir Gawain were sore at heart;
Yet they covered their care with countenance glad:
Many a mournful man made mirth for his sake.
So after supper soberly he speaks to his uncle
Of the hard hour at hand, and openly says,
545 "Now, liege lord of my life, my leave I take;
The terms of this task too well you know—
To count the cost over concerns me nothing.
But I am bound forth betimes to bear a stroke
From the grim man in green, as God may direct."
550 Then the first and foremost came forth in throng:[6]
Yvain and Eric and others of note,
Sir Dodinal le Sauvage, the Duke of Clarence,
Lionel and Lancelot and Lucan the good,
Sir Bors and Sir Bedivere, big men both,
555 And many manly knights more, with Mador de la Porte.
All this courtly company comes to the king
To counsel their comrade, with care in their hearts;
There was much secret sorrow suffered that day
That one so good as Gawain must go in such wise
560 To bear a bitter blow, and his bright sword
                                   lay by.
                    He said, "Why should I tarry?"
                    And smiled with tranquil eye;

---

4. The harvest moon at Michaelmas, on September 29.
5. All Saints' Day, on November 1, another holiday on which Arthur presided, crowned, over his court.
6. The following list would have recalled, especially to readers of French romances, other great quests and chal-lenges encountered by Arthur's knights. The list's order may also suggest later and more tragic episodes in the Arthurian narrative, ending with Bedivere who throws Excalibur into a lake after Arthur is mortally wounded.

"In destinies sad or merry,
565   True men can but try."

He dwelt there all that day, and dressed in the morning;
Asked early for his arms, and all were brought.
First a carpet of rare cost was cast on the floor
Where much goodly gear gleamed golden bright;
570   He takes his place promptly and picks up the steel,
Attired in a tight coat of Turkestan silk
And a kingly cap-à-dos, closed at the throat,
That was lavishly lined with a lustrous fur.
Then they set the steel shoes on his sturdy feet
575   And clad his calves about with comely greaves,
And plate well-polished protected his knees,
Affixed with fastenings of the finest gold.
Fair cuisses enclosed, that were cunningly wrought,
His thick-thewed thighs, with thongs bound fast,
580   And massy chain-mail of many a steel ring
He bore on his body, above the best cloth,
With brace burnished bright upon both his arms,
Good couters[7] and gay, and gloves of plate,
And all the goodly gear to grace him well
585   that tide.
        His surcoat blazoned bold;
        Sharp spurs to prick with pride;
        And a brave silk band to hold
        The broadsword at his side.

590   When he had on his arms, his harness was rich,
The least latchet or loop laden with gold;
So armored as he was, he heard a mass,
Honored God humbly at the high altar.
Then he comes to the king and his comrades-in-arms,
595   Takes his leave at last of lords and ladies,
And they clasped and kissed him, commending him to Christ.
By then Gringolet was girt with a great saddle
That was gaily agleam with fine gilt fringe,
New-furbished for the need with nail-heads bright;
600   The bridle and the bars bedecked all with gold;
The breast-plate, the saddlebow, the side-panels both,
The caparison and the crupper accorded in hue,
And all ranged on the red the resplendent studs
That glittered and glowed like the glorious sun.
605   His helm now he holds up and hastily kisses,
Well-closed with iron clinches, and cushioned within;
It was high on his head, with a hasp behind,
And a covering of cloth to encase the visor,
All bound and embroidered[8] with the best gems
610   On broad bands of silk, and bordered with birds,

---

7. Elbow-pieces.
8. The preceding technical language of armor is now
joined by an equally technical description of needlework,
for which English women were famous.

Parrots and popinjays preening their wings,
Lovebirds and love-knots as lavishly wrought
As many women had worked seven winters thereon,
                              entire.
615   The diadem costlier yet
             That crowned that comely sire,
             With diamonds richly set,
             That flashed as if on fire.

Then they showed forth the shield, that shone all red,
620   With the pentangle[9] portrayed in purest gold.
      About his broad neck by the baldric he casts it,
      That was meet for the man, and matched him well.
      And why the pentangle is proper to that peerless prince
      I intend now to tell, though detain me it must.
625   It is a sign by Solomon sagely devised
      To be a token of truth, by its title of old,
      For it is a figure formed of five points,
      And each line is linked and locked with the next
      For ever and ever, and hence it is called
630   In all England, as I hear, the endless knot.
      And well may he wear it on his worthy arms,
      For ever faithful five-fold in five-fold fashion
      Was Gawain in good works, as gold unalloyed,
      Devoid of all villainy, with virtues adorned
635   in sight.
             On shield and coat in view
             He bore that emblem bright,
             As to his word most true
             And in speech most courteous knight.

640   And first, he was faultless in his five senses,
      Nor found ever to fail in his five fingers,
      And all his fealty was fixed upon the five wounds
      That Christ got on the cross, as the creed tells;
      And wherever this man in melee took part,
645   His one thought was of this, past all things else,
      That all his force was founded on the five joys
      That the high Queen of heaven had in her child.[1]
      And therefore, as I find, he fittingly had
      On the inner part of his shield her image portrayed,
650   That when his look on it lighted, he never lost heart.
      The fifth of the five fives followed by this knight
      Were beneficence boundless and brotherly love
      And pure mind and manners, that none might impeach,
      And compassion most precious—these peerless five
655   Were forged and made fast in him, foremost of men.

9. A five-pointed star and symbol of perfection and eternity, since it can be drawn with an uninterrupted line
ending at the point of the star where it begins. Inscribed
within a circle, it was called Solomon's seal.

1. Poems and meditations on the Virgin's joys and sorrows
were widespread. Her five joys were the Annunciation,
Nativity, Resurrection, Ascension, and Assumption.

Now all these five fives were confirmed in this knight,
And each linked in other, that end there was none,
And fixed to five points, whose force never failed,
Nor assembled all on a side, nor asunder either,
660   Nor anywhere at an end, but whole and entire
However the pattern proceeded or played out its course.
And so on his shining shield shaped was the knot
Royally in red gold against red gules,
That is the peerless pentangle, prized of old
665   in lore.
                Now armed is Gawain gay,
                And bears his lance before,
                And soberly said good day,
                He thought forevermore.

670   He struck his steed with the spurs and sped on his way
So fast that the flint-fire flashed from the stones.
When they saw him set forth they were sore aggrieved,
And all sighed softly, and said to each other,
Fearing for their fellow, "Ill fortune it is
675   That you, man, must be marred, that most are worthy!
His equal on this earth can hardly be found;
To have dealt more discreetly had done less harm,
And have dubbed him a duke, with all due honor.
A great leader of lords he was like to become,
680   And better so to have been than battered to bits,
Beheaded by an elf-man, for empty pride!
Who would credit that a king could be counseled so,
And caught in a cavil in a Christmas game?"
Many were the warm tears they wept from their eyes
685   When goodly Sir Gawain was gone from the court
                                      that day.
                No longer he abode,
                But speedily went his way
                Over many a wandering road,
690   As I heard my author say.

Now he rides in his array through the realm of Logres,[2]
Sir Gawain, God knows, though it gave him small joy!
All alone must he lodge through many a long night
Where the food that he fancied was far from his plate;
695   He had no mate but his mount, over mountain and plain,
Nor man to say his mind to but almighty God,
Till he had wandered well-nigh into North Wales.
All the islands of Anglesey he holds on his left,
And follows, as he fares, the fords by the coast,
700   Comes over at Holy Head, and enters next

---

2. Identified with England in Geoffrey of Monmouth, elsewhere a vaguer term for Arthur's kingdom. Here, Gawain is heading northward through Wales, then along the coast of the Irish Sea and into the forest of Wirral in Cheshire—a wild area and resort of outlaws in the 14th century. Gawain thus moves into the area around Chester, where the poem may well have been written.

The Wilderness of Wirral—few were within
That had great good will toward God or man.
And earnestly he asked of each mortal he met
If he had ever heard aught of a knight all green,
705   Or of a Green Chapel, on ground thereabouts,
And all said the same, and solemnly swore
They saw no such knight all solely green
                    in hue.
          Over country wild and strange
710   The knight sets off anew;
          Often his course must change
          Ere the Chapel comes in view.

Many a cliff must he climb in country wild;
Far off from all his friends, forlorn must he ride;
715   At each strand or stream where the stalwart passed
'Twere a marvel if he met not some monstrous foe,
And that so fierce and forbidding that fight he must.
So many were the wonders he wandered among
That to tell but the tenth part would tax my wits.
720   Now with serpents he wars, now with savage wolves,
Now with wild men of the woods, that watched from the rocks,
Both with bulls and with bears, and with boars besides,
And giants that came gibbering from the jagged steeps.
Had he not borne himself bravely, and been on God's side,
725   He had met with many mishaps and mortal harms.
And if the wars were unwelcome, the winter was worse,
When the cold clear rains rushed from the clouds
And froze before they could fall to the frosty earth.
Near slain by the sleet he sleeps in his irons
730   More nights than enough, among naked rocks,
Where clattering from the crest the cold stream ran
And hung in hard icicles high overhead.
Thus in peril and pain and predicaments dire
He rides across country till Christmas Eve,
735   our knight.
          And at that holy tide
          He prays with all his might
          That Mary may be his guide
          Till a dwelling comes in sight.

740   By a mountain next morning he makes his way
Into a forest fastness, fearsome and wild;
High hills on either hand, with hoar woods below,
Oaks old and huge by the hundred together.
The hazel and the hawthorn were all intertwined
745   With rough raveled moss, that raggedly hung,
With many birds unblithe upon bare twigs
That peeped most piteously for pain of the cold.
The good knight on Gringolet glides thereunder
Through many a marsh and mire, a man all alone;

750   He feared for his default, should he fail to see
           The service of that Sire that on that same night
           Was born of a bright maid, to bring us His peace.
           And therefore sighing he said, "I beseech of Thee, Lord,
           And Mary, thou mildest mother so dear,
755   Some harborage where haply I might hear mass
           And Thy matins[3] tomorrow—meekly I ask it,
           And thereto proffer and pray my pater and ave
                          and creed."[4]
                He said his prayer with sighs,
760   Lamenting his misdeed;
                He crosses himself, and cries
                On Christ in his great need.

           No sooner had Sir Gawain signed himself thrice
           Than he was ware, in the wood, of a wondrous dwelling,
765   Within a moat, on a mound, bright amid boughs
           Of many a tree great of girth that grew by the water—
           A castle as comely as a knight could own,
           On grounds fair and green, in a goodly park
           With a palisade of palings planted about
770   For two miles and more, round many a fair tree.
           The stout knight stared at that stronghold great
           As it shimmered and shone amid shining leaves,
           Then with helmet in hand he offers his thanks
           To Jesus and Saint Julian,[5] that are gentle both,
775   That in courteous accord had inclined to his prayer;
           "Now fair harbor," said he, "I humbly beseech!"
           Then he pricks his proud steed with the plated spurs,
           And by chance he has chosen the chief path
           That brought the bold knight to the bridge's end
780   in haste.
                The bridge hung high in air;
                The gates were bolted fast;
                The walls well-framed to bear
                The fury of the blast.

785   The man on his mount remained on the bank
           Of the deep double moat that defended the place.
           The wall went in the water wondrous deep,
           And a long way aloft it loomed overhead.
           It was built of stone blocks to the battlements' height,
790   With corbels under cornices in comeliest style;
           Watch-towers trusty protected the gate,
           With many a lean loophole, to look from within:
           A better-made barbican the knight beheld never.[6]
           And behind it there hoved a great hall and fair:

---

3. First of the canonical hours of prayer and praise in monastic tradition, observed between midnight and dawn.
4. The Paternoster ("Our Father . . ."), Ave Maria ("Hail Mary . . ."), and Creed (the articles of the Christian faith).

5. Patron saint of hospitality.
6. The poet again revels in technical vocabulary, here architectural; this is a fashionable (if exaggerated) building of the 14th century.

795   Turrets rising in tiers, with tines[7] at their tops,
       Spires set beside them, splendidly long,
       With finials well-fashioned, as filigree fine.
       Chalk-white chimneys over chambers high
       Gleamed in gay array upon gables and roofs;
800   The pinnacles in panoply, pointing in air,
       So vied there for his view that verily it seemed
       A castle cut of paper for a king's feast.[8]
       The good knight on Gringolet thought it great luck
       If he could but contrive to come there within
805   To keep the Christmas feast in that castle fair
                             and bright.
                   There answered to his call
                   A porter most polite;
                   From his station on the wall
810   He greets the errant knight.

       "Good sir," said Gawain, "Wouldst go to inquire
       If your lord would allow me to lodge here a space?"
       "Peter!"[9] said the porter, "For my part, I think
       So noble a knight will not want for a welcome!"
815   Then he bustles off briskly, and comes back straight,
       And many servants beside, to receive him the better.
       They let down the drawbridge and duly went forth
       And kneeled down on their knees on the naked earth
       To welcome this warrior as best they were able.
820   They proffered him passage—the portals stood wide—
       And he beckoned them to rise, and rode over the bridge.
       Men steadied his saddle as he stepped to the ground,
       And there stabled his steed many stalwart folk.
       Now come the knights and the noble squires
825   To bring him with bliss into the bright hall.
       When his high helm was off, there hied forth a throng
       Of attendants to take it, and see to its care;
       They bore away his brand and his blazoned shield;
       Then graciously he greeted those gallants each one,
830   And many a noble drew near, to do the knight honor.
       All in his armor into hall he was led,
       Where fire on a fair hearth fiercely blazed.
       And soon the lord himself descends from his chamber
       To meet with good manners the man on his floor.
835   He said, "To this house you are heartily welcome:
       What is here is wholly yours, to have in your power
                             and sway."
                   "Many thanks," said Sir Gawain;
                   "May Christ your pains repay!"
840   The two embrace amain
                   As men well met that day.

7. Pinnacles.
8. Models in cut paper sometimes decorated elaborate

feasts such as that at the beginning of the poem.
9. Swearing by Saint Peter, keeper of the keys to heaven.

935 Gawain in gay attire goes thither soon;
     The lord catches his coat, and calls him by name,
     And has him sit beside him, and says in good faith
     No guest on God's earth would he gladlier greet.
     For that Gawain thanked him; the two then embraced
940 And sat together soberly the service through.
     Then the lady, that longed to look on the knight,
     Came forth from her closet with her comely maids.
     The fair hues of her flesh, her face and her hair
     And her body and her bearing were beyond praise,
945 And excelled the queen herself, as Sir Gawain thought.
     He goes forth to greet her with gracious intent;
     Another lady led her by the left hand
     That was older than she—an ancient, it seemed,
     And held in high honor by all men about.
950 But unlike to look upon, those ladies were,
     For if the one was fresh, the other was faded:
     Bedecked in bright red was the body of one;
     Flesh hung in folds on the face of the other;
     On one a high headdress, hung all with pearls;
955 Her bright throat and bosom fair to behold,
     Fresh as the first snow fallen upon hills;
     A wimple the other one wore round her throat;
     Her swart chin well swaddled, swathed all in white,
     Her forehead enfolded in flounces of silk
960 That framed a fair fillet, of fashion ornate,
     And nothing bare beneath save the black brows,
     The two eyes and the nose, the naked lips,
     And they unsightly to see, and sorrily bleared.
     A beldame, by God, she may well be deemed,
965   of pride!
                    She was short and thick of waist,
                    Her buttocks round and wide;
                    More toothsome, to his taste,
                    Was the beauty by her side.

970 When Gawain had gazed on that gay lady,
     With leave of her lord, he politely approached;
     To the elder in homage he humbly bows;
     The lovelier he salutes with a light embrace.
     He claims a comely kiss, and courteously he speaks;
975 They welcome him warmly, and straightway he asks
     To be received as their servant, if they so desire.
     They take him between them; with talking they bring him
     Beside a bright fire; bade then that spices
     Be freely fetched forth, to refresh them the better,
980 And the good wine therewith, to warm their hearts.
     The lord leaps about in light-hearted mood;
     Contrives entertainments and timely sports;
     Takes his hood from his head and hangs it on a spear,
     And offers him openly the honor thereof

985   Who should promote the most mirth at that Christmas feast;
        "And I shall try for it, trust me—contend with the best,
        Ere I go without my headgear by grace of my friends!"
        Thus with light talk and laughter the lord makes merry
        To gladden the guest he had greeted in hall
990   that day.
                    At the last he called for light
                    The company to convey;
                    Gawain says goodnight
                    And retires to bed straightway.

995   On the morn when each man is mindful in heart
        That God's son was sent down to suffer our death,
        No household but is blithe for His blessed sake;
        So was it there on that day, with many delights.
        Both at larger meals and less they were lavishly served
1000   By doughty lads on dais, with delicate fare;
        The old ancient lady, highest she sits;
        The lord at her left hand leaned, as I hear;
        Sir Gawain in the center, beside the gay lady,
        Where the food was brought first to that festive board,
1005   And thence throughout the hall, as they held most fit,
        To each man was offered in order of rank.
        There was meat, there was mirth, there was much joy,
        That to tell all the tale would tax my wits,
        Though I pained me, perchance, to paint it with care;
1010   But yet I know that our knight and the noble lady
        Were accorded so closely in company there,
        With the seemly solace of their secret words,
        With speeches well-sped, spotless and pure,
        That each prince's pastime their pleasures far
1015   outshone.
                    Sweet pipes beguile their cares,
                    And the trumpet of martial tone;
                    Each tends his affairs
                    And those two tend their own.

1020   That day and all the next, their disport was noble,
        And the third day, I think, pleased them no less;
        The joys of Saint John's Day[4] were justly praised,
        And were the last of their like for those lords and ladies;
        Then guests were to go in the gray morning,
1025   Wherefore they whiled the night away with wine and with mirth,
        Moved to the measures of many a blithe carol;[5]
        At last, when it was late, took leave of each other,
        Each one of those worthies, to wend his way.
        Gawain bids goodbye to his goodly host
1030   Who brings him to his chamber, the chimney beside,
        And detains him in talk, and tenders his thanks

4. December 27, traditionally given over to drinking and   5. A ring dance.
celebration.

And holds it an honor to him and his people
That he has harbored in his house at that holy time
And embellished his abode with his inborn grace.
1035 "As long as I may live, my luck is the better
That Gawain was my guest at God's own feast!"
"Noble sir," said the knight, "I cannot but think
All the honor is your own—may heaven requite it!
And your man to command I account myself here
1040 As I am bound and beholden, and shall be, come
                    what may."
          The lord with all his might
          Entreats his guest to stay;
          Brief answer makes the knight:
1045   Next morning he must away.

Then the lord of that land politely inquired
What dire affair had forced him, at that festive time,
So far from the king's court to fare forth alone
Ere the holidays wholly had ended in hall.
1050 "In good faith," said Gawain, "you have guessed the truth:
On a high errand and urgent I hastened away,
For I am summoned by myself to seek for a place—
I would I knew whither, or where it might be!
Far rather would I find it before the New Year
1055 Than own the land of Logres, so help me our Lord!
Wherefore, sir, in friendship this favor I ask,
That you say in sober earnest, if something you know
Of the Green Chapel, on ground far or near,
Or the lone knight that lives there, of like hue of green.
1060 A certain day was set by assent of us both
To meet at that landmark, if I might last,
And from now to the New Year is nothing too long,
And I would greet the Green Knight there, would God but allow,
More gladly, by God's son, than gain the world's wealth!
1065 And I must set forth to search, as soon as I may;
To be about the business I have but three days
And would as soon sink down dead as desist from my errand."
Then smiling said the lord, "Your search, sir, is done,
For we shall see you to that site by the set time.
1070 Let Gawain grieve no more over the Green Chapel;
You shall be in your own bed, in blissful ease,
All the forenoon, and fare forth the first of the year,
And make the goal by midmorn, to mind your affairs,
                    no fear!
1075   Tarry till the fourth day
          And ride on the first of the year.
          We shall set you on your way;
          It is not two miles from here."

Then Gawain was glad, and gleefully he laughed:
1080 "Now I thank you for this, past all things else!

Now my goal is here at hand! With a glad heart I shall
Both tarry, and undertake any task you devise."
Then the host seized his arm and seated him there;
Let the ladies be brought, to delight him the better,
1085 And in fellowship fair by the fireside they sit;
So gay waxed the good host, so giddy his words,
All waited in wonder what next he would say.
Then he stares on the stout knight, and sternly he speaks:
"You have bound yourself boldly my bidding to do—
1090 Will you stand by that boast, and obey me this once?"
"I shall do so indeed," said the doughty knight;
While I lie in your lodging, your laws will I follow."
"As you have had," said the host, "many hardships abroad
And little sleep of late, you are lacking, I judge,
1095 Both in nourishment needful and nightly rest;
You shall lie abed late in your lofty chamber
Tomorrow until mass, and meet then to dine
When you will, with my wife, who will sit by your side
And talk with you at table, the better to cheer
1100   our guest.
        A-hunting I will go
        While you lie late and rest."
        The knight, inclining low,
        Assents to each behest.

1105 "And Gawain," said the good host, "agree now to this:
Whatever I win in the woods I will give you at eve,
And all you have earned you must offer to me;
Swear now, sweet friend, to swap as I say,
Whether hands, in the end, be empty or better."
1110 "By God," said Sir Gawain, "I grant it forthwith!
If you find the game good, I shall gladly take part."
"Let the bright wine be brought, and our bargain is done,"
Said the lord of that land—the two laughed together.
Then they drank and they dallied and doffed all constraint,
1115 These lords and these ladies, as late as they chose,
And then with gaiety and gallantries and graceful adieux
They talked in low tones, and tarried at parting.
With compliments comely they kiss at the last;
There were brisk lads about with blazing torches
1120 To see them safe to bed, for soft repose
            long due.
        Their covenants, yet awhile,
        They repeat, and pledge anew;
        That lord could well beguile
1125   Men's hearts, with mirth in view.

Part 3

Long before daylight they left their beds;
Guests that wished to go gave word to their grooms,
And they set about briskly to bind on saddles,

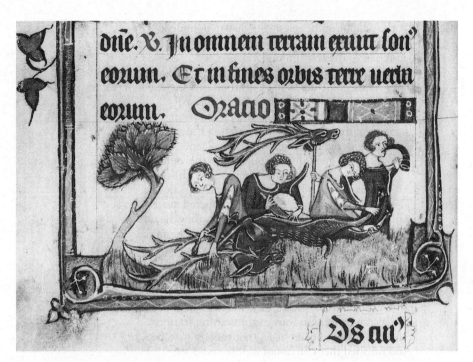

Courtly Women Hunting, from the *Taymouth Hours,* 14th century. Women in courtly dress dismember a stag, usually the work of aristocratic men.

Tend to their tackle, tie up trunks.
1130 The proud lords appear, appareled to ride,
Leap lightly astride, lay hold of their bridles,
Each one on his way to his worthy house.
The liege lord of the land was not the last
Arrayed there to ride, with retainers many;
1135 He had a bite to eat when he had heard mass;
With horn to the hills he hastens amain.[6]
By the dawn of that day over the dim earth,
Master and men were mounted and ready.
Then they harnessed in couples the keen-scented hounds,
1140 Cast wide the kennel-door and called them forth,
Blew upon their bugles bold blasts three;
The dogs began to bay with a deafening din,
And they quieted them quickly and called them to heel,
A hundred brave huntsmen, as I have heard tell,
1145   together.
Men at stations meet;
From the hounds they slip the tether;
The echoing horns repeat,
Clear in the merry weather.

6. The hunts that follow, for all their violent energy, are as ritualized in their procedure as the earlier feasts and games. The poet delights in describing still another area of knightly lore. A number of contemporary treatises on hunting survive.

1150 At the clamor of the quest, the quarry trembled;
       Deer dashed through the dale, dazed with dread;
       Hastened to the high ground, only to be
       Turned back by the beaters, who boldly shouted.
       They harmed not the harts, with their high heads,
1155 Let the bucks go by, with their broad antlers,
       For it was counted a crime, in the close season,
       If a man of that demesne should molest the male deer.
       The hinds were headed up, with "Hey!" and "Ware!"
       The does with great din were driven to the valleys.
1160 Then you were ware, as they went, of the whistling of arrows;
       At each bend under boughs the bright shafts flew
       That tore the tawny hide with their tapered heads.
       Ah! they bray and they bleed, on banks they die,
       And ever the pack pell-mell comes panting behind;
1165 Hunters with shrill horns hot on their heels—
       Like the cracking of cliffs their cries resounded.
       What game got away from the gallant archers
       Was promptly picked off at the posts below
       When they were harried on the heights and herded to the streams:
1170 The watchers were so wary at the waiting-stations,
       And the greyhounds so huge, that eagerly snatched,
       And finished them off as fast as folk could see
                         with sight.
                  The lord, now here, now there,
1175   Spurs forth in sheer delight.
                  And drives, with pleasures rare,
                  The day to the dark night.

       So the lord in the linden-wood leads the hunt
       And Gawain the good knight in gay bed lies,
1180 Lingered late alone, till daylight gleamed,
       Under coverlet costly, curtained about.
       And as he slips into slumber, slyly there comes
       A little din at his door, and the latch lifted,
       And he holds up his heavy head out of the clothes;
1185 A corner of the curtain he caught back a little
       And waited there warily, to see what befell.
       Lo! it was the lady, loveliest to behold,
       That drew the door behind her deftly and still
       And was bound for his bed—abashed was the knight,
1190 And laid his head low again in likeness of sleep;
       And she stepped stealthily, and stole to his bed,
       Cast aside the curtain and came within,
       And set herself softly on the bedside there,
       And lingered at her leisure, to look on his waking.
1195 The fair knight lay feigning for a long while,
       Conning in his conscience what his case might
       Mean or amount to—a marvel he thought it.
       But yet he said within himself, "More seemly it were
       To try her intent by talking a little."

1200   So he started and stretched, as startled from sleep,
           Lifts wide his lids in likeness of wonder,
           And signs himself swiftly, as safer to be,
                           with art.
                   Sweetly does she speak
1205   And kindling glances dart,
                   Blent white and red on cheek
                   And laughing lips apart.

           "Good morning, Sir Gawain," said that gay lady,
           "A slack sleeper you are, to let one slip in!
1210   Now you are taken in a trice—a truce we must make,
           Or I shall bind you in your bed, of that be assured."
           Thus laughing lightly that lady jested.
           "Good morning, good lady," said Gawain the blithe,
           "Be it with me as you will; I am well content!
1215   For I surrender myself, and sue for your grace,
           And that is best, I believe, and behooves me now."
           Thus jested in answer that gentle knight.
           "But if, lovely lady, you misliked it not,
           And were pleased to permit your prisoner to rise,
1220   I should quit this couch and accoutre me better,
           And be clad in more comfort for converse here."
           "Nay, not so, sweet sir," said the smiling lady;
           "You shall not rise from your bed; I direct you better:
           I shall hem and hold you on either hand,
1225   And keep company awhile with my captive knight.
           For as certain as I sit here, Sir Gawain you are,
           Whom all the world worships, whereso you ride;
           Your honor, your courtesy are highest acclaimed
           By lords and by ladies, by all living men;
1230   And lo! we are alone here, and left to ourselves:
           My lord and his liegemen are long departed,
           The household asleep, my handmaids too,
           The door drawn, and held by a well-driven bolt,
           And since I have in this house him whom all love,
1235   I shall while the time away with mirthful speech
                           at will.
                   My body is here at hand,
                   Your each wish to fulfill;
                   Your servant to command
1240   I am, and shall be still."

           "In good faith," said Gawain, "my gain is the greater,
           Though I am not he of whom you have heard;
           To arrive at such reverence as you recount here
           I am one all unworthy, and well do I know it.
1245   By heaven, I would hold me the happiest of men
           If by word or by work I once might aspire
           To the prize of your praise—'twere a pure joy!"
           "In good faith, Sir Gawain," said that gay lady,

"The well-proven prowess that pleases all others,
1250   Did I scant or scout it, 'twere scarce becoming.
But there are ladies, believe me, that had liefer far
Have thee here in their hold, as I have today,
To pass an hour in pastime with pleasant words,
Assuage all their sorrows and solace their hearts,
1255   Than much of the goodly gems and gold they possess.
But laud be to the Lord of the lofty skies,
For here in my hands all hearts' desire
                              doth lie."
                  Great welcome got he there
1260   From the lady who sat him by;
                  With fitting speech and fair
                  The good knight makes reply.

"Madame," said the merry man, "Mary reward you!
For in good faith, I find your beneficence noble.
1265   And the fame of fair deeds runs far and wide,
But the praise you report pertains not to me,
But comes of your courtesy and kindness of heart."
"By the high Queen of heaven" (said she) "I count it not so,
For were I worth all the women in this world alive,
1270   And all wealth and all worship were in my hands,
And I should hunt high and low, a husband to take,
For the nurture I have noted in thee, knight, here,
The comeliness and courtesies and courtly mirth—
And so I had ever heard, and now hold it true—
1275   No other on this earth should have me for wife."
"You are bound to a better man," the bold knight said,
"Yet I prize the praise you have proffered me here,
And soberly your servant, my sovereign I hold you,
And acknowledge me your knight, in the name of Christ."
1280   So they talked of this and that until 'twas nigh noon,
And ever the lady languishing in likeness of love.
With feat words and fair he framed his defense,
For were she never so winsome, the warrior had
The less will to woo, for the wound that his bane
1285   must be.
                  He must bear the blinding blow,
                  For such is fate's decree;
                  The lady asks leave to go;
                  He grants it full and free.

1290   Then she gaily said goodbye, and glanced at him, laughing,
And as she stood, she astonished him with a stern speech:
"Now may the Giver of all good words these glad hours repay!
But our guest is not Gawain—forgot is that thought."
"How so?" said the other, and asks in some haste,
1295   For he feared he had been at fault in the forms of his speech.
But she held up her hand, and made answer thus:
"So good a knight as Gawain is given out to be,

And the model of fair demeanor and manners pure,
Had he lain so long at a lady's side,
1300   Would have claimed a kiss, by his courtesy,
Through some touch or trick of phrase at some tale's end."
Said Gawain, "Good lady, I grant it at once!
I shall kiss at your command, as becomes a knight,
And more, lest you mislike, so let be, I pray."
1305   With that she turns toward him, takes him in her arms,
Leans down her lovely head, and lo! he is kissed.
They commend each other to Christ with comely words,
He sees her forth safely, in silence they part,
And then he lies no later in his lofty bed,
1310   But calls to his chamberlain, chooses his clothes,
Goes in those garments gladly to mass,
Then takes his way to table, where attendants wait,
And made merry all day, till the moon rose
              in view.
1315   Was never knight beset
           'Twixt worthier ladies two:
           The crone and the coquette;
           Fair pastimes they pursue.

And the lord of the land rides late and long,
1320   Hunting the barren hind over the broad heath.
He had slain such a sum, when the sun sank low,
Of does and other deer, as would dizzy one's wits.
Then they trooped in together in triumph at last,
And the count of the quarry quickly they take.
1325   The lords lent a hand with their liegemen many,
Picked out the plumpest and put them together
And duly dressed the deer, as the deed requires.
Some were assigned the assay of the fat:
Two fingers'-width fully they found on the leanest.
1330   Then they slit the slot open and searched out the paunch,
Trimmed it with trencher-knives and tied it up tight.
They flayed the fair hide from the legs and trunk,
Then broke open the belly and laid bare the bowels,
Deftly detaching and drawing them forth.
1335   And next at the neck they neatly parted
The weasand[7] from the windpipe, and cast away the guts.
At the shoulders with sharp blades they showed their skill,
Boning them from beneath, lest the sides be marred;
They breached the broad breast and broke it in twain,
1340   And again at the gullet they begin with their knives,
Cleave down the carcass clear to the breach;
Two tender morsels they take from the throat,
Then round the inner ribs they rid off a layer
And carve out the kidney-fat, close to the spine,
1345   Hewing down to the haunch, that all hung together,

7. The esophagus.

And held it up whole, and hacked it free,
And this they named the numbles,[8] that knew such terms
of art.
They divide the crotch in two,
1350 And straightway then they start
To cut the backbone through
And cleave the trunk apart.

With hard strokes they hewed off the head and the neck,
Then swiftly from the sides they severed the chine,
1355 And the corbie's bone[9] they cast on a branch.
Then they pierced the plump sides, impaled either one
With the hock of the hind foot, and hung it aloft,
To each person his portion most proper and fit.
On a hide of a hind the hounds they fed
1360 With the liver and the lights,[1] the leathery paunches,
And bread soaked in blood well blended therewith.
High horns and shrill set hounds a-baying,
Then merrily with their meat they make their way home,
Blowing on their bugles many a brave blast.
1365 Ere dark had descended, that doughty band
Was come within the walls where Gawain waits
at leisure.
Bliss and hearth-fire bright
Await the master's pleasure;
1370 When the two men met that night,
Joy surpassed all measure.

Then the host in the hall his household assembles,
With the dames of high degree and their damsels fair.
In the presence of the people, a party he sends
1375 To convey him his venison in view of the knight.
And in high good-humor he hails him then,
Counts over the kill, the cuts on the tallies,
Holds high the hewn ribs, heavy with fat.
"What think you, sir, of this? Have I thriven well?
1380 Have I won with my woodcraft a worthy prize?"
"In good earnest," said Gawain, "this game is the finest
I have seen in seven years in the season of winter."
"And I give it to you, Gawain," said the goodly host,
"For according to our covenant, you claim it as your own."
1385 "That is so," said Sir Gawain, "the same say I:
What I worthily have won within these fair walls,
Herewith I as willingly award it to you."
He embraces his broad neck with both his arms,
And confers on him a kiss in the comeliest style.
1390 "Have here my profit, it proved no better;
Ungrudging do I grant it, were it greater far."

8. Internal organs such as heart, liver, lungs.   of the hunt.
9. The gristle at the end of the breastbone was left for the   1. Lungs.
ravens ("corbies"), still another of the prescribed rituals

"Such a gift," said the good host, "I gladly accept—
Yet it might be all the better, would you but say
Where you won this same award, by your wits alone."
1395   "That was no part of the pact; press me no further,
For you have had what behooves; all other claims
                 forbear."
          With jest and compliment
          They conversed, and cast off care;
1400   To the table soon they went;
          Fresh dainties wait them there.

And then by the chimney-side they chat at their ease;
The best wine was brought them, and bounteously served;
And after in their jesting they jointly accord
1405   To do on the second day the deeds of the first:
That the two men should trade, betide as it may,
What each had taken in, at eve when they met.
They seal the pact solemnly in sight of the court;
Their cups were filled afresh to confirm the jest;
1410   Then at last they took their leave, for late was the hour,
Each to his own bed hastening away.
Before the barnyard cock had crowed but thrice
The lord had leapt from his rest, his liegemen as well.
Both of mass and their meal they made short work:
1415   By the dim light of dawn they were deep in the woods
               away.
          With huntsmen and with horns
          Over plains they pass that day;
          They release, amid the thorns,
1420   Swift hounds that run and bay.

Soon some were on a scent by the side of a marsh;
When the hounds opened cry, the head of the hunt
Rallied them with rough words, raised a great noise.
The hounds that had heard it came hurrying straight
1425   And followed along with their fellows, forty together.
Then such a clamor and cry of coursing hounds
Arose, that the rocks resounded again.
Hunters exhorted them with horn and with voice;
Then all in a body bore off together
1430   Between a mere in the marsh and a menacing crag,
To a rise where the rock stood rugged and steep,
And boulders lay about, that blocked their approach.
Then the company in consort closed on their prey:
They surrounded the rise and the rocks both,
1435   For well they were aware that it waited within,
The beast that the bloodhounds boldly proclaimed.
Then they beat on the bushes and bade him appear,
And he made a murderous rush in the midst of them all;
The best of all boars broke from his cover,
1440   That had ranged long unrivaled, a renegade old,

For of tough-brawned boars he was biggest far,
Most grim when he grunted—then grieved were many,
For three at the first thrust he threw to the earth,
And dashed away at once without more damage.
1445   With "Hi!" "Hi!" and "Hey!" "Hey!" the others followed,
Had horns at their lips, blew high and clear.
Merry was the music of men and of hounds
That were bound after this boar, his bloodthirsty heart
     to quell.
1450   Often he stands at bay,
  Then scatters the pack pell-mell;
  He hurts the hounds, and they
  Most dolefully yowl and yell.

Men then with mighty bows moved in to shoot,
1455   Aimed at him with their arrows and often hit,
But the points had no power to pierce through his hide,
And the barbs were brushed aside by his bristly brow;
Though the shank of the shaft shivered in pieces,
The head hopped away, wheresoever it struck.
1460   But when their stubborn strokes had stung him at last,
Then, foaming in his frenzy, fiercely he charges,
Hies at them headlong that hindered his flight,
And many feared for their lives, and fell back a little.
But the lord on a lively horse leads the chase;
1465   As a high-mettled huntsman his horn he blows;
He sounds the assembly and sweeps through the brush,
Pursuing this wild swine till the sunlight slanted.
All day with this deed they drive forth the time
While our lone knight so lovesome lies in his bed
1470   Sir Gawain safe at home, in silken bower
    so gay.
  The lady, with guile in heart,
  Came early where he lay;
  She was at him with all her art
1475   To turn his mind her way.

She comes to the curtain and coyly peeps in;
Gawain thought it good to greet her at once,
And she richly repays him with her ready words,
Settles softly at his side, and suddenly she laughs,
1480   And with a gracious glance, she begins on him thus:
"Sir, if you be Gawain, it seems a great wonder—
A man so well-meaning, and mannerly disposed,
And cannot act in company as courtesy bids,
And if one takes the trouble to teach him, 'tis all in vain.
1485   That lesson learned lately is lightly forgot,
Though I painted it as plain as my poor wit allowed."
"What lesson, dear lady?" he asked all alarmed;
"I have been much to blame, if your story be true."
"Yet my counsel was of kissing," came her answer then,

1490   "Where favor has been found, freely to claim
       As accords with the conduct of courteous knights."
       "My dear," said the doughty man, "dismiss that thought;
       Such freedom, I fear, might offend you much;
       It were rude to request if the right were denied."
1495   "But none can deny you," said the noble dame,
       "You are stout enough to constrain with strength, if you choose,
       Were any so ungracious as to grudge you aught."
       "By heaven," said he, "you have answered well,
       But threats never throve among those of my land,
1500   Nor any gift not freely given, good though it be.
       I am yours to command, to kiss when you please;
       You may lay on as you like, and leave off at will."
                        With this,
                 The lady lightly bends
1505   And graciously gives him a kiss;
                 The two converse as friends
                 Of true love's trials and bliss.

       "I should like, by your leave," said the lovely lady,
       "If it did not annoy you, to know for what cause
1510   So brisk and so bold a young blood as you,
       And acclaimed for all courtesies becoming a knight—
       And name what knight you will, they are noblest esteemed
       For loyal faith in love, in life as in story;[2]
       For to tell the tribulations of these true hearts,
1515   Why, 'tis the very title and text of their deeds,
       How bold knights for beauty have braved many a foe,
       Suffered heavy sorrows out of secret love,
       And then valorously avenged them on villainous churls
       And made happy ever after the hearts of their ladies.
1520   And you are the noblest knight known in your time;
       No household under heaven but has heard of your fame,
       And here by your side I have sat for two days
       Yet never has a fair phrase fallen from your lips
       Of the language of love, not one little word!
1525   And you, that with sweet vows sway women's hearts,
       Should show your winsome ways, and woo a young thing,
       And teach by some tokens the craft of true love.
       How! are you artless, whom all men praise?
       Or do you deem me so dull, or deaf to such words?
1530   Fie! Fie!
                 In hope of pastimes new
                 I have come where none can spy;
                 Instruct me a little, do,
                 While my husband is not nearby."

1535   "God love you, gracious lady!" said Gawain then;
       "It is a pleasure surpassing, and a peerless joy,

2. The lady compares Gawain's behavior to descriptions of courtly love in romances; the poem is mirrored within itself.

That one so worthy as you would willingly come
And take the time and trouble to talk with your knight
And content you with his company—it comforts my heart.
1540   But to take to myself the task of telling of love,
And touch upon its texts, and treat of its themes
To one that, I know well, wields more power
In that art, by a half, than a hundred such
As I am where I live, or am like to become,
1545   It were folly, fair dame, in the first degree!
In all that I am able, my aim is to please,
As in honor behooves me, and am evermore
Your servant heart and soul, so save me our Lord!"
Thus she tested his temper and tried many a time,
1550   Whatever her true intent, to entice him to sin,
But so fair was his defense that no fault appeared,
Nor evil on either hand, but only bliss
                        they knew.
            They linger and laugh awhile;
1555   She kisses the knight so true,
            Takes leave in comeliest style
            And departs without more ado.

Then he rose from his rest and made ready for mass,
And then a meal was set and served, in sumptuous style;
1560   He dallied at home all day with the dear ladies,
But the lord lingered late at his lusty sport;
Pursued his sorry swine, that swerved as he fled,
And bit asunder the backs of the best of his hounds
When they brought him to bay, till the bowmen appeared
1565   And soon forced him forth, though he fought for dear life,
So sharp were the shafts they shot at him there.
But yet the boldest drew back from his battering head,
Till at last he was so tired he could travel no more,
But in as much haste as he might, he makes his retreat
1570   To a rise on rocky ground, by a rushing stream.
With the bank at his back he scrapes the bare earth,
The froth foams at his jaws, frightful to see.
He whets his white tusks—then weary were all
Those hunters so hardy that hoved round about
1575   Of aiming from afar, but ever they mistrust
                        his mood.
            He had hurt so many by then
            That none had hardihood
            To be torn by his tusks again,
1580   That was brainsick, and out for blood.

Till the lord came at last on his lofty steed,
Beheld him there at bay before all his folk;
Lightly he leaps down, leaves his courser,
Bares his bright sword, and boldly advances;
1585   Straight into the stream he strides towards his foe.

The wild thing was wary of weapon and man;
His hackles rose high; so hotly he snorts
That many watched with alarm, lest the worst befall.
The boar makes for the man with a mighty bound
1590 So that he and his hunter came headlong together
Where the water ran wildest—the worse for the beast,
For the man, when they first met, marked him with care,
Sights well the slot, slips in the blade,
Shoves it home to the hilt, and the heart shattered,
1595 And he falls in his fury and floats down the water,
                    ill-sped.
          Hounds hasten by the score
          To maul him, hide and head;
          Men drag him in to shore
1600   And dogs pronounce him dead.

With many a brave blast they boast of their prize,
All hallooed in high glee, that had their wind;
The hounds bayed their best, as the bold men bade
That were charged with chief rank in that chase of renown.
1605 Then one wise in woodcraft, and worthily skilled,
Began to dress the boar in becoming style:
He severs the savage head and sets it aloft,
Then rends the body roughly right down the spine;
Takes the bowels from the belly, broils them on coals,
1610 Blends them well with bread to bestow on the hounds.
Then he breaks out the brawn in fair broad flitches,
And the innards to be eaten in order he takes.
The two sides, attached to each other all whole,
He suspended from a spar that was springy and tough;
1615 And so with this swine they set out for home;
The boar's head was borne before the same man
That had stabbed him in the stream with his strong arm,
                    right through.
          He thought it long indeed
1620   Till he had the knight in view;
          At his call, he comes with speed
          To claim his payment due.

The lord laughed aloud, with many a light word,
When he greeted Sir Gawain—with good cheer he speaks.
1625 They fetch the fair dames and the folk of the house;
He brings forth the brawn, and begins the tale
Of the great length and girth, the grim rage as well,
Of the battle of the boar they beset in the wood.
The other man meetly commended his deeds
1630 And praised well the prize of his princely sport,
For the brawn of that boar, the bold knight said,
And the sides of that swine surpassed all others.
Then they handled the huge head; he owns it a wonder,
And eyes it with abhorrence, to heighten his praise.

1635 "Now, Gawain," said the good man, "this game becomes yours
      By those fair terms we fixed, as you know full well."
      "That is true," returned the knight, "and trust me, fair friend,
      All my gains, as agreed, I shall give you forthwith."
      He clasps him and kisses him in courteous style,
1640 Then serves him with the same fare a second time.
      "Now we are even," said he, "at this evening feast,
      And clear is every claim incurred here to date,
                          and debt."
                "By Saint Giles!"³ the host replies,
1645   "You're the best I ever met!
               If your profits are all this size,
               We'll see you wealthy yet!"

      Then attendants set tables on trestles about,
      And laid them with linen; light shone forth,
1650 Wakened along the walls in waxen torches.
      The service was set and the supper brought;
      Royal were the revels that rose then in hall
      At that feast by the fire, with many fair sports:
      Amid the meal and after, melody sweet,
1655 Carol-dances comely and Christmas songs,
      With all the mannerly mirth my tongue may describe.
      And ever our gallant knight beside the gay lady;
      So uncommonly kind and complaisant was she,
      With sweet stolen glances, that stirred his stout heart,
1660 That he was at his wits' end, and wondrous vexed;
      But he could not in conscience her courtship repay,
      Yet took pains to please her, though the plan might
                          go wrong.
                When they to heart's delight
1665   Had reveled there in throng,
               To his chamber he calls the knight,
               And thither they go along.

      And there they dallied and drank, and deemed it good sport
      To enact their play anew on New Year's Eve,
1670 But Gawain asked again to go on the morrow,
      For the time until his tryst was not two days.
      The host hindered that, and urged him to stay,
      And said, "On my honor, my oath here I take
      That you shall get to the Green Chapel to begin your chores
1675 By dawn on New Year's Day, if you so desire.
      Wherefore lie at your leisure in your lofty bed,
      And I shall hunt hereabouts, and hold to our terms,
      And we shall trade winnings when once more we meet,
      For I have tested you twice, and true have I found you;
1680 Now think this tomorrow: the third pays for all;

---

3. A hermit and patron saint of woodlands.

Be we merry while we may, and mindful of joy,
For heaviness of heart can be had for the asking."
This is gravely agreed on and Gawain will stay.
They drink a last draught and with torches depart
1685   to rest.
                    To bed Sir Gawain went;
                    His sleep was of the best;
                    The lord, on his craft intent,
                    Was early up and dressed.

1690   After mass, with his men, a morsel he takes;
        Clear and crisp the morning; he calls for his mount;
        The folk that were to follow him afield that day
        Were high astride their horses before the hall gates.
        Wondrous fair were the fields, for the frost was light;
1695   The sun rises red amid radiant clouds,
        Sails into the sky, and sends forth his beams.
        They let loose the hounds by a leafy wood;
        The rocks all around re-echo to their horns;
        Soon some have set off in pursuit of the fox,
1700   Cast about with craft for a clearer scent;
        A young dog yaps, and is yelled at in turn;
        His fellows fall to sniffing, and follow his lead,
        Running in a rabble on the right track,
        And he scampers all before; they discover him soon,
1705   And when they see him with sight they pursue him the faster,
        Railing at him rudely with a wrathful din.
        Often he reverses over rough terrain,
        Or loops back to listen in the lee of a hedge;
        At last, by a little ditch, he leaps over the brush,
1710   Comes into a clearing at a cautious pace,
        Then he thought through his wiles to have thrown off the hounds
        Till he was ware, as he went, of a waiting-station
        Where three athwart his path threatened him at once,
                            all gray.
1715   Quick as a flash he wheels
                        And darts off in dismay;
                        With hard luck at his heels
                        He is off to the wood away.

        Then it was heaven on earth to hark to the hounds
1720   When they had come on their quarry, coursing together!
        Such harsh cries and howls they hurled at his head
        As all the cliffs with a crash had come down at once.
        Here he was hailed, when huntsmen met him;
        Yonder they yelled at him, yapping and snarling;
1725   There they cried "Thief!" and threatened his life,
        And ever the harriers at his heels, that he had no rest.
        Often he was menaced when he made for the open,
        And often rushed in again, for Reynard was wily;
        And so he leads them a merry chase, the lord and his men,

1730   In this manner on the mountains, till midday or near,
While our hero lies at home in wholesome sleep
Within the comely curtains on the cold morning.
But the lady, as love would allow her no rest,
And pursuing ever the purpose that pricked her heart,
1735   Was awake with the dawn, and went to his chamber
In a fair flowing mantle that fell to the earth,
All edged and embellished with ermines fine;
No hood on her head, but heavy with gems
Were her fillet and the fret[4] that confined her tresses;
1740   Her face and her fair throat freely displayed;
Her bosom all but bare, and her back as well.
She comes in at the chamber-door, and closes it with care,
Throws wide a window—then waits no longer,
But hails him thus airily with her artful words,
1745   with cheer:
          "Ah, man, how can you sleep?
          The morning is so clear!"
          Though dreams have drowned him deep,
          He cannot choose but hear.

1750   Deep in his dreams he darkly mutters
As a man may that mourns, with many grim thoughts
Of that day when destiny shall deal him his doom
When he greets his grim host at the Green Chapel
And must bow to his buffet, bating all strife.
1755   But when he sees her at his side he summons his wits,
Breaks from the black dreams, and blithely answers.
That lovely lady comes laughing sweet,
Sinks down at his side, and salutes him with a kiss.
He accords her fair welcome in courtliest style;
1760   He sees her so glorious, so gaily attired,
So faultless her features, so fair and so bright,
His heart swelled swiftly with surging joys.
They melt into mirth with many a fond smile,
And there was bliss beyond telling between those two,
1765   at height.
          Good were their words of greeting;
          Each joyed in other's sight;
          Great peril attends that meeting
          Should Mary forget her knight.

1770   For that high-born beauty so hemmed him about,
Made so plain her meaning, the man must needs
Either take her tendered love or distastefully refuse.
His courtesy concerned him, lest crass he appear,
But more his soul's mischief, should he commit sin
1775   And belie his loyal oath to the lord of that house.
"God forbid!" said the bold knight, "That shall not befall!"

4. Ornamental hairnet.

With a little fond laughter he lightly let pass
All the words of special weight that were sped his way;
"I find you much at fault," the fair one said,
1780   "Who can be cold toward a creature so close by your side,
Of all women in this world most wounded in heart,
Unless you have a sweetheart, one you hold dearer,
And allegiance to that lady so loyally knit
That you will never love another, as now I believe.
1785   And, sir, if it be so, then say it, I beg you;
By all your heart holds dear, hide it no longer
                              with guile."
              "Lady, by Saint John,"
              He answers with a smile,
1790   "Lover have I none,
              Nor will have, yet awhile."

"Those words," said the woman, "are the worst of all,
But I have had my answer, and hard do I find it!
Kiss me now kindly; I can but go hence
1795   To lament my life long like a maid lovelorn."
She inclines her head quickly and kisses the knight,
Then straightens with a sigh, and says as she stands,
"Now, dear, ere I depart, do me this pleasure:
Give me some little gift, your glove or the like,
1800   That I may think on you, man, and mourn the less."
"Now by heaven," said he, "I wish I had here
My most precious possession, to put it in your hands,
For your deeds, beyond doubt, have often deserved
A repayment far passing my power to bestow.
1805   But a love-token, lady, were of little avail;
It is not to your honor to have at this time
A glove as a guerdon from Gawain's hand,
And I am here on an errand in unknown realms
And have no bearers with baggage with becoming gifts,
1810   Which distresses me, madame, for your dear sake.
A man must keep within his compass: account it neither grief
                              nor slight."
              "Nay, noblest knight alive,"
              Said that beauty of body white,
1815   "Though you be loath to give,
              Yet you shall take, by right."

She reached out a rich ring, wrought all of gold,
With a splendid stone displayed on the band
That flashed before his eyes like a fiery sun;
1820   It was worth a king's wealth, you may well believe.
But he waved it away with these ready words:
"Before God, good lady, I forgo all gifts;
None have I to offer, nor any will I take."
And she urged it on him eagerly, and ever he refused,
1825   And vowed in very earnest, prevail she would not.

And she sad to find it so, and said to him then,
"If my ring is refused for its rich cost—
You would not be my debtor for so dear a thing—
I shall give you my girdle; you gain less thereby."

1830 She released a knot lightly, and loosened a belt
That was caught about her kirtle, the bright cloak beneath,
Of a gay green silk, with gold overwrought,
And the borders all bound with embroidery fine,
And this she presses upon him, and pleads with a smile,

1835 Unworthy though it were, that it would not be scorned.
But the man still maintains that he means to accept
Neither gold nor any gift, till by God's grace
The fate that lay before him was fully achieved.
"And be not offended, fair lady, I beg,

1840 And give over your offer, for ever I must
                              decline.
            I am grateful for favor shown
            Past all deserts of mine,
            And ever shall be your own

1845   True servant, rain or shine."

"Now does my present displease you," she promptly inquired,
"Because it seems in your sight so simple a thing?
And belike, as it is little, it is less to praise,
But if the virtue that invests it were verily known,

1850 It would be held, I hope, in higher esteem.
For the man that possesses this piece of silk,
If he bore it on his body, belted about,
There is no hand under heaven that could hew him down,
For he could not be killed by any craft on earth."

1855 Then the man began to muse, and mainly he thought
It was a pearl for his plight, the peril to come
When he gains the Green Chapel to get his reward:
Could he escape unscathed, the scheme were noble!
Then he bore with her words and withstood them no more,

1860 And she repeated her petition and pleaded anew,
And he granted it, and gladly she gave him the belt,
And besought him for her sake to conceal it well,
Lest the noble lord should know—and the knight agrees
That not a soul save themselves shall see it thenceforth

1865   with sight.
            He thanked her with fervent heart,
            As often as ever he might;
            Three times, before they part,
            She has kissed the stalwart knight.

1870 Then the lady took her leave, and left him there,
For more mirth with that man she might not have.
When she was gone, Sir Gawain got from his bed,
Arose and arrayed him in his rich attire;
Tucked away the token the temptress had left,

1875 Laid it reliably where he looked for it after.
 And then with good cheer to the chapel he goes,
 Approached a priest in private, and prayed to be taught
 To lead a better life and lift up his mind,
 Lest he be among the lost when he must leave this world.
1880 And shamefaced at shrift he showed his misdeeds
 From the largest to the least, and asked the Lord's mercy,
 And called on his confessor to cleanse his soul,
 And he absolved him of his sins as safe and as clean
 As if the dread Day of Judgment should dawn on the morrow.[5]
1885 And then he made merry amid the fine ladies
 With deft-footed dances and dalliance light,
 As never until now, while the afternoon wore
      away.
   He delighted all around him,
1890   And all agreed, that day,
   They never before had found him
   So gracious and so gay.

 Now peaceful be his pasture, and love play him fair!
 The host is on horseback, hunting afield;
1895 He has finished off this fox that he followed so long:
 As he leapt a low hedge to look for the villain
 Where he heard all the hounds in hot pursuit,
 Reynard comes racing out of a rough thicket,
 And all the rabble in a rush, right at his heels.
1900 The man beholds the beast, and bides his time,
 And bares his bright sword, and brings it down hard,
 And he blenches from the blade, and backward he starts;
 A hound hurries up and hinders that move,
 And before the horse's feet they fell on him at once
1905 And ripped the rascal's throat with a wrathful din.
 The lord soon alighted and lifted him free,
 Swiftly snatched him up from the snapping jaws,
 Holds him over his head, halloos with a will,
 And the dogs bayed the dirge, that had done him to death.
1910 Hunters hastened thither with horns at their lips,
 Sounding the assembly till they saw him at last.
 When that comely company was come in together,
 All that bore bugles blew them at once,
 And the others all hallooed, that had no horns.
1915 It was the merriest medley that ever a man heard,
 The racket that they raised for Sir Reynard's soul
      that died.
   Their hounds they praised and fed,
   Fondling their heads with pride,
1920   And they took Reynard the Red
   And stripped away his hide.

---

5. Gawain's confession and absolution are problematic, since he has just accepted the green girdle and resolved to break the covenant of exchange with his host.

And then they headed homeward, for evening had come,
Blowing many a blast on their bugles bright.
The lord at long last alights at his house,
1925   Finds fire on the hearth where the fair knight waits,
Sir Gawain the good, that was glad in heart.
With the ladies, that loved him, he lingered at ease;
He wore a rich robe of blue, that reached to the earth
And a surcoat lined softly with sumptuous furs;
1930   A hood of the same hue hung on his shoulders;
With bands of bright ermine embellished were both.
He comes to meet the man amid all the folk,
And greets him good-humoredly, and gaily he says,
"I shall follow forthwith the form of our pledge
1935   That we framed to good effect amid fresh-filled cups."
He clasps him accordingly and kisses him thrice,
As amiably and as earnestly as ever he could.
"By heaven," said the host, "you have had some luck
Since you took up this trade, if the terms were good."
1940   "Never trouble about the terms," he returned at once,
"Since all that I owe here is openly paid."
"Marry!" said the other man, "mine is much less,
For I have hunted all day, and nought have I got
But this foul fox pelt, the fiend take the goods!
1945   Which but poorly repays those precious things
That you have cordially conferred, those kisses three
          so good."
          "Enough!" said Sir Gawain;
          "I thank you, by the rood!"
1950   And how the fox was slain
          He told him, as they stood.

With minstrelsy and mirth, with all manner of meats,
They made as much merriment as any men might
(Amid laughing of ladies and light-hearted girls,
1955   So gay grew Sir Gawain and the goodly host)
Unless they had been besotted, or brainless fools.
The knight joined in jesting with that joyous folk,
Until at last it was late; ere long they must part,
And be off to their beds, as behooved them each one.
1960   Then politely his leave of the lord of the house
Our noble knight takes, and renews his thanks:[6]
"The courtesies countless accorded me here,
Your kindness at this Christmas, may heaven's King repay!
Henceforth, if you will have me, I hold you my liege,
1965   And so, as I have said, I must set forth tomorrow,
If I may take some trusty man to teach, as you promised,
The way to the Green Chapel, that as God allows
I shall see my fate fulfilled on the first of the year."
"In good faith," said the good man, "with a good will

6. Gawain's highly stylized leave-taking is typical of courtly romance and again emphasizes his command of fine manners.

1970 Every promise on my part shall be fully performed."
He assigns him a servant to set him on the path,
To see him safe and sound over the snowy hills,
To follow the fastest way through forest green
                    and grove.
1975   Gawain thanks him again,
           So kind his favors prove,
           And of the ladies then
           He takes his leave, with love.

Courteously he kissed them, with care in his heart,
1980 And often wished them well, with warmest thanks,
Which they for their part were prompt to repay.
They commend him to Christ with disconsolate sighs;
And then in that hall with the household he parts—
Each man that he met, he remembered to thank
1985 For his deeds of devotion and diligent pains,
And the trouble he had taken to tend to his needs;
And each one as woeful, that watched him depart,
As he had lived with him loyally all his life long.
By lads bearing lights he was led to his chamber
1990 And blithely brought to his bed, to be at his rest.
How soundly he slept, I presume not to say,
For there were matters of moment his thoughts might well
                    pursue.
           Let him lie and wait;
1995   He has little more to do,
           Then listen, while I relate
           How they kept their rendezvous.

Part 4

Now the New Year draws near, and the night passes,
The day dispels the dark, by the Lord's decree;
2000 But wild weather awoke in the world without:
The clouds in the cold sky cast down their snow
With great gusts from the north, grievous to bear.
Sleet showered aslant upon shivering beasts;
The wind warbled wild as it whipped from aloft,
2005 And drove the drifts deep in the dales below.
Long and well he listens, that lies in his bed;
Though he lifts not his eyelids, little he sleeps;
Each crow of the cock he counts without fail.
Readily from his rest he rose before dawn,
2010 For a lamp had been left him, that lighted his chamber.
He called to his chamberlain, who quickly appeared,
And bade him get him his gear, and gird his good steed,
And he sets about briskly to bring in his arms,
And makes ready his master in manner most fit.
2015 First he clad him in his clothes, to keep out the cold,
And then his other harness, made handsome anew,

His plate-armor of proof, polished with pains,
The rings of his rich mail rid of their rust,
And all was fresh as at first, and for this he gave thanks
2020   indeed.
           With pride he wears each piece,
           New-furbished for his need:
           No gayer from here to Greece;
           He bids them bring his steed.

2025   In his richest raiment he robed himself then:
His crested coat-armor, close-stitched with craft,
With stones of strange virtue on silk velvet set;
All bound with embroidery on borders and seams
And lined warmly and well with furs of the best.
2030   Yet he left not his love-gift, the lady's girdle;
Gawain, for his own good, forgot not that:
When the bright sword was belted and bound on his haunches,
Then twice with that token he twined him about.
Sweetly did he swathe him in that swatch of silk,
2035   That girdle of green so goodly to see,
That against the gay red showed gorgeous bright.
Yet he wore not for its wealth that wondrous girdle,
Nor pride in its pendants, though polished they were,
Though glittering gold gleamed at the tips,
2040   But to keep himself safe when consent he must
To endure a deadly dint, and all defense
                            denied.
           And now the bold knight came
           Into the courtyard wide;
2045   That folk of worthy fame
           He thanks on every side.

Then was Gringolet girt, that was great and huge,
And had sojourned safe and sound, and savored his fare;
He pawed the earth in his pride, that princely steed.
2050   The good knight draws near him and notes well his look,
And says sagely to himself, and soberly swears,
"Here is a household in hall that upholds the right!
The man that maintains it, may happiness be his!
Likewise the dear lady, may love betide her!
2055   If thus they in charity cherish a guest
That are honored here on earth, may they have His reward
That reigns high in heaven—and also you all;
And were I to live in this land but a little while,
I should willingly reward you, and well, if I might."
2060   Then he steps into the stirrup and bestrides his mount;
His shield is shown forth; on his shoulder he casts it;
Strikes the side of his steed with his steel spurs,
And he starts across the stones, nor stands any longer
                            to prance.
2065   On horseback was the swain
           That bore his spear and lance;

"May Christ this house maintain
And guard it from mischance!"

The bridge was brought down, and the broad gates
2070 Unbarred and carried back upon both sides;
He commended him to Christ, and crossed over the planks;
Praised the noble porter, who prayed on his knees
That God save Sir Gawain, and bade him good day,
And went on his way alone with the man
2075 That was to lead him ere long to that luckless place
Where the dolorous dint must be dealt him at last.
Under bare boughs they ride, where steep banks rise,[7]
Over high cliffs they climb, where cold snow clings;
The heavens held aloof, but heavy thereunder
2080 Mist mantled the moors, moved on the slopes.
Each hill had a hat, a huge cape of cloud;
Brooks bubbled and broke over broken rocks,
Flashing in freshets that waterfalls fed.
Roundabout was the road that ran through the wood
2085 Till the sun at that season was soon to rise,
                              that day.
              They were on a hilltop high;
              The white snow round them lay;
              The man that rode nearby
2090   Now bade his master stay.

"For I have seen you here safe at the set time,
And now you are not far from that notable place
That you have sought for so long with such special pains.
But this I say for certain, since I know you, sir knight,
2095 And have your good at heart, and hold you dear—
Would you heed well my words, it were worth your while—
You are rushing into risks that you reck not of:
There is a villain in yon valley, the veriest on earth,
For he is rugged and rude, and ready with his fists,
2100 And most immense in his mold of mortals alive,
And his body bigger than the best four
That are in Arthur's house, Hector[8] or any.
He gets his grim way at the Green Chapel;
None passes by that place so proud in his arms
2105 That he does not dash him down with his deadly blows,
For he is heartless wholly, and heedless of right,
For be it chaplain or churl that by the Chapel rides,
Monk or mass-priest or any man else,
He would as soon strike him dead as stand on two feet.
2110 Wherefore I say, just as certain as you sit there astride,
You cannot but be killed, if his counsel holds,

---

7. The grimness of this landscape, reminiscent of waste-lands in Anglo-Saxon poetry, swiftly returns the poem from the courtly world to the elemental challenge Gawain now faces.

8. Chief hero among the defenders of Troy and, like Arthur, one of the "Nine Worthies" celebrated for their heroic valor; or perhaps Arthur's knight Hector De Maris.

For he would trounce you in a trice, had you twenty lives
                         for sale.
              He has lived long in this land
2115   And dealt out deadly bale;
              Against his heavy hand
              Your power cannot prevail.

"And so, good Sir Gawain, let the grim man be;
Go off by some other road, in God's own name!
2120 Leave by some other land, for the love of Christ,
And I shall get me home again, and give you my word
That I shall swear by God's self and the saints above,
By heaven and by my halidom[9] and other oaths more,
To conceal this day's deed, nor say to a soul
2125 That ever you fled for fear from any that I knew."
"Many thanks!" said the other man—and demurring he speaks—
"Fair fortune befall you for your friendly words!
And conceal this day's deed I doubt not you would,
But though you never told the tale, if I turned back now,
2130 Forsook this place for fear, and fled, as you say,
I were a caitiff coward; I could not be excused.
But I must to the Chapel to chance my luck
And say to that same man such words as I please,
Befall what may befall through Fortune's will
2135   or whim.
              Though he be a quarrelsome knave
              With a cudgel great and grim,
              The Lord is strong to save:
              His servants trust in Him."

2140 "Marry," said the man, "since you tell me so much,
And I see you are set to seek your own harm,
If you crave a quick death, let me keep you no longer!
Put your helm on your head, your hand on your lance,
And ride the narrow road down yon rocky slope
2145 Till it brings you to the bottom of the broad valley.
Then look a little ahead, on your left hand,
And you will soon see before you that self-same Chapel,
And the man of great might that is master there.
Now goodbye in God's name, Gawain the noble!
2150 For all the world's wealth I would not stay here,
Or go with you in this wood one footstep further!"
He tarried no more to talk, but turned his bridle,
Hit his horse with his heels as hard as he might,
Leaves the knight alone, and off like the wind
2155   goes leaping.
              "By God," said Gawain then,
              "I shall not give way to weeping;
              God's will be done, amen!
              I commend me to His keeping."

9. "By my holy relics."

2160 He puts his heels to his horse, and picks up the path;
      Goes in beside a grove where the ground is steep,
      Rides down the rough slope right to the valley;
      And then he looked a little about him—the landscape was wild,
      And not a soul to be seen, nor sign of a dwelling,
2165 But high banks on either hand hemmed it about,
      With many a ragged rock and rough-hewn crag;
      The skies seemed scored by the scowling peaks.
      Then he halted his horse, and hoved there a space,
      And sought on every side for a sight of the Chapel,
2170 But no such place appeared, which puzzled him sore,
      Yet he saw some way off what seemed like a mound,[1]
      A hillock high and broad, hard by the water,
      Where the stream fell in foam down the face of the steep
      And bubbled as if it boiled on its bed below.
2175 The knight urges his horse, and heads for the knoll;
      Leaps lightly to earth; loops well the rein
      Of his steed to a stout branch, and stations him there.
      He strides straight to the mound, and strolls all about,
      Much wondering what it was, but no whit the wiser;
2180 It had a hole at one end, and on either side,
      And was covered with coarse grass in clumps all without,
      And hollow all within, like some old cave,
      Or a crevice of an old crag—he could not discern
                            aright.
2185   "Can this be the Chapel Green?
                Alack!" said the man, "Here might
                The devil himself be seen
                Saying matins at black midnight!"

      "Now by heaven," said he, "it is bleak hereabouts;
2190 This prayer-house is hideous, half-covered with grass!
      Well may the grim man mantled in green
      Hold here his orisons, in hell's own style!
      Now I feel it is the Fiend, in my five wits,
      That has tempted me to this tryst, to take my life;
2195 This is a Chapel of mischance, may the mischief take it!
      As accursed a country church as I came upon ever!"
      With his helm on his head, his lance in his hand,
      He stalks toward the steep wall of that strange house.
      Then he heard, on the hill, behind a hard rock,
2200 Beyond the brook, from the bank, a most barbarous din:
      Lord! it clattered in the cliff fit to cleave it in two,
      As one upon a grindstone ground a great scythe!
      Lord! it whirred like a mill-wheel whirling about!
      Lord! it echoed loud and long, lamentable to hear!
2205 Then "By heaven," said the bold knight, "That business up there
      Is arranged for my arrival, or else I am much
                            misled.

---

1. The barrow, perhaps a burial mound, seems to link the moment to ancient, probably pagan, inhabitants.

               Let God work! Ah me!
               All hope of help has fled!
2210   Forfeit my life may be
               But noise I do not dread."

Then he listened no longer, but loudly he called,
"Who has power in this place, high parley to hold?
For none greets Sir Gawain, or gives him good day;
2215   If any would a word with him, let him walk forth
And speak now or never, to speed his affairs."
"Abide," said one on the bank above over his head,
"And what I promised you once shall straightway be given."
Yet he stayed not his grindstone, nor stinted its noise,
2220   But worked awhile at his whetting before he would rest,
And then he comes around a crag, from a cave in the rocks,
Hurtling out of hiding with a hateful weapon,
A Danish ax[2] devised for that day's deed,
With a broad blade and bright, bent in a curve,
2225   Filed to a fine edge—four feet it measured
By the length of the lace that was looped round the haft.
And in form as at first, the fellow all green,
His lordly face and his legs, his locks and his beard,
Save that firm upon two feet forward he strides,
2230   Sets a hand on the ax-head, the haft to the earth;
When he came to the cold stream, and cared not to wade,
He vaults over on his ax, and advances amain
On a broad bank of snow, overbearing and brisk
                        of mood.
2235   Little did the knight incline
               When face to face they stood;
               Said the other man, "Friend mine,
               It seems your word holds good!"

"God love you, Sir Gawain!" said the Green Knight then,
2240   "And well met this morning, man, at my place!
And you have followed me faithfully and found me betimes,
And on the business between us we both are agreed:
Twelve months ago today you took what was yours,
And you at this New Year must yield me the same.
2245   And we have met in these mountains, remote from all eyes:
There is none here to halt us or hinder our sport;
Unhasp your high helm, and have here your wages;
Make no more demur than I did myself
When you hacked off my head with one hard blow."
2250   "No, by God," said Sir Gawain, "that granted me life,
I shall grudge not the guerdon, grim though it prove;
Bestow but one stroke, and I shall stand still,
And you may lay on as you like till the last of my part
                        be paid.

2. A long-bladed ax, associated with Viking raiders.

2255

> He proffered, with good grace,
> His bare neck to the blade,
> And feigned a cheerful face:
> He scorned to seem afraid.

2260

Then the grim man in green gathers his strength,
Heaves high the heavy ax to hit him the blow.
With all the force in his frame he fetches it aloft,
With a grimace as grim as he would grind him to bits;
Had the blow he bestowed been as big as he threatened,
A good knight and gallant had gone to his grave.

2265

But Gawain at the great ax glanced up aside
As down it descended with death-dealing force,
And his shoulders shrank a little from the sharp iron.
Abruptly the brawny man breaks off the stroke,
And then reproved with proud words that prince among knights.

2270

"You are not Gawain the glorious," the green man said,
"That never fell back on field in the face of the foe,
And now you flee for fear, and have felt no harm:
Such news of that knight I never heard yet!
I moved not a muscle when you made to strike,

2275

Nor caviled at the cut in King Arthur's house;
My head fell to my feet, yet steadfast I stood,
And you, all unharmed, are wholly dismayed—
Wherefore the better man I, by all odds,
>   must be."

2280

> Said Gawain, "Strike once more;
> I shall neither flinch nor flee;
> But if my head falls to the floor
> There is no mending me!"

"But go on, man, in God's name, and get to the point!

2285

Deliver me my destiny, and do it out of hand,
For I shall stand to the stroke and stir not an inch
Till your ax has hit home—on my honor I swear it!"
"Have at thee then!" said the other, and heaves it aloft,
And glares down as grimly as he had gone mad.

2290

He made a mighty feint, but marred not his hide;
Withdrew the ax adroitly before it did damage.
Gawain gave no ground, nor glanced up aside,
But stood still as a stone, or else a stout stump
That is held in hard earth by a hundred roots.

2295

Then merrily does he mock him, the man all in green:
"So now you have your nerve again, I needs must strike;
Uphold the high knighthood that Arthur bestowed,
And keep your neck-bone clear, if this cut allows!"
Then was Gawain gripped with rage, and grimly he said,

2300

"Why, thrash away, tyrant, I tire of your threats;
You make such a scene, you must frighten yourself."
Said the green fellow, "In faith, so fiercely you speak
That I shall finish this affair, nor further grace

allow."

2305   He stands prepared to strike
And scowls with both lip and brow;
No marvel if the man mislike
Who can hope no rescue now.

He gathered up the grim ax and guided it well:
2310   Let the barb at the blade's end brush the bare throat;
He hammered down hard, yet harmed him no whit
Save a scratch on one side, that severed the skin;
The end of the hooked edge entered the flesh,
And a little blood lightly leapt to the earth.
2315   And when the man beheld his own blood bright on the snow,
He sprang a spear's length with feet spread wide,
Seized his high helm, and set it on his head,
Shoved before his shoulders the shield at his back,[3]
Bares his trusty blade, and boldly he speaks—
2320   Not since he was a babe born of his mother
Was he once in this world one-half so blithe—
"Have done with your hacking—harry me no more!
I have borne, as behooved, one blow in this place;
If you make another move I shall meet it midway
2325   And promptly, I promise you, pay back each blow
                    with brand.
            One stroke acquits me here;
            So did our covenant stand
            In Arthur's court last year—
2330   Wherefore, sir, hold your hand!"

He lowers the long ax and leans on it there,
Sets his arms on the head, the haft on the earth,
And beholds the bold knight that bides there afoot,
How he faces him fearless, fierce in full arms,
2335   And plies him with proud words—it pleases him well.
Then once again gaily to Gawain he calls,
And in a loud voice and lusty, delivers these words:
"Bold fellow, on this field your anger forbear!
No man has made demands here in manner uncouth,
2340   Nor done, save as duly determined at court.
I owed you a hit and you have it; be happy therewith!
The rest of my rights here I freely resign.
Had I been a bit busier, a buffet, perhaps,
I could have dealt more directly, and done you some harm.
2345   First I flourished with a feint, in frolicsome mood,
And left your hide unhurt—and here I did well
By the fair terms we fixed on the first night;
And fully and faithfully you followed accord:
Gave over all your gains as a good man should.

---

3. Gawain, who has displayed so much courtly refinement and religious emotion, now shows himself a practiced fighter, swiftly pulling his armor into place.

2350 A second feint, sir, I assigned for the morning
You kissed my comely wife—each kiss you restored.
For both of these there behooved but two feigned blows
by right.
True men pay what they owe;
2355 No danger then in sight.
You failed at the third throw,
So take my tap, sir knight.

"For that is my belt about you, that same braided girdle,
My wife it was that wore it; I know well the tale,
2360 And the count of your kisses and your conduct too,
And the wooing of my wife—it was all my scheme!
She made trial of a man most faultless by far
Of all that ever walked over the wide earth;
As pearls to white peas, more precious and prized,
2365 So is Gawain, in good faith, to other gay knights.
Yet you lacked, sir, a little in loyalty there,
But the cause was not cunning, nor courtship either,
But that you loved your own life; the less, then, to blame."
The other stout knight in a study stood a long while,
2370 So gripped with grim rage that his great heart shook.
All the blood of his body burned in his face
As he shrank back in shame from the man's sharp speech.
The first words that fell from the fair knight's lips:
"Accursed be a cowardly and covetous heart!
2375 In you is villainy and vice, and virtue laid low!"
Then he grasps the green girdle and lets go the knot,
Hands it over in haste, and hotly he says:
"Behold there my falsehood, ill hap betide it!
Your cut taught me cowardice, care for my life,
2380 And coveting came after, contrary both
To largesse and loyalty belonging to knights.
Now am I faulty and false, that fearful was ever
Of disloyalty and lies, bad luck to them both!
and greed.
2385 I confess, knight, in this place,
Most dire is my misdeed;
Let me gain back your good grace,
And thereafter I shall take heed."

Then the other laughed aloud, and lightly he said,
2390 "Such harm as I have had, I hold it quite healed.
You are so fully confessed, your failings made known,
And bear the plain penance of the point of my blade,
I hold you polished as a pearl, as pure and as bright
As you had lived free of fault since first you were born.
2395 And I give you, sir, this girdle that is gold-hemmed
And green as my garments, that, Gawain, you may
Be mindful of this meeting when you mingle in throng

With nobles of renown—and known by this token
How it chanced at the Green Chapel, to chivalrous knights.
2400 And you shall in this New Year come yet again
And we shall finish out our feast in my fair hall,
                         with cheer."
              He urged the knight to stay,
              And said, "With my wife so dear
2405   We shall see you friends this day,
              Whose enmity touched you near."

"Indeed," said the doughty knight, and doffed his high helm,
And held it in his hands as he offered his thanks,
"I have lingered long enough—may good luck be yours,
2410 And He reward you well that all worship bestows!
And commend me to that comely one, your courteous wife,
Both herself and that other, my honored ladies,
That have trapped their true knight in their trammels so quaint.
But if a dullard should dote, deem it no wonder,
2415 And through the wiles of a woman be wooed into sorrow,
For so was Adam by one, when the world began,
And Solomon by many more, and Samson the mighty—
Delilah was his doom, and David thereafter
Was beguiled by Bathsheba, and bore much distress;[4]
2420 Now these were vexed by their devices—'twere a very joy
Could one but learn to love, and believe them not.
For these were proud princes, most prosperous of old,
Past all lovers lucky, that languished under heaven,
                         bemused.
2425   And one and all fell prey
              To women that they had used;
              If I be led astray,
              Methinks I may be excused.

"But your girdle, God love you! I gladly shall take
2430 And be pleased to possess, not for the pure gold,
Nor the bright belt itself, nor the beauteous pendants,
Nor for wealth, nor worldly state, nor workmanship fine,
But a sign of excess it shall seem oftentimes
When I ride in renown, and remember with shame
2435 The faults and the frailty of the flesh perverse,
How its tenderness entices the foul taint of sin;
And so when praise and high prowess have pleased my heart,
A look at this love-lace will lower my pride,
But one thing would I learn, if you were not loath,
2440 Since you are lord of yonder land where I have long sojourned
With honor in your house—may you have His reward
That upholds all the heavens, highest on throne!

---

4. Gawain suddenly erupts in a brief but fierce diatribe, including this list of treacherous women recognizable from contemporary misogynist texts.

How runs your right name?—and let the rest go."
"That shall I give you gladly," said the Green Knight then;
2445 "Bercilak de Hautdesert this barony I hold,
Through the might of Morgan le Fay,[5] that lodges at my house,
By subtleties of science and sorcerers' arts,
The mistress of Merlin, she has caught many a man,
For sweet love in secret she shared sometime
2450 With that wizard, that knows well each one of your knights
            and you.
        Morgan the Goddess, she,
        So styled by title true;
        None holds so high degree
2455   That her arts cannot subdue.

"She guided me in this guise to your glorious hall,
To assay, if such it were, the surfeit of pride
That is rumored of the retinue of the Round Table.
She put this shape upon me to puzzle your wits,
2460 To afflict the fair queen, and frighten her to death
With awe of that elvish man that eerily spoke
With his head in his hand before the high table.
She was with my wife at home, that old withered lady,
Your own aunt is she, Arthur's half-sister,
2465 The Duchess' daughter of Tintagel, that dear King Uther
Got Arthur on after, that honored is now.[6]
And therefore, good friend, come feast with your aunt;
Make merry in my house; my men hold you dear,
And I wish you as well, sir, with all my heart,
2470 As any mortal man, for your matchless faith."
But the knight said him nay, that he might by no means.
They clasped then and kissed, and commended each other
To the Prince of Paradise, and parted with one
            assent.
2475   Gawain sets out anew;
        Toward the court his course is bent;
        And the knight all green in hue,
        Wheresoever he wished, he went.

Wild ways in the world our worthy knight rides
2480 On Gringolet, that by grace had been granted his life.
He harbored often in houses, and often abroad,
And with many valiant adventures verily he met
That I shall not take time to tell in this story.

5. Morgan is Arthur's half-sister and ruler of the mysterious Avalon; she learned magical arts from Merlin. Her presence can bode good or ill. In some stories she holds a deep grudge against Guinevere, yet she carries off the wounded Arthur after his final battle, perhaps to heal him. The earlier Celtic Morrigan, possibly related, is queen of demons, sower of discord, and goddess of war.
6. The poem now recalls an earlier transgression of guest–host obligations, when Uther began to lust for Ygerne while her husband, Gorlois, was at his court; he later killed Gorlois and married Ygerne. See Geoffrey of Monmouth, pages 167–69.

The hurt was whole that he had had in his neck,
2485   And the bright green belt on his body he bore,
Oblique, like a baldric, bound at his side,
Below his left shoulder, laced in a knot,
In betokening of the blame he had borne for his fault;
And so to court in due course he comes safe and sound.
2490   Bliss abounded in hall when the high-born heard
That good Gawain was come, glad tidings they thought it.
The king kisses the knight, and the queen as well,
And many a comrade came to clasp him in arms,
And eagerly they asked, and awesomely he told,
2495   Confessed all his cares and discomfitures many,
How it chanced at the Chapel, what cheer made the knight,
The love of the lady, the green lace at last.
The nick on his neck he naked displayed
That he got in his disgrace at the Green Knight's hands,
2500   alone.
              With rage in heart he speaks,
              And grieves with many a groan;
              The blood burns in his cheeks
              For shame at what must be shown.

2505   "Behold, sir," said he, and handles the belt,
"This is the blazon of the blemish that I bear on my neck;
This is the sign of sore loss that I have suffered there
For the cowardice and coveting that I came to there;
This is the badge of false faith that I was found in there,
2510   And I must bear it on my body till I breathe my last.
For one may keep a deed dark, but undo it no whit,
For where a fault is made fast, it is fixed evermore."
The king comforts the knight, and the court all together
Agree with gay laughter and gracious intent
2515   That the lords and the ladies belonging to the Table,
Each brother of that band, a baldric should have,
A belt oblique, of a bright green,
To be worn with one accord for that worthy's sake.
So that was taken as a token by the Table Round,
2520   And he honored that had it, evermore after,
As the best book of knighthood bids it be known.
In the old days of Arthur this happening befell;
The books of Brutus' deeds bear witness thereto
Since Brutus, the bold knight, embarked for this land
2525   After the siege ceased at Troy and the city fared
                                  amiss.
              Many such, ere we were born,
              Have befallen here, ere this.
              May He that was crowned with thorn
2530   Bring all men to His bliss! Amen.

              Hony Soyt Qui Mal Pence

Sir Thomas Malory
c. 1410–1471

The full identity of Sir Thomas Malory shimmers just beyond our grasp. In several of his colophons—those closing formulas to texts—the author of the *Morte Darthur* says he is "a knyght presoner, sir Thomas Malleorré," and prays that "God sende hym good delyveraunce sone and hastely." Scholars have traced a number of such names in the era, among whom two seem particularly likely: Sir Thomas Malory of Newbold Revell, and Thomas Malory of Papworth. The former Thomas Malory had a scabrous criminal record and was long kept prisoner awaiting trial, while the latter had links to a rich collection of Arthurian books.

Another colophon provides the more useful information that "the hoole book of kyng Arthur and of his noble knyghtes of the Rounde Table" was completed in the ninth year of King Edward IV, that is 1469 or 1470. So whichever Malory wrote the *Morte Darthur*, he was certainly working in the unsettled years of the War of the Roses, in which the great ducal families of York and Lancaster battled for control of the English throne. As one family gained dominance, adherents of the other were often jailed on flimsy charges. The spectacle of a nation threatening to crumble into clan warfare provides much of the thematic weight of the *Morte Darthur*, while the declining chivalric order of the later fifteenth century underlies Malory's increasingly elegiac tone.

Whether he gained his remarkable knowledge of French and English Arthurian tradition in or out of jail, Malory infused his version of these stories with a darkening perspective very much his own. Malory sensed the high aspirations, especially the bonds of honor and fellowship in battle, that held together Arthur's realm. Yet he was also bleakly aware of how tenuous those bonds were and how easily undone by tragically competing pressures. These include the centuries-old Arthurian preoccupation with transgressive love, but Malory is more concerned with the conflicting claims of loyalty to clan or king, the urge to avenge the death of a fellow knight, and the resulting alienation even among the best of knights. Still more unnerving, agents of a virtually unmotivated or unexplained malice have ever more impact as the *Morte Darthur* progresses.

For all his initial energy and control, Malory's Arthur is increasingly a king forced to suppress knightly grievances, to deplore religious quest, even to overlook the adultery of his wife and his greatest knight, all in the interest of his fading hopes for chivalric honor and unity. Arthur's commitment to courtesy finally undoes his honor in the eyes of his own knights. As the Round Table is broken (an image Malory uses repeatedly) Arthur is put in the agonizing position of acting as judge in his wife's trial, making war on his early companion Lancelot, and finally engaging in single combat with his own treacherous son Mordred.

Malory would have found many of these themes in his sources. Twelfth-century Arthurian romances in French verse had explored the elevation and danger of courtly eroticism, and the theme was extended in the enormous French prose versions of the thirteenth century that Malory had read in great detail. In these prose romances, too, religious and chivalric themes converged around the story of the Grail. Malory also knew the alliterative *Morte Arthur* poems of fourteenth-century England, with their emphases on conquest, treachery, and the military details of Arthur's final battles.

Malory regularly acknowledges these sources, but his powers of synthesis and the stamp of his style make his *Morte Darthur* unique. While he occasionally writes a complex, reflective sentence, Malory's prose is typically composed of simple, idiomatic narrative statements, and speeches so brief as to be almost gnomic. On hearing of his brother's death, Gawain faints, then rises and says only "Alas!" Yet the grief of his cry resonates across the closing episodes of the work. Malory's imagery is similarly resonant. He tends to strip it of the explanations that had become frequent in the French prose works, and he concentrates its impact by an almost obsessive repetition. The later episodes of the work become almost an incantation of breakage and dispersal, blood and wounds, each image cluster reaching alternately toward religious experience or secular destruction.

These versions of chivalric ambition, sacred or secular, do not divide easily in the *Morte Darthur*. The saintly Galahad and the scheming Mordred may represent extremes of contrary ambition, but Malory is more preoccupied by the sadly mixed motives of Lancelot or Arthur himself. In three late episodes offered below, the reader is drawn into the perspective of lesser knights like Bors and Bedivere, who witness great moments while affecting them only marginally. They bring back to the world of lesser men stories of uncanny experience and oversee their conversion from verbal rumor to written form, whether in books or on tombs. Much of Malory's power and his continuing appeal come from his unresolved doubleness of perspective. Whether by way of his characters or his style, resonant and mysterious elements emerge from a narrative of gritty realism.

from MORTE DARTHUR
from Caxton's Prologue[1]

After that I had accomplysshed and fynysshed dyuers hystoryes as wel of° contemplacyon as of other hystoryal and worldly actes of grete conquerours and prynces, and also certeyn bookes of ensaumples° and doctryne, many noble and dyuers gentylmen of thys royame° of Englond camen and demaunded me many and oftymes, wherefore that I haue not do made and enprynte the noble hystorye of the Sayntgreal° and of the moost renomed° Crysten kyng, fyrst and chyef of the thre best Crysten[2] and worthy, Kyng Arthur, whyche ought moost to be remembred emonge vs Englysshemen tofore° al other Crysten kynges. * * *

To whome I answerd that dyuers men holde oppynyon that there was no suche Arthur, and that alle suche bookes as been maad of hym ben° but fayned and fables, bycause that somme cronycles make of hym no mencyon ne° remembre hym noothynge ne of his knyghtes.

Wherto they answerd, and one in specyal sayd, that in hym that shold say or thynke that there was neuer suche a kyng callyd Arthur myght wel be aretted° grete folye and blyndenesse; for he sayd that there were many euydences of the contrarye. Fyrst ye may see his sepulture° in the monasterye of Glastyngburye. And also in Polycronycon,[3] * * * where his body was buryed and after founden and translated into the sayd monasterye. Ye shal se also in th'ystory of Bochas, in his book De Casu Principum,[4] parte of his noble actes and also of his falle; also Galfrydus in his Brutysshe book[5] recounteth his lyf. And in dyuers places of Englond many remembraunces ben yet of

both about

moral tales

realm

Holy Grail / famed

before

are

nor

presumed

tomb

1. The first English printer, William Caxton exerted a major literary influence through his translations of French works and his pioneering editions of English writers, including Chaucer and Gower. In 1485 he published a version of *Le Morte Darthur*, probably based on a revision by Malory himself but different from the text edited by Eugène Vinaver (1947, 1975) and used here. Caxton's *Prologue* is interesting in its own right as an early response to Malory, even as Caxton takes the opportunity to promote interest in his book. To give a sense of early printed English, the passages from Caxton's *Prologue* are presented in unaltered spelling.
2. Arthur appears in the traditional list of "nine worthies," three heroes each from pagan, Jewish, and Christian narratives.
3. The *Polychronicon*, a universal history by the monk Ranulph Higden (d. 1364).
4. Boccaccio's *On the Fall of Princes*.
5. Geoffrey of Monmouth, *History of the Kings of Britain*, whose later versions were often called simply *Brut*.

hym and shall remayne perpetuelly, and also of his knyghtes. Fyrst in the Abbey of Westmestre at Saynt Edwardes Shryne remayneth the prynte of his seal in reed waxe closed in beryll, in which is wryton, PATRICIUS ARTHURUS BRITANNIE GALLIE GERMANIE DACIE IMPERATOR.[6] Item° in the Castel of Douer ye may see Gauwayns skulle and Cradoks mantel; at Wynchester, the Round Table; in other places, Launcelottes swerde, and many other thynges. *also*

Thenne, al these thynges consydered, there can no man reson-ably gaynsaye but there was a kyng of thys lande named Arthur. ✳ ✳ ✳

Thenne al these thynges forsayd aledged, I coude not wel denye but that there was suche a noble kynge named Arthur, and reputed one of the ix worthy, and fyrst and chyef of the Cristen men. And many noble volumes be made of hym and of his noble knyghtes in Frensshe, which I haue seen and redde beyonde the see, which been not had in our maternal tongue. But in Walsshe ben many, and also in Frensshe, and somme in Englysshe, but nowher nygh alle. Wherfore suche as haue late ben drawen oute bryefly° into Englysshe, I haue, after the symple connyng° that God hath sente to me, vnder the fauour and correctyon of al noble lordes and gentylmen, enprysed° to enprynte a book of the noble hystoryes of the sayd Kynge Arthur and of certeyn of his knyghtes, after a copye vnto me delyuerd, whyche copye Syr Thomas Malorye dyd take oute of certeyn bookes of Frensshe and reduced it into Englysshe. And I, accordyng to my copye, haue doon sette it in enprynte, to the entente° that noble men may see and lerne the noble actes of chyualrye, the ientyl° and vertuous dedes that somme knyghtes used in tho° dayes, by whyche they came to honour, and how they that were vycious were punysshed and ofte put to shame and rebuke. Humbly bysechyng al noble lordes and ladyes, wyth al other estates° of what estate or degree they been of, that shal see and rede in this sayd book and werke, that they take the good and honest actes in their remembraunce and to folowe the same, wherin they shalle fynde many ioyous and playsaunt hystoryes and noble and renomed actes of humanyte, gentylness, and chyualryes. For herein may be seen noble chyual-rye, curtosye, humanyte, frendlynesse, hardynesse, loue, frend-shyp, cowardyse, murdre, hate, vertue, and synne. Doo after the good and leue the euyl, and it shal brynge you to good fame and renommee.° *renown*

abridged / wit
undertaken
with the aim
noble
those
ranks

And for to passe the tyme thys book shal be plesaunte to rede in, but for to gyue fayth and byleue that al is trewe that is conteyned herin, ye be at your lyberte. But al is wryton for our doctryne and for to beware that we falle not to vyce ne synne, but t'excersyse° and folowe vertu, by whyche we may come and atteyne to good fame and renomme in thys lyf, and after thys shorte and transytorye lyf to come vnto euerlastyng blysse in heuen, the whyche He graunte vs that reygneth in heuen, the Blessyd Trynyte. Amen. *to practice*

6. The Noble Arthur, Emperor of Btitain, Gaul, Germany, Dacia.

The Miracle of Galahad[1]

Now saith the tale that Sir Galahad rode many journeys in vain, and at last he came to the abbey where King Mordrains was. And when he heard that, he thought he would abide to see him.

And so upon the morn, when he had heard mass, Sir Galahad came unto King Mordrains. And anon the king saw him, which had lain blind of long time, and then he dressed him against° him *rose to meet* and said,

"Sir Galahad, the servant of Jesu Christ and very° knight, whose *true* coming I have abiden° long, now embrace me and let me rest on thy *awaited* breast, so that I may rest° between thine arms! For thou art a clean *die* virgin above all knights, as the flower of the lily in whom virginity is signified. And thou art the rose which is the flower of all good virtue, and in colour of fire.[2] For the fire of the Holy Ghost is taken so in thee that my flesh, which was all dead of oldness, is become again young."

When Galahad heard these words, then he embraced him and all his body. Then said he,° *Mordrains*

"Fair Lord Jesu Christ, now I have my will! Now I require Thee, in this point° that I am in, that Thou come and visit me." *state*

And anon Our Lord heard his prayer, and therewith the soul departed from the body. And then Sir Galahad put him in the earth as a king ought to be, and so departed and came into a perilous forest where he found the well which boiled with great waves, as the tale telleth tofore.° *earlier*

And as soon as Sir Galahad set his hand thereto it ceased, so that it brent° no more, and anon the heat departed away. And cause *burned* why it brent, it was a sign of lechery that was that time much used. But that heat might not abide his pure virginity. And so this was taken in the country for a miracle, and so ever after was it called Galahad's Well.

So by adventure he came unto the country of Gore, and into the abbey where Sir Lancelot had been toforehand and found the tomb of King Bagdemagus; but he was founder thereof.[3] For there was the tomb of Joseph of Arimathea's son and the tomb of Simeon, where Lancelot had failed.[4] Then he looked into a croft° under the min- *crypt* ster,° and there he saw a tomb which brent full marvellously. Then *church* asked he the brethren what it was.

---

1. From *The Holy Grail*, in *King Arthur and His Knights*, ed. Eugène Vinaver (1975). Earlier in the text, Lancelot's saintly son Galahad had come to the Round Table and precipitated a brief apparition of the Holy Grail (the cup with which Christ had celebrated the Last Supper). One hundred fifty of Arthur's knights then took a vow to seek a fuller vision of the Grail, but in the mysterious adventures that followed, many died or despaired. Malory's attention now narrows to Lancelot and his partial vision of the Grail, and the continuing quest of Galahad, Perceval, and Bors. The blind King Mordrains is one of several maimed or aged kings cured by Galahad's presence.
2. Galahad's physical and spiritual purity are shown in a number of earlier episodes.
3. Gore, the mysterious realm of Bagdemagus, who had been gravely wounded when he presumed to take a shield intended for Galahad. Words may be missing from the final phrase.
4. In Arthurian tradition, Joseph of Arimathea was keeper of the Grail and used it to catch Christ's blood at the Crucifixion. His son Joseph was the first Christian bishop and carried both the faith and the Grail to England. Galahad is the last of their lineage. Lancelot's failure refers to an episode in the French source that Malory never tells, either inadvertently or because he assumed that many readers would know the story.

"Sir," said they, "a marvellous adventure that may not be brought to an end but by him that passeth of bounty and of knighthood all them of the Round Table."

"I would," said Sir Galahad, "that ye would bring me thereto."

"Gladly," said they, and so led him till° a cave. And he went down upon greses° and came unto the tomb. And so the flaming failed, and the fire staunched° which many a day had been great.

to
steps
was quenched

Then came there a voice which said,

"Much are ye beholden to thank God which hath given you a good hour,° that ye may draw out the souls of earthly pain and to put them into the joys of Paradise. Sir, I am of your kindred, which hath dwelled in this heat this three hundred winter and four-and-fifty to be purged of the sin that I did against Arimathea Joseph."

good luck

Then Sir Galahad took the body in his arms and bare it into the minster. And that night lay Sir Galahad in the abbey; and on the morn he gave him his service and put him in the earth before the high altar.

So departed he from thence, and commended the brethren to God, and so he rode five days till that he came to the Maimed King. And ever followed Perceval the five days asking where he had been, and so one told him how the adventures of Logres were achieved.[5] So on a day it befell that he came out of a great forest, and there they met at traverse with Sir Bors[6] which rode alone. It is no need to ask if they were glad! And so he salewed them, and they yielded to him° honour and good adventure, and everych told other how they had sped. Then said Sir Bors,

wished him

"It is more than a year and a half that I ne lay° ten times where men dwelled, but in wild forests and in mountains. But God was ever my comfort."

have not slept

Then rode they a great while till they came to the castle of Corbenic. And when they were entered within, King Pelles knew them. So there was great joy, for he wist well by their coming that they had fulfilled the Sankgreall.[7]

Then Eliazar, King Pelles' son, brought tofore them the broken sword wherewith Joseph was stricken through the thigh.[8] Then Bors set his hand thereto to essay if he might have sowded° it again; but it would not be. Then he took it to Perceval, but he had no more power thereto than he.

joined

"Now have ye it again," said Sir Perceval unto Sir Galahad, "for an° it be ever achieved by any bodily man, ye must do it."

if

And then he took the pieces and set them together, and seemed to them as it had never be broken, and as well as it was first forged. And when they within espied that the adventure of the sword was achieved, then they gave the sword to Sir Bors, for it might no better be set,° for he was so good a knight and a worthy man.

used

---

5. Perceval has followed Galahad's movements. Malory reduces a five-year period in his source to five days and omits the two knights' meeting.
6. Sir Bors has also been wandering in search of the Grail.
7. Pelles is the maimed king and keeper of Corbenic, the

Grail Castle. The past tense looks forward to events not yet achieved.
8. This sword had wounded Joseph of Arimathea; joining its broken halves is part of the Grail quest.

And a little before even the sword[9] arose, great and marvellous, and was full of great heat, that many men fell for dread. And anon alight a voice among them and said, "They that ought not to sit at the table of Our Lord Jesu Christ, avoid° hence! For now there shall very° knights be fed."

withdraw
true

So they went thence, all save King Pelles and Eliazar, his son, which were holy men, and a maid which was his niece. And so there abode these three knights and these three; else were no more. And anon they saw knights all armed come in at the hall door, and did off their helms and their arms, and said unto Sir Galahad,

"Sir, we have hied° right much for to be with you at this table where the holy meat shall be departed."°

hastened
distributed

Then said he, "Ye be welcome! But of whence be ye?"

So three of them said they were of Gaul, and other three said they were of Ireland, and other three said they were of Denmark.

And so as they sat thus, there came out a bed of tree° of° a chamber, which four gentlewomen brought; and in the bed lay a good man sick, and had a crown of gold upon his head. And there, in the midst of the palace, they set him down and went again. Then he lift up his head and said,

wood / from

"Sir Galahad, good knight, ye be right welcome, for much have I desired your coming! For in such pain and in such anguish as I have no man else° might have suffered long. But now I trust to God the term is come that my pain shall be allayed, and so I shall pass out of this world, so as it was promised me long ago."

no other man

And therewith a voice said, "There be two among you that be not in the quest of the Sankgreall, and therefore departeth!"

Then King Pelles and his son departed. And therewithal beseemed them° that there came an old man and four angels from heaven, clothed in likeness of a bishop, and had a cross in his hand. And these four angels bare him up in a chair and set him down before the table of silver whereupon the Sankgreall was. And it seemed that he had in midst of his forehead letters which said: "See ye here Joseph, the first bishop of Christendom, the same which Our Lord succoured[1] in the city of Sarras in the spiritual palace." Then the knights marvelled, for that bishop was dead more than three hundred year tofore.

it seemed

"Ah, knights," said he, "marvel not, for I was sometime an earthly man."

So with that they heard the chamber door open, and there they saw angels; and two bare candles of wax, and the third bare a towel,[2] and the fourth a spear which bled marvellously, that the drops fell within a box which he held with his other hand. And anon they set the candles upon the table, and the third the towel upon the vessel, and the fourth the holy spear even° upright upon the vessel.

straight

9. Malory misconstrues a phrase meaning "a wind."
1. Joseph of Arimathea was blessed by Christ.
2. In the French source, a veil of samite.

And then the bishop made semblaunt as though he would have
gone to the sacring° of a mass, and then he took an ubblie° which   *consecration /*
was made in likeness of bread. And at the lifting up there came a fig-   *wafer*
ure in likeness of a child, and the visage was as red and as bright as
any fire, and smote himself° into the bread, that all they saw it that   *impressed itself*
the bread was formed of a fleshly man. And then he put it into the
holy vessel again, and then he did that longed° to a priest to do mass.   *what was right*

And then he went to Sir Galahad and kissed him and bade him
go and kiss his fellows. And so he did anon.

"Now," said he, "the servants of Jesu Christ, ye shall be fed afore
this table with sweet meats that never knights yet tasted."

And when he had said he vanished away. And they set them at
the table in great dread and made their prayers. Then looked they
and saw a Man come out of the holy vessel that had all the signs of
the Passion of Jesu Christ, bleeding all openly, and said,

"My knights and my servants and my true children which be
come out of deadly life into the spiritual life, I will no longer cover
me from you, but ye shall see now a part of my secrets and of my hid
things. Now holdeth and receiveth the high order and meat which
ye have so much desired."

Then took He himself the holy vessel and came to Sir Galahad.
And he kneeled down and received his Saviour. And after him so
received all his fellows, and they thought it so sweet that it was marvellous to tell. Then said He to Sir Galahad,

"Son, wotest thou what I hold betwixt my hands?"

"Nay," said he, "but if ye tell me."

"This is," said He, "the holy dish wherein I ate the lamb on Easter Day, and now hast thou seen that thou most desired to see. But
yet hast thou not seen it so openly as thou shalt see it in the city of
Sarras, in the spiritual palace. Therefore thou must go hence and
bear with thee this holy vessel, for this night it shall depart from the
realm of Logres, and it shall nevermore be seen here. And knowest
thou wherefore? For he° is not served nother worshipped to his right°   *it / properly*
by them of this land, for they be turned to evil living, and therefore I
shall disinherit them of the honour which I have done them. And
therefore go ye three to-morn unto the sea, where ye shall find your
ship ready, and with you take the sword with the strange girdles,°   *belts*
and no more with you but Sir Perceval and Sir Bors. Also I will that
ye take with you of this blood of this spear for to anoint the Maimed
King, both his legs and his body, and he shall have his heal."

"Sir," said Galahad, "why shall not these other fellows go with us?"

"For this cause: for right as I depart° my apostles one here and   *separate*
another there, so I will that ye depart. And two of you shall die in
my service, and one of you shall come again and tell tidings."

Then gave He them His blessing and vanished away.

And Sir Galahad went anon to the spear which lay upon the
table and touched the blood with his fingers, and came after to the
maimed knight and anointed his legs and his body. And therwith he

clothed him anon, and start upon his feet out of his bed as an whole man, and thanked God that He had healed him. And anon he left the world and yielded himself to a place of religion of white monks,[3] and was a full holy man.

And that same night, about midnight, came a voice among them which said,

"My sons, and not my chief sons,[4] my friends, and not mine enemies, go ye hence where ye hope best to do, and as I bade you do."

"Ah, thanked be Thou, Lord, that Thou wilt whightsauf° to   *vouchsafe*
call us Thy sons! Now may we well prove that we have not lost our pains."

And anon in all haste they took their harness and departed; but the three knights of Gaul (one of them hight Claudine, King Claudas' son, and the other two were great gentlemen) then prayed° Sir   *asked*
Galahad to everych of them, that an° they come to King Arthur's   *if*
court, "to salew my lord Sir Lancelot, my father and them all of the Round Table"; and prayed them, an they came on that party,° not to   *to that region*
forget it.

Right so departed Sir Galahad, and Sir Perceval and Sir Bors with him, and so they rode three days. And then they came to a rivage° and found the ship whereof the tale speaketh of tofore.   *shore*
And when they came to the board° they found in the midst of the   *on board*
bed the table of silver which they had left with the Maimed King, and the Sankgreall which was covered with red samite.° Then were   *silk*
they glad to have such things in their fellowship; and so they entered and made great reverence thereto, and Sir Galahad fell on his knees and prayed long time to Our Lord, that at what time he asked he might pass out of this world. And so long he prayed till a voice said,

"Sir Galahad, thou shalt have thy request, and when thou asketh the death of thy body thou shalt have it, and then shalt thou have the life of thy soul."

Then Sir Perceval heard him a little, and prayed him of° fellow-   *for the sake of*
ship that was between them wherefore he asked such things.

"Sir, that shall I tell you," said Sir Galahad. "This other day, when we saw a part of the adventures of the Sankgreall, I was in such a joy of heart that I trow° never man was that was earthly. And therefore I   *believe*
wot° well, when my body is dead, my soul shall be in great joy to see   *know*
the Blessed Trinity every day, and the majesty of Our Lord, Jesu Christ."

And so long were they in the ship that they said to Galahad,

"Sir, in this bed ye ought to lie, for so saith the letters."°   *writings*

And so he laid him down, and slept a great while. And when he awaked he looked tofore him and saw the city of Sarras. And as they would have landed they saw the ship wherein Sir Perceval had put his sister in.

---

3. The white monks were Cistercians, whose spirituality   4. A confusing phrase, perhaps in error for "stepsons."
had some role in Malory's French sources.

"Truly," said Sir Perceval, "in the name of God, well hath my sister holden us covenant."[5]

Then they took out of the ship the table of silver, and he took it to Sir Perceval and to Sir Bors to go tofore, and Sir Galahad came behind, and right so they went into the city. And at the gate of the city they saw an old man crooked, and anon Sir Galahad called him and bade him help "to bear this heavy thing."

"Truly," said the old man, "it is ten year ago that I might not go but with crutches."

"Care thou not," said Galahad, "and arise up and show thy good will!"

And so he essayed, and found himself as whole as ever he was. Then ran he to the table and took one part against° Galahad.   *beside*

Anon arose there a great noise in the city that a cripple was made whole by knights marvellous that entered into the city. Then anon after the three knights went to the water and brought up into the palace Sir Perceval's sister, and buried her as richly as them ought a king's daughter.

And when the king of that country knew that and saw that fellowship (whose name was Estorause), he asked them of whence they were, and what thing it was that they had brought upon the table of silver. And they told him the truth of the Sankgreall, and the power which God hath set there.

Then this king was a tyrant, and was come of the line of paynims,° and took them and put them in prison in a deep hole. But as   *pagans* soon as they were there Our Lord sent them the Sankgreall, through whose grace they were alway fulfilled° while that they were   *fed* in prison.

So at the year's end it befell that this king lay sick and felt that he should die. Then he sent for the three knights, and they came afore him, and he cried them mercy of that he had done to them, and they forgave it him goodly, and he died anon.

When the king was dead all the city stood dismayed and wist° not   *knew* who might be their king. Right so as they were in council there came a voice among them, and made them choose the youngest knight of three to be their king, "for he shall well maintain you and all yours."

So they made Sir Galahad king by all the assent of the whole city, and else they would have slain him. And when he was come to behold his land he let make° above the table of silver a chest of gold   *had made* and of precious stones that covered the holy vessel, and every day early the three knights would come before it and make their prayers.

Now at the year's end, and the self Sunday after that Sir Galahad had borne the crown of gold, he arose up early and his fellows, and came to the palace, and saw tofore them the holy vessel and a man kneeling on his knees in likeness of a bishop that had about him a great fellowship of angels, as it had been Jesu Christ himself.

---

5. Kept her promise to us. In an earlier episode Perceval's sister died after giving a basin of her blood to heal a leper woman.

And then he arose and began a mass of Our Lady. And so he came to
the sacring, and anon made an end. He called Sir Galahad unto him
and said,

"Come forth, the servant of Jesu Christ, and thou shalt see that
thou hast much desired to see."

And then he began to tremble right hard when the deadly° flesh   *mortal*
began to behold the spiritual things. Then he held up his hands
toward heaven and said,

"Lord, I thank Thee, for now I see that that hath been my desire
many a day. Now, my Blessed Lord, I would not live in this wretched
world no longer, if it might please Thee, Lord."

And therewith the good man took Our Lord's Body[6] betwixt his
hands, proffered it to Sir Galahad, and he received it right gladly
and meekly.

"Now wotest thou what I am?" said the good man.

"Nay, Sir," said Sir Galahad.

"I am Joseph, the son of Joseph of Arimathea, which Our Lord
hath sent to thee to bear thee fellowship. And wotest thou wherefore He hath sent me more than any other? For thou hast resembled me in two things: that thou hast seen, that is the marvels of
the Sankgreall, and for thou hast been a clean maiden° as I have   *chaste virgin*
been and am."

And when he had said these words Sir Galahad went to Sir Perceval and kissed him and commended him to God. And so he went to Sir
Bors and kissed him and commended him to God, and said,

"My fair lord, salew me° unto my lord Sir Lancelot, my father,   *give my greeting*
and as soon as ye see him bid him remember of this world unstable."

And therewith he kneeled down tofore the table and made his
prayers. And so suddenly departed his soul to Jesu Christ, and a
great multitude of angels bare it up to heaven, even in the sight of
his two fellows.

Also these two knights saw come from heaven an hand, but
they saw not the body, and so it came right to the vessel, and took it,
and the spear, and so bare it up to heaven. And sithen° was there   *since then*
never man so hardy to say that he had seen the Sankgreall.

So when Sir Perceval and Sir Bors saw Sir Galahad dead they
made as much sorrow as ever did men. And if they had not been
good men they might lightly° have fallen in despair. And so people   *easily*
of the country and city, they were right heavy. But so he was buried,
and soon as he was buried Sir Perceval yielded him to an hermitage
out of the city and took religious clothing. And Sir Bors was alway
with him, but he changed never his secular clothing, for that he purposed him to go again into the realm of Logres.

Thus a year and two months lived Sir Perceval in the hermitage
a full holy life, and then passed out of the world. Then Sir Bors let   *consecrated*
bury him by[7] his sister and by Sir Galahad in the spiritualities.°   *ground*

---

6. The wafer of the Eucharist.   7. Had him buried next to.

So when Bors saw that he was in so far° countries as in the parts   *remote*
of Babylon, he departed from the city of Sarras and armed him and
came to the sea, and entered into a ship. And so it befell him, by
good adventure, he came unto the realm of Logres, and so he rode a
pace° till he came to Camelot where the king was.   *swiftly*

And then was there made great joy of him in all the court, for
they weened all he had been lost forasmuch as he had been so long
out of the country. And when they had eaten, the king made great
clerks to come before him, for cause they should chronicle of° the   *record*
high adventures of the good knights. So when Sir Bors had told him
of the high adventures of the Sankgreall such as had befallen him
and his three fellows, which were Sir Lancelot, Perceval, Sir Galahad and himself, then Sir Lancelot told the adventures of the
Sankgreall that he had seen. All this was made in great books and
put up in almeries° at Salisbury.   *libraries*

And anon Sir Bors said to Sir Lancelot,

"Sir Galahad, your own son, salewed you by me, and after you my
lord King Arthur and all the whole court, and so did Sir Perceval. For I
buried them with both mine own hands in the city of Sarras. Also, Sir
Lancelot, Sir Galahad prayed you to remember of this unsiker° world,   *uncertain*
as ye behight him° when ye were together more than half a year."   *promised*

"This is true," said Sir Lancelot; "now I trust to God his prayer
shall avail me."

Then Sir Lancelot took Sir Bors in his arms and said,

"Cousin, ye are right welcome to me! For all that ever I may do
for you and for yours, ye shall find my poor body ready at all times
while the spirit is in it, and that I promise you faithfully, and never
to fail. And wit ye well, gentle cousin Sir Bors, ye and I shall never
depart in sunder while our lives may last."

"Sir," said he, "as ye will, so will I."

THUS ENDETH THE TALE OF THE SANKGREALL THAT WAS BRIEFLY
DRAWN OUT OF FRENCH, WHICH IS A TALE CHRONICLED FOR ONE OF
THE TRUEST AND OF THE HOLIEST THAT IS IN THIS WORLD, BY SIR
THOMAS MALEORRÉ, KNIGHT.
O BLESSED JESU HELP HIM THROUGH HIS MIGHT! AMEN.

The Poisoned Apple[1]

So after the quest of the Sankgreall was fulfilled, and all knights that
were left on live were come home again unto the Table Round, as
The Book of the Sankgreall maketh mention, then was there great joy
in the court, and in especial King Arthur and Queen Guinevere
made great joy of the remnant that were come home. And passing
glad was the king and the queen of Sir Lancelot and of Sir Bors, for
they had been passing long away in the quest of the Sankgreall.

---

1. From the section titled *The Book of Sir Launcelot and Queen Guinevere*, in *King Arthur and His Knights*, ed. Eugène
Vinaver (1975).

Then, as the book saith, Sir Lancelot began to resort unto
Queen Guinevere again and forgat the promise and the perfection°   *of perfection*
that he made in the quest; for, as the book saith, had not Sir
Lancelot been in his privy° thoughts and in his mind so set inwardly   *secret*
to the queen as he was in seeming outward to God, there had no
knight passed him in the quest of the Sankgreall. But ever his
thoughts privily were on the queen, and so they loved together more
hotter than they did to forehand, and had many such privy draughts°   *meetings*
together that many in the court spake of it, and in especial Sir Agravain, Sir Gawain's brother, for he was ever open-mouthed.

So it befell that Sir Lancelot had many resorts of° ladies and   *entreaties from*
damsels which daily resorted unto him, that besought him to be
their champion. In all such matters of right Sir Lancelot applied him
daily to do for the pleasure of Our Lord Jesu Christ, and ever as
much as he might he withdrew him from the company of Queen
Guinevere for to eschew the slander and noise.° Wherefore the   *rumor*
queen waxed wroth with Sir Lancelot.

So on a day she called him unto her chamber and said thus:

"Sir Lancelot, I see and feel daily that your love beginneth to
slake,° for ye have no joy to be in my presence, but ever ye are out of   *cool*
this court, and quarrels and matters ye have nowadays for ladies,
maidens and gentlewomen, more than ever ye were wont to have
beforehand."

"Ah, madam," said Sir Lancelot, "in this ye must hold me excused
for divers causes. One is, I was but late in the quest of the Sankgreall,
and I thank God of His great mercy, and never of my deserving, that I
saw in that my quest as much as ever saw any sinful man living, and so
was it told me. And if that I had not had my privy thoughts to return
to your love again as I do, I had° seen as great mysteries as ever saw my   *should have*
son, Sir Galahad, Perceval, other Sir Bors. And therefore, madam, I
was but late in that quest, and wit you well, madam, it may not be yet
lightly forgotten, the high service in whom I did my diligent labour.

"Also, madam, wit you well that there be many men speaketh of
our love in this court, and have you and me greatly in await,° as this   *suspicion*
Sir Agravain and Sir Mordred.[2] And, madam, wit you well I dread
them more for your sake than for any fear I have of them myself, for I
may happen to escape and rid myself in a great need where, madam,
ye must abide all that will be said unto you. And then, if that ye fall
in any distress throughout° wilful folly, then is there none other help   *through*
but by me and my blood.°   *kinsmen*

"And wit you well, madam, the boldness of you and me will
bring us to shame and slander; and that were me loath to see you dis-
honoured. And that is the cause I take upon me more for to do for
damsels and maidens than ever I did toforn:° that men should under-   *before*
stand my joy and my delight is my pleasure to have ado for damsels
and maidens."

---

2. Mordred was Arthur's illegitimate son, by an incestuous encounter with his half-sister Morgause (or in some versions,
Morgan le Fay).

All this while the queen stood still and let Sir Lancelot say what he would; and when he had all said she brast out of weeping, and so she sobbed and wept a great while. And when she might speak she said,

"Sir Lancelot, now I well understand that thou art a false, recreant° knight and a common lecher, and lovest and holdest other ladies, and of me thou hast disdain and scorn. For wit thou well, now I understand thy falsehood I shall never love thee more, and look thou be never so hardy° to come in my sight. And right here I discharge thee this court, that thou never come within it, and I forfend° thee my fellowship, and upon pain° of thy head that thou see me nevermore!"

Right so Sir Lancelot departed with great heaviness that unneth° he might sustain himself for great dole-making.

Then he called Sir Bors, Ector de Maris and Sir Lionel, and told them how the queen had forfended him the court, and so he was in will to depart into his own country.

"Fair sir," said Bors de Ganis, "ye shall not depart out of this land by mine advice, for ye must remember you what ye are, and renowned the most noblest knight of the world, and many great matters ye have in hand. And women in their hastiness will do oftentimes that after them sore repenteth. And therefore, by mine advice, ye shall take your horse and ride to the good hermit here beside Windsor, that sometime was a good knight; his name is Sir Brastias. And there shall ye abide till that I send you word of better tidings."

"Brother," said Sir Lancelot, "wit you well I am full loath to depart out of this realm, but the queen hath defended° me so highly,° that meseemeth she will never be my good lady as she hath been."

"Say ye never so," said Sir Bors, "for many times or° this time she hath been wroth with you, and after that she was the first that repented it."

"Ye say well," said Sir Lancelot, "for now will I do by your counsel and take mine horse and mine harness and ride to the hermit Sir Brastias, and there will I repose me till I hear some manner of tidings from you. But, fair brother, in that° ye can get me the love of my lady, Queen Guinevere."

"Sir," said Sir Bors, "ye need not to move° me of such matters, for well ye wot I will do what I may to please you."

And then Sir Lancelot departed suddenly, and no creature wist where he was become° but Sir Bors. So when Sir Lancelot was departed the queen outward made no manner of sorrow in showing to none of his blood nor to none other, but wit ye well, inwardly, as the book saith, she took great thought;° but she bare it out with a proud countenance, as though she felt no thought nother danger.°

So the queen let make° a privy dinner in London unto the knights of the Round Table, and all was for to show outward that she had as great joy in all other knights of the Round Table as she had in

cowardly

bold

forbid / at the risk

scarcely

dismissed
angrily

before

so far as

persuade

had gone

grief
fear
had made

Sir Lancelot. So there was all only at that dinner Sir Gawain and his brethren, that is for to say Sir Agravain, Sir Gaheris, Sir Gareth and Sir Mordred, also there was Sir Bors de Ganis, Sir Blamore de Ganis, Sir Bleoberis de Ganis, Sir Galihad, Sir Eliodin, Sir Ector de Maris, Sir Lionel, Sir Palomides, Sir Safir, his brother, Sir La Cote Male Tayle, Sir Persaunt, Sir Ironside, Sir Braundiles, Sir Kay le Seneschal, Sir Mador de la Porte, Sir Patrise, a knight of Ireland, Sir Aliduke, Sir Ascamore, and Sir Pinel le Savage, which was cousin to Sir Lamorak de Galis, the good knight that Sir Gawain and his brethren slew by treason.[3]

And so these four-and-twenty knights should dine with the queen in a privy place by themselves, and there was made a great feast of all manner of dainties. But Sir Gawain had a custom that he used daily at meat and at supper, that he loved well all manner of fruit, and in especial apples and pears. And therefore whosomever dined other° feasted Sir Gawain would commonly purvey for° good fruit for him. And so did the queen; for to please Sir Gawain she let purvey for him all manner of fruit. For Sir Gawain was a passing hot° knight of nature, and this Sir Pinel hated Sir Gawain because of his kinsman Sir Lamorak's death, and therefore, for pure envy and hate, Sir Pinel enpoisoned certain apples for to enpoison Sir Gawain.

So this was well yet unto° the end of meat, and so it befell by misfortune a good knight Sir Patrise, which was cousin unto Sir Mador de la Porte, took an apple, for he was enchafed° with heat of wine. And it mishapped him to take a poisoned apple. And when he had eaten it he swall° sore till he brast,° and there Sir Patrise fell down suddenly° dead among them.

Then every knight leap from the board ashamed, and araged for° wrath out of their wits, for they wist not what to say; considering Queen Guinevere made the feast and dinner they had all suspicion unto her.

"My lady the queen!" said Sir Gawain. "Madam, wit you that this dinner was made for me and my fellows, for all folks that knoweth my condition understand that I love well fruit. And now I see well I had near been slain. Therefore, madam, I dread me lest ye will be shamed."

Then the queen stood still and was so sore abashed that she wist not what to say.

"This shall not so be ended," said Sir Mador de la Porte, "for here have I lost a full noble knight of my blood, and therefore upon this shame and despite° I will be revenged to the utterance!"°

And there openly Sir Mador appealed° the queen of the death of his cousin Sir Patrise.

Then stood they all still, that° none would speak a word against him, for they all had great suspicion unto the queen because she let make that dinner. And the queen was so abashed that she could

or / provide

hot-tempered

toward

inflamed

swelled / burst
instantly

enraged with

wrong / utmost
accused

for

---

3. This catalog draws together most of the Round Table knights who survived the Grail quest, except for Sir Bors, absent perhaps because his kinsman Lancelot is in disgrace with the queen.

none otherways do but wept so heartily that she fell on a swough. So
with this noise and cry came to them King Arthur, and when he wist
of the trouble he was a passing heavy° man. And ever Sir Mador   *sad*
stood still before the king, and appealed the queen of treason. (For
the custom was such at that time that all manner of shameful death
was called treason.)

"Fair lords," said King Arthur, "me repenteth of this trouble, but
the case is so I may not have ado° in this matter, for I must be a   *intervene*
rightful judge. And that repenteth me that I may not do battle[4] for
my wife, for, as I deem, this deed came never by her.° And therefore   *by her doing*
I suppose she shall not be all disdained° but that some good knight   *dishonored*
shall put his body in jeopardy for my queen rather than she should be
brent° in a wrong quarrel.° And therefore, Sir Mador, be not so   *burned / unjustly*
hasty; for, perdy,° it may happen she shall not be all friendless. And   *by God*
therefore desire thou thy day of battle, and she shall purvey her of°   *find herself*
some good knight that shall answer you, other else it were to me
great shame and to all my court."

"My gracious lord," said Sir Mador, "ye must hold me excused,
for though ye be our king, in that degree° ye are but a knight as we   *rank*
are, and ye are sworn unto knighthood as well as we be. And therefore I beseech you that ye be not displeased, for there is none of all
these four-and-twenty knights that were bidden to this dinner but all
they have great suspicion unto the queen. What say ye all, my
lords?" said Sir Mador.

Then they answered by and by and said they could not excuse
the queen for why she made the dinner, and other it must come by
her other by her servants.

"Alas," said the queen, "I made this dinner for a good intent and
never for none evil, so Almighty Jesu help me in my right,° as I was   *just cause*
never purposed to do such evil deeds, and that I report me unto God."[5]

"My lord the king," said Sir Mador, "I require you as ye be a
righteous king, give me my day that I may have justice."

"Well," said the king, "this day fifteen days look thou be ready
armed on horseback in the meadow beside Winchester. And if it so
fall° that there be any knight to encounter against you, there may   *happens*
you do your best, and God speed the right. And if so befall that there
be no knight ready at that day, then must my queen be brent, and
there she shall be ready to have her judgment."

"I am answered," said Sir Mador.

And every knight yode° where him liked.   *went*

So when the king and the queen were together the king asked
the queen how this case° befell. Then the queen said,   *misfortune*

"Sir, as Jesu be my help!" She wist not how nother° in what   *nor*
manner.

"Where is Sir Lancelot?" said King Arthur. "An° he were here   *if*
he would not grudge to do battle for you."

---

4. Malory refers to a procedure in law, archaic in his day,   innocence in a "trial by battle."
wherein an armed champion could vindicate a person's   5. I appeal to God to confirm.

"Sir," said the queen, "I wot not where he is, but his brother and his kinsmen deem that he be not within this realm."

"That me repenteth," said King Arthur, "for an he were here he would soon stint° this strife. Well, then I will counsel you," said the king, "that ye go unto Sir Bors, and pray him for to do battle for you for Sir Lancelot's sake, and upon my life he will not refuse you. For well I see," said the king, "that none of the four-and-twenty knights that were at your dinner where Sir Patrise was slain that will do battle for you, nother none of them will say well of you, and that shall be great slander to you in this court."

"Alas," said the queen, "an I may not do withall,[6] but now I miss Sir Lancelot, for an he were here he would soon put me in my heart's ease."

"What aileth you," said the king, "that ye cannot keep Sir Lancelot upon your side? For wit you well," said the king, "who hath Sir Lancelot upon his party° hath the most man of worship in this world upon his side. Now go your way," said the king unto the queen, "and require Sir Bors to do battle for you for Sir Lancelot's sake."

So the queen departed from the king and sent for Sir Bors into the chamber. And when he came she besought him of succour.

"Madam," said he, "what would ye that I did? For I may not with my worship° have ado in this matter, because I was at the same dinner, for dread of any of those knights would have you in suspicion. Also Madam," said Sir Bors, "now miss ye Sir Lancelot, for he would not a failed you in your right nother in your wrong, for when ye have been in right great dangers he hath succoured you. And now ye have driven him out of this country, by whom ye and all we were daily worshipped° by. Therefore, madam, I marvel how ye dare for shame to require me to do anything for you, insomuch ye have enchased out of your court by whom° we were upborne and honoured."

"Alas, fair knight," said the queen, "I put me wholly in your grace, and all that is amiss I will amend as ye will counsel me." And therewith she kneeled down upon both her knees, and besought Sir Bors to have mercy upon her, "other else I shall have a shameful death, and thereto I never offended."°

Right so came King Arthur and found the queen kneeling. And then Sir Bors took her up, and said,

"Madam, ye do me great dishonour."

"Ah, gentle knight," said the king, "have mercy upon my queen, courteous knight, for I am now in certain she is untruly defamed! And therefore, courteous knight," the king said, "promise her to do battle for her, I require you for the love ye owe unto Sir Lancelot."

"My lord," said Sir Bors, "ye require me the greatest thing that any man may require me. And wit you well, if I grant to do battle for the queen I shall wrath° many of my fellowship of the Table Round. But as for that," said Sir Bors, "I will grant° for my lord Sir Lancelot's

stop

faction

with honor

honored

the man by whom

did wrong

enrage

consent

---

6. If I cannot help it.

sake, and for your sake: I will at that day be the queen's champion unless that there come by adventures a better knight than I am to do battle for her."

"Will ye promise me this," said the king, "by your faith?"

"Yea sir," said Sir Bors, "of that I shall not fail you, nother her; but if there come a better knight than I am, then shall he have the battle."

Then was the king and the queen passing glad, and so departed, and thanked him heartily.

Then Sir Bors departed secretly upon a day, and rode unto Sir Lancelot thereas he was with Sir Brastias, and told him of all this adventure.

"Ah Jesu," Sir Lancelot said, "this is come happily as I would have it. And therefore I pray you make you ready to do battle, but look that ye tarry till ye see me come as long as ye may. For I am sure Sir Mador is an hot knight when he is enchafed for the more ye suffer him the hastier will he be to battle."

"Sir," said Sir Bors, "let me deal with him. Doubt ye not ye shall have all your will."

So departed Sir Bors from him and came to the court again. Then it was noised° in all the court that Sir Bors should do battle for the queen, wherefore many knights were displeased with him that he would take upon him to do battle in the queen's quarrel; for there were but few knights in all the court but they deemed the queen was in the wrong and that she had done that treason. So Sir Bors answered thus to his fellows of the Table Round.

"Wit you well, my fair lords, it were shame to us all an we suffered to see the most noble queen of the world to be shamed openly, considering her lord and our lord is the man of most worship christened, and he hath ever worshipped° us all in all places."

Many answered him again: "As for our most noble King Arthur, we love him and honour him as well as ye do, but as for Queen Guinevere we love her not, because she is a destroyer of good knights."

"Fair lords," said Sir Bors, "meseemeth ye say not as ye should say, for never yet in my days knew I never ne° heard say that ever she was a destroyer of good knights, but at all times as far as ever I could know, she was a maintainer of good knights; and ever she hath been large° and free of her goods to all good knights, and the most bounteous lady of her gifts and her good grace that ever I saw other heard speak of. And therefore it were shame to us all and to our most noble king's wife whom we serve an we suffered her to be shamefully slain. And wit ye well," said Sir Bors, "I will not suffer it, for I dare say so much, for the queen is not guilty of Sir Patrise's death: for she owed° him never none evil will nother none of the four-and-twenty knights that were at that dinner, for I dare say for good love she bade us to dinner, and not for no mal engine.° And that, I doubt not, shall be proved hereafter, for howsomever the game goeth, there was treason among us."

Then some said to Bors, "We may well believe your words." And so some were well pleased and some were not.

rumored

honored

nor

generous

felt towards

evil intent

So the day came on fast until the even that° the battle should be.   *evening before*
Then the queen sent for Sir Bors and asked him how he was
disposed.°   *resolved*

"Truly, madam," said he, "I am disposed in like wise as I
promised you, that is to say I shall not fail you unless there by adventure come a better knight than I am to do battle for you. Then,
madam, I am of° you discharged° of my promise."   *by / released*

"Will ye," said the queen, "that I tell my lord the king thus?"

"Do as it pleaseth you, madam."

Then the queen yode° unto the king and told the answer of   *went*
Sir Bors.

"Well, have ye no doubt," said the king, "of Sir Bors, for I call
him now that is living° one of the noblest knights of the world, and   *of those now alive*
most perfectest man."

And thus it passed on till the morn, and so the king and the
queen and all manner of knights that were there at that time drew°   *gathered*
them unto the meadow beside Winchester where the battle should
be. And so when the king was come with the queen and many
knights of the Table Round, so the queen was then put in the constable's award,° and a great fire made about an iron stake, that an Sir   *custody*
Mador de le Porte had the better, she should there be brent; for such
custom was used in those days: for favour, love, nother affinity°   *kinship*
there should be none other but righteous judgment, as well upon a
king as upon a knight, and as well upon a queen as upon another°   *any*
poor lady.

So this meanwhile came in Sir Mador de la Porte, and took his
oath before the king, how that the queen did this treason until° his   *toward*
cousin Sir Patrise, "and unto mine oath I will prove it with my body,
hand for hand, who that will say the contrary."

Right so came in Sir Bors de Ganis and said that as for Queen
Guinevere, "she is in the right, and that will I make good that she is
not culpable of this treason that is put upon her."

"Then make thee ready," said Sir Mador, "and we shall prove
whether thou be in the right or I."

"Sir Mador," said Sir Bors, "wit you well, I know you for a good
knight. Notforthen° I shall not fear you so greatly but I trust to God   *nevertheless*
I shall be able to withstand your malice. But thus much have I
promised my lord Arthur and my lady the queen, that I shall do battle for her in this cause to the utterest, unless that there come a better knight than I am and discharge° me."   *release*

"Is that all?" said Sir Mador. "Other come thou off and do battle
with me, other else say nay!"

"Take your horse," said Sir Bors, "and, as I suppose, I shall not
tarry long but ye shall be answered."

Then either departed to their tents and made them ready to
horseback° as they thought best. And anon Sir Mador came into the   *to mount*
field with his shield on his shoulder and his spear in his hand, and so
rode about the place crying unto King Arthur,

"Bid your champion come forth an he dare!"

Then was Sir Bors ashamed, and took his horse and came to the lists'° end. And then was he ware° where came from a wood there fast by a knight all armed upon a white horse with a strange shield of strange arms, and he came driving all that° his horse might run. And so he came to Sir Bors and said thus:

jousting field's / noticed

as fast as

"Fair knight, I pray you be not displeased, for here must a better knight than ye are have this battle. Therefore I pray you withdraw you, for wit you well I have had this day a right great journey and this battle ought to be mine. And so I promised you when I spake with you last, and with all my heart I thank you of your good will."

Then Sir Bors rode unto King Arthur and told him how there was a knight come that would have the battle to fight for the queen.

"What knight is he?" said the king.

"I wot not," said Sir Bors, "but such covenant he made with me to be here this day. Now, my lord," said Sir Bors, "here I am discharged."

Then the king called to that knight, and asked him if he would fight for the queen. Then he answered and said,

"Sir, therefore come I hither. And therefore, sir king, tarry° me no longer, for anon as I have finished this battle I must depart hence, for I have to do many battles elsewhere. For wit you well," said the knight, "this is dishonour to you and to all knights of the Round Table to see and know so noble a lady and so courteous as Queen Guinevere is, thus to be rebuked and shamed amongst you."

delay

Then they all marvelled what knight that might be that so took the battle upon him, for there was not one that knew him but if it were Sir Bors. Then said Sir Mador de la Porte unto the king:

"Now let me wit with whom I shall have ado."

And then they rode to the lists' end, and there they couched° their spears and ran together with all their mights. And anon Sir Mador's spear brake all to pieces, but the other's spear held and bare Sir Mador's horse and all backwards to the earth a great fall. But mightily and deliverly he avoided his horse from him and put his shield before him and drew his sword and bade the other knight alight and do battle with him on foot.

lowered

Then that knight descended down from his horse and put his shield before him and drew his sword. And so they came eagerly unto battle, and either gave other many sad° strokes, tracing and traversing and foining° together with their swords as it were wild boars, thus fighting nigh an hour; for this Sir Mador was a strong knight, and mightily proved in many strong battles. But at the last this knight smote Sir Mador grovelling upon the earth, and the knight stepped near him to have pulled Sir Mador flatling° upon the ground; and therewith Sir Mador arose, and in his rising he smote that knight through the thick of the thighs, that the blood brast out fiercely.

grievous
thrusting

at full length

And when he felt himself so wounded and saw his blood, he let him arise upon his feet, and then he gave him such a buffet upon the helm that he fell to the earth flatling. And therewith he strode to him to have pulled off his helm off his head. And so Sir Mador prayed that knight to save his life. And so he yielded him as overcome, and released the queen of his quarrel.° *accusation*

"I will not grant thee thy life," said the knight, "only that° thou *unless* freely release the queen forever, and that no mention be made upon Sir Patrise's tomb that ever Queen Guinevere consented to that treason."

"All this shall be done," said Sir Mador, "I clearly discharge my quarrel forever."

Then the knights parters° of the lists took up Sir Mador and led *stewards* him till his tent. And the other knight went straight to the stairfoot where sat King Arthur. And by that time was the queen came to the king, and either kissed other heartily.

And when the king saw that knight he stooped down to him and thanked him, and in like wise did the queen. And the king prayed him put off his helmet and to repose him and to take a sop of wine.

And then he put off his helm to drink, and then every knight knew him that it was Sir Lancelot. And anon as the king wist that, he took the queen in his hand and yode unto Sir Lancelot and said,

"Sir, gramercy of your great travail° that ye have had this day for *labor* me and for my queen."

"My lord," said Sir Lancelot, "wit you well I ought of right ever to be in your quarrel,° and my lady the queen's quarrel, to do battle; *on your side* for ye are the man that gave me the high Order of Knighthood, and that day my lady, your queen, did me worship.° And else I had been *honor* shamed, for that same day that ye made me knight through my hastiness I lost my sword, and my lady, your queen, found it, and lapped° *wrapped* it in her train, and gave me my sword when I had need thereto; and else had I been shamed among all knights. And therefore, my lord Arthur, I promised her at that day ever to be her knight in right other in wrong."

"Gramercy," said the king, "for this journey. And wit you well," said the king, "I shall acquit° your goodness." *reward*

And evermore the queen beheld Sir Lancelot and wept so tenderly that she sank almost to the ground for sorrow, that he had done to her so great kindness where she showed him great unkindness. Then the knights of his blood drew unto him, and there either of them made great joy of other. And so came all the knights of the Table Round that were there at that time and welcomed him.

And then Sir Mador was healed of his leechcraft,° and Sir *by surgery* Lancelot was healed of his play.° And so there was made great joy *wound* and many mirths there was made in that court.

And so it befell that the Damsel of the Lake that hight Ninive, which wedded the good knight Sir Pelleas, and so she came to the court, for ever she did great goodness unto King Arthur and to all his knights through her sorcery and enchantments. And so when she heard how the queen was grieved° for the death of Sir Patrise, then *blamed* she told it openly that she was never guilty, and there she disclosed by whom it was done, and named him Sir Pinel, and for what cause he did it. There it was openly known and disclosed, and so the queen was excused. And this knight Sir Pinel fled into his country, and was openly known that he enpoisoned the apples at that feast to that intent to have destroyed Sir Gawain, because Sir Gawain and his breathren destroyed Sir Lamorak de Galis which Sir Pinel was cousin unto.

Then was Sir Patrise buried in the church of Westminster in a tomb, and thereupon was written: "Here lieth Sir Patrise of Ireland, slain by Sir Pinel le Savage, that enpoisoned apples to have slain Sir Gawain, and by misfortune Sir Patrise ate one of the apples, and then suddenly he brast." Also there was written upon the tomb that Queen Guinevere was appealed° of treason of° the death of Sir *accused / for* Patrise by Sir Mador de la Porte, and there was made the mention how Sir Lancelot fought with him for Queen Guinevere and overcame him in plain battle. All this was written upon the tomb of Sir Patrise in excusing of the queen.

And then Sir Mador sued daily and long to have the queen's good grace, and so by the means of Sir Lancelot he caused him to stand in the queen's good grace, and all was forgiven.

[*In intervening episodes, Agravain and Mordred, nursing long-held grudges, connive to expose the adultery of Lancelot and Guinevere. Their brother, Gawain, reluctantly joins their plot. Mordred traps Lancelot at night in Guinevere's chamber, and in escaping Lancelot kills Agravain. Rescuing Guinevere as she is about to be burned at the stake, Lancelot kills another of Gawain's brothers, Gareth, thereby earning Gawain's implacable enmity. Arthur must now make war on Lancelot and, pressed by Gawain, repeats his siege even after Guinevere is returned to him. Arthur thus besieges Lancelot in his French domain, leaving Mordred as regent.*]

The Day of Destiny[1]

As Sir Mordred was ruler of all England, he let make° letters as *commissioned* though that they had come from beyond the sea, and the letters specified that King Arthur was slain in battle with Sir Lancelot. Wherefore Sir Mordred made a parliament, and called the lords together, and there he made them to choose him king. And so was he crowned at Canterbury, and held a feast there fifteen days.

And afterward he drew him unto Winchester, and there he took Queen Guinevere, and said plainly that he would wed her (which was his uncle's wife and his father's wife). And so he made ready for the feast, and a day prefixed that they should be wedded; wherefore Queen Guinevere was passing heavy,° but spake fair, and agreed to *sad* Sir Mordred's will.

---

1. From the section titled *The Most Piteous Tale of the Morte Arthur Saunz Guerdon*, in *King Arthur and His Knights*, ed. Eugène Vinaver (1975).

And anon she desired of Sir Mordred to go to London to buy all manner things that longed to the bridal. And because of her fair speech Sir Mordred trusted her and gave her leave; and so when she came to London she took the Tower of London and suddenly in all haste possible she stuffed it with all manner of victual, and well garnished° it with men, and so kept it.   *garrisoned*

And when Sir Mordred wist this he was passing wroth out of measure. And short tale to make, he laid a mighty siege about the Tower and made many assaults, and threw engines° unto them, and   *siege machines* shot great guns. But all might not prevail, for Queen Guinevere would never, for fair speech neither for foul, never to trust unto Sir Mordred to come in his hands again.

Then came the Bishop of Canterbury, which was a noble clerk and an holy man, and thus he said unto Sir Mordred:

"Sir, what will ye do? Will you first displease God and sithen°   *then* shame yourself and all knighthood? For is not King Arthur your uncle, and no farther but your mother's brother, and upon her he himself begat you, upon his own sister? Therefore how may you wed your own father's wife? And therefore, sir," said the Bishop, "leave this opinion,° other else I shall curse you with book, bell and candle."   *intention*

"Do thou thy worst," said Sir Mordred, "and I defy thee!"

"Sir," said the Bishop, "and wit you well I shall not fear me to do that me ought to do. And also ye noise° that my lord Arthur is slain,   *spread rumors* and that is not so, and therefore ye will make a foul work in this land!"

"Peace, thou false priest!" said Sir Mordred, "for an thou chafe°   *anger* me any more, I shall strike off thy head."

So the Bishop departed, and did the cursing in the most orgulust°   *defiant* wise that might be done. And then Sir Mordred sought the Bishop of Canterbury for to have slain him. Then the Bishop fled, and took part of his goods with him, and went nigh unto Glastonbury. And there he was a priest-hermit in a chapel, and lived in poverty and in holy prayers; for well he understood that mischievous war was at hand.

Then Sir Mordred sought upon Queen Guinevere by letters and sonds,° and by fair means and foul means, to have her to come out of   *messengers* the Tower of London; but all this availed nought, for she answered him shortly, openly and privily,[2] that she had liefer° slay herself than   *rather* be married with him.

Then came there word unto Sir Mordred that King Arthur had araised the siege from Sir Lancelot and was coming homeward with a great host to be avenged upon Sir Mordred; wherefore Sir Mordred made write writs° unto all the barony of this land, and much people   *summonses* drew unto him. For then was the common voice among them that with King Arthur was never other life but war and strife, and with Sir Mordred was great joy and bliss. Thus was King Arthur depraved° and evil said of; and many there were that King Arthur   *disparaged* had brought up of nought, and given them lands, that might not then say him a good word.

---

2. At once, publicly and privately.

Lo ye Englishmen, see ye not what a mischief° here was? For he   *evil*
that was the most kind and noblest knight of the world, and most
loved the fellowship of noble knights, and by him they all were
upholden, and yet might not these Englishmen hold them content
with him. Lo thus was the old custom and the usages of this land,
and men say that we of this land have not yet lost that custom. Alas!
this is a great default of us Englishmen, for there may no thing us
please no term.°   *length of time*

And so fared the people at that time: they were better pleased
with Sir Mordred than they were with the noble King Arthur, and
much people drew unto Sir Mordred and said they would abide with
him for better and for worse. And so Sir Mordred drew with a great
host to Dover, for there he heard say that King Arthur would arrive,
and so he thought to beat his own father from his own lands. And
the most party of all England held with Sir Mordred, for the people
were so new-fangle.°   *fond of new things*

And so as Sir Mordred was at Dover with his host, so came King
Arthur with a great navy of ships and galleys and carracks, and there
was Sir Mordred ready awaiting upon his landing, to let° his own   *stop*
father to land° upon the land that he was king over.   *from landing*

Then there was launching of great boats and small, and full of
noble men of arms; and there was much slaughter of gentle knights,
and many a full bold baron was laid full low, on both parties. But
King Arthur was so courageous that there might no manner of
knight let him to land, and his knights fiercely followed him. And so
they landed maugre° Sir Mordred's head° and all his power, and put   *against / will*
Sir Mordred aback, that he fled and all his people.

So when this battle was done King Arthur let search his people[3]
that were hurt and dead. And then was noble Sir Gawain found in a
great boat, lying more than half dead. When King Arthur knew that
he was laid so low he went unto him and so found him. And there
the king made great sorrow out of measure, and took Sir Gawain in
his arms, and thrice he there swooned. And then when he was
waked, King Arthur said,

"Alas! Sir Gawain, my sister son, here now thou liest, the man
in the world that I loved most. And now is my joy gone! For now,
my nephew, Sir Gawain, I will discover me unto° you, that in your   *disclose*
person and in Sir Lancelot I most had my joy and my affiance.° And   *trust*
now have I lost my joy of you both, wherefore all mine earthly joy is
gone from me!"

"Ah, mine uncle," said Sir Gawain, "now I will that ye wit that
my death-days be come! And all I may wite° mine own hastiness°   *blame / rashness*
and my wilfulness, for through my wilfulness I was causer of mine
own death; for I was this day hurt and smitten upon mine old wound
that Sir Lancelot gave me, and I feel myself that I must needs be
dead by the hour of noon. And through me and my pride ye have all
this shame and disease,° for had that noble knight, Sir Lancelot,   *sorrow*

---

3. Had his people searched for.

been with you, as he was and would have been, this unhappy war had never been begun; for he, through his noble knighthood and his noble blood, held all your cankered° enemies in subjection and danger.° And now," said Sir Gawain, "ye shall miss Sir Lancelot. But alas that I would not accord° with him! And therefore, fair uncle, I pray you that I may have paper, pen and ink, that I may write unto Sir Lancelot a letter written with mine own hand." *malignant* / *control* / *make peace*

So when paper, pen and ink was brought, then Sir Gawain was set up weakly° by King Arthur, for he was shriven a little afore. And then he took his pen and wrote thus, as the French book maketh mention: *gently*

"Unto thee, Sir Lancelot, flower of all noble knights that ever I heard of or saw by my days, I, Sir Gawain, King Lot's son of Orkney, and sister's son unto the noble King Arthur, send thee greeting, letting thee to have knowledge that the tenth day of May I was smitten upon the old wound that thou gave me afore the city of Benwick, and through that wound I am come to my death-day. And I will that all the world wit that I, Sir Gawain, knight of the Table Round, sought my death, and not through thy deserving, but mine own seeking. Wherefore I beseech thee, Sir Lancelot, to return again unto this realm and see my tomb and pray some prayer more other less for my soul. And this same day that I wrote the same cedle° I was hurt to the death, which wound was first given of thine hand, Sir Lancelot; for of a more nobler man might I not be slain. *letter*

"Also, Sir Lancelot, for all the love that ever was betwixt us, make no tarrying, but come over the sea in all the goodly haste that ye may, with your noble knights, and rescue that noble king that made thee knight, for he is full straitly bestead with° a false traitor which is my half-brother, Sir Mordred. For he hath crowned himself king and would have wedded my lady, Queen Guinevere; and so had he done, had she not kept the Tower of London with strong hand. And so the tenth day of May last past my lord King Arthur and we all landed upon them at Dover, and there he put that false traitor, Sir Mordred, to flight. And so it misfortuned me to be smitten upon the stroke that ye gave me of old. *hard-pressed by*

"And the date of this letter was written but two hours and a half before my death, written with mine own hand and subscribed with part of my heart blood. And therefore I require thee, most famous knight of the world, that thou wilt see my tomb."

And then he wept and King Arthur both, and swooned. And when they were awaked both, the king made Sir Gawain to receive his sacrament, and then Sir Gawain prayed the king for to send for Sir Lancelot and to cherish him above all other knights.

And so at the hour of noon Sir Gawain yielded up the ghost. And then the king let inter him° in a chapel within Dover Castle. And there yet all men may see the skull of him, and the same wound is seen that Sir Lancelot gave in battle. *had him buried*

Then was it told the king that Sir Mordred had pight a new field upon Barham Down.[4] And so upon the morn King Arthur rode thither to him, and there was a great battle betwixt them, and much people were slain on both parties. But at the last King Arthur's party stood best, and Sir Mordred and his party fled unto Canterbury.

And there the king let search all the downs for his knights that were slain and interred them; and salved them with soft salves° that full sore were wounded. Then much people drew unto   *ointments* King Arthur, and then they said that Sir Mordred warred upon King Arthur with wrong.

And anon King Arthur drew him with his host down by the sea-side westward, toward Salisbury. And there was a day assigned betwixt King Arthur and Sir Mordred, that they should meet upon a down beside Salisbury, and not far from the seaside. And this day was assigned on Monday after Trinity Sunday, whereof King Arthur was passing glad that he might be avenged upon Sir Mordred.

Then Sir Mordred araised much people about London, for they of Kent, Sussex and Surrey, Essex, Suffolk and Norfolk held the most party with Sir Mordred. And many a full noble knight drew unto him and also to the king; but they that loved Sir Lancelot drew unto Sir Mordred.

So upon Trinity Sunday at night King Arthur dreamed a wonderful dream, and in his dream him seemed that he saw upon a chaf-flet° a chair, and the chair was fast to a wheel, and thereupon sat   *platform* King Arthur in the richest cloth of gold that might be made. And the king thought there was under him, far from him, an hideous deep black water, and therein was all manner of serpents and worms° and   *dragons* wild beasts, foul and horrible. And suddenly the king thought that the wheel turned up-so-down, and he fell among the serpents, and every beast took him by a limb. And then the king cried as he lay in his bed, "Help! help!"

And then knights, squires and yeomen awaked the king, and then he was so amazed that he wist not where he was. And then so he awaked until it was nigh day, and then he fell on slumbering again, not sleeping nor thoroughly waking. So° the king seemed ver-   *to* ily that there came Sir Gawain unto him with a number of fair ladies with him. So when King Arthur saw him he said,

"Welcome, my sister's son, I weened° ye had been dead. And   *thought* now I see thee on live, much am I beholden unto Almighty Jesu. Ah, fair nephew, what been these ladies that hither be come with you?"

"Sir," said Sir Gawain, "all these be ladies for whom I have foughten for, when I was man living. And all these are those that I did battle for in righteous quarrels, and God hath given them that grace at their great prayer, because I did battle for them for their right, that they should bring me hither unto you. Thus much hath given me leave God for to warn you of your death: for an ye fight as

4. Set up a new battleground at Barham Down (southeast of Canterbury)

to-morn with Sir Mordred, as ye both have assigned, doubt ye not ye
shall be slain, and the most party of your people on both parties.
And for the great grace and goodness that Almighty Jesu hath unto
you, and for pity of you and many more other good men there shall
be slain, God hath sent me to you of His especial grace to give you
warning that in no wise ye do battle as to-morn, but that ye take a
treatise for a month-day.[5] And proffer you largely,° so that to-morn   *generously*
ye put in a delay. For within a month shall come Sir Lancelot with
all his noble knights, and rescue you worshipfully, and slay Sir Mordred and all that ever will hold with him."

Then Sir Gawain and all the ladies vanished, and anon the king
called upon his knights, squires, and yeomen, and charged° them   *ordered*
mightily to fetch his noble lords and wise bishops unto him. And
when they were come the king told them of his avision: that Sir
Gawain had told him and warned him that an he fought on the
morn he should be slain. Then the king commanded Sir Lucan the
Butler and his brother Sir Bedivere the Bold, with two bishops with
them, and charged them in any wise to take a treatise for a month-
day with Sir Mordred:

"And spare not, proffer him lands and goods as much as you
think reasonable."

So then they departed and came to Sir Mordred where he had
a grim° host of an hundred thousand. And there they entreated   *fierce*
Sir Mordred long time, and at the last Sir Mordred was agreed for
to have Cornwall and Kent by° King Arthur's days;° and after   *during / lifetime*
that all England, after the days of King Arthur. Then were they
condescended° that King Arthur and Sir Mordred should meet   *agreed*
betwixt both their hosts, and every each of them should bring
fourteen persons. And so they came with this word unto Arthur.
Then said he,

"I am glad that this is done," and so he went into the field.

And when King Arthur should depart he warned all his host
that an they see any sword drawn, "look ye come on fiercely and slay
that traitor, Sir Mordred, for I in no wise trust him." In like wise Sir
Mordred warned his host that "an ye see any manner of sword drawn
look that ye come on fiercely and so slay all that ever before you
standeth, for in no wise I will not trust for this treatise." And in the
same wise said Sir Mordred unto his host: "for I know well my father
will be avenged upon me."

And so they met as their pointment was, and were agreed and
accorded thoroughly. And wine was fette,° and they drank together.   *fetched*
Right so came out an adder of a little heath-bush, and it stang a
knight in the foot. And so when the knight felt him so stung, he
looked down and saw the adder; and anon he drew his sword to slay
the adder, and thought none other harm. And when the host on
both parties saw that sword drawn, then they blew beams,° trumpets,   *bugles*

5. Make a compact for a month from today.

and horns, and shouted grimly, and so both hosts dressed them
together.° And King Arthur took his horse and said, "Alas, this   *confronted each*
unhappy day!" And so rode to his party, and Sir Mordred in like wise.   *other*

And never since was there seen a more dolefuller battle in no
Christian land, for there was but rushing and riding, foining° and   *thrusting*
striking, and many a grim word was there spoken of either to other,
and many a deadly stroke. But ever King Arthur rode throughout the
battle° of Sir Mordred many times and did full nobly, as a noble king   *battle formation*
should do, and at all times he fainted never. And Sir Mordred did his
devour° that day and put himself in great peril.   *utmost effort*

And thus they fought all the long day, and never stinted° till   *ceased*
the noble knights were laid to the cold earth. And ever they fought
still till it was near night, and by then was there an hundred thou-
sand laid dead upon the earth. Then was King Arthur wood wroth°   *wild with rage*
out of measure, when he saw his people so slain from him.

And so he looked about him and could see no mo° of all his   *more*
host, and good knights left no mo on live but two knights: the tone°   *one*
was Sir Lucan de Butler and his brother, Sir Bedivere; and yet they
were full sore wounded.

"Jesu mercy!" said the king, "where are all my noble knights
become? Alas, that ever I should see this doleful day! For now," said
King Arthur, "I am come to mine end. But would to God," said he,
"that I wist now where were that traitor Sir Mordred that hath
caused all this mischief."°   *evil*

Then King Arthur looked about and was ware where stood Sir
Mordred leaning upon his sword among a great heap of dead men.

"Now, give me my spear," said King Arthur unto Sir Lucan, "for
yonder I have espied the traitor that all this woe hath wrought."

"Sir, let him be," said Sir Lucan, "for he is unhappy.° And if ye   *unlucky*
pass this unhappy day ye shall be right well revenged. And, good
lord, remember ye of your night's dream and what the spirit of Sir
Gawain told you to-night, and yet God of His great goodness hath
preserved you hitherto. And for God's sake, my lord, leave off this,
for, blessed be God, ye have won the field: for yet we been here three
on live, and with Sir Mordred is not one of live. And therefore if ye
leave off now, this wicked day of Destiny is past!"

"Now tide° me death, tide me life," said the king, "now I see   *befall*
him yonder alone, he shall never escape mine hands! For at a better
avail° shall I never have him."   *advantage*

"God speed you well!" said Sir Bedivere.

Then the king gat his spear in both his hands, and ran toward
Sir Mordred, crying and saying,

"Traitor, now is thy death-day come!"

And when Sir Mordred saw King Arthur he ran until° him   *toward*
with his sword drawn in his hand, and there King Arthur smote Sir
Mordred under the shield with a foin° of his spear throughout the   *thrust*
body more than a fathom. And when Sir Mordred felt that he had
his death wound he thrust himself with the might that he had up

to the burr° of King Arthur's spear, and right so he smote his   *hand guard*
father, King Arthur, with his sword holding in both his hands,
upon the side of the head, that the sword pierced the helmet and
the tay° of the brain. And therewith Mordred dashed down stark   *lining*
dead to the earth.

And noble King Arthur fell in a swough to the earth, and there
he swooned oftentimes, and Sir Lucan and Sir Bedivere oftentimes
hove° him up. And so weakly° betwixt them they led him to a little   *lifted / gently*
chapel not far from the sea, and when the king was there, him
thought him reasonably eased.

Then heard they people cry in the field.

"Now go thou, Sir Lucan," said the king, "and do me to wit°   *let me know*
what betokens that noise in the field."

So Sir Lucan departed, for he was grievously wounded in many
places; and so as he rode he saw and harkened by the moonlight how
that pillers° and robbers were come into the field to pille and to rob *plunderers*
many a full noble knight of brooches and bees° and of many a good   *bracelets*
ring and many a rich jewel. And who that were not dead all out,
there they slew them for their harness° and their riches.   *armor*

When Sir Lucan understood his work he came to the king as
soon as he might, and told him all what he had heard and seen.

"Therefore by my rede,"° said Sir Lucan, "it is best that we bring   *advice*
you to some town."

"I would it were so," said the king, "but I may not stand, my
head works° so. . . . Ah, Sir Lancelot!" said King Arthur, "this day   *aches*
have I sore missed thee! And alas, that ever I was against thee! For
now have I my death, whereof Sir Gawain me warned in my dream."

Then Sir Lucan took up the king the tone party° and Sir Bedi-   *on one side*
vere the other party, and in the lifting up the king swooned, and in
the lifting Sir Lucan fell in a swoon, that part of his guts fell out of
his body; and therewith the noble knight his heart brast. And when
the king awoke he beheld Sir Lucan, how he lay foaming at the
mouth and part of his guts lay at his feet.

"Alas," said the king, "this is to me a full heavy sight, to see this
noble duke so die for my sake, for he would have holpen° me that   *helped*
had more need of help than I! Alas, that he would not complain
him, for his heart was so set to help me. Now Jesu have mercy upon
his soul!"

Then Sir Bedivere wept for the death of his brother.

"Now leave this mourning and weeping, gentle knight," said the
king, "for all this will not avail° me. For wit thou well an I might live *aid*
myself, the death of Sir Lucan would grieve me evermore. But my
time passeth on fast," said the king. "Therefore," said King Arthur
unto Sir Bedivere, "take thou here Excalibur, my good sword, and go
with it to yonder water's side; and when thou comest there, I charge
thee throw my sword in that water, and come again and tell me what
thou seest there."

"My lord," said Sir Bedivere, "your commandment shall be
done, and lightly° bring you word again."   *I will quickly*

So Sir Bedivere departed. And by the way he beheld that noble sword, and the pomell° and the haft° was all precious stones. And then he said to himself, "If I throw this rich sword in the water, thereof shall never come good, but harm and loss." And then Sir Bedivere hid Excalibur under a tree, and so soon as he might he came again unto the king and said he had been at the water and thrown the sword into the water.

hand guard / handle

"What saw thou there?" said the king.

"Sir," he said, "I saw nothing but waves and winds."

"That is untruly said of thee," said the king. "And therefore go thou lightly again, and do my commandment as thou art to me lief° and dear: spare not but throw it in."

beloved

Then Sir Bedivere returned again and took the sword in his hand; and yet him thought sin and shame to throw away that noble sword. And so eft° he hid the sword and returned again and told the king that he had been at the water and done his commandment.

again

"What sawest thou there?" said the king.

"Sir," he said, "I saw nothing but waters wap° and waves wan."°

lapping / dark

"Ah, traitor unto me and untrue," said King Arthur, "now hast thou betrayed me twice! Who would ween° that thou who has been to me so lief and dear, and also named so noble a knight, that thou would betray me for the riches of this sword? But now go again lightly; for thy long tarrying putteth me in great jeopardy of my life, for I have taken cold. And but if° thou do now as I bid thee, if ever I may see thee, I shall slay thee mine own hands, for thou wouldest for my rich sword see me dead."

believe

unless

Then Sir Bedivere departed and went to the sword and lightly took it up, and so he went unto the water's side. And there he bound the girdle about the hilt, and threw the sword as far into the water as he might. And there came an arm and an hand above the water, and took it and cleight° it, and shook it thrice and brandished, and then vanished with the sword into the water.

clutched

So Sir Bedivere came again to the king and told him what he saw.

"Alas!" said the king, "help me hence, for I dread me I have tarried over long."

Then Sir Bedivere took the king upon his back and so went with him to the water's side. And when they were there, even fast by° the bank hoved° a little barge with many fair ladies in it, and among them all was a queen, and all they had black hoods. And all they wept and shrieked when they saw King Arthur.

next to / floated

"Now put me into that barge," said the king.

And so he did softly, and there received him three ladies with great mourning. And so they set him down, and in one of their laps King Arthur laid his head. And then the queen said,

"Ah, my dear brother!⁶ Why have you tarried so long from me? Alas, this wound on your head hath caught overmuch cold!"

---

6. The queen is thus revealed as Morgan le Fay, in whose story magical healing powers mixed with inveterate hostility to Guinevere and sometimes to Arthur himself.

And anon they rowed fromward° the land, and Sir Bedivere   *away from*
beheld all those ladies go fromward him. Then Sir Bedivere cried
and said,

"Ah, my lord Arthur, what shall become of me, now ye go from
me and leave me here alone among mine enemies?"

"Comfort thyself," said the king, "and do as well as thou mayst,
for in me is no trust for to trust in. For I must into the vale of Avalon
to heal me of my grievous wound. And if thou hear nevermore of
me, pray for my soul!"

But ever the queen and ladies wept and shrieked, that it was
pity to hear. And as soon as Sir Bedivere had lost sight of the
barge he wept and wailed, and so took° the forest and went all   *went into*
that night.

And in the morning he was ware, betwixt two holts hoar°, of a   *gray woods*
chapel and an hermitage. Then was Sir Bedivere fain°, and thither   *glad*
he went, and when he came into the chapel he saw where lay an
hermit grovelling° on all fours, fast thereby a tomb was new   *face down*
graven.° When the hermit saw Sir Bedivere he knew him well, for   *freshly dug*
he was but little tofore Bishop of Canterbury, that Sir Mordred
fleamed.°   *put to flight*

"Sir," said Sir Bedivere, "what man is there here interred that
you pray so fast° for?"   *intently*

"Fair son," said the hermit, "I wot not verily but by deeming.°   *guessing*
But this same night, at midnight, here came a number of ladies and
brought here a dead corse and prayed me to inter him. And here
they offered an hundred tapers, and gave me a thousand besants."°   *gold coins*

"Alas," said Sir Bedivere, "that was my lord King Arthur, which
lieth here graven° in this chapel."   *buried*

Then Sir Bedivere swooned, and when he awoke he prayed the
hermit that he might abide with him still, there to live with fasting
and prayers:

"For from hence will I never go," said Sir Bedivere, "by my will,
but all the days of my life here to pray for my lord Arthur."

"Sir, ye are welcome to me," said the hermit, "for I know you
better than ye ween that I do: for ye are Sir Bedivere the Bold, and
the full noble duke Sir Lucan de Butler was your brother."

Then Sir Bedivere told the hermit all as you have heard tofore,
and so he beleft° with the hermit that was beforehand Bishop of   *remained*
Canterbury. And there Sir Bedivere put upon him poor clothes, and
served the hermit full lowly in fasting and in prayers.

Thus of Arthur I find no more written in books that been
authorised, neither more of the very certainty of his death heard I
never read, but thus was he led away in a ship wherein were three
queens; that one was King Arthur's sister, Queen Morgan le Fay, the
tother was the Queen of North Galis, and the third was the Queen
of the Waste Lands.

Now more of the death of King Arthur could I never find, but
that these ladies brought him to his grave, and such one was interred
there which the hermit bare witness that sometime° Bishop of Can-   *was once*

terbury. But yet the hermit knew not in certain that he was verily
the body of King Arthur; for this tale Sir Bedivere, a knight of the
Table Round, made it to be written.

Yet some men say in many parts of England that King Arthur is
not dead, but had° by the will of our Lord Jesu into another place;   *was carried*
and men say that he shall come again, and he shall win the Holy
Cross. Yet I will not say that it shall be so, but rather I would say:
here in this world he changed his life. And many men say that there
is written upon the tomb this:

HIC IACET ARTHURUS REX QUONDAM REXQUE FUTURUS[7]

And thus leave I here Sir Bedivere with the hermit that
dwelled that time in a chapel beside Glastonbury, and there was his
hermitage. And so they lived in prayers and fastings and great
abstinence.

And when Queen Guinevere understood that King Arthur was
dead and all the noble knights, Sir Mordred and all the remnant,
then she stole away with five ladies with her, and so she went to
Amesbury. And there she let make herself° a nun, and weared white   *became*
clothes and black, and great penance she took upon her, as ever did
sinful woman in this land. And never creature could make her merry, but ever she lived in fasting, prayers and alms-deeds, that all
manner of people marvelled how virtuously she was changed.

━━◄❈►━━

Geoffrey Chaucer
c. 1340–1400

On Easter weekend 1300, the Italian poet Dante Alighieri had a vision in which he descended
to hell, climbed painfully through purgatory, and then attained a transcendent experience of
paradise. He tells his tale in his visionary, passionately judgmental *Divine Comedy*. One hundred years later, on 25 October 1400, Geoffrey Chaucer—the least judgmental of poets—died
quietly in his house at the outskirts of London. By a nice accident of history, these two great
writers bracket the last great century of the Middle Ages.

Of Chaucer's own life our information is abundant but often frustrating. Many documents
record the important and sensitive posts he held in government, but there are only faint hints of
his career as a poet. During his lifetime, he was frequently in France and made at least two trips
to Italy, which proved crucial for his own growth as a writer and indeed for the history of English
literature. He also served under three kings: the aging Edward III, his brilliant and sometimes
tyrannical grandson Richard II, and—at the very end of his life—Richard's usurper Henry IV.

Chaucer was born into a rising mercantile family, part of the growing bourgeois class that
brought so much wealth to England even while it disrupted medieval theories of social order.
Chaucer's family fit nowhere easily in the old model of the three estates: those who pray (the
clergy), those who fight (the aristocracy), and those who work the land (the peasants). Yet like
many of their class, they aspired to a role among the aristocracy, and in fact Chaucer's parents
succeeded in holding minor court positions. Chaucer himself became a major player in the

---

7. Here lies Arthur, once and future king.

cultural and bureaucratic life of the court, and Thomas Chaucer (who was very probably his son) was ultimately knighted.

Geoffrey was superbly but typically educated. He probably went to one of London's fine grammar schools, and as a young man he very likely followed a gentlemanly study of law at one of the Inns of Court. He shows signs of knowing and appreciating the topics debated in the university life of his time. His poems reflect a vast reading in classical Latin, French, and Italian (of which he was among the earliest English readers). *The Parliament of Fowls*, for instance, reveals the influence not only of French court poetry but also of Dante's *Divine Comedy*; and the frame-story structure of *The Canterbury Tales* may have been inspired by Boccaccio's *Decameron*.

By 1366 Chaucer had married Philippa de Roet, a minor Flemish noblewoman, and a considerable step up the social hierarchy. Her sister later became the mistress and ultimately the wife of Chaucer's great patron, John of Gaunt. Thus, when Gaunt's son Henry Boling-broke seized the throne from Richard II, the elderly Geoffrey Chaucer found himself a distant in-law of his king. Chaucer had been associated with Richard II and suffered reverses when Richard's power was restricted by the magnates. But he was enough of a cultural figure that Henry IV continued (perhaps with some prompting) the old man's royal annuities. Whatever Western literature owes to Chaucer (and its debts are profound), in his own life his writing made a place in the world for him and his heirs.

Despite his lifelong productivity as a writer, and despite the slightly obtuse narrative voice he consistently uses, Geoffrey Chaucer was a canny and ambitious player in the world of his time. He was a soldier, courtier, diplomat, and government official in a wide range of jobs. These included controller of the customs on wool and other animal products, a lucrative post, and later controller of the Petty Custom that taxed wine and other goods. Chaucer's frequent work overseas extended his contacts with French and Italian literature. He was ward of estates for several minors, a job that also benefited the guardian. Chaucer began to accumulate prop-erty in Kent, where he served as justice of the peace (an important judicial post) and then Member of Parliament in the mid-1380s.

Despite the comfortable worldly progress suggested by such activities, these were troubled years in the nation and in Chaucer's private life. Chaucer's personal fortunes were affected by the frequent struggles between King Richard and his magnates over control of the govern-ment. From another direction there exploded The Rising of 1381 (see pages 454–66), rocking all of English society. The year before that, Chaucer had been accused of *raptus* by Cecilia Champaigne, daughter of a baker in London. A great deal of nervous scholarship has been exercised over this case, but it becomes increasingly clear that in legal language *raptus* meant some form of rape. The case was settled, and there are signs of efforts to hush it up at quite high levels of government. The somewhat bland and bumbling quality of Chaucer's narrative per-sona would probably have seemed more artificially constructed and more ironic to Chaucer's contemporaries than it does at first glance today.

Chaucer was a Janus-faced poet, truly innovative at the levels of language and theme yet deeply involved with literary and intellectual styles that stretched back to Latin antiquity and twelfth- and thirteenth-century France. His early poems—the dream visions such as *The Parlia-ment of Fowls* and the tragic romance *Troilus and Criseyde*—derive from essentially medieval genres and continental traditions: the French poets Deschamps and Machaut and the Italians Dante, Boccaccio, and Petrarch. Yet in his reliance on the English vernacular, Chaucer was in a vanguard generation along with the *Gawain* poet and William Langland. English was indeed gain-ing importance in other parts of this world, such as in Parliament, some areas of education, and in the "Wycliffite" translations of the Bible. Chaucer's own exclusive use of English was particularly ambitious, though, for a poet whose patronage came from the court of the francophile Richard II.

The major work of Chaucer's maturity, *The Canterbury Tales*, founds an indisputably Eng-lish tradition. While he still uses the craft and allusions he learned from his continental mas-ters, he also experiments with the subject matter of everyday English life and the vocabularies

Portrait of Geoffrey the Canterbury Pilgrim, from the Ellesmere manuscript of *The Canterbury Tales,* early 15th century. This carefully produced and beautifully decorated manuscript reflects the speed with which Chaucer's works took on wide cultural prestige and were enshrined in luxury books for a wealthy, probably aristocratic audience.

of the newly valorized English vernacular. Moreover, starting with traditional forms and largely traditional models of society and the cosmos, Chaucer found spaces for new and sometimes disruptive perspectives, especially those of women and the rising mercantile class into which he had been born. Though always a court poet, Chaucer increasingly wrote in ways that reflected both the richness and the uncertainties of his entire social world. The *Tales* include a Knight who could have stepped from a twelfth-century heroic poem; yet they also offer the spectacle of the Knight's caste being aped, almost parodied, and virtually shouted down by a sword-carrying peasant, the Miller. And the entire notion of old writings as sources of authoritative wisdom is powerfully challenged by the illiterate or only minimally literate Wife of Bath.

The *Canterbury Tales* also differ from the work of many of Chaucer's continental predecessors in their deep hesitation to cast straightforward judgment, either socially or spiritually. Here we may return to Chaucer's connection with Dante. His *Divine Comedy* presented mortal life as a pilgrimage and an overt test in stable dogma, a journey along a dangerous road toward certain damnation or the reward of the heavenly Jerusalem. The *Canterbury Tales* are literally about a pilgrimage, and Chaucer presents the road as beautiful and fascinating in its own right. The greatness of the poem lies in its exploration of the variousness of the journey and that journey's reflection of a world pressured by spiritual and moral fractures. In depicting a mixed company of English men and women traveling England's most famous pilgrimage route and telling one another stories, Chaucer suggests not only the spiritual meaning of humankind's earthly pilgrimage, but also its overflowing beauties and attractions as well as the evils and temptations that lie along the way. The vision of the serious future, the day of judgment, is constantly attended in *The Canterbury Tales* by the troubling yet hilarious and distracting present.

Unlike Dante, however, Chaucer almost never takes it upon himself to judge, at least not openly. He records his characters with dizzying immediacy, but he never tells his reader quite what to think of them, leaving the gaps for us as readers to fill. He does end the *Tales* with a kind of sermon, the Parson's long prose treatise on the Christian vices and virtues. That coda by no means erases the humor and seriousness, sentiment and ribaldry, high spiritual love and unmasked carnal desire, profound religious belief and squalid clerical corruption that have been encountered along the way. Indeed, Chaucer's genius is to transmute the disorder of his world almost into an aesthetic of plenitude: "foyson" in Middle English. His poem overflows constantly with rich detail, from exquisite visions to squabbling pilgrims. His language overflows with its multiple vocabularies, Anglo-Saxon, Latin, and French. And finally, the tales themselves are notable for the range of genres used by the pilgrims: the Miller's bawdy fabliau, the Wife of Bath's romance, the Franklin's story of courtly love and clerkly magic, the Nun's Priest's beast fable, the Pardoner's hypocritical cautionary tale, as well as the Parson's sermon. *The Canterbury Tales* are an anthology embracing almost every important literary type of Chaucer's day.

None of this celebratory richness, however, fully masks the unresolved social and spiritual tensions that underlie the *Tales*. The notion of spiritual pilgrimage is deeply challenged by the very density of characterization and worldly detail that so enlivens the work. And the model of a competitive game, which provides the fictional pretext for the tales themselves, is only one version of what the critic Peggy Knapp has called Chaucer's "social contest" in the work as a whole. The traditional estates such as knight and peasant openly clash during the pilgrimage, and the estate of the clergy is more widely represented by its corrupt than by its virtuous members. Women, merchants, common landowners, and others from outside the traditional three estates bulk large in the tales. And their stories cast doubt upon such fundamental religious institutions as penance and such social institutions as marriage. For all their pleasures, *The Canterbury Tales* have survived, in part, because they are so riven by challenge and doubt.

Chaucer's Middle English

Grammar

The English of Chaucer's London, and particularly the English of government bureaucracy, became the source for the more standardized vernacular that emerged in the era of print at the close of the Middle Ages. As a result, Chaucer's English is easier to understand today than the dialect of many of his great contemporaries such as the *Gawain* poet, who worked far to the north. The text that follows preserves Chaucer's language, with some spellings slightly modernized and regularized by its editor, E. Talbot Donaldson.

The marginal glosses in the readings are intended to help the nonspecialist reader through Chaucer's language without elaborate prior study. It will be helpful, though, to explain a few key differences from Modern English.

Nouns: The possessive is sometimes formed without a final *-s*.

Pronouns: Readers will recognize the archaic *thou, thine, thee* of second-person singular, and *ye* of the plural. Occasional confusion can arise from the form *hir*, which can mean "her" or "their." *Hem* is Chaucer's spelling for "them," and *tho* for "those." Chaucer uses *who* to mean "whoever."

Adverbs: Formed, as today, with *-ly*, but also with *-liche*. Sometimes an adverb is unchanged from its adjective form: *fairly, fairliche, faire* can all be adverbs.

Verbs: Second-person singular is formed with *-est* (*thou lovest*, past tense *thou lovedest*); third-person singular often with *-eth* (*he loveth*); plurals often with *-n* (*we loven*); and infinitive with *-n* (*loven*).

Strong verbs/impersonal verbs: Middle English has many "strong verbs," which form the past and perfect by changing a vowel in their stem; these are usually recognizable by analogy with surviving forms in Modern English (*go, went, gone; sing, sang, sung;* etc.). Middle English also often uses "impersonal verbs" (*liketh,* "it pleases"; *as me thinketh,* "as I think"), in which case sometimes no obvious subject noun or pronoun occurs.

Pronunciation

A few guidelines will help approximate the sound of Chaucer's English and the richness of his versification. For fuller discussion, consult sources listed in the bibliography.

Pronounce all consonants: *knight* is "k/neecht" with a guttural *ch,* not "nite"; *gnaw* is "g/naw." Middle English consonants preserve many of the sounds of the language's Germanic roots: guttural *gh;* sounded *l* and *w* in words like *folk* or *write.* (Exceptions occur in some words that derive from French, like *honour* whose *h* is silent.)

Final *-e* was sounded in early Middle English. Such pronunciation was becoming archaic by Chaucer's time, but was available to aid meter in the stylized context of poetry.

The distinction between short and long vowels was greater in Middle English than today. Middle English short vowels have mostly remained short in Modern English, with some shift in pronunciation: short *a* sounds like the *o* in *hot,* short *o* like a quick version of the *aw* in *law,* short *u* like the *u* in *full.*

Long vowels in Middle English (here usually indicated by doubling, when vowel length is unclear by analogy to modern spelling) are close to long vowels in modern Romance languages. The chart shows some differences in Middle English long vowels.

Middle English	pronounced as in	Modern English
a (as in *name*)		*father*
open *e* (*deel*)		*swear, bread*
close *e* (*sweet*)		*fame*
i (*whit*)		*feet*
open *o* (*holy*)		*law*
close *o* (*roote*)		*note*
u (as in *town, aboute*)		*root*
u (*vertu*)		*few*

Open and close long vowels are a challenge for modern readers. Generally, open long *e* in Middle English (*deel*) has become Modern English spelling with *ea* (*deal*); close long *e* (*sweet*) has become Modern English spelling with *ee* (*sweet*). Open long *o* in Middle English has come to be pronounced as in *note;* close long *o* in Middle English has come to be pronounced *root.* This latter case illustrates the idea of "vowel shift" across the centuries, in which some long vowels have moved forward in the throat and palate.

Versification

All of Chaucer's poetry presented here is in a loosely iambic pentameter line, which Chaucer was greatly responsible for bringing into prominence in England. He is a fluid versifier, though, and often shifts stress, producing metrical effects that have come to be called trochees and spondees. Final *-e* is often pronounced within lines to provide an unstressed syllable and is typically pronounced at the end of each line. Yet final *-e* may also elide with a following word that begins with a vowel. The following lines from *The Nun's Priest's Tale* have a proposed scansion, but the reader will see that alternate scansions are possible at several places.

"Avoi," quod she, "fy on you, hertelees!
Allas," quod she, "for by that God above,
Now han ye lost myn herte and al my love!
I can nat love a coward, by my faith.
For certes, what so any womman saith,
We alle desiren, if it mighte be,
To han housbondes hardy, wise, and free,
And secree, and no nigard, ne no fool,
Ne him that is agast of every tool,
Ne noon avauntour. By that God above,
How dorste ye sayn for shame unto youre love
That any thing mighte make you aferd?
Have ye no mannes herte and han a beerd?

THE PARLIAMENT OF FOWLS   *The Parliament of Fowls* initially seems to be a rather conventional poem of dream and courtly love. Yet it swiftly draws into play a surprising exploration of cosmic harmony and social order, and then a delightful critique of aristocratic courtliness in the voice of other classes. This multiplication of challenging perspectives is especially daring in a poem that may well have at its core a sophisticated allegory of Richard II's negotiations to wed Anne of Bohemia, in which (like Chaucer's tercel eagle) he faced vocal competitors. Certainly Chaucer employs and may have helped initiate the courtly convention of love play and love poems on Saint Valentine's day. For all its nerve and range, the *Parliament* (written in the late 1370s or early 1380s) is the work of a court poet, attentive to his patrons and audience.

Chaucer extends a pattern he had established in earlier dream-vision poems, in which the worlds of books, dreams, and experience interpenetrate and question one another. The narrator is presented as a feckless, unsuccessful lover who hesitates before tough choices. (His dream guide finally has to shove him into the garden.) He reads Cicero's famed survey of social order and the cosmos, *The Dream of Scipio*, then falls into a dream of his own that seems to derive instead from the literary conventions of the enclosed garden of love. The worlds of book and dream are surrounded by the narrator's own limited waking experience, and the garden of the dream erupts, in the parliament of birds, into a class-specific debate about love and procreation. In this, Chaucer's audience would have recognized echoes of the divisive English Parliaments of their own time.

The convention of dream vision in an enclosed garden draws upon French love poetry of the thirteenth and fourteenth centuries. Equally, the summary of Cicero's *Dream*, as well as the poem's broader reference to number and harmony, engage a tradition of cosmological and natural speculation important in late antiquity and the twelfth century. This includes texts like Alan of Lille's *Complaint of Nature* (specifically mentioned in the poem) and numerous commentaries on *The Dream of Scipio* itself, beginning with that by Macrobius. One way the poem reflects these neoplatonic concerns is its elaborate numerical structure. Cosmic symbolism linked the number seven to the created world and ten to the divine. The poem is written in "rime royal" (seven-line stanzas rhyming ABABBCC) and totals 699 or 700 lines and 100 or 101 stanzas, depending on how the closing roundel is presented. At a more local level, the seven chapters of *The Dream of Scipio* are summarized in seven stanzas; and the nine spheres and their harmony are first mentioned in stanza nine. The platonic notion of creation as an expression of divine love and plenitude emerges in the poem's exuberant catalogs of trees and birds.

Together these elements lead the narrator through multiple versions of love. The poem's numerological structure encloses a dream that includes, on the one hand, the erotic servitude and superheated frustration of Venus's temple, and on the other hand the eagerly fecund birds gathered to mate on the goddess Nature's hill. Yet these persistently mix, too, as early as the double message of the garden gate and as late as the courtly debate of the tercel eagles. Both versions of desire occupy the same garden.

In the parliament of birds the poem fully breaks out of its inherited conventions. While love debates often focus on an arcane issue of love-service, the *"demande d'amours,"* Chaucer's birds move swiftly past such gestures, even parodying them. These birds mimic a range of human social classes; and even while Chaucer allows his reader space to condescend to lower classes (like the worm-fowl), their perspectives also result in a lively critique of courtly love. The parliament also raises wider, more immediate issues of social order, public good, and simple propagation of the species.

Each order of birds chooses a spokesman, and each speaker is wonderfully characterized, as seen in the slightly fussy traditionalism of the tercel eagles, the dismissive tone of the duck, and the cuckoo's indifference to the rest so long as he gets his own mate. Yet the *Parliament* finally returns, by now from a far different angle, to the issues of social harmony and "commune profit" raised in the opening cosmological journey. The notions of a circular cosmos whose concentric spheres generate a musical harmony returns, too, in the form of the lyric roundel that closes the poem.

The Parliament of Fowls

	The lif so short, the craft° so long to lerne,	*skill*
	Th'assay° so sharp, so hard the conqueringe,	*attempt*
	The dredful joye alway that slit° so yerne,°	*slides away / quickly*
	Al this mene I by Love, that my feelinge	
5	Astonieth[1] with his wonderful werkinge	
	So sore, ywis,° that whan I on him thinke,	*certainly*
	Nat woot° I wel wher° that I flete° or sinke.	*know / whether / float*
	For al be that I knowe nat Love in deede,	
	Ne woot how that he quiteth° folk hir hire,°	*repays / their wages*
10	Yit happeth me ful ofte in bookes rede	
	Of his miracles and his cruel ire;	
	That rede I wel, he wol be lord and sire:	
	I dar nat sayn—his strokes been so sore°—	*painful*
	But° "God save swich° a lord!"—I saye namore.	*except / such*
15	Of usage, what for lust and what for lore,[2]	
	On bookes rede I ofte, as I you tolde;	
	But wherfore° that I speke al this: nat yore°	*why / long*
	Agoon it happed me for to biholde	
	Upon a book, was write with lettres olde;	
20	And therupon, a certain thing to lerne,	
	The longe day ful faste I redde and yerne.°	*eagerly*
	For out of olde feeldes, as men saith,	
	Cometh al this newe corn from yeer to yere;	
	And out of olde bookes, in good faith,	
25	Cometh al this newe science that men lere.°	*learn*
	But now to purpos as of this matere:	
	To rede forth so gan me to delite	
	That al that day me thoughte but a lite.°	*little while*

---

1. Turns to stone, is astonished.

2. By habit, both for pleasure and for learning.

This book of which I make of mencioun
30 Entitled was al thus, as I shal telle:
"Tullius of the Dreem of Scipioun."[3]
Chapitres sevene it hadde, of hevene and helle
And erthe, and soules that therinne dwelle;
Of which as shortly as I can it trete,
35 Of his sentence° I wol you sayn the grete:°   *meaning / major part*

First telleth it when Scipion was come
In Affrike, how he meeteth Massinisse,[4]
That him for joye in armes hath ynome,[5]
Thanne telleth he[6] hir speeche, and of the blisse
40 That was bitwixe hem til that day gan misse;°   *disappeared*
And how his auncestre Affrican[7] so dere
Gan in his sleep that night to him appere.

Thanne telleth it that from a sterry° place   *starry*
How Affrican hath him Cartage shewed
45 And warned him biforn of al his grace,°   *destiny*
And saide what man, lered other lewed,°   *learned or unlearned*
That loved commune profit,° wel ythewed,[8]   *public good*
He sholde into a blisful place wende,°   *go*
Ther as joye is° that last withouten ende.   *where there is joy*

50 Thanne axed he if folk that now been dede
Han lif and dwelling in another place;
And Affrican saide, "Ye, withouten drede,°   *doubt*
And that oure present worldes lives space
Nis but a manere deeth, what way we trace.[9]
55 And rightful folk shul goon after they die
To hevene"; and shewed him the Galaxye.

Thanne shewed he him the litel erthe that here is,
At regard of° the hevenes quantitee;   *in comparison to*
And after shewed he him the nine speres;[1]
60 And after that the melodye herde he
That cometh of thilke° speres thries three,   *such*
That welle° is of musik and melodye   *source*
In this world here, and cause of armonye.°   *harmony*

Thanne bad he him, sin erthe was so lite,°   *small*
65 And deceivable,° and ful of harde grace,   *deceiving*
That he ne sholde him in the world delite.
Thanne tolde he him in certain yeres space
That every sterre sholde come into his place,
Ther it was first, and al sholde out of minde
70 That in this world is doon of al mankinde.

---

3. Marcus Tullius Cicero's *Dream of Scipio.*
4. Masinissa, King of Numidia.
5. Took him in his arms, embraced him.
6. Cicero, in the book.
7. Scipio's ancestor, Scipio Africanus, who fought against Hannibal in the Punic Wars.

8. Endowed with good qualities.
9. And that the length of our life in the present world / Is just a type of death, whatever path we take.
1. The seven planets, the sun, and the moon, thought to generate music through their revolutions around the earth.

Thanne prayed him Scipion to telle him al
The way to come into that hevene blisse;
And he saide, "Know thyself first immortal,
And looke ay bisily thou werke and wisse°   *instruct*
75   To commune profit, and thou shalt nat misse
To comen swiftly to this place dere,
That ful of blisse is, and of soules clere.°   *pure*

"But brekeres of the lawe, sooth° to sayne,   *truth*
And likerous° folk, after that they been dede   *lecherous*
80   Shul whirle aboute th'erthe alway in paine,
Til many a world be passed, out of drede,
And that° foryiven is hir wikked deede: *until*
Thanne shal they comen into this blisful place,
To which to comen, God sende thee his grace."

85   The day gan folwen° and the derke night,   *to follow*
That reveth° beestes from hir bisinesse,   *steals*
Birafte me my book for lak of light,
And to my bed I gan me for to dresse,
Fulfild of thought and bisy hevinesse:
90   For bothe I hadde thing which that I nolde,°   *did not want*
And eek I ne hadde that thing that I wolde.

But finally my spirit at the laste,
Forwery° of my labour al the day,   *exhausted*
Took reste, that made me to sleepe faste;
95   And in my sleep I mette,° as that I lay,   *dreamed*
How Affrican, right in the same array
That Scipion him saw bifore that tide,°   *time*
Was come, and stood right at my beddes side.

The wery hunter, sleeping in his bed,
100 To wode ayain his minde gooth anoon;
The juge dremeth how his plees been sped;
The cartere dremeth how his carte is goon;
The riche, of gold; the knight fight with his foon;°   *foes*
The sike met he drinketh of the tonne;°   *cask*
105 The lovere met he hath his lady wonne.

Can I nat sayn if that the cause were
For I hadde red of Affrican biforn,
That made me to mete that he stood there:
But thus saide he: "Thou hast thee so wel born
110 In looking of myn olde book totorn,°   *tattered*
Of which Macrobie roughte° nat a lite,   *reckoned*
That somdeel° of thy labour wolde I quite."°   *somewhat / repay*

Cytherea,° thou blisful lady sweete,   *Venus*
That with thy firbrand dauntest° whom thee lest,°   *subdue / it pleases*
115 And madest me this swevene° for to mete,   *dream*
Be thou myn help in this, for thou maist best;
As wisly° as I sawgh thee north-north-west   *certainly*
Whan I bigan my swevene for to write,
So yif° me might to ryme and eek t'endite.   *give*

120	This forsaide Affrican me hente° anoon,	seized
	And forth with him unto a gate broughte,	
	Right of a park walled with greene stoon,	
	And over the gates with lettres large ywroughte°	worked
	Ther were vers ywriten, as me thoughte,	
125	On either side, of ful greet difference,	
	Of which I shal now sayn the plein sentence:	

	"Thurgh me men goon into that blisful place	
	Of hertes hele° and deedly woundes cure;	health
	Thurgh me men goon unto the welle of grace,	
130	Ther greene and lusty May shal evere endure:	
	This is the way to al good aventure;	
	Be glad, thou redere, and thy sorwe of-caste;°	cast off
	Al open am I: passe in, and speed thee faste."	

	"Thurgh me men goon," thanne spak that other side,	
135	"Unto the mortal strokes of the spere	
	Of which Desdain and Daunger° is the gide,	Haughtiness
	That nevere yit° shal fruit ne leves bere;°	yet / nor leaves bear
	This streem you ledeth to the sorweful were°	net
	Ther as° the fissh in prison is al drye:	where
140	Th'eschewing° is only the remedye."	avoiding

	Thise vers of gold and blak ywriten were,	
	Of whiche I gan astonied to biholde,	
	Forwhy° that oon encreesed ay my fere,°	because / fear
	And with that other gan myn herte bolde.	
145	That oon me hette,° that other dide me colde:	heated me up
	No wit hadde I, for errour, for to chese°	choose
	To entre or fleen, or me to save or lese.°	lose

	Right as bitwixen adamantes° two	magnets
	Of evene might, a pece of iren set	
150	Ne hath no might to meve to ne fro—	
	For what that oon may hale,° that other let°—	welcome / stop
	Ferde° I, that niste° whether me was bet	acted / did not know
	To entre or leve, til Affrican my gide	
	Me hente, and shoof° in at the gates wide,	shoved

155	And saide, "It stant writen in thy face	
	Thyn errour, though thou telle it nat to me;	
	But dreed thee nat to come into this place,	
	For this writing nis no thing ment by thee,	
	Ne by noon but he Loves servant be;	
160	For thou of love hast lost thy tast, I gesse,	
	As sik man hath of sweete and bitternesse.	

	"But nathelees, although that thou be dul,
	Yit that thou canst nat do, yit maist thou see;
	For many a man that may nat stonde a pul,[2]
165	It liketh him at wrastling for to be,

2. Withstand a fall (at wrestling).

And deemen° yit wher he do bet or he.   *judge*
And ther, if thou haddest conning for t'endite,°   *compose*
I shal thee shewe matere for to write."

170   With that myn hand he took in his anoon,
Of which I confort caughte, and that as faste;
But Lord, so I was glad and wel bigoon,°   *in a good situation*
For overal wher that I mine yën° caste   *eyes*
Were trees clad with leves that ay° shal laste,   *forever*
Eech in his kinde, of colour fressh and greene
175   As emeraude, that joye was to seene.

The bildere ook,° and eek the hardy assh;   *oak for building*
The pilere elm, the cofre unto caraine,³
The boxtree pipere;° holm to whippes lassh;   *for flutes*
The sailing firre;⁴ the cypres, deeth to plaine;°   *to lament death*
180   The shetere ew;⁵ the asp° for shaftes plaine;°   *aspen / smooth arrows*
The olive of pees;° and eek the dronke° vine;   *peace / drunken*
The victour palm; the laurer to divine.⁶

A gardin saw I ful of blosmy boughes
Upon a river in a greene mede,°   *meadow*
185   Ther as the swetnesse everemore ynough is,
With flowres white, blewe, and yelowe, and rede,
And colde welle-stremes no thing dede,
That swimmen ful of smale fisshes lighte,
With finnes rede, and scales silver-brighte.

190   On every bough the briddes° herde I singe   *birds*
With vois of angel in hir armonye;
Some bisied hem hir briddes forth to bringe.
The litel conies° to hir play gonne hie;   *rabbits*
And ferther al aboute I gan espye
195   The dredful to, the buk, the hert, the hinde;⁷
Squireles, and beestes smale of gentil kinde.°   *noble nature*

Of instruments of stringes in accord
Herde I so playe a ravisshing swetnesse
That God, that Makere is of al and Lord,
200   Ne herde nevere bettre, as I gesse.
Therwith a wind, unnethe° it mighte be lesse,   *scarcely*
Made in the leves greene a noise softe
Accordant to the briddes song alofte.

The air of that place so attempre° was   *temperate*
205   That nevere was grevance of hoot ne cold;
Ther weex° eek every hoolsom spice and gras: *grew*
No man may there waxe sik ne old.°   *grow sick nor old*
Yit was ther joye more than a thousandfold

---

3. The elm for making pillars, boxwood for corpses (i.e.,
for coffins).
4. Fir tree for sailing (shipbuilding).
5. Yew for shooting (bows and arrows).

6. Laurel for divining oracles.
7. The timid female deer, the hart, the male red deer, the
female red deer.

Than man can telle; ne nevere wolde it nighte,
210   But ay cleer day to any mannes sighte.

Under a tree biside a welle I sey°   *saw*
Cupide oure lord his arwes forge and file;
And at his feet his bowe al redy lay,
And Wil his doughter tempered al this while
215   The hevedes° in the welle, and with hir wile°   *(arrow)heads / skill*
She couched° hem after they sholde serve,   *laid out*
Some for to slee, and some to wounde and kerve.°   *cut*

Tho was I war of Plesance anoon right,[8]
And of Array, and Lust,° and Curteisye,   *Desire*
220   And of the Craft that can and hath the might
To doon° by force a wight° to doon folye: *make / person*
Disfigurat was she, I nil nat lie.
And by hemself under an ook, I gesse,
Saw I Delit that stood by Gentilesse.°   *Nobility*

225   I saw Beautee withouten any attir,
And Youthe ful of game and jolitee,
Foolhardinesse, and Flaterye, and Desir,
Messagerye,[9] and Meede,° and othere three—   *Bribery, Reward*
Hir names shal nat here be told for me;
230   And upon pileres grete of jasper longe
I saw a temple of bras yfounded stronge.

Aboute that temple daunceden alway
Wommen ynowe,° of whiche some ther were   *enough*
Faire of hemself, and some of hem were gay;
235   In kirteles° al dischevele[1] wente they there: *frocks*
That was hir office° alway, yeer by yere.   *duty, business*
And on the temple of douves° white and faire   *doves*
Saw I sittinge many an hundred paire.

Bifore the temple-dore ful sobrely
240   Dame Pees sat with a curtin in hir hond,[2]
And by hir side, wonder discreetly,
Dame Pacience sitting ther I foond,
With face pale, upon an hil of sond;°   *sand*
And aldernext° withinne and eek withoute   *next of all*
245   Biheeste and Art, and of hir folk a route.[3]

Within the temple of sikes° hote as fir   *sighs*
I herde a swough° that gan aboute renne,   *groan*
Whiche sikes were engendred with desir,
That maden every auter° for to brenne°   *altar / burn*
250   Of newe flaumbe;° and wel espied I thenne   *flame*
That al the cause of sorwes that they drie°   *suffered*
Cometh of the bittre goddesse Jalousye.

8. The 19 virtues and vices that follow are allegorical figures common in the Garden of Earthly Delights since the
time of *The Romance of the Rose.*
9. Sending of messengers between lovers.
1. With hair hanging loose.

2. The "curtin" may be a royal emblem of peace or mercy,
the *cortina* or short sword used at the coronation of English kings, or alternately, the curtain in front of the Old
Testament tabernacle.
3. Promise and Craft, and a crowd of their folk.

The god Priapus[4] saw I, as I wente,
Within the temple in soverein place stonde,
255   In swich array as whan the asse him shente°[5]   *ruined*
With cry by night, and with his sceptre in honde;
Ful bisily men gonne assaye and fonde°   *attempt and strive*
Upon his heed to sette, of sondry hewe,
Gerlandes ful of flowres fresshe and newe.

260   And in a privee corner in disport
Foond I Venus and hir porter Richesse,
That was ful noble and hautain of hir port;°   *haughty in bearing*
Derk was the place, but afterward lightnesse
I saw a lite—unnethe it mighte be lesse;
265   And on a bed of gold she lay to reste,
Til that the hote sonne gan to weste.

Hire gilte heres° with a golden threed   *hairs*
Ybounden were, untressed° as she lay;   *unbraided*
And naked from the brest up to the heed
270   Men mighte hire seen; and soothly for to say,
The remenant was wel covered to my pay°   *pleasure*
Right with a subtil coverchief of Valence:[6]
Ther nas no thikker cloth of no defence.°   *of any protection*

The place yaf a thousand savours soote,°   *sweet smells*
275   And Bacus, god of win, sat hire biside,
And Ceres next that dooth of hunger boote,°   *remedy*
And as I saide, amiddes lay Cypride,°   *Venus*
To whom on knees two yonge folk ther cride
To been hir help; but thus I leet hire lie,
280   And ferther in the temple I gan espye,

That, in despit of Diane the chaste,
Ful many a bowe ybroke heeng on the wal,
Of maidenes swiche as gonne hir times waste
In hir service; and painted overal
285   Ful many a storye, of which I touche shal
A fewe, as of Caliste and Atalante,[7]
And many a maide of which the name I wante.°   *lack*

Semiramis,[8] Candace, and Ercules,
Biblis, Dido, Thisbe, and Pyramus,

---

4. Roman god of gardens and of fertility, often depicted with an enormous phallus.
5. In Ovid's *Fasti* (1.415–40), the braying of an ass awakens the nymph whom Priapus was preparing to deflower.
6. Valencia was a center for producing finely woven textiles.
7. Callisto and Atalanta, two of the virgins dedicated to the cult of Diana, who later became famous lovers.
8. Semiramis, queen of Babylon and wife of King Ninus, conceived an incestuous passion for her own son; Candace, queen of India, fell in love with Alexander the Great and was the cause of his death by poisoning; Ercules (Hercules) was inadvertently slain by his jealous wife, Deianira; Biblis fell in love with her brother Caunus; Dido, queen of Carthage, was abandoned by her lover Aeneas, a Trojan prince and ancestor of the Romans; Thisbe and Piramus were lovers who met their deaths during a secret tryst in ancient Babylon; Tristram and Isaude (Isolde) were adulterous lovers in Arthurian legend; Paris' abduction of Helen of Troy ("Elaine" in line 291) started the Trojan War; Achilles died in battle for love of Polyxena; Cleopatra lost her life and her kingdom in Egypt because of her love for Antony; Troilus died unhappily after his lover Criseyde left him; Sylla (Scylla), daughter of King Nisus of Athens, betrayed her city to her father's enemy, Minos, king of Crete, with whom she had fallen in love; the mother of Romulus was Rhea Silvia, a priestess of Diana.

290   Tristam, Isoude, Paris, and Achilles,
       Elaine, Cleopatre, and Troilus,
       Sylla, and eek the moder of Romulus:
       Alle thise were painted on that other side,
       And al hir love, and in what plit they dyde.

295   Whan I was come ayain unto the place
       That I of spak, that was so soote and greene,
       Forth welk° I tho° myselven to solace;   *walked / then*
       Tho was I war wher that ther sat a queene,
       That as of light the someres sonne sheene
300   Passeth the sterre, right so over mesure
       She fairer was than any creature.

       And in a launde° upon an hil of flowres   *meadow*
       Was set this noble goddesse Nature;
       Of braunches were hir halles and hir bowres,°   *bedrooms*
305   Ywrought after hir cast° and hir mesure;   *design*
       Ne was ther fowl that cometh of engendrure°   *procreation*
       That they ne were alle prest° in hir presence   *ready*
       To take hir doom,° and yive hire audience.   *pass judgment*

       For this was on Saint Valentines⁹ day,
310   Whan every brid cometh ther to chese his make,°   *mate*
       Of every kinde that men thinke may;
       And that so huge a noise gan they make,
       That erthe and air and tree and every lake
       So ful was that unnethe was ther space
315   For me to stonde, so ful was al the place.

       And right as Alain in the "Plainte of Kinde"¹
       Deviseth° Nature in array and face,   *describes*
       In swich array men mighte hire there finde.
       This noble emperesse, ful of grace,
320   Bad every fowl to take his owene place,
       As they were wont alway, from yeer to yere,
       Saint Valentines day, to stonden there.

       That is to sayn, the fowles of ravine°   *birds of prey*
       Were hyest set, and thanne the fowles smale
325   That eten as hem Nature wolde encline.
       As worm, or thing of which I telle no tale;
       And waterfowl sat lowest in the dale;
       But fowl that liveth by seed sat on the greene,
       And that so fele° that wonder was to seene.   *many*

330   Ther mighte men the royal egle finde,
       That with his sharpe look perceth the sonne;²

---

9. This is the first mention of Valentine's Day in English literature.
1. *De Planctu Naturae* (*The Complaint of Nature*) was a 12th-century Latin allegorical poem by Alan of Lille, in which the figure of Nature laments the irregularity of human sexual practices. Within the text, all other crea- tures are shown to obey her laws, including the birds, the "concilium avium" (the parliament of fowls), from which Chaucer derives the title of his work.
2. The eagle was believed to be able to look directly into the sun.

And othere egles of a lower kinde
Of whiche that clerkes wel devise conne;
Ther was the tyrant with his fetheres donne°   *brown*
335   And greye—I mene the goshawk—that dooth pine°   *cause pain*
To briddes for his outrageous ravine.

The gentil faucon that with his feet distraineth°   *seizes*
The kinges hand; the hardy sperhawk[3] eke,°   *also*
The quailes fo; the merlion[4] that paineth
340   Himself ful ofte the larke for to seeke;
Ther was the douve with hir yën° meeke;   *eyes*
The jalous swan, ayains° his deeth that singeth;   *at the point of*
The owle eek that of deeth the bode° bringeth;   *foreboding*

The crane, geant° with his trompes soun;°   *giant / trumpet call*
345   The theef, the chough,° and eek the jangling pie;[5]   *crow*
The scorning jay; the eeles fo, heroun;
The false lapwing, ful of trecherye;
The starling that the conseil can biwrye;°   *reveal (secrets)*
The tame rodok, and the coward kite;[6]
350   The cok, that orlogge is of thropes lite;[7]

The sparwe, Venus sone; the nightingale,
That clepeth° forth the greene leves newe;   *calls*
The swalwe, mortherere of the fowles smale°   *killer of bees*
That maken hony of flowres fresshe of hewe;
355   The wedded turtel,° with hir herte trewe;°   *turtledove / true*
The pecok, with his angeles clothes brighte;
The fesant, scornere of the cok by nighte;[8]

The wakere goos; the cokkou evere unkinde;[9]
The popinjay° ful of delicasye;   *parrot*
360   The drake, stroyere of his owene kinde;[1]
The stork,[2] the wrekere of avouterye;°   *adultery*
The hote° cormerant of glotonye;   *hot*
The raven wis: the crowe with vois of care;
The throstel° old; the frosty feeldefare.[3]   *thrush*

365   What sholde I sayn? Of fowles every kinde
That in this world hath fetheres and stature,
Men mighten in that place assembled finde,
Bifore the noble goddesse Nature;
And everich of hem dide his bisy cure°   *business*
370   Benignely to chese or for to take,
By hir accord, his formel° or his make.°   *female / mate*

---

3. Sparrowhawk, a smaller member of the falcon species.
4. Merlin, another type of falcon.
5. The chattering magpie.
6. The ruddock is a European robin; the kite is another kind of crow.
7. The rooster, that is the clock for little villages.
8. The pheasant was thought to mate with chickens during the night.

9. Geese were reputed to have wakened Rome against barbarian attack; the cuckoo was thought unnatural because it left its eggs in the nests of other birds.
1. Male ducks were thought to destroy their own offspring.
2. Storks were thought to kill their adulterous rivals.
3. Fieldfare, another kind of thrush.

But to the point: Nature heeld on hir hond
A formel° egle, of shap the gentileste   *female*
That evere she among hir werkes foond,
375   The most benigne and the goodlieste:
In hire was every vertu at his reste,
So ferforth that Nature hirself hadde blisse
To looke on hire, and ofte hir beek to kisse.

Nature, vicarye° of the Almighty Lord   *deputy*
380   That hoot, cold, hevy, light, and moist and dreye
Hath knit with evene nombres of accord,
In esy vois gan for to speke and saye,
"Fowles, take heede of my sentence, I praye;
And for youre ese, in forthering of youre neede,
385   As faste as I may speke, I wol you speede.

"Ye knowe wel how, Saint Valentines Day,
By my statut and thurgh my governaunce,
Ye come for to chese—and flee youre way—
Youre makes as I prike° you with plesaunce.   *goad*
390   But nathelees, my rightful ordinaunce
May I nat breke, for al this world to winne,
That he that most is worthy shal biginne.

"The tercelet° egle, as that ye knowe ful weel,   *young male*
The fowl royal aboven every degree,
395   The wise and worthy, secree,° trewe as steel,   *discreet*
Which I have formed, as ye may wel see,
In every part as it best liketh me—
It needeth nat his shap you to devise—
He shal first chese and speken in his gise.°   *manner*

400   "And after him by ordre shul ye chese,
After youre kinde, everich as you liketh,
And as youre hap is shul ye winne or lese—
But which of you that love most entriketh,°   *entraps*
God sende him hire that sorest for him siketh."°   *sighs*
405   And therwithal the tercel gan she calle,
And saide, "My sone, the chois is to you falle.

"But nathelees, in this condicioun
Moot° be the chois of everich that is here: *must*
That she agree to his eleccioun,
410   What so he be that sholde be hir fere.°   *companion*
This is oure usage alway, from yeer to yere:
And who so may at this time have his grace,
In blisful time he cam into this place."

With heed enclined and with humble cheere°   *expression*
415   This royal tercel spak and taried nought:
"Unto my soverein lady, and nat my fere,°   *equal*
I chese, and chese with wil and herte and thought,
The formel on your hand, so wel ywrought,
Whos I am al, and evere wil hire serve,
420   Do what hire list to do me live or sterve;°   *die*

"Biseeking hire of mercy and of grace,
As she that is my lady sovereine—
Or lat me die present in this place:
For certes, longe I may nat live in paine,
425   For in myn herte is corven° every veine;   *cut*
And having reward° only to my trouthe,°   *regard / faithfulness*
My dere herte, have of my wo som routhe.°   *pity*

"And if that I to hire be founde untrewe,
Disobeisant, or wilful necligent,
430   Avauntour,° or in proces[4] love a newe,   *boaster*
I praye to you, this be my juggement:
That with thise fowles be I al torent°   *torn apart*
That ilke day that evere she me finde
To hire untrewe, or in my gilt unkinde.

435   "And sin that hire loveth noon so wel as I—
Al be that she me nevere of love bihette°—   *promised*
Thanne oughte she be myn thurgh hir mercy,
For other bond can I noon on hire knette;°   *tie*
Ne nevere for no wo ne shal I lette°   *stop*
440   To serven hire, how fer so that she wende;
Saye what you list: my tale is at an ende."

Right as the fresshe, rede rose newe
Ayain the somer sonne coloured is,
Right so for shame al waxen gan the hewe°   *the color turned*
445   Of this formel, whan she herde al this.
She neither answerde wel, ne saide amis,
So sore abasshed° was she, til that Nature   *embarrassed*
Saide, "Doughter, drede you nought, I you assure."

Another tercel egle spak anoon,
450   Of lower kinde,° and saide, "That shal nat be!   *nature, lineage*
I love hire bet than ye doon, by saint John,
Or at the leeste I love as wel as ye,
And lenger have served hire in my degree:
And if she sholde have loved for long loving,
455   To me ful longe° hadde be the guerdoning.°   *long ago / reward*

"I dar eek sayn, if she me finde fals,
Unkinde,° or janglere,° or rebel in any wise,   *unnatural / gossip*
Or jalous, do me hangen by the hals;°   *neck*
And but I bere me in hir servise
460   As wel as that my wit can me suffise,
From point to point, hir honour for to save,
Take ye my lif, and al the good I have."

The thridde tercel egle answerde tho:
"Now, sires, ye seen the litel leiser° here,   *leisure*
465   For every fowl crieth out to been ago
Forth with his make, or with his lady dere;
And eek Nature hirself ne wol nat heere,

4. The course of time.

For tarying here, nat half that I wolde saye;
And but I speke, I moot for sorwe deye:°   *must die for sorrow*

470   "Of long service avaunte I me no thing—
      But as possible is me to die today
      For wo, as he that hath been languisshing
      This twenty yeer; and as wel happen may
      A man may serven bet, and more to pay,
475   In half a yeer, although it were no more,
      Than som man dooth that hath served ful yore.

      "I saye nat this by me, for I ne can
      Doon no service that may my lady plese;
      But I dar sayn I am hir trewest man,
480   As to my doom,° and fainest° wolde hire ese;   *judgment / gladly*
      At shorte wordes, til that deeth me sese,°   *seize*
      I wil been hires, whether I wake or winke,°   *sleep*
      And trewe in al that herte may bithinke."

      Of al my lif, sin that day I was born,
485   So gentil plee in love or other thing
      Ne herde nevere no man me biforn,
      Who that hadde leiser and conning
      For to reherce hir cheere and hir speking:
      And from the morwe° gan this speeche laste,   *morning*
490   Til downward drow the sonne wonder faste.

      The noise of fowles for to been delivered
      So loude roong: "Have doon, and lat us wende!"°   *go*
      That wel wende° I the wode hadde al toslivered.5   *thought*
      "Come of!" they criden, "allas, ye wole us shende.°   *ruin*
495   Whan shal youre cursed pleting° have an ende?   *pleading*
      How sholde a juge either partye leve,°   *believe*
      For ye or nay, withouten other preve?"

      The goos, the cokkou, and the doke also
      So cride, "Kek kek, cokkou, quek quek," hye
500   That thurgh mine eres the noise wente tho.
      The goos saide, "Al this nis nat worth a flye!
      But I can shape° herof a remedye: *arrange*
      And I wol saye my verdit° faire and swithe°   *verdict / quickly*
      For waterfowl, who so be wroth or blithe."°   *angry or happy*

505   "And I for wormfowl," quod the fool cokkou.
      "And I wol of myn owene auctoritee,
      For commune speed,° take on me the charge now: *profit*
      For to delivere us is greet charitee."
      "Ye may abide a while yit, pardee,"°   *by God*
510   Quod the turtel, "if it be youre wille:
      A wight may speke him were as fair been stille.6

---

5. Broken into slivers.

6. "A creature may express himself, though he would have done better to keep quiet."

"I am a seedfowl, oon the unworthieste,
That woot° I wel, and litel of conninge;°   *know / understanding*
But bet is that a wightes tonge reste
515   Than entremetten° him of swich doinge   *interfere*
Of which he neither rede° can ne singe.   *advise*
And who so dooth, ful foule himself accloyeth:°   *overburdens*
For office uncommitted° ofte anoyeth."   *unassigned*

Nature, which that alway hadde an ere
520   To murmur of the lewednesse° bihinde,   *the uneducated*
With facound° vois saide, "Holde youre tonges there,   *eloquent*
And I shal soone, I hope, a conseil finde
You to delivere, and from this noise unbinde;
I jugge of every folk men shul oon calle
525   To sayn the verdit for you fowles alle."

Assented was to this conclusioun
The briddes alle; and fowles of ravine
Han chosen first, by plain eleccioun,
The tercelet of the faucon to diffine°   *state*
530   Al hir sentence,° as hem liste to termine;°   *opinion / conclude*
And to Nature him gonne to presente,
And she accepteth him with glad entente.°   *intention*

The tercelet saide thanne, "In this manere
Ful hard were it to preve by resoun
535   Who loveth best this gentil formel here
For everich hath swich replicacioun,°   *reply*
That noon by skiles° may been brought adown.   *arguments*
I can nat see that arguments availe:
Thanne seemeth it ther moste be bataile."

540   "Al redy," quod thise egles tercels tho.
"Nay, sires," quod he, "if that I dorste it saye,
Ye doon me wrong, my tale is nat ydo.
For sires, ne taketh nat agrief, I praye,
It may nat goon as ye wolde in this waye:
545   Oure[7] is the vois that han the charge on honde,
And to the juges doom ye moten stonde.

"And therfore, pees; I saye, as to my wit,
Me wolde thinke how that the worthieste
Of knighthood, and lengest hath used it,
550   Most of estaat, of blood the gentileste,
Were sittingest° for hire, if that hire leste;   *most suitable*
And of thise three she woot hirself, I trowe,
Which that he be, for hire is light° to knowe."   *easy*

The waterfowles han hir hedes laid
555   Togidre; and of a short avisement,°   *deliberation*
Whan everich hadde his large golee° said,   *mouthful*
They saiden soothly, alle by oon assent,

---

7. Royal "we," indicating the tercelet.

How that the goos, with hir facounde gent,°   *noble eloquence*
"That so desireth to pronounce oure neede
560   Shal telle oure tale," and prayed God hire speede.

As for thise waterfowles tho bigan
The goos to speke, and in hir cakelinge
She saide, "Pees, now take keep,° every man,   *heed*
And herkneth which a reson I shal bringe:
565   My wit is sharp, I love no taryinge.
I saye, I rede° him, though he were my brother,   *counsel*
But° she wil love him, lat him take another."   *unless*

"Lo, here a parfit° reson of a goos,"   *perfect*
Quod the sperhawk. "Nevere mote she thee!°   *thrive*
570   Lo, swich it is to have a tonge loos!
Now pardee, fool, now were it bet for thee
Han holde thy pees than shewe thy nicetee.°   *simpleness*
It lith nat in his might ne in his wille,
But sooth is said, a fool can nat be stille."

575   The laughtre aroos of gentil fowles alle,
And right anoon the seedfowl chosen hadde
The turtel trewe, and gonne hire to hem calle,
And prayed hire for to sayn the soothe sadde°   *earnest truth*
Of this matere, and axed what she radde:°   *advised*
580   And she answerde that plainly hir entente
She wolde it shewe, and soothly what she mente.

"Nay, God forbede a lovere sholde chaunge,"
The turtel saide, and weex for shame al reed.°   *red*
"Though that his lady everemore be straunge,°   *reserved*
585   Yit lat him serve hire til that he be deed.
Forsoothe, I praise nat the gooses reed.°   *advice*
For though she dyde, I wolde noon other make:
I wil been hires til that the deeth me take."

"Wel bourded,"° quod the doke, "by myn hat!   *joked*
590   That men shal loven alway causelees—
Who can a reson finde or wit in that?
Daunceth he merye that is mirthelees?
What sholde I rekke° of him that is recchelees?   *care for*
Ye, queke," yit said the doke, ful wel and faire:
595   "Ther been mo sterres, God woot, than a paire."

"Now fy, cherl,"° quod the gentil° tercelet: *commoner / noble*
"Out of the donghil cam that word ful right.
Thou canst nat seen what thing is wel biset;°   *arranged*
Thou farest° by love as owles doon by light: *go about*
600   The day hem blent,° but wel they seen by night.   *blinds*
Thy kinde is of so lowe a wrecchednesse
That what love is thou canst nat seen ne gesse."

Tho gan the cokkou putte him forth in prees°   *in the midst*
For fowl that eteth worm, and saide blive,°   *quickly*

605   "So I," quod he, "may have my make in pees,

     I recche° nat how longe that ye strive.   *care*

     Lat eech of hem be solein° al hir live,   *single*

     This is my reed, sin they may nat accorde:

     This shorte lesson needeth nat recorde."°   *repeat*

610   "Ye, have the gloton fild ynough his paunche,

     Thanne are we wel," saide thanne a merlioun.

     "Thou mortherere of the haysoge° on the braunche   *hedge sparrow*

     That broughte thee forth, thou reweful° glotoun,   *pitiful*

     Live thou solein, wormes corrupcioun,

615   For no fors is of lak of thy nature:[8]

     Go, lewed° be thou whil that the world may dure."°   *ignorant / endure*

     "Now pees," quod Nature, "I comande heer,

     For I have herd al youre opinioun,

     And in effect yit be we nevere the neer.°   *no closer*

620   But finally, this is my conclusioun:

     That she hirself shal han the eleccioun

     Of whom hire list; and who be wroth or blithe,

     Him that she cheseth he shal hire have as swithe.°   *at once*

     "For sin it may nat here discussed be

625   Who loveth hire best, as saith the tercelet,

     Thanne wol I doon hire this favour, that she

     Shal have right him on whom hir herte is set,

     And he hire that his herte hath on hire knet.°   *joined*

     Thus jugge I, Nature, for I may nat lie:

630   To noon estaat have I noon other yë.

     "But as for conseil for to chese a make,

     If I were Reson, certes thanne wolde I

     Conseile you the royal tercel take—

     As saide the tercelet ful skilfully—

635   As for the gentileste and most worthy,

     Which I have wrought so wel to my pleasaunce

     That to you oughte it been a suffisaunce."°   *sufficient*

     With dredful° vois the formel tho answerde,   *timid*

     "Myn rightful lady, goddesse of Nature,

640   Sooth is that I am evere under youre yerde,°   *rod, authority*

     As is another lives creature,

     And moot been youre whil that my lif may dure;

     And therfore, graunteth me my firste boone,°   *request*

     And myn entente you wol I sayn wel soone."

645   "I graunte it you," quod she. And right anoon

     This formel egle spak in this degree:

     "Almighty queene, unto° this yeer be goon,   *until*

     I axe respit for to avise me,

     And after that to have my chois al free:

---

8. For it is no matter if your nature (lineage) disappears.

650 This al and som that I wol speke and saye;
Ye gete namore although ye do me deye.°   *kill me*

"I wol nat serve Venus ne Cupide
Forsoothe, as yit, by no manere waye."
"Now, sin it may noon otherwise bitide,"
655 Quod tho Nature, "here is namore to saye.
Thanne wolde I that thise fowles were awaye,
Eech with his make, for tarying° lenger here,"   *to avoid delaying*
And saide hem thus, as ye shul after heere.

"To you speke I, you tercelets," quod Nature.
660 "Beeth of good herte, and serveth alle three:
A yeer is nat so longe to endure,
And eech of you paine him in his degree
For to do wel; for God woot, quit° is she   *released*
Fro you this yeer, what after so bifalle:
665 This entremes⁹ is dressed° for you alle."   *prepared*

And whan this werk al brought was to an ende,
To every fowl Nature yaf his make
By evene accord,° and on hir way they wende.   *mutual agreement*
But Lord, the blisse and joye that they make,
670 For eech gan other in his winges take,
And with hir nekkes eech gan other winde,
Thanking alway the noble queene of Kinde.°   *Nature*

But first were chosen fowles for to singe—
As yeer by yere was alway the usaunce°—   *custom*
675 To singe a roundel¹ at hir departinge,
To doon to Nature honour and plesaunce.
The note, I trowe, ymaked was in Fraunce;
The wordes were swiche as ye may here finde
The nexte vers, as I now have in minde.

680 "Now welcome, somer, with thy sonne softe,
That hast thise wintres wedres° overshake,   *storms*
And driven away the large nightes blake.°   *long dark nights*

Saint Valentin, that art ful heigh on lofte,
Thus singen smale fowles for thy sake:
685 Now welcome, somer, with thy sonne softe,
That hast thise wintres wedres overshake,
And driven away the large nightes blake.

"Wel han they cause for to gladen ofte,
Sith° eech of hem recovered hath his make;   *since*
690 Ful blisful mowe° they singe whan they wake: *may*
Now welcome, somer, with thy sonne softe,
That hast thise wintres wedres overshake,
And driven away the large nightes blake."

9. Either food or an entertainment given in between main courses.
1. A song with repeating refrain which originated in France.

```
       And with the shouting, whan the song was do,
695    That fowles maden at hir flight away,
       I wook, and othere bookes took me to
       To rede upon, and yit I rede alway,
       In hope, ywis, to rede so somday,
       That I shal mete° somthing for to fare                          dream
700    The bet, and thus to rede I nil nat spare.°           will not refrain
```

from THE CANTERBURY TALES

THE GENERAL PROLOGUE   The twenty-nine "sondry folke" of the Canterbury company gather at the Tabard Inn, ostensibly with the pious intent of making a pilgrimage to England's holiest shrine, the tomb of Saint Thomas Becket at Canterbury. From the start in the raffish and worldly London suburb of Southwerk, though, the pilgrims' attentions and energy veer wildly between the sacred and the profane. The mild story-telling competition proposed by the Host also slides swiftly into a contest among social classes. Set in Chaucer's own time and place, *The Canterbury Tales* reflect both the dynamism and the uncertainties of a society still nostalgic for archaic models of church and state, yet riven by such crises as plague, economic disruption, and the new claims of peasants and mercantile bourgeois—claims expressed and repressed most violently in the recent Rising, or "Peasants' Revolt," of 1381.

Chaucer's *Prologue* has roots in the genre known as "estates satire." Such writings criticized the failure of the members of the three traditional "estates" of medieval society—the aristocracy, the clergy, and the commons—to fulfill their ordained function of fighting, praying, and working the land, respectively. From the beginning the pilgrims' portraits are couched in language fraught with class connotations. The Knight, the idealized (if archaic) representative of the aristocracy, is called *gentil* (that is, "noble, aristocratic") and is said never to have uttered any *vileynye*—speech characteristic of peasants or *villeyns*. Many of the pilgrims in the other two estates display aristocratic manners, among the clergy notably the Prioress, with her "cheere of court," and the Monk, who lives like a country gentleman, hunting with greyhounds and a stable full of fine horses. Both pilgrims contrast with the ideal of their estate, the Parson, who, though "*povre*" is "rich" in holy works.

The commons are traditionally the last of the "three estates," yet they bulk largest in the Canterbury company and fit least well in that model of social order. There are old-fashioned laborers on the pilgrimage, but many more characters from the emerging and disruptive world of small industry and commerce. They are commoners, but have ambitions that lead them both to envy and to mock the powers held by their aristocratic and clerical companions.

Among the group that traditionally comprised the commons, the peasants, Chaucer singles out one ideal, the Plowman, who is, significantly, the Parson's brother. He is characterized as a diligent *swynkere* (worker), in implicit contrast to the lazy peasants castigated in estates satire. Most of the rest of the commons, however, such as the Miller and the Cook, are presented as "churlish," and their tales have a coarse vigor that Chaucer clearly relishes even as he disassociates himself from their vulgarity.

In theory, women were treated as a separate category, defined by their sexual nature and marital role rather than by their class. Nevertheless, the Prioress and the Wife of Bath are both satirized as much for their social ambition as for the failings of their gender. The Prioress prides herself on her courtesy, and the commoner Wife of Bath aspires to the same social recognition as the guildsmen's upwardly mobile wives. Her portrait is complex, however, for she is simultaneously satirized and admired for challenging the expected roles of women at the time, with her economic independence (as a rich widow and a cloth-maker) and her resultant freedom to travel. The narrator's suggestion that she goes on many pilgrimages in order to find a sixth husband

bears out the stereotype of unbridled female sexuality familiar from estates satire, as her fondness of talking and laughing bears out the stereotype of female garrulousness.

Chaucer's satire is pointed but also exceptionally subtle, largely because of the irony
achieved through his use of the narrator, seemingly naive and a little dense. His deadpan narration leaves the readers themselves to supply the judgment.

from THE CANTERBURY TALES
The General Prologue

	Whan that April with his showres soote°	*sweet*
	The droughte of March hath perced to the roote,	
	And bathed every veine in swich licour,°	*such liquid*
	Of which vertu° engendred is the flowr;	*by whose strength*
5	Whan Zephyrus[1] eek° with his sweete breeth	*also*
	Inspired hath in every holt and heeth°	*wood and field*
	The tendre croppes, and the yonge sonne	
	Hath in the Ram° his halve cours yronne,	*the zodiac sign Aries*
	And smale fowles maken melodye	
10	That sleepen al the night with open yë°—	*eye*
	So priketh hem Nature in hir corages°—	*hearts, spirits*
	Thanne longen folk to goon on pilgrimages,	
	And palmeres[2] for to seeken straunge strondes°	*shores*
	To ferne halwes,° couthe° in sondry londes;	*far-off shrines / known*
15	And specially from every shires ende	
	Of Engelond to Canterbury they wende,°	*go*
	The holy blisful martyr[3] for to seeke	
	That hem hath holpen° whan that they were seke.°	*helped / sick*
	Bifel that in that seson on a day,	
20	In Southwerk[4] at the Tabard as I lay,	
	Redy to wenden on my pilgrimage	
	To Canterbury with ful devout corage,	
	At night was come into that hostelrye	
	Wel nine and twenty in a compaignye	
25	Of sondry folk, by aventure yfalle	
	In felaweshipe, and pilgrimes were they alle	
	That toward Canterbury wolden ride.	
	The chambres° and the stables weren wide,	*guestrooms*
	And wel we weren esed° at the beste.	*accommodated*
30	And shortly, whan the sonne was to reste,	
	So hadde I spoken with hem everichoon	
	That I was of hir felaweshipe anoon,	
	And made forward° erly for to rise,	*agreed*
	To take oure way ther as I you devise.°	*relate*
35	But nathelees, whil I have time and space,°	*opportunity*
	Er that I ferther in this tale pace,°	*proceed*

1. In Roman mythology Zephyrus was the demigod of the west wind, herald of warmer weather.
2. Pilgrims who had traveled to the Holy Land.
3. St. Thomas Becket, murdered in Canterbury Cathedral in 1170.
4. Southwark, a suburb of London south of the Thames and the traditional starting point for the pilgrimage to

Canterbury in Kent, was notorious as a center of gambling and prostitution. The Tabard Inn was an actual
public house at the time, named for the shape of its sign
which resembled the coarse, sleeveless outer garment
worn by members of the lower classes, monks, and foot
soldiers alike.

Me thinketh it accordant to resoun
To telle you al the condicioun°   *circumstances*
Of eech of hem, so as it seemed me,
40   And whiche they were, and of what degree,°   *social status*
And eek in what array that they were inne:
And at a knight thanne wol I first biginne.
     A Knight ther was, and that a worthy man,
That fro the time that he first bigan
45   To riden out, he loved chivalrye,
Trouthe and honour, freedom and curteisye.[5]
Ful worthy was he in his lordes werre,°   *war*
And therto hadde he riden, no man ferre,°   *farther*
As wel in Cristendom as hethenesse,°   *heathen lands*
50   And evere honoured for his worthinesse.
At Alisandre[6] he was whan it was wonne;
Ful ofte time he hadde the boord bigonne[7]
Aboven alle nacions in Pruce;
In Lettou had he reised,° and in Ruce,   *campaigned*
55   No Cristen man so ofte of his degree;
In Gernade at the sege eek hadde he be
Of Algezir, and riden in Belmarye;
At Lyeis was he, and at Satalye,
Whan they were wonne; and in the Grete See
60   At many a noble arivee° hadde he be.   *military landing*
     At mortal batailes[8] hadde he been fifteene,
And foughten for oure faith at Tramissene
In listes° thries, and ay° slain his fo.   *duels / always*
     This ilke° worthy Knight hadde been also   *same*
65   Somtime with the lord of Palatye
Again° another hethen in Turkye;   *against*
And everemore he hadde a soverein pris.°   *reputation*
And though that he were worthy, he was wis,
And of his port° as meeke as is a maide.   *bearing*
70   He nevere yit no vilainye° ne saide   *rudeness*
In al his lif unto no manere wight:°   *no kind of man*
He was a verray,° parfit,° gentil° knight.   *true / perfect / noble*
But for to tellen you of his array,°   *equipment*
His hors were goode, but he was nat gay.°   *gaily attired*
75   Of fustian° he wered a gipoun°   *coarse cloth / tunic*
Al bismotered with his haubergeoun,[9]
For he was late come from his viage,°   *expedition*
And wente for to doon his pilgrimage.
     With him ther was his sone, a yong Squier,
80   A lovere and a lusty bacheler,[1]

5. Fidelity and good reputation, generosity and courtliness.
6. The place-names Chaucer lists over the next 15 lines
were primarily associated with 14th-century Crusades
against both Muslims and Eastern Orthodox Christians.
Alisandre: Alexandria in Egypt; Pruce: Prussia; Lettou:
Lithuania; Ruce: Russia; Gernade and Algezir: Granada
and Algeciras in Spain; Belmarye: Ben-Marin near

Morocco; Lyeis: Ayash in Turkey; Satalye: Atalia in
Turkey; Grete See: Mediterranean; Tramissene: Tlemcen
near Morocco; Palatye: Balat in Turkey.
7. Held the place of honor at feasts.
8. Tournaments waged to the death.
9. Rust-stained from his coat of mail.
1. An unmarried and unpropertied younger knight.

With lokkes crulle° as they were laid in presse.   *curled*
Of twenty yeer of age he was, I gesse.
Of his stature he was of evene° lengthe,   *average*
And wonderly delivere,° and of greet strengthe.   *agile*
85   And he hadde been som time in chivachye°   *cavalry expedition*
In Flandres, in Artois, and Picardye,[2]
And born him wel as of so litel space,°   *time*
In hope to stonden in his lady grace.°   *lady's favor*
      Embrouded° was he as it were a mede,°   *embroidered / meadow*
90   Al ful of fresshe flowres, white and rede;
Singing he was, or floiting,° al the day: *playing the flute*
He was as fressh as is the month of May.
Short was his gowne, with sleeves longe and wide.
Wel coude he sitte on hors, and faire ride;
95   He coude songes make, and wel endite,°   *compose*
Juste° and eek daunce, and wel portraye° and write.   *joust / draw*
So hote he loved that by nightertale°   *nighttime*
He slepte namore than dooth a nightingale.
Curteis he was, lowely,° and servisable,°   *humble / attentive*
100   And carf° biforn his fader° at the table   *carved / father*
      A Yeman[3] hadde he° and servants namo   *i.e., the Knight*
At that time, for him liste° ride so;   *he liked*
And he was clad in cote and hood of greene.
A sheef of pecok arwes,° bright and keene,   *peacock arrows*
105   Under his belt he bar ful thriftily;
Wel coude he dresse° his takel° yemanly: *arrange / gear*
His arwes drouped nought with fetheres lowe.
And in his hand he bar a mighty bowe.
A not-heed° hadde he with a brown visage.°   *short haircut / face*
110   Of wodecraft° wel coude he al the usage.   *forestry*
Upon his arm he bar a gay bracer,°   *archer's armguard*
And by his side a swerd and a bokeler,°   *small shield*
And on that other side a gay daggere,
Harneised wel and sharp as point of spere;
115   A Cristophre[4] on his brest of silver sheene;
An horn he bar, the baudrik° was of greene.   *shoulder strap*
A forster° was he soothly,° as I gesse.   *gamekeeper / truly*
      Ther was also a Nonne, a Prioresse,
That of hir smiling was ful simple and coy.°   *quiet, shy*
120   Hir gretteste ooth was but by Sainte Loy![5]
And she was cleped° Madame Eglantine.°   *called / Brier-rose*
Ful wel she soong the service divine,
Entuned in hir nose ful semely;°   *becomingly*
And Frenssh she spak ful faire and fetisly,°   *elegantly*
125   After the scole of Stratford at the Bowe[6]

2. Regions in the north of France and in what is now Belgium, where the English and the French were fighting out
the Hundred Years' War.
3. A yeoman was a freeborn servant (not a peasant), who
looked after the affairs of the gentry. This particular yeoman was a forester and gamekeeper for the Knight.
4. Medal of St. Christopher, patron saint of travelers.

5. St. Eligius, patron saint of metalworkers, believed
never to have sworn an oath in his life.
6. From the school (i.e., after the manner of) Stratford, a
suburb of London where the prosperous convent of St.
Leonard's was located; her French is Anglo-Norman as
opposed to the French spoken on the Continent.

For Frenssh of Paris was to hire unknowe.
At mete° wel ytaught was she withalle: *meals*
She leet no morsel from hir lippes falle,
Ne wette hir fingres in hir sauce deepe;
130   Wel coude she carye a morsel, and wel keepe°   *safeguard*
That no drope ne fille upon hir brest.
In curteisye was set ful muchel hir lest.°   *her great pleasure*
Hir over-lippe° wiped she so clene   *upper lip*
That in hir coppe ther was no ferthing[7] seene
135   Of grece,° whan she dronken hadde hir draughte;   *grease*
Ful semely after hir mete she raughte.°   *reached for her food*
And sikerly° she was of greet disport,°   *certainly / good cheer*
And ful plesant, and amiable of port,
And pained hire to countrefete cheere°   *appearance*
140   Of court, and to been estatlich° of manere,   *stately*
And to been holden digne° of reverence.   *worthy*
But, for to speken of hir conscience,
She was so charitable and so pitous
She wolde weepe if that she saw a mous
145   Caught in a trappe, if it were deed or bledde.
Of smale houndes hadde she that she fedde
With rosted flessh,° or milk and wastelbreed;[8]   *meat*
But sore wepte she if oon of hem were deed,
Or if men smoot° it with a yerde° smerte;°   *hit / rod / painfully*
150   And al was conscience and tendre herte.
Ful semely hir wimpel[9] pinched was,
Hir nose tretis,° hir yën greye as glas,   *shapely*
Hir mouth ful smal, and therto softe and reed—
But sikerly she hadde a fair forheed:
155   It was almost a spanne[1] brood, I trowe,°   *believe*
For hardily,° she was nat undergrowe.°   *assuredly / short*
Ful fetis° was hir cloke, as I was war;   *elegant*
Of smal coral aboute hir arm she bar
A paire of bedes, gauded al with greene,[2]
160   And theron heeng a brooch of gold ful sheene,
On which ther was first writen a crowned A.[3]
And after, *Amor vincit omnia*.[4]
      Another Nonne with hire hadde she
That was hir chapelaine,° and preestes three.   *secretary*
165   A Monk ther was, a fair for the maistrye,°   *very good-looking*
An outridere[5] that loved venerye,°   *hunting*
A manly° man, to been an abbot able.   *courageous*
Ful many a daintee° hors hadde he in stable,   *fine*
And whan he rood, men mighte his bridel heere
170   Ginglen° in a whistling wind as clere   *jingling*

7. Spot the size of a farthing.
8. Bread of the finest quality.
9. A pleated headdress covering all but the face, such as nuns and married women wore.
1. A hand's width, 7 to 9 inches.
2. A set of rosary beads, marked off by larger beads (gauds) to indicate where the Paternosters should be said.

3. The letter "A" with a crown on top.
4. Love conquers all (Virgil, *Eclogues*, 10.69). Though pagan and secular in origin, the phrase was often used to refer to divine love as well.
5. A monk who worked outside the confines of the monastery.

	And eek as loude as dooth the chapel belle	
	Ther as this lord was kepere of the celle.[6]	
	The rule of Saint Maure or of Saint Beneit,[7]	
	By cause that it was old and somdeel strait°—	*somewhat strict*
175	This ilke Monk leet olde thinges pace,	
	And heeld after the newe world the space.°	*the times (customs)*
	He yaf nought of that text° a pulled° hen	*regulation / plucked*
	That saith that hunteres been nought holy men,	
	Ne that a monk, whan he is recchelees,°	*careless*
180	Is likned til a fissh that is waterlees—	
	This is to sayn, a monk out of his cloistre;	
	But thilke° text heeld he nat worth an oystre.	*that same*
	And I saide his opinion was good:	
	What sholde he studye and make himselven wood°	*crazy*
185	Upon a book in cloistre alway to poure,	
	Or swinke° with his handes and laboure,	*work*
	As Austin[8] bit?° How shal the world be served?	*orders*
	Lat Austin have his swink° to him reserved!	*toil*
	Therfore he was a prikasour° aright.	*hunter on horseback*
190	Grehoundes he hadde as swift as fowl in flight.	
	Of priking and of hunting for the hare	
	Was al his lust,° for no cost wolde he spare.	*pleasure*
	I sawgh his sleeves purfiled° at the hand	*fur-lined*
	With gris,° and that the fineste of a land;	*gray fur*
195	And for to festne his hood under his chin	
	He hadde of gold wrought a ful curious° pin:	*elaborate*
	A love-knotte[9] in the grettere° ende ther was.	*larger*
	His heed was balled,° that shoon as any glas,	*bald*
	And eek his face, as he hadde been anoint:	
200	He was a lord ful fat and in good point;°	*in good shape*
	His yën steepe,° and rolling in his heed,	*bright*
	That stemed as a furnais of a leed;[1]	
	His bootes souple,° his hors in greet estat[2]—	*supple*
	Now certainly he was a fair prelat.[3]	
205	He was nat pale as a forpined° gost:	*tormented*
	A fat swan loved he best of any rost.	
	His palfrey° was as brown as is a berye.	*saddle horse*
	A Frere° ther was, a wantoune[4] and a merye,	*Friar*
	A limitour,[5] a ful solempne man.	
210	In alle the ordres foure[6] is noon that can°	*knows*
	So muche of daliaunce° and fair langage:	*flirtation*
	He hadde maad ful many a mariage	
	Of yonge wommen at his owene cost;	

6. Supervisor of the outlying cell of the monastery.
7. St. Benedict (Beneit) was the founder of Western monasticism, and his Rule prohibited monks from leaving the grounds of the monastery without special permission. St. Maurus introduced the Benedictine order into France.
8. St. Augustine recommended that monks perform manual labor.
9. An elaborate knot.

1. Glowed like a furnace under a cauldron.
2. Excellent condition.
3. Prelate, important churchman.
4. Jovial, pleasure-seeking.
5. Friar licensed by his order to beg for alms within a given district.
6. The four orders of friars were the Carmelites, Augustinians, Dominicans, and Franciscans.

Unto his ordre he was a noble post.°   *pillar*

215   Ful wel biloved and familier was he
With frankelains[7] over al in his contree,
And with worthy wommen of the town—
For he hadde power of confessioun,
As saide himself, more than a curat,°   *parish priest*

220   For of his ordre he was licenciat.[8]
Ful swetely herde he confessioun,
And plesant was his absolucioun.
He was an esy man to yive penaunce
Ther as he wiste to have a good pitaunce;[9]

225   For unto a poore ordre for to yive
Is signe that a man is wel yshrive;°   *absolved*
For if he yaf, he dorste make avaunt°   *boast*
He wiste that a man was repentaunt;
For many a man so hard is of his herte

230   He may nat weepe though him sore smerte:°   *hurts*
Therfore, in stede of weeping and prayeres,
Men mote yive silver to the poore freres.
His tipet° was ay farsed° ful of knives   *scarf / packed*
And pinnes, for to yiven faire wives;

235   And certainly he hadde a merye note;
Wel coude he singe and playen on a rote;°   *fiddle*
Of yeddinges° he bar outrely the pris.[1]   *singing ballads*
His nekke whit was as the flowr-de-lis;[2]
Therto he strong was as a champioun.

240   He knew the tavernes wel in every town,
And every hostiler and tappestere,°   *innkeeper and barmaid*
Bet than a lazar or a beggestere.°   *a leper or a beggar*
For unto swich a worthy man as he
Accorded nat, as by his facultee,°[3]   *official position*

245   To have with sike° lazars aquaintaunce: *such*
It is nat honeste,° it may nought avaunce,°   *dignified / profit*
For to delen with no swich poraile,°   *poor people*
But al with riche, and selleres of vitaile;°   *food*
And over al ther as profit sholde arise,

250   Curteis he was, and lowely° of servise.   *humble*
Ther was no man nowher so vertuous:°   *capable*
He was the beste beggere in his hous.
And yaf a certain ferme for the graunt:[4]
Noon of his bretheren cam ther in his haunt.°   *territory*

255   For though a widwe hadde nought a sho,
So plesant was his *In principio*[5]
Yit wolde he have a ferthing er he wente;
His purchas° was wel bettre than his rente.°   *income / expense*
And rage° he coude as it were right a whelpe;°   *flirt / puppy*

---

7. Franklins, important property holders.
8. Licensed by the Church to hear confessions.
9. Where he knew he would get a good donation.
1. Utterly took the prize.
2. Lily, emblem of the royal house of France.

3. It was unbecoming to his official post.
4. And gave a certain fee for the license to beg.
5. "In the beginning," the opening line in Genesis and
the Gospel of John, popular for devotions.

260 In love-dayes⁶ ther coude he muchel helpe,
    For ther he was nat lik a cloisterer,
    With a thredbare cope, as is a poore scoler,
    But he was lik a maister° or a pope.   *professor*
    Of double worstede was his semicope,°⁷   *short cloak*
265 And rounded as a belle out of the presse.°   *bell-mold*
    Somwhat he lipsed for his wantounesse
    To make his Englissh sweete upon his tonge;
    And in his harping, whan that he hadde songe,
    His yën twinkled in his heed aright
270 As doon the sterres in the frosty night.
    This worthy limitour was cleped° Huberd.   *called*
        A Marchant was ther with a forked beerd,
    In motlee,° and hye on hors he sat,   *multicolored fabric*
    Upon his heed a Flandrissh° bevere hat,   *Flemish*
275 His bootes clasped faire and fetisly.°   *elegantly*
    His resons° he spak ful solempnely,   *opinions*
    Souning° alway th'encrees of his winning.   *announcing*
    He wolde the see were kept for any thing°   *protected at all costs*
    Bitwixen Middelburgh and Orewelle.⁸
280 Wel coude he in eschaunge sheeldes⁹ selle.
    This worthy man ful wel his wit bisette:°   *employed*
    Ther wiste° no wight° that he was in dette,   *knew / person*
    So estatly° was he of his governaunce,°   *dignified / management*
    With his bargaines, and with his chevissaunce.°   *borrowing*
285 Forsoothe° he was a worthy man withalle;   *in truth*
    But, sooth to sayn, I noot° how men him calle.   *do not know*
        A Clerk ther was of Oxenforde also
    That unto logik hadde longe ygo.°   *gone (studied)*
    As lene was his hors as is a rake,
290 And he was nought right fat, I undertake,
    But looked holwe,° and therto sobrely.   *emaciated*
    Ful thredbare was his overeste courtepy,°   *outer cloak*
    For he hadde geten him yit no benefice,°   *church income*
    Ne was so worldly for to have office.°   *secular employment*
295 For him was levere° have at his beddes heed   *he preferred*
    Twenty bookes, clad in blak or reed,
    Of Aristotle and his philosophye,
    Than robes riche, or fithele,° or gay sautrye.°   *fiddle / harp*
    But al be that he was a philosophre¹
300 Yit hadde he but litel gold in cofre;
    But al that he mighte of his freendes hente,°   *get*
    On bookes and on lerning he it spente,
    And bisily gan for the soules praye
    Of hem that yaf him wherwith to scoleye.°   *study*
305 Of studye took he most cure° and most heede.   *care*
    Nought oo° word spak he more than was neede,   *one*

---

6. Holidays for settling disputes out of court.
7. His short cloak was made of thick woolen cloth.
8. Middleburgh in the Netherlands and Orwell in Suffolk were major ports for the wool trade.

9. Unit of exchange, a credit instrument for foreign merchants.
1. A philosopher could be a scientist or alchemist.

And that was said in forme° and reverence,   *formally*
And short and quik, and ful of height sentence:°   *lofty meaning*
Souning in° moral vertu was his speeche,   *consonant with*
310   And gladly wolde he lerne, and gladly teche.
     A Sergeant of the Lawe,[2] war and wis,
That often hadde been at the Parvis[3]
Ther was also, ful riche of excellence.
Discreet he was, and of greet reverence—
315   He seemed swich, his wordes weren so wise.
Justice he was ful often in assise[4]
By patente and by plein commissioun.[5]
For his science° and for his heigh renown   *knowledge*
Of fees and robes hadde he many oon.
320   So greet a purchasour° was nowher noon;   *buyer of land*
Al was fee simple[6] to him in effect—
His purchasing mighte nat been infect.°   *invalidated*
Nowher so bisy a man as he ther nas;
And yit he seemed bisier than he was.
325   In termes hadde he caas and doomes° alle   *lawsuits and judgments*
That from the time of King William[7] were falle.
Therto he coude endite and make a thing,[8]
Ther coude no wight° pinchen° at his writing;   *person / find fault with*
And every statut coude he plein by rote.[9]
330   He rood but hoomly° in a medlee° cote,   *simply / multicolored*
Girt with a ceint° of silk, with barres° smale.   *belt / stripes*
Of his array telle I no lenger tale.
     A Frankelain[1] was in his compaignye:
Whit was his beerd as is the dayesye;°   *daisy*
335   Of his complexion he was sanguin.[2]
Wel loved he by the morwe a sop in win.[3]
To liven in delit° was evere his wone,°   *pleasure / custom*
For he was Epicurus owene sone,
That heeld opinion that plein° delit   *complete*
340   Was verray felicitee parfit.[4]
An housholdere and that a greet was he:
Saint Julian[5] he was in his contree.
His breed, his ale, was always after oon;°   *just as good*
A bettre envined° man was nevere noon.   *stocked with wine*
345   Withouten bake mete was nevere his hous,
Of fissh and flessh, and that so plentevous°   *plentiful*
It snewed° in his hous of mete and drinke,   *snowed*
Of alle daintees that men coude thinke.
After the sondry sesons of the yeer

---

2. A lawyer of the highest rank.
3. The porch of St. Paul's Cathedral, a meeting place for lawyers.
4. He was often judge in the court of assizes (civil court).
5. By letter of appointment from the king and by full jurisdiction.
6. Owned outright with no legal impediments.
7. Since the introduction of Norman law in England under William the Conqueror.

8. Compose and draw up a deed.
9. He knew entirely from memory.
1. A large landholder, freeborn but not belonging to the nobility.
2. In temperament he was sanguine (optimistic, governed by blood as his chief humor).
3. In the morning a sop of bread soaked in wine.
4. True and perfect happiness.
5. Patron saint of hospitality.

350   So chaunged he his mete and his soper.[6]
       Ful many a fat partrich° hadde he in mewe,°   *partridge / cage*
       And many a breem,° and many a luce° in stewe.°   *carp / pike / pond*
       Wo was his cook but if his sauce were
       Poinant° and sharp, and redy al his gere.   *pungent*
355   His table dormant[7] in his halle alway
       Stood redy covered al the longe day.
       At sessions[8] ther was he lord and sire.
       Ful ofte time he was Knight of the Shire.[9]
       An anlaas° and a gipser° al of silk   *dagger / purse*
360   Heeng at his girdel, whit as morne milk.
       A shirreve hadde he been, and countour.[1]
       Was nowher swich a worthy vavasour.[2]
           An Haberdasshere° and a Carpenter,   *hat-maker*
       A Webbe, a Dyere, and a Tapicer[3]—
365   And they were clothed alle in oo liveree°   *in the same uniform*
       Of a solempne and a greet fraternitee.°   *parish guild*
       Ful fresshe and newe hir gere apiked was;[4]
       Hir knives were chaped° nought with bras,   *mounted*
       But al with silver; wrought ful clene° and weel   *quite nicely made*
370   Hir girdles and hir pouches everydeel.°   *entirely*
       Wel seemed eech of hem a fair burgeis°   *townsperson*
       To sitten in a yeldehalle° on a dais.   *guildhall*
       Everich, for the wisdom that he can,°   *knows*
       Was shaply° for to been an alderman.°   *fit / mayor*
375   For catel° hadde they ynough and rente,°   *property / income*
       And eek hir wives wolde it wel assente—
       And elles certain were they to blame:
       It is ful fair to been ycleped° "Madame,"   *called*
       And goon to vigilies[5] al bifore,
380   And have a mantel royalliche ybore.
           A Cook they hadde with hem for the nones,°   *for the occasion*
       To boile the chiknes with the marybones,°   *marrowbones*
       And powdre-marchant tart and galingale.°   *aromatic spices*
       Wel coude he knowe a draughte of London ale.
385   He coude roste, and seethe,° and broile, and frye,   *boil*
       Maken mortreux,° and wel bake a pie.   *stews*
       But greet harm was it, as it thoughte me,
       That on his shine a mormal° hadde he.   *ulcer*
       For blankmanger,° that made he with the beste.   *thick stew*
390   A Shipman was ther, woning° fer by weste—   *dwelling*
       For ought I woot,° he was of Dertemouthe.[6]   *know*
       He rood upon a rouncy° as he couthe,   *nag*
       In a gowne of falding° to the knee.   *coarse brown cloth*
       A daggere hanging on a laas° hadde he   *strap*

---

6. For health he changed his diet according to the different seasons.
7. Left standing rather than dismantled between meals.
8. Meetings of the justices of the peace.
9. A representative of the district at Parliament.
1. He had been sheriff and auditor of the county finances.

2. Lower member of the feudal elite.
3. A weaver, dyer, and tapestry-maker, all members of the same commercial guild.
4. Their gear was decorated.
5. Feasts held the night before a holy day.
6. Dartmouth, a port on the southwestern coast.

395   Aboute his nekke, under his arm adown.
       The hote somer hadde maad his hewe al brown;
       And certainly he was a good felawe.
       Ful many a draughte of win hadde he drawe
       Fro Burdeuxward, whil that the chapman° sleep[7]:   *merchant*
400   Of nice° conscience took he no keep;°   *scrupulous / care*
       If that he faught and hadde the hyer hand,
       By water he sente hem hoom to every land.
       But of his craft, to rekene wel his tides,
       His stremes° and his daungers° him bisides,   *currents / hazards*
405   His herberwe° and his moone, his lodemenage,°   *harboring / navigation*
       Ther was noon swich from Hulle to Cartage.[8]
       Hardy he was and wis to undertake;
       With many a tempest hadde his beerd been shake;
       He knew alle the havenes as they were
410   Fro Gotlond to the Cape of Finistere,[9]
       And every crike° in Britaine° and in Spaine.   *inlet / Brittany*
       His barge ycleped was the Maudelaine.

            With us ther was a Doctour of Physik:°   *Medicine*
       In al this world ne was ther noon him lik
415   To speken of physik and of surgerye.
       For he was grounded in astronomye,°   *astrology*
       He kepte his pacient a ful greet deel
       In houres° by his magik naturel.   *astronomical hours*
       Wel coude he fortunen the ascendent[1]
420   Of his images° for his pacient.   *talismans*
       He knew the cause of every maladye,
       Were it of hoot or cold or moiste or drye,[2]
       And where engendred° and of what humour:[3]   *originated*
       He was a verray parfit praktisour.°   *practitioner*
425   The cause yknowe, and of his harm the roote,
       Anoon he yaf the sike man his boote.°   *remedy*
            Ful redy hadde he his apothecaries
       To senden him drogges and his letuaries,°   *medicines*
       For eech of hem made other for to winne:
430   Hir frendshipe was nought newe to biginne.
       Wel knew he the olde Esculapius,[4]
       And Deiscorides and eek Rufus,
       Olde Ipocras, Hali, and Galien,
       Serapion, Razis, and Avicen,
435   Averrois, Damascien, and Constantin,

---

7. On the trip back from Bordeaux while the merchant slept.
8. Hull, on the northeastern coast in Yorkshire; Cartage: Carthage in North Africa or Cartagena on the Mediterranean coast of Spain.
9. Gotland in the Baltic Sea; Finistere: Land's End in western Spain.
1. Calculate the ascendent (propitious moment).
2. The qualities of the four natural elements, corresponding to the humors of the body and the composition of the universe, needed to be kept in perfect balance.
3. Bodily fluids, or "humors," thought to govern moods

(blood, phlegm, black bile, yellow bile).
4. The Physician is acquainted with a full range of medical authorities from among the ancient Greeks (Aesculapius, Dioscorides, Rufus, Hippocrates, Galen, and Serapion), the Persians (Hali and Rhazes), the Arabs (Avicenna and Averroes), the Mediterranean transmitters of Eastern science to the West (John of Damascus, Constantine the African), and later medical school professors (Bernard of Gordon, who taught at Montpellier; John of Gaddesden, who taught at Merton College; and Gilbertus Anglicus, an early contemporary of Chaucer's).

Bernard, and Gatesden, and Gilbertin.
Of his diete mesurable° was he,   *moderate*
For it was of no superfluitee,
But of greet norissing and digestible.
His studye was but litel on the Bible.   440
In sanguin° and in pers° he clad was al,   *red / Persian blue*
Lined with taffata and with sendal;°   *silks*
And yit he was but esy of dispence;°   *thrifty*
He kepte that he wan in pestilence.
For gold in physik is a cordial,°   *tonic*   445
Therfore he loved gold in special.
   A good Wif was ther of biside Bathe,
But she was somdeel deef,° and that was scathe.°   *somewhat deaf / a pity*
Of cloth-making she hadde swich an haunt,°   *practice*
She passed hem of Ypres and of Gaunt.[5]   450
In al the parissh wif ne was ther noon
That to the offring[6] bifore hire sholde goon,
And if ther dide, certain so wroth° was she   *angry*
That she was out of alle charitee.
Hir coverchiefs ful fine were of ground[7]—   455
I dorste swere they weyeden° ten pound   *weighed*
That on a Sonday weren upon hir heed.
Hir hosen° weren of fin scarlet reed,   *stockings*
Ful straite yteyd,° and shoes ful moiste° and newe.   *tightly laced / supple*
Bold was hir face and fair and reed of hewe.   460
She was a worthy womman al hir live:
Housbondes at chirche dore she hadde five,
Withouten other compaignye in youthe—
But therof needeth nought to speke as nouthe.°   *for now*
And thries hadde she been at Jerusalem;   465
She hadde passed many a straunge streem;
At Rome she hadde been, and at Boloigne,[8]
In Galice at Saint Jame, and at Coloigne:
She coude° muchel of wandring by the waye.   *knew*
Gat-toothed° was she, soothly for to saye.   *gap-toothed*   470
Upon an amblere[9] esily she sat,
Ywimpled[1] wel, and on hir heed an hat
As brood as is a bokeler or a targe,°   *small shields*
A foot-mantel° aboute hir hipes large,   *riding skirt*
And on hir feet a paire of spores° sharpe.   *spurs*   475
In felaweshipe wel coude she laughe and carpe:
Of remedies of love she knew parchaunce,[2]
For she coude of that art the olde daunce.°   *tricks*
   A good man was ther of religioun,
And was a poore Person° of a town,   *parson*   480
But riche he was of holy thought and werk.
He was also a lerned man, a clerk,

5. Centers of Flemish cloth-making.
6. The collection of gifts at the consecration of the Mass.
7. Her linen kerchiefs were fine in texture.
8. Rome, Boulogne, Santiago Compostela, and Cologne
were major European pilgrimage sites.
9. A horse with a gentle pace.
1. Wearing a large headdress that covers all but the face.
2. She knew cures for lovesickness, as it happened.

That Cristes gospel trewely wolde preche;

His parisshens° devoutly wolde he teche.   *parishioners*

485   Benigne he was, and wonder diligent,

And in adversitee ful pacient,

And swich he was preved ofte sithes.

Ful loth were him to cursen for his tithes,[3]

But rather wolde he yiven, out of doute,

490   Unto his poore parisshens aboute

Of his offring and eek of his substaunce:°   *possessions*

He coude in litel thing have suffisaunce.

Wid was his parissh, and houses fer asonder,

But he ne lafte nought for rain ne thonder,

495   In siknesse nor in meschief, to visite

The ferreste in his parissh, muche and lite,[4]

Upon his feet, and in his hand a staf.

This noble ensample° to his sheep he yaf   *example*

That first he wroughte,° and afterward he taughte.   *did*

500   Out of the Gospel he tho° wordes caughte,   *those*

And this figure° he added eek therto: *saying*

That if gold ruste, what shal iren do?

For if a preest be foul, on whom we truste,

No wonder is a lewed° man to ruste.   *uneducated*

505   And shame it is, if a preest take keep,°   *is concerned*

A shiten° shepherde and a clene sheep.   *shit-covered*

Wel oughte a preest ensample for to yive

By his clennesse how that his sheep sholde live.

He sette nought his benefice to hire[5]

510   And leet his sheep encombred in the mire

And ran to London, unto Sainte Poules,

To seeken him a chaunterye for soules,

Or with a bretherhede to been withholde,

But dwelte at hoom and kepte wel his folde,

515   So that the wolf ne made it nought miscarye:

He was a shepherde and nought a mercenarye.

And though he holy were and vertuous,

He was to sinful men nought despitous,°   *scornful*

Ne of his speeche daungerous ne digne,°   *haughty*

520   But in his teching discreet and benigne,

To drawen folk to hevene by fairnesse

By good ensample—this was his bisinesse.

But it were any persone obstinat,

What so he were, of heigh or lowe estat,

525   Him wolde he snibben° sharply for the nones:°   *rebuke / on the spot*

A bettre preest I trowe° ther nowher noon is.   *believe*

He waited after° no pompe and reverence,   *expected*

Ne maked him a spiced° conscience,   *overly critical*

---

3. And so was he shown to be many times. / He was most unwilling to curse parishioners (with excommunication) if they failed to pay his tithes (a tenth of their income due to the Church).

4. The furthest away in his parish, great and small.

5. The priest did not rent out his parish to another in order to take a more profitable position saying masses for the dead at the chantries of St. Paul's in London or to serve as chaplain to a wealthy guild (bretherhede).

	But Cristes lore° and his Apostles twelve	*teaching*
530	He taughte, but first he folwed° it himselve.	*followed*
	With him ther was a Plowman, was his brother,	
	That hadde ylad of dong ful many a fother.[6]	
	A trewe swinkere° and a good was he,	*worker*
	Living in pees° and parfit° charitee.	*peace / perfect*
535	God loved he best with al his hoole herte	
	At alle times, though him gamed or smerte,[7]	
	And thanne his neighebor right as himselve.	
	He wolde thresshe, and therto dike and delve,°	*make ditches and dig*
	For Cristes sake, for every poore wight,°	*person*
540	Withouten hire,° if it laye in his might.	*pay*
	His tithes payed he ful faire and wel,	
	Bothe of his propre swink[8] and his catel.°	*possessions*
	In a tabard° rood upon a mere.°	*smock / mare*
	Ther was also a Reeve° and a Millere,	*estate manager*
545	A Somnour, and a Pardoner[9] also,	
	A Manciple,° and myself—ther were namo.	*Steward*
	The Millere was a stout carl° for the nones.	*fellow*
	Ful big he was of brawn and eek of bones—	
	That preved wel, for overal ther he cam	
550	At wrastling he wolde have alway the ram.[1]	
	He was short-shuldred, brood, a thikke knarre.°	*bully*
	Ther was no dore that he nolde heve of harre,°	*push off its hinges*
	Or breke it at a renning with his heed.	
	His beerd as any sowe or fox was reed,	
555	And therto brood, as though it were a spade;	
	Upon the cop° right of his nose he hade	*tip*
	A werte, and theron stood a tuft of heres,	
	Rede as the bristles of a sowes eres;	
	His nosethirles° blake were and wide.	*nostrils*
560	A swerd and a bokeler° bar° he by his side.	*small shield / carried*
	His mouth as greet was as a greet furnais.	
	He was a janglere and a Goliardais,[2]	
	And that was most of sinne and harlotries.°	*obscenities*
	Wel coude he stelen corn and tollen thries[3]—	
565	And yit he hadde a thombe of gold,[4] pardee.°	*by God*
	A whit cote and a blew hood wered he.	
	A baggepipe wel coude he blowe and soune,	
	And therwithal he broughte us out of towne.	
	A gentil Manciple was ther of a temple,°	*law school*
570	Of which achatours° mighte take exemple	*buyers*
	For to been wise in bying of vitaile;°	*food*
	For wheither that he paide or took by taile,°	*on credit*
	Algate he waited so in his achat[5]	

---

6. That had carried many a cartload of manure.
7. Enjoyed himself or suffered pain.
8. Money earned from his own work.
9. A Summoner, a server of summonses for the ecclesiastical courts; Pardoner: a seller of indulgences.
1. Awarded as a prize for wrestling.
2. He was a teller of dirty stories and a reveller.

3. Collect three times as much tax as was due.
4. It was proverbial that millers were dishonest and that an honest miller was as rare as one who had a golden thumb. The statement is meant ironically.
5. He was always so watchful for his opportunities to purchase.

	That he was ay biforn° and in good stat.°	*always ahead / well off*
575	Now is nat that of God a ful fair grace°	*blessing*
	That swich a lewed° mannes wit shal pace°	*uneducated / surpass*
	The wisdom of an heep of lerned men?	
	Of maistres° hadde he mo than thries ten	*scholars*
	That weren of lawe expert and curious,°	*skillful*
580	Of whiche ther were a dozeine in that house	
	Worthy to been stiwardes of rente° and lond	*managers of revenues*
	Of any lord that is in Engelond,	
	To make him live by his propre good°	*own wealth*
	In honour dettelees but if he were wood,°	*unless he were crazy*
585	Or live as scarsly° as him list° desire,	*thriftily / pleases*
	And able for to helpen al a shire	
	In any caas° that mighte falle° or happe,	*event / befall*
	And yit this Manciple sette hir aller cappe!°	*made fools of them all*
	The Reeve was a sclendre° colerik° man;	*lean / ill-tempered*
590	His beerd was shave as neigh° as evere he can;	*close*
	His heer was by his eres ful round yshorn;	
	His top was dokked° lik a preest biforn;°	*clipped / in front*
	Ful longe were his legges and ful lene,	
	Ylik° a staf, ther was no calf yseene.°	*like / visible*
595	Wel coude he keepe a gerner° a binne—	*granary*
	Ther was noon auditour coude on him winne.[6]	
	Wel wiste he by the droughte and by the rain	
	The yeelding of his seed and of his grain.	
	His lordes sheep, his neet,° his dayerye,°	*cattle / dairy cattle*
600	His swim, his hors, his stoor,° and his pultrye	*livestock*
	Was hoolly in this Reeves governinge,	
	And by his covenant° yaf the rekeninge,°	*contract / gave account*
	Sin that his lord was twenty yeer of age.	
	Ther coude no man bringe him in arrerage.°	*financial arrears*
605	Ther nas baillif, hierde, nor other hine,[7]	
	That he ne knew his sleighte° and his covine°—	*tricks / plotting*
	They were adrad of him as of the deeth.	
	His woning° was ful faire upon an heeth;°	*dwelling / meadow*
	With greene trees shadwed was his place.	
610	He coude bettre than his lord purchace.°	*buy property*
	Ful riche he was astored prively.°	*stocked in secret*
	His lord wel coude he plesen subtilly,	
	To yive and lene° him of his owene good,°	*lend / possessions*
	And have a thank,° and yit a cote and hood.	*gratitude*
615	In youthe he hadde lerned a good mister:°	*profession*
	He was a wel good wrighte, a carpenter.	
	This Reeve sat upon a ful good stot°	*stallion*
	That was a pomely° grey and highte° Scot.	*dappled / named*
	A long surcote° of pers° upon he hade,	*overcoat / blue*
620	And by his side he bar a rusty blade.	
	Of Northfolk[8] was this Reeve of which I telle,	
	Biside a town men clepen° Baldeswelle.	*call*

6. Gain anything (by catching him out).
7. There was no foreman, herdsman, or other farmhand.

8. Norfolk in the north of England. The Reeve is notable for his northern dialect and regionalisms.

Tukked[9] he was as is a frere aboute,

And evere he rood the hindreste° of oure route.°   *hindmost / group*

625   A Somnour was ther with us in that place

That hadde a fir-reed° cherubinnes° face,   *fire-red / cherub's*

For saucefleem° he was, with yën narwe,   *pimply*

And hoot he was, and lecherous as a sparwe,°   *sparrow*

With scaled° browes blake and piled[1] beerd: *scabby*

630   Of his visage children were aferd.°   *frightened*

Ther nas quiksilver, litarge, ne brimstoon,

Boras, ceruce, ne oile of tartre noon,[2]

Ne oinement that wolde clense and bite,

That him mighte helpen of his whelkes° white,   *blotches*

635   Nor of the knobbes° sitting on his cheekes.   *lumps*

Wel loved he garlek, oinons, and eek leekes,

And for to drinke strong win reed as blood.

Thanne wolde he speke and crye as he were wood;°   *crazy*

And whan that he wel dronken hadde the win,

640   Thanne wolde he speke no word but Latin:

A fewe termes hadde he, two or three,

That he hadde lerned out of som decree;

No wonder is—he herde it al the day,

And eek ye knowe wel how that a jay°   *parrot*

645   Can clepen "Watte"° as wel as can the Pope—   *call "Walter"*

But whoso coude in other thing him grope,°   *examine*

Thanne hadde he spent all his philosophye;

Ay *Questio quid juris*[3] wolde he crye.

He was a gentil harlot° and a kinde;   *rascal*

650   A bettre felawe sholde men nought finde:

He wolde suffre,° for a quart of win,   *allow*

A good felawe to have his concubin°   *mistress*

A twelfmonth, and excusen him at the fulle;

Ful prively a finch eek coude he pulle.[4]

655   And if he foond owher° a good felawe   *anywhere*

He wolde techen him to have noon awe

In swich caas of the Ercedekenes curs,[5]

But if a mannes soule were in his purs,°   *wallet*

For in his purs he sholde ypunisshed be.

660   "Purs is the Ercedekenes helle," saide he.

But wel I woot° he lied right in deede: *know*

Of cursing° oughte eech gilty man him drede,°   *excommunication / fear*

For curs wol slee° right as assoiling° savith—   *will kill / absolving*

And also war him of a *significavit*.[6]

665   In daunger hadde he at his owene gise[7]

The yonge girles of the diocise,

And knew hir conseil,° and was al hir reed.°   *secrets / advice*

---

9. He wore his clothes tucked up with a cinch as friars did.
1. With hair falling out.
2. There was not mercury, lead ointment, or sulphur, / Borax, white lead, nor any oil of tartar that could clean him.
3. "The question as to what point of law (applies)"; often used in ecclesiastical courts.
4. And secretly he also knew how to fool around.
5. In case of excommunication by the archdeacon.
6. Order of transfer from ecclesiastical to secular courts.
7. Under his control he had at his disposal.

A gerland hadde he set upon his heed
As greet as it were for an ale-stake;° _tavern sign_
670 A bokeler hadde he maad him of a cake.° _loaf of bread_
    With him ther rood a gentil Pardoner
Of Rouncival,[8] his freend and his compeer,° _companion_
That straight was comen fro the Court of Rome.
Ful loude he soong, "Com hider, love, to me."[9]
675 This Somnour bar to him a stif burdoun:° _a strong baritone_
Was nevere trompe° of half so greet a soun. _trumpet_
    This Pardoner hadde heer as yelow as wex,
But smoothe it heeng as dooth a strike of flex;° _clump of flax_
By ounces° heenge his lokkes that he hadde, _thin strands_
680 And therwith he his shuldres overspradde,
But thinne it lay, by colpons,° oon by oon; _strands_
But hood for jolitee° wered he noon, _fanciness_
For it was trussed up in his walet:° _pack_
Him thoughte he rood al of the newe jet.° _fashion_
685 Dischevelee° save his cappe he rood al bare. _loose-haired_
Swiche glaring yën hadde he as an hare.
A vernicle[1] hadde he sowed upon his cappe,
His walet biforn him in his lappe,
Bretful of pardon,[2] comen from Rome al hoot.
690 A vois he hadde as smal° as hath a goot;° _high-pitched / goat_
No beerd hadde he, ne nevere sholde have;
As smoothe it was as it were late yshave:
I trowe he were a gelding or a mare.[3]
But of his craft,° fro Berwik into Ware,[4] _skill_
695 Ne was ther swich another pardoner;
For in his male° he hadde a pilwe-beer° _bag / pillowcase_
Which that he saide was Oure Lady veil;
He saide he hadde a gobet° of the sail _chunk_
That Sainte Peter hadde whan that he wente
700 Upon the see, til Jesu Crist him hente.° _grabbed_
He hadde a crois of laton,° ful of stones, _brass cross_
And in a glas he hadde pigges bones,
But with thise relikes whan that he foond
A poore person° dwelling upon lond, _parson_
705 Upon a day he gat him more moneye
Than that the person gat in monthes twaye;° _two_
And thus with feined flaterye and japes° _tricks_
He made the person and the peple his apes.° _dupes_
But trewely to tellen at the laste,
710 He was in chirche a noble ecclesiaste;
Wel coude he rede a lesson and a storye,° _liturgical texts_
But alderbest° he soong an offertorye, _best of all_
For wel he wiste whan that song was songe,

---

8. A hospital at Charing Cross in London.
9. A popular ballad.
1. A pilgrim badge, reproducing St. Veronica's veil bearing the imprint of Christ's face.

2. Full to the brim with indulgences.
3. I believe he was a gelding (eunuch) or a mare (perhaps a passive homosexual).
4. Towns north and south of London.

He moste preche and wel affile° his tonge   *sharpen*
715 To winne silver, as he ful wel coude—
Therfore he soong the merierly and loude.
   Now have I told you soothly° in a clause°   *truly / briefly*
Th'estaat, th'array, the nombre, and eek the cause
Why that assembled was this compaignye
720 In Southwerk at this gentil hostelrye
That highte the Tabard, faste by the Belle;[5]
But now is time to you for to telle
How that we baren us that ilke° night   *same*
Whan we were in that hostelrye alight;
725 And after wol I telle of oure viage,°   *trip*
And al the remenant of oure pilgrimage.
   But first I praye you of youre curteisye
That ye n'arette° it nought my vilainye°   *consider / rudeness*
Though that I plainly speke in this matere
730 To telle you hir wordes and hir cheere,°   *comportment*
Ne though I speke hir wordes proprely;°   *accurately*
For this ye knowen also wel as I:
Who so shal telle a tale after a man
He moot reherce,° as neigh as evere he can,   *must repeat*
735 Everich a word, if it be in his charge,
Al speke he nevere so rudeliche° and large,°   *crudely / freely*
Or elles he moot telle his tale untrewe,
Or feine° thing, or finde wordes newe;   *invent, falsify*
He may nought spare although he were his brother:
740 He moot as wel saye oo word as another.
Crist spak himself ful brode° in Holy Writ,   *plainly*
And wel ye woot° no vilainye is it;   *know*
Eek Plato saith, who so can him rede,
The wordes mote be cosin° to the deede.   *closely related*
745   Also I praye you to foryive it me
Al° have I nat set folk in hir degree°   *although / rank*
Here in this tale as that they sholde stonde:
My wit is short, ye may wel understonde.
   Greet cheere made oure Host us everichoon,
750 And to the soper sette he us anoon.
He served us with vitaile at the beste.
Strong was the win, and wel to drinke us leste.°   *it pleased*
A semely° man oure Hoste was withalle   *apt*
For to been a marchal° in an halle;   *master of ceremonies*
755 A large man he was, with yën steepe;°   *glaring eyes*
A fairer burgeis was ther noon in Chepe°—   *Cheapside (in London)*
Bold of his speeche, and wis, and wel ytaught,
And of manhood him lakkede° right naught.   *he lacked*
Eek therto he was right a merye man,
760 And after soper playen he bigan,
And spak of mirthe amonges othere thinges—

5. Another tavern in Southwark.

Whan that we hadde maad oure rekeninges°—   *paid the bill*
And saide thus, "Now, lordinges, trewely,
Ye been to me right welcome, hertely.
765   For by my trouthe, if that I shal nat lie,
I sawgh nat this yeer so merye a compaignye
At ones in this herberwe° as is now.   *inn*
Fain wolde I doon you mirthe, wiste I how.
And of a mirthe I am right now bithought,
770   To doon you ese, and it shal coste nought.
     Ye goon to Canterbury—God you speede;
The blisful martyr quite° you youre meede.°   *repay / reward*
And wel I woot° as ye goon by the waye   *know*
Ye shapen° you to talen° and to playe,   *intend / tell tales*
775   For trewely, confort ne mirthe is noon
To ride by the waye domb as stoon;
And therfore wol I maken you disport
As I saide erst,° and doon you som confort;   *before*
And if you liketh alle, by oon assent,
780   For to stonden at my juggement,
And for to werken as I shal you saye,
Tomorwe whan ye riden by the waye—
Now by my fader soule that is deed,
But° ye be merye I wol yive you myn heed!   *unless*
785   Holde up youre handes withouten more speeche."
     Oure conseil was nat longe for to seeche;°   *seek*
Us thoughte it was nat worth to make it wis,°   *deliberate*
And graunted him withouten more avis,°   *opinions*
And bade him saye his voirdit° as him leste.   *verdict*
790   "Lordinges," quod he, "now herkneth for the beste;
But taketh it nought, I praye you, in desdain.
This is the point, to speken short and plain,
That eech of you, to shorte with oure waye
In this viage, shal tellen tales twaye°—   *two*
795   To Canterburyward, I mene it so,
And hoomward he shal tellen othere two,
Of aventures that whilom° have bifalle;   *long ago*
And which of you that bereth him best of alle—
That is to sayn, that telleth in this cas
800   Tales of best sentence° and most solas°—   *substance / pleasure*
Shal have a soper at oure aller cost,
Here in this place, sitting by this post,
Whan that we come again fro Canterbury.
And for to make you the more mury
805   I wol myself goodly° with you ride—   *gladly*
Right at myn owene cost—and be youre gide.
And who so wol my juggement withsaye°   *contradict*
Shal paye al that we spende by the waye.
And if ye vouche sauf° that it be so,   *grant*
810   Telle me anoon, withouten wordes mo,
And I wol erly shape° me therfore."   *prepare*

This thing was graunted and oure othes swore
With ful glad herte, and prayden him also
That he wolde vouche sauf for to do so,
815   And that he wolde been oure governour,
And of oure tales juge° and reportour,° — *judge / recordkeeper*
And sette a soper at a certain pris,° — *price*
And we wol ruled been at his devis,° — *plan*
In heigh and lowe; and thus by oon assent
820   We been accorded to his juggement.
And therupon the win was fet° anoon; — *fetched*
We dronken and to reste wente eechoon° — *everyone*
Withouten any lenger taryinge.
     Amorwe° whan that day bigan to springe — *next morning*
825   Up roos oure Host and was oure aller cok,° — *cock, wake-up call*
And gadred us togidres in a flok,
And forth we riden, a litel more than pas,° — *slow walk*
Unto the watering of Saint Thomas;[6]
And ther oure Host bigan his hors arreste,° — *stop*
830   And saide, "Lordes, herkneth if you leste:° — *it please*
     "Ye woot youre forward° and it you recorde:° — *agreement / remember*
If evensong and morwesong accorde,
Lat see now who shal telle the firste tale.
As evere mote I drinken win or ale,
835   Who so be rebel to my juggement
Shal paye for al that by the way is spent.
Now draweth cut° er that we ferrer twinne:° — *lots / separate furthur*
He which that hath the shorteste shal biginne.
     "Sire Knight," quod he, "my maister and my lord,
840   Now draweth cut, for that is myn accord.° — *wish*
Cometh neer," quod he, "my lady Prioresse,
And ye, sire Clerk, lat be youre shamefastnesse°— — *modesty*
Ne studieth nought. Lay hand to, every man!"
     Anoon to drawen every wight° bigan, — *person*
845   And shortly for to tellen as it was,
Were it by aventure, or sort, or cas,° — *luck, fate or chance*
The soothe° is this, the cut fil° to the Knight; — *truth / fell*
Of which ful blithe° and glad was every wight, — *happy*
And telle he moste his tale, as was resoun,
850   By forward and by composicioun,° — *agreement*
As ye han herd. What needeth wordes mo?
And whan this goode man sawgh that it was so,
As he that wis was and obedient
To keepe his forward by his free assent,
855   He saide, "Sin I shal biginne the game,
What, welcome be the cut, in Goddes name!
Now lat us ride, and herkneth what I saye."
And with that word we riden forth oure waye,
And he bigan with right a merye cheere° — *expression*
860   His tale anoon, and saide as ye may heere.

6. A brook two miles from London.

THE MILLER'S TALE   *The Miller's Tale* both answers and parodies *The Knight's Tale*, a long aristocratic romance about two knights in rivalry for the hand of a lady. While the Miller tells a nearly analogous story of erotic competition, his tale is radically shorter and explicitly sexual. Such brevity and physicality fit his tale's genre—a fabliau, or short comic tale, usually bawdy and often involving a clerk, a wife, and a cuckolded husband. Following the convention (if not the reality) that romances were written by and for the nobility and fabliaux by and for the commons, Chaucer suits *The Miller's Tale* to its teller as aptly as he does the Knight's. Slyly disclaiming responsibility for the tale, he explains its bawdiness by the Miller's class status: "the Millere is a cherle" and like his peer the Reeve who follows and "requites" him, tells "harlotrye."

The drunken Miller's insistence on telling his tale to requite the Knight's tale has been called a "literary peasants' revolt." Although the Miller, a free man, was not actually a peasant, yeomen of his status were active in the Rising of 1381, and millers in particular played a symbolic role in it (see the letters of John Ball, page 461). In fact, this tale is highly literate, with its echoes of the Song of Songs and its parody of the language of courtly love: an actual miller would have had neither the education nor the social sophistication to tell it. Yet a parody implies some degree of attachment to the very model being ridiculed, and *The Miller's Tale* is as much a claim upon the Knight's world as a repudiation of it. The Miller wants to "quiten" the Knight's tale, he says, using a word that can mean to repay or avenge, but also to fulfill. The tale's several plots converge brilliantly upon a single cry: "Water!" The tale's impact derives as well from its plenitude of pleasures (sexual, comic, even religious) after the austere and rigid desires of *The Knight's Tale*.

The Miller's Tale
The Introduction

	Whan that the Knight hadde thus his tale ytold,	
	In al the route° nas ther yong ne old	*group*
	That he ne saide it was a noble storye,	
	And worthy for to drawen° to memorye,	*recall*
5	And namely the gentils° everichoon.	*upper class*
	Oure Hoste lough° and swoor, "So mote I goon,[1]	*laughed*
	This gooth aright: unbokeled is the male.[2]	
	Lat see now who shal telle another tale.	
	For trewely the game is wel bigonne.	
10	Now telleth ye, sire Monk, if that ye conne,°	*know*
	Somwhat to quite° with the Knightes tale."	*repay*
	The Millere, that for dronken was al pale,	
	So that unnethe° upon his hors he sat,	*barely*
	He nolde avalen° neither hood ne hat,	*would not remove*
15	Ne abiden no man for his curteisye,	
	But in Pilates[3] vois he gan to crye,	
	And swoor, "By armes and by blood and bones,°	*(of Christ)*
	I can° a noble tale for the nones,	*know*
	With which I wol now quite the Knightes tale."	
20	Oure Hoste sawgh that he was dronke of ale,	
	And saide, "Abide,° Robin, leve° brother,	*wait / dear*
	Som bettre man shal telle us first another.	
	Abide, and lat us werken thriftily."°	*properly*
	"By Goddes soule," quod he, "that wol nat I,	

1. Thus I may proceed.
2. The bag is opened (i.e., the games are begun).

3. The role of Pilate was traditionally played in a loud and raucous voice in the mystery plays.

25	For I wol speke or elles go my way."
Oure Host answerde, "Tel on, a devele way!°	*in the devil's name*
Thou art a fool; thy wit is overcome."
"Now herkneth," quod the Millere, "alle and some.°	*one and all*
But first I make a protestacioun
30	That I am dronke: I knowe it by my soun.°	*sound*
And therfore if that I mis speke or saye,
Wite it° the ale of Southwerk, I you praye;	*blame it on*
For I wol telle a legende and a lif[4]
Bothe of a carpenter and of his wif,
35	How that a clerk hath set the wrightes cappe."[5]
The Reeve answerde and saide, "Stint thy clappe!°	*hold your tongue*
Lat be thy lewed° dronken harlotrye.°	*unlearned / obscenity*
It is a sinne and eek a greet folye
To apairen° any man or him defame,	*injure*
40	And eek to bringen wives in swich fame.
Thou maist ynough of othere thinges sayn."
This dronken Millere spak ful soone again,
And saide, "Leve brother Osewold,
Who hath no wif, he is no cokewold.°	*cuckold*
45	But I saye nat therfore that thou art oon.
Ther ben ful goode wives many oon,
And evere a thousand goode ayains oon badde.°	*against one bad*
That knowestou wel thyself but if thou madde.°	*go insane*
Why artou angry with my tale now?
50	I have a wif, pardee,° as wel as thou,	*by God*
Yet nolde I, for the oxen in my plough,[6]
Take upon me more than ynough
As deemen° of myself that I were oon:°	*judge / one (a cuckold)*
I wol bileve wel that I am noon.
55	An housbonde shal nought been inquisitif
Of Goddes privetee,° nor of his wif.	*secrets*
So he may finde Goddes foison° there,	*plenty*
Of the remenant needeth nought enquere."
What sholde I more sayn but this Millere
60	He nolde° his wordes for no man forbere,	*would not*
But tolde his cherles° tale in his manere.	*commoner's*
M'athinketh° that I shal reherce° it here,	*I regret / repeat*
And therfore every gentil wight° I praye,	*person*
Deemeth nought, for Goddes love, that I saye
65	Of yvel entente, but for° I moot° reherse	*because / must*
Hir tales alle, be they bet or werse,
Or elles falsen som of my matere.
And therfore, whoso list it nought yheere
Turne over the leef,° and chese° another tale,	*page / choose*
70	For he shal finde ynowe,° grete and smale,	*enough*
Of storial° thing that toucheth gentilesse,°	*historical / nobility*
And eek moralitee and holinesse:

4. The story of a saint's life.
5. Made a fool of the carpenter.

6. Yet I wouldn't, not even (in wager) for the oxen in my plough.

Blameth nought me if that ye chese amis.
The Millere is a cherl, ye knowe wel this,
75 So was the Reeve eek, and othere mo,
And harlotrye they tolden bothe two.
Aviseth you,° and putte me out of blame: be warned
And eek men shal nought maken ernest of game.°   treat jokes seriously

The Tale

Whilom° ther was dwelling at Oxenforde   long ago
80 A riche gnof° that gestes heeld to boorde,°   fool / took in boarders
And of his craft he was a carpenter.
With him ther was dwelling a poore scoler,
Hadde lerned art,[7] but al his fantasye°   fancy
Was turned for to lere° astrologye,   learn
85 And coude a certain of conclusiouns,°   predictions
To deemen by interrogaciouns,[8]
If that men axed° him in certain houres   asked
Whan that men sholde have droughte or elles showres,
Or if men axed him what shal bifalle
90 Of every thing—I may nat rekene° hem alle.   count
    This clerk was cleped° hende[9] Nicholas.   called
Of derne° love he coude, and of solas,[1]   secret
And therto he was sly and ful privee,°   secretive
And lik a maide meeke for to see.
95 A chambre hadde he in that hostelrye°   inn
Allone, withouten any compaignye,
Ful fetisly ydight with herbes swoote,[2]
And he himself as sweete as is the roote
Of licoris or any setewale.[3]
100 His Almageste[4] and bookes grete and smale,
His astrelabye,[5] longing for° his art,   belonging to
His augrim stones,° layen faire apart   abacus beads
On shelves couched° at his beddes heed;   arranged
His presse° ycovered with a falding° reed;   dresser / coarse cloth
105 And al above ther lay a gay sautrye,°   harp
On which he made a-nightes melodye
So swetely that al the chambre roong,
And Angelus ad Virginem[6] he soong,
And after that he soong the Kinges Note:[7]
110 Ful often blessed was his merye throte.
And thus this sweete clerk his time spente
After his freendes finding and his rente.[8]
    This carpenter hadde wedded newe a wif
Which that he loved more than his lif.

7. The arts curriculum (trivium).
8. To estimate by consulting (the stars).
9. Handsome, courteous, handy.
1. Pleasure, (sexual) comforts.
2. Elegantly decked out with sweet herbs.
3. Setwall, a gingerlike spice used as a stimulant.

4. An astrological treatise by Ptolemy.
5. Astrolabe, an astrological instrument.
6. A prayer commemorating the Annunciation.
7. A popular song.
8. According to what his friends gave him and his income.

115 Of eighteteene yeer she was of age;
Jalous he was, and heeld hire narwe in cage,
For she was wilde and yong, and he was old,
And deemed° himself been lik a cokewold.   *supposed*
He knew nat Caton,[9] for his wit was rude,
120 That bad men sholde wedde his similitude:°   *equal in age*
Men sholde wedden after hir estat,°   *station in life*
For youthe and elde is often at debat.
But sith that he was fallen in the snare,
He moste endure, as other folk, his care.
125   Fair was this yonge wif, and therwithal
As any wesele hir body gent and smal.[1]
A ceint° she wered, barred° al of silk;   *belt / striped*
A barmcloth° as whit as morne milk   *apron*
Upon hir lendes,° ful of many a gore;°   *loins / flounce*
130 Whit was hir smok,° and broiden° al bifore   *slip / embroidered*
And eek bihinde, on hir coler aboute,°   *around her collar*
Of col-blak silk, withinne and eek withoute;
The tapes° of hir white voluper°   *ribbons / cap*
Were of the same suite° of hir coler;   *pattern*
135 Hir filet° brood° of silk and set ful hye;   *headband / broad*
And sikerly she hadde a likerous yë;[2]
Ful smale ypulled° were hir browes two,   *plucked*
And tho° were bent, and blake as any slo.°   *they / plum*
She was ful more blisful on to see
140 Than is the newe perejonette° tree,   *pear*
And softer than the wolle is of a wether;°   *ram*
And by hir girdel° heeng a purs of lether,   *belt*
Tasseled with silk and perled° with latoun.°   *decorated / brass*
In al this world, to seeken up and down,
145 Ther nis no man so wis that coude thenche°   *imagine*
So gay a popelote° or swich a wenche.[3]   *doll*
Ful brighter was the shining of hir hewe
Than in the Towr the noble° yforged newe.[4]   *gold coin*
But of hir song, it was as loud and yerne°   *lively*
150 As any swalwe sitting on a berne.
Therto she coude skippe and make game
As any kide or calf folwing his dame.°   *mother*
Hir mouth was sweete as bragot or the meeth,°   *honey drinks*
Or hoord of apples laid in hay or heeth.°   *heather*
155 Winsing° she was as is a joly° colt,   *skittish / spirited*
Long as a mast, and upright° as a bolt.°   *strait / arrow*
A brooch she bar upon hir lowe coler
As brood as is the boos° of a bokeler;°   *boss / shield*
Hir shoes were laced on hir legges hye.
160 She was a primerole,° a piggesnye,[5]   *primrose*
For any lord to leggen in his bedde,

---

9. Cato, Latin author of a book of maxims used in elementary education.
1. Her body as delicate and slender as any weasel.
2. And certainly she had a wanton eye.

3. Woman of the working class.
4. Than the new-forged gold coin in the Tower (of London, the royal mint).
5. Pig's eye, a flower.

Or yet for any good yeman to wedde.

Now sire, and eft° sire, so bifel the cas   *again*
That on a day this hende Nicholas
165 Fil with this yonge wif to rage° and playe,   *sport*
Whil that hir housbonde was at Oseneye°   *Osney, near Oxford*
(As clerkes been ful subtil and ful quainte),°   *clever*
And prively he caughte hire by the queinte,[6]
And saide, "Ywis,° but if ich have my wille,   *certainly*
170 For derne° love of thee, lemman,° I spille,"°   *secret / sweetheart / die*
And heeld hire harde by the haunche-bones,
And saide, "Lemman, love me al atones,°   *at once*
Or I wol dien, also° God me save."   *so*
And she sproong as a colt dooth in a trave,[7]
175 And with hir heed she wried° faste away;   *twisted*
She saide, "I wol nat kisse thee, by my fay.°   *faith*
Why, lat be," quod she, "lat be, Nicholas!
Or I wol crye 'Out, harrow, and allas!'
Do way youre handes, for your curteisye!"
180   This Nicholas gan mercy for to crye,
And spak so faire, and profred him° so faste,   *pressed his case*
That she hir love him graunted atte laste,
And swoor hir ooth by Saint Thomas of Kent
That she wolde been at his comandement,
185 Whan that she may hir leiser° wel espye.   *opportunity*
"Myn housbonde is so ful of jalousye
That but ye waite wel and been privee,[8]
I woot° right wel I nam but deed,"° quod she.   *know / am no more than*
"Ye moste been ful derne° as in this cas."   *secret*
190   "Nay, therof care thee nought," quod Nicholas.
"A clerk hadde litherly biset his while,°   *wasted his time*
But if he coude a carpenter bigile."
And thus they been accorded and ysworn
To waite a time, as I have told biforn.
195 Whan Nicholas hadde doon this everydeel,
And thakked° hire upon the lendes° weel,   *patted / loins*
He kiste hire sweete, and taketh his sautrye,
And playeth faste, and maketh melodye.
    Thanne fil it thus, that to the parissh chirche,
200 Cristes owene werkes for to wirche,
This goode wif wente on an haliday:°   *holy day*
Hir forheed shoon as bright as any day,
So was it wasshen whan she leet° hir werk.   *left off*
    Now was ther of that chirche a parissh clerk,
205 The which that was ycleped° Absolon: *called*
Crul° was his heer, and as the gold it shoon,   *curly*
And strouted as a fanne[9] large and brode;
Ful straight and evene lay his joly shode.°   *part in his hair*

---

6. Literally "dainty part," slang for the female genitals.
7. A restraint for horses when they are being shod.
8. That unless you're very caurious and discreet.

9. And spread out like a winnowing fan (for separating wheat from chaff).

His rode° was reed, his y'n greye as goos.   *complexion*
210 With Poules window¹ corven° on his shoos,   *carved*
In hoses rede he wente fetisly.°   *elegantly*
Yclad he was ful smale° and proprely,   *fine*
Al in a kirtel° of a light waget°—   *tunic / blue*
Ful faire and thikke been the pointes° set—   *laces*
215 And therupon he hadde a gay surplis,°   *clerical robe*
As whit as is the blosme upon the ris.°   *twig*
A merye child° he was, so God me save.   *lad*
Wel coude he laten blood,² and clippe,° and shave,   *cut hair*
And maken a chartre of land, or acquitaunce;°   *legal release*
220 In twenty manere coude he trippe and daunce
After the scole of Oxenforde tho,
And with his legges casten° to and fro,   *fling*
And playen songes on a smal rubible;°   *fiddle*
Therto he soong somtime a loud quinible,°   *high treble*
225 And as wel coude he playe on a giterne:°   *guitar*
In al the town nas brewhous ne taverne
That he ne visited with his solas,³
Ther any gailard tappestere° was.   *saucy barmaid*
But sooth to sayn, he was somdeel squaimous°   *somewhat squeamish*
230 Of farting, and of speeche daungerous.°   *haughty*
This Absolon, that joly was and gay,
Gooth with a cencer° on the haliday,   *incense bowl*
Cencing the wives of the parissh faste,
And many a lovely look on hem he caste,
235 And namely on this carpenteres wif:
To looke on hire him thoughte a merye lif.
She was so propre and sweete and likerous,°   *sexy*
I dar wel sayn, if she hadde been a mous,
And he a cat, he wolde hire hente° anoon.   *catch*
240 This parissh clerk, this joly Absolon,
Hath in his herte swich a love-longinge
That of no wif ne took he noon offringe—
For curteisye he saide he wolde noon.
The moone, whan it was night, ful brighte shoon,
245 And Absolon his giterne hath ytake—
For paramours he thoughte for to wake—⁴
And forth he gooth, jolif° and amorous,   *pretty*
Til he cam to the carpenteres hous,
A litel after cokkes hadde ycrowe,
250 And dressed° him up by a shot-windowe°   *placed / hinged window*
That was upon the carpenteres wal.
He singeth in his vois gentil and smal,°   *high*
"Now dere lady, if thy wille be,
I praye you that ye wol rewe° on me,"   *take pity*
255 Ful wel accordant° to his giterninge.   *harmonizing*

---

1. The windows of St. Paul's Chapel were intricately patterned.
2. Let blood (a medical treatment performed by barbers).

3. Entertainment (also with sexual connotations).
4. For the sake of love he thought to keep a vigil.

This carpenter awook and herde him singe,
And spak unto his wif, and saide anoon,
"What, Alison, heerestou nought Absolon
That chaunteth thus under oure bowres° wal?"   *bedroom's*
260 And she answerde hir housbonde therwithal,
"Yis, God woot,° John, I heere it everydeel."°   *knows / every bit*
 This passeth forth. What wol ye bet than weel?[5]
Fro day to day this joly Absolon
So woweth° hire that him is wo-bigoon: *woos*
265 He waketh al the night and al the day;
He kembed° his lokkes brode° and made him gay; *combed / wide-spreading*
He woweth hire by menes and brocage,[6]
And swoor he wolde been hir owene page;°   *attendant*
He singeth, brokking° as a nightingale;   *trilling*
270 He sente hire piment,° meeth,° and spiced ale, *spiced wine / mead*
And wafres° piping hoot out of the gleede;°   *pastries / coals*
And for she was of towne, he profred meede°—   *bribes*
For som folk wol be wonnen for richesse,
And som for strokes,° and som for gentilesse.   *by force*
275 Somtime to shewe his lightnesse° and maistrye,° *agility / skill*
He playeth Herodes[7] upon a scaffold° hye.   *platform*
But what availeth him as in this cas?
She loveth so this hende Nicholas
That Absolon may blowe the bukkes horn;[8]
280 He ne hadde for his labour but a scorn.
And thus she maketh Absolon hir ape,°   *fool*
And al his ernest turneth til a jape.°   *joke*
Ful sooth° is this proverbe, it is no lie;   *true*
Men saith right thus: "Alway the nye slye°   *sly one nearby*
285 Maketh the ferre leve to be loth."[9]
For though that Absolon be wood° or wroth,° *crazy / angry*
By cause that he fer was from hir sighte,
This nye Nicholas stood in his lighte.°   *in the way*
 Now beer thee wel, thou hende Nicholas,
290 For Absolon may waile and singe allas.
  And so bifel it on a Saterday
This carpenter was goon til Oseney,
And hende Nicholas and Alisoun
Accorded been to this conclusioun,
295 That Nicholas shal shapen hem a wile°   *devise them a trick*
This sely° jalous housbonde to bigile,   *innocent*
And if so be this game wente aright,
She sholden sleepen in his arm al night—
For this was his desir and hire also.
300 And right anoon, withouten wordes mo,
This Nicholas no lenger wolde tarye,
But dooth ful softe unto his chambre carye

5. What more would you want?
6. He woos her with go-betweens and mediation.
7. In the English mystery plays, Herod was often por-

trayed as a bully.
8. Undertake a useless endeavor.
9. Makes the distant beloved seem hateful.

Bothe mete and drinke for a day or twaye,
And to hir housbonde bad hire for to saye,
305 If that he axed after Nicholas,
She sholde saye she niste° wher he was—   did not know
Of al that day she sawgh him nought with yë:
She trowed° that he was in maladye,   believed
For for no cry hir maide coude him calle,
310 He nolde° answere for no thing that mighte falle.°   would not / happen
     This passeth forth al thilke° Saterday   that same
That Nicholas stille in his chambre lay,
And eet, and sleep, or dide what him leste,°   he liked
Til Sonday that the sonne gooth to reste.
315   This sely carpenter hath greet mervaile°   wonder
Of Nicholas, or what thing mighte him aile,
And saide, "I am adrad,° by Saint Thomas,   afraid
It stondeth nat aright with Nicholas.
God shilde° that he deide sodeinly!   forbid
320 This world is now ful tikel,° sikerly:°   changeable / surely
I sawgh today a corps yborn to chirche
That now a Monday last I sawgh him wirche.°   working
Go up," quod he unto his knave° anoon,   manservant
"Clepe° at his dore or knokke with a stoon.   call
325 Looke how it is and tel me boldely."
     This knave gooth him up ful sturdily,
And at the chambre dore whil that he stood
He cride and knokked as that he were wood,
"What? How? What do ye, maister Nicholay?
330 How may ye sleepen al the longe day?".
But al for nought: he herde nat a word.
An hole he foond ful lowe upon a boord,
Ther as the cat was wont in for to creepe,
And at that hole he looked in ful deepe,
335 And atte laste he hadde of him a sighte.
     This Nicholas sat evere caping° uprighte   staring
As he hadde kiked° on the newe moone.   gazed
A down he gooth and tolde his maister soone
In what array° he saw this ilke° man.   condition / same
340   This carpenter to blessen him[1] bigan.
And saide, "Help us, Sainte Frideswide![2]
A man woot litel what him shal bitide.
This man is falle, with his astromye,
In som woodnesse° or in som agonye.°   madness / fit
345 I thoughte ay° wel how that it sholde be: always
Men sholde nought knowe of Goddes privetee.
Ye, blessed be alway a lewed° man   unlearned
That nought but only his bileve can.°   knows his creed
So ferde° another clerk with astromye: fared
350 He walked in the feeldes for to prye°   gaze
Upon the sterres, what ther sholde bifalle,

---

1. Bless himself (with the sign of the cross).   2. A saint venerated for her healing powers.

Til he was in a marle-pit° yfalle—   *clay-pit*
He saw nat that. But yet, by Saint Thomas,
Me reweth sore° for hende Nicholas.   *feel sorry*
355   He shal be rated° of his studying,   *scolded*
If that I may, by Jesus, hevene king!
Get me a staf that I may underspore,°   *pry upward*
Whil that thou, Robin, hevest up the dore.
He shal out of his studying, as I gesse."
360   And to the chambre dore he gan him dresse.°   *placed himself*
His knave was a strong carl° for the nones,°   *fellow / purpose*
And by the haspe° he haaf° it up atones: *hinge / heaved*
Into the floor the dore fil anoon.
This Nicholas sat ay as stille as stoon,
365   And evere caped up into the air.
This carpenter wende° he were in despair,   *thought*
And hente° him by the shuldres mightily,   *grabbed*
And shook him harde, and cride spitously,°   *vigorously*
"What, Nicholay, what, how! What! Looke adown!
370   Awaak and thenk on Cristes passioun!³
I crouche° thee from elves and fro wightes."°   *bless / evil spirits*
Therwith the nightspel° saide he anoonrightes   *charm*
On foure halves° of the hous aboute,   *sides*
And on the thresshfold on the dore withoute:
375   "Jesu Crist and Sainte Benedight,⁴
Blesse this hous from every wikked wight!
For nightes nerye° the White Pater Noster.⁵   *protect*
Where wentestou, thou Sainte Petres soster?"°   *sister*
And at the laste this hende Nicholas
380   Gan for to sike° sore, and saide, "Allas,   *sigh*
Shal al the world be lost eftsoones° now?"   *immediately*
    This carpenter answerde, "What saistou?
What, thenk on God as we doon, men that swinke."°   *work*
    This Nicholas answerde, "Fecche me drinke,
385   And after wol I speke in privetee
Of certain thing that toucheth me and thee.
I wol telle it noon other man, certain."
    This carpenter gooth down and comth again,
And broughte of mighty ale a large quart,
390   And whan that eech of hem hadde dronke his part,
This Nicholas his dore faste shette,°   *shut*
And down the carpenter by him he sette,
And saide, "John, myn hoste lief° and dere,   *beloved*
Thou shalt upon thy trouthe° swere me here   *word of honor*
395   That to no wight thou shalt this conseil° wraye;°   *advice / disclose*
For it is Cristes conseil that I saye,
And if thou telle it man, thou art forlore,°   *lost*
For this vengeance thou shalt have therfore,
That if thou wraye° me, thou shalt be wood."°   *reveal / mad*

---

3. Thinking about Christ's death and resurrection was   4. St. Benedict, founder of Western monasticism.
supposed to ward off evil spells.   5. The Lord's Prayer, used as a charm.

400   "Nay, Crist forbede it, for his holy blood,"
       Quod tho this sely man. "I nam no labbe,°   *am no blabbermouth*
       And though I saye, I nam nat lief° to gabbe.   *do not like*
       Say what thou wilt, I shal it nevere telle
       To child ne wif, by him that harwed helle."[6]
405   "Now John," quod Nicholas, "I wol nought lie.
       I have yfounde in myn astrologye,
       As I have looked in the moone bright,
       That now a Monday next, at quarter night,°   *near dawn*
       Shal falle a rain, and that so wilde and wood,°   *furious*
410   That half so greet was nevere Noees° flood.   *Noah's*
       This world," he saide, "in lasse than an hour
       Shal al be dreint,° so hidous is the showr.   *drowned*
       Thus shal mankinde drenche° and lese hir lif."°   *drown / lose their lives*
       This carpenter answerde, "Allas, my wif!
415   And shal she drenche? Allas, myn Alisoun!"
       For sorwe of this he fil almost adown,
       And saide, "Is there no remedye in this cas?"
       "Why yis, for Gode," quod hende Nicholas,
       "If thou wolt werken° after lore° and reed°—   *act / learning / advice*
420   Thou maist nought werken after thyn owene heed;
       For thus saith Salomon that was ful trewe,
       'Werk al by conseil and thou shalt nought rewe.'°   *regret*
       And if thou werken wolt by good conseil,
       I undertake, withouten mast or sail,
425   Yet shal I save hire and thee and me.
       Hastou nat herd how saved was Noee
       Whan that Oure Lord hadde warned him biforn
       That al the world with water sholde be lorn?"°   *lost*
       "Yis," quod this carpenter, "ful yore° ago."   *long*
430   "Hastou nat herd," quod Nicholas, "also
       The sorwe° of Noee with his felaweshipe?°   *sorrow / companions*
       Er that he mighte gete his wif to shipe,
       Him hadde levere,° I dar wel undertake,   *would have preferred*
       At thilke° time than alle his wetheres blake°   *that / black rams*
435   That she hadde had a ship hirself allone.[7]
       And therfore woostou° what is best to doone?   *do you know*
       This axeth haste, and of an hastif° thing   *urgent*
       Men may nought preche or maken tarying.
       Anoon go gete us faste into this in°   *inn*
440   A kneeding trough or elles a kimelin°   *brewing trough*
       For eech of us, but looke that they be large,
       In whiche we mowen swimme as in a barge,
       And han therinne vitaile suffisaunt°   *enough food*
       But for a day—fy on the remenaunt!
445   The water shal aslake° and goon away   *recede*
       Aboute prime° upon the nexte day.   *6 A.M.*
       But Robin may nat wite° of this, thy knave,   *know*

6. Christ, who harrowed hell upon his resurrection,   7. Noah's wife was traditionally portrayed in the mystery
releasing captive souls.   plays as a complaining wife who resisted boarding the ark.

Ne eek thy maide Gille I may nat save.
Axe nought why, for though thou axe me,
450   I wol nought tellen Goddes privetee.
Suffiseth thee, but if thy wittes madde,°   go mad
To han° as greet a grace as Noee hadde.   have
Thy wif shal I wel saven, out of doute.
Go now thy way, and speed thee heraboute.
455   But whan thou hast for hire and thee and me
Ygeten° us thise kneeding-tubbes three,   gotten
Thanne shaltou hangen hem in the roof ful hye,
That no man of oure purveyance° espye.   preparations
And whan thou thus hast doon as I have said,
460   And hast oure vitaile faire in hem ylaid,
And eek° an ax to smite° the corde atwo,   also / cut
Whan that the water comth that we may go,
And broke an hole an heigh° upon the gable   on high
Unto the gardinward,° over the stable,   toward the garden
465   That we may freely passen forth oure way,
Whan that the grete showr is goon away,
Thanne shaltou swimme as merye, I undertake,
As dooth the white doke° after hir drake.   female duck
Thanne wol I clepe,° 'How, Alison? How, John?   call out
470   Be merye, for the flood wol passe anoon.'
And thou wolt sayn, 'Hail, maister Nicholay!
Good morwe, I see thee wel, for it is day!'
And thanne shal we be lordes al oure lif
Of al the world, as Noee and his wif.
475   But of oo thing I warne thee ful right:
Be wel avised on that ilke night
That we been entred into shippes boord
That noon of us ne speke nought a word,
Ne clepe,° ne crye, but been in his prayere,   call out
480   For it is Goddes owene heeste° dete.   commandment
Thy wif and thou mote° hange fer atwinne,°   must / apart
For that bitwixe you shal be no sinne—
Namore in looking than ther shal in deede.
This ordinance is said: go, God thee speede.
485   Tomorwe at night whan men been alle asleepe,
Into oure kneeding-tubbes wol we creepe,
And sitten there, abiding Goddes grace.
Go now thy way, I have no lenger space°   time
To make of this no lenger sermoning.
490   Men sayn thus: 'Send the wise and say no thing.'
Thou art so wis it needeth thee nat teche:
Go save oure lif, and that I thee biseeche."
        This sely° carpenter gooth forth his way: single
Ful ofte he saide allas and wailaway,
495   And to his wif he tolde his privetee,
And she was war,° and knew it bet° than he,   aware / better
What al this quainte cast° was for to saye.°   clever trick / mean
But nathelees she ferde° as she wolde deye,   acted

And saide, "Allas, go forth thy way anoon.
500   Help us to scape,° or we been dede eechoon.   escape
I am thy trewe verray wedded wif:
Go, dere spouse, and help to save oure lif."
    Lo, which a greet thing is affeccioun!°   emotion
Men may dien,° of imaginacioun,°   die / fantasy
505   So deepe may impression be take.
This sely carpenter biginneth quake;
Him thinketh verrailiche° that he may see   truly
Noees flood come walwing° as the see   rolling in
To drenchen Alison, his hony dere.
510   He weepeth, waileth, maketh sory cheere;°   expression
He siketh° with ful many a sory swough,°   sighs / breath
And gooth and geteth him a kneeding-trough,
And after a tubbe and a kimelin,
And prively he sente hem to his in,
515   And heeng hem in the roof in privetee;
His owene hand he made laddres three,
To climben by the ronges and the stalkes°   uprights
Unto the tubbes hanging in the balkes,°   rafters
And hem vitailed, bothe trough and tubbe,
520   With breed and cheese and good ale in a jubbe,°   jug
Suffising right ynough as for a day.
But er that he hadde maad al this array,
He sente his knave, and eek his wenche also,
Upon his neede° to London for to go.   errand
525   And on the Monday whan it drow to nighte,
He shette his dore withouten candel-lighte,
And dressed° alle thing as it sholde be,   arranged
And shortly up they clomben alle three.
They seten stille wel a furlong way.[8]
530   "Now, Pater Noster, clum,"[9] saide Nicholay,
And "Clum" quod John, and "Clum" saide Alisoun.
This carpenter saide his devocioun,
And stille he sit and biddeth his prayere,
Awaiting on the rain, if he it heere.
535   The dede sleep, for wery bisinesse,
Fil on this carpenter right as I gesse
Aboute corfew time,° or litel more.   dusk
For travailing of his gost° he groneth sore,   spirit
And eft he routeth,° for his heed mislay.   snores
540   Down of the laddre stalketh Nicholay,
And Alison ful softe adown she spedde:
Withouten wordes mo they goon to bedde
Ther as the carpenter is wont to lie.
Ther was the revel and the melodye,
545   And thus lith Alison and Nicholas
In bisinesse of mirthe and of solas,

8. The length of time to travel a furlong.   9. Say the Lord's Prayer and hush.

Til that the belle of Laudes[1] gan to ringe,
And freres° in the chauncel° gonne singe.   *friars / chapel*
    This parissh clerk, this amorous Absolon,
550 That is for love alway so wo-bigoon,
Upon the Monday was at Oseneye,
With compaignye him to disporte and playe,
And axed upon caas° a cloisterer[2]   *by chance*
Ful prively after John the carpenter;
555 And he drow him apart out of the chirche,
And saide, "I noot:° I sawgh him here nought wirche°   *don't know / working*
Sith Saterday. I trowe that he be went
For timber ther oure abbot hath him sent.
For he is wont for timber for to go,
560 And dwellen atte grange° a day or two.   *outlying farm*
Or elles he is at his hous, certain.
Where that he be I can nought soothly° sayn."   *truly*
    This Absolon ful jolif was and light,°   *amorous and happy*
And thoughte, "Now is time to wake al night,
565 For sikerly,° I sawgh him nought stiringe   *surely*
Aboute his dore sin° day bigan to springe.°   *since / break*
So mote I thrive,° I shal at cokkes crowe   *may I prosper*
Ful prively knokken at his windowe
That stant ful lowe upon his bowres° wal.   *bedroom's*
570 To Alison now wol I tellen al
My love-longing, for yet I shal nat misse
That at the leeste way I shal hire kisse.
Som manere confort shal I have, parfay.°   *indeed*
My mouth hath icched° al this longe day: *itched*
575 That is a signe of kissing at the leeste.
Al night me mette° eek I was at a feeste.   *dreamed*
Therfore I wol go sleepe an hour or twaye,
And al the night thanne wol I wake and playe."
    Whan that the firste cok hath crowe, anoon
580 Up rist this joly lovere Absolon,
And him arrayeth gay at point devis.°   *fastidiously*
But first he cheweth grain[3] and licoris,
To smellen sweete, er he hadde kembd his heer.
Under his tonge a trewe-love[4] he beer.
585 For therby wende° he to be gracious.°   *supposed / attractive*
He rometh to the carpenteres hous,
And stille he stant under the shot-windowe—
Unto his brest it raughte,° it was so lowe—   *reached*
And ofte he cougheth with a semisoun.°   *soft noise*
590 "What do ye, hony-comb, sweete Alisoun,
My faire brid,° my sweete cinamome?   *bird or bride*
Awaketh, lemman° myn, and speketh to me.   *sweetheart*
Wel litel thinken ye upon my wo
That for your love I swete° ther I go.   *dissolve*

---

1. Lauds, daily church service before sunrise.
2. Member of the monastery.
3. Grain of paradise, an aromatic spice.
4. Four-leafed herb in the shape of a love knot.

595 No wonder is though that I swelte° and swete: *swelter*
    I moorne as dooth a lamb after the tete.
    Ywis,° lemman, I have swich love-longinge,   *certainly*
    That lik a turtle° trewe is my moorninge: *turtle-dove*
    I may nat ete namore than a maide."
600   "Go fro the windowe, Jakke fool," she saide.
    "As help me God, it wol nat be com-pa-me.°   *come kiss me*
    I love another, and elles I were to blame,
    Wel bet than thee, by Jesu, Absolon.
    Go forth thy way or I wol caste a stoon,
605 And lat me sleepe, a twenty devele way."[5]
        "Allas," quod Absolon, "and wailaway,
    That trewe love was evere so yvele biset.°   *badly done to*
    Thanne kis me, sin that it may be no bet,
    For Jesus love and for the love of me."
610   "Woltou thanne go thy way therwith?" quod she.
    "Ye, certes, lemman," quod this Absolon.
    "Thanne maak thee redy," quod she. "I come anoon."
    And unto Nicholas she said stille,
    "Now hust,° and thou shalt laughen al thy fille."   *hush*
615   This Absolon down sette him on his knees,
    And saide, "I am a lord at alle degrees,°   *in every way*
    For after this I hope ther cometh more.
    Lemman, thy grace, and sweete brid, thyn ore!"°   *mercy*
        The windowe she undooth, and that in haste.
620 "Have do," quod she, "com of and speed thee faste,
    Lest that oure neighebores thee espye."
        This Absolon gan wipe his mouth ful drye:
    Derk was the night as pich or as the cole,
    And at the windowe out she putte hir hole.
625 And Absolon, him fil no bet ne wers,
    But with his mouth he kiste hir naked ers,
    Ful savoury,° er he were war of this.   *enthusiastically*
    Abak he sterte, and thoughte it was amis,
    For wel he wiste a womman hath no beerd.
630 He felte a thing al rough and longe yherd,°   *haird*
    And saide, "Fy, allas, what have I do?"
    "Teehee," quod she, and clapte the windowe to.
    And Absolon gooth forth a sory pas.°   *with downcast step*
    "A beerd, a beerd!" quod hende Nicholas,
635 "By Goddes corpus,° this gooth faire and weel."   *body*
        This sely Absolon herde everydeel,
    And on his lippe he gan for anger bite,
    And to himself he saide, "I shal thee quite."°   *repay*
        Who rubbeth now, who froteth now his lippes
640 With dust, with sond, with straw, with cloth, with chippes,
    But Absolon, that saith ful ofte allas?
    "My soule bitake° I unto Satanas,   *hand over*
    But me were levere than[6] all this town," quod he,

---

5. In the name of 20 devils.   6. I would rather than (have).

"Of this despit° awroken° for to be.   insult / avenged
645   Allas," quod he, "allas I ne hadde ybleint!"°   turned aside
His hote love was cold and al yqueint,°   quenched
For fro that time that he hadde kist hir ers
Of paramours he sette nought a kers,[7]
For he was heled of his maladye.
650   Ful ofte paramours he gan defye,°   renounce
And weep as dooth a child that is ybete.°   beaten
A softe paas he wente over the streete
Until a smith men clepen daun° Gervais,   call Sir
That in his forge smithed plough harneis:°   equipment
655   He sharpeth shaar° and cultour° bisily.   plowshare / plough-blade
This Absolon knokketh al esily,°   softly
And saide, "Undo,° Gervais, and that anoon."   open up
    "What, who artou?" "It am I, Absolon."
    "What, Absolon? What, Cristes sweete tree!
660   Why rise ye so rathe?° Ey, benedicite,°   early / bless me
What aileth you? Som gay girl, God it woot,
Hath brought you thus upon the viritoot.°   on the prowl
By Sainte Note,[8] ye woot wel what I mene."
    This Absolon ne roughte nat a bene°   did not care a bean
665   Of al his play. No word again he yaf:°   gave
He hadde more tow on his distaf[9]
Than Gervais knew, and saide, "Freend so dere,
This hote cultour in the chimenee° here,   fireplace
As lene it me:[1] I have therwith to doone.
670   I wol bringe it thee again ful soone."
    Gervais answerde, "Certes, were it gold,
Or in a poke nobles alle untold,[2]
Thou sholdest have, as I am trewe smith.
Ey, Cristes fo,[3] what wol ye do therwith?"
675   "Therof," quod Absolon, "be as be may.
I shal wel telle it thee another day,"
And caughte the cultour by the colde stele.°   handle
Ful softe out at the dore he gan to stele,
And wente unto the carpenteres wal:
680   He cougheth first and knokketh therwithal
Upon the windowe, right as he dide er.°   before
    This Alison answerde, "Who is ther
That knokketh so? I warante° it a thief."   bet
    "Why, nay," quod he, "God woot, my sweete lief,°   dear
685   I am thyn Absolon, my dereling.
Of gold," quod he, "I have thee brought a ring—
My moder yaf it me, so God me save;
Ful fin it is and therto wel ygrave:°   engraved
This wol I yiven thee if thou me kisse."
690   This Nicholas was risen for to pisse,

7. Did not value as much as a piece of cress.
8. St. Noet, a ninth-century saint, with possible pun on
Noah.
9. Flax on his distaf (i.e., cares on his mind).

1. Be so good as to lend it to me.
2. Or in a pouch of uncounted gold coins.
3. By Christ's foe (i.e., the Devil).

And thoughte he wolde amenden al the jape:[4]	
He sholde kisse his ers er that he scape.	
And up the windowe dide he hastily,	
And out his ers he putteth prively,	
695 Over the buttok to the haunche-boon.°	*thigh*
And therwith spak this clerk, this Absolon,	
"Speek, sweete brid, I noot nought wher thou art."	
This Nicholas anoon leet flee° a fart	*let fly*
As greet as it hadde been a thonder-dent°	*thunderbolt*
700 That with the strook he was almost yblent,°	*blinded*
And he was redy with his iren hoot,	
And Nicholas amiddle the ers he smoot:	
Of gooth the skin an hande-brede° aboute;	*hand's width*
The hote cultour brende so his toute°	*backside*
705 That for the smert° he wende° for to die;	*pain / thought*
As he were wood for wo he gan to crye,	
"Help! Water! Water! Help, for Goddes herte!"	
This carpenter out of his slomber sterte,	
And herde oon cryen "Water!" as he were wood,	
710 And thoughte, "Allas, now cometh Noweles° flood!"	*Noah's*
He sette him up withoute wordes mo,	
And with his ax he smooth the corde atwo,	
And down gooth al: he foond neither to selle	
Ne breed ne ale til he cam to the celle,[5]	
715 Upon the floor, and ther aswoune° he lay.	*stunned*
Up sterte° hire Alison and Nicholay,	*leaped*
And criden "Out" and "Harrow" in the streete.	
The neighebores, bothe smale and grete,[6]	
In ronnen for to gauren° on this man	*stare*
720 That aswoune lay bothe pale and wan,	
For with the fal he brosten° hadde his arm;	*broken*
But stonde he moste unto his owene harm,	
For whan he spak he was anoon bore down°	*restrained*
With° hende Nicholas and Alisoun:	*by*
725 They tolden every man that he was wood°—	*crazy*
He was agast° so of Noweles flood,	*afraid*
Thurgh fantasye, that of his vanitee°	*folly*
He hadde ybought him kneeding-tubbes three,	
And hadde hem hanged in the roof above,	
730 And that he prayed hem, for Goddes love,	
To sitten in the roof, *par compaignye*.°	*for fellowship*
The folk gan laughen at his fantasye.	
Into the roof they kiken° and they cape,°	*peer / gape*
And turned al his harm unto a jape,	
735 For what so that this carpenter answerde,	
It was for nought: no man his reson herde;	
With othes grete he was so sworn adown,°	*refuted by oaths*
That he was holden wood in al the town,	

4. Make the joke even better.
5. He found no time to sell either bread or ale until he reached the floor (i.e., he fell to the ground too quickly to be aware of what was happening).
6. Lower- and upper-class people alike.

For every clerk anoonright heeld with other:
740   They saide, "The man was wood, my leve brother,"
And every wight° gan laughen at this strif.   *person*
Thus swived° was the carpenteres wif   *screwed*
For al his keeping and his jalousye,
And Absolon hath kist hir nether° yë,   *lower*
745   And Nicholas is scalded in the toute:
This tale is doon, and God save al the route!

THE WIFE OF BATH'S PROLOGUE AND TALE   Dame Alison, the Wife of Bath, is Chaucer's greatest contribution to the stock characters of Western culture. She has a long literary ancestry, most immediately in the Duenna of the thirteenth-century French poem, *The Romance of the Rose*, and stretching back to the Roman poet Ovid. Dame Alison stands out in bold relief, even among the vivid Canterbury pilgrims, partly because Chaucer gives her so rebellious and explicitly self-created a biography. She has out-lived five husbands, accumulated wealth from the first three, and made herself rich in the growing textile industry of her time. At once a great companion and greatly unnerving, Alison lives in constant battle with a secular and religious world mostly controlled by men and yet has a keen appetite both for the men and for the battle.

The Wife of Bath's *Prologue* and *Tale* seem only the current installments of a multifaceted struggle in which Dame Alison has long been engaged, at first through her body and social role and now, in the face of advancing years, through the remaining agency of retrospective storytelling. She battles a society in which many young women are almost chattels in a marital market, as was the twelve-year-old version of herself who first was married off to a wealthier, much older man. She battles him and later husbands for power within the marriage, and her ambition to social dominance, as the *General Prologue* reports, extends to life in her urban parish.

By the moment of the Canterbury pilgrimage, though, the Wife's adversaries are more daunting, less easily conquered. The *Wife's Prologue*, for all its autobiographical energy, is primarily a debate with the clergy and with "auctoritee"—the whole armature of learning and literacy by which the clergy (like her clerically educated fifth husband, Jankyn) seeks to silence her.

The *Wife's Tale*, too, can be seen as an angry riposte to the secular fantasies of Arthurian chivalry and genetic nobility. The Wife's well-born Arthurian knight is a common rapist, who finds himself at the mercy of a queen and then in the arms of a crone. The tale turns Arthurian conventions on their head, lays sexual violence in the open, and puts legal and magical power in the hands of women. It is explicitly a fantasy, but a powerful one.

Alison's final enemy, mortality itself, is what makes her both most desperate and most sympathetic. The husbands are gone. Even the fondly recalled Jankyn slips into a rosy glow and the past tense; so does her own best friend and "gossip," the odd mirror-double "Alisoun." The Wife of Bath keeps addressing other "wives" in her *Prologue*, but there are no others on the pilgrimage. Her very argument with the institutionalized church distances her from its comforts, and she is deeply aware that time is stealing her beauty as it has taken away the companions who made up her earlier life. If Alison's *Tale* closes with a delicious fantasy of restored youth, it is only a pendant to the much longer *Prologue* and its cheerful yet poignant acceptance of age.

The Wife of Bath's Prologue

Experience, though noon auctoritee[1]
Were in this world, is right ynough for me
To speke of wo that is in mariage:
For lordinges,° sith I twelf yeer was of age—   *gentlemen*

---

1. Even if no authority, textual precedent.

5   Thanked be God that is eterne on live—
         Housbondes at chirche dore I have had five
         (If I so ofte mighte han wedded be),
         And alle were worthy men in hir° degree.   *their*
         But me was told, certain, nat longe agoon is,
10   That sith that Crist ne wente nevere but ones°   *once*
         To wedding in the Cane of Galilee,[2]
         That by the same ensample taughte he me
         That I ne sholde wedded be but ones.
         Herke eek, lo, which a sharp word for the nones,°   *for the purpose*
15   Biside a welle, Jesus, God and man,
         Spak in repreve° of the Samaritan:[3]   *reproof*
         "Thou hast yhad five housbondes," quod he,
         "And that ilke° man that now hath thee   *same*
         Is nat thyn housbonde." Thus saide he certain.
20   What that he mente therby I can nat sayn,
         But that I axe why that the fifthe man
         Was noon housbonde to the Samaritan?
         How manye mighte she han in mariage?
         Yit herde I nevere tellen in myn age
25   Upon this nombre diffinicioun.
         Men may divine° and glosen° up and down,   *guess / interpret*
         But wel I woot,° expres,° withouten lie,   *know / manifestly*
         God bad us for to wexe° and multiplye: *increase*
         That gentil text can I wel understonde.
30   Eek wel I woot he saide that myn housbonde
         Sholde lete° fader and moder and take to me,   *leave*
         But of no nombre mencion made he—
         Of bigamye or of octogamye:
         Why sholde men thanne speke of it vilainye?°   *as churlish*
35   Lo, here the wise king daun° Salomon: *Lord*
         I trowe° he hadde wives many oon,   *believe*
         As wolde God it leveful° were to me   *lawful*
         To be refresshed half so ofte as he.
         Which yifte° of God hadde he for alle his wives!   *what a gift*
40   No man hath swich that in this world alive is.
         God woot° this noble king, as to my wit,°   *knows / understanding*
         The firste night hadde many a merye fit
         With eech of hem, so wel was him on live.
         Blessed be God that I have wedded five,
45   Of whiche I have piked° out the beste,   *picked*
         Bothe of hir nether purs and of hir cheste.[4]
         Diverse° scoles maken parfit° clerkes,   *different / accomplished*
         And diverse practikes in sondry werkes
         Maken the werkman° parfit sikerly:°   *craftsman / surely*
50   Of five housbondes scoleying° am I.   *studying*
         Welcome the sixte whan that evere he shal!

---

2. Cana, where Jesus performed his first miracle at a wedding feast (John 2.1).
3. The story of Jesus and the Samaritan woman is related
in John 4.6 ff.

4. Money chest, with a pun on body parts.

	For sith I wol nat keepe me chast in al,	
	Whan myn housbonde is fro the world agoon,	
	Som Cristen man shal wedde me anoon.	
55	For thanne th'Apostle[5] saith that I am free	
	To wedde, a Goddes half,[6] where it liketh° me.	*please*
	He said that to be wedded is no sinne:	
	Bet° is to be wedded than to brinne.°	*better / burn (in hell)*
	What rekketh° me though folk saye vilainye	*do I care*
60	Of shrewed° Lamech[7] and his bigamye?	*cursed*
	I woot wel Abraham was an holy man,	
	And Jacob eek, as fer as evere I can,°	*know*
	And eech of hem hadde wives mo than two,	
	And many another holy man also.	
65	Where can ye saye in any manere age	
	That hye God defended° mariage	*prohibited*
	By expres word? I praye you, telleth me.	
	Or where comanded he virginitee?	
	I woot as wel as ye, it is no drede,°	*doubt*
70	Th'Apostle, whan he speketh of maidenhede,°	*virginity*
	He saide that precept° therof hadde he noon:	*command*
	Men may conseile a womman to be oon,°	*single*
	But conseiling nis no comandement.	
	He putte it in oure owene juggement.	
75	For hadde God comanded maidenhede,	
	Thanne hadde he dampned° wedding with the deede;	*condemned*
	And certes, if ther were no seed ysowe,	
	Virginitee, thanne wherof sholde it growe?	
	Paul dorste nat comanden at the leeste	
80	A thing of which his maister yaf no heeste.°	*commandment*
	The dart° is set up for virginitee:	*prize*
	Cacche whoso may, who renneth° best lat see.	*runs*
	But this word is nought take° of every wight,°	*required / person*
	But ther as God list° yive it of his might.	*pleases*
85	I woot wel that th'Apostle was a maide,°	*virgin*
	But nathelees, though that he wroot or saide	
	He wolde that every wight were swich as he,	
	Al nis but° conseil to virginitee;	*it is only*
	And for to been a wif he yaf me leve	
90	Of indulgence; so nis it no repreve	
	To wedde me if that my make° die,	*mate*
	Withouten excepcion° of bigamye—	*legal objection*
	Al were it good no womman for to touche	
	(He mente as in his bed or in his couche,	
95	For peril is bothe fir and tow t'assemble[8]—	
	Ye knowe what this ensample may resemble).	
	This al and som,° he heeld virginitee	*all told*
	More parfit than wedding in freletee.°	*due to weakness*
	(Freletee clepe° I but if° that he and she	*call / except*

5. St. Paul, in Romans 7.2.
6. From God's perspective.
7. The earliest bigamist in the Bible (Genesis 4.19).
8. To bring together fire and flax.

100 Wolde leden al hir lif in chastitee).
I graunte it wel, I have noon envye
Though maidenhede preferre° bigamye: *surpasses*
It liketh hem to be clene in body and gost.°   *soul*
Of myn estaat° ne wol I make no boost;   *condition*
105 For wel ye knowe, a lord in his houshold
Ne hath nat every vessel al of gold:
Some been of tree,° and doon hir lord servise.   *wood*
God clepeth° folk to him in sondry wise,   *calls*
And everich hath of God a propre yifte,
110 Som this, som that, as him liketh shifte.⁹
Virginitee is greet perfeccioun,
And continence eek with devocioun,
But Crist, that of perfeccion is welle,°   *source*
Bad nat every wight° he sholde go selle   *person*
115 Al that he hadde and yive it to the poore,
And in swich wise folwe° him and his fore:°   *follow / footsteps*
He spak to hem that wolde live parfitly°—   *perfectly*
And lordinges, by youre leve, that am nat I.
I wol bistowe the flour of al myn age
120 In th'actes and in fruit of mariage.
    Telle me also, to what conclusioun°   *end*
Were membres maad of generacioun
And of so parfit wis a wrighte ywrought?¹
Trusteth right wel, they were nat maad for nought.
125 Glose whoso wol, and saye bothe up and down
That they were maked for purgacioun
Of urine, and oure bothe thinges smale
Was eek to knowe a femele from a male,
And for noon other cause—saye ye no?
130 Th'experience woot wel it is nought so.
So that the clerkes be nat with me wrothe,°   *angry*
I saye this, that they maked been for bothe—
That is to sayn, for office° and for ese°   *use / pleasure*
Of engendrure,° ther we nat God displese.   *procreation*
135 Why sholde men elles in hir bookes sette
That man shal yeelde° to his wif hir dette?°   *pay / marriage debt*
Now wherwith sholde he make his payement
If he ne used his sely° instrument?   *innocent*
Thanne were they maad upon a creature
140 To purge urine, and eek for engendrure.
    But I saye nought that every wight is holde,°   *bound*
That hath swich harneis° as I to you tolde,   *equipment*
To goon and usen hem in engendrure:
Thanne sholde men take of chastitee no cure.°   *heed*
145 Crist was a maide and shapen as a man,
And many a saint sith that the world bigan,
Yit lived they evere in parfit° chastitee.   *perfect*
I nil envye no virginitee:

9. As it pleases him to provide.   1. And created by so perfectly wise a Creator?

Lat hem be breed° of pured° whete seed,   *bread / refined*
150   And lat us wives hote° barly breed—   *be called*
And yit with barly breed, Mark telle can,
Oure Lord Jesu refresshed many a man.
In swich estaat as God hath cleped° us   *called*
I wol persevere: I nam nat precious.°   *am not fussy*
155   In wifhood wol I use myn instrument
As freely° as my Makere hath it sent.   *generously*
If I be daungerous,° God yive me sorwe:°   *withholding / sorrow*
Myn housbonde shal it han both eve and morwe,°   *morning*
Whan that him list come forth and paye his dette.
160   An housbonde wol I have, I wol nat lette,°   *forgo*
Which shal be bothe my dettour and my thral,°   *slave*
And have his tribulacion withal
Upon his flessh whil that I am his wif.
I have the power during al my lif
165   Upon his propre° body, and nat he: *own*
Right thus th'Apostle tolde it unto me,
And bad oure housbondes for to love us weel.
Al this sentence° me liketh everydeel.   *interpretation*

An Interlude

Up sterte° the Pardoner and that anoon: *started*
170   "Now dame," quod he, "by God and by Saint John,
Ye been a noble prechour° in this cas.   *preacher*
I was aboute to wedde a wif: allas,
What° sholde I bye° it on my flessh so dere?   *why / buy*
Yit hadde I levere° wedde no wif toyere."°   *rather / this year*
175   "Abid," quod she, "my tale is nat bigonne.
Nay, thou shalt drinken of another tonne,°   *barrel*
Er that I go, shal savoure wors than ale.
And whan that I have told thee forth my tale
Of tribulacion in mariage,
180   Of which I am expert in al myn age—
This is to saye, myself hath been the whippe—
Thanne maistou chese° wheither thou wolt sippe   *may you choose*
Of thilke° tonne that I shal abroche:°   *that same / open*
Be war of it, er thou too neigh approche,
185   For I shal telle ensamples mo than ten.
'Whoso that nile° be war by othere men,   *will not*
By him shal othere men corrected be.'
Thise same wordes writeth Ptolomee:[2]
Rede in his Almageste and take it there."
190   "Dame, I wolde praye you if youre wil it were,"
Saide this Pardoner, "as ye bigan,
Telle forth youre tale; spareth for no man,
And teche us yonge men of youre practike."
"Gladly," quod she, "sith it may you like;

2. Ptolemy, ancient Greek astronomer and author of the *Almageste*.

195 But that I praye to al this compaignye,
    If that I speke after my fantasye,°   *fancy*
    As taketh nat agrief° of that I saye,   *amiss*
    For myn entente nis but° for to playe."   *intent is only*

The Wife Continues

    Now sire, thanne wol I telle you forth my tale.
200 As evere mote I drinke win or ale,
    I shal saye sooth:° tho° housbondes that I hadde,   *truth / those*
    As three of hem were goode, and two were badde.
    The three men were goode, and riche, and olde;
    Unnethe° mighte they the statut holde   *scarcely*
205 In which they were bounden unto me—
    Ye woot wel what I mene of this, pardee.°   *by God*
    As help me God, I laughe whan I thinke
    How pitously anight I made hem swinke;°   *work*
    And by my fay,° I tolde of it no stoor:°   *faith / gave it no heed*
210 They hadde me yiven hir land and hir tresor;°   *wealth*
    Me needed nat do lenger diligence
    To winne hir love or doon hem reverence.
    They loved me so wel, by God above,
    That I ne tolde no daintee° of hir love.   *set no value on*
215 A wis womman wol bisye hire evere in oon°   *constantly*
    To gete hire love, ye, ther as she hath noon.
    But sith I hadde hem hoolly in myn hand,
    And sith that they hadde yiven me al hir land,
    What sholde I take keep° hem for to plese,   *care*
220 But it were for my profit and myn ese?
    I sette hem so awerke, by my fay,°   *faith*
    That many a night they songen wailaway.
    The bacon was nat fet° for hem, I trowe,   *collected*
    That some men han in Essexe at Dunmowe.[3]
225 I governed hem so wel after my lawe
    That eech of hem ful blisful was and fawe°   *glad*
    To bringe me gaye thinges fro the faire;
    They were ful glade whan I spak to hem faire,
    For God it woot, I chidde° hem spitously.°   *scolded / cruelly*
230   Now herkneth how I bar me proprely:
    Ye wise wives, that conne understonde,
    Thus sholde ye speke and bere him wrong on honde°—   *wrongly accuse*
    For half so boldely can ther no man
    Swere and lie as a woman can.
235 I saye nat this by wives that been wise,
    But if it be whan they hem misavise.°   *err*
    A wis wif, if that she can hir good,[4]
    Shal bere him on hande the cow is wood,[5]
    And take witnesse of hir owene maide

---

3. At Dunmowe, spouses who had spent a year without quarrelling were awarded a side of bacon.
4. Knows what's good for her.

5. Shall convince him the chough is mad. The chough, a crow-like bird, was fabled to reveal wives' infidelities.

240	Of hir assent.° But herkneth how I saide:	*as her accomplice*
	"Sire olde cainard,° is this thyn array?	*dotard*
	Why is my neighebores wif so gay?	
	She is honoured overal ther she gooth:	
	I sitte at hoom; I have no thrifty° cloth.	*decent*
245	What doostou at my neighebores hous?	
	Is she so fair? Artou so amorous?	
	What roune° ye with oure maide, benedicite?°	*whisper / bless us*
	Sire olde lechour, lat thy japes° be.	*tricks*
	And if I have a gossib° or a freend,	*confidante*
250	Withouten gilt ye chiden as a feend,	
	If that I walke or playe unto his hous.	
	Thou comest hoom as dronken as a mous,	
	And prechest on thy bench, with yvel preef.°	*bad luck to you*
	Thou saist to me, it is a greet meschief	
255	To wedde a poore womman for costage.°	*expense*
	And if that she be riche, of heigh parage,°	*breeding*
	Thanne saistou that it is a tormentrye	
	To suffre hir pride and hir malencolye.	
	And if that she be fair, thou verray knave,	
260	Thou saist that every holour° wol hire have:	*whoremonger*
	She may no while in chastitee abide	
	That is assailed upon eech a side.	
	"Thou saist som folk desiren us for richesse,	
	Som for oure shap, and som for oure fairnesse,	
265	And som for she can outher° singe or daunce,	*either*
	And som for gentilesse and daliaunce,°	*conversation*
	Som for hir handes and hir armes smale—	
	Thus gooth al to the devel by thy tale!⁶	
	Thou saist men may nat keepe a castel wal,	
270	It may so longe assailed been overal.	
	And if that she be foul, thou saist that she	
	Coveiteth° every man that she may see;	*desires*
	For as a spaniel she wol on him lepe,	
	Til that she finde som man hire to chepe.°	*take*
275	Ne noon so grey goos gooth ther in the lake,	
	As, saistou, wol be withoute make;°	*mate*
	And saist it is an hard thing for to weelde°	*control*
	A thing that no man wol, his thankes,° heelde.°	*willingly / hold*
	Thus saistou, lorel,° whan thou goost to bedde,	*scoundrel*
280	And that no wis man needeth for to wedde,	
	Ne no man that entendeth° unto hevene—	*expects (to go)*
	With wilde thonder-dint° and firy levene°	*thunderclap / lightning*
	Mote° thy welked° nekke be tobroke!°	*may / withered / broken*
	Thou saist that dropping° houses and eek smoke	*leaking*
285	And chiding wives maken men to flee	
	Out of hir owene houses: a, benedicite,	
	What aileth swich an old man for to chide?	
	Thou saist we wives wil oure vices hide	

6. According to what you say.

Til we be fast,° and thanne we wol hem shewe—   *bound (in marriage)*
290   Wel may that be a proverbe of a shrewe!°   *scoundrel*
Thou saist that oxen, asses, hors, and houndes,
They been assayed° at diverse stoundes;°   *tested / times*
Bacins,° lavours,° er that men hem bye,   *basins / wash bowls*
Spoones, stooles, and al swich housbondrye,
295   And so be pottes, clothes, and array—
But folk of wives maken noon assay°   *trial*
Til they be wedded—olde dotard shrewe!
And thanne, saistou, we wil oure vices shewe.
Thou saist also that it displeseth me
300   But if° that thou wolt praise my beautee,   *unless*
And but thou poure alway upon my face,
And clepe° me 'Faire Dame' in every place,   *call*
And but thou make a feeste on thilke° day   *that*
That I was born, and make me fressh and gay,
305   And but thou do to my norice° honour,   *nurse*
And to my chamberere° within my bowr,°   *chambermaid / bedroom*
And to my fadres folk, and his allies°—   *kinsmen*
Thus saistou, olde barel-ful of lies.
And yit of our apprentice Janekin,
310   For his crispe heer,° shining as gold so fin,   *curly hair*
And for he squiereth° me bothe up and down,   *chaperones*
Yit hastou caught a fals suspecioun;
I wil° him nat though thou were deed tomorwe.   *desire*
      "But tel me this, why hidestou with sorwe
315   The keyes of thy cheste away fro me?
It is my good as wel as thyn, pardee.°   *by God*
What, weenestou° make an idiot of oure dame?   *do you suppose*
Now by that lord that called is Saint Jame,[7]
Thou shalt nought bothe, though that thou were wood,°   *enraged*
320   Be maister of my body and of my good:
That oon thou shalt forgo, maugree thine yën.[8]
      "What helpeth it of me enquere and spyen?
I trowe thou woldest loke° me in thy cheste.   *lock*
Thou sholdest saye, 'Wif, go wher thee leste.°   *it pleases*
325   Taak youre disport.° I nil leve° no tales: *amusement / believe*
I knowe you for a trewe wif, dame Alis.'
We love no man that taketh keep° or charge   *notice*
Wher that we goon: we wol been at oure large.°   *liberty*
Of alle men yblessed mote he be
330   The wise astrologen daun Ptolomee,
That saith this proverbe in his Almageste:
'Of alle men his wisdom is the hyeste
That rekketh° nat who hath the world in honde.'   *cares*
By this proverbe thou shalt understonde,
335   Have thou ynough, what thar° thee rekke° or care   *need / be concerned*
How merily that othere folkes fare?°   *go about*

---

7. Santiago de Compostela, whose shrine in Spain the   8. In spite of your eyes (an oath).
Wife of Bath has already made a pilgrimage to visit.

For certes, olde dotard, by youre leve,
Ye shal han queinte° right ynough at eve: *sex*
He is too greet a nigard that wil werne°   *refuse*
340 A man to lighte a candle at his lanterne;
He shal han nevere the lasse lighte, pardee.°   *by God*
Have thou ynough, thee thar nat plaine thee.°   *complain*
         "Thou saist also that if we make us gay
With clothing and with precious array,
345 That it is peril of oure chastitee,
And yit with sorwe thou moste enforce thee,[9]
And saye thise wordes in th'Apostles name:
'In habit° maad with chastitee and shame   *clothing*
Ye wommen shal apparaile you,' quod he,
350 'And nat in tressed heer° and gay perree,°   *styled hair / jewels*
As perles ne with gold ne clothes riche.'
After thy text, ne after thy rubriche,[1]
I wol nat werke as muchel as a gnat.
Thou saidest this, that I was lik a cat:
355 For whoso wolde senge° a cattes skin,   *singe*
Thanne wolde the cat wel dwellen in his in;°   *inn*
And if the cattes skin be slik° and gay,   *sleek*
She wol nat dwelle in house half a day,
But forth she wol, er any day be dawed,°   *dawned*
360 To shewe her skin and goon a-caterwawed.°   *caterwauling*
This is to saye, if I be gay, sire shrewe,
I wol renne out, my borel° for to shewe.   *coarse cloth*
Sire olde fool, what helpeth thee t'espyen?
Though thou praye Argus[2] with his hundred yën
365 To be my wardecors,° as he can best,   *bodyguard*
In faith, he shal nat keepe me but me lest:
Yit coude I make his beerd,[3] so mote I thee.°   *so may I prosper*
         "Thou saidest eek that ther been thinges three,
The whiche thinges troublen al this erthe,
370 And that no wight° may endure the ferthe.°   *person / fourth*
O leve sire shrewe, Jesu shorte thy lif!
Yit prechestou and saist an hateful wif
Yrekened° is for oon of thise meschaunces.   *accounted*
Been ther nat none othere resemblaunces
375 That ye may likne youre parables to,
But if a sely° wif be oon of tho?   *innocent*
         "Thou liknest eek wommanes love to helle,
To bareine land ther water may nat dwelle;
Thou liknest it also to wilde fir—
380 The more it brenneth,° the more it hath desir   *burns*
To consumen every thing that brent wol be;
Thou saist right as wormes shende° a tree,   *destroy*
Right so a wif destroyeth hir housbonde—

---

9. Reinforce (your position).
1. Rubric, interpretive heading on a text.
2. Mythical hundred-eyed monster employed by Juno to

guard over Io, one of Jove's many lovers, whom the goddess turned into a cow.
3. Deceive him.

This knowen they that been to wives bonde."

385   Lordinges, right thus, as ye han understonde,
      Bar I stifly° mine olde housbondes on honde°   *firmly / swore*
      That thus they saiden in hir dronkenesse—
      And al was fals, but that I took witnesse
      On Janekin and on my nece° also.   *kinswoman*
390   O Lord, the paine I dide hem and the wo,
      Ful giltelees, by Goddes sweete pine!°   *suffering*
      For as an hors I coude bite and whine;
      I coude plaine and° I was in the gilt,°   *when / wrong*
      Or elles often time I hadde been spilt.°   *ruined*
395   Whoso that first to mille comth first grint.°   *grinds*
      I plained first: so was oure werre° stint.°   *war / stopped*
      They were ful glad to excusen hem ful blive°   *quickly*
      Of thing of which they nevere agilte° hir live.   *offended (in)*
      Of wenches wolde I beren hem on honde,
400   Whan that for sik they mighte unnethe° stonde,   *barely*
      Yit tikled I his herte for that he
      Wende° I hadde had of him so greet cheertee.°   *supposed / fondness*
      I swoor that al my walking out by nighte
      Was for to espye wenches that he dighte.°   *had sex with*
405   Under that colour° hadde I many a mirthe.   *pretense*
      For al swich wit is yiven us in oure birthe:
      Deceite, weeping, spinning God hath yive
      To wommen kindely° whil they may live.   *by nature*
      And thus of oo thing I avaunte° me: *boast*
410   At ende I hadde the bet in eech degree,
      By sleighte° or force, or by som manere thing,   *deception*
      As by continuel murmur° or grucching;°   *complaining / grumbling*
      Namely abedde° hadden they meschaunce:°   *in bed / misfortune*
      Ther wolde I chide and do hem no plesaunce;
415   I wolde no lenger in the bed abide
      If that I felte his arm over my side,
      Til he hadde maad his raunson° unto me;   *amends*
      Thanne wolde I suffre him do his nicetee.°   *lust*
      And therfore every man this tale I telle:
420   Winne whoso may, for al is for to selle;
      With empty hand men may no hawkes lure.
      For winning° wolde I al his lust endure,   *profit*
      And make me a feined appetit—
      And yit in bacon° hadde I nevere delit.   *old meat*
425   That made me that evere I wolde hem chide;
      For though the Pope hadde seten° hem biside,   *sat*
      I wolde nought spare hem at hir owene boord.°   *table*
      For by my trouthe, I quitte° hem word for word.   *repaid*
      As help me verray God omnipotent,
430   Though I right now sholde make my testament,
      I ne owe hem nat a word that it nis quit.°   *is not repaid*
      I broughte it so aboute by my wit
      That they moste yive it up as for the beste,
      Or elles hadde we nevere been in reste;

435	For though he looked as a wood leoun,°	crazed lion
	Yit sholde he faile of his conclusion.°	purpose
	Thanne wolde I saye, "Goodelief,° taak keep,	Sweetheart
	How mekely looketh Wilekin, oure sheep!	
	Com neer my spouse, lat me ba° thy cheeke—	kiss
440	Ye sholden be al pacient and meeke,	
	And han a sweete-spiced conscience,	
	Sith ye so preche of Jobes⁴ pacience;	
	Suffreth alway, sin ye so wel can preche;	
	And but ye do, certain, we shal you teche	
445	That it is fair to han a wif in pees.	
	Oon of us two moste bowen, doutelees,	
	And sith a man is more resonable	
	Than womman is, ye mosten been suffrable.°	patient
	What aileth you to grucche thus and grone?	
450	Is it for ye wolde have my queinte allone?	
	Why, taak it al—lo, have it everydeel.	
	Peter,° I shrewe° you but ye love it weel.	by St. Peter / curse
	For if I wolde selle my bele chose,⁵	
	I coude walke as fressh as is a rose;	
455	But I wol keepe it for youre owene tooth.°	taste
	Ye be to blame. By God, I saye you sooth!"	
	Swiche manere wordes hadde we on honde.	
	Now wol I speke of my ferthe housbonde.	
	My ferthe housbonde was a revelour—	
460	This is to sayn, he hadde a paramour°—	lover
	And I was yong and ful of ragerye,°	wantonness
	Stibourne° and strong and joly as a pie:°	stubborn / magpie
	How coude I daunce to an harpe smale,°	gracefully
	And singe, ywis,° as any nightingale,	certainly
465	Whan I hadde dronke a draughte of sweete win.	
	Metellius,⁶ the foule cherl,° the swin,	ruffian
	That with a staf birafte his wif hir lif	
	For she drank win, though I hadde been his wif,	
	Ne sholde nat han daunted me fro drinke;	
470	And after win on Venus moste I thinke,	
	For also siker° as cold engendreth hail,	certainly
	A likerous° mouth moste han a likerous° tail:	gluttonous / lecherous
	In womman vinolent° is no defence—	drunken
	This knowen lechours by experience.	
475	But Lord Crist, whan that it remembreth me	
	Upon my youthe and on my jolitee,	
	It tikleth me aboute myn herte roote°—	bottom of my heart
	Unto this day it dooth myn herte boote°	good
	That I have had my world as in my time.	
480	But age, allas, that al wol envenime,°	poison
	Hath me biraft my beautee and my pith°—	vigor

---

4. The biblical Job, who suffers patiently the trials imposed by God.
5. "Beautiful thing," a euphemism for female genitals.

6. Egnatius Metellius, whose actions are described in Valerius Maximus's *Facta et dicta memorabilia*, 6.3.

Lat go, farewel, the devel go therwith!
The flour is goon, ther is namore to telle:
The bren° as I best can now moste I selle;   bran
485   But yit to be right merye wol I fonde.°   try
Now wol I tellen of my ferthe housbonde.
  I saye I hadde in herte greet despit
That he of any other hadde delit,
But he was quit,° by God and by Saint Joce:°   repaid / St. Judocus
490   I made him of the same wode a croce°—   cross
Nat of my body in no foul manere—
But, certainly, I made folk swich cheere
That in his owene grece° I made him frye,   grease
For angre and for verray jalousye.
495   By God, in erthe I was his purgatorye,
For which I hope his soule be in glorye.
For God it woot, he sat ful ofte and soong
Whan that his sho° ful bitterly him wroong.°   shoe / pinched
Ther was no wight° save God and he that wiste   person
500   In many wise how sore I him twiste.
He deide whan I cam fro Jerusalem,
And lith ygrave° under the roode-beem,°   buried / crossbeam
Al is his tombe nought so curious°   carefully made
As was the sepulcre of him Darius,[7]
505   Which that Appelles wroughte subtilly:
It nis but wast to burye him preciously.°   expensively
Lat him fare wel, God yive his soule reste;
He is now in his grave and in his cheste.
  Now of my fifthe housbonde wol I telle—
510   God lete his soule nevere come in helle—
And yit he was to me the moste shrewe:
That feele I on my ribbes al by rewe,°   in a row
And evere shal unto myn ending day.
But in oure bed he was so fressh and gay,
515   And therwithal so wel coude he me glose°   flatter
Whan that he wolde han my bele chose,°   pretty thing
That though he hadde me bet° on every boon,°   beaten / bone
He coude winne again my love anoon.
I trowe I loved him best for that he
520   Was of his love daungerous° to me.   hard to get
We wommen han, if that I shal nat lie,
In this matere a quainte fantasye:
Waite° what thing we may nat lightly° have,   note that / easily
Therafter wol we crye al day and crave;
525   Forbede us thing, and that desiren we;
Presse on us faste, and thanne wol we flee.
With daunger oute we al oure chaffare:[8]
Greet prees° at market maketh dere ware,°   crowd / costly goods
And too greet chepe° is holden at litel pris.   bargain

7. Persian Emperor defeated by Alexander the Great, whose tomb was elaborately designed by the Jewish craftsman Apelles.
8. With coyness we spread out all our merchandise.

530　This knoweth every womman that is wis.
　　　　　My fifthe housbonde—God his soule blesse!—
　　　Which that I took for love and no richesse,
　　　He somtime was a clerk of Oxenforde,
　　　And hadde laft scole° and wente at hoom to boorde　　　　*left school*
535　With my gossib,° dwelling in oure town—　　　　*close friend*
　　　God have hir soule!—hir name was Alisoun;
　　　She knew myn herte and eek my privetee°　　　　*secrets*
　　　Bet than oure parissh preest, as mote I thee.
　　　To hire biwrayed° I my conseil° al,　　　　*revealed / thoughts*
540　For hadde myn housbonde pissed on a wal,
　　　Or doon a thing that sholde han cost his lif,
　　　To hire, and to another worthy wif,
　　　And to my nece which that I loved weel,
　　　I wolde han told his conseil everydeel;
545　And so I dide ful often, God it woot,
　　　That made his face often reed° and hoot°　　　　*red / hot*
　　　For verray shame, and blamed himself for he
　　　Hadde told to me so greet a privetee.
　　　　　And so bifel that ones in a Lente—
550　So often times I to my gossib wente,
　　　For evere yit I loved to be gay,
　　　And for to walke in March, Averil, and May,
　　　From hous to hous, to heere sondry tales—
　　　That Janekin clerk and my gossib dame Alis
555　And I myself into the feeldes wente.
　　　Myn housbonde was at London al that Lente:
　　　I hadde the better leiser° for to playe,　　　　*opportunity*
　　　And for to see, and eek for to be seye°　　　　*seen*
　　　Of lusty° folk—what wiste I wher my grace°　　　　*merry / luck*
560　Was shapen° for to be, or in what place?　　　　*destined*
　　　Therfore I made my visitaciouns
　　　To vigilies[9] and to processiouns,
　　　To preching eek, and to thise pilgrimages,
　　　To playes of miracles and to mariages,
565　And wered upon my gaye scarlet gites°—　　　　*robes*
　　　Thise wormes ne thise motthes ne thise mites,
　　　Upon my peril, frete° hem neveradeel:　　　　*devoured*
　　　And woostou why? For they were used weel.
　　　　　Now wol I tellen forth what happed me.
570　I saye that in the feeldes walked we,
　　　Til trewely we hadde swich daliaunce,°　　　　*flirtation*
　　　This clerk and I, that of my purveyaunce°　　　　*providence*
　　　I spak to him and saide him how that he,
　　　If I were widwe, sholde wedde me.
575　For certainly, I saye for no bobaunce°　　　　*boast*
　　　Yit was I nevere withouten purveyaunce
　　　Of mariage n'of othere thinges eek:
　　　I holde a mouses herte nought worth a leek

9. Services on the eve of holy days.

That hath but oon hole for to sterte° to,   *flee*
580 And if that faile thanne is al ydo.
I bar him on hand he hadde enchaunted me
(My dame taughte me that subtiltee);
And eek I saide I mette° of him al night: *dreamed*
He wolde han slain me as I lay upright,°   *facing up*
585 And al my bed was ful of verray blood—
"But yit I hope that ye shul do me good;
For blood bitokeneth gold, as me was taught."
And al was fals, I dremed of it right naught,
But as I folwed ay° my dames lore°   *always / teaching*
590 As wel of that as of othere thinges more.
But now sire—lat me see, what shal I sayn?
Aha, by God, I have my tale again.
      Whan that my ferthe housbonde was on beere,°   *funeral bier*
I weep algate,° and made sory cheere,   *constantly*
595 As wives moten, for it is usage,°   *custom*
And with my coverchief covered my visage;
But for that I was purveyed° of a make,°   *provided / mate*
I wepte but smale, and that I undertake.°   *vouch*
      To chirche was myn housbonde born amorwe°   *next morning*
600 With neighebores that for him maden sorwe,
And Janekin oure clerk was oon of tho.
As help me God, whan that I saw him go
After the beere, me thoughte he hadde a paire
Of legges and of feet so clene and faire,
605 That al myn herte I yaf unto his hold.°   *possession*
He was, I trowe, twenty winter old,
And I was fourty, if I shal saye sooth°—   *truth*
But yit I hadde alway a coltes tooth:°   *youthful tastes*
Gat-toothed° was I, and that bicam me weel;   *gap-toothed*
610 I hadde the prente° of Sainte Venus seel.°   *imprint / beauty mark*
As help me God, I was a lusty oon,
And fair and riche and yong and wel-bigoon,°   *well situated*
And trewely, as mine housbondes tolde me,
I hadde the beste quoniam° mighte be.   *you-know-what*
615 For certes I am al Venerien[1]
In feeling, and myn herte is Marcien:°   *governed by Mars*
Venus me yaf my lust, my likerousnesse,
And Mars yaf me my sturdy hardinesse.
Myn ascendent° was Taur° and Mars therinne—   *zodiac sign / Taurus*
620 Allas, allas, that evere love was sinne!
I folwed ay my inclinacioun
By vertu of my constellacioun;
That made me I coude nought withdrawe°   *withhold*
My chambre of Venus from a good felawe.
625 Yit have I Martes° merk upon my face,   *Mars's*
And also in another privee place.
For God so wis° be my savacioun,°   *surely / salvation*

1. Governed by Venus, the planet.

I loved nevere by no discrecioun,
But evere folwede° myn appetit,   *followed*
630 Al were he short or long or blak or whit;
I took no keep, so that he liked° me,   *pleased*
How poore he was, ne eek of what degree.
     What sholde I saye but at the monthes ende
This joly clerk Janekin that was so hende°   *courteous*
635 Hath wedded me with greet solempnitee,
And to him yaf I al the land and fee°   *property*
That evere was me yiven therbifore—
But afterward repented me ful sore:
He nolde suffre° no thing of my list.°   *would allow / pleasure*
640 By God, he smoot° me ones on the list°   *struck / ear*
For that I rente° out of his book a leef,°   *tore / page*
That of the strook myn ere weex° al deef.   *grew, became*
Stibourne I was as is a leonesse,
And of my tonge a verray jangleresse,°   *chatterbox*
645 And walke I wolde, as I hadde doon biforn,
From hous to hous, although he hadde it sworn;°   *prohibited*
For which he often times wolde preche,
And me of olde Romain geestes° teche,   *Latin stories*
How he Simplicius Gallus[2] lafte his wif,
650 And hire forsook for terme of al his lif,
Nought but for open-heveded° he hire sey°   *bareheaded / saw*
Looking out at his dore upon a day.
     Another Romain[3] tolde he me by name
That, for his wif was at a someres° game   *summer's*
655 Withouten his witing,° he forsook hire eke;   *knowledge*
And thanne wolde he upon his Bible seeke
That ilke proverbe of Ecclesiaste[4]
Where he comandeth and forbedeth faste
Man shal nat suffre his wif go roule° aboute;   *roam*
660 Thanne wolde he saye right thus withouten doute:
"Whoso that buildeth his hous al of salwes,°   *willow branches*
And priketh° his blinde hors over the falwes,°   *rides / open fields*
And suffreth his wif to go seeken halwes,°   *shrines*
Is worthy to be hanged on the galwes."
665 But al for nought—I sette nought an hawe[5]
Of his proverbes n'of his olde sawe;
N'I wolde nat of him corrected be:
I hate him that my vices telleth me,
And so doon mo, God woot, of us than I.
670 This made him with me wood al outrely:°   *utterly*
I nolde nought forbere° him in no cas.   *would not submit*
     Now wol I saye you sooth, by Saint Thomas,
Why that I rente out of his book a leef,
For which he smoot me so that I was deef.
675 He hadde a book that gladly night and day

2. Narrated in Valerius Maximus, *Facta et dicta memora-*
bilia 6.3.
3. P. Sempronius Sophus, as related in Valerius Maximus,

Facta 6.3.
4. Ecclesiasticus 25.25.
5. Hawthorn berry (i.e., little value).

For his disport° he wolde rede alway.   amusement
He cleped° it Valerie and Theofraste,[6]   called
At which book he lough° alway ful faste;   laughed
And eek ther was somtime a clerk at Rome,
680   A cardinal, that highte Saint Jerome,
That made a book again Jovinian;
In which book eek ther was Tertulan,
Crysippus, Trotula, and Helouis,
That was abbesse nat fer fro Paris;
685   And eek the Parables of Salomon,
Ovides Art, and bookes many oon—
And alle thise were bounden in oo volume.
And every night and day was his custume,°   custom
Whan he hadde leiser and vacacioun
690   From other worldly occupacioun,
To reden in this book of wikked wives.
He knew of hem mo legendes and lives
Than been of goode wives in the Bible.
For trusteth wel, it is an impossible°   impossibility
695   That any clerk wol speke good of wives,
But if it be of holy saintes lives,
N'of noon other womman nevere the mo—
Who painted the leon, tel me who?[7]
By God, if wommen hadden writen stories,
700   As clerkes han within hir oratories,
They wolde han writen of men more wikkednesse
Than al the merk of° Adam may redresse.   mark, sex
The children of Mercurye and Venus[8]
Been in hir werking° ful contrarious:°   deeds / contradictory
705   Mercurye loveth wisdom and science,
And Venus loveth riot° and dispence;°   celebration / expense
And for hir diverse disposicioun
Each falleth in otheres exaltacioun,[9]
And thus, God woot, Mercurye is desolat°   powerless
710   In Pisces wher Venus is exaltat,
And Venus falleth ther Mercurye is raised:
Therfore no womman of no clerk is praised.
The clerk, whan he is old and may nought do
Of Venus werkes worth his olde sho,°   shoe
715   Thanne sit he down and writ in his dotage
That wommen can nat keepe hir mariage.

6. Janekin's book is a collection of different works, nearly all of which are directed against women: Walter Map's fictitious letter entitled *Valerius's Dissuasion of Rufinus from Marrying* (Valerius); Theophrastus's *Golden Book on Marriage* (Theofraste); Saint Jerome's *Against Jovinian*; Tertullian's misogynist tracts on sexual continence (Tertulan); Crysippus's writings, mentioned by Jerome but otherwise unknown; *The Sufferings of Women*, an 11th-century book on gynecology by Trotula di Ruggiero, a female physician from Sicily (Trotula); the letters of the abbess Heloise to her lover Abelard (Helouis); the bibli-

cal Book of Proverbs (Parables of Salomon), and Ovid's *Art of Love*.
7. In one of Aesop's fables, a lion asked this question when confronted with a painting of a man killing a lion, indicating that if a lion had painted the picture, the scene would have been very different.
8. Followers of Mercury, the god of rhetoric (scholars, poets, orators); followers of Venus (lovers).
9. Astrologically, one planet diminishes in influence as the other ascends.

But now to purpos why I tolde thee
That I was beten for a book, pardee:°   *by God*
Upon a night Janekin, that was oure sire,°   *master of our house*
720   Redde on his book as he sat by the fire
Of Eva[1] first, that for hir wikkednesse
Was al mankinde brought to wrecchednesse,
For which that Jesu Crist himself was slain
That boughte° us with his herte blood again—   *redeemed*
725   Lo, heer expres of wommen may ye finde
That womman was the los° of al mankinde.   *ruin*
      Tho° redde he me how Sampson loste his heres:°   *then / hair*
Sleeping his lemman° kitte° it with hir sheres,   *lover / cut*
Thurgh which treson loste he both his yën.
730   Tho redde he me, if that I shal nat lien,
Of Ercules and of his Dianire,[2]
That caused him to sette himself afire.
      No thing forgat he the sorwe and wo
That Socrates hadde with his wives two—
735   How Xantippa[3] caste pisse upon his heed:
This sely man sat stille as he were deed;
He wiped his heed, namore dorste he sayn
But "Er° that thonder stinte,° comth a rain."   *before / stops*
      Of Phasipha[4] that was the queene of Crete—
740   For shrewednesse° him thoughte the tale sweete—   *wickedness*
Fy, speek namore, it is a grisly thing
Of hir horrible lust and hir liking.
      Of Clytermistra[5] for hir lecherye
That falsly made hir housbonde for to die,
745   He redde it with ful good devocioun.
      He tolde me eek for what occasioun
Amphiorax[6] at Thebes loste his lif:
Myn housbonde hadde a legende of his wif
Eriphylem, that for an ouche° of gold   *trinket*
750   Hath prively unto the Greekes told
Wher that hir housbonde hidde him in a place,
For which he hadde at Thebes sory grace.
      Of Livia[7] tolde he me and of Lucie:
They bothe made hir housbondes for to die,
755   That oon for love, that other was for hate;
Livia hir housbonde on an even late
Empoisoned hath for that she was his fo;
Lucia likerous loved hir housbonde so

---

1. Eve's temptation by the serpent was blamed for humanity's fall from grace and thus required Christ's incarnation to redeem the world.
2. Deianira gave her husband, Hercules, a robe which she believed was charmed with a love potion, but once he put it on, it burned his flesh so badly that he died.
3. Xanthippe was famous for nagging her husband, the philosopher Socrates.
4. Pasiphae, wife of Minos, became enamored of a bull, engendering the Minotaur.
5. Clytemnestra, queen of Mycenae, slew her husband Agamemnon when he returned from the Trojan War.
6. Amphiaraus died at the Siege of Thebes after listening to the advice of his wife, Eriphyle.
7. Livia poisoned her husband, Drusus, to satisfy her lover Sejanus; Lucia unwittingly poisoned her husband, the poet Lucretius, with a potion meant to keep him faithful.

That for he sholde alway upon hire thinke,
760   She yaf him swich a manere love-drinke
That he was deed er it were by the morwe.
And thus algates° housbondes han sorwe.   *continually*
      Thanne tolde he me how oon Latumius
Complained unto his felawe Arrius
765   That in his gardin growed swich a tree,
On which he saide how that his wives three
Hanged hemself for herte despitous.°   *cruel*
      "O leve brother," quod this Arrius,
"Yif° me a plante of thilke° blessed tree,   *give / that same*
770   And in my gardin planted shal it be."
      Of latter date of wives hath he red
That some han slain hir housbondes in hir bed
And lete hir lechour dighte° hire al the night,   *screw*
Whan that the cors° lay in the floor upright;°   *corpse / face up*
775   And some han driven nailes in hir brain
Whil that they sleepe, and thus they han hem slain;
Some han hem yiven poison in hir drinke.
He spak more harm than herte may bithinke,
And therwithal he knew of mo proverbes
780   Than in this world ther growen gras or herbes:
"Bet is," quod he, "thyn habitacioun
Be with a leon or a foul dragoun
Than with a wommman using° for to chide."   *accustomed*
"Bet is," quod he, "hye in the roof abide
785   Than with an angry wif down in the hous:
They been so wikked and contrarious,
They haten that hir housbondes loveth ay."°   *always*
He saide, "A womman cast hir shame away
Whan she cast of hir smok,"° and ferthermo,   *slip*
790   "A fair womman, but she be chast also,
Is lik a gold ring in a sowes nose."
Who wolde weene, or who wolde suppose
The wo that in myn herte was and pine?
      And whan I sawgh he wolde nevere fine°   *end*
795   To reden on this cursed book al night,
Al sodeinly three leves have I plight°   *plucked*
Out of his book right as he redde, and eke
I with my fist so took° him on the cheeke   *struck*
That in oure fir he fil bakward adown.
800   And up he sterte as dooth a wood° leoun,   *enraged*
And with his fist he smoot me on the heed
That in the floor I lay as I were deed.
And whan he sawgh how stille that I lay,
He was agast,° and wolde have fled his way,   *afraid*
805   Til atte laste out of my swough° I braide:°   *faint / arose*
"O hastou slain me, false thief?" I saide,
"And for my land thus hastou mordred me?
Er I be deed yit wol I kisse thee."

	And neer he cam and kneeled faire adown,	
810	And saide, "Dere suster Alisoun,	
	As help me God, I shal thee nevere smite.	
	That I have doon, it is thyself to wite.°	blame
	Foryif it me, and that I thee biseeke."	
	And yit eftsoones° I hitte him on the cheeke,	immediately
815	And saide, "Thief, thus muchel am I wreke.°	avenged
	Now wol I die: I may no lenger speke."	
	But at the laste with muchel care and wo	
	We fille accorded by us selven two.	
	He yaf me al the bridel° in myn hand,	bridle, control
820	To han the governance of hous and land,	
	And of his tonge and his hand also;	
	And made him brenne his book anoonright tho.	
	And whan that I hadde geten unto me	
	By maistrye° al the sovereinetee,°	skill / dominance
825	And that he saide, "Myn owene trewe wif,	
	Do as thee lust° the terme of al thy lif,	please
	Keep thyn honour, and keep eek myn estat,"	
	After that day we hadde nevere debat.	
	God help me so, I was to him as kinde	
830	As any wif from Denmark unto Inde,	
	And also trewe, and so was he to me.	
	I praye to God that sit in majestee,	
	So blesse his soule for his mercy dere.	
	Now wol I saye my tale if ye wol heere.	

Another Interruption

835	The Frere lough whan he hadde herd al this:	
	"Now dame," quod he, "so have I joye or blis,	
	This is a long preamble of a tale."	
	And whan the Somnour herde the Frere gale,°	exclaim
	"Lo," quod the Somnour, "Goddes armes two,	
840	A frere wol entremette him° everemo!	interfere
	Lo, goode men, a flye and eek a frere	
	Wol falle in every dissh and eek matere.	
	What spekestou of preambulacioun?	
	What, amble or trotte or pisse or go sitte down!	
845	Thou lettest° oure disport in this manere."	hinder
	"Ye, woltou so, sire Somnour?" quod the Frere.	
	"Now by my faith, I shal er that I go	
	Telle of a somnour swich a tale or two	
	That al the folk shal laughen in this place."	
850	"Now elles, Frere, I wol bishrewe thy face,"	
	Quod this Somnour, "and I bishrewe me,	
	But if I telle tales two or three	
	Of freres, er I come to Sidingborne,⁸	

8. Sittingbourne, a town about 40 miles from London.

That I shal make thyn herte for to moorne—
855   For wel I woot thy pacience is goon."
     Oure Hoste cride, "Pees, and that anoon!"
And saide, "Lat the womman telle hir tale:
Ye fare° as folk that dronken been of ale.   *behave*
Do, dame, tel forth youre tale, and that is best."
860   "Al redy, sire," quod she, "right as you lest°—   *it pleases*
If I have licence of this worthy Frere."
"Yis, dame," quod he, "tel forth and I wol heere."

The Wife of Bath's Tale

In th'olde dayes of the King Arthour,
Of which that Britouns° speken greet honour,   *Bretons*
865   Al was this land fulfild° of faïrye: *filled*
The elf-queene° with hir joly compaignye   *fairy queen*
Daunced ful ofte in many a greene mede°—   *meadow*
This was the olde opinion as I rede;
I speke of many hundred yeres ago.
870   But now can no man see none elves mo,
For now the grete charitee and prayeres
Of limitours,[1] and othere holy freres,
That serchen every land and every streem,
As thikke as motes° in the sonne-beem,   *dust particles*
875   Blessing halles, chambres, kichenes, bowres,°   *bedrooms*
Citees, burghes,° castels, hye towres,   *boroughs*
Thropes,° bernes,° shipnes,° dayeries— *villages / barns / stables*
This maketh that ther been no faïries.
For ther as wont° to walken was an elf   *where there used*
880   Ther walketh now the limitour himself,
In undermeles° and in morweninges,°   *afternoons / mornings*
And saith his Matins° and his holy thinges, *morning prayers*
As he gooth in his limitacioun.°   *prescribed district*
Wommen may go saufly° up and down: *safely*
885   In every bussh or under every tree
Ther is noon other incubus[2] but he,
And he ne wol doon hem but dishonour.
     And so bifel it that this King Arthour
Hadde in his hous a lusty bacheler,°   *young knight*
890   That on a day cam riding fro river,°   *hunting waterfowl*
And happed that, allone as he was born,
He sawgh a maide walking him biforn;
Of which maide anoon, maugree hir heed,° *against her will*
By verray force he rafte° hir maidenheed;   *stole*
895   For which oppression was swich clamour,
And swich pursuite° unto the King Arthour,   *petitioning*
That dampned° was this knight for to be deed *condemned*
By cours of lawe, and sholde han lost his heed—
Paraventure° swich was the statut tho°— *as it happens / then*

---

1. Friars licensed to beg within set districts.   2. Demon who fornicates with women.

900	But that the queene and othere ladies mo	
	So longe prayeden the king of grace,	
	Til he his lif him graunted in the place,	
	And yaf him to the queene, al at hir wille,	
	To chese° wheither she wolde him save or spille.°	decide / destroy
905	The queene thanked the king with al hir might,	
	And after this thus spak she to the knight,	
	Whan that she saw hir time upon a day:	
	"Thou standest yit," quod she, "in swich array°	situation
	That of thy lif yit hastou no suretee.°	guarantee
910	I graunte thee lif if thou canst tellen me	
	What thing it is that wommen most desiren:	
	Be war and keep thy nekke boon° from iren.°	bone / iron
	And if thou canst nat tellen me anoon,	
	Yit wol I yive thee leve for to goon	
915	A twelfmonth and a day to seeche° and lere°	seek out / learn
	An answere suffisant° in this matere,	satisfactory
	And suretee° wol I han er that thou pace,°	pledge / pass
	Thy body for to yeelden° in this place."	surrender
	Wo was this knight, and sorwefully he siketh.°	sighs
920	But what, he may nat doon al as him liketh,	
	And atte laste he chees him° for to wende,°	decided / travel
	And come again right at the yeres ende,	
	With swich answere as God wolde him purveye,°	provide
	And taketh his leve and wendeth forth his waye.	
925	He seeketh every hous and every place	
	Wher as he hopeth for to finde grace,	
	To lerne what thing wommen love most.	
	But he ne coude arriven in no coost°	country
	Wher as he mighte finde in this matere	
930	Two creatures according in fere.°	agreeing together
	Some saiden wommen loven best richesse;	
	Some saide honour, some saide jolinesse;°	pleasure
	Some riche array, some saiden lust abedde,	
	And ofte time to be widwe and wedde.	
935	Some saide that oure herte is most esed	
	Whan that we been yflatered and yplesed—	
	He gooth ful neigh the soothe,° I wol nat lie:	near the truth
	A man shal winne us best with flaterye,	
	And with attendance and with bisinesse°	attentive service
940	Been we ylimed,° bothe more and lesse.	ensnared
	And some sayen that we loven best	
	For to be free, and do right as us lest,°	pleases
	And that no man repreve° us of oure vice,	scold
	But saye that we be wise and no thing nice.°	foolish
945	For trewely, ther is noon of us alle,	
	If any wight wol clawe us on the galle,°	rub a sore spot
	That we nil kike° for he saith us sooth:°	kick / the truth
	Assaye° and he shal finde it that so dooth.	try
	For be we nevere so vicious withinne,	
950	We wol be holden° wise and clene of sinne.	considered

And some sayn that greet delit han we
For to be holden stable° and eek secree,°   *constant / discreet*
And in oo purpos stedefastly to dwelle,
And nat biwraye° thing that men us telle—   *reveal*
955   But that tale is nat worth a rake-stele.°   *rake handle*
Pardee,° we wommen conne no thing hele:°   *by God / conceal*
Witnesse on Mida.³ Wol ye heere the tale?
    Ovide, amonges othere thinges smale,
Saide Mida hadde under his longe heres,
960   Growing upon his heed, two asses eres,
The whiche vice° he hidde as he best mighte   *fault*
Ful subtilly from every mannes sighte,
That save his wif ther wiste of it namo.°   *no one else know*
He loved hire most and trusted hire also.
965   He prayed hire that to no creature
She sholde tellen of his disfigure.°   *deformity*
    She swoor him nay, for al this world to winne,
She nolde° do that vilainye or sinne   *would not*
To make hir housbonde han so foul a name:
970   She nolde nat telle it for hir owene shame.
But nathelees, hir thoughte that she dyde°   *would die*
That she so longe sholde a conseil° hide;   *secret*
Hire thoughte it swal so sore aboute hir herte
That nedely° som word hire moste asterte,°   *surely / come out*
975   And sith she dorste nat telle it to no man,
Down to a mareis° faste° by she ran—   *marsh / close*
Til she cam there hir herte was afire—
And as a bitore° bombleth° in the mire,   *heron / squawks*
She laide hir mouth unto the water down:
980   "Biwray° me nat, thou water, with thy soun,"°   *betray / sound*
Quod she. "To thee I telle it and namo:
Myn housbonde hath longe asses eres two.
Now is myn herte al hool, now is it oute.
I mighte no lenger keepe it, out of doute."
985   Here may ye see, though we a time abide,
Yit oute it moot:° we can no conseil hide.   *must*
The remenant of the tale if ye wol heere,
Redeth Ovide, and ther ye may it lere.°   *learn*
    This knight of which my tale is specially,
990   Whan that he sawgh he mighte nat come therby—
This is to saye what wommen loven most—
Within his brest ful sorweful was his gost,°   *spirit*
But hoom he gooth, he mighte nat sojurne:°   *linger*
The day was come that hoomward moste he turne.
995   And in his way it happed him to ride
In al this care under a forest side,
Wher as he sawgh upon a daunce go
Of ladies foure and twenty and yit mo;
Toward the whiche daunce he drow° ful yerne,°   *drew / gladly*

---

3. Midas's story is recounted in Ovid's *Metamorphoses* 9.

1000	In hope that som wisdom sholde he lerne.
	But certainly, er he cam fully there,
	Vanisshed was this daunce, he niste° where. *did not know*
	No creature sawgh he that bar lif,
	Save on the greene he sawgh sitting a wif—
1005	A fouler wight° ther may no man devise.° *creature / imagine*
	Again the knight this olde wif gan rise,
	And saide, "Sire knight, heer forth lith no way.° *road*
	Telle me what ye seeken, by youre fay.° *faith*
	Paraventure it may the better be:
1010	Thise olde folk conne° muchel thing," quod she. *know*
	"My leve moder,"° quod this knight, "certain, *dear mother*
	I nam but° deed but if that I can sayn *am no more than*
	What thing it is that wommen most desire.
	Coude ye me wisse,° I wolde wel quite youre hire."° *inform / repay you*
1015	"Plight° me thy trouthe° here in myn hand," quod she, *pledge / promise*
	"The nexte thing that I requere thee,
	Thou shalt it do, if it lie in thy might,
	And I wol telle it you er it be night."
	"Have heer my trouthe," quod the knight. "I graunte."
1020	"Thanne," quod she, "I dar me wel avaunte° *brag*
	Thy lif is sauf, for I wol stande therby.
	Upon my lif the queene wol saye as I.
	Lat see which is the pruddeste° of hem alle *proudest*
	That wereth on a coverchief or a calle° *headdress*
1025	That dar saye nay of that I shal thee teche.
	Lat us go forth withouten lenger speeche."
	Tho rouned° she a pistel° in his ere, *whispered / message*
	And bad him to be glad and have no fere.
	Whan they be comen to the court, this knight
1030	Saide he hadde holde his day as he hadde hight,° *promised*
	And redy was his answere, as he saide.
	Ful many a noble wif, and many a maide,
	And many a widwe—for that they been wise—
	The queene hirself sitting as justise,° *judge*
1035	Assembled been this answere for to heere,
	And afterward this knight was bode appere.
	To every wight comanded was silence,
	And that the knight sholde telle in audience
	What thing that worldly wommen loven best.
1040	This knight ne stood nat stille° as dooth a best,° *silent / beast*
	But to his question anoon answerde
	With manly vois that al the court it herde.
	"My lige° lady, generally," quod he, *liege*
	"Wommen desire to have sovereinetee
1045	As wel over hir housbonde as hir love,
	And for to been in maistrye him above.
	This is youre moste desir though ye me kille.
	Dooth as you list: I am here at youre wille."
	In al the court ne was ther wif ne maide
1050	Ne widwe that contraried that he saide,

But saiden he was worthy han his lif.
    And with that word up sterte that olde wif,
Which that the knight sawgh sitting on the greene;
"Mercy," quod she, "my soverein lady queene,
1055   Er that youre court departe, do me right.
I taughte this answere unto the knight,
For which he plighte me his trouthe there
The firste thing I wolde him requere
He wolde it do, if it laye in his might.
1060   Bifore the court thanne praye I thee, sire knight,"
Quod she, "that thou me take unto thy wif,
For wel thou woost° that I have kept° thy lif.   *know / saved*
If I saye fals, say nay, upon thy fay."
    This knight answerde, "Allas and wailaway,
1065   I woot° right wel that swich was my biheeste.°   *know / promise*
For Goddes love, as chees° a newe requeste: *choose*
Taak al my good and lat my body go."
    "Nay thanne," quod she, "I shrewe° us bothe two.   *curse*
For though that I be foul and old and poore,
1070   I nolde° for al the metal ne for ore   *would not wish*
That under erthe is grave° or lith above,   *buried*
But if thy wif I were and eek thy love."
    "My love," quod he. "Nay, my dampnacioun!
Allas, that any of my nacioun°   *lineage*
1075   Sholde evere so foule disparaged° be."   *degraded*
But al for nought, th'ende is this, that he
Constrained was: he needes moste hire wedde,
And taketh his olde wif and gooth to bedde.
    Now wolden some men saye, paraventure,
1080   That for my necligence I do no cure
To tellen you the joy and al th'array
That at the feeste was that ilke day.
To which thing shortly answere I shal:
I saye ther nas no joye ne feeste at al;
1085   Ther nas but hevinesse and muche sorwe.
For prively he wedded hire on morwe,°   *in the morning*
And al day after hidde him as an owle,
So wo was him, his wif looked so foule.
    Greet was the wo the knight hadde in his thought:
1090   Whan he was with his wif abedde brought,
He walweth° and he turneth to and fro.   *rolls over*
His olde wif lay smiling everemo,
And saide, "O dere housbonde, benedicite,°   *bless us*
Fareth° every knight thus with his wif as ye?   *behaves*
1095   Is this the lawe of King Arthures hous?
Is every knight of his thus daungerous?°   *reserved*
I am youre owene love and youre wif;
I am she which that saved hath youre lif;
And certes yit ne dide I you nevere unright.°   *injustice*
1100   Why fare° ye thus with me this firste night?   *behave*
Ye faren like a man hadde lost his wit.

What is my gilt? For Goddes love, telle it,
And it shal been amended if I may."
    "Amended!" quod this knight. "Allas, nay, nay,
1105 It wol nat been amended neveremo.
Thou art so lothly° and so old also,   *loathsome*
And therto comen of so lowe a kinde,°   *breeding*
That litel wonder is though I walwe and winde.°   *turn*
So wolde God myn herte wolde breste!"°   *burst*
1110   "Is this," quod she, "the cause of youre unreste?"
    "Ye, certainly," quod he. "No wonder is."
    "Now sire," quod she, "I coude amende al this,
If that me liste,° er it were dayes three,   *it pleased me*
So° wel ye mighte bere you° unto me.   *provided that / behave*
1115   "But for ye speken of swich gentilesse°   *nobility*
As is descended out of old richesse—
That therfore sholden ye be gentilmen—
Swich arrogance is nat worth an hen.
Looke who that is most vertuous alway,
1120 Privee and apert,° and most entendeth ay   *privately and publicly*
To do the gentil deedes that he can,
Taak him for the gretteste gentilman.
Crist wol° we claime of him oure gentilesse,   *wishes*
Nat of oure eldres for hir 'old richesse.'
1125 For though they yive us al hir heritage,
For which we claime to been of heigh parage,°   *noble lineage*
Yit may they nat biquethe for no thing
To noon of us hir vertuous living,
That made hem gentilmen ycalled be,
1130 And bad us folwen° hem in swich degree.   *to follow*
    "Wel can the wise poete of Florence,
That highte° Dant,[4] speken in this sentence;°   *was called / opinion*
Lo, in swich manere rym is Dantes tale:
'Ful selde° up riseth by his braunches[5] smale   *seldom*
1135 Prowesse° of man, for God of his prowesse   *excellence*
Wol that of him we claime oure gentilesse.'
For of oure eldres may we no thing claime
But temporel thing that man may hurte and maime.
Eek every wight woot° this as wel as I,   *person knows*
1140 If gentilesse were planted natureelly
Unto a certain linage down the line,
Privee and apert, thanne wolde they nevere fine°   *end*
To doon of gentilesse the faire office°—   *duty*
They mighte do no vilainye or vice.
1145   "Taak fir and beer° it in the derkeste hous   *bring*
Bitwixe this and the Mount of Caucasus,
And lat men shette° the dores and go thenne,°   *shut / thence*
Yit wol the fir as faire lie and brenne
As twenty thousand men mighte it biholde:

4. Dante Alighieri, the 13th-century Italian poet, ex-   5. Branches (of his family tree).
pressed similar views in his *Convivio*.

1150	His° office natureel ay° wol it holde,	*its / always*
	Up peril of my lif, til that it die.	
	Heer may ye see wel how that genterye°	*gentility*
	Is nat annexed° to possessioun,	*connected*
	Sith° folk ne doon hir operacioun°	*since / their work*
1155	Alway, as dooth the fir, lo, in his kinde.°	*nature*
	For God it woot, men may wel often finde	
	A lordes sone do shame and vilainye;	
	And he that wol han pris° of his gentrye,°	*esteem / noble birth*
	For he was boren of a gentil hous,	
1160	And hadde his eldres noble and vertuous,	
	And nil° himselven do no gentil deedes,	*will not*
	Ne folwen his gentil auncestre that deed is,	
	He nis nat gentil, be he duc or erl—	
	For vilaines sinful deedes maken a cherl.°	*ruffian*
1165	Thy gentilesse nis but renomee°	*reputation*
	Of thine auncestres for hir heigh bountee,°	*generosity*
	Which is a straunge° thing for thy persone.	*foreign*
	For gentilesse cometh fro God allone.	
	Thanne comth oure verray gentilesse of grace:	
1170	It was no thing biquethe us with oure place.	
	Thenketh how noble, as saith Valerius,[6]	
	Was thilke° Tullius Hostilius[7]	*that*
	That out of poverte roos to heigh noblesse.	
	Redeth Senek,[8] and redeth eek Boece:	
1175	Ther shul ye seen expres that no drede° is	*doubt*
	That he is gentil that dooth gentil deedes.	
	And therfore, leve housbonde, I thus conclude:	
	Al were it that mine auncestres weren rude,°	*lowborn*
	Yit may the hye God—and so hope I—	
1180	Graunte me grace to liven vertuously.	
	Thanne am I gentil whan that I biginne	
	To liven vertuously and waive° sinne.	*avoid*
	"And ther as ye of poverte me repreve,	
	The hye God, on whom that we bileve,	
1185	In wilful poverte chees to live his lif;	
	And certes every man, maiden, or wif	
	May understonde that Jesus, hevene king,	
	Ne wolde nat chese a vicious living.	
	Glad poverte is an honeste° thing, certain;	*honorable*
1190	This wol Senek and othere clerkes sayn.	
	Whoso that halt him paid of his poverte,[9]	
	I holde him riche al° hadde he nat a sherte.°	*although / shirt*
	He that coveiteth is a poore wight,	
	For he wolde han that is nat in his might;	
1195	But he that nought hath, ne coveiteth have,	
	Is riche, although we holde him but a knave.°	*servant*

6. The Roman historian Valerius Maximus, in his *Facta et dicta memorabilia* 3.4.

7. The legendary third king of Rome who started as a shepherd.

8. Seneca, the Stoic author, in his *Epistle* 44; Boece: Boethius in his *Consolation of Philosophy*.

9. Whoever is satisfied with poverty.

Verray poverte it singeth proprely.
Juvenal[1] saith of poverte, 'Merily
The poore man, whan he gooth by the waye,
1200   Biforn the theves he may singe and playe.'
Poverte is hateful good, and as I gesse,
A ful greet bringere out of bisinesse;°   *worldly cares*
A greet amendere eek of sapience°   *wisdom*
To him that taketh it in pacience;
1205   Poverte is thing, although it seeme elenge,°   *miserable*
Possession that no wight wol chalenge;
Poverte ful often, whan a man is lowe,
Maketh his God and eek himself to knowe;
Poverte a spectacle° is, as thinketh me,   *eyeglass*
1210   Thurgh which he may his verray freendes see.
And therfore, sire, sin that I nought you greve,
Of my poverte namore ye me repreve.
        "Now sire, of elde° ye repreve me: *old age*
And certes sire, though noon auctoritee
1215   Were in no book, ye gentils of honour
Sayn that men sholde an old wight° doon favour,   *person*
And clepe° him fader for youre gentilesse—   *call*
And auctours° shal I finden, as I gesse.   *authorities*
        "Now ther ye saye that I am foul and old:
1220   Thanne drede you nought to been a cokewold,°   *cuckold*
For filthe and elde, also mote I thee,
Been grete wardeins° upon chastitee.   *guardians*
But nathelees, sin I knowe your delit,
I shal fulfille youre worldly appetit.
1225   "Chees° now," quod she, "oon of thise thinges twaye: *choose*
To han me foul and old til that I deye
And be to you a trewe humble wif,
And nevere you displese in al my lif,
Or elles ye wol han me yong and fair,
1230   And take youre aventure° of the repair°   *chances / visits*
That shal be to youre hous by cause of me—
Or in som other place, wel may be.
Now chees youreselven wheither° that you liketh."   *whichever*
        This knight aviseth him° and sore siketh;°   *considers / sighs*
1235   But atte laste he saide in this manere:
"My lady and my love, and wif so dere,
I putte me in youre wise governaunce:
Cheseth youreself which may be most plesaunce
And most honour to you and me also.
1240   I do no fors° the wheither of the two,   *do not care*
For as you liketh it suffiseth° me."   *satisfies*
        "Thanne have I gete of you° maistrye," quod she,   *won from you*
"Sin I may chese and governe as me lest?"°   *it pleases*
        "Ye, certes, wif," quod he. "I holde it best."
1245   "Kisse me," quod she. "We be no lenger wrothe.°   *opposed*

1. The misogynist Roman poet in his *Satires* 10.21, 22.

For by my trouthe, I wol be to you bothe—
This is to sayn, ye, bothe fair and good.
I praye to God that I mote sterven wood,°   *die mad*
But I to you be al so good and trewe
1250   As evere was wif sin that the world was newe.
And but I be tomorn° as fair to seene   *in the morning*
As any lady, emperisse, or queene,
That is bitwixe the eest and eek the west,
Do with my lif and deeth right as you lest:
1255   Caste up the curtin, looke how that it is."
      And whan the knight sawgh verraily al this,
That she so fair was and so yong therto,
For joye he hente° hire in his armes two;   *seized*
His herte bathed in a bath of blisse;
1260   A thousand time arewe° he gan hire kisse,   *in a row*
And she obeyed him in every thing
That mighte do him plesance or liking.
And thus they live unto hir lives ende
In parfit° joye. And Jesu Crist us sende   *perfect*
1265   Housbondes meeke, yonge, and fresshe abedde—
And grace t'overbide° hem that we wedde.   *outlive*
And eek I praye Jesu shorte hir lives
That nought wol be governed by hir wives,
And olde and angry nigardes of dispence°—   *misers in spending*
1270   God sende hem soone a verray pestilence!

THE FRANKLIN'S TALE   A franklin was a wealthy landowner below the ranks of the nobility. Chaucer's Franklin claims that the tale he is about to tell is a Breton *lai*—a short narrative poem about chivalry, romantic love, and often magic, in the manner of Marie de France's *Lanval*. Though his tale does deal with such subject matter and is set in Brittany, it is not a Breton *lai* at all, but another of Chaucer's many unacknowledged adaptations of Boccaccio. This initial generic misidentification sets the tone for a sly and subversive poem, in which love and magic are viewed with a certain skepticism and things are seldom what they seem.

Although the tale has long been seen as part of an ongoing discussion of marriage initiated in the Wife of Bath's *Prologue* and *Tale*, few today would argue that it constitutes Chaucer's own ideal resolution of the issue. The tale's beginning claims to celebrate mutual respect and compromise in marriage. The rest of the story undercuts those values, though, as the young wife Dorigen becomes a pawn handed back and forth between two men—partly, it is true, as the result of her own rash promise to a would-be courtly lover, Aurelius. Her helplessness when he appears to fulfill the far-fetched condition of her promise suggests that the Franklin in fact sees Dorigen as a childlike figure in need of a wise husband's guidance.

Ultimately, the Franklin is less interested in the relation between the husband and wife than in that among the three men, and their different ranks—knight, squire, and clerk. He is particularly concerned with the comparative degrees of their "gentillesse," as seen in their three final acts of "freedom" or generosity to one another. His closing question—which of the men was most "free"—notably excludes Dorigen, whose conflicting promises (marriage vow and courtly vow) have lost her any further power to act in her own behalf.

The Franklin treats the issues of both gender and class relations with a certain amount of detachment. Dorigen's distraught account of classical women who killed themselves rather than submit to dishonor becomes more and more an obscure, even irrelevant, catalog, as if she were trying to stave off death with sheer verbiage. The narrative effect is to deflate the aristocratic idealism of romance with common sense.

The magic characteristic of romance is similarly debunked in the tale. After the magician—a university student turned astronomical entrepreneur—promises Aurelius to help him win his lady, his hard-nosed bargaining over the price of his service has a comic effect. It has been suggested that in dwelling on such issues the Franklin is revealing his class anxiety at a time when many members of the upper bourgeoisie were aspiring to the ranks of the nobility.

The Franklin's Tale
The Prologue

	Thise olde gentil Britons° in hir° dayes	*noble Bretons / their*
	Of diverse aventures maden layes,°	*poems*
	Rymeyed in hir firste° Briton tonge;°	*original / language*
	Whiche layes with hir instruments they songe,	
5	Or elles redden hem° for hir plesaunce;	*them*
	And oon of hem have I in remembraunce,	
	Which I shal sayn with good wil as I can.	
	But sires, by cause I am a burel° man,	*uneducated*
	At my biginning first I you biseeche	
10	Have me excused of my rude° speeche.	*rough*
	I lerned nevere retorike, certain:	
	Thing that I speke it moot° be bare and plain;	*must*
	I sleep nevere in the Mount of Parnaso,[1]	
	Ne lerned Marcus Tullius Scithero;[2]	
15	Colours° ne knowe I noon, withouten drede,°	*rhetorical figures / doubt*
	But swiche° colours as growen in the mede,°	*such / meadow*
	Or elles swiche as men dye or painte;	
	Colours of retorike been° too quainte:°	*are / obscure*
	My spirit feeleth nat of swich° matere.	*such*
20	But if you list, my tale shul ye heere.	

The Tale

	In Armorik,° that called is Britaine,°	*Armorica / Brittany*
	Ther was a knight that loved and dide his paine°	*made great effort*
	To serve a lady in his beste wise,°	*manner*
	And many a labour, many a greet emprise°	*undertaking*
25	He for his lady wroughte er° she were wonne,	*made before*
	For she was oon° the faireste under sonne,	*one of*
	And eek therto come of so heigh kinrede°	*such high kindred*
	That wel unnethes dorste° this knight for drede	*hardly dared*
	Telle hire his wo, his paine, and his distresse.	
30	But atte laste she for his worthinesse,	
	And namely for his meeke obeisaunce,°	*obedience*
	Hath swich a pitee caught of his penaunce°	*suffering*
	That prively she fil of° his accord	*fell in with*
	To taken him for hir housbonde and hir lord,	
35	Of swich lordshipe as men han over hir wives.	
	And for to lede the more in blisse hir lives,	
	Of his free wil he swoor hire as a knight	

---

1. Parnassus, home of the Muses.   2. Cicero, the Roman rhetorician.

That nevere in al his lif he day ne night
Ne sholde upon him take no maistrye°   *control*
40   Again hir wil, ne kithe° hire jalousye,   *show*
But hire obeye and folwe hir wil in al,
As any lovere to his lady shal—
Save that the name of sovereinetee,°   *sovereignty*
That wolde he have, for shame of his degree.°   *station*
45   She thanked him, and with ful greet humblesse
She saide, "Sire, sith of youre gentilesse°   *nobility*
Ye profre me to have so large a reine,
Ne wolde nevere God bitwixe° us twaine,°   *between / two*
As in my gilt, were outher werre° or strif.   *either war*
50   Sire, I wol be your humble, trewe wif—
Have heer my trouthe°—til that myn herte breste."   *troth, word of honor*
Thus been they bothe in quiete and in reste.
     For oo thing, sires, saufly dar I saye:
That freendes everich other moot° obeye,   *each other must*
55   If they wol longe holden compaignye.°   *stay together*
Love wol nat be constrained by maistrye:°   *domination*
Whan maistrye comth, the God of Love anoon°   *at once*
Beteth his winges and farewel, he is goon!
Love is a thing as any spirit free;
60   Wommen of kinde° desiren libertee,   *by nature*
And nat to been constrained as a thral°—   *slave*
And so doon men, if I sooth° sayen shal.   *truth*
Looke° who that is most pacient in love,   *see*
He is at his avantage al above.
65   Pacience is an heigh vertu, certain,
For it venquissheth,° as thise clerkes sayn,   *vanquishes*
Thinges that rigour° sholde nevere attaine.°   *power / overcome*
For every word men may nat chide or plaine:°   *complain*
Lerneth to suffre, or elles, so mote I goon,°   *as I may live*
70   Ye shul it lerne, wherso ye wol or noon.°   *whether you wish or not*
For in this world, certain, ther no wight° is   *person*
That he ne dooth or saith somtime amis:
Ire,° siknesse, or constellacioun,°   *anger / planetary influences*
Win, wo, or chaunging of complexioun°   *balance of humors*
75   Causeth ful ofte to doon amis or speken.
On every wrong a man may nat be wreken:°   *avenged*
After the time moste be temperaunce
To every wight that can on governaunce.³
And therfore hath this wise worthy knight
80   To live in ese suffrance hire bihight,°   *promised her toleration*
And she to him ful wisly gan to swere
That nevere sholde ther be defaute° in here.   *defect*
     Here may men seen an humble wis accord:
Thus hath she take hir servant and hir lord—
85   Servant in love and lord in mariage.
Thanne was he bothe in lordshipe and servage.°   *servitude*

---

3. To every person that is capable of self-control.

Servage? Nay, but in lordshipe above,

Sith° he hath bothe his lady and his love;   *since*

His lady, certes, and his wif also,

90   The which that lawe of love accordeth to.

And whan he was in this prosperitee,

Hoom with his wif he gooth to his contree,

Nat fer fro Pedmark⁴ ther his dwelling was,

Wher as he liveth in blisse and in solas.°   *delight*

95   Who coude telle but° he hadde wedded be   *unless*

The joye, the ese, and the prosperitee

That is bitwixe an housbonde and his wif?

A yeer and more lasted this blisful lif,

Til that the knight of which I speke of thus,

100   That of Kairrud⁵ was cleped° Arveragus,   *called*

Shoop° him to goon and dwelle a yeer or twaine°   *prepared / two*

In Engelond, that cleped was eek Britaine,

To seeke in armes worshipe and honour—

For al his lust° he sette in swich labour—   *desire*

105   And dwelled ther two yeer, the book saith thus.

Now wol I stinte° of this Arveragus,   *stop speaking*

And speke I wol of Dorigen his wif,

That loveth hir housbonde as hir hertes lif.

For his absence weepeth she and siketh,°   *sighs*

110   As doon thise noble wives whan hem liketh.°   *it pleases them*

She moorneth, waketh, waileth, fasteth, plaineth;

Desir of his presence hire so distraineth°   *afflicts*

That al this wide world she sette at nought.

Hir freendes, whiche that knewe hir hevy thought,

115   Conforten hire in al that evere they may:

They prechen hire, they telle hire night and day

That causelees she sleeth° hirself, allas;   *kills*

And every confort possible in this cas

They doon to hire with al hir bisinesse,°   *assiduousness*

120   Al for to make hire leve hir hevinesse.

By proces,° as ye knowen everichoon,°   *course of time / every one*

Men may so longe graven in° a stoon   *engrave on*

Til som figure therinne emprinted be:

So longe han they conforted hire til she

125   Received hath, by hope and by resoun,

The emprinting of hir consolacioun,

Thurgh which hir grete sorwe gan assuage:

She may nat alway duren° in swich rage.°   *remain / passion*

And eek° Arveragus in al this care   *also*

130   Hath sent hir lettres hoom of his welfare,

And that he wol come hastily again—

Or elles hadde this sorwe hir herte slain.

Hir freendes sawe hir sorwe gan to slake,°   *diminish*

And prayed hire on knees, for Goddes sake,

135   To come and romen hire in compaignye,

---

4. Penmarch, a town in Brittany.   5. Kerreu, a town in Brittany.

Away to drive hir derke fantasye,
And finally she graunted that requeste:
For wel she saw that it was for the beste.
    Now stood hir castel faste° by the see,   *close*
140   And often with hir freendes walketh she,
Hire to disporte° upon the bank an heigh,   *amuse*
Wher as she many a ship and barge seigh,°   *saw*
Sailing hir cours wher as hem liste go—
But thanne was that a parcel° of hir wo,   *part*
145   For of hirself ful ofte, "Allas!" saith she,
"Is ther no ship of so manye as I see
Wol bringen hoom my lord? Thanne were myn herte
Al warisshed° of his bittre paines smerte."   *recovered*
    Another time ther wolde she sitte and thinke,
150   And caste hir yën° downward fro the brinke;   *eyes*
But whan she sawgh the grisly rokkes blake,
For verray fere° so wolde hir herte quake   *fear*
That on hir feet she mighte hire nat sustene:
Thanne wolde she sitte adown upon the greene
155   And pitously into the see° biholde,   *sea*
And sayn right thus, with sorweful sikes° colde: *sighs*
    "Eterne God that thurgh thy purveyaunce°   *providence*
Ledest the world by certain governaunce,
In idel,° as men sayn, ye nothing make: *vain*
160   But Lord, thise grisly feendly° rokkes blake,   *hostile*
That seemen rather a foul confusioun
Of werk, than any fair creacioun
Of swich a parfit wis God and a stable,
Why han ye wrought this werk unresonable?
165   For by this werk south, north, ne° west ne eest,   *nor*
Ther nis yfostred° man ne brid° ne beest: *nourished / bird*
It dooth no good, to my wit, but anoyeth.
See ye nat, Lord, how mankinde it destroyeth?
An hundred thousand bodies of mankinde
170   Han rokkes slain, al be they nat in minde:[6]
Which mankinde is so fair part of thy werk
That thou it madest lik to thyn owene merk;°   *mark*
Thanne seemed it ye hadde a greet cheertee°   *charity*
Toward mankinde. But how thanne may it be
175   That ye swiche menes make it to destroyen?—
Whiche menes do no good, but evere anoyen.
I woot wel clerkes wol sayn as hem leste,
By arguments, that al is for the beste,
Though I ne can the causes nat yknowe.
180   But thilke God that made wind to blowe,
As keepe my lord! This my conclusioun.
To clerkes lete° I al disputisoun,°   *leave / disputation*
But wolde God that alle thise rokkes blake
Were sonken into helle for his sake!
185   Thise rokkes slain myn herte for the fere."

---

6. Though they are not remembered.

Thus wolde she sayn with many a pitous tere.
   Hir freendes sawe that it was no disport° *amusement*
To romen° by the see, but disconfort, *stroll*
And shopen for to playen somwher elles:
190 They leden hire by rivers and by welles,
And eek in othere places delitables;° *delightful*
They dauncen and they playen at ches and tables.
   So on a day, right in the morwetide,° *morning*
Unto a gardin that was ther biside,
195 In which that they hadde maad hir ordinaunce° *arrangements*
Of vitaile° and of other purveyaunce,° *food / provisions*
They goon and playe hem al the longe day.
And this was on the sixte morwe° of May, *morning*
Which May had painted with his softe showres
200 This gardin ful of leves and of flowres;
And craft° of mannes hand so curiously *skill*
Arrayed hadde this gardin trewely
That nevere was ther gardin of swich pris,° *excellence*
But if it were the verray Paradis.° *Garden of Eden*
205 The odour of flowres and the fresshe sighte
Wolde han maked any herte lighte
That evere was born, but if° too greet siknesse, *unless*
Or too greet sorwe heeld it in distresse,
So ful it was of beautee with plesaunce.° *pleasure*
210 At after-diner gonne they to daunce,
And singe also, save° Dorigen allone, *except*
Which made alway hir complainte and hir mone,
For she ne sawgh him on the daunce go
That was hir housbonde and hir love also.
215 But nathelees she moste a time abide,
And with good hope lete hir sorwe slide.
   Upon this daunce, amonges othere men,
Daunced a squier° bifore Dorigen *squire*
That fressher was and jolier of array,° *clothing*
220 As to my doom, than is the month of May.
He singeth, daunceth, passing any man
That is or was sith that the world bigan.
Therwith he was, if men him sholde descrive,
Oon of the beste-faring° man on live:° *best-looking / alive*
225 Yong, strong, right vertuous, and riche and wis,
And wel-biloved, and holden in greet pris.° *respect*
And shortly, if the soothe I tellen shal,
Unwiting of this Dorigen at al,
This lusty squier, servant to Venus,
230 Which that ycleped° was Aurelius, *called*
Hadde loved hire best of any creature
Two yeer and more, as was his aventure,
But nevere dorste° he tellen hire his grevaunce:° *dared / pain*
Withouten coppe he drank al his penaunce.[7]
235 He was despaired, no thing dorste he saye—

---

7. He suffered in silence.

Save in his songes somwhat wolde he wraye°   *betray*
His wo, as in a general complaining:
He saide he loved and was biloved no thing;°   *not at all*
Of which matere made he manye layes,°   *songs*
240   Songes, complaintes, roundels, virelayes,
How that he dorste nat his sorwe telle,
But languissheth as a furye dooth in helle;
And die he moste, he saide, as dide Ekko
For Narcisus that dorste nat telle hir wo.[8]
245   In other manere than ye heere me saye
Ne dorste he nat to hire his wo biwraye,°   *reveal*
Save that paraventure° som time at daunces,   *perhaps*
Ther yonge folk keepen hir observaunces,°   *observe their rituals*
It may wel be he looked on hir face
250   In swich a wise as man that asketh grace;
But no thing wiste° she of his entente.   *knew*
Nathelees it happed, er they thennes wente,
By cause that he was hir neighebour,
And was a man of worshipe and honour,
255   And hadde yknowen him of time yore,
They fille in speeche,° and forth more and more   *fell into conversation*
Unto his purpos drow Aurelius,
And whan he sawgh his time, he saide thus:
       "Madame," quod he, "by God that this world made,
260   So that I wiste it mighte youre herte glade,
I wolde that day that youre Arveragus
Wente over the see that I, Aurelius,
Hadde went ther° nevere I sholde have come again.   *where*
For wel I woot° my service is in vain: *know*
265   My gerdon° is but bresting° of myn herte.   *reward / bursting*
Madame, reweth° upon my paines smerte,   *take pity*
For with a word ye may me slee° or save.   *kill*
Here at youre feet God wolde that I were grave!°   *buried*
I ne have° as now no leiser° more to saye: *do not have / leisure*
270   Have mercy, sweete, or ye wol do° me deye."   *make*
       She gan to looke upon Aurelius:
"Is this youre wil?" quod she, "and saye ye thus?
Nevere erst,"° quod she, "ne wiste° I what ye mente.   *before / knew*
But now, Aurelie, I knowe youre entente,
275   By thilke God that yaf° me soule and lif,   *gave*
Ne shal I nevere been untrewe° wif,   *unfaithful*
In word ne werk, as fer as I have wit.
I wol be his to whom that I am knit:°   *joined*
Take this for final answere as of me."
280   But after that in play thus saide she:
       "Aurelie," quod she, "by hye God above,
Yit wolde I graunte you to been youre love,
Sin I you see so pitously complaine,
Looke what day that endelong° Britaine   *along*
285   Ye remeve° alle the rokkes, stoon by stoon,   *remove*

---

8. Echo was unable to convey her love for Narcissus and eventually died of woe.

That they ne lette° ship ne boot to goon.°   *prevent / from passing*
I saye, whan ye han maad the coost so clene
Of rokkes that ther nis no stoon yseene,
Thanne wol I love you best of any man—
290   Have heer my trouthe°—in al that evere I can.   *word of honor*
For wel I woot° that it shal nevere bitide.°   *know / happen*
Lat swiche folies out of youre herte slide!
What daintee° sholde a man han by his lif   *delight*
For to love another mannes wif,
295   That hath hir body whan so that him liketh?"°   *it pleases him*
    Aurelius ful ofte sore siketh:°   *sighs*
"Is ther noon other grace in you?" quod he.
"No, by that Lord," quod she, "that maked me."
Wo was Aurelie whan that he this herde,
300   And with a sorweful herte he thus answerde.
    "Madame," quod he, "this were an impossible.°   *impossibility*
Thanne moot I die of sodein° deeth horrible."   *sudden*
And with that word he turned him anoon.°   *at once*
Tho come hir othere freendes many oon,
305   And in the aleyes romeden° up and down,   *alleys strolled*
And no thing wiste of this conclusioun,
But sodeinly bigonne revel newe,°   *new revelry*
Til that the brighte sonne loste his hewe,
For th'orisonte° hath reft° the sonne his light—   *horizon / deprived of*
310   This is as muche to saye as it was night.
And hoom they goon in joye and in solas,
Save only wrecche° Aurelius, allas.   *wretched*
He to his hous is goon with sorweful herte;
He seeth° he may nat from his deeth asterte;°   *sees / escape*
315   Him seemed that he felte his herte colde;
Up to the hevene his handes he gan holde,
And on his knees bare he sette him down,
And in his raving saide his orisoun.°   *prayer*
For verray wo out of his wit he braide;°   *went*
320   He niste° what he spak, but thus he saide;   *did not know*
With pitous herte his plainte hath he bigonne
Unto the goddes, and first unto the sonne:
    He saide, "Appollo, god and governour
Of every plaunte, herbe, tree, and flowr,
325   That yivest° after thy declinacioun   *gives*
To eech of hem his time and his sesoun,
As thyn herberwe° chaungeth, lowe or hye;   *zodiacal position*
Lord Phebus,° cast thy merciable yë°   *Apollo / merciful eye*
On wrecche Aurelie which that am but lorn.°   *lost*
330   Lo, lord, my lady hath my deeth ysworn
Withouten gilt, but° thy benignitee°   *unless / good will*
Upon my deedly° herte have som pitee;   *dying*
For wel I woot, lord Phebus, if you lest,°   *if it pleases you*
Ye may me helpen, save my lady, best.⁹
335   Now voucheth sauf° that I may you devise°   *grant / relate*

---

9. Except for my lady, you may help me best.

How that I may been holpe,° and in what wise:°   *helped / manner*
    Youre blisful suster, Lucina° the sheene,°   *Diana (the moon) / beautiful*
That of the see is chief goddesse and queene—
Though Neptunus have deitee in the see.°   *sea*
340 Yit emperisse° aboven him is she—   *empress*
Ye knowen wel, lord, that right as hir desir
Is to be quiked° and lighted of youre fir,   *quickened*
For which she folweth you ful bisily,°   *constantly*
Right so the see desireth naturelly
345 To folwen hire, as she that is goddesse
Bothe in the see and rivers more and lesse;
Wherfore, lord Phebus, this is my requeste:
Do this miracle—or do° myn herte breste—   *make*
That now next at this opposicioun,°   *relation of sun and moon*
350 Which in the signe shal be of the Leoun,
As prayeth hite so greet a flood to bringe
That five fadme° at the leeste it overspringe°   *fathoms / overrun*
The hyeste rok in Armorik Britaine;
And lat this flood endure yeres twaine:°   *two years*
355 Thanne certes to my lady may I saye,
'Holdeth youre heeste,° the rokkes been awaye.'   *promise*
    Lord Phebus, dooth this miracle for me!
Praye hire she go no faster cours than ye—
I saye this, prayeth youre suster that she go
360 No faster cours than ye thise yeres two:[1]
Thanne shal she been evene at the fulle alway,
And spring-flood lasten bothe night and day.
And but she vouche sauf in swich manere
To graunte me my soverein lady dere,
365 Praye hire to sinken every rok adown
Into hir owene derke regioun
Under the ground ther Pluto dwelleth inne,
Or nevere mo shal I my lady winne.
Thy temple in Delphos° wol I barefoot seeke.   *Delphi*
370 Lord Phebus, see the teres on my cheeke,
And of my paine have som compassioun."
And with that word in swoune he fil adown,
And longe time he lay forth in a traunce.
    His brother, which that knew of his penaunce.°   *suffering*
375 Up caughte him, and to bedde he hath him brought.
Despaired in this torment and this thought
Lete° I this woful creature lie—   *leave*
Chese he° for me wher° he wol live or die.   *let him choose / whether*
    Arveragus with hele° and greet honour,   *prosperity*
380 As he that was of chivalrye the flowr,
Is comen hoom, and othere worthy men:
O, blisful artou now, thou Dorigen,
That hast thy lusty housbonde in thine armes.
The fresshe knight, the worthy man of armes,

---

1. This miracle would keep the sun and moon in perfect position for two years, so that the high tide would continue to cover the rocks.

385	That loveth thee as his owene hertes lif.	
	No thing list him to been imaginatif[2]	
	If any wight° hadde spoke whil he was oute	*person*
	To hire of love; he ne hadde of it no doute:	
	He nought entendeth to no swich matere.	
390	But daunceth, justeth,° maketh hire good cheere.	*jousts*
	And thus in joye and blisse I lete hem dwelle,	
	And of the sike Aurelius wol I telle.	
	In langour and in torment furious	
	Two yeer and more lay wreeche Aurelius,	
395	Er any foot he mighte on erthe goon.	
	Ne confort in this time hadde he noon,	
	Save of his brother, which that was a clerk:°	*scholar*
	He knew of al this wo and al this werk,	
	For to noon other creature, certain,	
400	Of this matere he dorste no word sayn.	
	Under his brest he bar it more secree°	*bore it more secretly*
	Than evere dide Pamphilus for Galathee.[3]	
	His brest was hool withoute for to seene,	
	But in his herte ay was the arwe° keene;	*arrow*
405	And wel ye knowe that of a sursanure[4]	
	In surgerye is perilous the cure,	
	But men mighte touche the arwe or come therby.	
	His brother weep and wailed prively,	
	Til at the laste him fil in remembrance°	*happened to remember*
410	That whiles he was at Orliens[5] in France,	
	As yonge clerkes that been likerous°	*desirous*
	To reden artes that been curious,	
	Seeken in every halke° and every herne°	*nook / cranny*
	Particuler° sciences for to lerne,	*out of the way*
415	He him remembred that, upon a day,	
	At Orliens in studye a book he sey°	*saw*
	Of magik naturel,° which his felawe,	*i.e., employing astronomy*
	That was that time a bacheler of lawe—	
	Al were he° ther to lerne another craft—	*although he was*
420	Hadde prively° upon his desk ylaft:°	*secretly / left*
	Which book spak muchel° of the operaciouns	*much*
	Touching the eighte and twenty mansiouns°	*daily positions*
	That longen° to the moone—and swich folye	*belong*
	As in oure dayes is nat worth a flye,	
425	For holy chirches faith in oure bileve°	*creed*
	Ne suffreth noon illusion° us to greve.°	*deception / vex*
	And whan this book was in his remembraunce,	
	Anoon for joye his herte gan to daunce,	
	And to himself he saide prively,	
430	"My brother shal be warisshed° hastily,	*cured*
	For I am siker° that ther be sciences°	*sure / knowledge*
	By whiche men make diverse apparences,°	*apparitions*

2. He did not at all wish to be curious.
3. Pamphilus is a lover who seduces Galatea in the 12th-century comedy *Pamphilus, De Amore.*

4. A wound healed only on the surface.
5. Orléans, site of schools known for the study of the liberal arts.

Swiche as thise subtile tregettoures° playe;   *magicians*
For ofte at feestes° have I wel herd saye   *feasts*
435   That tregettours withinne an halle large
Have maad come in a water and a barge,
And in the halle rowen up and down;
Som time hath seemed come a grim leoun;°   *lion*
Som time flowres springe as in a mede;°   *meadow*
440   Som time a vine and grapes white and rede;
Som time a castel al of lim° and stoon—   *lime*
And whan hem liked voided it° anoon: *made it disappear*
Thus seemed it to every mannes sighte.
       Now thanne conclude I thus: that if I mighte
445   At Orliens som old felawe yfinde
That hadde thise moones mansions in minde,
Or other magik naturel above,
He sholde wel make my brother han his love.
For with an apparence° a clerk may make   *illusion*
450   To mannes sighte that alle the rokkes blake
Of Britaine were yvoided° everichoon,   *removed*
And shippes by the brinke° comen and goon,   *coast*
And in swich forme enduren a day or two:
Thanne were my brother warisshed° of his wo;   *cured*
455   Thanne moste she needes holden hir biheeste,°   *promise*
Or elles he shal shame hire at the leeste."
       What sholde I make a lenger tale of this?
Unto his brotheres bed he comen is,
And swich confort he yaf° him for to goon   *gave*
460   To Orliens, that up he sterte° anoon,   *started*
And on his way forthward thanne is he fare,°   *has he traveled*
In hope for to been lissed° of his care.   *assuaged*
       Whan they were come almost to that citee,
But if° it were a two furlong or three,[6]   *unless*
465   A yong clerk roming° by himself they mette,   *strolling*
Which that in Latin thriftily° hem grette,°   *properly / greeted*
And after that he saide a wonder thing:
"I knowe," quod he, "the cause of your coming."
And er they ferther any foote wente,
470   He tolde hem al that was in hir entente.
       This Briton° clerk him axed of felawes,°   *Breton / about companions*
The whiche that he hadde knowe° in olde dawes,°   *known / days*
And he answerde him that they dede were;
For which he weep ful ofte many a tere.
475   Down of his hors Aurelius lighte anoon,
And with this magicien forth is he goon
Hoom to his hous, and maden hem wel at ese:
Hem lakked no vitaile° that mighte hem° plese;   *food / them*
So wel arrayed hous as ther was oon
480   Aurelius in his lif saw nevere noon.
       He shewed him er he wente to soper

6. Unless it were two or three furlongs (the length of one-eighth of a mile) away.

Forestes, parkes ful of wilde deer:

Ther saw he hertes° with hir hornes hye,   *harts*

The gretteste that evere were seen with yë;°   *eye*

485 He sawgh of hem an hundred slain with houndes,

And some with arwes° bledde of bittre woundes.   *arrows*

He saw, when voided° were thise wilde deer,   *removed*

Thise fauconers° upon a fair river,°   *falconers / river bank*

That with hir hawkes han° the heron slain.   *had*

490 Tho sawgh he knightes justing° in a plain.   *jousting*

And after this he dide him this plesaunce,

That he him shewed his lady on a daunce—

On which himself he daunced, as him thoughte.°   *as it seemed to him*

And whan this maister° that this magik wroughte   *Master of Arts*

495 Sawgh it was time, he clapte his handes two,

And farewel, al oure revel was ago.°   *gone*

And yit remeved they nevere out of the hous

Whil they sawe al this sighte merveilous,

But in his studye, ther° as his bookes be,°   *where / were*

500 They sitten stille, and no wight° but they three.   *person*

To him this maister called his squier

And saide him thus, "Is redy oure soper?

Almost an houre it is, I undertake,

Sith° I you bad oure soper for to make,   *since*

505 Whan that thise worthy men wenten with me

Into my studye, ther as my bookes be."

"Sire," quod this squier, "whan it liketh° you,   *pleases*

It is al redy, though ye wol° right now."   *wish*

"Go we thanne soupe," quod he, "as for the beste:

510 This amorous folk som time mote han hir reste."

At after-soper fille° they in tretee°   *fell / negotiations*

What somme° sholde this maistres gerdon° be   *sum / reward*

To remeven alle the rokkes of Britaine,

And eek from Gerounde° to the mouth of Seine: *Gironde River*

515 He made it straunge,° and swoor, so God him save,   *difficult*

Lasse than a thousand pound he wolde nat have,

Ne gladly for that somme he wolde nat goon.

Aurelius with blisful herte anoon

Answerde thus, "Fy on a thousand pound!

520 This wide world, which that men saye is round,

I wolde it yive, if I were lord of it.

This bargain is ful drive,° for we been knit.°   *concluded / agreed*

Ye shal be payed trewely, by my trouthe.°   *word of honor*

But looketh now, for no necligence or slouthe,°   *sloth*

525 Ye tarye us heer no lenger than tomorwe."

"Nay," quod this clerk, "have heer my faith to borwe."°   *as a pledge*

To bedde is goon Aurelius whan him leste,

And wel neigh al that night he hadde his reste:

What for his labour and his hope of blisse,

530 His woful herte of penance° hadde a lisse.°   *suffering / relief*

Upon the morwe, whan that it was day,

To Britaine tooke they the righte way,

Aurelius and this magicien biside,
And been descended ther they wolde abide;
535   And this was, as thise bookes me remembre,
The colde frosty seson of Decembre.
    Phebus wax old, and hewed lik latoun,[7]
That in his hote declinacioun[8]
Shoon as the burned gold with stremes brighte;
540   But now in Capricorn° adown he lighte,   *house of the goat*
Wher as he shoon ful pale, I dar wel sayn:
The bittre frostes with the sleet and rain
Destroyed hath the greene in every yeerd.°   *garden*
Janus[9] sit by the fir with double beerd,
545   And drinketh of his bugle horn the win;
Biforn him stant° brawn of the tusked swin,°   *stands / boar*
And "Nowel!"° crieth every lusty man.   *Noel (Christmas)*
    Aurelius in al that evere he can
Dooth to this maister cheere and reverence,
550   And prayeth him to doon his diligence
To bringen him out of his paines smerte,
Or with a swerd° that he wolde slitte his herte.   *sword*
    This subtil clerk swich routhe° hadde of this man   *pity*
That night and day he spedde him that he can
555   To waiten a time of his conclusioun[1]—
This is to sayn, to make illusioun
By swich an apparence° or jogelrye°   *apparition / magic*
(I ne can° no termes of astrologye)   *know*
That she and every wight sholde weene° and saye   *think*
560   That of Britaine the rokkes were awaye,
Or elles they were sonken under grounde.
So at the laste he hath his time yfounde
To maken his japes° and his wrecchednesse°   *tricks / miserable actions*
Of swich a supersticious cursednesse.
565   His tables tolletanes[2] forth hath he brought,
Ful wel corrected; ne ther lakked nought,
Neither his collect ne his expans yeres,°   *astrological tables*
Ne his rootes,° ne his othere geres,°   *astrological dates / gear*
As been his centres and his arguments,
570   And his proporcionels convenients,[3]
For his equacions in every thing;
And by his eighte spere[4] in his werking°   *operation*
He knew ful wel how fer Alnath was shove
Fro the heed of thilke fixe Aries above
575   That in the ninte spere considered is:[5]
Ful subtilly he calculed al this.
    When he hadde founde his firste mansioun,°   *position (of the moon)*

---

7. The sun became old, and colored like brass.
8. In his celestial position (Tropic of Cancer).
9. The two-headed god who looks forward and backward. His name is reflected in the word "January."
1. To watch for a time to conclude the matter.
2. Astronomical tables based on the latitude of Toledo, Spain.

3. Tables for astronomical calculation.
4. I.e., the sphere of the fixed stars.
5. He knew how far the star Alnath had moved / from the head of the fixed star Aries / that is held to be in the ninth sphere (the primum mobile).

He knew the remenant by proporcioun,°   *use of proportion*
And knew the arising of his moone weel,
580   And in whos face and terme and every deel,
And knew ful wel the moones mansioun
Accordant to his operacioun,
And knew also his othere observaunces°   *rules*
For swiche illusions and swiche meschaunces°   *mischief*
585   As hethen folk useden in thilke dayes;
For which no lenger maked he delayes,
But, thurgh his magik, for a wike° or twaye°   *week / two*
It seemed that alle the rokkes were awaye.
    Aurelius, which that yit° despaired is   *yet*
590   Wher° he shal han his love or fare amis,   *whether*
Awaiteth night and day on this miracle;
And whan he knew that there was noon obstacle,
That voided° were thise rokkes everichoon,°   *removed / every one*
Down to his maistres feet he fil anoon,
595   And saide, "I, woful wrecche Aurelius,
Thanke you, lord, and lady myn Venus,
That me han holpen° fro my cares colde."   *helped*
And to the temple his way forth hath he holde,
Wher as he knew he sholde his lady see.
600   And whan he saw his time, anoon right he,
With dredful° herte and with ful humble cheere,°   *fearful / manner*
Salued° hath his soverein lady dere.   *greeted*
    "My righte lady," quod this woful man,
"Whom I most drede and love as best I can,
605   And lothest° were of al this world displese,   *most unwilling*
Nere it° that I for you have swich disese°   *were it not / pain*
That I moste dien° heer at youre foot anoon,   *must die*
Nought wolde I telle how me is wo-bigoon.°   *how woebegone I am*
But certes, outher° moste I die or plaine:°   *either / complain*
610   Ye sleen° me giltelees for verray paine;   *slay*
But of my deeth though that ye have no routhe,°   *pity*
Aviseth° you er° that ye breke youre trouthe.°   *consider / before / pledge*
Repenteth you, for thilke God above,
Er ye me sleen by cause that I you love.
615   For Madame, wel ye woot° what ye han hight°—   *know / promised*
Not that I chalenge any thing of right
Of you, my soverein lady, but youre grace:
But in a gardin yond at swich a place,
Ye woot right wel what ye bihighten° me,   *promised*
620   And in myn hand youre trouthe plighten° ye   *pledged*
To love me best. God woot ye saiden so,
Al be that I unworthy am therto.
Madame, I speke it for the honour of you
More than to save myn hertes lif right now.
625   I have do so as ye comanded me,
And if ye vouche sauf,° ye may go see.   *grant (it)*
Dooth as you list,° have youre biheeste° in minde,   *wish / promise*
For quik° or deed right ther ye shal me finde.   *living*

In you lith° al to do° me live or deye: *lies / make*

630 But wel I woot the rokkes been awaye."

He taketh his leve and she astoned° stood: *astonished*

In al hir face nas° a drope of blood;   *there was not*

She wende° nevere have come in swich a trappe.   *thought*

"Allas," quod she, "that evere this sholde happe!°   *happen*

635 For wende I nevere by possibilitee

That swich a monstre° or merveile° mighte be;   *strange thing / marvel*

It is agains the proces° of nature."   *due course*

And hoom she gooth a sorweful creature.

For verray fere unnethe° may she go.°   *fear scarcely / walk*

640 She weepeth, waileth al a day or two,

And swouneth° that it routhe° was to see.   *swoons / pity*

But why it was to no wight tolde she,

For out of town was goon Arveragus.

But to hirself she spak and saide thus,

645 With face pale and with ful sorweful cheere,°   *countenance*

In hir complainte, as ye shal after heere:

"Allas," quod she, "on thee, Fortune, I plaine,

That unwar wrapped hast me in thy chaine,

For which t'escape woot° I no socour°—   *know / help*

650 Save only deeth or dishonour:

Oon of thise two bihoveth° me to chese.°   *it behooves / choose*

But nathelees yit have I levere to lese°   *would I rather lose*

My lif, than of my body to have a shame,

Or knowen myselven fals or lese my name,°   *reputation*

655 And with my deeth I may be quit,° ywis.   *freed from the dilemma*

Hath ther nat many a noble wif er this,°   *woman before now*

And many a maide, yslain hirself, allas,

Rather than with hir body doon trespas?°   *sin*

Yis, certes, lo, thise stories beren witnesse:

660 Whan thritty tyrants ful of cursednesse

Hadde slain Phidon[6] in Atthenes atte feeste,°   *at the feasting*

They comanded his doughtren for t'arreste,

And bringen hem biforn hem in despit°   *scorn*

Al naked, to fulfille hir foule delit,

665 And in hir fadres blood they made hem daunce

Upon the pavement—God yive hem meschaunce!°   *give them misfortune*

For which thise woful maidens, ful of drede,

Rather than they wolde lese hir maidenhede,

They prively been stert° into a welle,   *secretly leaped*

670 And dreinte° hemselven, as the bookes telle.   *drowned*

They of Messene lete enquere and seeke[7]

Of Lacedomye° fifty maidens eke,   *Sparta*

On whiche° they wolden doon hir lecherye;   *on whom*

But ther was noon of al that compaignye

675 That she nas° slain, and with a good entente   *was not*

---

6. The story of Phidon's daughter and the 30 tyrants, as well as the following stories, are from St. Jerome's tract against Jovinian, a heretical 4th-century monk.

7. I.e., the men of Messene (in the Peloponnesus) had inquiries made and sought.

Chees° rather for to die than assente   *chose*
To been oppressed° of hir maidenhede: *ravished*
Why sholde I thanne to die been in drede?°   *afraid*
   Lo, eek, the tyrant Aristoclides
680 That loved a maiden highte Stymphalides,°   *called Stymphalis*
Whan that hir fader slain was on a night,
Unto Dianes temple gooth she aright,
And hente° the image in hir handes two;   *seized*
Fro which image wolde she nevere go:
685 No wight ne mighte hir handes of it arace,°   *tear*
Til she was slain right in the selve° place.   *same*
Now sith that maidens hadden swich despit°   *indignation*
To been defouled with mannes foul delit,
Wel oughte a wif rather hirselven slee°   *slay*
690 Than be defouled, as it thinketh me.
   What shal I sayn of Hasdrubales[8] wif
That at Cartage birafte° hirself hir lif?   *took*
For whan she saw that Romains wan° the town,   *won*
She took hir children alle and skipte° adown   *jumped*
695 Into the fir, and chees rather to die
Than any Romain dide° hire vilainye.   *should do*
   Hath nat Lucrece yslain hirself, allas,
At Rome whan that she oppressed° was   *violated*
Of° Tarquin, for hire thoughte° it was a shame   *by / it seemed to her*
700 To liven whan that she hadde lost hir name?°   *reputation*
   The sevene maidens of Milesie[9] also
Han slain hemself for verray° drede and wo   *great*
Rather than folk of Gaule° hem sholde oppresse: *Galatia*
Mo than a thousand stories, as I gesse,
705 Coude I now telle as touching this matere.
   Whan Habradate was slain, his wif so dere
Hirselven slow,° and leet hir blood to glide   *slew*
In Habradates woundes deepe and wide,
And saide, 'My body at the leeste way°   *at least*
710 Ther shal no wight° defoulen, if I may.'°   *person / have power*
   What° sholde I mo ensamples° herof sayn?   *why / more examples*
Sith that so manye han hemselven slain
Wel rather than they wolde defouled be,
I wol conclude that it is bet° for me   *better*
715 To sleen° myself than been defouled thus: *slay*
I wol be trewe unto Arveragus,
Or rather slee myself in som manere—
As dide Demociones doughter dere,
By cause that she wolde nat defouled be.
720   O Cedasus,° it is ful greet pitee   *Scedasus*
To reden how thy doughtren° deide, allas,   *daughters*
That slowe hemself for swich manere cas.°   *such an occurrence*
   As greet a pitee was it, or wel moor,

8. Hasdrubal was the king of Carthage when it was   9. Miletus, a city in Asia Minor.
destroyed by the Romans.

The Theban maiden that for Nichanor°   *Nicanor*
725   Hirselven slow° right for swich manere wo.   *slew*
Another Theban maiden dide right so:
For° oon of Macedonie hadde hire oppressed,°   *because / violated*
She with hir deeth hir maidenhede redressed.°   *vindicated*
   What shal I sayn of Nicerates° wif   *Niceratus's*
730   That for swich caas birafte hirself hir lif?
   How trewe eek was to Alcebiades[1]
His love, that rather for to dien chees°   *chose*
Than for to suffre his body unburied be.
   Lo, which a wif was Alceste," quod she.
735   "What saith Omer° of goode Penolopee?   *Homer*
Al Greece knoweth of hir chastitee.
   Pardee, of Laodomia is writen thus,
That whan at Troye was slain Protheselaus,
No lenger wolde she live after his day.
740   The same of noble Porcia[2] telle I may:
Withoute Brutus coude she nat live,
To whom she hadde al hool hir herte yive.°   *given*
   The parfit° wifhood of Arthemesie°   *perfect / Artemisia*
Honoured is thurgh al the Barbarye.°   *heathendom*
745   O Teuta[3] queene, thy wifly chastitee
To alle wives may a mirour° be!   *model*
   The same thing I saye of Biliea,[4]
Of Rodogone, and eek Valeria."
Thus plained° Dorigen a day or twaye,°   *lamented / two*
750   Purposing evere that she wolde deye.
   But nathelees upon the thridde night
Hoom cam Arveragus, this worthy knight,
And axed° hire why that she weep° so sore,   *asked / wept*
And she gan weepen evere lenger the more.°   *always more and more*
755   "Allas," quod she, "that evere I was born:
Thus have I said," quod she; "thus have I sworn—"
And tolde him al as ye han herd bifore:
It needeth nat reherce it you namore.
   This housbonde with glad cheere° in freendly wise   *expression*
760   Answerde and saide as I shal you devise:°   *relate*
   "Is there ought° elles, Dorigen, but this?"   *anything*
   "Nay, nay," quod she, "God help me so as wis,°   *indeed*
This is too muche, and° it were Goddes wille."   *if*
   "Ye, wif," quod he, "lat sleepen that° is stille.°   *that which / quiet*
765   It may be wel paraunter° yit today.   *perhaps*
Ye shul youre trouthe° holden, by my fay,°   *word / faith*
For God so wisly have mercy upon me,
I hadde wel levere ystiked for to be,[5]

1. Alcibiades' mistress risked death for her loyalty to her
dead lover, but did not die to preserve her chastity; thus
this, like many of her other examples, does not support
Dorigen's point.
2. Portia swallowed hot coals on learning of Brutus's

death.
3. Teuta, Queen of Illyria.
4. Bilieia's sacrifice seems to have consisted in her enduring her husband's bad breath without complaining.
5. I'd rather be stabbed to death.

For verray love which that I to you have,

770 But if° ye sholde youre trouthe keepe and save: *unless*
Trouthe is the hyeste thing that man may keepe."
But with that word he brast anoon to weepe,°   *burst into weeping*
And saide, "I you forbede, up° paine of deeth,   *upon*
That nevere whil thee lasteth lif ne breeth,

775 To no wight° tel thou of this aventure.   *person*
As I may best I wol my wo endure,
Ne make no countenance of hevinesse,°   *show no sorrowful face*
That folk of you may deemen° harm or gesse."   *think*
    And forth he cleped° a squier and a maide: *called*

780 "Go forth anoon with Dorigen," he saide,
"And bringeth hire to swich a place anoon."
They tooke hir leve and on hir way they goon,
But they ne wiste° why they thider wente: *did not know*
He nolde° no wight tellen his entente.   *did not wish*

785 Paraventure° an heep° of you, ywis,°   *perhaps / many / certainly*
Wol holden him a lewed° man in this,   *foolish*
That he wol putte his wif in jupartye.°   *jeopardy*
Herkneth the tale er ye upon hire crye:°   *complain about her*
She may have bettre fortune than you seemeth,°   *it seems to you*

790 And whan that ye han herd the tale, deemeth.°   *judge*
    This squier which that highte° Aurelius,   *was called*
On Dorigen that was so amorous,
Of aventure happed° hire to meete   *by chance happened*
Amidde the town, right in the quikkest° streete,   *busiest*

795 As she was boun° to goon the way forth right   *about*
Toward the gardin ther as she hadde hight;°   *promised*
And he was to the gardinward° also,   *toward the garden*
For wel he spied whan she wolde go
Out of hir hous to any manere place.

800 But thus they meete of aventure or grace,°   *chance or good fortune*
And he salueth° hire with glad entente,°   *greets / cheerfully*
And axed° of hire whiderward° she wente.   *asked / in what direction*
    And she answerde half as she were mad,
"Unto the gardin as myn housbonde bad,°   *commanded*

805 My trouthe° for to holde, allas, allas!"   *pledge*
    Aurelius gan wondren° on this cas,°   *fell to wondering / event*
And in his herte hadde greet compassioun
Of hire and of hir lamentacioun,
And of Arveragus, the worthy knight,

810 That bad hire holden al that she hadde hight,°   *promised*
So loth him was his wif sholde breke hir trouthe;
And in his herte he caughte of this greet routhe,°   *took pity on this*
Considering the beste on every side
That fro his lust yit were him levere abide

815 Than doon so heigh a cherlissh wrecchednesse[6]
Agains franchise° and alle gentilesse;°   *generosity / nobility*

6. I.e., he would rather abstain from his lust / than commit such an extremely churlish act.

For which in fewe wordes saide he thus:
"Madame, sayeth to youre lord Arveragus
That sith° I see his grete gentilesse   *since*
820   To you, and eek° I see wel youre distresse,   *also*
That him were levere° han shame—and that were routhe—   *he would rather*
Than ye to me sholde breke thus youre trouthe,
I have wel levere° evere to suffre wo   *would much rather*
Than I departe° the love bitwixe you two.   *divide*
825   I you releesse, Madame, into youre hond,
Quit° every serement° and every bond   *discharged of / oath*
That ye han maad to me as herbiforn,°   *before*
Sith thilke° time which that ye were born.   *since that*
My trouthe I plighte,° I shal you nevere repreve°   *word I pledge / reproach*
830   Of no biheeste.° And here I take my leve,   *promise*
As of the treweste and the beste wif
That evere yit I knew in al my lif.
But every wif be war° of hir biheeste: *be careful*
On Dorigen remembreth at the leeste.°   *at the least*
835   Thus can a squier doon a gentil° deede   *noble*
As wel as can a knight, withouten drede."°   *doubt*
She thanketh him upon hir knees al bare,
And hoom unto hir housbonde is she fare,°   *has she gone*
And tolde him al as ye han herd me said.
840   And be ye siker,° he was so wel apaid°   *certain / pleased*
That it were impossible me to write.
What° sholde I lenger of this caas endite?°   *why / event relate*
Arveragus and Dorigen his wif
In soverein° blisse leden forth° hir lif.   *supreme / lead on*
845   Nevere eft° ne was ther angre hem bitweene: *again*
He cherisseth hire as though she were a queene,
And she was to him trewe for everemore.
Of thise two folk ye gete of° me namore.   *from*
Aurelius, that his cost° hath al forlorn,°   *expense / lost*
850   Curseth the time that evere he was born.
"Allas," quod he, "allas that I bihighte°   *promised*
Of pured° gold a thousand pound of wighte°   *refined / weight*
Unto this philosophre.[7] How shall I do?
I see namore but that I am fordo.°   *ruined*
855   Myn heritage° moot I needes selle   *inheritance*
And been a beggere. Here may I nat dwelle,
And shamen al my kinrede° in this place,   *kindred*
But° I of him may gete bettre grace.   *unless*
But nathelees° I wol of him assaye°   *nonetheless / endeavor*
860   At certain dayes° yeer by yere to paye,   *on extended terms*
And thanke him of his grete curteisye:
My trouthe wol I keepe, I nil° nat lie."   *will not*
With herte soor° he gooth unto his cofre,°   *painful / money chest*
And broughte gold unto this philosophre
865   The value of five hundred pound, I gesse,
And him biseecheth of° his gentilesse   *(out) of*

7. A practitioner of occult science.

To graunten him dayes of the remenaunt,[8]
And saide, "Maister, I dar wel make avaunt°   *boast*
I failed nevere of my trouthe as yit,
870   For sikerly° my dette shal be quit°   *surely / repaid*
Towardes you, how evere that I fare,°   *although I may go off*
To goon abegged° in my kirtel° bare.   *begging / shirt*
But wolde ye vouche sauf° upon suretee°   *grant / pledge*
Two yeer or three for to respiten me,°   *give me a delay*
875   Thanne were I wel, for elles moot° I selle   *otherwise must*
Myn heritage: ther is namore to telle."
     This philosophre sobrely answerde,
And saide thus, whan he thise wordes herde,
"Have I nat holden° covenant unto thee?"   *kept*
880   "Yis, certes,° wel and trewely," quod he.   *certainly*
"Hastou° nat had thy lady as thee liketh?"   *hast thou*
"No, no," quod he and sorwefully he siketh.°   *sighs*
"What was the cause? Tel me if thou can."
     Aurelius his tale anoon bigan,
885   And tolde him al as ye han herd bifore:
It needeth nat to you reherce it more.
     He saide, "Arveragus, of gentilesse,
Hadde levere° die in sorwe and in distresse   *rather*
Than that his wif were of hir trouthe fals,"
890   The sorwe of Dorigen he tolde him als.°   *also*
How loth hire was to been a wikked wif,
And that she levere hadde lost that day hir lif,
And that hir trouthe she swoor thurgh innocence:
She nevere erst° hadde herd speke of apparence.°   *before / illusion*
895   "That made me han of hire so greet pitee;
And right as freely° as he sente hire me,   *generously*
As freely sente I hire to him again:
This al and som,° ther is namore to sayn."   *the whole story*
     This philosophre answerde, "Leve° brother,   *dear*
900   Everich° of you dide gentilly to other.°   *each / nobly to the other*
Thou art a squier, and he is a knight:
But God forbede, for his blisful might,
But if° a clerk coude doon a gentil° deede   *unless / noble*
As wel as any of you, it is no drede.°   *doubt*
905   Sire, I releesse thee thy thousand pound,
As° thou right now were cropen° out of the ground,   *as if / had crept*
Ne nevere er° now ne haddest knowen me.   *before*
For sire, I wol nat take a peny of thee,
For al my craft° ne nought for my travaile.°   *skill / labor*
910   Thou hast ypayed° wel for my vitaile:°   *paid / food*
It is ynough.° And farewel, have good day."   *enough*
And took his hors and forth he gooth his way.
     Lordinges, this question thanne wol I axe now:
Which was the moste free,° as thinketh you?   *generous*
915   Now telleth me, er that ye ferther wende.
I can namore: my tale is at an ende.

---

8. Time to pay the remainder.

THE PARDONER'S PROLOGUE AND TALE   There is something in Chaucer's Pardoner to unnerve practically everyone. The Pardoner's physiology blurs gender itself, his apparent homosexuality challenges the dominant heterosexual ordering of medieval society, his *Prologue* subverts the notion that the intent and effect of words are connected, and his willingness to convert religious discourse into cash undermines the very bases of faith. He initiates a sequence of moments in the later tales that threaten to puncture or tear the social fabric of the Canterbury company.

The Pardoner and "his freend and his compeer," the Summoner, are the last two pilgrims described in *The General Prologue*, reflecting the distaste with which such marginal clergy were often regarded in the period. Summoners were the policing branch of the ecclesiastical courts, paid to bring in transgressors against the canon law. Pardoners had the job, criticized even within the church, of exchanging indulgences for cash. The sufferings of Christ and saintly martyrs, it was thought, had left the church with a legacy of goodness. This could be transferred to sinners, freeing them from a period in Purgatory, if they proved their penitence (among other ways) by gifts to support good works such as the hospital for which the Pardoner worked.

The Pardoner has turned this part of the structure of penitence into a profit center. In his own *Prologue*, the Pardoner is boastfully explicit about this:

> For myn entente is nat but for to winne,
> And no thing for correccion of sinne . . .

This merciless equation of his verbal power with cash profit deeply subverts the logic of Christian language and the priestly role in salvation. These are replaced by language working in a strange self-consuming circle: the Pardoner brilliantly achieves the very sin his sermon most vituperates.

The Pardoner's physiology—he has either lost his testicles or never had them—may emblematize this exploitation of language emptied of spiritual intention. His uncertain or incomplete gender, though, also challenges the fundamental distinctions of the body within the medieval social economy, as does his apparent homosexuality. The Pardoner's theatrical self-presentation, abetted by rhetorical techniques he lovingly describes, draws the fascinated if queasy attention of his audience and seems to provide him a monstrous though (as it turns out) fragile power.

The Pardoner's tale of three rioters and their encounter with death is actually folded into his Prologue as an exemplum, an illustrative story, in the sermon against cupidity he proposes to offer as a sample of his skills. Yet the Pardoner's obsession with bodies in extremity, seeking or denying death, skeletal or gorged, pulls against his tale as a parable of greed. The tale draws toward its close in a scene of rage, exposure, and angry silence, which threatens to undo the pilgrim society, rather as the Pardoner and his discourse have threatened so much of the broader social contract. The Knight steps in, though, and almost bullies the Host and the Pardoner into a kiss of peace. This ritual gesture, nearly as empty of real goodwill as any of the Pardoner's most cynical words, does allow the shaken group to continue on their way, even as it hints at the emptiness that may hide in other, less openly challenged systems of value in the tales and their world.

The Pardoner's Prologue
The Introduction

Oure Hoste gan to swere as he were wood;°   *mad*
"Harrow," quod he, "by nailes[1] and by blood,

This was a fals cherl° and a fals justice.°[2]   *villain / judge*
As shameful deeth as herte may devise
5   Come to thise juges and hir advocats.°   *lawyers*
Algate° this sely° maide is slain, allas!   *anyway / innocent*
Allas, too dere boughte she beautee!
Wherfore I saye alday° that men may see   *always*
The yiftes of Fortune and of Nature
10 Been cause of deeth to many a creature.
As bothe yiftes° that I speke of now,   *gifts*
Men han ful ofte more for harm than prow.°   *profit*
   "But trewely, myn owene maister dere,
This is a pitous tale for to heere.
15 But nathelees, passe over, is no fors:°   *concern*
I praye to God so save thy gentil° cors,°   *noble / body*
And eek thine urinals[3] and thy jurdones,°   *chamber pots*
Thyn ipocras and eek thy galiones,[4]
And every boiste° ful of thy letuarye°—   *box / medicine*
20 God blesse hem, and oure lady Sainte Marye.
So mote I theen,° thou art a propre man,   *so may I prosper*
And lik a prelat,° by Saint Ronian![5]   *Church officer*
Saide I nat wel? I can nat speke in terme.°   *jargon*
But wel I woot,° thou doost myn herte to erme°   *know / grieve*
25 That I almost have caught a cardinacle.°   *heart condition*
By corpus bones,[6] but if I have triacle,°   *medicine*
Or elles a draughte of moiste° and corny° ale,   *fresh / malted*
Or but I heere anoon a merye tale,
Myn herte is lost for pitee of this maide.
30   "Thou bel ami,[7] thou Pardoner," he saide,
"Tel us som mirthe or japes° right anoon."   *joke*
   "It shal be doon," quod he, "by Saint Ronian.
But first," quod he, "here at this ale-stake°   *tavern marker*
I wol bothe drinke and eten of a cake."°   *loaf of bread*
35   And right anoon thise gentils gan to crye,
"Nay, lat him telle us of no ribaudye.°   *obscenity*
Tel us som moral thing that we may lere,°   *learn*
Som wit, and thanne wol we gladly heere."
   "I graunte, ywis,"° quod he, "but I moot° thinke *certainly / must*
40 Upon som honeste° thing whil that I drinke."   *honorable*

The Prologue

Lordinges—quod he—in chirches whan I preche,
I paine me to han an hautein° speeche,   *loud*
And ringe it out as round as gooth a belle,
For I can al by rote° that I telle.   *know it all by heart*

---

2. Harry Baily, the host, is responding to *The Physician's Tale* and the story of a young woman named Virginia whose father kills her rather than surrender her to a wicked judge and his accomplice.
3. Physician's vessels for analyzing urine samples.
4. Medicines named after the ancient Greek physicians

Hippocrates and Galen.
5. St. Ronan, a Scottish saint, with a possible pun on "runnions," the male sexual organs.
6. A confused oath mixing God's body and God's bones.
7. Fair friend (French, affected).

45 My theme is alway oon,° and evere was: *the same*
    Radix malorum est cupiditas.[8]
    First I pronounce whennes that I come,
    And thanne my bulles° shewe I alle and some: *indulgences*
    Oure lige lordes seel[9] on my patente,°   *license*
50 That shewe I first, my body to warente,°   *safeguard*
    That no man be so bold, ne preest ne clerk,
    Me to destourbe of Cristes holy werk.
    And after that thanne telle I forth my tales—
    Bulles of popes and of cardinales,
55 Of patriarkes and bisshopes I shewe,
    And in Latin I speke a wordes fewe,
    To saffron° with my predicacioun,°   *season / preaching*
    And for to stire hem to devocioun.
        Thanne shewe I forth my longe crystal stones,°   *jars*
60 Ycrammed ful of cloutes° and of bones—   *rags*
    Relikes been they, as weenen they eechoon.°   *they all suppose*
    Thanne have I in laton° a shulder-boon   *brazened*
    Which that was of an holy Jewes sheep.
    "Goode men," I saye, "take of my wordes keep:°   *notice*
65 If that this boon be wasshe in any welle,
    If cow, or calf, or sheep, or oxe swelle,
    That any worm° hath ete or worm ystonge,   *snake*
    Take water of that welle and wassh his tonge,
    And it is hool° anoon. And ferthermoor,   *healthy*
70 Of pokkes° and of scabbe and every soor   *pox*
    Shal every sheep be hool that of this welle
    Drinketh a draughte. Take keep eek that I telle:
    If that the goode man that the beestes oweth°   *owns*
    Wol every wike,° er that the cok him croweth,   *week*
75 Fasting drinken of this welle a draughte—
    As thilke° holy Jew oure eldres taughte—   *that*
    His beestes and his stoor° shal multiplye.   *stock*
        "And sire, also it heleth jalousye:
    For though a man be falle in jalous rage
80 Lat maken with this water his potage,°   *soup*
    And nevere shal he more his wif mistriste,
    Though he the soothe° of hir defaute wiste,°   *truth / offense knows*
    Al hadde she taken preestes two or three.
        "Here is a mitein° eek that ye may see: *mitten*
85 He that his hand wol putte in this mitein
    He shal have multiplying of his grain,
    Whan he hath sowen, be it whete or otes—
    So that he offre pens° or elles grotes.°   *pennies / silver coins*
        "Goode men and wommen, oo thing warne I you:
90 If any wight° be in this chirche now   *person*
    That hath doon sinne horrible, that he
    Dar nat for shame of it yshriven° be,   *confessed*
    Or any womman, be she yong or old,

---

8. Greed is the root of all evil.   9. Seal of our liege lord (i.e., the Pope).

That hath ymaked hir housbonde cokewold,°   cuckold
95   Swich folk shal have no power ne no grace
To offren to my relikes in this place;
And whoso findeth him out of swich blame,
He wol come up and offre in Goddes name,
And I assoile° him by the auctoritee   absolve
100   Which that by bulle ygraunted was to me."
By this gaude° have I wonne, yeer by yeer,   trick
An hundred mark[1] sith I was pardoner.
I stonde lik a clerk in my pulpet,
And whan the lewed° peple is down yset,   ignorant
105   I preche so as ye han herd bifore,
And telle an hundred false japes° more.   tricks
Thanne paine I me to strecche forth the nekke,
And eest and west upon the peple I bekke°   nod
As dooth a douve,° sitting on a berne;°   dove / barn
110   Mine handes and my tonge goon so yerne°   fast
That it is joye to see my bisinesse.
Of avarice and of swich cursednesse
Is al my preching, for to make hem free°   generous
To yiven hir pens, and namely unto me,
115   For myn entente is nat but for to winne,°   profit
And no thing for correccion of sinne:
I rekke° nevere whan that they been beried°   care / buried
Though that hir soules goon a-blakeberied.[2]
For certes, many a predicacioun
120   Comth ofte time of yvel entencioun:
Som for plesance of folk and flaterye,
To been avaunced by ypocrisye,
And som for vaine glorye, and som for hate;
For whan I dar noon otherways debate,
125   Thanne wol I stinge him with my tonge smerte°   hurting
In preching, so that he shal nat asterte°   escape
To been defamed falsly, if that he
Hath trespassed to my bretheren or to me.
For though I telle nought his propre name,
130   Men shal wel knowe that it is the same
By signes and by othere circumstaunces.
Thus quite° I folk that doon us displesaunces;°   repay / trouble
Thus spete I out my venim under hewe°   color
Of holinesse, to seeme holy and trewe.
135   But shortly myn entente I wol devise:°   describe
I preche of no thing but for coveitise;°   greed
Therfore my theme is yit and evere was
Radix malorum est cupiditas.
Thus can I preche again that same vice
140   Which that I use, and that is avarice.
But though myself be gilty in that sinne,
Yit can I make other folk to twinne°   separate

---

1. About 66 pounds.   2. Looking for blackberries.

From avarice, and sore to repente—
But that is nat my principal entente:
145 I preche no thing but for coveitise.
Of this matere it oughte ynough suffise.
     Thanne telle I hem ensamples° many oon   *exemplary tales*
Of olde stories longe time agoon,
For lewed peple loven tales olde—
150 Swiche thinges can they wel reporte° and holde.°   *repeat / remember*
What, trowe° ye that whiles I may preche,   *believe*
And winne gold and silver for I teche,
That I wol live in poverte wilfully?
Nay, nay, I thoughte it nevere, trewely,
155 For I wol preche and begge in sondry landes;
I wol nat do no labour with mine handes,
Ne make baskettes and live therby,
By cause I wol nat beggen idelly.°   *in vain*
I wol none of the Apostles countrefete:°   *imitate*
160 I wol have moneye, wolle,° cheese, and whete,   *wool*
Al were it yiven of the pooreste page,°   *servant*
Or of the pooreste widwe in a village—
Al sholde hir children sterve° for famine.   *die*
Nay, I wol drinke licour of the vine
165 And have a joly wenche in every town.
But herkneth, lordinges, in conclusioun,
Youre liking is that I shal telle a tale:
Now have I dronke a draughte of corny ale,
By God, I hope I shal you telle a thing
170 That shal by reson been at youre liking;
For though myself be a ful vicious man,
A moral tale yit I you telle can,
Which I am wont to preche for to winne.
Now holde youre pees, my tale I wol biginne.

The Pardoner's Tale

175 In Flandres whilom° was a compaignye   *once*
Of yonge folk that haunteden° folye—   *practiced*
As riot, hasard, stewes,[1] and tavernes,
Wher as with harpes, lutes, and giternes°   *guitars*
They daunce and playen at dees° bothe day and night,   *dice*
180 And ete also and drinke over hir might,
Thurgh which they doon the devel sacrifise
Withinne that develes temple in cursed wise
By superfluitee° abhominable.   *overindulgence*
Hir othes been so grete and so dampnable
185 That it is grisly for to heere hem swere:
Oure blessed Lordes body they totere°—   *rip apart*
Hem thoughte that Jewes rente° him nought ynough.   *tore*
And eech of hem at otheres sinne lough.°   *laughed*

---

1. Such as carousing, gambling, brothels.

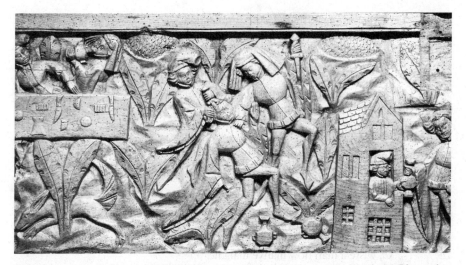

Detail from a carved chest, c. 1410. This large wooden panel is the surviving half of the front of a massive chest. It presents scenes from *The Pardoner's Tale*: at left, the youngest rioter buys wine; in the center, his two companions stab him to death; at right, they die from the wine their companion had poisoned. The composition and carving have much of the energy and economical narrative style of the tale itself. Produced about a decade after Chaucer's death, the panel reflects the impact of his tales in settings very different from those that supported such grand aristocratic productions as the Ellesmere manuscript, created around the same time (see Color Plate 9 and page 281).

	And right anoon thanne comen tombesteres,°	*dancing girls*
190	Fetis° and smale,° and yonge frutesteres,[2]	*elegant / slender*
	Singeres with harpes, bawdes,° wafereres°—	*pimps / cake sellers*
	Whiche been the verray develes officeres,	
	To kindle and blowe the fir of lecherye	
	That is annexed° unto glotonye:°	*connected / gluttony*
195	The Holy Writ take I to my witnesse	
	That luxure° is in win and dronkenesse.	*lechery*
	Lo, how that dronken Lot[3] unkindely°	*against nature*
	Lay by his doughtres two unwitingly:	
	So dronke he was he niste what he wroughte.°	*knew not what he did*
200	Herodes,[4] who so wel the stories soughte,	
	Whan he of win was repleet at his feeste,	
	Right at his owene table he yaf his heeste°	*command*
	To sleen° the Baptist John, ful giltelees.	*slay*
	Senek[5] saith a good word doutelees:	
205	He saith he can no difference finde	
	Bitwixe a man that is out of his minde	
	And a man which that is dronkelewe,°	*drunk*
	But that woodnesse, yfallen in a shrewe,[6]	

2. Girls selling fruit.
3. Lot, the nephew of Abraham, whose story is told in Genesis 19.30–38.
4. King Herod, who was enticed by Salome into bringing her the head of John the Baptist (Mark 6.17–29, Matthew 14.1–12).
5. The stoic author Seneca in his *Epistle* 83.18.493–97.
6. Madness, occurring in a wicked person.

Persevereth lenger than dooth dronkenesse.

210 O glotonye, ful of cursednesse!

O cause first of oure confusioun!°   *ruin*

O original of oure dampnacioun,

Til Crist hadde bought° us with his blood again!   *redeemed*

Lo, how dere, shortly for to sayn,

215 Abought was thilke° cursed vilainye;   *that*

Corrupt was al this world for glotonye:

Adam oure fader and his wif also

Fro Paradis to labour and to wo

Were driven for that vice, it is no drede.°   *doubt*

220 For whil that Adam fasted, as I rede,

He was in Paradis; and whan that he

Eet of the fruit defended° on a tree,   *forbidden*

Anoon he was out cast to wo and paine.

O glotonye, on thee wel oughte us plaine!°   *lament*

225   O, wiste a man how manye maladies

Folwen of° excesse and of glotonies,   *result from*

He wolde been the more mesurable°   *moderate*

Of his diete, sitting at his table.

Allas, the shorte throte, the tendre mouth,

230 Maketh that eest and west and north and south,

In erthe, in air, in water, men to swinke,°   *labor*

To gete a gloton daintee mete and drinke.

Of this matere, O Paul, wel canstou trete:°   *discuss*

"Mete unto wombe, and wombe° eek unto mete,   *belly*

235 Shal God destroyen bothe," as Paulus saith.[7]

Allas, a foul thing is it, by my faith,

To saye this word, and fouler is the deede

Whan man so drinketh of the white and rede°   *white and red wines*

That of his throte he maketh his privee°   *toilet*

240 Thurgh thilke cursed superfluitee.

   The Apostle[8] weeping saith ful pitously,

"Ther walken manye of which you told have I—

I saye it now weeping with pitous vois—

They been enemies of Cristes crois,°   *cross*

245 Of whiche the ende is deeth—wombe is hir god!"

O wombe, O bely, O stinking cod,°   *bag*

Fulfilled of dong° and of corrupcioun!   *dung*

At either ende of thee foul is the soun.°   *sound*

How greet labour and cost is thee to finde!°   *provide for*

250 Thise cookes, how they stampe and straine and grinde,

And turnen substance into accident[9]

To fulfillen al thy likerous talent!°   *greedy desire*

Out of the harde bones knokke they

The mary,° for they caste nought away   *marrow*

255 That may go thurgh the golet° softe and soote.°   *gullet / sweet*

---

7. St. Paul in 1 Corinthians 6.13.
8. St. Paul, in Philippians 3.18–19.
9. A learned joke about the Eucharist where, in Catholic

doctrine, the essence ("substance") of bread and wine is transformed into the body and blood of Christ, though their form ("accident") remains unchanged.

Of spicerye of leef and bark and roote
Shal been his sauce ymaked by delit,
To make him yit a newer appetit.
But certes, he that haunteth swiche delices°   *delicacies*
260   Is deed whil that he liveth in tho° vices.   *those*
         A lecherous thing is win, and dronkenesse
Is ful of striving° and of wrecchednesse.   *quarreling*
O dronke man, disfigured is thy face!
Sour is thy breeth, foul artou to embrace!
265   And thurgh thy dronke nose seemeth the soun
As though thou saidest ay° "Sampsoun, Sampsoun."   *always*
And yit, God woot,° Sampson drank nevere win.   *knows*
Thou fallest as it were a stiked swin;°   *stuck pig*
Thy tonge is lost, and al thyn honeste cure,°   *care for honor*
270   For dronkenesse is verray sepulture°   *grave*
Of mannes wit and his discrecioun.
In whom that drinke hath dominacioun
He can no conseil keepe, it is no drede.
Now keepe you fro the white and fro the rede—
275   And namely fro the white win of Lepe[1]
That is to selle in Fisshstreete or in Chepe:[2]
The win of Spaine creepeth subtilly[3]
In othere wines growing faste° by,   *close*
Of which ther riseth swich fumositee°   *vapors*
280   That whan a man hath dronken draughtes three
And weeneth that he be at hoom in Chepe,
He is in Spaine, right at the town of Lepe,
Nat at The Rochele ne at Burdeux town;
And thanne wol he sayn "Sampsoun, Sampsoun."
285   But herkneth, lordinges, oo word I you praye,
That alle the soverein actes,° dar I saye,   *excellent deeds*
Of victories in the Olde Testament,
Thurgh verray God that is omnipotent,
Were doon in abstinence and in prayere:
290   Looketh the Bible and ther ye may it lere.°   *learn*
         Looke Attilla, the grete conquerour,[4]
Deide in his sleep with shame and dishonour,
Bleeding at his nose in dronkenesse:
A capitain sholde live in sobrenesse.
295   And overal this, aviseth you right wel
What was comanded unto Lamuel[5]—
Nat Samuel, but Lamuel, saye I—
Redeth the Bible and finde it expresly,
Of win-yiving° to hem that han° justise: *wine-serving / dispense*
300   Namore of this, for it may wel suffise.
         And now that I have spoken of glotonye,

---

1. Wine-growing region in Spain.
2. Commercial districts in London.
3. Chaucer is referring to the illegal practice of using cheap wine (here, Spanish wine from Lepe) to dilute more expensive wines (from the neighboring French

provinces of La Rochelle and Bordeaux).
4. Attila the Hun died on his wedding night from excessive drinking.
5. Biblical king of Massa, warned against drinking in Proverbs 31.4.

Now wol I you defende hasardrye:°   *gambling*
Hasard is verray moder of lesinges,°   *lies*
And of deceite and cursed forsweringes,
305   Blaspheme of Crist, manslaughtre, and wast° also   *waste*
Of catel° and of time; and ferthermo,   *property*
It is repreve° and contrarye of honour   *reprobate*
For to been holden a commune hasardour,
And evere the hyer he is of estat
310   The more is he holden desolat.°   *dissolute*
If that a prince useth hasardrye,
In alle governance and policye
He is, as by commune opinioun,
Yholde the lasse in reputacioun.
315   Stilbon,[6] that was a wis embassadour,
Was sent to Corinthe in ful greet honour
Fro Lacedomye° to make hir alliaunce,   *Sparta*
And whan he cam him happede parchaunce
That alle the gretteste that were of that lond
320   Playing at the hasard he hem foond,
For which as soone as it mighte be
He stal him hoom again to his contree,
And saide, "Ther wol I nat lese° my name,   *lose*
N'I wol nat take on me so greet defame
325   You to allye unto none hasardours:
Sendeth othere wise embassadours,
For by my trouthe, me were levere° die   *I would rather*
Than I you sholde to hasardours allye.
For ye that been so glorious in honours
330   Shal nat allye you with hasardours
As by my wil, ne as by my tretee."
This wise philosophre, thus saide he.
        Looke eek that to the king Demetrius
The King of Parthes,[7] as the book saith us,
335   Sente him a paire of dees of gold in scorn,
For he hadde used hasard therbiforn,
For which he heeld his glorye or his renown
At no value or reputacioun.
Lordes may finden other manere play
340   Honeste ynough to drive the day away.
        Now wol I speke of othes false and grete
A word or two, as olde bookes trete:
        Greet swering is a thing abhominable,
And fals swering is yit more reprevable.°   *reprehensible*
345   The hye God forbad swering at al—
Witnesse on Mathew. But in special
Of swering saith the holy Jeremie,[8]
"Thou shalt swere sooth° thine othes and nat lie,   *truly*
And swere in doom° and eek in rightwisnesse,   *judgment*

---

6. Possibly referring to the Greek philosopher Stilbo or   7. Parthia in northern Persia.
Chilon.   8. The prophet Jeremiah (4.2).

350	But idel swering is a cursednesse."	
	Biholde and see that in the firste Table°	tablet
	Of hye Goddes heestes° honorable	commandments
	How that the seconde heeste of him is this:	
	"Take nat my name in idel or amis."	
355	Lo, rather° he forbedeth swich swering	sooner
	Than homicide, or many a cursed thing.	
	I saye that as by ordre thus it stondeth—	
	This knoweth that° his heestes understondeth	he who
	How that the seconde heeste of God is that.	
360	And fertherover, I wol thee telle al plat°	flatly
	That vengeance shal nat parten from his hous	
	That of his othes is too outrageous.	
	"By Goddes precious herte!" and "By his nailes!"	
	And "By the blood of Crist that is in Hailes,⁹	
365	Sevene is my chaunce, and thyn is cink and traye!"°	five and three
	"By Goddes armes, if thou falsly playe	
	This daggere shal thurghout thyn herte go!"	
	This fruit cometh of the bicche bones° two—	cursed dice
	Forswering, ire, falsnesse, homicide.	
370	Now for the love of Crist that for us dyde,	
	Lete° youre othes bothe grete and smale.	leave off
	But sires, now wol I telle forth my tale.	
	Thise riotoures° three of whiche I telle,	revelers
	Longe erst er° prime° ronge of any belle,	before / 6 A.M.
375	Were set hem in a taverne to drinke,	
	And as they sat they herde a belle clinke	
	Biforn a cors° was caried to his grave.	corpse
	That oon of hem gan callen to his knave:°	servant
	"Go bet,"° quod he, "and axe redily	quickly
380	What cors is this that passeth heer forby,	
	And looke that thou reporte his name weel."	
	"Sire," quod this boy, "it needeth neveradeel:¹	
	It was me told er ye cam heer two houres.	
	He was, pardee,° an old felawe of youres,	by God
385	And sodeinly he was yslain tonight,	
	Fordronke° as he sat on his bench upright;	very drunk
	Ther cam a privee° thief men clepeth° Deeth,	stealthy / call
	That in this contree al the peple sleeth,°	slays
	And with his spere he smoot his herte atwo,	
390	And wente his way withouten wordes mo.	
	He hath a thousand slain this pestilence.°	during this plague
	And maister, er ye come in his presence,	
	Me thinketh that it were necessarye	
	For to be war of swich an adversarye;	
395	Beeth redy for to meete him everemore:	
	Thus taughte me my dame.° I saye namore."	mother
	"By Sainte Marye," saide this taverner,	

---

9. Hales Abbey in Gloucestershire owned a relic of Christ's blood.

1. Is not necessary in the least.

"The child saith sooth,° for he hath slain this yeer,   *truth*

Henne° over a mile, within a greet village,   *from here*

400   Bothe man and womman, child and hine° and page.°   *farmhand / servant*

I trowe his habitacion be there.

To been avised° greet wisdom it were   *warned*

Er that he dide a man a dishonour."

    "Ye, Goddes armes," quod this riotour,

405   "Is it swich peril with him for to meete?

I shal him seeke by way and eek by streete,

I make avow to Goddes digne° bones.   *worthy*

Herkneth, felawes, we three been alle ones:

Lat eech of us holde up his hand to other

410   And eech of us bicome otheres brother,

And we wol sleen this false traitour Deeth.

He shal be slain, he that so manye sleeth,

By Goddes dignitee, er it be night."

    Togidres han thise three hir trouthes° plight°   *words of honor / pledged*

415   To live and dien eech of hem with other,

As though he were his owene ybore° brother.   *born*

And up they sterte, al dronken in this rage,

And forth they goon towardes that village

Of which the taverner hadde spoke biforn.

420   And many a grisly ooth thanne han they sworn,

And Cristes blessed body they torente:°   *tore apart*

Deeth shal be deed if that they may him hente.°   *capture*

    Whan they han goon nat fully, half a mile,

Right as they wolde han treden° over a stile,   *stepped*

425   An old man and a poore with hem mette;

This olde man ful mekely hem grette,°   *greeted*

And saide thus, "Now lordes, God you see."°   *look after*

    The pruddeste° of thise riotoures three   *proudest*

Answerde again, "What, carl with sory grace,°   *unlucky fellow*

430   Why artou al forwrapped° save thy face?   *bundled up*

Why livestou so longe in so greet age?"

    This olde man gan looke in his visage,

And saide thus, "For I ne can nat finde

A man, though that I walked into Inde,

435   Neither in citee ne in no village,

That wolde chaunge his youthe for myn age;

And therfore moot I han° myn age stille,   *I must have*

As longe time as it is Goddes wille.

    "Ne Deeth, allas, ne wol nat have my lif.

440   Thus walke I lik a restelees caitif,°   *wretch*

And on the ground which is my modres° gate   *mother's*

I knokke with my staf bothe erly and late,

And saye, 'Leve° moder, leet me in: *dear*

Lo, how I vanisshe, flessh and blood and skin.

445   Allas, whan shal my bones been at reste?

Moder, with you wolde I chaunge° my cheste°   *exchange / strongbox*

That in my chambre longe time hath be,

Ye, for an haire-clout° to wrappe me.'   *winding sheet*

But yit to me she wol nat do that grace,

450 For which ful pale and welked° is my face.   *withered*
    But sires, to you it is no curteisye
    To speken to an old man vilainye,°   *discourtesy*
    But he trespasse in word or elles in deede.
    In Holy Writ ye may yourself wel rede,
455 'Agains an old man, hoor° upon his heed,   *grey*
    Ye shal arise.' Wherfore I yive you reed,°   *advice*
    Ne dooth unto an old man noon harm now,
    Namore than that ye wolde men dide to you
    In age, if that ye so longe abide.
460 And God be with you wher ye go or ride:
    I moot go thider as I have to go."
        "Nay, olde cherl, by God thou shalt nat so,"
    Saide this other hasardour anoon.
    "Thou partest nat so lightly,° by Saint John!   *easily*
465 Thou speke right now of thilke traitour Deeth,
    That in this contree alle oure freendes sleeth:
    Have here my trouthe, as thou art his espye,
    Tel wher he is, or thou shalt it abye,°   *pay for*
    By God and by the holy sacrament!
470 For soothly thou art oon of his assent°   *in league with him*
    To sleen us yonge folk, thou false thief."
        "Now sires," quod he, "if that ye be so lief°   *eager*
    To finde Deeth, turne up this crooked way,
    For in that grove I lafte him, by my fay,
475 Under a tree, and ther he wol abide:
    Nat for youre boost he wol him no thing hide.
    See ye that ook?° Right ther ye shal him finde.   *oak*
    God save you, that boughte again° mankinde,   *redeemed*
    And you amende." Thus saide this olde man.
480   And everich of thise riotoures ran
    Til he cam to that tree, and ther they founde
    Of florins° fine of gold ycoined rounde   *gold coins*
    Wel neigh an eighte busshels as hem thoughte—
    Ne lenger thanne after Deeth they soughte,
485 But eech of hem so glad was of the sighte,
    For that the florins been so faire and brighte,
    That down they sette hem by this precious hoord.
    The worste of hem he spak the firste word:
        "Bretheren," quod he, "take keep what that I saye:
490 My wit is greet though that I bourde° and playe.   *joke*
    This tresor hath Fortune unto us yiven
    In mirthe and jolitee oure lif to liven,
    And lightly as it cometh so wol we spende.
    Ey, Goddes precious dignitee, who wende°   *would suppose*
495 Today that we sholde han so fair a grace?
    But mighte this gold be caried fro this place
    Hoom to myn hous—or elles unto youres—
    For wel ye woot that al this gold is oures—
    Thanne were we in heigh felicitee.°   *happiness*
500 But trewely, by daye it mighte nat be:
    Men wolde sayn that we were theves stronge,°   *flagrant*

And for oure owene tresor doon us honge.°   *have us hanged*
This tresor moste ycaried be by nighte,
As wisely and as slyly as it mighte.
505 Therfore I rede° that cut° amonges us alle   *advise / lots*
Be drawe, and lat see wher the cut wol falle;
And he that hath the cut with herte blithe°   *happy*
Shal renne to the town, and that ful swithe,°   *swiftly*
And bringe us breed and win ful prively;
510 And two of us shal keepen subtilly
This tresor wel, and if he wol nat tarye,
Whan it is night we wol this tresor carye
By oon assent wher as us thinketh best."
That oon of hem the cut broughte in his fest°   *fist*
515 And bad hem drawe and looke wher it wol falle;
And it fil on the yongeste of hem alle,
And forth toward the town he wente anoon.
And also soone as that he was agoon,
That oon of hem spak thus unto that other:
520 "Thou knowest wel thou art my sworen brother;
Thy profit wol I telle thee anoon:
Thou woost wel that oure felawe is agoon,
And here is gold, and that ful greet plentee,
That shal departed° been among us three.   *divided*
525 But nathelelees, if I can shape° it so   *arrange*
That it departed were among us two,
Hadde I nat doon a freendes turn to thee?"
    That other answerde, "I noot° how that may be: *do not know*
He woot° that the gold is with us twaye.   *knows*
530 What shal we doon? What shal we to him saye?"
    "Shal it be conseil?"° saide the firste shrewe.°   *secret / villain*
"And I shal telle in a wordes fewe
What we shul doon, and bringe it wel aboute."
    "I graunte," quod that other, "out of doute,
535 That by my trouthe I wol thee nat biwraye."°   *betray*
    "Now," quod the firste, "thou woost wel we be twaye,
And two of us shal strenger be than oon:
Looke whan that he is set that right anoon
Aris as though thou woldest with him playe,
540 And I shal rive° him thurgh the sides twaye,   *stab*
Whil that thou strugelest with him as in game,
And with thy daggere looke thou do the same;
And thanne shal al this gold departed be,
My dere freend, bitwixe thee and me.
545 Thanne we may bothe oure lustes° al fulfille,   *desires*
And playe at dees right at oure owene wille."
And thus accorded been thise shrewes twaye
To sleen the thridde, as ye han herd me saye.
    This yongeste, which that wente to the town,
550 Ful ofte in herte he rolleth up and down
The beautee of thise florins newe and brighte.
"O Lord," quod he, "if so were that I mighte
Have al this tresor to myself allone,

Ther is no man that liveth under the trone°   *throne*
555   Of God that sholde live so merye as I."
      And at the laste the feend oure enemy
      Putte in his thought that he sholde poison beye,°   *buy*
      With which he mighte sleen his felawes twaye—
      Forwhy° the feend foond him in swich livinge   *wherefore*
560   That he hadde leve° him to sorwe° bringe: *permission / sorrow*
      For this was outrely his fulle entente,
      To sleen hem bothe, and nevere to repente.
            And forth he gooth—no lenger wolde he tarye—
      Into the town unto a pothecarye,°   *druggist*
565   And prayed him that he him wolde selle
      Som poison that he mighte his rattes quelle,°   *kill*
      And eek ther was a polcat° in his hawe°   *weasel / yard*
      That, as he saide, his capons° hadde yslawe,°   *chickens / slain*
      And fain° he wolde wreke° him if he mighte   *gladly / avenge*
570   On vermin that destroyed him by nighte.
            The pothecarye answerde, "And thou shalt have
      A thing that, also° God my soule save,   *so*
      In al this world ther is no creature
      That ete or dronke hath of this confiture°—   *concoction*
575   Nat but the mountance° of a corn° of whete—   *amount / grain*
      That he ne shal his lif anoon forlete.°   *lose*
      Ye, sterve° he shal, and that in lasse while   *die*
      Than thou wolt goon a paas° nat but a mile,   *walking*
      The poison is so strong and violent."
580   This cursed man hath in his hand yhent°   *taken*
      This poison in a box and sith he ran
      Into the nexte streete unto a man
      And borwed of him large botels three,
      And in the two his poison poured he—
585   The thridde he kepte clene for his drinke,
      For al the night he shoop° him for to swinke°   *prepared / work*
      In carying of the gold out of that place.
      And whan this riotour with sory grace
      Hadde filled with win his grete botels three,
590   To his felawes again repaireth he.
            What needeth it to sermone of it more?
      For right as they had cast° his deeth bifore,   *planned*
      Right so they han him slain, and that anoon.
      And whan that this was doon, thus spak that oon:
595   "Now lat us sitte and drinke and make us merye,
      And afterward we wol his body berye."
      And with that word it happed him par cas°   *by chance*
      To take the botel ther the poison was,
      And drank, and yaf his felawe drinke also,
600   For which anoon they storven bothe two.
            But certes I suppose that Avicen²
      Wroot nevere in no canon ne in no *fen*

---

2. The 12th-century Arab philosopher Avicenna composed a *Canon of Medicine*, divided into sections called "fens."

Mo wonder signes of empoisoning
Than hadde thise wrecches two er hir ending:
605   Thus ended been thise homicides two,
And eek the false empoisonere also.
       O cursed sinne of alle cursednesse!
O traitours homicide, O wikkednesse!
O glotonye, luxure,° and hasardrye!   *lechery*
610   Thou balsphemour of Crist with vilainye
And othes grete of usage° and of pride!   *habit*
Allas, mankinde, how may it bitide
That to thy Creatour which that thee wroughte,
And with his precious herte blood thee boughte,
615   Thou art so fals and so unkinde,° allas?   *unnatural*
       Now goode men, God foryive you youre trespas,
And ware° you fro the sinne of avarice: *guard*
Myn holy pardon may you alle warice°—   *save*
So that ye offre nobles or sterlinges,°   *gold or silver coins*
620   Or elles silver brooches, spoones, ringes.
Boweth your heed under this holy bulle!
Cometh up, ye wives, offreth of youre wolle!°   *wool*
Youre name I entre here in my rolle: anoon
Into the blisse of hevene shul ye goon.
625   I you assoile° by myn heigh power—   *absolve*
Ye that wol offre—as clene and eek as cleer°   *pure*
As ye were born.—And lo, sires, thus I preche.
And Jesu Crist that is oure soules leeche°   *physician*
So graunte you his pardon to receive,
630   For that is best—I wol you nat deceive.

The Epilogue

"But sires, oo word forgat I in my tale:
I have relikes and pardon in my male°   *bag*
As faire as any man in Engelond,
Whiche were me yiven by the Popes hond.
635   If any of you wol of devocioun
Offren and han myn absolucioun,
Come forth anoon, and kneeleth here adown,
And mekely receiveth my pardoun,
Or elles taketh pardon as ye wende,°   *travel*
640   Al newe and fressh at every miles ende—
So that ye offre alway newe and newe°   *over and over*
Nobles or pens whiche that be goode and trewe.
It is an honour to everich that is heer
That ye mowe have a suffisant° pardoner   *competent*
645   T'assoile you in contrees as ye ride,
For aventures whiche that may bitide:
Paraventure ther may falle oon or two
Down of his hors and breke his nekke atwo;
Looke which a suretee° is it to you alle   *safeguard*
650   That I am in youre felaweshipe yfalle
That may assoile you, bothe more and lasse,

Whan that the soule shal fro the body passe.
I rede° that oure Hoste shal biginne,   *advise*
For he is most envoluped in sinne.
655   Com forth, sire Host, and offre first anoon,
And thou shalt kisse the relikes everichoon,
Ye, for a grote:° unbokele anoon thy purs."   *fourpence coin*
          "Nay, nay," quod he, "thanne have I Cristes curs!
Lat be," quod he, "it shal nat be, so theech!°   *may I prosper*
660   Thou woldest make me kisse thyn olde breech
And swere it were a relik of a saint,
Though it were with thy fundament° depeint.°   *bowels / stained*
But, by the crois° which that Sainte Elaine³ foond,   *cross*
I wolde I hadde thy coilons° in myn hond,   *testicles*
665   In stede of relikes or of saintuarye.°   *container of relics*
Lat cutte hem of: I wol thee helpe hem carye.
They shal be shrined in an hogges tord."°   *turd*
          This Pardoner answerde nat a word:
So wroth° he was no word ne wolde he saye.   *angry*
670   "Now," quod oure Host, "I wol no lenger playe
With thee, ne with noon other angry man."
          But right anoon the worthy Knight bigan,
Whan that he sawgh that al the peple lough,
"Namore of this, for it is right ynough.
675   Sire Pardoner, be glad and merye of cheere,
And ye, sire Host that been to me so dere,
I praye you that ye kisse the Pardoner,
And Pardoner, I praye thee, draw thee neer,
And as we diden lat us laughe and playe."
680   Anoon they kiste and riden forth hir waye.

THE NUN'S PRIEST'S TALE   Of all his varied and ambitious output, *The Nun's Priest's Tale* may be Chaucer's most impressive tour de force. At its core is a wonderful animal fable, free of the conventionality and sometimes easy moralities this ancient form had taken on by the fourteenth century. The fable of Chauntecleer and Pertelote achieves quite extraordinary density, further, because of the multiple frames—structural and thematic—that surround it.

As part of the Canterbury tale-telling competition, the priest's fable plays a role in that broadest contest of classes and literary genres. More locally, it is one of many moments in which the Host, Harry Bailey, demands a tale from a male pilgrim in a style that also suggests a sexual challenge, and then adjusts his estimate of the teller's virility (even his social position) to suit. The fable itself is surrounded by an intimate portrait of Chauntecleer's peasant owner and her simple life, content with "hertes suffisaunce," a marked contrast to courtly values.

The central story of Chauntecleer's dream, danger, and escape works within a subtle and funny exploration of relations between the sexes. This is conditioned by courtly love conventions, literacy and education, and even the vocabulary of Pertelote's mostly Anglo-Saxon diction and Chauntecleer's love of French. This linguistic competition has its high point when Chauntecleer condescendingly mistranslates a misogynist Latin tag. Linguistic vanity, though, is exactly what puts Chauntecleer most in jeopardy. It is not the destiny Chauntecleer thinks he glimpses in his dream that almost costs his life, but rather another verbal competition, and an almost Oedipal challenge to his father.

---

3. St. Helen, who was said to have found the True Cross on which Jesus was crucified.

Much of the story's energy, however, derives not from its frames but from the explosion of those frames—literary, spatial, even social—enacted and recalled at the heart of the tale. The chickens are simultaneously, and hilariously, both courtly lovers and very realistic fowl. When Chauntecleer is carried off, the whole world of the tale—widow, daughters, dogs, even bees—bursts outward in pursuit. In the midst of mock-epic and mock-romance comparisons to this joyful disorder, Chaucer even inserts one of his very few direct references to the greatest disorder of his time, the Rising of 1381.

The Nun's Priest's Tale is a comedy as well as a fable, reversing a lugubrious series of tragedies in the preceding Monk's Tale. In the end, it is a story of canniness, acquired self-knowledge, and self-salvation. Woven into the priest's humor are a gentle satire and a quiet assertion that free will is the final resource of any agent, avian or human.

The Nun's Priest's Tale
The Introduction

	"Ho!" quod the Knight, "good sire, namore of this:	
	That ye han said is right ynough, ywis,°	*indeed*
	And muchel more, for litel hevinesse	
	Is right ynough to muche folk° I gesse:[1]	*for most folks*
5	I saye for me it is a greet disese,	
	Wher as men han been in greet welthe and ese,	
	To heeren of hir sodein° fal, allas;	*sudden*
	And the contrarye is joye and greet solas,°	*comfort*
	As whan a man hath been in poore estat,	
10	And climbeth up and wexeth° fortunat,	*becomes*
	And there abideth in prosperitee:	
	Swich thing is gladsom, as it thinketh° me,	*seems to*
	And of swich thing were goodly for to telle."	
	"Ye," quod oure Host, "by Sainte Poules° belle,	*Paul's*
15	Ye saye right sooth:° this Monk he clappeth° loude.	*truly / chatters*
	He spak how Fortune covered with a cloude—	
	I noot nevere what.° And als of a tragedye	*I don't know what*
	Right now ye herde, and pardee,° no remedye	*by God*
	It is for to biwaile ne complaine	
20	That that is doon, and als° it is a paine,	*also*
	As ye han said, to heere of hevinesse.	
	"Sire Monk, namore of this, so God you blesse:	
	Youre tale anoyeth al this compaignye;	
	Swich talking is nat worth a boterflye,	
25	For therinne is ther no disport ne game.	
	Wherfore, sire Monk, or daun° Piers by youre name,	*Master*
	I praye you hertely telle us somwhat elles:	
	For sikerly, nere clinking of youre belles,[2]	
	That on youre bridel hange on every side,	
30	By hevene king that for us alle dyde,	
	I sholde er this have fallen down for sleep,	
	Although the slough° hadde nevere been so deep.	*mud*
	Thanne hadde youre tale al be told in vain;	

---

1. The Monk has just told a series of stark and repetitive "tragedies"—the falls of men both ancient and modern.   2. For truly, were it not for the jingling of your bells.

For certainly, as that thise clerkes sayn,
35 Wher as a man may have noon audience,
Nought helpeth it to tellen his sentence;°   *statement*
And wel I woot° the substance is in me,   *know*
If any thing shal wel reported be.
Sire, saye somwhat of hunting, I you praye."
40   "Nay," quod this Monk, "I have no lust° to playe.   *wish*
Now lat another telle, as I have told."
        Thanne spak oure Host with rude speeche and bold,
And saide unto the Nonnes Preest anoon,
"Com neer, thou Preest,³ com hider, thou sire John:
45 Tel us swich thing as may oure hertes glade.°   *gladden our hearts*
Be blithe,° though thou ride upon a jade!°   *happy / nag*
What though thyn hors be bothe foul and lene?°   *thin*
If he wol serve thee, rekke nat a bene.°   *don't care a bean*
Looke that thyn herte be merye everemo."
50   "Yis, sire," quod he, "yis, Host, so mote I go,
But I be merye, ywis, I wol be blamed."
And right anoon his tale he hath attamed,°   *begun*
And thus he saide unto us everichoon,
This sweete Preest, this goodly man sire John.

The Tale

55 A poore widwe somdeel stape° in age   *well along*
Was whilom° dwelling in a narwe cotage,   *once upon a time*
Biside a grove, stonding in a dale:
This widwe of which I telle you my tale,
Sin° thilke° day that she was last a wif,   *since / that*
60 In pacience ladde a ful simple lif.
For litel was hir catel° and hir rente,°   *property / income*
By housbondrye° of swich as God hire sente   *management*
She foond° hirself and eek hir doughtren two.   *provided for*
Three large sowes hadde she and namo,
65 Three kin,° and eek a sheep that highte° Malle.   *cows / was named*
Ful sooty was hir bowr° and eek hir halle,   *bedroom*
In which she eet ful many a sclendre meel;
Of poinant° sauce hire needed neveradeel: *pungent*
No daintee morsel passed thurgh hir throte—
70 Hir diete was accordant to hir cote.°   *cottage*
Repleccioun° ne made hire nevere sik: *gluttony*
Attempre° diete was al hir physik,   *moderate*
And exercise and hertes suffisaunce.
The goute lette hire nothing for to daunce,⁴
75 N'apoplexye shente° nat hir heed.   *hurt*
No win ne drank she, neither whit ne reed:
Hir boord° was served most with whit and blak,   *table*
Milk and brown breed, in which she foond no lak;°   *fault*

---

3. The Host uses the familiar, somewhat condescending   4. Did not keep her from dancing.
"thou," then contemptuously calls the priest "Sir John."

	Seind° bacon, and somtime an ey° or twaye,°	*singed / egg / two*
80	For she was as it were a manere daye.°	*dairy maid*
	A yeerd° she hadde, enclosed al withoute	*yard*
	With stikkes, and a drye dich aboute,	
	In which she hadde a cok heet° Chauntecleer:	*called*
	In al the land of crowing nas his peer.	
85	His vois was merier than the merye orgon	
	On massedayes that in the chirche goon;°	*is played*
	Wel sikerer° was his crowing in his logge°	*surer / dwelling*
	Than is a clok or an abbeye orlogge;°	*timepiece*
	By nature he knew eech ascensioun	
90	Of th'equinoxial⁵ in thilke town:	
	For whan degrees fifteene were ascended,	
	Thanne crew he that it mighte nat been amended.°	*surpassed*
	His comb was redder than the fin coral,	
	And batailed° as it were a castel wal;	*crenellated*
95	His bile° was blak, and as the jeet° it shoon;	*beak / jet*
	Like asure° were his legges and his toon;°	*azure / toes*
	His nailes whitter than the lilye flowr,	
	And lik the burned° gold was his colour.	*burnished*
	This gentil cok hadde in his governaunce	
100	Sevene hennes for to doon al his plesaunce,	
	Whiche were his sustres and his paramours,°	*lovers*
	And wonder like to him as of colours;	
	Of whiche the faireste hewed° on hir throte	*colored*
	Was cleped° faire damoisele Pertelote:	*called*
105	Curteis she was, discreet, and debonaire,°	*gracious*
	And compaignable,° and bar hirself so faire,	*sociable*
	Sin thilke° day that she was seven night old,	*that*
	That trewely she hath the herte in hold	
	Of Chauntecleer, loken in every lith.⁶	
110	He loved hire so that wel was him therwith.	
	But swich a joye was it to heere hem singe,	
	Whan that the brighte sonne gan to springe,	
	In sweete accord "My Lief is Faren in Londe"⁷—	
	For thilke time, as I have understonde,	
115	Beestes and briddes° couden speke and singe.	*birds*
	And so bifel that in a daweninge,	
	As Chauntecleer among his wives alle	
	Sat on his perche that was in the halle,	
	And next him sat this faire Pertelote,	
120	This Chauntecleer gan gronen in his throte,	
	As man that in his dreem is drecched° sore.	*disturbed*
	And whan that Pertelote thus herde him rore,	
	She was agast, and saide, "Herte dere,	
	What aileth you to grone in this manere?	
125	Ye been a verray° slepere, fy, for shame!"	*true*

5. The points marking the celestial hours.
6. Locked in every limb (i.e., thoroughly).

7. A popular ballad, "My Love Has Gone to the Country."

                And he answerde and saide thus, "Madame,
                I praye you that ye take it nat agrief.°   *amiss*
                By God, me mette° I was in swich meschief   *I dreamed*
                Right now, that yit myn herte is sore afright.
130   Now God," quod he, "my swevene recche aright,[8]
                And keepe my body out of foul prisoun!
                Me mette how that I romed up and down
                Within oure yeerd, wher as I sawgh a beest,
                Was lik an hound and wolde han maad arrest°   *taken captive*
135   Upon my body, and han had me deed.
                His colour was bitwixe yelow and reed,
                And tipped was his tail and bothe his eres
                With blak, unlik the remenant of his heres;°   *the rest of his hair*
                His snoute smal, with glowing yën twaye.
140   Yit of his look for fere almost I deye:
                This caused me my groning, doutelees."
                    "Avoi,"° quod she, "fy on you, hertelees!°   *Have done! / coward*
                Allas," quod she, "for by that God above,
                Now han ye lost myn herte and al my love!
145   I can nat love a coward, by my faith.
                For certes, what so any womman saith,
                We alle desiren, if it mighte be,
                To han housbondes hardy, wise, and free,°   *generous*
                And secree,° and no nigard, ne no fool,   *discreet*
150   Ne him that is agast° of every tool,°   *afraid / weapon*
                Ne noon avauntour.° By that God above,   *braggart*
                How dorste ye sayn for shame unto youre love
                That any thing mighte make you aferd?
                Have ye no mannes herte and han a beerd?
155   Allas, and conne ye been agast of swevenes?
                No thing, God woot,° but vanitee° in swevene is!   *knows / illusion*
                Swevenes engendren of replexiouns,°   *surfeits*
                And ofte of fume° and of complexiouns,°   *gas / bodily humors*
                Whan humours been too habundant in a wight.°   *creature*
160   Certes, this dreem which ye han met tonight
                Comth of the grete superfluitee
                Of youre rede colera,[9] pardee,°   *by God*
                Which causeth folk to dreden in hir dremes
                Of arwes,° and of fir with rede lemes,°   *arrows / flames*
165   Of rede beestes, that they wol hem bite,
                Of contek,° and of whelpes° grete and lite—   *strife / dogs*
                Right as the humour of malencolye[1]
                Causeth ful many a man in sleep to crye
                For fere of blake beres or boles° blake,   *bulls*
170   Or elles blake develes wol hem take.
                Of othere humours coude I telle also
                That werken many a man in sleep ful wo,

8. Intepret my dream correctly.   1. Black bile, thought to produce dark thoughts.
9. Coleric bile, thought to overheat the body.

But I wol passe as lightly as I can.
Lo, Caton,[2] which that was so wis a man,
175   Saide he nat thus? 'Ne do no fors° of dremes.'   *pay no attention to*
Now, sire," quod she, "whan we flee° fro the bemes,°   *fly / rafters*
For Goddes love, as take som laxatif.
Up° peril of my soule and of my lif,   *upon*
I conseile you the beste, I wol nat lie,
180   That bothe of colere and of malencolye
Ye purge you; and for ye shal nat tarye,
Though in this town is noon apothecarye,
I shal myself to herbes techen you,
That shal been for youre hele° and for youre prow,°   *health / profit*
185   And in oure yeerd tho° herbes shal I finde,   *then*
The whiche han of hir propretee by kinde°   *nature*
To purge you binethe and eek above.
Foryet nat this, for Goddes owene love.
Ye been ful colerik of complexioun;
190   Ware° the sonne in his ascencioun   *beware lest*
Ne finde you nat repleet° of humours hote;°   *full / hot*
And if it do, I dar wel laye[3] a grote°   *fourpence*
That ye shul have a fevere terciane,[4]
Or an agu° that may be youre bane.°   *fever / death*
195   A day or two ye shul han digestives
Of wormes, er ye take youre laxatives
Of lauriol, centaure, and fumetere,[5]
Or elles of ellebor that groweth there,
Of catapuce, or of gaitres beries,
200   Of herbe-ive growing in oure yeerd ther merye is.°   *where it is pleasant*
Pekke hem right up as they growe and ete hem in.
Be merye, housbonde, for youre fader kin!
Dredeth no dreem: I can saye you namore."
        "Madame," quod he, "graunt mercy of youre lore.°   *learning*
205   But nathelees, as touching daun Catoun,
That hath of wisdom swich a greet renown,
Though that he bad no dremes for to drede,
By God, men may in olde bookes rede
Of many a man more of auctoritee
210   Than evere Caton was, so mote I thee,°   *so may I prosper*
That al the revers sayn of his sentence,°   *opinion*
And han wel founden by experience
That dremes been significaciouns
As wel of joye as tribulaciouns
215   That folk enduren in this lif present.
Ther needeth make of this noon argument:
The verray preve° sheweth it in deede.   *proof*
        "Oon of the gretteste auctour that men rede
Saith thus, that whilom two felawes wente

---

2. Marcus Porcius Cato, ancient author of a book of
proverbs used by schoolchildren.
3. Bet (with a pun on egg-laying).

4. Recurring fever.
5. These and the following are bitter herbs that produce
hot and dry sensations and lead to purging.

220 On pilgrimage in a ful good entente,
And happed so they comen in a town,
Wher as ther was swich congregacioun
Of peple, and eek so strait of herbergage,°   *short of lodging*
That they ne founde as muche as oo° cotage   *one*
225 In which they bothe mighte ylogged be;
Wherfore they mosten of necessitee
As for that night departe compaignye.
And eech of hem gooth to his hostelrye,
And took his logging as it wolde falle.
230 That oon of hem was logged in a stalle,
Fer in a yeerd, with oxen of the plough;
That other man was logged wel ynough,
As was his aventure or his fortune,
That us governeth alle as in commune.
235 And so bifel that longe er it were day,
This man mette in his bed, ther as he lay,
How that his felawe gan upon him calle,
And saide, 'Allas, for in an oxes stalle
This night I shal be mordred° ther I lie!   *murdered*
240 Now help me, dere brother, or I die!
In alle haste com to me,' he saide.
    "This man out of his sleep for fere abraide,°   *bolted up*
But whan that he was wakened of his sleep,
He turned him and took of this no keep:°   *heed*
245 Him thoughte his dreem nas° but a vanitee.   *was not*
Thus twies in his sleeping dremed he,
And atte thridde time yit his felawe
Cam, as him thoughte, and saide, 'I am now slawe:°   *slain*
Bihold my bloody woundes deepe and wide.
250 Aris up erly in the morwe tide°   *morning time*
And atte west gate of the town,' quod he,
'A carte ful of dong° ther shaltou see,   *dung*
In which my body is hid ful prively:
Do thilke° carte arresten° boldely.   *that / have seized*
255 My gold caused my mordre, sooth° to sayn'—   *truth*
And tolde him every point how he was slain,
With a ful pitous face, pale of hewe.
And truste wel, his dreem he foond ful trewe,
For on the morwe as soone as it was day,
260 To his felawes in he took the way,
And whan that he cam to this oxes stalle,
After his felawe he bigan to calle.
    "The hostiler° answerde him anoon,   *innkeeper*
And saide, 'Sire, youre felawe is agoon:
265 As soone as day he wente out of the town.'
    "This man gan fallen in suspecioun,
Remembring on his dremes that he mette;
And forth he gooth, no lenger wolde he lette,°   *delay*
Unto the west gate of the town, and foond
270 A dong carte, wente as it were to donge° lond,   *spread manure on*

That was arrayed in that same wise
As ye han herd the dede man devise;
And with an hardy herte he gan to crye,
'Vengeance and justice of this felonye!
275   My felawe mordred is this same night,
And in this carte he lith gaping upright!°   *facing up*
I crye out on the ministres,'° quod he,   *magistrates*
'That sholde keepe and rulen this citee.
Harrow, allas, here lith my felawe slain!'
280   What sholde I more unto this tale sayn?
The peple up sterte and caste the carte to grounde,
And in the middel of the dong they founde
The dede man that mordred was al newe.°   *just recently*
   "O blisful God that art so just and trewe,
285   Lo, how that thou biwrayest° mordre alway!   *reveal*
Mordre wol out, that see we day by day:
Mordre is so wlatsom° and abhominable   *loathsome*
To God that is so just and resonable,
That he ne wol nat suffre it heled° be,   *concealed*
290   Though it abide a yeer or two or three.
Mordre wol out: this my conclusioun.
And right anoon ministres of that town
Han hent° the cartere and so sore him pined,°   *seized / tortured*
And eek the hostiler so sore engined,
295   That they biknewe° hir wikkednesse anoon,   *confessed*
And were anhanged by the nekke boon.
Here may men seen that dremes been to drede.
   "And certes, in the same book I rede—
Right in the nexte chapitre after this—
300   I gabbe° nat, so have I joye or blis—   *lie*
Two men that wolde han passed over see
For certain cause into a fer contree,
If that the wind ne hadde been contrarye
That made hem in a citee for to tarye,
305   That stood ful merye upon an haven° side—   *harbor*
But on a day again° the even tide   *toward*
The wind gan chaunge, and blewe right as hem leste:°   *they wanted*
Jolif° and glad they wenten unto reste,   *merry*
And casten hem° ful erly for to saile.   *decided*
310   "But to that oo man fil a greet mervaile;
That oon of hem, in sleeping as he lay,
Him mette a wonder dreem again the day:
Him thoughte a man stood by his beddes side,
And him comanded that he sholde abide,
315   And saide him thus, 'If thou tomorwe wende,°   *travel*
Thou shalt be dreint:° my tale is at an ende.'   *drowned*
   "He wook and tolde his felawe what he mette,
And prayed him his viage to lette;°   *put off his journey*
As for that day he prayed him to bide.
320   His felawe that lay by his beddes side
Gan for to laughe, and scorned him ful faste.

'No dreem,' quod he, 'may so myn herte agaste
That I wol lette for to do my thinges.°   *business*
I sette nat a straw by thy dreminges,
325 For swevenes been but vanitees and japes:°   *tricks*
Men dreme alday° of owles or of apes,   *constantly*
And of many a maze° therwithal—   *delusion*
Men dreme of thing that nevere was ne shal.
But sith° I see that thou wolt here abide,   *since*
330 And thus forsleuthen° wilfully thy tide,   *waste due to sloth*
Good woot, it reweth me; and have good day.'
And thus he took his leve and wente his way.
But er that he hadde half his cours ysailed—
Noot° I nat why ne what meschaunce it ailed°—   *know / went wrong*
335 But casuelly° the shippes botme rente,°   *by accident / split apart*
And ship and man under the water wente,
In sighte of othere shippes it biside,
That with hem sailed at the same tide.
And therfore, faire Pertelote so dere,
340 By swiche ensamples olde maistou lere°   *may you learn*
That no man sholde been too recchelees°   *careless*
Of dremes, for I saye thee doutelees
That many a dreem ful sore is for to drede.
    "Lo, in the lif of Saint Kenelm[6] I rede—
345 That was Kenulphus sone, the noble king
Of Mercenrike—how Kenelm mette a thing
A lite° er he was mordred on a day.   *little while*
His mordre in his avision° he sey.°   *dream / saw*
His norice° him expounded everydeel   *nurse*
350 His swevene, and bad him for to keepe him° weel   *guard against*
For traison, but he nas but seven yeer old,
And therfore litel tale hath he told°   *he cared little for*
Of any dreem, so holy was his herte.
By God, I hadde levere than my sherte°   *would give my shirt*
355 That ye hadde rad his legende as have I.
    "Dame Pertelote, I saye you trewely,
Macrobeus,[7] that writ the Avisioun
In Affrike of the worthy Scipioun,
Affermeth° dremes, and saith that they been   *confirms*
360 Warning of thinges that men after seen.
    "And ferthermore, I praye you looketh wel
In the Olde Testament of Daniel,
If he heeld dremes any vanitee.[8]
    "Rede eek of Joseph and ther shul ye see
365 Wher° dremes be somtime—I saye nat alle—   *whether*
Warning of thinges that shul after falle.
    "Looke of Egypte the king daun Pharao,
His bakere and his botelere° also,   *butler*

6. St. Cenhelm, son of Cenwulf, a 9th-century child-king
in Mercia who was murdered at his sister's orders.
7. Macrobius, a 4th-century author, wrote an extensive
commentary on Cicero's *Dream of Scipio*.
8. Daniel interprets the pagan King Nebuchadnezzar's
dream, which foretells his downfall (Daniel 4).

Wher they ne felte noon effect in dremes.[9]
370 Whoso wol seeke actes of sondry remes°   *various kingdoms*
May rede of dremes many a wonder thing.
    "Lo Cresus, which that was of Lyde° king,   *Lydia*
Mette he nat that he sat upon a tree,
Which signified he sholde anhanged be?
375   "Lo here Andromacha, Ectores° wif,   *Hector of Troy*
That day that Ector sholde lese° his lif,   *lose*
She dremed on the same night biforn
How that the lif of Ector sholde be lorn,
If thilke day he wente into bataile;
380 She warned him, but it mighte nat availe:
He wente for to fighte nathelees,
But he was slain anoon of Achilles.
But thilke tale is al too long to telle,
And eek it is neigh day, I may nat dwelle.
385 Shortly I saye, as for conclusioun,
That I shal han of this avisioun
Adversitee, and I saye ferthermoor
That I ne telle of laxatives no stoor,°   *hold no regard for*
For they been venimes,° I woot° it weel: *poisons / know*
390 I hem defye, I love hem neveradeel.
    "Now lat us speke of mirthe and stinte° al this.   *stop*
Madame Pertelote, so have I blis,
Of oo thing God hath sente me large grace:
For whan I see the beautee of youre face—
395 Ye been so scarlet reed aboute youre yën—
It maketh al my drede for to dien.
For also siker° as *In principio,*[1]   *certain*
Mulier est hominis confusio.[2]
Madame, the sentence° of this Latin is,   *meaning*
400 'Womman is mannes joye and al his blis.'
For whan I feele anight youre softe side—
Al be it that I may nat on you ride,
For that oure perche is maad so narwe, allas—
I am so ful of joye and of solas°   *delight*
405 That I defye bothe swevene and dreem."
And with that word he fleigh down fro the beem,
For it was day, and eek° his hennes alle,   *also*
And with a "chuk" he gan hem for to calle,
For he hadde founde a corn lay in the yeerd.
410 Real° he was, he was namore aferd:°   *regal / afraid*
He fethered Pertelote twenty time,
And trad° hire as ofte er it was prime.[3]   *mounted*
He looketh as it were a grim leoun,°   *lion*
And on his toes he rometh up and down:
415 Him deined nat to sette his foot to grounde.
He chukketh whan he hath a corn yfounde,

9. Joseph interpreted dreams for the pharaoh's chief baker and butler (Genesis 40–41).
1. "In the beginning," the opening verse of the Book of Genesis and the Gospel of John.
2. "Woman is the ruination of mankind."
3. First hour of the day.

And to him rennen thanne his wives alle.
Thus royal, as a prince is in his halle,
Leve I this Chauntecleer in his pasture,
420   And after wol I telle his aventure.
       Whan that the month in which the world bigan,
That highte March, whan God first maked man,
Was compleet, and passed were also,
Sin March biran,° thritty days and two,[4]   *finished*
425   Bifel that Chauntecleer in al his pride,
His sevene wives walking him biside,
Caste up his yën to the brighte sonne,
That in the signe of Taurus hadde yronne
Twenty degrees and oon and somwhat more,
430   And knew by kinde,° and by noon other lore,   *nature*
That it was prime, and crew with blisful stevene.°   *voice*
"The sonne," he saide, "is clomben up on hevene
Fourty degrees and oon and more, ywis.°   *indeed*
Madame Pertelote, my worldes blis,
435   Herkneth thise blisful briddes° how they singe,   *birds*
And see the fresshe flowres how they springe:
Ful is myn herte of revel and solas."
But sodeinly him fil a sorweful cas,°   *event*
For evere the latter ende of joye is wo—
440   God woot that worldly joye is soone ago,
And if a rethor° coude faire endite,°   *rhetorician / compose*
He in a cronicle saufly° mighte it write,   *safely*
As for a soverein notabilitee.
Now every wis man lat him herkne me:
445   This storye is also° trewe, I undertake,   *as*
As is the book of Launcelot de Lake,[5]
That wommen holde in ful greet reverence.
Now wol I turne again to my sentence.°   *topic*
       A colfox° ful of sly iniquitee,   *black fox*
450   That in the grove° hadde woned° yeres three,   *woods / lived*
By heigh imaginacion forncast,[6]
The same night thurghout the hegges brast°   *burst*
Into the yeerd ther Chauntecleer the faire
Was wont, and eek his wives, to repaire;
455   And in a bed of wortes° stille he lay   *cabbages*
Til it was passed undren° of the day,   *midmorning*
Waiting his time on Chauntecleer to falle,
As gladly doon thise homicides alle,
That in await liggen to mordre men.
460   O false mordrour, lurking in thy den!
O newe Scariot! Newe Geniloun![7]
False dissimilour!° O Greek Sinoun,[8]   *dissembler*
That broughtest Troye al outrely° to sorwe!   *entirely*

4. The date is thus May 3.
5. The adventures of the Arthurian knight.
6. Predicted (in Chauntecleer's dream).
7. Judas Iscariot, who handed Jesus over to the Roman authorities for execution; Ganelon, a medieval traitor who betrayed the hero Roland to his Saracen enemies.
8. The Greek who tricked the Trojans into accepting the Trojan horse behind the city walls.

O Chauntecleer, accursed be that morwe
465   That thou into the yeerd flaugh fro the bemes!
Thou were ful wel ywarned by thy dremes
That thilke day was perilous to thee;
But what that God forwoot moot° needes be,   *foreknew must*
After the opinion of certain clerkes:
470   Witnesse on him that any parfit° clerk is   *accomplished*
That in scole is greet altercacioun
In this matere, and greet disputisoun,
And hath been of an hundred thousand men.
But I ne can nat bulte it to the bren,[9]
475   As can the holy doctour Augustin,
Or Boece, or the bisshop Bradwardin[1]—
Wheither that Goddes worthy forwiting°   *foreknowledge*
Straineth° me nedely for to doon a thing   *compels*
("Nedely" clepe I simple necessitee),
480   Or elles if free chois be graunted me
To do that same thing or do it nought,
Though God forwoot it er that I was wrought;°   *made*
Or if his witing straineth neveradeel,
But by necessitee condicionel[2]—
485   I wol nat han to do of swich matere:
My tale is of a cok, as ye may heere,
That took his conseil of his wif with sorwe,
To walken in the yeerd upon that morwe
That he hadde met the dreem that I you tolde.
490   Wommenes conseils been ful ofte colde,°   *disastrous*
Wommanes conseil broughte us first to wo,
And made Adam fro Paradis to go,
Ther as he was ful merye and wel at ese.
But for I noot° to whom it mighte displese   *do not know*
495   If I conseil of wommen wolde blame,
Passe over, for I saide it in my game—
Rede auctours° where they trete of swich matere,   *authors*
And what they sayn of wommen ye may heere—
Thise been the cokkes wordes and nat mine:
500   I can noon harm of no womman divine.°   *guess at*
     Faire in the sond° to bathe hire merily   *sand*
Lith° Pertelote, and alle hir sustres by,   *lies*
Again the sonne, and Chauntecleer so free
Soong merier than the mermaide in the see—
505   For Physiologus[3] saith sikerly
How that they singen wel and merily.
     And so bifel that as he caste his yë
Among the wortes on a boterflye,°   *butterfly*
He was war of this fox that lay ful lowe.
510   No thing ne liste him° thanne for to crowe,   *he wanted*

---

9. Sift it from the husks (i.e., discriminate).
1. St. Augustine, the ancient writer Boethius, and the 14th-century Archbishop of Canterbury Thomas Bradwardine attempted to explain how God's predestination

of events still allowed for humans to have free will.
2. Boethius argued only for conditional necessity, which still permitted for much exercise of free will.
3. Said to have written a bestiary.

But cride anoon "Cok cok!" and up he sterte,
As man that was affrayed in his herte—
For naturelly a beest desireth flee
Fro his contrarye° if he may it see,   *natural enemy*
515 Though he nevere erst° hadde seen it with his yë.   *before*
This Chauntecleer, whan he gan him espye,
He wolde han fled, but that the fox anoon
Saide, "Gentil sire, allas, wher wol ye goon?
Be ye afraid of me that am youre freend?
520 Now certes, I were worse than a feend°   *devil*
If I to you wolde harm or vilainye.
I am nat come youre conseil for t'espye,
But trewely the cause of my cominge
Was only for to herkne how that ye singe:
525 For trewely, ye han as merye a stevene°   *voice*
As any angel hath that is in hevene.
Therwith ye han in musik more feelinge
Than hadde Boece,⁴ or any that can singe.
My lord your fader—God his soule blesse!—
530 And eek youre moder, of hir gentilesse,°   *gentility*
Han in myn hous ybeen, to my grete ese.
And certes sire, ful fain° wolde I you plese.   *gladly*
    But for men speke of singing, I wol saye,
So mote I brouke° wel mine yën twaye,   *use*
535 Save ye, I herde nevere man so singe
As dide youre fader in the morweninge.
Certes, it was of herte° al that he soong.   *heartfelt*
And for to make his vois the more strong,
He wolde so paine him that with bothe his yën
540 He moste winke,° so loude wolde he cryen;   *shut his eyes*
And stonden on his tiptoon therwithal,
And strecche forth his nekke long and smal;
And eek he was of swich discrecioun
That ther nas no man in no regioun
545 That him in song or wisdom mighte passe.°   *surpass*
I have wel rad in Daun Burnel the Asse.⁵
Among his vers how that ther was a cok,
For° a preestes sone yaf him a knok   *because*
Upon his leg whil he was yong and nice,°   *foolish*
550 He made him for to lese his benefice.⁶
But certain, ther nis no comparisoun
Bitwixe the wisdom and discrecioun
Of youre fader and of his subtiltee.
Now singeth, sire, for sainte° charitee!   *holy*
555 Lat see, conne ye youre fader countrefete?"°   *imitate*
    This Chauntecleer his winges gan to bete,
As man that coude his traison nat espye,
So was he ravisshed with his flaterye.

---

4. In addition to theology, Boethius also wrote a music textbook.
5. The hero of a 12th-century satirical poem, *Speculum* *Stultorum*, by Nigel Wirecker, Brunellus was a donkey who traveled around Europe trying to educare himself.
6. Lose his commission (because he overslept).

	Allas, ye lordes, many a fals flatour
560	Is in youre court, and many a losengeour,°
	That plesen you wel more, by my faith,
	Than he that soothfastnesse° unto you saith!
	Redeth Ecclesiaste[7] of flaterye.
	Beeth war, ye lordes, of hir trecherye.
565	This Chauntecleer stood hye upon his toos,
	Strecching his nekke, and heeld his yën cloos,
	And gan to crowe loude for the nones;°
	And daun Russel the fox sterte up atones,°
	And by the gargat° hente° Chauntecleer,
570	And on his bak toward the wode him beer,
	For yit ne was ther no man that him sued.
	O destinee that maist nat been eschued!°
	Allas that Chauntecleer fleigh fro the bemes!
	Allas his wif ne roughte° nat of dremes!
575	And on a Friday[8] fil al this meschaunce!
	O Venus that art goddesse of plesaunce,
	Sin that thy servant was this Chauntecleer,
	And in thy service dide al his power—
	More for delit than world° to multiplye—
580	Why woldestou suffre him on thy day to die?
	O Gaufred,[9] dere maister soverein,
	That, whan thy worthy king Richard was slain
	With shot,° complainedest his deeth so sore,
	Why ne hadde I now thy sentence and thy lore,
585	The Friday for to chide as diden ye?
	For on a Friday soothly° slain was he.
	Thanne wolde I shewe you how that I coude plaine°
	For Chauntecleres drede and for his paine.
	Certes, swich cry ne lamentacioun
590	Was nevere of ladies maad whan Ilioun°
	Was wonne, and Pyrrus[1] with his straite° swerd,
	Whan he hadde hent King Priam by the beerd
	And slain him, as saith us Eneidos,°
	As maden alle the hennes in the cloos,°
595	Whan they hadde seen of Chauntecleer the sighte.
	But sovereinly Dame Pertelote shrighte°
	Ful louder than dide Hasdrubales wif[2]
	Whan that hir housbonde hadde lost his lif,
	And that the Romains hadden brend Cartage:
600	She was so ful of torment and of rage
	That wilfully unto the fir she sterte,
	And brende hirselven with a stedefast herte.
	O woful hennes, right so criden ye

Glosses (right margin):
- 560 *deceiver*
- 562 *truth*
- 567 *for the purpose*
- 568 *at once*
- 569 *throat / seized*
- 572 *avoided*
- 574 *cared*
- 579 *population*
- 583 *(of an arrow)*
- 586 *truly*
- 587 *lament*
- 590 *Troy*
- 591 *drawn*
- 593 *Virgil's Aeneid*
- 594 *yard*
- 596 *shrieked*

---

7. The Book of Ecclesiasticus.
8. Venus's day, but also an ominous day of the week.
9. Geoffrey of Vinsauf, who wrote a poem when King Richard the Lion-Hearted died, cursing the day of the week on which he died, a Friday.
1. Pyrrhus, the son of Achilles, who slew Troy's King Priam.
2. Hasdrubal was King of Carthage when it was defeated by the Romans during the Punic Wars.

As, whan that Nero³ brende the citee
605   Of Rome, criden senatoures wives
For that hir housbondes losten alle hir lives:
Withouten gilt this Nero hath hem slain.
Now wol I turne to my tale again.
      The sely° widwe and eek hir doughtres two   *innocent*
610   Herden thise hennes crye and maken wo,
And out at dores sterten they anoon,
And sien° the fox toward the grove goon,   *saw*
And bar upon his bak the cok away,
And criden, "Out, harrow, and wailaway,
615   Ha, ha, the fox," and after him they ran,
And eek with staves many another man;
Ran Colle oure dogge, and Talbot and Gerland,⁴
And Malkin with a distaf in hir hand,
Ran cow and calf, and eek the verray hogges,
620   Sore aferd for berking of the dogges
And shouting of the men and wommen eke.
They ronne so hem thoughte hir herte breke;
They yelleden as feendes doon in helle;
The dokes° criden as men wolde hem quelle;°   *ducks / kill*
625   The gees for fere flowen over the trees;
Out of the hive cam the swarm of bees;
So hidous was the noise a, benedicite,
Certes, he Jakke Straw⁵ and his meinee
Ne made nevere shoutes half so shrille
630   Whan that they wolden any Fleming kille,
As thilke day was maad upon the fox:
Of bras they broughten bemes° and of box,°   *trumpets / boxwood*
Of horn, of boon, in whiche they blewe and pouped,°   *puffed*
And therwithal they skriked and they houped—
635   It seemed as that hevene sholde falle.
      Now goode men, I praye you herkneth alle:
Lo, how Fortune turneth sodeinly
The hope and pride eek of hir enemy.
This cok that lay upon the foxes bak,
640   In al his drede unto the fox he spak,
And saide, "Sire, if that I were as ye,
Yit sholde I sayn, as wis° God helpe me,   *certainly*
'Turneth ayain, ye proude cherles° alle!   *ruffians*
A verray pestilence upon you falle!
645   Now am I come unto this wodes side,
Maugree° your heed,° the cok shal here abide.   *despite / planning*
I wol him ete, in faith, and that anoon.'"
      The fox answerde, "In faith, it shal be doon."
And as he spak that word, al sodeinly

---

3. The Emperor Nero set fire to Rome, killing many of his senators.
4. Common names for dogs.

5. Jack Straw was one of the leaders of the Peasants' Revolt of 1381, which was directed in part against the Flemish traders in London.

650   The cok brak from his mouth deliverly,°   *nimbly*
       And hye upon a tree he fleigh anoon.
           And whan the fox sawgh that he was agoon,
       "Allas," quod he, "O Chauntecleer, allas!
       I have to you," quod he, "ydoon trespas,
655   In as muche as I maked you aferd
       Whan I you hente and broughte out of the yeerd.
       But sire, I dide it in no wikke° entente: *wicked*
       Come down, and I shal telle you what I mente.
       I shal saye sooth to you, God help me so."
660   "Nay thanne," quod he, "I shrewe° us bothe two: *curse*
       But first I shrewe myself, bothe blood and bones,
       If thou bigile me ofter than ones;
       Thou shalt namore thurgh thy flaterye
       Do° me to singe and winken with myn yë.   *make*
665   For he that winketh whan he sholde see,
       Al wilfully, God lat him nevere thee."°   *prosper*
           "Nay," quod the fox, "but God yive him meschaunce
       That is so undiscreet of governaunce
       That jangleth° whan he sholde holde his pees."   *chatters*
670   Lo, swich it is for to be recchelees°   *careless*
       And necligent and truste on flaterye.
       But ye that holden this tale a folye
       As of a fox, or of a cok and hen,
       Taketh the moralitee, goode men.
675   For Saint Paul saith that al that writen is
       To oure doctrine° it is ywrit, ywis:°   *instruction / indeed*
       Taketh the fruit, and lat the chaf be stille.
       Now goode God, if that it be thy wille,
       As saith my lord, so make us alle goode men,
680   And bringe us to his hye blisse. Amen.

The Epilogue

       "Sire Nonnes Preest," oure Hoste saide anoon,
       "Yblessed be thy breech° and every stoon:°   *buttocks / testicle*
       This was a merye tale of Chauntecleer.
       But by my trouthe, if thou were seculer°   *a layman*
685   Thou woldest been a tredefowl° aright: *a cock*
       For if thou have corage° as thou hast might   *desire*
       Thee were neede of hennes, as I weene,°   *suppose*
       Ye, mo than sevene times seventeene.
       See whiche brawnes° hath this gentil preest—   *muscles*
690   So greet a nekke and swich a large breest.
       He looketh as a sperhawk° with his yën;   *sparrowhawk*
       Him needeth nat his colour for to dyen
       With brasil ne with grain of Portingale[6]
       Now sire, faire falle you for youre tale."
695   And after that he with ful merye cheere
       Saide unto another as ye shul heere.

6. Two types of red dye, the latter from Portugal.

THE PARSON'S TALE Although *The Canterbury Tales* remain unfinished and even the order of the tales is unclear, we know that Chaucer's plan was to end them with *The Parson's Tale*, just as it was to begin them with the pilgrimage to Canterbury in *The General Prologue*. Thus, when the Parson responds to the Host's request for a final tale by praying Jesus to show the way to the "glorious pilgrimage" called "Jerusalem celestial," there is a sense of closure in his return to an idea that has been obscured during the tale-telling. His shift of the destination from Canterbury to the heavenly city, however, gives us pause. The view that life on earth is a pilgrimage to heaven was a Christian commonplace, but was it Chaucer's view? The three parts of *The Parson's Tale* included here raise questions about how Chaucer's religious beliefs relate to his art. What is his final judgment of the artful, but often sinful, tales he has been telling?

In the introduction, the Parson rejects the idea of poetry entirely, scornfully refusing to tell a "fable" or to adorn his tale with alliteration or rhyme; instead, he will tell what he refers to as a "merye tale in prose," which turns out to be a forty-page treatise on penitence. Thus Chaucer specifically attributes to him an ascetic view of art which is hard to reconcile with his own extraordinary poetry. Does the Parson speak for Chaucer? Although he has a measure of authority as the only exemplary member of the clergy on the pilgrimage, he is nevertheless a fictional character. Since, however, Chaucer is thought to have written the introduction to this tale as well as the *Retraction* at the end of his life, perhaps he could have come to share the Parson's aesthetic views.

The Parson begins his tale proper with a second reference to celestial Jerusalem, stating that the route to it is through penitence. The tale, which Chaucer had translated at an earlier period, belongs to a common type of manuals of confession for either clergy or laity. Included in it is an analysis of the seven deadly sins—pride, envy, anger, sloth, avarice, gluttony, and lechery—in an order that suggests that Chaucer, like Dante, considered the last to be the least serious, although still worthy of damnation. The passage on lechery excerpted here offers an opportunity to measure *The Parson's Tale* against the tales that have gone before, particularly such "sinful" works as *The Miller's Tale* and *The Wife of Bath's Prologue*.

Whatever conclusion we draw about the relevance of *The Parson's Tale* to the tales preceding, the *Retraction* appended to it is troubling yet intriguing. In it Chaucer repudiates much of the work for which he is most loved and admired, such "worldly vanitees" as *Troilus and Criseyde*, *The Parliament of Fowls*, and those *Canterbury Tales* that "sounen [lead] into sinne." On the other hand, he thanks God for his works of "moralitee," including his translation of Boethius and his saints' legends, works that are seldom read today. He himself is engaged in penance—repentance, confession, and satisfaction—thus connecting his own spiritual experience with the manual he has translated. However disappointing it is to read this rejection of his most artistically satisfying tales, we must remember that a concept of art for art's sake would have been historically unavailable to him. Perhaps his last tale was indeed his last word.

from The Parson's Tale
The Introduction

	By that° the Manciple hadde his tale al ended,	*by that time*
	The sonne fro the south line[1] was descended	
	So lowe, that he nas nat to my sighte	
	Degrees nine and twenty as in highte.	
5	Four of the clokke it was, so as I gesse,	
	For elevene foot,° or litel more or lesse,	*feet*
	My shadwe was at thilke° time as there,	*that*
	Of swich feet as my lengthe parted were	
	In sixe feet equal of proporcioun.	
10	Therwith the moones exaltacioun°—	*dominant influence*
	I mene Libra[2]—alway gan ascende,	

---

1. Astronomical marking parallel to the celestial equator.   2. Seventh sign in the Zodiac, the Scales.

As we were entring at a thropes ende.°   *village boundary*
For which oure Host, as he was wont to gie°   *lead*
As in this caas oure joly compaignye,
15   Saide in this wise, "Lordinges everichoon,
Now lakketh us no tales mo than oon:
Fulfild is my sentence° and my decree;   *design*
I trowe° that we han herd of eech degree;   *believe*
Almost fulfild is al myn ordinaunce.
20   I praye to God, so yive him right good chaunce
That telleth this tale to us lustily.
Sire preest," quod he, "artou a vicary,°   *vicar*
Or arte a Person?° Say sooth, by thy fay.°   *parish priest / faith*
Be what thou be, ne breek thou nat oure play,
25   For every man save thou hath told his tale.
Unbokele and shew us what is in thy male!°   *bag*
For trewely, me thinketh by thy cheere°   *expression*
Thou sholdest knitte up wel a greet matere.
Tel us a fable anoon, for cokkes bones!"[3]
30   This Person answerde al atones,
"Thou getest fable noon ytold for me,
For Paul, that writeth unto Timothee,[4]
Repreveth hem that waiven soothfastnesse,°   *truth*
And tellen fables and swich wrecchednesse.
35   Why sholde I sowen draf° out of my fest,°   *chaff / fist*
Whan I may sowen whete if that me lest?°   *it pleases*
For which I saye that if you list to heere
Moralitee and vertuous matere,
And thanne that ye wol yive me audience,
40   I wol ful fain,° at Cristes reverence,   *gladly*
Do you plesance leveful° as I can.   *lawfully*
But trusteth wel, I am a southren man:[5]
I can nat geeste° Rum-Ram-Ruf by lettre—   *tell stories*
Ne, God woot,° rym holde° I but litel bettre.   *knows / appreciate*
45   And therfore, if you list, I wol nat glose;°   *adorn my speech*
I wol you telle a merye tale in prose,
To knitte up al this feeste and make an ende.
And Jesu for his grace wit me sende
To shewe you the way in this viage°   *journey*
50   Of thilke parfit° glorious pilgrimage   *that perfect*
That highte Jerusalem celestial.
And if ye vouche-sauf,° anoon I shal   *agree*
Biginne upon my tale, for which I praye
Telle youre avis:° I can no bettre saye.   *opinion*
55   But nathelees, this meditacioun
I putte it ay° under correccioun   *always*
Of clerkes, for I am nat textuel:°   *a literalist*
I take but the sentence,° trusteth wel.   *sense*
Therfore I make protestacioun

---

3. Cock's bones, a euphemism for God's bones.
4. St. Paul's Epistle to Timothy.
5. The parson, like Chaucer himself, comes from the south of England and so is not accustomed to telling stories in the alliterative meter used traditionally in the north. Rum-Ram-Raf is an example of alliteration.

60   That I wol stonde to correccioun."
         Upon this word we han assented soone,
      For, as it seemed, it was for to doone
      To enden in som vertuous sentence,°   *topic*
      And for to yive him space° and audience;   *time*
65   And bede oure Host he sholde to him saye
      That alle we to telle his tale him praye.
         Oure Hoste hadde the wordes for us alle:
      "Sire preest," quod he, "now faire you bifalle:
      Telleth," quod he, "youre meditacioun.
70   But hasteth you, the sonne wol adown.
      Beeth fructuous, and that in litel space,
      And to do wel God sende you his grace.
      Saye what you list, and we wol gladly heere."
      And with that word he saide in this manere.

from *The Tale*

Oure sweete Lord God of Hevene, that no man wol perisse[1] but wol
that we comen alle to the knowliche of him and to the blisful lif
that is perdurable,° amonesteth° us by the prophete Jeremie[2] that   *enduring / warns*
saith in this wise: "Stondeth upon the wayes and seeth and axeth of
olde pathes (that is to sayn, of olde sentences)° which is the goode   *opinions*
way, and walketh in that way, and ye shul finde refresshing for youre
soules."
   Manye been the wayes espirituels that leden folk to oure Lord
Jesu Crist and to the regne of glorye: of whiche wayes ther is a ful
noble way and a ful covenable° which may nat faile to man ne to   *suitable*
womman that thurgh sinne hath misgoon fro the righte way of
Jerusalem celestial; and this way is cleped° Penitence. * * *   *called*

THE REMEDY FOR THE SIN OF LECHERY

Now cometh the remedye agains Lecherye, and that is generally
Chastitee and Continence that restraineth alle the desordainee
mevinges° that comen of flesshly talents.° And evere the gretter   *impulses / desires*
merite shal he han that most restraineth the wikkede eschaufinges°   *inflammations*
of the ardure of this sinne. And this is in two maneres: that is to
sayn, chastitee in mariage and chastitee of widwehood.
   Now shaltou understonde that matrimoine is leeful° assembling   *lawful*
of man and of womman that receiven by vertu of the sacrement the
bond thurgh which they may nat be departed in al hir life—that is to
sayn, whil that they liven bothe. This, as saith the book, is a ful greet
sacrement: God maked it, as I have said, in Paradis, and wolde himself be born in mariage. And for to halwen° mariage, he was at a   *bless*
wedding where as he turned water into win, which was the firste
miracle that he wroughte in erthe biforn his disciples. Trewe effect
of mariage clenseth fornicacion and replenisseth Holy Chirche of
good linage° (for that is the ende of mariage), and it chaungeth   *offspring*

1. Who wishes no man to perish.   2. Jeremiah 6.16.

deedly sinne[3] into venial sinne bitwixe hem that been ywedded, and maketh the hertes al oon° of hem that been ywedded, as wel as the bodies.   *united*

This is verray mariage that was establissed by God er that sinne bigan, whan naturel lawe was in his right point° in Paradis;   *order*
and it was ordained that oo man sholde have but oo womman, and oo womman but oo man (as saith Saint Augustine) by manye resons: First, for mariage is figured° bitwixe Crist and Holy   *represented*
Chirche; and that other is for a man is heved° of a womman—   *head*
algate,° by ordinance it sholde be so. For if a womman hadde mo   *at least*
men than oon, thanne sholde she have mo hevedes than oon, and that were an horrible thing biforn God; and eek a womman ne mighte nat plese to many folk at ones. And also ther ne sholde nevere be pees ne reste amonges hem, for everich wolde axen his owene thing. And fortherover, no man sholde knowe his owene engendrure,° ne who sholde have his heritage, and the womman   *offspring*
sholde been the lesse biloved fro the time that she were conjoint to manye men.

Now cometh how that a man sholde bere him with his wif, and namely in two thinges, that is to sayn, in suffrance° and in rever-   *obedience*
ence, as shewed Crist whan he made first womman. For he ne made hire nat of the heved of Adam for she sholde nat claime too greet lorshipe: for ther as womman hath the maistrye she maketh too greet desray° (ther needen none ensamples of this: the experience of day   *disorder*
by day oughte suffise). Also, certes, God ne made nat womman of the foot of Adam, for she ne sholde nat be holden too lowe, for she can nat paciently suffre. But God made womman of the rib of Adam for womman sholde be felawe unto man. Man sholde bere him to his wif in faith, in trouthe, and in love, as saith Sainte Paul, that a man sholde loven his wif as Crist loved Holy Chirche, that loved it so wel that he deide for it. So sholde a man for his wif, if it were neede.

Now how that a womman sholde be subjet to hir housbonde, that telleth Sainte Peter: First, in obedience. And eek, as saith the decree, a womman that is a wif, as longe as she is a wif, she hath noon auctoritee° to swere ne to bere witnesse withoute leve of hir   *power*
housbonde that is hir lord—algate, he sholde be so by reson. She sholde eek serven him in alle honestee, and been attempree° of hir   *moderate*
array; I woot wel that they sholde setten hir entente° to plesen hir   *purpose*
housbondes, but nat by hir quaintise of array:° Saint Jerome saith   *flamboyant attire*
that wives that been apparailed in silk and in precious purpre ne mowe nat clothen hem in Jesu Crist. What saith Saint John eek in this matere? Saint Gregorye eek saith that no wight° seeketh precious   *person*
array but only for vaine glorye to been honoured the more biforn the peple. It is a greet folye a womman to have a fair array outward and in hireself be foul inward. A wif sholde eek be mesurable° in looking   *modest*
and in bering and in laughing, and discreet in alle hir wordes and hir deedes. And aboven alle worldly thinges she sholde loven hir hous- bonde with al hir herte, and to him be trewe of hir body (so sholde

---

3. Sex remains a minor sin even within marriage, but it is a more serious sin outside of marriage.

an housbonde eek be to his wif): for sith that° al the body is the *since*
housbondes, so sholde hir herte been, or elles ther is bitwixe hem
two as in that no parfit mariage.

Thanne shul men understonde that for three thinges a man and
his wif flesshly mowen° assemble. The firste is in entente of engen- *may*
drure of children to the service of God: for certes, that is the cause
final of matrimoine. Another cause is to yeelden everich° of hem to *each*
other the dette of hir bodies, for neither of hem hath power of his
owene body. The thridde is for to eschewe lecherye and vilainye.
The ferthe is, for soothe, deedly sinne. As to the firste, it is merito-
rye; the seconde also, for, as saith the decree, that she hath merite of
chastitee that yeeldeth to hir housbonde the dette of hir body, ye,
though it be again hir liking and the lust of hir herte. The thridde
manere is venial sinne—and, trewely, scarsly may any of thise be
withoute venial sinne, for the corrupcion and for the delit. The ferthe
manere is for to understonde if they assemble only for amorous love
and for noon of the forsaide causes, but for to accomplice thilke
brenning delit—they rekke° nevere how ofte—soothly, it is deedly *care*
sinne. And yit with sorwe some folk wol painen hem° more to doon *trouble*
than to hir appetit suffiseth. * * * *themselves*

Another remedye agains lecherye is specially to withdrawen
swiche thinges as yive occasion to thilke vilainye, as ese,° eting, and *leisure*
drinking: for certes, whan the pot boileth strongly, the beste remedye is
to withdrawe the fir. Sleeping longe in greet quiete is eek a greet
norice° to lecherye. Another remedye agains lecherye is that a man or a *nurse*
womman eschewe the compaignye of hem by whiche he douteth° to be *suspects*
tempted: for al be it so that the deede be withstonden, yit is ther greet
temptacion. Soothly, a whit wal,° although it ne brenne nought fully by *wall*
stiking of a candele, yit is the wal blak of the leit.° Ful ofte time I rede *from the flame*
that no man truste in his owene perfeccion but he be stronger than
Sampson, holier than David, and wiser than Salomon.

Chaucer's Retraction

Here Taketh the Makere of This Book His Leve

Now praye I to hem alle that herkne this litel tretis° or rede,° that if *treatise / advice*
ther be any thing in it that liketh° hem, that therof they thanken *pleases*
oure Lord Jesu Crist, of whom proceedeth al wit and al goodnesse.
And if ther be any thing that displese hem, I praye hem also that
they arrette° it to the defaute of myn unconning,° and nat to my wil, *attribute / inability*
that wolde ful fain° have said bettre if I hadde had conning. For oure *gladly*
book saith, "Al that is writen is writen for oure doctrine," and that is
myn entente. Wherfore I biseeke you mekely, for the mercy of God,
that ye praye for me that Crist have mercy on me and foryive me my
giltes,° and namely of my translacions and enditinges° of worldly *sins / writings*
vanitees, the whiche I revoke in my retraccions:[4] as is the book of

4. Here Chaucer repents having written most of his major works: *Troilus and Criseyde, The Book* (or *House*) *of Fame, The Legend of Good Women, The Book of the Duchess, The Parliament of Fowls,* and various of *The Canterbury Tales. The Book of the Lion* has not been preserved. Chaucer's translation of Boethius's *Consolation of Philosophy* is excepted.

Troilus; the book also of Fame; the book of the five and twenty
Ladies; the book of the Duchesse; the book of Saint Valentines Day
of the Parlement of Briddes; the tales of Canterbury, thilke that
sounen° into sinne; the book of the Leon; and many another book, if   *lead*
they were in my remembrance, and many a song and many a lecch-
erous lay: that Crist for his grete mercy foryive me the sinne. But
of the translacion of Boece *de Consolatione*, and othere bookes of
legendes of saintes, and omelies, and moralitee, and devocion, that
thanke I oure Lord Jesu Crist and his blisful Moder and alle the
saintes of hevene, biseeking hem that they from hennes forth unto
my lives ende sende me grace to biwaile° my giltes and to studye to   *repent*
the salvacion of my soule, and graunte me grace of verray penitence,
confession, and satisfaccion to doon in this present lif, thurgh the
benigne grace of him that is king of kinges and preest over alle
preestes, that boughte° us with the precious blood of his herte, so that   *redeemed*
I may been oon of hem at the day of doom° that shulle be saved. *Qui*   *judgment*
cum patre et Spiritu Sancto vivis et regnas Deus per omnia saecula. Amen.[5]

To His Scribe Adam[1]

Adam scrivain,° if evere it thee bifalle   *copyist*
Boece[2] or Troilus for to writen newe,
Under thy longe lokkes thou moste have° the scalle,°   *may you get / mange*
But after my making thou write more trewe,[3]
So ofte a day I moot° thy werk renewe,   *must*
It to correcte, and eek to rubbe and scrape:
And al is thurgh thy necligence and rape.°   *haste*

Complaint to His Purse[1]

To you, my purs, and to noon other wight,°   *creature*
Complaine I, for ye be my lady dere
I am so sory, now that ye be light,°   *empty, wanton*
For certes, but if° ye make me hevy cheere,[2]   *unless*

---

5. You who live with the Father and the Holy Spirit and
reign as God through all the centuries. Amen.
1. Given his position at court, Chaucer was asked to write
many lyrics and occasional poems, such as this poem and
the one that follows. In both, he wittily bemoans the
conditions of authorship under which he was forced to
work, depending on scribes to reproduce his poetry and
on patrons to support it. In *To His Scribe Adam*, he strikes
a pose of affectionate raillery toward his scribe, whose
occupation writers widely scorned. Perhaps he sees it as
fitting to curse Adam with a skin disease which will make
him scratch his scalp, just as Chaucer has had to scratch
out the errors from his manuscripts. However, the poem
has a serious undertone too. In fearing that Adam will
miscopy his great romance, *Troilus and Criseyde*, he
echoes a concern for the accurate reproduction of his
work, which he voiced at the end of *Troilus* itself: he
prays God that, in view of the great dialectal "diversitee /
in Englissh, and in writing of oure tonge," no one "mis-
write" his book (5.1793–94).

2. Chaucer's translation of Boethius's *Consolation of Philosophy*.
3. Unless you make a more reliable copy of what I have
composed.
1. This is a traditional "begging" poem, based on French
models. The request for money is presented humorously,
as a parody of a courtly love complaint to a cruel mistress.
The parallel takes on ironic force when one recalls
Chaucer's presentation of himself, in such early poems as
The Parliament of Fowls, as a failed lover. This is one of
Chaucer's last poems, written a year before his death. It
was addressed to Henry IV when he took the throne in
1399, to request a renewal of the annuity Chaucer had
received from the deposed Richard II. The flattering
"envoy" to Henry at the end alludes to the tradition dating from Geoffrey of Monmouth that Britain was founded
by Brutus, the grandson of Aeneas, the exiled prince of
Troy and founder of Rome.
2. Serious expression (in a person); full weight (in a
purse).

5   Me were as lief° be laid upon my beere;°   *I would prefer / bier*
       For which unto youre mercy thus I crye:
       Beeth hevy again, or elles moot° I die.   *must*

       Now voucheth sauf° this day er it be night   *grant*
       That I of you the blisful soun may heere,
10   Or see youre colour, lik the sonne bright,
       That of yelownesse hadde nevere peere.
       Ye be my lif, ye be myn hertes steere,°   *guide*
       Queene of confort and of good compaignye:
       Beeth hevy again, or elles moot I die.

15   Ye purs, that been to me my lives light
       And saviour, as in this world down here,
       Out of this tonne° helpe me thurgh your might,   *dark situation*
       Sith that ye wol nat be my tresorere;
       For I am shave as neigh° as any frere.[3]   *close*
20   But yit I praye unto youre curteisye:
       Beeth hevy again, or elles moot I die.

                        Envoy to Henry IV[4]

       O conquerour of Brutus Albioun,[5]
       Which that by line° and free eleccioun   *inheritance*
       Been verray king, this song to you I sende:
25   And ye, that mowen° alle oure harmes amende,   *may*
       Have minde upon my supplicacioun.

                         ⤏ ✦ ⤎

William Langland
c. 1330–1387

Little is known of William Langland. On the basis of evidence in his best-known work, *Piers Plowman*, he is thought to have been a clerk in minor orders whose career in the church was curtailed by his marriage. He may have come from the Malvern Hills in the west of England, but he spent much of his professional life in London. He was clearly learned, using many Latin quotations from the Bible (given below primarily in English translation and designated by italics), and the style of his poem in many ways resembles sermon rhetoric.

   Piers Plowman is an ambitious and multilayered allegory, an attempt to combine Christian history, social satire, and an account of the individual soul's quest for salvation. It is presented as a dream vision whose hero is a humble plowman, and whose narrator, the naive dreamer named Will, may only be a convenient fiction. Even its first audience sometimes reacted to this mysterious poem in surprising ways. *Piers Plowman* was so inspiring to the leaders of the peasants who led the Rising of 1381 that they saw Piers not as a fictional character but as an

3. Friar (with a bald tonsure).
4. The "envoy" is the traditional close of a ballad, usually directed to its addressee.

5. According to legend, Brutus conquered the kingdom of Albion and renamed it "Britain," after himself.

actual seditious person, as can be seen in the letter of radical priest John Ball in the readings following this poem (page 461). This interpretation of the poem is remarkable given Langland's profound conservatism; despite his scathing social satire, he offers no program for social change. In fact, he supports the model of the three estates, whereby the king and knights protect the body politic, the clergy prays for it, and the commons provide its food. Although he was sympathetic toward the poor and scornful of the rich and powerful, he felt that what ailed society was that *none* of the three estates was performing its proper role.

Piers Plowman survives in many manuscripts, a fact that suggests a large audience, which most likely included secular readers in the government and law as well as the clergy. Most of John Ball's followers would have been unable to read it. The poem exists in three versions—known as the A-, B-, and C-texts—and their history throws light on the poem's role in the Rising of 1381. The short A-text was expanded into the B-text some time between 1377 and 1381, when John Ball and other rebel leaders referred to it, while the C-text is generally agreed to reflect Langland's attempt to distance himself from the radical beliefs of the rebels. Nevertheless, the poem remained popular for the next two centuries as a document of social protest and was ultimately regarded as a prophecy of the English Reformation. Langland's social criticism, however, is only part of his project, for he considered individual salvation to be equally important. A strictly political reading of *Piers Plowman*—whether in the fourteenth century or the twenty-first—misses a great deal of its originality and its power.

Piers Plowman is a challenge to read: it is almost surrealistic in its rapid and unexplained transitions, its many dreams, and its complex use of allegory. It is as confusing to people reading it in its entirety as to those reading it in excerpts, as here. Nevertheless, the poem does have a kind of unity, of a thematic rather than a narrative sort. It is held together by the dreamer's vision of the corruption of society and his personal quest to save his own soul. This quest is loosely structured by the metaphor of the journey, which is reflected in the poem's subdivision into parts called *passūs*—Latin for "steps." The poem is further unified by the allegorical character of Piers the plowman: a literal fourteenth-century English farmer when we first meet him, in the course of the poem he becomes a figural representation of Saint Peter, the first pope and founder of the church, and of Christ himself.

The five passages included here suggest the connection between the social and spiritual aspects of the poem. In the *Prologue*, the dreamer has a vision of a tower on a hill (later explained as the seat of Truth, i.e., God), a hellish dungeon beneath, and between them, a "field full of folk," representing various professions from the three estates, who are later said to be more concerned with their material than their spiritual welfare. A final fable of rats trying to bell a cat shows great dissatisfaction with the king's governance but simultaneously expresses skepticism about the ability of the commons to govern themselves.

Passus 2 is the first of three on the marriage of Lady Meed, an ambiguous allegorical figure whose name can mean "just reward," "bribery," or the profit motive generally, the last being a cause for anxiety as England moved from a barter economy to one based on money. The dreamer is invited by Lady Holy Church to Meed's marriage to "False Fickle Tongue." Members of all three estates approve this event (a sign of corruption on every social level), except for the king, who arrests Lady Meed and her fiancé, who then run away.

Langland sees greed as a sin of the poor as well as the rich, and in a comic passage of personification allegory represents the seven deadly sins as members of the commons. Included here from *Passus 5* is the vividly realized portrait of Glutton, who revels in his sin as he confesses it. Langland discusses the issues of poverty and work most directly in *Passus 6*, where Piers Plowman insists that the assembled people help him plow his half-acre before he will agree to lead them on a pilgrimage to Truth. Piers supports the traditional division of labor, explicitly exempting the knight from producing food, as long as he protects the commons and clergy from "wasters"—lazy shirkers. He insists, however, that the knight treat peasants well—in part because roles may be reversed in heaven, and earthly underlings can become heavenly masters. Yet Langland is not simply taking the workers' side. The knight turns out to be too courteous to control wasters, and Hunger must be called in to offer an incentive to work. When Piers takes pity on the poor and sends Hunger away, Waster refuses to work and the laborers demand more money, cursing the king for the statutes that have instituted wage freezes.

The spiritual climax of the poem takes place in *Passus 18*, which depicts Christ's crucifixion, harrowing of hell (release of the souls of Adam and other Old Testament figures), and resurrection. After many *passūs* of theological debate about his own salvation, the dreamer falls asleep on Palm Sunday and dreams of a man entering Jerusalem on a donkey. The dreamer thinks the man looks like Piers the Plowman, until he recognizes him as Jesus. This man is presented as a young knight going to be dubbed: he will joust against the devil in Piers's armor ("human nature") for the "fruit of Piers the Plowman" (human souls).

Before Christ can release the souls from hell, a lively debate takes place among the "four daughters of God"—Mercy and Truth, Righteousness and Peace—homely "wenches" who embody the words of Psalm 84.11: "Mercy and Truth have met together, Righteousness and Peace have kissed each other." They concede that forgiveness can take precedence over retribution, whereupon Jesus, having "jousted well," leads out the patriarchs and prophets in victory. As church bells ring to signal the resurrection, the dreamer awakes and calls his wife and daughter to church to celebrate Easter with him, thus connecting the grand scheme of salvation history to his personal experience.

The remainder of the poem, *Passūs 19–20*, which are not included here, recount the foundation of the church (by Piers as Saint Peter), and offer an apocalyptic vision of its subsequent corruption by the friars and its attack by Antichrist. There are no answers: the poem ends inconclusively with the allegorical figure of Conscience setting out on a pilgrimage in search of Piers Plowman.

Langland did not write French-inspired rhymed poetry, which was fashionable in London and used by Chaucer; instead, he composed old-fashioned alliterative poetry, which survived from Old English. The so-called Alliterative Revival was divided into two traditions, one based in the north of England and featuring romances in the alliterative "high" style, such as *Sir Gawain and the Green Knight*, and the other based in the south and west, and tending to social protest poems in a plain style. Langland's subject matter and style link him to the latter tradition, which includes satirical poems such as *Richard the Redeless*, *Mum and the Sothsegger*, and *Jack Upland*. In Middle English alliterative poetry, each line contains at least four major stressed syllables, with the first three usually beginning with the same sound. The translations of alliterative poems in this anthology—including *Beowulf* and *Sir Gawain*, as well as *Piers Plowman*—all sufficiently retain the alliteration to convey its flavor in modern English. The following passage from *Piers Plowman* in Middle English, the description of Lady Meed in her gaudy clothes, makes the point more clearly. The dreamer, with naive admiration, reports that he

> . . . was war of a womman wonderliche yclothed,
> Purfiled with Pelure, the pureste on erthe,
> Ycorouned in a coroune, the kyng hath noon bettre.
> Fetisliche hire fyngres were fretted with gold wyr
> And theron riche Rubyes as rede as any gleede,
> And Diamaundes of derrest pris and double manere saphires,
> Orientals and Ewages enuenymes to destroye.
> Hire Robe ful riche, of reed scarlet engreyned,
> With Ribanes of reed gold and of riche stones.
> Hire array me rauysshed; swich richesse saugh I neuere.*

(B 2.8–17)

---

*The passage is taken from *Piers Plowman: The B-Text*, ed. George Kane and E. Talbot Donaldson (1975).

Although Langland generally uses the plainer alliterative style of southern protest poetry, here he uses the high style of northern alliterative romances, for satirical purposes. Meed's dress recalls that of Bercilak's lady in *Sir Gawain*, in "rich red rayled" (line 952), as well as the elegant clothing of the Green Knight, "with pelure pured apert, the pane ful clene" (154). In contrast to the clothing of Lady Holy Church, whom Langland introduces in *Passus* 1 simply as "a lady lovely of look, clothed in linen," the robes of lady Meed seem dangerously seductive, thus underscoring a sexual metaphor for bribery which Langland consistently develops. Thus, in a more subtle fashion than some of his followers, such as the Wycliffite author of *Pierce the Ploughman's Crede*, Langland was able to use the specialized language of alliterative poetry in the service of social criticism.

from Piers Plowman[1]
Prologue

In a summer season when the sun was mild
I clad myself in clothes as I'd become a sheep;
In the habit of a hermit unholy of works
Walked wide in this world, watching for wonders.
5   And on a May morning, on Malvern Hills,[2]
There befell me as by magic a marvelous thing:
I was weary of wandering and went to rest
At the bottom of a broad bank by a brook's side,
And as I lay lazily looking in the water
10   I slipped into a slumber, it sounded so pleasant.
There came to me reclining there a most curious dream
That I was in a wilderness, nowhere that I knew;
But as I looked into the east, up high toward the sun,
I saw a tower on a hill-top, trimly built,
15   A deep dale beneath, a dungeon tower in it,
With ditches deep and dark and dreadful to look at.
A fair field full of folk I found between them,
Of human beings of all sorts, the high and the low,
Working and wandering as the world requires.
20   Some applied themselves to plowing, played very rarely,
Sowing seeds and setting plants worked very hard;
Won what wasters gluttonously consume.
And some pursued pride, put on proud clothing,
Came all got up in garments garish to see.
25   To prayers and penance many put themselves,
All for love of our Lord lived hard lives,
Hoping thereafter to have Heaven's bliss—
Such as hermits and anchorites[3] hold to their cells,
Don't care to go cavorting about the countryside,
30   With some lush livelihood delighting their bodies.
And some made themselves merchants—they managed better,
As it seems to our sight that such men prosper.
And some make mirth as minstrels can

1. Translated by E. Talbot Donaldson.
2. These hills in the west of England were probably Langland's original home.
3. Both were vowed to a religious life of solitude, hermits in the wilderness and anchorites walled in a tiny dwelling.

And get gold for their music, guiltless, I think.
35   But jokers and word jugglers, Judas' children,
Invent fantasies to tell about and make fools of themselves,
And have whatever wits they need to work if they wanted.
What Paul preaches of them I don't dare repeat here:
Qui loquitur turpiloquium[4] is Lucifer's henchman.
40   Beadsmen[5] and beggars bustled about
Till both their bellies and their bags were crammed to the brim;
Staged flytings° for their food, fought over beer.   *insult contests*
In gluttony, God knows, they go to bed.
And rise up with ribaldry, those Robert's boys.°   *robbers*
45   Sleep and sloth pursue them always.
     Pilgrims and palmers[6] made pacts with each other
To seek out Saint James[7] and saints at Rome.
They went on their way with many wise stories,
And had leave to lie all their lives after.
50   I saw some that said they'd sought after saints:
In every tale they told their tongues were tuned to lie
More than to tell the truth—such talk was theirs.
A heap of hermits with hooked staffs
Went off to Walsingham,[8] with their wenches behind them.
55   Great long lubbers that don't like to work
Dressed up in cleric's dress to look different from other men
And behaved as they were hermits, to have an easy life.
I found friars there—all four of the orders[9]—
Preaching to the people for their own paunches' welfare,
60   Making glosses of the Gospel that would look good for themselves;
Coveting copes,° they construed it as they pleased.   *monk's capes*
Many of these Masters° may clothe themselves richly,   *Divinity*
For their money and their merchandise march hand in hand.
Since Charity has proved a peddler and principally shrives[1] lords,
65   Many marvels have been manifest within a few years.
Unless Holy Church and friars' orders hold together better,
The worst misfortune in the world will be welling up soon.
     A pardoner[2] preached there as if he had priest's rights,
Brought out a bull° with bishop's seals,   *papal license*
70   And said he himself could absolve them all
Of failure to fast, of vows they'd broken.
Unlearned men believed him and liked his words,
Came crowding up on knees to kiss his bulls.
He banged them with his brevet° and bleared their eyes,   *pardoner's license*
75   And raked in with his parchment-roll rings and brooches.
Thus you give your gold for gluttons' well-being,

4. Who speaks filthy language; not Paul, though (cf. Ephesians 5.3–4).
5. People who said prayers, often counting on rosary beads, for the souls of those who gave them alms.
6. "Professional" pilgrims who took advantage of the hospitality offered them in order to travel.
7. That is, his shrine at Compostela, in Spain.
8. English town, site of a famous shrine to the Virgin Mary.

9. The four orders of friars—Franciscans, Dominicans, Carmelites, and Augustinians. In 14th-century England they were much satirized for their corruption (cf. the friar in the *General Prologue* to Chaucer's *Canterbury Tales*).
1. Confesses. Confession and the remission of sins (shrift) is the "merchandise" cynically sold by the friars.
2. An official empowered to pass on from the pope absolution for the sins of people who had given money to charity.

And squander it on scoundrels schooled in lechery.
If the bishop were blessed and worth both his ears,
His seal should not be sent out to deceive the people.
80   —It's nothing to the bishop that the blackguard preaches,
And the parish priest and the pardoner split the money
That the poor people of the parish would have but for them.
     Parsons and parish priests complained to the bishop
That their parishes were poor since the pestilence-time,[3]
85   Asked for license and leave to live in London,
And sing Masses there for simony,[4] for silver is sweet.
Bishops and Bachelors, both Masters and Doctors,[5]
Who have cures under Christ and their crowns shaven
As a sign that they should shrive their parishioners,
90   Preach and pray for them, and provide for the poor,
Take lodging in London in Lent and other seasons.
Some serve the king and oversee his treasury,
In the Exchequer and in Chancery[6] press charges for debts
Involving wards' estates and city-wards, waifs and strays.
95   And some like servants serve lords and ladies
And in the stead of stewards° sit and make judgments.   *estate managers*
Their Masses and their matins and many of their Hours[7]
Are done undevoutly: there's dread that in the end
Christ in his consistory will condemn full many.
100   I pondered on the power that Peter had in keeping
To bind and unbind as the Book tells,[8]
How he left it with love as our Lord commanded
Among four virtues, most virtuous of all,
That are called "cardinals"—and closing gates
105   Of the kingdom of Christ, who may close and lock them,
Or else open them up and show Heaven's bliss.
But as for the cardinals at court that thus acquired their name
And presumed they had the power to appoint a pope
Who should have the power that Peter had—well I'll not impugn them,
110   For the election belongs to love and to learning:
Therefore I can and cannot speak of court further.
     Then there came a king, knighthood accompanied him,
Might of the community made him a ruler.
And then came Kind Wit, and he created clerks
115   To counsel the king and keep the commons safe.
The king in concert with knighthood and with clergy as well
Contrived that the commons should provide their commons[9] for them.
The commons with Kind Wit contrived various crafts,
And for profit of all the people appointed plowmen
120   To till and to toil as true life requires.

3. Since 1349 England had suffered a number of epidemics of the Black Death (i.e., the bubonic plague).
4. Buying and selling church offices or spiritual functions.
5. Bachelors and Doctors of Divinity.
6. The Exchequer was a royal commission that received revenue and audited accounts; Chancery dealt with petitions addressed to the king.
7. Clerics organized their day around seven canonical "hours," of which matins was the first.
8. Matthew 16.18–20 recounts Christ's giving Peter and the succeeding popes the authority to make pronouncements on earth that will also be binding in Heaven.
9. The first occurrence of "commons" in this line means "the common people"; the second, "food."

The king and the commons and Kind Wit the third
Defined law and lewte°—for every kind of life, known limits.   *justice*
Then a lunatic looked up—a lean one at that—
And counseled the king with clerkly words, kneeling before him:
125   "Christ keep you, sir King, and the kingdom you rule
And grant you to lead your land so that Lewte loves you,
And for your righteous ruling be rewarded in Heaven."
And after in the air on high an angel of Heaven
Came low to speak in Latin, for illiterate men lacked
130   The jargon or the judgment to justify themselves,
But can only suffer and serve; therefore said the angel:
"'I'm a king. I'm a prince!'—Neither perhaps when you've gone hence.
You, King, who're here to save the special laws that King Christ gave.
To do this better you will find it's well to be less just than kind.
135   *By you law's naked truth wants to be clothed in ruth.°*   *mercy*
Such seeds as you sow, such a crop will grow.
If you strip law bare, bare law will be your share.
If you sow pity, you'll be sitting pretty."
Then a Goliard[1] grew angry, a glutton of words,
140   And to the angel on high answered after:
"Since the name of king, rex, comes from regere, 'to rule,'
Unless he law directs, he's a wright without a tool."
Then all the commons commenced to cry in Latin verse
To the king's council—let who will construe it:
145   *"What the king ordains is to us the law's chains."*
With that there ran a rabble of rats together,
And little mice along with them, no less than a thousand,
Came to a council for their common profit;
For a cat of court came when he pleased
150   And leapt lightly over them and when he liked seized them,
And played with them perilously, and pushed them about.
"For dread of various deeds we hardly dare move,
And if we grumble at his games he will grieve us all,
Scratch us or claw us or catch us in his clutches.
155   So that we'll loathe life before he lets us go.
If by any wit we might withstand his will
We could be lofty as lords and live at our ease."
A rat of renown, most ready of tongue,
Said as a sovereign salve for them all:
160   "I've seen creatures," he said, "in the city of London
Bear chains full bright about their necks,
And collars of fine craftsmanship; they come and go without leashes
Both in warren and in wasteland, wherever they please;
And at other times they are in other places, as I hear tell.
165   If there were a bell to clink on their collars, by Christ, I think
We could tell where they went and keep well out of their way.
And right so," said the rat, "reason tells me
To buy a bell of brass or of bright silver
And clip it on a collar for our common profit

---

1. A wandering student or cleric. Goliards were known for satirical songs and poetry that attacked the clerical establishment.

170   And hang it over the cat's head; then we'd be able to hear
        Whether he's riding or resting or roving out to play.
        And if he desires sport we can step out
        And appear in his presence while he's pleased to play.
        And if he's angry we'll take heed and stay out of his way."
175   This whole convention of vermin was convinced by this advice,
        But when the bell was brought and bound to the collar
        There was no rat in the rabble, for all the realm of France,
        That dared bind the bell about the cat's neck
        Or hang it over his head to win all England;
180   But they held themselves faint-hearted and their whole plan foolish,
        And allowed all their labor lost, and all their long scheming.
        A mouse that knew much good, as it seemed to me then,
        Strode forth sternly and stood before them all,
        And to the rats arrayed there recited these words:
185   "Though we killed the cat, yet there would come another
        To scratch us and all our kind though we crept under benches.
        Therefore I counsel all the commons to let the cat alone,
        And let's never be so bold as to show the bell to him.
        While he's catching conies° he doesn't crave our flesh,   rabbits
190   But feeds himself on rich food—let's not defame him.
        For a little loss is better than a long sorrow:
        We'd all be muddling through a maze though we'd removed one foe.
        For I heard my sire say, seven years ago,
        Where the cat is a kitten, the court is wholly wretched.
195   That's how Holy Writ reads, whoever wants to look:
        Woe to the land where the king is a child![2]
        For no creature may rest quiet because of rats at night,
        And many a man's malt we mice would destroy,
        And also you rabble of rats would ruin men's clothing
200   If it weren't for the court-cat that can outleap you.
        For if you rats held the reins, you couldn't rule yourselves.
        I speak for myself," said the mouse, "I foresee such trouble later,
        That by my counsel neither cat nor kitten shall be grieved—
        And let's have no carping of this collar, that cost me nothing.
205   And though it had cost me money, I'd not admit it had—
        But suffer as himself wishes to slay what he pleases,
        Coupled and uncoupled let them catch what they will.
        Therefore I warn every wise creature to stick to what's his own."
        —What this dream may mean, you men that are merry,
210   You divine, for I don't dare, by dear God in Heaven.
              Yet scores of men stood there in silken coifs
        Who seemed to be law-sergeants[3] that served at the bar,
        Pleaded cases for pennies and impounded the law,
        And not for love of our Lord once unloosed their lips:
215   You might better measure mist on Malvern Hills
        Than get a "mum" from their mouths till money's on the table.

---

2. Ecclesiastes 10.16. A reference to the boy-king Richard II.

3. Important lawyers; a silk scarf, or "coif," was a lawyer's badge of office.

Barons and burgesses and bondmen[4] also
I saw in this assemblage, as you shall hear later;
Bakers and brewers and butchers aplenty,
220   Weavers of wool and weavers of linen,
Tailors, tinkers, tax-collectors in markets,
Masons, miners, many other craftsmen.
Of all living laborers there leapt forth some,
Such as diggers of ditches that do their jobs badly,
225   And dawdle away the long day with *"Dieu save dame Emme."*[5]
Cooks and their kitchen-boys kept crying, "Hot pies, hot!
Good geese and pork! Let's go and dine!"
Tavern-keepers told them a tale of the same sort:
"White wine of Alsace and wine of Gascony,
230   Of the Rhine and of La Rochelle, to wash the roast down with."
All this I saw sleeping, and seven times more.

Passus 2

[THE MARRIAGE OF LADY MEAD]

Still kneeling on my knees I renewed my plea for grace
And said, "Mercy, madam, for Mary's love in heaven,
Who bore the blissful babe that bought° us on the Cross,   *redeemed*
Teach me some talent to distinguish the false."
5   "Look on your left side, and lo, where he stands,
Both False and Favel[1] and lots of fellows of theirs."
I looked on my left side as the lady told me
And was aware of a woman wonderfully dressed.
Her gown was faced with fur, the finest on earth;
10   Crowned with a coronet—the king has none better.
Her fingers were filigreed fancifully with gold,
And rich rubies on them, as red as hot coals,
And diamonds most dear of cost, and two different kinds of sapphires,
Pearls and precious water-stones to repel poisons.
15   Her robe was most rich, dyed with red-scarlet,
With ribbons of red gold and with rich stones.
Her array ravished me—I'd seen such riches nowhere.
I wondered who she was and whose wife she might be.
    "Who is this woman," said I, "so worthily attired?"
20   "That is Meed[2] the maid who has harmed me very often
And maligned my lover—Lewte° is his name—   *Justice*
And has told lords who enforce laws lies about him.
In the Pope's palace she's as privileged as I am,
But Soothness[3] would not have it so, for she is a bastard,
25   And her father was false—he has a fickle tongue
And never told the truth since the time he came to earth.

---

4. Barons were members of the higher aristocracy; burgesses were town-dwellers with full rights as citizens; and bondmen were peasants who held their land from a lord in return for services or rent.
5. Presumably a popular song.
1. "Lying"; the name of characters representing deceit in

Old French literature.
2. A richly ambiguous word referring to a wide variety of "reward," both positive and negative, including just reward, heavenly salvation, recompense, the profit motive, graft, and bribery.
3. Truth, truthfulness, fidelity.

And Meed has manners like his, as men say is natural:
> Like father, like son. A good tree brings forth good fruit.
I ought to be higher than she: I came of better parentage.
My father is the great God, the giver of all graces,
30   One God without beginning, and I'm his good daughter.
And he's granted me that I might marry Mercy as my own,
And any man who's merciful and loves me truly
Shall be my lord and I his love, aloft in Heaven;
And the man who takes Meed—I'll bet my head on it—
35   Shall lose for her love a lump of *caritatis*.[4]
What does David the King declare of men that crave meed
And of the others on earth who uphold truth,
And how you shall save yourselves? The Psalter[5] bears witness:
> Lord, who shall dwell in thy tabernacle? etc.
40   And now this Meed is being married to a most accursed wretch,
To one False Fickle-Tongue—a fiend begot him.
Favel through his fair speech has these folk under enchantment,
And it's all by Liar's leadership that this lady is thus wedded.
Tomorrow will be made the maiden's bridal,
45   If you wish you may witness there who they all are
That belong to that lordship, the lesser and the greater.
Acquaint yourself with them if you can, and keep clear of them all,
And don't malign them but let them be until Lewte becomes justice
And has power to punish them—then put forth your evidence.
50   Now I commend you to Christ," said she, "and to Christ's pure mother,
And don't let your conscience be overcome by coveting Meed."
    Thus that lady left me lying asleep,
And how Meed was married was shown me in a dream—
How all the rich retinue that rule with False
55   Were bidden to the bridal for both sides of the match,
Of all manner of men, the moneyless and the rich;
To marry off this maiden many men were assembled,
Including knights and clerks and other common people,
Such as assizers and summoners, sheriffs and their clerks,
60   Beadles and bailiffs and brokers of merchandise,
Harbingers and hostelers and advocates of the Arches[6]—
I can't reckon the rabble that ran about Meed.
But Simony and Civil[7] and assizers of courts
Were most intimate with Meed of any men, I thought.
65   But Favel was the first that fetched her from her bedroom
And like a broker brought her to be joined to False.
    When Simony and Civil saw the couple's wish
They assented for silver to say as both wanted.
Then Liar leaped forth and said, "Lo, here's a charter
70   That Guile with his great oaths has given them jointly."
And he prayed Simony to inspect it and Civil to read it.
Simony and Civil both stand forth

---

4. Of love (Latin).
5. The book of Psalms.
6. The officials in this and the two preceding lines had jobs that made them particularly open to bribery.

7. Simony is the buying and selling of church offices or spiritual functions; Civil is civil as opposed to criminal law (especially noted for its bribery and corruption).

And unfold the conveyance that False has made;
Then these characters commence to cry on high:
      Let men now living and those to come after know, etc.[8]
75   "Let all who are on earth hear and bear witness
That Meed is married more for her property
Than for any goodness or grace or any goodly parentage.
Falseness fancies her for he knows she's rich,
And Favel with his fickle speech enfeoffs[9] them by this charter
80   That they may be princes in pride and despise Poverty,
Backbite and boast and bear false witness,
Scorn and scold and speak slander,
Disobedient and bold break the Ten Commandments;
And the Earldom of Envy and Ire together,
85   With the Castelet[1] of Quarreling and uncurbed Gossip,
The County of Covetousness and the countryside about,
That is Usury and Avarice—all I grant them
In bargainings and brokerings with the Borough of Theft,
With all the Lordship of Lechery in length and in breadth,
90   As in works and in words and with watching of eyes,
And in wild wishes and fantasies and with idle thoughts,
When to do what their wills would they want° the strength."   lack
Gluttony he gave them too and great oaths together,
And to drink all day at diverse taverns,
95   And to jabber there, and joke, and judge their fellow-Christians;
And to gobble food on fasting days before the fitting time,
And then to sit supping till sleep assails them,
And grow portly as town-pigs, and repose in soft beds,
Till sloth and sleep sleek their sides;
100   And then they'll wake up with Wanhope,[2] with no wish to amend,
For he believes he's lost—this is their last fortune.
"And they to have and to hold and their heirs after them
A dwelling with the Devil, and be damned forever,
With all the appurtenances of Purgatory, into the pain of hell,
105   Yielding for this thing at some year's end
Their souls to Satan, to suffer pain with him,
And to live with him in woe while God is in Heaven."
To witness which thing Wrong was the first,
And Piers the pardoner of Pauline doctrine,
110   Bart the beadle of Buckinghamshire,
Reynold the reeve of Rutland district,
Mund the miller and many more besides.
"In the date of the Devil this deed is sealed
In sight of Sir Simony and with Civil's approval."
115   Then Theology grew angry when he heard all this talk,
And said to Civil, "Now sorrow on your books,
To permit such a marriage to make Truth angry;
And before this wedding is performed, may it befall you foul!

8. The formula for the beginning of a charter, a legal document often conveying rights or property.
9. Grants them territory in the manner of a feudal lord, to
be specifically held by them as his liegemen, in return for

military and other service.
1. Little castle.
2. Despair, considered the ultimate development of sloth,
one of the seven deadly sins.

Since Meed is *mulier*³—Amends is her parent—
120 God granted to give Meed to truth,
And you've bestowed her on a deceiver, now God send you sorrow!
The text does not tell you so, Truth knows what's true,
For *dignus est operarius*⁴ to have his hire.
And you've fastened her to False—fie on your law!
125 For you live wholly by lies and by lecherous acts.
Simony and yourself are sullying Holy Church;
The notaries⁵ and you are noxious to the people.
You shall both make amends for it, by God that made me!
You know well, you wastrels, unless your wits are failing,
130 That False is unflaggingly fickle in his deeds,
And like a bastard born of Beëlzebub's° kindred.   *Satan's*
And Meed is *mulier*, a maiden of property:
She could kiss the king for cousin if she wished.
Work with wisdom and with your wit as well:
135 Lead her to London where law is determined—
If it's legally allowable for them to lie together.
And if the Justice judges it's right to join her with False,
Yet be wary of the wedding, for Truth is wise and discerning,
And Conscience is of his council and knows all your characters,
140 And if he finds that you've offended and are one of False's followers,
It shall beset your soul most sourly in the end."
      Civil assents to this, but Simony was unwilling
Till he had silver for his seal and the stamps of the notaries.
Then Favel fetched forth florins° enough   *gold coins*
145 And bade Guile, "Go give gold all about,
And don't neglect the notaries, see that they need nothing.
And fee False Witness with florins enough,
For he may overmaster Meed and make her obey me."
When this gold had been given, there was great thanking
150 To False and Favel for their fair gifts.
And they all came to comfort False from the care that afflicted him,
And said, "Be sure we shall never cease our efforts
Till Meed is your wedded wife through wit of us all,
For we've overmastered Meed with our merry speech
155 So that she grants to go with a good will
To London to learn whether law would
Judge you jointly in joy forever."
Then False felt well pleased and Favel was glad,
And they sent to summon all men in shires about,
160 And bade them all be ready, beggars and others,
To go with them to Westminster to witness this deed.
And then they had to have horses to haul them thither;
Then Favel fetched foals of the best;
Set Meed on a sheriff shod all new;
165 And False sat on an assizer that softly trotted,

---

3. Literally, "woman"; technically, a woman of legitimate
birth.
4. Worthy is the laborer (Luke 10.7).

5. Officials charged with drawing up important documents, also the clerks or secretaries of important persons.

And Favel on Fair Speech, clad in feigning clothes.
Then notaries had no horses, and were annoyed also
Because Simony and Civil should walk on foot.
But then Simony swore and Civil as well
170 That summoners[6] should be saddled and serve them all:
"And let these provisors[7] be put into palfrey's harness;
Sir Simony himself shall sit on their backs.
Deans and subdeans,[8] you draw together,
Archdeacons and officials and all your registrars,
175 Let them be saddled with silver to suffer our sins
Such as adultery and divorce and clandestine usury,[9]
To bear bishops about, abroad on visitations.
Pauline's people, for complaints in the consistory,[1]
Shall serve myself, Civil is my name.
180 And let the commissary[2] be cart-saddled and our cart pulled by him,
And he must fetch us victuals from *fornicatores.*°   *fornicators*
And make a long cart of Liar, loaded with all the rest,
Such as twisters and tricksters that trot on their feet."
False and Favel fare forth together,
185 And Meed in the midst and her serving men behind.
I've no opportunity to tell of the tail of the procession,
Of many manner of men that move over this earth.
But Guile was foregoer and guided them all.
    Soothness saw them well and said but a little,
190 And pressed ahead on his palfrey and passed them all
And came to the King's court and told Conscience about it,
And Conscience recounted it to the King afterward.
"By Christ!" said the King, "if I can catch
False or Favel or any of his fellows,
195 I'll be avenged on those villains that act so viciously,
And have them hanged by the neck, and all who support them.
Shall no bondsman be allowed to go bail for the least,
But whatever law will allot, let it fall on them all."
And he commanded a constable that came straightway
200 To "detain those tyrants, despite their treasure, I say;
Fetter Falseness fast no matter what he gives you,
And get Guile's head off at once—let him go no farther;
And bring Meed to me no matter what they do.
Simony and Civil, I send to warn them
205 That their actions will hurt Holy Church forever.
And if you lay hand on Liar, don't let him escape
Before he's put in the pillory, for any prayer he makes."
    Dread stood at the door and heard this declaration,
How the King commanded constables and sergeants

---

6. Officials who served summons to the ecclesiastical courts, which dealt with matters of private morality. They were much feared because of their power to blackmail and demand bribes.
7. Clerics nominated to their benefices directly by the pope; petitions for such offices were regularly accompanied by bribes.
8. Clerics in charge of a body of priests generally attached to a cathedral; thought to be open to bribery.
9. Lending money for interest.
1. A bishop's court.
2. The bishop's official representative in part of his diocese.

210   That Falseness and his fellowship should be fettered and bound.
       Then Dread came away quickly and cautioned the False
       And bade him flee for fear and his fellows too.
       Then Falseness for fear fled to the friars;
       And Guile in dread of death dashed away fast.
215   But merchants met with him and made him stay
       And shut him up in their shop to show their wares,
       Appareled him as an apprentice to wait on purchasers.
       Lightly Liar leapt away then,
       Lurking through lanes, belabored by many:
220   Nowhere was he welcome for his many tales,
       Everywhere hunted out and ordered to pack,
       Till pardoners took pity and pulled him indoors;
       Washed him and wiped him and wound him in cloths,
       And sent him on Sundays with seals[3] to church,
225   Where he gave pardon for pennies by the pound about.
       Then doctors were indignant and drafted letters to him
       That he should come and stay with them to examine urine.
       Apothecaries wanted to employ him to appraise their wares,
       For he was trained in their trade and could distinguish many gums.[4]
230   But minstrels and messengers met with him once
       And had him with them half a year and eleven days.
       Friars with fair speech fetched him thence;
       To keep him safe from the curious they coped him as a friar
       But he has leave to leap out as often as he pleases,
235   And is welcome to come when he wants, and he stays with them often.
       All fled for fear and flew into corners;
       Except for Meed the maid none remained there.
       But truly to tell she trembled for dread
       And twisted about tearfully when she was taken into custody.

from *Passus 5*

[THE CONFESSION OF GLUTTON]

       Now Glutton begins to go to shrift
       And takes his way towards the Church to tell his sins.
       But Betty the brewer bade him good morning
       And she asked him where he was going.
300   "To Holy Church," he said, "to hear Mass,
       And then I shall be shriven and sin no more."
       "I've got good ale, old friend," she said. "Glutton, will you try it?"
       "Have you," he asked, "any hot spices?"
       "I have pepper and peony and a pound of garlic,
305   A farthingworth of fennel seed[1] for fasting days."
       Then Glutton goes in, and great oaths after.
       Cissy the seamstress was sitting on the bench,
       Wat the warren-keeper and his wife too,

---

3. A pardoner needed the bishop's seal on the document that gave him license to preach and collect money for indulgences in a particular diocese or district.

4. Gums used as perfumes, spices, and medicines.
1. An herb thought to be good for someone drinking on an empty stomach.

Tim the tinker and two of his servants,
310   Hick the hackneyman and Hugh the needle-seller,
Clarice of Cock's Lane[2] and the clerk of the church,
Sir Piers of Pridie and Parnel of Flanders,
Dave the ditch-digger and a dozen others,
A rebeck-player,[3] a rat-catcher, a street-raker of Cheapside,
315   A rope-maker, a redingking and Rose the dish vendor,
Godfrey of Garlickhithe and Griffin the Welshman,
A heap of old-clothesmen early in the morning
Gladly treated Glutton to drinks of good ale.
    Clement the cobbler took the cloak off his back
320   And put it up as a prize for a player of "New Fair."[4]
Then Hick the ostler took off his hood
And bade Bart the butcher to be on his side.
Then peddlers were appointed to appraise the goods:
For his cloak Clement should get the hood plus compensation.
325   They went to work quickly and whispered together
And appraised these prize items apart by themselves.
There were heaps of oaths for any one to hear.
They couldn't in conscience come to an agreement
Till Robin the roper was requested to rise
330   And named as an umpire so no quarrel should break out.
Then Hick the ostler had the cloak
In covenant that Clement should have the cup filled
And have Hick the ostler's hood, and call it a deal;
The first to regret the agreement should get up straightway
335   And greet Sir Glutton with a gallon of ale.
There was laughing and louring and "Let go the cup!"
They began to make bets and bought more rounds
And sat so till evensong[5] and sang sometimes
Till Glutton had gulped down a gallon and a gill.
340   His guts began to grumble like two greedy sows;
He pissed four pints in a Paternoster's length;[6]
And on the bugle of his backside he blew a fanfare
So that all that heard that horn held their noses after
And wished it had been waxed up[7] with a wisp of gorse.
345   He had no strength to stand before he had his staff in hand,
And then he made off moving like a minstrel's bitch[8]
Some times sideways and some times backwards,
Like some one laying lines to lime birds with.
But as he started to step to the door his sight grew dim;
350   He fumbled for the threshold and fell on the ground.
Clement the cobbler caught him by the waist.
To lift him aloft and laid him on his knees.
But Glutton was a large lout and a load to lift,
And he coughed up a custard in Clement's lap.

---

2. Clarice and Parnel (of the next line) are prostitutes.
3. Fiddle-player.
4. An elaborate game involving the exchange of clothing.
5. Vespers, the evening prayer service said just before sunset.

6. The time it takes to say the Paternoster, the Lord's Prayer.
7. Sealed up with gorse, a shiny shrub.
8. Trained dog performing on her hind legs.

355　There's no hound so hungry in Hertfordshire
　　That would dare lap up that leaving, so unlovely the taste.
　　　With all the woe in this world his wife and his maid
　　Brought him to his bed and bundled him in it.
　　And after all this excess he had a fit of sloth
360　So that he slept Saturday and Sunday till the sun set.
　　When he was awake and wiped his eyes,
　　The first word he spoke was, "Where is the bowl?"
　　His spouse scolded him for his sin and wickedness,
　　And right so Repentance rebuked him at that time.
365　"As with words as well as with deeds you've done evil in your life,
　　Shrive yourself and be ashamed, and show it with your mouth."
　　"I, Glutton," he began, "admit I'm guilty of this:
　　That I've trespassed with my tongue, I can't tell how often;
　　Sworn by God's soul and his sides and 'So God help me!'
370　When there was no need for it nine hundred times.
　　And over-stuffed myself at supper and sometimes at midday,
　　So that I, Glutton, got rid of it before I'd gone a mile,
　　And spoiled what might have been saved and dispensed to the hungry;
　　Over-indulgently on feast days I've drunk and eaten both;
375　And sometimes sat so long there that I slept and ate at once;
　　To hear tales in taverns I've taken more drink;
　　Fed myself before noon on fasting days."
　　"This full confession," said Repentance, "will gain favor for you."
　　Then Glutton began to groan and to make great lament
380　For the life he had lived in so loathsome a way,
　　And vowed he would fast, what for hunger or for thirst:
　　"Shall never fish on Friday be fed to my belly
　　Till Abstinence my aunt has given me leave,
　　And yet I have hated her all my lifetime."

Passus 6

[PIERS PLOWING THE HALF-ACRE]

　　"This would be a bewildering way unless we had a guide
　　Who could trace our way foot by foot": thus these folk complained.
　　Said Perkin[1] the Plowman, "By Saint Peter of Rome!
　　I have a half-acre to plow by the highway;
5　If I had plowed this half-acre and afterwards sowed it,
　　I would walk along with you and show you the way to go."
　　"That would be a long delay," said a lady in a veil.
　　"What ought we women to work at meanwhile?"
　　"Some shall sew sacks to stop the wheat from spilling.
10　And you lovely ladies, with your long fingers,
　　See that you have silk and sendal[2] to sew when you've time
　　Chasubles° for chaplains for the Church's honor.　　　　　　　　robes
　　Wives and widows, spin wool and flax;
　　Make cloth, I counsel you, and teach the craft to your daughters.

---

1. A nickname for Piers, or Peter.　　　　　　2. A thin, rich form of silk.

Plowmen, from the *Luttrell Psalter,* early 14th century.

15   The needy and the naked, take note how they fare:
Keep them from cold with clothing, for so Truth wishes.
For I shall supply their sustenance unless the soil fails
As long as I live, for the Lord's love in Heaven.
And all sorts of folk that feed on farm products,
20   Busily abet him who brings forth your food."
"By Christ!" exclaimed a knight then, "your counsel is the best.
But truly, how to drive a team has never been taught me.
But show me," said the knight, "and I shall study plowing."
"By Saint Paul," said Perkin, "since you proffer help so humbly,
25   I shall sweat and strain and sow for us both,
And also labor for your love all my lifetime,
In exchange for your championing Holy Church and me
Against wasters and wicked men who would destroy me.
And go hunt hardily hares and foxes,
30   Boars and bucks that break down my hedges,
And have falcons at hand to hunt down the birds
That come to my croft° and crop my wheat."   *field*
Thoughtfully the knight then spoke these words:
"By my power, Piers, I pledge you my word
35   To uphold this obligation though I have to fight.
As long as I live I shall look after you."
"Yes, and yet another point," said Piers, "I pray you further:
See that you trouble no tenant unless Truth approves,
And though you may amerce° him, let Mercy set the fine,   *fine*
40   And Meekness be your master no matter what Meed does.
And though poor men proffer you presents and gifts,
Don't accept them for it's uncertain that you deserve to have them.
For at some set time you'll have to restore them
In a most perilous place called purgatory.
45   And treat no bondman badly—you'll be the better for it;
Though here he is your underling, it could happen in Heaven
That he'll be awarded a worthier place, one with more bliss:
      Friend, go up higher.[3]

3. Luke 14.10.

For in the charnelhouse[4] at church churls are hard to distinguish,
Or a knight from a knave: know this in your heart.
50   And see that you're true of your tongue, and as for tales—hate them
Unless they have wisdom and wit for your workmen's instruction.
Avoid foul-mouthed fellows and don't be friendly to their stories,
And especially at your repasts shun people like them,
For they tell the Fiend's fables—be very sure of that."
55   "I assent, by Saint James," said the knight then,
"To work by your word while my life lasts."
"And I shall apparel myself," said Perkin, "in pilgrims' fashion
And walk along the way with you till we find Truth."
He donned his working-dress, some darned, some whole,
60   His gaiters and his gloves to guard his limbs from cold,
And hung his seed-holder behind his back instead of a knapsack:
"Bring a bushel of bread-wheat for me to put in it,
For I shall sow it myself and set out afterwards
On a pilgrimage as palmers[5] do to procure pardon.
65   And whoever helps me plow or work in any way
Shall have leave, by our Lord, to glean my land in harvest-time,
And make merry with what he gets, no matter who grumbles.
And all kinds of craftsmen that can live in truth,
I shall provide food for those that faithfully live,
70   Except for Jack the juggler and Jonette from the brothel,
And Daniel the dice-player and Denot the pimp,
And Friar Faker and folk of his order,
And Robin the ribald for his rotten speech.
Truth told me once and bade me tell it abroad:
75   *Deleantur de libro viventium.*[6] I should have no dealings with them,
For Holy Church is under orders to ask no tithes[7] of them.
        For let them not be written with the righteous.[8]
Their good luck has left them, the Lord amend them now."
Dame-Work-When-It's-Time-To was Piers's wife's name;
His daughter was called Do-Just-So-Or-Your-Dame-Will-Beat-You;
80   His son was named Suffer-Your-Sovereigns-To-Have-Their-Will-
Condemn-Them-Not-For-If-You-Do-You'll-Pay-A-Dear-Price-
Let-God-Have-His-Way-With-All-Things-For-So-His-Word-Teaches.
"For now I am old and hoary and have something of my own,
To penance and to pilgrimage I'll depart with these others;
85   Therefore I will, before I go away, have my will written:
'In Dei nomine, amen,'[9] I make this myself.
He shall have my soul that has deserved it best,
And defend it from the Fiend—for so I believe—
Till I come to his accounting, as my Creed teaches me—
90   To have release and remission I trust in his rent book.
The kirk° shall have my corpse and keep my bones,   *church*
For of my corn and cattle it craved the tithe:

---

4. Crypt for dead bodies.
5. "Professional" pilgrims.
6. Let them be blotted out of the book of the living. (Psalms 68.29).
7. Because the money they make is illegitimate, they do

not owe the church the customary tithes, or ten percent of their income.
8. Psalms 68.29.
9. In the name of God, amen; customary beginning of a will.

I paid it promptly for peril of my soul;
It is obligated, I hope, to have me in mind
95 And commemorate me in its prayers among all Christians.
My wife shall have what I won with truth, and nothing else,
And parcel it out among my friends and my dear children.
For though I die today, my debts are paid;
I took back what I borrowed before I went to bed.'
100 As for the residue and the remnant, by the Rood of Lucca,[1]
I will worship Truth with it all my lifetime,
And be his pilgrim at the plow for poor men's sake.
My plowstaff shall be my pikestaff and push at the roots
And help my coulter° to cut and cleanse the furrows."   slow blade
105 Now Perkin and the pilgrims have put themselves to plowing.
Many there helped him to plow his half-acre.
Ditchers and diggers dug up the ridges;
Perkin was pleased by this and praised them warmly.
There were other workmen who worked very hard:
110 Each man in his manner made himself a laborer,
And some to please Perkin pulled up the weeds.
At high prime[2] Piers let the plow stand
To oversee them himself; whoever worked best
Should be hired afterward, when harvest-time came.
115 Then some sat down and sang over ale
And helped plow the half-acre with "Ho! trolly-lolly!"[3]
"Now by the peril of my soul!" said Piers in pure wrath,
"Unless you get up again and begin working now,
No grain that grows here will gladden you at need,
120 And though once off the dole you die let the Devil care!"
Then fakers were afraid and feigned to be blind;
Some set their legs askew as such loafers can
And made their moan to Piers, how they might not work:
    "We have no limbs to labor with, Lord, we thank you;
125 But we pray for you, Piers, and for your plow as well,
That God of his grace make your grain multiply,
And reward you for whatever alms you will give us here,
For we can't strain and sweat, such sickness afflicts us."
    "If what you say is so," said Piers, "I'll soon find out.
130 I know you're ne'er-do-wells, and Truth knows what's right,
And I'm his sworn servant and so should warn him
Which ones they are in this world that do his workmen harm.
You waste what men win with toil and trouble.
But Truth shall teach you how his team should be driven,
135 Or you'll eat barley bread and use the brook for drink;
Unless you're blind or broken-legged, or bolted° with iron—   braced
Those shall eat as well as I do, so God help me,
Till God of his goodness gives them strength to arise.
But you could work as Truth wants you to and earn wages and bread

---

1. Ornate crucifix in the Italian city of Lucca, which was
a popular object of pilgrimage.
2. Nine in the morning, after a substantial amount of

work has been done.
3. Probably the refrain of a popular song.

140   By keeping cows in the field, the corn from the cattle,
        Making ditches or dikes or dinging° on sheaves,   *beating*
        Or helping make mortar, or spreading much afield.
        You live in lies and lechery and in sloth too,
        And it's only for suffrance that vengeance has not fallen on you.
145   But anchorites and hermits that eat only at noon
        And nothing more before the morrow, they shall have my alms,
        And buy copes at my cost—those that have cloisters and churches.
        But Robert Runabout shall have no rag from me,
        Nor 'Apostles' unless they can preach and have the bishop's permission.
150   They shall have bread and boiled greens and a bit extra besides,
        For it's an unreasonable religious life that has no regular meals."
            Then Waster waxed angry and wanted to fight;
        To Piers the Plowman he proffered his glove.
        A Breton, a braggart, he bullied Piers too,
155   And told him to go piss with his plow, peevish wretch.
        "Whether you're willing or unwilling, we will have our will
        With your flour and your flesh, fetch it when we please,
        And make merry with it, no matter what you do."
        Then Piers the Plowman complained to the knight
160   To keep him safe, as their covenant was, from cursed rogues,
        "And from these wolfish wasters that lay waste the world,
        For they waste and win nothing, and there will never be
        Plenty among the people while my plow stands idle."
        Because he was born a courteous man the knight spoke kindly to Waster
165   And warned him he would have to behave himself better:
        "Or you'll pay the penalty at law, I promise, by my order!"
        "It's not my way to work," said Waster, "I won't begin now!"
        And made light of the law and lighter of the knight,
        And said Piers wasn't worth a pea or his plow either,
170   And menaced him and his men if they met again.
            "Now by the peril of my soul!" said Piers, "I'll punish you all."
        And he whooped after Hunger who heard him at once.
        "Avenge me on these vagabonds," said he, "that vex the whole world."
        Then Hunger in haste took hold of Waster by the belly
175   And gripped him so about the guts that his eyes gushed water.
        He buffeted the Breton about the cheeks
        That he looked like a lantern all his life after.
        He beat them both so that he almost broke their guts.
        Had not Piers with a pease loaf prayed him to leave off
180   They'd have been dead and buried deep, have no doubt about it.
        "Let them live," he said, "and let them feed with hogs,
        Or else on beans and bran baked together."
        Fakers for fear fled into barns
        And flogged sheaves with flails from morning till evening,
185   So that Hunger wouldn't be eager to cast his eye on them.
        For a potful of peas that Piers had cooked
        A heap of hermits laid hands on spades
        And cut off their copes and made short coats of them
        And went like workmen to weed and to mow,
190   And dug dirt and dung to drive off Hunger.

Blind and bedridden got better by the thousand;
Those who sat to beg silver were soon healed,
For what had been baked for Bayard[4] was boon to many hungry,
And many a beggar for beans obediently labored,
195 And every poor man was well pleased to have peas for his wages,
And what Piers prayed them to do they did as sprightly as sparrowhawks.
And Piers was proud of this and put them to work,
And gave them meals and money as they might deserve.
        Then Piers had pity and prayed Hunger to take his way
200 Off to his own home and hold there forever.
"I'm well avenged on vagabonds by virtue of you.
But I pray you, before you part," said Piers to Hunger,
"With beggars and street-beadsmen[5] what's best to be done?
For well I know that once you're away, they will work badly;
205 Misfortune makes them so meek now,
And it's for lack of food that these folk obey me.
And they're my blood brothers, for God bought us all.
Truth taught me once to love them every one
And help them with everything after their needs.
210 Now I'd like to learn, if you know, what line I should take
And how I might overmaster them and make them work."
        "Hear now," said Hunger, "and hold it for wisdom:
Big bold beggars that can earn their bread,
With hounds' bread and horses' bread hold up their hearts,
215 And keep their bellies from swelling by stuffing them with beans—
And if they begin to grumble, tell them to get to work,
And they'll have sweeter suppers once they've deserved them.
And if you find any fellow-man that fortune has harmed
Through fire or through false men, befriend him if you can.
220 Comfort such at your own cost, for the love of Christ in Heaven;
Love them and relieve them—so the law of Kind[6] directs.
        Bear ye one another's burdens[7]
And all manner of men that you may find
That are needy or naked and have nothing to spend,
With meals or with money make them the better.
225 Love them and don't malign them; let God take vengeance.
Though they behave ill, leave it all up to God
        Vengeance is mine and I will repay.[8]
And if you want to gratify God, do as the Gospel teaches,
And get yourself loved by lowly men: so you'll unloose his grace."
        Make to yourselves friends of the mammon of unrighteousness.[9]
"I would not grieve God," said Piers, "for all the goods on earth!
230 Might I do as you say without sin?" said Piers then.
"Yes, I give you my oath," said Hunger, "or else the Bible lies:
Go to Genesis the giant, engenderer of us all:
In sudore[1] and slaving you shall bring forth your food

4. A generic name for a horse; a bread made of beans and   8. Romans 12.19.
bran was fed to horses.   9. Luke 16.9.
5. Paid prayer-sayers.   1. In the sweat [of thy brow thou shalt eat bread] (Gene-
6. Nature (an aspect of God).   sis 3.19).
7. Galatians 6.2.

And labor for your livelihood, and so our Lord commanded.
235   And Sapience says the same—I saw it in the Bible.
Piger propter frigus[2] would plow no field;
He shall be a beggar and none abate his hunger.
Matthew with man's[3] face mouths these words:
'Entrusted with a talent, *servus nequam*[4] didn't try to use it,
240   And earned his master's ill-will for evermore after,
And he took away his talent who was too lazy to work,
And gave it to him in haste that had ten already;
And after he said so that his servants heard it,
He that has shall have, and help when he needs it,
245   And he that nothing has shall nothing have and no man help him,
And what he trusts he's entitled to I shall take away.'
Kind Wit wants each one to work,
Either in teaching or tallying or toiling with his hands,
Contemplative life or active life; Christ wants it too.
250   The Psalter says in the Psalm of *Beati omnes*,[5]
The fellow that feeds himself with his faithful labor,
He is blessed by the Book in body and in soul."
        The labors of thy hands, etc.[6]
"Yet I pray you," said Piers, "*pour charité*,[7] if you know
Any modicum of medicine, teach me it, dear sir.
255   For some of my servants and myself as well
For a whole week do not work, we've such aches in our stomachs."
"I'm certain," said Hunger, "what sickness ails you.
You've munched down too much: that's what makes you groan,
But I assure you," said Hunger, "if you'd preserve your health,
260   You must not drink any day before you've dined on something.
Never eat, I urge you, ere Hunger comes upon you
And sends you some of his sauce to add savor to the food;
And keep some till suppertime, and don't sit too long;
Arise up ere Appetite has eaten his fill.
265   Let not Sir Surfeit sit at your table;
Love him not for he's a lecher whose delight is his tongue,
And for all sorts of seasoned stuff his stomach yearns.
And if you adopt this diet, I dare bet my arms
That Physic for his food will sell his furred hood
270   And his Calabrian cloak with its clasps of gold,
And be content, by my troth, to retire from medicine
And learn to labor on the land lest livelihood fail him.
There are fewer physicians than frauds—reform them, Lord!—
Their drinks make men die before destiny ordains."
275   "By Saint Parnel," said Piers, "these are profitable words.
This is a lovely lesson; the Lord reward you for it!
Take your way when you will—may things be well with you always!"
"My oath to God!" said Hunger, "I will not go away

2. The sluggard [will not plow] by reason of the cold (Proverbs 20.4).
3. Each of the four Evangelists was represented by a different symbol; Matthew was represented by a man.
4. The wicked servant (Luke 19.22); a talent is a unit of money.
5. Blessed [are] all [who] (Psalms 127.1).
6. Psalms 127.2.
7. For charity.

Till I've dined this day and drunk as well."

280   "I've no penny," said Piers, "to purchase pullets,

And I can't get goose or pork; but I've got two green cheeses,

A few curds and cream and a cake of oatmeal,

A loaf of beans and bran baked for my children.

And yet I say, by my soul, I have no salt bacon

285   Nor any hen's egg, by Christ, to make ham and eggs,

But scallions aren't scarce, nor parsley, and I've scores of cabbages,

And also a cow and a calf, and a cart-mare

To draw dung to the field while the dry weather lasts.

By this livelihood I must live till Lammass[8] time

290   When I hope to have harvest in my garden.

Then I can manage a meal that will make you happy."

All the poor people fetched peasepods;

Beans and baked apples they brought in their skirts,

Chives and chervils and ripe cherries aplenty,

295   And offered Piers this present to please Hunger with.

Hunger ate this in haste and asked for more.

Then poor folk for fear fed Hunger fast,

Proffering leeks and peas, thinking to appease him.

And now harvest drew near and new grain came to market.

300   Then poor people were pleased and plied Hunger with the best;

With good ale as Glutton taught they got him to sleep.

Then Waster wouldn't work but wandered about,

And no beggar would eat bread that had beans in it,

But the best bread or the next best, or baked from pure wheat,

305   Nor drink any half-penny ale in any circumstances,

But of the best and the brownest that barmaids sell.

Laborers that have no land to live on but their hands

Deign not to dine today on last night's cabbage.

No penny-ale can please them, nor any piece of bacon,

310   But it must be fresh flesh or else fried fish,

And that *chaud* or *plus chaud*[9] so it won't chill their bellies.

Unless he's hired at high wages he will otherwise complain;

That he was born to be a workman he'll blame the time.

Against Cato's counsel he commences to murmur:

315   *Remember to bear your burden of poverty patiently.*[1]

He grows angry at God and grumbles against Reason,

And then curses the king and all the council after

Because they legislate laws that punish laboring men.

But while Hunger was their master there would none of them complain

320   Or strive against the statute,[2] so sternly he looked.

But I warn you workmen, earn wages while you may,

For Hunger is hurrying hitherward fast.

With waters he'll awaken Waster's chastisement;

Before five years are fulfilled such famine shall arise.

---

8. The harvest festival, August 1, when a loaf made from the first wheat of the season was offered at mass.
9. Hot or very hot.
1. From Cato's *Distichs*, a collection of phrases used to teach Latin to beginning students.

2. The Statutes of Laborers, passed after 1351, when the Black Death depopulated the countryside and a labor shortage ensued. They were intended to control the mobility and the wages of laborers.

325   Through flood and foul weather fruits shall fail,
       And so Saturn[3] says and has sent to warn you:
       When you see the moon amiss and two monks' heads,
       And a maid have the mastery, and multiply by eight,
       Then shall Death withdraw and Dearth be justice,
330   And Daw the diker° die for hunger,   *ditch-digger*
       Unless God of his goodness grants us a truce.

Passus 18

[THE CRUCIFIXION AND THE HARROWING OF HELL]

       Wool-chafed and wet-shoed I went forth after
       Like a careless creature unconscious of woe,
       And trudged forth like a tramp, all the time of my life,
       Till I grew weary of the world and wished to sleep again,
5   And lay down till Lent, and slept a long time,
       Rested there, snoring roundly, till *Ramis-Palmarum*.[1]
       I dreamed chiefly of children and cheers of *"Gloria, laus!"*[2]
       And how old folk to an organ sang *"Hosanna!"*
       And of Christ's passion and pain for the people he had reached for.
10   One resembling the Samaritan and somewhat Piers the Plowman
       Barefoot on an ass's back bootless came riding
       Without spurs or spear: sprightly was his look,
       As is the nature of a knight that draws near to be dubbed,
       To get himself gilt spurs and engraved jousting shoes.
15   Then was Faith watching from a window and cried, "A, *fili David!*"[3]
       As does a herald of arms when armed men come to joust.
       Old Jews of Jerusalem joyfully sang,
               "Blessed is he who cometh in the name of the Lord."[4]
       And I asked Faith to reveal what all this affair meant,
       And who was to joust in Jerusalem. "Jesus," he said,
20   "And fetch what the Fiend claims, the fruit of Piers the Plowman."
       "Is Piers in this place?" said I; and he pierced me with his look:
       "This Jesus for his gentleness will joust in Piers's arms,
       In his helmet and in his hauberk, *humana natura*,[5]
       So that Christ be not disclosed here as *consummatus Deus*.[6]
25   In the plate armor of Piers the Plowman this jouster will ride,
       For no dint will do him injury as in *deitate Patris*.[7]
       "Who shall joust with Jesus," said I, "Jews or Scribes?"[8]
       "No," said Faith, "but the Fiend and False-Doom-To-Die.
       Death says he will undo and drag down low
30   All that live or look upon land or water.
       Life says that he lies, and lays his life in pledge

3. Planet thought to influence the weather, generally perceived to be hostile.
1. Palm Sunday (literally, "branches of palms"): this part of the poem reflects the biblical account of Christ's entry into Jerusalem.
2. "Glory, praise [and honor]": the first words of an anthem sung by children on Palm Sunday.
3. On the first Palm Sunday, crowds greeted Christ crying "Hosanna [line 8] to the son of David."

4. Matthew 21.9.
5. A hauberk is a coat of mail; in the Incarnation Christ assumed human nature, to redeem humankind.
6. The perfect (triune) God.
7. In the godhead of the Father: as God Christ could not suffer, but as man he could.
8. Scribes were persons who made a strict literal interpretation of the Old Law and hence rejected Christ's teaching of the New.

That for all that Death can do, within three days he'll walk
And fetch from the Fiend the fruit of Piers the Plowman,
And place it where he pleases, and put Lucifer in bonds,
35   And beat and bring down burning death forever.
          O death, I will be thy death."[9]
        Then Pilate came with many people, *sedens pro tribunali,*[1]
To see how doughtily Death should do, and judge the rights of both.
The Jews and the justice were joined against Jesus,
And all the court cried upon him, "*Crucifige!*"[2] loud.
40   Then a plaintiff appeared before Pilate and said,
"This Jesus made jokes about Jerusalem's temple,
To have it down in one day and in three days after
Put it up again all new—here he stands who said it—
And yet build it every bit as big in all dimensions,
45   As long and as broad both, above and below."
"*Crucifige!*" said a sergeant, "he knows sorcerer's tricks."
"*Tolle! tolle!*"[3] said another, and took sharp thorns
And began to make a garland out of green thorn,
And set it sorely on his head and spoke in hatred,
50   "*Ave, Rabbi,*"[4] said that wretch, and shot reeds° at him;   arrows
They nailed him with three nails naked on a Cross,
And with a pole put a potion up to his lips
And bade him drink to delay his death and lengthen his days,
And said, "If you're subtle, let's see you help yourself.
55   If you are Christ and a king's son, come down from the Cross!
Then we'll believe that Life loves you and will not let you die."
"*Consummatum est,*"[5] said Christ and started to swoon,
Piteously and pale like a prisoner dying.
The Lord of Life and of Light then laid his eyelids together.
60   The day withdrew for dread and darkness covered the sun;
The wall wavered and split and the whole world quaked.
Dead men for that din came out of deep graves
And spoke of why that storm lasted so long:
"For a bitter battle," the dead body said;
65   "Life and Death in this darkness, one destroys the other.
No one will surely know which shall have the victory
Before Sunday about sunrise"; and sank with that to earth.
Some said that he was God's son that died so fairly:
          Truly this was the Son of God.[6]
        And some said he was a sorcerer: "We should see first
70   Whether he's dead or not dead before we dare take him down."
Two thieves were there that suffered death that time
Upon crosses beside Christ; such was the common law.
A constable came forth and cracked both their legs
And the arms afterward of each of those thieves.

---

9. Hosea 13.14.
1. Sitting as a judge (Matthew 27.19).
2. Crucify! (John 19.6).
3. "Away with him! Away with him!" (John 19.15).
4. "Hail, Rabbi [i.e., Master]" (Matthew 26.49): the

words Judas spoke when he kissed Christ to identify him
to the arresting officers.
5. "It is finished" (John 19.30).
6. Matthew 27.54.

75   But no bastard was so bold as to touch God's body there;
      Because he was a knight and a king's son, Nature decreed that time
      That no knave should have the hardiness to lay hand on him.
      But a knight with a sharp spear was sent forth there
      Named Longeus[7] as the legend tells, who had long since lost his sight;
80   Before Pilate and the other people in that place he waited on his horse.
      For all that he might demur, he was made that time
      To joust with Jesus, that blind Jew Longeus.
      For all who watched there were unwilling, whether mounted or afoot,
      To touch him or tamper with him or take him down from the cross,
85   Except this blind bachelor that bore him through the heart.
      The blood sprang down the spear and unsparred° his eyes.   opened
      The knight knelt down on his knees and begged Jesus for mercy.
      "It was against my will, Lord, to wound you so sorely."
      He sighed and said, "Sorely I repent it.
90   For what I here have done, I ask only your grace.
      Have mercy on me, rightful Jesu!" and thus lamenting wept.
      Then Faith began fiercely to scorn the false Jews,[8]
      Called them cowards, accursed forever.
      "For this foul villainy, may vengeance fall on you!
95   To make the blind beat the dead, it was a bully's thought.
      Cursed cowards, no kind of knighthood was it
      To beat a dead body with any bright weapon.
      Yet he's won the victory in the fight for all his vast wound,
      For your champion jouster, the chief knight of you all,
100   Weeping admits himself worsted and at the will of Jesus.
      For when this darkness is done, Death will be vanquished,
      And you louts have lost, for Life shall have the victory;
      And your unfettered freedom has fallen into servitude;
      And you churls and your children shall achieve no prosperity,
105   Nor have lordship over land or have land to till,
      But be all barren and live by usury,°   money-lending
      Which is a life that every law of our Lord curses.
      Now your good days are done as Daniel prophesied;
      When Christ came their kingdom's crown should be lost:
          When the Holy of Holies comes your anointing shall cease.[9]
110   What for fear of this adventure and of the false Jews
      I withdrew in that darkness to Descendit-ad-Inferna[1]
      And there I saw surely Secundum Scripturas[2]
      Where out of the west a wench, as I thought,
      Came walking on the way—she looked toward hell.
115   Mercy was that maid's name, a meek thing withal,
      A most gracious girl, and goodly of speech.
      Her sister as it seemed came softly walking
      Out of the east, opposite, and she looked westward,
      A comely creature and cleanly: Truth was her name.
120   Because of the virtue that followed her, she was afraid of nothing.

7. Longeus (usually Longinus) appears in the apocryphal Gospel of Nicodemus, which was the principal source of this account of Christ's harrowing of hell.
8. This and the next 18 lines are an example of late medieval antisemitism.
9. Compare with Daniel 9.24.
1. He descended into hell (from the Apostles' Creed).
2. According to the Scriptures.

When these maidens met, Mercy and Truth,
Each of them asked the other about this great wonder,
And of the din and of the darkness, and how the day lowered,
And what a gleam and a glint glowed before hell.

125 "I marvel at this matter, by my faith," said Truth,
"And am coming to discover what this queer affair means."
"Do not marvel," said Mercy, "it means only mirth.
A maiden named Mary, and mother without touching
By any kind of creature, conceived through speech

130 And grace of the Holy Ghost; grew great with child;
With no blemish to her woman's body brought him into this world.
And that my tale is true, I take God to witness,
Since this baby was born it has been thirty winters,
Who died and suffered death this day about midday.

135 And that is the cause of this eclipse that is closing off the sun,
In meaning that man shall be removed from darkness
While this gleam and this glow go to blind Lucifer.
For patriarchs and prophets have preached of this often
That man shall save man through a maiden's help,

140 And what a tree took away a tree shall restore,[3]
And what Death brought down a death shall raise up."
"What you're telling," said Truth, "is just a tale of nonsense.
For Adam and Eve and Abraham and the rest,
Patriarchs and prophets imprisoned in pain,

145 Never believe that yonder light will lift them up,
Or have them out of hell—hold your tongue, Mercy!
Your talk is mere trifling. I, Truth, know the truth,
For whatever is once in hell, it comes out never.
Job the perfect patriarch disproves what you say:
        Since in hell there is no redemption."[4]

150   Then Mercy most mildly uttered these words:
"From observation," she said, "I suppose they shall be saved,
Because venom destroys venom, and in that I find evidence
That Adam and Eve shall have relief.
For of all venoms the foulest is the scorpion's:

155 No medicine may amend the place where it stings
Till it's dead and placed upon it—the poison is destroyed,
The first effect of the venom, through the virtue it possesses.
So shall this death destroy—I dare bet my life—
All that Death did first through the Devil's tempting.

160 And just as the beguiler with guile beguiled man first,
So shall grace that began everything make a good end
And beguile the beguiler—and that's a good trick:
        A trick by which to trick trickery."
        "Now let's be silent," said Truth. "It seems to me I see
Out of the nip° of the north, not far from here,   *chill*

165 Righteousness come running—let's wait right here,
For she knows far more than we—she was here before us both."

---

3. The first tree bore the fruit that Adam and Eve ate, thereby damaging humankind; the second tree is the cross on which Christ was crucified, thereby redeeming humankind.

4. Compare with Job 7.9.

"That is so," said Mercy, "and I see here to the south
Where Peace clothed in patience comes sportively this way.
Love has desired her long: I believe surely
170   That Love has sent her some letter, what this light means
That hangs over hell thus: she will tell us what it means."
When Peace clothed in patience approached near them both,
Righteousness did her reverence for her rich clothing
And prayed Peace to tell her to what place she was going,
175   And whom she was going to greet in her gay garments.
"My wish is to take my way," said she, "and welcome them all
Whom many a day I might not see for murk of sin.
Adam and Eve and the many others in hell,
Moses and many more will merrily sing,
180   And I shall dance to their song: sister, do the same.
Because Jesus jousted well, joy begins to dawn.
        Weeping may endure for a night, but joy cometh in the morning.[5]
Love who is my lover sent letters to tell me
That my sister Mercy and I shall save mankind,
And that God has forgiven and granted me, Peace, and Mercy
185   To make bail for mankind for evermore after.
Look, here's the patent,"[6] said Peace: "*In pace in idipsum:*
And that this deed shall endure, *dormiam et requiescam.*"[7]
"What? You're raving," said Righteousness. "You must be really drunk.
Do you believe that yonder light might unlock hell
190   And save man's soul? Sister, don't suppose it.
At the beginning God gave the judgment himself
That Adam and Eve and all that followed them
Should die downright and dwell in torment after
If they touched a tree and ate the tree's fruit.
195   Adam afterwards against his forbidding
Fed on that fruit and forsook as it were
The love of our Lord and his lore too,
And followed what the Fiend taught and his flesh's will
Against Reason. I, Righteousness, record this with Truth,
200   That their pain should be perpetual and no prayer should help them,
Therefore let them chew as they chose, and let us not chide, sisters,
For it's misery without amendment, the morsel they ate."
"And I shall prove," said Peace, "that their pain must end,
And in time trouble must turn into well-being;
205   For had they known no woe, they'd not have known well-being;
For no one knows what well-being is who was never in woe,
Nor what is hot hunger who has never lacked food.
If there were no night, no man, I believe,
Could be really well aware of what day means.
210   Never should a really rich man who lives in rest and ease
Know what woe is if it weren't for natural death.
So God, who began everything, of his good will
Became man by a maid for mankind's salvation

---

5. Psalms 29.6.
6. Document conferring authority.

7. In peace in the self-same: . . . I will find rest (Psalms 4.9).

And allowed himself to be sold to see the sorrow of dying.

215 And that cures all care and is the first cause of rest,

For until we meet *modicum*,° I may well avow it, *a little*

No man knows, I suppose, what 'enough' means.

Therefore God of his goodness gave the first man Adam

A place of supreme ease and of perfect joy,

220 And then he suffered him to sin so that he might know sorrow,

And thus know what well-being is—to be aware of it naturally.

And afterward God offered himself, and took Adam's nature,

To see what he had suffered in three separate places,

Both in Heaven and on earth, and now he heads for hell,

225 To learn what all woe is like who has learned of all joy.

So it shall fare with these folk: their folly and their sin

Shall show them what sickness is—and succor from all pain.

No one knows what war is where peace prevails,

Nor what is true well-being till 'Woe, alas!' teaches him."

230 Then was there a wight° with two broad eyes: *creature*

Book was that beaupere's[8] name, a bold man of speech.

"By God's body," said this Book, "I will bear witness

That when this baby was born there blazed a star

So that all the wise men in the world agreed with one opinion

235 That such a baby was born in Bethlehem city

Who should save man's soul and destroy sin.

And all the elements," said the Book, "hereof bore witness.

The sky first revealed that he was God who formed all things:

The hosts in Heaven took *stella comata*[9]

240 And tended her like a torch to reverence his birth.

The light followed the Lord into the low earth.

The water witnessed that he was God for he walked on it;

Peter the Apostle perceived his walking

And as he went on the water knew him well and said,

'Bid me come unto thee on the water.'[1]

245 And lo, how the sun locked her light in herself

When she saw him suffer that made sun and sea.

The earth for heavy heart because he would suffer

Quaked like a quick thing, and the rock cracked all to pieces.

Lo, hell might not hold, but opened when God suffered,

250 And let out Simeon's sons[2] to see him hang on Cross.

And now shall Lucifer believe it, loath though he is,

For Jesus like a giant with an engine[3] comes yonder

To break and beat down all that may be against him,

And to have out of hell every one he pleases.

255 And I, Book, will be burnt unless Jesus rises to life

In all the mights of a man and brings his mother joy,

And comforts all his kin, and takes their cares away,

And all the joy of the Jews disjoins and disperses;

And unless they reverence his Rood° and his resurrection *cross*

---

8. Fine fellow; Book's two broad eyes suggest the Old and New Testaments.
9. Hairy star (i.e., comet).
1. Matthew 14.28.

2. According to the apocryphal Gospel of Nicodemus, Simeon's sons were raised from the dead at the time of Christ's crucifixion.
3. A military device, perhaps like a giant slingshot.

260 And believe on a new law be lost body and soul."
    "Let's be silent," said Truth, "I hear and see both
A spirit speaks to hell and bids the portals be opened."
        Lift up your gates.[4]
    A voice loud in that light cried to Lucifer,
265 "Princes of this place, unpin and unlock,
For he comes here with crown who is King of Glory."
Then Satan[5] sighed and said to hell,
"Without our leave such a light fetched Lazarus away:[6]
Care and calamity have come upon us all.
If this King comes in he will carry off mankind
270 And lead it to where Lazarus is, and with small labor bind me.
Patriarchs and prophets have long prated of this,
That such a lord and a light should lead them all hence."
"Listen," said Lucifer, "for this lord is one I know;
Both this lord and this light, it's long ago I knew him.
275 No death may do this lord harm, nor any devil's trickery,
And his way is where he wishes—but let him beware of the perils.
If he bereaves me of my right he robs me by force.
For by right and by reason the race that is here
Body and soul belongs to me, both good and evil.
280 For he himself said it who is Sire of Heaven,
If Adam ate the apple, all should die
And dwell with us devils: the Lord laid down that threat.
And since he who is Truth himself said these words,
And since I've possessed them seven thousand winters,
285 I don't believe law will allow him the least of them."
"That is so," said Satan, "but I'm sore afraid
Because you took them by trickery and trespassed in his garden,
And in the semblance of a serpent sat upon the apple tree
And egged them to eat, Eve by herself,
290 And told her a tale with treasonous words;
And so you had them out, and hither at the last."
"It's an ill-gotten gain where guile is at the root,
For God will not be beguiled," said Goblin, "nor tricked.
We have no true title to them, for it was by treason they were damned."
295 "Certainly I fear," said the Fiend, "lest Truth fetch them out.
These thirty winters, as I think, he's gone here and there and preached.
I've assailed him with sin, and sometimes asked
Whether he was God or God's son: he gave me short answer.
And thus he's traveled about like a true man these two and thirty winters.
300 And when I saw it was so, while she slept I went
to warn Pilate's wife what sort of man was Jesus,
For some hated him and have put him to death.
I would have lengthened his life, for I believed if he died
That his soul would suffer no sin in his sight.

---

4. The first words from Psalms 23.9, which reads in the Latin Bible, "Lift up your gates, O princes, and be ye lifted up, ye everlasting doors, and the King of Glory shall come in."

5. Satan pictures hell as populated by a number of devils: Satan, Lucifer, Goblin, Belial, and Astoreth.
6. Compare with John 11.

305   For the body, while it walked on its bones, was busy always
     To save men from sin if they themselves wished.
     And now I see where a soul comes descending hitherward
     With glory and with great light; God it is, I'm sure.
     My advice is we all flee," said the Fiend, "fast away from here.

310   For we had better not be at all than abide in his sight.
     For your lies, Lucifer, we've lost all our prey.
     Through you we fell first from Heaven so high:
     Because we believed your lies we all leapt out.
     And now for your latest lie we have lost Adam,

315   And all our lordship, I believe, on land and in hell."
          Now shall the prince of this world be cast out.[7]
        Again the light bade them unlock, and Lucifer answered,
        "*Who is that?*[8]
     What lord are you?" said Lucifer. The light at once replied,
        "*The King of Glory.*
     The Lord of might and of main and all manner of powers:
        The Lord of Powers.
     Dukes of this dim place, at once undo these gates

320   That Christ may come in, the Heaven-King's son."
     And with that breath hell broke along with Belial's bars;
     For any warrior or watchman the gates wide opened.
     Patriarchs and prophets, *populus in tenebris*,[9]
     Sang Saint John's song, *Ecce agnus Dei*.[1]

325   Lucifer could not look, the light so blinded him.
     And those that the Lord loved his light caught away,
     And he said to Satan, "Lo, here's my soul in payment
     For all sinful souls, to save those that are worthy.
     Mine they are and of me—I may the better claim them.

330   Although Reason records, and right of myself,
     That if they ate the apple all should die,
     I did not hold out to them hell here forever.
     For the deed that they did, your deceit caused it;
     You got them with guile against all reason.

335   For in my palace Paradise, in the person of an adder,
     You stole by stealth something I loved.
     Thus like a lizard with a lady's face
     Falsely you filched from me; the Old Law confirms
     That guilers be beguiled, and that is good logic:
          A tooth for a tooth and an eye for an eye.[2]

340   *Ergo*[3] soul shall requite soul and sin revert to sin,
     And all that man has done amiss, I, man, will amend.
     Member for member was amends in the Old Law,
     And life for life also, and by that law I claim
     Adam and all his issue at my will hereafter.

345   And what Death destroyed in them, my death shall restore

---

7. John 12.31; "prince of this world" is a title of the devil.
8. This phrase and the next two translated from Latin come from Psalms 23.8.
9. People in darkness (Matthew 4.16, citing Isaiah 9.2).

1. Behold the Lamb of God (John 1.36).
2. Matthew 5.38, citing Exodus 21.14.
3. "Therefore," a central term in scholastic argument, used to introduce the logical conclusion to an argument.

And both quicken[4] and requite what was quenched through sin.
And that grace destroy guile is what good faith requires.
So don't believe it, Lucifer, against the law I fetch them,
But by right and by reason here ransom my liegemen.
  I have not come to destroy the law but to fulfill it.[5]

350 You fetched mine in my place unmindful of all reason
Falsely and feloniously; good faith taught me
To recover them by reason and rely on nothing else.
So what you got with guile through grace is won back.
You, Lucifer, in likeness of a loathsome adder

355 Got by guile those whom God loved;
And I, in likeness of a mortal man, who am master of Heaven,
Have graciously requited your guile: let guile go against guile!
And as Adam and all died through a tree
Adam and all through a tree return to life,

360 And guile is beguiled and grief has come to his guile:
  And he is fallen into the ditch which he made.[6]
And now your guile begins to turn against you,
And my grace to grow ever greater and wider.
The bitterness that you have brewed, imbibe it yourself
Who are doctor of death, the drink you made.

365 "For I who am Lord of Life, love is my drink
And for that drink today I died upon earth.
I struggled so I'm thirsty still for man's soul's sake.
No drink may moisten me or slake my thirst
Till vintage time befall in the Vale of Jehoshaphat,[7]

370 When I shall drink really ripe wine, *Resurrectio mortuorum.*[8]
And then I shall come as a king crowned with angels
And have out of hell all men's souls.
Fiends and fiendkins shall stand before me
And be at my bidding, where best it pleases me.

375 But to be merciful to man then, my nature requires it.
For we are brothers of one blood, but not in baptism all.
And all that are both in blood and in baptism my whole brothers
Shall not be damned to the death that endures without end.
  Against thee only have I sinned, etc.[9]
It is not the custom on earth to hang a felon

380 Oftener than once, even though he were a traitor.
And if the king of the kingdom comes at that time
When a felon should suffer death or other such punishment,
Law would he give him life if he looks upon him.
And I who am King of Kings shall come in such a time

385 Where doom to death damns all wicked,
And if law wills I look on them, it lies in my grace
Whether they die or do not die because they did evil.
And if it be any bit paid for, the boldness of their sins,

---

4. Bring to life.
5. Matthew 5.17.
6. Psalms 7.16.
7. On the evidence of Joel 3.2, 12, the Last Judgment was

to take place at the Vale of Jehosaphat.
8. The resurrection of the dead (from the Nicene Creed).
9. Psalms 50.6.

I may grant mercy through my righteousness and all my true words;

390 And though Holy Writ wills that I wreak vengeance on those that
wrought evil,
No evil unpunished, etc.[1]
They shall be cleansed and made clear and cured of their sins
In my prison purgatory till *Parce!*° says 'Stop!'   spare
And my mercy shall be shown to many of my half-brothers,
For blood-kin may see blood-kin both hungry and cold,

395 But blood-kin may not see blood-kin bleed without his pity:
I heard unspeakable words which it is not lawful for a man to utter.[2]
But my righteousness and right shall rule all hell
And mercy rule all mankind before me in Heaven.
For I'd be an unkind king unless I gave my kin help,
And particularly at such a time when help was truly needed.
Enter not into judgment with thy servant.[3]

400 Thus by law," said our Lord, "I will lead from here
Those I looked on with love who believed in my coming;
And for your lie, Lucifer, that you lied to Eve,
You shall buy it back in bitterness"—and bound him with chains.
Ashtoreth and all the gang hid themselves in corners;

405 They dared not look at our Lord, the least of them all,
But let him lead away what he liked and leave what he wished.
Many hundreds of angels harped and sang,
Flesh sins, flesh redeems, flesh reigns as God of God.[4]
Then Peace piped a note of poetry:
As a rule the sun is brighter after the biggest cloud; After hostilities
love is brighter.[5]
"After sharp showers," said Peace, "the sun shines brightest;

410 No weather is warmer than after watery clouds;
Nor any love lovelier, or more loving friends,
Than after war and woe when Love and peace are masters.
There was never war in this world nor wickedness so sharp
That Love, if he liked, might not make a laughing matter.

415 And peace through patience puts an end to all perils."
"Truce!" said Truth, "you tell the truth, by Jesus!
Let's kiss in covenant and each of us clasp other."
"And let no people," said Peace, "perceive that we argued;
For nothing is impossible to him that is almighty."

420 "You speak the truth," said Righteousness, and reverently kissed her,
Peace, and Peace her, *per saecula saeculorum:*[6]
Mercy and Truth have met together; Righteousness and Peace
have kissed each other.[7]
Truth sounded a trumpet then and sang *Te Deum Laudamus,*[8]
And then Love strummed a lute with a loud note:

1. [He is a just judge who leaves] no evil unpunished [and
no good unrewarded] (from Pope Innocent III's tract *Of
Contempt for the World*; see 4.143–44).
2. In 2 Corinthians 12.4, St. Paul tells of how in a mystical vision he was caught up to heaven, where he saw
things that cannot be repeated.
3. Psalms 142.2.

4. From a medieval Latin hymn.
5. From Alain de Lille, a 12th-century poet and philosopher.
6. Forever and ever (the liturgical formula).
7. Psalms 84.11.
8. We praise thee, God (a celebrated Latin hymn).

Behold how good and how pleasant, etc.[9]
Till the day dawned these damsels caroled.
425   When bells rang for the Resurrection, and right then I awoke
And called Kit my wife and Calote my daughter:
"Arise and go reverence God's resurrection,
And creep to the Cross on knees, and kiss it as a jewel,
For God's blessed body it bore for our good,
430   And it frightens the Fiend, for such is its power
That no grisly ghost may glide in its shadow."

❂ "PIERS PLOWMAN" AND ITS TIME ❂
The Rising of 1381

The event previously known as the "Peasants' Revolt" is generally referred to by today's historians as the "Rising of 1381," since it is now recognized that it included many members of the commons who were not peasants but rather middle-class landholders, artisans, and so forth. William Langland had a rather ambiguous relation to the rising, for while deploring the conditions that caused it, he refused to endorse its radical social program. When the rebels invoked his character Piers as a cultural hero, he revised Piers Plowman for a second time (the so-called C-text), thus disassociating himself from them. This section brings together a number of documents that record the events of the rising, and more importantly, reveal the subjective responses of contemporary writers to it.

The causes of the rising were varied. Among them was the "Statute of Laborers" enacted by Parliament in 1351 to freeze wages and restrict laborers' mobility, both of which had been increasing as a result of the depopulation caused by the Black Death. The more immediate catalyst, however, was a flat poll tax enacted in 1380, which hurt the poor disproportionately and which the government collected in a particularly ruthless way.

The rising itself was astonishingly brief, beginning at the end of May 1381 and collapsing by the end of July. From the prosperous southern counties of Essex and Kent the rebels marched to London, swearing loyalty to one another and to Richard II. Their hostility was directed against the church hierarchy and the feudal lords rather than against the monarchy. In London they burned the Savoy Palace, the local residence of the powerful John of Gaunt, Duke of Lancaster and uncle of King Richard. The king, then only fourteen years old, found his advisers ineffectual, and so retreated with them to the Tower of London.

Having agreed to meet the Essex contingent outside the city, at Mile End, the king acceded to their demands of an end to villeinage (serfdom), and ordered his office of chancery to make multiple copies of charters to that effect. During this meeting, some rebels broke into the Tower of London and beheaded two of the most hated men in the kingdom, Simon Sudbury (the king's chancellor and Archbishop of Canterbury) and Robert Hales (his treasurer). Afterward, they displayed their heads on London Bridge, as a sign that they were traitors to the commons.

The next day the king met with the Kentish rebels, again outside the city, at Smithfield. Here their captain Wat Tyler demanded not only the abolition of villeinage but fixed rents, partial disendowment of the church and dispersal of its goods to the poor, and punishment of all "traitors" held to be responsible for the poll tax. In the course of a scuffle, the Lord Mayor of London, William Walworth, stabbed Tyler and mortally wounded him; thereupon, the king

9. Psalms 132.1.

Adam and Eve, detail of a misericord, c. 1379. Misericords were shallow seats in the choir stalls of medieval churches, on which worshipers could rest, still standing, during the long celebrations of the Mass and Daily Office. Their undersides were often carved with animal grotesques and scenes of common life, both seen in this depiction of Adam and Eve from a misericord in Worcester Cathedral. Eve spins and Adam digs, in a moment reminiscent of the couplet from John Ball's sermon : "Whan Adam dalf and Eve span, / who was thanne a gentilman?"

rode before the rebels and declared himself their new captain, successfully leading them off the field.

Tyler's death broke the will of the rebels, and the king promptly revoked the charters freeing the serfs. In a series of trials, he prosecuted the instigators, among them John Ball, the priest who had shortly before preached to the rebels at Blackheath the famous sermon challenging the division of society into three estates: "Whan Adam dalf and Eve span, / who was thanne a gentilman?" Ball was found guilty of treason, and drawn, hanged, and quartered. Aside from such punishments, there were few apparent effects of the rising, although the nobles and the clergy relented in their treatment of the commons, and in the long run, the institution of villeinage declined. For the ruling class itself, the rising caused intense anxiety. John Gower, in his allegorized account, *The Voice of One Crying*, reports hiding in the woods to escape the peasants. Like him, the monastic chroniclers like Thomas of Walsingham generally present the rebels as mad beasts.

What is perhaps most significant about the written reception of the rising is the languages—Latin, French, and English—in which it occurs. Like Gower's *Voice of One Crying*, the chronicles are generally written in Latin, although the *Anonimalle Chronicle*, from which a passage is included here, is in French. Langland and Chaucer wrote in English, while the short poem below, *The Course of Revolt*, is macaronic, alternating English lines with Latin ones. Although there is little written evidence in the voice of the rebels themselves (who were generally illiterate), there are two tantalizing scraps identified as John Ball's letters, written in English although embedded in hostile Latin chronicle accounts of Ball's trial and execution. It has been suggested recently that the most important fact about the rebel speeches and writings is their "vernacularity"—the fact that they appear in a language that the common people could understand.

from *The Anonimalle Chronicle*[1]

[Wat Tyler's Demands to Richard II, and His Death]

At this time a great body of the commons[2] went to the Tower of London to speak with the king. As they could not get a hearing from him, they laid siege to the Tower from the side of Saint Katherine's, towards the south. Another group of the commons, who were within the city, went to the Hospital of Saint John, Clerkenwell, and on their way they burned the place and houses of Roger Legett, questmonger,[3] who had been beheaded in Cheapside, as well as all the rented property and tenements of the Hospital of Saint John they could find. Afterwards they came to the beautiful priory of the said hospital, and set on fire several fine and pleasant buildings within it—a great and horrible piece of damage to the priory for all time to come. They then returned to London to rest or to do more mischief.

At this time the king was in a turret of the great Tower of London, and saw the manor of the Savoy[4] and the Hospital of Clerkenwell, and the houses of Simon Hosteler near Newgate, and John Butterwick's place, all in flames. He called all the lords about him into a chamber, and asked their counsel as to what should be done in such a crisis. But none of them could or would give him any counsel; and so the young king said that he would order the mayor of the city to command the sheriffs and aldermen to have it cried within their wards that everyone between the age of fifteen and sixty, on pain of life and limb, should go next morning (which was Friday) to Mile End, and meet him there at seven of the bell. He did this in order that all the commons who were stationed around the Tower would be persuaded to abandon the siege, and come to Mile End to see him and hear him, so that those who were in the Tower could leave safely at their will and save themselves as they wished. But it came to nothing, for some of them did not have the good fortune to be saved.

Later that Thursday, the said feast of Corpus Christi, the king, remaining anxiously and sadly in the Tower, climbed on to a little turret facing Saint Katherine's, where a large number of the commons were lying. He had it proclaimed to them that they should all go peaceably to their homes, and he would pardon them all their different offenses. But all cried with one voice that they would not go before they had captured the traitors within the Tower, and obtained charters to free them from all manner of serfdom, and certain other points which they wished to demand. The king benevolently granted their requests and made a clerk write a bill in their presence in these terms: "Richard, king of England and France, gives great thanks to his good commons, for that they have so great a desire to see and maintain their king; and he grants them pardon for all manner of trespasses and misprisions and felonies done up to this hour, and wills and commands that every one should now quickly return to his own home: He wills and commands that everyone should put his grievances in writing, and have them sent to him; and he will provide, with the aid of his loyal lords and his good council, such remedy as shall be profitable both to him and to them, and to the kingdom." He put his signet seal to this document in their presence and then sent the said bill by the hands of two of his knights to the people around Saint Katherine's. And he caused it to be read to them, the man who read it standing up on

1. This gripping account describes the rebel Wat (Walter) Tyler's confrontation with the King. Written in French rather than Latin, *The Anonimalle Chronicle* is considered to be more contemporary and more balanced than judgmental Latin accounts like that of Thomas of Walsingham. Translated by R. B. Dobson.

2. The common people as opposed to the nobility or the clergy; the third estate.
3. One who made a business of conducting inquests.
4. The beautiful palace of John of Gaunt, the King's powerful uncle.

an old chair above the others so that all could hear. All this time the king remained in the Tower in great distress of mind. And when the commons had heard the bill, they said that it was nothing but a trifle and mockery. Therefore they returned to London and had it cried around the city that all lawyers, all the men of the Chancery and the Exchequer and everyone who could write a writ or a letter should be beheaded,[5] wherever they could be found. At this time they burnt several more houses within the city. The king himself ascended to a high garret of the Tower to watch the fires; then he came down again, and sent for the lords to have their counsel. But they did not know how to advise him, and were surprisingly abashed.

On the next day, Friday, the commons of the country and the commons of London assembled in fearful strength, to the number of a hundred thousand or more, besides some four score who remained on Tower Hill to watch those who were within the Tower. Some went to Mile End, on the way to Brentwood, to wait for the king's arrival, because of the proclamation that he had made. But others came to Tower Hill, and when the king knew that they were there, he sent them orders by a messenger to join their companions at Mile End, saying that he would come to them very soon. And at this time of the morning he advised the archbishop of Canterbury and the others who were in the Tower, to go down to the little water-gate, and take a boat and save themselves. And the archbishop proceeded to do this; but a wicked woman raised a cry against him, and he had to turn back to the Tower, to his own confusion.

And by seven of the bell the king himself came to Mile End, and with him his mother in a carriage, and also the earls of Buckingham, Kent, Warwick and Oxford, as well as Sir Thomas Percy, Sir Robert Knolles, the mayor of London and many knights and squires; and Sir Aubrey de Vere carried the royal sword. And when the king arrived and the commons saw him, they knelt down to him, saying "Welcome our Lord King Richard, if it pleases you, and we will not have any other king but you." And Wat Tyghler, their master and leader, prayed on behalf of the commons that the king would suffer them to take and deal with all the traitors against him and the law. The king granted that they should freely seize all who were traitors and could be proved to be such by process of law. The said Walter and the commons were carrying two banners as well as pennons and pennoncels[6] while they made their petition to the king. And they required that henceforward no man should be a serf nor make homage or any type of service to any lord, but should give four pence for an acre of land. They asked also that no one should serve any man except at his own will and by means of regular covenant. And at this time the king had the commons arrayed in two lines, and had it proclaimed before them that he would confirm and grant that they should be free, and generally should have their will; and that they could go through all the realm of England and catch all traitors and bring them to him in safety, and then he would deal with them as the law demanded.

Because of this grant Wat Tyghler and the commons took their way to the Tower, to seize the archbishop and the others while the king remained at Mile End. Meanwhile the archbishop had sung his mass devoutly in the Tower, and confessed the prior of the Hospital of Clerkenwell and others; and then he heard two or three masses and chanted the *Commendatio*, and the *Placebo* and *Dirige*, and the Seven Psalms, and the Litany; and when he was at the words "*Omnes sancti orate*

---

5. Chancery held the archives of public record and the Exchequer dealt with the collection of revenue. The Latin chroniclers saw the rising as a threat to writing itself; Thomas of Walsingham, for example, reports that the rebels gleefully burned records they saw as guaranteeing the lords' legal power over them.

6. Small flags and streamers borne on a lance.

pro nobis" [All saints pray for us], the commons entered and dragged him out of the chapel of the Tower, and struck and hustled him roughly, as they did also the others who were with him, and led them to Tower Hill. There they cut off the heads of Master Simon of Sudbury, archbishop of Canterbury, of Sir Robert Hales,[7] High Prior of the Hospital of Saint John's of Clerkenwell, Treasurer of England, of Brother William of Appleton, a great physician and surgeon, and one who had much influence with the king and the duke of Lancaster. And some time after they beheaded John Legge, the king's serjeant-at-arms, and with him a certain juror. At the same time the commons had it proclaimed that whoever could catch any Fleming[8] or other aliens of any nation, might cut off their heads; and so they did accordingly. Then they took the heads of the archbishop and of the others and put them on wooden poles, and carried them before them in procession through all the city as far as the shrine of Westminster Abbey, to the contempt of themselves, of God and of Holy Church: for which reason vengeance descended on them shortly afterwards. Then they returned to London Bridge and set the head of the archbishop above the gate, with the heads of eight others they had executed, so that all who passed over the bridge could see them. This done, they went to the church of Saint Martin's in the Vintry, and found therein thirty-five Flemings, whom they dragged outside and beheaded in the street. On that day there were beheaded 140 or 160 persons. Then they took their way to the places of Lombards and other aliens, and broke into their houses, and robbed them of all their goods that they could discover. So it went on for all that day and the night following with hideous cries and horrible tumult.

At this time, because the Chancellor had been beheaded, the king made the earl of Arundel Chancellor for the day, and entrusted him with the Great Seal; and all that day he caused various clerks to write out charters, patents, and letters of protection, granted to the commons in consequence of the matters before mentioned, without taking any fines for the sealing or transcription.

On the next day, Saturday, great numbers of the commons came into Westminster Abbey at the hour of Tierce,[9] and there they found John Imworth, Marshal of the Marshalsea and warden of the prisoners, a tormentor without pity; he was near the shrine of Saint Edward, embracing a marble pillar, hoping for aid and succor from the saint to preserve him from his enemies. But the commons wrenched his arms away from the pillar of the shrine, and dragged him into Cheap, and there beheaded him. And at the same time they took from Bread Street a valet named John of Greenfield, merely because he had spoken well of Brother William Appleton and the other murdered persons; and they brought him into Cheap and beheaded him. All this time the king was having it cried through the city that every one should go peaceably to his own country and his own house, without doing more mischief; but to this the commons would not agree.

And on this same day, at three hours after noon, the king came to Westminster Abbey and about two hundred persons with him. The abbot and convent of the said abbey, and the canons and vicars of Saint Stephen's Chapel, came to meet him in procession, clothed in their copes and their feet bare, halfway to Charing Cross; and they brought him to the abbey, and then to the high altar of the church. The king made his

---

7. Sudbury and Hales were especially hated by the rebels—the former, as chancellor of England, for instituting the poll tax, and the latter, as treasurer, for collecting it.

8. Immigrants from Flanders, who had become wealthy in

the London wool trade; they were particular targets of the rebels (see Chaucer, *The Nun's Priest's Tale*, line 576).

9. The third of seven canonical "hours" around which clerics organized their day; usually, the third hour after sunrise.

prayers devoutly, and left an offering for the altar and the relics. Afterwards he spoke with the anchorite,[1] and confessed to him, and remained with him some time. Then the king caused a proclamation to be made that all the commons of the country who were still within the city should come to Smithfield[2] to meet him there; and so they did.

And when the king with his retinue arrived there, he turned to the east, in a place before Saint Bartholomew's a house of canons: and the commons arrayed themselves in bands of great size on the west side. At this moment the mayor of London, William of Walworth, came up, and the king ordered him to approach the commons, and make their chieftain come to him. And when he was called by the mayor, this chieftain, Wat Tyghler of Maidstone by name, approached the king with great confidence, mounted on a little horse so that the commons might see him. And he dismounted, holding in his hand a dagger which he had taken from another man; and when he had dismounted he half bent his knee and took the king by the hand, shaking his arm forcefully and roughly, saying to him, "Brother, be of good comfort and joyful, for you shall have, in the fortnight that is to come, forty thousand more commons than you have at present, and we shall be good companions." And the king said to Walter, "Why will you not go back to your own country?" But the other answered, with a great oath, that neither he nor his fellows would leave until they had got their charter as they wished to have it with the inclusion of certain points which they wished to demand. Tyghler threatened that the lords of the realm would rue it bitterly if these points were not settled at the commons' will. Then the king asked him what were the points which he wished to have considered, and he should have them freely and without contradiction, written out and sealed. Thereupon the said Wat rehearsed the points which were to be demanded; and he asked that there should be no law except for the law of Winchester[3] and that henceforward there should be no outlawry[4] in any process of law, and that no lord should have lordship in future, but it should be divided among all men, except for the king's own lordship. He also asked that the goods of Holy Church should not remain in the hands of the religious, nor of parsons and vicars, and other churchmen; but that clergy already in possession should have a sufficient sustenance and the rest of their goods should be divided among the people of the parish. And he demanded that there should be only one bishop in England and only one prelate, and all the lands and tenements of the possessioners should be taken from them and divided among the commons, only reserving for them a reasonable sustenance. And he demanded that there should be no more villeins[5] in England, and no serfdom nor villeinage but that all men should be free and of one condition. To this the king gave an easy answer, and said that Wat should have all that he could fairly grant, reserving only for himself the regality of his crown. And then he ordered him to go back to his own home, without causing further delay.

During all the time that the king was speaking, no lord or counselor dared or wished to give answer to the commons in any place except for the king himself. Presently Wat Tyghler, in the presence of the king, sent for a jug of water to rinse his mouth, because of the great heat that he felt; and as soon as the water was brought he rinsed out his mouth in a very rude and villainous manner before the king. And then he made them bring him a jug of ale, and drank a great draught, and then, in the presence of the king, climbed on his horse again. At that time a certain valet from Kent, who was among the

---

1. A religious recluse who lived enclosed in a tiny dwelling.
2. An area outside the walls of the city of London.
3. The reference is unclear; it may refer to a claim by the

rebels to the rights of tenants on royal lands.
4. Condition of being outside traditional legal protection.
5. Serfs tied to the land; bondmen.

king's retinue, asked to see the said Wat, chieftain of the commons. And when he saw him, he said aloud that he was the greatest thief and robber in all Kent. Wat heard these words, and commanded the valet to come out to him, shaking his head at him as a sign of malice; but Wat himself refused to go to him for fear that he had of the others there. But at last the lords made the valet go out to Wat, to see what the latter would do before the king. And when Wat saw him he ordered one of his followers, who was mounted on horseback and carrying a banner displayed, to dismount and behead the said valet. But the valet answered that he had done nothing worthy of death, for what he had said was true, and he would not deny it, although he could not lawfully debate the issue in the presence of his liege lord, without leave, except in his own defense: but that he could do without reproof, for whoever struck him would be struck in return. For these words Wat wanted to strike the valet with his dagger, and would have slain him in the king's presence; but because he tried to do so, the mayor of London, William of Walworth, reasoned with the said Wat for his violent behavior and contempt, done in the king's presence, and arrested him. And because he arrested him, the said Wat stabbed the mayor with his dagger in the body in great anger. But, as it pleased God, the mayor was wearing armor and took no harm, but like a hardy and vigorous man drew his dagger and struck back at the said Wat, giving him a deep cut in the neck, and then a great blow on the head. And during this scuffle a valet of the king's household drew his sword, and ran Wat two or three times through the body, mortally wounding him. Wat spurred his horse, crying to the commons to avenge him, and the horse carried him some four score paces, and then he fell to the ground half dead. And when the commons saw him fall, and did not know for certain how it happened, they began to bend their bows and to shoot. Therefore the king himself spurred his horse, and rode out to them, commanding them that they should all come to him at the field of Saint John of Clerkenwell.

Meanwhile the mayor of London rode as hastily as he could back to the city, and commanded those who were in charge of the twenty-four wards to have it cried round their wards, that every man should arm himself as quickly as he could, and come to the king's aid in Saint John's Fields, where the commons were, for he was in great trouble and necessity. But at this time almost all of the knights and squires of the king's household, and many others, were so frightened of the affray that they left their liege lord and went each his own way.

Afterwards, when the king had reached the open fields, he made the commons array themselves on the west side. And presently the aldermen came to him in a body, bringing with them the keepers of the wards arrayed in several bands, a fine company of well-armed men in great strength. And they enveloped the commons like sheep within a pen. Meanwhile, after the mayor had sent the keepers of the town on their way to the king, he returned with a good company of lances to Smithfield in order to make an end of the captain of the commons. And when he came to Smithfield he failed to find there the said captain Wat Tyghler, at which he marveled much, and asked what had become of the traitor. And he was told that Wat had been carried by a group of the commons to the hospital for the poor near Saint Bartholomew's, and put to bed in the chamber of the master of the hospital. The mayor went there and found him, and had him carried out to the middle of Smithfield, in the presence of his companions, and had him beheaded. And so ended his wretched life. But the mayor had his head set on a pole and carried before him to the king, who still remained in the field. And when the king saw the head he had it brought near him to subdue the commons, and thanked the mayor greatly for what he had done. And when the commons saw that their chieftain, Wat Tyghler, was dead in such a manner, they fell to the ground there among the corn, like beaten men, imploring the king for mercy for their misdeeds. And the king benevolently granted them mercy, and most of them took to flight.

Three Poems on the Rising of 1381
John Ball's First Letter[1]

John Ball Saint Mary Priest, greeteth well all manner of men, and biddeth them in name of the Trinitie, Father, Sonne, & holy Ghost, stand manlike together in truth, & helpe truth, and truth shall helpe you:

now raygneth pride in price,	
couetise° is holden° wise	*greed / held*
lechery without shame,	
gluttonie without blame,	
enuye raygneth° with reason,	*reigns*
and sloath is taken in great season,	
God doe boote° for nowe is time. Amen.	*make amends*

John Ball's Second Letter[2]
LITTERA IOHANNIS BALLE MISSA COMMUNIBUS ESTSEXIE
[THE LETTER OF JOHN BALL TO THE ESSEX COMMONS]

Iohan schep, som-tyme seynte marie prest of york, and now of colchestre, Greteth wel Iohan nameles & Iohn the mullere and Iohon cartere, and biddeth hem thei bee war of gyle [treachery] in borugh, and stondeth to-gidere in godes name, and biddeth Pers ploughman / go to his werk and chastise wel hobbe the robbere; and taketh with yow Iohan Trewman and alle hijs felawes and no mo, and loke schappe you to on heued[3] and no mo.

Iohan the mullere hath y-grounde smal, smal, smal.	
The kynges sone of heuene schal paye for al.	
be war or the be wo.°	*beware or be sorry*
knoweth your freend fro your foo.	
haueth y-now & seith hoo!	
and do wel and bettre and fleth° synne,	*flee*
and seketh pees and hold yow ther-inne.	
and so biddeth Iohan trewaman and alle his felawes.	

1. This and the piece following can only provisionally be called "poems," despite their rhymed couplets and sporadic alliteration. The court that tried and convicted Ball regarded them as actual directions to his followers, and modern scholarship has tended to concur. If so they are directions in code, for they are, in the words of one chronicler, "full of enigmas." In this poem the complaint about the seven deadly sins running rampant is conventional, but the conclusion, "God do bote for neow is time" (God make amends, for now is the time) is highly unusual in its call to action. Significantly, the sin of anger is absent from the list.

2. According to the chronicle from which this "letter" was taken, Ball sent it to "the leaders of the commons in Essex . . . in order to urge them to finish what they had begun," and it was "afterwards found in the sleeve of a man about to be hanged for disturbing the peace." It appears in Thomas Walsingham's Latin *Historia Anglicana*, where it is included as evidence of the treason for which Ball was hanged. In the prose introduction to the poem, John the "shep," priest of Colchester, is the assumed name of John Ball (as "pastor"), while John Carter and John the Miller are both generic occupational names often ascribed to the leaders of the rebels. The reference to "Pers Ploughman" in the poem's introduction indicates that the rebels interpreted Langland's conservative poem for their own purposes. It presents Piers not as Langland's patient laborer, but as one who should get to his "work" of punishing "robbers," perhaps "Hobbe" (Robert) Hales, the treasurer of the king, beheaded by the rebels for his role in collecting the poll tax.

3. Take one head for yourself; possibly a reference to the rebels' loyalty to Richard II as opposed to the nobles.

Hanc litteram Idem Iohannes balle confessus est scripsisse, et communibus transmisisse, et plura alia fatebatur et fecit; propter-que, ut diximus, traitus, suspensus, et decollatus apud sanctum albanum Idibus Iulij, presente rege, et cadauer eius quadripertitum quatuor regni cuntatibus missum est. [John Ball confessed that he wrote this letter and sent it to the commons, and said and did many other things. For which reason, as we have said, he was drawn, hanged, and beheaded before the king at Saint Albans, on the ides of July; and his body was quartered and sent to four cities in the kingdom.]

The Course of Revolt[4]

The taxe hath tened° vs alle,	*harmed*
probat hoc mors tot validorum;°	*this death tests so many of the strong[?]*
The Kyng therof had small,	
ffuit in manibus cupidorum.°5	*it was in the hands of the greedy ones*
5 yt had ful hard hansell,°	*bad omen*
dans causam fine dolorum;°	*giving cause to an end of sorrows*
vengeaunce nedes most° fall,	*must*
propter peccata malorum.°	*on account of the sins of the wicked*
In Kent care° be-gan,[6]	*troubles*
10 *mox infestando potentes;*°	*soon attacking the rulers*
On rowtes° tho Rebawdes° they ran,	*crowds / rascals*
Sua turpida arma ferentes.°	*bearing their shameful weapons*
ffoles° they dred no man,	*fools*
Regni Regem, neque gentes;°	*neither king of the realm, nor the people*
15 laddes° they were there Cheveteyns,°	*churls / captains*
Sine iure fere superantes.°	*lawlessly rising above their station*
laddes° lowde they lowght,°	*churls / laughed*
Clamantes voce sonora,°	*shouting in a loud voice*
The bischop[7] wan they slowght,°	*slew*
20 *Et corpora plura decora.*°	*and many handsome people*
Maners down they drowght,°	*they threw down manor houses*
In regno non meliora;°	*there were none better in the kingdom*
Harmes they dyde y-nowght;°	*enough*
habuerunt libera lora.°	*they had free rein*
25 Iak strawe[8] made yt stowte°	*swaggered*
Cum profusa comitiua,°	*with a captain's munificence*
And seyd al schuld hem lowte,°	*bow down to them*
Anglorum corpora viua.°	*the living community of Englishmen*
Sadly° can they schowte,°	*vigorously / shouted*
30 *pulsant pietatis oliua,*°	*they beat the olive branch of pity*

---

4. Unlike the two preceding letters, there is no doubt that this piece is a poem: it is written in six- or eight-line stanzas of English alternating with Latin, with a rhyme scheme *ababab* (*ab*). The masculine rhymes of the English (alle, small, etc.) contrast with the feminine rhymes of the Latin (validorum, cupidorum, etc.) to give it a lilting quality. The poem laments the violence of the rising, although it opens with a recognition of the rebels' grievances: the poll tax of 1377, 1379, and 1380–1381 "hath tened [harmed] vs alle."

5. Much of the tax revenue was diverted to collectors rather than returned to the king.

6. The rising actually began in Essex and spread to Kent.

7. Simon Sudbury, Archbishop of Canterbury.

8. Jack Straw was a fictional character believed to have been a leader of the rising; see Chaucer, *Nun's Priest's Tale*, lines 628–31.

The wycche were wont to lowte,°   *those who used to skulk*
   aratrum traducere stiua.°   *disgrace the plough and plough handle*

Hales,[9] that dowghty° knyght,   *brave*
   quo splenduit Anglia tota,°   *in whom all England shone*

35 dolefully° he was dyght,°   *pitiably / cut down*
   Cum stultis pace remota.°   *when removed from peace by fools*

There he myght not fyght,
   nec Christo soluere vota.°   *nor say his prayers to Christ*

Savoy[1] semely set°   *beautifully built*

40 *heu! funditus igne cadebat.*°   *alas, it was given over to the fire*

Arcan don there they bett,[2]
   Et eos virtute premebat.°   *and threatened them with force*

deth was ther dewe dett,
   qui captum quisque ferebat.°   *whoever carried off stolen goods*

45 Oure kyng myght have no rest,
   Alii latuere cauerna;°   *others hid in caves*

To ride he was ful prest,
   recolendo gesta paterna.°   *remembering his father's deeds*

Iak straw dovn they cast[3]

50 *Smethefeld virtute superna.*°   *at Smithfield with superior strength*

god, as thou may best,
   Regem defende, guberna.°   *defend the kingdom and govern it*

John Gower
from *The Voice of One Crying*[1]
from PROLOGUE

In the beginning of this work, the author intends to describe how the lowly peasants violently revolted against the freemen and nobles of the realm. And since an event of this kind was as loathsome and horrible as a monster, he reports that in a dream he saw different throngs of the rabble transformed into different kinds of domestic animals. He

9. Sir Robert Hales, treasurer of England and therefore closely associated with the collection of the poll tax. He was beheaded at the Tower of London during the rising.
1. John of Gaunt's London residence.
2. A reference to Achan (Joshua 7), who transgressed the law of God by stealing valuables from Jericho. Several chronicles mention the rebels' restraint in not looting the houses of the nobles.
3. It was not (the fictional) Jack Straw, but Wat Tyler who was mortally wounded at Smithfield.
1. Gower grew up in Kent (one of the counties where the Rising of 1381 started), in a well-connected family, and both Richard II and Henry IV were his patrons. He was a friend of Chaucer, who refers to him as "moral Gower." The immorality of contemporary society, particularly the refusal of the three estates to work together, is in fact the unifying theme of Gower's work. Of his three long poems (written in the three languages of the period, English, Anglo-Norman, and Latin), the Middle English *Lover's Confession* (*Confessio amantis*), though primarily a dream vision exploring the frustrations and folly of human

divine love, is set a framing complaint about the three estates, and the Anglo-Norman *Mirror of Man* (*Mirour de l'Omme*) is based on such a complaint.
   Gower's Latin *Voice of One Crying* (*Vox Clamantis*) laments the failure of the three estates in a more prophetic way: the speaker identifies himself with John the Baptist, crying in the wilderness of 14th-century England. Like *Piers Plowman*, the poem takes the form of an allegorical dream vision. Like Langland, Gower revised his work in response to the revolt. He had written Books 2–7 by 1378 as a general complaint about the three estates, though he blamed the peasants in particular. Their refusal to produce food "by the sweat of their brow" as God decreed shows their laziness, and their demand of higher wages shows their wickedness and greed (bk. 5.9). After the Rising of 1381 occurred, he composed what is now Book 1 to decry the violence, which he saw as led by the devil; in it, he casts the peasants as beasts lacking reason, and their leader, Wat Tyler, as a rabble-rousing jackdaw, or jay (bk. 1.9). Translated by Eric W. Stockton.

says, moreover, that those domestic animals deviated from their true nature and took on the barbarousness of wild beasts. In accordance with the separate divisions of this book, which is divided into seven parts (as will appear more clearly below in its headings), he treats furthermore of the causes for such outrages taking place among men. * * *

[Wat Tyler as a Jackdaw Inciting the Peasants to Riot][2]

> Here he says that in his dream he saw that when all the aforementioned madmen stood herded together, a certain Jackdaw (in English a Jay, which is commonly called Wat) assumed the rank of command over the others. And to tell the truth of the matter, this Wat was their leader.

When this great multitude of monsters like wild beasts stood united, a multitude like the sands of the sea, there appeared a Jackdaw, well instructed in the art of speaking, which no cage could keep at home. While all were looking on, this bird spread his wings and claimed to have top rank, although he was unworthy. Just as the Devil was placed in command over the army of the lower world, so this scoundrel was in charge of the wicked mob. A harsh voice, a fierce expression, a very faithful likeness to a death's head—these things gave token of his appearance. He checked the murmuring and all kept silent so that the sound from his mouth might be better heard. He ascended to the top of a tree, and with the voice from his open mouth he uttered such words as these to his compeers:

"O you low sort of wretches, which the world has subjugated for a long time by its law, look, now the day has come when the peasantry will triumph and will force the freemen to get off their lands. Let all honor come to an end, let justice perish, and let no virtue that once existed endure further in the world. Let the law give over which used to hold us in check with its justice, and from here on let our court rule."

The whole mob was silent and took note of the speaker's words, and they liked every command he delivered from his mouth. The rabble lent a deluded ear to his fickle talk, and it saw none of the future things that would result. For when he had been honored in this way by the people, he quickly grabbed all the land for himself. Indeed, when the people had unadvisedly given themselves into servitude, he called the populace together and gave orders. Just as a billow usually grows calm after a stiff breeze, and just as a wave swells by the blast of a whirlwind, so the Jackdaw stirred up all the others with his outrageous shouting, and he drew the people's minds toward war. The stupid portion of the people did not know what its "court" might be, but he ordered them to adopt the laws of force. He said, "Strike," and one man struck. He said, "Kill," and another killed. He said, "Commit crime"; everyone committed it, and did not oppose his will. Everyone he called to in his madness listened with ears pricked up, and once aroused to his voice, pursued the [prescribed] course. Thus many an unfortunate man, driven by his persuasive raving, stuck his hand into the fire again and again. All proclaimed in a loud voice, "So be it," so that the sound was like the din of the sea. Stunned by the great noise of their voice, I now could scarcely lift my trembling feet. Yet from a distance I observed how they made their mutual arrangements by clasping their hands. For they said this, that the mob from the country would destroy whatever was left of the noble class in the world.

With these words, they all marched together in the same fashion, and the wicked ruler of hell led the way. A black cloud mingled with the furies of hell

2. From Book 1.

approached, and every wickedness poured into their hearts rained down. The earth was so thoroughly soaked with the dew of hell that no virtue could flourish from that time forth. But every vice that a worthy man abhors flourished and filled men's hearts from that time on. Then at midday the Devil attacked and his hard-shot arrow flew during that painful day. Satan himself was freed and on hand, together with all the sinful band of servile hell. Behold, the untutored heart's sense of shame was lost, and it no longer feared the terrors of crime or punishment. And so when I saw the leaders of hell ruling the world, the rights of heaven were worth nothing. The more I saw them, the more I judged I ought to be afraid of them, not knowing what sort of end would be bound to come.

[THE LAZINESS AND GREED OF PLOUGHMEN][3]

Now that he has spoken of those of knightly rank who ought to keep the state unharmed, it is necessary to speak of those who are under obligation to enter into the labors of agriculture, which are necessary for obtaining food and drink for the sustenance of the human race.

Now you have heard what knighthood is, and I shall speak in addition of what the guiding principle for other men ought to be. For after knighthood there remains only the peasant rank; the rustics in it cultivate the grains and vineyards. They are the men who seek food for us by the sweat of their heavy toil, as God Himself has decreed. The guiding principle of our first father Adam, which he received from the mouth of God on high, is rightly theirs. For God said to him, when he fell from the glories of Paradise, "O sinner, the sweat and toil of the world be thine; in them shalt thou eat thy bread."[4] So if God's peasant pays attention to the plowshare as it goes along, and if he thus carries on the work of cultivation with his hand, then the fruit which in due course the fertile field will bear and the grape will stand abundant in their due seasons. Now, however, scarcely a farmer wishes to do such work; instead, he wickedly loafs everywhere.

An evil disposition is widespread among the common people, and I suspect that the servants of the plow are often responsible for it. For they are sluggish, they are scarce, and they are grasping. For the very little they do they demand the highest pay. Now that this practice has come about, see how one peasant insists upon more than two demanded in days gone by. Yet a short time ago one performed more service than three do now, as those maintain who are well acquainted with the facts. For just as the fox seeks his hole and enters it while the woods are echoing on every side of the hole, so does the servant of the plow, contrary to the law of the land, seek to make a fool of the land. They desire the leisures of great men, but they have nothing to feed themselves with, nor will they be servants. God and Nature have ordained that they shall serve, but neither knows how to keep them within bounds. Everyone owning land complains in his turn about these people; each stands in need of them and none has control over them. The peasants of old did not scorn God with impunity or usurp a noble worldly rank. Rather, God imposed servile work upon them, so that the peasantry might subdue its proud feelings; and liberty, which remained secure for freemen, ruled over the serfs and subjected them to its law.

The experience of yesterday makes us better informed as to what perfidy the unruly serf possesses. As the teasel[5] harmfully thins out the standing crops if it is not

---

3. From Book 5.
4. Genesis 3.19.

5. A bristly plant like a thistle.

thinned out itself, so does the unruly peasant weigh heavily upon the well-behaved ones. The peasant strikes at the subservient and soothes the troublesome, yet the principle which the old order of things teaches is not wrong: let the law accordingly cut down the harmful teasels of rabble, lest they uproot the nobler grain with their stinging. Unless it is struck down first, the peasant race strikes against freemen, no matter what nobility or worth they possess. Its actions outwardly show that the peasantry is base, and it esteems the nobles the less because of their very virtues. Just as lopsided ships begin to sink without the right load, so does the wild peasantry, unless it is held in check.

God and our toil confer and bestow everything upon us. Without toil, man's advantages are nothing. The peasant should therefore put his limbs to work, as is proper for him to do. Just as a barren field cultivated by the plowshare fails the granaries and brings home no crop in autumn, so does the worthless churl, the more he is cherished by your love, fail you and bring on your ruin. The serfs perform none of their servile duties voluntarily and have no respect for the law. Whatever the serf's body suffers patiently under compulsion, inwardly his mind ever turns toward utter wickedness. Miracles happen only contrary to nature; only the divinity of nature can go against its own powers. It is not for man's estate that anyone from the class of serfs should try to set things right.

END OF "PIERS PLOWMAN" AND THE RISING OF 1381

MYSTICAL WRITINGS

Throughout the Middle Ages, religious belief was communally expressed in the great public liturgies: the mass and the Divine Office—those prayers, hymns, and readings performed, especially by monastic communities, at the eight liturgical "hours" from dawn until dark. Private devotion, however, also had a continuous place in medieval Christianity. The British Isles enjoyed a particularly rich and ancient tradition of lives led in holy solitude and of texts and collections intended for private devotion by both clergy and laity. Such early works were enriched in the late eleventh century by the influential *Prayers or Meditations* of Anselm, Archbishop of Canterbury.

Anselm's prayers and related works were collected into portable books. Beginning in the thirteenth century, England also produced distinguished, sometimes elaborately decorated psalters—collections of psalms and other prayers—that were often privately owned. Toward the middle of the thirteenth century, an Oxford workshop produced the earliest of the decorated Books of Hours, a form that was to prove enormously popular across Europe for the rest of the Middle Ages.

Books of Hours typically contained the "Little Hours of the Virgin," an abbreviated version of the Divine Office that allowed for private commemoration of the holy hours, as well as other prayers, extracts from the gospels, and the "seven penitential psalms." Psalters and Books of Hours both featured texts devoted to the Virgin Mary, only one manifestation of a widespread English tradition. Many were explicitly intended for use by women, both lay and clerical, and emphasize female readership in their illustrations, as in the scene of women reading from the Bedford Hours (see Color Plate 10). Psalters and especially Books of Hours played a key role in the growth of lay literacy during the later Middle Ages.

By the fourteenth century, then, England had an ancient tradition of private religious devotion and varied books created especially for that purpose as well as a growing readership, lay and clerical. Two further, related elements added to the growth in that century of works that have been grouped, largely retrospectively, as "mystical." First, across Europe there was a renewed expression of "affective spirituality," the emotionally, even physically empathetic contemplation of the crises of salvation, especially the crucifixion of Christ and the sufferings of the Virgin Mary. This is reflected in the vision of the crucifixion in *Passus* 18 of Langland's *Piers Plowman*, and in many lyrics, as well as in sculpture and drawings like that on page 517. Second, widespread dissatisfaction with the established church—or a more diffuse sense of spiritual needs left unfulfilled there—led a growing number of Christians to explore more immediate and often private avenues of religious experience. The quest for a mystical union with Christ or God the Father is a particularly ambitious aspect of such exploration.

This search was often exercised, particularly in the lay community and among religious women, in the recently invigorated vernacular, which (whether French or English) had long had a place along with Latin in Books of Hours. Among these expressions were the "Wycliffite" translations of the Bible into Middle English (see pages 516–19), as well as texts intended for religious recluses and for people seeking mystical experience even as they remained active in the mundane world. These emergent religious aspirations, as well as some of their accompanying fears and tensions, are expressed below in Julian of Norwich's *Book of Showings* and the Companion Readings that follow it.*

◆━━◆═◆━━◆

Julian of Norwich
1342–c. 1420

Dame Julian of Norwich was an anchoress, a woman dedicated to prayer and contemplation who lived separate from the world, literally enclosed in a modest residence and symbolically "dead" to the secular world. Yet Julian also lived in the midst of the world. Her anchorhold at the church of Saint Julian—hence her name—was in a busy market neighborhood of Norwich. Dame Julian's lifelong stability as an anchoress, and her persistent rhetoric of humility (she most often speaks of herself only as a "creature"), may have masked or softened the daring of her theology. This she developed from decades of meditation on a sequence of sixteen visions of the Crucifixion—"showings"—that she received in extreme illness at age thirty.

The urban space and domestic arrangements of Julian's anchorhold serve as an emblem for her theology and her place in the spiritual world. She had a maidservant, and received and spoke to guests. Some of those encounters were reported, as for example by Margery Kempe from nearby Lynn, whose own work appears later in this anthology (page 530). Julian brought eminence to the churches of Norwich without threatening their hierarchy; she lived under the direction of a priestly confessor, made no claim to worldly power, and insisted upon her orthodoxy. Yet a visitor like Margery Kempe could use Julian's approval as a defense for her own more mobile and subversive quest for holiness.

Dame Julian used her own background of household and family as images to create a complex and subtle domestic theology of the trinity and especially of the sacrifice of Christ. Julian's metaphors for the divine are not exclusively intimate or domestic, however. She repeatedly speaks of God in socially conservative terms, as a great secular lord whose grace is a form of public "courtesy." Her revelation of the soul as a great citadel (ch. 68) features Jesus as its bishop, king, and lord.

Julian probably dictated the two versions of her *Book of Showings*, although it is clear that she was deeply versed in the Bible and liturgy, and in the writings of English and Continental mystics. The earlier version is largely focused on the visions themselves, while the very much

* The editors express their gratitude to Professor Nicholas Watson for his advice on this section.

longer version (selections from which follow) reflects the ensuing decades of theological spec-ulations to which Julian's visions led her. She will often expound a statement by Christ in one of her visions with all the nuance that contemporary theologians would apply to a line from the Bible. In an extraordinary series of reflections, Julian at once meditates upon key moments in her initial visions, and explores the role of Christ in mankind and in the Trinity through the multifaceted image of the Lord as mother. Julian exploits all the moments of mother-hood—conception, labor, breast-feeding, nurture, and upbringing—to articulate the place of Christ in the scheme of salvation and the necessity of sin. At the same time, other aspects of motherhood also serve Julian to explore the other persons of the Trinity, God the Father and the Holy Spirit, as well as the sufferings and joys of the Virgin Mary.

Even more than Richard Rolle or the *Cloud of Unknowing* (selections from which follow as Companion Readings), Julian is explicitly concerned with the love and salvation of all the faithful, not just private communion with the divine. She addresses herself, more broadly than her predecessors, to the entire community of the faithful. She explicitly does not privilege her-self above those of simple belief, and again uses the imagery of a nurturing mother to urge the sinful soul's recourse to the Holy Church.

from A Book of Showings[1]
[THREE GRACES. ILLNESS. THE FIRST REVELATION]
CHAPTER 2

This revelation was made to a simple, unlettered creature, living in this mortal flesh, the year of our Lord one thousand, three hundred and seventy-three, on the thir-teenth day of May;[2] and before this the creature had desired three graces by the gift of God. The first was recollection of the Passion. The second was bodily sickness. The third was to have, of God's gift, three wounds. As to the first, it seemed to me that I had some feeling for the Passion of Christ, but still I desired to have more by the grace of God. I thought that I wished that I had been at that time with Mag-dalen and with the others who were Christ's lovers, so that I might have seen with my own eyes the Passion which our Lord suffered for me, so that I might have suf-fered with him as others did who loved him. Therefore I desired a bodily sight, in which I might have more knowledge of our savior's bodily pains, and of the compas-sion of our Lady and of all his true lovers who were living at that time and saw his pains, for I would have been one of them and have suffered with them. I never desired any other sight of God or revelation, until my soul would be separated from the body, for I believed that I should be saved by the mercy of God. This was my intention, because I wished afterwards, because of that revelation, to have truer rec-ollection of Christ's Passion. As to the second grace, there came into my mind with contrition—a free gift which I did not seek—a desire of my will to have by God's gift a bodily sickness. I wished that sickness to be so severe that it might seem mortal, so that I might in it receive all the rites which Holy Church has to give me, whilst I myself should think that I was dying, and everyone who saw me would think the same; for I wanted no comfort from any human, earthly life in that sickness. I wanted to have every kind of pain, bodily and spiritual, which I should have if I had died, every fear and temptation from devils, and every other kind of pain except the departure of the spirit. I intended this because I wanted to be purged by God's mercy,

1. Translated by Edmund Colledge and James Walsh.
2. Julian provides the biographical setting of her visions

in this chapter. By "unlettered" she may mean that she was not formally schooled; it is clear she was literate.

and afterwards live more to his glory because of that sickness; because I hoped that this would be to my reward when I should die, because I desired soon to be with my God and my Creator.

These two desires about the Passion and the sickness which I desired from him were with a condition, for it seemed to me that this was not the ordinary practice of prayer; therefore I said: Lord, you know what I want, if it be your will that I have it, and if it be not your will, good Lord, do not be displeased, for I want nothing which you do not want. When I was young I desired to have this sickness when I would be thirty years old. As to the third, by the grace of God and the teaching of Holy Church I conceived a great desire to receive three wounds in my life, that is, the wound of true contrition, the wound of loving compassion, and the wound of longing with my will for God. Just as I asked for the other two conditionally, so I asked urgently for this third without any condition. The two desires which I mentioned first passed from my mind, and the third remained there continually.

CHAPTER 3

And when I was thirty and a half years old, God sent me a bodily sickness in which I lay for three days and three nights, and on the third night I received all the rites of Holy Church, and did not expect to live until day. And after this I lay for two days and two nights, and on the third night I often thought that I was on the point of death, and those who were with me often thought so. And yet in this I felt a great reluctance to die, not that there was anything on earth which it pleased me to live for, or any pain of which I was afraid, for I trusted in the mercy of God. But it was because I wanted to live to love God better and longer, so that I might through the grace of that living have more knowledge and love of God in the bliss of heaven. Because it seemed to me that all the time that I had lived here was very little and short in comparison with the bliss which is everlasting, I thought: Good Lord, can my living no longer be to your glory? And I understood by my reason and the sensation of my pains that I should die; and with all the will of my heart I assented to be wholly as was God's will.

So I lasted until day, and by then my body was dead from the middle downwards, as it felt to me. Then I was helped to sit upright and supported, so that my heart might be more free to be at God's will, and so that I could think of him whilst my life would last. My curate was sent for to be present at my end; and before he came my eyes were fixed upwards, and I could not speak. He set the cross before my face, and said: I have brought the image of your savior; look at it and take comfort from it. It seemed to me that I was well, for my eyes were set upwards towards heaven, where I trusted that I by God's mercy was going; but nevertheless I agreed to fix my eyes on the face of the crucifix if I could, and so I did, for it seemed to me that I would hold out longer with my eyes set in front of me rather than upwards. After this my sight began to fail. It grew as dark around me in the room as if it had been night, except that there was ordinary light trained upon the image of the cross, I did not know how. Everything around the cross was ugly and terrifying to me, as if it were occupied by a great crowd of devils.

After this the upper part of my body began to die, until I could scarcely feel anything. My greatest pain was my shortness of breath and the ebbing of my life. Then truly I believed that I was at the point of death. And suddenly at that moment all my pain was taken from me, and I was as sound, particularly in the upper part of my body, as ever I was before. I was astonished by this sudden change, for it seemed to me that it was by God's secret doing and not natural; and even so, in this ease which I felt, I had no more confidence that I should live, nor was the ease I felt complete for me, for I thought that I would rather have been delivered of this world, because that was what my heart longed for.

Then suddenly it came into my mind that I ought to wish for the second wound as a gift and a grace from our Lord, that my body might be filled full of recollection and feeling of his blessed Passion, as I had prayed before, for I wished that his pains might be my pains, with compassion which would lead to longing for God. So it seemed to me that I might with his grace have the wounds which I had before desired; but in this I never wanted any bodily vision or any kind of revelation from God, but the compassion which I thought a loving soul could have for our Lord Jesus, who for love was willing to become a mortal man. I desired to suffer with him, living in my mortal body, as God would give me grace.

CHAPTER 4

And at this, suddenly I saw the red blood running down from under the crown, hot and flowing freely and copiously, a living stream, just as it was at the time when the crown of thorns was pressed on his blessed head.[3] I perceived, truly and powerfully, that it was he who just so, both God and man, himself suffered for me, who showed it to me without any intermediary.

And in the same revelation, suddenly the Trinity filled my heart full of the greatest joy, and I understood that it will be so in heaven without end to all who will come there. For the Trinity is God, God is the Trinity. The Trinity is our maker, the Trinity is our protector, the Trinity is our everlasting lover, the Trinity is our endless joy and our bliss, by our Lord Jesus Christ and in our Lord Jesus Christ. And this was revealed in the first vision and in them all, for where Jesus appears the blessed Trinity is understood, as I see it. And I said: Blessed be the Lord! This I said with a reverent intention and in a loud voice, and I was greatly astonished by this wonder and marvel, that he who is so to be revered and feared would be so familiar with a sinful creature living in this wretched flesh.

I accepted it that at that time our Lord Jesus wanted, out of his courteous love, to show me comfort before my temptations began; for it seemed to me that I might well be tempted by devils, by God's permission and with his protection, before I would die. With this sight of his blessed Passion, with the divinity which I saw in my understanding, I knew well that this was strength enough for me, yes, and for all living creatures who were to be saved, against all the devils of hell and against all their spiritual enemies.

In this he brought our Lady Saint Mary to my understanding. I saw her spiritually in her bodily likeness, a simple, humble maiden, young in years, grown a little taller than a child, of the stature which she had when she conceived.[4] Also God showed me part of the wisdom and the truth of her soul, and in this I understood the reverent contemplation with which she beheld her God, who is her Creator, marveling with great reverence that he was willing to be born of her who was a simple creature cre-

---

3. This begins the first of Julian's 16 revelations.
4. Julian will have two further visions of the Virgin Mary

in different manifestations: as mother mourning at the Crucifixion and as ascended saint.

ated by him. And this wisdom and truth, this knowledge of her Creator's greatness and of her own created littleness, made her say very meekly to Gabriel: Behold me here, God's handmaiden. In this sight I understood truly that she is greater, more worthy and more fulfilled, than everything else which God has created, and which is inferior to her. Above her is no created thing, except the blessed humanity of Christ, as I saw.

CHAPTER 5

At the same time as I saw this sight of the head bleeding, our good Lord showed a spiritual sight of his familiar love. I saw that he is to us everything which is good and comforting for our help. He is our clothing, who wraps and enfolds us for love, embraces us and shelters us, surrounds us for his love, which is so tender that he may never desert us. And so in this sight I saw that he is everything which is good, as I understand.

And in this he showed me something small, no bigger than a hazelnut, lying in the palm of my hand, as it seemed to me, and it was as round as a ball. I looked at it with the eye of my understanding and thought: What can this be? I was amazed that it could last, for I thought that because of its littleness it would suddenly have fallen into nothing. And I was answered in my understanding: It lasts and always will, because God loves it; and thus everything has being through the love of God.

In this little thing I saw three properties. The first is that God made it, the second is that God loves it, the third is that God preserves it. But what did I see in it? It is that God is the Creator and the protector and the lover. For until I am substantially united to him, I can never have perfect rest or true happiness, until, that is, I am so attached to him that there can be no created thing between my God and me.

This little thing which is created seemed to me as if it could have fallen into nothing because of its littleness. We need to have knowledge of this, so that we may delight in despising as nothing everything created, so as to love and have uncreated God. For this is the reason why our hearts and souls are not in perfect ease, because here we seek rest in this thing which is so little, in which there is no rest, and we do not know our God who is almighty, all wise and all good, for he is true rest. God wishes to be known, and it pleases him that we should rest in him; for everything which is beneath him is not sufficient for us. And this is the reason why no soul is at rest until it has despised as nothing all things which are created. When it by its will has become nothing for love, to have him who is everything, then is it able to receive spiritual rest.

And also our good Lord revealed that it is very greatly pleasing to him that a simple soul should come naked, openly and familiarly. For this is the loving yearning of the soul through the touch of the Holy Spirit, from the understanding which I have in this revelation: God, of your goodness give me yourself, for you are enough for me, and I can ask for nothing which is less which can pay you full worship. And if I ask anything which is less, always I am in want; but only in you do I have everything.

And these words of the goodness of God are very dear to the soul, and very close to touching our Lord's will, for his goodness fills all his creatures and all his blessed works full, and endlessly overflows in them. For he is everlastingness, and he made us only for himself, and restored us by his precious Passion and always preserves us in his blessed love; and all this is of his goodness.

CHAPTER 9

I am not good because of the revelations, but only if I love God better; and inasmuch as you love God better, it is more to you than to me. I do not say this to those who are wise, because they know it well. But I say it to you who are simple, to give you comfort and strength; for we are all one in love, for truly it was not revealed to me that God loves me better than the humblest soul who is in a state of grace. For I am sure that there are many who never had revelations or visions, but only the common teaching of Holy Church, who love God better than I. If I pay special attention to myself, I am nothing at all; but in general I am, I hope, in the unity of love with all my fellow Christians. For it is in this unity that the life of all men consists who will be saved. For God is everything that is good, as I see; and God has made everything that is made, and God loves everything that he has made. And he who has general love for all his fellow Christians in God has love towards everything that is. For in mankind which will be saved is comprehended all, that is to say all that is made and the maker of all. For God is in man and in God is all. And he who loves thus loves all. And I hope by the grace of God that he who may see it so will be taught the truth and greatly comforted, if he has need of comfort.

I speak of those who will be saved, for at this time God showed me no one else. But in everything I believe as Holy Church preaches and teaches. For the faith of Holy Church, which I had before I had understanding, and which, as I hope by the grace of God, I intend to preserve whole and to practice, was always in my sight, and I wished and intended never to accept anything which might be contrary to it. And to this end and with this intention I contemplated the revelation with all diligence, for throughout this blessed revelation I contemplated it as God intended.

All this was shown in three parts,[5] that is to say, by bodily vision and by words formed in my understanding and by spiritual vision. But I may not and cannot show the spiritual visions as plainly and fully as I should wish. But I trust in our Lord God almighty that he will, out of his goodness and for love of you, make you accept it more spiritually and more sweetly than I can or may tell it.

[LAUGHING AT THE DEVIL]

CHAPTER 13[6]

And after this, before God revealed any words, he allowed me to contemplate him for a fitting length of time, and all that I had seen, and all the significance that was contained in it, as well as my soul's simplicity could accept it. And then he, without voice and without opening of lips, formed in my soul this saying: With this the fiend is overcome. Our Lord said this to me with reference to his blessed Passion, as he had shown it before. In this he showed a part of the fiend's malice, and all of his impotence, because he showed that his Passion is the overcoming of the fiend. God showed me that the fiend has now the same malice as he had before the Incarnation, and he works as hard, and he sees as constantly as he did before that all souls who will be saved escape him to God's glory by the power of our Lord's precious Passion. And that is the devil's sorrow, and he is put to terrible shame, for everything which God permits him to do turns to joy for us and to pain and shame for him. And he has as much sorrow when God permits him to work as when he is not working. And that is because he can never do as much evil as he would wish, for his power is all locked in

---

God's hands. But in God there can be no anger, as I see it, and it is with power and justice, to the profit of all who will be saved, that he opposes the damned, who in malice and malignity work to frustrate and oppose God's will.

Also I saw our Lord scorn his malice and despise him as nothing, and he wants us to do so. Because of this sight I laughed greatly, and that made those around me to laugh as well; and their laughter was pleasing to me. I thought that I wished that all my fellow Christians had seen what I saw. Then they would all have laughed with me; but I did not see Christ laughing, but I know well that it was the vision he showed me which made me laugh, for I understood that we may laugh, to comfort ourselves and rejoice in God, because the devil is overcome. And when I saw our Lord scorn his malice, that was through the fixing of my understanding on him, that is, that this was an interior revelation of his truth, in which his demeanour did not change. For as I see it, this is an attribute of God which must be honoured, and which lasts forever.

And after this I became serious again, and said: I see three things: sport and scorn and seriousness. I see sport, that the devil is overcome; and I see scorn, that God scorns him and he will be scorned; and I see seriousness, that he is overcome by the blessed Passion and death of our Lord Jesus Christ, which was accomplished in great earnest and with heavy labour. And when I said that he is scorned, I meant that God scorns him, that is, because he sees him now as he will forever. For in this God revealed that the devil is damned. And I meant this when I said that he ought to be scorned; for I saw that on Judgment Day he will be generally scorned by all who will be saved, of whose salvation he has had great envy. For then he will see that all the woe and tribulation which he has caused them will be changed into the increase of their eternal joy. And all the pain and the sorrow that he wanted to bring them into will go forever with him to hell.

[CHRIST DRAWS JULIAN IN THROUGH HIS WOUND]

CHAPTER 24[7]

With a kindly countenance our good Lord looked into his side, and he gazed with joy, and with his sweet regard he drew his creature's understanding into his side by the same wound;[8] and there he revealed a fair and delectable place, large enough for all mankind that will be saved and will rest in peace and in love. And with that he brought to mind the dear and precious blood and water which he suffered to be shed for love. And in this sweet sight he showed his blessed heart split in two, and as he rejoiced he showed to my understanding a part of his blessed divinity, as much as was his will at that time, strengthening my poor soul to understand what can be said, that is the endless love which was without beginning and is and always shall be.

And with this our good Lord said most joyfully: See how I love you, as if he had said, my darling, behold and see your Lord, your God, who is your Creator and your endless joy; see your own brother, your savior; my child, behold and see what delight and bliss I have in your salvation, and for my love rejoice with me.

And for my greater understanding, these blessed words were said: See how I love you, as if he had said, behold and see that I loved you so much, before I died for you, that I wanted to die for you. And now I have died for you, and willingly suffered what I could. And now all my bitter pain and my hard labor is turned into everlasting joy

7. This chapter recounts Julian's tenth revelation.   8. The spear wound in Christ's side.

and bliss for me and for you. How could it now be that you would pray to me for any-thing pleasing to me which I would not very gladly grant to you? For my delight is in your holiness and in your endless joy and bliss in me.

This is the understanding, as simply as I can say it, of these blessed words: See how I loved you. Our Lord revealed this to make us glad and joyful.

CHAPTER 25[9]

And with this same appearance of mirth and joy our good Lord looked down on his right, and brought to my mind where our Lady stood at the time of his Passion, and he said: Do you wish to see her? And these sweet words were as if he had said, I know well that you wish to see my blessed mother, for after myself she is the greatest joy that I could show you, and the greatest delight and honor to me, and she is what all my blessed creatures most desire to see. And because of the wonderful, exalted and singular love that he has for this sweet maiden, his blessed mother, our Lady Saint Mary, he reveals her bliss and joy through the sense of these sweet words, as if he said, do you wish to see how I love her, so that you could rejoice with me in the love which I have in her and she has in me?

And for greater understanding of these sweet words our good Lord speaks in love to all mankind who will be saved, addressing them all as one person, as if he said, do you wish to see in her how you are loved? It is for love of you that I have made her so exalted, so noble, so honorable; and this delights me. And I wish it to delight you. For next to him, she is the most blissful to be seen. But in this matter I was not taught to long to see her bodily presence whilst I am here, but the virtues of her blessed soul, her truth, her wisdom, her love, through which I am taught to know myself and rev-erently to fear my God.

And when our good Lord had revealed this, and said these words: Do you wish to see her? I answered and said: Yes, good Lord, great thanks, yes, good Lord, if it be your will. Often times I had prayed for this, and I had expected to see her in a bodily like-ness; but I did not see her so. And Jesus, saying this, showed me a spiritual vision of her. Just as before I had seen her small and simple, now he showed her high and noble and glorious and more pleasing to him than all creatures. And so he wishes it to be known that all who take delight in him should take delight in her, and in the delight that he has in her and she in him.

And for greater understanding he showed this example, as if, when a man loves some creature particularly, more than all other creatures, he will make all other crea-tures to love and delight in that creature whom he loves so much. And in these words which Jesus said: Do you wish to see her? it seemed to me that these were the most delectable words which he could give me in this spiritual vision of her which he gave me. For our Lord showed me no particular person except our Lady Saint Mary, and he showed her on three occasions. The first was as she conceived, the second was as she had been under the Cross, and the third was as she is now, in delight, honor and joy.

CHAPTER 26[1]

And after this our Lord showed himself to me, and he appeared to me more glorified than I had seen him before, in which I was taught that our soul will never have rest till it comes into him, acknowledging that he is full of joy, familiar and courteous and blissful and true life. Again and again our Lord said: I am he, I am he, I am he who is

---

9. The eleventh revelation.   1. The twelfth revelation.

highest. I am he whom you love. I am he in whom you delight. I am he whom you serve. I am he for whom you long. I am he whom you desire. I am he whom you intend. I am he who is all. I am he whom Holy Church preaches and teaches to you. I am he who showed himself before to you. The number of the words surpasses my intelligence and my understanding and all my powers, for they were the most exalted, as I see it, for in them is comprehended I cannot tell what; but the joy which I saw when they were revealed surpasses all that the heart can think or the soul may desire. And therefore these words are not explained here, but let every man accept them as our Lord intended them, according to the grace God gives him in understanding and love.

[THE NECESSITY OF SIN, AND OF HATING SIN]

CHAPTER 27[2]

And after this our Lord brought to my mind the longing that I had for him before, and I saw that nothing hindered me but sin, and I saw that this is true of us all in general, and it seemed to me that if there had been no sin, we should all have been pure and as like our Lord as he created us. And so in my folly before this time I often wondered why, through the great prescient wisdom of God, the beginning of sin was not prevented. For then it seemed to me that all would have been well.

The impulse to think this was greatly to be shunned; and nevertheless I mourned and sorrowed on this account, unreasonably, lacking discretion. But Jesus, who in this vision informed me about everything needful to me, answered with these words and said: Sin is necessary, but all will be well, and all will be well, and every kind of thing will be well. In this naked word "sin," our Lord brought generally to my mind all which is not good, and the shameful contempt and the direst tribulation which he endured for us in this life, and his death and all his pains, and the passions, spiritual and bodily, of all his creatures. For we are all in part troubled, and we shall be troubled, following our master Jesus until we are fully purged of our mortal flesh and all our inward affections which are not very good.

And with the beholding of this, with all the pains that ever were or ever will be, I understood Christ's Passion for the greatest and surpassing pain. And yet this was shown to me in an instant, and it quickly turned into consolation. For our good Lord would not have the soul frightened by this ugly sight. But I did not see sin, for I believe that it has no kind of substance, no share in being, nor can it be recognized except by the pain caused by it. And it seems to me that this pain is something for a time, for it purges and makes us know ourselves and ask for mercy; for the Passion of our Lord is comfort to us against all this, and that is his blessed will. And because of the tender love which our good Lord has for all who will be saved, he comforts readily and sweetly, meaning this: It is true that sin is the cause of all this pain, but all will be well, and every kind of thing will be well.

These works were revealed most tenderly, showing no kind of blame to me or to anyone who will be saved. So it would be most unkind of me to blame God or marvel at him on account of my sins, since he does not blame me for sin.

2. The thirteenth revelation.

And in these same words I saw hidden in God an exalted and wonderful mystery, which he will make plain and we shall know in heaven. In this knowledge we shall truly see the cause why he allowed sin to come, and in this sight we shall rejoice forever.

CHAPTER 40

And this is a supreme friendship of our courteous Lord, that he protects us so tenderly whilst we are in our sins; and furthermore he touches us most secretly, and shows us our sins by the sweet light of mercy and grace. But when we see ourselves so foul, then we believe that God may be angry with us because of our sins. Then we are moved by the Holy Spirit through contrition to prayer, and we desire with all our might an amendment of ourselves to appease God's anger, until the time that we find rest of soul and ease of conscience. And then we hope that God has forgiven us our sin; and this is true. And then our courteous Lord shows himself to the soul, happily and with the gladdest countenance, welcoming it as a friend, as if it had been in pain and in prison, saying: My dear darling, I am glad that you have come to me in all your woe. I have always been with you, and now you see me loving, and we are made one in bliss.

So sins are forgiven by grace and mercy, and our soul is honorably received in joy, as it will be when it comes into heaven, as often as it comes by the operation of grace of the Holy Spirit and the power of Christ's Passion.

Here I truly understood that every kind of thing is made available to us by God's great goodness, so much so that when we ourselves are at peace and in charity we are truly safe. But because we cannot have this completely whilst we are here, therefore it is fitting for us to live always in sweet prayer and in loving longing with our Lord Jesus. For he always longs to bring us to the fullness of joy, as has been said before, where he reveals his spiritual thirst. But now, because of all this spiritual consolation which has been described, if any man or woman be moved by folly to say or to think "If this be true, then it would be well to sin so as to have the greater reward, or else to think sin less important," beware of this impulse, for truly, should it come, it is untrue and from the fiend.

For the same true love which touches us all by its blessed strength, that same blessed love teaches us that we must hate sin only because of love. And I am sure by what I feel that the more that each loving soul sees this in the courteous love of our Lord God, the greater is his hatred of sinning and the more he is ashamed. For if it were laid in front of us, all the pain there is in hell and in purgatory and on earth, death and all the rest, we should choose all that pain rather than sin. For sin is so vile and so much to be hated that it can be compared with no pain which is not itself sin. And no more cruel hell than sin was revealed to me, for a loving soul hates no pain but sin; for everything is good except sin, and nothing is evil except sin. And when by the operation of mercy and grace we set our intention on mercy and grace, we are made all fair and spotless.

And God is as willing as he is powerful and wise to save man. And Christ himself is the foundation of all the laws of Christian men, and he taught us to do good in return for evil. Here we may see that he is himself this love, and does to us as he teaches us to do; for he wishes us to be like him in undiminished, everlasting love towards ourselves and our fellow Christians. No more than his love towards us is withdrawn because of our sin does he wish our love to be withdrawn from ourselves or from our fellow Christians; but we must unreservedly hate sin and endlessly love the soul as God loves it. Then we should hate sin just as God hates it, and love the soul as God loves it. For these words which God said are an endless strength: I protect you most truly.

CHAPTER 58

God the blessed Trinity, who is everlasting being, just as he is eternal from without beginning, just so was it in his eternal purpose to create human nature, which fair nature was first prepared for his own Son, the second person; and when he wished, by full agreement of the whole Trinity he created us all once. And in our creating he joined and united us to himself, and through this union we are kept as pure and as noble as we were created. By the power of that same precious union we love our Creator and delight in him, praise him and thank him and endlessly rejoice in him. And this is the work which is constantly performed in every soul which will be saved, and this is the godly will mentioned before.

And so in our making, God almighty is our loving Father, and God all wisdom is our loving Mother,[3] with the love and the goodness of the Holy Spirit, which is all one God, one Lord. And in the joining and the union he is our very true spouse and we his beloved wife and his fair maiden, with which wife he was never displeased; for he says: I love you and you love me, and our love will never divide in two.

I contemplated the work of all the blessed Trinity, in which contemplation I saw and understood these three properties: the property of the fatherhood, and the property of the motherhood, and the property of the lordship in one God. In our almighty Father we have our protection and our bliss, as regards our natural substance, which is ours by our creation from without beginning; and in the second person, in knowledge and wisdom we have our perfection, as regards our sensuality, our restoration and our salvation, for he is our Mother, brother and savior; and in our good Lord the Holy Spirit we have our reward and our gift for our living and our labor, endlessly surpassing all that we desire in his marvelous courtesy, out of his great plentiful grace. For all our life consists of three: In the first we have our being, and in the second we have our increasing, and in the third we have our fulfillment. The first is nature, the second is mercy, the third is grace.

As to the first, I saw and understood that the high might of the Trinity is our Father, and the deep wisdom of the Trinity is our Mother, and the great love of the Trinity is our Lord; and all these we have in nature and in our substantial creation. And furthermore I saw that the second person, who is our Mother, substantially the same beloved person, has now become our mother sensually, because we are double by God's creating, that is to say substantial and sensual. Our substance is the higher part, which we have in our Father, God almighty; and the second person of the Trinity is our Mother in nature in our substantial creation, in whom we are founded and rooted, and he is our Mother of mercy in taking our sensuality. And so our Mother is working on us in various ways, in whom our parts are kept undivided; for in our Mother Christ we profit and increase, and in mercy he reforms and restores us, and by the power of his Passion, his death and his Resurrection, he unites us to our substance. So our Mother works in mercy on all his beloved children who are docile and

---

3. The image of God as a wise woman draws from an ancient tradition of the female Sophia, Holy Wisdom, who figures in the apocryphal book of Ecclesiasticus (ch. 24).

obedient to him, and grace works with mercy, and especially in two properties, as it was shown, which working belongs to the third person, the Holy Spirit. He works, rewarding and giving. Rewarding is a gift for our confidence which the Lord makes to those who have labored; and giving is a courteous act which he does freely, by grace, fulfilling and surpassing all that creatures deserve.

Thus in our Father, God almighty, we have our being, and in our Mother of mercy we have our reforming and our restoring, in whom our parts are united and all made perfect man, and through the rewards and the gifts of grace of the Holy Spirit we are fulfilled. And our substance is in our Father, God almighty, and our substance is in our Mother, God all wisdom, and our substance is in our Lord God, the Holy Spirit, all goodness, for our substance is whole in each person of the Trinity, who is one God. And our sensuality is only in the second person, Christ Jesus, in whom is the Father and the Holy Spirit; and in him and by him we are powerfully taken out of hell and out of the wretchedness on earth, and gloriously brought up into heaven, and blessedly united to our substance, increased in riches and nobility by all the power of Christ and by the grace and operation of the Holy Spirit.

CHAPTER 59

And we have all this bliss by mercy and grace, and this kind of bliss we never could have had and known, unless that property of goodness which is in God had been opposed, through which we have this bliss. For wickedness has been suffered to rise in opposition to that goodness; and the goodness of mercy and grace opposed that wickedness, and turned everything to goodness and honor for all who will be saved. For this is that property in God which opposes good to evil. So Jesus Christ, who opposes good to evil, is our true Mother. We have our being from him, where the foundation of motherhood begins, with all the sweet protection of love which endlessly follows.

As truly as God is our Father, so truly is God our Mother, and he revealed that in everything, and especially in these sweet words where he says: I am he; that is to say: I am he, the power and goodness of fatherhood; I am he, the wisdom and the lovingness of motherhood; I am he, the light and the grace which is all blessed love; I am he, the Trinity; I am he, the unity; I am he, the great supreme goodness of every kind of thing; I am he who makes you to love; I am he who makes you to long; I am he, the endless fulfilling of all true desires. For where the soul is highest, noblest, most honorable, still it is lowest, meekest and mildest.

And from this foundation in substance we have all the powers of our sensuality by the gift of nature, and by the help and the furthering of mercy and grace, without which we cannot profit. Our great Father, almighty God, who is being, knows us and loved us before time began. Out of this knowledge, in his most wonderful deep love, by the prescient eternal counsel of all the blessed Trinity, he wanted the second person to become our Mother, our brother and our savior. From this it follows that as truly as God is our Father, so truly is God our Mother. Our Father wills, our Mother works, our good Lord the Holy Spirit confirms. And therefore it is our part to love our God in whom we have our being, reverently thanking and praising him for our creation, mightily praying to our Mother for mercy and pity, and to our Lord the Holy Spirit for help and grace. For in these three is all our life: nature, mercy and grace, of which we have mildness, patience and pity, and hatred of sin and wickedness; for the virtues must of themselves hate sin and wickedness.

And so Jesus is our true Mother in nature by our first creation, and he is our true Mother in grace by his taking our created nature. All the lovely works and all the sweet loving offices of beloved motherhood are appropriated to the second person, for in him we have this godly will, whole and safe forever, both in nature and in grace, from his own goodness proper to him.

I understand three ways of contemplating motherhood in God. The first is the foundation of our nature's creation; the second is his taking of our nature, where the motherhood of grace begins; the third is the motherhood at work. And in that, by the same grace, everything is penetrated, in length and in breadth, in height and in depth without end; and it is all one love.

CHAPTER 60

But now I should say a little more about this penetration, as I understood our Lord to mean: How we are brought back by the motherhood of mercy and grace into our natural place, in which we were created by the motherhood of love, a mother's love which never leaves us.

Our Mother in nature, our Mother in grace, because he wanted altogether to become our Mother in all things, made the foundation of his work most humbly and most mildly in the maiden's womb. And he revealed that in the first revelation, when he brought that meek maiden before the eye of my understanding in the simple stature which she had when she conceived; that is to say that our great God, the supreme wisdom of all things, arrayed and prepared himself in this humble place, all ready in our poor flesh, himself to do the service and the office of motherhood in everything. The mother's service is nearest, readiest and surest: nearest because it is most natural, readiest because it is most loving, and surest because it is truest. No one ever might or could perform this office fully, except only him. We know that all our mothers bear us for pain and for death. O, what is that? But our true Mother Jesus, he alone bears us for joy and for endless life, blessed may he be. So he carries us within him in love and travail, until the full time when he wanted to suffer the sharpest thorns and cruel pains that ever were or will be, and at the last he died. And when he had finished, and had borne us so for bliss, still all this could not satisfy his wonderful love. And he revealed this in these great surpassing words of love: If I could suffer more, I would suffer more. He could not die any more, but he did not want to cease working; therefore he must needs nourish us, for the precious love of motherhood has made him our debtor.

The mother can give her child to suck of her milk, but our precious Mother Jesus can feed us with himself, and does, most courteously and most tenderly, with the blessed sacrament, which is the precious food of true life; and with all the sweet sacraments he sustains us most mercifully and graciously, and so he meant in these blessed words, where he said: I am he whom Holy Church preaches and teaches to you. That is to say: All the health and the life of the sacraments, all the power and the grace of my word, all the goodness which is ordained in Holy Church for you, I am he.

The mother can lay her child tenderly to her breast, but our tender Mother Jesus can lead us easily into his blessed breast through his sweet open side, and show us there a part of the godhead and of the joys of heaven, with inner certainty of endless bliss. And that he revealed in the tenth revelation, giving us the same understanding in these sweet words which he says: See, how I love you, looking into his blessed side, rejoicing.

This fair lovely word "mother" is so sweet and so kind in itself that it cannot truly be said of anyone or to anyone except of him and to him who is the true Mother of life and of all things. To the property of motherhood belong nature, love, wisdom and knowledge, and this is God. For though it may be so that our bodily bringing to birth is only little, humble and simple in comparison with our spiritual bringing to birth, still it is he who does it in the creatures by whom it is done. The kind, loving mother who knows and sees the need of her child guards it very tenderly, as the nature and condition of motherhood will have. And always as the child grows in age and in stature, she acts differently, but she does not change her love. And when it is even older, she allows it to be chastised to destroy its faults, so as to make the child receive virtues and grace. This work, with everything which is lovely and good, our Lord performs in those by whom it is done. So he is our Mother in nature by the operation of grace in the lower part, for love of the higher part. And he wants us to know it, for he wants to have all our love attached to him; and in this I saw that every debt which we owe by God's command to fatherhood and motherhood is ful-filled in truly loving God, which blessed love Christ works in us. And this was revealed in everything, and especially in the great bounteous words when he says: I am he whom you love.

CHAPTER 61

And in our spiritual bringing to birth he uses more tenderness, without any compari-son, in protecting us. By so much as our soul is more precious in his sight, he kindles our understanding, he prepares our ways, he eases our conscience, he comforts our soul, he illumines our heart and gives us partial knowledge and love of his blessed divinity, with gracious memory of his sweet humanity and his blessed Passion, with courteous wonder over his great surpassing goodness, and makes us to love every-thing which he loves for love of him, and to be well satisfied with him and with all his works. And when we fall, quickly he raises us up with his loving embrace and his gracious touch. And when we are strengthened by his sweet working, then we will-ingly choose him by his grace, that we shall be his servants and his lovers, constantly and forever.

And yet after this he allows some of us to fall more heavily and more grievously than ever we did before, as it seems to us. And then we who are not all wise think that everything which we have undertaken was all nothing. But it is not so, for we need to fall, and we need to see it; for if we did not fall, we should not know how fee-ble and how wretched we are in ourselves, nor, too, should we know so completely the wonderful love of our Creator.

For we shall truly see in heaven without end that we have sinned grievously in this life; and notwithstanding this, we shall truly see that we were never hurt in his love, nor were we ever of less value in his sight. And by the experience of this falling we shall have a great and marvelous knowledge of love in God without end; for enduring and marvelous is that love which cannot and will not be broken because of offenses.

And this was one profitable understanding; another is the humility and meekness which we shall obtain by the sight of our fall, for by that we shall be raised high in heaven, to which raising we might never have come without that meekness. And therefore we need to see it; and if we do not see it, though we fell, that would not prof-it us. And commonly we first fall and then see it; and both are from the mercy of God.

The mother may sometimes suffer the child to fall and to be distressed in various ways, for its own benefit, but she can never suffer any kind of peril to come to her child, because of her love. And though our earthly mother may suffer her child to perish, our heavenly Mother Jesus may never suffer us who are his children to perish, for he is almighty, all wisdom and all love, and so is none but he, blessed may he be.

But often when our falling and our wretchedness are shown to us, we are so much afraid and so greatly ashamed of ourselves that we scarcely know where we can put ourselves. But then our courteous Mother does not wish us to flee away, for nothing would be less pleasing to him; but he then wants us to behave like a child. For when it is distressed and frightened, it runs quickly to its mother; and if it can do no more, it calls to the mother for help with all its might. So he wants us to act as a meek child, saying: My kind Mother, my gracious Mother, my beloved Mother, have mercy on me. I have made myself filthy and unlike you, and I may not and cannot make it right except with your help and grace.

And if we do not then feel ourselves eased, let us at once be sure that he is behaving as a wise Mother. For if he sees that it is profitable to us to mourn and to weep, with compassion and pity he suffers that until the right time has come, out of his love. And then he wants us to show a child's characteristics, which always naturally trusts in its mother's love in well-being and in woe. And he wants us to commit ourselves fervently to the faith of Holy Church, and find there our beloved Mother in consolation and true understanding, with all the company of the blessed. For one single person may often be broken, as it seems to him, but the entire body of Holy Church was never broken, nor ever will be without end. And therefore it is a certain thing, and good and gracious to will, meekly and fervently, to be fastened and united to our mother Holy Church, who is Christ Jesus. For the flood of mercy which is his dear blood and precious water is plentiful to make us fair and clean. The blessed wounds of our savior are open and rejoice to heal us. The sweet gracious hands of our Mother are ready and diligent about us; for he in all this work exercises the true office of a kind nurse, who has nothing else to do but attend to the safety of her child.

It is his office to save us, it is his glory to do it, and it is his will that we know it; for he wants us to love him sweetly and trust in him meekly and greatly. And he revealed this in these gracious words: I protect you very safely.

[THE SOUL AS CHRIST'S CITADEL]

CHAPTER 68

And then our good Lord opened my spiritual eye, and showed me my soul in the midst of my heart. I saw the soul as wide as if it were an endless citadel, and also as if it were a blessed kingdom, and from the state which I saw in it, I understood that it is a fine city. In the midst of that city sits our Lord Jesus, true God and true man, a handsome person and tall, highest bishop, most awesome king, most honourable lord. And I saw him splendidly clad in honours. He sits erect there in the soul, in peace and rest, and he rules and guards heaven and earth and everything that is. The humanity and the divinity sit at rest, the divinity rules and guards, without instrument or effort. And the soul is wholly occupied by the blessed divinity, sovereign power, sovereign wisdom and sovereign goodness.

The place which Jesus takes in our soul he will nevermore vacate, for in us is his home of homes and his everlasting dwelling. And in this he revealed the delight that he has in the creation of man's soul; for as well as the Father could create a creature and as well as the Son could create a creature, so well did the Holy Spirit want man's spirit to be created, and so it was done. And therefore the blessed Trinity rejoices without end in the creation of man's soul, for it saw without beginning what would delight it without end.

Everything which God has made shows his dominion, as understanding was given at the same time by the example of a creature who is led to see the great nobility and the rulership which is fitting to a lord, and when it had seen all the nobility beneath, then in wonder it was moved to seek up above for that high place where the lord dwells, knowing by reason that his dwelling is in the most honourable place. And thus I understood truly that our soul may never have rest in anything which is beneath itself. And when it comes above all creatures into itself, still it cannot remain contemplating itself; but all its contemplation is blessedly set in God, who is the Creator, dwelling there, for in man's soul is his true dwelling.

And the greatest light and the brightest shining in the city is the glorious love of our Lord God, as I see it. And what can make us to rejoice more in God than to see in him that in us, of all his greatest works, he has joy? For I saw in the same revelation that if the blessed Trinity could have created man's soul any better, any fairer, any nobler than it was created, the Trinity would not have been fully pleased with the creation of man's soul. But because it made man's soul as beautiful, as good, as precious a creature as it could make, therefore the blessed Trinity is fully pleased without end in the creation of man's soul. And it wants our hearts to be powerfully lifted above the depths of the earth and all empty sorrows, and to rejoice in it.

This was a delectable sight and a restful showing, which is without end, and to contemplate it while we are here is most pleasing to God and very great profit to us. And this makes the soul which so contemplates like to him who is contemplated, and unites it in rest and peace. And it was a singular joy and bliss to me that I saw him sitting, for the truth of sitting revealed to me endless dwelling; and he gave me true knowledge that it was he who had revealed everything to me before. And when I had contemplated this with attention, our Lord very humbly revealed words to me, without voice and without opening of lips, just as he had done before, and said very sweetly: Know it well, it was no hallucination which you saw today, but accept and believe it and hold firmly to it, and comfort yourself with it and trust in it, and you will not be overcome.

These last words were said to me to teach me perfect certainty that it is our Lord Jesus who revealed everything to me; and just as in the first words which our good Lord revealed, alluding to his blessed Passion: With this the fiend is overcome, just so he said in the last words, with perfect fidelity, alluding to us all: You will not be overcome. And all this teaching and this true strengthening apply generally to all my fellow Christians, as is said before, and so is the will of God.

And these words: You will not be overcome, were said very insistently and strongly, for certainty and strength against every tribulation which may come. He did not say: You will not be troubled, you will not be belaboured, you will not be disquieted; but he said: You will not be overcome. God wants us to pay attention to these words, and always to be strong in faithful trust, in well-being and in woe, for he loves us and delights in us, and so he wishes us to love him and delight in him and trust greatly in him, and all will be well.

And soon all was hidden, and I saw no more after this.

[THE MEANING OF THE VISIONS IS LOVE]

CHAPTER 86

This book is begun by God's gift and his grace, but it is not yet performed, as I see it. For charity, let us all join with God's working in prayer, thanking, trusting, rejoicing, for so will our good Lord be entreated, by the understanding which I took in all his own intention, and in the sweet words where he says most happily: I am the foundation of your beseeching. For truly I saw and understood in our Lord's meaning that he revealed it because he wants to have it better known than it is. In which knowledge he wants to give us grace to love him and to cleave to him, for he beholds his heavenly treasure with so great love on earth that he will give us more light and solace in heavenly joy, by drawing our hearts from the sorrow and the darkness which we are in.

And from the time that it was revealed, I desired many times to know in what was our Lord's meaning. And fifteen years after and more, I was answered in spiritual understanding, and it was said: What, do you wish to know your Lord's meaning in this thing? Know it well, love was his meaning. Who reveals it to you? Love. What did he reveal to you? Love. Why does he reveal it to you? For love. Remain in this, and you will know more of the same. But you will never know different, without end.

So I was taught that love is our Lord's meaning. And I saw very certainly in this and in everything that before God made us he loved us, which love was never abated and never will be. And in this love he has done all his works, and in this love he has made all things profitable to us, and in this love our life is everlasting. In our creation we had beginning, but the love in which he created us was in him from without beginning. In this love we have our beginning, and all this shall we see in God without end.

Thanks be to God. Here ends the book of revelations of Julian the anchorite of Norwich, on whose soul may God have mercy.[4]

May Jesus grant us this. Amen. So ends the revelation of love of the blessed Trinity, shown by our savior Jesus Christ for our endless comfort and solace, and also that we may rejoice in him in the passing journey of this life. Amen. Jesus. Amen. I pray almighty God that this book may not come except into the hands of those who wish to be his faithful lovers, and those who will submit themselves to the faith of Holy Church and obey the wholesome understanding and teaching of men who are of virtuous life, settled age and profound learning; for this revelation is exalted divinity and wisdom, and therefore it cannot remain with him who is a slave to sin and to the devil. And beware that you do not accept one thing which is according to your pleasure and liking, and reject another, for that is the disposition of heretics. But accept it all together, and understand it truly; it all agrees with Holy Scripture, and is founded upon it, and Jesus, our true love and light and truth, will show this to all pure souls who meekly and perseveringly ask this wisdom from him. And you to whom this book will come, give our savior Christ Jesus great and hearty thanks that he made these showings and revelations for you and to you out of his endless love, mercy and goodness, for a safe guide and conduct for you and us to everlasting bliss, which may Jesus grant us. Amen. Here end the sublime and wonderful revelations of

---

4. What follows is a lengthy version of the traditional "colophon" in which the author takes leave of the work and its audience; expressions of inadequacy and appeals to God are common elements.

the unutterable love of God, in Jesus Christ vouchsafed to a dear lover of his, and in her to all his dear friends and lovers whose hearts like hers do flame in the love of our dearest Jesus.

☙

COMPANION READINGS
Richard Rolle: from The Fire of Love[1]

It is obvious to those who are in love that no one attains the heights of devotion at once, or is ravished with contemplative sweetness. In fact it is only very occasionally—and then only momentarily—that they are allowed to experience heavenly things; their progress to spiritual strength is a gradual one. When they have attained the gravity of behavior so necessary and have achieved a certain stability of mind—as much as changing circumstances permit—a certain perfection is acquired after great labor. It is then that they can feel some joy in loving God.

Notwithstanding, it appears that all those who are mighty performers in virtue immediately and genuinely experience the warmth of uncreated or created charity, melt in the immense fire of love, and sing within their hearts the song of divine praise. For this mystery is hidden from the many, and is revealed to the few, and those the most special. So the more sublime such a level is, the fewer—in this world—are those who find it. Rarely in fact have we found a man who is so holy or even perfect in this earthly life endowed with love so great as to be raised up to contemplation to the level of jubilant song. This would mean that he would receive within himself the sound that is sung in heaven, and that he would echo back the praises of God as it were in harmony, pouring forth sweet notes of music and composing spiritual songs as he offers his heavenly praises, and that he would truly experience in his heart the genuine fire of the love of God. It would be surprising if anyone without such experience should claim the name of contemplative when the psalmist, speaking in character as the typical contemplative, exclaims, *I will go into the house of the Lord, with the voice of praise and thanksgiving.*[2] The praise, of course, is the praise offered by the banqueter, one who is feeding on heavenly sweetness.

Further, perfect souls who have been caught up into this friendship—surpassing, abundant, and eternal!—discover that life is suffused with imperishable sweetness from the glittering chalice of sweet charity. In holy happy wisdom they inhale joyful heat into their souls, and as a result are much cheered by the indescribable comfort of God's healing medicine. Here at all events is refreshment for those who love their high and eternal heritage, even though in their earthly exile distress befell them. However they think it not unfitting to endure a few years' hardship in order to be raised to heavenly thrones, and never leave them. They have been selected out of all mankind to be the beloved of their Maker and to be crowned with glory, since, like the seraphim in highest heaven, they have been inflamed with the same love. Physi-

---

1. Richard Rolle (c. 1300–1349) studied at Oxford and then spent part of his life as a hermit, but he also acted as spiritual director for women engaged in solitary contemplation. In seeking to express and draw his readers toward the ineffable experience of the divine, Rolle made particularly intensive use of the imagery of bodily sensation and action—warmth, sweetness, and song. Well-known biblical texts such as the Song of Songs provided both a precedent and a language for Rolle's explorations. Unlike more rigorous mystics, he presents at least the earlier stages of the mystical ascent as an almost spontaneous, if also conflict-ridden, rising of the soul like a spark toward God. Rolle wrote a number of English lyrics and meditations; *The Fire of Love* is his most famous treatise in Latin. The passage here, taken from ch. 2, is translated by Clifton Wolters.

2. Psalms 42.4.

cally they may have sat in solitary state, but in mind they have companied with angels, and have yearned for their Beloved. Now they sing most sweetly a prayer of love everlasting as they rejoice in Jesus:

> O honeyed flame, sweeter than all sweet, delightful beyond all creation!
> My God, my Love, surge over me, pierce me by your love, wound me with your
>> beauty.
> Surge over me, I say, who am longing for your comfort.
> Reveal your healing medicine to your poor lover.
> See, my one desire is for you; it is you my heart is seeking.
> My soul pants for you; my whole being is athirst for you.
>> Yet you will not show yourself to me; you look away;
>> you bar the door, shun me, pass me over;
> You even laugh at my innocent sufferings.
> And yet you snatch your lovers away from all earthly things.
> You lift them above every desire for worldly matters.
> You make them capable of loving you—
>> and love you they do indeed.
> So they offer you their praise in spiritual song
>> which bursts out from that inner fire;
>> they know in truth the sweetness of the dart of love.
> Ah, eternal and most lovable of all joys,
>> you raise us from the very depths,
>> and entrance us with the sight of divine majesty so often!
> Come into me, Beloved!
> All ever I had I have given up for you;
>> I have spurned all that was to be mine,
>> that you might make your home in my heart,
>> and I your comfort.
> Do not forsake me now, smitten with such great longing,
>> whose consuming desire is to be amongst those who love you.
> Grant me to love you, to rest in you, that in your kingdom I may be worthy
>> to appear before you world without end.

from *The Cloud of Unknowing*[1]

CHAPTER 3

Lift up your heart to God with humble love: and mean God himself, and not what you get out of him. Indeed, hate to think of anything but God himself, so that nothing occupies your mind or will but only God. Try to forget all created things that he ever made, and the purpose behind them, so that your thought and longing do not turn or reach out to them either in general or in particular. Let them go, and pay no attention to them. It is the work of the soul that pleases God most. All saints and angels rejoice over it, and hasten to help it on with all their might. All the fiends, however, are furious at what you are doing, and try to defeat it in every conceivable

---

1. Written toward the end of the 14th century, *The Cloud of Unknowing* draws upon an influential tradition of Neoplatonic Christianity. One strand of this tradition extolled the *via negativa*: the approach to union with God by emptying the mind of worldly consciousness, and entering instead a dark place of uncertainty, a "cloud of unknowing." Though informed by a very private notion of disciplined spiritual quest, the *Cloud* nevertheless insists that the mystic's work serves the salvation of all the faithful. At the same time, the text also betrays considerable anxiety about, even hostility to, the spread of an undirected and body-oriented spirituality in its time. It particularly warns against the danger of demonic influence in those seeking too eagerly some bodily sign of the divine. It mentions the sensation of heat and other enthusiastic bodily manifestations, which may recall the affective imagery of Rolle. The translation here is by Clifton Wolters.

way. Moreover, the whole of mankind is wonderfully helped by what you are doing, in ways you do not understand. Yes, the very souls in purgatory find their pain eased by virtue of your work. And in no better way can you yourself be made clean or virtuous than by attending to this. Yet it is the easiest work of all when the soul is helped by grace and has a conscious longing. And it can be achieved very quickly. Otherwise it is hard and beyond your powers.

Do not give up then, but work away at it till you have this longing. When you first begin, you find only darkness, and as it were a cloud of unknowing. You don't know what this means except that in your will you feel a simple steadfast intention reaching out towards God. Do what you will, this darkness and this cloud remain between you and God, and stop you both from seeing him in the clear light of rational understanding, and from experiencing his loving sweetness in your affection. Reconcile yourself to wait in this darkness as long as is necessary, but still go on longing after him whom you love. For if you are to feel him or to see him in this life, it must always be in this cloud, in this darkness. And if you will work hard at what I tell you, I believe that through God's mercy you will achieve this very thing.

FROM CHAPTER 4

So that you may make no mistake, or go wrong in this matter, let me tell you a little more about it as I see it. This work does not need a long time for its completion. Indeed, it is the shortest work that can be imagined! It is no longer, no shorter, than one atom, which as a philosopher of astronomy will tell you is the smallest division of time. It is so small that it cannot be analyzed: it is almost beyond our grasp. Yet it is as long as the time of which it has been written, "All the time that is given to thee, it shall be asked of thee how thou hast spent it." And it is quite right that you should have to give account of it. It is neither shorter nor longer than a single impulse of your will, the chief part of your soul. * * *

So pay great attention to this marvelous work of grace within your soul. It is always a sudden impulse and comes without warning, springing up to God like some spark from the fire. An incredible number of such impulses arise in one brief hour in the soul who has a will to this work! In one such flash the soul may completely forget the created world outside. Yet almost as quickly it may relapse back to thoughts and memories of things done and undone—all because of our fallen nature. And as fast again it may rekindle.

This then, in brief, is how it works. It is obviously not make-believe, nor wrong thinking, nor fanciful opinion. These would not be the product of a devout and humble love, but the outcome of the pride and inventiveness of the imagination. If this work of grace is to be truly and genuinely understood, all such proud imaginings must ruthlessly be stamped out!

For whoever hears or reads about all this, and thinks that it is fundamentally an activity of the mind, and proceeds then to work it all out along these lines, is on quite the wrong track. He manufactures an experience that is neither spiritual nor physical. He is dangerously misled and in real peril. So much so, that unless God in his great goodness intervenes with a miracle of mercy and makes him stop and submit to the advice of those who really know, he will go mad, or suffer some other dreadful form of spiritual mischief and devilish deceit. Indeed, almost casually as it were, he may be lost eternally, body and soul. So for the love of God be careful, and do not attempt to achieve this experience intellectually. I tell you truly it cannot come this way. So leave it alone.

Do not think that because I call it a "darkness" or a "cloud" it is the sort of cloud you see in the sky, or the kind of darkness you know at home when the light is out. That kind of darkness or cloud you can picture in your mind's eye in the height of summer, just as in the depth of a winter's night you can picture a clear and shining light. I do not mean this at all. By "darkness" I mean "a lack of knowing"—just as anything that you do not know or may have forgotten may be said to be "dark" to you, for you cannot see it with your inward eye. For this reason it is called "a cloud," not of the sky, of course, but "of unknowing," a cloud of unknowing between you and your God.

Chapter 52

The madness I speak of is effected like this: they read and hear it said that they should stop the "exterior" working with their mind, and work interiorly. And because they do not know what this "interior" work means, they do it wrong. For they turn their actual physical minds inwards to their bodies, which is an unnatural thing, and they strain as if to see spiritually with their physical eyes, and to hear within with their outward ears, and to smell and taste and feel and so on inwardly in the same way. So they pervert the natural order, and with this false ingenuity they put their minds to such unnecessary strains that ultimately their brains are turned. And at once the devil is able to deceive them with false lights and sounds, sweet odors and wonderful tastes, glowing and burning in their hearts or stomachs, backs or loins or limbs.

In all this make-believe they imagine they are peacefully contemplating their God, unhindered by vain thoughts. So they are, in a fashion, for they are so stuffed with falsehood that a little extra vanity cannot disturb them. Why? Because it is the same devil that is working on them now as would be tempting them if they were on the right road. You know very well that he will not get in his own way. He does not remove all thought of God from them, lest they should become suspicious.

⌒∞⌒

[END OF MYSTICAL WRITINGS]

MEDIEVAL CYCLE DRAMA

Medieval drama is very entertaining, but it was meant to instruct as well. It developed not from classical drama, which virtually died out in the Middle Ages, but from the church liturgy. Although it originated on the Continent, its greatest flowering was in England, in the plays of the Corpus Christi cycle performed from the end of the fourteenth to the end of the sixteenth century. So called because they were put on during the feast of Corpus Christi in midsummer, these plays portray the entire cycle of sacred history from Creation to the Last Judgment, including such events as the Fall of Lucifer, Noah's flood, the Nativity, and Christ's Crucifixion and Resurrection. The plays are given coherence by a pattern of typology whereby Satan's deception and Adam's sin are redeemed by Christ's sacrifice. Old Testament events and characters predict and are fulfilled by New Testament ones—for instance, Isaac and Moses being types of Christ, and Cain, Pharaoh, and Herod being types of Satan.

The cycle plays exist in four versions, which are almost complete and come primarily from the north of England: the Chester, N-Town, York, and Wakefield (or Towneley) cycles. They were generally performed outdoors, in partnership with the church, by craft guilds, associations of tradesmen who represented a newly prosperous mercantile class. Often they sponsored plays whose subject matter was specifically appropriate to their craft—for instance, the butchers putting on the killing of Abel and the water-drawers the play of Noah.

The popularity of the plays in the Corpus Christi cycle—as well as their function as a surrogate Bible for the poor—can be seen in Chaucer's *Miller's Tale*. The Miller himself insists on telling his tale out of order in "Pilate's voice," the ranting manner of Pontius Pilate in the Passion plays, and the foppish Absolon woos his beloved Alison by playing the role of the tyrant Herod on a scaffold. More importantly, the chief trick of this fabliau—the clerk Nicholas's arranging to be alone with Alison by frightening her husband with the threat of a second flood—relies on the old man's sketchy knowledge of the play of Noah.

Nicholas's invocation of a sacred story to pursue a profane goal walks a thin line between comedy and blasphemy. So too did many of the Corpus Christi plays, but for a more obviously sacred purpose. The Wakefield *Annunciation*, for instance, presents Joseph in fabliau fashion as an old man fearing that he has been cuckolded when he discovers that Mary, his young bride-to-be, is pregnant. Only at the end does he come to understand the divine purpose behind her condition.

+—+ ☰◊☰ +—+

The Second Play of the Shepherds

Nowhere are the sacred and profane paired as brilliantly as in the Nativity play known as the *Second Play of the Shepherds*, one of the Wakefield plays, named after the prosperous Yorkshire town in which they were performed. It was written or revised by an artist of great imagination and skill, no doubt a cleric, known as the Wakefield Master. His great achievement is his ability to make biblical stories relevant to fifteenth-century England in such a way that daily life takes on typological significance. The prime example is the parallel between Mak's stolen sheep, hidden in swaddling clothes in a cradle, and the newborn Christ child whom the shepherds visit at the end of the play. The mercy that the shepherds show to Mak by tossing him in a blanket rather than delivering him to be hanged prefigures the mercy that the Christ child will bring into the world.

No matter how neatly the typological scheme works, however, the author does not present the birth of Christ as entirely nullifying the complaints of the characters in the play. With his guileful assault on the sheep fold and his concealment of a "horned lad" swaddled in a cradle, Mak may be a type of the devil, but his complaints of poverty (he stole the sheep to feed his rapidly expanding family) are real. So too are those of the shepherds that they echo, to which the first 180 lines of the play are devoted. The shepherds' opening complaints against taxes, lords and their condescending servants, and nagging, prolific wives reflect the power of the wool and cloth trade that enriched medieval England in the fourteenth and fifteenth centuries but impoverished farmers by driving landlords to enclose individually owned lands in order to convert them to profitable sheep farming. These complaints cannot simply be dismissed as the grumbling of fallen men who fail to understand their need for divine grace. Nor can the complaints of Mak's wife Gill against women's work be seen as simply setting her up as a contrast with the patient Virgin Mary at the end of the play.

The Second Play of the Shepherds

[*Scene: Field near Bethlehem.*]

I PASTOR: Lord, what these weathers are cold!   And I am ill happed.[1]

    I am near hand dold,°   so long have I napped;   *almost numb*

    My legs they fold,   my fingers are chapped.

---

1. Clothed.

It is not as I would,   for I am all lapped°   *tied up*
5   In sorrow.
In storms and tempest,
Now in the east, now in the west,
Woe is him has never rest
Mid-day nor morrow!

10   But we sely° shepherds   that walks on the moor,   *poor*
In faith we are near hands   out of the door.
No wonder, as it stands,   if we be poor,
For the tilthe of our lands   lies fallow as the floor,
As ye ken.°   *know*
15   We are so hamed,°   *hamstrung*
For-taxed° and ramed,°   *overburdened / oppressed*
We are made hand tamed
With these gentlery men.°   *gentry, aristocrats*

Thus they reave° us our rest,   our Lady them wary!°   *rob / curse*
20   These men that are lord-fest,[2]   they cause the plow tarry.
That men say is for the best,   we find it contrary.
Thus are husbandys° opprest,   in point to miscarry   *farmhands*
On live.
Thus hold they us hunder;°   *under*
25   Thus they bring us in blonder;°   *trouble*
It were great wonder
And ever should we thrive.

For may he get a paint slefe°   or a broche now on days,   *painted sleeve*
Woe is him that him grefe°   or once again says!   *troubles*
30   Dare noman him reprefe,°   what mastry° he mays,   *reprove / power*
And yet may noman lefe°   one word that he says,   *believe*
No letter.
He can make purveance°   *provision*
With boast and bragance,
35   And all is through maintenance
Of men that are greater.

There shall come a swane   as proud as a po,[3]
He must borrow my wane,°   my plow also,   *wagon*
Then I am full fane°   to grant or he go.   *pleased*
40   Thus live we in pain,   anger, and woe,
By night and day.
He must have if he langed,°   *desired*
If I should forgang° it;   *forgo*
I were better be hanged
45   Then once say him nay.

It does me good, as I walk   thus by mine one,
Of this world for to talk   in manner of moan.
To my sheep will I stalk,   and hearken anone,°   *awhile*
There abide on a balk,°   or sit on a stone,   *ridge*

2. Bound to their lords.   3. A servant as proud as a peacock.

50   Full soon.
        For I trowe,° perde,°   believe / by God
        True men if they be,
        We get more company
        Or° it be noon.   before

        [*The Second Shepherd enters without noticing the First.*]

II PASTOR: Benste and Dominus!⁴   What may this bemean?
        Why fares this world thus?   Oft have we not seen?
        Lord, these weathers are spytus,°   and the winds full keen,   spiteful
        And the frosts so hideous   they water my eyes—
        No lie.
60   Now in dry, now in wete,
        Now in snow, now in sleet;
        When my shoen° freeze to my feet,   shoes
        It is not all easy.

        But as far as I ken,   or yet as I go,
65   We sely wedmen   dre mekyll woe;⁵
        We have sorrow then and then: it falls oft so.
        Sely Copple,⁶ our hen,   both to and fro
        She cackles;
        But begin she to croak,
70   To groan or to cluck,
        Woe is him is of our cock,
        For he is in the shackels.

        These men that are wed   have not all their will;
        When they are full hard sted,°   they sigh full still;   placed
75   God wayte° they are led   full hard and full ill;   knows
        In bower° nor in bed   they say nought there till,°   bedroom / thereto
        This tide.°   time
        My part have I fun;°   found
        I know my lesson.
80   Woe is him that is bun,°   bound in marriage
        For he must abide.

        But now late in our lives   a marvel to me,
        That I think my heart rives°   such wonders to see.   breaks
        What that destiny drives   it should so be;
85   Some men will have two wives   and some men three,
        In store;
        Some are woe that has any,
        But so far can I,
        Woe is him that has many,
90   For he felys° sore.   suffers

        But young men of a-wooing,   for God that you bought,°   redeemed
        Be well ware of wedding,   and think in your thought,
        "Had I wist"°   is a thing   it serves of nought;   known

---

4. Corruption of a Latin blessing, *Benedicite ad Dominum*.   6. A copple is the crest on a bird's head.
5. We poor, innocent married men suffer much.

	Mekyll° still° mourning has wedding home brought,	*much / constant*
95	And griefs,	
	With many a sharp shower;	
	For thou may catch in an hour	
	That shall savour fulle sour	
	As long as thou lives.	
100	For, as ever read I pistill[7] I have one to my fere,°	*mate*
	As sharp as a thistle, as rough as a brere;	
	She is browed like a bristle with a sour-loten cheer;[8]	
	Had she once wet her whistle she could sing full clear	
	Her *Paternoster*.°	*Lord's Prayer*
105	She is as great as a whale;	
	She has a gallon of gall.	
	By him that died for us all,	
	I would I had run to° I had lost her.	*until*

I PASTOR: God look over the raw![9]   Full deafly ye stand.

II PASTOR: Yea, the devil in thy maw,°   so tariand.°   *mouth / slow*

Saw thou awre° of Daw?[1]   *anywhere*

I PASTOR: Yea, on a ley land°   *fallow ground*

Hard I him blaw.[2]   He comes here at hand,

Not far.

Stand still.

II PASTOR: Why?

I PASTOR: For he comes, hope I.

II PASTOR: He will make us both a lie

But if° we beware.   *unless*

[Enter Third Shepherd.]

III PASTOR: Christ's cross me speed,   and Saint Nicholas!

There of had I need;   it is worse than it was.

120	Whoso could take heed and let the world pass,	
	It is ever in dread and brekill° as glass,	*brittle*
	And slithes.°	*slides away*
	This world fowre° never so,	*fared*
	With marvels mo and mo,	
125	Now in weal, now in woe,	
	And all thing writhes.°	*turns about*
	Was never sin° Noah's flood such floods seen;	*since*
	Winds and rains so rude, and storms so keen;	
	Some stammerd, some stood in doubt,° as I ween;	*fear*
130	Now God turn all to good! I say as I mean,	
	For° ponder.	*to*
	These floods so they drown,	
	Both fields and in town,	
	And bears all down,	
135	And that is a wonder.	

---

7. [St. Paul's] Epistle.
8. Sour-looking face.
9. Let God pay attention to his audience (row), i.e., God

attend me.
1. The Third Shepherd.
2. I just blew by him.

We that walk on the nights,   our cattle to keep,
We see sudden sights   when other men sleep.
Yet me think my heart lights;   I see shrews peep;[3]
Ye are two ill wights.   I will give my sheep
140 A turn.
But full ill have I meant;
As I walk on this bent,
I may lightly repent,
My toes if I spurn.

145 Ah, sir, God you save,   and master mine!
A drink fain would I have,   and somewhat to dine.
I PASTOR: Christ's curse, my knave,   thou art a leder hine!°   *lazy servant*
II PASTOR: What, the boy list rave!   Abide unto sine;[4]
We have made it.[5]
150 Ill thrift on thy pate!
Though the shrew came late,
Yet is he in state
To dine, if he had it.

III PASTOR: Such servants as I,   that sweats and swinks,°   *works*
155 Eats our bread full dry,   and that me forthinks;°   *upsets*
We are oft wet and weary   when master-men winks;°   *sleeps*
Yet comes full lately   both diners and drinks,
But nately.°   *thoroughly*
Both our dame and our sire,
160 When we have run in the mire,
They can nip° at our hire,°   *trim / wages*
And pay us full lately.

But here my troth, master: for the fare that ye make,
I shall do therafter,   work as I take;
165 I shall do a little, sir,   and emang ever lake,[6]
For yet lay my supper   never on my stomach
In fields.
Whereto should I threpe?°   *wrangle*
With my staff can I leap,
170 And men say "Light cheap°   *little cost*
Letherly for-yields."°   *poorly yields*

I PASTOR: Thou were an ill lad   to ride a-wooing
With a man that had   but little of spending.
II PASTOR: Peace, boy, I bade.   No more jangling,°   *chattering*
175 Or I shall make there full rad,°   by the heavens king!   *quickly*
With thy gauds°—   *tricks*
Where are our sheep, boy?—we scorn.°   *despise*
III PASTOR: Sir, this same day at morn
I them left in the corn,
180 When they rang lauds.[7]

---

3. I see villains peeping out.
4. The boy is crazy; wait a while.
5. We have already eaten.

6. Keep playing besides.
7. The first church service of the day.

They have pasture good,   they cannot go wrong.

I PASTOR: That is right, by the roode!⁸   these nights are long,

Yet I would, or we yode,°   one gave us a song.   *went*

II PASTOR: So I thought as I stood,   to mirth us among.

III PASTOR: I grant.

I PASTOR: Let me sing the tenory.

II PASTOR: And I treble so hee.

III PASTOR: Then the meyne° falls to me: *middle*

Let see how ye chant.

[*They sing.*]

*Tunc intrat Mak in clamide se super togam vestitus.*⁹

MAK: Now, Lord, for thy names vii,¹   that made both moon and starns°   *stars*

Well mo then can I neven°   thy will, Lord, of me tharns;²   *say*

I am all uneven,   that moves oft my harness.

Now would God I were in heaven,   for there weep no barnes°   *babies*

So still.

I PASTOR: Who is that pipes so poor?

MAK: Would God ye wist how I foor!°   *fared*

Lo, a man that walks on the moor,

And has not all his will!

II PASTOR: Mak, where has thou gone?   Tell us tiding.

III PASTOR: Is he comme? Then ylkon°   take heed to his thing.   *everyone*

*Et accipit clamidem ab ipso.*³

MAK: What! Ich be a yoman,⁴   I tell you, of the king;

The self and the same,   sond° from a great lording,   *messenger*

And sich.°   *such like*

Fy on you! Goeth hence

205   Out of my presence!

I must have reverence;

Why, who be ich?

I PASTOR: Why make ye it so quaint?⁵   Mak, ye do wrang.

II PASTOR: But, Mak, list ye saint?   I trow that ye lang.⁶

III PASTOR: I trow the shrew can paint,   the devill might him hang!

MAK: Ich shall make complaint, and make you all to thwang⁷

At a word,

And tell even how ye doth.

I PASTOR: But, Mak, is that sooth?

215   Now take out that southren tooth,°   *accent*

And set in a turd!

II PASTOR: Mak, the devil in your eye!   A stroke would I lean° you.   *lend*

III PASTOR: Mak, know ye not me?   By God, I could teen° you.   *rage at*

MAK: God look you all three!   Me thought I had seen you;

220   Ye are a fair company.

---

8. Cross; the humor here, as with the other oaths, is based on the anachronism that Jesus has not yet been born, much less crucified.

9. Then Mak enters, wearing a cloak over his garment.

1. Seven (written by the copyist as the roman numeral).

2. Is lacking.

3. And he takes his cloak from him.

4. Freeborn property-holder.

5. Why act so elegant?

6. Do you want to be a saint? I think you long to be.

7. Be beaten.

I PASTOR: Can ye now mean you?
II PASTOR: Shrew, pepe![8]
        Thus late as thou goes,
        What will men suppose?
        And thou has an ill nose°   reputation
225   Of steeling of sheep.

MAK: And I am true as steel,   all men waytt,°   know
        But a sickness I feel   that holds me full haytt;°   hot
        My belly fares not weel;   it is out of estate.
III PASTOR: Seldom lies the devil   dead by the gate.[9]
MAK: Therfore
        Full sore am I and ill,
        If I stand stone still;
        I eat not an nedill°   scrap
        This month and more.

I PASTOR: How fares thy wife? By my hood,   how fares sho?°   she
MAK: Lies waltering,° by the rood,   by the fire, lo!   collapsed
        And a house full of brood.°   She drinks well, too;   children
        Ill spede° other good   that she will do!   success
        But sho
240   Eats as fast as she can,
        And ilk° year that comes to man   each
        She brings forth a lakan,°   baby
        And some years two.

        But were I not more gracious   and richer by far;
245   I were eaten out of house   and of harbar;°   home
        Yet is she a foul dowse,°   if ye come nar;   wench
        There is none that trowse°   nor knows a war°   imagines / worse
        Than ken I.
        Now will ye see what I proffer,
250   To give all in my coffer
        To morn at next to offer
        Her hed mas-penny.[1]

II PASTOR: I wote so forwaked°   is none in this shire: sleepless
        I would sleep if I taked   less to my hire.
III PASTOR: I am cold and naked,   and would have a fire.
I PASTOR: I am weary, for-rakyd,°   and run in the mire.   exhausted
        Wake thou!
II PASTOR: Nay, I will lyg° down by,   lie
        For I must sleep truly.
III PASTOR: As good a man's son was I
        As any of you.

        But, Mak, come hither! Between   shall thou lyg down.
        [*Mak lies down with the Shepherds.*]
MAK: Then might I let you bedene   of that ye would rowne,[2]

---

8. Villain, look around!
9. Proverbial: The devil seldom lies dead by the wayside;
i.e., the devil is not often an innocent victim.

1. Penny offering for a mass for the dead.
2. That way I can readily prevent you from whispering
together.

No drede.
265 From my top to my toe,
Manus was commendo,
Poncio Pilato;[3]
Christ cross me speed!
Tunc surgit, pastoribus dormientibus, et dicit[4]

Now were time for a man   that lacks what he would
270 To stalk privily than   unto a fold,
And nimbly to work than,   and be not too bold,
For he might aby the bargain,   if it were told
At the ending.
Now were time for to reyll;°   *revel*
275 But he needs good counsel
That fain would fare well,
And has but little spending.

But about you a circle,   as round as a moon,
Too I have done that I will,   till° that it be noon,[5]   *until*
280 That ye lyg stone still   to that I have done,
And I shall say theretill   of good words a foyne.°   *a few*
"On hight
Over your heads my hand I lift;
Out go your eyes! Fordo° your sight!"   *ruin*
285 But yet I must make better shift,
And it be right.

Lord, what they sleep hard!   That may ye all here;
Was I never a shepherd,   but now will I lere.°   *learn*
If the flock be scared,   yet shall I nip near.
290 How, drawes° hitherward!   Now mends our cheer   *come*
From sorrow:
A fat sheep, I dare say,
A good fleece, dare I lay,
Eft-whyte when I may,[6]
295 But this will I borrow.
[*Mak goes home to his wife.*]

How, Gill, art thou in?   Get us some light.
UXOR EIUS:[7] Who makes such din   this time of the night?
I am set for to spin;   I hope not[8] I might
Rise a penny to win,°   I shrew° them on height!   *gain / curse*
300 So fares
A housewife that has been
To be raised° thus between: *disturbed*
Here may no note° be seen   *scrap*
For such small chares.°   *chores*

---

3. An amusing corruption of two Bible verses: "Into your hands I commend my soul" and "I wash my hands of this man."
4. Then Mak arises, while the shepherds are sleeping, and speaks.

5. Mak is casting a spell on the shepherds in the form of a fairy circle to keep them from waking.
6. I will pay it back when I can.
7. His wife.
8. I don't expect that.

MAK: Good wife, open the hek!° Sees thou not what I bring?   *inner door*
UXOR: I may thole the dray the snek.⁹ Ah, come in, my sweeting!
MAK: Yea, thou thar not rek° of my long standing.   *care*
UXOR: By the naked neck art thou like for to hing.
MAK: Do way:
310   I am worthy my meat,°   *supper*
   For in a strait° can I get   *tight spot*
   More than they that swink° and sweat   *work*
   All the long day.

   Thus it fell to my lot, Gill, I had such grace.
UXOR: It were a foul blot to be hanged for the case.
MAK: I have skaped, Jelot,¹ oft as hard a glase.°   *blow*
UXOR: But so long goes the pot to the water, men says,
   At last
   Comes it home broken.
MAK: Well know I the token,
   But let it never be spoken;
   But come and help fast.

   I would he were flayn;° I lyst° well eat: *skinned / wish*
   This twelvemonth was I not so fain of one sheep mete.
UXOR: Come they or° he be slain, and hear the sheep bleat—   *before*
MAK: Then might I be tane.° That were a cold sweat!   *taken*
   Go spar°   *lock*
   The gate-door.
UXOR: Yes, Mak,
   For and° they come at thy back—   *if*
MAK: Then might I buy, for all the pack,²
   The devil of the war.

UXOR: A good bowrde° have I spied, sin thou can none.   *trick*
   Here shall we him hide to° they be gone;   *until*
335   In my cradle abide. Let me alone,
   And I shall lyg beside in childbed, and groan.
MAK: Thou red;°   *get ready*
   And I shall say thou was light°   *delivered*
   Of a knave child this night.
UXOR: Now well is me day bright,
340   That ever was I bred.

   This is a good gise° and a far cast;   *way*
   Yet a woman avise helps at the last.
   I wote° never who spies, agane° go thou fast.   *know / back*
MAK: But I come or they rise, else blows a cold blast!
345   I will go sleep.
   [*Mak returns to the Shepherds and lies down.*]
   Yet sleeps all this meneye,°   *household*
   And I shall go stalk privily

9. I will let you draw the latch.
1. Affectionate nickname for "Gill."
2. Then I may have the worse, for there are such a pack of them.

As it had never been I
That carried there sheep.

I PASTOR: *Resurrex a mortruis!*[3]   Have hold my hand.
     Iudas carnas dominus![4]   I may not well stand:
     My foot sleeps, by Jesus,   and I water fastand.[5]
     I thought that we had laid us   full near England.

II PASTOR: Ah ye!
355   Lord, what I have slept well;
     As fresh as an eel,
     As light I me feel
     As leaf on a tree.

III PASTOR: Benste° be here in!   So my heart quakes,   *a blessing*
360   My heart is out of skin,°   what so it makes.   *(body)*
     Who makes all this din?   So my brows blakes°   *darkens*
     To the door will I win.   Hark, fellows, wakes!
     We were four:
     See ye awre° of Mak now?   *anywhere*

I PASTOR: We were up or thou.
II PASTOR: Man, I give God a vow,
     Yet yede° he nawre.°   *went / nowhere*

III PASTOR: Me thought he was lapt,°   in a wolf skin.   *clothed*
I PASTOR: So are many hapt°   now namely within.   *covered*
II PASTOR: When we had long napped,   me thought with a gyn°   *trap*
     A fat sheep he trapped,   but he made no din.
III PASTOR: Be still:
     Thy dream makes thee woode:°   *mad*
     It is but phantom, by the roode.°   *cross*
I PASTOR: Now God turn all to good,
     If it be his will.

II PASTOR: Rise, Mak, for shame!   Thou lies right long.
MAK: Now Christ's holy name   be us among!
     What is this? For Saint Jame,   I may not well gang!
380   I trow I be the same.   Ah, my neck has lain wrong
     Enough.
     Mekill,° thanks syn° yister even,   *many / since*
     Now, by Saint Steven,
     I was flayd° with a sweven,°   *frightened / dream*
385   My heart out of slough.°   *skin*

I thought Gill began to croak   and travail° full sad,   *struggle*
     Welner° at the first cock,   of a young lad   *nearly*
     For to mend our flock.   Then be I never glad;
     I have tow° on my rock°   more then ever I had.   *flax / distaff*
390   Ah, my head!
     A house full of young tharms;°   *children*

3. Corruption from the Latin Bible of "He rose from the dead."
4. A corruption into Latin gibberish, "Judas lord of the flesh."
5. Stagger from lack of food.

The devil knock out their harns!°   *brains*
Woe is him has many barns,
And thereto little bread!

395   I must go home, by your leave,   to Gill, as I thought.
I pray you looke,° my sleeve   that I steal nought: *inspect*
I am loath you to grieve, or from you take ought.
III PASTOR: Go forth, ill might thou chefe!° Now would I we sought,   *fare*
This morn,
400   That we had all our store.
I PASTOR: But I will go before;
Let us meet.
II PASTOR: Whore?
III PASTOR: At the crooked thorn.
    [*The Shepherds leave. Mak knocks at his door.*]
MAK: Undo this door! Who is here?   How long shall I stand?
UXOR EIUS: Who makes such a bere?°   Now walk in the wenyand.⁶   *noise*
MAK: Ah Gill, what cheer?   It is I, Mak, your husband.
UXOR: Then may we be here   the devil in a band,
Sir Gyle:⁷
Lo, he comes with a lote°   *noise*
410   As he were holden° in the throat.   *held*
I may not sit at my note,°   *work*
A hand-lang° while.   *little*

MAK: Will ye hear what fare she makes   to get her a glose?⁸
And does nought but lakes°   and claws her toes.   *plays*
UXOR: Why, who wanders, who wakes?   Who commes, who goes?
Who brews, who bakes?   What makes me thus hose?°   *hoarse*
And than,
It is rewthe° to behold,   *pitiful*
Now in hot, now in cold,
420   Full woeful is the household
That wants a woman.
But what end has thou made   with the herds, Mak?
MAK: The last word that thay said   when I turned my back,
They would look that they had   their sheep, all the pack.
425   I hope⁹ they will not be well paid   when they their sheep lack,
Perde!
But how so the game goes,
To me they will suppose,
And make a foul noise,
430   And cry out upon me.

But thou must do as thou hight.°   *said*
UXOR: I accord me there till.
I shall swaddle him right   in my cradle;
If it were a greater sleight,°   yet could I help till.   *trick*

I will lyg down straight.   Come hap me.

MAK: I will.

UXOR: Behind!
    Come Coll[1] and his maroo,°   *mate*
    They will nyp° us full naroo.°   *pinch / hard*

MAK: But I may cry out "Haroo!"
    The sheep if they find.

UXOR: Harken ay when they call;   they will come onone.°   *soon*
    Come and make ready all   and sing by thine one;
    Sing "lullay" thou shall,   for I must groan,
    And cry out by the wall   on Mary and John,
    For sore.
445   Sing "lullay" on fast
    When thou hears at the last;
    And but I play a false cast,°   *trick*
    Trust me no more.

[*At the crooked thorn.*]

III PASTOR: Ah, Coll, good morn.   Why sleeps thou not?
I PASTOR: Alas, that ever was I born!   We have a foul blot.
    A fat wether° have we lorne.°   *ram / lost*

III PASTOR: Mary, God's forbot!

II PASTOR: Who should do us that scorn?°   That were a foul spot.   *harm*

I PASTOR: Some shrewe.°   *villain*
    I have sought with my dogs
455   All Horbury[2] shrogs,°   *hedges*
    And of xv° hogs   *fifteen*
    Found I but one ewe.

III PASTOR: Now trow me, if ye will,   by Saint Thomas of Kent,
    Either Mak or Gill   was at that assent.°   *affair*

I PASTOR: Peace, man, be still!   I saw when he went;
    Thou slanders him ill;   thou ought to repent,
    Good speed.

II PASTOR: Now as ever might I the,°   *thrive*
    If I should even here die,
465   I would say it were he,
    That did that same deed.

III PASTOR: Go we thither, I read,   and run on our feet.
    Shall I never eat bread   the sothe to I wytt.[3]

I PASTOR: Nor drink in my head   with him till I meet.

II PASTOR: I will rest in no stead   till that I him greet,
    My brother.
    One I will hight:°   *promise*
    Till I see him in sight
    Shall I never sleep one night
475   There I do another.

---

1. The First Shepherd.   3. Until I know the truth.
2. A town south of Wakefield.

[*They approach Mak's house.*]

III PASTOR: Will ye hear how they hack?[4]   Our sire list croon.

I PASTOR: Heard I never none crack   so clear out of toon;
      Call on him.

II PASTOR: Mak,   undo your door soon.

MAK: Who is that spake,   as it were noon
480   On loft?
      Who is that, I say?

III PASTOR: Good felows, were it day.

MAK: As far as ye may,
      Good, speaks soft,

485   Over a sick woman's head   that is at malaise;
      I had lever° be dead   or she had any disease.   *rather*

UXOR: Go to another stead!   I may not well qweasse.°   *breathe*
      Each foot that ye tread   goes through my nese,°   *nose*
      So hee!°   *loudly*

I PASTOR: Tell us, Mak, if ye may,
      How fare ye, I say?

MAK: But are ye in this town to-day?
      Now how fare ye?

      Ye have run in the mire,   and are wet yit:
495   I shall make you a fire,   if you will sit.
      A nurse would I hire.   Think ye on yit,
      Well quit is my hire[5]—   my dream this is it—
      A season.
      I have barns, if ye knew,
500   Well mo then enewe,
      But we must drink as we brew,
      And that is but reason.
      I would ye dined or ye yode.[6]   Me think that ye sweat.

II PASTOR: Nay, neither mends our mood   drink nor meat.

MAK: Why, sir, ails you ought but good?

III PASTOR: Yea, our sheep that we get,
      Are stolen as they yode.   Our loss is great.

MAK: Sirs, drinks!
      Had I been there,
      Some should have bought it full sore.

I PASTOR: Mary, some men trowes° that ye wore,   *believes*
      And that us forthinks.°   *disturbs*

II PASTOR: Mak, some men trowys   that it should be ye.

III PASTOR: Either ye or your spouse,   so say we.

MAK: Now if ye have suspowse°   to Gill or to me,   *suspicion*
515   Come and ripe° our house,   and then may ye see   *search*
      Who had her;
      If I any sheep fot,°   *took*

4. Sing (badly).   6. I would like you to eat before you go.
5. My wages are paid; i.e., his dream has been fulfilled.

Either cow or stot;°   heifer
And Gill, my wife, rose not
520   Here sin she laid her.

As I am true and leal,°   to God here I pray,   loyal
That this be the first meal   that I shall eat this day.
I PASTOR: Mak, as have I ceyll,°   advise thee, I say;   heaven
He learned timely to steal   that could not say nay.
UXOR: I swelt!°   die
Out, thieves, from my wonys!°   home
Ye come to rob us for the nonys.°   for the purpose
MAK: Here ye not how she groans?
Your hearts should melt.

UXOR: Out, thieves, from my barn!   Nigh him not thor!°   there
MAK: Wist ye how she had farn,°   your hearts would be sore.   fared
Ye do wrong, I you warn,   that thus comes before
To a woman that has farn—   but I say no more.
UXOR: Ah, my medill!°   middle
535   I pray to God so mild,
If ever I you beguiled,
That I eat this child
That lies in this cradle.

MAK: Peace, woman, for God's pain,   and cry not so:
540   Thou spills thy brain,   and makes me full woe.
II PASTOR: I trow our sheep be slain.   What find ye two?
III PASTOR: All work we in vain;   as well may we go.
But hatters,°   (an oath)
I can find no flesh,
545   Hard nor nesh,°   soft
Salt nor fresh,
But two tome° platters.   empty
Whik° cattle but this,   tame nor wild,   living
None, as have I bliss,   as loud as he smiled.°   smelled
UXOR: No, so God me bliss,   and give me joy of my child!
I PASTOR: We have marked amiss;   I hold us beguiled.
II PASTOR: Sir, don,°   it is done
Sir, our Lady him save,
Is your child a knave?[7]
MAK: Any lord might him have
This child to his son.

When he wakens he kips,°   that joy is to see.   snatches
III PASTOR: In good time to his hips,   and in cele.°   heaven
But who was his gossips°,   so soon rede?°   godparents / ready
MAK: So fair fall their lips!
I PASTOR: Hark now, a le.°   lie
MAK: So God them thank,

---

7. Boy-child (of the serving-class).

Parkin, and Gibon Waller I say,
And gentle John Horne,[8] in good fay,
He made all the garray,°   *noise*
565   With the great shank.°   *leg*

II PASTOR: Mak, friends will we be,   for we are all one.
MAK: We? Now I hold for me,   for mends° get I none.   *profit*
        Farewell all three!   All glad were ye gone.
    [*The Shepherds depart.*]
III PASTOR: Fair words may there be,   but love is there none
570   This year.
I PASTOR: Gave ye the child anything?
II PASTOR: I trow not one farthing.
III PASTOR: Fast again will I fling,°   *hurry*
        Abide ye me there.
    [*Returns to the house.*]

575   Mak, take it to no grief   if I come to thy barn.°   *baby*
MAK: Nay, thou does me great reproof,   and foul has thou farn.° *done*
III PASTOR: The child will it not grief,   that little daystarn.[9]
        Mak, with your leaf,   let me give your barn
        But vi° pence.   *six*
MAK: Nay, do way: he sleeps.
III PASTOR: Me think he peeps.
MAK: When he wakens he weeps.
        I pray you go hence.
    [*The other Shepherds return.*]

III PASTOR: Give me leave him to kiss,   and lift up the clout.°   *cloth*
585   What the devil is this?   He has a long snout.
I PASTOR: He is marked amiss.   We wat° ill about.   *watch*
II PASTOR: Ill-spun weft, iwys,   ay comes foul out.[1]
        Aye, so!
        He is like to our sheep!
III PASTOR: How, Gyb,° may I peep?   *the Second Shepherd*
I PASTOR: I trow kind° will creep   *Nature*
        Where it may not go.°   *walk*

II PASTOR: This was a quaint gawde,°   and a far cast.   *clever trick*
        It was a high fraud.
III PASTOR: Yea, sirs, was't.
595   Let bren° this bawd,   and bind her fast.   *burn*
        A false skawd°   hang at the last;   *scold*
        So shall thou.
        Will ye see how they swaddle
        His four feet in the middle?
600   Saw I never in a cradle
        A horned lad[2] or° now.   *before*

---

8. Parkin, Gibon Waller, and John Horne are the names of the shepherds in the First Play of the Shepherds, possibly referring to actual townspeople.
9. Little day star; a term also used for the Christ child

later in the play, indicating a parallel with Mak's baby.
1. Badly spun thread always makes poor cloth.
2. A horned child (devil).

MAK: Peace bid I. What,   let be youre fare;
    I am he that him gat,°   and yond woman him bare.   *begat*
I PASTOR: What devil shall he hat,°   Mak? Lo, God, Mak's heir.   *be called*
II PASTOR: Let be all that.   Now God give him care,
    I sagh.°   *saw*
UXOR: A pretty child is he
    As sits on a woman's knee;
    A dillydown,° perde,   *darling*
610   To gar° a man laugh.   *make*

III PASTOR: I know him by the earn mark: that is a good token.
MAK: I tell you, sirs, hark!—   his nose was broken.
    Sithen° told me a clerk   that he was forspoken.°   *since / bewitched*
I PASTOR: This is a false work;   I would fain be wroken.°   *avenged*
615   Get wepyn.
UXOR: He was taken with° an elf;   *by*
    I saw it myself.
    When the clock struck twelve
    Was he forshapen.°   *changed*

II PASTOR: Ye two are well feft°   sam° in a stead.   *endowed / together*
III PASTOR: Sin they maintain their theft,   let do them to dead.
MAK: If I trespass eft,°   gird° off my head.   *again / cut*
    With you will I be left.
I PASTOR: Sirs, do my read.°   *advice*
    For this trespass,
625   We will neither ban ne flite,°   *curse nor quarrel*
    Fight nor chite,°   *chide*
    But have done as tite,°   *quickly*
    And cast him in canvas.

    [*They toss Mak in a sheet.*]
    Lord, what I am sore, in point for to brist.
630   In faith I may no more; therefore will I rist.
II PASTOR: As a sheep of vii score³   he weighed in my fist.
    For to sleep ay-whore°   me think that I list.   *anywhere*
III PASTOR: Now I pray you,
    Lyg down on this green.
I PASTOR: On these thieves yet I mene.°   *speak*
III PASTOR: Whereto should ye tene?°   *be angry*
    Do as I say you.
    [*The Shepherds sleep.*]
    Angelus cantat "Gloria in excelsis"; *postea dicat* ⁴

ANGELUS: Rise, herd-men heynd!   For now is he born
    That shall take fro the fiend   that Adam had lorn;°   *lost*
640   That warloo° to shend,°   this night is he born.   *devil / destroy*
    God is made your friend   now at this morn.
    He behestys°   *orders*

3. Seven score pounds (140 lbs).
4. The Angel sings "Glory to God in the highest," and   afterward says.

At Bedlem° go see: *Bethlehem*
There lies that fre°   *lord*
645   In a crib full poorly,
Betwyx two bestys.

I PASTOR: This was a quaint steven°   that ever yet I heard.   *voice*
It is a marvel to neven,°   thus to be scared.   *mention*
II PASTOR: Of God's son of heaven   he spake upward.°   *on high*
650   All the wood on a leven   me thought that he gard
Appear.[5]
III PASTOR: He spake of a barn
In Bedlem, I you warn.
I PASTOR: That betokens yond starn.°   *star*
655   Let us seek him there.

II PASTOR: Say, what was his song?   Heard ye not how he cracked° it? *roared*
Three breves to a long.[6]
III PASTOR: Yea, marry, he hakt° it.   *sang*
Was no crochett° wrong,   nor nothing that lacked it.   *note*
I PASTOR: For to sing us among   right as he knacked° it,   *sang*
660   I can.
II PASTOR: Let se how ye croon.
Can ye bark at the moon?
III PASTOR: Hold your tongues, have done!
I PASTOR: Hark after than.
    [*Sings.*]

II PASTOR: To Bedlem he bade   that we should gang:
I am full fard°   that we tarry too lang.   *afraid*
III PASTOR: Be merry and not sad;   of mirth is our sang;
Ever-lasting glad   to mede° may we fang,°   *reward / get*
Without noise.
I PASTOR: Hie we thither for-thy;°   *therefore*
If we be wet and weary,
To that child and that lady,
We have it not to lose.

II PASTOR: We find by the prophecy—   let be your din—
675   Of David and Isay,[7]   and mo than I min,
They prophesied by clergy   that in a virgin
Should he light and lie,   to sloken° our sin   *remove*
And slake it,
Our kynd° from woe;   *humankind*
680   For Isay said so,
Ecce virgo
Concipiet[8] a child that is naked.

III PASTOR: Full glad may we be,   and abide that day
That lovely to see,   that all mights may.
685   Lord, well were me,   for once and for ay,

5. I thought he lit up the woods like lightning.   7. The prophet Isaiah.
6. Three short notes to one long.   8. Behold, a virgin conceives (Isaiah 7.14).

Might I kneel on my knee,   some word for to say
To that child.
But the angel said
In a crib was he laid;
690   He was poorly arrayed,
Both mener° and milde.   poor

I PASTOR: Patriarchs that has been,   and prophets beforn,
They desired to have seen   this child that is born.
They are gone full clean,°   that have they lorn.°   entirely / lost
695   We shall see him, I ween,   or it be morn,
To token.°   as proof
When I see him and feel,
Then wot I full weel
It is true as steel
700   That prophets have spoken:

To so poore as we are   that he would appear,
First find, and declare   by his messenger.
II PASTOR: Go we now, let us fare;   the place is us near.
III PASTOR: I am ready and yare;°   go we in fere°   prepared / together
705   To that bright.
Lord, if thy wills be,
We are lewde° all three,   unschooled
Thou grant us somkyns glee°   some kind of joy
To comfort thy wight.°   creature
[They enter the stable.]

I PASTOR: Hail, comely and clean!   Hail, young child!
Hail, maker, as I mean,   of a maiden so mild!
Thou has waryd,° I ween,   the warlo° so wild;   cursed / devil
The false gyler° of teen°   now goes he beguiled.   deceiver / anger
Lo, he merries!
715   Lo, he laughs, my sweeting!
A well fair meeting!
I have holden my heting;°   kept my promise
Have a bob° of cherries.   bunch

II PASTOR: Hail, sovereign saviour,   for thou has us sought!
720   Hail, freely food and flour,⁹   that all thing has wrought!
Hail, full of favour,   that made all of nought!
Hail! I kneel and I cower.   A bird have I brought
To my barn.
Hail, little tyne mop!°   tiny baby
725   Of our creed thou art crop:°   fruit, fulfillment
I would drink on thy cop,°   cup
Little day starn.°   star

III PASTOR: Hail, darling dear,   full of Godhede!
I pray thee be near   when that I have need.
730   Hail, sweet is thy cheer!   My heart would bleed

9. Noble child and flower.

To see thee sit here   in so poor weed,°   *clothing*
With no pennies.
Hail, put forth thy dall!°   *hand*
I bring thee but a ball:
735   Have and play thee with all,
And go to the tenys.°   *tennis*

MARIA: The Father of heaven,   God omnipotent,
That set all on seven,[1]   his son has he sent.
My name could he neven,°   and light or he went.   *name*
740   I conceived him full even   through might, as he ment,°   *intended*
And now is he born.
He keep you from woe!
I shall pray him so.
Tell forth as ye go,
745   And myn° on this morn.   *remember*

I PASTOR: Farewell, lady,   so fair to behold,
With thy child on thy knee.
II PASTOR: But he lies full cold.
Lord, well is me!   Now we go, thou behold.
III PASTOR: Forsooth already   it seems to be told
750   Full oft.
I PASTOR: What grace we have fun!°   *found*
II PASTOR: Come forth: now are we won.
III PASTOR: To sing are we bun:°   *bound*
Let take on loft![2]
[*They go out singing.*]
                                        Explicit pagina Pastorum.[3]

The York Crucifixion

The York *Crucifixion* serves as a counterpoint to the Wakefield *Second Play of the Shepherds*, focusing not on the beginning of Christ's earthly life but on its end. Like the Wakefield play, it was shaped by an anonymous playwright of great literary skill, a master of concrete detail, colloquial speech, and grotesque humor. He is known as the "York Realist."

As with many of the cycle plays, the York *Crucifixion* was produced by a guild whose business bore some relation to the subject at hand. In this case, it is the pinners—the makers of wooden pegs—which is a source of grim irony. The soldiers carrying out the Crucifixion joke about their task, as they boast of the technology of their craft, but are incompetent to pursue it. In their ignorance of the larger significance of their actions, they can be seen as representing fallen mankind in need of Christ's forgiveness.

In striking contrast to the buffoonery of the soldiers is the dignified demeanor of Christ. He speaks only twice, first to accept the sacrifice of his life, and second to beg God's forgiveness for his torturers. His portrayal reflects a balance of two conflicting images: the heroic

---

1. Made everything in seven days.   3. The play of the Shepherds is finished.
2. Let us sing on high.

Christ who defeats Satan and the human Christ who suffers. The former "Romanesque" image dates from the early Middle Ages and can be seen in the Old English *Dream of the Rood*, while the latter "gothic" image can be seen in the religious lyrics and mystical writings of the later Middle Ages, whose purpose was to inspire the laity to meditation by focusing on Christ's wounds. Much of the power of the York *Crucifixion* comes from the fact the audience does not see Christ until the end of the play, so that its attention is focused on the soldiers fumbling with their mechanical task. As the cross is lifted, however, spectators receive the shock of seeing Christ and recognizing their complicity in the Crucifixion. Thus the play's "realism" can be seen to have a profound and symbolic purpose.

The York Play of the Crucifixion

SOLDIER 1:	Sir knights, take heed hither in hie,°	*in haste*
	This deed on dreigh we may not draw.[1]	
	Ye wot° yourselves as well as I	*know*
	How lords and leaders of our law	
5	Have given doom° that this dote° shall die.	*judgment / fool*
SOLDIER 2:	Sir, all their counsel well we know.	
	Since we are come to Calvary	
	Let ilk° man help now as him owe.°	*each / ought*
SOLDIER 3:	We are all ready, lo,	
10	That foreward° to fulfil.	*undertaking*
SOLDIER 4:	Let hear how we shall do,	
	And go we tite theretill.°	*quickly thereto*
SOLDIER 1:	It may not help here for to hone°	*delay*
	If we shall any worship° win.	*honor*
SOLDIER 2:	He must be dead needlings° by noon.	*necessarily*
SOLDIER 3:	Then is good time that we begin.	
SOLDIER 4:	Let ding° him down, then is he done—	*knock*
	He shall not dere° us with his din.	*harm*
SOLDIER 1:	He shall be set and learned soon,[2]	
20	With care° to him and all his kin.	*sorrow*
SOLDIER 2:	The foulest death of all	
	Shall he die for his deeds.	
SOLDIER 3:	That means cross° him we shall.	*crucify*
SOLDIER 4:	Behold, so right he redes.°	*he advises well*
SOLDIER 1:	Then to this work us must take heed,	
	So that our working be not wrong.	
SOLDIER 2:	None other note° to neven° is need,	*matter / mention*
	But let us haste him for to hang.°	*crucify*
SOLDIER 3:	And I have gone for gear good speed,°	*with haste*
30	Both hammers and nails large and long.	
SOLDIER 4:	Then may we boldly do this deed.	
	Come on, let kill this traitor strong.	
SOLDIER 1:	Fair might ye fall in fere[3]	

---

1. We may not draw this task out too long.   3. Good fortune to all of you.
2. He shall be put in his place and taught a lesson.

That has wrought on this wise.
SOLDIER 2: Us needs not for to lere[4]
    Such faitours° to chastise.   *traitors*

SOLDIER 3: Since ilka° thing is right arrayed,°   *every / prepared*
    The wiselier° now work may we.   *more wisely*
SOLDIER 4: The cross on ground is goodly graid°   *prepared*
40   And bored° even as it ought to be.   *drilled*
SOLDIER 1: Look° that the lad on length be laid   *see to it*
    And made me° then unto this tree.°   *fastened / cross*
SOLDIER 2: For all his fare° he shall be flayed,°   *deeds / tortured*
    That on assay° soon shall ye see.   *by trial*
SOLDIER 3: Come forth, thou cursed knave,
    Thy comfort soon shall keel.°   *turn cold*
SOLDIER 4: Thine hire° here shall thou have.   *reward*
SOLDIER 1: Walk on—now work we well.

JESUS: Almighty God, my Father free,°   *gracious*
50   Let these matters be made in mind:
    Thou bade° that I should buxom° be, *commanded / willing*
    For Adam's plight for to be pined.°   *tormented*
    Here to death I oblige me,°   *pledge myself*
    For that sin for to save mankind,
55   And sovereignly beseech I thee
    That they for me may favour find.
    And from the fiend° them fend,°   *devil / defend*
    So that their souls be safe
    In wealth° without end—   *joy*
60   I keep° nought else to crave.°   *care / ask for*
SOLDIER 1: We, hark sir knights, for Mahound's° blood, *Muhammad's*
    Of Adam's kind° is all his thought.   *offspring*
SOLDIER 2: The warlock waxes war than wood;[5]
    This doleful° death ne dreadeth° he nought. *terrible / fears*
SOLDIER 3: Thou should have mind,° with main° and mood, *recall / might*
    Of wicked works that thou hast wrought.
SOLDIER 4: I hope° that he had been as good   *think*
    Have ceased of saws° that he upsought.° *sayings / thought up*
SOLDIER 1: Tho saws shall rue him° sore,   *words he will regret*
70   For all his sauntering,° soon.   *babbling*
SOLDIER 2: Ill speed them° that him spare   *bad luck (to) them*
    Till he to death be done.

SOLDIER 3: Have done belive, boy, and make thee boun,[6]
    And bend thy back unto this tree.
SOLDIER 4: Behold, himself has laid him down
    In length and breadth as he should be.
SOLDIER 1: This traitor here tainted° of treason,   *convicted*

---

4. We do not need to be taught.   6. Be done quickly, wretch, and make yourself ready.
5. The sorcerer grows worse than mad.

Go fast and fetter him then ye three;
And since he claimeth kingdom with crown,
80   Even as a king here hang shall he.
SOLDIER 2: Now, certes,° I shall not fine°   *indeed / stop*
        Ere° his right hand be fast.°   *before / tightly tied*
SOLDIER 3: The left hand then is mine—
        Let see who bears him best.

SOLDIER 4: His limbs on length then shall I lead,°   *stretch*
        And even unto the bore° them bring.   *bored holes*
SOLDIER 1: Unto his head I shall take heed,
        And with mine hand help him to hang.
SOLDIER 2: Now since we four shall do this deed
90   And meddle with this unthrifty° thing,   *unprofitable*
        Let no man spare for° special speed   *refrain from (using)*
        Till that we have made ending.
SOLDIER 3: This foreward° may not fail;   *deed*
        Now are we right arrayed.°   *prepared*
SOLDIER 4: This boy° here in our bail°   *rascal / custody*
        Shall bide° full bitter braid.°   *suffer / torment*

SOLDIER 1: Sir knights, say, how work we now?
SOLDIER 2: Yes, certes,° I hope° I hold this hand,   *indeed / think*
        And to the bore° I have it brought   *bored holes*
100   Full buxomly° without band.°   *obediently / ropes*
SOLDIER 1: Strike on then hard, for him thee bought.°   *redeemed*
SOLDIER 2: Yes, here is a stub° will stiffly stand,   *thick nail*
        Through bones and sinews it shall be sought°—   *found*
        This work is well, I will warrand.°   *warrant*
SOLDIER 1: Say sir, how do we there?
        This bargain° may not blin.°   *business / cease*
SOLDIER 3: It fails a foot and more,°   *i.e., is too short*
        The sinews are so gone in.°   *shrunken*

SOLDIER 4: I hope that mark amiss° be bored.°   *wrongly / drilled*
SOLDIER 2: Then must he bide° in bitter bale.°   *suffer / torment*
SOLDIER 3: In faith, it was over-scantily scored,°   *too sloppily marked*
        That makes it foully° for to fail.   *badly*
SOLDIER 1: Why carp° ye so? Fast on° a cord   *speak / fasten*
        And tug° him to, by top and tail.°   *stretch / head and feet*
SOLDIER 3: Yah, thou commands lightly° as a lord;   *effortlessly*
        Come help to haul, with ill hail.°   *bad luck to you*
SOLDIER 1: Now certes that shall I do—
        Full snelly° as a snail.   *quickly*
SOLDIER 3: And I shall tache° him to,°   *attach / to (the cross)*
120   Full nimbly with a nail.

        This work will hold, that dare I hete,°   *promise*
        For now are fest° fast both his hend.°   *fasten / hands*
SOLDIER 4: Go we all four then to his feet,

So shall our space° be speedily spend.°   *time / usefully spent*
SOLDIER 2: Let see what bourd his bale might beet,[7]
    Thereto my back now would I bend.
SOLDIER 4: Oh, this work is all unmeet°—   *out of place*
    This boring must all be amend.°   *corrected*
SOLDIER 1: Ah, peace man, for Mahound,°   *by Muhammad*
130   Let no man wot° that wonder,°   *know about / miracle*
    A rope shall rug° him down   *yank*
    If° all his sinews go asunder.   *even if*

SOLDIER 2: That cord full kindly° can I knit,°   *fittingly / fasten*
    The comfort of this carl° to keel.°   *churl / cool, lessen*
SOLDIER 1: Fast° on then fast, that all be fit,°   *fasten / ready*
    It is no force° how fell° he feel.   *matter / terrible*
SOLDIER 2: Lug° on ye both a little yet.   *pull*
SOLDIER 3: I shall not cease, as I have sele.°   *joy*
SOLDIER 4: And I shall fond° him for to hit.   *try*
SOLDIER 2: Oh, hale!°   *haul*
SOLDIER 4:   Whoa, now, I hold it well.
SOLDIER 1: Have done, drive in that nail,
    So that no fault be found.
SOLDIER 4: This working would not fail
    If four bulls here were bound.

SOLDIER 1: These cords have evil° increased his pains,   *sorely*
    Ere he were to the borings° brought.   *bored holes*
SOLDIER 2: Yea, asunder are both sinews and veins
    On ilka° side, so have we° sought.   *each / as we have*
SOLDIER 3: Now all his gauds nothing him gains,[8]
150   His sauntering shall with bale be bought.[9]
SOLDIER 4: I will go say to our sovereigns
    Of all these works how we have wrought.
SOLDIER 1: Nay sirs, another thing
    Falls first to you and me,
155   They bade we should him hang
    On high, that men might see.

SOLDIER 2: We wot° well so° their words were,   *know / what*
    But sir, that deed will do us dere.°   *harm*
SOLDIER 1: It may not mend° for to moot° more,   *help / argue*
160   This harlot° must be hanged here.   *rascal*
SOLDIER 2: The mortice° is made fit° therefore.   *slot / ready*
SOLDIER 3: Fast° on your fingers then, in fere.°   *fasten / together*
SOLDIER 4: I ween° it will never come° there—   *believe / rise*
    We four raise° it not right to-year.°   *will raise / this year*
SOLDIER 1: Say man, why carps° thou so?   *talk*

---

7. Let us see what joke might lighten his sorrow.   9. His babbling shall be paid for with pain.
8. Now all his tricks gain him nothing.

        Thy lifting was but light.°   *weak*
SOLDIER 2: He means there must be more
        To heave him up on height.

SOLDIER 3: Now certes, I hope it shall not need°   *be necessary*
170   To call to us more company.°   *help*
        Methink we four should do this deed
        And bear him to yon hill on high.
SOLDIER 1: It must be done, without dread.°   *doubt*
        No more, but look ye be ready,
175   And this part° shall I lift and lead;   *(the head)*
        On length he shall no longer lie.
        Therefore now make you boun,°   *ready*
        Let bear him to yon hill.
SOLDIER 4: Then will I bear here down,
180   And tent his toes until.°   *attend to his toes*

SOLDIER 2: We two shall see to either side,
        For else this work will wry° all wrong.   *go awry*
SOLDIER 3: We are ready.
SOLDIER 4:   Good sirs, abide,
        And let me first his feet up fang.°   *take up*
SOLDIER 2: Why tent ye so to tales this tide?[1]
SOLDIER 1: Lift up!
SOLDIER 4:   Let see!
SOLDIER 2:   Oh, lift along.
SOLDIER 3: From all this harm he should him hide°   *protect himself*
        And° he were God.   *if*
SOLDIER 4:   The devil him hang!
SOLDIER 1: For-great harm have I hent,°   *received*
190   My shoulder is in sunder.°   *asunder*
SOLDIER 2: And certes, I am near shent,°   *ruined*
        So long have I borne under.°   *lifted up*

SOLDIER 3: This cross and I in two must twin,°   *separate*
        Else breaks my back in sunder° soon.   *asunder*
SOLDIER 4: Lay down again and leave° your din,°   *stop / noise*
        This deed for us will never be done.
SOLDIER 1: Assay,° sirs, let see if any gin°   *try / device*
        May help him up without hone,°   *delay*
        For here should wight men worship win,
200   And not with gauds° all day to gone.°   *tricks / spend*
SOLDIER 2: More wighter° men than we   *stronger*
        Full few I hope° ye find.   *expect*
SOLDIER 3: This bargain° will not be,°   *job / (ever) be done*
        For certes, me wants wind.°   *I am winded*

---

1. Why are you paying so much attention to talk at this time (i.e., instead of working)?

SOLDIER 4: So will° of work never we were—   *bewildered*
    I hope this carl some cautels cast.[2]
SOLDIER 2: My burden sat° me wonder sore,   *distressed*
    Unto the hill I might not last.
SOLDIER 1: Lift up, and soon he shall be there,
210   Therefore fast on° your fingers fast.   *fasten*
SOLDIER 3: Oh, lift!
SOLDIER 1:   We, lo!
SOLDIER 4:   A little more.
SOLDIER 2: Hold then!
SOLDIER 1:   How now?
SOLDIER 2:   The worst is past.
SOLDIER 3: He weighs a wicked weight.
SOLDIER 2: So may we all four say,
215   Ere he was heaved on height°   *aloft*
    And raised in this array.°   *fashion*

SOLDIER 4: He made us stand as° any stones,   *as (still) as*
    So boistous° was he for to bear.   *awkward*
SOLDIER 1: Now raise him nimbly for the nonce
220   And set him by this mortice° here,   *slot*
    And let him fall in all at once,
    For certes, that pain shall have no peer.
SOLDIER 3: Heave up!
SOLDIER 4:   Let down, so all his bones
    Are asunder now on sides sere.°   *in many places*
SOLDIER 1: This falling was more fell°   *cruel*
    Than all the harms he had.
    Now may a man well tell°   *easily count*
    The least lith° of this lad.   *smallest limbs*

SOLDIER 3: Methinketh this cross will not abide°   *hold firm*
230   Ne stand still in this mortice° yet.   *slot*
SOLDIER 4: At the first time was it made over-wide;
    That makes it wave,° thou may well wit.°   *wobble / know*
SOLDIER 1: It shall be set on ilka° side   *each*
    So that it shall no further flit.°   *move*
235   Good wedges shall we take this tide°   *time*
    And fast the foot,° then is all fit.   *fasten the base*
SOLDIER 2: Here are wedges arrayed°   *ready*
    For that, both great and small.
SOLDIER 3: Where are our hammers laid
240   That we should work withal?°   *with*

SOLDIER 4: We have them even here at our hand.
SOLDIER 2: Give me this wedge, I shall it in drive.
SOLDIER 4: Here is another yet ordained.°   *ready*

---

2. I think this churl has devised some tricks.

SOLDIER 3: Do take it me hither belive.°   *to me quickly*

SOLDIER 1: Lay on then fast.

SOLDIER 2:   Yes, I warrand.°   *warrant*

    I thring them sam, so mote I thrive.³

    Now will this cross full stably° stand,   *firmly*

    All if° he rave they will not rive.°   *even if / split*

SOLDIER 1: Say sir, how likes you now,

250   This work that we have wrought?

SOLDIER 4: We pray you say° us how   *tell*

    Ye feel, or faint ye aught.°   *if you feel faint at all*

JESUS: All men that walk by way or street,

    Take tent ye shall no travail tine.⁴

255   Behold mine head, mine hands, and my feet,

    And fully feel now, ere ye fine,°   *before you finish*

    If any mourning may be meet,°   *matched with*

    Or mischief measured° unto mine.   *misfortune compared*

    My father, that all bales° may beet,°   *sorrows / remedy*

260   Forgive these men that do me pine.°   *pain*

    What they work,° wot° they not;   *do / know*

    Therefore, my father, I crave,

    Let never their sins be sought,°   *examined*

    But see° their souls to save.   *see that*

SOLDIER 1: We, hark, he jangles° like a jay.   *chatters*

SOLDIER 2: Methink he patters like a pie.°   *magpie*

SOLDIER 3: He has been doing all this day,

    And made great moving of° mercy.   *reference to*

SOLDIER 4: Is this the same that gan us say°   *is said to us*

270   That he was God's son almighty?

SOLDIER 1: Therefore he feels full fell affray,°   *cruel assault*

    And deemed° this day for to die.   *was judged*

SOLDIER 2: *Vath, qui destruis templum!*⁵

SOLDIER 3: His saws° were so, certain.   *words*

SOLDIER 4: And sirs, he said to some

    He might raise it again.

SOLDIER 1: To muster° that he had no might,   *manifest*

    For all the cautels° that he could cast.   *spells*

    All if he were in word so wight,⁶

280   For all his force now is he fast.°   *bound*

    As Pilate deemed is done and dight,°   *dealt with*

    Therefore I rede° that we go rest.   *advise*

SOLDIER 2: This race° mun be rehearsed° right,   *action / reported*

    Through the world both east and west.

SOLDIER 3: Yea, let him hang there still

    And make mows on° the moon.   *faces at*

---

3. I'll thrust them together, so I may prosper.   6. Even though his words were so bold.
4. Take heed that you miss none of my suffering.
5. Ah! thou who destroyeth the temple! (Mark 14:58,
John 2:19).

SOLDIER 4: Then may we wend at will.°   *go when we please*
SOLDIER 1: Nay, good sirs, not so soon.

      For certes us needs another note:°   *we have other business*
290   This kirtle° would I of you crave.   *garment*
SOLDIER 2: Nay, nay, sir, we will look by lot°   *draw lots*
      Which of us four falls it to° have.   *it falls to*
SOLDIER 3: I rede° we draw cut° for this coat—   *advise / straws*
      Lo, see how soon—all sides to save.°   *to satisfy all parties*
SOLDIER 4: The short cut shall win, that well ye wot,°   *know*
      Whether it fall to knight or knave.
SOLDIER 1: Fellows, ye tharf° not flite,°   *need / quarrel*
      For this mantle is mine.
SOLDIER 2: Go we then hence tite,°   *quickly*
300   This travail° here we tine.°   *effort / waste*

            [END OF MEDIEVAL CYCLE DRAMA]

❖

Vernacular Religion and Repression

As Middle English religious writers were fond of pointing out, Christ's apostles preached and wrote in the mother tongues of their audiences. The early Western church used Latin, the dominant world language of late-imperial Rome. With the passing centuries, though, the Latin of the church was less and less accessible to most laypeople. They heard a liturgy they understood mostly through vernacular explanations and visual images in the church. Preaching and the translation of biblical and other sacred texts certainly continued in all the emerging European vernaculars. On the other hand, Latin became a protective bulwark for clerical authority and the institutional church. Increasingly, this control of the Bible and doctrine accompanied an anxiety among clerics about laypeople reading or interpreting religious texts in the absence of ecclesiastical oversight. Other aspects of the church, such as its great wealth and varying degrees of clerical corruption, also alienated many laypeople in England and elsewhere.

Throughout the Middle Ages, both the established church and its critics were aware of these problems. One response was a persistent call for more and better preaching in local vernaculars. Yet the learning and energies of parish clergy were very uneven. Such "secular" clergy needed books of simple instruction and sample sermons in English for the whole church year. Toward this end, John Mirk wrote a lively and very popular sermon cycle, the *Festial*, toward the end of the fourteenth century. The later thirteenth and fourteenth centuries also witnessed a growing desire among laypeople for more intimate religious experience: "affective piety" as it has been called. Expressive and intense depictions of scriptural events such as the Crucifixion (see page 515) invited intense and expressive response, such as we will witness, in highly exaggerated form, in *The Book of Margery Kempe*.

In the midst of this religious yearning, dissatisfaction, and incomplete response by the church, there arrived the disruptive brilliance of John Wyclif. Wyclif came to public notice at Oxford by the 1350s, initially as a superb though radical practitioner of the technical scholastic theology of his day. He took increasingly extreme positions on a number of religious issues, key among them the nature of the Eucharist. Wyclif maintained—against established orthodoxy—that eucharistic bread was not utterly transformed into the body of Christ ("transubstantiated") when blessed by the priest. Perhaps more challenging to the everyday work of the

Crucifixion Scene, from a manuscript of Michael de Massa's *On the Passion of Our Lord,* 1405.
This illumination is found at the beginning of a narrative of the Passion written in Latin and Middle English. Delicate yet emotive, it evokes much of the "affective spirituality" of its era. The drawing is in pale brown ink and wash, which only renders more emphatic and disturbing the bright red of Christ's elaborately detailed wounds. The weeping Virgin Mary sways, nearly fainting, while Mary Magdalene kneels and clutches Christ's legs. Even the angels look down in sorrow, though the men at right are more restrained. Late-medieval worshipers were encouraged to imagine themselves as if present at such scenes of high pathos. Here, the author of the text, Michael de Massa, is depicted among the witnesses of Christ's suffering; the scroll hanging from his desk contains the first words of his book: *Angeli pacis . . .*

church, he held that a man in a state of sin could not be a priest—that the priestly role was vested in the individual, not his enactment of the sacraments.

Wyclif vigorously supported ecclesiastical poverty. He argued that tithes could be withheld and used charitably elsewhere, even that the vast accumulated wealth of the church should be "disendowed" and placed in the hands of the secular government. The first notion appealed to many common people, and the latter intrigued a royal court plagued by debt. Wyclif was brought to London by John of Gaunt in 1376 to preach his views about disendowment. The church tried to condemn him as a heretic in 1377, but Gaunt deflected their efforts. Wyclif's evolving view of the Eucharist was harder to defend, though, and another church council in 1381 found that and other positions heretical; Wyclif retired from Oxford to his parish church, where he continued to write at a great pace until his death in 1384. Despite the church's condemnation, though, Wyclif's ideas gained followers (called "Lollards" by the late 1380s) at every level of society, and noble sympathizers were influential in the household of Richard II.

Wyclif insisted throughout his life that laypeople had a right to understand, even enter into, theological debate. And that meant they needed access to the fundamental work of all Christian belief, the Bible, in English. A group of his learned adherents undertook an enormous and complex project toward this end. They translated the Bible but also wrote extensive English commentaries based on Latin tradition and produced a full cycle of sermons urging Lollard doctrines; one is included below. Of course, laypeople had always heard biblical passages in English, since they were the basis of most sermons. The great threat of Wyclif and his followers was that they felt the Bible could be used to criticize and correct the church, that it stood outside of its institutional settings and interpretations. Along with the impressively organized text production mentioned above, there were Lollard schools, and a network of household "cells" where Lollard texts and ideas were studied and discussed. Taken all together, the outlines of something like a shadow church emerge. The 1430 "confession" of Hawisia Moone, included here, reflects many of these activities, and suggests the major beliefs (not all of them originating with Wyclif) that Lollards supported.

All of this was profoundly unnerving to the institutional church. Writing around 1390, the monastic chronicler Henry Knighton mentions the English Bible and comments: "that, which formerly belonged to those clergy who were sufficiently learned and intelligent, was made available to any lay person, even women, who knew how to read." Knighton thus sees the Lollard danger not just in terms of theology, but also of class and especially gender. It was relatively easy to condemn Wyclif's own beliefs and remove him from Oxford, even to burn other Lollards, but far harder to locate and suppress the network of local Lollard groups. And in a culture where church and state were so intimately linked, Lollard religious beliefs soon posed a political threat. Knighton also says Wyclif was inspired by John Ball, the priest who helped lead the Rising of 1381 (see pages 454–66). The movement lost virtually all its aristocratic support after a rebellion against Henry V in 1413, led by the Lollard Sir John Oldcastle.

Repression of Lollard beliefs had been in the air since the church council that condemned Wyclif in 1381. By 1401, Parliament passed a statute (excerpted here) that called for the burning of unrepentant heretics. In the somewhat paranoid atmosphere of a threatened church and a king (Henry IV) who had usurped the throne, almost any vernacular religious writings might smell of heresy and political subversion. "Lollard" came to mean almost anyone outside of holy orders who spoke or acted religiously beyond narrow community norms, as we see in the case of Margery Kempe. The 1409 Constitutions enacted under Archbishop Thomas Arundel officially restricted preaching, writing, or translation in English. All these activities had to be licensed by a bishop or his council. Mere possession of some vernacular books, including the Bible, was a ground for arrest and examination. Rumor too could lead to ecclesiastical inquiry, as happened repeatedly to Margery Kempe. The closing passages of the Confession of Hawisia Moone suggest the sort of surveillance culture that the religious world of late medieval England had become.

Archbishop Arundel and the church did not oppose all religious reading in the vernacular, however. For instance, Arundel patronized the translation (by Nicholas Love) of a long tract of meditations on the life of Christ. This was a form of meditation recommended to laypeople because knowing the story of Christ's life did not require direct knowledge of the Bible, nor did it involve questions of doctrine or the institutional church. Several other passages in this section were written by people of clear orthodoxy, and texts like *The Holy Prophet David Saith* instruct laypeople in humbly reading the Bible. Nonetheless, popular Lollardy continued through the end of the Middle Ages, and over 240 medieval copies of the Wycliffite Bible survive, more than any other Middle English text.

from The Wycliffite Bible
John 10.11–18[1]

I am a good shepherd. A good shepherd giveth his life for his sheep. But a hired hyne,[2] and that is not the shepherd, whose are not the sheep his own,[3] seeth a wolf coming, and he leaveth the sheep and fleeth, and the wolf ravisheth and disparpleth[4] the sheep. And the hired hyne fleeth for he is an hired hyne, and it pertaineth not to him of the sheep. I am a good shepherd and I know my sheep and my sheep know me, as the father hath known me and I know the father, and I put[5] my life for my sheep. I have other sheep that are not of this fold; and it behoveth me to bring them together; and they shall hear my voice, and it shall be made one fold and one shepherd. Therefore the father loveth me for I put my life that eftsoon[6] I take it. No man takith it from me, but I put it of myself; I have power to put it, and I have power to take it again. This commandment I have taken of my father.

from A Wycliffite Sermon on John 10.11–18[1]

Ego sum pastor bonus.   Johannis X[2]

Christ telleth in his gospel the manners of a good herd,[3] so that hereby we may wit[4] how our herds fail now. And default of such herds is most peril in the church for, as right office of them should most bring men to heaven, so default in this office draweth men most to hell. Christ telleth of himself how *he is a good herd.* For he is the best herd that mankind may have, for he is good by himself and may no way fail, for he is both God and man, and God may no way sin. And thus we have the measure to know a good herd and an evil, for the more that a herd is like to Christ he is the better, and the more that he straungeth[5] from him he is the worse in this office.

And eft,[6] when Christ hath given the measure to know good herds, he telleth the highest property that falleth to a good herd: *a good herd,* as Christ saith, *putteth his life for his sheep,* for more charity may none have than to put his life for his friends, and, if he worketh wisely, for to bring these sheep to heaven, for thus the herd hath most pain and the sheep most profit. Thus may we see who is a good herd and who faileth in this office. For as Christ putteth wisely his own life for his

---

1. The process that resulted in the "Wycliffite" Bible is complex and still unclear. The translation was the work of followers of Wycliffite ideas, but Wyclif himself did not participate in it. It was also a huge and well-organized undertaking, that involved study of the Latin original aided by learned commentaries. The later and more colloquial version is given here. We have modernized spellings but altered vocabulary as little as possible, to retain the syntax and rhythms of the original Middle English.
2. Servant.
3. An awkward construction, derived from close adherence to the Latin.

4. Seizes and scatters.
5. Lay down, commit.
6. Another time.
1. Dating from the later 14th century, this is only one sermon from a huge sermon cycle produced in connection with the Wycliffite Bible. Note the rhetorically effective use of alliteration in parts of the sermon.
2. I am a good shepherd (Latin). John 10.
3. Shepherd, priest.
4. Know.
5. Differs.
6. Again.

sheep, so Antichrist putteth proudly many lives for his foul life; as, if the fiend led the pope to kill many thousand men to hold his worldly state, he sued[7] Antichrist's manners * * *

And thus seem our religious[8] to be exempt from charity, for, need a man never so much to have help of such goods, yea if they[9] have stones or jewels that harm them, they will not give such goods nor their value to help their brethren, nor cease to annoy[1] themselves in building of high houses, nor to gather such vain goods if it do harm to their brethren. Such avaricious men are far from manners of a good herd. And so these new religious[2] that the fiend hath tolled[3] in, by color to help the former herds, harm them many gates,[4] and letten[5] this office in the church, for true preaching and worldly goods are spoiled by such religious. And therefore teacheth Christ to flee them, for they are ravishing wolves: some will as briars tear the wool of sheep and make them cold in charity, and some will sturdily as thorns slay the sheep of holy church.

And thus is our mother shend[6] for default of man's help. And more meed[7] might no man have than to help this sorry widow, for princes of priests and Pharisees that called Christ a beguiler croched[8] to themselves the choosing of many herds in the church, and they are taught by Antichrist to choose his herds and not Christ's. And thus faileth Christ's church. Lord, since herds should pass[9] their sheep as men pass bleating sheep, how should Christ's church fare if these herds were turned to wolves? But Christ saith thus it fareth among the herds of the church, that many of them *are hired hynes and not herds over the sheep, for the sheep are not their own,* and so they love too little the sheep. For, if they have their temporal hire,[1] they reckon not how their flock fare. And thus do all these curates that tell more by[2] worldly winning than by virtues of their subjects or soul's heal[3] to come to heaven.

Such are not herds of sheep but of the dung and wool of them, and these shall not have in heaven joy of the sheep that they keep. *Such hynes see wolves coming to flocks that they should keep, and they flee* for dread of nought. *And these wolves ravish these sheep and scatter them* for this end, that then they may sooner perish. And this moved Paul to found no order,[4] for Christ's order is enough, and then should all Christian men be more surely in one flock. Lord, if cowardice of such hynes be damned of Christ, how much more should wolves be damned that are put to keep Christ's sheep? But Christ saith a clean[5] cause why *this hired hyne fleeth* thus: *for he is an hired hyne and the sheep pertain not to him,* but the dung of such sheep and this dung sufficeth to him, however the sheep fare. Some are wolves without, and some are wolves within and these are more perilous, for homely[6] enemies are the worst * * *

But *Christ saith he is a good herd and knoweth his sheep and they him,* for the office that falleth to herds maketh him known among them. *As my father knoweth me and I again know my father,* so, saith Christ, *I put my life to keep my sheep* against wolves. And as this knowing might not quench[7] betwixt Christ and his father, so should these herds watch upon their sheep, and they should know him, not by bodily feasts nor other signs[8] that he doth, but by three offices of a herd that Christ hath limited[9]

7. He (the pope) followed, imitated.
8. Clerics.
9. I.e., the clerics.
1. Trouble, injure.
2. Friars.
3. Lured.
4. In many ways.
5. Hinder.
6. Ruined.
7. Reward.
8. Seized.

9. Surpass.
1. Wages.
2. Consider more important.
3. Their salvation.
4. I.e., no religious order such as monks or friars.
5. Simple.
6. Familiar.
7. Be extinguished.
8. I.e., liturgical rituals.
9. Assigned.

to him. It falleth to a good herd to lead his sheep in wholesome pastures, and when his sheep are hurt or scabbed to heal them and grease them, and when other evil beasts assail them then help them. And hereto should he put his life to save his sheep from such beasts. The pasture is God's law that evermore is green in truth, and rotten pastures are other laws and other fables without ground. And cowardice of such herds that dare not defend God's law witnesseth that they fail in two offices suing[1] after: for he that dare not, for world's dread, defend the law of his God, how should he defend his sheep for love that he hath to them? And if they bring in new laws contrary to God's law, how should they not fail after in other offices that they should have?

But Christ that is head of herds saith that *he hath other sheep that are not yet of this flock, and them must he bring together and teach them to know his voice. And so shall there be one flock and one herd* over them all. These sheep are heathen men or Jews that Christ will convert, for all these shall make one flock, the which flock is holy church—but far from this understanding that all men shall be converted.[2]

John Mirk

from *Festial*[1]

Hortamur vos, ne in vacuum graciam Dei recipiatis. Corinthians VI.[2]

Good men and women, these words that I have said in Latin be thus to say in English: "We admonish you that ye take not the grace of God in vain." These be the words of St. Paul, Christ's holy apostle, that be read in the epistle of this day. By the which word this holy apostle chargeth all good people that they take heed what grace God sendeth them and that they take not that grace in vain. God giveth grace to man all times; but, for a man needeth more his grace this time than another, therefore, of his high mercy, he giveth nowadays more abundance of Lent than any other time. The which grace he parteth in three ways; that is to say, in way of gracious abiding, in way of gracious deeming,[3] and in way of gracious amends-making. These three ways God sendeth his grace to you.

Wherefore, right as St. Paul admonisheth his disciples, right so I admonish you that be my children in God, that ye take not this grace of God in vain.

Ye have a common saying among you and say that God's grace is worth a new fair. Then taketh heed how much worth God's grace is. For, though any of you had as much gold as a fair is worth, but he had God's grace with it, it should turn him more into shameship than into worship. Thus ye may see by very reason that God's grace is more worth than any fair. But yet ye shall know further. For, though a man had never so much riches and prosperity here, that cometh all of God's grace. But-if[4] he take that grace well and please his God withal, it shall turn him into damnation.

But, for the poor plaineth on the rich and say they be unkind to God and do not as God biddeth them do and full elder[5] see a mote in another man's eye that cannot see a beam their own; therefore, ye shall know well that it is a special grace of God when he maketh a man rich and some man poor. He maketh them rich that they with

1. Following.
2. The preacher does not agree with the opinion that all mankind will convert.
1. Even as Wyclif's followers were attacking the secular clergy for their failure to preach, efforts were being made to supply parish priests of limited education with model sermons. John Mirk's *Festial*, c. 1390, is a sermon cycle organized around the church year and the calendar of the saints. At least in part it is a response to Lollard ideas,

especially Lollard opposition to religious images. While it has none of the zeal of Wycliffite sermons, the *Festial* gives some impression of what was being heard when priests did try to educate their flock. Modern English version by William Matthews.
2. 2 Corinthians 6.1.
3. Judging.
4. Unless.
5. Quickly.

their riches should succour the poor in their need, and so with their goods buy them heaven. And some he maketh poor that their poverty shall be their salvation. For God knoweth well, if they were rich they would forget their God and so spill[6] themself.

Wherefore, we admonish you, both rich and poor, that ye take not this grace of God in idle nor in vain. But he that is rich, set not his heart thereupon, but ever be in dread, lest he misspend it, and thank God of his grace. And he that is poor, grouch he not against his God, ne deem he not the rich, but take his poverty in patience, and thank God of his grace; for, at the last he shall have that for the best.

But a man, be he rich or be he poor, if he have grace of God to see how much he taketh of God and how little he giveth again, very reason will tell that he is more worth damnation than salvation. But, for God is full of grace and sheweth his grace to all his handiwork, and for he knoweth our frailty, he hath compassion of us and giveth us his grace in abiding of amendment. That is: though thou trespass sore against him, he will not smite anon, but graciously abideth, for he hath much liever for to do grace than vengeance. And that is for two causes, as St. Augustine saith.

One is: if God had done vengeance, anon the world had been ended many a day ago, and so many had been unborn that now be holy saints in heaven.

That other cause is: for to shew how full he is of grace, and how fain he will do grace and mercy to all that will leave the evil and take the good. Wherefore he saith thus by his prophet: *Nolo mortem peccatoris, sed ut magis convertatur et vivat:* "I will not," he says, "that a sinful man be dead, but I will rather that he turn to good life."

Thus ye heareth how gracious God is in abiding. Wherefore, I admonish you that ye take not this grace in vain, but thinketh well how he hath spared you from Easter hitherto, whereas he might, by right, have smitten you with his sword of vengeance each day. For, as St. Anselm saith, the least sin that a man doth, it unworshippeth[7] God. Then, if a man did anything that unworshipped his worldly king, he were worthy to take his death, much more is a man worth the death that unworshippeth him that is King of Heaven and lord and king over all kings. But, right as he passeth all in dignity, right so he passeth all in grace and bounty. But, though ye feelen him gracious, be never the bolder to lie in sin, but hieth you for to cleanse you thereof. For though he abide long, at the last He will smite such that will not amend them. And when he smiteth, he smiteth sore.

I read that there was a knight that had no rents of his own, but he had gotten much good in wars. And, when he had all spent out, he yode[8] and wedded a lady of that country that was rich enough. And though he was poor, he was a seemly man of person.

She said to him thus: I wot well that thou art a seemly man of body, but for thou art poor I may not, for shame, take thee but-if thou have much gold or many rents. But for thou hast no gold, do as I teach thee, and get gold. Go into such a place where many rich merchants come, and get thee gold, and then thou shalt have me."

Then went he thither. And it happened that there came a rich merchant that way. And he anon took him, and bare forth his gold, and slew him and buried him. And then after came to the lady and said, "Lo!—the sum of gold I have gotten of such a man, and buried him there!"

Then said the lady, "Go again tonight and look if thou aught hear."

Then yede he that night and stood by the dead man's grave. And at midnight there came a light from heaven down to the grave, and then the grave opened, and the corpse sat up and held up his hands to God, and said, "Lord that art righteous judge, do thou wreke[9] me upon this man that hath thus falsely slain me for my true chattel."

---

6. Destroy.
7. Dishonors.

8. Went.
9. Avenge.

And therewith came a voice from heaven and said, "This day thirty winter thou shalt have vengeance." And then the corpse thanked God and lay down in his grave again.

Then was this knight sore afeared, and went to this lady and told her all, and how the voice said how, that day thirty winter, he should have vengeance.

Then said the lady, "Yea," quoth she, "Much may fall in thirty winter! Go we together and be wedded!"

So they lived y-fere[1] twenty year, in prosperity and weal. But ever this knight was adread of this vengeance, and said to the lady, "Now twenty year be passed, and the ten will hie fast. What is thy best counsel?"

Then she said, "We will make this castle as secure and as strong as we may. And, that same day, we shall gather all our friends and stuff[2] us with men enow, and so we shall scape well enough.

And so they did. When the day came, they gathered a great sum of men into the castle, and set them to the meat, and made all the mirth that they could. Then was there a harper, and harped always at the meat.

But, for there may no wicked spirit come there ne have no powsty[3] as far as the harp is heard, there came out of the kitchen a brothel,[4] bawded with grease, and rubbed his strings with his bawdy hands. Then was this harper wonder wroth, and with his harp would have smitten this brothel. But, for he flew fast away, the harper sued[5] him out of the castle. And, when he came out, this brothel vanished away.

Then this harper turned again—and saw this castle sink into the earth, all afire.

Thus ye may see, though God abide long, at the last he smiteth sore. Wherefore, I admonish you that ye take not his grace of abiding in vain, but bethinketh you well of your misdeeds and cometh betimes and cleanseth you. For God giveth you all an high grace of deeming, for thereas he is truth and righteousness, and he may not deem but with righteousness. And then shall none scape undamned,[6] for, as Job saith, "Though we would strive with him, we may not answer of one good deed for a thousand that he giveth us."

from The Statute "On Burning the Heretic," 1401[1]

Also, whereas it is shown to our sovereign lord the king on behalf of the prelates and clergy of his realm of England in this present parliament, that although the catholic faith built upon Christ, and by his apostles and the holy church sufficiently determined, declared, and approved, has hitherto been most devoutly observed by good and holy and most noble progenitors and predecessors of the king, and the church of England laudably endowed by his most noble forebears and sustained in all her rights

1. Together.
2. Provide.
3. Power.
4. Low fellow.
5. Followed.
6. Unjudged.
1. Drafted in 1401 under the Latin title *De Heretico Comburendo*. Henry IV came to the throne of England in 1400, after the deposition of Richard II. Among the supporters of Henry's shaky new reign was the Archbishop of Canterbury, Thomas Arundel, an implacable opponent of the Lollards. (This statute is also called "Contra Lollardos.") As part of his political payback, and in some contrast to his earlier positions, Henry supported several pieces of parliamentary legislation that made the surveillance, interrogation, and punishment of heretics far more aggressive; those who had recanted but relapsed could now be burned. This statute gave legal support, after the fact, to the first burning of a Lollard in England earlier in the year. It also marks a new stage in the transformation of Wyclif's followers from purely doctrinal to equally political subversives. The translation by A. R. Myers omits much of the legal wordiness of the original Latin. We have eliminated the translator's numerous ellipsis points for the sake of readability; interested readers may consult *English Historical Documents* (Oxford University Press).

and liberties yet nevertheless divers false and perverse persons of a certain new sect, thinking in a damnable way of the said faith, of the sacraments of the church, and the authority of the same, and usurping the office of preaching against the law of God and of the church, do perversely and maliciously in divers places within the realm under the colour of dissembled holiness, preach and teach these days openly and privily new doctrines, and heretical opinions contrary to the same faith and blessed determinations of holy church; and they make unlawful conventicles and confederacies, they hold and exercise schools, they make and write books, they do wickedly instruct and inform people, and stir them to sedition and insurrection, and make great strife and division among the people by which sect not only very great peril of souls but also many more other perils might come to this realm, unless it be more speedily helped by the king especially since the diocesans of the realm cannot by their spiritual jurisdiction, without the help of the royal majesty, sufficiently correct these false and perverse persons because they go from diocese to diocese, and will not appear before the diocesans, but do utterly despise the diocesans and their spiritual jurisdiction. Upon which novelties and excesses being recited, the prelates and clergy and also the commons of the said realm have prayed our sovereign lord the king that his royal highness would vouchsafe in parliament to provide a convenient remedy.

Our sovereign lord the king, graciously considering the premises has ordained, from henceforth firmly to be observed, that none within the realm, or any other dominions subject to his royal majesty, presume to preach openly or privily, without the licence of the diocesan of the same place first required and obtained, curates in their own churches, and persons hitherto privileged only excepted; and that none henceforth preach, hold, teach or instruct anything openly or secretly, or make or write any book contrary to the catholic faith nor make conventicles nor hold schools, and also that none henceforth shall in any way favour such and that all and singular having such books or writings of such wicked doctrines or opinions shall deliver such books and writings to the diocesan of the same place within forty days from the time of the proclamation of this ordinance and statute. And if any person or persons henceforth attempt anything against the royal ordinance and statute aforesaid then the diocesan of the same place may cause such persons to be arrested and to be detained under safe custody in his prisons until he or they do canonically purge themselves of the articles laid against them in this behalf or abjure such wicked sect and doctrines. And if any person in any case above expressed be convicted, then the diocesan may cause to be kept in his prison the said person so convicted according to the quality of his offence and to make the same person pay the king a pecuniary fine. And if any person within the realm and dominions, upon these wicked preachings, doctrines, schools, etc. be convicted by sentence before the diocesan of the same place or his commissaries and do refuse duly to abjure the same wicked preachings, etc., or after abjuration be pronounced relapsed then the sheriff of the county of the same place, and mayor and sheriffs or sheriff, or mayor and bailiffs of the city, town, and borough of the same county nearest to the said diocesan or his commissioners, shall be personally present at the passing of such sentences by the diocesan and his commissaries against such persons when they shall be required and after such a sentence is promulgated, they shall receive such persons and cause them to be burnt before the people in a conspicuous place; that such punishment may strike fear into the minds of others, so that no such wicked doctrines or their supporters may be in any way tolerated.

Preaching and Teaching in the Vernacular[1]

Since Christ bade his disciples and other preachers and teachers of God's law to teach the gospel to every man and woman in every language, there may no prelate arten nor letten[2] preaching and teaching of the gospel in English; but every prelate and preacher is bound to preach and teach the gospel of Christ and his law to the people after the conning[3] that God hath sent to them. And therefore, though it be these days defended[4] and inhibited by some prelates that men should teach the gospel in English, I answer and say to them as the apostles said to Annas and Caiaphas and to the prelates and to the bishops and the masters[5] of the Jews which defended the apostles for to preach the gospel, *Obedire oportet Deo magis quam hominibus.*[6] * * * And, leve[7] friend, since it is lawful to preach the gospel in English, it is lawful to write it in English, both to the teacher and to the hearer if he con writing,[8] for by writing is most sure examination of man's speech and by writing God's law may best be cowd[9] and best kept in mind. And therefore, leve friend, although some prelates have defended me to teach the gospel and to write it in English, yet none of them hath defended you nor may defend you to con the gospel in English that is your kindly[1] language. * * * And since I have written the gospel to you in well great dread and persecution, ye that be in such security that no prelate may letten you nor distress you for conning nor for keeping of the gospel, conneth it and keepeth it with good devotion. * * * And, as ye may hear, now preaching and teaching of the gospel and of God's law is arted and letted[2] more than it was wont to be, therefore taketh goodly the teaching that cometh to you freely. And though the persecution of Diocletian and Maximian[3] be now newly begun to letten teaching and preaching of God's word and God's law and to compel men to worship graven images of stone and of tree, stand ye stiff in the faith. * * *

Christ said not to him,[4] as prelates and men of holy church do these days to men and women that ask them questions of holy writ, of conscience and of God's law, "Oh thou borel clerk, what entermettest thou thee[5] with holy writ and with God's law? Say thy Pater Noster and thy Creed, and it is enough to thee!" and though they[6] con neither their Pater Noster nor their Creed—for they understand it not, but say it as a starling or a jay—and many men say it not so well. This is the teaching of prelates and of men of holy church these days. And cause is for[7] many prelates and men of holy church be so lewed[8] that they can nought answer, nor they con well their Creed, and therefore they defend English books of God's law. * * * They love no

---

1. From a series of sermons (or discussions of scripture) written by a friar in the early 15th century and probably meant for private reading by a lay aristocrat. The same writer is author of a popular vernacular dialogue on religion, *Dives and Pauper,* "Rich Man and Poor Man." The author is orthodox, especially regarding key issues such as the Eucharist and confession; as a friar, he is a natural enemy of Lollards. Yet he opposes the Arundel Constitutions of 1409, castigates the corruption of the church, criticizes enclosed orders like monks, and opposes the worship of images. All these positions were dangerous at the time—the Constitutions forbid criticism of the clergy to a lay audience—and the writer is careful to associate himself with his powerful lay patron and "leve friend." Mere ownership of *Dives and Pauper* was sometimes considered a sign of heretical leanings. We have modernized spellings but altered vocabulary as little as possible, to retain the syntax and rhythms of the original Middle English.

2. Blame nor hinder.
3. Understanding.
4. Forbidden.
5. Teachers.
6. It is more important to obey God than men (Acts 5.29).
7. Dear.
8. Knows how to write.
9. Known.
1. Natural, inborn.
2. Blamed and hindered.
3. Roman emperors who persecuted Christians.
4. A questioner.
5. Oh you uneducated layman, why do you concern yourself.
6. Even though they (the laymen).
7. The cause is that.
8. Ignorant.

multiplication[9] of God's law, for they would not be asked nor opposed; and for many of them be well lewed, therefore they would keep the people in overdone lewedness,[1] that themselves in their lewedness might seem wise.

from The Holy Prophet David Saith[1]
[SIX POINTS ON LAY READING OF SCRIPTURE]

But leave we all these cursednesses beforesaid, and comfort we Christian people to take trustily[2] and devoutly the text of Holy Writ and the true understanding thereof. Christian men should pray devoutly to God, author of all wisdom and conning,[3] that he give to them true understanding of Holy Writ. Thus saith the wise man: "Lord, give thou to me wisdom that standeth about thy seats,"[4] that I wit what faileth to me[5] and what is pleasant before thee in all time.[6] The second time,[7] they should meek[8] themselves to God in doing penance, that God open to them the true understanding of his law, as he opened wit to his apostles to understand Holy Scripture. The third, that they should subject themselves to the will of God, and believe steadfastly that his law is true, and trust faithfully in God's help; and for this they shall have the blessing of God and the bliss of heaven, and shall graciously be heard in their prayer. For God despiseth not the prayer of meek men, and he heareth the desire of poor men that know verily that they have no good but of God. The fourth time, they should meek themselves to their brethren, and inquire meekly of every learned man—and specially of well-willed men, and well-living—the true understanding of Holy Writ; and be they not obstinate in their own wit but give stead and credence to wiser men that have the spirit of wisdom and of grace. The fifth time, read they busily[9] the text of the New Testament and take they example of the holy life of Christ and of his apostles, and trust they fully to the goodness of the Holy Ghost, which is special teacher of well-willed men. For Christ saith in the Gospel to his disciples, "The Holy Ghost shall teach you all truth that is necessary to health of souls."[1] And John saith in his epistle, "That anointing"—that is, grace of the Holy Ghost—"teacheth you of all things that pertaineth to health of soul."[2] The sixth time, they should see and study the true and open exposition of holy doctors[3] and other wise men as they may easily and goodly come thereto.

Let Christian men travail faithfully in these six ways, and be not too much afeared of objections of enemies saying that "the letter slaith."[4] These enemies mean thus: that the letter of Holy Writ is harmful to men, and false and reprievable,[5] since that it slaith men by death of sin.[6] But sikerly[7] they mistake the words of Holy Writ,

9. Dissemination.

1. Excessive ignorance.

1. Written between the 1380s and 1420s, this text typifies many treatises that appeared in reaction to the production of the Wycliffite Bible, but not always therefore Wycliffite in their leanings, which justify English translation and provide both advice and warning about scriptural and doctrinal study. In other passages, *The Holy Prophet* attacks study merely in pursuit of pride and worldly profit, attributing such motives mostly to clerics. In the passage here, he helps less learned, lay readers with the understanding of sacred text. The treatise survives in one manuscript, which circulated among pious merchants in London. From *The Idea of the Vernacular: An Anthology of Middle English Literary Theory, 1280–1520*, ed. Jocelyn Wogan-Browne et al. (University Park, PA: Pennsylvania State University Press, 1999), pages 151–52. We have modernized spellings but altered vocabulary as little as possible, to retain the syntax and rhythms of the original Middle English.

2. Faithfully.

3. Learning.

4. Book of Wisdom 9.4.

5. That I may know what I am lacking.

6. In all points.

7. Second point.

8. Humble.

9. Intently.

1. John 16.13.

2. John 2.27.

3. Authoritative commentators.

4. Opponents to biblical translation often objected to laypeople receiving the mere "letter" of the Bible, its literal sense as opposed to its spiritual meaning, to which clerics tried to claim exclusive access.

5. Blameworthy.

6. I.e., by leading them into error, hence mortal sin.

7. Certainly.

and their mistaking and wayward meaning, and their wicked living bring in death of soul; that is sin. But against their false meaning Christ saith in the Gospel of John, "The words which I have spoken to you are spirit and life," and in the same chapter Saint Peter saith to Christ, "Lord, thou hast words of everlasting life."[8] Paul saith, that the Lord Jesus "by the spirit of his mouth"—that is, his holy and true words—"shall slay Antichrist,"[9] and the prophet Isaiah saith, that "God by the spirit of his lips shall slay the wicked man"[1]—that is, Antichrist. Then since the words of Christ be words of everlasting life—that is, bring true men to everlasting bliss—and since these words shall slay Antichrist, the words of Christ be full holy and full mighty and full profitable to true men. But Paul meaneth thus, by authority of the Holy Ghost, when he saith "the letter slaith," that ceremonies either[2] sacrifices of the old law, without ghostly[3] understanding of the new law, slaith man by error of misbelief. * * * Therefore Paul saith, "the spirit quickeneth"[4]—that is, ghostly understanding of ceremonies and sacrifices of Moses' law quickeneth men of right belief that now, instead of bodily circumcision, take baptism taught and commanded of Christ, and, instead of sacrifices of beasts in the old law, take now Christ and his passion and hope to be saved thereby with His mercy and their own good living.[5] Also, the letter of the New Testament slaith rebel men that live thereagainst customably[6] without amending in this life. * * * Then though the letter slaith in manner beforesaid, it sueth[7] not therefore that the letter is false and harmful to men, as it sueth not that God is false and harmful in his kind,[8] though he slaith justly by death of body and of soul them that rebel finally against his law. Also this sentence, "the letter slaith," should more make afeared proud clerics, that understand the truth of God's law and live customably thereagainst, than simple men of wit that little understand the law of Christ and busy themselves to live well in charity to God and man. For these proud clerics, the more they connen[9] God's law the more they make themselves damnable for their high conning[1] and their wicked living; and the simple men for their little conning ground themselves the more in meekness, and busy themselves to learn the way of salvation. Thus, though they have not time and leisure to turn and turn again the books of God's law to con the letter thereof, they have and keep the fruit and the very sentence[2] of all the law of God by keeping of double charity.

Nicholas Love

from *The Mirror of the Blessed Life of Jesus Christ*[1]

But now furthermore for to speak of the blessed birth of Jesus and of that clean and holy deliverance[2] of his dear mother Mary, as it is written in part by revelation of our lady

8. John, ch. 6.
9. 2 Thessalonians 2.8.
1. Isaiah 11.14.
2. Or.
3. Spiritual.
4. Gives life.
5. The explicit reference to baptism and probable reference to the Eucharist would both suggest a non-Lollard author.
6. Against it habitually.
7. Follows.
8. Nature.
9. Know.
1. Learning.
2. True meaning.
1. At the same time that the Arundel Constitutions were suppressing much vernacular theological and mystical writing, the Carthusian Nicholas Love (d. 1424) was adapting into English the thirteenth-century Latin *Meditations on the*

Life of Christ, widely attributed to Bonaventure (but actually by another Franciscan). The *Mirror* draws from all the gospels, but also from later legends, to narrate Christ's life; Love adds elements directed specifically against Lollards. He offers detailed tableaux for meditation and devotion but omits much of Christ's teaching. The *Meditations* thereby invite pious reflection in "those of simple understanding" but draw the reader away from issues of the church and its doctrines. As is reported in many manuscripts of the *Mirror*, it was submitted to Archbishop Arundel under the terms of the 1409 Constitutions; he "commended it, ordering it to be published for the edification of the faithful and the confutation of heretics and Lollards." Appealing to the same affective piety seen in much late medieval religious art, the *Mirror* was widely read and copied. We have modernized spellings but altered vocabulary as little as possible, to retain the syntax and rhythms of the original Middle English.
2. Delivery.

made hereof to a devout man, when time of that blessed birth was come, that is to say the Sunday at midnight, God's son of heaven, as he was conceived in his mother's womb by the Holy Ghost, without seed of man, so going out of that womb without travail or sorrow, suddenly was upon hay at his mother's feet. And anon she, devoutly inclining with sovereign joy, took him in her arms, and sweetly clipping[3] and kissing, laid him in her barm,[4] and with a full pap, as she was taught of the Holy Ghost, washed him all about with her sweet milk, and so wrapped him in the kerchief of her head, and laid him in the crèche.[5] And anon, the ox and the ass, kneeling down, laid their mouths on the crèche, breathing at their noses upon the child, as they knew by reason that in that cold time the child so simply hiled[6] had need to be hot in that manner. And then his mother kneeling down worshipped and loved God, inwardly thanking and saying in this manner: "Lord God, holy father of heaven, I thank thee with all my might that hast given me thy dear son, and I honor thee, almighty God, God's son and mine." Joseph, also honoring and worshipping the child, God and man, took the saddle of the ass and made thereof a cushion our lady to sit on and a suppoyle[7] to lean to. And so sat the lady of all the world in that simple array beside the crèche, having her mild mode[8] and her lovely eyes, with her inward affection, upon her sweet dearworth[9] child.

But in this poor and simple worldly array what ghostly riches and inward comfort and joy she had may no tongue tell. Wherefore if we will feel the true joy and comfort of Jesus, we must with him and with his mother love poverty, meekness, and bodily penance, as he gave us example of all these here in this birth and first coming into this world.

For of the first, that is poverty, saint Bernard in a sermon of the Nativity of our lord, telling how he was born to comfort of mankind, saith in this manner: "God's son comforteth his people. Wilt thou know his people? That is of whom speaketh David in the psalter and saith: *Lord, to thee is belaft the poor people.*[1] And he[2] himself saith in the gospel: *Woe to you rich men that have your comfort here.*[3] How should he comfort them that have their own comfort? Wherefore Christ's innocence and childhood comforteth not janglers and great speakers, Christ's weeping and tears comforteth not dissolute laughers, his simple clothing comforteth not them that go in proud clothing, and his stable and crèche comforteth not them that love first seats and worldly worship. And also the angels in Christ's nativity appearing to the waking shepherds comfort none other but the poor travailers,[4] and to them tell they the joy of new light, and not to the rich men that have their joy and comfort here."

Also as to the second, we may see at this birth both in Christ and in his mother perfect meekness. For they were not squeamish of the stable, nor of the beasts, nor of hay and other such abject simpleness. But this virtue of meekness both our lord and our lady kept perfectly in all their deeds, and commend it sovereignly to us. Wherefore be we about[5] with all our might to get this virtue, knowing that without it is no salvation. For there is no work or deed of us that may please God with pride.

Also as to the third we may see in them both, and namely[6] in the child Jesus not a little bodily penance. Of the which saint Bernard saith thus: "God's son, when he would be born, that had in his own free will to choose what time he would take[7]

---

3. Embracing.
4. Lap.
5. Manger.
6. Clothed.
7. A prop.
8. Manner.
9. Precious.

1. Psalm 10.14.
2. I.e., Christ.
3. Luke 6.24.
4. Laborers.
5. Let us endeavor.
6. Especially.
7. Choose.

thereto, he chose the time that was most noisome and hard, as the cold winter, namely to a young child and a poor woman's son, that scarcely had clothes to wrap him in, and a crèche as for a cradle to lay him in."

from The Confession of Hawisia Moone of Loddon[1]

In the name of God tofore you, the worshipful father in Christ, William by the grace of God bishop of Norwich, I Hawise Moone, the wife of Thomas Moone of Loddon of your diocese, your subject, knowing, feeling, and understanding that before this time I have been right homely and privy with many heretics, knowing them for heretics. And them I have received and harbored in our house, and them I have concealed, comforted, supported, maintained and favored with all my power. Which heretics' names be these: Sir William Whyte, Sir William Caleys, Sir Huwe Pye, Sir Thomas Pert—priests—John Waddon, John Fowlyn, John Gray, William Everden, William Bate of Sethyng, Bartholomew Cornmonger, Thomas Burell and Betty his wife, William Wardon, John Pert, Edmond Archer of Loddon, Richard Belward, Niclas Belward, Bartholomew Monk, William Wright and many other.[2] Wich have oft times kept, held, and continued schools of heresy in privy chambers and privy places of ours, in the which schools I have heard, conceived, learned and reported the errors and heresies which be written and contained in these indentures. That is to say:

First, that the sacrament of baptism done in water in form customed in the church is but a trifle and not to be pondered, for all Christ's people is sufficiently baptized in the blood of Christ. And so Christ's people needeth none other baptism. Also that the sacrament of confirmation done by a bishop is of none avail nor necessary to be had, for as much as when a child hath discretion, and can and will understand the word of God, it is sufficiently confirmed by the Holy Ghost and needeth none other confirmation. Also that confession should be made only to God and to none other priest, for no priest hath power to remit sin nor to assoile[3] a man of any sin. Also that no man is bound to do no[4] penance which any priest enjoineth him to do for their sins which they have confessed unto the priest, for sufficient penance for all manner of sin is every person to abstain him from lying, backbiting and evil doing, and no man is bound to do none other penance. Also that no priest hath power to make Christ's very[5] body at mass in form of bread, but that, after the sacramental words said at mass of the priest, there remaineth only material bread. Also that the pope of Rome is father[6] Antichrist, and false in all his working, and hath no power of God more than any other lewed man, but if[7] he be more holy in living; nor the pope hath no power to make bishops, priests nor none other orders. And he that the people call pope of Rome is no pope, but a false extortioner and a deceiver of the people. Also that he only that is most holy and most perfect in living in earth is very pope. And these sing-masses that be cleped[8] priests are no priests, but they be lecherous

---

1. Hawisia Moone's confession is among records of heresy trials kept for Bishop William Alnwick from 1428 to 1431. Most of the accused are, like Hawisia, from a cluster of villages on the border of Norfolk and Suffolk. We have modernized spellings but altered vocabulary as little as possible, to retain the syntax and rhythms of the original Middle English.

2. These names suggest that Hawisia Moone was part of a Wycliffite cell based on a network of family and local connections, but linked across England by itinerant

preachers such as the famous William White, who preached in Kent as well as Norfolk and Suffolk. Among those listed by Hawisia, White, Pye, and Waddon were all burned for heresy.

3. Absolve.

4. Any.

5. True.

6. I.e., father of.

7. Any other layman, unless.

8. Are called.

and covetous men, and false deceivers of the people; and with their subtle teaching and preaching, singing and reading, piteously they pile[9] the people of their good, and therewith they sustain their pride, their lechery, their sloth and all other vices; and always they make new laws and new ordinances to curse and kill cruelly all other persons that hold against their vicious living.[1] Also that only consent of love betwixt man and woman, without contract of words and without solemnization in church and without symbred asking[2] is sufficient for the sacrament of matrimony. Also it is but a trifle to anoint a sick man with material oil consecrated by a bishop,[3] for it sufficeth every man at his last end only to have mind of God. Also that every man may lawfully withdraw and withhold tithes and offerings from priests and curates and give them to the poor people; and that is more pleasing to God. Also that the temporal lords and temporal men may lawfully take all possessions and temporal goods from men of holy church, and from all bishops and prelates, both horse and harness, and give their goods to poor people; and thereto the temporal men be bound in pain of deadly sin.[4] Also that it is no sin any person to do the contrary of the precepts of holy church. Also that every man and every woman being in good life out of sin is as good a priest and hath as much power of God in all things as any priest ordered,[5] be he pope or bishop. Also that censures of holy church, sentences and cursings nor of suspending given by prelates or ordinaries[6] be not to be dreaded nor to be feared, for God blesseth the cursings of bishops and ordinaries. Also that it is not lawful to swear in any case[7] nor it is not lawful to pletyn[8] for any thing. Also that it is not lawful to slay a man for any cause, nor by process of law to damn any traitor or any man for any treason or felony to death, nor to put any man to death for any cause, but every man should remit all vengeance only to the sentence of God. Also that no man is bound to fast in Lent, Ember days,[9] Fridays nor vigils of saints, but all such days and times it is lawful to all Christ's people to eat flesh and all manner meats indifferently at their own lust[1] as often as they have appetite as well as any other days which be not commanded to be fasted. Also that no pilgrimage oweth to be done nor be made, for all pilgrimage-going serveth of nothing but only to give priests goods that be too rich, and to make gay tapsters and proud hostelers. Also that no worship nor reverence ought be done to any images of the crucifix, of our Lady nor of none other saints, for all such images be but idols, and made by working of man's hand; but worship and reverence should be done to the image of God, which only is man. Also that all prayer ought be made only to God and to none other saints, for it is doubt if there be any such saints in heaven as these sing-masses approve[2] and command to be worshipped and prayed to here in earth.

Because of which and many other errors and heresies I am called tofore you, worshipful father, which have cure of my soul, and by you fully informed that the said[3] my affirming, believing, and holding be open errors and heresies, and contrary to the determination[4] of the church of Rome. Wherefore I willingly follow and sue the doctrine of holy church and depart from all manner of error and heresy, and turn with

9. Rob.
1. Moone's words, initially in legal form and rather terse, now begin to echo the tone (and frequent alliteration) of some Wycliffite sermons.
2. Reading of banns.
3. I.e., to administer last rites.
4. Since worldly possessions corrupt the true church, Moone implies, secular lords are religiously obligated to undo that corruption by disendowing the church.
5. Ordained.

6. The prelates' deputies.
7. I.e., legal case.
8. Sue in court of law.
9. Periods of fasting in each of the four seasons of the church year.
1. Pleasure.
2. Attest.
3. Aforesaid.
4. Doctrine.

good will and heart to the onehead[5] of the church, considering that holy church spareth not her bosom to him that will turn again, nor god wishe not the death of a sinner but rather that he be turned and live, with a pure heart I confess, detest and despise my said errors and heresies, and these said opinions I confess hereticous and erroneous, and to the faith of the church of Rome and all universal holy church repugnant. And, for as much as by the said things that I so held, believed and affirmed, I showed myself corrupt and unfaithful, that from henceforth I show me uncorrupt and faithful, the faith and doctrine of holy church truly to keep I promise, * * * and swear by these holy gospels by me bodily touched, that from henceforth I shall never hold error nor heresy, * * * nor no such things I shall obstinately defend. * * * I shall never after this time be no recettour, fautour,[6] counselor or defender of heretics or of any person suspect of heresy, nor shall I never trowe to them,[7] nor wittingly I shall fellowship with them nor be homely with them, nor give them counsel, succor, favor nor comfort. If I know any heretics, or of heresy any persons suspect, or of them fau-tours, comforters, counselors or defenders or of any person making privy conventicles or assemblies, or holding any diverse or singular opinions from the common doctrine of the church, I shall let you, worshipful father, or your vicar general in your absence, or the diocesans of such persons have soon and ready knowing, so help me God at holy doom and these holy gospels! In witness of which thing I subscribe here with my own hand a cross ✝ and to this part indented to remain in your register I set my signet; and that other part indented I receive under your seal to abide with me unto my life's end.[8] Given at Norwich in the chapel of your palace the iiii day of the month of August, the year of our Lord a thousand four hundred and thirty.

Margery Kempe
c. 1373–after 1439

Margery Kempe's religious life—its temptations, visions, ecstasies, and pilgrimages—was unusual in intensity, but not in kind, for her time. She was very much in the mainstream of later medieval affective piety. What gained Margery both admiration and contempt, to the extent of endangering her life, was her drive to express these experiences publicly and have them acknowledged within an official hierarchy that had very little place for her. *The Book of Margery Kempe* is only one aspect of a lifetime of religious performance—from "holy conversa-tion" and the vexed dictation of her book, through the kinds of bodily gestures, weeping, and roaring that Margery knew to be almost theatrical in their impact.

The daughter of a mayor in the prosperous market town of Lynn, Margery began her adult life quite traditionally, married to the burger John Kempe. The mental and religious crisis follow-ing the birth of her first child inspired her to pursue a holier form of life. To create this mixed life of secular marriage and sacred quest, Margery Kempe had to struggle and negotiate with a hierar-chy of male authority. By canon law, her husband could demand the rights of the marriage bed, and did so for many years. She approached her local confessors for permission to undertake pil-grimages. Only a bishop could allow the weekly Eucharist for which Margery yearned, or officially approve her wearing white clothes. Hostile officials and clerics at all levels repeatedly attempted

---

5. Unity.
6. Harborer, supporter.
7. Believe in them.
8. An indented document had two copies of the same

text on a single sheet of parchment, which was then authenticated by a seal and cut unevenly (indented) in two, to be retained by the two parties to the document.

to misrepresent or silence her. She depended on male readers for her knowledge of other mystics, and on a sequence of recalcitrant male amanuenses for the very writing of her book.

Kempe's activities enraged political and ecclesiastical authorities, alienated her fellow pilgrims, and angered people at home. Yet those same activities gained her many admirers, increasingly among common laypeople. Her weeping and noisy mourning for the sufferings of Christ intruded upon daily life and often interrupted religious ceremonies. Just as daringly in the anxious and repressive religious climate of her day, Kempe spoke about her experiences without clerical mediation, and defended herself effectively before the highest clerics in England, including the Archbishop of York. She did not even hesitate to criticize them. She was repeatedly accused and taken into custody as a Lollard heretic, although she was doctrinally quite conservative (almost radically orthodox), as she ably and repeatedly proved under hostile examination.

Along with this pattern of negotiation and striving with a largely male ecclesiastical establishment, Kempe engaged more quietly with a network of female religious. She knew she had predecessors among married women who experienced visions and moved into a holy life while still living in the secular world. She specifically mentions "Saint Bride"—Bridget of Sweden (c. 1303–1373), who like Margery had many children and took up the holy life (once widowed), traveled to Rome and Jerusalem, and engaged in prophecy. Margery may also have known about the Blessed Angela of Foligno (1248–1309), whose temptations, weeping, and conversations with Christ are similar to Margery's own. She records a visit and long conversation with the mystic and anchoress Julian of Norwich. During her arrest by agents of the Duke of Bedford, local women sympathize with Margery, bring her wine, and listen to her religious discourse. Indeed, it seems that the Duke had Margery arrested because he suspected her of having encouraged a woman cousin to leave her own husband and pursue a religious life.

It is possible, though, to exaggerate Kempe's struggle with male power, secular and ecclesiastical. She was warmly supported by a number of holy men including the bishop of Lincoln. She met the Archbishop of Canterbury and gained at least his qualified approval. For all the conflicts within her marriage, Margery often expressed a wry and affectionate sense of John Kempe's indulgence, and sympathy for his weakness. Indeed, when John became ill and senile in later years, Margery suspended her life of prayer and returned to their home to care for him. Much of the domestic imagery of the *Book* derives from this fractious but loving relationship with her husband.

Perhaps the most appealing aspects of Kempe's religious imagery derive in fact from urban and domestic life. Money is a constant hindrance to her ambitions, and figures in her conversations with Christ. Her understanding of mystical language is often highly literal. If Jesus becomes her mystic lover, he does so very much as a husband, inviting her embraces; and when Kempe has a vision of Christ's birth she bustles about like a midwife. Her concentration on the Eucharist is continuous with her experience of meals (and fasting) within the family and in society. Indeed, a long negotiation with her husband, crucial to Margery's pursuit of chastity, centers upon the heat and thirst of travel, a cake and a bottle of beer. The humble meal that caps their agreement has clear eucharistic implications. Whatever the spectacle of her religious expression, and the struggle to maintain and record it, Margery Kempe's religion and sense of her own limits are grounded in the very life she was eager to abjure.

from The Book of Margery Kempe[1]
The Preface

A short treatise of a creature set in great pomp and pride of the world, who later was drawn to our Lord by great poverty, sickness, shame, and great reproofs in many diverse countries and places, of which tribulations some shall be shown hereafter, not

---

1. Translated by B. A. Windeatt.   2. Alan of Lynne, a Carmelite.

in the order in which they befell, but as the creature could remember them when they were written.

For it was twenty years and more from the time when this creature had forsaken the world and busily cleaved to our Lord before this book was written, notwithstanding that this creature had much advice to have her tribulations and her feelings written down, and a White Friar[2] freely offered to write for her if she wished. And she was warned in her spirit that she should not write so soon. And many years later she was bidden in her spirit to write.

And then it was written first by a man who could neither write English nor German well, so that it could not be read except by special grace alone, for there was so much obloquy and slander of this creature that few men would believe her.

And so at last a priest was greatly moved to write this treatise, and he could not read it for four years together. And afterwards, at the request of this creature, and compelled by his own conscience, he tried again to read it, and it was much easier than it was before. And so he began to write in the year of our Lord 1436, on the next day after Mary Magdalene,[3] after the information of this creature.

[EARLY LIFE AND TEMPTATIONS, REVELATION, DESIRE FOR FOREIGN PILGRIMAGE]

CHAPTER 1

When this creature was twenty years of age, or somewhat more, she was married to a worshipful burgess and was with child within a short time, as nature would have it. And after she had conceived, she was troubled with severe attacks of sickness until the child was born. And then, what with the labor-pains she had in childbirth and the sickness that had gone before, she despaired of her life, believing she might not live. Then she sent for her confessor, for she had a thing on her conscience which she had never revealed before that time in all her life. For she was continually hindered by her enemy—the devil—always saying to her while she was in good health that she didn't need to confess but to do penance by herself alone, and all should be forgiven, for God is merciful enough. And therefore this creature often did great penance in fasting on bread and water, and performed other acts of charity with devout prayers, but she would not reveal that one thing in confession.

And when she was at any time sick or troubled, the devil said in her mind that she should be damned, for she was not shriven of that fault.[4] Therefore, after her child was born, and not believing she would live, she sent for her confessor, as said before, fully wishing to be shriven of her whole lifetime, as near as she could. And when she came to the point of saying that thing which she had so long concealed, her confessor was a little too hasty and began sharply to reprove her before she had fully said what she meant, and so she would say no more in spite of anything he might do. And soon after, because of the dread she had of damnation on the one hand, and his sharp reproving of her on the other, this creature went out of her mind and was amazingly disturbed and tormented with spirits for half a year, eight weeks and odd days.

And in this time she saw, as she thought, devils opening their mouths all alight with burning flames of fire, as if they would have swallowed her in, sometimes pawing at her, sometimes threatening her, sometimes pulling her and hauling her about both

3. July 23.
4. Margery had not completed the stages of penance: contrition, confession, restitution (or other act of repentance), absolution. She never says openly what her unconfessed sin was.

night and day during the said time. And also the devils called out to her with great threats, and bade her that she should forsake her Christian faith and belief, and deny her God, his mother, and all the saints in heaven, her good works and all good virtues, her father, her mother, and all her friends. And so she did. She slandered her husband, her friends, and her own self. She spoke many sharp and reproving words; she recognized no virtue nor goodness; she desired all wickedness; just as the spirits tempted her to say and do, so she said and did. She would have killed herself many a time as they stirred her to, and would have been damned with them in hell,[5] and in witness of this she bit her own hand so violently that the mark could be seen for the rest of her life. And also she pitilessly tore the skin on her body near her heart with her nails, for she had no other implement, and she would have done something worse, except that she was tied up and forcibly restrained both day and night so that she could not do as she wanted.

And when she had long been troubled by these and many other temptations, so that people thought she should never have escaped from them alive, then one time as she lay by herself and her keepers were not with her, our merciful Lord Christ Jesus—ever to be trusted, worshiped be his name, never forsaking his servant in time of need—appeared to his creature who had forsaken him, in the likeness of a man, the most seemly, most beauteous, and most amiable that ever might be seen with man's eye, clad in a mantle of purple silk, sitting upon her bedside, looking upon her with so blessed a countenance that she was strengthened in all her spirits, and he said to her these words: "Daughter, why have you forsaken me, and I never forsook you?"

And as soon as he had said these words, she saw truly how the air opened as bright as any lightning, and he ascended up into the air, not hastily and quickly, but beautifully and gradually, so that she could clearly behold him in the air until it closed up again.

And presently the creature grew as calm in her wits and her reason as she ever was before, and asked her husband, as soon as he came to her, if she could have the keys of the buttery to get her food and drink as she had done before. Her maids and her keepers advised him that he should not deliver up any keys to her, for they said she would only give away such goods as there were, because she did not know what she was saying, as they believed.

Nevertheless, her husband, who always had tenderness and compassion for her, ordered that they should give her the keys. And she took food and drink as her bodily strength would allow her, and she once again recognized her friends and her household, and everybody else who came to her in order to see how our Lord Jesus Christ had worked his grace in her—blessed may he be, who is ever near in tribulation. When people think he is far away from them he is very near through his grace. Afterwards this creature performed all her responsibilities wisely and soberly enough, except that she did not truly know our Lord's power to draw us to him.

Chapter 2

And when this creature had thus through grace come again to her right mind, she thought she was bound to God and that she would be his servant. Nevertheless, she would not leave her pride or her showy manner of dressing, which she had previously been used to, either for her husband, or for any other person's advice. And yet she

---

5. Suicide was considered a mortal sin.

knew full well that people made many adverse comments about her, because she wore gold pipes on her head,[6] and her hoods with the tippets were fashionably slashed. Her cloaks were also modishly slashed and underlaid with various colors between the slashes, so that she would be all the more stared at, and all the more esteemed.

And when her husband used to try and speak to her, to urge her to leave her proud ways, she answered sharply and shortly, and said that she was come of worthy kindred—he should never have married her—for her father was sometime mayor of the town of N., and afterwards he was alderman of the High Guild of the Trinity in N.[7] And therefore she would keep up the honor of her kindred, whatever anyone said.

She was enormously envious of her neighbors if they were dressed as well as she was. Her whole desire was to be respected by people. She would not learn her lesson from a single chastening experience, nor be content with the worldly goods that God had sent her—as her husband was—but always craved more and more.

And then, out of pure covetousness, and in order to maintain her pride, she took up brewing, and was one of the greatest brewers in the town of N. for three or four years until she lost a great deal of money, for she had never had any experience in that business. For however good her servants were and however knowledgeable in brewing, things would never go successfully for them. For when the ale had as fine a head of froth on it as anyone might see, suddenly the froth would go flat, and all the ale was lost in one brewing after another, so that her servants were ashamed and would not stay with her. Then this creature thought how God had punished her before—and she could not take heed—and now again by the loss of her goods; and then she left off and did no more brewing.

And then she asked her husband's pardon because she would not follow his advice previously, and she said that her pride and sin were the cause of all her punishing, and that she would willingly put right all her wrongdoing. But yet she did not entirely give up the world, for she now thought up a new enterprise for herself. She had a horse-mill. She got herself two good horses and a man to grind people's corn, and thus she was confident of making her living. This business venture did not last long, for shortly afterwards, on the eve of Corpus Christi,[8] the following marvel happened. The man was in good health, and his two horses were strong and in good condition and had drawn well in the mill previously, but now, when he took one of those horses and put him in the mill as he had done before, this horse would not pull in the mill in spite of anything the man might do. The man was sorry, and tried everything he could think of to make his horse pull. Sometimes he led him by the head, sometimes he beat him, and sometimes he made a fuss of him, but nothing did any good, for the horse would rather go backwards than forwards. Then this man set a pair of sharp spurs on his heels and rode on the horse's back to make him pull, but it was no better. When this man saw it was no use, he put the horse back in his stable, and gave him food, and the horse ate well and freshly. And afterwards he took the other horse and put him in the mill. And just as his fellow had done so did he, for he would not pull for anything the man might do. And then this man gave up his job and would not stay any longer with the said creature.[9]

6. Margery wore the fashionable *crespine*, a horned headdress of wire, often in gold or silver.

7. Margery here uses an initial for her town; later she openly calls it Lynn.

8. A feast day toward midsummer commemorating the Eucharist; marked by the performance of mystery plays in major mercantile towns such as York.

9. Popular superstition can be glimpsed behind the failure in brewing and milling, and the servants' refusal to stay with Margery thereafter.

Then it was noised about in the town of N. that neither man nor beast would serve the said creature, and some said she was accursed; some said God openly took vengeance on her; some said one thing and some said another. And some wise men, whose minds were more grounded in the love of our Lord, said it was the high mercy of our Lord Jesus Christ that called her from the pride and vanity of this wretched world.

And then this creature, seeing all these adversities coming on every side, thought they were the scourges of our Lord that would chastise her for her sin. Then she asked God for mercy, and forsook her pride, her covetousness, and the desire that she had for worldly dignity, and did great bodily penance, and began to enter the way of everlasting life as shall be told hereafter.

CHAPTER 3

One night, as this creature lay in bed with her husband, she heard a melodious sound so sweet and delectable that she thought she had been in paradise.[1] And immediately she jumped out of bed and said, "Alas that ever I sinned! It is full merry in heaven." This melody was so sweet that it surpassed all the melody that might be heard in this world, without any comparison, and it caused this creature when she afterwards heard any mirth or melody to shed very plentiful and abundant tears of high devotion, with great sobbings and sighings for the bliss of heaven, not fearing the shames and contempt of this wretched world. And ever after her being drawn towards God in this way, she kept in mind the joy and the melody that there was in heaven, so much so that she could not very well restrain herself from speaking of it. For when she was in company with any people she would often say, "It is full merry in heaven!"

And those who knew of her behavior previously and now heard her talk so much of the bliss of heaven said to her, "Why do you talk so of the joy that is in heaven? You don't know it, and you haven't been there any more than we have." And they were angry with her because she would not hear or talk of worldly things as they did, and as she did previously.

And after this time she never had any desire to have sexual intercourse with her husband, for paying the debt of matrimony was so abominable to her that she would rather, she thought, have eaten and drunk the ooze and muck in the gutter than consent to intercourse, except out of obedience.

And so she said to her husband, "I may not deny you my body, but all the love and affection of my heart is withdrawn from all earthly creatures and set on God alone." But he would have his will with her, and she obeyed with much weeping and sorrowing because she could not live in chastity. And often this creature advised her husband to live chaste and said that they had often (she well knew) displeased God by their inordinate love, and the great delight that each of them had in using the other's body, and now it would be a good thing if by mutual consent they punished and chastised themselves by abstaining from the lust of their bodies. Her husband said it was good to do so, but he might not yet—he would do so when God willed. And so he used her as he had done before, he would not desist. And all the time she prayed to God that she might live chaste, and three or four years afterwards, when it pleased our Lord, her husband made a vow of chastity, as shall be written afterwards, by Jesus's leave.

1. Compare Richard Rolle's discussion of heavenly music, page 484–85.

And also, after this creature heard this heavenly melody, she did great bodily penance. She was sometimes shriven two or three times on the same day, especially of that sin which she had so long concealed and covered up, as is written at the beginning of this book. She gave herself up to much fasting and keeping of vigils; she rose at two or three of the clock and went to church, and was there at her prayers until midday and also the whole afternoon. And then she was slandered and reproved by many people because she led so strict a life. She got herself a hair-cloth from a kiln— the sort that malt is dried on—and put it inside her gown as discreetly and secretly as she could, so that her husband should not notice it. And nor did he, although she lay beside him every night in bed and wore the hair-shirt every day, and bore him children during that time.

Then she had three years of great difficulty with temptations, which she bore as meekly as she could, thanking our Lord for all his gifts, and she was as merry when she was reproved, scorned or ridiculed for our Lord's love, and much more merry than she was before amongst the dignities of this world. For she knew very well that she had sinned greatly against God and that she deserved far more shame and sorrow than any man could cause her, and contempt in this world was the right way heavenwards, for Christ himself chose that way. All his apostles, martyrs, confessors and virgins, and all those who ever came to heaven, passed by the way of tribulation, and she desired nothing as much as heaven. Then she was glad in her conscience when she believed that she was entering upon the way which would lead her to the place that she most desired.

And this creature had contrition and great compunction, with plentiful tears and much loud and violent sobbing, for her sins and for her unkindness towards her maker. She reflected on her unkindness since her childhood, as our Lord would put it into her mind, very many times. And then when she contemplated her own wickedness, she could only sorrow and weep and ever pray for mercy and forgiveness. Her weeping was so plentiful and so continual that many people thought that she could weep and leave off when she wanted, and therefore many people said she was a false hypocrite, and wept when in company for advantage and profit. And then very many people who loved her before while she was in the world abandoned her and would not know her, and all the while she thanked God for everything, desiring nothing but mercy and forgiveness of sin.

CHAPTER 5

Then on a Friday before Christmas Day, as this creature was kneeling in a chapel of Saint John, within a church of Saint Margaret in N., weeping a very great deal and asking mercy and forgiveness for her sins and her trespasses, our merciful Lord Christ Jesus—blessed may he be—ravished her spirit and said to her, "Daughter, why are you weeping so sorely? I have come to you, Jesus Christ, who died on the cross suffering bitter pains and passion for you. I, the same God, forgive you your sins to the uttermost point. And you shall never come into hell nor into purgatory, but when you pass out of this world, within the twinkling of an eye, you shall have the bliss of heaven, for I am the same God who has brought your sins to your mind and caused you to be shriven of them. And I grant you contrition until your life's end.

"Therefore, I command you, boldly call me Jesus, your love, for I am your love and shall be your love without end. And, daughter, you have a hair-shirt on your back. I want you to leave off wearing it, and I shall give you a hair-shirt in your heart which shall please me much more than all the hair-shirts in the world. But also, my beloved daughter, you must give up that which you love best in this world, and that is the eating of meat. And instead of meat you shall eat my flesh and my blood, that is the true body of Christ in the sacrament of the altar. This is my will, daughter, that you receive my body every Sunday, and I shall cause so much grace to flow into you that everyone shall marvel at it.[2]

"You shall be eaten and gnawed by the people of the world just as any rat gnaws the stockfish.[3] Don't be afraid, daughter, for you shall be victorious over all your enemies. I shall give you grace enough to answer every cleric in the love of God. I swear to you by my majesty that I shall never forsake you whether in happiness or in sorrow. I shall help you and protect you, so that no devil in hell shall ever part you from me, nor angel in heaven, nor man on earth—for devils in hell may not, nor angels in heaven will not, nor man on earth shall not.

"And daughter, I want you to give up your praying of many beads, and think such thoughts as I shall put into your mind. I shall give you leave to pray until six o'clock to say what you wish. Then you shall lie still and speak to me in thought, and I shall give you high meditation and true contemplation.[4] And I command you to go to the anchorite at the Preaching Friars and tell him my confidences and counsels which I reveal to you, and do as he advises, for my spirit shall speak in him to you."

Then this creature went off to see the anchorite as she was commanded, and revealed to him the revelations that had been shown to her. Then the anchorite, with great reverence and weeping, thanking God, said, "Daughter, you are sucking even at Christ's breast, and you have received a pledge of paradise.[5] I charge you to receive such thoughts—when God will give them—as meekly and devoutly as you can, and then come and tell me what they are, and I shall, by the leave of our Lord Jesus Christ, tell you whether they are from the Holy Ghost or else from your enemy the devil."

CHAPTER 11

It happened one Friday, Midsummer Eve,[6] in very hot weather—as this creature was coming from York carrying a bottle of beer in her hand, and her husband a cake tucked inside his clothes against his chest—that her husband asked his wife this question: "Margery, if there came a man with a sword who would strike off my head unless I made love with you as I used to do before, tell me on your conscience—for you say you will not lie—whether you would allow my head to be cut off, or else allow me to make love with you again, as I did at one time?"

"Alas, sir," she said, "why are you raising this matter, when we have been chaste for these past eight weeks?"

"Because I want to know the truth of your heart."

And then she said with great sorrow, "Truly, I would rather see you being killed, than that we should turn back to our uncleanness."

2. Weekly communion was uncommon, and required special ecclesiastical permission. Margery may have known that an admired predecessor, St. Bridget of Sweden, took weekly communion.
3. Dried cod.
4. Christ thus promises Margery the mystic way, without the ecclesiastical mediation of set prayers.

5. The image of Christ as mother particularly recalls Julian of Norwich, whom Margery later visits.
6. Probably 23 June 1413. The feast of Corpus Christi fell on the previous day, and it is likely that Margery and her husband had seen the great cycle of mystery plays traditionally performed in York on that day.

And he replied, "You are no good wife."

And then she asked her husband what was the reason that he had not made love to her for the last eight weeks, since she lay with him every night in his bed. And he said that he was made so afraid when he would have touched her, that he dared do no more.

"Now, good sir, mend your ways and ask God's mercy, for I told you nearly three years ago that your desire would suddenly be slain—and this is now the third year, and I hope yet that I shall have my wish. Good sir, I pray you to grant what I shall ask, and I shall pray for you to be saved through the mercy of our Lord Jesus Christ, and you shall have more reward in heaven than if you wore a hair-shirt or wore a coat of mail as a penance. I pray you, allow me to make a vow of chastity at whichever bishop's hand that God wills."

"No," he said, "I won't allow you to do that, because now I can make love to you without mortal sin, and then I wouldn't be able to."

Then she replied, "If it be the will of the Holy Ghost to fulfill what I have said, I pray God that you may consent to this; and if it be not the will of the Holy Ghost, I pray God that you never consent."

Then they went on towards Bridlington[7] and the weather was extremely hot, this creature all the time having great sorrow and great fear for her chastity. And as they came by a cross her husband sat down under the cross, calling his wife to him and saying these words to her: "Margery, grant me my desire, and I shall grant you your desire. My first desire is that we shall still lie together in one bed as we have done before; the second, that you shall pay my debts before you go to Jerusalem; and the third, that you shall eat and drink with me on Fridays as you used to do."

"No, sir," she said, "I will never agree to break my Friday fast as long as I live."

"Well," he said, "then I'm going to have sex with you again."

She begged him to allow her to say her prayers, and he kindly allowed it. Then she knelt down beside a cross in the field and prayed in this way, with a great abundance of tears: "Lord God, you know all things. You know what sorrow I have had to be chaste for you in my body all these three years, and now I might have my will and I dare not, for love of you. For if I were to break that custom of fasting from meat and drink on Fridays which you commanded me, I should now have my desire. But, blessed Lord, you know I will not go against your will, and great is my sorrow now unless I find comfort in you. Now, blessed Jesus, make your will known to my unworthy self, so that I may afterwards follow and fulfill it with all my might."

And then our Lord Jesus Christ with great sweetness spoke to this creature, commanding her to go again to her husband and pray him to grant her what she desired: "And he shall have what he desires. For, my beloved daughter, this was the reason why I ordered you to fast, so that you should the sooner obtain your desire, and now it is granted to you. I no longer wish you to fast, and therefore I command you in the name of Jesus to eat and drink as your husband does."

Then this creature thanked our Lord Jesus Christ for his grace and his goodness, and afterwards got up and went to her husband, saying to him, "Sir, if you please, you shall grant me my desire, and you shall have your desire. Grant me that you will not come into

7. On the coast, east of York.

my bed, and I grant you that I will pay your debts before I go to Jerusalem. And make my body free to God, so that you never make any claim on me requesting any conjugal debt after this day as long as you live—and I shall eat and drink on Fridays at your bidding."[8]

Then her husband replied to her, "May your body be as freely available to God as it has been to me."

This creature thanked God greatly, rejoicing that she had her desire, praying her husband that they should say three paternosters in worship of the Trinity for the great grace that had been granted them. And so they did, kneeling under a cross, and afterwards they ate and drank together in great gladness of spirit. This was on a Friday, on Midsummer's Eve.

Then they went on to Bridlington and also to many other places, and spoke with God's servants, both anchorites and recluses, and many other of our Lord's lovers, with many worthy clerics, doctors and bachelors of divinity as well, in many different places. And to various people amongst them this creature revealed her feelings and her contemplations, as she was commanded to do, to find out if there were any deception in her feelings.

[MEETING WITH BISHOP OF LINCOLN AND ARCHBISHOP OF CANTERBURY]

CHAPTER 15

This creature, when our Lord had forgiven her her sin (as has been written before), had a desire to see those places where he was born, and where he suffered his Passion and where he died, together with other holy places where he was during his life, and also after his resurrection.

While she was feeling these desires, our Lord commanded her in her mind— two years before she went[9]—that she should go to Rome, to Jerusalem, and to Santiago de Compostela, and she would gladly have gone, but she had no money to go with.

And then she said to our Lord, "Where shall I get the money to go to these holy places with?"

Our Lord replied to her, "I shall send you enough friends in different parts of England to help you. And, daughter, I shall go with you in every country and provide for you. I shall lead you there and bring you back again in safety, and no Englishman shall die in the ship that you are in. I shall keep you from all wicked men's power. And, daughter, I say to you that I want you to wear white clothes and no other color, for you shall dress according to my will."[1]

"Ah, dear Lord, if I go around dressed differently from how other chaste women dress, I fear people will slander me. They will say I am a hypocrite and ridicule me."

"Yes, daughter, the more ridicule that you have for love of me, the more you please me."

Then this creature dared not do otherwise than as she was commanded in her soul. And so she set off on her travels with her husband, for he was always a good and easygoing man with her. Although he sometimes—out of groundless fear—left her on her own for a while, yet he always came back to her again, and felt sorry for her,

---

8. Margery may have received an inheritance from her father by now, giving her the financial leverage to strike a deal, in effect, for her chastity.

9. Probably 1411.

1. White dress implied special holiness or virginity.

and spoke up for her as much as he dared for fear of other people. But all others that went along with her forsook her, and they most falsely accused her—through temptation of the devil—of things that she was never guilty of.

And so did one man in whom she greatly trusted, and who offered to travel with her, at which she was very pleased, believing he would give her support and help her when she needed it, for he had been staying a long time with an anchorite, a doctor of divinity and a holy man, and that anchorite was this woman's confessor.

And so his servant—at his own inward stirring—took his leave to travel with this creature; and her own maidservant went with her too, for as long as things went well with them and nobody said anything against them.

But as soon as people—through the enticing of our spiritual enemy, and by permission of our Lord—spoke against this creature because she wept so grievously, and said she was a false hypocrite and deceived people, and threatened her with burning, then this man, who was held to be so holy, and in whom she trusted so much, rebuked her with the utmost force and scorned her most foully, and would not go any further with her. Her maidservant, seeing discomfort on every side, grew obstreperous with her mistress. She would not do as she was told, or follow her mistress's advice. She let her mistress go alone into many fine towns and would not go with her.

And always, her husband was ready when everybody else let her down, and he went with her where our Lord would send her, always believing that all was for the best, and would end well when God willed.

And at this time, he took her to speak with the Bishop of Lincoln, who was called Philip,[2] and they stayed for three weeks before they could speak to him, for he was not at home at his palace. When the Bishop came home, and heard tell of how such a woman had waited so long to speak to him, he then sent for her in great haste to find out what she wanted. And then she came into his presence and greeted him, and he warmly welcomed her and said he had long wanted to speak with her, and he was very glad she had come. And so she asked him if she might speak with him in private and confide in him the secrets of her soul, and he appointed a convenient time for this.

When the time came, she told him all about her meditations and high contemplations, and other secret things, both of the living and the dead, as our Lord revealed to her soul.[3] He was very glad to hear them, and graciously allowed her to say what she pleased, and greatly commended her feelings and her contemplations, saying they were high matters and most devout matters, and inspired by the Holy Ghost, advising her seriously that her feelings should be written down.

And she said that it was not God's will that they should be written so soon, nor were they written for twenty years afterwards and more.

And then she said furthermore, "My Lord, if it please you, I am commanded in my soul that you shall give me the mantle and the ring, and clothe me all in white clothes. And if you clothe me on earth, our Lord Jesus Christ shall clothe you in heaven, as I understand through revelation."[4]

Then the Bishop said to her, "I will fulfill your desire if your husband will consent to it."

---

2. Philip Repyngdon, Bishop of Lincoln 1405–1419. This journey occurred after their private agreement of chastity in June 1413.

3. Margery had some prophetic visions, though on a smaller scale than those of her predecessor St. Bridget of Sweden.

4. By clothing her, the bishop would acknowledge Margery and John's vow of chastity. In the Book if Revelation, the saints in heaven are clothed in white robes.

Then she said to the Bishop, "I pray you, let my husband come into your presence, and you shall hear what he will say."

And so her husband came before the Bishop, and the Bishop asked him, "John, is it your will that your wife shall take the mantle and the ring and that you live chaste, the two of you?"

"Yes, my lord," he said, "and in token that we both vow to live chaste I here offer my hands into yours," and he put his hands between the Bishop's hands.

And the Bishop did no more with us on that day, except that he treated us very warmly and said we were most welcome. * * * [5]

CHAPTER 16

Then this creature went on to London with her husband, to Lambeth,[6] where the Archbishop was in residence at that time. And as they came into the hall in the afternoon, there were many of the Archbishop's clerks about and other heedless men, both squires and yeomen, who swore many great oaths and spoke many thoughtless words, and this creature boldly rebuked them, and said they would be damned unless they left off their swearing and the other sins they practised.[7]

And with that there came forward a woman of that town dressed in a pilch[8] who reviled this creature, cursed her, and said very maliciously to her in this way: "I wish you were in Smithfield,[9] and I would bring a bundle of sticks to burn you with—it is a pity that you are alive."

This creature stood still and did not answer, and her husband endured it with great pain and was very sorry to hear his wife so rebuked.

Then the Archbishop sent for this creature to come to him in his garden.[1] When she came into his presence she made her obeisances to him as best she could, praying him, out of his gracious lordship, to grant her authority to choose her confessor and to receive communion every Sunday—if God would dispose her to this—under his letter and his seal throughout all his province. And he granted her with great kindness her whole desire without any silver or gold, nor would he let his clerks take anything for the writing or sealing of the letter.

When this creature found this grace in his sight, she was much comforted and strengthened in her soul, and so she told this worshipful lord about her manner of life, and such grace as God wrought in her mind and in her soul, in order to discover what he would say about it, and if he found any fault with either her contemplation or her weeping.

And she also told him the cause of her weeping, and the manner in which our Lord conversed with her soul. And he did not find fault at all, but approved her manner of life, and was very glad that our merciful Lord Christ Jesus showed such grace in our times—blessed may he be.

Then this creature spoke to him boldly about the correction of his household, saying with reverence, "My lord, our Lord of all, Almighty God, has not given you

---

5. The Bishop instructs Margery to approach the Archbishop of Canterbury, England's highest prelate, and obtain his permission to receive the mantle and ring. She agrees to go but says she will not ask the archbishop for that particular gift.
6. Lambeth Palace was (and is) the Archbishop's home nearest London.
7. Margery frequently reproaches people for swearing.

8. A garment of animal skin with the hair still on it.
9. This is not an idle threat. Lollard heretics were put to death in Margery's lifetime, beginning in 1401 when William Sawtry (formerly a priest at Lynn) was burned at Smithfield outside London.
1. Thomas Arundel (Archbishop of Canterbury 1396–1414) was a vigorous opponent of Lollards.

your benefice and great worldly wealth in order to maintain those who are traitors to him, and those who slay him every day by the swearing of great oaths. You shall answer for them, unless you correct them or else put them out of your service."

In the most meek and kindly way he allowed her to say what was on her mind and gave her a handsome answer, she supposing that things would then be better. And so their conversation continued until stars appeared in the sky. Then she took her leave, and her husband too.

Afterwards they went back to London, and many worthy men wanted to hear her converse, for her conversation was so much to do with the love of God that those who heard it were often moved to weep very sadly.

And so she had a very warm welcome there—and her husband because of her— for as long as they wished to stay in the city. Afterwards they returned to Lynn, and then this creature went to the anchorite at the Preaching Friars in Lynn and told him how she had been received, and how she had got on while she was travelling round the country. And he was very pleased at her homecoming and held it to be a great miracle, her coming and going to and fro.

And he said to her: "I have heard much evil talk of you since you went away, and I have been strongly advised to leave you and not to associate with you any more, and great friendships are promised me on condition that I give you up. And I answered for you in this way: 'If you were still the same as you were when we parted, I certainly dared say you were a good woman, a lover of God, and highly inspired with the Holy Ghost. I will not forsake her for any lady in this realm, if speaking with the lady means leaving her, for I would rather leave the lady and speak with Margery, if I might not do both, than do the contrary.'" (Read first the twenty-first chapter and then this chapter after that.)

[VISIT WITH JULIAN OF NORWICH]
CHAPTER 17

One day long before this time, while this creature was bearing children and was newly delivered of a child, our Lord Christ Jesus said to her that she should bear no more children, and therefore he commanded her to go to Norwich. * * *

CHAPTER 18

This creature was charged and commanded in her soul that she should go to a White Friar in the same city of Norwich, who was called William Southfield, a good man who lived a holy life, to reveal to him the grace that God had wrought in her, as she had done to the good Vicar before. She did as she was commanded and came to the friar one morning, and was with him in a chapel for a long time, and told him her meditations and what God had wrought in her soul, in order to know if she were deceived by any delusions or not.[2]

This good man, the White Friar, all the time that she told him of her feelings, held up his hands and said, "Jesus, mercy, and thanks be to Jesus."

"Sister," he said, "have no fear about your manner of life, for it is the Holy Ghost plentifully working his grace in your soul. Thank him highly of his goodness, for we are all bound to thank him for you, who now in our times inspires you with his grace,

---

2. Southfield was a Carmelite friar who received visions of the Virgin Mary. Many mystical texts warn against the possibility that visions may be of demonic origin; see selections from *The Cloud of Unknowing*, pages 485–87.

to the help and comfort of all of us who are supported by your prayers and by others such as you. And we are preserved from many misfortunes and troubles which we should deservedly suffer for our trespasses, were there not such good creatures among us. Blessed be Almighty God for his goodness.

"And therefore, sister, I advise you to dispose yourself to receive the gifts of God as lowly and meekly as you can, and put up no obstacle or objections against the goodness of the Holy Ghost, for he may give his gifts where he will, and the unworthy he makes worthy, the sinful he makes righteous. His mercy is always ready for us unless the fault be in ourselves, for he does not dwell in a body subject to sin. He flies from all false pretense and falsehood; he asks of us a low, a meek, and a contrite heart, with a good will.[3] Our Lord says himself, 'My spirit shall rest upon a meek man, a contrite man, and one who fears my words.'[4]

"Sister, I trust to our Lord that you have these conditions either in your will or in your affections or else in both, and I do not consider that our Lord allows to be endlessly deceived those who place their trust in him, and seek and desire nothing but him only, as I hope you do. And therefore believe fully that our Lord loves you and is working his grace in you. I pray God increase it and continue it to his everlasting worship, for his mercy."

The said creature was much comforted both in body and in soul by this good man's words, and greatly strengthened in her faith.

And then she was commanded by our Lord to go to an anchoress in the same city who was called Dame Julian.[5] And so she did, and told her about the grace, that God had put into her soul, of compunction, contrition, sweetness and devotion, compassion with holy meditation and high contemplation, and very many holy speeches and converse that our Lord spoke to her soul, and also many wonderful revelations, which she described to the anchoress to find out if there were any deception in them, for the anchoress was expert in such things and could give good advice.

The anchoress, hearing the marvelous goodness of our Lord, highly thanked God with all her heart for his visitation, advising this creature to be obedient to the will of our Lord and fulfill with all her might whatever he put into her soul, if it were not against the worship of God and the profit of her fellow Christians.[6] For if it were, then it were not the influence of a good spirit, but rather of an evil spirit. "The Holy Ghost never urges a thing against charity, and if he did, he would be contrary to his own self, for he is all charity. Also he moves a soul to all chasteness, for chaste livers are called the temple of the Holy Ghost,[7] and the Holy Ghost makes a soul stable and steadfast in the right faith and the right belief.

"And a double man in soul is always unstable and unsteadfast in all his ways.[8] He that is forever doubting is like the wave of the sea which is moved and borne about with the wind, and that man is not likely to receive the gifts of God.[9]

"Any creature that has these tokens may steadfastly believe that the Holy Ghost dwells in his soul. And much more, when God visits a creature with tears of contrition, devotion or compassion, he may and ought to believe that the Holy Ghost is in

3. Psalm 51.17.
4. Isaiah 66.2.
5. Julian of Norwich; see selections from her *Book of Showings*, pages 468–84.
6. This concern with the whole community of the faithful, a new note in Kempe's book, is highly characteristic of Julian's spirituality.

7. 1 Corinthians 6.19. The density of biblical reference in this passage suggests not only Dame Julian's learning but also Kempe's powerful memory for Scripture and theology. It is important that such biblical justification comes to Kempe through another holy woman.
8. James 1.8.
9. James 1.6–7.

his soul. Saint Paul says that the Holy Ghost asks for us with mourning and weeping unspeakable;[1] that is to say, he causes us to ask and pray with mourning and weeping so plentifully that the tears may not be numbered. No evil spirit may give these tokens, for Saint Jerome says that tears torment the devil more than do the pains of hell. God and the devil are always at odds, and they shall never dwell together in one place, and the devil has no power in a man's soul.

"Holy Writ says that the soul of a righteous man is the seat of God,[2] and so I trust, sister, that you are. I pray God grant you perseverance. Set all your trust in God and do not fear the talk of the world, for the more contempt, shame and reproof that you have in this world, the more is your merit in the sight of God.[3] Patience is necessary for you, for in that shall you keep your soul."[4]

Great was the holy conversation that the anchoress and this creature had through talking of the love of our Lord Jesus Christ for the many days that they were together.

This creature revealed her manner of life to many a worthy clerk, to honored doctors of divinity, both religious men and others of secular habit, and they said that God wrought great grace in her and bade her not to be afraid—there was no delusion in her manner of living. They counseled her to be persevering, for their greatest fear was that she would turn aside and not keep her perfection. She had so many enemies and so much slander, that it seemed to them that she might not bear it without great grace and a mighty faith. * * *

[PILGRIMAGE TO JERUSALEM]

CHAPTER 28[5]

* * * And so they went on into the Holy Land until they could see Jerusalem. And when this creature saw Jerusalem—she was riding on an ass—she thanked God with all her heart, praying him for his mercy that, just as he had brought her to see this earthly city of Jerusalem, he would grant her grace to see the blissful city of Jerusalem above, the city of heaven. Our Lord Jesus Christ, answering her thought, granted her her desire.

Then for the joy that she had and the sweetness that she felt in the conversation of our Lord, she was on the point of falling off her ass, for she could not bear the sweetness and grace that God wrought in her soul. Then two German pilgrims went up to her and kept her from falling—one of them was a priest, and he put spices in her mouth to comfort her, thinking she was ill. And so they helped her onwards to Jerusalem, and when she arrived there she said, "Sirs, I beg you, don't be annoyed though I weep bitterly in this holy place where our Lord Jesus Christ lived and died."

Then they went to the Church of the Holy Sepulchre in Jerusalem, and they were let in on the one day at evensong time, and remained until evensong time on the next day. Then the friars lifted up a cross and led the pilgrims about from one place to another where our Lord had suffered his pains and his Passion, every man and woman carrying a wax candle in one hand.[6] And the friars always, as they went

---

1. Romans 8.26.
2. 2 Corinthians 6.16, Revelation 21.3.
3. Luke 6.22–23.
4. Luke 21.19.
5. In autumn 1413, Margery sets out to the Holy Land. Her party of pilgrims repudiates Margery, and she is helped by the Papal legate at Constance, an English friar. She continues her travel toward Italy with an elderly

Englishman. She rejoins the English pilgrims at Bologna, but continues to suffer their hostility because of her austere diet and dramatic displays of religious emotion.
6. Although Jerusalem was under Islamic control, Franciscan friars had negotiated permission to keep a convent next to the Church of the Holy Sepulchre and to guide pilgrims around a number of holy sites.

about, told them what our Lord suffered in every place. And this creature wept and sobbed as plenteously as though she had seen our Lord with her bodily eyes suffering his Passion at that time. Before her in her soul she saw him in truth by contemplation, and that caused her to have compassion. And when they came up on to the Mount of Calvary, she fell down because she could not stand or kneel, but writhed and wrestled with her body, spreading her arms out wide, and cried with a loud voice as though her heart would have burst apart, for in the city of her soul she saw truly and freshly how our Lord was crucified. Before her face she heard and saw in her spiritual sight the mourning of our Lady, of Saint John and Mary Magdalene, and of many others that loved our Lord.

And she had such great compassion and such great pain to see our Lord's pain, that she could not keep herself from crying and roaring though she should have died for it. And this was the first crying that she ever cried in any contemplation. And this kind of crying lasted for many years after this time, despite anything that anyone might do, and she suffered much contempt and much reproof for it. The crying was so loud and so amazing that it astounded people, unless they had heard it before, or else knew the reason for the cryings. And she had them so often that they made her very weak in her bodily strength, and specially if she heard of our Lord's Passion.

And sometimes, when she saw the crucifix, or if she saw a man had a wound, or a beast, whichever it were, or if a man beat a child before her or hit a horse or other beast with a whip, if she saw or heard it, she thought she saw our Lord being beaten or wounded, just as she saw it in the man or in the beast, either in the fields or in the town, and alone by herself as well as among people.

When she first had her cryings at Jerusalem, she had them often, and in Rome also. And when she first came home to England her cryings came but seldom, perhaps once a month, then once a week, afterwards daily, and once she had fourteen in one day, and another day she had seven, just as God would visit her with them, sometimes in church, sometimes in the street, sometimes in her chamber, sometimes in the fields, when God would send them, for she never knew the time nor hour when they would come. And they never came without surpassingly great sweetness of devotion and high contemplation.

And as soon as she perceived that she was going to cry, she would hold it in as much as she could, so that people would not hear it and get annoyed. For some said it was a wicked spirit tormented her; some said it was an illness; some said she had drunk too much wine; some cursed her; some wished she was in the harbor; some wished she was on the sea in a bottomless boat; and so each man as he thought. Other, spiritually inclined men loved her and esteemed her all the more. Some great clerks said our Lady never cried so, nor any saint in heaven, but they knew very little what she felt, nor would they believe that she could not stop herself from crying if she wanted.

And therefore, when she knew that she was going to cry, she held it in as long as she could, and did all that she could to withstand it or else to suppress it, until she turned the color of lead, and all the time it would be seething more and more in her mind until such time as it burst out. And when the body might no longer endure the spiritual effort, but was overcome with the unspeakable love that worked so fervently in her soul, then she fell down and cried astonishingly loud. And the more that she labored to keep it in or to suppress it, so much the more would she cry, and the louder.

And thus she did on the Mount of Calvary, as it is written before: she had as true contemplation in the sight of her soul as if Christ had hung before her bodily eye in his manhood.[7] And when through dispensation of the high mercy of our sovereign savior, Christ Jesus, it was granted to this creature to behold so truly his precious tender body, all rent and torn with scourges, more full of wounds than a dovecote ever was of holes, hanging upon the cross with the crown of thorns upon his head, his blessed hands, his tender feet nailed to the hard wood, the rivers of blood flowing out plenteously from every limb, the grisly and grievous wound in his precious side shedding out blood and water for her love and her salvation, then she fell down and cried with a loud voice, twisting and turning her body amazingly on every side, spreading her arms out wide as if she would have died, and could not keep herself from crying and these physical movements, because of the fire of love that burned so fervently in her soul with pure pity and compassion.[8]

[ARREST BY DUKE OF BEDFORD'S MEN; MEETING WITH ARCHBISHOP OF YORK]
CHAPTER 53[9]

Afterwards that good man who was her escort brought her out of the town, and they went on to Bridlington to her confessor, who was called Sleytham, and spoke with him and with many other good men who had encouraged her previously and done much for her. Then she would not stay there, but took her leave to walk on upon her journey. And then her confessor asked her if she dared not stay because of the Archbishop of York, and she said, "No, truly."

Then the good man gave her silver, begging her to pray for him. And so she went on to Hull. And there, on one occasion, as they went in procession, a great woman treated her with utter contempt, and she said not a word in reply. Many other people said that she ought to be put in prison and made great threats. And notwithstanding all their malice, a good man still came and asked her to a meal, and made her very welcome. Then the malicious people who had despised her before came to this good man, and told him that he ought not do her any kindness, for they considered that she was not a good woman. On the next day, in the morning, her host escorted her out to the edge of town, for he dared not keep her with him any longer.

And so she went to Hessle and would have crossed over the Humber.[1] Then she happened to find there two Preaching Friars, and two yeomen of the Duke of Bedford's.[2] The friars told the yeomen which woman she was, and the yeomen arrested her as she was about to board her boat, and also arrested a man who travelled with her.

"For our lord," they said, "the Duke of Bedford, has sent for you, and you are held to be the greatest Lollard in all this part of the country, or around London either. We have sought you in many a part of the land, and we shall have a hundred pounds for bringing you before our lord."

7. The detailed rendering of Christ's suffering corresponds to Julian of Norwich's visions and to depictions of the Crucifixion in later medieval art. Margery's gestures reinforce the pattern of imitation of Christ seen throughout her book.
8. Margery's images of the dovecote and the fire of love echo Richard Rolle.
9. Margery returns from pilgrimage to Santiago de Compostela. Traveling from Bristol to York, she has twice been detained by civil and clerical authorities, and questioned as a suspected Lollard. Each time she establishes her orthodoxy, most recently to the Archbishop of York, who nevertheless has her escorted from his archdiocese.
1. By crossing the Humber, Margery would have passed beyond the authority of the Archbishop of York, and closer to the Bishop of Lincoln, who had been sympathetic to her.
2. John, third son of King Henry IV, first Duke of Bedford, 1389–1435; at this time he was Lieutenant of the kingdom. (See the Book of Hours made for him, Color Plate 10.)

She said to them, "With a good will, sirs, I shall go with you wherever you will lead me."

Then they brought her back to Hessle, and there men called her Lollard, and women came running out of their houses with their distaffs, crying to the people, "Burn this false heretic."

So as she went on towards Beverley with the said yeomen and friars, they many times met with men of that district who said to her, "Woman, give up this life that you lead, and go and spin, and card wool, as other women do, and do not suffer so much shame and so much unhappiness. We would not suffer so much for any money on earth."

Then she said to them, "I do not suffer as much sorrow as I would do for our Lord's love, for I only suffer cutting words, and our merciful Lord Christ Jesus—worshipped be his name—suffered hard strokes, bitter scourgings, and shameful death at the last, for me and for all mankind, blessed may he be. And therefore, it is truly nothing that I suffer, in comparison to what he suffered."

And so, as she went along with the said men, she told them good stories, until one of the Duke's men who had arrested her said to her, "I rather regret that I met with you, for it seems to me that you speak very good words."

Then she said to him, "Sir, do not regret nor repent that you met with me. Do your lord's will, and I trust that all shall be for the best, for I am very well pleased that you met with me."

He replied, "If ever you're a saint in heaven, lady, pray for me."

She answered, saying to him, "Sir, I hope you will be a saint yourself, and every man that shall come to heaven."

So they went on till they came into Beverley, where lived the wife of one of the men who had arrested her. And they escorted her there and took away from her her purse and her ring. They provided her with a nice room and a decent bed in it, with all the necessaries, locking the door with a key, and bearing the key away with them. * * *

* * * Then she stood looking out at a window, telling many edifying tales to those who would hear her, so much so that women wept bitterly, and said with great heaviness of heart, "Alas, woman, why should you be burned?"

Then she begged the good wife of the house to give her a drink, for she was terribly thirsty. And the good wife said her husband had taken away the key, because of which she could not come in to her, nor give her a drink. And then the women took a ladder and set it up against the window, and gave her a pint of wine in a pot, and also a cup, begging her to conceal the pot and cup, so that when the good man came back he might not notice it.

CHAPTER 54

The said creature, lying in her bed on the following night, heard with her bodily ears a loud voice calling, "Margery." With that voice she awoke, greatly frightened, and, lying still in silence, she said her prayers as devoutly as she could at that time. And soon our merciful Lord, everywhere present, comforting his unworthy servant, said to her, "Daughter, it is more pleasing to me that you suffer scorn and humiliation, shame and rebukes, wrongs and distress, than if your head were struck off three times a day every day for seven years. And therefore, daughter, do not fear what any man can say to you. But in my goodness, and in your sorrows that you have suffered, you have great cause to rejoice, for when you come home to heaven, then shall every sorrow be turned into joy for you."

On the next day she was brought into the Chapterhouse of Beverley,[3] and there was the Archbishop of York, and many great clerics with him, priests, canons, and secular men. Then the Archbishop said to this creature, "What, woman, have you come back again? I would gladly be rid of you."

And then a priest brought her before him, and the Archbishop said, in the hearing of all present, "Sirs, I had this woman before me at Cawood, and there I with my clerics examined her in her faith and found no fault in her. Furthermore, sirs, I have since that time spoken with good men who hold her to be a perfect woman and a good woman. Notwithstanding all this, I gave one of my men five shillings to lead her out of this part of the country, in order to quieten the people down. And as they were going on their journey they were taken and arrested, my man put in prison because of her; also her gold and her silver was taken away from her, together with her beads and her ring, and she is brought before me again here. Is there any man here who can say anything against her?"

Then other men said, "Here is a friar who knows many things against her."

The friar came forward and said that she disparaged all men of Holy Church—and he uttered much evil talk about her that time. He also said that she would have been burnt at Lynn, had his order—that was the Preaching Friars—not been there. "And, sir, she says that she may weep and have contrition when she will."

Then came the two men who had arrested her, saying with the friar that she was Cobham's daughter, and was sent to carry letters about the country.[4] And they said she had not been to Jerusalem, nor in the Holy Land, nor on other pilgrimage, as she had been in truth. They denied all truth, and maintained what was wrong, as many others had done before. When they had said enough for a long while, they held their peace.

Then the Archbishop said to her, "Woman, what do you say to all this?"

She said, "My lord, saving your reverence, all the words that they say are lies."

Then the Archbishop said to the friar, "Friar, the words are not heresy; they are slanderous words and erroneous."

"My lord," said the friar, "she knows her faith well enough. Nevertheless, my lord of Bedford is angry with her, and he will have her."[5] * * *

A short time afterwards the Archbishop sent for her, and she was led into his chamber, and even up to his bedside. Then she, bowing, thanked him for his gracious favour that he had shown her before.

"Yes, yes," said the Archbishop, "I am told worse things of you than I ever was before."

She said, "My lord, if you care to examine me, I shall avow the truth, and if I be found guilty, I will be obedient to your correction."

Then a Preaching Friar came forward, who was Suffragan[6] to the Archbishop, to whom the Archbishop said, "Now, sir, as you said to me when she was not present, say now while she is present."

"Shall I do so?" said the Suffragan.

"Yes," said the Archbishop.

---

3. Just north of the Humber.
4. Sir John Oldcastle, Lord Cobham, a leading Lollard, had mounted an unsuccessful rising against Henry V. He was executed, in the presence of the Duke of Bedford, 14 December 1417.

5. Margery becomes part of a potential dispute over jurisdiction between clergy and laity.
6. A subsidiary bishop, usually assisting a bishop or archbishop in local matters.

Then the Suffragan said to this creature, "Woman, you were at my Lady Westmorland's."[7]

"When, sir?" said she.

"At Easter," said the Suffragan.

She, not replying, said, "Well, sir?"

Then he said, "My Lady herself was well pleased with you and liked your talk, but you advised my Lady Greystoke to leave her husband,[8] and she is a baron's wife, and daughter to my Lady of Westmorland. And now you have said enough to be burned for." And so he multiplied many sharp words in front of the Archbishop—it is not fitting to repeat them.

At last she said to the Archbishop, "My lord, if it be your will, I have not seen my Lady Westmorland these two years and more. Sir, she sent for me before I went to Jerusalem[9] and, if you like, I will go to her again for a testimonial that I prompted no such matter."

"No," said those who stood round about, "let her be put in prison, and we will send a letter to the noble lady, and, if it be the truth that she is saying, let her go free, without any grudging."

And she said she was quite satisfied that it should be so.

Then a great cleric who stood a little to one side of the Archbishop said, "Put her in prison forty days, and she will love God the better for the rest of her life."

The Archbishop asked her what tale it was that she told the Lady of Westmorland when she spoke with her.

She said, "I told her a good tale of a lady who was damned because she would not love her enemies, and of a bailiff who was saved because he loved his enemies and forgave them their trespasses against him, and yet he was held to be an evil man."

The Archbishop said it was a good tale. Then his steward said, and many others with him, crying with a loud voice to the Archbishop, "My lord, we pray you, let her go from here this time, and if she ever comes back again, we will burn her ourselves."

The Archbishop said, "I believe there was never woman in England so treated as she is, and has been."

Then he said to this creature, "I do not know what I shall do with you."

She said, "My lord, I pray you, let me have your letter and your seal as a record that I have vindicated myself against my enemies, and that nothing admissible is charged against me, neither error nor heresy that may be proved against me, our Lord be thanked. And let me have John, your man, again to bring me over the water."

And the Archbishop very kindly granted her all she desired—our Lord grant him his reward—and delivered to her her purse with her ring and beads, which the Duke of Bedford's men had taken from her before. The Archbishop was amazed at where she got the money to travel about the country with, and she said good men gave it her so that she would pray for them.

Then she, kneeling down, received his blessing and took her leave with a very glad heart, going out of his chamber. And the Archbishop's household asked her to pray for them, but the Steward was angry because she laughed and was so cheerful, saying to her, "Holy folk should not laugh."

---

7. Joan de Beaufort (d. 1440), daughter of John of Gaunt and at this time wife of Ralph Neville, first Earl of Westmorland. She was the Duke of Bedford's aunt.
8. Elizabeth, Lady Greystoke, daughter of Joan de Beau-

fort, hence a relative of the Duke of Bedford. Margery had already been accused of encouraging the wives of urban commoners to leave their husbands.
9. At least four years earlier.

She said, "Sir, I have great cause to laugh, for the more shame and scorn I suffer, the merrier I may be in our Lord Jesus Christ."

Then she came down into the hall, and there stood the Preaching Friar who had caused her all that unhappiness. And so she passed on with a man of the Archbishop's, bearing the letter which the Archbishop had granted her for a record, and he brought her to the River Humber, and there he took his leave of her, returning to his lord and bearing the said letter with him again, and so she was left alone, without any knowledge of the people.[1]

All the aforesaid trouble befell her on a Friday, God be thanked for everything.[2]

CHAPTER 55

When she had crossed the River Humber, she was immediately arrested as a Lollard and led towards prison. There happened to be a person there who had seen her before the Archbishop of York, and he got her leave to go where she wanted, and excused her to the bailiff, and undertook for her that she was no Lollard. And so she escaped away in the name of Jesus. * * *

Middle English Lyrics

Although many Middle English lyrics have a beguilingly fresh and unselfconscious tone, they owe much to learned and sophisticated continental sources—the medieval Latin lyrics of the "Goliard poets" and the Provençal and French lyrics of the Troubadours and Trouvères. Most authors were clerics, aware of the similarities between earthly and divine love, and fond of punning in Latin or English.

The anonymity of the Middle English lyrics prevents us from seeing them as part of a single poet's *oeuvre*, as we can, for instance, with the poems of Chaucer, Dunbar, and Dafydd ap Gwilym. Rather, we must rely on more general contexts, such as genre, to establish relationships among poems. One of the most popular genres among the secular lyrics was the *reverdie*, a poem celebrating the return of spring. The early thirteenth-century *Cuckoo Song* ("Sumer is icumen in") joyfully invokes the bird's song, and revels in the blossoming of the countryside and the calls of the animals to their young. More typical examples of the *reverdie* are *Alisoun* and *Spring*, whose male speakers ruefully contrast the burgeoning of nature with the stinginess of their beloveds; in *Spring*, flowers bloom, birds sing, animals mate—but one woman remains unmoved. In the genre of the love complaint, *My Lefe Is Faren in a Lond* and *Fowls in the Frith* express erotic loss and frustration with great succinctness.

Frustration was not the only attitude in Middle English love lyrics, however. A stance more boasting than adoring or despairing is taken in the witty lyric *I Have a Noble Cock*. Furthermore, clerical misogyny is expressed in *Abuse of Women*, which ostensibly praises women by absolving them of the vices—gossip, infidelity, shrewishness—typically attributed to them in satires against women; yet the refrain first praises women as the best of creatures but then undercuts this claim in Latin, which few women would have been able to understand.

Although most of the Middle English lyrics are in the male voice, there are a few "women's songs"—most likely written by men—which convey female experience. Occasionally

---

1. At the southern edge of the archbishop's territory, Margery is again left alone and without the document that would guarantee her orthodoxy.

2. Margery's greatest trials often occur on a Friday, connecting her sufferings to events of the Crucifixion.

these songs are invitations (for instance, the enigmatic *Irish Dancer*), but more often they are laments by an abandoned, and often pregnant, woman. A *Forsaken Maiden's Lament* is punctuated by the regretful refrain: "Were it undo that is ido, / I wolde bewar." Two of the women's songs, while concluding with laments about pregnancy, stress the cleverness and charm of the clerical seducers, perhaps suggesting that churchmen were their audience as well as their authors. *The Wily Clerk* attributes a young man's skill at deception to his scholarly training, as does *Jolly Jankin*, whose clerk engages in multilingual word play, turning the "Kyrie Eleison" into a request for mercy from the woman herself, "Alison."

The majority of Middle English lyrics were not secular but religious. Songs in praise of the Virgin Mary or Christ, however, employ the same erotic language as the secular lyrics, often in conjunction with typological figures linking events in the Old Testament to those in the New. In *Adam Lay Ibounden*, for instance, the poet follows a statement of the "fortunate Fall"—that Adam's sin was necessary to permit Christ's redemption—with a courtly compliment to the Virgin Mary. Similarly, *I Sing of a Maiden* draws on the typological significance of Gideon's fleece in Judges 6 (the soaking of the fleece by dew figuring Mary's impregnation by the Holy Spirit) while also employing the courtly imagery of a poet "singing of a maiden" who "chooses" Christ as her son, as if he were a lover. In a much longer poem in praise of the Virgin, the poet—casting himself as Mary's "knight" caught in the bonds of love—begs her mercy and also compliments her by contrasting her with her antitype, Eve.

Occasionally the Middle English religious lyric uses secular motifs and genres in a way that approaches parody. For instance, the second stanza of the Nativity poem *Mary Is with Child* resembles a pregnancy lament by a young girl. Mary, however, explains that her condition will be a source of joy rather than shame, when she will sing a lullaby to her "darling." This Middle English poet, far from blaspheming, was trying to humanize the mystery of the Nativity and relate it to daily life.

Other religious poems either celebrate Christ or reject the world. The poems to Christ, in their tenderness and immediacy, resemble those to Mary. In only four lines, *Now Goeth Sun Under Wood* evokes nature's oneness with Christ (the setting sun figuring the crucifixion) and the poet's empathy with the Virgin mother. Poets used erotic language in poems to Christ as well as those to Mary, as in *Sweet Jesus, King of Bliss* and *Jesus, My Sweet Lover*. Finally, in a different vein, the *Contempt of the World* questions the values of courtly life, with the *"ubi sunt"* ("where are") motif. "Where beth they biforen us weren?" it asks, evoking the lovely women who enjoyed their paradise on earth and now suffer the eternal fires of hell.

The Cuckoo Song

	Sumer is icumen in,°	*spring has come in*
	Lhude° sing, cuccu!°	*loudly / cuckoo*
	Groweth sed° and bloweth° med°	*seed / blooms / meadow*
	And springth° the wude° nu.°	*grows / forest / now*
5	Sing, cuccu!	
	Awe° bleteth after lomb,	*ewe*
	Lhouth° after calve° cu,°	*lows / calf / cow*
	Bulluc sterteth,° bucke ferteth.°	*leaps / farts*
	Murie° sing, cuccu!	*merrily*
10	Cuccu, cuccu,	
	Wel singes thu, cuccu.	
	Ne swik° thu naver° nu!	*cease / never*
	Sing cuccu nu, sing cuccu!	
	Sing cuccu, sing cuccu nu!	

This page contains the words and music to one of the earliest and best loved of Middle English lyrics, *The Cuckoo Song* ("Sumer is icumen in"). The lyric is a *reverdie*, or spring song, but its joyful description of nature's rebirth is given a more sober allegorical interpretation by the interlinear Latin gloss, apparently to be sung to the same tune. The gloss parallels the lyric's celebration of the reawakening landscape with an account of the "heavenly farmer" (*celicus agricola*) whom "rot on the vine" (*vitis vicio*) leads to sacrifice his Son. The fact that the manuscript was copied at a monastery reminds us that this song, like much other early English secular poetry, survives only because it was seen to have religious relevance.

Spring

	Lenten° is come with love to toune,°	*spring / town*
	With blosmen° and with briddes° roune,°	*flowers / birds' / song*
	That all this blisse bringeth.	
	Dayeseyes° in this° dales,	*daisies / these*
5	Notes swere of nightegales—	
	Uch° foul° song singeth.	*each / bird*
	The threstelcok him threteth o;[1]	
	Away is here° winter wo	*their*
	When woderove° springeth.°	*woodruff / grows*
10	This foules° singeth ferly fele,°	*birds / wonderfully much*
	And wliteth on here winne wele,[2]	
	That all the wode ringeth.	
	The rose raileth hire rode,°	*puts on her rosy hue*
	The leves on the lighte° wode	*bright*
15	Waxen° all with wille.°	*grow / pleasure*

---

1. The song thrush contends always.   2. And chirp their wealth of joys.

The mone mandeth hire bleo,[3]
The lilie is lossom° to seo,°   *lovely / see*
   The fenil° and the fille.°   *fennel / chervil*
Wowes° this° wilde drakes;   *woo / these*
20 Miles murgeth here makes,[4]
   Ase strem that striketh° stille.°   *flows / softly*
Mody meneth, so doth mo;[5]
Ichot° ich° am one of tho,°   *I know / I / those*
   For love that likes° ille.   *pleases*

25 The mone mandeth hire light;
So doth the semly,° sonne bright,   *lovely*
   When briddes singeth breme.°   *loudly*
Deawes donketh the dounes;[6]
Deores with here derne rounes,[7]
30   Domes for to deme;[8]
Wormes woweth under cloude,°   *the soil*
Wimmen waxeth° wounder° proude,   *become / wondrously*
   So well it wol hem° seme.°   *to them / appear*
If me shall wonte wille of on,[9]
35 This wunne weole° I wole forgon   *wealth of joys*
   And wight° in wode be fleme.°   *quickly / exile*

Alisoun

Bitwene Mersh° and Averil°   *March / April*
When spray° biginneth to springe,°   *twig / grow*
The lutel° fowl° hath hire° will   *little / bird / her*
On° hire lud° to singe.   *in / language*
5 Ich° libbe° in love-longinge   *I / live*
For semlokest° of alle thinge: *fairest*
He° may me blisse bringe;   *she*
Ich° am in hire baundoun.°   *I / power*
   An hendy hap ich habbe ihent![1]
10 *Ichot° from hevene it is me sent;*   *I know*
  From alle wimmen my love is lent,°   *taken away*
  And light° on Alisoun.[2]   *settled*

On hew° hire her° is fair inogh,   *color / hair*
Hire browe browne, hire eye blake;
15 With lossum chere he on me logh,[3]
With middel° small and well imake.°   *waist / made*
Bote° he me wolle° to hire take   *unless / will*
For to ben hire° owen° make,°   *her / own / mate*
Longe to liven ichulle° forsake,°   *I will / refuse*
20 And feye° fallen adoun.   *doomed*

3. The moon sends forth her light.
4. Beasts gladden their mates.
5. The high-spirited man mourns, so do others.
6. Dew moistens the downs (hills).
7. Animals with their secret whispers.
8. Speak their opinions.

9. If I shall lack the pleasure of one.
1. A fair destiny I have received.
2. Alison is a stock name for a country woman, shared by the wife in Chaucer's *Miller's Tale* and by his Wife of Bath.
3. With lovely manner she laughed at me.

> *An hendy hap ich habbe ihent!*
> *Ichot from hevene it is me sent;*
> *From alle wimmen my love is lent,*
> *And light on Alisoun.*

25 Nightes° when I wende° and wake—   at night / turn
Forthy min wonges waxeth won[4]—
Levedy,° all for thine sake   lady
Longinge is ilent° me on.   come
In world nis non so witer° mon   wise
30 That all hire° bounte° telle con: her / excellence
Hire swire° is whittore° then the swon,   neck / whiter
And feirest may° in toune.   maiden
> *An hendy hap ich habbe ihent!*
> *Ichot from hevene it is me sent;*
35 > *From alle wimmen my love is lent,*
> *And light on Alisoun.*

Ich am for wowing all forwake,[5]
Wery so water in wore[6]
Lest eny reve° me my make°   steal / mate
40 Ich habbe iyerned yore.[7]
Betere is tholien while sore[8]
Then mournen evermore.
Geynest° under gore,°   kindest / petticoat
Herkne to my roun!°   song
45 > *An hendy hap ich habbe ihent!*
> *Ichot from hevene it is me sent;*
> *From alle wimmen my love is lent,*
> *And light on Alisoun.*

I Have a Noble Cock

I have a gentil° cok,   noble
    Croweth° me day;   who crows
He doth° me risen erly,   makes
    My matins for to say.

5 I have a gentil cok,
    Comen he is of gret;°   a great family
His comb is of red corel,
    His tayel is of jet.

I have a gentil cok,
10   Comen he is of kinde;°   good lineage
His comb is of red corel,
    His tail is of inde.°   indigo

His legges ben of asor,°   azure
    So gentil and so smale;

---

4. Therefore my cheeks become pale.   7. (For whom) I have long yearned.
5. I am for wooing all sleepless.   8. It is better to suffer sorely for a time.
6. Weary as water in a troubled pool.

15   His spores° arn of silver white,   *spurs*
          Into the worte-wale.°   *root of cock's spur*

      His eynen° arn of cristal,   *eyes*
          Loken° all in aumber;   *set*
      And every night he percheth him
20   In min ladyes chaumber.

My Lefe Is Faren in a Lond[9]

      My lefe is faren in a lond[1]—
      Alas! why is she so?
      And I am so sore bound
      I may nat com her to.
      She hath my hert in hold,°   *imprisoned*
      Where-ever she ride or go,
      With trew love a thousandfold.

Fowls in the Frith

      Foweles° in the frith,°   *birds / wood*
      The fisses° in the flod,°   *fishes / river*
      And I mon° waxe° wod.°   *must / become / mad*
      Mulch° sorw° I walke with   *much / sorrow*
      For beste[2] of bon° and blod.°   *bone / blood*

Abuse of Women

          Of all creatures women be best:
          Cuius contrarium verum est.[3]

      In every place ye may well see
      That women be trewe as tirtil° on tree,   *turtledove*
5   Not liberal° in langage, but ever in secree,°   *licentious / secrecy*
      And gret joye amonge them is for to be.

          Of all creatures women be best:
          Cuius contrarium verum est.

      The stedfastnes of women will never be don,
10   So jentil, so curtes they be everychon,[4]
      Meke as a lambe, still as a stone,
      Croked° nor crabbed find ye none!   *perverse*

          Of all creatures women be best:
          Cuius contrarium verum est.

15   Men be more cumbers° a thousand fold,   *troublesome*
      And I mervail how they dare be so bold

---

9. Chaucer alludes to this poem in *The Nun's Priest's*   2. Either "beast" or "best."
Tale, line 112.   3. Latin for "The opposite of this is true."
1. My beloved has gone away.   4. So well-bred, so courteous is each one.

Against women for to hold,
Seeing them so pacient, softe, and cold.

    Of all creatures women be best:
20   *Cuius contrarium verum est.*

For tell a woman all your counsaile,
And she can kepe it wonderly well;
She had lever go quik° to hell,   *alive*
Than to her neighbour she wold it tell!

25   *Of all creatures women be best:*
    Cuius contrarium verum est.

For by women men be reconsiled,
For by women was never man begiled,
For they be of the condicion of curtes Grisell,[5]
30   For they be so meke and milde.

    Of all creatures women be best:
    Cuius contrarium verum est.

Now say well by° women or elles be still,   *about*
For they never displesed man by ther will;
35   To be angry or wroth they can° no skill,   *have*
For I dare say they think non ill.

    Of all creatures women be best:
    Cuius contrarium verum est.

Trow° ye that women list° to smater,°   *think / like / chatter*
40   Or against ther husbondes for to clater?
Nay, they had lever° fast bred and water,   *rather*
Then for to dele in suche a mater.

    Of all creatures women be best:
    Cuius contrarium verum est.

45   Though all the paciens in the world were drownd,
And non were lefte here on the ground,
Again in a woman it might be found,
Suche vertu in them dothe abound!

    Of all creatures women be best:
50   *Cuius contrarium verum est.*

To the tavern they will not go,
Nor to the alehous never the mo,°   *more*
For, God wot,° ther hartes wold be wo, knows   *knows*
To spende ther husbondes money so.

55   *Of all creatures women be best:*
    Cuius contrarium verum est.

---

5. Griselda, the long-suffering wife of Chaucer's *Clerk's Tale*; the tale ends with the observation that there are no more Griseldas left.

If here were a woman or a maid,
That list for to go freshely arayed,
Or with fine kirchers° to go displayed,   *kerchiefs*
60   Ye wold say, "They be proude": it is ill said.

> *Of all creatures women be best:*
> *Cuius contrarium verum est.*

The Irish Dancer

Ich° am of Irlaunde,   *I*
And of the holy londe
Of Irlande.
Gode° sire, pray ich thee,   *good*
For of sainte° charitee,°   *holy / charity*
Come and daunce wit me
In Irlaunde.

A Forsaken Maiden's Lament

> *Were it undo° that is ido,°*   *undone / done*
> *I wolde bewar.*

I lovede a child° of this cuntree,   *young man*
And so I wende° he had do me;   *thought*
5   Now myself the sothe° I see,   *truth*
     That he is far.

> *Were it undo that is ido,*
> *I wolde bewar.*

He seide to me he wolde be trewe,
10   And change me for non other newe;
Now I sikke° and am pale of hewe,   *sigh*
     For he is far.

> *Were it undo that is ido,*
> *I wolde bewar.*

15   He seide his sawes° he wolde fulfille: *promises*
Therfore I lat him have all his wille;
Now I sikke and morne stille,°   *quietly*
     For he is far.

> *Were it undo that is ido,*
20   *I wolde bewar.*

The Wily Clerk

A, dere God, what I am fayn,
For I am madyn now gane![6]

This enther° day I mete a clerke,°   *other / cleric*
And he was wily in his werke;

---

6. Ah, dear God, how worthless I am, / For I am no longer a virgin.

5   He prayd me with° him to herke,°   *to / listen*
        And his counsel all for to layne.°   *conceal*

A, dere God, what I am fayn,
For I am madyn now gane!

    I trow° he coud° of gramery;[7]   *believe / knew*
10   I shall now telle a good skill° why: *reason*
    For what I hade siccurly,°   *certainly*
      To warne° his will had I no mayn.°   *resist / strength*

A, dere God, what I am fayn,
For I am madyn now gane!

15   Whan he and me brout° un° us the schete,°   *brought / on / sheet*
    Of all his will I him lete;°   *permitted*
    Now will not my girdil met—°   *meet*
      A, dere God, what shall I sayn?

A, dere God, what I am fayn,
20   *For I am madyn now gane!*

    I shall sey to man and page°   *youth*
    That I have bene of pilgrimage.
    Now will I not lete° for no rage°   *permit / lust*
      With me a clerk for to pleyn.°   *play*

25   *A, dere God, what I am fayn,*
    For I am madyn now gane!

Jolly Jankin

"Kyrie,"° so "Kyrie,"   *Lord*
Jankin[8] singeth merie,°   *merrily*
With "aleison."[9]

    As I went on Yol° Day in our procession,   *Yule (Christmas)*
5   Knew I joly Jankin be° his mery ton.°   *by / tone*
      Kyrieleison.

"Kyrie," so "Kyrie,"
Jankin singeth merie,
With "aleison."

10   Jankin began the offis° on the Yol Day,   *church service*
    And yet me thinketh[1] it dos me good, so merie gan he say
      Kyrieleison.

"Kyrie," so "Kyrie,"
Jankin singeth merie,
15   With "aleison."

7. Latin, learning, or magic—indicates the magical power which the speaker attributes to the clergy, who could read Latin.
8. "Johnny," a stock name. Also the name of Chaucer's Wife of Bath's fifth husband, who was a clerk.

9. "*Kyrie eleison,*" Greek for "Lord have mercy upon us" (an early part of the Mass). The poem puns on "Alison," supposedly the speaker's name (a stock female name).
1. It seems to me.

Jankin red the pistil° full fair and full well,   *Epistle*
And yet me thinketh it dos me good, as evere have I sell.°   *luck*
    Kyrieleison.

20   "Kyrie," so "Kyrie,"
Jankin singeth merie,
With "aleison."

Jankin at the *Sanctus* craked° a merie note,   *uttered*
And yet me thinketh it dos me good—I payed for his cote.
    Kyrieleison.

25   "Kyrie," so "Kyrie,"
Jankin singeth merie,
With "aleison."

Jankin craked notes an hundered on a knot,°   *at once*
And yet he hakked hem smaller than wortes[2] to the pot.
30   Kyrieleison.

"Kyrie," so "Kyrie,"
Jankin singeth merie,
With "aleison."

Jankin at the *Angnus* bered the *pax-brede*;[3]
35 He twinkeled, but said nout, and on min fot he trede.[4]
    Kyrieleison.

"Kyrie," so "Kyrie,"
Jankin singeth merie,
With "aleison."

40 *Benedicamus Domino*,[5] Crist fro° schame me schilde.°   *from / shield*
Deo gracias,[6] therto—alas, I go with childe!
    Kyrieleison.

"Kyrie," so "Kyrie,"
Jankin singeth merie,
45 With "aleison."

Adam Lay Ibounden

Adam lay ibounden,°   *bound*
Bounden in a bond;
Foure thousand winter
Thowt° he not too long.   *thought*
5 And all was for an appil,
An appil that he took,
As clerkes finden wreten
In here° book.   *their*

---

2. Vegetables.
3. At the *Agnus Dei* (at the later part of the Mass), Jankin
carried the *pax-brede*, an article signalling the exchanging
of the kiss of peace.

4. He winked, but said nothing, and on my foot he
stepped.
5. Let us bless the Lord.
6. Thanks be to God.

	Ne° hadde the appil take° ben,	*if not / taken*
10	The appil taken ben,	
	Ne° hadde never our lady	*not*
	A ben hevene quen.[7]	
	Blissed be the time	
	That appil take was!	
15	Therfore we moun° singen	*may*
	"Deo gracias!"°	*Thanks be to God!*

I Sing of a Maiden

	I sing of a maiden	
	That is makeles,[8]	
	King of alle kinges	
	To° here° sone she ches.°	*for / her / chose*
5	He cam also° stille°	*as / quietly*
	Ther° his moder was	*where*
	As dew in Aprille	
	That falleth on the gras.	
	He cam also stille	
10	To his moderes bowr	
	As dew in Aprille	
	That falleth on the flour.	
	He cam also stille	
	Ther his moder lay	
15	As dew in Aprille	
	That falleth on the spray.°	*twigs*
	Moder and maiden	
	Was never non but she:	
	Well may swich° a lady	*such*
20	Godes moder be.	

In Praise of Mary

	Edi° be thu, Hevene Quene,	*blessed*
	Folkes froure° and engles° blis,	*comfort / angels'*
	Moder unwemmed° and maiden clene,	*unspotted*
	Swich° in world non other nis.°	*such / is*
5	On thee it is well eth° sene°	*easily / seen*
	Of alle wimmen thu havest that pris.°	*prize*
	My swete Levedy,° her my bene,°	*Lady / prayer*
	And rew° of me yif° thy wille is.	*take pity / if*
	Thu asteye° so° the dais-rewe°	*climb / as / dawn's ray*
10	The° deleth° from the derke night;	*that / separates*
	Of thee sprong a leme° newe light	*light*
	That all this world haveth ilight.°	*illuminated*

---

7. Have been heaven's queen.   8. Spotless, matchless, and mateless.

Nis non maide of thine hewe
So fair, so shene,° so rudy, so bright.   *beautiful*
15   Swete Levedy, of me thu rewe,
And have mercy of thine knight.

Spronge° blostme° of one rote,°   *sprung / blossom / root*
The Holy Ghost thee reste upon;
That wes for monkunnes° bote,°   *mankind's / healing*
20   And here° soule to alesen° for on.   *their / deliver*
Levedy milde, softe and swote,°   *sweet*
Ic° crye thee mercy: ic am thy mon,°   *I / man*
Bothe to honde and to fote,
On alle wise° that ic con.°   *way / can*

25   Thu ert° erthe° to° gode sede;   *art / earth / for*
On thee lighte° the Hevene° dews;   *came down / of heaven*
Of thee sprong the edi° blede—°   *blessed / fruit*
The Holy Ghost hire on thee sews.°   *sowed it*
Thu bring us ut of care, of drede,°   *fear*
30   That Eve bitterliche us brews.
Thu shalt us into Hevene lede—
Welle° swete is the ilke° dews.   *most / same*

Moder, full of thewes° hende,°   *virtues / gracious*
Maide, dreigh° and well itaught,°   *patient / taught*
35   Ic em in thine lovebende,°   *bonds of love*
And to thee is all my draught.°   *leaning*
Thu me shilde° from the Fende,°   *shield / Fiend*
Ase thu ert fre,° and wilt° and maught:°   *noble / will / can*
Help me to my lives ende,
40   And make me with thine sone isaught.°   *reconciled*

Thu ert icumen° of heghe° cunne,°   *come / high / lineage*
Of David the riche king.
Nis non maiden under sunne
The° mey be thine evening,°   *that / equal*
45   Ne that so derne° loviye cunne,°   *secretly / can*
Ne non so trewe of alle thing.
Thy love us broughte eche° wunne:°   *eternal / bliss*
Ihered° ibe° thu, swete thing!   *praised / be*

Selcudliche ure Louerd it dighte[9]
50   That thu, maide, withute were,°   *mate*
That all this world bicluppe ne mighte,°   *could not encompass*
Thu sholdest of thine boseme° bere.°   *womb / bear*
Thee ne stighte,° ne thee ne prighte,°   *stabbing / pricking*
In side, in lende° ne elleswhere:°   *loins / elsewhere*
55   That wes° with full muchel° righte,   *was / much*
For thu bere° thine Helere.°   *bore / Savior*

Tho° Godes sune alighte wolde°   *when / wished*
On erthe, all for ure° sake,   *our*

<hr>

9. Marvellously our Lord arranged it.

	Herre° teyen° he him nolde	*higher / servant*
60	Thene° that maide to ben° his make:°	*than / be / mate*
	Betere ne mighte he, thaigh° he wolde,	*though*
	Ne swetture thing on erthe take.	
	Levedy,° bring us to thine bolde°	*Lady / abode*
	And shild° us from helle wrake.°	*shield / vengeance*
	Amen.	

Mary Is with Child

	Nowel! nowel! nowel!	
	Sing we with mirth!	
	Christ is come well	
	With us to dwell,	
5	*By his most noble birth.*	
	Under a tree	
	In sporting me,	
	Alone by a wod-side,°	*side of a wood*
	I hard° a maid[1]	*heard*
10	That swetly said,	
	"I am with child this tide.°	*time*
	"Graciously	
	Conceived have I	
	The Son of God so swete:	
15	His gracious will	
	I put me till,	
	As moder him to kepe.	
	"Both night and day	
	I will him pray,	
20	And her° his lawes taught,	*hear*
	And every dell°	*in every way*
	His trewe gospell	
	In his apostles fraught.°	*carried*
	"This ghostly° case°	*spiritual / act*
25	Doth me embrace,	
	Without despite or mock;	
	With my derling,	
	'Lullay,'° to sing,	*lullabye*
	And lovely him to rock.	
30	"Without distress	
	In grete lightness	
	I am both night and day.	
	This hevenly fod°	*child*
	In his childhod	
35	Shall daily with me play.	

---

1. A poem that opens with the speaker in the countryside overhearing a woman's lament raises expectations that we will hear a *chanson d'aventure*, with erotic connotations.

"Soone must I sing
With rejoicing,
For the time is all ronne°   *run out*
That I shall child,°   *give birth to*
40   All undefil'd,
The King of Heven's Sonne."

Sweet Jesus, King of Bliss

Swete Jesu, king of blisse,
Min herte° love, min herte lisse,°   *heart's / joy*
Thou art swete mid iwisse.°   *certainly*
Wo is him that thee shall misse!

5   Swete Jesu, min herte light,
Thou art day withoute night,
Thou geve° me streinthe and eke° might   *may you give / also*
For to lovien thee aright.

Swete Jesu, min herte bote,°   *remedy*
10   In min herte thou sete° a rote°   *may you set / root*
Of thy love, that is so swote,°   *sweet*
And leve° that it springe mote.°   *grant / may grow*

Swete Jesu, min herte gleem,°   *light*
Brightore then the sonnebeem,
15   Ibore° thou were in Bedleheem;   *born*
Thou make me here thy swete dreem.[2]

Swete Jesu, thy love is swete;
Wo is him that thee shall lete!°   *abandon*
Gif me grace for to grete°   *cry*
20   For my sinnes teres° wete.°   *with tears / wet*

Swete Jesu, king of londe,
Thou make me fer° understonde   *to*
That min herte mote° fonde°   *may / experience*
How swete beth° thy love-bonde.   *is*

25   Swete Jesu, Louerd° min,   *Lord*
My lif, min herte, all is thin;°   *yours*
Undo° min herte and light° therin,   *open / alight*
And wite° me from fendes° engin.°   *guard / the Devil's / trick*

Swete Jesu, my soule° fode,   *soul's*
30   Thin werkes beth° bo° swete and gode;   *are / both*
Thou boghtest° me upon the rode;°   *redeemed / cross*
For me thou sheddest thy blode.

Swete Jesu, me reoweth° sore   *I regret*
Gultes that I ha wroght yore;[3]
35   Therfore I bidde° thin milse° and ore;°   *beg / mercy / grace*
Mercy, Lord, I nul° namore.   *will not*

---

2. May thou make me hear thy sweet melody.   3. The sins that I have committed in the past.

Swete Jesu, Louerd God,
Thou me boghtest with thy blod;
Out of thin herte orn° the flod;   *ran*
40   Thy moder° it segh° that thee by stod.   *mother / saw*

Swete Jesu, bright and shene,°   *beautiful*
I preye thee thou here my bene°   *prayer*
Thourgh ernding° of the hevene quene,   *intercession*
That thy love on me be sene.°   *seen*

45   Swete Jesu, berne° best,   *of men*
With thee ich hope habbe° rest;   *to have*
Whether I be south other° west,   *or*
The help of thee be me nest.°   *nearest*

Swete Jesu, well may him be
50   That thee may in blisse see.
With love-cordes drawe thou me
That I may comen and wone° with thee.   *dwell*

Swete Jesu, hevene king,
Feir and best of alle thing,
55   Thou bring me of° this longing   *out of*
To come to thee at min ending.

Swete Jesu, all folkes reed,°   *counsel*
Graunte us er we buen° ded   *are*
Thee underfonge° in fourme of bred,   *to receive*
60   And sethe° to heovene thou us led.°   *later / may lead*

Now Goeth Sun under Wood

Now goth° sonne under wod:°   *goes / forest*
Me reweth,[4] Marye, thy faire rode.°   *face*
Now goth sonne under tree:
Me reweth, Marye, thy sone and thee.

Jesus, My Sweet Lover

Jesu Christ, my lemmon° swete,   *lover*
That diyedest on the Rode° Tree,   *Cross*
With all my might I thee beseche,
For thy woundes two and three,
That also° faste mot° thy love   *as / may*
Into mine herte fitched° be   *fixed*
As was the spere into thine herte,
Whon thou soffredest deth for me.

Contempt of the World

Where beth° they biforen us weren?   *are*
Houndes ladden° and hawkes beren,°   *led / bore*
And hadden feld and wode;

4. I feel pity for.

	The riche levedies° in here° bour,°	*ladies / their / bower*
5	That wereden° gold in here° tressour,°	*wore / head-dress*
	With here° brighte rode:°	*their / face*
	Eten and drounken and maden hem° glad;	*themselves*
	Here lif was all with gamen° ilad.°	*sport / spent*
	Men keneleden° hem° biforen;	*kneeled / them*
10	They beren hem well swithe° heye—°	*very / high*
	And in a twinkling of an eye	
	Here soules weren forloten.°	*lost*
	Where is that laughing and that song,	
	That trailing⁵ and that proude gong,°	*gait*
15	Tho hawkes and tho° houndes?	*those*
	All that joye is went away,	
	That wele° is comen to weylaway,°	*prosperity / woe*
	To manye harde stoundes.°	*times*
	Here° paradis hy° nomen° here,	*their / they / took*
20	And now they lien° in helle ifere;°	*lie / together*
	The fuir° it brennes° evere.	*fire / burns*
	Long is "ah!" and long is "oh!"	
	Long is "wy!" and long is "wo!"	
	Thennes° ne cometh they nevere.	*thence*
25	Drey° here, man, thenne, if thou wilt,	*suffer*
	A litel pine that me thee bit;⁶	
	Withdraw thine eyses° ofte.	*comforts*
	They° thy pine° be unrede,°	*though / pain / severe*
	And° thou thenke° on thy mede,°	*if / think / reward*
30	It shall thee thinken° softe.	*seem*
	If that fend,° that foule thing,	*the Devil*
	Thorou wikke roun, thorou fals egging,°	*counsel*
	Nethere° thee haveth icast, down	*down*
	Up and be good chaunpioun!	
35	Stond, ne fall namore adoun	
	For a litel blast.	
	Thou tak the rode° to° thy staf,	*cross / as*
	And thenk on him that thereonne gaf°	*gave*
	His lif that wes so lef.°	*dear*
40	He it gaf for thee; thou yelde° it him;	*give back*
	Agein° his fo that staf thou nim°	*against / take*
	And wrek° him of that thef.°	*avenge / thief*
	Of righte bileve° thou nim that sheld,	*belief*
	The whiles that thou best° in that feld,	*are*
45	Thin hond to strengthen fonde;°	*try*
	And kep thy fo with° staves° ord,°	*at / staff's / point*
	And do° that traitre seyen that word.	*make*
	Biget° that murie° londe.	*win / happy*

---

5. Walking with trailing garments.   6. A little pain that one enjoins.

Thereinne is day withouten night,
50   Withouten ende strengthe and might,
And wreche° of everich fo;   punishment
Mid° God himselven eche° lif,   with / eternal
And pes° and rest withoute strif,   peace
Wele° withouten wo.   happiness

55   Maiden moder,° hevene° quene,   mother / heaven's
Thou might and const and owest to bene[7]
Oure sheld agein the fende;°   Devil
Help us sunne° for to flen,°   sin / flee
That we moten° they sone° iseen°   may / Son / see
60   In joye withouten ende.

The Tale of Taliesin

The Tale of Taliesin extends a series of very ancient legends about the great bard Taliesin, placing him about a generation after the time of King Arthur. Yet this version was not written down until the sixteenth century, by the antiquarian Elis Grufydd, who expresses occasional doubt about the truth and orthodoxy of his story. Nonetheless, the tale's coherence, its references to pagan Welsh myth, and its depiction of bardic practice at royal courts all reflect the extraordinary continuity of ancient and medieval Welsh culture. Like Celtic culture in Ireland, Welsh literature and art display remarkable tenacity as well as flexibility. The Britons and their Welsh successors absorbed wave after wave of cultural, religious, and ethnic influence: Latin, Christian, Roman, Saxon, and Norman. Yet they folded these elements into cultural expressions that remained distinctive in style and structure. As a people, too, the Welsh clung to beliefs that they were as ancient as the Trojans, and to prophecies that they would one day reconquer the Anglo-Saxon and Norman parvenus.

Especially in its reverence for the nearly supernatural role of the poet-prophet, *The Tale of Taliesin* is a genuine survival of medieval, even pagan, Welsh culture. Taliesin was regarded as the founder of Welsh poetry (for poems attributed to him, see pages 146–50), and as his reputation grew, so did his image. In this story Taliesin is a magician, trickster, shape-shifter, and prophet, an incarnation of bards and wise men from both the Celtic and Mediterranean past. Miraculously reborn, he is more the product of the elements than the child of mortal parents, and his consciousness crosses both time and space. He has the poetic learning of his ancestors, yet knows what is happening to his patron Elphin at a distant royal court. He can loose chains and render other bards dumb; and his keen powers of observation enable him to solve the mystery of a severed finger.

At the same time, the story deftly extends Taliesin's wisdom to encompass Old Testament prophecy, Roman myth, Christian practices such as the Eucharist, and the major languages of late medieval England. All this is done with lightness and wit, and the occasional (if still delighted) demur of the copyist. The tale also registers historical developments throughout Britain, though—not only by listing the competitor languages (Latin, French, and English) but also by acknowledging wryly that French is now the language of royal largesse.

---

7. You may and can and ought to be.

The Tale of Taliesin[1]

In the days when Maelgwn Gwynedd[2] was holding court in Castell Deganwy, there was a holy man named Cybi living in Môn.[3] Also in that time there lived a wealthy squire near Caer Deganwy, and the story says he was called Gwyddno Garanhir[4] (he was a lord). The text says that he had a weir on the shore of the Conway adjacent to the sea, in which was caught as much as ten pounds[5] worth of salmon every eve of All Hallows. The tale also says that Gwyddno had a son called Elphin son of Gwyddno, who was in service in the court of King Maelgwn. The text says that he was a noble and generous man, much loved among his companions, but that he was an incorrigible spendthrift—as are the majority of courtiers. As long as Gwyddno's wealth lasted, Elphin did not lack for money to spend among his friends. But as Gwyddno's riches began to dwindle, he stopped lavishing money on his son. The latter regretfully informed his friends that he was no longer able to maintain a social life and keep company with them in the manner he had been accustomed to in the past, because his father had fallen on hard times. But as before, he asked some of the men of the court to request the fish from the weir as a gift to him on the next All Hallow's eve; they did that and Gwyddno granted their petition.

And so when the day and the time arrived, Elphin took some servants with him, and came to set up and watch the weir, which he tended from high tide until the ebb.

When Elphin and his people came within the arms of the weir, they saw there neither head nor tail of a single young salmon; its sides were usually full of such on that night. But the story says that on this occasion he saw nothing but some dark hulk within the enclosure. On account of that, he lowered his head and began to protest his ill-fortune, saying as he turned homeward that his misery and misfortune were greater than those of any man in the world. Then it occurred to him to turn around and see what the thing in the weir was. Immediately, he found a coracle or hide-covered basket, wrapped from above as well as from below. Without delay, he took his knife and cut a slit in the hide, revealing a human forehead.

As soon as Elphin saw the forehead, he said, "behold the radiant forehead!"[6] To those words the child replied from the coracle, "Tal-iesin he is!" People suppose that this was the spirit of Gwion Bach, who had been in the womb of Ceridwen;[7] after she was delivered of him, she had cast him into fresh water or into the sea, as the present work shows above. He had been in the pouch, floating about in the sea, from the beginning of Arthur's time until about the beginning of Maelgwn's time—and that was approximately forty years.

Indeed, this is far from reason and sense. But as before, I will keep to the story, which says that Elphin took the bundle and placed it in a basket upon one of the horses. Thereupon, Taliesin sang the stanzas known as *Dehuddiant Elphin*, or, *Elphin's Consolation*, saying as follows:

---

1. From *The Mabinogi and Other Medieval Welsh Tales*, translated by Patrick K. Ford.
2. "*Mael-goon Gwi-neth*," a 6th-century king of Gwynedd, in northwestern Wales.
3. Pronounced "moan," the island of Anglesey, off northwestern Wales.
4. "*Gwith-no Ga-ron-hir*."
5. A great deal of money at the time.
6. In Welsh, *tal iesin*. This is only one of the legends that cluster around Taliesin; see page 146.
7. Gwion Bach ("Little Gwion") gained three magical drops, conferring wisdom, which the magician Ceridwen had intended for her son. Enraged, she pursued Gwion; when he took the form of a grain of wheat, she became a hen, swallowed him, and nine months later gave birth to him. Unwilling to kill the infant, she launched him in a small boat—a coracle.

Fair Elphin, cease your weeping!
  Despair brings no profit.
  No catch in Gwyddno's weir
  Was ever as good as tonight's.
  Let no one revile what is his.
  Man sees not what nurtures him;
  Gwyddno's prayers shall not be in vain.
  God breaks not his promises.

Fair Elphin, dry your cheeks!
  It does not become you to be sad.
  Though you think you got no gain
  Undue grief will bring you nothing—
  Nor will doubting the miracles of the Lord.
  Though I am small, I am gifted.
  From the sea and the mountain, from rivers' depths
  God sends bounty to the blessed.

Elphin of the cheerful disposition—
  Meek is your mind—
  You must not lament so heavily.
  Better God than gloomy foreboding.
  Though I am frail and little
  And wet with the spume of Dylan's sea,
  I shall earn in a day of contention
  Riches better than three score for you.

Elphin of the remarkable qualities.
  Grieve not for your catch.
  Though I am frail here in my bunting,
  There are wonders on my tongue.
  You must not fear greatly
  While I am watching over you.
  By remembering the name of the Trinity
  None can overcome you.

Together with various other stanzas which he sang to cheer Elphin along the path from there toward home, where Elphin turned over his catch to his wife. She raised him lovingly and dearly.

From that moment on, Elphin's wealth increased more and more each succeeding day, as well as his favor and acceptance with the king. Some while after this, at the feast of Christmas, the king was holding open court at Deganwy Castle, and all his lords—both spiritual and temporal—were there, with a multitude of knights and squires. Their conversation grew, as they queried one another, saying:

"Is there in the entire world a man as powerful as Maelgwn? Or one to whom the heavenly father has given as many spiritual gifts as God has given him: beauty, shape, nobility, and strength, besides all the powers of the soul?" And with these gifts, they proclaimed that the Father had given him an excellent gift, one that surpassed all of the others, namely, the beauty, appearance, demeanor, wisdom, and faithfulness of his queen. In these virtues, she excelled all the ladies and daughters of the nobility in the entire land. Beside that, they asked themselves: "whose men are more valiant? Whose horses and hounds are swifter and fairer? Whose bards more proficient and wiser than Maelgwn's?"

At that time poets were received with great esteem among the eminent ones of the realm. And in those days, none of whom we now call "heralds" were appointed to that office, unless they were learned men, and not only in the proper service of kings and princes, but steeped and skilled in pedigrees, arms, the deeds of kings and princes of foreign kingdoms as well as the ancestors of this kingdom, especially in the history of the chief nobility. Furthermore, each of these bards had to have their responses readily prepared in various languages, such as Latin, French, Welsh, and English, and in addition, be a great historian and good chronicler, be skilled in the composition of poetry and ready to compose metrical stanzas in each of these languages. On this feast, there was in the court of Maelgwn no less than twenty-four of these; chief among them was the one called Heinin Fardd the Poet.

And so after everyone had spoken in praise of the king and his blessings, Elphin happened to say this: "Indeed, no one can compete with a king except another king; but, truly, were he not a king, I would surely say that I had a wife as chaste as any lady in the kingdom. Furthermore, I have a bard who is more proficient than all the king's bards."

Some time later, the king's companions told him the extent of Elphin's boast, and the king commanded that he be put into a secure prison until he could get confirmation of his wife's chastity and his poet's knowledge. And after putting Elphin in one of the castle towers with a heavy chain on his feet (some people say that it was a silver chain that was put upon him, because he was of the king's blood), the story says that the king sent his son Rhun to test the continence of Elphin's wife. It says that Rhun was one of the lustiest men in the world, and that neither woman nor maiden with whom he had spent a diverting moment came away with her reputation intact.

As Rhun was hastening toward Elphin's residence, fully intending to despoil Elphin's wife, Taliesin was explaining to her how the king had thrown his master into prison and how Rhun was hurrying there with the intention of corrupting her virtue. Because of that he had his mistress dress one of the scullery maids in her own garb. The lady did this cheerfully and unstintingly, adorning the maid's fingers with the finest rings that she and her husband possessed. In this guise, Taliesin had his mistress seat the girl in her own chamber to sup at her own table and in her own place; Taliesin had made the girl look like his mistress, his mistress like the girl.

As they sat most handsomely at their supper in the manner described above, Rhun appeared suddenly at the court of Elphin. He was received cheerfully, for all the servants knew him well. They escorted him without delay to their mistress's chamber. The girl disguised as the mistress rose from her supper and greeted him pleasantly, then sat back down to her meal, and Rhun with her. He began to beguile the girl with seductive talk, while she preserved the mien of her mistress.

The story says that the maiden got so inebriated that she fell asleep. It says that Rhun had put a powder in her drink that made her sleep so heavily—if the tale can be believed—that she didn't even feel him cutting off her little finger, around which was Elphin's signet ring that he had sent to his wife as a token a short time before. In this way he did his will with the maiden, and afterwards, he took the finger—with the ring on it—to the king as proof. He told him that he had violated her chastity, explaining how he had cut off her finger as he left, without her awakening.

The king took great delight in this news, and, because of it, summoned his council, to whom he explained the whole affair from one end to the other. Then he had Elphin brought from the prison to taunt him for his boast, and said to him as follows:

"It should be clear to you, Elphin, and beyond doubt, that it is nothing but foolishness for any man in the world to trust his wife in the matter of chastity any farther than he can see her. And so that you may harbor no doubts that your wife broke her marriage vows last night, here is her finger as evidence for you, with your own signet ring on it; the one who lay with her cut it off her hand while she slept. So that there is no way that you can argue that she did not violate her fidelity."

To this Elphin replied, "with your permission, honorable king, indeed, there is no way I can deny my ring, for a number of people know it. But, indeed, I do deny vehemently that the finger encircled by my ring was ever on my wife's hand, for one sees there three peculiar things not one of which ever characterized a single finger of my wife's hands. The first of these is that—with your grace's permission—wherever my wife is at this moment, whether she is sitting, standing, or lying down, this ring will not even fit her thumb! And you can easily see that it was difficult to force the ring over the knuckle of the little finger of the hand from which it was cut. The second thing is that my wife has never gone a single Saturday since I have known her without paring her nails before going to bed. And you can see clearly that the nail of this finger has not been cut for a month. And the third thing, indeed, is that the hand from which this finger was cut kneaded rye dough within the past three days, and I assure you, your graciousness, that my wife has not kneaded rye dough since she became my wife."

The story says that the king became more outraged at Elphin for standing so firmly against him in the matter of his wife's fidelity. As a result, the king ordered him to be imprisoned again, saying that he would not gain release from there until he proved true his boast about the wisdom of his bard as well as about the fidelity of his wife.

Those two, meanwhile, were in Elphin's palace, taking their ease. Then Taliesin related to his mistress how Elphin was in prison on account of them. But he exhorted her to be of good cheer, explaining to her how he would go to the court of Maelgwn to free his master. She asked him how he could set his master free, and he replied as follows:

> I shall set out on foot,
>   Come to the gate,
>   And make for the hall.
> I shall sing my song
>   And proclaim my verse,
>   And the lord's bards I shall inhibit:
> Before the chief one
> I shall make demands,
> And I shall overcome them.
>
>   And when the contention comes
>   In the presence of the chieftains,
>   And a summons to the minstrels
>   For precise and harmonious songs
>   In the court of the scions of nobles,
>   Companion to Gwion,
>   There are some who assumed the appearance
>   Of anguish and great pains.

They shall fall silent by rough words,
   If it grows ever worse, like Arthur, Chief of givers,
   With his blades long and red
   From the blood of nobles;
   The king's battle against his enemies,
   Whose gentles' blood flows
   From the battle of the woods in the distant North.

May there be neither blessing nor beauty
   On Maelgwn Gwynedd,
   But let the wrong be avenged—
   And the violence and the arrogance—finally,
   For the act of Rhun his offspring:
   Let his lands be desolate,
   Let his life be short,
   Let the punishment last long
   On Maelgwn Gwynedd.

And after that he took leave of his mistress, and came at last to the court of Maelgwn Gwynedd. The latter, in his royal dignity, was going to sit in his hall at supper, as
kings and princes were accustomed to do on every high feast in those days. And as
soon as Taliesin came into the hall, he saw a place for himself to sit in an inconspicu-
ous corner, beside the place where the poets and minstrels had to pass to pay their
respects and duty to the king—as is still customary in proclaiming largess in the courts
on high holidays, except that they are proclaimed now in French. And so the time
came for the bards or the heralds to come and proclaim the *largesse*, power, and might
of the king. They came past the spot where Taliesin sat hunched over in the corner,
and as they went by, he puckered his lips and with his finger made a sound like *blerum
blerum*. Those going past paid no attention to him, but continued on until they stood
before the king. They performed their customary curtsy as they were obliged to do; not
a single word came from their mouths, but they puckered up, made faces at the king,
and made the *blerum blerum* sound on their lips with their fingers as they had seen the
lad do it earlier. The sight astonished the king, and he wondered to himself whether
they had had too much to drink. So he ordered one of the lords who was administering
to his table to go to them and ask them to summon their wits and reflect upon where
they were standing and what they were obliged to do. The lord complied.

But they did not stop their nonsense directly, so he sent to them again, and a
third time, ordering them to leave the hall; finally, the king asked one of the squires
to clout their chief, the one called Heinin Fardd. The squire seized a platter and
struck him over the head with it until he fell back on his rump. From that spot, he
rose up onto his knees whence he begged the king's mercy and leave to show him that
it was neither of the two failings on them—neither lack of intelligence nor drunkenness—but due to some spirit that was inside the hall. And then Heinin said as follows:
"O glorious king! Let it be known to your grace, that it is not from the pickling effect
of a surfeit of spirits that we stand here dumb, unable to speak properly, like drunk-
ards, but because of a spirit, who sits in the corner yonder, in the guise of a little man."

Whereupon, the king ordered a squire to fetch him. He went to the corner
where Taliesin sat, and brought him thence before the king, who asked him what sort
of thing he was and whence he came. He answered the king in verse, and spoke as
follows:

Official chief-poet
    to Elphin am I,
And my native abode
    is the land of the Cherubim.

Then the king asked him what he was called, and he answered him saying this:

Johannes the prophet
    called me Merlin,[8]
But now all kings
    call me Taliesin.

Then the king asked him where he had been, and thereupon he recited his history to the king, as follows here in this work:

I was with my lord
    in the heavens
When Lucifer fell
    into the depths of hell;
I carried a banner
    before Alexander;
I know the stars' names
    from the North to the South
I was in the fort of Gwydion,[9]
    in the Tetragramaton;[1]
I was in the canon
    when Absalon was killed;
I brought seed down
    to the vale of Hebron;
I was in the court of Dôn
    before the birth of Gwydion;
I was patriarch
    to Elijah and Enoch;
I was head keeper
    on the work of Nimrod's tower;
I was atop the cross
    of the merciful son of God;
I was three times
    in the prison of Arianrhod;[2]
I was in the ark
    with Noah and Alpha;
I witnessed the destruction
    of Sodom and Gomorrah;
I was in Africa
    before the building of Rome;
I came here
    to the survivors of Troy.[3]

8. Taliesin claims still another poetic incarnation as Merlin, and links him in turn to John the Baptist.
9. The magician Gwydion, son of the goddess Dôn.
1. The four Hebrew letters that spell God's name, Yahweh. The text continues its playful combination of ancient Celtic and Christian references.
2. A daughter of the goddess Dôn.
3. As descendants of the ancient Britons (founded by Brutus), the Welsh claimed Trojan lineage and an antiquity as great as the Romans.

And I was with my lord
        in the manger of oxen and asses;
I upheld Moses
        through the water of Jordan;
I was in the sky
        with Mary Magdalen;
I got poetic inspiration
        from the cauldron of Ceridwen;[4]
I was poet-harper
        to Lleon Llychlyn;
I was in Gwynfryn
        in the court of Cynfelyn;
In stock and fetters
        a day and a year.

I was revealed
        in the land of the Trinity;
And I was moved
        through the entire universe;
And I shall remain till doomsday,
        upon the face of the earth.
And no one knows what my flesh is—
        whether meat or fish.

And I was nearly nine months
        in the womb of the witch Ceridwen;
I was formerly Gwion Bach,
        but now I am Taliesin.

And the story says that this song amazed the king and his court greatly. Then he sang a song to explain to the king and his people why he had come there and what he was attempting to do, as the following poem sets forth.

Provincial bards! I am contending!
        To refrain I am unable.
        I shall proclaim in prophetic song
        To those that will listen.
        And I seek that loss
        That I suffer:
        Elphin, from the punishment
        Of Caer Deganwy.

And from him, my lord will pull
        The binding chain.
        The Chair of Caer Deganwy—
        Mighty is my pride—
        Three hundred songs and more
        Are the songs I shall sing;
        No bard that knows them not

---

4. Ceridwen prepared the three drops conferring wisdom in a great cauldron; it cried out and burst when the drops fell on Gwion Bach.

Shall merit spear
Nor stone nor ring,
Nor remain about me.

Elphin son of Gwyddno
Suffers torment now,
'Neath thirteen locks
For praising his master-bard.

And I am Taliesin,
Chief-poet of the West,
And I shall release Elphin
From the gilded fetters.

After this, as the text shows, he sang a song of succor, and they say that instantly a tempestuous wind arose, until the king and his people felt that the castle would fall upon them. Because of that, the king had Elphin fetched from prison in a hurry, and brought to the side of Taliesin. He is said to have sung a song at that moment that resulted in the opening of the fetters from around his feet—indeed, in my opinion, it is very difficult for anyone to believe that this tale is true. But I will continue the story with as many of the poems by him as I have seen written down.

Following this, he sang the verses called "Interrogation of the Bards," which follows herewith.

What being first
Made Alpha?
What is the fairest refined language
Designed by the Lord?

What food? What drink?
Whose raiment prudent?
Who endured rejection
From a deceitful land?

Why is a stone hard?
Why is a thorn sharp?
Who is hard as a stone,
And as salty as salt?

Why is the nose like a ridge?
Why is the wheel round?
Why does the tongue articulate
More than any one organ?

Then he sang a series of verses called "The Rebuke of the Bards," and it begins like this:

If you are a fierce bard
Of spirited poetic-inspiration,
Be not testy
In your king's court,
Unless you know the name for *rimin*,[5]

5. A nonsense word, as are *ramin, rimiad,* and *ramiad* in the lines that follow.

And the name for *ramin*,
And the name for *rimiad*,
And the name for *ramiad*,
And the name of your forefather
Before his baptism.

And the name of the firmament,
And the name of the element,
And the name of your language,
And the name of your district.

Company of poets above,
Company of poets below;
My darling is below
'Neath the fetters of Aranrhod.
You certainly do not know
The meaning of what my lips sing,
Nor the true distinction
Between the true and the false.
Bards of limited horizons,
Why do you not flee?
The bard who cannot shut me up
Shall have no quiet
Till he come to rest
Beneath a gravelly grave.
And those who listen to me,
Let God listen to them.

And after this follows the verses called "The Satire on the Bards."

Minstrels of malfeasance make
    Impious lyrics; in their praise
    They sing vain and evanescent song,
    Ever exercising lies.
    They mock guileless men
    They corrupt married women,
    They despoil Mary's chaste maidens.
    Their lives and times they waste in vain,
    They scorn the frail and the guileless,
    They drink by night, sleep by day,
    Idly, lazily, making their way.
    They despise the Church
    Lurch toward the taverns;
    In harmony with thieves and lechers,
    They seek out courts and feasts,
    Extol every idiotic utterance,
    Praise every deadly sin.
    They lead every manner of base life,
    Roam every village, town, and land.
    The distresses of death concern them not,
    Never do they give lodging or alms.
    Excessive food they consume.
    They rehearse neither the psalms nor prayer,

Pay neither tithes nor offerings to God,
Worship not on Holy Days nor the Lord's day,
Fast on neither Holy Days nor ember days.
   Birds fly,
   Fish swim,
   Bees gather honey,
   Vermin crawl;
   Everything bustles
   To earn its keep
   Except minstrels and thieves, the lazy and worthless.

I do not revile your minstrelsy.
For God gave that to ward off evil blasphemy;
But he who practices it in perfidy
Reviles Jesus and his worship.

After Taliesin had freed his master from prison, verified the chastity of his mistress, and silenced the bards so that none of them dared say a single word, he asked Elphin to wager the king that he had a horse faster and swifter than all the king's horses. Elphin did that.

On the day, time, and place determined—the place known today as Morfa Rhianedd—the king arrived with his people and twenty-four of the swiftest horses he owned. Then, after a long while, the course was set, and a place for the horses to run. Taliesin came there with twenty-four sticks of holly, burnt black. He had the lad who was riding his master's horse put them under his belt, instructing him to let all the king's horses go ahead of him, and as he caught up with each of them in turn, to take one of the rods and whip the horse across his rump, and then throw it to the ground. Then take another rod and do in the same manner to each of the horses as he overtook them. And he instructed the rider to observe carefully the spot where his horse finished, and throw down his cap on that spot.

The lad accomplished all of this, both the whipping of each of the king's horses as well as throwing down his cap in the place where the horse finished. Taliesin brought his master there after his horse won the race, and he and Elphin set men to work to dig a hole. When they had dug the earth to a certain depth, they found a huge cauldron of gold, and therewith Taliesin said, "Elphin, here is payment and reward for you for having brought me from the weir and raising me from that day to this." In that very place there stands a pool of water, which from that day to this is called "Cauldon's Pool."

After that, the king had Taliesin brought before him, and asked for information concerning the origin of the human race. Forthwith, he sang the verses that follow here below, and that are known today as one of the four pillars of song. They begin as follows:

Here begin the prophecies of Taliesin.

   The Lord made
   In the midst of Glen Hebron
   With his blessed hands,
      I know, the shape of Adam.

5   He made the beautiful;
   In the court of paradise,
   From a rib, he put together
      Fair woman.

Seven hours they
10 Tended the Orchard
Before Satan's strife,
    Most insistent suitor.

Thence they were driven
Through cold and chill
15 To lead their lives
    In this world.

To bear in affliction
Sons and daughters,
To get tribute
20   From the land of Asia.

One hundred and eight
Was she fertile,
Bearing a mixed brood,
    Masculine and feminine.

25 And then, openly,
When she bore Abel
And Cain, unconcealable,
    Most unredeemable.

To Adam and his mate
30 Was given a digging shovel
To break the earth
    To gain bread.

And shining white wheat
To sow, the instrument
35 To feed all men
    Until the great feast.

Angels sent
From God Almighty
Brought the seed of growth
40   To Eve.

She hid
A tenth of the gift
So that not all did
    The whole garden enclose.

45 But black rye was had
In place of the fine wheat,
Showing the evil
    For stealing.

Because of that treacherous turn,
50 It is necessary, says Sattwrn,
For each to give his tithe
    To God first.

From crimson red wine
Planted on a sunny day,

55   And the moon's night prevails
      Over white wine.

   From wheat of true privilege,
   From red wine generous and privileged.
   Is made the finely molded body
60   Of Christ son of Alpha.

   From the wafer is the flesh.
   From the wine is the flow of blood.
   And the words of the Trinity
      Consecrated him.

65   Every sort of mystical book
   Of Emmanuel's work
   Rafael brought
      To give to Adam.

   When he was in ferment,
70   Above his two jaws
   Within the Jordan River
      Fasting.

   Moses found,
   To guard against great need,
75   The secret of the three
      Most famous rods.

   Samson got
   Within the tower of Babylon
   All the magical arts
80   Of Asia land.

   I got, indeed,
   In my bardic song,
   All the magical arts
      Of Europe and Africa.

85   And I know whence she emanates
   And her home and her hospitality,
   Her fate and her destiny
      Till Doomsday.

   Alas, God, how wretched,
90   Through excessive plaint,
   Comes the prophecy
      To the race of Troy.

   A coiled serpent,
   Proud and merciless,
95   With golden wings
      Out of Germany.

   It shall conquer
   England and Scotland,
   From the shore of the Scandinavian Sea
100   To the Severn.

Then shall the Britons be
Like prisoners,
With status of aliens,
    To the Saxons.

105   Their lord they shall praise.
Their language preserve,
And their land they will lose—
    Save wild Wales.

Until comes a certain period
110   After long servitude,
When shall be of equal duration
    The two proud ones.

Then will the Britons gain
Their land and their crown,
115   And the foreigners
    Will disappear.

And the words of the angels
On peace and war
Will be true
120   Concerning Britain.

And after this he proclaimed to the king various prophecies in verse, concerning the world that would come hereafter.

Dafydd ap Gwilym

Widely regarded as the greatest Welsh poet, Dafydd ap Gwilym flourished in the fourteenth century, during a period of relative peace between two failed rebellions—that of Llywelyn, the last native prince of Wales, in 1282, and that of Owain Glyn Dwr (Owen Glendower), in 1400. A member of an upper-class family whose ancestors had served the English king, he wrote for a sophisticated audience of poets and patrons.

Dafydd drew inspiration from both continental and Welsh poetry but not, significantly, from English. (Influence, if any, went the other way, for the Middle English Harley lyrics, composed near the Welsh border, may owe their intricate rhyme scheme and ornamental alliteration to Welsh poetry; see *Spring* and *Alisoun*, pages 551–53). Among continental poets, the Roman Ovid is the greatest influence, whether directly or through twelfth-century Latin adaptations. He is the only foreign poet whom Dafydd mentions by name (*One Saving Place*, line 39). Dafydd is also indebted to medieval French and Provençal lyric genres—the *aubade* (dawn song), and the *reverdie* (spring song)—as well as to the *fabliau*.

Much of Dafydd's charm comes from his undercutting and transforming inherited poetic conventions through his personal revelations. His most endearing device, the self-deprecating persona, has been compared to that of his younger contemporary, Geoffrey Chaucer. There is an important difference, however, for while Chaucer in early love poems like *The Parliament of Fowls* presents himself as a failed lover, Dafydd often boasts of his success. Although he gives comic accounts of romantic failures in such anecdotal poems as *The Girls of Llanbadarn* (in which the women he ogles in church scornfully dismiss him) and the *Tale of a Wayside Inn* (in which a tryst ends in disaster when he goes to the wrong room), these are as often due to external obstacles as to his own inadequacy. In fact, Dafydd's persona is much more akin to Ovid's than to Chaucer's, with *The Hateful Husband* echoing the exasperated and scheming lover of *Amores* 1.4 and 1.6. In *The Ruin*, Dafydd gives an erotic twist to the ascetic Christian motif of the impermanence of worldly pleasures (as in the Old English *Wanderer*, page 150, and the Middle English *Contempt of the World*, page 563) by recalling that he once made love in a cottage that is now abandoned. He concludes his complaint *The Winter* with the observation that he would not venture out in such snowy weather for the sake of any girl.

Dafydd's poetry owes an equal debt to the rich poetic tradition of Wales. He shows familiarity with characters from the Arthurian tradition, which was originally Celtic although transformed by French adaptations by the time it reached him (see *The Tale of Taliesin*, page 565). In the poems included here, he often emphasizes the local Welsh setting. In *One Saving Place*, for instance, he lists all the locales where he sought his beloved Morvith, or she refused him—places with names like Meirch, Eleirch, Rhiw, and Cwcwll hollow. In *The Winter*, it is specifically in north Wales that he is assailed by snow. Finally, part of the humor in the *Tale of a Wayside Inn* derives from Dafydd's self-presentation as a "Welshman" whose accidental presence in their bedroom is discovered by three coarse Englishmen.

Dafydd's work is also distinguished by the poetic techniques of Welsh poetry, which are extraordinarily complex. His *cywyddau* (lyric poems) are written in the traditional lines of seven syllables, which rhyme in couplets, with the rhyming syllables alternately stressed and unstressed. He applies further ornamentation with a technique called *cynghanned*—internal alliteration or rhyme, which he sometimes extends over many lines. Although such an intricate style is impossible to capture in English, Rolfe Humphries has tried to approximate it in the translations given here. Easier to reproduce are Daffyd's *dyfalu*—strings of fanciful comparisons, such as the metaphors for snow used in *The Winter*:

> The snowflakes wander,
> A swarm of white bees.
> Over the woods
> A cold veil lies.
> A load of chalk
> Bows down the trees.
>
> * * *
>
> Will someone tell me
> What angels lift
> Planks in the flour-loft
> Floor of heaven
> Shaking down dust?
> An angel's cloak
> Is cold quicksilver.

In extending the virtuoso techniques of the native tradition, Dafydd set the standard for Welsh poets for the next two centuries.

Aubade[1]

> It seemed as if we did not sleep
> One wink that night; I was sighing deep.
> The cruellest judge in the costliest court

1. The aubade or dawn song is a genre of love lyric with a long European tradition, in which two lovers lament the necessity of parting at dawn. Chaucer uses the aubade, as later do Shakespeare (in *Romeo and Juliet*) and John Donne in *The Sun Rising*.

Could not condemn a night so short.
5   We had the light out, but I know,
Each time I turned, a radiant glow
Suffused the room, and shining snow
Alit from Heaven's candle-fires
Illuminated our desires.

10   But the last time I held her, strong,
Excited, closest, very long,
Something started going wrong.
The edge of dawn's despotic veil
Showed at the eastern window-pale
15   And there it was,—the morning light!
Gwen[2] was seized with a fearful fright,
Became an apparition, cried,
"Get up, go now with God, go hide!

"Love is a salt, a gall, a rue,
20   A vinegar-vintage. *Dos y Ddw,*
Vaya con Dios,[3] quickly, too!"
"Ah, not yet, never yet, my love;
The stars and moon still shine above."
"Then why do the raucous ravens talk
25   With such a loud insistent squawk?"
"Crows always cry like that, when fleas
Nibble their ankles, nip their knees."

"And why do the dogs yip, yammer, yell?"
"They think they've caught a fox's smell."
30   "Poet, the wisdom of a fool
Offers poor counsel as a rule.
Open the door, open it wide
As fast as you can, and leap outside.
The dogs are fierce when they get untied."
35   "The woods are only a bound from here,
And I can outjump a deer, my dear!"

"But tell me, best beloved of men,
Will you come again? Will you come again?"
"Gwen, you know I'm your nightingale,
40   And I'll be with you, without fail,
When the cloud is cloak, and the dark is sky,
And when the night comes, so will I."

One Saving Place

What wooer ever walked through frost and snow,
Through rain and wind, as I in sorrow?
My two feet took me to a tryst in Meirch[1]

---

2. Along with Morvith and Dovekie, a woman's name
which recurs in many of Dafydd's love poems.
3. "Go with God"; this Spanish phrase represents license,
on the part of the translator, in the spirit of Dafydd's

playfulness.
1. This and other Welsh place names are listed by Dafydd
in his account of his search for his beloved, Morvith.

	No luck; I swam and waded the Eleirch,
5	No golden loveliness, no glimpse of her;
	Night or day, I came no nearer
	Except in Bleddyn's arbors, where I sighed
	When she refused me, as she did beside
	Maesalga's murmuring water-tide.
10	I crossed the river, Bergul, and went on
	Beyond its threatening voices; I have gone
	Through the mountain-pass of Meibion,
	Came to Camallt, dark in my despair,
	For one vision of her golden hair.
15	All for nothing. I've looked down from Rhiw,
	All for nothing but a valley view,
	Kept on going, on my journey through
	Cyfylfaen's gorge, with rock and boulder,
	Where I had thought to ermine-cloak her shoulder.
20	Never; not here, there, thither, thence,
	Could I ever find her presence.
	Eagerly on summer days I'd go
	Brushing my way through Cwcwll hollow,
	Never stopped, continued, skirting
25	Gastell Gwrgan and its ring
	Where the red-winged blackbirds sing,
	Tramped across fields where goslings feed
	Below the cat-tail and the reed.
	I have limped my way, a weary hound,
30	In shadow of the walls that bound
	Adail Heilyn's broken ground.
	I have hidden, like a friar,
	In Ifor's Court, among the choir,
	Sought to seek my sweet one there,
35	But there was no sign of her.
	On both sides of Nant-y-glo
	There's no vale, no valley, no
	Stick or stump where I failed to go,
	Only Gwynn of the Mist for guide,
40	Without Ovid[2] at my side.
	Gwenn-y-Talwrn!—there I found
	My hand close on hers, on ground
	Where no grass was ever green,
	Where not even a shrub was seen,
45	There at last I made the bed
	For my Morvith,[3] my moon-maid,
	Underneath the dark leaf-cloak
	Woven by saplings of an oak.
	Bitter, if a man must move
50	On his journeys without love.
	Bitter, if soul's pilgrimage

2. See introduction for Dafydd's indebtedness to the Roman love poet.

3. The lady most frequently mentioned in Dafydd's love poems, apparently married.

Must be like the body's rage,
Must go down the desolate road
Midway through the darkling wood.

The Girls of Llanbadarn[1]

I am one of passion's asses,
Plague on all these parish lasses!
Though I long for them like mad,
Not one female have I had,
5   Not a one in all my life,
Virgin, damsel, hag, or wife.
What maliciousness, what lack,
What does make them turn their back?
Would it be a shame to be
10   In a bower of leaves with me?
No one's ever been so bitched,
So bewildered, so bewitched
Saving Garwy's[2] lunatics
By their foul fantastic tricks.
15   So I fall in love, I do,
Every day, with one or two,
Get no closer, any day,
Than an arrow's length away.
Every single Sunday, I,
20   Llanbadarn can testify,
Go to church and take my stand
With my plumed hat in my hand,
Make my reverence to the altar,
Find the right page in my psalter,
25   Turn my back on holy God,
Face the girls, and wink, and nod
For a long, long time, and look
Over feather, at the folk.
Suddenly, what do I hear?
30   A stage whisper, all too clear,
A girl's voice, and her companion
Isn't slow at catching on?
"See that simple fellow there,
Pale and with his sister's hair
35   Giving me those leering looks
Wickeder than any crook's?"
"Don't you think that he's sincere?"
Asks the other in her ear.

"All I'll give him is *Get out!*
40   Let the Devil take the lout!"
Pretty payment, in return
For the love with which I burn.

---

1. A village near the busy Welsh market town of   2. A legendary lover.
Aberystwyth.

Burn for what? The bright girl's gift
Offers me the shortest shrift.
45   I must give them up, resign
These fear-troubled hopes of mine:
Better be a hermit, thief,
Anything, to bring relief.
Oh, strange lesson, that I must
50   Go companionless and lost,
Go because I looked too long,
I, who loved the power of song.

Tale of a Wayside Inn

With one servant, I went down
To a sportive sort of town
Where a Welshman might secure
Comely welcome, and pleasure.
5   There we found the book to sign
In the inn, and ordered wine.

But whatever did I see
But the loveliest lady
Blooming beautiful and bright,
10   Blossom stemming from sunlight,
Graceful as the gossamer.
I said, "Let me banquet her!"
Feasting's a fine way, it seems,
For fulfilling young men's dreams.

15   So, unshy, she took her seat
At my side, and we did eat,
Sipped our wine, and smiled and dallied
Like a man and maid, new-married.
Bold I was, but whispering,
20   And the others heard nothing.

Troth and tryst we pledged, to keep
When the others were asleep.
I should find my way, and come
Through the darkness to her room.
25   Love would haul my steps aright
Down the hallways of the night;
Love would steer my steps,—alas,
This was not what came to pass.
For, by some outrageous miss,
30   What I got was not a kiss,
But a stubble-whiskered cheek
And a triple whiskey-reek,
Not one Englishman, but three,
(What a Holy Trinity!)
35   Diccon, 'Enry, Jerk-off Jack,
Each one pillowed on his pack.

One of them let out a yell,
"What's that thing I think I smell?
There's a Welshman must have hid
40 In the closet or under t' bed,
Come to cut our throats with knives,
Guard your wallets and your lives,
They're all thieves, beyond all doubt,
Throw the bloody bugger out!"

45 None too nimble for my need,
First I found how shins will bleed
When you bark them in your haste
On a stool that's been misplaced
By some ostler-stupid fool,
50 Then the sawney of a stool
Squealed its pig-stuck tattle-tale
After my departing trail.

By good luck, I never got
Wet-foot from the chamber-pot.
55 That was all I saved myself,
Knocked my noggin on a shelf,
Overturned the table-trestles,
Down came all the pans and kettles.
As I dove to outer dark,
60 All the dogs began to bark.

Asses bray, and scullions rouse
Every sleeper in the house.
I could hear the hunt come round me,
Scowl-faced scoundrels, till they found me.
65 I could feel their stones and sticks,
So I clasped my crucifix,
Jesu, Jesu, Jesu dear,
Don't let people catch me here!

Since my prayer was strong, I came
70 Through the mercy of His name
Safely to my room at last,
All my perils over-passed.
No girl's love to ease my plight,
Only God's that dreadful night,
75 To the saints be brought the praise,
And the Good Lord mend my wicked ways.

The Hateful Husband

'Tis sorrow and pain,
'Tis endless chagrin
For Dafydd to gain
His dark-haired girl.
5 Her house is a jail,
Her turnkey a vile,

Sour, yellow-eyed, pale,
Odious churl.

She cannot go out
10   Unless he's about,
The blackguard, the lout,
The stingy boor.
The look in her eye
Of fondness for me—
15   God bless her bounty!—
He can't endure.

I know he hates play:
The greenwood in May,
The birds' roundelay
20   Are not for him.
The cuckoo, I know,
He'd never allow
To sing on his bough,
Light on his limb

25   The flash of the wing,
The swell of the song,
Harp-music playing
Draw his black looks.
The hounds in full cry,
30   A race-horse of bay,
He cannot enjoy
More than the pox.

My heart would be glad
At seeing him laid
35   All gray in his shroud;
How could I grieve?
Should he die this year,
I'd give him with cheer
Good oak for his bier,
40   Sods for his grave.

O starling, O swift,
Go soaring aloft,
Come down to the croft
By Dovekie's home.
45   This message give her,
Tell her I love her,
And I will have her,
All in good time.

The Winter

Across North Wales
The snowflakes wander,
A swarm of white bees.
Over the woods

5   A cold veil lies.
       A load of chalk
       Bows down the trees.

       No undergrowth
       Without its wool,
10   No field unsheeted;
       No path is left
       Through any field;
       On every stump
       White flour is milled.

15   Will someone tell me
       What angels lift
       Planks in the flour-loft
       Floor of heaven
       Shaking down dust?
20   An angel's cloak
       Is cold quicksilver.

       And here below
       The big drifts blow,
       Blow and billow
25   Across the heather
       Like swollen bellies.
       The frozen foam
       Falls in fleeces.

       Out of my house
30   I will not stir
       For any girl
       To have my coat
       Look like a miller's
       Or stuck with feathers
35   Of eider down.

       What a great fall
       Lies on my country!
       A wide wall, stretching
       One sea to the other,
40   Greater and graver
       Than the sea's graveyard.
       When will rain come?

The Ruin

       Nothing but a hovel now
       Between moorland and meadow,
       Once the owners saw in you
       A comely cottage, bright, new,
5   Now roof, rafters, ridge-pole, all
       Broken down by a broken wall.

A day of delight was once there
For me, long ago, no care
When I had a glimpse of her
10   Fair in an ingle-corner.
Beside each other we lay
In the delight of that day.

Her forearm, snowflake-lovely,
Softly white, pillowing me,
15   proferred a pleasant pattern
For me to give in my turn,
And that was our blessing for
The new-cut lintel and door.

"Now the wild wind, wailing by,
20   Crashes with curse and with cry
Against my stones, a tempest
Born and bred in the East,
Or south ram-batterers break
The shelter that folk forsake."

25   Life is illusion and grief;
A tile whirls off, as a leaf
Or a lath goes sailing, high
In the keening of kite-kill cry.
Could it be, our couch once stood
30   Sturdily under that wood?

"Pillar and post, it would seem
Now you are less than a dream.
Are you that, or only the lost
Wreck of a riddle, rune-ghost?"

35   "Dafydd, the cross on their graves
Marks what little it saves,
Says, *They did well in their lives.*"

MIDDLE SCOTS POETS

In the late fifteenth and early sixteenth centuries, Scotland enjoyed a brief flowering of poetry centered in a sophisticated court society. Relations with England were fraught with irony, marked, on the one hand, by royal alliance (James IV married Margaret Tudor, daughter of England's Henry VII in 1503) and on the other by disastrous warfare (James IV also, in alliance with France, invaded England and perished with most of the Scottish nobility at the Battle of Flodden in 1513). The poets of this period have been variously known as the "Scottish Chaucerians," the "Middle Scots Poets," and the "Makars"—each term privileging a significant, though only partial, aspect of their work. The first conveys the debt that William Dunbar, Robert Henryson, and Gavin Douglas (to name the three most famous) owed to Chaucer's subject matter, rhetorical style, and techniques of parody. The second suggests their equal debt to a native Scottish tradition, which includes such overtly nationalist works as Barbour's *Bruce* and Blind Harry's *Wallace.* The best term to describe these poets is perhaps the one used by Dunbar himself—"Makars" (makers)—for it suggests their powerful and self-conscious artistry.

William Dunbar

Of all the Makars, Dunbar is the greatest virtuoso, intoxicated with language, whether it be the elevated vocabulary borrowed from Latin, or the Germanic diction of alliterative poetry, whose tradition was kept alive in Scotland a century after it had died out in England. He was versatile in his choice of genres, writing occasional poems (such an an allegory in celebration of the marriage of James IV and Princess Margaret), divine poems, and parodies such as *The Tretis of Two Mariit Wemen and the Wedo*, a bawdy satire on the morals of court ladies written in the traditional alliterative long line. Included here are a meditation on death (*Lament for the Makars*), an Easter hymn (*Done Is a Battell*) and a parody of the courtly genre of the *chanson d'aventure* (*In Secreit Place This Hyndir Nycht*).

Lament for the Makars[1]

	I that in heill° wes° and gladnes	*health / was*
	Am trublit now with gret seiknes	
	And feblit with infermite:	
	Timor mortis conturbat me.[2]	
5	Our plesance heir is all vane glory,	
	This fals warld is bot transitory,	
	The flesche is brukle,° the Fend° is sle:°	*frail / Devil / sly*
	Timor mortis conturbat me.	
	The stait of man dois change and vary,	
10	Now sound, now seik, now blith, now sary,	
	Now dansand mery, now like to dee:°	*die*
	Timor mortis conturbat me.	
	No stait in erd° heir standis sickir;°	*on earth / secure*
	As with the wynd wavis the wickir,	
15	Wavis this warldis vanite:	
	Timor mortis conturbat me.	
	On to the ded gois all estatis,	
	Princis, prelotis,° and potestatis,°	*prelates / rulers*
	Baith riche and pur of al degre:	
20	*Timor mortis conturbat me.*	
	He takis the knychtis° in to feild,°	*knights / the field*
	Anarmit° under helme and scheild; armed	*armed*
	Victour he is at all mellie:°.	*battles*
	Timor mortis conturbat me.	

---

1. This poem reflects the late medieval fascination with death. The speaker wistfully observes that beautiful ladies, brave knights, and wise clerks have had their lives cut short but gives most of his attention to poets. He lists 23 of these—three English (Chaucer, Gower, and Lydgate) and 20 Scots, only half of whom modern scholars can identify. Since Death has taken all his "brothers," he regards himself as next and resolves to prepare himself for the next world. The poem was printed in 1508 by Walter Chepman and Andrew Myllar, who introduced the printing press to Scotland.
2. Fear of death shakes me (from the liturgical Office of the Dead).

I have be° the very mene° for yowr restitucion.　　　　　　　*been / true means*
Mercy is my name, that mournith for yowr offence.
Diverte not yowrsilffe in time of temptacion,
20　　That ye may be acceptable to Gode at yowr going hence.°　　*at your death*
The grett mercy of Gode, that is of most preemminence,
By mediacion of Owr Lady, that is ever habundaunte
To the sinfull creature that will repent his necligence.[5]
I prey Gode, at yowr most nede, that mercy be yowr
　　defendawnte.

25　　In goode werkys I avise yow, soverence,° to be perseveraunte　　*masters*
To purifye yowr sowlys, that they be not corrupte;
For yowr gostly° enmy will make his avaunte,°　　　　*spiritual / boast*
Yowr goode condicions° if he may interrupte.　　　　　　*habits*

O ye soverens[6] that sitt, and ye brothern[7] that stonde right
　　uppe,
30　　Prike° not yowr felicites in thingys transitorye!　　　　*Place*
Beholde not the erth, but lifte yowr eye uppe!
Se how the hede the members° daily do magnifye.°[8]　*members, limbs / worship*
Who is the hede, forsoth, I shall yow certifye:
I mene owr Saviowr, that was likynnyde° to a lambe;　　　*likened*
35　　Ande his saintys° be the members that daily he doth
　　satisfye　　　　　　　　　　　　　　　　　　　　　*saints, believers*
With the preciose rever° that runnith from his wombe.°[9]　*river / abdomen*

Ther is none such foode, by water nor by londe,°　　　*i.e., anywhere*
So preciouse, so gloriouse, so nedefull to owr entent;°　　*purpose*
For it hath dissolvyde° mankinde from the bitter bonde　*dissolved, freed*
40　　Of the mortall enmye, that venimousse° serpente—　　*venomous*
From the whiche Gode preserve yow all at the Last Jugement!
For sekirly° ther shall be a strait° examinacion:　　*surely / strict*
The corn° shall be savyde, the chaffe shall be brente.°　*grain / burned*
I besech yow hertily, have this in premeditacion.°　*bear this in mind*
　　[*Enter Mischief.*]

MISCHEFFE: I beseche yow hertily, leve yowr calculacion!
Leve yowr chaffe, leve yowr corn, leve yowr daliacion!°　　*idle talk*
Yowr witt is lityll, yowr hede is mekyll, ye are full of
　　predicacion.°　　　　　　　　　　　　　　　　　*preaching*
But, ser, I prey you this question to clarifye:
Misse-masche, driff-draff,[1]
50　　Sume° was corn and sume was chaffe,　　　　　　*Some*
My dame seyde my name was Raffe;
On-schett° yowr lokke and take an halpenye.　　*Unshut, open*

---

5. The great mercy of God, which is preeminent, is always abundant by means of Our Lady's intercession to the sinful man who will repent his waywardness.
6. Rich masters with seats.
7. Comrades, those of lower status who are standing.

8. See (by way of analogy) how the body's limbs defer to the head (as we should worship God).
9. I.e., Christ's blood, issuing from the wound made by a spear.
1. Nonsense verse.

25   That strang unmercifull tyrand
      Takis, on the moderis° breist sowkand,°   *mother's / sucking*
      The bab full of benignite:
          Timor mortis conturbat me.

      He takis the campion° in the stour,°   *champion / conflict*
30   The capitane closit in the tour,
      The lady in bour° full of bewte: *bower*
          Timor mortis conturbat me.

      He sparis no lord for his piscence,°   *power*
      Na clerk for his intelligence;
35   His awfull strak° may no man fle: *stroke*
          Timor mortis conturbat me.

      Art magicianis and astrologgis,
      Rethoris,° logicianis and theologgis,   *rhetoricians*
      Thame helpis no conclusionis sle:°   *clever*
40   *Timor mortis conturbat me.*

      In medicyne the most practicianis,
      Lechis,° surrigianis,° and phisicianis,   *doctors / surgeons*
      Thame self fra ded° may not supple:°   *death / deliver*
          Timor mortis conturbat me.

45   I se that makaris° amang the laif°   *poets / remainder*
      Playis heir ther pageant, syne gois to graif;°   *grave*
      Sparit° is nocht ther faculte: *spared*
          Timor mortis conturbat me.

      He hes done petuously devour
50   The noble Chaucer of makaris flour,°   *flower of poets*
      The Monk of Bery,³ and Gower, all thre:
          Timor mortis conturbat me.

      The gude Syr Hew of Eglintoun,⁴
      And eik Heryot, and Wyntoun,⁵
55   He hes tane out of this cuntre:
          Timor mortis conturbat me.

      That scorpion fell° hes done infek°   *fierce / infect*
      Maister Johne Clerk and James Afflek⁶
      Fra ballat making and tragidie:
60   *Timor mortis conturbat me.*

      Holland and Barbour⁷ he hes berevit;
      Allace,° that he nocht with us levit   *alas*
      Schir Mungo Lokert of the Le:⁸
          Timor mortis conturbat me.

3. John Lydgate, monk of Bury St. Edmunds, a minor poet who was an imitator of Chaucer. He also used the *"timor mortis"* refrain in a poem on the same subject.
4. Brother-in-law of Robert II and not otherwise known as a poet.
5. Andrew of Wyntoun, author of the *Oryginale Chronykil of Scotland.*

6. These two are unknown, as are the other poets in this list not identified.
7. Sir Richard Holland, author of the allegorical *Buke of the Howlat* (c. 1450), and John Barbour, author of the patriotic *Actes and Life . . . of Robert Bruce* (1376).
8. This Scotsman (d. 1489?) is not otherwise known as a poet.

65   Clerk of Tranent eik he hes tane,
      That maid the Anteris° of Gawane;   *adventures*
      Schir Gilbert Hay endit hes he:[9]
          Timor mortis conturbat me.

      He hes Blind Hary and Sandy Traill
70   Slaine with his schour° of mortall haill,   *shower*
      Quhilk Patrik Johnestoun[1] mycht nocht fle:
          Timor mortis conturbat me.

      He hes reft° Merseir his endite°   *taken from / talent*
      That did in luf so lifly° write,   *in a lively manner*
75   So schort, so quyk, of sentence hie:
          Timor mortis conturbat me.

      He hes tane Roull of Aberdene
      And gentill Roull of Corstorphin;
      Two bettir fallowis did no man se:
80   *Timor mortis conturbat me.*

      In Dunfermelyne he hes done roune°   *held conversation*
      With Maister Robert Henrisoun.[2]
      Schir Johne the Ros enbrast° hes he: *embraced*
          Timor mortis conturbat me.

85   And he hes now tane last of aw
      Gud gentill Stobo and Quintyne Schaw,[3]
      Of quham all wichtis hes pete:[4]
          Timor mortis conturbat me.

      Gud Maister Walter Kennedy[5]
90   In° poynt of dede° lyis veraly;°   *on / death / truly*
      Gret reuth° it wer that so suld be: *pity*
          Timor mortis conturbat me.

      Sen he hes all my brether tane
      He will nocht lat me lif alane;
95   On forse° I man his nyxt pray be: *of necessity*
          Timor mortis conturbat me.

      Sen for the deid remeid° is none,   *remedy*
      Best is that we for dede dispone°   *prepare*
      Eftir our deid that lif may we:
          Timor mortis conturbat me.

9. The "clerk of Tranent" is unknown, but Arthurian romances focusing on Gawain were popular in Scotland; Sir Gilbert Hay (d. 1456) translated the poem *The Buik of Alexander* from French.
1. Blind Harry is credited with writing the Scots epic *Wallace* (c. 1475); Patrick Johnstoune was a producer of stage entertainments at court in the late 1400s.
2. Henryson was a major Middle Scots poet; see his *Robene and Makyne*, page 594.
3. John Reid, known as Stobo, was priest and secretary to James II, James III, and James IV; Schaw was a minor Scots poet.
4. On whom all people have pity.
5. Known for his *Flyting* (poem of ritual insult) with Dunbar.

Done Is a Battell[1]

Done is a battell on° the dragon blak,   with
Our campioun° Chryst confountet hes his force;   champion
The yettis° of hell ar brokin with a crak,   gates
The signe triumphall rasit is of the croce,°   cross
5   The divillis trymmillis° with hiddous voce,   trembles
The saulis° ar borrowit° and to the blis can go,   souls / redeemed
Chryst with his blud our ransonis dois indoce:°   endorse
Surrexit dominus de sepulchro.[2]

Dungin° is the deidly dragon Lucifer,   beaten
10   The crewall° serpent with the mortall stang,°   cruel / sting
The auld kene tegir with his teith on char°   ajar
Quhilk° in a wait hes lyne° for us so lang,   which / lain
Thinking to grip us in his clowis strang:
The mercifull lord wald° nocht that it wer so,   would
15   He maid him for to felye° of that fang:°   fail / booty
Surrexit dominus de sepulchro.

He for our saik that sufferit to be slane
And lyk a lamb in sacrifice wes dicht,°   prepared
Is lyk a lyone° rissin up agane,   lion
20   And as a gyane raxit him on hicht.[3]
Sprungin° is Aurora radius° and bricht,   arisen / radiant
On loft° is gone the glorius Appollo,[4]   aloft
The blisfull day depairtit° fro the nycht: separated
Surrexit dominus de sepulchro.

25   The grit victour agane is rissin on hicht
That for our querrell to the deth wes woundit;
The sone that wox° all paill now schynis bricht,   became
And, dirknes clerit, our fayth is now refoundit:°   reestablished
The knell of mercy fra the hevin is soundit,[5]
30   The Cristin ar deliverit of thair wo,
The Jowis° and thair errour ar confoundit: Jews
Surrexit dominus de sepulchro.

The fo is chasit, the battell is done ceis,°   ceased
The presone brokin, the jevellouris fleit and flemit,[6]
35   The weir° is gon, confermit is the peis,°   war / peace
The fetteris lowsit° and the dungeoun temit,°   loosed / emptied
The ransoun maid, the presoneris° redemit,°   prisoners / redeemed
The feild is win,° ourcummin° is the fo,   won / overcome
Dispulit° of the tresur that he yemit:°   despoiled / kept
Surrexit dominus de sepulchro.

1. This Easter hymn heroically portrays Christ's Resurrection as a battle with the devil, drawing on the account of the harrowing of hell in the apocryphal Gospel of Nicodemus, in which Christ journeys to hell to release worthy souls who had been born before his coming. It gains much of its power from the juxtaposition of alliterative diction from the Scots tradition with Latinate vocabulary. As in the *Lament for the Makars,* the Latin refrain fits within the overall English rhyme scheme.
2. The Lord is risen from the tomb. From the opening of the service for matins on Easter Sunday.
3. And like a giant stretched himself on high. A reference to Sampson, who in bearing off the gates of Gaza was seen as a type of Christ breaking the gates of hell.
4. Christ, the sun (and Son) of righteousness, is identified with Apollo, the sun god, which explains the reference to Aurora, goddess of the dawn.
5. An allusion to the ringing of the bells on Easter morning.
6. The prison broken, the jailers fled and banished.

In Secreit Place This Hyndir Nycht[1]

In secreit place this hyndir° nycht	last
I hard ane beyrne° say till ane bricht,°	man / fair lady
"My huny, my hart, my hoip, my heill,[2]	
I have bene lang° your luifar° leill°	long / lover / loyal
5 And can of yow get confort nane:°	none
How lang will ye with danger deill?[3]	
Ye brek my hart, my bony ane."°	pretty one
His bony beird was kemmit and croppit,[4]	
Bot all with cale° it was bedroppit,°	soup / smeared
10 And he wes townysche, peirt and gukit.[5]	
He clappit fast, he kist and chukkit[6]	
As with the glaikis° he wer ouirgane;°	lust / overcome
Yit be his feirris° he wald have fukkit:	manner
"Ye brek my hart, my bony ane."	
15 Quod he, "My hairt, sweit° as the hunye,	sweet
Sen that I borne wes of my mynnye°	mother
I never wowit° weycht° bot yow;	wooed / creature
My wambe° is of your luif sa fow°	belly / full
That as ane gaist° I glour° and grane,°	ghost / glower / groan
20 I trymble° sa, ye will not trow:°	tremble / believe
Ye brek my hart, my bony ane."	
"Tehe,"° quod scho, and gaif ane gawfe;°	Teehee / guffaw
"Be still my tuchan[7] and my calfe,	
My new spanit howffing fra the sowk,[8]	
25 And all the blythnes° of my bowk;°	joy / body
My sweit swanking,° saif yow allane	fine fellow
Na leid° I luiffit° all this owk:°	no man / loved / week
Full leifis° me° your graceles gane."°	dear / to me / face
Quod he, "My claver° and my curldodie,°	clover / a plant
30 My huny soppis, my sweit possodie,°	sheep's head broth
Be not oure bosteous° to your billie,°	rough / sweetheart
Be warme hairtit° and not evill willie;°	hearted / ill-willed
Your heylis quhyt as quhalis bane,[9]	
Garris ryis° on loft my quhillelillie:°	makes rise / penis
35 Ye brek my hart, my bony ane."	
Quod scho, "My clype, my unspaynit gyane[1]	
With moderis° mylk yit in your mychane,°	mother's / mouth

1. This comic account of the wooing of a kitchen maid by a boorish man parodies the *chanson d'aventure*, a genre in which the speaker overhears a dialogue between two lovers. Dunbar undercuts the poem's courtly language, which he has used seriously elsewhere, with overtly sexual references. In addition to words familiar to modern readers, the poem features terms of endearment from colloquial Scots which have long since been lost.
2. My honey, my heart, my hope, my salvation.
3. Ladies were expected to be "dangerous" (reluctant) in a courtship situation.

4. His handsome beard was combed and trimmed.
5. And he was townish (uncourtly), pert, and foolish.
6. He fondled fast, kissed, and chucked her under the chin.
7. Calf skin stuffed with straw, to encourage a cow to give milk.
8. My clumsy fellow newly weaned from nursing.
9. Your neck white as whale's bone; a common alliterative phrase in the conventional love poetry.
1. Said she, "My big soft fellow, my unweaned giant."

	My belly huddrun,° my swete hurle bawsy,[2]	*big-bellied glutton*
	My huny gukkis,° my slawsy gawsy,	*sweet fool*
40	Your musing waild perse° ane hart of stane:	*would pierce*
	Tak gud confort, my grit heidit° slawsy,	*great-headed*
	Full leifis me your graceles gane."	
	Quod he, "My kid, my capirculyoun,°	*woodgrouse*
	My bony baib° with the ruch° brylyoun,	*babe / rough*
45	My tendir gyrle, my wallie gowdye,°	*pretty goldfinch*
	My tyrlie myrlie, my crowdie mowdie,°	*milky porridge*
	Quhone° that oure mouthis dois meit° at ane	*when / do meet*
	My stang dois storkyn with your towdie:[3]	
	Ye brek my hairt, my bony ane."	
50	Quod scho, "Now tak me be the hand,	
	Welcum, my golk° of Marie° land,	*cuckoo / fairy*
	My chirrie and my maikles munyoun,[4]	
	My sowklar° sweit as ony unyoun,°	*suckling / any onion*
	My strumill stirk yit new to spane,[5]	
55	I am applyit° to your opunyoun:°	*inclined / opinion*
	I luif rycht weill° your graceles gane."	*love right well*
	He gaiff to hir ane apill rubye;°	*apple red*
	Quod scho, "Gramercye,° my sweit cowhubye.°"	*thanks / fool*
	And thai tway to ane play began	
60	Quhilk° men dois call the dery dan,[6]	*which*
	Quhill° that thair myrthis° met baythe in ane:	*while / pleasure*
	"Wo is me," quod scho, "Quhair will ye,° man?	*where will you go*
	Best now I luif° that graceles gane."	*love*

Robert Henryson

We know little about Robert Henryson, although he is said to have been a schoolmaster at the town of Dumferline, and Dunbar implies that he was dead by 1506, when he mentions him in the *Lament for the Makars*. Unlike Dunbar, he wrote not for the Scottish court but for the literate middle class, which gives his poetry a more moralistic and less witty tone. Henryson is a "Scottish Chaucerian" with a somber cast, for his major work, the *Testament of Crisseid*, picks up where Chaucer's great romance, *Troilus and Criseide*, leaves off, depicting the faithless heroine as punished with leprosy, achieving redemption, and entering a nunnery. *Robene and Makyne*, however, is a much more lighthearted poem. Like Dunbar's *In Secret Place*, it is a chanson d'aventure which parodies the language of courtly love, though its shepherd and shepherdess are far more appealing than Dunbar's grimy lovers. The roles are comically reversed, with the shepherdess Makyne, offering to instruct the shepherd Robene in the "ABCs" of love's lore, while he, in his ignorance, resists. After Robene dutifully departs with his sheep, he has regrets and returns, only to have Makyne tell him that he has delayed too long. She states the poem's moral, *carpe diem*:

---

2. An obscure term of endearment, as are several other phrases in the following lines.
3. My pole does stiffen by your thing.

4. My cherry and my matchless darling.
5. My stumbling bullock still newly weaned.
6. A dance (i.e., copulation).

The man that will nocht quhen he may
Sall haif nocht quhen he wald.

Robyn is thus left to repeat in vain couttly love sentiments that he learned from her.

Robene and Makyne[1]

	Robene sat on gud grene hill	
	Kepand° a flok of fe;°	*keeping / sheep*
	Mirry Makyne said him till:°	*to*
	"Robene, thow rew° on me!	*have pity*
5	I haif the luvit lowd and still[2]	
	Thir yeiris° two or thre;	*these years*
	My dule in dern bot gif thow dill,[3]	
	Dowtless but dreid° I de."	*surely*
	Robene ansuerit: "Be the Rude,°	*by the Cross*
10	Nathing of lufe I knaw,	
	Bot keipis my scheip under yone° wude—	*yonder*
	Lo quhair thay raik on raw![4]	
	Quhat° hes marrit° the in thy mude,°	*what / harmed / mind*
	Makyne, to me thow schaw:°	*declare*
15	Or quhat is lufe, or to be lude?°	*loved*
	Fane° wald I leir° that law."	*gladly / learn*
	"At luvis lair gife thow will leir,[5]	
	Tak thair ane ABC:	
	Be heynd, courtas and fair of feir,[6]	
20	Wyse, hardy° and fre;°	*brave / generous*
	So that no denger° do the deir,°	*disdain / do harm*
	Quhat dule in dern thow dre,[7]	
	Preiss° the with pane at all poweir°—	*strive / effort*
	Be patient and previe."°	*discreet*
25	Robene anserit hir agane:	
	"I wait° nocht quhat is luve,	*know*
	Bot I haif mervell° in certane	*wonder*
	Quhat makis the this wanrufe;°	*restless*
	The weddir is fair and I am fane,°	*happy*
30	My scheip gois haill aboif;[8]	
	And we wald play° us in this plane°	*disport / valley*
	Thay wald us bayth reproif."	
	"Robene, tak tent° unto my taill,°	*heed / advice*
	And wirk° all as I reid,°	*do / advise*
35	And thow sall haif my hairt all haill,°	*entirely*
	Eik° and my madinheid:	*also*

---

1. In Scots, as in Middle English poetry, Makyn (or Malkin) was a conventional name for a rustic girl, as Robin was for a boy.
2. I have loved thee openly and secretly.
3. Unless you relieve my secret pain.
4. See how they wander afield!
5. Of love's learning if you would learn.

6. Be gentle, courteous, and fair of manners (these and the qualities that follow are conventional attributes of the courtly lover; cf. Chaucer's *Nun's Priest's Tale*, page 402).
7. What sorrow in secret you suffer.
8. Are all around me on this hill.

Sen God sendis bute° for baill°   *cure / pain*
And for murnyng° remeid,°   *sorrow / remedy*
I dern with the bot gif I daill,[9]
40 Dowtles I am bot deid.[1]

"Makyne, tomorne this ilka° tyde,°   *same / time*
And° ye will meit me heir,   *if*
Peraventure my scheip ma gang besyd° *fend for themselves*
Quhill we haif liggit full neir[2]—
45 Bot mawgre haif I and I byd,[3]
Fra° thay begin to steir;°   *when / stray*
Quhat lyis on hairt° I will nocht hyd;° *lies in my heart / not*
Makyn, than mak gud cheir."

"Robene, thow reivis° me roif° and rest— *rob / tranquility*
50 I luve bot the allone."
"Makyne, adew; the sone gois west,
The day is neir-hand gone."
"Robene, in dule° I am so drest°   *to pain / resigned*
That lufe wil be my bone."°   *bane*
55 "Ga lufe, Makyne, quhairever thow list,[4]
For lemman° I lue° none."   *lover / love*

"Robene, I stand in sic a styll;°   *such a plight*
I sicht°—and that full sair."°   *sigh / painfully*
"Makyne, I haif bene heir this quhyle;° *while*
60 At hame God gif I wair![5]
"My huny Robene, talk ane quhill,°   *a while*
Gif thow will do na mair."
"Makyne, sum uthir man begyle,[6]
For hamewart° I will fair."°   *homeward / go*

65 Robene on his wayis went
Als licht as leif of tre;[7]
Mawkin murnit° in hir intent   *mourned*
And trowd° him nevir to se;°   *expected / see*
Robene brayd attour the bent;[8]
70 Than Mawkyne cryit on hie:°   *loudly*
"Now ma thow sing, for I am schent!° *ruined*
Quhat alis° lufe at me?"   *ails*

Mawkyne went hame withowttin faill;
Full wery eftir cowth weip:[9]
75 Than Robene in a ful fair daill°   *very neat order*
Assemblit all his scheip.
Be that, sum pairte of Mawkynis aill° *pain*
Outthrow his hairt cowd creip;[1]

9. Unless in secret I deal (i.e., have sex) with you.
1. Conventionally, the courtly lover threatens to die unless his lady takes pity on him.
2. While we have lain nearby.
3. But yet I am uneasy if I wait.
4. Go love, Makyn, wherever you wish.

5. I wish to God I were at home!
6. Seduce some other man.
7. As light as a leaf on a tree.
8. Bounded across the field.
9. Wearily afterward wept.
1. Entered his heart.

He fallowit fast thair till assaill,[2]
80   And till hir tuke gude keip.°   *paid good heed*

"Abyd, abyd, thow fair Makyne!
A word for ony thing!
For all my luve it sal be thyne,
Withowttin depairting.°   *wholly*
85   All haill° thy harte for till haif myne   *whole*
Is all my cuvating;
My scheip tomorne quhill houris nyne°   *until nine o'clock*
Will neid of no keiping."

"Robene, thow hes hard° soung and say   *hast heard*
90   In gestis° and storeis auld,   *legends*
The man that will nocht quhen° he may   *when*
Sall haif nocht quhen he wald.°   *would*
I pray to Jesu every day
Mot eik thair cairis cauld[3]
95   That first preiss° with the to play   *strives*
Be firth,° forrest or fawld."°   *wood / sheepfold*

"Makyne, the nicht° is soft and dry,   *night*
The wedder° is warme and fair,   *weather*
And the grene woid° rycht° neir us by   *wood / right*
100   To walk attour° allquhair;°   *across / everywhere*
Thair ma na janglour[4] us espy,
That is to lufe contrair;
Thairin, Makyne, bath ye and I
Unsene we ma repair."

105   "Robene, that warld is all away
And quyt° brocht° till ane end,   *entirely / brought*
And nevir agane thairto perfay,°   *by my faith*
Sall it be as thow wend:°   *think*
For of my pane thow maid it play,[5]
110   And all in vane I spend:°   *made an effort*
As thow hes done, sa sall I say:
Murne° on! I think to mend."   *grieve*

"Mawkyne, the howp° of all my heill°,[6]   *hope / salvation*
My hairt on the° is sett,   *thee*
115   And evirmair to the be leill,°   *loyal*
Quhill I may leif but lett;[7]
Nevir to faill—as utheris feill—
Quhat grace° that evir I gett."   *favor*
"Robene, with the I will nocht deill;[8]
120   Adew!° For thus we mett."   *adieu*

2. He went back to accost her there.
3. That he might make them too suffer.
4. Gossip; "janglours" were a stock threat to courtly lovers.

5. For you made fun of my pain.
6. Robene uses the religious metaphors of courtly love.
7. Unceasingly, while I live.
8. Robene, I will not have dealings (i.e., sex) with you.

Malkyne went hame blyth annewche°   *blithe enough*
Attour the holttis hair:[9]
Robene murnit, and Malkyne lewche,°   *laughed*
Scho sang,° he sichit sair°—   *sang / sighed sorely*
125   And so left him bayth wo° and wrewche,°   *sad / troubled*
In dolour° and in cair,   *sorrow*
Kepand his hird under a huche,°   *hovel*
Amangis° the holtis hair.   *among*

[END OF MIDDLE SCOTS POETS]

LATE MEDIEVAL ALLEGORY

The end of the Middle Ages saw an extraordinary flowering of allegory, a literary mode that at its simplest is a narrative in which a symbolic meaning runs parallel to, but distinct from, a literal one. Gone, for the most part, was the elaborate multileveled allegory based on biblical exegesis that had held sway in earlier centuries, to be replaced by the more transparent personification allegory, which embodies an abstract quality in a person or a thing, often to convey a spiritual quest or psychological conflict. This volume contains passages from the greatest English allegory of the time, William Langland's *Piers Plowman*, which uses personification as well as other types of allegory to convey the quest of its hero and its critique of society. The poem's dreamer/narrator "Will" stands for the errant human will as well as the author's nickname, and the flamboyant Lady Meed stands for monetary reward, whether just or unjust. Borrowing techniques from contemporary sermons, Langland makes many of his personifications grotesquely "realistic." When Gluttony goes to confess his sin to Repentance, for instance, he is portrayed as a fourteenth-century churl who is lured into a tavern, eats and drinks so much that he vomits, and ultimately is carried home to bed.

By the mid-fifteenth century, when the examples of allegory included in this section were written or translated into English, personification allegory was even more prominent. John Lydgate's *Pilgrimage of the Life of Man* features a protagonist locked in a spiritual struggle between vice (Wrath, Sloth, etc.) and virtue (Grace Dieu, representing the Church). Similarly, the hero of *Mankind* finds himself caught between Mercy (a priest) and Nowadays, New-Guise, and Nought (the personifications of novelty), until he chooses the correct path. Christine de Pizan's protagonist, dismayed by the Church's misogynist tradition, receives comfort from three allegorical ladies: Reason, Rectitude, and Justice. Two of these works use the common allegorical image of the building to clarify their points, Lydgate's pilgrim seeking the New Jerusalem, and Christine, at her mentors' behest, constructing a fortified city to honor women.

Allegory, with its tendency to abstraction, has been generally seen as supporting the status quo. This is certainly true in the case of Lydgate, whose pilgrim ultimately resists the temptation of the seven deadly sins and accepts the values of the Church. Christine's *City of Ladies* and *Mankind*, however, use allegory in more subversive ways, as had *Piers Plowman* when criticizing the corruption of the clergy. Christine's protagonist learns to take pride in the achievements of women rather than to accept the limitations of her gender. And while *Mankind* rejects the temptations of Nowadays, New-Guise, and Nought, these exuberant vice figures in effect steal the show, making Mercy, the Church's spokesman, look pedantic and ineffectual. However one chooses to read these particular texts, personification allegory as a mode proved flexible enough to respond to the social changes of the later Middle Ages and to persist into the Renaissance and Reformation. Its influence can be seen in Bunyan's *Pilgrim's Progress*, Spenser's *Faerie Queene*, and Shakespeare's plays—most memorably in his villains.

9. Across the woods gray (a traditional alliterative phrase).

+ ⇥⬧⇤ +

John Lydgate
c. 1370–1449

John Lydgate has often been accused (with some reason) of lacking great poetic gifts. What he did have were the gifts of good connections and remarkable diligence. For the last four decades of his life, Lydgate was the chief poet of a quasi-official English language culture under the Lancastrian kings, Henry IV, V, and VI. Fueled by noble and royal commissions, he churned out, across his career, as much as 150,000 lines of verse. His poetry consolidated the influence of Chaucerian style, though he rarely matched it, and extended that style to a huge range of projects.

Born in the village from which he took his name, Lydgate entered the great Benedictine abbey of Bury St. Edmunds during his boyhood. He was educated there and would eventually return there for the last fifteen years of his long life. In between, he spent some time at Oxford and many more years in aristocratic and royal households. Lydgate's writing under Lancastrian patronage included huge narrative poems about ancient empire, especially the *Troy Book*, perhaps his best sustained work. Lydgate also produced many religious poems and some political writing. He wrote "occasional" works as well, to mark royal entries such as Henry VI's arrival in London, or official celebrations of wealthy mercantile groups like the Goldsmiths. In many of these poems, Lydgate pursues an "aureate" style, importing into English richly polysyllabic words derived from French and Latin. Not all his work falls into such categories, though; Lydgate often writes in a humorous colloquial vein, or in a rather simple didactic style.

The latter tone characterizes the lengthy allegorical *Pilgrimage of the Life of Man*, translated between 1426 and 1428 from the early fourteenth-century work of a French monk, Guillaume de Deguileville. The *Pilgrimage* explores the struggle of virtues and vices in the path through earthly life, both at the level of the individual "Pilgrim" and of larger institutions. Beginning with a visionary dream of the New Jerusalem, the poem follows the Pilgrim through a long series of encounters with such personified figures as "Grace Dieu"; these often display Lydgate's talent for dramatic settings and exchanges. Grace Dieu initially rejects the Pilgrim from her house, and he is lured into danger by characters like Youth and Sloth. Surviving these temptations, he meets Grace Dieu once again. She takes him to a ship (the church), its structure endangered by loosened bindings (hoops and willow shoots) but provided with defensive "castles"—perhaps the monastic orders. He later meets Sickness and Age and prepares himself for a final encounter with Death, aided by Prayer. The genre of the allegorical pilgrimage has a strong literary heritage, perhaps best known in John Bunyan's *Pilgrim's Progress*.

from Pilgrimage of the Life of Man
[THE PILGRIM HAS A DREAM OF THE NEW JERUSALEM.]

This said year (who will, take keep°)   *note*
I was advised in my sleep,
Excited too, and that anon,
To Jerusalem to be gone.
5   Greatly moved in my courage°   *heart*
For to do my pilgrimage,
And thereto steered inwardly.
And to tell the cause why,
Was, that I thought I had a sight
10   Within a mirror large and bright,
Of that heavenly fair city—
Which represented unto me

Thereof wholly the manner,
Within the glass full bright and clear.
15   And verily, as seemed to me
It excelled of beauty
All other in comparison;
For God himself was the mason
Who made it fair, at his device.°   *at his pleasure*
20   For workman was there none so wise
It to conceive in his intent;°   *design*
For all the ways and pavement
Were paved all of gold.
And in the psalter it is told
25   How the first foundation,
On hills of devotion,
The masonry wrought full clean°   *completely*
Of living stones bright and sheen,°   *shining*
With a closure° round about   *fence*
30   From enemies, there was no doubt.
For Angels the watch kept,
The which, day nor night they slept,
Keeping so strongly the entry,
That no men came in that city,
35   But pilgrims, day nor night,
Who thither went, even right.°   *quite rightly*
      And there were many mansions,
Places, and habitations;
And there was also all gladness,
40   Joy without heavyness.
And plainly, who that had grace
For to enter in that place,
found, unto his pleasaunce,°   *delight*
Of joy all manner suffisaunce°   *sufficiency*
45   That any heart can devise.
And yet the entry in such wise
Was strongly kept for coming in;°   *guarded to prevent*
For the angel Cherubin
Of the gate was chief porter,
50   Having a sword, flaming as clear
As any fire, right at the gate;
And who that would, early or late,
Pass the wall, he was slain.
                              * * *

[Grace Dieu Takes the Pilgrim to Her Ship "Religion"]

Then Grace Dieu,° with good cheer   *Grace of God*
Led me down to the river;
And there we have a ship found.
With great bonds it was bound;
5   But the bonds sat not closed;
The most part of them were loosed;

The small osiers,° here and yonder,   *willow shoots*
Were broken then, and went asunder,
The hoops about the vessel,
10   Because they were not bound well;
Yet the hoops (with no denial)
Were strong enough when put to trial;
Default in them was found none;
But since the osiers, nigh each one,
15   Were broken first (as it is found),
Therefore the hoops were unbound.

The Pilgrim:

"Madam," said I, "without blame,°   *finding fault*
Of your ship, tell me the name,
And who that should it well govern;°   *steer*
20   For soothly, as I can discern,
The governor° is not wise,   *captain*
(As it seems in my avise°)   *opinion*
Who will allow (in his folly)
The bonds to break so recklessly
25   In midst of the perilous sea,
In which there is no surety.

Grace Dieu answers:

This ship (as by description)
Called is Religion,
Which is bound with circumstances,
30   And freighted with diverse observances.
And while that it is bound well,
It may perish neveradel;°   *not at all*
Except by young folks negligent,
That enter this ship of intent,
35   And, through their misgovernances,
Keep not the observances
That were made by folks old,
For to break them they're full bold:
First, the osiers small,
40   They tell of them but little tale,°   *pay them no heed*
Cast them behind at their back,
Whereby the ship goes all to wrack:
They break the small circumstances,
And farewell the great observances!
45   For if the small commandments
Be not kept in their intents,
The great (in conclusion)
Go unto destruction.
The small (both in cold and heat)
50   Are wardens of the great;
And if the small truly fail,
Aright this ship may not sail.

Break the small here and yonder,
And the great must go asunder.
55 Thus the ship of religion
Goes often to destruction.
So, would God that their living
Were now like their beginning,
The ship should the better prove,
60 Against all tempest itself relieve:
It were a charity, by the rood.°   *cross*
Yet I hope some are good,
Such as to holiness intend;
and who doth not, god him amend!
65 God give them grace so to dress°   *raise*
The mast upward, by holiness,
and that they may, to their avail,
By grace, so to the cross sail,
That in the wind be no debate
70 To make their passage fortunate;
That readily they may, and blyve,°   *quickly*
At the haven up arrive,
Where Joy and bliss (who can discern)
Is endlessly, and life etern.°   *eternally*
75 Now choose freely, after my law,
To which castle thou wilt draw,
And in my ship, they are each one
Built full fair, of lime and stone.

Mankind

c. 1465–1470

The chief example of medieval allegory included here, *Mankind*, belongs to the genre of moral-ity play—a dramatic representation of the spiritual crisis of a representative man as he strug-gles to achieve redemption. (Other examples include the *Castle of Perseverance*, *Wisdom*, and most famously, *Everyman*.) Such plays were produced in the same milieu as the cycle plays, and like them were the product of the wealth of late medieval English cities. The primary differ-ence lies in the fact that their narrative focus is not on salvation history, but on the life of an individual Christian as he is assailed by personified vices and virtues.

   The plot of *Mankind* concerns a simple farmer so frustrated by the difficulties of surviv-ing that he succumbs to the temptation of the Devil, Titivillus, and the seductions of three personifications of novelty—Nowadays, New-Guise (trendy behavior) and Nought. They lead him to temporarily forsake his protector Mercy in order to pursue worldly pleasures, until he sees his error and repents. Such a bald summary, however, fails to convey the raucous humor of the play, which derives largely from its language. When the only virtuous character in the play, Mercy, speaks in an ornate, Latinate style of English which would have been asso-ciated with the priesthood, the vice figures mock his "Latin English." They themselves express their scorn of authority in a highly colloquial, occasionally obscene style that lends the play great humor and energy.

Such linguistic virtuosity raises a question that is relevant to medieval English drama generally: to what extent do the comic characters undercut or support the status quo? The traditional view is that since the church generally used drama to inculcate Christian virtues, the comic characters in *Mankind* are used to support the status quo. Certainly the ostensible moral is that the Christian soul should resist the temptation to novelty and hew to the old approved ways. Nevertheless, the association of the personified vices with social mobility may have made the play resonate with the newly prosperous middle classes. Although Mercy has the last word, his pedantic language has made him look foolish, possibly compromising the conservative message toward which allegory generally aims.

Unlike the cycle plays, the moralities continued to flourish into the early modern period. In particular *Mankind*, whose characters are not consistently allegorical but keep threatening to break into realism, can be seen as a link to early modern drama. The devil Titivillus may lie behind Shakespearean villains such as Iago in *Othello* and Edmund in *King Lear*, while the more benign personifications of novelty—New-Guise, Nowadays, and Nought—suggest the exuberant and unrepentant Falstaff in *Henry IV, Part 1*.

The annotations to the text here are by David Bevington.

Mankind

Dramatis Personae

MANKIND	MISCHEFF
MERCY	NEW-GUISE
TITIVILLUS	NOWADAYS
NOUGHT	

[*Enter Mercy.*]

MERCY: The very fownder and beginner of owr first creacion,
    Amonge us sinfull wrechys He oweth° to be magnifiede,°   *ought / worshiped*
    That for owr disobedience He hade none indignacion°   *did not disdain*
    To sende His own son to be torn and crucifiede.
5   Owr obsequiouse° service to Him shulde be apliede,   *dutiful*
    Where He was Lorde of all and made all thinge of nought,
    For the sinnfull sinnere to hade him revivyde,°   *revived*
    And, for his° redempcion, sett His own son at nought.[1]   *his (man's)*

    It may be seyde and verifiede: mankinde was dere bought.°   *dearly ransomed*
10   By the pituose° deth of Jhesu he hade his remedye.   *piteous*
    He was purgyde of his defawte, that wrechydly hade
        wrought,[2]
    By His glorius Passion, that blissyde lavatorye.°   *source of cleansing*
    O soverence,° I beseche yow yowr condicions to rectifye,   *masters (the audience)*
    Ande with humilité and reverence to have a remocion°   *an inclination*
15   To this blissyde prince that owr nature doth glorifye,[3]
    That ye may be participable of His retribucion.[4]

---

1. Our dutiful worship should be devoted to God, forasmuch as He, who is Lord of all and made all creation out of a void, sacrificed (set at nought) His own son in order to revive sinful man and bring about man's redemption.

2. Man, who had acted culpably, was purged of his sin.
3. Who glorifies our nature.
4. That you may be able to share in His heavenly reward.

MERCY: Why com ye hethyr, brother? Ye were not dysiryde.°   *desired*

MISCHEFF: For a winter corn-threscher, ser, I have hiryde,°   *hired myself out*

55   Ande ye saide the corn shulde be savyde and the chaff

            shulde be feryde.°   *burned*

          Ande he[2] provith nay, as it schewth° by this verse: *shows, is proven*

          "*Corn servit bredibus, chaffe horsibus, straw firybusque.*"[3]

          This is as moche to say, to yowr lewde° undyrstondinge,   *ignorant*

          As: the corn shall serve to brede at the nexte bakinge;

60   "*Chaff horsibus," et reliqua,*°   *and the rest*

          The chaff to horse shall be goode provente;°   *provender*

          When a man is for-colde,° the straw may be brent,°   *very cold / burned*

          And so forth, *et cetera.*

MERCY: Avoide,° goode brother! Ye ben° culpable   *Be gone / are*

65   To interrupte thus my talking delectable.

MISCHEFF: Sere,° I have nother° horse nor sadyll,   *Sir / neither*

          Therfor I may not ride.[4]

MERCY: Hie yow forthe on fote,° brother, in Godys name!   *foot*

MISCHEFF: I say, ser, I am cumme hedyr° to make yow game.°   *come hither / sport*

70   Yet bade ye me not go out in the devillys name,

          Ande I will abide.[5]

MERCY: ...... [*A leaf is lost in the* MS. *In the interim, Mischief evidently departs, leav-*
          ing the tormenting of Mercy to three rowdies, New-Guise, Nowadays, and Nought,
          with minstrels. The first two are badgering Nought to dance energetically; Nought views
          the proposition as risky.]

NEW-GUISE: Ande how,° minstrellys, pley the comyn trace!°   *ho! / common dance*

          Ley on with thy ballys° till his bely breste![6]   *bagpipe bellows or switch (?)*

NOUGHT: I putt case I breke my neke:° how than?   *i.e., Suppose I break*

NEW-GUISE: I giff no force,° by Sent Tanne!°   *I don't care / Anne*

NOWADAYS: Leppe° about lively! Thou art a wight° man.   *Leap / agile*

          Lett us be mery whill we be here.

NOUGHT: Shall I breke my neke to schew yow sporte?

NOWADAYS: Therfor ever beware of thy reporte.°[7]   *talk*

NOUGHT: I beschrew ye all! Here is a schrewde sorte.°[8]   *a rascally lot*

          Have theratt, then,° with a mery chere!   *Let's go then*

          Here they daunce. Mercy seyth:

MERCY: Do wey!° do wey this revell, sers, do wey!   *Do away, stop*

NOWADAYS: Do wey, goode Adam,° do wey?   *Adam, old man*

          This is no parte of thy pley.[9]

---

2. The imagined author of the burlesqued Latin verse following.
3. Doggerel Latin for: Wheat serves for breads, chaff for
horses, and straw for fires. (Mischief then proceeds to parody biblical exegesis in his "translation.")
4. I.e., I haven't any means of leaving your company.
5. I.e., Since you didn't invoke the devil to chase me out,
I'll stay.

6. (According to Eccles, ed., *The Macro Plays*, New-Guise
may be urging Nowadays to flog Nought with a switch
until his belly bursts, in order to make him dance.)
7. I.e., Watch what you say.
8. (Nought evidently feels the others are urging him on,
expecting him to hurt himself; see lines 96–97, below.)
9. I.e., this doesn't concern you.

NOUGHT: Yis, mary,° I prey yow, for I love not this revelinge.   *marry, indeed*
　　　　Cum forth, goode fader, I yow prey!¹
　　　　By a lityll ye may assay.²
　　　　Anon, off with yowr clothes, if ye will play.
　　　　Go to! for I have hade a praty scottlinge.°   *fine little caper (ironic)*

MERCY: Nay, brother, I will not daunce.
NEW-GUISE: If ye will, ser, my brother° will make yow to   *i.e., Nowadays*
　　　　prawnce.
NOWADAYS: With all my herte, ser, if I may yow avaunce.°³   *assist*
　　　　Ye may assay by a lityll trace.°   *try a little dance*
NOUGHT: Yea, ser, will ye do well?⁴
95　　　Trace° not with them, by my cownsell,   *Dance*
　　　　For I have tracyde sumwhat too fell°—   *vigorously*
　　　　I tell you it is a narow space!°   *room*

　　　　But ser, I trow, of us thre I herde yow speke.
NEW-GUISE: Cristys curse hade ye therfor! for I was in slepe.
NOWADAYS: And I hade the cuppe in my honde, redy to goo
　　　　to mete.°⁵   *to dine*
　　　　Therfor, ser, curtly grett yow well.°   *briefly we greet you*
MERCY: Few wordys, few and well sett!°   *well placed (ironic)*
NEW-GUISE: Ser, it is the new guise and the new jett:°   *fashion*
　　　　Many wordys, and schortely sett°—   *curtly offered*
105　　　This is the new guise, every dele.°   *deal, bit*

MERCY: Lady,° helpe! How wrechys delighte in ther simpull weys!   *i.e., Our Lady*
NOWADAYS: Say nought ageyn° the new guise nowadays!   *nothing against*
　　　　Thou shall finde us schrewys° at all assays.°⁶   *rascals / trials*
　　　　Beware, ye may soon like a bofett!°   *taste a blow*
MERCY: He was well occupiede that browghte yow brether!⁷
NOUGHT: I harde° yow call "New-Guise, Nowadays,   *heard*
　　　　Nought," all these thre togethere.
　　　　If ye sey that I lie, I shall make yow to slither:°   *slide, fall*
　　　　Lo, take yow here a trepett!° [*Trips him up.*]   *tripping*

MERCY: Say me yowr namys. I know yow not.
NEW-GUISE: New-Guise, I.
NOWADAYS:　　　　　　I, Nowadays.
NOUGHT:　　　　　　　　　　I, Nought.
MERCY: By Jhesu Crist, that me dere bowghte,° Ye betray many   *who dearly*
　　　　men.   *ransomed me*
NEW-GUISE: Betray? Nay, nay, ser, nay, nay!

1. (Nought may mean that he's tired of being forced to dance, and wants Mercy to take his place as the butt.)
2. For a little while you can try (to dance).
3. (Nowadays mockingly agrees to assist Mercy to dance by whipping him and making him prance, as he did Nought.)
4. I.e., Do you want my advice?
5. (The three indicate they have been summoned like evil spirits by Mercy's sermonizing against the degenerate new fashions they represent. The summons has interrupted their fleshly pursuits of sleeping and eating.)
6. You'll find us tough rascals if you provoke us to a test.
7. I.e., (sarcastically) He who brought you together (or here) as comrades was certainly making good use of his time!

We make them both fresch and gay.
120   But of yowr name, ser, I yow prey,
That we may yow ken.°   *know*

MERCY: "Mercy" is my name by denominacion.
I conseive° ye have but a lityll favour° in my communicacion.   *realize / comfort*
NEW-GUISE: Ey, ey, yowr body is full of Englisch Laten![8]
125   I am aferde it will brest.°   *burst*
"Pravo te,"° quod the bocher° onto me   *I curse you / butcher*
When I stale° a leg a motun.°[9]   *stole / of mutton*
NOWADAYS: Ye are a strong cunning clerke;°   *very learned divine*
I prey yow hertily, worschippfull clerke,
130   To have this Englisch mad in:° Laten   *translate this English into*

"I have etun° a disch-full of curdys,°   *eaten / curds*
Ande I have schetun° yowr mowth full of turdys."—   *shitten*
Now, opyn yowr sachell with Laten wordys
Ande sey me this in clericall manere![1]
135   Also, I have a wife—her name is Rachell—
Betwix her and me was a gret batell,
Ande fain° of yow I wolde here° tell   *gladly / hear*
Who was the most master.

NOUGHT: Thy wife Rachell, I dare ley° twenty lise.°   *wager / lice*
NOWADAYS: Who spak to thee, foll?° Thou art not wise.   *fool*
Go and do that longith° to thine office: *that which belongs*
Osculare fundamentum!°   *Kiss my ass*
NOUGHT: Lo, master, lo, here is a pardon[2] bely-mett°—   *satisfying*
It is grawntyde of° Pope Pokett: *granted by*
145   If ye will putt yowr nose in his wiffys sokett,°   *vagina*
Ye shall have forty days of pardon.

MERCY: This idyll language ye shall repent!
Out of this place I wolde ye went.
NEW-GUISE: Goo we hens° all thre with one assent.   *hence*
150   My fadyr° is irke of owr eloquence;   *(spiritual) father, priest*
Therfor I will no lenger tary.
Gode bringe yow, master, and blissyde Mary,
To the number of the demonicall frairy!°[3]   *friary*
. . . .

NOWADAYS: Cum winde, cum reyn,
155   Thowgh I cumme never ageyn.[4]

---

8. New-Guise pokes fun at Mercy's stilted and redundant choice of "aureate" terms coined from the Latin, such as "denominacion."
9. (New-Guise cites another instance of "English Latin" being used absurdly out of context, by a butcher. But this stanza is metrically imperfect and may be obscure.)
1. And translate what I've just said into learned Latin.
2. A document granting remission of sin, granted in this case by the imaginary and absurd Pope Pocket (i.e., Money-purse).
3. May God and blessed Mary bring you, master, to the company of the brotherhood of devils. (A line is evidently missing to complete the stanza.)
4. I.e., Let the weather be what it please, for all I'll ever come again. (Proverbial.)

The devill put out both yowr eyn!°   *eyes*
Felowse, go we hens tight.°   *hence quickly*

NOUGHT: Go we hens, a devill wey!°   *i.e., in the devil's name*
Here is the dore, here is the wey. [*To Mercy.*]

160   Farwell, jentyll Jaffrey,
I prey Gode gif yow goode night!
Exiant simul. Cantent.[5]

MERCY: Thankyde be Gode we have a fayer diliverance°   *good riddance*
Of these thre onthrifty gestys!°   *profligate guests*
They know full lityll what is ther ordinance.°   *ordained place*
165   I preve,° by reson, they be wers then bestys:°   *prove / worse than beasts*

A best doth after° his naturall institucion;°   *according to / function*
Ye may conseive,° by there° disporte and behavour,   *understand / their*
Ther° joy ande delite is in derision   *(That) their*
Of ther owyn Criste, to his dishonur.

170   This condicion of leving, it is prejudiciall—
Beware therof! It is wers than ony° felony or treson.   *any*
How may it be excusyde befor the Justice° of all,   *Judge*
When for every idyll worde we must yelde° a reson?   *yield, give*

They have grett ease; therfor they will take no thought.
175   But how then, when the angell of hevyn shall blow the
trumpe
Ande sey to the transgressors that wikkydly hath wrought:°   *who have sinned*
"Cum forth onto yowr juge, and yelde yowr acownte"?

Then shall I, Mercy, begin sore to wepe.
Nother° comfort nor cownsell ther shall non[e] be hade,   *Neither*
180   But such as they have sowyn,° such shall they repe.°   *sown / reap*
They be wanton° now, but then shall they be sade.   *jovial*

The goode new guise nowadays I will not disalow;
I discomende the viciouse guise. I prey have me excusyde,
I nede not to speke of it; yowr reson will tell it yow.
185   Take that° is to be takyn, and leve that is to be refusyde.[6]   *that which*
[*Enter Mankind with a spade.*]

MANKIND: Of the erth and of the cley we have owr propagacion.
By the providens of Gode thus be we derivatt°—   *derived*
To whose mercy I recomende this wholl congrygacion.
I hope, onto° his blisse ye be all predestinatt!°   *unto / destined*

190   Every man, for his degré, I trust shall be participatt,[7]
If we will mortifye owr carnall condicion

---

5. Let them go out together. Let them sing.
6. I disapprove of the vicious new fashion only. I pray that you'll excuse me for speaking laboriously of what your reason tells you plainly. Use moderately those things God intended you to enjoy, and refuse what should be refused.
7. Every man according to his spiritual condition will, I trust, be a participant (in God's bliss).

Ande owr voluntarye° dysires, that ever be pervercionatt°—   *willful / perverse*
To renunce them, and yelde us under° Godys provicion.   *submit ourselves to*

My name is "Mankinde." I have my composicion
195   Of a body and of a soull, of condicion contrarye—
Betwix them tweyn is a grett division.
He° that shulde be subjecte, now he hath the victory.[8]   *He (the body)*

This is to me a lamentable story,
To se my flesch of my soull to have governance.
200   Wher the goode-wyff° is master, the goodeman° may be   *wife / husband*
     sory.
I may both syth° and sobbe; this is a pituose remembrance.   *sigh*

O thou my soull, so sotyll° in thy substance,   *subtle, delicate*
. . . .
Alasse, what was thy fortune and thy chaunce°   *why was it your fate*
To be associat with my flesch, that stinking dungehill?

205   Lady,° helpe! Soverens, it doth my soull myche° ill   *i.e., Our Lady / much*
To se the flesch prosperouse, and the soull trodyn under
     fote.
I shall go to yondyr man, and asay him° I will.   *appeal to him*
I trust of gostly° solace he will be my bote.°   *spiritual / help*
[*He goes to Mercy, and kneels.*]

All heyll, semely father, ye be welcom to this house!
210   Of the very° wisdam ye have participacion.[9]   *true*
My body with my soull is ever querulose;°   *quarrelsome*
I prey yow, for sent° charité, of yowr supportacion!°   *holy / support*

I beseche yow hertily of° yowr gostly° comforte.   *for / spiritual*
I am onstedfast in livinge; my name is "Mankinde."
215   My gostly enmy, the devill, will have a grett disporte°   *amusement*
In sinfull guidinge° if he may se me ende.   *conduct*

MERCY: Crist sende yow goode comforte! Ye be welcum, my
     frende.
Stonde uppe on yowr fete. I prey yow, arise.
My name is "Mercy." Ye be to me full hende;°   *gracious*
220   To eschew vice I will yow avise.

MANKINDE: O Mercy, of all grace and vertu ye are the well!°   *fountain*
I have herde° tell, of° right worschippfull clerkys,°   *heard / from / divines*
Ye° be approximatt to Gode and nere of his consell;   *(That) you*
He hath institut° you above all his werkys.   *instituted, established*

---

8. He (my body), who should be subordinate (to my   9. You share in and partake of the true wisdom (of God).
soull), is instead dominant.

225   O, yowr lovely wordys to my soull are swetere then hony!
MERCY: The temptacion of the flesch ye must resist like a man,
        For ther is ever° a batell betwix the soull and the body: *constantly*
        Vita hominis est militia super terram.[1]

        Oppresse yowr gostly enmy and be Cristys own knight!
230   Be never a cowarde ageyn° yowr adversary: *against*
        If ye will be crownyde, ye must nedys° fight.   *must needs, must*
        Intende well, and Gode will be yow adjutory.°   *helpful to you*

        Remember, my frende, the time of continuance:°   *of (life's) duration*
        So helpe me Gode, it is but a chery time![2]
235   Spende it well. Serve Gode with hertys affiance.°   *loyalty of heart*
        Distempure not yowr brain with goode ale nor with wine.

        "Mesure° is tresure"; I forbidde yow not the use.   *Moderation*
        Mesure yowrsylf ever. Beware of excesse.
        The superfluouse guise I will that ye refuse;
240   When nature is suffisyde, anon that ye sesse.°   *cease at once*

        If a man have an hors, and kepe him not too hye,°   *too well-fed*
        He may then reull° him at his own dysiere;°   *rule / desire*
        If he° be fede over-well he will disobey   *he (the horse)*
        Ande, in happe,° cast his master in the mire.   *perchance*
        [*New-Guise, Nowadays, and Nought, who have been eavesdropping, speak from
        backstage or from some concealed position where Mercy and Mankind cannot observe
        them.*]

NEW-GUISE: Ye sey trew, ser; ye are no faitour:°   *liar*
        I have fedde my wiff so well till sche is my master!
        I have a grett wounde on my hede, lo! and theron leyth° a   *lies*
            playster;
        Ande another ther° I pisse° my peson.[3]   *where / pease*
        Ande° my wife were yowr hors, sche wolde yow all   *If*
            tobanne.°   *curse you all*
250   Ye fede yowr hors in mesure; ye are a wise man!
        I trow, and° ye were the kingys palfrey-man   *if*
        A goode horse shulde be gesunne.°[4]   *scarce*

MANKINDE: Wher spekys this felow? Will he not com nere?
MERCY: All too sone, my brother, I fere me, for yow.°   *for your sake*
255   He was here right now—by him that bowghte me dere!°—   *dearly ransomed me*
        With other of his felowse. They kan° moche sorow.   *They're acquainted with*

1. The life of man on earth is a battle, a struggle. (Job 7:1.)
2. Cherry time (i.e., brief).
3. (New-Guise has plaster bandages on his head and genitals from sparring with his bossy wife.)
4. (Sarcastically) You're a clever one to starve your horse, in the name of "moderation"! I bet that if you were keeper of the king's horses, there'd be few horses left unruined (by your parsimony).

They will be here right sone,° if I owght° departe.   soon / at all
Thinke on my doctrine! It shall be yowr defence.
Lerne whill I am here; sett my wordys in herte.
260 Within a schorte space I must nedys hens.°   Soon I must go

NOWADAYS [*unseen*]: The sooner the lever,° and° it be evyn   better / if
          anon!⁵
     I trow yowr name is "Do-lityll," ye be so long fro hom.
     If ye wolde go hens, we shall cum everychon,°   everyone
     Mo then a goode sorte.°   More than a great many
265 Ye have leve,° I dare well say;   leave (to go)
     When ye will, go forth yowr wey.
     Men have lityll deynté of° yowr pley   pleasure in
     Because ye make no sporte.

NOUGHT [*unseen*]: Yowr potage° shall be for-colde,° ser. When   soup / entirely cold
          will ye go dine?
270 I have sen a man lost twenty noblys° in as lityll time⁶—   gold coins
     Yet it was not I, by Sent Qwintyn!
     For I was never worth a pottfull a wortys sithyn° I was   of cabbages since
          born.
     My name is "Nought." I love well to make mery!
     I have be sethen° with the comyn tapster of Bury   been before now
275 And pleyde so longe the foll° that I am evyn very wery°—   fool / weary
     Yit shall I be ther ageyn to-morn.°   tomorrow

MERCY [*to Mankind*]: I have moche care for yow, my own frende.
     Yowr enmys will be here anon; they make ther avaunte.°   their boast
     Thinke well in yowr hert: yowr name is "Mankinde";
280 Be not unkinde to Gode, I prey yow! Be his servante.

     Be stedefast in condicion; se ye be not variant.
     Lose not thorowgh foly that° is bowghte so dere!°   that which / dearly
     Gode will prove° yow sone;° ande, if that ye be constant,   test / soon
     Of his blisse perpetuall ye shall be partener.

285 Ye may not have yowr intent at yowr first dysiere.°   desire
     Se the grett pacience of Job in tribulacion:
     Like as the smith trieth ern° in the fiere,°   refines iron / fire
     So was he triede by Godys visitacion.

     He was of yowr nature° and of yowr fragilité.   i.e., human nature
290 Folow the steppys of him, my own swete son,
     Ande sey, as he seyde, in yowr trobyll and adversité:
     "*Dominus dedit, Dominus abstulit; sicut sibi placuit,
          ita factum est; sit nomen Domini benedictum.*"⁷

---

5. The sooner the better, even if it's right now!
6. I.e., Hurry home to your dinner. I've seen a man lose 20
gold coins (at gambling) in the time you're taking to go.

7. "The Lord gave, and the Lord has taken away; as it was
pleasing to him, so it was done; blessed be the name of
the Lord." (Job 1.21.)

Moreover, in speciall I give yow in charge:
Beware of New-Guise, Nowadays, and Nought!
295   Nise° in ther aray, in language they be large.°   *Wanton / licentious*
To perverte yowr condicions, all ther menys° shall be   *their means*
    sowghte.

Gode° son, intromitt° not yowrsylff in ther cumpeny!   *Good / intermix*
They harde° not a masse this twelmonyth,° I dare well say.   *heard / year*
Giff them none audience; they will tell yow many a lie.
300   Do truly yowr labure, and kepe yowr haly° day.   *holy*

Beware of Titivillus—for he lesith° no wey°—8   *loses / means, device*
That° goth invisibull and will not be sen.°   *Who / seen*
He will ronde° in yowr ere,° and cast a nett befor yowr ey.9   *whisper / ear*
He is worst of them all, Gode lett him never then!°   *thrive*
305   If ye disples° Gode, aske mercy anon,   *displease*
Ellys° Mischeff will be redy to brace° yow in his bridyll.   *Or else / fasten*
Kisse me now, my dere darlinge. Gode schelde° yow from   *shield*
    yowr fon!°   *foes*
Do truly yowr labure, and be never idyll.
The blissinge of Gode be with yow and with all these
    worschippfull men!°   [*Exit.*]   *i.e., the audience*
MANKINDE: Amen, for sent° charité, amen!   *holy*

Now, blissyde be Jhesu! My soull is well saciatt°   *satiated, filled*
With the mellifluose doctrine of this worschippfull man.
The rebellion of my flesch, now it is superatt,°   *conquered*
Thankinge be Gode of the comminge that I kam.1

315   Here will I sitt, and tityll° in this papyr   *write down*
The incomparable astat of my promicion.° [*Sits and writes.*]   *my promised bliss*
[*To the audience.*] Worschipfull soverence, I have wretyn here
The gloriouse remembrance of my nobyll condicion.

To have remors and memory of mysylff thus wretyn it is,2
320   To defende me from all supersticious charmys:
"Memento, homo, quod cinis es, et in cinerem reverteris."3
[*He points to the cross depicted on his breast.*]
    Lo, I bere on my bryst the bagge° of mine armys.   *badge*
[*New-Guise approaches from his place of concealment.*]

NEW-GUISE: The wether is colde. Gode sende us goode ferys!°   *fires*
    "Cum sancto sanctus eris, et cum perverso perverteris."

---

8. (For the name Titivillus—"all vile things"—see the Wakefield Judgment pageant.)
9. I.e., to render Titivillus invisible.
1. Thanks be to God for my coming hither (to this holy man, Mercy).

2. It is written as follows, to cause me to have remorse (for my fleshly frailty).
3. "Remember, O man, that you are dust, and to dust you will return." (See Job 34.15.)

325   "Ecce quam bonum et quam jocundum," quod the devill to
            the frerys,°   *friars*
        "Habitare fratres in unum."[4]

MANKINDE: I her° a felow speke. With him I will not mell.°   *hear / concern myself*
        This erth, with my spade, I shall assay to delffe.°   *delve, dig*
        To eschew idullnes, I do it mine own selffe.
330   I prey Gode sende it his fusion!° [*Digs.*]   *foison, fruition*
    [*Nowadays and Nought approach, making their way through the audience.*]

NOWADAYS: Make rom, sers, for we have be longe!°   *been long absent*
        We will cum gif yow a Cristemes songe.

NOUGHT: Now I prey all the yemandry° that is here   *yeomanry, folk*
        To singe with us, with a mery chere!
    [*He sings a line at a time; New-Guise and Nowadays lead the audience in singing after
    him.*]

335   It is wretyn with a coll, it is wretyn° with a cole,°   *written / coal*
NEW-GUISE *and* NOWADAYS: It is wretyn with a colle, it is
            wretyn [with a cole],
NOUGHT: He that schitith with his hoyll, he that schitith with
            his hoyll,°   *hole*
NEW-GUISE, NOWADAYS: He that schitith with his hoyll,
        [he that schitith with his hoyll],
NOUGHT: But° he wippe his ars clen, but he [wipe his ars clen],   *Unless*
NEW-GUISE, NOWADAYS: But he wipe his ars clen, but he
        [wipe his ars clen],
NOUGHT: On his breche° it shall be sen, on his breche [it shall   *breeches*
        be sen],
NEW-GUISE, NOWADAYS: On his breche it shall be sen, on
        his [breche it shall be sen].
        Cantant omnes:°   *All sing*
        Hoylyke, holyke, holyke! holyke, holyke, holyke!

NEW-GUISE: Ey, Mankinde, Gode spede yow with yowr spade!
345   I shall tell yow of a mariage:
        I wolde yowr mowth and his ars, that this made,[5]
        Wer mariede junctly° together.   *jointly*
MANKINDE: Hey° yow hens, felowse, with bredinge!°   *Hasten / reproach*
        Leve yowr derision and yowr japing!°   *mocking*
350   I must nedys labure—it is my livinge.
NOWADAYS: What, ser? We cam but late hethyr.°[6]   *only lately hither*
        Shall all this corn° grow here[7]   *grain*

---

4. "With the holy you will show yourself holy; and with
the wicked you will show yourself wicked." (Psalms
18.25–26.) "Behold how good and how pleasant it is for
brethren to dwell together in unity" (Psalms 133.1), said
the devil to the friars.

5. That made this (perhaps referring to excrement or
stained breeches, as in the song).
6. I.e., We've only just arrived, and don't quite understand what you're doing.
7. Nowadays implies that Mankind's field is terribly small.

That ye shall have the nexte yere?

If it be so, corn hade nede be dere,° *better be high in price*

355   Ellys ye shall have a pore liffe.° *you'll be poor*

NOUGHT: Alasse, goode fadere,[8] this labor fretith° yow to the *frets, consumes*
bone!

But, for yowr croppe I take grett mone:° *feel great sorrow*

Ye shall never spende° it alone! *finish*

I shall assay to geett° yow a wiffe. *get*

360   How many acres suppose ye here, by estimacion?

NEW-GUISE: Ey, how ye turne the erth uppe and down!

I have be in my days° in many goode town, *been during my life*

Yett saw I never such another tillinge.

MANKINDE: Why stonde ye idyll? It is pety that ye were born!

NOWADAYS: We shall bargen with yow, and nother moke° nor *neither mock*
scorne:

Take a goode carte in hervest, and lode it with yowr corne,

Ande what shall we gif° yow for the levinge?° *pay / crop*

NOUGHT: He is a goode starke° laburrer—he wolde fain do well![9] *strong*

He hath mett with the goode man Mercy, in a schrowde
sell!°[1] *bad time*

370   For all this, he may have many a hungry mele.° *meal*

Yit, woll ye se? He is politike:° *shrewd, prudent*

Here shall be goode corn—he may not misse it.° *he can't fail*

If he will have reyn,° he may over-pisse it;° *rain / piss on it*

Ande if he will have compasste,° he may over-blisse it *compost*

375   A lityll with his ars, like.°[2] *similarly*

MANKINDE: Go and do yowr labur—Gode lett yow never the!°— *prosper*

Or with my spade I shall yow dinge,° by the holy Trinité! *strike*

Have ye none other man to moke° but ever° me? *mock / always*

Ye wolde have me of yowr sett?° *group, gang*

380   Hie° yow forth lively, for hens I will yow driffe!° *Hasten / drive*
[He beats them with his spade.]

NEW-GUISE: Alas, my jewellys!° I shall be schent of my wiffe![3] *testicles*

NOWADAYS: Alasse, and I am like° never for to thrive, I have *likely*
such a buffett!

MANKINDE: Hens I sey, New-Guise, Nowadays, and Nowghte!

385   It was seyde beforn,° all the menys° shuld be sought *previously (that) / means*

To perverte my condicions and bringe me to nought.

Hens, thevys! Ye have made many a lesinge.° *lie*

NOUGHT: Marryde° I was for colde, but now am I warme![4] *Marred, suffering*

---

8. (Condescendingly) old fellow.
9. (Said sarcastically.)
1. I.e., It was an evil hour when he met Mercy.
2. And similarly, if he needs compost he can bestow a

blessing on his land with his arse.
3. Alas, my testicles! I'll be in disgrace with my wife (because I'm impotent).
4. I.e., I was cold until that beating warmed me up.

Ye are evill-avisyde,° ser, for ye have don harme.   *ill-advised*
390   By Cokkys body sakyrde,° I have such a peyn in my arme   *God's consecrated body*
I may not chonge a man a ferthinge!⁵

[*The three rogues start out. Mankind kneels.*]

MANKINDE: Now I thanke Gode, knelinge on my kne.
Blissyde be his name! He is of hye° degré.   *high*
By the subsidé° of his grace that he hath sente me,   *help*
395   Thre of mine enmys I have putt to flight. [*Holds up his spade.*]
Yit this instrument, soverens, is not made to defende.
Davide seyth, "*Nec in hasta, nec in gladio, salvat Dominus.*"

NOUGHT [*over his shoulder*]: No, mary, I beschrew yow, it is *in
spadibus!*⁶
Therfor Cristys curse cum on yowr hedibus,°   *i.e., head*
400   To sende yow lesse might!° *Exiant.*   *strength*

MANKINDE: I promitt° yow, these felowse will no more cum here;   *promise*
For summe of them, certenly, were summewhat too nere!⁷
My fadyr Mercy avisyde° me to be of a goode chere   *advised*
Ande again° my enmys manly for to fight.   *against*

405   I shall convicte° them, I hope, everychon.   *conquer*
Yet I say amisse; I do it not alon:
With the helpe of the grace of Gode, I resist my fon°   *foes*
Ande ther° maliciouse herte.   *their*
With my spade I will departe, my worschippfull soverence,
410   Ande live ever with labure, to corecte my insolence.
I shall go fett corn° for my londe. I prey yow of pacience;   *fetch grain seed*
Right sone I shall reverte.°   *return*

[*He goes out to get his seed. Enter Mischief.*]

MISCHEFF: Alas, alasse, that ever I was wrought!
Alasse the whill,° I [am] wers then° nought!   *while, time / worse than*
415   Sithyn° I was here, by Him that me bought,°   *Since / ransomed*
I am utterly ondon.
I, Mischeff, was here at the beginninge of the game,
Ande arguyde with Mercy—Gode giff him schame!
He hath taught Mankinde, whill I have be vane,°   *been absent*
420   To fight manly ageyn° his fon.°   *against / foes*

For with his spade, that was his wepyn,°   *weapon*
New-Guise, Nowadays, and Nought hath [he] all tobetyn°—   *beaten utterly*
I have grett pité to se them wepyn.°   *weep*
Will ye list?° I here° them crye. *Clamant.*°   *listen / hear / they cry*

[*New-Guise, Nowadays, and Nought enter, sobbing, as Mischief
calls to them solicitously.*]
425   Alasse, alasse, cum hether! I shall be yowr borow.°   *protector*

---

5. I can't buy or sell from men worth a farthing (quarter-penny); i.e., I'm incapacitated.
6. David says, "The Lord saves neither with the spear nor with the sword." (Cf. 1 Samuel 17.47.)—No, indeed, curse you, he saves "with spades"!
7. I.e., came too close for their own good.

Alack, alack! *Vene,*° *vene!* Cum hethere, with sorowe!   *Come*
Pesse,° fayer babys! Ye shall have a nappyll°—tomorow.   *Peace, hush / apple*
Why grete° ye so, why?   *weep*

NEW-GUISE: Alasse, master, alasse, my privité!°   *privy parts*
MISCHEFF: A, wher? Alacke, fayer babe, ba me!°   *kiss me*
    Abide! Too sone I shall it se.[8]
NOWADAYS: Here, here, se my hede, goode master!
MISCHEFF: Lady,° helpe! Sely° darlinge, *vene, vene!*   *(Our) Lady / Poor*
    I shall helpe thee of thy peyn:
435   I shall smitte off thy hede and sett it on again.
NOUGHT: By Owr Lady, ser, a fayer playster![9]

    Will ye off with his hede? It is a schrewde charme!°   *i.e., harsh cure*
    As for me, I have none harme—
    I were loth to forbere° mine arme.   *do without*
440   Ye pley: *In nomine patris,* choppe!
NEW-GUISE: Ye shall not choppe my jewellys, and° I may.[1]   *if*
NOWADAYS: Ye, Cristys crose!° Will ye smight° my hede awey?   *cross / smite*
    Ther, wher, on and on? Oute! Ye shall not assay°—   *try*
    I might well be callyde a foppe.[2]

MISCHEFF: I kan choppe it off and make it again.°   *make it (whole)*
NEW-GUISE: I hade a schrewde *recumbentibus,*° but I fele no   *a knockdown blow*
    peyn.[3]
NOWADAYS: Ande my hede is all save° and wholl again.—   *safe, well*
    Now, towchinge° the mater of Mankinde,   *concerning*
    Lett us have an interleccion,° sithen ye be cum hethere.   *consultation*
450   It were goode to have an ende.[4]

MISCHEFF: How, how? A minstrell! Know ye ony ought?°   *any at all*
NOUGHT: I kan pipe in a Walsingham whistill, I, Nought,
    Nought.
MISCHEFF: Blow apase, and thou shall bring him in with a
    flowte.°[5]   *flute*
[*Nought plays. The voice of Titivillus is heard offstage.*]
TITIVILLUS: I com, with my leggys under me!
MISCHEFF: How, New-Guise, Nowadays, herke or° I goo: *ere*
    When owr hedys wer togethere, I spake of *si dedero.*[6]

8. I.e., Wait, don't show me the wound in your genital region; I'll see it all too soon anyway.
9. By the Virgin Mary, that would call for a fair-sized wound-plaster!
1. I.e., As for me, my wound is a mere scratch; I'd be most unwilling to do without my arm! (Nought minimizes his wound because he suspects that Mischief would resort to amputation, as he has threatened with Nowadays.) Your way is to say a quick prayer, and start cutting.—You won't castrate me if I can prevent it.
2. I.e., Cutting right and left, one after another? Curse it! I won't let you try; I might look foolish without my head.

3. (New-Guise and Nowadays still pretend, in order to avoid Mischief's treatment, that they need no medical attention.)
4. It would be good to bring this matter (of tempting Mankind) to a successful conclusion.
5. (It occurs to them that the answer to their problem—Titivillus—can best be fetched by playing music to attract him.)
6. When we conferred earlier, I spoke of taking up a collection. (*Si dedero:* If I give you something [I'll expect payment].)

NEW-GUISE: Ye, go thy wey, we shall gather mony onto°—   *for the purpose*
Ellys ther shall no man him° se.   *him (Titivillus)*

[*To the audience.*]
Now gostly° to owr purpos, worschipfull soverence,   *devoutly*
460   We intende to gather mony, if it plesse yowr necligence,[7]
For a man with a hede that [is] of grett omnipotens—
NOWADAYS: Kepe yowr tayll,[8] in goodnes I prey yow, goode
brother!
He[9] is a worschippfull man, sers, saving yowr reverens.°   *begging your pardon*
He lovith no grotys,° nor pens of two-pens:°   *groats / two-penny coin*
465   Gif us rede reyallys,° if ye will se his abhominabull   *royals, gold coins*
presens.
NEW-GUISE: Not so! Ye that mow° not pay the ton,° pay the
tother.   *may, can / one*
[*They pass among the audience, taking up a collection.*]

At the goode-man° of this house first we will assay.   *master, host*
Gode blisse yow, master! Ye sey us ill, yet ye will not sey
"nay."
Lett us go by and by, and do them pay.[1]
470   Ye pay all alike. Well mut ye fare!°   *May you have good luck*
[*When they have finished collecting, they return to the stage.*]
NOUGHT: I sey, New-Guise, Nowadays, *Estis vos pecuniatus?*°   *Are you moneyed?*
I have criede a fayer will, I beschrew yowr patus!°   *pate, head*
[*Nowadays turns to call in Titivillus.*]
NOWADAYS: *Ita vere, magister,* cumme forth now yowr gatus!°[2]   *gate, door*
He is a goodly man, sers; make space, and beware!
[*Enter Titivillus, arrayed as a devil with a net in his hand. He addresses the
audience.*]

TITIVILLUS: *Ego sum dominantium dominus,*[3] and my name is
Titivillus.
Ye that have goode hors,° to yow I sey *"caveatis"*:°   *horses / beware*
Here is an abyll felyschippe to trise hem° out at yowr   *snatch them*
gatis![4]
Ego probo sic:°   *I demonstrate it thus*
(*Loquitur ad New-Guise.*°)   *He speaks to New-Guise*
Ser New-Guise, lende me a peny.
NEW-GUISE: I have a grett purse, ser, but I have no monay:
480   By the masse, I faill° two farthingys of an halpeny.[5]   *I am short*
Yit hade I ten pound this night° that was.   *last night*

---

7. An insolent term used instead of "reverence."
8. *Kepe yowr tayll:* watch what you say (addressed to New-Guise, interrupting him; or, keep proper custody of your reckoning, money collection).
9. Titivillus.
1. God bless you for your contribution, sir! Even though you say disparaging things about us players, you won't refuse to pay. Let us pass among the others and get them to pay.

2. I have begged (for money) a long time, with a curse on your head!—Truly therefore, master, now make your entrance.
3. I am lord of lords.
4. (To the audience) Here is a fellowship (these villains on stage) able to snatch your horses from your very doors!
5. A halfpenny. (New-Guise claims to have not a cent even after taking up the collection, thereby proving Titivillus' contention that he is a thief and scoundrel.)

TITIVILLUS (*loquitur ad Nowadays*): What is in thy purse?
    Thou art a stout velan.°   *valiant fellow*
NOWADAYS: The devill have [the] qwitt!° I am a clen   *bit*
    jentyllman.°6   *penniless*
    I prey Gode I be never wers storyde° then I am.   *worse supplied*
485   It shall be otherwise, I hope, or° this night passe.   *ere*
TITIVILLUS (*loquitur ad Nought*): Herke now, I say, thou hast
    many a peny.
NOUGHT: *Non nobis, domine, non nobis,*7 by Sent Deny!°   *Saint Denis*
    The devill may daunce in my purse for ony peny;
    It is as clen as a birdys ars.

TITIVILLUS [*to the audience*]: Now I say yet ageyn, "*caveatis*":
    Her is an abyll felyschippe to trise hem° out of yowr gatis!—   *them (horses)*
    Now I sey, New-Guise, Nowadays, and Nought,
    Go and serche the contré: anon [that] it be sowghte,
    Summe here, summe ther, what if° ye may cache owghte.8   *to see if*

495   If ye faill of hors,° take what ye may ellys.°   *don't find horses / otherwise*
NEW-GUISE: Then speke to Mankinde for the *recumbentibus*°   *knockdown blow /*
    of my jewellys!°   *on my testicles*
NOWADAYS: Remember my brokyn hede in the worschippe
    of the five vowellys.9
NOUGHT: Yea, goode ser, and the siatica in my arme!
TITIVILLUS: I know full well what Mankinde dide to yow;
500   Mischiff hath informyde [me] of all the matere thorow.°   *thoroughly*
    I shall venge yowr quarell, I make Gode a vow.
    Forth, and espye where ye may do harme!
    Take William Fyde,1 if ye will have ony mo.°   *any more (companions)*
    I sey, New-Guise, whethere° art thou avisyde° to go?   *whither / determined*

NEW-GUISE: First I shall begin at Master Huntington of
    Sauston.°   *Sawston*
    Fro thens I shall go to William Thurlay of Hauston,°   *Hauxton*
    Ande so forth to Picharde of Trumpington—
    I will kepe me to these thre.
NOWADAYS: I shall goo to Williham Bakere of Walton,
510   To Richerde Bollman of Gayton.
    I shall spare Master Woode of Fullburn°—   *Fulbourn*
    He is a "*noli me tangere.*"°2   *touch me not*

NOUGHT: I shall goo to William Patrike of Massingham;
    I shall spare Master Alington of Bottisham,
515   Ande Hamonde of Swoffeham,

---

6. May the devil have the whole lot! I'm penniless.
7. Not to us, O Lord, not to us. (Psalms 115.1, profanely quoted out of context.)
8. Some searching in one place and some in another, to see whether you can steal anything.
9. Perhaps an error for "seven devils," or a reference to

Christ's five wounds.
1. This and the following names doubtless made topical reference to the play's original audience in Cambridgeshire and Norfolk near Cambridge and Lynn, where all the towns mentioned are located.
2. I.e., an irascible fellow.

For drede of "*in manus tuas*, qweke!"[3]
Felows, cum forth and go we hens togethyr.

NEW-GUISE: Sith° we shall go, lett us be well ware wethere.°[4]   *Since / whither*
If we may be take,° we com no more hethyr.   *taken, captured*
520   Lett us con° well owr neke verse,[5] that we have not   *memorize*
a cheke.°   *disaster*

TITIVILLUS: Goo yowr wey, a devill wey,° go yowr wey all!   *in the devil's name*
I blisse yow with my lyfte[6] honde—foull yow befall!°   *bad luck to you*
Com again, I werne,° as sone as I yow call,   *admonish*
And bringe yowr avantage° into this place.   *your booty*
[*Exeunt. Manet Titivillus.*]
525   To speke with Mankinde I will tary here this tide,°   *at this time*
Ande assay his goode purpose for to sett aside.[7]
The goode man Mercy shall no lenger be his guide.
I shall make him to dawnce° another trace!   *dance*

Ever I go invisibull—it is my jett°—   *fashion*
530   Ande befor his ey thus I will hange my nett
To blench° his sight. I hope to have his fote-mett!°[8]   *blind / take his measure*
To irke him of his labur I shall make a frame:°   *a plot*
This borde° shall be hidde under the erth prevely.°   *board / secretly*
[*Titivillus places a board in Mankind's field.*]
His spade shall enter, I hope, onredily!°   *unreadily*
535   By then° he hath assayde,° he shall be very angry   *By the time / tried*
Ande lose his paciens—peyn of° schame.   *(on) penalty of*
I shall menge° his corne with drawke° and with durnell;   *mix / weeds*
It shall not be like° to sow nor to sell.   *suitable*
Yondyr he commith. I prey of cownsell.°   *Keep my secret*
540   He shall wene grace were wane!°   *think grace is lacking*
[*Enter Mankind with a sack of grain.*]

MANKIND: Now Gode, of his mercy, sende us of his sonde!°   *message, counsel*
I have brought sede here to sow° with my londe.   *with which to sow*
Qwhill I over-dylve it,° here it shall stonde.   *While I dig (the land)*
[*He sets the grain down, and Titivillus goes out with it while Mankind is using the spade.*]
In nomine Patris et Filii et Spiritus Sancti, now I will begin.
[*His spade strikes Titivillus' board in the earth.*]
545   This londe is so harde it makith [me] unlusty and irke!°   *tired and irritated*
I shall sow my corn at vyntur,° and lett Gode werke.   *at venture, random*
[*He turns to get his sack of grain.*]
Alasse, my corn is lost! Here is a foull werke!
I se well, by tillinge lityll shall I win.
[*He throws down the spade in disgust.*]

---

3. Into your hands (Christ's last words, and hence the final prayer of a man about to be hanged). *qweke*: a choking sound.
4. Since we're going, let's be very careful where we go.
5. The first verse of the fifty-first Psalm, the recitation of which in court enabled a defendant to claim right of clergy and so avoid the gallows.
6. Left (in the devil's blessing, everything is inverted).
7. And try to set aside his good intentions.
8. I.e., I hope to ensnare him.

Here I giff uppe my spade, for now and forever!

550   To occupye my body I will not put me in dever.°   *I won't endeavor*

[*Here Titivillus goth out with the spade.*]

I will here° my evynsonge here, or I dissever.°   *hear / ere I leave*

This place I assing° as for my kirke;°   *assign / church*

Here, in my kerke, I knell on my kneys. [*Prays, with beads.*]

Pater noster,° *qui es in caelis.*   (*The Lord's Prayer*)

TITIVILLUS [*re-entering*]: I promes yow, I have no lede° on my   *lead*
helys!°⁹   *heels*

I am here ageyn to make this felow irke.

Qwhist!° Pesse! I shall go to his ere and tityll° therin.   *Whist, quiet / whisper*

[*He goes up to Mankind and whispers in his ear.*]

A schorte preyere thirlith hevyn.° Of thy preyere blin.°   *pierces heaven / cease*

Thou art holier then ever was ony° of thy kin.   *any*

560   Arise and avent the[e]!° Nature compellys.   *relieve yourself*

[*Mankind rises, and excuses himself to the audience.*]

MANKIND: I will into this yerde, soverens, and cum ageyn sone.

For drede of the colike, and eke of the stone,°   *kidney-stone*

I will go do that nedys must° be done.   *that which must*

My bedys° shall be here for whosummever will ellys.¹   *beads*

Exiat [*leaving his prayer-beads behind*].

TITIVILLUS: Mankinde was besy in his prayere, yet I dide°   *caused*
him arise;

He is conveyde°—by Crist!—from his divine service.   *removed*

Whethere° is he, trow ye? Iwisse, I am wonder° wise: *Whither / wondrously*

I have sent him forth to schitte lesinges.°²   *lies*

Iff ye have ony silver, in happe° pure brasse,   *perchance*

570   Take a lityll powder of Parisch and cast over his° face,   *its (the coin's)*

Ande evyn in the howll-flight° let him passe.   *owl-flight (the dark)*

Titivillus kan lerne° yow many praty° thingys!³   *teach / pretty, crafty*

I trow Mankinde will cum ageyn sone,°   *soon*

Or ellys, I fere° me, evynsonge will be done!⁴   *fear*

575   His bedys shall be trisyde° aside, and that anon.   *thrown*

Ye shall° a goode sport, if ye will abide: *You will (have)*

Mankinde cummith ageyn—well fare he!⁵

I shall answere him *ad omnia quare.*°⁶   *at every "why"*

Ther shall be sett abroche° a clericall mater.°   *stirred up / controversy*

580   I hope of his purpose to sett him aside.⁷

[*Reenter Mankind.*]

---

9. I.e., I assure you, I move quickly.

1. My beads will be here for whoever else wants them.

2. I.e., I've sent him to learn the devil's lies by means of his bowels.

3. (Titivillus teaches the audience one of his magic spells. A brass coin coated with Paris-powder is to be passed—i.e., excreted?—at night.)

4. I.e., (sardonically) Otherwise I'm afraid he'll be too late for vespers.

5. Good luck to him (ironic).

6. I.e., I'll answer all his questions.

7. I trust to turn him aside from his purpose.

MANKIND: Evynsong hath be° in the sayinge, I trow, a   been
          fayer while!⁷ᴬ
     I am irke of it. It is too longe, by one mile.
     Do wey! I will no more so oft over the chirche-stile;⁸
     Be as be may, I shall do another.°   otherwise
585 Of labure and preyer, I am nere irke of both;
     I will no more of it, thowgh Mercy be wroth.
     My hede is very hevy, I tell yow, forsoth.
     I shall slepe full my bely,° and° he were my brother.⁹   my bellyfull / even if
[Goes to sleep and snores. Titivillus gloats to the audience.]

TITIVILLUS: Ande° ever ye dide, for me kepe now yowr   If
           silence!
590 Not a worde, I charge yow, peyn of forty pens!°   on pain of forfeiture
     A praty° game shall be schewde° yow, or° ye hens.   crafty / showed / ere
     Ye may here° him snore—he is sade° aslepe.   hear / sound
     Qwhist! Pesse! The devill is dede, I shall goo ronde°   whisper
         in his ere.¹
[He goes to Mankind and whispers in his ear.]
     Alasse, Mankinde, alasse, Mercy stown a mere!°   has stolen a mare
595 He is runn away fro his master, ther wot no man°   no one knows
         where.
     Moreover, he stale° both a hors and a nete!°   stole / neat, ox or cow

     But yet I herde° sey he brake his neke as he rode in   heard
         Fraunce;
     But I thinke he ridith on the galows, to lern for to°   how to
         daunce,²
     Bicause of his theft—that is his governance!³
600 Trust no more on him: he is a marryde° man.   marred, ruined
     Mekill° sorow with thy spade beforn° thou hast   Much / heretofore
         wrought;⁴
     Arise and aske mercy of New-Guise, Nowadays, and
         Nought.
     They cun° avise thee for the best. Lett ther° goode   can / their
         will be sought;
     Ande thy own wiff brethell,° and take thee a lemman.° deceive / mistress

[To the audience.]
605 For-well, everychon,° for I have don my game,   Farewell everyone
     For I have brought Mankinde to mischeff and to schame!
[Exit Titivillus. Mankind awakes.]

7A. Vespers has taken a long while in the saying (or   1. Hush! I'm going to whisper in Mankind's ear that
singing).   Mercy is dead (?).
8. To hell with it! No more will I climb over the steps in 2. I.e., swing at the end of a noose.
the churchyard wall (leading to church) as I have done so   3. That's how he conducts himself.
often.   4. You've caused much sorrow (to New-Guise, etc.)
9. I'll get my bellyfull of sleep, even if Mercy were my   heretofore with your spade.
brother (and thus would have a special claim on my loyalty).

MANKIND: Whope! who! Mercy hath brokyn his nekekicher,
     avows,°⁵   *(he) avows*
   Or he hangith by the neke hye upp on the gallowse!
   Adew, fayer masters,° I will hast me to the ale-house   *i.e., audience*
610   Ande speke with New-Guise, Nowadays, and Nought,
   And geett° me a lemman with a smattringe° face.   *get / kissable(?)*
[*New-Guise comes running in with a broken noose around his neck, shouting to the audience.*]
NEW-GUISE: Make space, for Cokkys° body sakyrde,° make   *God's / consecrated*
     space!
   A ha, well over-ron, Gode giff him evill grace!⁶
   We were nere Sent Patrikes Wey, by Him that me
     bought;°   *ransomed*

615   I was twichyde° by the neke—the game was begunne!   *twitched*
   A grace was, the halter brast° asonder: *Ecce signum!*°   *burst / Behold the proof*
   The halff is abowte my neke. We hade a nere runne!°   *narrow escape*
   "Beware," quod° the goode-wiff when sche smote off   *said*
     her husbondys hede, "beware!"
   Mischeff is a convicte, for he coude° his neke-verse.⁷   *knew*
620   My body gaff° a swinge when I hinge° uppon the   *gave / hung*
     casse.°   *gibbet-frame*
   Alasse, he will hange such a lighly° man and a ferse⁸   *likely, handsome*
   For stelinge of an horse—I prey Gode gif him care!°   *sorrow*

   Do wey° this halter! What devill doth Mankinde here,   *Take off*
     with sorrow?⁹
   Alasse, how my neke is sore, I make avowe!°   *I swear*
MANKIND: Ye be welcom, New-Guise. Ser, what chere with yow?°   *how goes it*
NEW-GUISE: Well, ser; I have no cause to mourn.
MANKIND: What was that abowte yowr neke, so Gode yow
     amende?°   *may God help you*
NEW-GUISE: In feyth, Sent Audrys holy bende.°¹   *neck-band*
   I have a lityll dishes,° as it plesse Gode to sende,   *disease*
630   With a runninge ringe-worme.
[*Enter Nowadays laden with stolen church furnishings, including the sacrament.*]

NOWADAYS: Stonde a-rom,° I prey thee, brother mine!   *Make room*
   I have laburryde all this night. When shall we go dine?

5. Whoop! Whoop! Mercy has broken his neck (literally, neckerchief), he (Titivillus) avows.
6. Well outrun (i.e., making good an escape), may God condemn him (the hangman)!
7. I.e., My head was in the noose—the jig was up. Fortunately, the noose parted in two: see, here's the proof, half of it still around my neck. We had a narrow escape! As the wife said when she was about to behead her husband (giving him a ludicrously ineffectual warning), "Watch out!" Mischief has been found guilty and imprisoned rather than executed because he was able to recite his neck-verse (see line 520 and note).
8. Alas that the hangman would hang such a handsome and fierce fellow.
9. (To the audience still) Take off this noose! What the devil is Mankind doing here, with sorrow to him? (New-Guise remembers his beating.)
1. (New-Guise, still mistrusting Mankind, evasively pretends that his broken noose is a necklace-charm against disease, gotten from a shrine.)

A chirche here-beside° shall pay for ale, brede, and wine: *nearby*
Lo, here is stoff° will serve.   *furnishing (that)*
NEW-GUISE: Now, by the holy Mary, thou art better marchande
    then I!
    [*Enter Nought.*]
NOUGHT: Avante,° knavys, lett me go by!   *Out of the way*
    I kannot geet,° and° I shulde sterve!   *get, steal / even if*
    [*Enter Mischief with a pair of fetters.*]

MISCHEFF: Here cummith a man of armys!° Why stonde ye so   *a soldier*
    still?[2]
    Of murder and manslawghter I have my bely-fill.
NOWADAYS: What, Mischeff, have ye ben in presun? And° it   *If*
    be yowr will,
    Me semith ye have scouryde° a peyr° of fetters.[3]   *scoured / pair*
MISCHEFF: I was chenyde° by the armys—lo, I have them here.   *chained*
    The chenys I brast° asundyr, and killyde the jailere,   *burst*
    Yea, ande his fayer wiff halsyde° in a cornere—   *embraced*
645   A, how swetly I kissyde the swete mowth of hers!

    When I hade do,° I was mine owyn bottler: *done, finished*
    I brought awey with me both disch and dublere.°   *plate*
    Here is anow° for me. Be of goode chere! [*He offers*   *enough*
        refreshment.]
    Yet well fare the new chesaunce![4]
MANKINDE [*kneeling*]: I aske mercy of New-Guise, Nowadays,
        and Nought.
    Onys° with my spade I remember that I faught;   *Once*
    I will make yow amendys if I hurt yow ought,
    Or dide ony grevaunce.

NEW-GUISE: What a devill likith thee to be of this disposicion?[5]
MANKINDE: I drempt Mercy was hange—this was my vision—
    Ande that to yow thre I shulde have recors and remocion.°   *inclination*
    Now I prey yow hertily of yowr goode will:
    I crye yow mercy of all that I dide amisse.
NOWADAYS [*aside*]: I sey, New-Guise, Nought: Titivillus made°   *caused*
    all this;
660   As sekyr° as Gode is in hevyn, so it is!   *sure*
NOUGHT [*to Mankind*]: Stonde uppe on yowr feet! Why stonde
    ye so still?°   *motionless*

NEW-GUISE: Master Mischeff, we will yow exort
    Mankindys name in yowr bok for to report.[6]

2. I.e., Why do you look so surprised?
3. Have you been in prison, Mischeff? If you don't mind my saying so, it seems to me you've scoured (polished by wearing) a pair of fetters.
4. I.e., Good luck to our new venture.
5. I.e., What the devil makes you want to change your mind (about us)?
6. (Mischief is urged to set down Mankind's name in his list of loyal followers. Mischief decides the apprenticeship needs the legal and ritual sanction of a manor-court session.)

MISCHEFF: I will not so; I will sett a corte.°   *convene a court*
665   Nowadays, mak proclamacion,
           And do it *sub forma juris*,° dastarde!°   *in legal form / fool*
NOWADAYS: Oy-yt,° oy-yit, oyet! All manere of men and   *Oyez*
           comun women
           To the cort of Mischiff othere° cum or sen!°   *either / send (excuses)*
           Mankinde shall retorn; he is one of owr men.
MISCHEFF: Nought, cum forth. Thou shall be stewerde.[7]

NEW-GUISE: Master Mischeff, his side gown° may be solde;   *long coat*
           He may have a jakett therof, and mony tolde.°[8]   *counted*
MANKINDE: I will do for the best, so° I have no colde.[9]   *so long as*
           [*He takes off his gown reluctantly.*]
675   Holde, I prey yow, and take it with yow,
           Ande let me have it ageyn in ony wise.° *Nought*   *in any case*
               scribit.°   *Nought is busy writing*
NEW-GUISE: I promitt° yow a fresch jakett, after the new   *promise*
               guise.
MANKINDE: Go and do that longith° to yowr office,   *that which pertains*
           And spare that ye mow!°   *save what you can*
           [*New-Guise goes out with Mankind's coat. Nought shows what he has written to
           Mischief.*]

NOUGHT: Holde, master Mischeff, and rede this!
MISCHEFF: Here is [*reads*] "*Blottibus in blottis, Blottorum blottibus
               istis.*"
           I beshrew yowr erys,° a fayer hande!   *ears*
NOWADAYS: Yea, it is a goode renninge fist;°   *cursive hand*
           Such an hande may not be mist.°[1]   *missed*
NOUGHT: I shulde have don better, hade I wist.°   *known*
MISCHEFF: Take hede, sers, it stoude you° on hande: [*reads.*]   *it behooves you*

           "*Curia tenta generalis,*[2]
           In a place ther° goode ale is,   *where*
           Anno regni regitalis
690   *Edwardi nullateni,*[3]
           On yestern day, in Feverere, the yere passith fully;°   *completely ends*
           As Nought hath writyn—here is owr Tully°—   *Cicero*
           Anno regni regis nulli."[4]

NOWADAYS: What how,° New-Guise, thou makist moche   *What ho*
               taryinge!
695   That jakett shall not be worth a ferthinge.

---

7. Recorder of a manor court.
8. I.e., money left over (because the long coat is large
enough to cut a jacket and have cloth left).
9. I.e., I'll do what you think best, as long as I don't get
cold. (Mankind correctly fears that the new fashion
won't keep him warm.)

1. (Sarcastically) Such a handwriting is indispensable.
2. "The general court having been held" (the usual heading for the record of manor-court proceedings).
3. "In the regnal year of King Edward the Nothing[th]."
4. As Nought, our expert writer in Latin, has written: "In
the regnal year of no king."

[*New-Guise returns with Mankind's coat drastically abbreviated. He elbows the audience aside.*]

NEW-GUISE: Out of my wey, sers, for drede of fightinge!
　　Lo, here is a feet° taill, light to leppe abowte!⁵　　　　*feat, elegant shape*
NOUGHT: It is not schapyn° worth a morsell of brede!　　　　*shaped*
　　Ther is too moche cloth—it weys as ony lede.°　　　　*weighs heavy as lead*
700　　I shall goo and mende it, ellys° I will lose my hede.°　　　　*or else / head*
　　Make space, sers, lett me go owte!
[*He goes out through the audience, with Mankind's coat.*]

MISCHEFF: Mankinde, cum hethere—God sende yow the
　　　　gowte!
　　Ye shall goo to all the goode felowse in the cuntré aboute,
　　Onto the goode-wiff when the goode-man° is owte.　　　　*husband*
705　　"I will," say ye.
MANKIND:　　　　　I will, ser.
NEW-GUISE: There arn but sex dedly sinnys; lechery is non,
　　As it may be verefiede by us brethellys everychon.°　　　　*rogues everyone*
　　Ye shall goo robbe, stell,° and kill as fast as ye may gon.　　　　*steal*
　　"I will," sey ye.
MANKIND:　　　　　I will, ser.

NOWADAYS: On Sundays, on the morow° erly betime,　　　　*morning*
　　Ye shall with us to the alle-house° erly to go dine,　　　　*ale-house*
　　And forbere° masse and matens, howres and prime.°　　　　*forbear / canonical*
　　"I will," sey ye.　　　　　　　　　　　　　　　　　　　　　　*hours*
MANKIND:　　　　　I will, ser.
MISCHEFF: Ye must have by yowr side a longe *da pacem*,°　　　　*"give peace," a dagger*
715　　As trew men ride by the wey, for to onbrace them.⁶
　　Take ther monay, kitt ther° throtys! Thus overface them.　　　　*cut their*
　　"I will," sey ye.
MANKIND:　　　　　I will, ser.
[*Nought returns with Mankind's coat reduced to a ridiculously short jacket.*]

NOUGHT: Here is a joly jakett! How sey ye?
NEW-GUISE:　　It is a goode jaket of fence° for a mannys body!⁷　　　　*defense*
[*They put it on Mankind.*]
720　　Hay, doog! hay, whoppe!° whoo! Go yowr wey lightly!°　　　　*whoop! / quickly*
　　Ye are well made for to ren.°⁸　　　　　　　　　　　　　　　　*run*
[*Mercy enters at a distance.*]
MISCHEFF:　　Tidingys, tidingys! I have aspyede one.
　　Hens° with yowr stuff,° fast we were gon!⁹　　　　*Hence / plunder*
　　I beshrew the last shall° com to his hom.　　　　*(who) shall*
　　Dicant omnes:°　　　　　　　　　　　　　　　　　*Let all say*
ALL:　　Amen!

---

5. Lo, here's an elegant shape in which to go leaping about nimbly!
6. To unbrace (i.e., rob and carve up) honest men as they ride on journeys.
7. I.e., (sarcastically) It's a fine short jacket to defend a man's body against the cold!
8. (In his new coat, Mankind evidently reminds New-Guise of a racing dog.)
9. Get going with your plunder; let's be off quickly!

MERCY: What, how, Mankinde, fle that felyschippe, I yow prey!

MANKINDE: I shall speke with [thee] another time—to-morn,
  or the next day.

    We shall goo forth together, to kepe my faders yer-day.° *death anniversary*
    A tapster, a tapster! Stow, statt,° stow!¹ *Whoa woman*

MISCHEFF: A mischeff go with!° Here I have a foull fall. *with (you)*
    Hens, awey fro me, or I shall beschitte yow all.

NEW-GUISE: What, how, hostlere,° hostlere, lende us a football! *innkeeper*
    Whoppe,° whow! a-now, a-now, a-now, a-now! *Whoop*

[*The rogues go off, taking Mankind with them.*]

MERCY: My minde is dispersyde,° my body trymmelith° as the *distracted / trembles*
    aspen leffe!

735 The terys shuld trekyll down by my chekys, were not
    yowr reverrence.²

    It were° to me solace, the cruell visitacion of deth! *It would be*
    Without rude behaver, I kan[not] expresse this
    inconveniens.° *misfortune*
    Wepinge, sythinge,° and sobbinge were my sufficiens;° *sighing / sustinence*
    All naturall nutriment to me as caren is odibull.° *is odious as carrion*

740 My inwarde afflixcion yeldith me° tediouse unto yowr *makes me*
    presens.
    I kannot bere it evynly° that Mankinde is so flexibull! *with equanimity*

    Man on-kinde,° wherever thou be! For, all this world *unnatural*
    was not aprehensible° *could not see how*
    To discharge thine originall offence, thraldam, and
    captivité,
    Till Godys own welbelovyde son was obedient and
    passible.° *willing to suffer*

745 Every droppe of his bloode was schede to purge thine
    iniquité.
    I discomende and disalow thine oftyn mutabilité!° *changeability*
    To every creature thou art dispectuose° and odible.° *contemptible / odious*
    Why art thou so on-curtess, so inconsideratt?° Alasse, *unkind*
    who° is me! *woe*
    As the fane° that turnith with the winde, so thou *weathervane*
    art convertible.

750 In trust is treson; thy promes is not credible.
    Thy perversiose° ingratitude I cannot rehers!°³ *perverse / speak*
    To God and to all the holy corte of hevyn thou art
    despectible,° *despicable*
    As a nobyll versifier makith mencion in this verse:
    "Lex et natura, Cristus et omnia jura
755 Damnant ingratum; lugent eum fore natum."⁴

---

1. (Mankind and his companions respond to Mercy's presence by indulging in a frenetic roughhouse, in which Mischief is tripped up.)
2. The tears would trickle down my cheeks, were it not for the respect I owe you (the audience).
3. I.e., Those whom we trust will betray us; your promises cannot be trusted. Your perverse ingratitude is more than I can say.
4. "Law and nature, Christ and all justice condemn the ingrate; they lament that he was born." (The author is unidentified.)

O goode Lady and Mother of Mercy, have pety° and compassion   *pity*

Of° the wrechydnes of Mankinde, that is so wanton and so fraill!   *On*

Lett° Mercy excede Justice, dere Mother! Admitt this supplicacion: *Grant*

Equité to be leyde onparty,° and Mercy to prevaill.   *set aside*

760   To sensuall livinge is reprovable that is nowadays,

As by the comprehence° of this mater it may be specifiede.[5]   *contents*

New-Guise, Nowadays, Nought, with ther allectuose° ways   *alluring*

They have pervertyde Mankinde, my swet sun, I have well espyede.

A, with these cursyde caityfs, and° I may, he shall not long indure!   *if*

765   I, Mercy, his father gostly, will procede forth and do my propyrté.°   *special task*

Lady, helpe! This maner of livinge is a detestabull plesure.

Vanitas vanitatum,° all is but a vanité.[6]   *Vanity of vanities*

Mercy shall never be convicte of° his oncurtes condicion;   *conquered by / Man's*

With wepinge terys,° by nighte and by day, I will goo, and never sesse.°   *tears / cease*

770   Shall I not finde him? Yes, I hope. Now Gode be my proteccion!

[*He calls aloud.*]

My predilecte° son, wher be ye? Mankinde, *ubi es?*°   *greatly beloved / where are you*

[*He goes off, crying "Ubi es?" Enter Mischief.*]

MISCHEFF: My prepotent fadere, when ye sowpe,° sowpe out yowr messe!   *sup*

Ye are all to-gloriede in yowr termys—ye make many a lesse.°[7]   *lie*

Will ye here?° He crieth ever° "Mankinde, *ubi es?*"   *Do you hear / constantly*

[*Enter New-Guise. Nowadays and Nought, who have been relieving themselves, follow soon after.*]

NEW-GUISE: Hic,° hic, hic, hic, hic, hic, hic, hic!   *Here*

That is to sey, here, here, here, ny dede° in the cryke!°[8]   *nearly dead / creek*

If ye° will have him, goo and syke,° syke, syke!   *ye (Mercy) / seek*

Syke not over-long, for losinge of yowr minde.

5. Sensual living can be blamed for what goes on nowadays, as may be proven by the contents of this edifying story.
6. (Ecclesiastes 1.2.)
7. My greatly powerful father, when you sup, drink up your portion! (A nonsense parody of Mercy's parting statement.) You are excessively puffed up (i.e., Latinate, aureate) in your vocabulary—you tell many a lie.
8. (New-Guise mockingly suggests how Mankind might answer Mercy's call: "Here I am, nearly dead in a creek.")

NOWADAYS: If ye will have Mankinde—how, *Domine, Domine,*
    Dominus!°—   *Lord*
780   Ye must speke to the schrive for a *cape corpus,*°   *"take his body"*
    Ellys ye must be fain to retorn with *non est inventus.*°   *"he is not found"*
    How sey ye, ser? My bolte° is schett.°   *bolt, arrow / shot*
NOUGHT: I am doinge of my nedingys;° beware how ye schott!⁹   *moving my bowels*
    Fy, fy, fy! I have fowll arayde my fote.°   *foully soiled my foot*
785   Be wise for schotinge with yowr takyllys,° for, Gode   *weapons*
    wott,¹
    My fote is fowly over-schett.°   *covered with shit*

MISCHEFF: A parlement, a parlement! Cum forth, Nought,
    behinde;°   *from behind*
    A cownsell belive!° I am aferde° Mercy will him finde.   *quickly / afraid*
    How sey ye? And what sey ye? How shall we do with
    Mankinde?
NEW-GUISE: Tische,° a flyes weyng!° Will ye do well?²   *Tush / wing*
    He wenith° Mercy were honge for steling of a mere.°   *thinks / mare*
    Mischeff, go sey to him that Mercy sekith everywhere:
    He will honge himselff, I undyrtake,° for fere.°   *wager / fear (of a ghost)*
MISCHEFF: I assent therto. It is wittily seyde, and well.

NOWADAYS: Qwippe° it in thy cote; anon it were don!   *Whip, put*
    Now, Sent Gabriellys modyr save the clothes° of thy   *clouts*
    schon!³
    All the bokys in the worlde,° if they hade be undon,°   *books / been ransacked*
    Kowde° not a° cownselde us bett.°   *Could / have / better*
    Hic° exit Mischeff. [*He returns with Mankind, now*   *Here*
    in despair.]
MISCHEFF: How, Mankinde, cumm and speke with Mercy!
    He is here fast by.°   *nearby*
MANKINDE: A roppe, a rope, a rope! I am not worthy.
MISCHEFF: Anon, anon, anon! I have it here redy,
    With a tre° also that I have gett.°   *gallows-tree / gotten*
[*They bring forth a rope and gallows.*]

    Holde the tre, Nowadays; Nought, take hede and be wise!
NEW-GUISE: Lo, Mankinde, do as I do: this is thy new guise.
805   Giff° the roppe just to thye neke, this is mine avise.   *Give, adjust*
[*New-Guise demonstrates with his own neck in the noose. Mercy enters at a*
distance.]

---

9. If you want to find Mankind—O, Lord, Lord, Lord!
(Nowadays mimics Mercy's prayerful entreaties)—you
must speak to the sheriff for a writ of arrest, or else you
must be content to come back with a sheriff's certifica-
tion that the prisoner cannot be found. (Mankind has
evidently been getting into trouble with the law.) How
do you like the way I've shot my bolt, i.e., practiced my
wit at Mercy's expense (with an added meaning of
"relieved myself")?—Nought (who has apparently been
the target of this "shot" in a literal sense): Watch where

you're shooting while I'm moving my bowels!
1. Watch where you're aiming with your weapon (perhaps in the obscene sense), for, God knows.
2. Tush, a fly's wing (or weight; a trifle). Do you want my
idea as to how we'll succeed?
3. Put it quickly in your kirtle (i.e., the rope for
Mankind?); let it be done immediately! Now, may Saint
Gabriel's mother save the clouts or cleats of your shoes!
(a hyperbolical oath of appreciation).

MISCHEFF: Helpe thysylff, Nought! Lo, Mercy is here!
   He skarith us° with a bales;° we may no lengere tary!   *drives us off / scourge*
  [*They run away. New-Guise, forgetting the rope, hangs himself.*]
NEW-GUISE: Qweke, qweke, qweke! Alass, my thrott!
   I beschrew yow, mary![4]
   A, Mercy, Cristys coppyde° curse go with yow—and   *heaped-up*
   Sent Davy!
810 Alasse, my wesant!° Ye were sumwhat too nere.   *throat*
  [*They return and release him.*] *Exiant.* [*Mankind falls, despairing.*]

MERCY: Arise, my preciose redempt son! Ye be to me full dere.—
   He is so timerouse, me semith° his vitall sprit doth exspire.   *it seems to me*
MANKINDE: Alasse, I have be° so bestially disposyde I dare   *been*
   not apere!
   To se yowr solayciose° face I am not worthy to dysiere.° *solace-giving / desire*

MERCY: Yowr criminose compleynt° woundith my hert as a   *confession of guilt*
   lance!
   Dispose yowrsylff mekly to aske mercy, and I will assent.
   Yelde° me nethyr golde nor tresure, but yowr humbyll   *Yield, give*
   obeisiance—
   The voluntary subjeccion of yowr hert—and I am content.

MANKIND: What, aske mercy yet onys again? Alas, it were a
   vile peticion!
820 Evyr to offend and ever to aske mercy, it is a puerilité.°   *childish way*
   It is so abhominabyll to rehers my iterat° transgrescion,   *repeated*
   I° am not worthy to have mercy by no possibilité.   *(That) I*

MERCY: O Mankend, my singler solas,° this is a lamentabyll   *special solace*
   excuse!
   The dolorus° terys of my hert, how they begin to a-mownt!° *sorrowful / mount*
825 O pirssid° Jhesu, help thou this sinfull sinner to redouce!° *pierced / lead back*
   Nam haec est mutatio dexterae Excelsi: vertit impios, et non
   sunt.[5]

   Arise and aske mercy, Mankend, and be associat to me.
   Thy deth schall be my hevinesse. Alas, tis pety it schuld
   be thus!
   Thy obstinacy will exclude [thee] fro the glorius perpetuité.° *eternity*
830 Yet, for my lofe,° ope° thy lippys and sey "*Miserere mei,* *love / open*
   Deus!"[6]
MANKEND: The egall° justise of God will not permitte sych a   *evenhanded*
   sinfull wrech
   To be revivyd and restoryd ageyn; it were impossibyll.

---

4. Sound of choking. *mary:* marry, indeed.   (Psalms 77.10 and Proverbs 12.7.)
5. For this is the change of the right hand of the Most   6. Have mercy upon me, O God.
High: he overthrows the wicked, and they are no more.

MERCY: The justice of God will° as I will, as himsylfe doth preche: *will do*
        Nolo mortem peccatoris, inquit, iff he will be redusible.°[7]   *recoverable*

MANKEND: Than° mercy, good Mercy! What is a man withowte   *Then*
        mercy?
        Lityll is our parte of paradise, where mercy ne were.°   *if mercy were lacking*
        Good Mercy, excuse the inevitabyll objeccion° of my   *assault*
        gostly enmy.
        The proverbe seyth, "The trewth tryith the sylfe." Alas,
        I have mech care!°   *much sorrow*

MERCY: God will not make yow prevy onto his Last Jugement.[8]
840   Justice and equité shall be fortifyid,° I will not denye;   *strong in argument*
        Trowthe° may not so cruelly procede in his streyt°   *(Yet) Truth / strict*
        argument
        But that Mercy schall rewle the mater, withowte
        contraversye.°   *doubtless*

        Arise now, and go with me in this deambulatorye.°   *walking area, cloister*
        Incline yowyr capacité; my doctrine is convenient.[9]
845   Sinne not in hope of mercy![1] That is a crime notary.°   *notorious*
        To truste overmoche in a prince, it is not expedient.

        In hope, when ye sin, ye thinke to have mercy: beware
        of that aventure!
        The good Lord seyd to the lecherus woman of Chanane°—   *Canaan*
        The holy Gospell is the autorité, as we rede in Scripture—
850   *"Vade, et iam amplius noli peccare."*[2]

        Crist preservyd this sinfull woman takyn in avowtry;°   *adultery*
        He seyde to her theis° wordys, "Go and sin no more."   *these*
        So to yow: "Go, and sin no more." Beware of veyn°   *vain*
        confidens of° mercy!   *in*
        Offend not a prince on trust° of his favour, as I seyd   *in trust*
        before.

855   If ye fele° yoursylfe trappyd in the snare of your gostly   *feel*
        enmy,
        Aske mercy anon;° beware of the continuance!°   *at once / continuing in sin*
        Whill a wound is fresch, it is provyd curabyll by
        surgery,
        That,° if it procede ovyrlong, it is cawse of gret grevans.   *Which*

---

7. I do not wish the sinner's death, he said (see Ezekiel 33.11), if he is willing to be recovered.
8. I.e., Good Mercy, forgive my fall as the result of the unavoidable assault of my spiritual enemy. As the proverb says, "The truth proclaims itself." Alas, I have great sorrow!—God won't share with you the secret intentions of his Last Judgment. (Mercy hereupon describes the debate of the four daughters of God, as in *Perseverance,* although he doesn't actually name Peace.)
9. Submit your understanding to my teaching; it is befitting, agreeable.
1. Beware of sinning in hope of mercy. (See Ecelesiasticus 5.4–7.)
2. Go and sin no more. (John 8.11.)

MANKEND: To aske mercy and to have, this is a liberall°   *precious*
        possescion.
860   Schall this expedicius peticion ever be alowyd, as ye
        have insight?
MERCY: In this present life, mercy is plenté, till deth makith
        his division.
        But, whan ye be go,° *usque ad minimum quadrantem* ye   *gone, dead*
        schall rekyn your right.³

        Aske mercy, and have, whill the body with the sowle
        hath his annexion;
        If ye tary till your discesse,° ye may hap of your desire   *decease*
        to misse.
865   Be repentant here! Trust not the howr of deth. Thinke
        on this lessun:
        Ecce nunc tempus acceptabile, ecce nunc dies salutis.

        All the vertu in the world if° ye might comprehend,°   *even if / attain*
        Your meritys were not premiabyll° to the blis above—   *deserving of reward*
        Not to the lest joy of hevyn, of your propyr° efforte to   *your own*
        ascend.⁴
870   With mercy, ye may. I tell yow no fabyll; Scripture
        doth prove.

MANKEND: O Mercy, my suavius° solas and singuler°   *sweet / sole*
        recreatory,°   *restorer*
        My predilecte° spesiall! Ye are worthy to have my love.   *dearly beloved*
        For, withowte deserte and menys supplicatorye,
        Ye be compacient° to my inexcusabyll reprove.°⁵   *compassionate / shame*

875   A, it swemith° my hert to think how onwisely I have   *grieves*
        wrought!
        Titivillus, that goth° invisibele, hing° his nett before   *who goes / hung*
        my eye,
        And by his fantasticall visionys sediciously sowght,
        To New-Guise, Nowadayis, Nowght causyd me to obey.⁶

MERCY: Mankend, ye were oblivious of my doctrine monitorye:°   *admonitory*
880   I seyd before, Titivillus wold asay yow a bronte.°   *try an attack on you*
        Beware fro hensforth of his fablys delusory!
        The proverbe seyth: "*Jacula praestita minus laedunt.*"⁷

3. To ask for and receive mercy is a precious thing. Will this hastily-presented request ever be granted, as you understand the situation?—As long as you're alive, mercy is still plentifully available (i.e., it is never too late to repent during life). But when you die, you'll have to reckon up your just reward to the uttermost farthing (literally, smallest fourth part of a coin). (See Matthew 5.26.)
4. Behold, now is the accepted time, behold, now is the day of salvation. (2 Corinthians 6.2.) Even if you could attain to all the virtues in the world, your merits would not entitle you to the least joy of heaven, to ascend by your own efforts to heavenly bliss.
5. For you are compassionate toward my inexcusable shame—I who am without deserving or means of imploring you for help.
6. And by his supernatural illusions seditiously endeavored to cause me to obey New-Guise, Nowadays, and Nought.
7. "Anticipated darts wound less."

Ye have thre adversaryis and he is mayster of hem° all: *them*
That is to sey, the Devell, the World, the Flesch and
    the Fell.°   *Skin*

885   The New-Guise, Nowadayis, Nowgth, the "World" we
    may hem call;
And propyrlly Titivillus singnifith the Fend of helle;

The Flesch—that is the unclene concupissens of your body.
These be your thre gostly enmyis, in whom ye have put
    your confidens.
They browght yow to Mischeffe, to conclude your temporall
    glory—
890   As it hath be schewyd° before this worcheppfyll audiens.   *been showed*

Remembyr how redy I was to help yow; fro swheche° I was   *from such*
    not dangerus.[8]
Wherfore, good sunne, absteyne fro sin evermore after this!
Ye may both save and spill° yowr sowle, that is so precius;   *destroy*
Libere welle, libere nolle God may not deny, iwis.[9]

895   Beware of Titivillus with his net, and of all his envious will,
Of your sinfull delectacion° that grevith your gostly substans.°   *pleasure / soul*
Your body is your enmy. Let him not have his will!
Take your leve° whan ye will—God send yow good   *Depart*
    perseverans!

MANKIND: Sith I schall departe, blisse me, fader, here then I go.°   *ere I go*
    God send us all plenté of his gret mercy!
MERCY: *Dominus custodit te ab omni malo!*[1]
    In nomine Patris, et Filii, et Spiritus Sancti. Amen.

    Hic° exit Mankend. [*Mercy speaks the epilogue.*]   *Here*

Wyrschepfyll sofereyns, I have do my propirté:°   *my special task*
Mankind is deliveryd by my faverall patrocinye.°   *benevolent protection*
905   God preserve him fro all wickyd captivité,
And send him grace his sensuall condicions° to mortifye!   *disposition*

Now, for His love that for us receivyd His humanité,°   *i.e., took human form*
Serche your condicions with dew° examinacion!   *due, thorough*
Thinke and remembyr the world is but a vanité,
910   As it is provyd daly by diverse transmutacion.

Mankend is wrechyd, he hath sufficient prove;°   *sufficently proven*
Therefore God [grant] yow all *per suam misericordiam*°   *through his mercy*
That ye may be pley-ferys° with the angellys above,   *companions*
And have to your porcion *vitam aeternam.*° Amen!   *life everlasting*
    Finis.

---

8. From such (encounters) I was not standoffish, reluctant.   choose, truly.
9. You have free will to choose salvation or damnation;   1. (May) the Lord preserve you from all evil. (Psalms
God may not deny you freely to choose or freely not to   121.7.)

Christine de Pizan
c. 1364–c. 1430

Christine de Pizan is an epochal figure in the history of European literature, not only for the quality and influence of her many works, but equally because she was Europe's first profession-al woman of letters. There were many important women writers in the Middles Ages, several of them represented in this anthology, but Christine—widowed in 1389 with three children and no family money—was the first to make writing the sole source of her income. She was well aware of this and wove her unique perspective, as a woman engaged with a largely male (and often misogynist) intellectual tradition, into much of her writing.

Like many late medieval writers, Christine de Pizan spent a good part of her energies translating, adapting, and consolidating earlier works on a wide range of topics, from moral and political treatises (such as the *Book of Peace*) to texts on religion (*Prayers to Our Lady*) and the conduct of war (*Book of the Deeds of Arms and Chivalry*). She wrote love poetry in traditional forms such as the ballade, but innovated by writing lyrics on widowhood as well. Like other writers of her time, too, Christine frames many of her books as dream-visions populated by alle-gorical figures, especially teachers or guides, such as the three ladies (Reason, Rectitude, and Justice) whom she encounters in the *Book of the City of Ladies*. Also like her contemporaries, Christine had to seek patronage in the noble and royal courts of France (where she spent most of her life) and Burgundy, as well as England. She was an innovator here as well, though, care-fully supervising the scribes and painters who produced splendid manuscripts of her works for presentation to her patrons.

Christine innovated most of all, however, by persistently reacting to her cultural inheri-tance from the perspective of women. At the turn of the fifteenth century, she was a major voice in the debate surrounding the famous but often misogynist *Romance of the Rose*. Classical and medieval Latin had an even greater store of works hostile to women; Christine began her intervention in that tradition around 1400 by inventing a quasi-classical goddess, Othea, to instruct the Trojan prince Hector in the *Letter of Othea*. It is with the *Book of the City of Ladies*, though, that Christine offers a systematic response to the depiction of women in biblical and classical texts. The three allegorical ladies who appear to her as the book opens instruct Chris-tine to build a walled city—a typical space of allegorical narrative—of and for the virtuous women of her cultural past. In doing so, Christine radically reinterprets women's histories as they have been recorded by men, and imagines a symbolic space from which a female literary tradition might emanate.

The works of Christine de Pizan were widely known in England in her own lifetime and well into the early modern period. Splendid manuscripts of her French works came into the hands of English kings and nobles. Her elder son was raised for three years in the household of the Duke of Salisbury, an influential member of the court of Richard II. Christine's *Letter of Othea* was translated three times in the fifteenth century; and Thomas Hoccleve, a late con-temporary of Chaucer, adapted her *Letter of the God of Love*—a feminist response to courtly love—as the *Letter of Cupid*. England's first printer, William Caxton, translated and published yet other of her works (some by royal commission) in the 1480s, as did early sixteenth-century printers like Henry Pepwell, who published Brian Anslay's 1521 translation of the *Book of the City of Ladies*, which is used here.

Her role in England places Christine de Pizan within several key transitions there. The ongoing translations of her works reflect the importation of Continental texts into an increasingly English-language literary and political culture under the Lancastrian and Yorkist kings. The numerous early printings of these translations is part of a massive dissemination of late medieval texts made possible by the rise of print. And in turn, this widespread access to

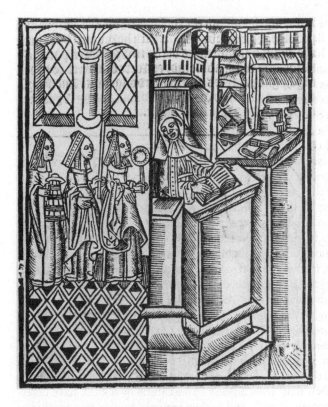

Illustration from Brian
Anslay's English translation
of *Book of the City of Ladies*,
1521

later medieval literary modes carried their influences—not least, that of allegory—into early
modern culture in England. Works like the *Book of the City of Ladies* lie behind the allegorized, often female-controlled cities and castles of early modern works like Spenser's *Faerie
Queene*.

from *Book of the City of Ladies*[1]

[In the first chapter Christine presents herself surrounded by books in her study, and
is dismayed to read philosophers and poets all claiming that women are full of vice.
While such a view is contrary to her perception of herself and of other women she
has known, she concludes that so many famous men cannot be wrong. She is so overwhelmed by sorrow that she asks God why he created women, if they are so vile, and
why he did not make her a man, so that she might serve him better.]

[PART 1, CHAPTER 2]

*Christine telleth how three ladies appeared to her, and how she that went before rea-
soned with her first, and comforted her of the displeasure that she had.*

As I was in this sorrowful thought, my head downcast as a shameful person, the eyes
full of tears, holding mine hand under my cheek, leaning upon the pommel of my

1. Translated by Brian Anslay (1521); edited with modernized spelling by Christopher Baswell.

chair, suddenly I saw come down upon my lap a streaming of light, as it were of the sun. And I, that was in a dark place in which the sun might not shine at that hour, started then as though I had been wakened of a dream; and dressing[2] the head to behold this light from whence it might come, I saw before me standing three ladies, crowned, of right sovereign reverence. Of the which the shining of their clear faces gave light unto me and to all the place. Threat I was marveling—neither man nor woman with me, considering the door closed upon me, and they thither came—doubting lest it had been some fantasy for to have tempted me, made the sign of the cross on my forehead, full of dread. And then she which was the first of the three in laughing began thus to reason with me. "Dear Daughter dread thee nought, for we be not come hither for nothing that is contrary unto thee, nor to do thee to be encumbered,[3] but for to comfort thee as those that have pity of thy trouble; and to put thee out of the ignorance that so much blindeth thine understanding, and that thou puttest from thee that thou knowest of very certain science,[4] to give faith to the contrary—to that which thou feelest not, nor seest not, nor knowest otherwise than by plurality[5] of strange opinions. Thou resemblest the fool of the which was made a jape,[6] which was sleeping in the mill and was clothed in the clothing of a woman; and to make resemblance[7] those that mocked him witnessed he was a woman, and so he believed more their false sayings than the certainty of his being. How is it, fair daughter, and where is thy wit become? Hast thou forgotten now how the fine gold proveth him[8] in the furnace, that he changeth not his virtue but is more pliant to be brought into diverse fashions? And knowest thou not that the most marvelous things be most debated and most argued, if thou wilt advise thee? In the same wise to[9] the most high things that be, that is to know, the celestial things. Behold if these great philosophers, that hath been that[1] thou arguest against thine own kind, have determined false and to the contrary of truth, and as they repugne[2] one against another as thou thyself hast seen in the book of *Metaphysics* whereas Aristotle reproveth their opinions, and rehearseth the same wise of[3] Plato and of others. And note this again, if[4] Saint Augustine and other doctors of the church have done so the same wise Aristotle in some parties,[5] albeit that he be called the prince of philosophers, and in whom philosophy, natural and moral, was sovereignly. And it seemeth thou trowest[6] that all the words of philosophers be articles of the faith of Jesus Christ, and that they may not err. And as to these poets of which thou speakest, knowest not thou well that they have spoken in many things in manner of fables, and intend so much to the contrary of that that their sayings showeth? And it may be taken after the rule of grammar the which is named Antiphrasis, the which intendeth thus, as thou knowest well: as one should say sith[7] one is a shrew, that is to say that he is good; and so by the contrary. So I counsel thee that thou do thy profit of[8] their sayings and thou understand it so, whatsoever be their intent in such places whereas they blame women. And peradventure[9] this same man that is Matheolus in his book[1] understood the

2. Turning.
3. Troubled.
4. (The ignorance) that makes you reject what you know through sure knowledge.
5. Multiplicity.
6. Joke.
7. To trick him.
8. Is tested.
9. This applies to.
1. The reason that.

2. How they contradict.
3. Makes the same point about.
4. How.
5. Done the same thing to Aristotle in some passages.
6. Believe.
7. Since.
8. Interpret positively.
9. Perhaps.
1. *The Book of the Lamentations of Matheolus*, the misogynist work that most troubled Christine in her study.

same. For there be many things, whoso taketh them after the letter, it should be pure heresy and shame to him that saith it, and not only to him but to others. And the same wise of the *Romance of the Rose* on whom is put great faith, because of the authority of the maker of [2] the order of marriage, which is an holy estate and worshipful and ordained of God. This thing proveth clearly by experience that the contrary is true of the shrewdness that they purpose and saith to be in that estate, to great charge and blame of women. For who was ever that husband that ever suffered such mastery of [3] his wife that she should have leave to say so many villainies and injuries as they put upon women that they should say? I believe whatsoever thou hast seen in writing thou sawest it never at the eye. So they be pure lesyngs[4] right shrewdly colored. Thus I say in concluding, my lief [5] friend, that folly caused thee this present opinion. Now come again to thyself and take thy wit and trouble thee no more for such fantasies. For know well that all this evil sayings generally of women hurteth the sayers and not the women.

[PART 1, CHAPTER 3]

Christine saith how that the lady that reasoned with her devised[6] what was her property and whereof she served, and told her how she should build a city with the help of the three ladies.

This famous lady saying these words to me, with the presence of whom I can not say which of my wits was most undertaken[7]: in mine hearing, in hearkening of her worthy words; where that my sight was[8] in beholding her great beauty, her attire, her reverent port and her right worshipful countenance. And the same wise of the others, and wist[9] not which of them to behold. For so much these three ladies resembled either other, that of pain[1] I might know that one from that other, but that I should have been deceived. And she of the less authority than that other had her cheer so fierce that whom her eyes beheld was not so hardy but that he should be undertaken[2] with great dread. For it seemed that she menaced the evil doers. So I was before them standing up from my siege[3] for their reverence, beholding them without saying of any word, as that person that was so overtaken that could not sound a word. And I had great marvel in my heart, thinking who they might be, and right gladly if I had durst, I would have asked their names and their being, and what was the signifying of the different scepters that each of them held in their right hands, which were of right great richesse, and wherefore they were come thither. Yet when I had thought me not worthy to reason with them in such demands—so high ladies as they appeared unto me—I durst in no manner, but continued my sight upon them, half afeared, and half assured by the words that I had heard them say, which hath cast me out of my first thought. Yet that right wise lady that reasoned with me, which knew my thought in spirit, as she that hath sight in all things, answered to my thought saying thus. "Dear daughter, know ye that the providence of God, that nothing leaveth vain, commandeth us to estable[4]—though that we know celestial things to be[5]—and to

---

2. Because of the respect accorded its writer regarding (his knowledge of).
3. By.
4. Lies.
5. Dear.
6. Explained.
7. Overcome.
8. Or whether my sight was (more overcome).

9. [I] knew.
1. With difficulty.
2. Whomever she looked at was not so brave that he would not be overcome.
3. Seat.
4. Commands us to remain. (The 1521 printing here reads "ne cometh not us to estable," an apparent error.)
5. Though we are celestial beings.

haunt among the people of this base world, to the intent[6] to put in order and to hold in equity the stablements[7] made by ourself after the will of God in diverse offices, to the which god we three be daughters and of him borne. So it is mine office to redress[8] men and women when they are out of the way, to put them again in the right way. And I come to them privily, in spirit all covertly, and I preach them and teach them in showing their error and that in which they fail, I assign them to the causes, and after, I teach them the manner to follow, that that is to do, and how they should flee that that is to be left. And for that[9] I serve to show clearly, and make to see in conscience their deeds, to every man and woman, and their proper taches[1] and defaults, thou seest me hold instead of a scepter this bright glass or mirror that I bear in my right hand. Know this for truth that there is no person that looketh this mirror but he may know every creature what he is clearly. O! my mirror, it is of so great dignity that it is not without great cause that he is so environed of so[2] rich precious stones as thou seest it. For by him these beings, qualities, proportion, and measures of all things be known; nor without him may nothing be well made nor done. And forthy[3] that thou desirest to know also the offices of mine other two sisters that thou seest here, to that intent that the witnessing of us may be to thee more certain, each of them in their own person shall answer of their name and of their property. Yet the cause and the moving of our coming shall be declared by me right here. I make thee to understand that as there shall be done nothing without good cause, our appearing is nothing here in vain. For though that we be not commonly in many places, and that the knowledge of us cometh not unto all people, nevertheless for the great love the which thou hast for to enquire after things by very long and continual study, by the which thou dost yield thyself here solitary and thou withdrawest thee out of the world, thou hast deserved and thou deservest to be visited and to be comforted of us in thy trouble and sorrow as right a dear friend, and that thou be made clearly seeing those things that defoul and trouble thy courage[4] in the darkness of thought. Also there is a greater cause of our coming and a more special that thou shalt know by our revelation; so understand to that intent[5] that this error might be destroyed, we would that these ladies and all worshipful women might have from henceforth some manner of place to come to, or a cloister of defense against all those that would assail them. For the default of which all these foresaid ladies and famous women have long time be left unclosed,[6] as a field without hedge, without finding of any champion that for their defense might compare sufficiently,[7] notwithstanding these noblemen that by ordinance of right ought to defend them, which by negligence and no force hath suffered them to be defouled. By the which it is no marvel though their envious enemies and the outrage of villainies assailed them by diverse crafts, and have had the victory against them in their war for default of defense. Where is the city so strong that might not soon be taken if there be not found resistance? Nor so unjust a cause but it might be gotten by continuance of him that pleadeth without party?[8] Right so these simple and debonair ladies, to[9] the example of patience which God commandeth, hath suffered friendly[1] these great injuries, that[2] so much by the mouth of so many

---

6. With the purpose.
7. Enactments.
8. Correct.
9. Since.
1. Defects.
2. Surrounded by such.
3. Because.
4. Spirit.

5. To that purpose.
6. Unenclosed.
7. Be an adequate fighter.
8. Who makes a legal case without opposition.
9. By.
1. Cheerfully.
2. (These ladies) who.

and their hands' writing have suffered so much wrong, though they report them to God of their good right.[3] Yet now it is time that their just cause be put out of the hands of Pharaoh. And therefore between us three ladies that thou sees here, moved by pity, we be come to tell thee of a certain building made in the manner of a cloister, of a city strongly wrought by masons' hands and well builded which is predestinate to thee for to make, and to stable[4] it by our help and counsel, in the which shall none inhabit but only ladies of good fame and women worthy of praisings. For to them where virtue shall not be found, the walls of our city shall be strongly shut.

[PART 1, CHAPTER 4]

Christine telleth how the lady devised to her the city that was committed to her to make, and that she was stabled[5] to help her to begin the walls and the cloister about, and after told her her name.

Thus, fair daughter, the prerogative is given to thee among all other women to make and fortify the city of ladies, for the which thou shall take upon thee to make the foundation and perfectly conclude him.[6] And thou shalt receive of us three wine and water as of a clear well. And we shall deliver to thee matter enough, more stronger and more durable than any marble, and as for cement there shall be no better than thou shall have. So shall thy city be right fair without peer and of perpetual during[7] to the world. Hast ye not read that the king of Troy founded the great city of Troy by the help of Apollo, Minerva, and Neptune, which the people at that time trowed them as[8] gods? And also how Cadmus founded the city of Thebes by the ministration of gods? And for all that, those cities by space of time were overthrown and then turned into ruin. But I prophesy to thee, as very Sibyl, that never this city which thou shall found shall be brought to nought, nor shall not fall, but always endure in prosperity, malgre[9] all his envious enemies. Though that he be fought withal by many diverse assaults, so she shall never be taken nor overcome.[1] Sometime the realm of Amazony was begun by the ordinance and enterprise of diverse women of great courage, which despised bondage, so as the histories beareth witness. And long time by them it was maintained under signories[2] of diverse queens, right noble ladies which they chose themselves, and governed right fair and well, and by great strength maintained the lordship. And nevertheless though they were of great might and puissance, and that in the time of their domination conquered great part of the orient and all the lands nigh them put them in dread,[3] and in the same wise the country of Greece doubted[4] them, which that time was the flower of all countries of the world, and not forthy[5] within process of time the puissance of the realm [declined[6]]; by the same manner as it is of all other worldly lordships, there is not biden[7] in this time as now but only the name. But this city shall be of much more stronger building that thou hast to make, for the which to begin I am committed, by the deliberation among us all three ladies together, to deliver the mortar durable and without corruption to make the strong

---

3. Though they (the attackers) appeal to God for their good right to do so. (The translator or printer has become confused by Christine's syntax here; the 1521 text reads "thus they report.")
4. Establish.
5. Prepared.
6. Complete it.
7. Duration.
8. Believed to be.

9. Despite.
1. The city changes gender, "he" to "she," in the 1521 text.
2. Rule.
3. Terrified all the lands near them.
4. Feared.
5. Yet nevertheless.
6. The printer has dropped a word in the 1521 text.
7. Abided, survived.

fundaments[8] and the great walls all about, and to lift up the high, large, and great towers and strong castles, diked, bastiled,[9] and barred as much as it pertaineth to a city of great defense. And by our device thou shalt set it in great deepness to endure the longer. And after, thou shalt lift up the walls so high that all the world shall dread them. Daughter, thus I have now told thee the causes of our coming, to the intent that thou take the more credence to my saying. Now I will that thou learn my name, by the sound of which only thou shalt know that thou hast in me, if thou wilt follow mine ordinances, a ministress in thy need to do that thou might not yestereven.[1] I am named Dame Reason: now advise thee then if thou be in good conduit.[2] So I say no more to thee at this time.

[In the following chapters, the other two ladies identify themselves as "Rightwisenesse" (Rectitude) and Justice. Just as Lady Reason had carried a mirror signifying self-knowledge, Rightwisenesse carries a ruler signifying the distinction of right from wrong, and offers to help Christine measure her City of Ladies with it. Lady Justice carries a gold flask from which she portions out justice to all, and promises to help Christine populate her city. The remainder of the book describes Christine's questions to the three ladies about the achievements of women. Countering charges of physical weakness and cowardice, Lady Reason cites the bravery of the Amazons Hippolyta and Penthesilea. As examples of women's intelligence and learning, she offers the wisdom of Sappho and (more problematically) the cleverness of Medea and Circe. Lady Rectitude absolves women of the charge of lustfulness with the biblical examples of Susannah, Sarah, and Rebecca, and the Greek example of Penelope. After praising Christine's construction work, Lady Justice welcomes the Virgin Mary into the City of Ladies, to rule as queen. In the final chapter, Christine offers advice to women of all marital conditions and social stations on how to bear their lot.]

[PART 3, CHAPTER 19]

Here Christine speaketh unto the ladies in the end of the book.

My right redoubted[3] ladies, worshipped be God, now is our City well achieved and made perfect, in the which all ye that loveth honor, virtue, and praising may be lodged with great worship, as well those that are past as those that be now, and those that be to come. For it is founded and made for every woman of worship. And my right dear ladies, it is a thing natural to man's heart to rejoice him when he findeth him that he hath the victory of any enterprise, and that his enemies be confounded. So have ye cause, all ye my ladies, to rejoice you now virtuously in God and in good conditions by this new city, to see it perfect, which may not be only the refuge of all you—that is to understand of virtuous women—but also the defense and ward against your enemies and assailers, if ye keep it well. ✳ ✳ ✳ So use ye not of this new heritage as these proud people which become so full of pride when their prosperity increaseth and are mounted in richesse, but by the example of your queen the sovereign virgin, which after so great worship that the angel brought to her as to be the mother of the son of God, she so much more meeked her[4] in calling her the handmaiden of God. So my ladies, as be it true that the more the virtues be, the more ye ought to yield you humble and benign, and this City be cause unto you to love good

---

8. Foundations.
9. Fortified.
1. Last night.

2. So consider what good guidance you are under.
3. Honored.
4. Acted meekly.

manners, and to be virtuous and humble. And have ye not in despite, ye ladies that be married, to be so subjects to your husbands. For it is not sometimes best to a creature to be free out of subjection, and that witnesseth the tongue of our lord God where he saith to Ezra the prophet: those (he saith) that use their free will falleth in sin, and despise their lord, and defouleth the just people, and therefore they perish. So be ye humble and patient and the grace of God shall increase in you, and ye shall be given in praising to the world. For Saint Gregory saith that patience is the entry of paradise and the way of Jesus Christ. And among you virgins in the state of maidenhood, be ye clean, simple, coy,[5] and without idleness. For the gins[6] of evil men be set against you. So be ye armed with virtuous strength against their cautels,[7] to eschew their frequentation.

And to lady widows, be honest in habit and countenance and in word, devout in deed and in conversation, prudent in governance, patient in that where need is, in meekness and in charity. And to all generally—great, mean, and little—will ye always to be set in defense against the enemies of your worship and chastity. See, my ladies, how these that accuseth you maketh all them liars that blameth you. And put aback these losengers[8] which by diverse draughts[9] hurteth and withdraweth that that ye ought to keep so well, that is to understand, your worships. O, the lewd love of which they counsel you and steereth you thereto, flee it for God's love, flee it, for be ye certain, though that the semblant[1] be fair it is deceivable, that at all times the end of it is prejudice to you. And think not the contrary, for otherwise it may not be. Remember how they call you frail and false, and always they seek engines right strange and deceivable, with great pain and travail for to take you, so as one doth to take wild beasts. Flee their gins, my ladies, flee their acquaintance under laughing of whom is lapped[2] venom right full of anguish which bringeth one lightly to the death. And thus that it please you, my right redoubted ladies, to draw to the virtues and flee vices, to increase and multiply our City, and ye to rejoice in well doing. And me your servant to be recommended unto you in praying God, which by his grace in this world grant me for to live and persevere in his holy service, and at the end to be piteous to my great defaults, and grant both unto you and me the Joy which endures evermore. Amen.

Here endeth the third and the last party of the book of the City of Ladies. Imprinted at London in Paul's Churchyard at the sign of the Trinity by Henry Pepwell. In the year of our Lord .M.CCCCC .xxi. The .xxvi. day of October. And the .xii. year of our sovereign lord king Henry the .viii.

[END OF LATE MEDIEVAL ALLEGORY]

5. Quiet.
6. Traps.
7. Stratagems.
8. Deceivers.

9. Plots.
1. Appearance.
2. Hidden.

LITERARY AND CULTURAL TERMS*

Absolutism. In criticism, the belief in irreducible, unchanging values of form and content that underlie the tastes of individuals and periods and arise from the stability of an absolute hierarchical order.

Accent. Stress or emphasis on a syllable, as opposed to the syllable's length of duration, its quantity. *Metrical accent* denotes the metrical pattern ($\smile$ –) to which writers fit and adjust accented words and rhetorical emphases, keeping the meter as they substitute word-accented feet and tune their rhetoric.

Accentual Verse. Verse with lines established by counting accents only, without regard to the number of unstressed syllables. This was the dominant form of verse in English until the time of Chaucer.

Acrostic. Words arranged, frequently in a poem or puzzle, to disclose a hidden word or message when the correct combination of letters is read in sequence.

Aestheticism. Devotion to beauty. The term applies particularly to a 19th-century literary and artistic movement celebrating beauty as independent from morality, and praising form above content; art for art's sake.

Aesthetics. The study of the beautiful; the branch of philosophy concerned with defining the nature of art and establishing criteria of judgment.

Alexandrine. A six-foot iambic pentameter line.

Allegorical Meaning. A secondary meaning of a narrative in addition to its primary meaning or literal meaning.

Allegory. A story that suggests another story. The first part of this word comes from the Greek *allos*, "other." An allegory is present in literature whenever it is clear that the author is saying, "By this I also mean that." In practice, allegory appears when a progression of events or images suggests a translation of them into conceptual language.

Alliteration. "Adding letters" (Latin *ad* + *littera*, "letter"). Two or more words, or accented syllables, chime on the same initial letter (*l*ost *l*ove *a*lone; *a*fter *a*pple-picking) or repeat the same consonant.

Alliterative Verse. Verse using alliteration on stressed syllables for its fundamental structure.

Allusion. A meaningful reference, direct or indirect, as when William Butler Yeats writes, "Another Troy must rise and set," calling to mind the whole tragic history of Troy.

Amplification. A restatement of something more fully and in more detail, especially in oratory, poetry, and music.

Analogy. A comparison between things similar in a number of ways; frequently used to explain the unfamiliar by the familiar.

Anapest. A metrical foot: $\smile \smile$ –.

Anaphora. The technique of beginning successive clauses or lines with the same word.

Anatomy. Greek for "a cutting up": a dissection, analysis, or systematic study. The term was popular in titles in the 16th and 17th centuries.

Anglo-Norman (Language). The language of upper-class England after the Norman Conquest in 1066.

Anglo-Saxon. The people, culture, and language of three neighboring tribes—Jutes, Angles, and Saxons—who invaded England, beginning in 449, from the lower part of Denmark's Jutland Peninsula. The Angles, settling along the eastern seaboard of central and northern England, developed the first literate culture of any Germanic people.

---

*Adapted from *The Harper Handbook to Literature* by Northrop Frye, Sheridan Baker, George Perkins, and Barbara M. Perkins, 2d edition (Longman, 1997).

Antagonist. In Greek drama, the character who opposes the protagonist, or hero: therefore, any character who opposes another. In some works, the antagonist is clearly the villain (Iago in *Othello*), but in strict terminology an antagonist is merely an opponent and may be in the right.

Anthropomorphism. The practice of giving human attributes to animals, plants, rivers, winds, and the like, or to such entities as Grecian urns and abstract ideas.

Antithesis. (1) A direct contrast or opposition. (2) The second phase of dialectical argument, which considers the opposition—the three steps being *thesis, antithesis, synthesis*. (3) A rhetorical figure sharply contrasting ideas in balanced parallel structures.

Aphorism. A pithy saying of known authorship, as distinguished from a folk proverb.

Apology. A justification, as in Sir Philip Sidney's *The Apology for Poetry* (1595).

Apostrophe. (Greek, "a turning away"). An address to an absent or imaginary person, a thing, or a personified abstraction.

Archaism. An archaic or old-fashioned word or expression—for example, *o'er, ere,* or *darkling*.

Archetype. (1) The first of a genre, like Homer's *Iliad*, the first heroic epic. (2) A natural symbol imprinted in human consciousness by experience and literature, like dawn symbolizing hope or an awakening; night, death or repose.

Assonance. Repetition of middle vowel sounds: *fight, hive; pane, make*.

Aubade. Dawn song, from French *aube*, for dawn. The aubade originated in the Middle Ages as a song sung by a lover greeting the dawn, ordinarily expressing regret that morning means parting.

Avant-Garde. Experimental, innovative, at the forefront of a literary or artistic trend or movement. The term is French for *vanguard*, the advance unit of an army. It frequently suggests a struggle with tradition and convention.

Ballad. A narrative poem in short stanzas, with or without music. The term derives by way of French *ballade* from Latin *ballare*, "to dance," and once meant a simple song of any kind, lyric or narrative, especially one to accompany a dance.

Ballad Stanza. The name for common meter as found in ballads: a quatrain in iambic meter, alternating tetrameter and trimeter lines, usually rhyming *abcb*.

Bard. An ancient Celtic singer of the culture's lore in epic form; a poetic term for any poet.

Baroque. (1) A richly ornamented style in architecture and art. Founded in Rome by Frederigo Barocci about 1550, and characterized by swirling allegorical frescoes on ceilings and walls, it flourished throughout Europe until 1700. (2) A chromatic musical style with strict forms containing similar exuberant ornamentation, flourishing from 1600 to 1750. In literature, Richard Crashaw's bizarre imagery and the conceits and rhythms of John Donne and other metaphysical poets are sometimes called baroque, sometimes mannerist.

Bathos. (1) A sudden slippage from the sublime to the ridiculous. (2) Any anticlimax. (3) Sentimental pathos. (4) Triteness or dullness.

Blank Verse. Unrhymed iambic pentameter. *See also* Meter.

Bloomsbury Group. An informal social and intellectual group associated with Bloomsbury, a London residential district near the British Museum, from about 1904 until the outbreak of World War II. Virginia Woolf was a principal member. The group was loosely knit, but famed, especially in the 1920s, for its exclusiveness, aestheticism, and social and political freethinking.

Burden. (1) A refrain or set phrase repeated at intervals throughout a song or poem. (2) A bass accompaniment, the "load" carried by the melody, the origin of the term.

Burlesque. (1) A ridicule, especially on the stage, treating the lofty in low style, or the low in grandiose style. (2) A bawdy vaudeville, with obscene clowning and stripteasing.

Caesura. A pause in a metrical line, indicated by punctuation, momentarily suspending the beat (from Latin "a cutting off"). Caesuras are *masculine* at the end of a foot, and *feminine* in mid-foot.

Canon. The writings accepted as forming a part of the Bible, of the works of an author, or of a body of literature. Shakespeare's canon consists of works he wrote, which may be distinguished from works attributed to him but written by others. The word derives from Greek *kanon*, "rod" or "rule," and suggests authority. Canonical authors and texts are those taught most frequently, noncanonical are those rarely taught, and in between are disputed degrees of canonicity for authors considered minor or marginalized.

Canto. A major division in a long poem. The Italian expression is from Latin *cantus*, "song," a section singable in one sitting.

Caricature. Literary cartooning, depicting characters with exaggerated physical traits such as huge noses and bellies, short stature, squints, tics, humped backs, and so forth.

Catalog. In literature, an enumeration of ancestors, of ships, of warriors, of a woman's beauties, and the like; a standard feature of the classical epic.

Celtic Revival. In the 18th century, a groundswell of the Romantic movement in discovering the power in ancient, primitive poetry, particularly Welsh and Scottish Gaelic, as distinct from that of the classics.

Chiasmus. A rhetorical balance created by the inversion of one of two parallel phrases or clauses; from the Greek for a "placing crosswise," as in the Greek letter χ (chi).

Chronicle. A kind of history, with the emphasis on *time* (Greek *chronos*). Events are described in order as they occurred. The chronicles of the Middle Ages provided material for later writers and serve now as important sources of knowledge about the period.

Chronicle Play. A play dramatizing historical events, as from a chronicle.

Classical Literature. (1) The literature of ancient Greece and Rome. (2) Later literature reflecting the qualities of classical Greece or Rome. *See also,* Classicism; Neoclassicism. (3) The classic literature of any time or place, as, for example, classical American literature or classical Japanese literature.

Classicism. A principle in art and conduct reflecting the ethos of ancient Greece and Rome: balance, form, proportion, propriety, dignity, simplicity, objectivity, rationality, restraint, unity rather than diversity. In English literature, classicism emerged with Erasmus (1466–1536) and his fellow humanists. In the Restoration and 18th century, classicism, or neoclassicism, expressed society's deep need for balance and restraint after the shattering Civil War and Puritan commonwealth. Classicism continued in the 19th century, after the Romantic period, particularly in the work of Matthew Arnold. T. E. Hulme, Ezra Pound, and T. S. Eliot expressed it for the 20th century.

Cliché. An overused expression, once clever or metaphorical but now trite and timeworn.

Closed Couplet. The heroic couplet, especially when the thought and grammar are complete in the two iambic pentameter lines.

Closet Drama. A play written for reading in the "closet," or private study.

Cockney. A native of the East End of central London. The term originally meant "cocks' eggs," a rural term of contempt for city softies and fools. Cockneys are London's ingenious street peddlers, speaking a dialect rich with an inventive rhyming slang, dropping and adding aitches.

Comedy. One of the typical literary structures, originating as a form of drama and later extending into prose fiction and other genres as well. Comedy, as Susanne Langer says, is the image of Fortune; tragedy, the image of Fate.

Comedy of Humors. Comedy based on the ancient physiological theory that a predominance of one of the body's four fluids (humors) produces a comically unbalanced personality: (1) blood—sanguine, hearty, cheerful, amorous; (2) phlegm—phlegmatic, sluggish; (3) choler (yellow bile)—angry, touchy; (4) black bile—melancholic.

Comedy of Manners. Suave, witty, and risqué, satire of upper-class manners and immorals, particularly that of Restoration masters like George Etherege and William Congreve.

Common Meter. The ballad stanza as found in hymns and other poems: a quatrain (four-line stanza) in iambic meter, alternating tetrameter and trimeter, rhyming *abcb* or *abab*.

Complaint. A lyric poem, popular in the Middle Ages and the Renaissance, complaining of unrequited love, a personal situation, or the state of the world.

Conceit. Any fanciful, ingenious expression or idea, but especially one in the form of an extended metaphor.

Concordia Discors. "Discordant harmony," a phrase expressing for the 18th century the harmonious diversity of nature, a pleasing balance of opposites.

Concrete Poetry. Poetry that attempts a concrete embodiment of its idea, expressing itself physically apart from the meaning of the words. A recent relative of the much older *shaped poem*, the concrete poem places heavy emphasis on the picture and less on the words, so that the visual experience may be more interesting than the linguistic.

Connotation. The ideas, attitudes, or emotions associated with a word in the mind of speaker or listener, writer or reader. It is contrasted with the *denotation*, the thing the word stands for, the dictionary definition, an objective concept without emotional coloring.

Consonance. (1) Repetition of inner or end consonant sounds, as, for example, the *r* and *s* sounds from Gerard Manley Hopkins's *God's Grandeur:* "broods with warm breast." (2) In a broader sense, a generally pleasing combination of sounds or ideas.

Couplet. A pair of rhymed metrical lines, usually in iambic tetrameter or pentameter. Sometimes the two lines are of different length.

Cynghanedd. A complex medieval Welsh system of rhyme, alliteration, and consonance, to which Gerard Manley Hopkins alluded to describe his interplay of euphonious sounds, actually to be heard in any rich poet, as in the Welsh Dylan Thomas: "The force that through the green fuse drives the flower / Drives my green age."

Dactyl. A three-syllable metrical foot: – ⌣ ⌣ . It is the basic foot of dactylic hexameter, the six-foot line of Greek and Roman epic poetry.

Dactylic Hexameter. The classical or heroic line of the epic. A line based on six dactylic feet, with spondees substituted, and always ending – ⌣ ⌣ | – – .

Dead Metaphor. A metaphor accepted without its figurative picture: "a jacket," for the paper around a book, with no mental picture of the human coat that prompted the original metaphor.

Decasyllabic. Having ten syllables. An iambic pentameter line is decasyllabic.

Deconstruction. The critical dissection of a literary text's statements, ambiguities, and structure to expose its hidden contradictions, implications, and fundamental instability of meaning. Jacques Derrida originated deconstruction in *Of Grammatology* (1967) and *Writing and Difference* (1967).

Decorum. Propriety, fitness, the quality of being appropriate.

Defamiliarization. Turning the familiar to the strange by disrupting habitual ways of perceiving things. Derived from the thought of Victor Shklovsky and other Russian formalists, the idea is that art forces us to see things differently as we view them through the artist's sensibility, not our own.

Deism. A rational philosophy of religion, beginning with the theories of Lord Herbert of Cherbury, the "Father of Deism," in his *De Veritate* (1624). Deists generally held that God, the supreme Artisan, created a perfect clock of a universe, withdrew, and left it running, not to return to intervene in its natural works or the life of humankind; that the Bible is a moral guide, but neither historically accurate nor divinely authentic; and that reason guides human beings to virtuous conduct.

Denotation. The thing that a word stands for, the dictionary definition, an objective concept without emotional coloring. It is contrasted with the *connotation*, ideas, attitudes, or emotions associated with the word in the mind of user or hearer.

Dénouement. French for "unknotting": the unraveling of plot threads toward the end of a play, novel, or other narrative.

Determinism. The philosophical belief that events are shaped by forces beyond the control of human beings.

Dialect. A variety of language belonging to a particular time, place, or social group, as, for example, an 18th-century cockney dialect, a New England dialect, or a coal miner's dialect. A language other than one's own is for the most part unintelligible without study or translation; a dialect other than one's own can generally be understood, although pronunciation, vocabulary, and syntax seem strange.

Dialogue. Conversation between two or more persons, as represented in prose fiction, drama, or essays, as opposed to *monologue*, the speech of one person.

Diatribe. Greek for "a wearing away": a bitter and abusive criticism or invective, often lengthy, directed against a person, institution, or work.

Diction. Word choice in speech or writing, an important element of style.

Didactic. Greek for "teaching": instructive, or having the qualities of a teacher. Literature intended primarily for instruction or containing an important moralistic element is didactic.

Dirge. A lamenting funeral song.

Discourse. (1) A formal discussion of a subject. (2) The conventions of communication associated with specific areas, in usages such as "poetic discourse," "the discourse of the novel," or "historical discourse."

Dissenter. A term arising in the 1640s for a member of the clergy or a follower who dissented from the forms of the established Anglican church, particularly Puritans. Dissenters generally came from the lower middle classes.

Dissonance. (1) Harsh and jarring sound; discord. It is frequently an intentional effect, as in the poems of Robert Browning. (2) Occasionally a term for half rhyme or slant rhyme.

Distich. A couplet, or pair of rhymed metrical lines.

Dithyramb. A frenzied choral song and dance to honor Dionysus, Greek god of wine and the power of fertility. Any irregular, impassioned poetry may be called *dithyrambic*.

Doggerel. (1) Trivial verse clumsily aiming at meter, usually tetrameter. (2) Any verse facetiously low and loose in meter and rhyme.

Domesday Book. The recorded census and survey of landholders that William the Conqueror ordered in 1085; from "Doomsday," the Last Judgment.

Dramatic Irony. A character in drama or fiction unknowingly says or does something in ironic contrast to what the audience or reader knows or will learn.

Dramatic Monologue. A monologue in verse. A speaker addresses a silent listener, revealing, in dramatic irony, things about himself or herself of which the speaker is unaware.

Eclogue. A short poem, usually a pastoral, and often in the form of a dialogue or soliloquy.

Edition. The form in which a book is published, including its physical qualities and its content. A *first edition* is the first form of a book, printed and bound; a *second edition* is a later form, usually with substantial changes in content.

Edwardian Period (1901–1914). From the death of Queen Victoria to the outbreak of World War I, named for the reign of Victoria's son, Edward VII (1901–1910), a period generally reacting against Victorian propriety and convention.

Elegiac Stanza. An iambic pentameter quatrain rhyming *abab*, taking its name from Thomas Gray's *Elegy Written in a Country Churchyard* (1751).

Elegy. Greek for "lament": a poem on death or on a serious loss; characteristically a sustained meditation expressing sorrow and, frequently, an explicit or implied consolation.

Elision. Latin for "striking out": the omission or slurring of an unstressed vowel at the end of a word to bring a line of poetry closer to a prescribed metrical pattern.

Elizabethan Drama. English drama of the reign of Elizabeth I (1558–1603). Strictly speaking, drama from the reign of James I (1603–1625) belongs to the Jacobean period and that from the reign of Charles I (1625–1642) to the Caroline period, but the term *Elizabethan* is sometimes extended to include works of later reigns, before the closing of the theaters in 1642.

Elizabethan Period (1558–1603). The years marked by the reign of Elizabeth I.

Ellipsis. The omission of words for rhetorical effect: "*Drop dead*" for "You drop dead."

Emblem. (1) A didactic pictorial and literary form consisting of a word or phrase (*mot* or *motto*), a symbolic woodcut or engraving, and a brief moralistic poem (*explicatio*). Collections of emblems in book form were popular in the 16th and 17th centuries. (2) A type or symbol.

Emendation. A change made in a literary text to remove faults that have appeared through tampering or by errors in reading, transcription, or printing from the manuscript.

Empathy. Greek for "feeling with": identification with the feelings or passions of another person, natural creature, or even an inanimate object conceived of as possessing human attributes.

Emphasis. Stress placed on words, phrases, or ideas to show their importance, by *italics*, **boldface**, and punctuation "!!!"; by figurative language, meter, and rhyme; or by strategies of rhetoric, like climactic order, contrast, repetition, and position.

Empiricism. Greek for "experience": the belief that all knowledge comes from experience, that human understanding of general truth can be founded only on observation of particulars. Empiricism is basic to the scientific method and to literary naturalism.

Enclosed Rhyme. A couplet, or pair of rhyming lines, enclosed in rhyming lines to give the pattern *abba*.

Encomium. Originally a Greek choral song in praise of a hero; later, any formal expression of praise, in verse or prose.

End Rhyme. Rhyme at the end of a line of verse (the usual placement), as distinguished from *initial rhyme*, at the beginning, or *internal rhyme*, within the line.

Enjambment. Run-on lines in which grammatical sense runs from one line of poetry to the next without pause or punctuation. The opposite of an end-stopped line.

Enlightenment. A philosophical movement in the 17th and 18th centuries, particularly in France, characterized by the conviction that reason could achieve all knowledge, supplant organized religion, and ensure progress toward happiness and perfection.

Envoy (or Envoi). A concluding stanza, generally shorter than the earlier stanzas of a poem, giving a brief summary of theme, address to a prince or patron, or return to a refrain.

Epic. A long narrative poem, typically a recounting of history or legend or of the deeds of a national hero. During the Renaissance, critical theory emphasized two assumptions: (1) the encyclopedic knowledge needed for major poetry, and (2) an aristocracy of genres, according to which epic and tragedy, because they deal with heroes and ruling-class figures, were reserved for major poets.

Epic Simile. Sometimes called a *Homeric simile*: an extended simile, comparing one thing with another by lengthy description of the second, often beginning with "as when" and concluding with "so" or "such."

Epicurean. Often meaning hedonistic (*see also* Hedonism), devoted to sensual pleasure and ease. Actually, Epicurus (c. 341–270 B.C.) was a kind of puritanical Stoic, recommending detachment from pleasure and pain to avoid life's inevitable suffering, hence advocating serenity as the highest happiness, intellect over the senses.

Epigram. (1) A brief poetic and witty couching of a home truth. (2) An equivalent statement in prose.

Epigraph. (1) An inscription on a monument or building. (2) A quotation or motto heading a book or chapter.

Epilogue. (1) A poetic address to the audience at the end of a play. (2) The actor performing the address. (3) Any similar appendage to a literary work, usually describing what happens to the characters in the future.

Epiphany. In religious tradition, the revelation of a divinity. James Joyce adapted the term to signify a moment of profound or spiritual revelation. For Joyce, art was an epiphany.

Episode. An incident in a play or novel; a continuous event in action and dialogue.

Episodic Structure. In narration, the incidental stringing of one episode upon another, with no necessary causal connection or plot.

Epistle. (1) A letter, usually a formal or artistic one, like Saint Paul's Epistles in the New Testament, or Horace's verse *Epistles*, widely imitated in the late 17th and 18th centuries, most notably by Alexander Pope. (2) A dedication in a prefatory epistle to a play or book.

Epitaph. (1) An inscription on a tombstone or monument memorializing the person, or persons, buried there. (2) A literary epigram or brief poem epitomizing the dead.

Epithalamium (or Epithalamion). A lyric ode honoring a bride and groom.

Epithet. A term characterizing a person or thing: e.g., *Richard the Lion-Hearted*.

Epitome. (1) A summary, an abridgment, an abstract. (2) One that supremely represents an entire class.

Essay. A literary composition on a single subject; usually short, in prose, and nonexhaustive. The word derives from French *essai* "an attempt," first used in the modern sense by Michel de Montaigne, whose *Essais* (1580–1588) are classics of the genre.

Estates. The "three estates of the realm," recognized from feudal times onward: the clergy (Lords Spiritual), the nobility (Lords Temporal), and the burghers (the Commons). The Fourth Estate is now the press and other media.

Eulogy. A speech or composition of praise, especially of a deceased person.

Euphemism. Greek for "good speech": an attractive substitute for a harsh or unpleasant word or concept; figurative language or circumlocution substituting an indirect or oblique reference for a direct one.

Euphony. Melodious sound, the opposite of cacophony. A major feature of verse, but also a consideration in prose, euphony results from smooth-flowing meter or sentence rhythm as well as attractive sounds.

Euphuism. An artificial, highly elaborate affected style that takes its name from John Lyly's *Euphues: The Anatomy of Wit* (1578). Euphuism is characterized by the heavy use of rhetorical devices such as balance and antithesis, by much attention to alliteration and other sound patterns, and by learned allusion.

Excursus. (1) A lengthy discussion of a point, appended to a literary work. (2) A long digression.

Exegesis. A detailed analysis, explanation, and interpretation of a difficult text, especially the Bible.

Exemplum. Latin for "example": a story used to illustrate a moral point. *Exempla* were a characteristic feature of medieval sermons.

Existentialism. A philosophy centered on individual existence as unique and unrepeatable, hence rejecting the past for present existence and its unique dilemmas. Existentialism rose to prominence in the 1930s and 1940s, particularly in France after World War II.

Expressionism. An early 20th-century movement in art and literature, best understood as a reaction against conventional realism and naturalism, and especially as a revolt against conventional society. The expressionist looked inward for images, expressing in paint, on stage, or in prose or verse a distorted, nightmarish version of reality.

Eye Rhyme. A rhyme of words that look but do not sound the same: *one, stone; word, lord; teak, break.*

Fable. (1) A short, allegorical story in verse or prose, frequently of animals, told to illustrate a moral. (2) The story line or plot of a narrative or drama. (3) Loosely, any legendary or fabulous account.

Falling Meter. A meter beginning with a stress, running from heavy to light.

Farce. A wildly comic play, mocking dramatic and social conventions.

Feminine Ending. An extra unstressed syllable at the end of a metrical line, usually iambic.

Feminine Rhyme. A rhyme of both the stressed and the unstressed syllables of one feminine ending with another.

Feudalism. The political and social system prevailing in Europe from the ninth century until the 1400s. It was a system of independent holdings (*feud* is Germanic for "estate") in which autonomous lords pledged fealty and service to those more powerful in exchange for protection, as did villagers to the neighboring lord of the manor.

Fiction. An imagined creation in verse, drama, or prose. Fiction is a thing made, an invention. It is distinguished from nonfiction by its essentially imaginative nature, but elements of fiction appear in fundamentally nonfictional constructions such as essays, biographies, autobiographies, and histories. Although any invented person, place, event, or condition is a fiction, the term is now most frequently used to mean "prose fiction," as distinct from verse or drama.

Figurative Language. Language that is not literal, being either metaphorical or rhetorically patterned.

Figure of Speech. An expression extending language beyond its literal meaning, either pictorially through metaphor, simile, allusion, and the like, or rhetorically through repetition, balance, antithesis, and the like. A figure of speech is also called a *trope*.

Fin de Siècle. "The end of the century," especially the last decade of the 19th. The term, acquired with the French influence of the symbolists Stéphane Mallarmé and Charles Baudelaire, connotes preciosity and decadence.

First-Person Narration. Narration by a character involved in a story.

Flyting. Scottish for "scolding": a form of invective, or violent verbal assault, in verse; traditional in Scottish literature, possibly Celtic in origin. Typically, two poets exchange scurrilous and often exhaustive abuse.

Folio. From Latin for "leaf." (1) A sheet of paper, folded once. (2) The largest of the book sizes, made from standard printing sheets, folded once before trimming and binding.

Folktale. A story forming part of the folklore of a community, generally less serious than the stories called *myths*.

Foot. The metrical unit; in English, an accented syllable with accompanying light syllable or syllables.

Formula. A plot outline or set of characteristic ingredients used in the construction of a literary work or applied to a portion of one.

Foul Copy. A manuscript that has been used for printing, bearing the marks of the proofreader, editor, and printer, as well as, frequently, the author's queries and comments.

Four Elements. In ancient and medieval cosmology, earth, air, fire, and water—the four ultimate, exclusive, and eternal constituents that, according to Empedocles (c. 493–c. 433 B.C.) made up the world.

Fourteeners. Lines of 14 syllables—7 iambic feet, popular with the Elizabethans.

Frame Narrative. A narrative enclosing one or more separate stories. Characteristically, the frame narrative is created as a vehicle for the stories it contains.

Free Verse. French *vers libre;* poetry free of traditional metrical and stanzaic patterns.

Genre. A term often applied loosely to the larger forms of literary convention, roughly analogous to "species" in biology. The Greeks spoke of three main genres of poetry—lyric, epic, and drama.

Georgian. (1) Pertaining to the reigns of the four Georges—1714–1830, particularly the reigns of the first three, up to the close of the 18th century. (2) The literature written during the early years (1910–1914) of the reign of George V.

Georgic. A poem about farming and annual rural labors, after Virgil's *Georgics*.

Gloss. An explanation (from Greek *glossa* "tongue, language"); originally, Latin synonyms in the margins of Greek manuscripts and vernacular synonyms in later manuscripts as scribes gave the reader some help.

Glossary. A list of words, with explanations or definitions.

Gothic. Originally, pertaining to the Goths, then to any Germanic people. Because the Goths began warring with the Roman empire in the 3rd century A.D., eventually sacking Rome itself, the term later became a synonym for "barbaric," which the 18th century next applied to anything medieval, of the Dark Ages.

Gothic Novel. A type of fiction introduced and named by Horace Walpole's *Castle of Otranto, A Gothic Story* (1764). Walpole introduced supernatural terror, with a huge mysterious helmet, portraits that walk abroad, and statues with nosebleeds. Mary Shelley's *Frankenstein* (1818) transformed the Gothic into moral science fiction.

Grotesque. Anything unnaturally distorted, ugly, ludicrous, fanciful, or bizarre; especially, in the 19th century, literature exploiting the abnormal.

Hedonism. A philosophy that sees pleasure as the highest good.

Hegelianism. The philosophy of G. W. F. Hegel (1770–1831), who developed the system of thought known as Hegelian dialectic, in which a given concept, or *thesis*, generates its opposite, or *antithesis*, and from the interaction of the two arises a *synthesis*.

Heroic Couplet. The closed and balanced iambic pentameter couplet typical of the heroic plays of John Dryden; hence, any closed couplet.

Heroic Quatrain. A stanza in four lines of iambic pentameter, rhyming *abab* (*see also* Meter). Also known as the *heroic stanza* and the *elegiac stanza*.

Hexameter. Six-foot lines.

Historicism. (1) Historical relativism. (2) An approach to literature that emphasizes its historical environment, the climate of ideas, belief, and literary conventions surrounding and influencing the writer.

Homily. A religious discourse or sermon, especially one emphasizing practical spiritual or moral advice.

Hubris. From Greek *hybris*, "pride": prideful arrogance or insolence of the kind that causes the tragic hero to ignore the warnings that might turn aside the action that leads to disaster.

Humors. The *cardinal humors* of ancient medical theory: blood, phlegm, yellow bile (choler), black bile (melancholy). From ancient times until the 19th century, the humors were believed largely responsible for health and disposition. In literature, especially during the early modern period, characters were portrayed according to the humors that dominated them, as in the comedy of humors.

Hyperbole. Overstatement to make a point, as when a parent tells a child "I've told you a thousand times."

Iambus (or Iamb). A metrical foot: ⌣ – .

Idealism. Literary idealism follows from philosophical precepts, emphasizing a world in which the most important reality is a spiritual or transcendent truth not always reflected in the world of sense perception.

Idyll. A short poem of rustic pastoral serenity.

Image. A concrete picture, either literally descriptive, as in "Red roses covered the white wall," or figurative, as in "She is a rose," each carrying a sensual and emotive connotation.

Impressionism. A literary style conveying subjective impressions rather than objective reality, taking its name from the movement in French painting in the mid–19th century.

Industrial Revolution. The accelerated change, beginning in the 1760s, from an agricultural-shopkeeping society, using hand tools, to an industrial-mechanized one.

Influence. The apparent effect of literary works on subsequent writers and their work, as in Robert Browning's influence on T. S. Eliot.

Innuendo. An indirect remark or gesture, especially one implying something derogatory; an insinuation.

Interlocking Rhyme. Rhyme between stanzas; a word unrhymed in one stanza is used as a rhyme for the next, as in terza rima: *aba bcb cdc* and so on.

Internal Rhyme. Rhyme within a line, rather than at the beginning (*initial rhyme*) or end (*end rhyme*); also, rhyme matching sounds in the middle of a line with sounds at the end.

Intertextuality. (1) The relations between one literary text and others it evokes through such means as quotation, paraphrase, allusion, parody, and revision. (2) More broadly, the relations between a given text and all other texts, the potentially infinite sum of knowledge within which any text has its meaning.

Inversion. A reversal of sequence or position, as when the normal order of elements within a sentence is inverted for poetic or rhetorical effect.

Irony. In general, irony is the perception of a clash between appearance and reality, between *seems* and *is*, or between *ought* and *is*. The myriad shadings of irony seem to fall into three categories: (1) *Verbal irony*—saying something contrary to what it means; the appearance is what the words say, the reality is their contrary meaning. (2) *Dramatic irony*—saying or doing something while unaware of its ironic contrast with the whole truth; named for its frequency in drama, dramatic irony is a verbal irony with the speaker's awareness erased. (3) *Situational irony*—events turning to the opposite of what is expected or what should be.

Italian Sonnet (or Petrarchan Sonnet). A sonnet composed of an octave and sestet, rhyming *abbaabba cdecde* (or *cdcdcd* or some variant, without a closing couplet).

Italic (or Italics). Type slanting upward to the right. *This sentence is italic.*

Jacobean Period (1603–1625). The reign of James I, *Jacobus* being the Latin for "James." A certain skepticism and even cynicism seeped into Elizabethan joy.

Jargon. (1) Language peculiar to a trade or calling, as, for example, the jargon of astronauts, lawyers, or literary critics. (2) Confused or confusing language.

Jeremiad. A lament or complaint, especially one enumerating transgressions and predicting destruction of a people, of the kind found in the Book of Jeremiah.

Juvenilia. Youthful literary products.

Kenning. A compound figurative metaphor, a circumlocution, in Old English and Old Norse poetry: "whale-road," for the sea.

Lament. A grieving poem, an elegy, in Anglo-Saxon or Renaissance times. *Deor's Lament* (c. 980) records the actual grief of a scop, or court poet, at being displaced in his lord's hall.

Lampoon. A satirical, personal ridicule in verse or prose.

Lay (or Lai). (1) A ballad or related metrical romance originating with the Breton lay of French Brittany and retaining some of its Celtic magic and folklore.

Lexicon. A word list, a vocabulary, a dictionary.

Libretto. "The little book" (Italian): the text of an opera, cantata, or other musical drama.

Litany. A prayer with phrases spoken or sung by a leader alternated with responses from congregation or choir.

Literal. According to the letter (of the alphabet): the precise, plain meaning of a word or phrase in its simplest, original sense, considered apart from its sense as a metaphor or other figure of speech. Literal language is the opposite of figurative language.

Literature. Strictly defined, anything written. Therefore the oral culture of a people—its folklore, folk songs, folktales, and so on—is not literature until it is written down. The movies are not literature except in their printed scripts. By the same strict meaning, historical records, telephone books, and the like are all literature because they are written in letters of the alphabet, although they are not taught as literature in schools. In contrast to this strict, literal meaning, literature has come to be equated with *creative writing* or works of the imagination: chiefly poetry, prose fiction, and drama.

Lollards. From Middle Dutch, literally, "mumblers": a derisive term applied to the followers of John Wyclif (c. 1328–1384), the reformer behind the Wyclif Bible (1385), the first in English. Lollards preached against the abuses of the medieval church, setting up a standard of poverty and individual service as against wealth and hierarchical privilege.

Lyric. A poem, brief and discontinuous, emphasizing sound and pictorial imagery rather than narrative or dramatic movement.

Macaronic Verse. (1) Strictly, verse mixing words in a writer's native language with endings, phrases, and syntax of another language, usually Latin or Greek, creating a comic or burlesque effect. (2) Loosely, any verse mingling two or more languages.

Mannerism, Mannerist. Literary or artistic affectation; a stylistic quality produced by excessively peculiar, ornamental, or ingenious devices.

Manners. Social behavior. In usages like comedy of manners and novel of manners, the term suggests an examination of the behavior, morals, and values of a particular time, place, or social class.

Manuscript. Literally, "written by hand": any handwritten document, as, for example, a letter or diary; also, a work submitted for publication.

Marginalia. Commentary, references, or other material written by a reader in the margins of a manuscript or book.

Masculine Ending. The usual iambic ending, on the accented foot: ⌣ –.

Masculine Rhyme. The most common rhyme in English, on the last syllable of a line.

Masque. An allegorical, poetic, and musical dramatic spectacle popular in the English courts and mansions of the 16th and early 17th centuries. Figures from mythology, history, and romance mingled in a pastoral fantasy with fairies, fauns, satyrs, and witches, as masked amateurs from the court (including kings and queens) participated in dances and scenes.

Materialism. In philosophy, an emphasis upon the material world as the ultimate reality. Its opposite is *idealism*.

Melodrama. A play with dire ingredients—the mortgage foreclosed, the daughter tied to the railroad tracks—but with a happy ending.

Menippean Satire. Satire on pedants, bigots, rapacious professional people, and other persons or institutions perceiving the world from a single framework. Typical ingredients include a rambling narrative; unusual settings; displays of erudition; and long digressions.

Metaphor. Greek for "transfer" (*meta* and *trans* meaning "across"; *phor* and *fer* meaning "carry"): to carry something across. Hence a metaphor treats something as if it were something else. Money becomes a *nest egg*; a sandwich, a *submarine*.

Metaphysical Poetry. Seventeenth-century poetry of wit and startling extended metaphor.

Meter. The measured pulse of poetry. English meters derive from four Greek and Roman quantitative meters (*see* also Quantitative Verse), which English stresses more sharply, although the patterns are the same. The unit of each pattern is the *foot*, containing one stressed syllable and one or two light ones. *Rising meter* goes from light to heavy; *falling meter*, from heavy to light. One meter—iambic—has dominated English poetry, with the three others lending an occasional foot, for variety, and producing a few poems.

Rising Meters

> Iambic: ⌣ – (the iambus)
> Anapestic: ⌣ ⌣ – (the anapest)

Falling Meters

> Trochaic: – ⌣ (the trochee)
> Dactylic: – ⌣ ⌣ (the dactyl)

The number of feet in a line also gives the verse a name:

> 1 foot: monometer
> 2 feet: dimeter
> 3 feet: trimeter
> 4 feet: tetrameter
> 5 feet: pentameter
> 6 feet: hexameter
> 7 feet: heptameter

All meters show some variations, and substitutions of other kinds of feet, but three variations in iambic writing are virtually standard:

Inverted foot: – ‿ (a trochee)
Spondee: – –
Ionic double foot: ‿ ‿ – –

The *pyrrhic foot* of classical meters, two light syllables (‿ ‿), lives in the English line only in the Ionic double foot, although some prosodists scan a relatively light iambus as pyrrhic.

Examples of meters and scansion:

Iambic Tetrameter
An-ni- | hil-a- | ting all | that's made |
To a | green thought | in a | green shade. |

Andrew Marvell, "The Garden"

Iambic Tetrameter
(with two inverted feet)
Close to | the sun | in lone- | ly lands, |
Ringed with | the az- | ure world, | he stands. |

Alfred, Lord Tennyson, "The Eagle"

Iambic Pentameter
Love's not | Time's fool, | though ros- | y lips | and cheeks |
Within | his bend- | ing sick- | le's com- | pass come |

William Shakespeare, Sonnet 116

When to | the ses- | sions of | sweet si- | lent thought |

William Shakespeare, Sonnet 30

Anapestic Tetrameter
(trochees substituted)
The pop- | lars are felled; | farewell | to the shade |
And the whis- | pering sound | of the cool | colonnade |

William Cowper, "The Popular Field"

Trochaic Tetrameter
Tell me | not in | mournful | numbers |

Henry Wadsworth Longfellow, "A Psalm of Life"

Dactylic Hexameter
This is the | forest prim- | eval. The | murmuring | pines and the | hemlocks |
Bearded with | moss . . . .

Henry Wadsworth Longfellow, "Evangeline"

Metonymy. "Substitute naming." A figure of speech in which an associated idea stands in for the actual item: "The *pen* is mightier than the *sword*" for "Literature and propaganda accomplish more and survive longer than warfare."

Metrics. The analysis and description of meter; also called *prosody*.

Middle English. The language of England from the middle of the 12th century to approximately 1500. English began to lose its inflectional endings and accepted many French words into its vocabulary, especially terms associated with the new social, legal, and governmental structures (*baron, judge, jury, marshal, parliament, prince*), and those in common use by the French upper classes (*mansion, chamber, veal, beef*).

Mimesis. A term meaning "imitation." It has been central to literary criticism since Aristotle's *Poetics*. The ordinary meaning of *imitation* as creating a resemblance to something else is clearly involved in Aristotle's definition of dramatic plot as *mimesis praxeos*, the imitation of an action.

Miracle Play. A medieval play based on a saint's life or story from the Bible.

Miscellany. A collection of various things. A literary miscellany is therefore a book collecting varied works, usually poems by different authors, a kind of anthology.

Mock Epic. A poem in epic form and manner ludicrously elevating some trivial subject to epic grandeur.

Modernism. A collective term, generally associated with the first half of the 20th century, for various aesthetic and cultural attempts to place a "modern" face on experience. Modernism arose from a sense that the old ways were worn out.

Monodrama. (1) A play with one character. (2) A closet drama or dramatic monologue.

Monody. (1) A Greek ode for one voice. (2) An elegiac lament, a dirge, in poetic soliloquy.

Monologue. (1) A poem or story in the form of a soliloquy. (2) Any extended speech.

Motif (or Motive). (1) A recurrent thematic element—word, image, symbol, object, phrase, action. (2) A conventional incident, situation, or device like the unknown knight of mysterious origin and low degree in the romance, or the baffling riddle in fairy tales.

Muse. The inspirer of poetry, on whom the poet calls for assistance. In Greek mythology the Muses were the nine daughters of Zeus and Mnemosyne ("Memory") presiding over the arts and sciences.

Mystery Play. Medieval religious drama; eventually performed in elaborate cycles of plays acted on pageant wagons or stages throughout city streets, with different guilds of artisans and merchants responsible for each.

Mysticism. A spiritual discipline in which sensory experience is expunged and the mind is devoted to deep contemplation and the reaching of a transcendental union with God.

Myth. From Greek *mythos*, "plot" or "narrative." The verbal culture of most if not all human societies began with stories, and certain stories have achieved a distinctive importance as being connected with what the society feels it most needs to know: stories illustrating the society's religion, history, class structure, or the origin of peculiar features of the natural environment.

Narrative Poem. One that tells a story, particularly the epic, metrical romance, and shorter narratives, like the ballad.

Naturalism. (1) Broadly, according to nature. (2) More specifically, a literary movement of the late 19th century; an extension of realism, naturalism was a reaction against the restrictions inherent in the realistic emphasis on the ordinary, as naturalists insisted that the extraordinary is real, too.

Neoclassical Period. Generally, the span of time from the restoration of Charles II to his father's throne in 1660 until the publication of William Wordsworth and Samuel Taylor Coleridge's *Lyrical Ballads* (1798). Writers hoped to revive something like the classical Pax Romana, an era of peace and literary excellence.

Neologism. A word newly coined or introduced into a language, or a new meaning given to an old word.

New Criticism. An approach to criticism prominent in the United States after the publication of John Crowe Ransom's *New Criticism* (1941). Generally, the New Critics were agreed that a poem or story should be considered an organic unit, with each part working to support the whole. They worked by close analysis, considering the text as the final authority, and were distrustful, though not wholly neglectful, of considerations brought from outside the text, as, for example, from biography or history.

New Historicism. A cross-disciplinary approach fostered by the rise of feminist and multicultural studies as well as a renewed emphasis on historical perspective. Associated in particular with work on the early modern and the romantic periods in the United States and England, the approach emphasizes analysis of the relationship between history and literature, viewing writings in both fields as "texts" for study. New Historicism has tended to note political influences on literary and historical texts, to illuminate the role of the writer against the backdrop of social customs and assumptions, and to view history as changeable and interconnected instead of as a linear progressive evolution.

Nocturne. A night piece; writing evocative of evening or night.

Nominalism. In the Middle Ages, the belief that universals have no real being, but are only names, their existence limited to their presence in the minds and language of humans. This belief was opposed to the beliefs of medieval realists, who held that universals have an independent existence, at least in the mind of God.

Norman Conquest. The period of English history in which the Normans consolidated their hold on England after the defeat of the Saxon King Harold by William, Duke of Normandy, in 1066. French became the court language and Norman lords gained control of English lands, but Anglo-Saxon administrative and judicial systems remained largely in place.

Novel. The extended prose fiction that arose in the 18th century to become a major literary expression of the modern world. The term comes from the Italian *novella*, the short "new" tale of intrigue and moral comeuppance most eminently disseminated by Boccaccio's *Decameron* (1348–1353). The terms *novel* and *romance*, from the French *roman*, competed interchangeably for most of the 18th century.

Novella. (1) Originally, a short tale. (2) In modern usage, a term sometimes used interchangeably with short novel or for a fiction of middle length.

Octave. (1) The first unit in an Italian sonnet: eight lines of iambic pentameter, rhyming *abbaabba. See also* Meter. (2) A stanza in eight lines.

Octavo (Abbreviated 8vo). A book made from sheets folded to give signatures of eight leaves (16 pages), a book of average size.

Octet. An octastich or octave.

Octosyllabic. Eight-syllable.

Ode. A long, stately lyric poem in stanzas of varied metrical pattern.

Old English. The language brought to England, beginning in 449, by the Jute, Angle, and Saxon invaders from Denmark; the language base from which modern English evolved.

Omniscient Narrative. A narrative account untrammeled by constraints of time or space. An omniscient narrator perspective knows about the external and internal realities of characters as well as incidents unknown to them, and can interpret motivation and meaning.

Onomatopoeia. The use of words formed or sounding like what they signify—*buzz, crack, smack, whinny*—especially in an extensive capturing of sense by sound.

Orientalism. A term denoting Western portrayals of Oriental culture. In literature it refers to a varied body of work beginning in the 18th century that described for Western readers the history, language, politics, and culture of the area east of the Mediterranean.

Oxymoron. A pointed stupidity: *oxy*, "sharp," plus *moron*. One of the great ironic figures of speech—for example, "a fearful joy," or Milton's "darkness visible."

Paleography. The study and interpretation of ancient handwriting and manuscript styles.

Palimpsest. A piece of writing on secondhand vellum, parchment, or other surface carrying traces of erased previous writings.

Panegyric. A piece of writing in praise of a person, thing, or achievement.

Pantheism. A belief that God and the universe are identical, from the Greek words *pan* ("all") and *theos* ("god"). God is all; all is God.

Pantomime. A form of drama presented without words, in a dumb show.

Parable. (1) A short tale, such as those of Jesus in the gospels, encapsulating a moral or religious lesson. (2) Any saying, figure of speech, or narrative in which one thing is expressed in terms of another.

Paradox. An apparently untrue or self-contradictory statement or circumstance that proves true upon reflection or when examined in another light.

Paraphrase. A rendering in other words of the sense of a text or passage, as of a poem, essay, short story, or other writing.

Parody. As comedy, parody exaggerates or distorts the prominent features of style or content in a work. As criticism, it mimics the work, borrowing words or phrases or characteristic turns of thought in order to highlight weaknesses of conception or expression.

Passion Play. Originally a play based on Christ's Passion; later, one including both Passion and Resurrection.

Pastiche. A work created by assembling bits and pieces from other works.

Pastoral. From Latin *pastor*, a shepherd. The first pastoral poet was Theocritus, a Greek of the 3rd century B.C. The pastoral poem is not really about shepherds, but about the complex society the poet and readers inhabit.

Pathetic Fallacy. The attribution of animate or human characteristics to nature, as, for example, when rocks, trees, or weather are portrayed as reacting in sympathy to human feelings or events.

Pathos. The feeling of pity, sympathy, tenderness, compassion, or sorrow evoked by someone or something that is helpless.

Pedantry. Ostentatious book learning.

Pentameter. A line of five metrical feet. (*See* Meter.)

Peripeteia (or Peripetia, Peripety). A sudden change in situation in a drama or fiction, a reversal of luck for good or ill.

Periphrasis. The practice of talking around the point; a wordy restatement; a circumlocution.

Peroration. (1) The summative conclusion of a formal oration. (2) Loosely, a grandiloquent speech.

Persona. A mask (in Latin); in poetry and fiction, the projected speaker or narrator of the work—that is, a mask for the actual author.

Personification. The technique of treating abstractions, things, or animals as persons. A kind of metaphor, personification turns abstract ideas, like love, into a physical beauty named Venus, or conversely, makes dumb animals speak and act like humans.

Petrarchan Sonnet. Another name for an Italian sonnet.

Phoneme. In linguistics, the smallest distinguishable unit of sound. Different for each language, phonemes are defined by determining which differences in sound function to signal a difference in meaning.

Phonetics. (1) The study of speech sounds and their production, transmission, and reception. (2) The phonetic system of a particular language. (3) Symbols used to represent speech sounds.

Picaresque Novel. A novel chronicling the adventures of a rogue (Spanish: *picaro*), typically presented as an autobiography, episodic in structure and panoramic in its coverage of time and place.

Picturesque, The. A quality in landscape, and in idealized landscape painting, admired in the second half of the 18th century and featuring crags, a torrent or winding stream, ruins, and perhaps a quiet cottage and cart, with contrasting light and shadow.

Plagiarism. Literary kidnapping (Latin *plagiarius*, "kidnapper")—the seizing and presenting as one's own the ideas or writings of another.

Plain Style. The straightforward, unembellished style of preaching favored by 17th-century Puritans as well as by reformers within the Anglican church, as speaking God's word directly from the inspired heart as opposed to the high style of aristocratic oratory and courtliness, the vehicle of subterfuge. Plain style was simultaneously advocated for scientific accuracy by the Royal Society.

Platonism. Any reflection of Plato's philosophy, particularly the belief in the eternal reality of ideal forms, of which the diversities of the physical world are but transitory shadows.

Poetics. The theory, art, or science of poetry. Poetics is concerned with the nature and function of poetry and with identifying and explaining its types, forms, and techniques.

Poet Laureate. Since the 17th century, a title conferred by the monarch on English poets. At first, the laureate was required to write poems to commemorate special occasions, such as royal birthdays, national celebrations, and the like, but since the early 19th century the appointment has been for the most part honorary.

Poetry. Imaginatively intense language, usually in verse. Poetry is a form of fiction—"the supreme fiction," said Wallace Stevens. It is distinguished from other fictions by the compression resulting from its heavier use of figures of speech and allusion and, usually, by the music of its patterns of sounds.

Postmodernism. A term first used in relation to literature in the late 1940s by Randall Jarrell and John Berryman to proclaim a new sensibility arising to challenge the reigning assumptions and practices of modernism. Intruding into one's own fiction to ponder its powers became a hallmark of the 1960s and 1970s.

Poststructuralism. A mode of literary criticism and thought centered on Jacques Derrida's concept of deconstruction. Structuralists see language as the paradigm for all structures. Poststructuralists see language as based on differences—hence the analytical deconstruction of what seemed an immutable system. What language expresses is already absent. Poststructuralism invites interpretations through the spaces left by the way words operate.

Pragmatism. In philosophy, the idea that the value of a belief is best judged by the acts that follow from it—its practical results.

Preciosity. An affected or overingenious refinement of language.

Predestination. The belief that an omniscient God, at the Creation, destined all subsequent events, particularly, in Calvinist belief, the election for salvation and the damnation of individual souls.

Pre-Raphaelite. Characteristic of a small but influential group of mid-19th-century painters who hoped to recapture the spiritual vividness they saw in medieval painting before Raphael (1483–1520).

Presbyterianism. John Calvin's organization of ecclesiastical governance not by bishops representing the pope but by elders representing the congregation.

Proscenium. That part of the stage projecting in front of the curtain.

Prose. Ordinary writing patterned on speech, as distinct from verse.

Prose Poetry. Prose rich in cadenced and poetic effects like alliteration, assonance, consonance, and the like, and in imagery.

Prosody. The analysis and description of meters; metrics (*see also* Meter). Linguists apply the term to the study of patterns of accent in a language.

Protagonist. The leading character in a play or story; originally the leader of the chorus in the agon ("contest") of Greek drama, faced with the antagonist, the opposition.

Pseudonym. A fictitious name adopted by an author for public use.

Psychoanalytic Criticism. A form of criticism that uses the insights of Freudian psychology to illuminate a work.

Ptolemaic Universe. The universe as perceived by Ptolemy, a Greco-Egyptian astronomer of the 2nd century A.D., whose theories were dominant until the Renaissance produced the Copernican universe. In Ptolemy's system, the universe was world-centered, with the sun, moon, planets, and stars understood as rotating around the earth in a series of concentric spheres.

Puritanism. A Protestant movement arising in the mid-16th century with the Reformation in England. Theocracy—the individual and the congregation governed directly under God through Christ—became primary, reflected in the centrality of the Scriptures and their exposition, and the direct individual experience of God's grace.

Quadrivium. The more advanced four of the seven liberal arts as studied in medieval universities: arithmetic, geometry, astronomy, and music.

Quantitative Verse. Verse that takes account of the quantity of the syllables (whether they take a long or short time to pronounce) rather than their stress patterns.

Quarto (Abbreviated 4to, 4o). A book made from sheets folded twice, giving signatures of four leaves (eight pages).

Quatrain. A stanza of four lines, rhymed or unrhymed. With its many variations, it is the most common stanzaic form in English.

Rationalism. The theory that reason, rather than revelation or authority, provides knowledge, truth, the choice of good over evil, and an adequate understanding of God and the universe.

Reader-Response Theory. A form of criticism that arose during the 1970s; it postulates the essential active involvement of the reader with the text and focuses on the effect of the process of reading on the mind.

Realism (in literature). The faithful representation of life. Realism carries the conviction of true reports of phenomena observable by others.

Realism (in philosophy). (1) In the Middle Ages, the belief that universal concepts possess real existence apart from particular things and the human mind. Medieval realism was opposed to nominalism. (2) In later epistemology, the belief that things exist apart from our perception of them. In this sense, realism is opposed to idealism, which locates all reality in our minds.

Recension. The text produced as a result of reconciling variant readings.

Recto. The right-hand page of an open book; the front of a leaf as opposed to the *verso* or back of a leaf.

Redaction. (1) A revised version. (2) A rewriting or condensing of an older work.

Refrain. A set phrase, or chorus, recurring throughout a song or poem, usually at the end of a stanza or other regular interval.

Relativism. The philosophical belief that nothing is absolute, that values are relative to circumstances. In criticism, relativism is either personal or historical.

Reversal. The thrilling change of luck for the protagonist at the last moment in comedy or tragedy.

Rhetoric. From Greek *rhetor*, "orator": the art of persuasion in speaking or writing.

Rhetorical Figure. A figure of speech employing stylized patterns of word order or meaning for purposes of ornamentation or persuasion.

Rhetorical Question. A question posed for effect, usually with a self-evident answer.

Rhyme (sometimes Rime, an older spelling). The effect created by matching sounds at the ends of words. The functions of rhyme are essentially four: pleasurable, mnemonic, structural, and rhetorical. Like meter and figurative language, rhyme provides a pleasure derived from fulfillment of a basic human desire to see similarity in dissimilarity, likeness with a difference.

Rhyme Royal. A stanza of seven lines of iambic pentameter, rhyming *ababbcc* (*see also* Meter).

Rhythm. The measured flow of repeated sound patterns, as, for example, the heavy stresses of accentual verse, the long and short syllables of quantitative verse, the balanced syntactical arrangements of parallelism in either verse or prose.

Romance. A continuous narrative in which the emphasis is on what happens in the plot, rather than on what is reflected from ordinary life or experience. Thus a central element in romance is adventure.

Romanticism. A term describing qualities that colored most elements of European and American intellectual life in the late 18th and early 19th centuries, from literature, art, and music, through architecture, landscape gardening, philosophy, and politics. The Romantics stressed the separateness of the person, celebrated individual perception and imagination, and embraced nature as a model for harmony in society and art.

Roundheads. Adherents of the Parliamentary, or Puritan, party in the English Civil War, so called from their short haircuts, as opposed to the fashionable long wigs of the Cavaliers, supporters of King Charles I.

Rubric. A heading, marginal notation, or other section distinguished for special attention by being printed in red ink or in distinctive type.

Run-on Line. A line of poetry whose sense does not stop at the end, with punctuation, but runs on to the next line.

Satire. Poking corrective ridicule at persons, types, actions, follies, mores, and beliefs.

Scop. An Anglo-Saxon bard, or court poet, a kind of poet laureate.

Semiotics. In anthropology, sociology, and linguistics, the study of signs, including words, other sounds, gestures, facial expressions, music, pictures, and other signals used in communication.

Senecan Tragedy. The bloody and bombastic tragedies of revenge inspired by Seneca's nine closet dramas.

Sensibility. Sensitive feeling, emotion. The term arose early in the 18th century to denote the tender undercurrent of feeling in the neoclassical period.

Sequel. A literary work that explores later events in the lives of characters introduced elsewhere.

Serial. A narration presented in segments separated by time. Novels by Charles Dickens and other 19th-century writers were first serialized in magazines.

Shakespearean Sonnet (or English Sonnet). A sonnet in three quatrains and a couplet, rhyming *abab cdcd efef gg*.

Signified, Signifier. In structural linguistics, the *signified* is the idea in mind when a word is used, an entity separate from the *signifier*, the word itself.

Simile. A metaphor stating the comparison by use of *like, as,* or *as if.*

Slang. The special vocabulary of a class or group of people (as, for example, truck drivers, jazz musicians, salespeople, drug dealers), generally considered substandard, low, or offensive when measured against formal, educated usage.

Sonnet. A verse form of 14 lines, in English characteristically in iambic pentameter and most often in one of two rhyme schemes: the *Italian* (or *Petrarchan*) or *Shakespearean* (or *English*). An Italian sonnet is composed of an octave, rhyming *abbaabba,* and a sestet, rhyming *cdecde* or *cdcdcd,* or in some variant pattern, but with no closing couplet. A Shakespearean sonnet has three quatrains and a couplet, and rhymes *abab cdcd efef gg*. In both types, the content tends to follow the formal outline suggested by rhyme linkage, giving two divisions to the thought of an Italian sonnet and four to a Shakespearean one.

Sonnet Sequence. A group of sonnets thematically unified to create a longer work.

Spondee. A metrical foot of two long, or stressed, syllables: – –.

Sprung Rhythm. Gerard Manley Hopkins's term to describe his variations of iambic meter to avoid the "same and tame." His feet, he said, vary from one to four syllables, with one stress per foot, on the first syllable.

Stanza. A term derived from an Italian word for "room" or "stopping place" and used, loosely, to designate any grouping of lines in a separate unit in a poem: a verse paragraph. More strictly, a stanza is a grouping of a prescribed number of lines in a given meter, usually with a particular rhyme scheme, repeated as a unit of structure.

Stereotype. A character representing generalized racial or social traits repeated as typical from work to work, with no individualizing traits.

Stichomythia. Dialogue in alternate lines, favored in Greek tragedy and by Seneca and his imitators among the Elizabethans—including William Shakespeare.

Stock Characters. Familiar types repeated in literature to become symbolic of a particular genre, like the hard-boiled hero of the detective story.

Stoicism. (1) Generally, fortitude, repression of feeling, indifference to pleasure or pain. (2) Specifically, the philosophy of the Stoics, who, cultivating endurance and self-control, restrain passions such as joy and grief that place them in conflict with nature's dictates.

Stress. In poetry, the accent or emphasis given to certain syllables, indicated in scansion by a *macron* (–). In a trochee, for example, the stress falls on the first syllable: *sūmmĕr*. *See also* Meter.

Structuralism. The study of social organizations and myths, of language, and of literature as structures. Each part is significant only as it relates to others in the total structure, with nothing meaningful by itself.

Structural Linguistics. Analysis and description of the grammatical structures of a spoken language.

Sublime. In literature, a quality attributed to lofty or noble ideas, grand or elevated expression, or (the ideal of sublimity) an inspiring combination of thought and language. In nature or art, it is a quality, as in a landscape or painting, that inspires awe or reverence.

Subplot. A sequence of events subordinate to the main story in a narrative or dramatic work.

Syllabic Verse. Poetry in which meter has been set aside and the line is controlled by a set number of syllables, regardless of stress.

Symbol. Something standing for its natural qualities in another context, with human meaning added: an eagle, standing for the soaring imperious dominance of Rome.

Symbolism. Any use of symbols, especially with a theoretical commitment, as when the French Symbolists of the 1880s and 1890s stressed, in Stéphane Mallarmé's words, not the thing but the effect, the subjective emotion implied by the surface rendering.

Syncopation. The effect produced in verse or music when two stress patterns play off against one another.

Synecdoche. The understanding of one thing by another—a kind of metaphor in which a part stands for the whole, or the whole for a part: *a hired hand* meaning "a laborer."

Synesthesia. Greek for "perceiving together": close association or confusion of sense impressions, as in common phrases like "blue note" and "cold eye."

Synonyms. Words in the same language denoting the same thing, usually with different connotations: *female, woman, lady, dame; male, masculine, macho*.

Synopsis. A summary of a play, a narrative, or an argument.

Tenor and Vehicle. I. A. Richards's terms for the two aspects of metaphor, *tenor* being the actual thing projected figuratively in the *vehicle*. "She [tenor] is a rose [vehicle]."

Tercet (or Triplet). A verse unit of three lines, sometimes rhymed, sometimes not.

Terza Rima. A verse form composed of tercets with interlocking rhyme (*aba bcb cdc*, and so on), usually in iambic pentameter. Invented by Dante for his *Divine Comedy*.

Third-Person Narration. A method of storytelling in which someone who is not involved in the story, but stands somewhere outside it in space and time, tells of the events.

Topos. A commonplace, from Greek *topos* (plural *topoi*), "place." A rhetorical device, similarly remembered as a commonplace.

Tragedy. Fundamentally, a serious fiction involving the downfall of a hero or heroine. As a literary form, a basic mode of drama. Tragedy often involves the theme of isolation, in which a hero, a character of greater than ordinary human importance, becomes isolated from the community.

Tragic Irony. The essence of tragedy, in which the most noble and most deserving person, because of the very grounds of his or her excellence, dies in defeat. *See also* Irony.

INDEX